DATE DUE

~~AC 2 '05~~			
MR 1 2 '09			

DEMCO 38-296

12

A-I
VOLUME 1

John G. Maurer

Joel M. Shulman

Marcia L. Ruwe

Richard C. Becherer

ENCYCLOPEDIA
OF BUSINESS

Gale Research

An ITP Information/Reference Group Company

I(T)P

Changing the Way the World Learns

NEW YORK • LONDON • BONN • BOSTON • DETROIT
MADRID • MELBOURNE • MEXICO CITY • PARIS
SINGAPORE • TOKYO • TORONTO • WASHINGTON
ALBANY NY • BELMONT CA • CINCINNATI OH

, John G. Maurer, Marcia L. Ruwe, Joel M. Shulman, *Managing Editors*

Gale Research Staff:

Jane Cousins Malonis, *Editor/Project Coordinator*

Shawn Brennan, Donna Craft, Deborah S. Fennell, Carol T. Gaffke, Jeff Lehman, Susan Boyles Martin, Kimberley A. McGrath, Bradley J. Morgan, Terrance W. Peck, Stefanie Scarlett, Lia Watson, *Contributing Editors*

Donald P. Boyden, *Managing Editor*

Glenn Wolfe, *Fact Checker*

Marlene Hurst, *Permissions Supervisor*
Margaret McAvoy-Amato, *Permissions Assistant*

Mary Beth Trimper, *Production Director*
Pamela Galbreath, *Art Director*
Tracey Rowens, *Graphic Designer*

Benita L. Spight, *Data Entry Services Manager*
Gwendolyn Tucker, *Data Entry Supervisor*
Lysandra Davis and Elizabeth Pilette, *Data Entry Associates*

Since this page cannot legibly accommodate all copyright notices,
the acknowledgements constitute an extension of the copyright notice.

Library of Congress Cataloging-in-Publication Data
Encyclopedia of business / John G. Maurer . . . [et al.], editors. — 1st ed.
     p. cm.
     Includes bibliographical references and index.
     ISBN 0-8103-9187-2
     1. Business—Encyclopedia. 2. Commerce—Encyclopedia.
     3. Finance—Encyclopedia. 4. North America—Commerce—
     Encyclopedia. 5. Finance—North America—Encyclopedia.
     I. Maurer, John G., 1937– .

     HF1001.E466 1995
     650′.103—dc20   95-33676
                                                                   CIP

 The paper used in this publication meets the minimum requirements of American National Standard for Information Sciences—Permanence Paper for Printed Library Materials, ANSI Z39.48-1984.

ISBN 0-8103-9187-2 (set), ISBN 0-8103-9188-0 (V1), ISBN 0-8103-9189-9 (V2)

Printed in the United States of America

I(T)P™   Gale Research, an ITP Information/Reference Group Company.
          ITP logo is a trademark under license.

10 9 8 7 6 5 4 3 2 1

CONTENTS

During this project's gestation, the world of business has witnessed many milestone events. From the historic signing of multinational trade agreements to the normalization of U.S. trade relations with Vietnam on the international front, to the savings & loan bailout and the U.S. government's designation of Empowerment Zones on the domestic front. The sphere of private enterprise has been impacted not only by the sweeping stroke of government decisions, but as well by the changing demands of consumers, the increasingly diverse nature of the labor force, and the breakneck pace of new technological innovation. In the four years since EOB was first conceived, the worldwide business climate has continued to evolve, and with that evolution so has grown the base of knowledge required to make sense of it.

The *Encyclopedia of Business*'s combined practical and theoretical approach offers readers a solid explanation of relevant concepts, issues, and terms, covering both current and classical areas of interest and concern. As the global business community is drawn into ever closer proximity by the broadening accessibility of electronic communication, the need for such information—and the ability to access it in understandable language—is becoming increasingly underscored. *EOB* provides an exemplary starting point for the fulfillment of this need.

COMPILATION METHODS USED

To create a truly authoritative work that can rightfully be designated "encyclopaedic" is no small task. *EOB* could never have successfully been created in a vacuum; indeed, the level of insight and opinion solicited by the publisher from business and informa-tion experts domestically and abroad has been no less than impressive. Our distinguished panel of *EOB* Advisors proved instrumental in helping to develop, define the scope of, and refine the list of business topics deemed essential for inclusion in these volumes. To these individuals, whose names are listed after this Preface and User's Guide, we express our sincere appreciation.

Once topic selection was determined, we turned to our Managing Editor Team, comprised of four tireless and highly esteemed business academicians. They are: John G. Maurer, Professor of Management, School of Business Administration, Wayne State University, Detroit, MI; Richard C. Becherer, Professor, Clarence E. Harris Chair of Excellence in Business and Entrepreneurship, University of Tennessee at Chattanooga, TN; Marcia L. Ruwe, Academic Dean, LeMoyne College, Syracuse, NY; and Joel M. Shulman, Robert Weissman Chair of Entrepreneurship, Babson College, Babson Park, MA. Their primary mission—carried out admirably despite heavy professional commitments—was to carefully review and critique each essay for accuracy, relevance, comprehensiveness, and source originality. We turned to them frequently for clarification and guidance throughout the course of this project. Their contribution to *EOB* was significant and can hardly be overstated. The head of this team, John G. Maurer, is owed a particular debt of gratitude.

With the Managing Editor Team in place, the task at hand entailed the selection and engagement of highly qualified contributors to compose the specific essays. Again, suggestions of possible candidates provided by the *EOB* Advisors as well as the Managing

Editor Team proved invaluable. The dozens of essayists chosen are either distinguished professional educators—many of whom are renowned in their respective fields—active and prominent members of the business community, or exceptionally skilled freelance writers with the appropriate subject matter expertise. To these individuals, whose names are listed after the Advisors', we express our deep appreciation.

USER'S GUIDE

The *Encyclopedia of Business* has been designed for ease of use. Comprised of two volumes, the signed, original essays are arranged alphabetically from A–Z by topic throughout the set. Average entry length is approximately 2,500 words. At the back of the second volume are two important features: the Discipline Index and the General Index.

Special features found within ENTRIES include the following:

Bolded Terms point the reader toward related entries within *EOB* that might be of interest

"See Also" references, included at the end of many entries, appear when direct reference to related entries are not indicated by bolded terms within the text; these, also, refer the reader to further topics that may be of interest

Charts, Graphs, Tables, and **Formulae** are included as illustrative examples whenever appropriate

"Further Reading" sections are included at the end of most entries; these bibliographic citations point the reader toward a variety of essential sources for further study.

"See" References serve to guide the reader toward the location of entries that may be recognized by more than one commonly used term. For example, upon turning to the term "Revenue," a "SEE" Reference will direct the user to search under the more inclusive "Income and Revenue." Another example is the broad use of the term "Employment Discrimination"; readers searching under this term will be guided toward a selection of several more specific topic entries with titles ranging from "Affirmative Action" to "Americans with Disabilities Act" to "Sexual Discrimination."

The **Discipline Index** offers subject access by way of 31 broadly encompassing business disciplines; all essays pertinent to a given discipline are listed accordingly. For example, under the discipline term "Finance," one could expect to find reference to dozens of essays covering aspects of investments, corporate finance, interest rates, and the like. Similarly, under "Management," one could expect to find essay titles such as International Management, Management Science, and Organizational Management—among many others.

The **General Index** contains alphabetical references to the following, as mentioned in *EOB* entries: important or unusual terms; names of companies, institutions, organizations, and associations; key government agencies; specific legislation; relevant court cases; names of prominent individuals; titles of groundbreaking literature (ie., business "bibles") and studies. Using this index, readers can easily locate all such references to the above mentioned items as they appear throughout both *EOB* volumes.

COMMENTS AND SUGGESTIONS

Questions, comments, and suggestions regarding the Encyclopedia of Business are invited and welcomed. Please contact:

Jane A. Malonis
Editor/Project Coordinator
Encyclopedia of Business
Gale Research Inc.
Ste. 835, Penobscot Bldg.
645 Griswold Ave.
Detroit, MI 48226-2242

Telephone: (313) 961-2242
Toll-Free Phone: 800-347-GALE
Toll-Free FAX: 800-339-3374

A number of recognized experts provided invaluable assistance in the preparation of this book. Our panel of advisors helped us shape this publication into its final form, and we would like to express our sincere appreciation to them:

Karel Cool
Professor of Strategic Management
Institut Europeen d'Administration des Affaires (INSEAD)
Fontainebleau, France

Thomas J. Kearney
Vice President
World Trade Centers Association
New York, NY

Leslie Pearlman
Professor of Healthcare Finance
Graduate School of Health Studies
Simmons College
Boston, MA
Adjunct Professor of Financial Management in Nonprofit
  Organizations
John F. Kennedy School of Government
Harvard University
Cambridge, MA

Charles J. Popovich
Head Business Librarian
The Ohio State University
Columbus, OH

Jone Rymer
Professor of Marketing
School of Business Administration
Wayne State University
Detroit, MI

Jean Scanlan
Director
Information Center
Price Waterhouse
Boston, MA

Guy F. Tozzoli
President
World Trade Centers Association
New York, NY

John E. Tropman
Professor of Nonprofit Management and Organizational
  Behavior
University of Michigan
Ann Arbor, MI

Pier A. Abetti
Rensselaer Polytechnic University
Troy, NY

Roger J. AbiNader

Paula M. Ard
Durham, NC

Susan Bard Hall

Virginia L. Barnstorff
Bloomfield, NJ

Christopher C. Barry
Price Waterhouse
Boston, MA

Laurence Barton
Freelance Writer
Schaumburg, IL

Linda Beamer

Brad Bernatek
Ann Arbor, MI

David P. Bianco

Paul Bolster, PhD
Associate Professor of Finance
Northeastern University
Boston, MA

Karen Leslie Boyd

John Burnett
Marketing Department
University of Denver
Denver, CO

Bruce D. Buskirk
Valdosta, GA

Boyd Childress
Auburn University Library
Auburn, AL

Rick A. Cooper, Ph.D.
Vice President
State Street Global Advisors
Boston, MA

Raymond A. K. Cox
Professor of Finance
Central Michigan University
Mount Pleasant, MI

William H. Coyle, PhD
Babson College
Babson Park, MA

James Cuene
Plymouth, MN

Richard Cuthie
South Boston, MA

Aldona Cytraus
Case Western Reserve University
Cleveland, OH

Dr. Lawrence Dandurand
Department of Marketing
University of Nevada-Las Vegas
Las Vegas, NV

William Delaney
Freelance Writer
San Diego, CA

Louis J. Drapeau
Adjunct Professor
Department of Finance and Business
    Economics
Wayne State University
Detroit, MI
Manager, Insurance and Risk
    Management
Budd Company
Troy, MI

Sina Dubovoy
Bethesda, MD

Arthur A. DuRivage
Livonia, MI

Ahmad K. Elshennawy
Associate Professor
Department of Industrial Engineering
    and Management Systems
University of Central Florida
Orlando, FL

Jeffrey A. Fadiman
Professor of Global Marketing and
    Transcultural Communications
San Jose State University
San Jose, CA

Jack Fiorito
Florida State University
Tallahassee, FL

William Fisher
School of Library and Information
    Science
San Jose State University
San Jose, CA

Nanette Fondas
Fuqua School of Business
Duke University
Durham, NC

Martin S. Fridson, C.F.A.
Chief High Yield Strategist
Merrill Lynch & Co.
New York, NY

Andrea Gacki
Bay City, MI

Dr. Graham Gal
School of Management
University of Massachusetts
Amherst, MA

April Dougal Gasbarre
University Heights, OH

Jim Gerhardinger
University of Toledo
Toledo, OH

Roger Gledhill
Associate Professor of Decision
  Sciences
Eastern Michigan University
Contact at:
  4959 Miller Road
  Ann Arbor, MI 48103

Edmund R. Gray
Professor of Management
Loyola Marymount University
Los Angeles, CA

Lin Grensing-Pophal
Freelance Writer
Chippewa Falls, WI

Kathryn Harrigan
Henry R. Kravis Professor of
  Business Leadership
Columbia University
New York, NY

Henry Hecht
Editorial Consultant
Teaneck, NJ

Heather Behn Hedden
Information Access Company
Foster City, CA

Tona Henderson
Business Librarian
The Pennsylvania State University
University Park, PA

Ned C. Hill
Joel C. Peterson Professor of
  Business Administration
Brigham Young University
Provo, UT

Laurie Collier Hillstrom, M.B.A.
Co-founder
Northern Lights Writers Group
Pleasant Ridge, MI

Ronald M. Horwitz
Professor, Department of Finance
Oakland University
Rochester, MI

Cynthia Iannarelli, Ph.D.

Frederick C. Ingram
Freelance Writer
Johnson City, TN

George C. Jackson, PhD
Department of Marketing and
  Logistics
Wayne State University
Detroit, MI

Clint Johnson
Business Writer
Winston-Salem, NC

Susan M. Kasuba, CPA
Chief Financial Officer
NELINET
Newton, MA

Daniel King
Monroe, NY

Robert T. Kleiman, Ph.D.
Oakland University
Rochester, MI

Timothy J. Kloppenborg
Project Management Professional
Associate Professor of Operations
  Management
Department of Management and
  Entrepreneurship
Xavier University
Cincinnati, OH

Michael Knes
Freelance Writer

David C. Kucera

John J. Lawler
Associate Professor
Institute of Labor and Industrial
  Relations
University of Illinois at Urbana-
  Champaign
Champaign, IL

Joan Leotta
Business Writer
Burke, VA

Anne C. Levy
Associate Professor of Law, Public
  Policy, and Business
Michigan State University
East Lansing, MI

Cary M. Lichtman
Industrial Psychology Graduate
  Program
Wayne State University
Detroit, MI

Thomas E. Love
Department of Operations Research
Case Western Reserve University
Cleveland, OH

James T. Low, PhD, CPIM
Department of Marketing
School of Business Administration
Wayne State University
Detroit, MI

John G. Maurer
Professor of Management
School of Management
Wayne State University
Detroit, MI

Donald O. Mayer
Associate Professor
Department of Management and
  Marketing
Oakland University
Rochester, MI

Evylyne Meier

Carl B. McGowan Jr.
Department of Management and
  Finance
California State University
Hayward, CA

Bruce Meyer
Managing Editor
Rubber and Plastics News
Akron, OH

Sharon Michaels
President
Sharon Michaels and Associates
Birmingham, MI

David Mote
Freelance Business Writer
Software Developer
Indianapolis, IN

John E. Oliver
Department of Management and
  Information Systems
Valdosta State University
Valdosta, GA

Ruth Pittman
Freelance Writer
Milford, OH

Richard Rump

Anandi P. Sahu
Associate Professor of Economics
School of Business Administration
Oakland University
Rochester, MI

Susan Salter
Freelance Writer
Walled Lake, MI

John Sarich
Freelance Writer
Albany, NY

Arthur G. Sharp
Business Faculty Member
Naugatuck Valley Community/
  Technical College
Waterbury, CT

John Simley
Chicago, IL

Kathryn D. Snavely
Freelance Writer
Raleigh, NC

David Sprinkle
New Orleans, LA

Paulette L. Stenzel
Professor of Business Law and
    Public Policy
Michigan State University
East Lansing, MI

John E. Tropman
University of Michigan
Ann Arbor, MI

David E. Upton
Virginia Commonwealth University
Richmond, VA

Divakara K. (Dik) Varma
Librarian Emeritus
York University
North York, ON, Canada

David A. Victor, PhD
Professor of Management
Eastern Michigan University
Ypsilanti, MI

Etan Vlessing
Canadian Bureau Chief for the
    Hollywood Reporter
Los Angeles, CA

Mark A. Vonderembse
Professor of Manufacturing
    Management
University of Toledo
Toledo, OH

Dorothy Walton
Chicago, IL

Peter B. Webb
Department of Economics
Xavier University
Cincinnati, OH

Mark A. White, Ph.D.

Valerie E. Wilson
Technologist
Lufkin Industries
Lufkin, TX

Roberta H. Winston
Writer/Editor
Belmont, WA

Charles J. Woelfel

Gillian Wolf
Freelance Writer
Evanston, IL

Glenn Wolfe
Associate Professor of Finance
University of Toledo
Toledo, OH

Judith A. Zimmerman
Schaumburg, IL

ACKNOWLEDGMENTS

The charts, graphs, and tables contained in this book are original works or were created using U.S. government data unless noted below.

The chart on page 1122 in the essay "Organizational Development" is copyright ©1991 by The Regents of the University of California. Reprinted from the **California Management Review**, Volume 33, Number 4. By permission of The Regents.

The chart on page 1128 in the essay "Organizational Life Cycle" is from "Tightening the Life Cycle Construct: A Taxonomic Study of Growth Stages and Configurations in High-Technology Organizations," by S. Hanks, C. Watson, E. Jansen, and G. Chandler, from **Entrepreneurship Theory and Practice**, 18 (2), Winter, 1993. Reprinted by permission of Baylor University.

The chart on page 1129 in the essay "Organizational Life Cycle" is reprinted by permission of **Harvard Business Review**. An exhibit from "Organization Practices During Evolution in the Five Phases of Growth" by L. Greiner, July/August 1972. Copyright ©1972 by the President and Fellows of Harvard College. All rights reserved.

Welcome to the *Encyclopedia of Business*. Business is defined as the creation, production, and distribution of goods or services for a profit. Businesses engage in these three core activities in order to satisfy customer or client needs and desires, including the resolution of their problems. In order to survive and prosper in a competitive environment, businesses must perform these core activities in an efficient and effective manner. This means they must continually search for and adopt better, faster, and cheaper ways of creating, producing, and distributing goods and services.

The *Oxford English Dictionary* defines encyclopedia as ''an elaborate and exhaustive repertory of information on all branches of some particular art or department of knowledge.'' The business ''department of knowledge'' is enormous in scope. It is important first to recognize that businesses operate within a larger system. They are directly or indirectly influenced by elements in their external environment. These external elements are: the general economy; local, state, and federal governments; conditions in the industry within which they compete; financial markets and institutions; societal values and beliefs; and the international environment. To attempt to understand business behavior by focusing only on the internal activities of businesses will provide only partial understanding. One must include in the analysis how the outside world affects the internal life of a business. The *Encyclopedia of Business* provides hundreds of entries covering this broad spectrum.

The internal and external functions of a business are numerous. They include such areas as: accounting; business ethics and social responsibility; decision sciences/operations research; finance; management; management information systems; marketing; and research, innovation, and technology. All of these areas, and many more, are well represented throughout *EOB*.

MAJOR ISSUES

Among the major issues addressed by the *Encyclopedia of Business* are four which promise to remain very important as we enter the twenty-first century; entrepreneurship/small business, the globalization of business, quality, and diversity.

In addition to essays detailing entrepreneurship and small business, the reader is alerted to entries that discuss business incubators, family-owned business enterprises, S corporations, self-employment, venture capital, and women entrepreneurs.

Over sixty entries address the globalization of business issue. Representative among these are essays on international organizations and agreements, international marketing, and emerging markets. Several entries provide excellent coverage of what it's like to engage in business activity in an unfamiliar culture; included among these are Managing Machismo, Doing Business in Africa, and Doing Business in the Third World, in addition to many others.

''Quality'' means that output must confirm to certain standards. ''High quality'' means defect-free output. This issue is addressed via such topics such as: benchmarking; Japanese manufacturing, and management techniques; project management; quality circles, quality control, and Total Quality Management

(TQM); statistical process control; Taguchi methods; teams; and theory of constraints.

Workforce diversity refers to the cultural and demographic differences among employees. Understanding these differences, managing them, and using them to create competitive advantage is a major concern of today's managers. A small sampling of the many entries on this topic are: Affirmative Action Programs; Career and Family; Child Care/Elder Care; Diversity Culture; Equal Opportunity; Gender and Leadership; Illiteracy in the Workplace; Multicultural Workforce; Sexual Harrassment in the Workplace; and Women in Business.

OBJECTIVES OF THE *ENCYCLOPEDIA OF BUSINESS*

There were three primary objectives which guided the production of *EOB:*

1. To create a fundamental and comprehensive reference book on business.

2. To provide current and authoritative information on business terms, ideas, issues, concepts, theories, models, and techniques of importance.

3. To present the information in a clear and concise fashion to our readers, be they students of business, entrepreneurs, information specialists, or lay people.

I worked closely with three Associate Managing Editors and I thank them for their important contributions: Professors Richard Becherer, Marcia Ruwe, and Joel Shulman. On behalf of the Managing Editor staff, I thank the entry contributors who worked very hard in helping to bring this book concept to life.

John G. Maurer
Senior Managing Editor
Wayne State University
Detroit, Michigan

A-I

VOLUME 1

ENCYCLOPEDIA
OF BUSINESS

A

ABSENTEEISM

An absentee is an employee of a company who does not come to work due to scheduled time off, illness, injury, or just not showing up. This phenomenon is called absenteeism.

The cost of absenteeism to business, usually expressed in terms of lost productivity, is difficult to determine. Studies from government sources such as the U.S. Bureau of the Census and U.S. Bureau of Labor Statistics put the direct losses at more than $40 billion a year. Various private studies and polls studying particular elements of absenteeism sometimes put the figure much higher. One recent Gallup poll did not put a price tag on the sniffles and swollen eyes, but claimed more than three million work days per year are lost when working people stay home when their allergies act up. The Massachusetts Institute of Technology released a study in 1994 claiming that clinical depression alone resulted in more than 213 million lost work days, costing $24 billion.

There is no long written history of absenteeism in business literature, probably because until this century businesses had a simple rule, "No work; no pay." The practice of offering paid "sick days" did not become popular until unions forced companies into contracts recognizing that illness may be a legitimate reason for staying home from work. While practices vary among companies and union contracts, an average of four to 10 sick days per year appears to be standard.

The problem of absenteeism is addressed directly by some companies and some handle the situation better than others. One recent study involved a television man-ufacturer which operates with a lean staff. Every hourly employee scheduled to work must be on the floor, or a substitute must be found. The union negotiated with the company to reduce the number of annual excused absences allowable from 24 days to 18. Employees with more than 18 absences could be terminated. The company thought that this reduction in absences before termination would show how serious it was about keeping employees on the line. However, the company made a mistake in its negotiations. It also allowed some vacation days to be applied toward those absences.

After the new contract went into effect there was a 45% decline in the number of unexcused absences and a 22% drop in excused absences, which was good. The use of vacation time to compensate for absences jumped 81%, however. The net effect was that there was a jump of 12% in the hours people were off work.

In the past, employees had been forced to schedule vacation days well in advance of taking them, allowing supervisors to schedule replacements. Under the new policy, employees could take a day off without warning their supervisor. By allowing employees the right to use vacation time to make up for absences, the company had inadvertently created a last minute opportunity for employees not to come to work.

In the next round of labor negotiations, the company eliminated the vacation day substitution practice. It also told employees desiring to move into different jobs that they must have had a good attendence record the previous year. As an additional incentive, the company also began a perfect attendance bonus of $200. In one year 127 employees qualified for the bonus. The previous year, before the bonus was created, only 27 employees had perfect attendance records.

The experience of this company showed how important it was to research absenteeism to discover its abuses and patterns. Once those abuses and patterns were discovered, the company developed strategies with the cooperation of the union to encourage work attendance.

Some companies have approached the problem by eliminating sick leave altogether. Instead of "vacation time" and "sick leave," the companies have developed "paid-leave banks." In one study of 464 hospitals using seven different methods of controlling absenteeism, only the "paid-leave bank" consistently showed a positive effect in controlling absenteeism.

Often, companies have halved the amount of time previously set aside for sick leave and added those days to the "bank." At the start of the year employees understand they have a certain number of days that can be taken, whether for a three-week trip to Europe or a two-week trip to the Grand Canyon and a one-week bout with the flu. No "sick days" are allotted. If a person uses his or her bank time and is out sick, they are not paid for the first several days. If they are legitimately ill and still cannot return to work, short term disability payments start. One company using such a policy found its employees' reporting of illness absences dropped by more than 30% in one year.

Some companies have tried what might be a surprisingly simple solution to the problem of chronic absenteeism: they have the worst offenders counsel each other. In one research study patterned after drug and alcohol abuser programs, a company paired valued employees who had high absence problems with each other. If one felt like skipping work, he or she was encouraged to call the "buddy" to talk it out. During the study, their absence rates dropped by nearly 50%. Once they stopped the "absence intervention" program, their absence levels increased, but they remained lower than they had been before peer counseling.

The employees who participated in the study found that they could talk freely about the reasons behind their absences with each other. The buddy would help talk through the problems, and encourage the wavering employee to return to work.

One other piece of information came up in the study. The absentee workers claimed to have little idea how much time they were really off from work. They knew they were taking "too much" time, but until the buddy started tracking it for them, they were unaware how their absence was affecting the company. All in all, the best practices seem to include company awareness of employees' non-work needs and employee awareness of company needs.

[Clint Johnson]

FURTHER READING:

Goodman, Paul S. *Absenteeism*. Jossey-Bass, 1984.

Rhodes, Susan. *Managing Employee Absenteeism*. Addison-Wesley, 1990.

ACCOUNTING

Accounting has been defined as "the language of business" because it is the basic tool for recording and reporting economic events and transactions that affect business enterprises. Other concepts of accounting view accounting as an historical record, a mirror of current economic reality, a subset of a total business information system, and a commodity that is the product of economic activity.

A committee of the American Institute of Certified Public Accountants (AICPA) defined accounting as follows:

Accounting is the art of recording, classifying in a significant manner and in terms of money, transactions and events which are, in part at least, of a financial character, and interpreting the results thereof.

This definition emphasizes the work that the accountant performs but makes little reference to the users of the information that the accountant provides. In 1970, the AICPA developed the following definition:

Accounting is a service activity. Its function is to provide quantitative information, primarily financial in nature, about economic activities that is intended to be useful in making economic decisions—making reasoned choices among alternative courses of action.

This definition is goal-oriented rather than process-oriented or function oriented. It emphasizes economic decision-making activities.

Accounting deals with numbers and measurable quantities as well as with qualitative data about an enterprise. Its basic functions include the accumulation, measurement, and communication of data. The accounting system accumulates data related primarily to completed transactions and events; it quantifies business transactions and events by measurements, primarily in terms of a monetary unit such as the dollar; and it communicates relevant and reliable information to investors, creditors, managers, and others for internal and external decision-making purposes.

Financial decisions which often require the use of accounting information include buying, holding, or selling a particular security and extending or not extending credit. Useful accounting information relates to such matters as the return on investments, risk, financial flexibility, liquidity, and operating capability.

Accounting can be broadly described in terms of financial accounting and management accounting. Financial accounting is a branch of accounting that provides external users with qualitative information regarding an enterprise's economic resources, obligations, financial performance, and cash flows. Management accounting is a branch of accounting which provides internal users with information relating to an enterprise's resources, obligations, financial performance, budgets, and other significant operating, financing, and investing activities.

HISTORY OF ACCOUNTING

By 5000 B.C., records in Babylon of inventories of grains, precious metals, and workers were maintained by scribes who made their marks on stone, papyrus, and wax tablets. The growth of empires and commerce throughout Egypt, Greece, Rome and through subsequent generations down to modern times made record keeping, the percussor of accounting, a prerequisite for progress and development. The earliest records typically belonged to persons in authority or to temples.

During the Renaissance of art, literature, and philosophy, a major breakthrough was made in Venice in 1494 when Luca Pacioli (1445?-1514?), a Franciscan friar, developed the first complete description of a method of keeping business records. This method, which was to be become known as the double-entry form of **bookkeeping**, also became the basis of modern accounting procedures.

With the Industrial Revolution in England and Europe, there was a large expansion of business activity. Industrial and commercial enterprises emerged and flourished. Many of these companies or corporations were owned by shareholders rather than by the persons who managed the enterprise. Accounting then began to serve as a communicating process for shareholders rather than just a way of keeping records.

Through the 19th and 20th centuries, corporations have become more important, larger, and more complex. The imposition of the federal income tax and governmental regulations with all of their complexities increased the necessity for the skills of accountants. Standard setting for the accounting profession has been maintained primarily in the private sector.

ECONOMIC ENVIRONMENT OF ACCOUNTING

Accounting operates within an economic, legal, political, and social environment. In the United States, accounting serves a private, free enterprise, capitalistic economy. In a free enterprise system, private citizens are free to own and operate a business. The means of production (land, factories, equipment) are privately owned although government does own and operate some enterprises such as the postal system. Incentive for investors and businesses is the profit motive and competition is a characteristic of the marketplace. Accounting serves the free enterprise system by providing useful financial data for making the economic choices that an enterprise or person must make, especially as the choices relate to the allocation of an enterprise's or investor's economic resources.

The users of accounting information in a free enterprise system are numerous and diverse but they have a common interest in the prediction of future cash flow. Securities markets are well-developed, tend to allocate scarce resources efficiently, and consume vast amounts of capital. The capital markets respond expeditiously to the release of accounting information and are quite capable of interpreting data provided by accounting through financial reporting.

The economic environment of accounting places constraints on what accounting can and should do. The economic environment identifies persons and institutions for whom an accounting is to be made and determines what is to be accounted for.

Economics is concerned with the production, distribution, exchange, and consumption of goods and services. The issues raised by any economic system which affect accounting include:

(1) What kinds and amounts of goods and services shall be produced (the production function)?

(2) For whom are goods and services to be produced (income distribution function)?

(3) How are goods and services traded or exchanged for other economic resources (the exchange function)?

(4) How is the output of the production process to be used (the consumption function)?

A business entity is an economic organization. Economic events and transactions are the life blood of the accounting system. The objectives of accounting relate to the making of economic decisions concerning the use of limited economic resources. Accounting and economics deal with many of the same elements: economic resources (assets), economic obligations (liabilities), stores of wealth (money), flows of wealth (income), prices, costs, cash flows, savings investments, and the allocation of scarce resources. This linkage reflects the economic environment in which accounting functions.

Accounting reports and financial statements can have economic consequences for decision makers, especially creditors and investors. Economic consequences refer primarily to the costs and benefits resulting from compliance with financial reporting requirements. Accountants are not held accountable for the effects that accounting might have on the decisions of users of accounting information. Accounting principles and methods, and their application, however, can have a significant impact on the decision-making process. Most accountants take the position that accounting policies and standards should not be developed to encourage or discourage economic transactions. This does not imply that standard setters should not be aware of the economic consequences of their actions.

ACCOUNTING PROFESSION

A profession is an association of individuals engaged in a vocation or occupation that typically:

(1) renders essential services to society;

(2) depends upon a body of specialized knowledge acquired through formal education;

(3) has developed a language of its own;

(4) has established requirements for admission to the profession which are regulated by law; and

(5) governs it members by ethical principles which emphasize the virtues of honesty, probity, and attention to the welfare of those served.

The accounting profession is subdivided into public accountants who function as independent experts and perform services for non-accountant clients and for accountants who work for a particular entity. The profession can be further subdivided as follows:

Public accountant	Internal (or private) accountant
External auditor	Financial or general accountant
Tax specialist	
Management consultant	Cost accountant
	Tax accountant
	Systems analyst
	Internal auditing
	Budgeting

A **certified public accountant** (CPA) is an accountant who has fulfilled certain education and experience requirements established by a state law for the practice of public accounting and an acceptable score on a written national examination. Such people be-

come licensed to practice public accounting in a particular state. The largest U.S. accounting firms, commonly referred to as the Big Six, have extensive international connections, include (in alphabetical order):

1. Arthur Andersen & Co.

2. Coopers & Lybrand

3. Deloitte and Touche

4. Ernst & Young

5. KPMG Peat Marwick

6. Price Waterhouse

The American Institute of Certified Public Accountants (AICPA) is the national professional organization of CPAs. The American Accounting Association is an organization that is composed primarily of accounting educators.

ACCOUNTING SYSTEM

An accounting system is a management information system that is responsible for the collection and processing of data to produce information useful to decision-makers in planning and controlling the activities of an organization. The data processing cycle of an accounting system can be conceptualized as the total structure of records and procedures associated with five activities: collection or recording; classifying; processing (including calculating and summarizing); maintenance or storage; and output or reporting.

The accounting system initially records transactions and events in a journal, a chronological list of the financial activities of an enterprise. The information is then posted (transferred) to a ledger, a book of accounts. An account is a form or place used to collect and record data arising from transactions affecting a single item, such as cash, inventory, accounts receivable, buildings, etc. Periodically, a trial balance is taken of the ledger account balances. Adjusting entries are usually required to update account balances before financial statements are prepared. Financial statements are prepared to communicate financial information about an enterprise primarily to external parties.

The accounting equation describes the relationships among assets, liabilities, and owners' equity.

$$\text{Assets} = \text{Liabilities} + \text{Owners' equity}$$

This equation represents the basic accounting model and provides a framework for the accounting system. It is the basis for recording transactions and events in the accounting records and for the preparation of the balance sheet. The equation is maintained in balance. The left side of the equation summarizes the economic resources of the entity while the right side summarizes the claims upon, or sources of, the economic resources.

OBJECTIVES OF FINANCIAL REPORTING

The objectives of financial reporting apply primarily to general purpose external financial reporting, especially that which is directed toward the common interests of users who lack the authority to obtain the information they want and who must rely on information provided by management. Simply put, financial reporting is designed to meet the needs of investors and creditors for decision making purposes. They are summarized as follows based on the FASB Statement of Financial Accounting Concepts No. 1, ''Objectives of Financial Reporting by Business Enterprises,'' prepared by the **Financial Accounting Standards Board (FASB)**:

- Provide information that is useful to investors, creditors, and other users in making rational investment, credit, and similar decisions.

- Provide information to help investors, creditors, and others in assessing the amounts, timing, and uncertainty of prospective net cash inflows to the related enterprisebecause their prospects for receiving cash from investments, from loans to, or from other participation in the enterprise depend significantly on cash flow prospects.

- Provide information to help investors, creditors, and others in assessing the amounts, timing, and uncertainty of prospective net cash inflows to the related company.

- Provide information about the economic resources of an enterprise, the claims to those resources, obligations of the enterprise to transfer resources to other entities and owners' equity, and the effects of transactions, events, and circumstances that change resources and claims to those resources.

The specific objectives of financial reporting give guidance about the kinds of information financial reporting should provide which include the following: provide information about a company's economic resources, obligations, and owners' equity; provide information about a company's comprehensive income and its components; provide information about a company's cash flows.

Financial statements individually and collectively contribute to meeting objectives of financial reporting. No single statement is likely to provide all the financial statement information that is useful for a particular kind of decision. The financial statements are said to articulate or relate one to another and are derived from the same underlying data

GENERALLY ACCEPTED ACCOUNTING PRINCIPLES (GAAP)

Generally accepted accounting principles (GAAP) are the guidelines, rules, and procedures necessary to define accepted accounting practice used in recording and reporting accounting information in audited financial statements. Various organizations have influenced the development of generally accepted accounting principles. Among these are the American Institute of Certified Public Accountants (AICPA), the Financial Accounting Standards Board (FASB), and the **Securities and Exchange Commission** (SEC). The first two are private sector organizations; the SEC is a federal government agency.

The AICPA played a major role in the development of accounting standards from 1937 to 1973. In 1937, the AICPA created the Committee on Accounting Procedures (CAP), which issued a series of *Accounting Research Bulletins (ARB)* with the purpose of standardizing accounting practices. In 1959, this committee was replaced by the Accounting Principles Board (APB). The APB continued the series of ARBs and began to publish a new set of pronouncements, referred to as Opinions of the Accounting Principles Board. In mid-1973, an independent private board, the Financial Accounting Standards Board, replaced the APB and assumed responsibility for the issuance of financial accounting standards. The FASB is currently the primary source for the determination of financial accounting standards in the United States.

The Financial Accounting Standards Board has seven members who serve full-time and are fully remunerated. The FASB identifies financial accounting issues, conducts research related to these issues, and is charged with resolving the issues. A super-majority vote (i.e., at least five to two) is required before Statements of Financial Accounting Standards are issued. These statements establish generally accepted accounting principles. Steps involved in the promulgation of Statements of Financial Accounting Standards can include the following:

- Prepare and issue a Discussion Memorandum.

- Receive public comment.

- Appoint a Task Force to research the issue.

- Issue an exposure draft.

- Receive public comments.

- Issue a Statement of Financial Accounting Standards.

The Financial Accounting Foundation is the parent organization to FASB. The foundation is governed by a 16-member Board of Trustees appointed from the memberships of eight organizations: the AICPA, Financial Executives Institute, Institute of Management

Accountants, Financial Analysts Federation, American Accounting Association, Securities Industry Association, Government Finance Officers Association, and National Association of State Auditors. A Financial Accounting Standards Advisory Council (approximately 30 members) advises the FASB. An Emerging Issues Task Force (EITF) was established in 1984 to provide timely guidance to the FASB on new accounting issues.

The Securities and Exchange Commission, an agency of the federal government, has the legal authority to prescribe accounting principles and reporting practices for all companies issuing publicly traded securities. The SEC has seldom used this authority, however, although it has intervened or expressed its views from time to time. The law requires that companies subject to the jurisdiction of the SEC make reports to the SEC giving detailed information about their operations. The SEC has broad powers to require public disclosure in a fair and accurate manner in financial statements and to protect investors. The SEC establishes accounting principles with respect to the information contained within reports it requires of registered companies including the following:

- Form S-X, a registration statement.

- Form 1O-K, an annual report.

- Form 1O-Q, a quarterly report of operations.

- Form S-K, a report used to describe significant events that may affect the company.

- Proxy Statements, reports used when management requests the right to vote through proxies for shareholders.

The **Internal Revenue Service (IRS)** prescribes rules, methods, ad regulations for the determination of taxable income. These pronouncements conflict at times with the accounting principles and methods acceptable for financial reporting, but the IRS's requirements must be followed when filing tax returns.

ACCOUNTING ASSUMPTIONS

Accounting assumptions are broad concepts that underlie generally accepted accounting principles and serve as a foundation for these principles. Major accounting assumptions include the following:

1. Economic entity assumption. Information is recorded and reported about each separate economic entity that is a particular unit of accountability, e.g., First National Bank, AT&T, John Doe, Chicago, IL.

2. Going-concern assumption. A company is assumed to continue operations, unless substantial evidence to the contrary exists.

3. Monetary unit assumption. The national currency of a company is used as a stable unit of measure in preparing financial reports. The purchasing power of money is not reported in the financial statements.

4. Timely and periodic reporting assumption. Information is reported in the financial statements at least on an annual basis.

Other significant accounting conventions include accrual accounting, the historical cost principle, the revenue realization principles, the matching principle, conservatism, and full disclosure. Accrual accounting recognizes the financial effects of transactions, events, and circumstances having cash consequences to the period in which they occur rather than when the cash receipt or payment occurs.

The historical cost principle requires that the exchange price at the time of an acquisition of an asset or liability is retained in the accounting records as the value of an item until it is consumed, sold, or liquidated, and subsequently removed from the accounting records. The acquisition cost of an asset or liability is its historical cost. Historical cost is considered to be objective and verifiable.

The revenue realization principle requires that revenue is recognized in the financial statements when 1) it is earned and 2) when it is realizable or realized. Revenue is considered earned when the entity has substantially accomplished what it must do to be entitled to the benefits represented by the revenues. Revenue is realized or realizable when it is convertible into cash. The matching principle (expense recognition) reflects the practice of letting the expense follow, match, or be associated with the revenue earned during a period whenever it is reasonable and practicable to do so.

Conservatism requires that uncertainties and risks related to a company be reflected in its accounting reports and that the financial statements reflect prudence or caution in financial reporting. Similarly, the full disclosure principle requires that circumstances and events that make a difference to financial statement users be adequately disclosed in the statements.

The economic substance of a transaction is considered more significant than the legal form of the transaction for reporting purposes. For example, consolidated financial statements are usually considered more relevant than are the separate statements of members of the affiliated group. Consolidated financial statements do not represent the legal statements of any accounting entity, however, they do represent an accounting entity.

Comparability is the quality of information that enables users to identify similarities in and differences between two sets of economic phenomena. Consistency is the conformity from period to period with unchanging policies and procedures. Materiality is the magnitude of an omission or misstatement of accounting information that, in the light of surrounding circumstances, makes it probable that the judgment of a reasonable person relying on the information would have been changed or influenced by the omission or misstatement.

ELEMENTS OF ACCOUNTING

The elements of accounting are the building blocks with which financial statements are constructed, i.e., the classes of items that are presented in the financial statements. FASB Concepts Statement No. 3, ''Elements of Financial Statements of Business Enterprises'' defines the elements that are directly related to measuring performance and the financial position of a business enterprise.

Assets are probable future economic benefits obtained or controlled by a particular entity as a result of past transactions or events.

Comprehensive income is the change in equity (net assets) of an entity during a period from transactions and other events and circumstances from nonowner sources. Comprehensive income includes all changes in equity during a period except those resulting from investments by owners and distributions to owners.

Distributions to owners are decreases in equity (net assets) of a particular enterprise resulting from transferring assets, rendering services, or incurring liabilities to owners.

Equity is the residual interest in the assets of an entity that remains after deducting liabilities. In a business entity, equity is the ownership interest.

Expenses are events that expend assets or incur liabilities during a period from delivering or providing goods or services and carrying out other activities that constitute the entity's ongoing major or central operation.

Gains are increases in equity (net assets) from peripheral or incidental transactions. Gains also come from other transactions, events, and circumstances affecting the entity during a period except those that result from revenues or investments by owners. Investments by owners are increases in net assets resulting from transfers of valuables from other entities to obtain or increase ownership interests (or equity) in it.

Liabilities are probable future sacrifices of economic benefits arising from present obligations to transfer assets or provide services to other entities in the future as a result of past transactions or events.

Losses are decreases in equity (net assets) from peripheral or incidental transactions of an entity and from all other transactions, events, and circumstances affecting the entity during a period. Losses do not include equity drops that result from expenses or distributions to owners.

Revenues are inflows or other enhancements of assets, settlements of liabilities, or a combination of both during a period from delivering or producing goods, rendering services, or conducting other activities that constitute the entity's ongoing major or central operations.

FINANCIAL STATEMENTS

Financial statements are the most comprehensive way of communicating financial information about an enterprise provided on its reports. General purpose financial statements have been developed to meet the needs of the many users of financial statements, primarily the needs of investors and creditors. The information provided by financial statements is primarily financing in nature quantified and expressed in units of money. The information presented pertains to individual business enterprises, government entities, and other accounting entities, but not to industries or consumers. The information provided on the statements is often approximated or estimated rather than exact. The measures involve classifications, summarizations, judgments, and allocations. The information provided generally reflects the financial effects of transactions and events that have already happened.

The basic outputs of the financial accounting process are presented in the following interrelated general purposes of financial statements.

1. A balance sheet (or statement of financial position) summarizes the financial position of an accounting entity at a particular point in time as represented by its economic resources (assets), economic obligations (liabilities), and equity.

2. An income statement summarizes the results of operations for a given period of time.

3. A statement of cash flows summarizes the impact of an enterprise's cash flows on its operating, financing, and investing activities over a given period of time.

4. A statement of retained earnings shows the increases and decreases in earnings retained by the company over a given period of time.

5. A statement of changes in stockholders' equity discloses the changes in the separate stockholders' equity account of an entity including investments by distributions to owners during the period.

Notes to financial statements are considered an integral part of a complete set of financial statements. Notes typically provide additional information at the end of the statement and concern such matters as depreciation and inventory methods used in the statements, details of long-term debt, pensions, leases, income taxes, contingent liabilities, methods of consolidation, and other matters. Significant accounting policies are usually disclosed as the initial note or as a summary preceding the notes to the financial statements. Accounting principles and their method of application are considered particularly important in the following areas:

1. A selection from existing alternatives (for example, inventory methods such as LIFO, FIFO, and average methods).

2. Areas that are peculiar to a particular industry which the company operates.

3. Unusual and innovative applications of generally accepted accounting principles.

FINANCIAL CAPITAL MAINTENANCE

Current financial statements are based on the concept of financial capital maintenance. Financial capital is the monetary value of the net assets contributed by stockholders and the value of the increase in net assets resulting from earnings retained by the corporation. According to this theory, income results from the increase in the number of nominal dollars representing capital. An enterprise receives a return only after its capital has been maintained or recovered. A return on financial capital results only if the money amount of an enterprise's net assets at the end of a period exceeds the financial amount of net assets at the beginning of the period after excluding the effects of transactions with owners (such as additional investments or withdrawals of capital and dividends). The effect of price changes on assets held and liabilities owed during a period are recognized, they are considered holding gains and losses and are included in the return on capital (and are included in the determination of income for the period). The concept of capital maintenance can be illustrated as follows:

Ending net assets	$90,000
Less: Additional investment	$10,000
Ending net assets excluding additional investments	$80,000
Less: Beginning net assets	$34,000
Total income for the year	$46,000

Note that capital must be maintained before a corporation earns income on that capital.

FINANCIAL STATEMENT ANALYSIS

Financial statement analysis is a method for evaluating the financial statements of an entity to determine the strengths, weaknesses, and the future operating prospects of a company. Major techniques of financial statement analysis include horizontal analysis, vertical analysis, common-size income statements, and ratio analysis. Horizontal analysis spotlights trends and establishes relationships between items that appear on the same row of a comparative financial statement and discloses changes on items in the statements over time. Vertical analysis involves the conversion of the number of appearances in statement columns into terms of percentages of a base figure showing the relative significance of the items in order to facilitate comparisons. For example, individual items such as net income and expenses reported on the income statement can be expressed as a percentage of sales. Common-size financial statements translate dollar amounts into percentages, which indicate the relative size of an item in proportion to the whole. A common size balance sheet shows assets, liabilities, and owners' equity as a percentage of total assets. Common-size income statements express revenue and expenses as a percentage of sales revenues.

Ratio analysis involves the computation of ratios of items appearing on financial statements. The elements which constitute the ratio must express a meaningful relationship. Rations can be classified as follows:

1. Liquidity ratios measure the ability of the enterprise to pay its debts as they mature. For example:

$$\text{Current ratio} = \frac{\text{Current assets}}{\text{Current liabilities}}$$

This equation measures ability to pay current liabilities from current assets.

2. Activity (or turnover) ratios measure how effectively the enterprise is using its assets. For example:

$$\text{Inventory turnover} = \frac{\text{Cost of goods sold}}{\text{Average inventory}}$$

This equation indicates salability of inventory.

3. Profitability ratios which measure management's success in generating returns for those who provide capital to the enterprise. For example:

$$\text{Return on sales} = \frac{\text{Net income}}{\text{Net sales}}$$

This equation shows the percentage of each sales dollar earned as a percentage of net income.

4. Coverage ratios measure the protection for long-term creditors and investors. For example:

$$\text{Debt ratio} = \frac{\text{Total liabilities}}{\text{Total assets}}$$

This equation indicates the percentage of assets financed through borrowing.

Financial statement analysis is not an end in itself but is performed for the purpose of providing information that is useful in making lending and investing decisions. An understanding of analytical methods associated with financial statement analysis is extremely useful when interpreting and analyzing financial reports.

[Charles Woelfel]

FURTHER READING:

Beam, F. A. *Advanced Accounting*. Prentice Hall, latest edition.

Financial Accounting Standards Board. *Statements of Financial Accounting Concepts*. Irwin, 1987.

Jarnagin, B. D. *Financial Accounting Standards*. Commerce Clearing House, latest edition.

Kieso, D. E. and J. J. Weyugandt. *Intermediate Accounting*. John Wiley & Sons, latest edition.

Harrison, W. T., Jr. and C. T. Horngren. *Financial Accounting*. Prentice Hall, latest edition.

Hendriksen, E. S. and M. F. Van Breda. *Accounting Theory*. Irwin, latest edition.

Nikolai, L. A. and J. D. Bazley. *Intermediate Accounting*. South-Western, latest edition.

Woelfel, C. J. *Financial Statement Analysis*. Probus, 1994.

Wolk, H. I., et al. *Accounting Theory: A Conceptual and Institutional Approach*. South-Western, 1992.

ACQUISITIONS

SEE: Mergers and Acquisitions

ACTIVE MANAGEMENT (FIXED INCOME)

Active **bonds** portfolio management attempts to take advantage of either superior bond selection or superior market timing. The former requires a bond portfolio manager who is capable of identifying mispriced bonds. The bond portfolio manager can buy underpriced bonds or sell overpriced bonds. The latter strategy requires a bond portfolio manager capable of predicting interest rate changes. Bond portfolio managers use swaps to implement either strategy.

A substitution swap replaces one bond with another bond that has very similar characteristics, such as coupon rate, time to maturity, rating quality, and call and **sinking fund** features. A bond is purchased if it is overpriced or sold if it is underpriced. The bond that is replaced is properly priced. The bond portfolio manager profits when the mis-priced bond moves to the proper equilibrium price.

An inter-market spread swap results when the bond portfolio manager shifts from one sector of the bond market to another sector of the bond market. U.S. Treasury bonds, federal agency bonds, corporate bonds, state and municipal bonds, and mortgage-backed bonds each constitute a sector of the bond market. As market risk perceptions change, the risk premium between the U.S. Treasury bond market and the risky bond sector changes. If the bond portfolio manager can determine the direction of the change in the spread, the composition of the bond portfolio can be shifted to the market sector that will increase in price.

An interest rate anticipation swap depends on the bond portfolio manager's ability to forecast interest rate changes. If the bond portfolio manager anticipates that **interest rates** will rise (fall) the duration of the bond portfolio is decreased (increased).

A pure yield pickup swap is implemented by moving from bonds with lower coupon payments to bonds with higher coupon payments. This provides a higher current yield and yield to maturity. The added return leads to higher risk, since the high coupon bond is more likely to be called.

[Carl B. McGowan, Jr.]

FURTHER READING:

Reilly, Frank K. *Investment Analysis and Portfolio Management*. 3rd ed., Chicago: Dryden Press, 1989.

ADVERTISING

Advertising is a paid form of communication from the manufacturer of a product or provider of a service that helps sell that product or service to consumers or other companies. It is a $150 billion a year business in the United States. Traditional advertising includes print advertisements in magazines and newspapers, commercials on local and cable television stations and national television networks, radio commercials, and outdoor billboards; may also include other speciality marketing concepts such as product promotions and **direct marketing**.

Over the past decade at least two new forms of advertising have emerged to rival the older forms: 30-minute television infomercials, and interactive advertising, which is emerging on computer on-line services.

HISTORY OF ADVERTISING

The history of advertising is as old as business itself. In the American colonies, certain craftsmen—such as cobblers, tinsmiths, and gunsmiths—erected signs outside their homes that depicted their trade. The signs were usually much larger than life so out-of-town visitors knew that the man with the four-foot-long wooden shoe hanging by his door could repair a worn sole.

Print advertising in the United States started in colonial-era newspapers and broadsheets as small, word-only ads, similar in concept to today's newspaper classified ads. Sometimes the ads would appear on the front page (a practice that has only recently been revived by *USA Today*). In time, the use of illustrations to actually show the products for sale began to appear.

At first the ads were created by the publisher of the newspaper as a service to the advertiser. After the American Civil War, an idea that first emerged in the 1840s began to grow in popularity. Advertising agents, supposedly independent creators of ads that would go into newspapers, started acting as middlemen and marketing advisers between the newspapers and advertising merchants. The first heavily advertised products were patent medicines.

One of the first true agencies and the oldest one still in business is N.W. Ayer & Son. Ayer was founded in 1869 by Francis Wayland Ayer who, like legions of admen after him, recognized the value of the illusion of permanence. Ayer named his agency after his father because it sounded as if the firm was older than it actually was. Ayer's father was not in the ad business, but his name looked good on the company letterhead.

The first true copywriter in advertising came along in 1880 when retailer John Wanamaker hired John E. Powers to write ads for the Grand Depot department stores in Philadelphia. Powers wrote simple ads, hated "catchy" headlines and illustrations, and once said that the key to advertising was to "have the attention of the reader. That means to be interesting. The next thing is to stick to the truth, and that means rectifying whatever's wrong in the merchant's business. If the truth isn't tellable, fix it so it is. That is about all there is to it."

ELEMENTS OF ADVERTISING

Powers's intuitive assessment of what makes good advertising has remained constant throughout the past 130 years of modern advertising. Research repeatedly confirms that a "basic selling proposition" is the most important variable in determining an advertisement's success in attracting the attention and trust of buyers. If consumers can easily find the reasons they should buy the product or service, are convinced the ad is truthful, and are motivated to act, the ad or commercial has served its purpose. One study found that an ad with good execution but an inferior selling proposition had a 60 percent likelihood to have an inferior persuasive score, while an ad with so-so execution but a superior selling proposition had a 75 percent likelihood of getting a high persuasive score.

Two of the strongest elements of a good selling proposition are a convincing introduction of a new product or adding of new features to an existing product, and a skillful differentiation between the advertised brand and competing brands. Advertisers who demonstrate that their product is "new and improved," or better than the competing brand sell product.

CURRENT STATE OF ADVERTISING

Advertising continues to undergo drastic changes. In 1980 two-thirds of every marketing dollar went into traditional advertising. By 1990 that figure had shrunk to one-third. Another study says brand loyalty, so lovingly built by advertising since the 1950s, is declining. Some studies suggest that more than a third of the people who consider themselves brand loyalists today could pick another brand the next time they buy, maybe for as simple a reason as a 50-cents-off coupon.

The biggest change affecting advertising is that the mass merchandising of all consumer goods over network television, which was the way to go for the past 40 years, may no longer be applicable. There is no longer just one mass market reached by three coast-to-coast TV networks. The choice of three network channels has evolved into 50-plus cable choices with more to come. VCRs allow people to tape the shows they want to watch, then zip past the commercials. Some ethnic or racial groups have their own networks, which removes a large number of people races out of the audience mix once promised to advertisers.

The change in mass marketing can be confusing. While some consumers are happily zapping the commercials they taped on "free TV," some of the same people are tuning in and buying from home-shopping stations, which offer nothing but commercials.

Changes in advertising practices are being felt in local communities as well. The local television network affiliates also have to compete with low-power, low-cost cable stations. Daily newspapers are mounting campaigns to get people to read their news, rather than get all of it from television and radio. Trade and professional magazines, always affected when the industries they cover go into or recover from recessions, have only recently started to pick up sales. Only in the past year have advertising rates and space sales held steady or even gone up a bit, indicating a slowing or end to an advertising recession.

Technology has created even more opportunities—or obstacles—to reaching the public. Advertising executives are trying to figure out what role advertising will play in reaching people who regularly use computers at work and home. This is a growing market of affluent, educated consumers willing to spend money, but until recently they have been reached only through traditional means. The big question is if these consumers will accept advertising over the computers they use.

TYPES OF ADVERTISING AND THEIR EFFECTIVENESS

NETWORK TELEVISION. The most expensive advertising is network television commercials where 30-second spots can cost a vast amount of money, depending on which highly rated shows they appear. These commercials, designed to appeal to the large, multicultural, mass audience that supposedly watches television, are also the most in danger of dying according to advertising prognosticators. In the spring of 1994 Edwin L. Artzt, CEO of Procter and Gamble (P&G), which spends more than $3 billion a year on television advertising, stunned advertising agency executives when he said that he was not sure advertising-supported television would be around much longer.

Artzt was making the point that the traditional network television viewership is slowly, but adily, dropping as the audience uses its remote control to sample cable offerings, or turn the set off in pursuit of other forms of entertainment. He predicted that mass market merchandisers such as P&G may one day return to a practice common in early television of totally sponsoring shows rather than buying 30-second commercials during the show. A modern-day model may be Hallmark Cards Inc., which occasionally sponsors shows that attract the same people who enjoy buying sentimental greeting cards.

Some ad-effectiveness research studies seem contradictory, particularly with television commercials. One recent study found that commercials with children are the most popular, with 61 percent of people surveyed saying they enjoyed them, followed by commercials with humor, and commercials with celebrities. At the bottom of the list of popularity were "endorsement from experts" (17 percent) and "product demonstrations" (17 percent). That research seems to fly in the face of other studies listing the "selling proposition" as the most important persuasive element in advertising. Another study released by a different organization found that 50 percent of television watchers do something other than watch television during commercial breaks. Only 22 percent of the people in this survey say they watch commercials closely and 26 percent say they are annoyed by commercials. The most faithful television commercial watchers are those older than 60 and those with the lowest incomes. These are the same two groups that most national television advertisers do not target.

LOCAL TELEVISION. Almost every city of any size either has its own local network affiliate or is reached by a neighboring city. Commercial time rates vary by size of the market (how many television viewing households can be reached by the signal) and how much of that market competing stations already have. Local stations sell commercials during network shows, and local news broadcasts, and during syndicated shows that are generally grouped around the late afternoon news hour until network television begins. Most local television stations can themselves produce commercials for low-budget customers, although it is probably better for both advertiser and station to involve an ad agency with television commercial experience.

LOCAL CABLE TELEVISION. "Spot buys" are possible on several stations when dealing with a cable operator. For example, a local car dealer pushing four-wheel-drive pickup trucks with a target market of young men may show the same commercial on different cable stations carrying professional football, wrestling, and a Chuck Norris film festival. Like local network affiliates, cable television stations can sometimes produce commercials for local advertisers on a budget.

RADIO ADVERTISING. While advertising agencies sometimes disdain it, radio is a favorite of advertisers and the public alike. Once thought to be slowly dying, AM radio has made a dramatic comeback over the last several years as "talk radio" stars such as Rush Limbaugh have come to dominate the airwaves, while most music stations are now FM. One nationally respected rating bureau found that 96 percent of Americans over the age of 12 listen to the radio daily. The same study found that over the last decade the amount of time spent listening to radio has risen almost 2 hours to 24 hours a week. During that same decade, ad revenues have doubled to nearly $10 billion, although radio's share of the advertising dollar has stayed constant with nearly 7 percent of the market.

Most of radio's ad dollars are spent locally with just $1 billion a year spent on network radio buys. The most expensive buys are purchased around "drive time" in the morning and evening when people are listening on their way to and from work.

Radio ad rates are generally considered inexpensive compared to print since they can be targeted by type of audience that listens to the station. Rates vary depending on size of the market reached, which is determined both by the power of the station's transmitter and the popularity of its talk or music format.

One recent study touted by the industry demonstrated the power of radio to extend the effect of television campaigns at much lower costs. The study found that radio "transfers and magnifies" images first seen on television when the listener hears a similar ad on radio. The researchers found that 60 percent of the people who listened to a radio spot made a connection with a similar sounding television commercial. Devout radio listeners were 12 percent more likely to "transfer image" to the intended television spot.

NEWSPAPER ADVERTISING. Except for *USA Today*, the *Wall Street Journal*, and *Investors Business Daily*, there are few national daily publications that try to reach all newspaper readers. Almost all newspaper advertising is either for local merchants and professionals (local department stores and accountants at tax time) or for national products and services that are available through a local source (airline tickets, grocery stores).

Before television, newspapers and magazines shared media dominance. Throughout the early 1990s, however, newspapers have seen slack ad rates and declining readership. Today, newspapers account for about 12 percent of advertising expenditures.

Taking a cue from *USA Today*, most local newspapers have been fighting back by revamping their design to appeal to younger readers. They are adding color and more features that they think will appeal to the 20-somethings.

Newspapers have also been pursuing their own studies to prove that newspapers deliver the buying public, even if the overall subscription numbers are down. One study showed a 50 percent increase in the sale of a popular brand of cookie after a one-third page, color ad ran for a month in one newspaper. Over an 11-week study period, the sale of the cookie was up 38 percent. Sales for a particular brand of cat food jumped 11 percent after its ad ran.

One recent survey conducted by a Canadian newspaper chain reconfirmed what advertising agencies have been telling their clients for years: bigger is good and with color is even better. The study found a half-page ad was 80 percent as effective in attracting attention as a full-page ad. A quarter-page ad was 60 percent as effective as a full-page ad. Using a second color boosted attention, but running full-color ads did not have a major effect in attracting more readers. That was a surprising finding to publishers who have been investing in color presses. Not surprisingly, awareness of individual ads decreased as the number of ads on the page increased. The only research finding that may surprise advertisers is that there appeared to be no effect on the placement of ads on the right or left page or above or below the fold. The standing belief is that ads placed on the right side are noticed more by readers.

The key finding in the study that cheered newspaper publishers was that readers who noticed the ads were 77 percent more likely to buy advertised products compared to those who had not seen the ads. The "intent to purchase" was somewhat higher among ad readers, which implies that shoppers in the market for certain products search out and study ads to help them make a purchase.

COOPERATIVE ADVERTISING. According to the Newspaper Association of America, more than $10 billion in advertising funds available to local retailers each year goes unused. That money is for cooprative ("co-op") campaigns that manufacturers of products set aside to reimburse retailers who mention their specific products in local ads. Many manufacturers will allocate between 3and 10 percent of a retailer's dollar purchases to co-op advertising that the retailer can draw against to help promote the local store and the manufacturer's product line.

Retailers do not always use the money because they do not always know it is there, or they do not wish to keep up with the manufacturer's bookkeeping requests to prove that the money was spent advertising its product line. The Newspaper Association suggested that most newspaper sales representative would be happy to help with the paperwork since it might mean another sale.

OUTDOOR ADVERTISING. Billboard advertising always seems to be under attack by one activist group or another. The main objections are that they distract drivers, frequently advertise controversial products such as liquor and cigarettes, and detract from the landscape.

Billboards work, however, if the execution is unusual and the message simple. One study found that highway billboards were remembered much more often than those on surface streets; that those on the right side of the highway were seen more than those on the left; and that black and white signs drew just as much attention as color. Simple messages were recalled best. Billboards with fewer than seven words were most often remembered.

FAX ADVERTISING. It may sound like a good idea to fax a personalized ad to a business, but it may be violating a 1992 **Federal Communications Commission** ban on unsolicited fax advertising. Still, many companies continue the practice and enforcement has been lax. The FCC rule says fax advertisers should stop if the company receiving their faxes sends a letter requesting that the unsolicited faxes stop.

INFOMERCIALS. The Hodgepodge of half-hour infomercials—from beef-jerky makers to wonder car polishes to finding true love seminars—work and are a growing part of advertising. In 1994 there were some 200 infomercials playing on cable television, accounting for about one-quarter of the programming time on cable systems. One trade association estimates consumers have bought nearly $1 billion worth of goods and services advertised on these programs.

Infomercial industry executives predict that the medium's content will grow in sophistication as cable television stations proliferate. The executives believe there will be channels that may show nothing but infomercials touting cars, boats, computers, or other high-ticket items. Production values will no doubt improve as consumers will expect broadcast quality television commercials that sells them expensive items.

ON-LINE COMPUTER ADVERTISING. Computers may be the new frontier for advertising, but it is a completely unknown frontier. By late 1994, advertising agencies and advertisers were still trying to figure out how, and if, they should put advertising on computer networks such as the global **Internet**. Early attempts by some new Internet users to advertise have met with angry resistance from veteran users, who consider the network to be purely a system for exchanging information.

ADVERTISING AGENCIES AND WHAT THEIR CLIENTS REALLY WANT

A study of companies by the North American Advertising Agency Network found that the clients of advertising agencies believe agency efficiency in carrying out advertiser orders is more valuable than "creativity." Clients prefer agencies that come in on time and on budget rather than those who spend more time and money trying to think of new ways to dazzle the customer.

The same study found that advertisers are continuing to shift to the idea that agencies should be compensated by a negotiated fee or for hours billed. Until recent years, agencies had traditionally tacked a 15 percent commission on their media purchases for their major means of compensation. Advertisers have been cutting that commission as a cost-savings measure. Large agencies, faced with a fragmented marketplace

that no longer produces large commissions from huge network television buys, are agreeing. The years-old debate on how much advertising is worth continues.

CREATIVITY AT ADVERTISING AGENCIES

"Breaking through the clutter" is the standard term advertising agencies use when trying to sell their clients on new campaigns. The "clutter," of course, is all those other advertisements that they have created for other clients. Trying to find a technique that will make potential buyers pay attention is a constantly changing process. Sometimes agencies find the key is to make fun of the commercials themselves—which is how the Energizer bunny was born several years ago. The bunny would interrupt fake commercials with its selling proposition that its power allowed it "to keep going and going and going."

In recent years creativity has reigned as agencies have searched for ways to make people look and listen. Much advertising now uses computer-generated images in order to attract attention. Today, television features tango-dancing gas pumps instead of a pitchman explaining how his brand of gasoline is the best. At the opposite end of the technology scale, but still high on the creative meter, is the frame-by-frame process of claymation where clay raisins were given personalities to sell dried grapes.

Creativity has its downside. In 1993 and 1994 advertising creative directors in both print and television launched an assault on the visual senses by using multiple hard-to-read typefaces in ads in the belief that the unusual look to the ads attracted attention. On television, the typefaces were put in motion, scrolling in all directions across the screen, sometimes too fast to read. The result was the opposite of what creative directors intended. One study showed that only 11 percent of magazine readers bothered to read the jumbled copy of a cosmetics ad, which was 19 percent below the average for the category. A supposedly stylish athletic shoe ad drew only 12 percent of the potential magazine readers, 43 percent below what that category normally attracts. Such results demonstrate that while creativity attracts attention, the majority of consumers will ignore ads that are difficult to listen to, view, or read.

BRAND LOYALTY CAN MEAN BIG PROFITS

No matter how creative advertising is, most advertising agencies and manufacturers agree that the consuming public falls into what is commonly called "the 80-20" rule. This theory, which seems to crop up no matter what is being sold, says that 80 percent of the product will be bought by 20 percent of the potential consumers. The other 80 percent of buyers fall into other categories. They may sample products with the potential of establishing a brand loyalty, are already brand loyalists with another product, or they will buy whatever is on sale or discounted by use of a special offer such as a coupon.

The figures might vary by the product being sold, but a core of loyal customers will always buy their favorite product unless its manufacturer drives them away by drastically changing it or raising the price too much. To that end, much advertising—particularly for consumable products—is designed to attract people who will become brand loyalists. Advertisers know much of this money is wasted on the majority of people, but they believe nothing else will establish brand loyalty like frequent advertising.

Once this brand loyalty is established, manufacturers often keep it by shifting some advertising dollars into promotion dollars. Known customers might be offered discounts or direct mail coupons for increased purchases. Advertising's real effect on brand loyalty itself is more difficult to measure. Some studies suggest that brand loyalists pay even more attention to advertising once they have bought because they are reassuring themselves that they made the right decision. This is particularly true of high-ticket items such as cars, kitchen appliances, and computers.

Finding consumers who want more information is a trend advertisers believe will allow them to better target some of their ad dollars, rather than try to hit everyone in the mass market. The process is called ''self-selection,'' where potential buyers notice some advertising then request more information. Requesting that information indicates interest, which allows the advertiser to identify a potential customer who might need more persuasive communications than is possible in early advertising. This is the sort of advertising push that results when a potential buyer writes or calls for more information such as an explanatory videotape. For instance, a car buyer who requests the full-color brochure after seeing a magazine ad, is likely to be studying cars in anticipation of buying one soon.

[Clint Johnson]

AFFIRMATIVE ACTION

Affirmative action refers to concrete steps that are taken not only to eliminate discrimination, whether in **employment**, education, or contracting, but also to attempt to redress the effects of past discrimination. The underlying motive for affirmative action is the principle of equal opportunity, which holds that all persons have the right to equal access to self-development, such that persons with equal abilities come to have equal opportunities.

Affirmative action programs differ widely in the extent to which they attempt to overturn discrimination. Some programs might simply institute reviews of the hiring process for women, minorities, and other affected groups. Other affirmative action programs might explicitly prefer members of affected groups. In such programs, minimum job requirements are used to create a pool of qualified applicants from which members of affected groups are given preference.

The interpretation and implementation of affirmative action has been contested since its origins in the 1960s. A central issue of contention was the definition of discriminatory employment practices. As the interpretation of affirmative action evolved, employment practices that were not intentionally discriminatory but that nevertheless had a ''disparate impact'' on affected groups were considered a violation of affirmative action regulations. Another central issue was whether members of affected groups could receive preferential treatment and, if so, the means by which they could be preferred. This issue is sometimes referred to as the debate over quotas. Though affirmative action programs came under heavy attack during the Reagan and Bush administrations, the principles of affirmative action were reaffirmed by the **Civil Rights Act of 1991**.

Affirmative action has its roots in the post-war civil rights movement. In March of 1961, President John F. Kennedy signed Executive Order 10925, which established the President's Commission on Equal Employment Opportunity. The Order stated that contractors doing business with the government ''will take affirmative action to ensure that applicants are employed, and employees are treated during their employment, without regard to their race, creed, color, or national origin.'' The Order did not advocate preferential treatment of affected groups but rather sought to eliminate discrimination in the traditional sense.

The legal status of the affirmative action was solidified by the Civil Rights Act of 1964. This landmark legislation prohibited discrimination in voting, public education and accommodations, and employment in firms with more than fifteen employees. Title VII of the Civil Rights Act offered a similar understanding of affirmative action as Executive Order 10925, stating that the Act was not designed ''to grant preferential treatment to any group because of race, color, religion, sex, or national origin.'' In an effort to break an eighty-two day filibuster by southern senators, the Act's sponsors had to assure that preferential treatment of affected groups would not become law. In an Interpretive Memorandum of Title VII, Senators

Joseph Clark and Clifford Case emphasized this non-preferential interpretation of affirmative action. They wrote: "There is no requirement in Title VII that an employer maintain a racial balance in his workforce. On the contrary, any deliberate attempt to maintain a racial balance, whatever such a balance may be, would involve a violation of Title VII, because maintaining such a balance would require an employer to hire or refuse to hire on the basis of race."

The Civil Rights Act did not provide criminal penalties for employers that discriminated, nor did the civil remedies established by the Act include compensation for pain and suffering or punitive damages. Rather the Act sought to establish a conciliation process by which victims would be restored to the situation they would have had in the absence of discrimination. To carry out the conciliation process, the Act created a new federal agency as a branch of the U.S. Department of Labor, the **Equal Employment Opportunity Commission (EEOC)**. The EEOC acts as a facilitator between plaintiffs and private employers and also pressures violating employers to provide compensation, whether in the form of back pay or restitution. The EEOC also provides legal support for plaintiffs should the plaintiffs pursue their grievances in court.

Two important issues became contested in the wake of the Civil Rights Act of 1964: whether unintentional or structural discrimination constituted violation of the principle of equal opportunity and the extent to which preferential treatment should be given to affected groups. These issues came to the forefront during the Johnson administration. In a 1965 commencement speech, President Johnson argued that equality of opportunity required more than simply ending discrimination. Rather he argued for a more active interpretation of affirmative action that would assure "equality as a result."

Johnson's Executive Order 11246 of 1965 established guidelines for firms contracting with the federal government and was enforced by the U.S. Department of Labor's newly created Office of Federal Contract Compliance (OFCC). As a consequence, all firms contracting with the federal government that had more than fifty employees and $50,000 or more in federal contracts were expected to implement affirmative action in hiring that would result in a greater number of minority hires.

In 1966, the U.S. Department of Labor began collecting employment records with breakdowns by race in order to evaluate hiring practices, overturning earlier policies of the Eisenhower and Kennedy administrations. In 1968, the Office of Federal Contract Compliance issued regulations which required, for the first time, that specific targets be set by which the effects of affirmative action programs could be evaluated. The regulations stated that "the contractor's program shall provide in detail for specific steps to guarantee equal employment opportunity keyed to the problems and needs of minority groups, including, when there are deficiencies, the development of specific goals and timetables for the prompt achievement of full and equal employment opportunity" It was in these regulations and analogous measures by the Equal Employment Opportunity Commission that the debate over affirmative action quotas had its origins.

Goals and timetables were established by the U.S. Department of Labor using "utilization analysis," which statistically compared the proportion of employed women and minorities in a firm with the proportion of women and minorities in the regional workforce, deriving a measure of what the Department called "disparate impact." In the absence of discrimination, it was assumed that these proportions would be roughly equal and furthermore that they should be roughly equal. Since these regulations focused on results and not intent, the structural nature of discrimination was officially recognized. In addition, these regulations provided an official and measurable basis for the preferential treatment of affected groups.

The future of affirmative action was in doubt when Richard Nixon took office in 1969, as Nixon had run against Johnson's Great Society programs. However with the appointment of George Shultz, later Ronald Reagan's Secretary of State, as head of the U.S. Department of Labor, the implementation of affirmative action program continued. Key among the Nixon era measures was the implementation of the Philadelphia Plan. The Plan was initially conceived by the Johnson administration as a means to address the highly segregated construction industry of Philadelphia. Attacked by the construction industry, construction unions, and the Controller General, the Plan languished at the end of the Johnson administration. In 1969, Shultz revived the Plan, calling for specific percentages of minorities to be hired. In 1970 the U.S. Department of Labor issued Order No. 4 and in 1971 Revised Order No. 4, new sets of affirmative action regulations that clarified and consolidated the Department's regulations of 1968.

In the landmark *Griggs v. Duke Power Co.* case of 1971, the Supreme Court unanimously ruled against Duke's requirement of high school diplomas or I.Q. tests for those applying for unskilled jobs. The decision held that "Title VII forbids not only practices adopted with a discriminatory motive, but also practices which, though adopted without discriminatory intent, have a discriminatory effect on minorities and women." The ruling provided a legal foundation for cases of "disparate impact," asserting that employers may not use job requirements that adversely affect women and minorities unless required by what it termed "business necessity." (For example, in the case of serious health or safety threats to co-workers or customers.)

The Equal Employment Opportunity Commission was strengthened by the Equal Employment Opportunity Act of 1972, enabling the Commission to file class action suits. Shortly thereafter, the EEOC challenged the employment practices of AT&T Corp., which was compelled to pay $15 million in back pay to 13,000 women and 2,000 minority men.

Under the Carter administration, the Uniform Guidelines on Employee Selection Procedures were established under which the "four-fifths rule" was established. This rule was significant in that it gave an explicit benchmark to determine disparate impact, which had been left vague in earlier U.S. Department of Labor regulations. The four-fifths rule held that firms contracting with the federal government should not be allowed to hire any race, sex, or ethnic group at a rate below four-fifths that of any other group.

Another significant Supreme Court ruling on affirmative action came in the 1978 case, *Regents of the University of California v. Bakke*. Under the University of California at Davis's admission policies, 16 of 100 places were set aside for minority applicants. Allan Bakke was a white applicant who was denied enrollment to Davis's medical school, even though his test scores were higher than the minority students who were admitted. Casting the deciding vote, Justice Lewis Powell held that Bakke should be admitted to the program since Davis's policies constituted a rigid quota, but that, nonetheless, Davis could continue to favor minorities in its admission practices and that it had a "compelling state interest" to attain a diversified educational environment.

The tide favoring affirmative action began to turn in the 1980s during the Reagan and Bush administrations. In the 1980 campaign, Reagan stated, "We must not allow the noble concept of equal opportunity to be distorted into federal guidelines or quotas which require race, ethnicity, or sex—rather than ability and qualifications—to be the principal factor in hiring or education." Through court appointments, hiring and firing decisions, and budget cuts, the Reagan administration sought to end affirmative action as it had evolved since the Johnson administration. Between 1981 and 1983, the budget of the Equal Employment Opportunity Commission (EEOC) was cut by 10 percent and the staff by 12 percent. The Office of Federal Contract Compliance was hit harder yet, with budget cuts of 24 percent and staff cuts of 34 percent during these same years.

Two important Supreme Court rulings in the late-1980s also acted to substantially weaken affirmative action. The 1988 case *Watson v. Fort Worth Bank and Trust* overturned the landmark 1971 *Griggs v. Duke Power Co.*, shifting the burden of proof in employ-

ment discrimination cases from employers to plaintiffs. In the 1989 case *Wards Cove Packing Company v. Antonio*, the Court ruled that a plaintiff could not simply show disparate impact to prove discrimination, but must demonstrate that a specific employment practice created the existing disparity.

In an effort to fight the dramatic rollback of affirmative action, Congress proposed the Civil Rights Act of 1990. The Act was passed by large majorities in the House and Senate, but was vetoed by President Bush. One year later, Congress passed the **Civil Rights Act of 1991**, which Bush reluctantly signed into law. The Act returned the burden of proof to employers in disparate impact cases, requiring employers to prove that employment practices that resulted in disparate impact were "job related" and "consistent with business necessity." The Act thus overturned the Supreme Court's rulings in *Watson v. Fort Worth Bank and Trust* and *Wards Cove Packing Company v. Antonio*. In short, the view of affirmative action advocated by the Johnson administration has won out to the present. In addition, the Civil Rights Act of 1991 addressed issues of unlawful harassment and intentional discrimination, allowing minority and female victims of intentional discrimination to be awarded up to $300,000 in compensatory damages in addition to back pay and restitution.

The **Americans with Disabilities Act** of 1990 extended protection from employment discrimination to disabled Americans. The employment provisions of the Act went into effect in 1992 and covered all private firms with more than twenty-five employees. The Act's employment regulations were enforced by the Equal Employment Opportunity Commission or the Office of Federal Contract Compliance.

In addition to the U.S. Department of Labor's Equal Opportunity Commission and the Office of Federal Contract Compliance, a host of agencies operate to regulate affirmative action at the state and local level. These include state attorney generals, human rights commissions, and 40 state-level versions of the EEOC. Prior to issuing rulings, the EEOC and OFCC, along with their state and local analogues, are required to submit proposed rulings to the public the affected industry to elicit their response.

The EEOC can refer violations of consent decrees (settlements agreed to by a firm accused of employment discrimination) to the U.S. Department of Justice for criminal prosecution. Regulating agencies can visit work sites and issue subpoenas, although some court rulings have held that the agency must have a reasonable basis for conducting such investigations. Though the EEOC and OFCC can initiate class action suits, instances of suspected employment discrimination can also be tried in administrative hearings. These hearings are generally open to the public and are conducted by the agencies law judge, who gives the agency's staff and the employer's attorney equal time to make their case. The hearing is concluded with the decision of the judge, and employers who are dissatisfied with the judge's ruling can appeal to either the head of the agency or to a court of law. The regulating agencies may also attempt less formal methods of resolution, including conciliation meetings.

Under Title VII of the Civil Rights Act of 1964, plaintiffs must file charges with the EEOC within 180 days of the alleged violation, or within 300 days if the plaintiff initially contacted a state or local equal opportunity employment agency. Title VII also requires that EEOC-approved notices be posted in a prominent place at the place of employment. The EEOC generally requires that plaintiffs take up their grievances with state and local agencies before it will undertake an investigation. The EEOC also encourages that plaintiffs seek to settle disputes out of court.

In 1994, the **Federal Communications Commission** (FCC) initiated one of the largest affirmative action programs ever. The FCC voted unanimously to set aside 1,000 of 2,000 new radio licenses for small businesses, women, and minorities. These licenses are for businesses serving the rapidly growing number of users of pocket-size telephones, fax machines, pagers, and hand-held computers. Small companies owned by women or minorities could receive up to a 60 percent discount on the cost of these liscenses, which federal officials estimated have a total market value of $10 billion. One of the concerns expressed about the FCC ruling is that it will enable the rise of companies that are only nominally headed by women or minorities. This could occur as a result of the acquisition provisions of the ruling, which allow a large corporation to acquire up to 75 percent of the equity and 49.9 percent of the voting stock of a small firm and for that firm to still qualify for licensing discounts.

SEE ALSO: Sex Discrimination (Employment)

[David Kucera]

FURTHER READING:

Andrews, Edmund L. "F.C.C. to Reserve Licenses in Affirmative Action Move," *New York Times*. June 30, 1994.

Bequai, August. *Every Manager's Legal Guide to Hiring*. Dow Jones-Irwin, 1990.

Fletcher, Meg. "Firms Fault ADA-Related Job Regulations," *Business Insurance*. February 22, 1993.

Fosu, Augustin. "Occupational Mobility of Black Women, 1958-1981: The Impact of Post-1964 Antidiscrimination Measures," *Industrial and Labor Relations Review*. January 1992, pp. 281-294.

Green, Kathanne W. *Affirmative Action and Principles of Justice*. Greenwood Press, 1989.

"How to Write an Affirmative Action Plan," *American Demographics*. March 1993, p. 56.

Leonard, Jonathan S. "Women and Affirmative Action," *Journal of Economic Perspectives*. Winter 1989, pp. 61-75.

Leonard, Jonathan S. "The Impact of Affirmative Action Regulation and Equal Employment Law on Black Employment," *Journal of Economic Perspectives*. Fall 1990, pp. 47-63.

Mills, Nicolaus, ed. *Debating Affirmative Action: Race, Gender, Ethnicity, and the Politics of Inclusion*. Dell Publishing, 1994.

1991 Guidebook to Fair Employment Practices. Commerce Clearing House, 1991.

Taylor, Bron Raymond. *Affirmative Action at Work: Law, Politics, and Ethics*. University of Pittsburgh Press, 1991.

Uri, Noel, et al. "Impact of Equal Employment Opportunity and Affirmative Action Programs on the Employment of Women in the U.S." *Labour*. Autumn 1991, pp. 89-104.

AFRICA, DOING BUSINESS IN

Among Americans, the neglect of Black African business practice now enters its fourth decade. This is evident from even cursory glances at current business literature on global commerce. Books on Asia and Europe are common. Middle Eastern, South American, and (now) East European titles are expanding. Africa has almost disappeared. "Global" titles are perhaps the most misleading. One book teaches ways to "Do Business Like A Pro Around The World," meaning Europe, Asia, South America, and the Middle East. A second, speaks to "international business women of the 1990s," suggesting ways to cope with (male) Europeans, Latins, Arabs, and Asians. A third analyzes anti-American feeling in Europe, Pakistan, China, Russia, and even Canada. In 1993 the Annual World Economic Forum, a respected gathering of leading policy analysts, corporate executives, and political leaders, convened to consider the most pressing problems of every global region—except Africa.

Black Africa is our commercial blind spot. One writer calls it "the most exotic place Americans can imagine—and the last place to contemplate doing business." In fact, Africa is a "closet millionaire," hiding both mineral wealth and agricultural potential. Gold, diamonds, chromium, platinum, manganese, uranium, "sweet" oil, hydroelectric power, and millions of acres in farmland permit us to spend $10 billion yearly for goods from that continent including one-third of our imported oil. In short, Africa was always wealthy. As a consequence, its businessmen developed complex, sophisticated business traditions that go back a thousand years. Surely they have something to teach.

There are two reasons we ignore African commercial methods. First, some lie outside the normal range of American commercial thought. We simply have no parallels for what they do and can't see why they do it. Most African firms are structured, for instance, along lines of an extended family, rather than along the chain of vertical command we draw from military models. Company interactions are thus based on kinship obligations, rather than the supervisor/subordinate relationships we internalize and expect. Few U.S. business people have extended families, thus few know how they function. Lacking these parallels, how can they understand the operation of an African extended family-firm, where 300 employees may be related? And lacking that understanding, how can they deal with that type of firm effectively?

We also object to the African tradition of commercial ambiguity. When doing business, Americans seek precision and predictable results. Therefore we formalize business procedures to make them predictable. This is true in our workplaces, where we insist on machines that work as advertised. It is true in our commercial proposals, which we compose expecting predictable results. It is even true with our subordinates, whom we train to behave in predictable fashion. It is reflected in our rising need to quantify even obviously intangible data, both to forecast future actions and evaluate the past. We take pride in commercial predictability.

In contrast, Africans take equal pride in commercial ambiguity. Certain facets of their historical, literary, and social tradition actually work against being specific. Oratorical traditions, for instance, encourage verbal ambiguity as a form of verbal art. Thus, business is most artfully conducted through the use of proverbs, with each side delighting in its ability to decipher hidden meanings thus permitting speech to flow at several levels. West Africans consider it a mark of eloquence to flavor speech with them. East Africans feel that stating an exact amount (whether cattle, commercial goods or contraband) will bring calamity. Central Africans learn that stating specifics is abrupt and rude, while adding verbal ambiguities lends ''spice'' and ''grace'' to conversation. In each case, the verbal goal—for which we once more have no parallel—is not commercial efficiency but conversational skill.

Africans cite solid social reasons to justify these customs. For Americans to dismiss them in favor of our ways may simply create anxiety among African counterparts. Intellectually they know what we expect. Emotionally they prefer their ways. That makes us anxious in turn. One option is to continue to ignore African commercial traditions. A second is to adjust to them and deal with African firms by learning how they do business.

IS THERE A "TYPICAL AFRICAN FIRM?"

Few African firms can be considered ''typical'' because each one displays peculiarities reflective of its region, tribe, linguistic group, and even family background. Thus, firms from our research zones in Central, West, and Eastern Africa do differ. Nonetheless, many African companies organize, finance, manage, and market their commercial concepts in surprisingly similar ways, all of which are rooted in centuries of common tradition. Five of these traits, however, are of particular interest to U.S. Business.

AFRICAN FIRM EQUALS AFRICAN (EXTENDED) FAMILY

Many African firms are structured like African families. In Africa, however, families are defined as all people descended from a single founder. Many families trace their ancestors back 20 generations. Thus, ''families'' extend outward to include scores or even hundreds of members, each of whom knows their precise relationship to everyone else. At one point, many of these ''extended'' families entered commerce, first locally, and then across borders. Today, many operate across several African regions and have extended their commercial reach into Europe and America. These firms are neither small nor primitive. They do not match the global scope of U.S. mega-corporations, nonetheless, they are large enough to have acquired international sophistication.

RURAL ROOTS/URBAN ADAPTATION

Many of these ''extended family firms'' use business methods taken from earlier eras, where rural families learned to work together in times of need. In those days, the crises were mainly agricultural. Nowadays, they are commercial, as families left the land and migrated to what they called ''the city.'' In fact, most migrate only to the outskirts of cities, settling within a point along the outer edges already inhabited by migrants from a related tribe.

Surrounded by urban neighbors with the same languages, culture, and commercial values, founding members of future firms began to adapt their rural methods to the new surroundings. These rural methods were reshaped gradually, initially to meet urban needs and subsequently those of trans-national markets. Thus, one extended family firm in Senegal markets gold in Paris, and another wood carving firm (actually a clan) exports ''fake masks'' from West Africa to New York for the American antique trade. These methods, although rooted in Africa's collective past, work too effectively within contemporary commerce for us to ignore them.

WHITE SKIN/BLACK (AFRICAN) HEART

Some Americans believe that African firms they deal with operate along Western lines, using methods learned from former colonizers. Here, appearances deceive. Centuries of contact with foreign commerce have often blurred differences between African business traditions and the foreign practices with which they must contend. As a result, some firms have fully Westernized. Others, however, function best by blending local and foreign ideas. Informants describe this type of firm as having a "White skin and Black (African) heart." Sometimes, both styles function simultaneously. In others, one style (eg: punctuality) dominates in foreign interactions, while the other is reserved for personnel in-house. Thus, the American visiting an extended family firm in Ghana is likely to be met in Western-furnished offices, by Western educated counterparts with Western business titles. Nonetheless, he will not be dealing with a Western-oriented firm. Outside the offices and behind the scenes, the decision making process will be African.

Indeed, local commercial ideals remain intact within the minds of even the most "Westernized" African businessmen. This is particularly true of the current generation, nearly all of whom grew up in rural, tradition-ruled environments. Like Americans, they are programmed by their early upbringing with values that carry over into their commercial lives. These values "pull" at their emotions, offering intangible counterweights to foreign practices. It can be commercially useful for us to recognize this inner conflict, acknowledge Africa's collective lifestyle, then ponder how to modify our business strategies to work with it.

EXTERNAL STRUCTURE: THE KINSHIP FACTOR

Compare, for example, the external structure of U.S. firms with those in West/Central Africa. U.S. firms are structured like U.S. armies. We use a vertical pyramid, with a single head and clearly defined, linear chains of command. Within them, we prefer equally well defined divisions of labor, with each individual restricted to specific tasks. We define superior/subordinate obligations by written contract. Ideally, employment and promotion come solely through commercial merit. Many of us not only consider this the most effective structure but the only effective one, dismissing others as comparatively primitive.

In contrast, most African firms are structured like most African villages: where we might see clusters of dwellings, they see clusters of related households, holding an extended family. We perceive the outer structures; they see the inner relationships that bind them. As a result, they find it hard to explain their managerial structure in terms we understand. We expect commercial phrasing; they prefer kinship terminology. In short, there is no common frame of verbal reference.

One way to bridge that gap is by analogy. An extended family forms a firm in somewhat the same way as a clan might form a village over time, as a series of concentric circles. The founder, older and (usually) male, forms the core. He is surrounded by an inner circle of "age-mates," men of his own generation who have shared his life and a common body of commercial wisdom. A "middle" circle lies beyond them, consisting of their (middle age) sons. Members of the middle circle may have acquired modern commercial expertise and Western commercial languages, but they remain subordinate to their elders' wisdom. The criteria for advancement within this structure is not commercial merit but age.

This chronologically organized core is surrounded by increasingly fictional fringes. The firm may have several outer circles. Never neatly organized, they may overlap or hold more than one type of employee. Nearer ones include more distant blood kin (cousins, etc.), ritually created kin (in-laws, etc.) and fictional kin (comrades, etc.) who behave as if they were members of the founding family. More distant circles may hold "homeboys" (common background), tribal members, and anyone else with ties close enough to the firm to perceive it as family. The further from center, the more fictional this family membership becomes, with subordinates "acting out" kinship obligations without truly being kin.

Recast in commercial terms, this type of firm can be envisioned in five tiers. Imagine the founder at the peak surrounded by a "board of elders" who function as advisors and directors. The second level consists of middle aged supervisors ("sons," etc.), each heading departments composed largely of those related (as kin or comrades) to themselves. The third includes skilled workers (in-laws, old friends, home-boys, etc.), whose internal hierarchy is based less on kinship ties and age. Outside that is a level of apprentices, either grandsons or youngsters hired from allied families. Thus, this type of firm becomes the commercial reflection of a specific, extended family. The principle stays unchanged even if the firm expands, modernizes, and globalizes, evolving into a "kin-based corporation." Regardless of size, it functions according to the rules used for family relationships.

It seems prudent, therefore, for Americans considering African ventures to consider kinship as a business factor when first making contact with African firms. It can prove particularly important when financial and/or contractual obligations are first considered by both sides. If dealing with a single individual, for instance, why not ask to whom he/she is related? A person without kin may be an errant genius, but might also be an outcast on the social margins of his own community. If so, he may be cut off from many of the normal sources of data, supply, credit, advice, etc. that make commercial ventures grow.

If dealing with a group—be it family, clan or ethnic guild—the kinship factor can bring two other advantages. The commercial reliability of individuals are hard to judge, but the sheer viability of an extended family may make it easier to form opinions. Thereafter, once agreement is reached, the uniquely African combination of familial and communal pressures may do more to insure that its clauses will be followed than either written contracts or appeals to courts. Ultimately, you have nothing more to lose than capital; they will have an on-site reputation to retain.

IN-HOUSE AUTHORITY: THE AGE FACTOR

In U.S. firms, the main criteria for leadership is merit, whether derived from education, training, commercial effectiveness, or project know-how. In African firms, the primary criterion for leadership is age. Each of the concentric circles that make up a company is composed entirely of members older than their subordinates. As a result, in-house authority flows solely from older to younger employees, making no exceptions for those with foreign language-skills, commercial training, university education or even business know-how.

This pattern is based on a philosophy that equates greater age with greater experience and thus greater wisdom. Africans across the continent believe that aging cools the blood, thus permitting elders to consider problems rationally rather than in the heat of emotion. Socially, this means the task of elders is to cool the conflicts invariably generated by the hotter blood (emotionalism) of youth. Thus, within contemporary firms as within traditional societies, the young create conflicts while the aged use their greater wisdom to cool and resolve them.

The wisdom of age is also based on both intuition and emotion. This contrasts with U.S. beliefs. We believe that both intuition and emotions interfere with business. We try to suppress them in commercial settings so as to decide each issue rationally and even quantitatively. Africans disagree, believing wisdom acquired through a lifetime of experience may be best expressed in terms of how they feel about specific business projects, as well as the proposers. Such feelings need not be based on commercial expertise. Rather, they emerge intuitively through extensive in-house consultation among those concerned with each projected venture. Their shared lifetime experiences will provide increasingly accurate intuition as to how to behave.

Americans contemplating African ventures might thus consider age as a commercial factor. It could prove particularly useful when selecting personnel to launch the venture, once agreements are reached. Initially, that means considering the age of the potential project head. Would African counterparts consider him (or her) an elder, thus capable of wise decisions? Gender is no barrier to commercial respect in much of Africa. Youth, however, even when backed by expertise, will not be considered a substitute for age. A Kenya proverb declares:

"Show me a people where calves teach (the) bulls and I will show you (a nation of) madmen."

It is also wise to consider the age of those Africans with whom you deal. Ask what authority they hold in their own firm because key managerial, promotional, or marketing posts may be held by younger men—appointed for commercial, technical, or linguistic expertise. They may be particularly prominent in posts requiring contact with foreigners. Nonetheless, these youngsters may be partial (or even total) figureheads, outside the actual chain of command. In practice, the currents of in-house authority may flow back and forth among elders. It can prove useful, therefore, to request introductions to "older" members of the firm, even if translation is required. You might also refocus the terms of each proposal to appeal to "elder" personnel, since they must make final decisions.

DECISION-MAKING: THE TIME FACTOR

U.S. firms do not cope well with African **decision-making**. Two elements in that process clash with our expectations.

The first is that we seek individual decision makers, especially within commercial settings. Americans admire the ability to make decisions individually and seek that same capacity in those with whom we trade. We dismiss decisions made collectively as too difficult to achieve.

We also desire timeliness. Americans admire speed and decisiveness even within unstructured situations. In our slang, "to wing it" and "think on our feet" are considered praiseworthy. In contrast, most African businessmen prefer decisions to emerge through consultation. To be sure, a single **CEO** may make individual decisions as swiftly and with as much authority as executives in other cultures. In so doing, however, the CEO remains aware of membership in an extended family, and thus of obligations to both its current members and collective past. In acting alone, a single executive may flaunt his family's collective wisdom by accidentally ignoring the traditions that say he must consult. Conversely, by consulting significant comrades and kin, he can fulfill communal obligations. In sum, most Africans simply find it psychologically more satisfying to make decisions by consulting others.

Unfortunately, this method causes problems for Americans, who may not see the similarities with procedures of their own. Let us thus consider it in detail.

Stage One: Commercial Proposal. Assume, for instance, a U.S. project head proposes a potential venture to a Congolese firm. To do this by African standards, the American must first identify and then work through an introducer, someone already connected as kin or comrade to significant members of the targeted corporation's family. If the introducer holds that family's trust, it will be his recommendation that opens the commercial door. Ideally, the introducer would also teach the American the proper etiquette required to initiate a business contact, including presentation of traditionally expected gifts. In fact, all three elements (introduction, etiquette, gifts) may be prerequisite to initiating an appropriate commercial relationship. Traditionally, these acts symbolize the outsider's wish to "join" the family.

Stage Two: Outsider "Lisanga" (Consultation). At this stage, Americans fall victim to their expectations with regard to time. Having completed rituals of introduction, most Americans instantly present their proposal. That done, they expect a timely and decisive reply. In contrast, Africans expect to spend this stage in "lisanga" (consolation) with the outsider in order to evaluate both the proposer and the proposal. They place a higher value both on interpersonal relations and proper performance of specific social and ritual activities; they are prerequisites to important decisions. Both the relationships and rites surrounding a proposed economic transaction are as important as the proposal itself. Thus participation by both sides is prerequisite to creation of commercial trust.

To facilitate this, most Africans prefer their visitors to simply spend the next few days (or even weeks) in conversation, most often visiting and perhaps hosting elder members of the firm. Their goal is to lay the groundwork for a future business venture by seeking values both sides hold in common. This is most often done, according to a Congo proverb, by "sharing liquor, laughter and soft words." Unfortunately, many Americans regard such use of time as non-commercial and non-profitable. The prospect of spending days in conversation may dismay them. Angered at what seems to be indefinite procrastination, they may retire to hotels, not realizing there may be solid business reasons for such delay.

One reason is to let the lisanga take its course. As Americans idealize haste, Africans prefer a more deliberate tempo. The Congo proverb "night is the wisest advisor," reflects the wisdom inherent in taking ones problems home, to debate at leisure with family and friends. Thus, African executives may delay their response to a proposal for as long as required for the consultative process to debate both proposal and proposer.

Stage Three: In-House Lisanga (Consultation). Americans might describe this stage as "in-house consultation." Africans call it "ndaba" (Zulu), "baraza" (Swahili), or "lisanga" (Congo). In each case it means a gathering of elders, each of whom is a spokesman for a larger group, to decide what action to take on a specific issue. In this example, the Congo CEO would convoke a "lisanga" of in-house elders, whom we might describe as a board of directors. They would assemble subjective opinions as well as hard data concerning both project and project head, with each "director" consulting relevant section heads and these consulting senior employees.

The lisanga process is simultaneously repeated outside the firm. We might call this "outside consultation." Thus, those who feel night is indeed the best advisor may seek advice from significant age-mates male elders, spiritual leaders, and "home-boys," as well as significant female elders/kin. This may include older wives, mothers, aunts, and grandmothers who may then consult other females outside the family.

Stage Four: Commercial Decision. African decision-making has neither a predictable rate of progress nor a predictable point of termination. We assume it will be slow. That need not be. The first three stages of lisanga can occur simultaneously and may also move swiftly. Conversely, the process may take as long as required to reach a decision benefiting all members of the group. Thus, it will not have a predictable termination time, despite the wishes of Americans—for it is their inability to predict when a decision will be made that draws our anger.

Thus, time must be considered as a commercial factor in every projected African venture. Once abroad, we joke bitterly about "African time," redefining it to mean indefinite delay and condemning those who use it. Instead, we might consider using time on African terms. When presenting a commercial proposal, for example, the following adjustments may be useful:

1. Initially, take time to both identify and cultivate an introducer. Choose someone with social class and family standing to compliment your own. Thereafter, take more time to nurture a relationship. Your goal is not to convince him of the quality of your product but of yourself.

2. Take still more time to understand, practice, and even actively prolong the rituals of introduction. Africans attach a higher value than Americans to both social and ceremonial activities. Many of these are religious, since Africans everywhere believe in ritually nurturing the existing bonds between objects, humans, and the supernatural. For Americans to regard these rituals as inciden-

tal, time-wasting, primitive, pagan, or non-commercial would be a serious error. In fact, the emotion generated by such rituals may prove critical in binding the participants to whatever future commitments will be made.

3. Take the most time to market yourself as well as your proposal. Follow local traditions: visit, play host, and converse. Learn local etiquette and local rituals as well as courtesies within the local language. Share not just food and drink, but something of your inner self. In Africa, this is doing business. You are sending a signal that you care for those with whom you hope to deal. In so doing, you create the groundwork for future business interaction.

STAFFING: THE NEPOTISM FACTOR

Equating the African firm with a fictional African family applies to both hiring and firing. Both are based on what we call nepotism. Work relations among employees are psychologically conditioned by pre-existing family relationships. In consequence, all members of a work group relate to one another in terms of family status rather than written contract. Thus in hiring, the firm simply extends its existing family structure, either to incorporate additional members of its own group, or those from allied groups it feels may become useful.

Under these circumstances, filling a post falls into the category of doing a favor. An in-house vacancy may exist, however, it may also be created as a favor to a kinsman, colleague, or comrade outside the firm who simply asks the appropriate in-house executive to hire someone to whom the outsider has ties. In such cases, rather than adapting the new worker to the post, the job itself may be reshaped to fit him. If he is skillful, it may expand. If not, it may diminish to allow him to be of more limited service.

Thus, few African firms employ by merit. Nor do they use Western ways to fill vacancies. They find no need for either written advertisements or standardized job interviews. Westerners may stigmatize this process as **nepotism**, but Africans call it caring for one's family.

Informants give three reasons for an African CEO to hire on request. One is to do a favor for the solicitor, thus placing him under future obligation. A second is to return a favor, thereby discharging a prior obligation. The third, and more complicated for U.S. observers, is to discharge an earlier obligation incurred by ones' parents or grandparents. Thus, a CEO can hire a youngster in return for a favor the boy's father did for his own father years ago. Neither elder might be alive; yet, the debt would be recalled on both

sides. A Zulu proverb expresses this succinctly: "To give is to store for your self."

Kenya provides one illustration of the system's effectiveness. The White owner of a large firm (120 employees) briefly left the region. He placed the company under an elderly Luo (African) supervisor. On leaving, 40 Luo were employed. On returning, 60 more were hired, jobs were redistributed by age and the firm ran along Luo lines. To the owner's surprise, employee turnover, customer complaints, and property damage fell steadily as the new corporate culture took hold. The arrangement was retained.

There are clear, commercial reasons for this type of staffing. A constant exchange of favors creates relationships and then alliances between potentially competitive groups. Two firms whose CEOs hire one another's kin are likely to find other areas in which to cooperate. Other favors can be exchanged in times of need: credit lines open, costs are shared, etc. In short, firms who hire their own kin extend their commercial reach; firms who hire the kin of friends may double it. Conversely, firing anyone can diminish that reach. In nations where other jobs are almost non-existent, terminating an employee stops support of an extended family. Thus, releasing individuals will not only harm them, but all others who rely on them. Worse, it will shame those kinsmen who originally requested their employment, thus eliminating them as future allies. I knew a Swazi colleague, for instance, who categorically refused to work. Unfortunately, those kin who asked my CEO to hire her were so useful to our venture that he dared not let her go. Instead, she was given increasingly symbolic tasks, to maintain her commercial dignity. In that instance, as in similar cases across Africa, firing can cost your firm relationships and consequently commercial harm.

Americans involved in Africa may therefore wish to re-examine their ideas on nepotism. In African settings, it is a valued business tool. Once you start to launch the venture, for example, your local partners may offer "help" in choosing your subordinates, using criteria unacceptable to most Americans. One option is to reject their advice, selecting staff according to U.S. criteria. A wiser alternative is to accept the fact that nepotism works within specific foreign settings and consequently can work for you.

Nepotistic hiring can, for instance, become a useful on-site business tool by allowing you to place your partners under an initial obligation. By hiring their kin you do them favors, which magnify if you subsequently provide hands-on training in U.S. business skills. Hiring their kin can also solidify your own work place relationships, by acting along African lines. From that perspective, you can become a "second father" to those new subordinates. They, in turn, can become work place sons.

These relationships are not symbolic; they are quite real to those involved. Failure to maintain them, even in industrial settings, causes instant complaint. One Nigerian supervisor, for instance, was called before his own elders to answer formal charges by a kinsman in his firm. The complaint was that the supervisor did not treat him like a kinsman when at work. By hiring kinsmen of your partners and treating them as family, you place their sponsors under double obligation. They will react with corresponding favors at your request. If you respond in turn, relationships will gradually develop. Over time, you will discover you have gained not only business partners but genuine allies.

CLIENT RELATIONS: THE MARKETING FACTOR

African firms use three marketing methods to gain and retain clientele. Like staffing, these are based on the premise that new clients (like new employees) represent additions to the family. Each client represents a new relationship. Each new relationship represents an extension of the firm's commercial reach. The more extensive that reach, the more secure its members feel. A Congolese proverb expresses this ideal: "Money cannot carry you. Money cannot bury you. Only people can." When Americans do business, they seek new sources of long-term profit. When Africans do this, they seek new, long-term relationships. In their system, wealth is not only tallied in currency, but also in the number of people who will aid each other on request.

THE HOMEBOY STRATEGY. One favored strategy is to market primarily to (and through) "homeboys." A homeboy is one with whom an individual shares elements of a common past, such as common values, ideals, and commercial aspirations. Thus, homeboys across Africa base this relationship on having shared:

- Childhood (Congo: "We have shared the same shirt.").

- Transition to adulthood (Kenya: "We have shared the same knife [i.e. circumcision]").

- Education/military training (same schools, military units, etc.).

- Dialect or language; village or region; tribe or nation.

Homeboys address each other both with this term and family names (e.g., "brother"), thus reflecting the obligation to treat one another as kin. This means they also accept kinship obligations. Like kin, any homeboy may ask (and must grant) favors of another. Thus, Africans seeking business favors turn first to kin and then to homeboys. Like real kin, they feel obligated to assist, even at inconvenience to themselves.

They do this for personal, social, and commercial reasons. Personally, each relationship they form intensifies their economic security. Socially, they gain the "moral satisfaction of making (our) ancestors proud."

Nowadays, however, the homeboy system also generates commercial benefits. The mother of a Congolese informant, for example, unexpectedly became CEO of her family's trucking firm. She began with little capital, driving through the countryside to collect produce to sell in the city. Wherever she went, farmers dropped their normal prices by half. On a personal level, they did so to help her get started. On a deeper, more communal level, they did it to repay favors done them (over decades) by her father and grandfather who had helped them as needed. Her time of crisis (in starting small) provided an opportunity to repay. Of course, the kindness carried the expectation that she would repay, as her suppliers (or their children) moved into crisis in their turn.

The homeboy system also operates in urban business settings, where homeboys may exchange business favors or simply become clientele. Africans become involved, on an intensely personal level, with all suppliers, distributors, clients, distant government bureaucrats, and anyone else who might affect their firm. They feel unable to control these people, unless they are involved in relationships that make them family. U.S. firms must realize that this need for involvement may also work for them. Those who display respect for the existing system and learn to play by local rules may find they are creating homeboy status for themselves.

THE FUTURE FAVOR STRATEGY. A second strategy to acquire clients is through use of the future favor. More complex than a simple exchange of services, this system adds dimensions of kinship and time that have no American parallels. One method is to exchange favors between equals. It begins when one person provides another with a favor on request, without asking for repayment. The recipient, though grateful, may not return a comparable favor until asked. Such an appeal may not come for weeks, months, years, or entire generations. When it does, however, the recipient (or his descendants) will feel a moral obligation to respond. That response does not cancel the interaction, as it would in the United Sates. Rather, it re-obligates the original provider to reciprocate in turn, thus continuing an exchange of services explicitly intended to last indefinitely.

Relationships emerge from the inner feelings generated by this constant giving and receiving, reflecting ties far stronger than those that would result from payment. Assume, for instance, that a U.S. project head seeks high level contacts within a Gambian ministry. If he pays a Gambian a preset fee to introduce him, the firm incurs no further obligation because the act of payment ends the relationship. If the Gambian refuses the fee, however, he has performed a favor. In consequence, the relationship between both men has changed. The American incurs an obligation. He can return the favor and thus eliminate both obligation and relationship. But if the Gambian, familiar with local business practice, provides a steady trickle of new favors, essentially guiding the American through the social and commercial minefields of local commerce, logically, the American's sense of obligation should intensify. Nonetheless, as his own familiarity with local business practice expands, his methods of reciprocation should grow more refined as well. As that occurs, the Gambian should feel obligated in his turn. Ideally, since both the U.S. and the African firms receive family benefit from the alliance, the relationship should continue throughout their business lives.

ENFORCED OBLIGATION: THE "BIG MAN" STRATEGY. Future favors can also be exchanged between a superior and a subordinate. In Northern Nigeria, for instance, the wealthy follow what Americans might call a "big man" strategy. This means they strive to gain communal (and thus commercial) status through self-serving generosity, providing gifts and favors to a group of "little brothers" explicitly intended to place them permanently under obligation. It is this generosity that separates "big men" from merely wealthy ones. Rich men live in isolation; "big men" live in communal splendor, symbolically surrounded by an entourage of "little brothers" who help them socially and commercially upon request.

There is no shame, however, in the little brother role. It connotes no inferiority. Inequalities of wealth are part of life. In consequence, subordinates play out their roles with pride; the very act of reciprocity provides social status. Unable to monetarily repay the big man's greater generosity, they respond with smaller but continuous acts of deference, service, and support in order to remind society that they remain aware of larger obligations. They also periodically reaffirm their subordinate status by asking favors: loans, advice, protection, etc. Meanwhile, their time, skills, and political support are at their patron's beck and call.

WORKING THE SYSTEM

The homeboy, favors, and Big Man strategies are clearly interwoven. On a personal level, they function as recruiting tools, drawing useful individuals into potentially profitable groups. On a communal level, they maintain harmony within those groups by forging obligations among members so as to generate good will. On a more modern, commercial level, they strengthen family firms through methods (unknown in the West) that generate cooperation, alliance, and

even merger with other commercial units. Most important, on an international level these methods provide tools we can use to work within the system.

There is a logical first step for Americans to take when starting a venture in Africa. If they lack first-hand knowledge of local markets, they can begin by enlisting key foreign contacts as company allies. Many U.S. personnel ignore this option, focusing on product presentation from the moment they arrive. In contrast, Africans focus first upon the marketing environment wherein their product must survive, seeking to identify both local rules and major players. Their interest is on forming ties that will allow them to fit in. Only then do they consider positioning their product.

In cultures where placing others under obligation has become a business tool, consider using generosity to generate allies. There are only two effective rules:

GIVE FIRST. By providing an initial favor, whether personal or commercial, Americans can show they seek long term relationships instead of short term sales. By placing others under obligation, they show their wish for an alliance in the form of other favors in the future.

KEEP GIVING. We find it easy to give, but harder to keep giving. U.S. recipients must reciprocate or givers will feel exploited. However, few cultures share this pattern. In nations marked by massive gaps between rich and poor, it is recurrent acts of generosity that symbolize wealth and confer status. When U.S. firms that mean to market in these countries have wealth and seek status, it seems wiser to give than to receive. Moreover, it seems best to give often, if by so doing, we both show respect for local customs and seek to form alliances on local terms.

When forming an alliance, most Americans prefer the big man role. Notwithstanding, that of little brother may prove more useful. On arrival in a foreign zone, use on-site inexperience as a business tool. Spend your first weeks asking about local rules and active players. Ask questions. Ask favors. Take on obligations. By playing little brother you allow your hosts to become big men, guiding you across the shoals of local commerce. By doing that, you do them honor. Rest assured you will eventually be paid in kind.

Consider linking your firm with one (or more) African companies, on their terms. Seek to develop local relationships into lifetime bonds. While it is true that homeboys share a common past, that need not shut out Americans. One former Peace Corps friend is ex-teacher and current homegirl to 90 Gambians. If you lack a common past, however, try to create a common present: become family to members of a local firm, then let bonds grow deeper of their own accord. That, in turn, will mean approaching African business from an African perspective, an attitude that can be expressed most clearly with one final Congo proverb:

Your son is my son. Your friend is my friend.

Your cares are my cares. Are we not brothers?

SEE ALSO: East African Community (EAC); Economic Community of West African States (ECOWAS)

[Jeffrey Andrew Fadiman]

FURTHER READING:

Ahiauzu, A.I. "The Theory: A System of Work Organization for the Modern African Workplace," *International Studies of Management & Organization*. 1989.

Ahiauzu, A.I. "The African Thought System & Work Behavior of the African Industrial Man," *International Studies of Man & Organization*. 1986.

Blunt, Peter. "Organizational Theory & Behaviour," *Modern Management in Africa*. Longman.

Chesanow, N. *The World Class Executive: How To Do Business Like a Pro Around the World*. Rawson Associates, 1985.

Dia, Mamadou. "Development & Cultural Values in Sub-Saharan Africa," *Finance & Development, International Monetary Fund & World Bank*. Dec., 1991.

Jones, M.L. "Management Development: An African Focus," *International Studies of Management & Organization*. 1989.

Rossman, M.L. *The International Businesswoman of the 1990s*. Praeger, 1986.

Schissel, Howard. "Africa's Underground Economy," *Africa Report*. Jan.-Feb., 1989.

AGE AND EMPLOYMENT

Historically, the issue of age has been a factor in employment in several ways. One way is the minimum age for employment. The set of laws governing this circumstance are the Child Labor Laws. States have child labor provisions and the federal government's statutory requirements governing the age of entrance into the labor market are the child Labor Laws, a part of the **Fair Labor Standards Act of 1938**.

Age is also a factor for retirement (i.e., leaving the workforce either on a voluntary or involuntary basis). Prior to 1994, companies could set mandatory retirement ages. Certain professions requiring a high degree of physical agility, such as law enforcement and fire fighting could set standards.

For many years the positive or negative treatment of employees based on their age was not a recognized area for complaint under federal law, but with the passage of the Age Discrimination in Employment Act (ADEA) in 1967, the issue of discrimination in the workplace on the basis of age has become a significant factor in complaints of discrimination in the workforce. An April 1994 article in INC. magazine indicated that over the last 20 years litigation under the ADEA and similar legislation has increased over 2,000%. The cost to employers of the litigation and to employees in the form of lost income and benefits has been immense.

More and more the phrase "age and employment" has come to mean how older workers are treated on the job. This issue has become more significant over the years because of the dollars involved in litigation by workers who claim that they have suffered age discrimination.

The Equal Employment Opportunity Commission (EEOC) reported in the December 13, 1993 *New York Times* that it handled 19,884 complaints of discrimination based on age during the 1993 fiscal year (ending Sept. 30, 1993). This figure represented a 32% increase over the 1989 fiscal year. The *New York Times* attributed this increase in complaints by older workers to the restructuring of corporations and the economic slump of the late 1980s and early 1990s.

Legal protection for workers on the basis of age is guaranteed for American workers through three pieces of federal law in addition to whatever other provisions a particular State may make. Part of the purpose of the already mentioned ADEA (Public Law 90-202) was, according to the Congressional mandate included in the law, "to promote employment of older persons on their ability rather than age [and] to prohibit arbitrary age discrimination in employment." The ADEA prohibits age discrimination in hiring, discharge, pay, promotions, and other areas. Retaliation by the employer against someone who brings a complaint under the ADEA or who participates in an investigation of a complaint brought under the act is also expressly designated as illegal. The law applies to private employers of 20 or more persons and to federal, state, and local governments and labor organizations with 25 or more members. As of 1988, the law also protected pension benefits for older workers under certain conditions. The ADEA, in section 12(c)(1), does not prohibit the compulsory retirement of certain bona fide executives or high policymakers, however.

Originally the administration of the enforcement of the ADEA was a function of the U.S. Department of Labor. Effective January 1, 1979 all functions relating to the administration and enforcement of the ADEA were transferred to the Equal Employment Opportunity Commission (EEOC) under the President's Reorganization Plan No. 1. The EEOC was created by Congress to enforce the Title VII provisions of the Civil Rights Act of 1964. The EEOC receives and investigates employment discrimination charges based not only on age, but also on race, color, religion, sex, national origin, and disability for both private and public employees.

The Older Workers Benefit Protection Act (OWBPA), enacted 10-16-90 and effective 4-15-91, clarified that employee benefits and pension plans are subject to the ADEA and codified EEOC regulations relating to age discrimination.

Since the passage of the ADEA and the OWPBA, the issue of age discrimination has continued to be studied by both employer and employee groups. The extended longevity predicted for today's worker means that more older workers will be physically capable of remaining in the labor market for a longer period of time.

The book *New Work Opportunities for Older Americans* documents the continued presence of older people in the workplace both for necessity and due to a genuine desire to work. The book also is a guide to resources for older people wishing to prolong their stay in the workplace or seeking to reenter after an absence.

Quoting from data published by The Commonwealth Fund, the books' author notes that 9.9 million Americans 55 and older are working full time, and another 4.4 million are working part time. Of the 26.4 million he finds not working, the data showed that 6.3 million were unable to work, but 5.4 million were willing and able to work.

Older women in particular reenter the workforce in large numbers. Their economic need to do so is cited in Menchin's book: women comprise nearly 70 percent of the 4 million persons over 65 years of age who live in poverty in America.

At one time the ideal for older Americans was depicted as a blissful time of leisure: days of golf, bocci, and bridge were easily funded with a social security check and possibly a private pension. Now the elderly need to reenter the workforce for monetary reasons and may, according to Menchin, also reenter for mental stimulation, prestige, a sense of involvement, or to reclaim their identity.

The need for continued vigilance against Age discrimination as late as 1994, almost 30 years after the passage of the age discrimination legislation, is noted by several cases and a 1994 study by the American Association of Retired Persons (AARP). The January 19, 1994 Boston Globe newspaper reported on a case of age discrimination involving women applying for jobs at four of Boston's retailers. Women over 45 years of age found few offers while at the same stores, women in their 20s found plenty of job offers. On February 23, 1994, the *Wall Street Journal* (WSJ) reported on the AARP's most recent study of job discrimination. The results showed that older people are being discriminated against in job offers. The

AARP had sent almost identical resumes for two people to 775 large corporations. The AARP found that a little over twenty-five percent of the companies discriminated against the fictional older person.

HOW TO FILE AN AGE DISCRIMINATION CLAIM

Each particular protection administered and enforced by the EEOC has its own set of regulations governing the time frames for filing a complaint and procedures to be followed. Under the ADEA, charges may be filed by an aggrieved individual or by another person on behalf of that individual . But the charges must be filed within 180 days of the alleged discriminatory act. If a State has a discrimination law, then a proceeding must be filed first with the authorizing State agency as a prerequisite to a private suit under ADEA. In those cases where there is a State filing, the time limits for filing with EEOC change to within 300 days of the alleged discriminatory act or 30 days after the State terminates its processing of the charge, whichever is earlier.

The ADEA offers confidentiality to the aggrieved individual. Charges may be filed with the EEOG by the aggrieved party or a representative in person, by mail, or by telephone. There are EEOC offices located around the country. For a list of offices and a publication explaining protection under the ADEA and the other laws that the EEOC enforces, call toll free 1-800-669-4000 or TDD 800-800-3302. Regional offices can be found by looking in the local telephone directory in the federal government section. The "Information for the Private Sector and State and Local Governments-EEOC, EEOC-BRP-E" booklet is available in large print, Braille, or on tape and may be requested by mail as well as in writing from the Office of Equal Employment Opportunity.

THE BUSINESS WORLD AND DISCRIMINATION

A very comprehensive article, from the business person's viewpoint, on the issue of discrimination in the workplace and its cost to business appeared in the April 1994 issue of INC. magazine. The article concluded that while there is still discrimination in the workplace, the awards granted in these cases often have been ruinous and an abuse of the legal system. The article posits that a drop in labor-union memberships left the federal discrimination laws as the only recourse for what normally would have been settled in the union grievance procedure. The four areas where INC. sees most of the legal activity is Title VII, ADEA, Americans with Disabilities Act and the Civil Rights Act of 1991. The INC. article concludes that while there is no way to "lawyer-proof" a company, the best defense is to implement a comprehensive preventive strategy. An example is Community Bank of Homestead. The bank, located in a hurricane-ravaged suburb south of Miami, has developed a strategy that has allowed it to remain out of court, despite the need for layoffs, at least through the date of the article. The strategy includes screening for new applicants including a test that measures detail attention, patience and competitiveness. The interviewer knows what questions cannot be asked and does not ask them. These include such things as age, marital status, and even if the prospect owns a car. Instead, the interviewer concentrates on open-ended questions that allow people to talk about themselves and sets forth the ground rules for working at the bank in a handbook. Futhermore the bank has a progressive system of evaluation, documentation, and action to be followed by all supervisors. Finally, and what is noted in the article as most important, the bank tries to create a good working environment. As the interviewer says, ''Our philosophy is that if we're good to our employees, they are going to be good to our customers.'' Good employee relations equal good business—on both sides of the counter.

SEE ALSO: Child Labor

[Joan Leotta]

FURTHER READING:

Menchir, Robert S. *New Work Opportunities for Older Americans*. Prentice Hall, 1993.

AGENCY FOR INTERNATIONAL DEVELOPMENT (AID)

The Agency for International Development (AID) is part of the U.S. International Development Corporation Agency and both organizations share a common chief administrator. AID was organized under Re-Organization Plan No. 2 of 1979 (5 U.S.C. app.) and Executive Order # 12163 of September 1979. AID administers programs under authorization of the Foreign Assistance Act of 1961 and is overseen by the U.S. Department of State.

The purpose of AID is to administer and promote economic assistance to developing countries around the globe. The agency is divided into three geographic bureaus: Africa, Latin America (which includes the Caribbean region), and Asia. With the disintegration of the Soviet Union, AID has also begun programs in eastern and central Europe and some of the former Soviet republics. Overall, AID administers programs in nearly 100 countries.

AID programs are administered at four different levels depending on the scope of involvement. An AID Mission directs programs in countries which receive major programs and multiple types of assistance. AID Offices are established in countries receiving moderate aid or are involved in programs with limited objectives. AID Offices and Missions are downgraded to Sections of Embassy when programs are being phased out or for small scale programs with immediate or narrowly defined objectives. AID Offices for Multi-Country Programs administer programs involving the cooperation of more than one country. There is also a Development Assistance Coordination and Representation Office which serves as a liaison with international organizations. The Audit and Investigations Office is responsible for on-site audits and inspections and reports to the Office of the Inspector General.

AID programs for economic and human resource development operate under the aegis of four beliefs. A market economy and free fomarket forces are necessary for the stimulation of internal economic growth and for encouraguing American private sector investment. Economic growth is dependent upon sound economic decision making and rational policy formulation on the part of the host country. Institutional development within the host country such as the implementation of training centers, funding for colleges and universities, and the structuring of new and relevant government agencies is often necessary. Finally, economic expansion is dependent upon technology transfer from more developed nations.

Within a framework of democracy and market economics, AID programs attempt to focus on various areas of activity at the grass roots level. Health care is a major focus of AID programs especially pediatric health care. In this regard AID assistance focuses on preventive medicine especially immunization, sanitation, and public health programs. AID is also active in HIV/AIDS prevention and educational programs. AID also promotes necessary changes in those institutions that are responsible for health care in the host country.

AID has programs which deal with the population problems of developing countries. Host countries are prioritized as to the severity of their over-population problems and AID resources are focused on countries most in need of assistance. Birth control and family planning are then vigorously promoted in high priority countries. The overall goal of these programs, however, is to deal with overpopulation as a global problem and not to isolate the problem to one particular country.

AID also has programs promoting environmental awareness, natural resource management, agricultural utilization of developing bio-technology, human nutrition, energy utilization, and housing development. AID has policies which encourage private sector development and a Food for Peace program which provides U.S. agricultural commodities for famine areas and countries whose population is suffering from acute malnutrition. AID also has a unique International Disaster Assistance Program which coordinates aid to victims of natural and man-made disasters.

[Michael Knes]

AGENCY THEORY

Agency theory suggests that the firm can be viewed as a nexus of contracts between resource holders. An agency relationship arises whenever one or more individuals, called principals, hire one or more other individuals, called agents, to perform some service and then delegate decision-making authority to the agents. The primary agency relationships are those (1) between stockholders and managers and (2) between debtholders and stockholders. Accordingly, agency theory has emerged as a dominant model in the financial economics literature.

CONFLICTS BETWEEN MANAGERS AND SHAREHOLDERS

Agency theory raises a fundamental problem in organizations—self-interested behavior. A corporation's managers may have personal goals that compete with the owner's goal of maximization of shareholder wealth. Since the shareholders authorize managers to administer the firm's assets, a potential conflict of interest is created between the two groups.

Agency theory suggests that, in imperfect labor and capital markets, managers will seek to maximize their own utility at the expense of corporate shareholders. Agents have the ability to operate in their own self-interest rather than in the best interests of the firm because of asymmetric information or uncertainty. Evidence of self-interested managerial behavior includes the consumption of some of the corporate resources in the form of perquisites and the avoidance of optimal risk positions whereby risk-averse managers bypass profitable opportunities in which the firm's shareholders would prefer they invest. Outside investors recognize that the firm will make decisions contrary to their best interests. Accordingly, investors will discount the prices they are willing to pay for the firm's securities.

A potential agency conflict arises whenever the manager of a firm owns less than 100 percent of the firm's common stock. If a firm is a sole proprietorship managed by the owner, the owner-manager will undertake actions to maximize his or her own welfare. The owner-manager will probably measure utility by personal wealth, but may trade off other considera-

tions, such as leisure and perquisites, against personal wealth. If the owner-manager forgoes a portion of his or her ownership by selling some of the firm's stock to outside investors, a potential conflict of interest, called an agency conflict, arises. For example, the owner-manager may now prefer a more leisurely lifestyle and not work as vigorously to maximize shareholder wealth, because less of the wealth will now accrue to the owner-manager. In addition, the owner-manager may decide to consume more perquisites, because some of the cost of the consumption of benefits will now be borne by the outside shareholders.

In the majority of large publicly traded corporations, agency conflicts are potentially quite significant because the firm's managers generally own only a small percentage of the common stock. Therefore, shareholder wealth maximization could be subordinated to an assortment of other managerial goals. For instance, managers may have a fundamental objective of maximizing the size of the firm. By creating a large, rapidly growing firm, executives increase their own status, create more opportunities for lower- and middle-level managers and salaries, and enhance their job security because an unfriendly takeover is less likely. As a result, incumbent management may pursue diversification at the expense of the shareholders who can easily diversify their individual portfolios simply by buying shares in other companies.

Managers can be encouraged to act in the stockholders' best interests through incentives, constraints, and punishments. These methods, however, are effective only if shareholders can observe all of the actions taken by managers. A moral hazard problem, whereby agents take unobserved actions in their own self interests, originates because it is infeasible for shareholders to monitor all managerial actions. To reduce the moral hazard problem, stockholders must incur agency costs.

Agency costs are defined as those costs borne by shareholders to encourage managers to maximize shareholder wealth rather than behave in their own self-interests. There are three major types of agency costs: (1) expenditures to monitor managerial activities, such as audit costs; (2) expenditures to structure the organization in a way that will limit undesirable managerial behavior, such as appointing outside members to the board of directors; and (3) opportunity costs which are incurred when shareholder-imposed restrictions, such as requirements for shareholder votes on specific issues, limit the ability of managers to take actions that advance shareholder wealth.

In the absence of efforts by shareholders to alter managerial behavior, there will typically be some loss of shareholder wealth due to inappropriate managerial actions. On the other hand, agency costs would be excessive if shareholders attempted to ensure that every managerial action conformed with shareholder interests. Therefore, the optimal amount of agency costs to be borne by shareholders should be viewed in a cost-benefit context—agency costs should be increased as long as each incremental dollar spent results in at least a dollar increase in shareholder wealth.

MECHANISMS FOR DEALING WITH SHAREHOLDER-MANAGER CONFLICTS

There are two polar positions for dealing with shareholder-manager agency conflicts. At one extreme, the firm's managers are compensated entirely on the basis of stock price changes. In this case, agency costs will be low because managers have great incentives to maximize shareholder wealth. It would be extremely difficult, however, to hire talented managers under these contractual terms because the firm's earnings would be affected by economic events that are not under managerial control. At the other extreme, stockholders could monitor every managerial action, but this would be extremely costly and inefficient. The optimal solution lies between the extremes, where executive compensation is tied to performance, but some monitoring is also undertaken. In addition to monitoring, the following mechanisms encourage managers to act in shareholders' interests: (1) performance-based incentive plans, (2) direct intervention by shareholders, (3) the threat of firing, and (4) the threat of takeover.

Most publicly traded firms now employ performance shares, which are shares of stock given to executives on the basis of performances as defined by financial measures such as earnings per share, return on assets, return on equity, and stock price changes. If corporate performance is above the performance targets, the firm's managers earn more shares. If performance is below the target, however, they receive less than 100 percent of the shares. Incentive-based compensation plans, such as performance shares, are designed to satisfy two objectives. First, they offer executives incentives to take actions that will enhance shareholder wealth. Second, these plans help companies attract and retain managers who have the confidence to risk their financial future on their own abilities—which should lead to better performance.

An increasing percentage of common stock in corporate America is owned by institutional investors such as insurance companies, pension funds, and mutual funds. The institutional money managers have the clout, if they choose, to exert considerable influence over a firm's operations. Institutional investors can influence a firm's managers in two primary ways. First, they can meet with a firm's management and provide suggestions regarding the firm's operations. Second, institutional shareholders can sponsor a proposal which must be voted on at the annual stockholders' meeting, even though the proposal is opposed by management. Although such shareholder-sponsored proposals are nonbinding and involve issues outside day-to-day operations, the results of these votes clearly influence management opinion.

In the past, the likelihood of a large company's management being ousted by its stockholders was so remote that it posed little threat. This was true because the ownership of most firms was so widely distributed, and management's control over the voting mechanism so strong, that it was almost impossible for dissident stockholders to obtain the necessary votes required to remove the managers. In recent years, however, the chief executive officers at American Express Co., General Motors Corp., IBM, and Kmart have all resigned in the midst of institutional opposition and speculation that their departures were associated with their companies' poor operating performance.

Hostile takeovers, which occur when management does not desire to sell the firm, are most likely to develop when a firm's stock is undervalued relative to its potential because of inadequate management. In a hostile takeover, the senior managers of the acquired firm are typically dismissed, and those who are retained lose the independence they had prior to the acquisition. The threat of a hostile takeover disciplines managerial behavior and induces managers to attempt to maximize shareholder value.

STOCKHOLDERS VERSUS CREDITORS: A SECOND AGENCY CONFLICT

In addition to the agency conflict between stockholders and managers, there is a second class of agency conflicts—those between creditors and stockholders. Creditors have the primary claim on part of the firm's earnings in the form of interest and principal payments on the debt as well as a claim on the firm's assets in the event of bankruptcy. The stockholders, however, (through the firm's managers) have control of the operating decisions that affect the cash flows and risk of the firm. Creditors lend capital to the firm at rates that are based on the riskiness of the firm's existing assets and on the firm's existing capital structure of debt and equity financing, as well as on expectations concerning changes in the riskiness of these two variables.

The shareholders, acting through management, have an incentive to induce the firm to take on new projects that have a greater risk than was anticipated by the firm's creditors. The increased risk will raise the required rate of return on the firm's debt, which in turn will cause the value of the outstanding bonds to fall. If the risky capital investment project is successful, all of the benefits will go to the firm's stockholders, because the bondholders' returns are fixed at the original low-risk rate. If the project fails, however, the bondholders are forced to share in the losses. On the other hand, shareholders may be reluctant to finance beneficial investment projects. Shareholders of firms undergoing financial distress are unwilling to raise additional funds to finance positive net present value projects because these actions will benefit bondholders more than shareholders by providing additional security for the creditors' claims.

Managers can also increase the firm's level of debt, without altering its assets, in an effort to leverage up stockholders' return on equity. If the old debt is not senior to the newly issued debt, its value will decrease, because a larger number of creditors will have claims against the firm's cash flows and assets. Both the riskier asset and the increased leverage transactions have the effect of transferring wealth from the firm's bondholders to the stockholders.

Shareholder-creditor agency conflicts can result in situations in which a firm's total value declines but its stock price rises. This occurs if the value of the firm's outstanding debt falls by more than the increase in the value of the firm's common stock. If stockholders attempt to expropriate wealth from the firm's creditors, bondholders will protect themselves by placing restrictive covenants in future debt agreements. Furthermore, if creditors believe that a firm's managers are trying to take advantage of them, they will either refuse to provide additional funds to the firm or will charge an above-market interest rate to compensate for the risk of possible expropriation of their claims. Thus, firms which deal with creditors in an inequitable manner either lose access to the debt markets or face high-interest rates and restrictive covenants, both of which are detrimental to shareholders.

Management actions which attempt to usurp wealth from any of the firm's other stakeholders, including its employees, customers, or suppliers are handled through similar constraints and sanctions. For example, if employees believe that they will be treated unfairly, they will demand an above-market wage rate to compensate for the unreasonably high likelihood of job loss.

[Robert T. Kleiman]

FURTHER READING:

Fama, Eugene, and Michael Jensen. "Agency Problems and Residual Claims." *Journal of Law and Economics.* 26, 1983, pp. 327-349.

Jensen, Michael C., and William H. Meckling. "Theory of the Firm, Managerial Behavior, Agency Costs, and Ownership Structure." *Journal of Financial Economics.* 3, October 1976, pp. 305-360.

Myers, Stewart, and Nicholas Majluf. "Corporate Financing and Investment Decisions When Firms Have Information That Investors Do Not Have." *Journal of Financial Economics.* 13, June 1984, pp. 187-221.

AGRIBUSINESS

Agribusiness is a broader term than agriculture. It combines production operations on the farm, the manufacture and distribution of supplies and equipment to be used on the farm, and the processing and distribution of farm commodities and items made from them. Its economic impact is significant; agribusiness is almost two times as large as the sum of all manufacturing enterprises (measured in total assets); it represents 40 percent of all consumer spending; and it employs 37 percent of the labor force.

The term "agribusiness" was coined by John Herbert Davis (1893-1967)and Ray A. Goldberg to reflect the two-way interdependence between businesspeople and farmers in the dual roles of suppliers and purchasers. Business firms that serve agriculture rely on farmers for their markets and for some of their supplies. By the same token, farms could not operate without businesses that manufacture farm supplies and those that store, process, and merchandise farm commodities.

In the early nineteenth century, agriculture was a self-contained industry. The typical farm family produced its own food, fuel, shelter, draft animals, feed, tools, implements, and even clothing. Only a few necessities had to be bartered for or purchased off the farm. The farm family performed virtually all operations pertaining to the production, processing, storage, and distribution of farm commodities. In the ensuing years, however, agriculture evolved from self-sufficiency to intricate interdependence with other segments of the economy, particularly those relating to the manufacture of production supplies and the processing and distribution of food and fiber products.

The agribusiness approach is a method of examining old problems or farm problems in a new and more comprehensive setting. One benefit from this approach has been the release of workers—farm manpower—from agriculture for employment in new non-farm occupations—including the armed forces during wars or the threats of war. This has resulted in tremendous economic growth and development and an improved standard of living.

Agribusiness consists of several million farm units and several thousand business units, each an independent entity, free to make its own decisions. Agribusiness is the sum total of hundreds of trade associations, commodity organizations, farm organizations, quasi-research bodies, conference bodies, and committees, each concentrating on its own interests. The U.S. government also is a part of agribusiness to the degree that it is involved in research, the regulation of food and fiber operations, and the ownership and trading of farm commodities. Land-grant colleges with their teaching, experiment stations, and extension functions form another sector of agribusiness. In summary, agribusiness exists in a vast mosaic of decentralized entities, functions, and operations relating to food and fiber.

The evolution from agricultural to agribusiness has brought with it numerous benefits. These include reduced drudgery for laborers; the release of workers for non-agricultural endeavors; a better quality of food and fibers; a greater variety of products; improved nutrition; and increased mobility of people. The release of farm manpower and the creation of new, off-the-farm jobs have been the basis for the country's economic growth and development for the last 150 years. The key to this growth and development has been increased worker productivity, which in turn spurs creativity, new products and wealth. This translates into risk captial, new factories, new jobs, and increased consumer purchasing power.

By releasing farm laborers and generating new, off-the-farm jobs in industries that manufacture farm supplies and process and distriute food and fiber products, the standard of living for all economic groups has gradually risen. This improved standard of living, in turn, means greater food value can be purchased and less drudgery is required for the preparation of food at home.

In the fibers area, agribusiness technology has reduced the price of clothing (in terms of what an hour's wage will buy); increased the variety of fabrics (from natural to synthetics); popularized affordable, ready-made clothing; and provided fabrics for numerous industrial uses. Living standards have improved by reducing back-bendng labor and increasing time for education and recreation.

SEE ALSO: Commodities

[Susan Bard Hall]

FURTHER READING:

Davis, John Herbert, and Ray A. Goldberg. *A Concept of Agribusiness*, Boston: Harvard University, Division of Research, Graduate School of Business Administration, 1957.

AIDS IN THE WORKPLACE

Acquired immune deficiency syndrome (AIDS) is a disease that impairs the human immune system and renders it susceptible to infections that would be repelled by a functioning immune system. AIDS, the terminal stage of the human immune deficiency virus (HIV), is transmitted by contamination of the bloodstream with HIV-infected body fluids, specifically blood, semen, breast milk, and vaginal fluid. The virus is principally spread through vaginal or anal intercourse, by the transfusion of virus-contaminated blood, by the sharing of HIV-infected intravenous needles, or by breast-feeding. U.S. Centers for Disease Control (CDC) literature emphasizes that "no additional routes of transmission have been recorded, despite a national sentinel system designed to detect just such an occurrence." AIDS is not spread by casual physical contact, biting insects, or airborne means, and transmission through body fluids such as saliva and tears has never occurred. Once infected, the incubation period for people between five and six years old averages eight years before symptoms appear.

As of 1993, the World Health Organization estimated that eight to ten million people worldwide were infected with HIV. Through December 31, 1993, the CDC had received 361,509 reports of AIDS cases, including 317,106 cases in males and 44,403 cases in females. The CDC estimated that approximately one million Americans, or one in 250, were infected with HIV at that time. Over 220,800 Americans have died of the disease by 1994. The virus carries many legal and ethical implications for businesses.

First conclusively identified in 1981, the disease was known as "gay cancer" or GRID (gay related immuno-deficiency) in the United States because it appeared to be limited to male homosexuals. Its subsequent spread to intravenous drug users, hemophiliac recipients of contaminated transfusions (the U.S. blood supply was not screened for HIV until 1985), heterosexual females whose sexual partners had contracted AIDS, and their children contradicted that theory. Although homosexual males still comprise the majority of AIDS cases, it is clearly no longer limited to that segment of the population.

Estimates compiled by the CDC predicted that at least 40 million people worldwide would be infected with HIV by the turn of the 21st century. An economic analysis by DRI/McGraw-Hill, Inc. projected that "the potential worldwide economic impact of the worst-case scenario" could equal 1.4 percent of the global gross domestic product annually, "roughly equivalent to the entire economy of Australia or India today."

The majority of infected Americans in the early 1990s were between 25 and 44 years old, and members of that age group were most likely to be infected in the future. For the nation's businesses, this meant that 50 percent of the workforce was at risk. In the early 1990s, HIV/AIDS was the third leading cause of death among 25- to 44 year-olds, and the sixth leading cause of death among 15- to 24- year-olds.

Given a supportive work environment and early detection, however, people with HIV and AIDS could continue to be productive members of the workforce. Studies showed that for half of the people who had HIV, it would take more than a decade to develop AIDS. With medical treatment, many of them could manage the infection as a chronic, long-term condition, similar to many other medical disorders. The numbers of people with HIV and their extended life expectancy, presaged more employees on the job with HIV in the future. This, in turn, foreshadowed the fact that most, if not all, businesses would eventually have to deal directly with HIV-infected and AIDS-afflicted employees.

The Business Responds to AIDS (BRTA) program was formed December 1, 1992 as a public-private partnership among the CDC, the public health sector, other organizations and agencies, and business and labor to provide workplace education and community services in order to prevent the spread of HIV. The BRTA program assists businesses of all sizes in the creation and implementation of workplace-based HIV and AIDS policies. In addition to education, service, and prevention of the spread of HIV, the program's goals are to prevent discrimination and foster community service and volunteerism both in the workplace and in the community. In order to achieve these goals, the BRTA has developed materials and technical assistance to assist businesses in forming comprehensive HIV and AIDS programs including: policy development, training for management and labor leaders; education for employees and their families; community involvement; and volunteerism.

Many authorities, including the BRTA, advise that employers formulate a well thought out AIDS policy to preempt problems. Such a policy would incorporate a position statement and outline such issues as education, employee safety, and employee rights.

Corporate HIV and AIDS policies and practices should comply with federal, state, and local legislation and **Occupational Safety and Health Administration** (OSHA) guidelines. Federal laws regarding AIDS in the workplace include: Occupational Safety and Health Act of 1970 (OSHA), 29 U.S.C. Section 651, et seq.; The Vocational Rehabilitation Act of 1973 (VRA), 29 U.S.C. Section 701, et seq.; Section 510 of the Employee Retirement Income Security Act of 1974 (ERISA), 29 U.S.C. Section 10001 et seq.; The U.S. Consolidated Omnibus Budget Reconciliation Act of 1986 (COBRA), Pub. L. No. 99-272, Section 10001, et seq.; and Section 5 (a) of the **Americans with Disabilities Act** of 1990, Pub. L. No. 101-336. Section 101, et seq.

The July 1992 passage of the Americans with Disabilities Act (ADA), which applied to any company with 25 or more employees, was a watershed of federal legislation. This landmark law forbade discrimination against any employee affected by a disability or chronic disease, specifically AIDS. It defends people who are infected, people perceived to be at high risk, relatives and caregivers of people with AIDS, and employees, from hiring to promotion to resignation or retirement. Over and above the legal stipulations of the ADA, authorities recommend that corporate HIV/AIDS policies preserve employee confidentiality, discourage discrimination, evaluate benefits programs, promote prevention, and foster an environment of understanding through the dissemination of the most up-to-date, accurate information.

Some more corporations that have composed HIV/AIDS policies include: Levi Strauss, Pacific Bell, Bank of America, Honeywell, Kimberly-Clark, Westinghouse Electric Corp., Goodyear Tire and Rubber Company, Chrysler Corp., Lotus Development Corp., Apple Computer, Inc., Nike, RJR Nabisco, Time Warner, General Motors Corp., and Pacific Gas & Electric. Digital Equipment Corp. (DEC) went so far as to create an HIV/AIDS Program Office, the first full-time corporate department devoted to AIDS awareness.

Specifically, employers and coworkers should strive to approach HIV and AIDS as illnesses, not moral issues. One of the most important concepts employers can convey is that there is no known risk of HIV transmission to co-workers, clients, or consumers from contact in most industries. Even in the riskiest occupational category, health care workers, the CDC had only documented 39 cases of HIV contraction following on-the-job exposures as of September 30, 1993. Conversely, there has been only one confirmed instance of patients being infected by a health care worker; this involved HIV transmission from an infected dentist to five patients. Investigations by the CDC of more than 15,000 patients of 32 HIV-infected doctors and dentists identified no other cases of this type of transmission.

Unfortunately, and in spite of the massive public service campaigns of the BRTA and hundreds of agencies across the nation, misinformation has continued to disrupt productivity and cause unnecessary anxiety as the AIDS epidemic progresses through its second decade. In the early 1990s, the Center for Work Performance Problems at the Georgia Institute of Technology reported the results of a survey of 2,000 full time workers that illustrated the scope of workers' fear of AIDS infection from casual contact. Two-thirds of the workers surveyed had reservations about using the same bathroom as co-workers with AIDS; 40 percent were concerned about using the same cafeteria; and over one-third of those surveyed were reluctant to use the same equipment as a co-worker with AIDS. The National Leadership Coalition on AIDS, a consortium of more than 200 businesses, found that two out of three adults still mistakenly believed they could contract the virus by working near, or being touched by, a person with AIDS.

A 1993 *American Management Association Survey on HIV and AIDS-Related Policies* can serve as a ''progress report'' on AIDS in the workplace. The AMA survey reported the responses of 630 companies on their experiences and activities. The percentage of companies reporting a case of HIV infection or AIDS rose 13 percent from 1991 to 1993, to 36 percent. The proportion of companies that terminated HIV-positive employees fell from 1.3 percent to zero over the same period. The percentage of companies that reassigned the employee decreased from 14.1 percent to 13 percent, the proportion of companies that took no action increased two percent to 17.4 percent, while 13 percent reported cases ending in a legal action.

Despite repeated and ongoing prodding from government and private agencies, the survey revealed that most companies continued to assume a reactive, rather than proactive, stance on HIV and AIDS. Three-quarters of the companies surveyed had reviewed their human resources policies, but nearly half determined that a policy was not necessary. They elected to treat AIDS as another catastrophic illness. Just over half, however, claimed to be prepared with policy provisions, educational materials, and other resources to work with potential cases of HIV infection or AIDS. Only 15 percent had explicit AIDS policies, and 3.3 percent were in the process of formulating them.

For further information, contact: Business Responds to AIDS Resource Service, P.O. Box 6003, Rockville, MD 20849-6003. By telephone: (800) 458-5231. The National Leadership Coalition on AIDS can be reached by dialing (202) 429-0930.

[April Dougal Gasbarre]

FURTHER READING:

Goldbeck, Willis B. ''AIDS and the Workplace,'' *Futurist*. March, 1988, pp. 18-19.

Knotts, Rose and J. Lynn Johnson. ''AIDS in the Workplace: The Pandemic Firms Want to Ignore,'' *Business Horizons*. July/August, 1993, pp. 5-9.

Pogash, Carol. ''Risky Business: Sooner or Later, Everyone Will Deal with AIDS in the Workplace,'' *Working Woman*. October, 1992, pp. 74-77, 102.

Romano, Catherine. ''Experience Drives Corporate AIDS Policies,'' *Management Review*. December, 1993, p. 7.

Squire, Madelyn C. ''The Fear of AIDS: A Just Cause Dilemma?'' *Dispute Resolution Journal*. December, 1993, pp. 46-50.

ALGORITHMS

The word algorithm comes from the name of an eighth century Arab mathematician, al-Khwarizmi. The original meaning of the word is a rule of procedure or set of steps for the solution of a mathematical problem, such as the procedure for finding a square root. More recently, a set of instructions making up a computer program has come to be described as an algorithm. At present, the word is used generally to describe any procedure or set of rules for accomplishing a task. Typically, the task might be analyzing and/or solving a problem, or making some type of decision. In many situations, algorithm refers to a formalized or codified set of precise rules or steps, but may also be applied to informal or general procedures of varying precision. Thus, application of the net present value technique for capital budgeting might be described as an algorithm.

BENEFITS OF ALGORITHMS

The use of algorithms provides a number of benefits. One of these benefits is in the development of the procedure itself. By breaking down the task into a series of steps, the problem is reduced in size. Problems that would be difficult or impossible to solve wholesale can be approached as a series of small, solvable subproblems. Just as importantly, developing an algorithm allows and even forces examination of the solution process in a rational manner. The required specification aids in the identification and reduction of subconscious biases. By using an algorithm, **decision making** becomes a more rational process.

In addition to making the process more rational, use of an algorithm will make the process more efficient and more consistent. Efficiency is an inherent result of the analysis and specification process. Consistency comes from both the use of the same specified process and increased skill in applying the process. Importantly, the algorithm serves as a mnemonic device and helps ensure that variables or parts of the problem are not ignored. Presenting the solution process as an algorithm allows more precise communication, and often permits delegation of some or all of the task.

A final benefit of the use of an algorithm comes from the improvement it makes possible. If the problem solver does not know what was done, he or she will not know what was done wrong. As time goes by and results are compared with goals, the existence of a specified solution process allows identification of weaknesses and errors in the process.

Reduction of a task to a specified set of steps through the use of an algorithm is an important part of analysis, control, and evaluation.

[David E. Upton]

ALIENS, EMPLOYMENT OF

An alien is any foreign born person who is neither a citizen nor national (that is, permanent resident) of the United States. The employment of aliens in the United States has generated controversy since the first great wave of Irish immigrants began arriving in this country in the late 1840s. Each successive wave of immigrants—Chinese and Japanese, east Europeans, Italians—has been met with suspicion and outright hostility. They were accused of depriving native born Americans of jobs. Nevertheless, there was no distinction made between "legal" and "illegal" aliens until the first restrictive immigration law was passed by Congress in the 1920s. While immigration laws since World War II have dropped specific restrictions against certain racial and ethnic groups, they have become more selective as to the skills that foreigners might bring with them, with the focus on American economic needs.

Aliens always have been permitted to work in the United States. However, there are many rules and restrictions pertaining to the employment of aliens in this country, both at the state and federal level. The landmark immigration law of 1986, or the Immigration Reform and Control Act (IRCA), legalized three million aliens in this country who had been living here illegally since January 1, 1982. With the passage of IRCA, however, anyone hiring an illegal alien (someone who had no authorization to work) became subject to fines or criminal penalties if s/he repeatedly broke the law prohibiting such hiring. Only "documented" aliens with authorization to work can now be considered for employment.

Four years later, the Immigration Act of 1990 tightened sanctions and made it easier for American businesses to hire of highly qualified aliens and allow them to work in the United States for a longer period of time—up to seven years. It also greatly expanded the number of visas issued to "desirable" aliens, mainly highly trained or highly educated foreigners with sponsors, from 54,000 to 140,000 per year.

Despite the passage of these two restrictive, highly selective immigration acts, the flow of immigrants to this country continues at all time highs—nearly 800,000 per year. Nor has the threat of sanctions against employers hiring illegal aliens had much effect. The flow of "illegal" aliens continues unabated. Intolerable economic or political conditions in their own country continues to motivate many aliens to emigrate to this country, legally or illegally. Contrary to popular perception, numerous studies indicate that the vast majority of the immigrants (legal and illegal) who arrive in the United States annually come here to work and do end up with jobs. The lucky 12 percent who fall into the "desirable" categories of the 1990 Immigration Act help to fill the critical gaps in the U.S. economy, like the medical and non medical science professions; the rest, including illegal aliens, contribute to income tax revenues and boost the demand for goods and services of all kinds.

Even the most favored categories of aliens face more restrictions than their American counterparts. An alien has little flexibility in his employment: a foreign scientist in the United States, for instance, cannot obtain permission to work on projects in sensitive areas, such as in American defense or in intelligence. Federal jobs are open only to U.S. citizens, although there are some exceptions. Many states have their own restrictions. For instance, most states prohibit aliens from employment as school teachers or police officers. A vast category of aliens—nonimmigrants such as tourists and students—are not permitted to work at all, even though they are legally in this country legally. Exceptions are made for students who obtain permission from the Immigration and Naturalization Service to work. Aliens with work permits are eligible for Social Security cards.

In the past 200 years, approximately 55 million immigrants have entered this country to live and work. The right of aliens to employment over time has been seriously restricted and regulated. Nonetheless, the United States opens its doors to more immigrants than any nation on earth, testimony to the contributions aliens make to the economic life and health of this country.

[Sina Dubovoy]

FURTHER READING:

American Civil Liberties Union. *The Rights of Aliens and Refugees: The Basic ACLU Guide to Alien and Refugee Rights.* Southern Illinois University Press, 1990.

Fierman, Jaclyn. "Is Immigration Hurting the U.S.?" *Fortune.* August 9, 1993.

Freeman, Richard B. "Immigration From Poor to Wealthy Countries: Experience of the United States," *European Economic Review.* April, 1993.

Groban, Robert S. "The Immigration Act of 1990: an Employer's Primer of Its New Provisions," *Employee Relations Law Journal.* Winter 1991/1992.

AMERICANS WITH DISABILITIES ACT (ADA)

The Americans with Disabilities Act (ADA) represents new and revolutionary civil rights legislation. The law is designed to protect the civil rights of people who have physical and mental disabilities, in a manner similar to the way that previous civil rights laws have protected people who are of various races, religions, and ethnic backgrounds. The ADA mandates changes in the way that both private businesses and the government conduct **employment** practices and provide products and services to the general public to ensure that all Americans have full access to and can fully participate in all aspects of society. It is the first federal law that requires privately-financed businesses to provide physical accessibility in existing buildings. The ADA requires the removal of barriers that deny individuals with disabilities equal opportunity and access to jobs, public accommodations, government services, public transportation, and telecommunications.

On July 26, 1990, President George Bush signed the ADA into law. The legal structure of the ADA is based on the legal structure of the Civil Rights Act of 1964 and the Rehabilitation Act of 1973.

The ADA uses concepts of disability, accessibility, and employment which were introduced in the Architectural Barriers Act of 1968 and the Rehabilitation Act of 1973. These two federal laws were the predecessors of the ADA that mandated a level of accessibility in federally-funded buildings and programs. The concepts of ''Reasonable Accommodation'' and ''Undue Burdens,'' which are found in Title I and Title III of the ADA came from Section 501 of the Rehabilitation Act. The concept of ''Program Accessibility'' using changes in services, policies, or programs to provide equal access came from Section 504 of the Rehabilitation Act. The ADA extends these service concepts to all state and local facilities and programs in Title II, and to private businesses in Title III. The architectural accessibility provisions of Title III extend to commercial buildings, including studios, factories, office buildings, and warehouses that are not open to the public.

It is estimated that 43 million people have a disability—one of every five. The ability of such people to participate in the mainstream of society has gradually increased during the last 30 years as a result of improvements in assistive technology and auxiliary aids and services, as well as expanding requirements for accessibility in newly-constructed facilities. As defined in the ADA, the term ''disability'' has a three-part definition:

(1) people who have a physical or mental impairment that substantially limits one or more major life activity;

(2) people who have a record of an impairment which substantially limits major life activities; and

(3) people who may be regarded by others as having such an impairment.

The ADA consists of five separate parts or titles: Title I - Employment; Title II - Public Services; Title III - Public Accommodations and Commercial Facilities; Title IV - Telecommunications; and Title V - Miscellaneous.

TITLE I. Employment, prohibits **discrimination** against qualified individuals with disabilities with regard to employment. For employers with 25 or more employees, the requirements became effective on July 26, 1992. For employers with 15 to 24 employees, the requirements became effective on July 26, 1994.

TITLE II. Public Services, prohibits discrimination in programs, services, or activities of public entities (state and local governments), including public transportation operated by public entities. The provisions of Title II which do not involve public transportation became effective on January 26, 1992.

TITLE III. Public Accommodations and Commercial Facilities, requires that private businesses that are open to the public—including restaurants, department stores, convenience stores and specialty shops, and hotels and motels—allow individuals with disabilities to participate equally in the goods and services that they offer. This title also requires that all future construction of commercial facilities, including office buildings, factories, warehouses, as well as places of public accommodation, be constructed so that the building is accessible to individuals with disabilities.

Title III also mandates modifications in policies, practices and procedures; the provision of auxiliary aids and services; the provision of accessible transportation services when transportation services are offered, and the removal of architectural and communications barriers. As of August 26, 1990, all newly-ordered or leased vehicles for fixed route systems with 17 seats or more (including the driver) must be accessible; this includes accessibility to persons in wheelchairs.

As of January 26, 1992, fixed route or on demand transportation services when viewed as a whole must be accessible. This includes accessibility to persons in wheelchairs, and would include hotel to airport shuttles and similar shuttle services.

As of the same date, existing places of public accommodation must modify policies, practices, and procedures; they must provide auxiliary aids and services; and they must remove certain architectural and communications barriers, where readily achievable.

Also as of January 26, 1992, alteration for which construction began must meet the applicable requirements of the ADA Accessibility Guidelines, regardless of the permit or permit application date.

As of January 26, 1993, new facilities designed and constructed for first occupancy after this date must comply with Title III requirements.

TITLE IV. Telecommunications, requires telephone companies to make relay services available for persons with hearing and speech impairments. This will provide equal opportunity for people with speech or hearing impairments to use telephone services. The requirements became effective on July 26, 1993 for provision of operator relay services.

TITLE V. Miscellaneous, ties the ADA to the Civil Rights Act of 1964 and its amendments. It includes a variety of legal and technical provisions, including a provision that stipulates that the ADA does not override or limit the remedies, rights, or procedures of any federal, state, or local law which provides greater or equal protection for the rights of individuals with disabilities.

A few of the key terms and definitions in the ADA are "Public Accommodation," "Reasonable Accommodations," and "Readily Achievable." As defined in the ADA, the term "Public Accommodation" refers to any private place of business that is open to the public for the sale or lease of goods and services. The Act lists 12 general categories of public accommodation:

1. places of lodging;
2. places serving food or drink;
3. places of exhibition and/or entertainment;
4. places of public gathering;
5. sales or rental establishments;
6. service establishments;
7. stations used for specified public transportation;
8. places of public display or collection;
9. places of recreation;
10. places of education;
11. social service center establishments; and
12. places of exercise or recreation.

As defined in the ADA, there are two distinctions between "Reasonable Accommodations" and "Readily Achievable." "Reasonable Accommodations" has to do with employees, and no modifications must be undertaken to fulfill the "Reasonable Accommodations" requirement until a qualified individual with a disability has been hired. "Reasonable Accommodations" must be made unless they impose a significant difficulty or expense. "Readily Achievable" has to do with clients or guests. "Readily Achievable" means easily accomplishable and able to be carried out without much difficulty or expense. "Readily Achievable" modifications must be made in anticipation of a disabled guest's or client's needs, before they ever arrive on the premises.

SEE ALSO: Civil Rights Act of 1991

[Susan Bard Hall]

FURTHER READING:

Saimen, John P.S. *Accommodating All Guests: The Americans with Disabilities Act and the Edging Industry.* American Hotel & Motel Association, December 1992, pp. 1-8, 11, 29.

U.S. Department of Justice, Civil Rights Division. *The Americans with Disabilities Act - Title II Technical Assistance Manual.* Washington, D.C.: GPO.

AMORTIZATION

Amortization, an accounting concept similar to **depreciation**, is the gradual reduction of an asset or liability by some periodic amount. In the case of an asset, it involves expensing the item over the time period it is thought to be consumed. For a liability, the amortization takes place over the time period the item is repaid or earned. It is essentially a means to allocate categories of **assets** and liabilities to their pertinent time period.

The key difference between depreciation and amortization is the nature of the items to which they apply. The former is generally used in the context of tangible assets, such as buildings, machinery, and equipment. The latter is more commonly associated with intangible assets, such as **copyright**s, goodwill, **patents**, and **capitalized costs** (e.g. product development costs). On the liability side, amortization is commonly applied to deferred revenue items such as premium income or subscription revenue, where the cash payment is often received in advance of the earning process, and therefore must be recognized as income ratably over some future time.

Amortization is a means by which accountants apply the period concept in accrual-based financial statements: income and expenses are recorded in the periods affected, rather than when the cash actually changes hands. The importance of spreading transactions across several periods becomes more clear when considering long-livd assets of substantial cost. Just as it would be inappropriate to expense the cost of a new facility in the year of its acquisition, it would be wrong to fully expense an intangible asset in the first year. Intangible assets generally benefit many future periods, and accordingly their expense should be spread over the time period the company will use the asset or generate revenue therefrom.

The periods over which intangible assets are amortized varies widely from a few years to 40 years. Leasehold interests with remaining lives of three years, for example, would be mortized over the following three years. The costs incurred with establishing and protecting patent rights would generally be amortized over 17 years. The goodwill recorded in connection with an acquisition of a subsidiary could be amortized over as long as 40 years past the author's death, should also be limited to 40 years under accounting rules. The general rule is that the asset should be amortized over its useful life.

It is important to realize that not all assets are consumed by their use or by the passage of time. A good example of tangible asset that is not depreciated is land; its value generally is not degraded by time or use. Within the intangible arena, trademarks can have idenfinite lives, and therefore are often not amortized. The cost of acquiring customer lists, if properly maintained, can also be argued to not decline in value.

The term amortization is also used in connection with loans. The amortization of a loan is the rate at which the principal balance will be paid down over time, given the term and interest rate of the note. Shorter not periods will have higher amounts amortized with each payment or period.

The loans most people are familiar with are car or mortgage loans, where 5 and 30 year terms, respectively, are fairly standard. In the case of a 30 year fixed rate mortgage, the loan will amortize at an increasing rate over the 360 months' payments. Although the monthly payments will remain constant, the amount allocated to interest and principal will shift as time passes, with increasing amounts applied toward principal repayment and decreasing amounts applied to interest. For example, a 30 year mortgage of $100,000 at eight percent will have equal monthly payments of $734. The first month's payment will consist of $667 interest and $67 of principal amortization, whereas the last payment will be very little interest and substantially all principal.

Another type of amortization involves the discount or premium frequently arising with the issuance of bonds. In the case of a discount, the bond issuer will record the original bond discount as an aset (a deferred cost) and amortize it ratably over the bond's term. The expense created by this amortization will effectively increase the interest expense above that from the pure coupon rate of interet, reflecting the fact that the issuer was forced to pay a higher interest rate (accept less cash from the bond buyer than originally contemplated by the bond deal.

SEE ALSO: Intangible Assets

[Christopher Barry]

ANNUAL REPORTS

Annual reports are formal **financial statements** that are published yearly and sent to company stock-holders and various other interested parties. The reports assess the year's operations and discuss the companies' view of the upcoming year and the companies' place and prospects in their industries. Both for-profit and not-for-profit organizations produce annual reports, with this discussion focusing on for-profit businesses.

THE BASICS

Annual reports are a **Securities and Exchange Commission** (SEC) requirement for businesses owned by the public. Companies meet this requirement, however, in many ways. At its most basic, an annual report includes:

- Audited statements of **income and revenue**, financial position and **cash flow statement** and notes to the statements providing details for various line items.

- A management's discussion and analysis (MD&A) of financial condition and the results of the company for the past two years.

- A brief description of the company's business in the most recent year, a description that should give a general understanding of the company.

- Information related to a company's business segments, segments that the company has chosen as appropriate for how it reports its operating results.

- A listing of the company's directors and executive officers. The list includes their principal occupations, and, if a director, the principal business of the company that employs him or her.

- Market price of the company's stock and **dividends** paid.

Some companies provide only this minimum amount of information. Annual reports of this type usually are only a few pages in length, printed in one color—black, and produced in an inexpensive fashion, often closely resembling photocopying. For these companies, the primary purpose of an annual report is simply to meet legal requirements.

A MARKETING TOOL

A wider group of companies views the annual report as a **marketing** tool. It is a forum through which a company can relate, influence, preach, opine, and discuss any number of issues and topics. A "Letter to Shareholders" most often sets the tone of the annual report. Two to four pages is a typical letter length. The chairman of the board of directors, the **chief executive officer**, the president, the chief operating officer or a combinaton of these four sign the letter on behalf of company **management**. The message of the letter will often focus on topics such as the past year's results, strategies, market conditions, new management and directors, and company initiatives. The letter sometimes is no more than a sounding board for the person leading the company. Some letters have run a dozen or more pages, contained several photos of the CEO in different poses and expounded on a wide variety of topics that apparently have some interest to the CEO, if not readers of annual reports. A letter that actually reads like a letter, and reads as if the person signing the letter may have actually penned it himself or herself, is one format known to appeal to readers. This contrasts with letters that read like an accounting treatise pieced together by an eclectic team.

Annual reports usually advance a theme or concept. Catch phrases such as ''Poised for the Twenty-first century'' or ''Meeting the Realities of the Nineties'' can unify a company's annual report message. In any year, a particular event or economic condition will create a theme adopted by a wide range of companies. For example, when the Berlin Wall fell in 1989, several reports focused on the opening of Eastern European markets. There was a similar response when the European Economic Community formed to unite Western Europe, when restructuring and reengineering dominated business, and, more recently, when the **North American Free Trade Agreement (NAFTA)** and **General Agreement on Tariffs and Trade (GATT)** opened previously restricted markets.

Companies also have used a milestone anniversary, such as 100 years of doing business, to unify a report. Promoting a long, successful track record can be appealing to shareholders and various audiences. Still other companies have developed a tried-and-true format that they use year after year with little change except updating the data. Whatever the theme, concept, or format, Wall Street will consider the most successful reports ones that clearly delineate a company's strategies for profitable growth.

AUDIENCES

Shareholders and potential shareholders remain the primary audiences for annual reports. Employees (who today are also likely to be shareholders), customers, suppliers, community leaders, and the community-at-large, however, are also targeted audiences. Companies will address other publics, depending on their objectives.

EMPLOYEES. The annual report serves many purposes with employees. It often relates the company's goals. Employee innovation, quality, teamwork, and commitment are all critical to achieving company goals, so it is essential that employees and management share the same focus.

An annual report is also a vehicle for relating the company's successes—a new contract, a new product, cost-saving initiatives, new applications of products, expansions into new geographies—all of which have had employee involvement. Seeing a successful project or initiative profiled in the annual report gives reinforcement to the employee **team**, operating division, operating group, and/or operating company responsible for the success.

The annual report can help increase employee understanding of the different parts of the company. Many **manufacturing** locations are in remote areas, and an employee's understanding of the company often does not go beyond the facility where he or she works. An annual report can be a source for learning about each of a company's product lines, its operating locations, and who is leading the various operations. Other copy can relate success stories from each of the divisions. The annual report can show employees how they fit into the ''big picture.''

Employees also are often shareholders. So, like other shareholders, these employees can use the annual report to help gauge their investment in the company. In this case, they also realize that the work they are doing in making products or providing a service is having an impact on how Wall Street values the company's stock.

CUSTOMERS. Customers want to work with quality suppliers, and an annual report can help a company promote its image with customers. Publishing management positions such as the company's mission and core values is one idea. Describing company initiatives such as projects to improve manufacturing processes, reduce **costs**, create quality, or enhance service can illustrate a company's customer orientation.

The annual report also will show the company's financial strength. Customers are reducing their number of suppliers, and one evaluation criterion is financial strength. They want committed and capable suppliers, and ones that are going to be around for the long term.

Often a supplier's annual report can be a marketing tool for the customer, as well. When a supplier highlights a customer in its annual report, it is giving the customer some free positive publicity.

SUPPLIERS. A company's capability to meet its customers' requirements is only as good as its suppliers' capabilities. One-hundred percent on-time delivery to customers is not possible if the company's suppliers are only responding with 60 percent on-time delivery. Therefore, successful companies today want to work with suppliers committed to the same quality standards. An annual report can help with this process by highlighting quality, innovation, and commitment. This will show a company leading by example and reinforce the type of response the company expects from its suppliers. Sometimes an annual report will even offer a profile of a supplier that the company has found exemplary so other suppliers have a better understanding of the level of service desired.

THE COMMUNITY. Especially in the communities where it does business, a company wants to be perceived as a corporate citizen making a valued contribution. An annual report can help with this marketing. Many annual reports discuss companies' community initiatives such as community renovation projects, charitable contributions for human services organizations, and programs to help protect the environment. The objective is to present the company as a proactive member of the community.

This sort of publicity also can be valuable when a company is making plans to move into a new community. Companies seek warm welcomes in new communities (including tax breaks and other incentives). Communities will woo a company perceived as a ''good'' corporate citizen more zealously than one that is not. The good corporate citizen also will receive less resistance from local interest groups. The company's annual report will be one document that all affected parties will pore over in evaluating the company.

READING AN ANNUAL REPORT

The wide variety of audiences means people read annual reports for different purposes and at different levels. Generalizations, however, are difficult. The stockholder with five shares might be as careful and discriminate a reader of an annual report as the financial analyst representing a firm owning one million shares.

It may require an MBA to understand all the details buried in an annual report's footnotes. Nevertheless, a good understanding of a company is possible by focusing on some key sections of the report.

COMPANY DESCRIPTION. Most companies will include a description of their business segments that includes products and markets served. Formats vary from a separate fold-out descriptive section to a few words on the inside front cover. Reviewing this section gives at least a basic understanding of what the company does.

THE LETTER. The Letter to Shareholders, Chairman's Message, or whatever a company may call it, should provide some informative data on how the past year went and what the prospects for the future are. As stated above, if the company has put in the time and thought, the language of the letter should be easy to follow and understand.

MANAGEMENT'S DISCUSSION AND ANALYSIS (MD&A). This section can be dry, full of accounting jargon and boring, but the MD&A gives in a succinct package an overview of what happened with the company over the past three years. It makes a comparison of the most recent year with the year previous, and then compares this latter year with the year previous to it. It discusses sales, manufacturing income and margin, operating income, net income, and the things that led to the reported numbers. A section discusses capital expenditures, cash flow, changes in working capital, and anything ''special'' that happened during the years. The MD&A is also supposed to be forward-looking, discussing anything the company may be aware of that could negatively or positively affect results. An MD&A can be written at all different levels of comprehension, but with even a little **accounting** understanding, the reader can get valuable insights.

FINANCIAL SUMMARY. Most companies will include either a five-, six-, ten-, or eleven-year summary of financial data. Sales, income, **dividends** paid, shareholders' equity, number of employees, and many other line items may also be included. This section summarizes key data from the statements of income, financial position, and cash flow for a number of years.

MANAGEMENT/DIRECTORS. A page or more of an annual report will list the management of the company and its board of directors. By reviewing the management list, one often can get a sense of the management team's background, diversity, and experience. The same is true of the director list. Number of directors, diversity, and the directors' positions within their respective companies all can help the reader evaluate the quality of company **leadership**.

INVESTOR INFORMATION. There almost always is a page that lists the company's address and phone number, the stock transfer agent, dividend and stock price information, and the next annual meeting date. This information is helpful for anyone wanting additional data on the company or more information about stock ownership.

PACKAGING THE ANNUAL REPORT

For most companies, the words and message are the most important aspect of an annual report. Companies also want to be sure, however, that their targeted audiences are going to read and understand the message. Thirty pages of monotonous, uninviting small type is not going to attract a lot of interest. At the same time, turning the message over to a designer who is more intent on creating a visual, aesthetic monument is likely to have a similar negative effect.

The challenge becomes attracting the reader's interest and, once accomplishing this, holding that interest long enough for the reader to get the company's message. Estimates are that the average annual report reader spends only a couple of minutes looking through a report. So the challenge is very real. Subheads, call-outs, and other snippets are helpful in getting across concepts to the report skimmer. Visually appealing photography also can help gain reader attention. Combining an appealing photo that illustrates a **strategy** or initiative with a short narrative can be an even more effective tool.

A report designer can work with type styles, point sizes, and a variety of other techniques to enhance appearance, always cautious of overdesigning that can hinder interest and readability. To a certain extent, the kind of company will dictate the design format. For example, the design of an industrial company's annual report will probably differ from that of a fashion, entertainment, or trendy consumer services company. The key is choosing a design that will best convey the company's message.

Costs also influence the production of an annual report. Companies will weigh the printer it uses, contracting for new photography or using "pick-up" photos, whether to write in-house or out, and even the type of paper used for the report. All will affect whether the report costs a few thousand dollars or several hundred-thousand dollars.

SUMMARY ANNUAL REPORTS

Few major trends have jarred the tradition of annual reports, but one is the "summary annual report." In 1987, the SEC eased its annual reporting requirements. It allowed companies to produce a summary annual report, rather than the traditional report with audited statements and footnotes. Full-blown financial data are still a requirement. Nevertheless, filing a Form 10-K containing this information and including audited financial data and other required material within a company's proxy statement—another SEC-mandated document for shareholders—met the requirement. Promoters of the summary annual report see it as a way to make the annual report a true marketing publication without the cumbersome, detailed financial data. Financial data is still included, but in a condensed form in a supporting role. The summary annual report has not gained widespread support. Initially, about 25 companies adopted the format. Today, several companies are still finding the format useful.

In some respects, annual reports are like fashions. Certain techniques, formats, and designs are popular for a few years and then new ideas displace the old. Several years later, the old ideas are back in vogue again. Other formats are "classic," never seeming to go out of style or lose their power. A key to a successful annual report is not getting caught up in a trend, and instead deciding what works best for conveying the message.

[Richard Rump]

ANTITRUST ACTS AND LAWS

Federal antitrust law is not only composed of statutes, it is also composed of administrative regulations, court decisions, and enforcement actions, all designed to regulate business activity and competition. Furthermore, most states have their own antitrust laws, which vary in effectiveness but are largely designed to complement the federally established antitrust mechanisms. The purpose of these laws is to ensure that the U.S. economy can reach equilibrium on its own and is not unduly influenced by the activities of large companies or groups of companies. Specifically, to protect the economy, antitrust laws prohibit monopolistic, conspiratorial, and exclusionary practices that obstruct **competition**. Activities such as these can drive up prices and reduce the supply and/or quality of the products affected. Unlike other types of economic regulation, antitrust laws do not directly dictate industry or corporate output, prices, rates, or services.

Antitrust laws show a predilection for free, open markets where price and quantity are set by competition and where there is no artificial monopoly or **restraint of trade** guiding market conditions. A monopoly is a dominant firm within a market that has the power to set prices and market conditions while excluding all potential competition. There are three basic activities classified as restraint of trade . . . they are agreements between industry competitors: to withhold patronage or refuse to do business with parties not participating in the agreement; to assign customers and/or markets; and to set prices. In theory, consumers served by an economy free of these restraints are able to maximize their satisfaction by choosing products and services in the open market.

EARLY HISTORY OF ANTITRUST ACTS AND LAWS

Modern antitrust acts and laws have their origins in English and American common laws—laws largely based on court decisions—that were passed in response to activities restraining trade and furthering monopolies. Before the first U.S. federal antitrust act was passed in 1890, these laws varied significantly between states and jurisdictions; in fact, there was no uniform body of U.S. common law at the time. These early English and American laws generally rested on individual court precedents dealing with contracts and conspiracies attempting to restrain trade.

After the Civil War, Americans moved west, the economy boomed, and the Industrial Revolution enabled U.S. production to increase to meet the new, rising demands. Indeed, U.S. technology expanded product development so drastically that, for the first time, supply often exceeded demand for many products. Facing new and intense competition, many companies in the late nineteenth century sought to better their market positions. Initially, these companies tended to enter into loose **cartel** arrangements with their existing competitors to exclude entry into their markets by new competitors. Later, as competitive forces strengthened, many of these same companies took more extreme actions to restrain trade, such as merging with other large competitors and/or forming **trusts** or **holding companies**.

A particularly abusive trust, known as a "pool," was formed by railroads in the early 1870s. Under the pool, railroads worked together and divided up their markets—activities resulting in price discrimination and, subsequently, ridiculously high prices. All types of people—from farmers to tradespeople—felt the effects of the railroad pool and similar restraints of trade undertaken by other industries. Thus, by the 1880s, these new trusts were gaining considerable public attention. Eventually, the negative public outcry became so loud that states passed new antitrust laws. The public, however, was not satisfied by state actions alone; the public pressured the U.S. Congress to adopt federal antitrust legislation. The result of this pressure was the Sherman Antitrust Act of 1890.

THE LEGACY OF THE SHERMAN ANTITRUST ACT OF 1890. Although the Sherman Act contained nothing drastically new, it did make some substantial contributions to halting restraint of trade and monopolization. Specifically, the Sherman Act made these activities crimes against the federal government, requiring enforcement by federal officials and allowing penalties to be imposed.

Unlike many acts of Congress, the significant passages of the Sherman Act are short and straightforward:

Sec. 1. Every contract, combination in the form of a trust or otherwise, or conspiracy, in restraint of trade or commerce among the several states, or with foreign nations, is hereby declared to be illegal.

Sec. 2. Every person who shall monopolize, or attempt to monopolize, or combine or conspire with any other person or persons, to monopolize any part of the trade or commerce among the several states, or with foreign nations, shall be deemed guilty of a misdemeanor.

At the time, if convicted, parties had to pay fines up to $5,000 and/or face prison sentences of up to one year. No significant antitrust acts were passed for the next 24 years.

THE CLAYTON ANTITRUST ACT OF 1914 AND THE FEDERAL TRADE COMMISSION ACT OF 1914. Two other acts, the Clayton Antitrust Act and the Federal Trade Commission Act of 1914, are considered to be almost as important in antitrust legislation as the Sherman Act. During the Cleveland and McKinley presidencies, the Sherman Act was rarely used because its broad language allowed for loose judicial interpretations. Subsequently, participants in many industries, notably those of steel and farm machinery, were involved in activities considered by many people to be conflicting with the idea of free markets; not surprisingly, antitrust legislation was a large issue in the presidential election of 1912.

Under newly-elected President Wilson, the Clayton and Federal Trade Commission Acts were passed in 1914. While the Clayton Act did not include any provisions that could not be addressed under the Sherman Act, it attempted to fill in language gaps found in the Sherman Act by citing activities seen as against free markets and specifically forbidding them. Some of the items addressed by the act are: price discrimination, exclusionary dealing practices, and certain types of **mergers and acquisitions**.

The Federal Trade Commission Act established the **Federal Trade Commission**, an agency that was charged with policing "unfair methods of competition in commerce, and unfair or deceptive acts or practices in commerce." Preventing unfair methods of competition, and unfair acts and practices in commerce has been the task of the FTC since its inception; defining these actions, however, has been more elusive. Basically, this act seeks to prevent price fixing, **boycotts**, and other restraints of trade, while bolstering the Sherman Act. Interestingly, this act also can be used to prosecute companies found guilty of deceptive advertising practices.

INTERPRETATION OF ANTITRUST LAWS

Since the turn of the century, the interpretation and enforcement of antitrust laws has varied significantly, reflecting the strength of the economy and the changing U.S. political attitudes and public sentiment. Ever since the passage of the Sherman Act, the purpose of these laws has been under debate. Some people are of the opinion that the laws are designed to protect the economy and maximize social wealth. Other people disagree and believe that these laws, by freeing consumers from the consequences of concentrated private economic powers, were passed to promote more equitable wealth distribution and more equal business opportunities.

Because the interpretation of antitrust legislation often changes with the economy and public opinion, certain mechanisms have arisen that give judges the ability to interpret applications of antitrust laws more narrowly, according to the specifics of a particular case. For example, the concept of restraint of trade has been the subject of much debate and has been modified by a "rule of reason." Under the rule of reason, a restraint of trade can be judged as reasonable and, thus, a company can try to use it to exempt itself from an antitrust suit. Specifically, whenever two parties enter into any contract, they basically have decided to deal primarily with each other at the exclusion of other parties for a short period in a limited way. Depending on the given situation, a judge could use the "rule of reason" to justify seemingly exclusionary practices taken by one or more firms, saying that the actions were reasonable given the industry or circumstances. Use of the rule of reason tends to increase whenever government and public opinion are permissive of business consolidations. The result of this rule is increased power in lower federal courts, which typically are sympathetic to local businesses.

The opposite of the rule of reason is the per se rule. Under the per se rule, competitor agreements that restrain trade are wrong per se. These offensives cannot be justified by any evidence attempting to show that the action is reasonable. The most basic per se rule is price fixing. This rule, obviously, is used more frequently when public sentiment is in favor of more restrictive business practices.

ENFORCEMENT OF ANTITRUST LAWS

The majority of antitrust cases are settled by consent decrees, where a private party or the government receives an often substantial sum of money in damages from a company or companies found guilty of violating the spirit of these laws. Furthermore, the U.S.Department of Justice can uphold antitrust laws through criminal prosecution and through civil suits attempting to get a court-ordered damage settlement. The Federal Trade Commission has similar enforcement capabilities through administrative "cease and desist orders" that often occur with civil penalties. Private citizens can also seek damages in federal court from companies that they perceive violate these laws. Additionally, legislation was enacted in 1976 permitting the state, acting on behalf of it citizens, to bring damage antitrust actions in federal court.

Antitrust cases can be brought to any federal court and further appealed to any federal appellate court. Because of this, there is no coordination among the typically differing decisions by local courts and agencies. Furthermore, no sole agency has complete control of antitrust policy. Thus, antitrust cases are usually not considered to be settled until they are decided upon by the Supreme Court of the United States. The Court has broad powers to interpret these laws but, because these suits often take a long time, the court accepts very few such cases each year. Therefore, the decisions that the Court does make have wide-reaching implications.

MERGERS AND ACQUISITIONS

Just as a company should consider applicable corporate, tax, or securities laws, any company planning to buy some or all of the stock or **assets** of another company should carefully research the possible applicability of antitrust laws. While these laws do not forbid all mergers and acquisitions, they are backed up by an extensive range of penalties against companies making illegal acquisitions. Some possible punishments are: divestiture of the securities or assets purchased, restoring the purchased company as a **going concern**, court orders against future mergers, and criminal penalties.

There are four basic types of mergers are horizontal, market extension, vertical, and conglomerate. A horizontal merger involves one company purchasing all or part of another company selling the same goods or services in the same market. Because the two companies involved would no longer be competitors, the test for the legality of this kind of merger is the amount of competition that is eliminated relative to the existing market. A market extension merger is very similar to a horizontal merger, as it involves one company acquiring assets of another company offering similar goods and services, but operating in a different market. Since the two companies were not previously in competition with each other, no competition would be eliminated. A vertical merger occurs when a company acquires either its supplier or customer. If a company purchases one of its suppliers, it is referred to as backward vertical integration. Similarly, if a company buys a customer, it is called forward vertical integration. A conglomerate merger involves one company purchasing another company operating in an entirely different business.

The type of merger that occurs definitely influences the chances of its being ruled illegal. In judging the legality of a merger, the most important law is the Clayton Act. As stated earlier, this act asserts that when a corporation engaged in interstate commerce purchases another corporation also engaged in interstate commerce, the merger is illegal whenever competition can potentially be substantially reduced.

RECENT CHANGES IN ANTITRUST LAWS AND POLICIES

During the past 25 years, increased competition from foreign companies has led to a prevailing sentiment that government should not regulate business stringently. The reason behind this sentiment is fear that strict government regulation will make it impossible for U.S. businesses to compete effectively with foreign companies entering U.S. markets. In this competitive environment, much of the recent interpretation and enforcement of antitrust laws has been in support of business. In fact, certain activities that were previously viewed with great suspicion, such as horizontal and vertical arrangements, are now seen as positive activities enhancing businesses' efficiency. While the Supreme Court continues to use the per se rule in making decisions on some activities, it has reduced the frequency with which it uses this rule and has expanded its use of a more generous rule of reason.

In this light, while recent court decisions have looked at reductions in competition brought on by mergers, they have also taken note of increases in efficiency associated with mergers. Furthermore, the Supreme Court has become a bit more lenient in its approach to mergers, requiring a more extensive economic assessment of the likely impacts on competition before a merger can be found illegal. The Court's new sympathetic position reflects a more lenient enforcement policy by the U.S. Department of Justice. Although still concerned with the potential to restrain trade, the Department of Justice has adopted revised guidelines that accentuate the potential economic advantages of merger activities. Thus, there is a much higher threshold for antitrust challenges than existed in the past.

The government has not initiated any major antitrust cases since 1982, when a suit against IBM was dismissed and another against AT&T was settled. Interestingly, the AT&T settlement resulted in the company's local services being separated from its long distance services—the largest divestiture in the history of antitrust litigation.

[Kathryn Snavely]

FURTHER READING:

Baldwin, William L. *Market Power, Competition, and Antitrust Policy*. Homewood, IL: Irwin Publications, 1987.

Geroski, Paul, Richard J. Gilbert, and Alexis Jacquemin. *Barriers to Entry and Strategic Competition*. New York: Harwood Academic Publishers, 1990.

Hall, Kermit L., ed. *The Oxford Companion to the Supreme Court of the United States*. New York: Oxford University Press, 1992.

Kintner, Earl W. *An Antitrust Primer.* New York: Macmillan Co., 1964.

Levy, Leonard W., ed. *Encyclopedia of the American Constitution*. New York: MacMillan Publishing Company, 1987.

Mansfield, Edwin. *Monopoly Power and Economic Performance.* 4th ed. New York: W.W. Norton & Company, 1978.

APPRENTICESHIP PROGRAMS

Apprenticeship programs are occupational training programs that combine on-the-job work experience with technical or classroom study. Such programs are designed to develop useful skills in individuals who are not planning to attend or have not attended college. They also address the need for better trained entry-level workers and help young people make the transition from school to work. From an employer's point of view, apprenticeship programs can help reduce the high cost of training inexperienced workers.

There are more than 800 occupations in the United States for which apprenticeships are available. Many of them are in the skilled trades and crafts, notably in occupations related to the construction industry. In many states apprenticeship programs are required to obtain occupational licensing or certification. The U.S. Department of Labor, Bureau of Apprenticeship and Training, maintains a registry of apprenticeship programs and the occupations that are covered.

In the United States there is currently no national apprenticeship program. In 27 states apprenticeship programs are regulated by the state. Apprenticeship programs may be sponsored by employers, a group of employers, or a union. Trade and other nonprofit organizations also sponsor apprenticeship programs within certain industries. Unions and employers often form joint apprenticeship committees to administer the programs. Such committees are concerned with determining an industry's particular needs and developing standards for the apprenticeship programs. Apprenticeship programs are usually registered with the federal or state government to ensure that the programs meet standards relating to job duties, instruction, wages, and safety and health conditions.

Individuals who are interested in entering an apprenticeship program must meet certain qualifications. Because of **child labor** laws in the United States, most apprenticeship programs in the United States require applicants to be at least 16 or 18 years of age. While some states have apprenticeship programs for high school juniors and seniors, most apprenticeship programs require a high school diploma. Other requirements relate to aptitude and physical condition.

Once an individual has been accepted into an apprenticeship program, he or she usually signs an agreement with the program's sponsor. The agreement covers such matters as the sponsor's compliance with the program's standards and the apprentice's performance of the required work and completion of the necessary studies. While enrolled in the program the apprentice works under the supervision of a fully qualified journeyperson as a paid, full-time employee. Apprentices are usually paid about half of what a journeyperson makes, and also receive relevant instruction outside of regular working hours, either in a classroom or through at-home study. The program may last from one to six years, depending on the occupation and other requirements. Journey certification or some other type of credential is usually granted upon successful completion of an apprenticeship program.

Recent presidential administrations, notably those of George Bush and Bill Clinton, have recognized the desirability of establishing some type of national apprenticeship program in the United States. Such a program, which would provide apprenticeship training and job skills certification at the national level, would help to reduce the wage gap between college graduates and those who do not attend college. It would also provide for better trained entry-level workers. With only 25 to 30 percent of all high school graduates projected to finish college, the need for apprenticeship programs is greater than ever.

In Europe, Germany's national apprenticeship program has been cited as a model on which to build an American program. Denmark, Holland, and Switzerland also have national training programs in place. Many aspects of the German program, however, would probably not be culturally acceptable in America. For example, in Germany's highly successful program, students are separated into one of three tracks at the relatively early age of eleven, and by the age of fourteen they know whether they will attend a university or enter an apprenticeship program. If the United States is to implement a national apprenticeship program, it will likely be one that meets the needs of employers and employees while taking into account the interests of state government and organized labor.

SEE ALSO: On-the-Job Training

[David Bianco]

FURTHER READING:

Couch, Kenneth A. "Germans and Job Training, Education and Us." *The American Enterprise*. November/December, 1993, pp. 12-14.

Couch, Kenneth A. "The German Apprenticeship Experience." *Current*. May, 1994, pp. 11-14.

Gitter, Robert J. "Apprenticeship-Trained Workers: United States and Great Britain." *Monthly Labor Review*. April, 1994, pp. 38-43.

Glazer, Nathan. "A Human Capital Policy for the Cities." *Public Interest*. Summer, 1993, pp. 27-49.

Kiester, Edwin. "Germany Prepares Kids for Good Jobs; We Were Preparing Ours for Wendy's." *Smithsonian*. March 1993, pp. 44-50.

Szabo, Joan C. "Training Workers for Tomorrow." *Nation's Business*. March 1993, pp. 22-25.

ARAB COMMON MARKET

The Arab Common Market (ACM) was established in 1964 as part of the Council for Economic Unity. The purpose of the ACM is to promote the uninhibited movement of capital and labor between member states. Founding members of the organization are Egypt, Iraq, Jordan, and Syria. ACM is open to all members of the Arab League but as of 1993, only Egypt, Libya, Mauritania, Iraq, Jordan, Syria, and Yemen were members. As a long term goal, ACM seeks to do away with customs duties on agricultural products and natural resources. The ACM also seeks to integrate members' economies on a limited basis through common external tariffs. The ACM also hopes to achieve more coordinated foreign economic planning among its members.

[Michael Knes]

ARAB MONETARY FUND (AMF)

The Arab Monetary Fund (AMF) was created on April 27, 1976 at Rabat, Morocco as a result of soaring oil prices in the early 1970s. Oil producing Arab nations created the AMF with money from oil sales to provide low interest loans to less prosperous Arab nations in order to ease their balance of payment problems. Later the AMF instituted a program to provide funds for pan-Arab development projects at a higher interest rate than balance of payment loans. The AMF is currently an agency of the Arab League, an umbrella organization encompassing most of the Arab world.

The AMF's goal is to integrate the economies of all member countries. The fund aggressively loans money for pan-Arab development projects, helps to stabilization Arab currency exchange rates, coordinates the international aspects of Arab economic activity. The AMF sponsors banking and monetary policy seminars and advises member states on long range economic planning through its Economic Policy Institute. The AMF also eases internal economic problems of member countries that result from high oil prices such as commodity price fluctuations. In addition, the fund has instituted an Arab Trade Financing Program that works in conjunction with other Arab organizations to encourage pan-Arab trade.

Arab Monetary Fund policy is set by a Board of Governors consisting of a governor and a deputy governor from each member state. The day-to-day operations of the AMF are controlled by a director general and eight financial and economic professionals who make up the Board of Executive Directors. The directors serve for three years and come from member countries.

Membership in the AMF consists of the Palestine Liberation Organization PLO and 19 Arab countries: Algeria, Bahrain, Egypt, Iraq, Jordan, Kuwait, Lebanon, Libya, Mauritania, Morocco, Oman, Qatar, Saudi Arabia, Somalia, Sudan, Syria, Tunisia, United Arab Emirates and Yemen. The memberships of Iraq, Somalia, and Sudan were suspended in early 1993 for arrears in loan payments.

The amount of money loaned by the AMF varies greatly from year to year. In 1989 the fund loaned almost $290 million but in 1990 loaned only $67 million. Total loans outstanding are nearly $2.5 billion. The fund is threatened by defaults on loans as evidenced by Iraq, Somalia, and Sudan's suspension.

[Michael Knes]

FURTHER READING:

Clements, Frank. *Arab Regional Organizations*. Transaction Publishers, 1992.

ARAB WORLD, DOING BUSINESS IN THE

Few areas have received more attention from business people in the industrialized world in recent decades than the Arab World. While Europeans have long held an interest in the Arab World, the United States had been relatively unaware of the region until after World War II. Even the European interest has historically been adversarial (as in the Crusades of the European Dark Ages or the European Catholic struggle for the control of Spain after 700 years of Arab civilization there) or subjugative (in the form of the nineteenth-century European colonization of much of the Arab World following the French conquest of Algeria in 1841, and lasting in some regions until the 1970s). The significance of the current attention to the Arab World is that—in business terms at least—the Arabic countries are being viewed as a source of potential partners and as equals.

In part, the reason for this has to do with a shift of control of the rich natural resources of North Africa and the Arabian peninsula in the 1970s from U.S.- and European-owned natural resource companies (most notably petroleum) to domestically run operations in the Arab oil-producing states. This also has to do with the growing recognition of the richness and venerability of Arabic culture, a culture as distinctive as any business culture in the industrialized world. Finally, the geographic location of the Arab World, sitting at the crossroads of three continents, has helped to place it at the center of an increasingly integrated world economy.

The very term "Arab World" is a questionable one. An Arab is a member of a linguistic group—that is, one who speaks Arabic. The Arab World, then, can best be defined as the region in which people predominantly speak Arabic. Yet throughout what would be considered the Arab World, tens of thousands of people speak languages other than Arabic, ranging from the numerous dialects of Berber on the African coast of the Mediterranean to Kurdish and Armenian in southwest Asia; from Nuer and Dinka in the Sudan to Fula and Wolof in Mauritania and so on.

The modern Arab World consists of between 19 and 21 nations. Listed in eastward geographic order 19 of these are indisputable: Algeria, Bahrain, Djibouti, Egypt, Iraq, Jordan, Kuwait, Lebanon, Libya, Mauritania, Morocco, Oman, Qatar, Saudi Arabia, the Sudan, Syria, Tunisia, the United Arab Emirates (itself consisting of seven emirates), and Yemen. Additionally, Palestine won self-rule in 1994 in the formerly Israeli administered West Bank and Gaza. Finally, Somalia—though Arabic there is a minority language with the majority of people speaking Somali—has been a member of the Arab League since 1974.

Moreover, it is important to note that the constituent parts of the Arab World are themselves quite diverse. Geographically, they cover a region spanning all of North Africa from the Atlantic coasts of Mauritania and Morocco in the west well into southwest Asia with Iraq, south into Sudan, and into the nations of the Arabian peninsula. Religiously, nations such as Saudi Arabia and Libya are almost exclusively Islamic, while other nations contain substantial Christian and Jewish populations. Over 10 million Arabs are Christian and 40,000 Arabs are Jews. Numerous other religions, such as the Druze of Lebanon and Syria, have ancient communities while the large number of Indian foreign workers in the Gulf countries of Qatar, Oman, Kuwait and the United Arab Emirates have led to substantial resident Hindu communities. In several parts of the Arab World, different religious groups live in peaceful integration, such as the Islamic, Jewish, and Christian communities of Morocco, while in Lebanon for decades nearly equipollent Christian and Moslem have fought in civil war with one another.

Nor is the Arab World particularly unified in political terms. Iraq's Gulf War invasion of Kuwait and attacks on Saudi Arabia are only the most dramatic illustration of this point, but other less belligerent tensions also exist.

Another definition of the Arab World is historical, as its members share certain common attributes of culture derived from a shared history. Most of the Arab World was united in a period ranging roughly from the eighth to the thirteenth centuries A.D. under an empire that at its height exceeded in size ancient Rome. The historic Arab Empire, however, included much of what is today no longer part of the Arab World. In the east, it stretched to the Chinese border (and so included Iran and much of south central Asia, none of which are Arabic). In the north it included the Italian islands of Sardinia and Sicily, and virtually all of present-day Spain and Portugal. Still, much of the borders of the historic Arab Empire match the region of the modern Arab World.

Though the Arab World is not easy to define, the combination of Arab language, North African and southwest Asian geography, and historical and cultural ties to the Arab Empire may present a working definition of the region.

HISTORY

The history of the region of the Arab World certainly predates the Arab Empire, but not as Arabic history.

Egypt was united in 3200 B.C. and has remained a single entity to the present. Mesopotamia—in modern-day Iraq—was the seat of the first civilization to perfect writing. Significantly, the Mesopotamians invented writing in order to carry out business.

The Phoenician trading empire of the eastern Mediterranean gave the entire Arab World a sense of the importance of international trade in ancient times, flowering in Carthage in North Africa with an empire rivaling Rome and eventually destroyed by the Romans. The region was also unified under the Byzantine Empire after the fall of Rome.

Still, the history of the Arab World is the history of the Arab Empire. In the seventh century A.D. Islam began to spread very rapidly from the Arabian peninsula where Mohammed had lived and founded the religion as its Prophet. From the death of Mohammed in 632 A.D., it took Arab armies only three generations to form an empire reaching as far west as Spain and as far east as China. Many factors contributed to the rapid spread of Islam, including the pre-existing trade routes, the popularity of the monotheistic message of Islam and its accompanying tenets of the equality of all believers, the tolerance Islam preached for Jews and Christians as "people of the book," and the fragmented leadership of much of the region where it spread.

With the spread of Islam and the conquest of the Arab armies came unity under Arabic government. Although the area of the domain included many languages, the language uniting this vast empire for trade and government was Arabic. This in turn spread Arabic culture in the empire. The importance in Islam of pilgrimage to Mecca also served as a unifying element since it promoted travel across the region and with it the exchange of ideas and awareness of cultural practices.

The seat of the Arab empire shifted from the Arabian peninsula early on to Baghdad in modern-day Iraq. Baghdad was the center of the medieval Arab World for over 500 years. Because Islam places great value on learning, the Arabs were able to avoid much of the struggle between faith and reason that acted as an obstacle to trade and science in Christian Europe at the same time. Out of this respect for learning the Arabs built up enormous libraries, saving in the process the writings of the ancient world and reintroducing them to Europe, laying the foundation of the Renaissance.

Only after the invasion by the Mongols, including the destruction of Baghdad in the thirteenth century, did the golden age of the Arab Empire begin to decline. With its decline, several factional groups rose in the fourteenth and fifteenth centuries, most notably the Mamluks. By the early fifteenth century, however, the Ottoman Turks—a non-Arabic but still Islamic people—had conquered Egypt (1517) and extended their rule over most of the Arab World (with the exceptions of Oman, Bahrain, and Morocco) in the next 100 years. The Ottomans held sway over most of the Arab World for the next two centuries when their rule, weakened by internal difficulties, was increasingly challenged by European colonizers.

Beginning in the first third of the nineteenth century, Europe began to divide the Arab World (along with much of the rest of the globe) in a policy of imperialism. As early as 1839, Britain established a base on the Arabian peninsula to protect its Indian trade routes. It was, however, France which began the occupation of the Arab World in earnest when it wrested Algeria from the Ottomans after over a decade of warfare in 1841. Britain established an exclusive treaty—negotiating its occupation—with the formerly independent Bahrain in 1861. France then took over Tunisia outright from the Ottomans in 1881, and Britain occupied Egypt the next year in 1882. Britain set up more exclusive treaties, first with independent Oman in 1891, but then with Ottoman controlled areas of the United Arab Emirates (1892) and Kuwait

(1899) over which they then assumed administration, effectively transferring control. In 1911, Italy declared Libya a protectorate. Soon after, France conquered the formerly independent Morocco in 1912. In 1916, Britain entered into one of its last exclusive treaties, negotiating the occupation of Qatar.

The Ottoman Empire—what remained of it—entered World War I on the German side, and lost. Following World War I, the victorious French and British divided the rest of the Arab World with France, taking Lebanon and Syria while Britain took over Iraq, Palestine, and Jordan.

Resentment of colonial occupation led to independence movements throughout the Arab World. This resistance led to rather rapid return to at least partial self-rule in the British territories of Egypt (1922), Jordan (1923), and a bit later in Iraq (1932) in the interwar years. Still, it was not until after World War II that Britain gave up its military control and at least partial political governance.

After World War II, the European powers were substantially weakened and the Arab World broke away in a series of independence struggles. Italy, which had lost the war, was the weakest and its colony Libya was the first to achieve postwar independence (1951). Tunisia and Morocco broke free of France in 1956. Independence, however, had to wait until the 1960s for Mauritania, Kuwait, and Yemen; and even the 1970s for Bahrain, Qatar, and the United Arab Emirates. The last colony, Djibouti, received independence from France only in 1977.

While retaining much of the unity of a shared culture and even gaining a new commonality in its hatred of colonial occupation, the Arab World emerged from occupation as fragmented as the myriad colonies the Europeans had carved out of the Ottoman Empire.

With the last vestige of colonialism only thrown off in the 1970s, it is not surprising that a re-emergence of nationalism among many former European colonies, including Arab nationalism, also resurfaced in the period following World War II. With this new nationalism came the desire on the part of the former colonies to reclaim control of their natural resources. In 1960, several oil producing nations joined together to form the Organization of Petroleum Exporting Countries (OPEC). Since OPEC only included ected producers and since roughly half of these nations were non-Arab, an additional Organization of Arab Oil Producing Countries was formed in 1968. Both OPEC and OAPEC helped coordinate pricing of petroleum exports.

It was during the 1970s, however, that the most significant shift in the control of oil took place. First Libya, and then Iraq and Algeria, nationalized their foreign oil companies. During the same decade, both Saudi Arabia and Kuwait purchased controlling interest of theirs. Before this shift in control, eight major companies based in the United States, Britain, and France controlled virtually all of the profits derived from the production of oil in the Arab World. Indeed, both Britain and the United States made more in taxes on oil from the Arab countries than the combined money made by all the Arab countries themselves.

Concurrent with this shift in control of the key natural resource of petroleum from U.S. and European interests to those of the Arab nations, a predictable shift in attention to doing business in the Arab World followed. With this background in mind, the following section touches on some of the major characteristics of doing business in the Arab nations.

LANGUAGE

The Arabic language is the foremost unifier of the nations of the Arab World. It is the official language of all of the Arab nations, by definition. Arabic is also an official language of the United Nations; it is a greater unifier of the Arab World than any other characteristic joining together such ethnically and racially diverse groups of people.

While Arabic is spoken as a first language by millions of Christians as well as thousands of Jews and Druzes, it remains a language of religious importance far beyond its approximately 190 million native speakers since it is the holy language of the world's approximately one billion followers of Islam.

Because of the colonial experience, many Arabs speak at least one European language. English and French are extremely widespread among the educated elite, many of whom were educated in Europe, Canada, or the United States. Nevertheless, the value of speaking Arabic is significant. Because many of the former colonial French and British occupiers of the Arab World felt that speaking Arabic was beneath them and failed to appreciate the richness of Arabic culture, speaking English or French without making any effort to learn even a little Arabic may well carry with it negative feelings. On the other hand, even speaking a small amount of Arabic is usually very much appreciated and establishes the English or French speaker's respect for Arabic culture.

The Arabic script is the lettering system of Arabic as well as dozens of other African and Asian languages such as Farsi and Urdu.

Arabic script is relatively easy to master for non-native speakers as it is phonetic with a particularly consistent system of spelling. Nevertheless, several vowels in Arabic—as with its sister Semitic language Hebrew—are indicated by non-letter marks (e.g., dashes) that are present only in formal writing. As a result, the writing of everyday life may be somewhat difficult for those learning to read the language in a structured setting.

Arabic is based on a root system of words. Words are formed around a root of three consonants. This is both a help and a hindrance to the speaker of Arabic as a second language. It is a help as a single root will open up dozens of related words, allowing the rapid acquisition of a vocabulary and a fairly accurate method for guessing the meaning of words not yet learned. It is a hindrance because Arab dictionaries are organized by root, not alphabetically as in European languages. This makes looking up new words difficult for the novice.

Modern Standard Arabic is taught in schools throughout the Arab World. Nevertheless, dialect differences are significant. Not all dialects are fully understandable to all others. The business person translating documents into Arabic would be safe in using Modern Arabic Standard. The marketer trying to reach a local market, by contrast, would do well to employ a translator familiar with the dialect of the targeted region.

ENVIRONMENT AND TECHNOLOGY

The Arab World is at once resource poor and resource rich. The economic success of the Arab World rests in its richness of natural resources—especially petroleum. Yet the majority of Arab nations have little other natural resources. The majority of the Arab countries are very dry with limited agriculture.

Additionally, most Arab nations are painfully dependent on a single commodity. Ten of the Arab nations rely on petroleum for over 50 percent of their export revenues: Algeria, Bahrain, Iraq, Kuwait, Libya, Oman, Qatar, Saudi Arabia, Syria, and the United Arab Emirates. Additionally, two more Arab nations depend on a single resource other than petroleum for over fifty percent of their export revenues: Morocco (fertilizer) and Mauritania (iron ore). Thus, over half of the Arab nations are extremely dependent on a single non-renewable commodity. To this end, Arab business culture is centered on trading this diminishing natural resource for a long-term benefit.

The traditional Arabic view of technology may be called a subjugation attitude. Much of Arab culture has been heavily influenced by Islamic tradition. While Islam has long favored education and was the bastion of science when Christian Europe had abandoned it during the Middle Ages, Islam also teaches acceptance with the way they were divinely made. Technological innovations are welcome as long as they act to serve God's will; long-term planning or change may be resisted in some strongly Islamic nations—including those outside of the Arab World—because it threatens to disrupt the divine will. This does not mean that numerous Arabic companies—especially in the Gulf countries—do not have the latest in computer technology and other technological devices; it does mean that the ramifications of how technology is used is more likely to be considered in the Arab World than in the West.

SOCIAL ORGANIZATION

FAMILY TIES. The concept of family in the Arab World is generally much broader than that of the United States and northern Europe. Close family ties exist between cousins, in-laws, and many other familial relationships considered to be distant in the United States. The number of close relations—akin to the loyalty of nuclear families in North America——in many Arab families often exceeds 100.

This family concept becomes important in business because, as Margaret Nydell explains, "Family loyalty and obligations take precedence over loyalty to friends or the demands of the job."

Family ties, in turn, influence those with whom one does business. Nepotism, which carries a negative stigma in the United States, is considered a positive virtue in most of the Arab World. Hiring one's own relatives ensures loyalty and trust. "The family in turn," Michael Field writes, "is the foundation of the intensely personal view of the world that Arabians have.... People—individuals and families—are much more real to Arabians than institutions." Field goes on to note, speaking particularly of the countries of the Arabian peninsula, "Arabians do not see society as a vast, impersonal mass of people containing a few individuals whom they will meet at various times in their lives and with whom they will form business or personal relationships. Rather, their world is made up of a web of communities, tribes and families—some they know personally, but all they know of."

RELIGION. Many people outside of the Arab world do not see its religious diversity. Nearly 14 million Arabs are Christian. Large Arabic Christian populations exist in Lebanon, Syria and Sudan, representing sizable percentages of the overall population. Although the percentage of the total population is smaller due to its greater overall population, the largest Arabic Christian community is in Egypt, center of the 6 million strong Coptic Church. Numerous other Eastern Rite Christian churches are primarily comprised of Arabs, most notably the Assyrian Church of the East, the Syrian Orthodox and the Armenian Orthodox. Non-Eastern Rite Churches also have large followings, notably the Maronite Catholics of Lebanon and the numerous Eastern Rite Catholics recognizing the Pontiff in Rome.

Additionally, ancient communities of Jews live in Morocco, where they are well integrated into society. Less well accepted communities of Jews also form a sizeable minority in Syria and Egypt.

Still, the overwhelming majority of Arabs follow Islam as their religion. Over 90 percent of the people in 17 of the Arab countries—excluding foreign workers—practice Islam.

It is important to note that while Islam is the predominant religion in much of the Arab world, Islam is much more widespread than the Arab World. Indeed, of the five nations with the largest Moslem populations, none is Arab: Indonesia, Pakistan, Bangladesh, India, and Turkey. This is not to deny that the Arab world is very important to Moslems worldwide. Arabic is the language of the Koran. Mecca, the holiest city of Islam, is in Saudi Arabia, and the Haj—or pilgrimage to Mecca—is one of the five pillars of Islam required of Moslem.

Islam, in many of the Arab countries, pervades all aspects of life making no distinction between the secular and the religious. Islam is as much a lifestyle as a religion in this respect.

Prohibitions of certain products (for example, those containing alcohol) can play a factor in business. Non-Moslems are banned from Mecca and Medina, the holy cities of Saudi Arabia, a fact that made the initial installation and maintenance of those cities' telecommunication systems difficult for workers of Bell Canada. The discussion of religion is more likely to be assumed in heavily Islamic countries since it is so much a part of life. Not being Moslem is, however, less a detriment than not believing in a religion. Being a Christian or Jew, for example, is not only understood but recognized in the Koran; being an atheist or agnostic may exceed belief and would certainly undercut one's respect.

GENDER ROLES. Gender roles are strongly differentiated in the Arab World. Considerable diversity exists among how women are treated from one Arab country to another. Education for women is one area in which particularly rapid advances have been made. In Egypt, for example, many women hold advanced degrees in a variety of fields and teach in university level positions. Several Egyptian women have held positions at the United Nations. Women have held high positions at universities and organizations in other Arab countries as well, but these individuals represent the exceptions.

While many writers suggest that Islam is at the root of the secondary role of women in most Arab nations, this is not fully true. Islam itself lays out gender differentiation, but Islam does not teach subjugation to a secondary role. Moreover, there are millions of Arab Christian women who must be considered separately from such generalizations.

Nevertheless, many Arab women are relegated to a secondary status. While they may be honored and cherished in their household roles, the business world is customarily prohibited to most Arab women. Socially, women are protected from scandal by chaperoning in public. Indeed, in Saudi Arabia women are prohibited from driving.

CONTEXTING AND FACE-SAVING

Arab culture is what Edward T. Hall termed "high context"; the United States is a "low context" culture. The more highly contexted a culture is, the more the context of what is communicated matters and the less the actual words used matter. The more low contexted a culture is, the less important the situation surrounding the message is and the more important the actual words communicated are.

Since Arab culture is high context, the amount of stored information needed to communicate effectively in business is quite extensive in order to form a context by which to judge any individual communication exchange. The actual new information needed to communicate, by contrast, is relatively small since most of what is communicated is shared through stored information. By contrast, the U.S. business person is accustomed to low context information where one needs to know little or nothing about the person with whom one communicates since virtually all of one's meaning is transmitted directly through explicit words.

The clash of low and high context communication can cause serious misunderstandings. Arabs, as high context communicators in the eyes of many U.S. business people, are seemingly concerned with irrelevant or personal details (building a context) while unduly vague and indirect (since the context, not the words themselves, convey the meaning). By contrast, U.S. business people in the eyes of many Arab business people are seemingly overly direct and require to have even the most obvious details explained to them (that is, they can only understand what they are told since they cannot effectively read the contexted information).

Arab culture also tends to place great value on how well something is said. The rhetorical value in how one words one's point is important. Since context allows the receiver of a message to understand what is really meant, one is free to exaggerate for rhetorical effect. This elaboration for eloquence's sake is often misunderstood by U.S. business people in the Arab World as lying. Conversely, the U.S. business person's failure to elaborate may make his or her presentation of the information appear dull, uninspired, and ultimately unconvincing.

Like most high context cultures, face-saving is very important in the Arab World. Victor defines "face-saving as the act of preserving one's prestige or outward dignity." The need to show adequate respect often leads to the exchange of formalized politeness. The U.S. business person is thus usually taken back by the extreme hospitality of his or her Arab hosts, but is unable to differentiate true politeness from the expected exchange of niceties. Moreover, the Arab businessperson must accommodate the lack of concern for face so widespread in the United States and other low context cultures or risk misreading what may be a series of unmeant slights as intentional.

NONVERBAL BEHAVIOR

Nonverbal behavior shifts dramatically from country to country. Arab and U.S. nonverbal behavior shifts most noticeably in the following areas.

DRESS. Arab dress differs radically in many parts of the Arab World. In Lebanon and Syria, Western-style clothing is commonplace. In Saudi Arabia and the Gulf States, the ghutra (head cloth) and thobe (long, generally white, flowing robe) are the standard. The U.S. business person would do well to learn to recognize distinctions in the clothing of the region he or she is in to tell appropriate dress from inappropriate and to tell clan or nationality indicators. It is also useful to determine when an Arab associate has dressed in Western garb because it is customary for him to do so or because he is attempting to make his Western counterpart feel more at ease.

It is not necessary for Westerners to dress in traditional Arabic outfits. Few Arab business people would expect this or even desire it. It is, however, necessary to make sure that one's own outfit is customarily modest. While levels of modesty vary from one part of the Arab world to the next, exposure of bare skin in shorts or short-sleeve shirts would almost universally be inappropriate for men or women. One should look closely to the materials one has brought along as well. It is not uncommon to have brochures or reports with models dressed immodestly posed next to a product or to have people in standard U.S. work situations or leisure time activities photographed in outfits that would be considered inappropriate.

BODY SPACE. Body space or proxemics shifts dramatically between U.S. and Arab standards. Most people speaking face to face in business situations in the United States stand at approximately arm's length. Most Arabs consider about one quarter of that distance to be appropriate. It is not uncommon to feel the breath of the other party on one's face in the proper Arab distance.

The customary U.S. distance is misread as being too stand-offish by Arabs. The average Arab distance is misread as being too aggressive and pushy by their U.S. counterparts.

HAPTICS. Haptics or touching behavior also differs radically between the United States and the Arabic World. Arabs of the same gender are very haptic, that is they touch extensively when speaking. Arm-patting and even knee-touching is not uncommon. Men often walk hand in hand in many parts of the Arab world. Greetings are usually accompanied by hugs and gestured kisses between men. Virtually all of these behaviors make most U.S. business people uncomfortable. The United States is essentially an ahaptic or non-touching culture. Aside from the handshake—which by Arabic greeting standards is very brief and attenuated—virtually no touching among the same gender is tolerable.

Touching between genders in much of the Arab World is, by contrast, totally forbidden in public. While some Arab countries (most notably Lebanon) do not hold handshaking as taboo and while most business men accustomed to Western business women may be willing to shake hands with Western women in business situations, such behavior is usually a concession and should be viewed as such. Refusal to touch a woman does not mean that the Arab business man is sexist or refuses to deal with Western business women; it is a moral breach for him. Western men and women should also take care to avoid moral breaches by, for example, taking care regarding kissing or hand-holding in public.

TIME CONCEPTION

The Arab World runs on what Edward Hall has called "polychronic" time; the United States on "monochronic" time.

In the Arab conception, time is fluid; in the United States, time is concrete. In the Arab world, as in all polychronic cultures, preset schedules are subordinate to interpersonal relations so that personal ties affect the schedule. In short, the schedule is flexible. In monochronic societies such as the United States, the schedule dominates interpersonal relations. The preset schedule, not the people involved, coordinates the length of time people will meet. In other words, the schedule is rigid.

In the Arab conception of time, each task is handled through completion and as a result multiple tasks can be undertaken simultaneously. Because the person in authority must give the person who is with him as much time as needed to complete the task at hand, Arab culture relies heavily on people who screen for these people. This in turn encourages personal relationships at work in order to receive preferential treatment and not be screened out.

The United States, by contrast, is organized on exactly the opposite conception of time. The schedule precludes any preferential treatment based on personal relationships. Indeed, personal relationships at work are looked on with suspicion since they may subvert maintaining one's schedule. One's appointment—not one's personal relationship—is what determines when one person sees another in the schedule.

The resulting friction deriving from these two conceptions of time and personal relationships can be quite severe in U.S.-Arab interactions. U.S. business people are seen as having no concept of personal relationships; Arab business people are seen as having no concept of schedule.

While the Arab world is a highly diverse combination of various peoples, many characteristics are shared in history and culture that affect the work place. The reader is urged to seek further sources of information on the specific countries in which he or she will do business. The United States maintains consulates in most of the Arab countries which can provide further information on specific countries. Also, most of the Arab nations have consulates in the United States. Many Arab countries have Chambers of Commerce and many U.S. Chambers of Commerce exist in several Arab countries as well. Several organizations, such as the Arab Information Centers in Washington and New York, and the Arab Studies departments of many universities, are also good sources of information. Finally, several major U.S. cities such as Detroit with substantial Arab American populations have American Arab Chambers of Commerce that are also useful sources of information for research on Arab subjects.

SEE ALSO: Cross-Cultural/International Business Communication

[David A. Victor]

FURTHER READING:

Field, Michael. *The Merchants: The Big Business Families of Saudi Arabia and the Gulf States.* New York: Overlook Press, 1984.

Hall, Edward T. *The Dance of Life: The Other Dimensions of Time.* Garden City, New York: Anchor Press/Doubleday, 1983.

Lamb, David. *The Arabs.* New York: Vintage, 1987.

Nydell, Margaret. *Understanding Arabs: A Guide for Westerners.* Yarmouth, Maine: Intercultural Press, 1987.

Victor, David A. *International Business Communication.* New York: HarperCollins, 1992.

ARBITRAGE

Arbitrage, in the context of financial markets, refers to earning money from either a current or expected inconsistency in the pricing of an asset or group of **assets**. For example, consider a dual-listed stock selling for $30 on one stock exchange and $40 on another. To make a guaranteed profit one only needs to buy the $30 stock and sell it for $40 on the other exchange. This is an example of an immediate arbitrage opportunity. Situations in which an asset has two different expected payoffs form expected arbitrage opportunities. Such a situation seems to occur at the casino. The casino's owners know that the odds of a customer winning on a roulette wheel by betting on either red or black are not 50 percent, but they pay out one for one on the amount gambled. This means that on any given spin the owners may lose money, but on average they will win.

Nevertheless, viewed in a more general context, the casino example may not be arbitrage. This is because the owners view the roulette wheel strictly as a long-term money-making proposition. The players, though, may derive some pleasure from the gamble itself and are willing to pay for the time spent having fun. Viewed from this perspective there may be little or no arbitrage. In general, apparent expected arbitrages must be examined carefully, to check whether what appears to be mispricing is not actually a risk premium (when one party transfers risk to another), or a utility providing service (when one party derives increased happiness from a transaction that the other does not).

Arbitrage is very closely tied to the concept of market efficiency. Proponents of the efficient market hypothesis (EMH) maintain that the only way to reliably earn more than the risk-free bond return in the market is to accept economic risk. The only way this can be true is if the market is free of opportunities for traders to earn arbitrage profits (this condition is necessary for efficient markets, but not sufficient). The rationale for arguing against the existence of arbitrage lies in the assumption that there exist large numbers of well-informed analysts. The moment an arbitrage opportunity presents itself, the potential arbitragers respond and drive it from the marketplace. Of course, this cannot literally be true or there would not be enough analysts earning money from looking for mispriced securities to keep the markets efficient. Determining the degree to which markets display efficiency, and hence the degree to which arbitrage opportunities exist in the marketplace, is a ongoing topic of research. Few researchers maintain that the market is perfectly efficient, and few maintain that arbitrage opportunities exist for long periods before the actions of arbitragers remove them.

When investing money, a portfolio manager's beliefs about the existence of arbitrage opportunities will greatly affect his or her management style. At the one extreme a manager may choose to invest according to the **capital asset pricing model** (CAPM) or the arbitrage pricing theory (APT). These models rely solely on quantifying economic risk as the vehicle for making investment decisions. Furthermore, they look only at average long-term results, completely ignoring the possibility that the market may occasionally have inconsistencies and mispricing. In fact, the APT derives its name from one of its central assumptions that no arbitrage is possible. On the other extreme are arbitrageurs. These are people who look exclusively for market mispricings and inconsistencies to make investment decisions. Arbitrageurs do not consider economic risk since their plan is to make investments that profit without taking such risk. Also, it is usually the case that arbitrageurs are considering too short an investment period for economic risk to have any real meaning.

Arbitragers look for opportunities in many different markets. One of the most common is in **foreign exchange**. For example, if the German deutsche mark to U.S. dollar exchange rate is 1.5 and the French franc to U.S. dollar exchange rate is 5.0, then the German deutsche mark to French franc rate must be 1.5/5.0 = 0.3 or else there is arbitrage. To illustrate, suppose the German deutsche mark (DM) to French franc (Fr) rate is actually at 0.4. An arbitrageur could sell $1,000,000 to receive Fr 5,000,000. Then the arbitrageur could sell the Fr 5,000,000 to receive DM 2,000,000. Finally, the arbitrageur could sell the DM 2,000,000 to receive $1,333,333.33. Since all transactions are done at the same time, the transaction is self-financing and nets $333,333.33 with no risk. Needless to say, in the real world the discrepancies rarely get this large and exist for a very short time before buying the cheap asset and selling the expensive one causes the gap to close.

Derivative securities are also favorite tools of arbitrageurs. Important relationships among the **futures**, **options**, **bonds**, stocks, and currencies markets exist, which if violated signal an arbitrage opportunity. One such relationship, called interest rate parity, links the futures and spot markets in a currency to the interest rate differential between the two countries. If the percentage difference between the futures market and spot markets exchange rates is greater or less than the percentage difference in **interest rates** between the two countries, the arbitrageur has a money-making opportunity. For example, say that German deutsche marks are currently 1.5 per dollar, and a futures contract obligates the holder to pay 1.2 in three months. Now, suppose the interest rates for three months are 3 percent (.03) in the United States and 2 percent (.02) in Germany. An arbitrageur would borrow $1,000,000 and invest DM 1,500,000. The arbitrageur would also enter a futures contract. In three months, the arbitrageur would receive DM 1,530,000 that could be converted back at 1.2 to $1,275,000. The U.S. loan is paid back for $1,030,000 leaving a riskless profit of $245,000.

The preceding examples are immediate arbitrage opportunities. Market mispricing allows immediate riskless profits to be realized. Two types of expected arbitrage opportunities are index arbitrage and interest rate arbitrage. Index arbitrage arises when the futures price of a stock index moves out of line with the cost of buying the index today plus the foregone interest on the money tied up in buying the index, less the expected **dividends**

$$ F \neq S + I - D $$

The arbitrageur buys the cheaper position and sells the more expensive one to make a profit. The problem is that dividends paid in the futures are uncertain so one can expect the profit but not guarantee it. To make this kind of arbitrage profit, the arbitrageur must have very good **forecasting** ability.

Interest rate arbitrage uses the government bond market and the treasury futures markets. Treasury futures markets provide prices for government debt in the future and hence can be used to estimate future interest rates. The actual bond market, however, may also be used to estimate future interest rates. For example, if one year bonds are at 8.0 percent and two-year bonds are at 9.0 percent then a good estimate of next year's one-year rate should be about 10 percent, since 8 percent plus 10 percent would average to 9 percent for the two years. If, however, the estimated interest rate from the futures contract did not indicate 10 percent for the second year, the arbitrageur would attempt to capitalize on the pricing discrepancy. Once again, the arbitrageur must be a good forecaster, and may or may not be actually accepting economic risk.

[Rick A. Cooper]

FURTHER READING:

Chance, Don M. *An Introduction to Derivatives.* 3rd ed. Fort Worth, TX: Dryden, 1994.

Elton, Edwin J., and Martin J. Gruber. *Modern Portfolio Theory and Investment Analysis.* 4th ed. New York: Wiley, 1991.

Haugan, Robert A. *Modern Investment Theory.* 3rd ed. Englewood Cliffs, NJ: Prentice-Hall, 1993.

Ingersoll, Jonathon E. *Theory of Financial Decision Making.* Totawa, NJ: Rowman & Littlefield, 1987.

Radcliffe, Robert C. *Investment: Concepts, Analysis, Strategy.* 4th ed. New York: HarperCollins, 1994.

Stoll, Hans R., and Robert E. Whaley. *Futures and Options: Theory and Applications.* Cincinnati, OH: South-Western, 1993.

ARBITRATION AND MEDIATION

Arbitration and mediation are parts of the labor relations process. Arbitration is the procedure by which parties agree to submit their disputes to an independent neutral third party, known as an arbitrator. Although there are several types of arbitration, labor arbitration is the dispute resolution procedure used in labor relations. Mediation also involves the active participation of a neutral third party whose role is to facilitate the dispute resolution process and to suggest solutions to resolve disputes. The term conciliation is often used interchangeably with mediation, but conciliation generally refers to the third party who brings the disputing parties together. While the mediator suggests possible solutions to the disputing parties, the arbitrator makes a final decision on the labor dispute which is binding on the parties.

As a process, arbitration predates English common law and has been called the oldest form of dispute settlement. King Solomon was an arbitrator and arbitration was utilized for settling differences during the Greco-Roman period. George Washington was an advocate of arbitration and, in his will, mandated using the process if disputes arose over his estate. The use of arbitration in labor disputes was a common practice in the late 19th century but developed more rapidly after World War II as a substitute for work stoppages. In the collective bargaining process, labor arbitration is generally the final stage of resolution.

Labor unions and management develop a collective bargaining agreement that details the rights of labor, the responsibilities of management, and the ultimate relationship between the two. Nearly all (96 percent) of these collective bargaining agreements provide for arbitration as the final step in dispute resolution. Arbitration can represent either all employees covered by the agreement or a specific individual on one side and management concerns on the other. Arbitration holds advantages over both strikes and litigation as a means of resolving disputes. Even the U.S. Supreme Court has determined that arbitration is the preferred method of resolution in reaching a workable solution to labor problems.

During World War II, the National War Labor Board gave great impetus to the use of arbitration. The Board heard over 20,000 labor disputes during the war and frequently mandated that future cases utilize arbitration. The President's National Labor-Management Conference of 1945 also recommended the application of the arbitration process to settle labor disputes. A major advantage to arbitration is the cost, especially when compared to the expense of litigation.

There are several organizations and agencies directly involved in arbitration and arbitration issues including the National Academy of Arbitrators (NAA), the American Arbitration Association (AAA), and the **Federal Mediation and Conciliation Service (FMCS)**. The NAA was founded in 1947 as a non-profit organization to foster high standards for arbitration and arbitrators and to promote the process. Through seminars, annual conferences, and educational programs, the NAA works to attain its objectives. The AAA is also non-profit and offers its services for voluntary arbitration to meet the objective to promote the use of arbitration in all fields. Meetings and educational programs highlight AAA efforts, although the organization does not arbitrate. The FMCS maintains a roster from which arbitrators can be selected and suggests procedures and guides to enhance the arbitration process.

The labor arbitration process involves an arbitrator and representatives of both labor and management. The arbitrator is either a permanent arbitrator, an independent arbitrator selected by the two parties to resolve a particular grievance, or an arbitrator selected through the procedures of the AAA or FMCS. A board of arbitrators can also be used in a hearing. After selection, the arbitrator then hears from both sides of the issue with testimony and evidence provided in much the same way as a court proceeding. Upon completion of the arbitration hearing, the arbitrator reviews the evidence, testimony, and the collective bargaining agreement, considers principles of arbitration, and makes a decision. The arbitrator's decision is generally rendered within 60 days, and, when all parties agree, is submitted for possible publication by one of several commercial publishers, either the U.S. Bureau of National Affairs (*Labor Arbitration Reports*), the Commerce Clearing House (*Labor Arbitration Awards*), or other sources. Fewer than 10 percent of these decisions are published. While intended to be binding or a final decision, arbitration findings can be appealed, but few are overturned.

Labor arbitration is used to describe the process briefly detailed above. There are several other types or forms of labor arbitration, briefly defined as follows:

- Compulsory arbitration is a dispute resolution which is required by law. Widely accepted in Australia and New Zealand, compulsory arbitration was practiced by the National War Labor Board during World War II. This is a binding process.

- Expedited arbitration is a process intended to speed up the arbitration process with an informal hearing and awards generally rendered within five days. It was first used in 1971 in settling disputes in the steel industry. Expedited arbitration was also designed as a cost-saving method of dispute resolution.

- Interest arbitration is the use of an arbitrator or arbitrator board to render a binding decision in resolving a dispute over new contract terms (also called nonjusticiable arbitration).

- Final offer selection arbitration is an interest arbitration process in which the arbitrator or arbitrator board selects either the union or management proposal to the solution. There can be no compromised decisions. This process is also termed either-or arbitration.

- Tripartite arbitration is a process wherein a three member panel of arbitrators is used to reach a decision. Both labor and management select an arbitrator and the third is selected by the other two arbitrators or the parties to the dispute as a neutral participant.

In contrast to arbitration, mediation is a process whereby the parties involved have to solve the dispute, although the mediator does suggest various proposals to help the parties find solutions. In mediation, the various needs of the conflicting sides of an issue are identified, and ideas and concepts are exchanged until a viable solution is proposed by either of the parties or the mediator. Rarely does the mediator exert pressure to accept a solution. The role, rather, is to encourage communication and exchange in order to resolve the dispute. The key to the concept of mediation is neutrality.

Like arbitration, mediation is deeply rooted in history. Essayist and scientist Francis Bacon (1561-1626) advocated the mediation of disputes. Since the essence of mediation is compromise, it could be said that much of American history is the history of mediating disputes. As a process in labor disputes, mediation is a basic tenet of the development of our society in the 20th century. Congress created the Federal Mediation Conciliation Service (FMCS) in 1947 to cut down on strikes and ease tension in labor disputes. Over the last 15 years, the popularity of mediation as a means of dispute resolution has grown enormously, and mediation impacts problems other than labor disputes. In 1980, for example, the state of California adopted mediation in child custody and visitation conflicts. A disagreement over a proposed flood control dam in the state of Washington was addressed by mediation in 1983. Over 160 environmental disputes before 1985 involved the use of mediators. The obvious success of the concept has been cited as the best hope for eliminating racial violence and lesser crimes. Many police departments and law enforcement agencies now employ mediators as a regular means to solving disputes. Many attorneys see mediation as having unlimited potential in what has become a litigious society. Although mediation's critics have been quick to level sharp barbs at its weaknesses, the process may well shape the future of conflict resolution on all fronts.

In labor disputes, the terms grievance mediation and preventive mediation are commonly used. Grievance mediation is an attempt to ward off arbitration

generally, involving fact finding with the objective of promoting dialogue. Preventive mediation dates to the **Taft-Hartley Act** (1947) and is an FMCS program intended to avoid deeper divisions between labor and management over labor issues. Also termed as technical assistance, the program encompasses training, education, consultation, and analysis of union-management disputes.

In the long and often bitter history of labor disputes in our nation, arbitration and mediation have been widely utilized as means of dispute resolution. Unions and companies hoping to avoid a legal solution to a labor dispute generally resort to one of these methods. The processes are now integral parts of our business environment and in use far more commonly than the general public realizes.

Other than labor arbitration, there are two other types of arbitration. These are commercial arbitration, which is used as a substitute for litigation in the settlement of disputes between businesspeople or businesses, and international arbitration, which involves the resolution of differences between nations—disputes which, if left unsolved, could lead to war. Historically, commercial arbitration developed as an alternative to a court settlement while labor arbitration was utilized to avoid strikes or work stoppages. In recent years, international commercial arbitration has become a popular means of settling disputes between businesses internationally.

[Boyd Childress]

FURTHER READING:

Elkouri, Frank and Edna Asper. *How Arbitration Works*. U.S. Bureau of National Affairs, 1985.

Kagel, Sam and Kathy Kelly. *The Anatomy of Mediation: What Makes it Work*. Bureau of National Affairs, 1989.

ARTIFICIAL INTELLIGENCE

Scientists are trying to create computers that can "think," i.e., act with human-like intelligence. It is a daunting task, one which has eluded them so far. There have been some successes, but there must be many more before computers can actually think. The research has created a great deal of controversy, since the imminence of true "thinking" machines has prompted critics to wonder whether artificial intelligence (AI) will ultimately lead to the demise of society, or, at best, impact individuals' lives adversely. Today, computers are far from being able to conceptualize or reason—but that will someday change.

WHAT IS ARTIFICIAL INTELLIGENCE?

Defining AI is very difficult. One area of agreement is that artificial intelligence is a field of scientific inquiry, rather than an end product. AI is difficult to define with any preciseness partially because several different groups of researchers with drastically different motivations are working in the field. Perhaps the best definition is that coined by M.L. Minsky, "Artificial intelligence is the science of making machines do things that would require intelligence if done by men."

HISTORY OF ARTIFICIAL INTELLIGENCE

Charles Babbage, (1792-1871) an English mathematician, is generally acknowledged to be the "Father of Modern Computing." Around 1823 he invented a working model of the world's first practical mechanical calculator. Then, he began work on his "analytical engine," which had the basic elements of a modern-day computer. Unfortunately, he was unable to raise the funds needed to build his machine. Nevertheless, his ideas lived on.

Herman Hollerith, (1860-1929) an American inventor, actually created the first working calculating machine, which was used to tabulate the results of the 1890 U.S. census. There ensued a series of rapid improvements to machines which allegedly "thought." The first true electronic computer, the Electronic Numerical Integrator and Computer (ENIAC), was developed in 1946. The so-called "giant brain" replaced mechanical switches with glass vacuum tubes. ENIAC used 17,468 vacuum tubes and occupied 1,800 square feet—the size of an average house. It weighed 30 tons! Scientists began at once to build smaller computers.

In 1959, scientists at Bell Laboratories invented the transistor, which marked the beginning of the second generation of computers. Transistors replaced vacuum tubes and sped up processing considerably. They also made possible a large increase in computer memory. Ten years later, International Business Machines Corp. (IBM) created third-generation computers. When they replaced transistors with integrated circuits. A single integrated circuit could replace a large number of transistors in a silicon chip less than one-eighth of an inch square! More importantly, integrated circuits allowed manufacturers to dramatically reduce the size of computers. New software which made use of increased speed and memory complemented these third-generation computers—which themselves proved to be short lived.

Only two years after the appearance of integrated circuits, Intel Corp. introduced microprocessor chips. One chip contained a computer's central processing unit. Prior to that time, computers contained specialized chips for functions such as logic and programming. Intel's invention placed all of the computers' functions on one chip. Scientists continued to improve on computers.

Miniaturization of chips led to large-scale integrated circuitry (LSI) and very-large-scale integrated circuitry (VLSI). LSI and VLSI enabled software and printers to react faster with each other and with computers. They also contributed to the invention of microcomputers, which revolutionized the role of computers in business. More importantly, LSI and VLSI heightened scientists' interest in the development of AI.

DEVELOPMENTS IN THE STUDY OF ARTIFICIAL INTELLIGENCE

AI is the construction and/or programming of computers to imitate human thought processes. Scientists are trying to design computers capable of processing natural languages and reasoning. They believe that once machines can process natural languages such as English or Spanish, humans will be able to give instructions and ask questions without learning special computer languages. When that day arrives, machines, like humans, will be able to learn from past experience and apply what they have learned to solve new problems. Scientists have a long way to go, but they have made what they believe is a giant step in that direction with the invention of "fuzzy logic."

Since their inception, computers have always acted on a "yes" or "no" basis. They simply have not been able to recognize "maybe." Even the most sophisticated computers, capable of performing millions of calculations per second, can not distinguish between "slightly" or "very." This simple difference has confused AI scientists for years. However, an American researcher, Dr. Lofti A. Zadeh, of the University of California, presented a possible answer, which he termed "fuzzy logic."

The concept is based on feeding the computer "fuzzy sets," i.e., groupings of concrete information and relative concepts. For example, in a fuzzy set for industrial furnaces, a temperature of 1,000 degrees might have a "membership" (relative value) of 0.95, while a temperature of 600 might have a membership of 0.50. A computer program might then utilize instructions such as . . . "the higher the temperature, the lower the pressure must be." This solution means that programmers can teach machines to compute with words, instead of numbers.

Historically, most complex mathematical models developed by programmers compute strictly with numbers. However, the "fuzzy logic" approach to AI did not catch on in the American scientific community. It did, however, among the Japanese.

The Japanese company Hitachi developed an artificial intelligence system based on "fuzzy logic" that allowed an automated subway system in Sendai, Japan, to brake more swiftly and smoothly than it could under human guidance. The Japanese Ministry of International Trade and Industry budgeted $36 million in 1990 to subsidize the initial operation of a Laboratory for International Fuzzy Engineering. Development of ''fuzzy engineering'' also took hold in China, Russia, and much of Western Europe. American scientists, however, pursued other.

In the early 1990s, a University of North Carolina professor developed a micro-processor type chip using an all-digital architecture, which would allow it to run in conventional computers. The chip can handle 580,000 ''if-then'' decisions per second, which is more than 100 times faster than the best Japanese ''fuzzy logic'' chip can operate. Many U.S. companies have been experimenting with this and similar chips. The Oak Ridge National Laboratory is using the chip in robots to be employed in radioactive areas of nuclear power plants. The Oricon Corporation has used ''fuzzy logic'' in a signal analysis system for submarines. NASA has also experimented with using ''fuzzy logic'' to help dock spacecraft. Other AI applications are also in use; one is the so-called expert system.

Expert systems are computer-based systems that apply the substantial knowledge of a computer specialist to help solve complex problems. In developing such systems, designers usually work with experts to determine the information and decision rules (heuristics) that the experts use when confronted with particular types of problems. In essence, these programs are simply attempting to imitate human behavior, rather than solving problems by themselves.

There are several advantages to expert systems. For example, they give novices ''instant expertise'' in a particular area. They capture knowledge and expertise that might be lost if an expert retires or dies. Expert systems are not subject to human problems of illness or fatigue. These benefits make them particularly attractive to businesses.

Companies use expert systems for training and analysis. For instance, General Electric developed a system called Delta, which helps maintenance workers identify and correct malfunctions in locomotives. Digital Equipment Corporation uses XCON (expert CONfigurer) to match customers' needs with the most appropriate combination of computer input, output, and memory devices. The system uses more than 3,000 decision rules and 5,000 product descriptions to analyze sales orders and design layouts, ensuring that the company's equipment will work when it arrives at customers' sites. XCON catches most configuration errors, and eliminates the need for completely assembling a computer system for testing and then breaking it down again for shipment to the customer. The system is expensive, however. DEC spends $2

million per year just to update XCON. In fact, cost is one of the most prohibitive factors involved in the development of AI systems.

A moderate-sized system, comprised of about 300 decision rules, generally costs between $250,000 and $500,000 to design. That is a great deal of money to spend on creating systems that do little more than play chess—which was what some designers did back in the 1960s.

Scientists in the 1960s developed machines that could play chess in an attempt to create machines that could think by themselves. They made tremendous strides in developing sophisticated decision trees that could map out possible moves, but those programs included so many potential alternatives that even contemporary supercomputers cannot assess them within a reasonable amount of time. They reduced the number of alternatives, which allowed the machines to play at the chess master level. But, they still could not get the machines to think. All the computers were doing was processing large amounts of data on alternative moves. It is this concept that AI scientists are trying to address, i. e., creating computers that can actually think. Once they achieve this goal, there is no limit to the number of uses AI can serve.

APPLICATIONS OF AI IN THE BUSINESS WORLD

AI is being used extensively in the business world, despite the fact that the discipline itself is still in the embryonic stages of development. Its applications cross a wide spectrum. For example, AI is being applied in management and administration, science, engineering, manufacturing, financial and legal areas, military and space endeavors, medicine, and diagnostics.

Some of the implemented AI applications include natural language processing, database retrieval, expert consulting systems, theorem proving, robotics, automatic programming, scheduling1 and solving perceptual problems. Management is relying more and more on knowledge work systems, which are systems used to aid professionals such as architects, engineers, and medical technicians in the creation and dissemination of new knowledge and information. One such system is in use at Square D, an electrical component manufacturer. A computer does the design work for giant units of electrical equipment. The units generally share the same basic elements but vary in required size, specifications, and features. However, as is the case with most AI-type systems, human intervention is still required. An engineer is needed to check the computer-produced drawing before the equipment is put into production.

Senior management in many companies uses AI-based strategic planning systems to assist in functions like competitive analysis, technology deployment, and resource allocation. They also use programs to assist in equipment configuration design, product distribution, regulatory compliance advisement, and personnel assessment. AI is contributing heavily to management's organization, planning, and controlling operations, and will continue to do with more frequency as scientists refine their programs.

AI is also influential in science and engineering. The applications developed were used to organize and manipulate the ever-increasing amounts of information available to scientists and engineers. AI has been used in complex processes such as mass spectometry analysis, biological classifications, and the creation of semiconductor circuits and automobile components. AI has been used with increasing frequency in diffraction and image analysis, power plant and space station design, and robot sensing, control and programming. It is the increased use of robotics in business that is alarming many critics of artificial intelligence.

Robots are being utilized more frequently in the business world. In 1990, over 200,000 robots were in use in U.S. factories. Experts predict that by the year 2025 robots could potentially replace humans in almost all manufacturing jobs. This includes not only the mundane tasks, but also those requiring specialized skills. They will be performing jobs such as shearing sheep, scraping barnacles from the bottoms of ships, and sandblasting walls. However, there are jobs that robots will never be able to perform, such as surgery. This creates some hope that robots will never replace humans entirely. Of course, there will still be a need for individuals to design, build, and maintain robots. Yet, once scientists develop robots that can think, as well as act, there may be less of a need for human intervention. Thus, the social ramifications of AI is of major concern to people today.

THE SOCIAL COSTS OF ARTIFICIAL INTELLIGENCE

One of the most significant impacts of AI on society is its effects on employment. For example, banks are utilizing more and more automated teller machines (ATMs), which eliminates thousands of jobs. Companies are installing state-of-the-art switchboards to replace receptionists and secretaries. What impact this trend will have on society in the future is difficult to analyze now, but it is a cause for concern for government planners, sociologists, and psychologists. There are also causes for concern regarding the use of AI in government and education.

For instance, many critics fear that governments will use AI-based systems to store information regarding citizens' private lives and use it to impinge on their rights. At the least, government officials can make decisions based on computerized information

without consulting citizens. Whether dire predictions of such events come to pass is yet to be decided.

Yet another area of concern is education. Many AI opponents suggest that machines will replace teachers, causing students to suffer from a lack of interactive education. Again, this may not come to pass. AI-based systems have reached classrooms, but their effect to date has not destroyed the education system. Again, though, concerns about AI's impact are growing—particularly as researchers get closer and closer to developing true ''thinking'' machines.

THE FUTURE OF ARTIFICIAL INTELLIGENCE

There is little doubt that AI will play a greater role in business and society in the coming years. Although workers displaced by robots and other types of automation today are in many cases being retrained for different jobs, that might not always be the case. And, AI is being used in more and more disciplines. For example, the use of computer-aided design and computer-aided manufacturing systems is increasing in the manufacturing design and production processes. So is the use of flexible manufacturing systems, which combine automated equipment, computer control, and automated material handling to create flexibility in production. Exactly what impact the increasing uses of AI will have on the future is impossible to predict today.

It is important to note that scientists still have not developed the true ''thinking'' machine. Until that day comes, society will continue to rely on rely on computers to a great extent as aids in the business process. In that respect, AI is still a servant of humanity, not its master. It is an important cog in the manufacturing and service processes—and will no doubt continue to be so well into the future.

[Arthur G. Sharp]

FURTHER READING:

Cohen, John. *Human Robots in Myth and Science*. London: Allen and Unwin, 1966.

McCorduck, Pamela. *Machines Who Think*. New York: W.H. Freeman and Company, 1979.

Nillson, Nils J. *Principles of Artificial Intelligence*. Palo Alto: Tioga Publishing Co., 1980.

Rich, Elaine. *Artificial Intelligence*. New York: McGraw Hill, 1983.

Schoen, Sy and Wendell Sykes. *Putting Artificial Intelligence to Work*. New York: John Wiley & Sons, Inc., 1987.

Yazdani, M. and A. Narayanan, eds. *Artificial Intelligence: Human Effects*. Chichester, England: Ellis Horwood Limited, 1984.

ASIAN TIGERS

SEE: Five Tigers

ASSEMBLY LINE METHODS

An assembly line is a line of factory workers and equipment that produce a product as it moves consecutively from station to station on the line until completed. Assembly line methods have become considerably more sophisticated since the first moving assembly lines were introduced in the automobile industry in the early part of the twentieth century. Assembly line methods were originally introduced to increase productivity and efficiency by reducing the amount of manufacturing time required to produce a finished product. Advances in assembly line methods have the same objective—to increase throughput, or the number of products produced in a given period of time. While assembly line methods apply primarily to **manufacturing** processes, they can also be applied to other areas of business ranging from product development to management.

A look at the introduction of the moving assembly line in Ford Motor Co.'s Highland Park (Michigan) plant in 1913 and 1914 reveals some of the basic principles and objectives involved in the development of assembly line methods throughout the 20th century. As assembly line methods were introduced, manufacturing tasks became minutely divided and closely timed. Manufacturing became a highly mechanized process in which mass manufacturing was performed largely by unskilled workers. The assembly line cut down on human handling, and machines were designed to handle multiple tasks.

A key factor in the development of the moving assembly line was the mechanization of materials handling. Before power-driven conveyors were introduced to move materials in the automobile industry, they were commonly used in such industries as brewing, milling, canning, and meatpacking. The first power driven conveyors in the Ford factory transported materials to individual work stations. Later they moved parts while workers worked on them.

Moving conveyors were first applied to Ford assembly operations in 1913 in the flywheel magneto assembly, part of the car's electrical system. Originally one worker took 20 minutes to assembly one unit. Ford's production managers looked at the operation and broke it into 29 separate operations that could be laid out along a moving belt. Assembly time dropped dramatically to only 13 minutes, then to five minutes after additional adjustments were made.

After Ford's success in applying assembly line methods to the flywheel magneto, as many manufacturing processes as possible were divided into a series of single work tasks that could be performed along a moving conveyor. By April 1914 Ford had introduced an electrically driven endless-chain conveyor that moved the auto chassis down the line. This enabled Ford to increase production from about 475 cars in a nine-hour day to more than 1200 auto assemblies in an eight-hour day. Ford tripled its **production** and reduced labor time per vehicle by nearly 90 percent.

The increased throughput at Ford's Highland Park plant required the installation of power-driven supply lines. Subassembly lines were laid out to feed into the main assembly line. When Ford built its famous River Rouge plant, automobile manufacturing became one continuously moving process, from the unloading of raw materials to the loading of completed vehicles onto railroad cars.

Using modern assembly line methods, manufacturing has become a highly refined process in which value is added to parts along the line. Assembly line manufacturing is characterized by concurrent processes, or multiple parallel activities that feed into a final assembly stage. These processes require a well planned flow of materials and the development of an advanced materials and supply infrastructure.

Just-in-time (JIT) manufacturing methods have been developed to reduce the cost of carrying parts and supplies as inventory. Under a JIT system, manufacturing plants carry only one or a few days' worth of inventory in the plant, relying on suppliers to provide parts and materials on an ''as needed'' basis. Future developments in this area may call for suppliers to establish operations within the manufacturing facility itself to provide for a more efficient supply of materials and parts.

Modular assembly is another advanced assembly line method that is designed to improve throughput by increasing the efficiency of parallel subassembly lines feeding into the final assembly line. As applied to automobile manufacturing, modular assembly would involve assembling separate modules—chassis, interior, body—on their own assembly lines, then joining them together on a final assembly line.

The recognized efficiency of machines performing multiple tasks has evolved into cell manufacturing. Cells of machines can be run by one operator or a multi-person work cell. In these machine cells it is possible to link older machines with newer ones, thus reducing the amount of investment required for new machinery. Cell operators can handle three or four tasks, and robots are used for such operations as materials handling and welding.

Team style production is another development in assembly line methods. Where workers used to work at one- or two-person work stations and perform repetitive tasks, now **teams** of workers can follow a job down the assembly line through its final quality checks. Team production creates greater worker involvement and was adopted by Swedish automakers Saab and Volvo in the early 1980s. On the recently introduced Sportster line at the Harley-Davidson, Inc. plant in Milwaukee, ten three-person teams follow the motorcycle through 20 assembly stations and its final check.

As new assembly line methods are introduced into manufacturing processes, business managers look at the techniques for possible application to other areas of business. New methods all share the common goal of improving throughput by reducing the amount of time individual workers and their machines spend on specific tasks. By reducing the amount of time required to produce an item, be it an automobile, a new product, or a report, assembly line methods have made it possible to produce more with less.

[David Bianco]

ASSESSMENT CENTERS

Assessment centers are used in many different types of organizations to evaluate personnel. Assessment centers may be established for a variety of **human resources** applications, from recruiting and hiring to determining training needs in the organization. While the specifics of assessment centers vary with their application, they share certain characteristics. These include a trained group of assessors, situational tests or exercises that participants must complete, and an assessment method that involves pooling the judgments of the assessors to reach a final evaluation of each participant.

Assessment centers function as integral parts of an organization's human resources management system. When an assessment center is being set up, it must be designed with a specific purpose in mind. A preliminary statement of organizational objectives may be drawn up, indicating who is to be assessed, who the assessors will be, what target positions will be tested for, and other considerations.

Once the basic objectives have been determined, the first step in creating an assessment center is called job analysis. The requirements of the target job or position are defined, as are the dimensions required for success in the target job. These dimensions include such factors as skills, qualities, attributes, motivation, knowledge, and tasks. The job analysis provides a basis for building situational exercises, observing behavior of the participants, evaluating their effectiveness, and giving feedback.

Once the job analysis has been completed, situational exercises are designed. These are simulations that portray important aspects of the target job. Typical exercises used in assessment centers include preparing written reports, making oral presentations, answering mail or memos, and talking with customers about a complaint. The situational tests or exercises provide assessors with an opportunity to observe different behaviors of the participants that are related to the target position. Thus, it is important that the situational exercises represent essential features of the target job, but not necessarily the entire job.

An essential feature of assessment centers is that the situational exercises must elicit some form of behavior from the participants that is consistent with the performance required on the job. The participants must display overt behavior, rather than covert behavior that is characteristic of taking an exam, for example. Typically there is some interaction between participants, as in a group discussion or oral presentation. The participants' overt behavior provides assessors with a basis for evaluation. Assessors should not need to make any inferences about covert behavior, such as what the participants were thinking.

The situational exercises should be complex enough that assessors are able to use multiple assessment techniques. Participants are expected to engage in complex behavior, and that behavior is observed by trained assessors. The assessors' observations consist of specific statements about observable behavior, without any inferences or interpretations. For example, an assessor may report that a participant spoke loudly (observable behavior), but not that the participant was angry (an inference).

It is essential that multiple assessors be involved in an assessment center, and that each participant be evaluated by more than one assessor. In this way the effect of any bias among the assessors is minimized. After the situational exercises have been completed and the assessors have completed their evaluations, all of the assessments are then pooled.

There are different methods for pooling assessments. The two major methods that are used are group discussion and statistical integration. When group discussion is used, the assessors meet and discuss their evaluations of each participant. Discrepancies between different evaluations are noted and discussed. Ultimately, a consensus is reached and a final evaluation produced for each participant. The group discussion process is highly judgmental, with individual judgments playing an important role throughout the pooling process.

Some organizations prefer using statistical integration to pool the different assessments and reach a final evaluation of the participants. Under this method, a five-point scale is typically used, and assessors rank participants for each dimension they are evaluating. Each dimension may be weighted in terms of its relative importance to the target position. At the end of the session, the weighted rankings are mathematically combined to reach a final evaluation for each participant.

Assessment centers have proven to be successful for a variety of human resources applications. Assessment centers have been set up to show job applicants from outside the company what they would experience under the company's management, to show them what management entails, and to discover their own managerial strengths. They can be used to select job applicants and identify those most likely to succeed on the job. They can be used to place new employees in the most appropriate departments. They have been used to diagnose employee deficiencies and identify areas that need additional training.

In the area of **performance appraisal**, assessment centers can be used to certify the competence of individuals to perform specific technical skills. They can be used to evaluate candidates for managerial positions, usually in combination with current performance appraisals. When layoffs are necessary, assessment centers can give employees the opportunity to demonstrate their qualifications for other positions with the company.

[David Bianco]

ASSETS

SEE: Financial Statements

ASSOCIATION OF SOUTH EAST ASIAN NATIONS (ASEAN)

The Association of South East Asian Nations (ASEAN) was formed in 1967 in Bangkok, Thailand as a result of the Bangkok Declaration. The organization, headquartered in Djakarta, Indonesia, promotes economic cooperation and cultural exchange programs between member states. Indonesia, Malaysia, the Philippines, Singapore, and Thailand founded ASEAN, and Brunei joined in 1984. Laos, Papua, New Guinea, and Vietnam have observer status. Jointly, ASEAN member nations have a land area of three million square kilometers (one million square miles) and a total population of nearly 333 million people.

In the early 1960s, various regional movements among the non-communist states of southeast Asia promoted regional economic cooperation. Early efforts were short-lived, but in 1965 Indonesia's leader, Sukarno, lost all but nominal power to an anti-communist military takeover. This change in the Indonesian government opened the door for the Bangkok Declaration, the formal beginning of ASEAN. The association grew rapidly and expanded its activities, eventually becoming a significant global organization. By 1976 the first ASEAN regional summit took place in Pattaya, Thailand. As a result of the Pattayan summit, ASEAN began an economic dialogue with the United States, the former Soviet Union, Australia, Canada, China, India, the European Community, Japan, the Republic of Korea, and New Zealand.

Subsequent ASEAN meetings and conferences have reinforced its original anti-communist stance including continued calls for economic cooperation among members through further reduction of tariffs and expanded economic projects. Although not a member, Japan has contributed to the expansion of ASEAN by offering low interest investment loans to ASEAN members, sponsoring technical training institutes, and participating in numerous ASEAN-Japanese industrial ventures.

In 1990 ASEAN had $48 billion worth of trade with the United States which made ASEAN America's fifth largest trading partner. The United States exports capital goods, transportation equipment, chemicals, and agricultural goods to ASEAN countries and imports natural rubber, tin, petroleum, sugar, palm oil, textiles, and electronic products and components.

ASEAN offers investors marketplace oriented economies, low labor costs, and abundant natural resources. There is, however, strong competition to American business from Japan and Taiwan. Most U.S. investments to the ASEAN region are administered by the Overseas Private Investment Corporation ($600 million total investments as of 1991) and the United States Export-Import Bank ($2.4 billion total investments as of 1991). The U.S. **Agency for International Development** (AID) also has many projects in the region. There is a United States-ASEAN Council for Business and Technology and an ASEAN-Washington Committee comprised of ASEAN ambassadors to the United States.

In its own statement of purpose, ASEAN says it seeks to provide for ''economic growth, social progress and cultural development . . .'' in southeast Asia. ASEAN additionally seeks to achieve regional political stability by promoting intra-ASEAN trade and ASEAN directed trade with non-member world markets. The association also encourages regional cooperation in technology, communications, tourist promotion, and educational and cultural exchanges among member nations. There is, however, lingering concern about joining the Asian-Pacific Economic Cooperation Forum (APEC) group. This is a loose economic coalition between ASEAN members and Australia, Canada, South Korea, Japan, the United States and New Zealand. Some members fear that the regional influence of ASEAN will be diluted by agreeing to a pact with such strong Asian and western economic powers. In 1992 in an effort to relieve this anxiety, the ASEAN Free Trade Area was created. This move further reduced regional tariffs and promoted regional investment.

As part of its social and political agenda, ASEAN actively works to aid refugees (especially the nearly 125,000 Vietnamese ''boat people''), improve the status of women, and stabilize the political situation in Cambodia. ASEAN has established bureaus of Economics, Narcotic Matters, Public Information, Technology and Science, and Social and Cultural. In addition, these committees address areas of specific concern: Culture and Information, Finance and Banking, Food, Agriculture and Forestry, Industry, Minerals and Energy, Science and Technology, Social Development, Trade and Tourism, Transportation, and Communications.

[Michael Knes]

FURTHER READING.

Broinowski, Alison. *ASEAN Into the 1990s.* Macmillan, 1990.

Broinowski, Alison. *Understanding ASEAN.* St. Martins Press, 1982.

U.S. Department of State, Bureau of Public Affairs, Office of Public Communication. *Background Notes, ASEAN.* Government Printing Office, 1992.

ASSOCIATIONS

SEE: Professional and Trade Associations

AUDITING

An audit is a systematic process of objectively obtaining and evaluating the accounts or financial records of a governmental, business, or other entity. Handled by a trained independent accountant, an audit and the auditor's report provide additional assurance to users of financial statements concerning the validity of the information presented in financial statements. The work performed by the auditor is referred to as auditing.

TYPES OF AUDITS

Major types of audits conducted by external auditors include the financial statements audit, the operational audit, and the **compliance audit**. A financial statement audit (or attest audit) examines financial statements, records, and related operations to ascertain adherence to generally accepted accounting principles. An operational audit examines an organization's acitivities in order to assess performances and develop recommendations for improvements, or further action. A compliance audit has as its objective the determination of whether an organization is following established procedures or rules. Auditors also perform statutory audits, which are performed to comply with the requirements of a governing body, such as a federal, state, or city government or agency.

TYPES OF AUDITORS

Auditors are either internal or independent. Internal auditors are employees of the organization whose activities are being examined and evaluated. The primary goal of internal auditing is to determine the extent to which the organization adheres to managerial policies, procedures, and requirements.

The independent auditor is not an employee of the organization. He or she performs an examination with the objective of issuing a report containing an opinion on a client's financial statements. The attest function of external auditing refers to the auditor's expression of an opinion on a company's financial statements. Generally, the criteria for judging an auditor's financial statements are generally-accepted accounting principles. The typical independent audit leads to an attestation regarding the fairness and dependability of the statements. This is communicated to the officials of the audited entity in the form of a written report accompanying the statements.

The audit committee of an enterprise is a major committee of the board of directors or the board of trustees. The committee is often composed of outside directors who nominate the independent auditors and react to the auditor's report and findings. Matters that the auditor believes should be brought to the attention of the shareholders are usually be first brought before the audit committee.

AUDITING STANDARDS

The auditing process is based on standards, concepts, procedures, and reporting practices, primarily imposed by the American Institute of Certified Public Accountants (AICPA). The auditing process relies on evidence, analysis, conventions, and informed professional judgment. General standards are brief statements relating to such matters as training, independence, and professional care. AICPA general standards are:

1. The examination is to be performed by a person or persons having adequate technical training and proficiency as an auditor.

2. In all matters relating to the assignment, an independence in mental attitude is to be maintained by the auditor or auditors.

3. Due professional care is to be exercised in the performance of the examination and the preparation of the report.

Standards of fieldwork provide basic planning standards to be followed during audits.

AICPA standards of field work are:

1. The work is to be adequately planned and assistants, if any, are to be properly supervised.

2. There is to be a proper study and evaluation of the existing internal control as a basis for reliance thereon and for the determination of the resultant extent to which auditing procedures are to be restricted.

3. Sufficient competent evidential matter is to be obtained through inspection, observation, inquiries, And confirmation to afford a reasonable basis for an opinion regarding the financial statements under examination.

Standards of reporting describe auditing standards relating to the audit report and its requirements. AICPA standards of reporting are:

1. The report shall state whether the financial statements are presented in accordance with generally-accepted accounting principles.

2. The report shall state whether such principles have been consistently observed in the current period in relation to the preceding period.

3. Informative disclosures to the financial statements are to be regarded as reasonably adequate unless otherwise stated in the report.

4. The report shall contain either an expression of opinion Regarding the financial statements, taken as a whole or an assertion to the effect that an opinion cannot be expressed. When an overall opinion cannot be expressed, the reasons therefore should be stated. In all cases where an auditor's name

is associated with financial statements, the report should contain a clear-cut indication of the character of the auditor's examination, if any, and the degree of responsibility he or she is taking.

THE AUDITING PROCESS

The auditor generally proceeds with an audit according to a set process with three steps: planning, gathering evidence, and issuing a report.

In planning the audit, the auditor develops an audit program that identifies and schedules audit procedures that are to be performed to obtain the evidence. Audit evidence is proof obtained to support the audit's conclusions. Audit procedures include those activities undertaken by the auditor to obtain the evidence. Evidence-gathering procedures include observation, confirmation, calculations, analysis, inquiry, inspection, and comparison. An audit trail is a chronological record of economic events or transactions that have been experienced by an organization. The audit trail enables an auditor to evaluate the strengths and weaknesses of internal controls, system designs, and company policies and procedures.

THE AUDIT REPORT

The independent audit report sets forth the independent auditor's opinion regarding the financial statements. That is, whether the financial statements are fairly presented in conformity with generally-accepted accounting principles, applied on a basis consistent with that of the preceding year (or in conformity with some other comprehensive basis of accounting that is appropriate for the entity). A fair presentation of financial statements is generally understood by accountants to refer to whether:

1. The accounting principles used in the statements have general acceptability.

2. The accounting principles are appropriate in the circumstances.

3. The financial statements are prepared so they can be used, understood, and interpreted.

4. The information presented in the financial statements is classified and summarized in a reasonable manner.

5. The financial statements reflect the underlying events and transactions in a way that presents the financial position, results of operations, and cash flows within reasonable and practical limits.

The auditor's unqualified report contains three paragraphs. The introductory paragraph identifies the financial statements audited, states that management is responsible for those statements, and asserts that the auditor is responsible for expressing an opinion on them. The scope paragraph describes what the auditor has done and specifically states that the auditor has examined the financial statements in accordance with generally-accepted auditing standards and has performed appropriate tests. The opinion paragraph expresses the auditor's opinion on whether the statements are in accordance with generally-accepted accounting principles.

Various audit opinions are defined by the AICPA's Auditing Standards Board as follows:

1. Unqualified opinion: An unqualified opinion states that the financial statements present fairly, in all material respects, the financial position, results of operations, and cash flows of the entity in conformity with generally-accepted accounting principles.

2. Explanatory language added to the auditor's standard report: Circumstances may require that the auditor add an explanatory paragraph (or other explanatory language) to his or her report.

3. Qualified opinion: A qualified opinion states that, except for the effects of the matter(s) to which the qualification relates, the financial statements present fairly, in all material respects, the financial position, results of operations, and cash flows of the entity in conformity with generally-accepted accounting principles.

4. Adverse opinion: An adverse opinion states that the financial statements do not represent fairly the financial position, results of operations, or cash flows of the entity in conformity with generally-accepted accounting principles.

5. Disclaimer of opinion: A disclaimer of opinion states that the auditor does not express an opinion on the financial statements.

The fair presentation of financial statements does not mean that the statements are fraud-proof. The independent auditor has the responsibility to search for errors or irregularities within the recognized limitations of the auditing process. An auditor is subject to risks that material errors or irregularities, if they exist, will not be detected.

Investors should examine the auditor's report for citations of problems such as debt-agreement violations or unresolved lawsuits. "Going-concern" references can suggest that the company may not be able to survive as a functioning operation. If an "except for" statement appears in the report the investor should understand that there are certain problems or depar-

tures from generally-accepted accounting principles in the statements that question whether the statements present fairly the company's financial statements and that will require the company to resolve the problem or somehow make the accounting treatment acceptable.

LEGAL RESPONSIBILITIES

The legal responsibilities of the auditor are determined primarily by the following:

1. Specific contractual obligations undertaken.

2. Statutes and common law governing the conduct and responsibilities of public accountants.

3. Rules and regulations of voluntary professional organizations.

SEE ALSO: Accounting; Balance Sheet; Financial Statements; Income Statement

[Charles Woelfel]

FURTHER READING:

American Institute of Certified Public Accountants. *AICPA Professional Standards*. Chicago, IL: Commerce Clearing House, Inc.

Delaney, P. R. *CPA Examination Review: Auditing*. New York: John Wiley & Sons, 1994.

Taylor, D. H., and G. W. Glazen. *Auditing: Integrated Concepts and Procedures*. New York: John Wiley & Sons.

AUSTRALIA, DOING BUSINESS IN

"Down Under" aptly describes Australia's physical location, which is almost at the bottom of the world. It definitely does not describe the economy or future prospects of this unique country, almost the size of the continental United States. With its seventeen million people, Australia (from the Latin word "australis," or southern) is an integral part of the Asian Pacific region, and shares in this region's economic growth, the fastest in the world.

Besides being a continent in its own right, the offshore island of Tasmania also belongs to Australia, and constitutes a separate state. Together, they lie entirely within the southern hemisphere. The interior of Australia proper is an arid desert. Because the climate of the country is warm year round, and its vast coastline boasts among the most beautiful, uncrowded beaches in the world, Australia has always been a mecca for tourists. Tourism is the fastest-growing industry in the country.

In part because of the many similarities between Australia and the United States, and the affinity of

Australians for many American products, American business has been investing heavily in Australia for many decades. Currently it is the twelfth largest export market for the United States. American businesses invest approximately $40 billion a year in Australia, making the U.S. Australia's principal foreign business partner. Moreover, there are few investment barriers, and those that still exist—government protected industries and high tariffs—are rapidly being eliminated, factors that are also encouraging substantial Japanese investment. The greatest **foreign investment** occurs in the tourist industry and in the development of **real estate** (residential and commercial) property.

While cultural and linguistic similarities between Australia and the U.S. help explain the country's attractiveness to American business, more salient reasons include Australia's historically stable government and economy, as well as the high living standards.

Reasons for Australia's enviable political and economic stability are not hard to find. Modern Australian history began only with the arrival of the first Europeans to its shores in 1788. While it is a fact that Great Britain used its Australian colony as a dumping ground for convicts, liberal British political institutions and a highly developed free enterprise economic system were introduced wholesale into Australia, along with free schools and a high degree of literacy. The number of convicts dwindled as the immigrant population rose, mainly from Great Britain and Ireland.

The country's extreme remoteness from the "developed" world made it dependent on foreign investment and trade from the start. The British introduced merino sheep into Australia in the early nineteenth century, which were ideally suited to Australia's climate and geography. For much of the nineteenth century, until the great economic crash of the 1890s, wool was Australia's chief industry.

Australia's extreme geographic remoteness also precluded rapid population growth, perhaps a major factor explaining why Australians never rebelled against British colonial rule as did Americans. Instead, the small population of whites in Australia—there would only be seven million at the outbreak of World War II—identified in every possible way with Great Britain. During the nineteenth century, Australia was a prime exporter of raw materials to Great Britain in exchange for its finished manufactured goods. However, Australian industry also developed in response to heavy British investment. Unlike the United States, the Australian colonial government took an active role in furthering Australia's economy, especially in terms of regulating wages, establishing **central banks**, and instituting a highly restrictive protective trade policy that lasted well into the twentieth century. In addition, there were many state-owned industries, such as textile factories, fisheries, and quarries.

Australia achieved independence from Great Britain, and became a commonwealth, in 1901. By then, Great Britain was buying up 75 percent of Australia's exports, besides investing in other ways, which greatly stimulated the Australian economy and contributed to the high educational and living standards. As early as 1891, over two thirds of the Australian population lived in urban areas. Mining was beginning to vie with wool as the country's most important industry. The future president of the United States, Herbert Hoover, spent years in Australia in the late nineteenth century as a mining engineer, and was impressed with the mineral wealth of the island continent.

American investment, especially in the exploitation of Australia's abundant mineral wealth, was beginning to be so extensive that the Australian economy collapsed following the New York stock market crash in 1929. After the Second World War, the United States replaced Great Britain as the leading investor and importer of Australian goods. The war stimulated heavy industry and **manufacturing**, especially the iron, steel, and automobile industries. Presently tourism, mining, and agriculture (especially meat and dairy products) are the country's main industries. To this day, Australia has not become an exporter of capital, but avidly seeks to import it by offering an array of incentives to foreign investors.

Because of its historic dependence on world trade, Australia has readily joined the developed nations of the world in major trade conferences and become a member of such international treaties and organizations as **General Agreement on Tariffs and Trade (GATT)**, the **International Monetary Fund**, and the International Bank for Reconstruction and Development, actions which have further deepened its ties to the United States.

Australia's highly developed economy, stable political and economic institutions, and sophisticated **infrastructure** have made the country a haven for foreign investors, despite the high tariffs that have prevailed throughout most of its history. By the mid-1970s, approximately one-third of Australia's manufacturing industry, especially oil refining, chemicals and pharmaceuticals, was directly owned by foreign business interests, with an even higher percentage of foreign ownership of the mineral industry.

Hence the man, woman or company wishing to do business in Australia will be competing less with Australian business than with other foreigners, particularly other Americans. Historically this has always been the case, and probably will continue to be the dominant trend well into the twenty-first century.

How, then, does one go about doing business with Australia? Australia has always been dependent on and open to foreign capital and foreign imports. Lately, the financial climate has become even more "free," with barriers being lifted even against foreign banks doing business in the country. Pertinent questions include: What is the government's relationship to foreign business? What incentives might one expect if one is thinking of investing in Australia? What, if any, barriers to trade still exist? What steps would an individual or a company take to establish a business in Australia?

The government in Australia is parliamentary, and the country is a constitutional monarchy. Because Australians identify less and less with Great Britain and increasingly with their neighbors in the Pacific Rim, the government will in all likelihood opt to turn the country into a republic in the near future. The government, regardless of which party is in power, is seeking a stable financial environment and is determined to implement **free trade** policies. Even the **telecommunications** industry, government owned since its inception, has had to face deregulation in the 1990s. American telecommunications companies are gearing up for the momentous changes that will follow when the government owned monopoly Telecom Australia is sold to private interests in the near future. While there still remain certain "protected" industries, such as shoe manufacturing, and the automobile and railroad industries, even these cannot count on government protection for long.

Because of what many Australians perceived as the foreign "takeover" of major Australian enterprises, the Australian parliament passed the Foreign Acquisitions and Takeovers Act in 1975. This legislation defined the "national interest" and gave the Treasurer the right to prohibit certain investments or limit them if they ran counter to that interest. Moreover, penalties for failure to disclose business transactions (or false disclosures) were set for the first time. While the Foreign Investment Review Board (FIRB) and the Treasurer review the investment proposals of foreign businesses according to the criteria established in the Act, the vast majority of these proposals are accepted and the Act has had little, if any, restrictive effect on the flow of foreign capital into Australia. In fact, the government in 1992 exempted many foreign projects from review by the FIRB, and eliminated the last restrictions on the acquisition of new mines by foreign investors. The need to attract foreign capital and reduce the huge Australian deficit is of prime importance to government and business in Australia.

There are many government—federal and state—incentives to encourage foreign investment. To begin with, anyone wishing to set up a business in the vast underdeveloped Northern Territory will find that it has been established as a free trade zone. That means that there are no customs **duties** on raw materials (as long as the final product is exported) as well as exemptions on many other taxes and land is available cheaply for the purpose of setting up a business or factory.

Other government incentives are known as bounty payments, or bounties, for **research and development** projects carried out in Australia, or direct payments to manufacturers of such items as bedsheeting, textile yarns, printed fabrics, computers, and other products. Because the list of products is subject to change, you need to inquire about the status of the current list. In addition, foreign banks get an incentive, in the form of exemption from Australian interest withholding tax, for establishing a branch in Australia. There are many other incentives and incentive programs for foreign investors, large and small. The Australian Trade Commission, of which there are seven branches in the United States, has the most current information on incentive programs.

Once an entrepreneur knows which business he wishes to establish and where to set it up in Australia, he would then proceed as if he were doing business in the United States. This would include an extensive market study, which might entail traveling to the area in which the business is to be set up. Australia still has a visa system in place, which is valid for a six month stay in the country. A consultant in Australia may be hired to provide quickly the needed investment information. There are a number of American **accounting** firms with branches in Australia, among the largest being Price Waterhouse, which publishes well known information guides on "Doing Business in Australia." For those unable to afford the luxury of private consultants, every state capital in Australia has an American Australian Chamber of Commerce that freely dispenses advice and can point one to other sources of information. The American Chamber of Commerce in Australia publishes a *USA/Australia Trade Directory* that provides an exhaustive list of information on doing business in Australia. Since most people probably are not intending to emigrate to Australia and operate their own business, it is also necessary to hire local Aussies (they must reside in the state or territory in which the business is located), which means complying with federal and state labor regulations. Some Americans are shocked at the very high wages, even for service jobs, that are at least twice what similar jobs pay in the United States. Labor **costs** are usually a company's greatest expense. Unlike the United States, health insurance is less of a headache for companies, since a government **health**

insurance plan covers all Australians, regardless of employment status.

Those businesses desiring to export a product or products to Australia can do all of their research the United States. The accounting and consulting firm Price Waterhouse publishes a handy "Guide to Australian Customs/Excise Duties and Government Assistance." However, since Australian tariff and customs regulations change frequently, it is best to receive updated information from to the Australian trade representatives in the United States.

After market studies are completed, most American businesses or individuals form a company, either private or public, which can then be incorporated in the Australian state or territory in which it will be situated. This is done through the Corporate Affairs Commission of that state or territory, a process which does entail some expense. First, most investors must file a proposal with the Foreign Investment Review Board. The FIRB must see to it that the proposal for doing business in Australia complies with the 1975 Foreign Acquisitions and Takeovers Act. This act is very liberally interpreted and foreign investment proposals are frequently exempted from review. In addition, one hundred percent ownership of a company in Australia is legal. There are, still some industries and enterprises that are restricted to Australians or where foreign businesses are allowed only a minimal financial stake, as in the Australian broadcasting and television industry. One should obtain the most current to date list of industries that are off limits to foreign investment, such as power generation, postal systems (although private companies in the 1990s have been allowed to compete with the state system), and urban transit systems, to name only a few. In the case of book publishing, the reverse has happened: what once was a trade dominated by the British and Americans in Australia has now been made extremely difficult for foreigners, thanks to the stringent copyright law passed by parliament in 1992. Henceforth, Australian book publishers will dominate in this industry and the price of books in Australia will decline precipitously, the reason for the popularity of the new law. This kind of "reverse to protectionism" is not the trend but an exception to it.

Publicly owned foreign companies wishing to set up a branch in Australia must comply with stringent financial disclosure regulations, which require no extraordinary legal or **audit**ing practices or procedures, although the person or persons auditing a company must be independent and preferably Australian (or whose licenses comply with Australian auditing standards). The approval of one's business proposal, along with registering the business with the state or territorial government completes the basic process of doing business in Australia.

Once a business is established, whether it is a branch of a huge multinational corporation or a small private enterprise, the taxes paid are levied only on income earned in Australia (for Australians, taxes are levied on all sources of income). This is yet another incentive for foreigners to do business in the country.

Australia is becoming the country that attracts more outside multinational investors than any on earth, with the possible exception of Canada. While the United States is the biggest foreign investor in Australia and Australia's biggest trading partner, that relationship may not last into the twenty-first century. The Asian-Pacific rim is already the second largest investor in Australia, with more than half of Australia's total exports going to East Asia (primarily Japan). The elimination of trade barriers of all kinds and Australia's history of economic and political stability will continue to attract major foreign capital into the country.

[Sina Dubovoy]

FURTHER READING:

Altfeld, Simone. "New Economic Initiatives Make Doing Business Easier," *Business America.* April 6, 1992, p. 35.

An American Guide to Doing Business in Australia. Burbank, CA: PacRim Publishers, 1994.

Baker, John F. "Gloomy Seminar on New Aussie Copyright Law," *Publisher's Weekly,* March 23, 1992, p. 9.

Byrt, William. *Business and Government in Australia.* Melbourne: Macmillan Company of Australia, 1991.

"Doing Business in Australia," New York: Price Waterhouse, 1991.

Dyster, Barrie, and David Meredith. *Australia in the International Economy in the Twentieth Century.* Sydney: Univ. of New South Wales, 1990.

Golike, William R. "Australia: Don't Overlook the Export Opportunities Down Under," *Business America.* April 19, 1993, p. 55.

"How to Tap Australia's Potential," *Global Trade.* August, 1990, p. 40.

Hand, Michael J. "There's a Dynamic Marketplace 'Down Under,' " *Business America.* Nov.30/Dec.14, 1992, p. 23.

Kramer, Hugh E. "Doing Business in Germany and Australia," *Management Decision.* July, 1992, p. 52.

Legal Aspects of Doing Business With Australia. Practising Law Institute, 1984.

McCalla, John. "They're Coming Back, Mate!," *Global Trade.* Nov., 1992, p. 10.

Wright, Edward J. *Doing Business in Australia.* New York: M. Bender, 1992.

AUTOMATED OFFICE SECURITY

Automated office security protects office resources from hazard by using electromechanical or computer devices to minimize loss. Hazards include threats to office resources from deliberate crime or accidental damage. The assessment of these hazards in developing a security system rests on the general idea of risk. Actions to diminish risk include alarms, access controls, intrusion detection, biometric technology, and informational protections. Alarms, such as fire and smoke, provide security from natural disaster. Access control measures such as keypads and keycards prevent unauthorized access to vital office materials. Intrusion detection devices, such as proximity sensors and closed-circuit television, likewise discourage unauthorized access. Contemporary biometric technology enhances automatic identification using eye, voice, and fingerprint recognition. Increasingly prevalent measures detect and secure digitized information itself by incorporating encryption, password management, and security software.

HISTORY OF AUTOMATED OFFICE SECURITY

In the 1950s, electronic locks preceded the modern access key and card control of the 1990s. These early electronic locks required keys that were independent of the individual users. Anyone with the correct key could access locked materials. Personal identification numbers (PINs), in the 1960s, remedied this weakness by tying together facility access and individual password codes. The further development of smart cards incorporated individual access rights— optically or magnetically coded onto a card—and featured access options such as automatic logging and multiple access levels. These keys and individual codes were both required to gain access to resources. Biometric access controls developed in the mid-1970s as a result of concern with errors in PINs and coded information. Both keys and codes could be stolen. By examining unique human characteristics, biometric access controls provide more accurate identification and are less easily counterfeited. With the advent of digital business information, such **computer security** measures as passwords and encrypted (coded) information developed as critical functions to protect office electronic information.

RISK ANALYSIS

As it applies to automated office security, risk includes understanding and assessing threats from natural disaster and unauthorized access. Overall vulnerabilities to theft of office equipment, theft of information, destruction of resources and access to computers are all important considerations. Specifically, risk analysis in the office environment addresses four basic factors: (1) the assets in need of protection, (2) the kinds of threats to these assets, (3) the probability of these threats occurring, and (4) the impact or effect if

loss occurs. In response, an automated security system integrates a number of products and functions to distribute security measures more widely and afford more complete prevention. These security packages minimize unauthorized access, theft, and destruction in a variety of ways.

TYPES OF AUTOMATED OFFICE SECURITY SYSTEMS

FIRE ALARMS. Physical alarms that trigger when fire, smoke, or heat are detected provide protection against loss due to fire. Smoke, heat, and flame detectors offer early warning using audible sounds and signals to central control units. Automatic sprinkler systems respond by attempting to quench the growth of a fire until the fire department responds.

ACCESS CONTROL. Access control measures ensure appropriate entry and reduce criminal and mischievous hazards to office resources. Keypads, cards, and proximity systems provide the most common automated interface between access system and personnel. Access controls are a part of increasingly sophisticated security management systems within the office environment.

KEYPADS AND KEYCARDS. A keypad system is a combination lock usually appearing as a plastic input device with at least ten numbered keys. The correct sequence of numbers must be selected on a set of push-buttons to gain entry. The level of security provided is a function of the number of combinations available. The more combinations available, the more secure the lock. Computer-controlled keypads are composed of local and centralized devices that accept input and coded information. Keypad systems are vulnerable to brute force attacks when all possible numerical combinations have been tried. When keypad systems are in isolated areas, unauthorized attempts at entry might remain unnoticed for long periods. Even when keypads are located in well-lighted and public areas, long-term probing (attempts to guess codes over a long time) might also go unnoticed. Keypad systems overcome weaknesses in access by incorporating visible and well-lighted locations as well as frequent code changes, time penalties, and error alarms. Frequent code changes, while effective in minimizing long-term probing, require notification to all authorized entrants. Time penalties freeze or lock up the system for a period of time when an erroneous code has been entered while, combination times require that codes be entered, within a specified time period. This penalty significantly increases the amount of time required to break into the keypad system by generating all possible combinations. Error alarms sound when incorrect codes are entered.

Keycards are often used in conjunction with keypad systems to provide another layer of security. Keycards, or smart cards, contain magnetic or optically etched information that act as a key to a computerized lock. Many companies use keycard access to buildings, parking areas, and offices. In one widespread example in the banking industry, automated teller machines (ATMs) combine keycard and keypad to require a user to present a keycard as a prerequisite to using the keypad. Locks and keys can be lost or stolen, but the combined use of personal identification numbers and cards creates a two-step process that improves security effectiveness.

PROXIMITY SYSTEMS. Proximity alarm or reaction systems rely on a sensor-based reaction to a signal. Proximity systems are either initiated by the user (sending a signal) or activated by a sensor (detecting a signal). Proximity systems fall into four basic transmission categories. First, passive proximity devices contain no power devices and rely on the radio waves of the initial signal to return transmission through a process called reradiation. This type of passive proximity device bases the relay process on the presence of crystalline materials that are agitated by incoming radio waves. The return of a signal using these crystalline materials is called surface acoustic wave technology. The second type, of field-powered devices, use a power supply and internal circuitry to transmit signals. A third type, the transponder, is a complete package of receiver, transmitter, antenna, code, and battery. Finally, a continuous transmission device features ongoing radio transmission and electronic recognition within selected proximate areas.

INTRUSION DETECTION. Intrusion detection devices use sensors, a control unit, and proximity alarms to discourage unauthorized entry. Early devices such as physical trip wires were clumsy and questionable deterrents. In the late 1960s and early 1970s, automated improvements in photoelectric beams and ultrasonic signals heralded rapid advances in the 1980s and early 1990s. Using a type of sensor and a detection signal, intrusion alarms deter intruders. Integrated systems may also include planning for alarm verification, response time, and delaying actions. Intrusion detection systems work on the principles of breaking circuits, interrupting light beams, detecting sound and vibration, detecting motion, detecting proximity, or detecting heat.

Sensors that rely on broken circuits include magnetic contact switches, electrical switches, and pressure mats. Contact switches create a magnetic field or electrical current when closed and activate when the contact is interrupted. Pressure mats are weight-sensitive floor coverings that activate when stepped on. The reverse pressure mat activates when an object or weight is removed from the mat.

Sound sensors identify vibrations by using microphones to detect forced or unauthorized entry. Devices placed on floors and walls and valuable objects relay sound and activate alarms. Sound sensors perform most effectively when background noise is minimal.

Light sensors activate when a light beam is interrupted by an intruder. Intruders may see the sensor, however, and step over it or crawl under it to evade detection. Additionally, light sensors perform erratically in adverse weather conditions such as rain and snow and in dusty areas.

Motion detectors employ microwave and ultrasonic technology to sense movement. Both use analysis of acoustical patterns of energy to identify spatial distortions that accompany movement. Motion can also be detected using a capacitance or electronic proximity field. In the electrostatic field created around an object or entry, intruders unbalance the field and activate an alarm.

CLOSED-CIRCUIT TELEVISION. Closed-circuit television (CCTV) employs cameras, lenses, signal transmission, video recorders, monitors, and other accessories to monitor office locations for access and intrusion. Two generic types of CCTV include tube and solid-state sensors. Tube cameras use electron beams to scan the area, while solid-state cameras use charge-coupling techniques in which electrical charges collected by the camera are transferred to a video signal using electronic synchronization. The integration of CCTV with other automated office security measures can significantly reduce intrusion and deter theft or damage.

BIOMETRICS. Biometrics refers to access controls based on human physical and behavioral characteristics such as retina pattern, fingerprint, and signature verification. The technologies, while still immature, represent an enormous breakthrough in access control. All biometric systems rely on a baseline image of the palm, fingerprint, retina, voice, or signature. Each instance of access is then compared to the baseline image for verification. Biometric technology remains more expensive than traditional access controls since large amounts of digital storage and processing are required to match or verify biometric input.

INFORMATION SECURITY. Securing the informational resources of the office plays an increasingly important role in automated office security. In general, both transactional and transformational resources are employed. Transactional security involves using passwords to access digital information or systems. Password security enhancements include automatic quota systems that allow only a limited number of log-on attempts before the user is logged off the system and two-stage passwords that require a project and a personal password. Transformational security strategies involve encrypting or coding information. Encrypted information, even when obtained, cannot be read without decryption. Scrambling information combined with password protection and security software to measure and monitor computer activities form a powerful informational security system.

SEE ALSO: Data Security

[Tona Henderson]

FURTHER READING:

Addis, Karen. ''Floored by Security.'' *Security Management.* July, 1993, pp. 18-20.

Betts, Curt P. ''The Intrusion Detection Misconception.'' *Security Management.* June 1990, pp. 79-83.

Bowers, Dan M. ''Control and Security Systems in the Office.'' *Modern Office Technology.* November, 1989, pp. 41-42.

Fay, John J., ed. *Encyclopedia of Security Management.* Boston: Butterworth-Heinemann, 1993.

Harowitz, Sherry L. ''More Than Meets the Eye.'' *Security Management.* February, 1993, pp. 24-28.

Keenan, Thomas P. ''Emerging Vulnerabilities in Office Automation Security.'' *Computers & Security.* May, 1989, pp. 223-227.

Phelps, E. Floyd. ''Balancing Security System and Procedure.'' *Security Management.* September, 1994, pp. 118-123.

Ronne, George. E. ''Devising a Strategy Keyed to Locks.'' *Security Management.* March, 1994, pp. 55-56.

San Luis, Ed, Louis A. Tyska, and Lawrence J. Fennelly. *Office and Office Building Security.* Boston: Butterworth-Heinemann, 1994.

Sherman, Robin L. ''Biometrics: The Right Look Can Open Doors.'' *Security Management.* October, 1992, pp. 83-85.

Silanger, Raymond P. *Introduction to Business and Industrial Security and Loss Control.* Springfield, IL: Charles C. Thomas, 1991.

Vaughn, Rayford B., Jr. ''A Survey of Security Issues in Office Computation and the Application of Secure Computing Models to Office Systems.'' *Computers & Security.* February, 1993, pp. 79-97.

Vollmart, Sarah. ''How to Implement a PC Security System.'' *Office.* February, 1992, pp. 42-43.

AUTOMATED TELLER MACHINES (ATMS)

Automated teller machines (ATMs) are mechanical devices that can provide a variety of routine banking services without the aid of a human teller. While the specific services that ATMs can provide are determined by the institutions that own them and any applicable legal restrictions, ATMs typically allow customers to withdraw cash from their checking or savings accounts and to deposit cash or checks into those same accounts. Some ATMs also accept bill payments and make small loans.

Upon their introduction ATMs had to overcome the initial reluctance of consumers to make full use of them. **Banks** mounted advertising campaigns to promote ATM usage, stressing their convenience, reliability, and security. ATMs offered bank customers the convenience of conducting routine banking transactions at any hour of the day. With the growth of ATMs and ATM networks, customers were given additional locations beside their local branch at which to make withdrawals from and deposits into their bank accounts.

In the decade from 1982 to 1992 ATMs became widely accepted by consumers. Average annual ATM transactions rose from approximately 2.1 billion in 1982 to 7.2 billion in 1992. Approximately 40-45 percent of all adults between the ages of 18 and 59 have an ATM card, according to statistics compiled by the Roper Organization and reported in the September 1993 issue of *American Demographics.* In adults 60 and over, only 27 percent reportedly have ATM cards. Comparable statistics on credit card usage revealed that approximately 65 percent of all adults 30 and older have at least one credit card, and the average card holder has nine different credit cards.

Consumer acceptance of ATMs was undoubtedly helped by the passage of the Electronic Funds Transfer Act (EFTA). Among others things EFTA limits consumer liability for all bank accounts linked to ATMs. In the case of unauthorized transfers, consumer liability is limited to $50 as long as the consumers report the unauthorized transfer within 60 days from the date their bank statement is postmarked. In some cases the 60-day limit may be extended. In the case of a lost or stolen ATM card, consumers must inform their bank within two days of discovering the loss (not two days from when it was actually stolen or lost) in order to limit their liability to $50. If more than two days elapses, then the ATM cardholder may be subject to a maximum liability of $500.

Local, regional, national, and international ATM networks allow cardholders to use their ATM cards virtually anywhere in the world. Individual banks that issue ATM cards to their customers generally belong to one or more of these networks. The bank's ATM customers can then use their cards at any ATM that is part of a network to which their bank belongs. The two largest international networks are CIRRUS and PLUS.

Mature markets such as the United States and Western Europe have nearly reached a saturation point with respect to ATMs. Most installations of ATMs in these markets are to replace existing equipment. In the emerging markets of Latin America and Eastern Europe, the installation of new ATMs is rapidly increasing. Internationally, the United States accounts for approximatley 25 percent of all ATM installations, Europe 31 percent, Japan 31 percent, Canada 4 percent, and in other countries 9 percent, as of 1994.

Recent trends in ATM installations include placing ATMs at more remote locations, such as major shopping malls, large supermarkets, and transportation centers. Locating ATMs at sites away from bank offices gives banks a marketing presence in those locations and allows them to provide banking services at places that are located more conveniently to their customers.

ATMs may eventually develop into fully automated bank branches. Adding new technologies to ATMs will allow them to offer a greater range of services. By adding imaging technology, for example, ATMs could accept a variety of bill payments. Interactive video conferencing and multimedia capabilities are other features that may be found in ATMs of the future.

[David Bianco]

AUTOMATIC IDENTIFICATION SYSTEMS

The term automatic identification refers to the electronic identification of a physical object. Physical objects include components, products, files and records. The accurate and timely identification of these physical objects plays a critical role in sales, inventory, and management. The manual process of identifying a physical object suffers from problems in human error and speed. People make mistakes when they attempt to identify objects. These mistakes fall into two general categories: inaccurate description and erroneous identification. Inaccurate descriptions, or transcriptive errors, occur when an object is correctly identified but inadvertently misdescribed. Erroneous identification reflects human error in the original identification of an object. Both mistakes are costly. Limitations in human speed also increase costs of manual identification. Two major advantages of automatic identification systems include reductions in data entry costs and improvements in the accuracy of the data entry. The technologies related to automatic identification vary but frequently include **bar codes**, **optical character recognition (OCR)**, magnetic ink, voice identification, radio frequency (RF), touch screens, light pens, and smart cards.

The most popular automatic identification systems currently use a bar code technology. Bar codes began to enjoy popularity in the early 1970s with the advent of the Universal Product Code (UPC) system for grocery systems. A bar code is a combination of printed bars and spaces representing letters or num-

bers. More than 50 different bar code structures offer considerable choice and variety for business use. Normally the bar code includes a start and stop character and a parity or check character. These characters enable the bar code to become a self-contained identification label. While bar codes essentially signal presence or absence of print, they are more properly considered a type of font. A font characterizes or categorizes printed alphabetical or numerical characters based on size and style. Because bar codes contain lines and spaces of varying widths, they resemble font specifications. The smallest width of any bar code is called the X dimension or, alternatively, the module width. Bar codes are also frequently characterized by a multi-directional nature. They can be read in either direction, top to bottom or bottom to top, left to right or right to left.

While bar codes rely on a finite set of pre-existing symbols to identify physical objects. optical character recognition (OCR) artificially identifies the features of an object. Using a combination of computer equipment and special software, OCR facilitates the identification of text and graphic material. With roots well into the early 1900s, OCR's first appeared with Emmanuel Goldberg's device to convert characters to telegraph cards in 1912. All OCR products rely on a recognition algorithm scheme. An algorithm is a set of concrete steps and procedures necessary to accomplish a designated task. For OCR, three recognition algorithms predominate: template matching, feature extraction, and topological analysis. These three algorithms form the foundation of the software component of OCR. Template matching employs the recognition and matching of pre-loaded font templates. Feature extraction maps loops, lines, and other characteristics of generic types to character tables. Finally, topological analysis also indexes type features but subsequently matches them to a classification algorithm which, in turn, refers to tables of many different fonts. OCR readers either convert print pages or extract print text strings for use with the recognition algorithm.

Other types of automated identification technologies include magnetic ink, voice recognition, radio frequency, smart cards, and touch screens or light pens. Magnetic ink technologies are primarily used by banks and financial institutions to identify checks and other signature based forms. Electromagnetic recordings on a strip of magnetic recording medium create the basic digital document. Decoded by some form of magnetic ink character recognition (MICR) software, the automated identification of materials using magnetic ink offers both advantages and disadvantages. Large amounts of identifying information can be stored with magnetic ink in a practically invisible form. However, magnetic ink can be accidentally destroyed and has a limited physical durability.

Voice recognition relies on the digitization of verbal expression to identify people and spoken commands, comments, and conversations. A microphone sends continuous electronic symbols of audible pitch to a mapping table of digital values. These values are then decoded by some form of template or feature analysis. Many voice recognition systems accommodate single discrete words. However, problems arise when digitizing connected or continuous words.

Radio frequency utilizes a radio transmitter to send digitally encoded information over radio waves. A unique radio signal is assigned to each informational object. This radio tag is actively powered by some form of battery or passively powered by the reader technology. A transceiver receives the relayed information and decodes it into machine readable format.

Smart cards consist of a microchip embedded into plastic cards. The digital memory of the microchip can be either read only or write and read memory. Frequently, three zones of information contain the smart cards database: secret zone, a private zone, and a public zone. Public zones track transactional information. Private zones contain user identified passwords. Secret zones contain information from the card issuer that can provide access and other restrictions. By prescribing the user interface and available choices, automated identification technologies like touch screens and light pens are a hybrid of manual and digital identification techniques.

Based on a simple yes or no scheme of decision making, employees improve accuracy based on fewer opportunities to make mistakes. Touch screens offer specialized graphic display formats that recognize pressure points. Light pens use light recognition to pinpoint choices, labels, or other identifying information presented to the user.

[Tona Henderson]

FURTHER READING:

Adams, Russ. *Sourcebook of Automatic Identification and Data Collection.* Van Nostrand Reinhold, 1990.

Angelo, Jean Marie. "From Mail to Phone to FAX to ... Wand?" *Catalog Age.* January 1992, p. 16.

Keller, Don. "High-Speed OCR Systems Have Flexibility and Accuracy." *Document Image Automation.* Spring 1993, pp. 28-29.

Khoshatefeh, Ramin. "9 Steps to Bar Code Competence." *Industrial Distribution.* August 1992, pp. 40-42.

Parker, Kevin. "RF Data Transmission Aids JIT Implementation." *Manufacturing Systems.* February 1992, pp. 20-24.

Robins, Gary. "Auto ID Technologies: An Update." *Stores.* May 1993, pp. 54-57.

Seidman, Stephan. "TV's to Toll Booths: Smart Card Capabilities." *Security Management.* April 1994, pp. 47-52.

Sharp, Kevin R. *Automatic Identification: Making It Pay.* Van Nostrand Reihold, 1990.

Suetens, Paul et al. "Computational Strategies for Object Recognition." *ACM Computing Surveys*, March 1992, pp. 5-61.

AUTOMATION

Automation refers to the use of computers and other automated machinery for the execution of tasks that a human laborer normally performs. Automated machinery may range from simple sensing devices to robots and other sophisticated equipment. Automation of operations may range from the automation of a single operation to the automation of an entire factory.

There are many different reasons to automate. Increased productivity is normally the major reason for many companies desiring a competitive advantage. Automation also offers low operational variability. Variability is directly related to quality and productivity. Other reasons to automate include the presence of a hazardous working environment and the high cost of human labor. The decision regarding automation is often associated with some economic and social considerations.

Automation is mostly notable in **manufacturing**. In recent years, the manufacturing field has witnessed the development of major automation alternatives. Some of these major automation alternatives include:

- Computer-aided manufacturing (CAM)
- Numerically control (NC) equipment
- Robots
- **Flexible manufacturing systems** (FMS)
- Computer integrated manufacturing (CIM)

Computer-aided manufacturing (CAM) refers to the use of computers in the different functions of production planning and control. Computer-aided manufacturing includes the use of numerically controlled machines, robots, and other automated systems for the manufacture of products. Computer-aided manufacturing also includes computer-aided process planning (CAPP), group technology (GT), production scheduling, and manufacturing flow analysis. Computer aided process planning (CAPP) means the use of computers to generate process plans for the manufacture of different products. Group technology (GT) is a manufacturing philosophy that aims at grouping different products and creating different manufacturing cells for the manufacture of each group.

Numerically controlled (NC) machines are a programmed version of machine tools that execute in operational sequence on parts or products. Individual machines may have their own computers for that purpose and they are normally known to be computerized numerical controlled (CNC) machines. In other cases, many machines may share the same computer and are normally referred to as direct numerical controlled machines.

Robots are automated equipment that, through programming, may execute different tasks that are normally handled by a human operator. In manufacturing, robots are used to handle a number of tasks that include assembly, welding, painting, loading and unloading, inspection and testing, and finishing operations.

Flexible manufacturing systems (FMS) may simply be defined as a group of computer numerically controlled machine tools, robots, and an automated material handling system that are used for the manufacture of a number of similar products or components using different routings among the machines. Flexible manufacturing systems have proved to increase manufacturing productivity by at least fifty percent.

A computer integrated manufacturing (CIM) system is a system where many manufacturing functions are linked through an integrated computer network. These manufacturing or manufacturing related functions include production planning and control, shop floor control, quality control, computer aided manufacturing, computer aided design, purchasing, marketing, and possibly other functions. The objective of a computer integrated manufacturing system is to allow changes in product design, to reduce costs, and to optimize production requirements.

[Ahmad K. Elshennawy, PhD]

FURTHER READING:

Hitomi, K. *Manufacturing Systems Engineering*. London: Taylor and Fracis, Ltd, 1979.

B

BALANCE SHEET

A balance sheet is a financial report that shows the financial position of an entity or enterprise at a specific time, including the firm's economic resources (**assets**), economic obligations (**liabilities**), and the residual claims of owners (owners' equity). The term balance sheet refers to the fact that on the statement assets equals (or balances) liabilities plus owners' equity. The balance sheet is also referred to as a statement of financial position or a statement of financial condition. The balance sheet is usually presented in one of the following formats:

- Assets = Liabilities + Owners' equity

- Assets − Liabilities = Owners' equity

In the report form of the balance sheet, asset accounts are listed first, and the liability and stockholders' equity accounts are listed in sequential order directly below the assets. In the account form, the balance sheet is organized in a horizontal manner, with the asset accounts listed on the left side and the liabilities and stockholders' equity accounts listed on the right side.

CONTENT OF THE STATEMENT

The balance sheet discloses major classes and amounts of an entity's assets as well as major classes and amounts of its financial structure, including liabilities and equity. Major classifications used in the statement include the following:

1. Assets—probable future economic benefits obtained or controlled by a business entity as a result of past transactions or events:

   - Current assets (including cash, marketable securities, accounts receivable, inventory, and prepaid expenses.

   - Investments

   - Property, plant, and equipment

   - Intangible assets (**patents**, **copyrights**, goodwill)

   - Deferred charges or other assets

2. Liabilities—probable future sacrifices of economic benefits arising from present obligations of a business entity to transfer assets or provide services to other entities in the future as a result of past transactions or events:

   - Current liabilities (accounts payable, notes payable, wages payable, and taxes payable)

   - Long-term liabilities (bonds payable, pensions, and lease obligations)

   - Other liabilities

3. Owners' equity—the residual interest in the assets of a business entity that remains after deducting its liabilities:

   - Capital stock

   - Other paid-in capital in excess of par or stated value

   - Retained earnings

The essential characteristics of an asset include the following: (1) it embodies a probable future benefit that involves a capacity, singly or in combination with other assets, to contribute directly or indirectly to future net cash inflows; (2) a particular entity can obtain the benefits and control others' access to it; and (3) the transaction or other event giving rise to the entity's right to or control of the benefits has already occurred. The essential characteristics of a liability include the following: (1) it embodies a present duty or responsibility to one or more entities that entails settlement by future transfer or use of assets at a specified or determinable date, an occurrence of a specified event, or on demand; (2) the duty or responsibility obligates a particular entity, leaving it little or no discretion to avoid the future sacrifices; and (3) the transaction or other event obliging the entity has already happened.

Current assets are cash and other assets that are expected to be converted into cash, sold, or consumed either in the year or in the operating cycle of the business, whichever is longer. Current liabilities are the obligations that are reasonably expected to be liquidated either through the use of current assets or the creation of other current liabilities. Working capital is the excess of current assets over current liabilities and can be computed from data shown on the balance sheet. **Working capital** is significant in determining the ability of the entity to finance current operations and to meet obligations as they mature. The relationship of current assets to current liabilities is referred to as the current ratio and is a measure of the liquidity of the entity.

Assets are classified in the balance sheet from most liquid to least liquid. Liabilities are classified in the order of maturity. Owners' equity items are classified according to source and in their decreasing order of permanence.

The heading of the balance sheet contains the name of the **accounting** entity, the name of the statement, and the date of the statement as of the close of business on that date.

Balance sheets are usually presented in comparative form. Comparative financial statements include the current year's statement and statements of one or more of the preceding accounting periods. Comparative statements are useful in evaluating and analyzing trends and relationships.

Notes to the balance sheet provide additional information not included in the accounts on the **financial statements**. Notes are consider to be an integral part of the statement. Additional information can be disclosed by means of supporting schedules or parenthetical notation.

RECOGNITION AND MEASUREMENT

For an item to be recognized in a balance sheet, the item and information about it must: (1) meet the definition of an element of accounting (the broad classes of items comprising the balance sheet), (2) be measurable (**valuation**), (3) be relevant, and (4) be reliable.

Assets and liabilities are measured or reported on the balance sheet by different attributes (for example, historical cost, current replacement cost, current market value, net realizable value, and present value of future cash flows), depending upon the nature of the item and the relevance and reliability of the attribute measured. The valuation method primarily used in balance sheets currently is historical cost because it is measurable and provides information that has a relatively high degree of reliability. Historical cost is the exchange price of the asset when it was acquired. Current cost is the amount of cash or cash equivalent required to obtain the same asset at the balance sheet date. Current market value or exit value is the amount of cash that may be obtained at the balance sheet date from selling the asset in an orderly liquidation. Net realizable value is the amount of cash that can be obtained as a result of future sale of an asset. Present value is the expected exit value discounted to the balance sheet date.

CONSOLIDATED BALANCE SHEET

Consolidated financial statements represent the financial position of single entity, even though there may be one or more separate legal entities. A consolidated balance sheet is presumed to present more meaningful information than separate financial statements of the affiliated entities and must be used in substantially all cases in which a parent directly or indirectly controls the majority voting stock (over 50 percent) of a subsidiary. Consolidated financial statements should not be prepared in those cases in which the parent's control of the subsidiary is temporary or where there is significant doubt concerning the parent's ability to control the subsidiary.

USES AND LIMITATION

The balance sheet assists external users of financial statements in assessing the entity's liquidity, financial flexibility, and operating capabilities; and in evaluating the earnings performance for the period. Liquidity describes the amount of time that is expected to elapse until an asset is realized or otherwise converted into cash or until a liability has to be paid. Financial flexibility is the ability of an enterprise to take effective action to alter the amounts and timing of cash flows so it can respond to unexpected needs and opportunities. Operating and performance capabilities refer to the capability and effectiveness of an entity related to its major or ongoing revenue producing activities.

The balance sheet has major limitations. The balance sheet does not necessarily reflect the fair market value of assets because accountants typically apply the historical cost principle in valuing and reporting assets and liabilities. The balance sheet omits many items that have financial significance. Furthermore, professional judgment and estimates are often used in the preparation of balance sheets which can possibly impair the usefulness of the statements.

SEE ALSO: Auditing, Income Statement

[Charles Woelfel]

FURTHER READING:

Eskew, R. K., and D. L. Jensen. *Financial Accounting.* New York: McGraw-Hill.

Financial Accounting Standards Board. *Statements of Financial Accounting Concepts.* Homewood, IL: Irwin, 1987.

Miller, Martin A. *HBJ Miller Comprehensive GAAP Guide 1991 College Edition* Fort Worth, TX: Harcourt Brace College Publishers, 1990.

BALANCE OF TRADE

The balance of trade of a nation is the difference between values of its exports and imports. When exports are greater than imports, the nation is said to have a balance of trade surplus. On the other hand, if imports are greater than exports, the nations is said to have a balance of **trade deficit**. Exports and imports that figure in the balance of trade concept arise in the context of trade with other countries. Exports are the value of goods and services produced in the United States and sold to other countries—in other words, exports are expenditures on American goods and services by the residents of foreign countries. A Jeep Cherokee produced in Detroit and sold to a Canadian resident in Toronto is an example of a U.S. export. Imports, on the other hand, are the value of goods and services produced in other countries and bought by the United States—in other words, imports are expenditures by the residents of the United States on goods and services produced by foreign countries. A Sony television manufactured in Japan and bought by an American living in Los Angeles is an example of a U.S. import. Since the balance of trade arises in the context of foreign trade, the balance of trade surplus is also called the foreign trade surplus and the balance of trade deficit is also called the foreign trade deficit. Also, since the balance of trade surplus or deficit is defined as the difference between exports and imports, it as also called net exports.

The foreign trade surplus or deficit is considered to play an important part in the economic growth of a nation, and thus it has implications for jobs created within the country or jobs lost to other nations. As a result, this topic is often debated in an emotionally charged atmosphere. Below is a brief history of balance of trade in the United States, as well as a summary of the economic implications of running a foreign trade surplus or deficit.

THE RISE AND FALL OF THE U.S. TRADE DEFICIT

Up until 1982, the foreign trade deficit was not a serious problem for the United States. The trade deficit started rising dramatically in 1983, from about $38 billion in 1982 to a peak of approximately $170 billion in 1987. Moreover, the trade deficit has remained at relatively high levels since 1982—hovering well over $100 billion per year for most of the 1988-94 period.

One of the reasons for the emergence of the balance of trade deficit in 1983-84 was the increase in **interest rates** in the United States. The early 1980s experienced higher nominal interest rates (the ordinary interest rates as quoted, by financial institutions) and higher real interest rates (nominal interest rates when adjusted for inflation). The interest rate is one of the major determinants of the exchange rate. The exchange rate, in turn, is the value of the U.S. dollar in relation to the currencies of other countries—often, it is expressed as the value of one U.S. dollar in terms of the number of units of the currency of another nation. For example, if one U.S. dollar is equal to 100 Japanese yen (the Japanese currency), then the exchange rate between the U.S. dollar and the Japanese yen is 1:100. Of course, the exchange rate of the U.S. dollar can also be expressed the other way around—that is, the number of U.S. dollars equal to one Japanese yen. The U.S. dollar will be characterized as being strong in relation to the Japanese yen if a large number of yens are equal to one U.S. dollar, whereas the dollar will be considered weak, if one U.S. dollar equals fewer yens.

The exchange rate is like the price of any commodity that responds to forces of demand and supply. If the demand for the U.S. dollar rises relative to another currency, its price in terms of that currency rises—that is, the exchange rate (of the dollar) appreciates. On the other hand, if the supply for the U.S. dollar rises relative to another currency, its price in terms of that currency falls—that is, the exchange rate (of the dollar) depreciates. The rise in interest rates experienced in the United States during the early 1980s made investment in the United States more attractive, relative to investments in other countries. As a result, foreign residents rushed to convert their financial assets (held in their own domestic currencies) into U.S. dollars for investment in the United States. This raised the demand for the U.S. dollar and the supply of foreign currencies, raising the value of the U.S. dollar. This appreciation in the U.S. dollar had adverse effects on the U.S. foreign trade deficit, since it reduced U.S. exports to other countries and increased imports from these countries.

The way changes in the exchange rate affect exports and imports can be briefly explained as follows. When the U.S. dollar appreciates, foreign goods (expressed in U.S. dollars) become cheaper and U.S. goods (expressed in foreign currencies) become more expensive. Assume, for example, that one U.S. dollar was equal to 100 Japanese yen and a Sony television is priced at 15,000 yen in Japan—implying that the television is worth $150 in the United States. Now, assume that the U.S. dollar appreciates so that one dollar equals 150 yen. The stronger dollar implies that the Sony television set will now cost only $100 in the United States. The lower price of the television set (in terms of the U.S. dollar) leads to increased sales of Sony television sets in the United States—that is, an increase in imports into the United States. Now, consider an item that the United States exports, for example, a Jeep Cherokee. Suppose that the Jeep costs $10,000 in the United States. When one dollar equals 100 yen, a Jeep Cherokee will sell for 1,000,000 yen in Japan. When the U.S. dollar appreciates to 150 yen to a dollar, the Jeep will sell for 1,500,000 yen in Japan. Thus, due to the appreciation of the U.S. dollar, a Jeep Cherokee becomes more expensive in Japan, reducing its demand—this translates into reduced exports from the United States. The exchange rate appreciation thus serves as the double-edged sword—reducing exports and increasing imports simultaneously. This is what happened in the 1980s; the rise in the value of the U.S. dollar was the main culprit behind the dramatic rise in the U.S. foreign trade deficit. The U.S. dollar has gradually declined in value since then, as has the trade deficit, but not to the level that existed in 1982.

THE U.S. BUDGET AND TRADE DEFICITS. For most of the 1980s, the U.S. economy faced both federal budget deficits and foreign trade deficits, often called the twin deficits. This was, however, no mere coincidence. As explained above, higher interest rates had pushed up the foreign exchange rate and the foreign trade deficit increased dramatically. Higher interest rates in the United States were, in turn, at least partly, caused by the U.S. budget deficit. An existence of a budget deficit implies that the government is spending more than it is receiveing in tax revenue. As a result, the government has to borrow to meet the shortfall in tax revenue. Such government borrowing adds to the demand for credit in the debt (financial) market which, in turn, raises the cost of borrowing, the inter-

est rate. This phenomenon is often called the international crowding out. U.S. budget deficits were in large part financed by investors from abroad (lured by higher interest rates in the United States relative to interest rates in their home countries). Thus, the simultaneous existence of budget and trade deficits appeared convenient and painless for the U.S. economy—the overspending on foreign goods and services (the negative net exports) were largely financed by borrowings from abroad.

This seemingly odd arrangement works as follows. The U.S. needs to pay for importing more than **exporting** (equal to the value of net exports). When foreign nationals invest in the United States by buying U.S. Treasury bonds, they lend funds to the U.S. government to finance the federal budget deficits. This inflow of funds from foreign nationals to buy the Treasury bonds (called the inflow of capital and deemed to be a part of the capital account), however, offsets the outflow of funds from the United States that would have been necessary to pay for the excess of imports over exports (often referred to as activities on the current account). The need for the payment by the United States on account of the current account is avoided due to the offsetting transaction on the capital account. Nevertheless, the net result of the twin deficits was that the U.S. dependence on foreign funds grew, and so did the U.S. foreign debt. In fact, the United States turned into a debtor nation for the first time during the Reagan administration—that is, the United States owed more to other countries than other nations owed to the United States. Foreign debt is not simply a matter of national prestige. It has certain economic implications. Sudden withdrawal of funds from the United States, by foreign nationals (for example, due to a lack of confidence in U.S. currency), can destabilize the U.S. and world financial markets.

DETERMINANTS OF THE BALANCE OF TRADE

There are three major determinants of the trade balance or net exports: Foreign exchange rates, national incomes, and domestic and foreign price levels.

EFFECTS OF THE FOREIGN EXCHANGE RATE. The way the foreign exchange rate affects exports and imports has already been discussed in fair detail. In a nutshell, if the U.S. dollar appreciates (the dollar becomes stronger and the foreign exchange rate increases), exports decline and imports increase, causing the foreign trade deficit to rise. If the dollar depreciates (the dollar becomes weaker and the foreign exchange rate decreases), the foreign trade deficit falls.

EFFECTS OF CHANGES IN DOMESTIC AND FOREIGN INCOMES. Changes in national incomes in foreign countries as well as in the United States have an important effect on net exports. If national incomes in foreign countries rise, foreign residents demand greater amounts of goods and services, some of which can be bought from the United States. As a result, an increase in incomes in foreign countries leads to an increase in U.S. exports, causing the foreign trade deficit to rise (assuming other factors do not change). If national incomes in foreign countries fall, U.S. exports to these countries will decline, leading to a decline in the foreign trade deficit as well.

If the U.S. national income rises, U.S. consumers demand more goods and services, and some of this increased demand is for goods and services produced in other countries. As a result, a rise in U.S. income increases U.S. imports, causing the foreign trade deficit to rise. On the other hand, if the U.S. national income declines, the demand for goods and services by U.S. consumers falls, so does the demand for imported goods and services—this leads to a decrease in the foreign trade deficit.

From the preceding discussion, it follows that changes in net exports are also tied to rates of economic growth, both home and abroad. While U.S. policy makers have some control over the rate of economic growth in the United States, they cannot unilaterally influence rates of economic growth in foreign countries. As a result, U.S. policy makers do not have complete control of the behavior of U.S. net exports.

PRICES IN THE UNITED STATES AND IN FOREIGN COUNTRIES. Even if the foreign exchange rate and the domestic and foreign economic growth rates remain unchanged, changes in price levels can affect U.S. net exports. Let us first look at the effects of a change in the price level in the United States. Suppose that the U.S. inflation rate is equal to 10 percent per annum. This means that prices of goods and services in the United States are rising at the annual rate of 10 percent, on average. As a result, a Jeep Cherokee that costs $10,000 this year will cost $11,000 next year. Also, let us assume that foreign prices do not change and that one U.S. dollar is equal to 100 Japanese yen, and this exchange rate will not change next year. Now, look at the effect of the U.S. price increase on the price of a Jeep Cherokee in terms of Japanese yen, the price most relevant to a prospective Japanese buyer of a Jeep Cherokee. This year the Jeep Cherokee costs 1,000,000 yen ($10,000*100) to a Japanese buyer, but it will cost 1,100,000 yen next year. Due to an increase in the price in yen, the export of Jeep Cherokees to Japan would decline as the demand for the vehicle declines in Japan (given that other factors do not change). Thus, in general, an increase in U.S. price levels will hurt U.S. exports.

An increase in U.S. price levels will also affect U.S. imports of foreign goods and services. In the above example, we assume that the U.S. price level rises and the Japanese price level does not. Thus, a Japanese-made Toyota costs the same amount in U.S. dollars this year as it will next year (since the foreign exchange rate is also assumed to remain unchanged), but a Jeep Cherokee sold in the United States will cost 10 percent more. This implies that the next year, a Japanese-made Toyota will become cheaper relative to a Jeep Cherokee—thus, a Toyota will become relatively more attractive to a prospective U.S. car buyer the next year. In general, therefore, U.S. price increases also increase U.S. imports. The price increases serve as a double-edged sword that reduces exports and increase imports simultaneously, causing net exports to decline—that is, the foreign trade deficit becomes worse or the magnitude of the foreign trade surplus declines.

One can see that changes in foreign price levels will have analogous effects. If foreign prices increase and the U.S. price level does not increase (given that other factors do not change also), U.S. exports will rise and imports will fall, causing the U.S. foreign trade deficit to shrink or the foreign trade surplus to grow, as the case may be.

ECONOMIC IMPLICATIONS OF FOREIGN TRADE DEFICITS

As alluded to in a previous section, increasing U.S. foreign trade deficits contributed, at least passively, to mounting U.S. foreign debts, with implications for the stability of U.S. financial markets. Foreign trade deficits have other serious economic implications.

A COMPONENT OF AGGREGATE DEMAND. When exports exceed imports, it implies that foreign demand for U.S. goods and services is greater than U.S. demand for goods and services of other countries. In other words, there is a net positive demand for U.S. goods and services from abroad. The foreign demand adds to the total domestic demand from all sectors—primarily, made up of consumer spending, business investment, and government spending on goods and services. Thus, a net positive foreign demand augments the aggregate demand for U.S. goods and services. The aggregate demand is simply the sum of consumer spending, business investment, government spending, and net exports. An increase in the aggregate demand, due to positive net exports, has roughly the same implications for the U.S. economy as an increase in one of the other three components of the aggregate demand.

On the other hand, when imports exceed imports, it implies that foreign demand for U.S. goods and services is less than U.S. demand for goods and services of other countries. In other words, there is a net negative demand for U.S. goods and services from abroad. The net negative foreign demand subtracts from the total domestic demand from all sectors. Thus, a net negative foreign demand reduces the aggregate demand for U.S. goods and services. A decrease in the aggregate demand, due to negative net exports, has roughly the same implications for the U.S. economy as a reduction in one of the other three components of the aggregate demand.

There are three major effects on the economy of an increase or decrease in the aggregate demand: (1) it affects the output and income in the economy; (2) it influences the level of employment and **unemployment** in the economy; and (3) it affects the price level and the inflation rate in the economy.

NET EXPORTS AND THE OUTPUT AND INCOME IN THE ECONOMY. When an increase in net exports leads to an increase in the aggregate demand, it also increases the output (often called the real **gross domestic product** or real GDP) and income (often called the real national income) in the economy. This can be explained in terms of Keynesian macroeconomic theory. When aggregate demand in the economy increases, producers increase the output of goods and services to meet the increased demand. The increased production of goods and services in the economy generates additional income in the economy. Thus, net exports can be a source of economic growth for an economy. If the economy is very large, relative to the magnitude of the change in the net exports, effects of changes in net exports may not be very conspicuous. Nevertheless, an export-dependent small economy can experience visible influences on its economic growth if net exports increase sharply. The Taiwanese economy provides a good example of such an economy where growth in the aggregate demand was fueled by exports to other countries.

Just as an increase in net exports has favorable effects on the economic growth of a nation, a decrease in net exports will have the opposite effect on the growth of its output and income.

NET EXPORTS AND THE EMPLOYMENT LEVEL. The fact that changes in net exports have an effect on the economy's gross domestic product and economic growth has an obvious implication for the employment level in the economy. If, for example, net exports in the United States increase and the output of U.S. goods and services increases as a result, producers will need to hire more workers in order to increase output which, in turn, raises the level of employment of the labor force. This normally translates into a lower unemployment rate in the economy, a much sought after economic outcome. It is true, however, that the employment level may increase only with a lag—as the aggregate demand level rises (such as due to an increase in net exports) in the economy, producers first resort to the use of overtime from existing workers before adding to the number of workers

employed. Once the increase in the aggregate demand level is deemed to be relatively permanent, however, they hire additional permanent workers.

A decrease in net exports will have the opposite effect on the level of employment in the economy—a reduction in net exports leads to a decline in aggregate demand and a consequent decrease in output and employment.

NET EXPORTS AND THE PRICE LEVEL. A rise in net exports is mixed blessing. While an increase in the foreign trade balance leads to an increase in gross domestic product, spurs economic growth, and generates jobs, it is also deemed to be inflationary. When net exports rise, the aggregate demand for goods and services increases. As producers rush to increase production to meet the increased demand, they put an upward pressure on wages and other input prices, leading to an increase in the cost of production. An increase in the cost of production, in turn, leads to an increase in the retail prices of goods and services paid by domestic consumers. In addition to the upward pressure put on the domestic prices due to an increase in the cost of production, an increase in foreign demand for U.S. goods makes U.S. producers of these goods more tempted to increase the prices of these products. Overall, an increase in net exports will tend to put an upward pressure on the domestic price level—the extent of the price increase will depend on how far the economy is from full employment. The U.S. economy is considered to have achieved the full employment, or the potential output level, when the economy experiences a 6 percent rate of unemployment and a plant capacity utilization rate of 86 percent. The closer the economy is to full employment, the greater is the pressure on the price level.

A decline in net exports or a shrinking foreign trade balance has the opposite effect on the domestic price level—it puts downward pressure on the price level. A decline in net exports leads to a decline in aggregate demand in the economy. This puts downward pressure on the domestic price level for two reasons—it puts a downward pressure on the cost of production, and it makes it harder for the domestic producers to raise the prices of their products.

As is apparent from the preceding discussion, a rising foreign trade deficit is rather good from the point of view of individual consumers—they end up paying lower prices for goods at the retail level (presumably, they also have a wider choice of products, since more foreign products, and greater quantities of them, are available).

MACROECONOMIC POLICIES AND THE FOREIGN TRADE DEFICIT. All capitalist economies, including the United States, attempt to stabilize the economy around full employment, using monetary and fiscal policies. Nevertheless, a macroeconomic policy that is good for the domestic economy does not necessarily improve the foreign trade balance. Consider, for example, that the United States conducts expansionary monetary policy which raises the domestic aggregate demand (by spurring domestic consumption and investment). Since the monetary policy leads to an economic expansion, output and income rise in the United States. This rise in the U.S. income, in turn, generates greater demand for imported goods, causing an existing foreign trade deficit to become worse. Thus, policy makers often face a policy dilemma—the possible adverse effects of a macroeconomic policy on the foreign trade balance.

THE POLITICS AND ECONOMICS OF FOREIGN TRADE

As is clear from the preceding discussions, foreign trade, even if it results in a deficit on the foreign trade balance, is not all bad. While a foreign trade deficit can be held responsible for some lost jobs, it also provides consumers with lower prices and greater choice. Debates on the foreign trade deficit in the popular media is often unbalanced. During the **North American Free Trade Agreement** (NAFTA) debates in the United States, opponents of the agreement put a lot of emphasis on the ''sucking sounds'' of jobs lost to Mexico. The trade deficit with Japan is also often debated in a politically charged atmosphere, frequently resulting in Japan-bashing.

A foreign trade deficit essentially creates a classic conflict between two groups—workers and consumers. Workers as a group may tend to lose due to lost jobs (but not all workers lose since jobs are created in imports-related industries). Consumers, on the other hand, gain as explained above. Which group's interest will the government keep in mind in dealing with trade issues? The answer to this question often boils down to whichever group has the greater political influence. It so happens that workers tend to be better organized and they are, thus, able to influence government trade policy in their favor.

[Anandi P. Sahu]

FURTHER READING:

Froyen, Richard T. *Macroeconomics: Theories and Policies*. 4th ed. New York: Macmillan Publishing Company, 1993.

Gordon, Robert J. *Macroeconomics*. 6th ed. New York: Harper-Collins College Publishers, 1993.

BANANA REPUBLIC

''Banana Republic'' is a derogatory term for countries under the economic control of foreign-owned companies or industries. The term originated in the late 1800s when American fruit companies controlled the economic, political, and social development of many Central American nations. Since then the phrase has grown to signify any country that is economically dependent on foreign-owned companies and foreign markets. The term implies that the host country has a corrupt government.

BANANA REPUBLICS TAKE HOLD

The nation of Honduras is most closely identified with the term ''Banana Republic.'' In the late 1870s, a liberal reform government came to power in Honduras and, in an effort to alleviate some of the country's economic problems, aggressively sought foreign investment. The government saw mineral exploitation as a possible solution but after some initial success the mining ventures failed when the price of silver on the world market collapsed. Next, banana cultivation became a means of luring foreign investment. The Honduran government saw American companies as an attractive partner in this venture because of their ready capital, steamships, marketing capabilities, and access to home markets; they tempted the businesses with exaggerated promises of easy profits.

Minor Keith and the United Fruit Company are a classic example of a Banana Republic from the business standpoint. Keith was an American railroad engineer who built railroad lines in Costa Rica. Along the railroad right-of-ways he planted banana trees as a cash crop. Already familiar with banana culture and Central American politics, Keith formed the Tropical Trading and Transport Company. Since he was already a large stockholder in the Boston Tropical Fruit Trading Company, he merged the two into a new concern called the United Fruit Company. Keith's political influence in Central America was made even stronger when he married into an influential Costa Rican family.

GOVERNMENT FAILS TO LIMIT CORPORATIONS

In 1893 the Honduran government, in an effort to support local growers and make the banana industry more competitive, put restrictions on the manner in which buying, selling, and transporting could occur within the country. The government also put a two cent tax on each stem of bananas for education and infrastructure improvements. By 1912, however, Keith's United Fruit Company was largely in control of Honduran politics and the tax was repealed, costing the Honduran government $121 million through the first half of the twentieth century. In addition, though the Honduran government had implemented policies preventing the large fruit companies from increasing the size of their land holdings at the expense of small growers, the United Fruit Company forced small growers to sell their holdings by controlling irrigation machinery, pesticide allocation, and various marketing practices. The fruit company executives soon became political power brokers, especially after their companies diversified into other areas of the Honduran economy.

While the fruit companies did bring some development, infrastructure improvement, and comparatively high wages to the countries in which they operated they also left a trail of exploitation and corruption.

[Michael Knes]

FURTHER READING:

Acker, Alison. *Honduras: The Making of a Banana Republic.* South End Press, 1988.

Stewart, Watt. *Keith and Costa Rica: A Biographical Study of Minor Cooper Keith.* University of New Mexico Press, 1964.

BANKING ACT OF 1933

The Glass-Steagall Act, or Banking Act, was passed by Congress in June, 1933, in the face of vociferous opposition from the American banking community. Six decades later, aspects of the Act are still unpopular in banking and brokerage circles. Prohibiting commercial banks from using their own **assets** to invest in securities (i.e., **stocks** and **bonds**) is a principal provision of the Glass-Steagall Act. This was meant to correct the abusive practices of the largest commercial **banks** in the 1920s that contributed to the uncontrollable speculation responsible for the **stock market** crash in 1929. Even more important than this provision, was the establishment of the **Federal Deposit Insurance Corporation**, or FDIC. The FDIC insures bank deposits up to a given amount; this not only restored the public's confidence in the nation's banks, but provided a life-giving flow of **capital** to the thousands of banks that had failed between 1929 and 1933. Six months after the inauguration of the FDIC in January 1934, bank failures that were so characteristic of the Depression came to a halt.

The Depression had given rise to the severest crisis in banking history. In a span of three years (1930-1933), over 9,000 banks had closed their doors. 90 percent of these small community (i.e. "unit") banks failed because frightened customers drained their bank accounts, and capital shriveled up, due in part to a 90 percent decline in private domestic investment. By 1933, the banking system was a wreck. Critics blamed banks for the nation's economic problems. Congressional hearings in early 1933 revealed gross irresponsibility on the part of major banks, which had used billions of dollars of deposit funds to

acquire stocks and bonds, and had made unsound loans to inflate the prices of these securities. The public's venom against banks and stock brokers was so great that many predicted imminent revolution.

As a result, one of the highest priorities of President Franklin D. Roosevelt's new administration was to resolve the banking dilemma. After congressional hearings took place in the spring, the Banking Act of 1933 (or Glass-Steagall Act), the first of many major laws regulating the nation's finances, was passed on June 16. Even before FDR had taken his oath of office, the Glass-Steagall bill had been in the works. Representative Henry Steagall had proposed deposit insurance as a means of saving failed banks. This was not a new idea. Several states had initiated deposit insurance schemes in the 1920s, when bank failures were on the rise. With the Crash, however, even states were too bankrupt to help out their own state chartered banks, to say nothing of the many smaller banks. Steagall realized that opposition to a federally insured deposit system would come from the large banks, which would resent parting with **revenue** for the sake of their weaker competitors. By the spring of 1933 even the major banks were willing to support this idea, rather than risk a more radical restructuring of the banking system.

Far more controversial was Senator Carter Glass's proposal, incorporated in the Banking Act, to separate investment from commercial banking. Only a handful of commercial banks had been guilty of financial transgressions, chiefly the misuse of depositors' funds to acquire and trade stocks and bonds. Nonetheless, there was evidence that these banks had made over eight billion dollars in **loans** to brokers and dealers in the 1920s, fueling stock market speculation and compromising their integrity as they attempted to lure their own customers to invest in the bank's security holdings. By using depositors' funds to invest in stocks and bonds, these banks imperiled savings and other deposits, given that these could be withdrawn on demand.

The passage of the Glass-Steagall bill into law strengthened the regulatory power of the **Federal Reserve**. Member banks would have to report on all investment transactions and loans. Those banks which were not members of the Federal Reserve had to be deemed in sound financial condition in order to join the FDIC (membership in FDIC became mandatory for those banks belonging to the Federal Reserve), which condemned weak banks to oblivion, but strengthened sound ones. Henceforth banks were not only subject to greater public scrutiny and compliance, but were compelled to a higher standard. The result was that by mid-1934, bank failures had stopped, banks by the thousands had reopened after joining the FDIC, and banking stability was never again to be so seriously jeopardized.

The United States has remained unique in the developed world in its separation of commercial from investment banking.

[Sina Dubovoy]

FURTHER READING:

Benston, George J. *The Separation of Commercial and Investment Banking; The Glass-Steagall Act Revisited and Reconsidered*. New York: Oxford University Press, 1990.

Bruchey, Stuart. *The Wealth of the Nation; An Economic History of the United States*. New York: Harper & Row, 1988.

Fearon, Peter. *War, Prosperity & Depression; The U.S. Economy, 1917-45*. University Press of Kansas, 1987.

BANKRUPTCY

SEE: Business Failure

BANKS AND BANKING

A bank is an institution that provides financial services to consumers, businesses, and governments. One major type of bank is the commercial bank, which has fewer restrictions on its services than other types of banks. Commercial banks profit by taking deposits from customers, for which they typically pay a relatively low rate of interest, and lending the deposits at a higher rate of interest to borrowers. These borrowers may be individuals purchasing homes, cars, and other things or they may be businesses financing **working capital** needs, equipment purchases, etc. Banks may also generate revenue from services such as asset management, investment sales, and mortgage loan maintenance. About 10,000 U.S. commercial banks with 60,000 branches existed in the early 1990s. Those banks controlled about 25 percent of all U.S. assets.

In addition to **commercial banks**, major types of banks include savings banks, trust companies, and **central banks**. Savings banks are similar to commercial banks but they are geared toward serving individuals rather than businesses. They take deposits primarily from individuals, and their investment activity is limited by the federal government to specific non-commercial investments, such as home mortgage loans. Trust companies act as trustees, managing assets that they transfer between two parties according to the wishes of the trustor. Trust services are often offered by departments of commercial banks. Central banks are usually government-controlled institutions that serve regulatory and monetary management roles.

Among other activities, central banks may issue their nation's currency, help to determine **interest rates**, collect and disburse government resources, and issue and redeem government debt.

Most commercial banks are operated as corporate holding companies, which may own one or several banks. Because of regulatory constraints, banks that are not associated with **holding companies** must operate under restrictions that often put them at a disadvantage compared with other financial institutions. Holding companies are often used as vehicles to circumvent legal restrictions and to raise capital by otherwise unavailable means. For instance, many banks can indirectly operate branches in other states by organizing their entity as a holding company. Banks are also able to enter, and often effectively compete in, related industries through holding company subsidiaries. In addition, holding companies are able to raise **capital** using methods from which banks are restricted, such as issuing **commercial paper**. Multibank holding companies may also create various **economies of scale** related to advertising, bookkeeping, and reporting, among other business functions.

BACKGROUND

Financial intermediaries that safeguard funds, lend money, and guarantee the exchange of money have existed since ancient times. The modern banking industry, however, is rooted in European institutions established in the 1700s. Early in that century, English goldsmiths discovered that they were consistently storing large amounts of gold owned by their customers. They found that they could temporarily lend some of the gold to other people in exchange for a promissory note for interest. Importantly, these early bankers found that the value of their **promissory notes** could exceed the value of their stored gold—in effect, they were creating money that could be used to expand the economy. That pivotal banking approach, known as fractional-reserve banking, is credited with making Western industrialization possible. Among the first major modern banks to use fractional-reserve banking were the Riksbank, founded in Sweden in 1656, and the Bank of England, created in 1694.

Similar banking industries sprang up throughout the world during the 1700s and 1800s. For example, one of the first banks in the United States—the Bank of the United States—was formed in 1791. Despite their important social and economic function, depositors considered banks a relatively risky investment until the mid-1900s. In fact, bank failures, such as those occurring throughout the late 1800s and during the Great Depression of the 1930s, effectively wiped out millions of dollars of depositors' savings. Following those disasters, most countries developed a system of government insurance for bank deposits. In the

United States, that insurance resulted from the Banking Acts of 1933 and 1935, which created the **Federal Deposit Insurance Corporation**. Those and similar efforts resulted in greater bank stability and increased use of banks, particularly by individuals, during the mid-1990s.

BANKING TODAY

Commercial banking in the United States during the 1970s and through the early 1990s has been characterized by: (1) a proliferation of competition from other financial service industries, such as **mutual funds** and leasing companies; (2) the growth of multibank holding companies; and (3) new technology that has changed the way that banks conduct business. The first two developments are closely related. Indeed, as new types of financial institutions have emerged to meet specialized needs, banks have increasingly turned to the holding company structure to increase their competitiveness. In addition, a number of laws passed since the 1960s have favored the multibank holding company format. As a result the U.S. banking industry had become highly concentrated in the hands of bank holding companies by the early 1990s. By 1993, in fact, the approximately 1,000 U.S. multibank holding companies controlled more than 90 percent of the entire banking industry's assets. Furthermore, the top 100 multibank corporations accounted for a full 80 percent of all bank assets.

Electronic information technology, the third major factor in the recent evolution of banking, is evidenced most visibly by the proliferation of electronic transactions. Electronic fund transfer systems, automated teller machines (ATMs), and computerized home-banking services all combined to transform the way that banks conduct business. By the mid-1990s, there were nearly 100,000 ATMs operating in the United States—far surpassing the number of bank branches—and an additional 200,000 worldwide. Such technological gains have served to reduce labor demands and intensify the trend toward larger and more centralized banking organizations. They have also diminished the role that banks have traditionally played as personal financial service organizations. Finally, electronic systems have made possible nationwide, and even globally, banking systems with nearly instant information access.

SEE ALSO: Savings and Loan Associations

[Dave Mote]

FURTHER READING:

Kamerschen, David R. *Money and Banking*. Cincinnati: South-Western Publishing Co., 1988.

McClellan, Hassell H. *Managing One Bank Holding Companies*. New York: Praeger Publishers, 1981.

Roussakis, Emmanuel N. *Commercial Banking in an Era of Deregulation*. New York: Praeger Publishers, 1989.

U.S. Department of Commerce. *U.S. Industrial Outlook 1993*. Washington, DC: GPO, 1993.

BAR CODING

Bar coding is an automatic identification technology that allows data to be collected rapidly and extremely accurately. Because of these attributes, bar coding has been used for a wide range of applications in almost every aspect of business. Bar codes provide a simple method of encoding text information that can be easily read by inexpensive electronic readers called scanners. A bar code consists of a series of parallel, adjacent bars and spaces. Predefined bar and space patterns, or symbologies, are used to code character data into a printed symbol. Bar codes might be considered a printed version of the Morse code, with narrow bars representing dots and wide bars representing dashes. A bar-code reading device decodes a bar code by scanning a light source across it and measuring the intensity of the light reflected back to the device. The pattern of reflected light produces an electronic signal that exactly matches the printed bar-code pattern and is easily decoded into the original data by inexpensive electronic circuits. Because of the design of most bar-code symbologies, scanning a bar code from right to left or from left to right makes no difference. The basic structure of a bar code consists of a leading and trailing quiet zone, a start pattern, one or more data characters, one or two optional check characters, and a stop pattern.

In the early 1990s, a variety of different types of bar-code encoding schemes, or symbologies, were developed to fulfill specific needs in specific industries. Several of these symbologies grew into de facto standards that have become universally used throughout most industries.

A bar-code reader works by scanning a dot of light across a bar-code symbol. As the dot scans the bar code, light is reflected back to the bar-code reader by the light areas and is absorbed by the dark areas. The scanner electronically measures the intensity of the reflected light to produce a digitized waveform that can be decoded back to the original message, similar to the way in which Morse code dots and dashes were decoded by a receiver. Factors influencing the readability of a bar code include: an adequate print contrast between the light and dark bars; all bar and space dimensions within the tolerances for the symbology; sharp bar edges; few or no spots or voids; a smooth surface; and clear margins or quiet zones at either end of the printed symbol.

Bar-code scanners come with different resolutions to enable them to read differently-sized bar codes. The scanner's resolution is measured by the size of the dot of light, which has to be equal to, or slightly smaller than, the narrowest element width (the ''X'' dimension). If the dot is wider than the width of the narrowest bar or space, then the scanner may become confused because of the dot's overlapping two or more bars at a time. If the dot is too small, then any spots or voids in the bars may be misinterpreted as light areas, thus rendering a bar code unreadable.

First utilized in supermarkets and libraries, bar coding has grown over the years to have applications in many fields. In combination with a record-tracking system (composed of a symbology, a scanner, decoding software, and labels), bar coding is an important tool in advanced file-room and record-center environments, allowing for speedier, more accurate data entry, improved document tracking, and increased productivity at lower cost.

In 1993 with bar-code applications increasing, the Uniform Code Council (UCC) and bar-code experts urged higher print quality in corrugated materials to ensure the readability of bar codes. These two groups believed that standardization was the best solution; they did not, however, take into consideration the fact that recycled corrugated materials were darker and that, therefore, contrast would prove more difficult. Many industry analysts believe that a variety of solutions will demand scrutiny as more and more employees are trained in the bar-code printing process.

Because these symbologies eliminated the human factors that could often lead to inaccuracies in keyboard data entry, bar codes are absolutely trustworthy. Moreover, bar codes have to pass a series of tests before the symbol can be decoded. The encoded data can also be structured in order to minimize data entry. One of the world's leading manufacturing companies of bar-code-scanning equipment is Symbol Technologies, Inc., in Bohemia, New York, which was founded in 1973 under the leadership of chairman Jerome Swartz, a former physics professor with a background in laser diodes. Nineteen years later, in 1992, the firm held a 40 percent share of the worldwide bar-code scanning equipment market. In that year, the company also commanded about 80 percent of the market in hand-held scanning devices, whose technology was pioneered by Symbol in 1983. Sales revenues for the fiscal year 1991 were $317 million, a growth of 37 percent.

In 1994, the technology of bar-code scanning was used widely in retail stores for basic functions, including price verification and inventory control. Hundreds of new applications, however, are under development. Other major users include the U.S. Postal Service, which applies the technology to route letters to their correct ZIP codes and to track packages (along with competitors United Parcel Service and Federal Express); publishing companies, which use bar coding to identify newspapers, magazines, and books and to keep records of sales; libraries, which utilize the technology for inventory and charging-out of materials; airlines, which enhance bar coding to allow the preparation of shipping labels as well as the tracing and monitoring of cargoes by shippers and freight-forwarding agents; automobile manufacturers, who track the cars they ship by using an automated identification system based on bar codes appearing on the windshields of automobiles; and banks, which are testing a bar-code-based computerized check-processing system to track the movement of bar-coded courier bags of checks between a bank's branches and its operating centers.

BAR-CODING SOFTWARE

In 1994, one of the leading software programs for bar-coding was B-Coder, manufactured by T.A.L. Enterprises in Philadelphia, Pennsylvania. Not only is B-Coder powerful; it is extremely easy to use, as well. While most other bar-code software packages are strictly label-design programs that force the user to employ his or her own label design tools, B-Coder allows the user to incorporate bar codes into any Windows application program. The primary types of bar codes generated by this software include Universal Product Codes (UPCs: UPC-A, UPC-E, and UPC Supplementals); PDF417; European Article Numbers (EANs: EAN-8, EAN-13, and EAN Supplementals); Code 39 (Normal and Full ASCII versions); codabars; Code 128; EAN/UCC 128; POSTNET (POSTal Numeric Encoding Technique); and Postal FIM (Facing Identification Marks). Other widely-used bar codes include Interleaved 2 of 5, Discrete 2 of 5, and Code 93.

UPCS. UPCs (Universal Product Codes) are used principally for retail purposes. UPC-A, a 12-digit numeric symbology used in retail applications, consists of 11 data digits and 1 check digit. The first digit is a number-system digit that usually represents the type of product being identified. The next 5 digits are a manufacturer's code, and the following 5 digits are used to identify a specific product. UPCs are also emblazoned on manufacturers' coupons, with the last 3 of the second set of 5 digits sometimes indicating the monetary value of the cash-off; when the vendor coupon is scanned, the amount of the cents-off is automatically deducted from the customer's bill, and misredemption is mitigated. Assigned to specific products and manufacturers by the Uniform Code Council (UCC), UPC numbers may be applied for by contacting the UCC.

UPC-E, a smaller, 6-digit UPC symbology for number system 0, is often used for small retail items.

UPC-E is also called "zero-suppressed" because UPC-E compresses a normal 12-digit UPC-A code into a 6-digit code by "suppressing" the number system digit, trailing zeros in the manufacturer's code, and leading zeros in the product identification part of the bar code. A seventh check digit is encoded into a parity pattern for the 6 main digits. Thus, UPC-E may be uncompressed into a standard UPC-A 12-digit number. Both UPC-A and UPC-E allow for a supplemental two- or 5-digit number to be appended to the main bar-code symbol. Designed for use on publications and periodicals, the Supplemental is simply a small additional bar code placed on the right side of a standard UPC symbol, which provides more precise product identification.

PDF417. Forging a path beyond that traveled by UPCs, Symbol Technologies in 1992 unveiled a new "smart" bar code. Not only does it identify the product—it also gives information about its source, destination, and proper handling. Whereas the ordinary bar code is one-dimensional, linear, and may contain 20 to 30 symbols per inch, the new bar code is two-dimensional and uses height and width to convey information. One small square of the new bar code may contain data equal in amount to a 20-foot strip of the old. T.A.L. Enterprises' high-density, two-dimensional bar-code symbology; it is called PDF417 and essentially consists of a stacked set of smaller bar codes. The B-Coder is capable of enclosing the entire (255-character) ASCII set. PDF stands for Portable Data File because the symbology can encode as many as 2,725 data characters in a single bar code. The complete specification for PDF417 provides many encoding options, including data compaction, error detection and correction, and variable size and aspect ratio symbols. Software analysts believe that the development of national standards for the technology will provide the impetus for its acceptance by industries.

EANS AND EAN SUPPLEMENTALS. A European version of the UPC, the EAN, or European Article Number system (also called JAN in Japan), uses the same size requirements and a similar encoding scheme as for UPC codes. EAN-8 encodes 8 numeric digits consisting of 2 country code digits, 5 data digits, and 1 check digit. EAN-13 is the European version of UPC-A, the former differing from the latter only insofar as that it encodes a 13th digit into the parity pattern of the left 6 digits of a normal UPC-A symbol. This 13th digit, in combination with the 12th digit, defines 2 flag characters that represent a country code. Both EAN-8 and EAN-13 allow for a supplemental 2- or 5-digit number to be appended to the main bar-code system. Designed for use on publications and periodicals, the Supplemental is simply a small additional bar code appended to the right side of a standard EAN symbol. EAN bar-code numbers are assigned to specific products and manufacturers by an organization called ICOF located in Brussels, Belgium.

EAN-13 is adopted as the standard in the publishing industry for encoding the ISBN number on books. An ISBN (International Standard Book Number) bar code is simply an EAN-13 symbol consisting of the ISBN number preceded by the digits 978. Thus, the supplemental message in an ISBN bar code is simply the retail price of the book preceded by the digit 5. For example, if the ISBN number were 1-23456-789-2 and the price of the book were $22.95, then one would enter 978123456789 as the bar-code message and 52295 as the supplemental message.

CODE 39. The Normal Code 39 is a variable-length symbology that can encode the following 43 characters: 1234567890ABCDEFGHIJKLMNOPQRSTU VWXYZ-.*$/+%. The most popular symbology in the nonretail world, Code 39 is used extensively in manufacturing, military, and health applications. Each Code 39 bar code is framed by a start/stop character represented by an asterisk (*). Code 39 allows for a check character in cases where data security is important. Consequently, the health-care industry adopted the use of this check character for health-care administration purposes. Another feature of Code 39 allows for concatenation (linkage) of two or more bar codes.

The Full ASCII version of Code 39 is a modification of the Normal (Standard) version that can encode the complete 128 ASCII character set (including asterisks). Also, the Full ASCII version is implemented by using the four characters "$/+%" as shift characters to change the meanings of the rest of the characters in the Normal Code 39 character set. Because the Full ASCII version uses shift characters to represent data not in the Normal Code 39 character set, each nonstandard character requires twice the width of a standard character in a printed symbol.

POSTAL SERVICE BAR CODES. Used by the U.S. Postal Service to encode ZIP code information for automatic mail sorting by ZIP code, POSTNET (POSTal Numeric Encoding Technique), a 5-, 9-, or 11-digit numeric-only bar-code symbology, is able to represent a 5-digit ZIP Code (32 bars), a 9-digit ZIP+4 Code (52 bars), or an 11-digit Delivery Point Code (62 bars). Unlike other bar codes, POSTNET features data encoded in the height of the bars instead of in the width of the bars and spaces; tall bars represented bits of 1, short bars bits of 0. As a result, most standard bar-code readers cannot decipher POSTNET. Chosen by the U.S. Postal Service in 1976 because it was extremely easy to print on almost any type of printer and was extremely easy to be modified, POSTNET is a fixed-dimension symbology, in that the height, width, and spacing of all bars has to fit within exact tolerances. The symbology is called a "clocked" bar code because the lower portion may be used as a standard "clock" and the reader does not require a completely steady scan for accurate results.

FIM (Facing Identification Mark) patterns are another type of bar code used by the U.S. Postal Service in automated mail processing. Utilized for automatic facing and canceling of mail which does not contain a stamp or meter imprint (business-reply mail, penalty mail, etc.), FIMs also provide a means of separating business- and courtesy-reply mail from other letters. FIM patterns in use in 1994 were: FIM-A, used on courtesy-reply mail that had been preprinted with POSTNET bar codes; FIM-B, used on business-reply penalty and franked (government) mail that was not preprinted with POSTNET bar codes; and FIM-C, used on business-reply, penalty, and franked mail that had been preprinted with POSTNET bar codes. The FIM pattern is placed in the upper right corner of the piece of mail, along the top edge, and two inches in from the right edge of letters and cards.

OTHER BAR CODES. Other bar codes widely used in 1994 included the codabar, the Interleaved 2 of 5, the Discrete 2 of 5, Code 93, Code 128, and EAN/UCC 128. Commonly used in libraries, blood banks, and the air-parcel business, the codabar is a variable-length symbology that allows encoding of the following 20 characters: 0123456789$:/-.+ABCD. The Interleaved 2 of 5 is a high-density, variable-length, numeric-only symbology that encodes digit pairs in an interleaved manner, with the odd-position digits encoded in the bars and the even-position digits encoded in the spaces. Discrete 2 of 5, very similar to Interleaved 2 of 5, is a variable-length numeric symbology which encodes data only in the bars. Code 93, a variable-length symbology that can encode the complete 128 ASCII character set, was developed as an enhancement to the Code 39 symbology by providing a slightly higher character density than does Code 39. Code 93 also incorporates two check digits as an added measure of security. While Code 93 is considered more robust than Code 39, it has never enjoyed the same popularity as the latter. Code 128, a variable-length high-density alphanumeric symbology, contains 106 different bit and space patterns, each of which can have one of three different meanings, depending upon which of three character sets are employed. The EAN/UCC 128 symbology, designed primarily for use in product-identification applications, is a variation of the original Code 128 symbology.

FUTURE PREDICTIONS FOR BAR CODING

With bar coding proliferating in the digital information age, a great deal of effort has been put forth in an attempt to establish industry-wide bar-code standards. For instance, in 1992, the Automotive Industry Action Group (AIAG) promulgated a document describing the requirements for bar-code symbols on transport packages and unit leads.

Although bar coding is expanding by 20 percent annually, the technology did not grow as much as it could have in 1994 because it was not being used in information systems (IS) departments. Many IS executives are reluctant to take a leadership role in the application of the technology because the bar-code systems often do not follow corporate standards for software and hardware development. Thus, many industry analysts believe that in spite of the potential payoffs of increased accuracy and timeliness, bar coding is unlikely to be adopted by IS professionals and that its penetration into American business will be minimal. In 1994, however, this scenario began to change as some IS professionals began learning about bar coding via just-in-time inventory systems, while other IS professionals were learning by being included on bar-coding project teams. The future of bar coding, therefore, seems somewhat more hopeful than that which many industry observers had first presumed.

[Virginia L. Barnstorff]

FURTHER READING:

"Airline's Customer Service Goals Aided by Automated Curbside Luggage Check-In." *Industrial Engineering.* June, 1992, p. 20.

Alpert, Mark. "Building a Better Bar Code." *Fortune.* June 15, 1992, p. 101.

"At BISAC Meeting, Questions about Bar Codes." *Publishers' Weekly.* January 27, 1992, p. 20.

"Automobile Carrier Uses Bar Code to Speed Delivery." *Industrial Engineering.* October, 1991, p. 27.

"Bar-Code Scanning Network Improves Product Configuration." *Industrial Engineering.* October, 1993, p. 31.

"Bar Code Speeds Bill Processing." *Modern Office Technology.* May, 1992, p. 78.

Betts, Mitch. "IS Must Get a Handle on Bar Coding: Business Opportunities Missed As Management Fails to Take Technology Leadership Role." *Computerworld.* September 9, 1991, p. 57.

Bhargava, Sunita Wadekar. "Beyond the Supermarket: Symbol Technologies, Inc., Dominates Growing Bar-Code Scanning Equipment Market." *Business Week.* February 3, 1992, p. 80A.

"Big Bad Bar Code: Two-Dimensional Bar Codes and Advances in Data Collection Technology Promise to Deliver More Operational Data to Decision Makers." *Computerworld.* May 25, 1992, p. 81.

Deogun, Nikhil. "UPS Unveils an Alternative to Bar Codes." *Atlanta Business Chronicle.* November 28, 1993, p. 28

"Expanded Bar Code Makes Grade." *Supermarket News.* February 7, 1994, p. 38.

Fales, James F. "Can You Really Bank on Bar-Coded Data?" *Industrial Engineering.* October, 1992, p. 40.

Filipczak, Bob. "Bar Coding: Not Just for Groceries Anymore." *Training.* December, 1992, p. 75.

"Gaining Control and Shrinking Expenses through Automation." *Modern Office Technology.* May, 1992, p. 42.

Geisler, Jennie. "Scan This: UCC and Bar-Code Experts Still Wrestling with Natural Kraft Issues." *Paperboard Packaging.* September, 1993, p. 20.

"The Generalist vs. the Specialist: How to Decide Which Printer Is Best for Your Application." *Modern Office Technology.* February, 1992, p. 44.

Goltz, Rick. "2-D Bar Codes Put Carriers in Your EDI Loop." *Transportation and Distribution.* May, 1993, p. 76.

Heidkamp, Maria. "BISAC Bats around Bar Codes." *Publishers Weekly.* June 29, 1994, p. 27.

Lustig, Theodore. "Bar Codes Shape Up Ink Shipments." *Graphic Arts Monthly.* April, 993, p. 95.

Lyons, Daniel J. "Bar-Code Printers Produce Coded Labels; Encrypted Information is Simplifying Retail Inventory Processes, Law-Enforcement Tasks." *PC Week.* January 6, 1992, p. 77.

———. "Bar-Code System Sees Bookkeeping for Alaskan Fish-Packing Company." *PC Week.* January 6, 1992, p. 77.

Mark, Teri J. "Decoding the Bar Code." *Records Management Quarterly.* January, 1994, p. 22.

Munro, Jay. "The POSTNET Bar Code." *PC Magazine.* December 8, 1992, p. 406.

———. "Using A CASS-Certified Address List." *PC Magazine.* December 8, 1992, p. 410.

Mutter, John. "At BISAC: Bar Codes and More." *Publishers Weekly.* April 5, 1993, p. 21.

———. "EAN Bar Codes to Appear on Back of Mass Market Titles." *Publishers Weekly.* February 15, 1993, p. 16.

———. "Wholesalers Issue Bar-Code Ultimatum to Publishers." *Publishers Weekly.* March 28, 1994, p. 20.

Nannery, Matt. "Optical Disks, Bar Codes Pay Off at Price Chopper." *Supermarket News.* August 2, 1993, p. 15.

Panchak, Patricia L. "Specialized Printers Expedite Nonstandard Applications." *Modern Office Technology.* February, 1992, p. 42.

Pavely, Richard W. "Postal Changes and Mailroom Management." *The Office.* January, 1992, p. 41.

Reese, K. M. "Checking the Accuracy of Identification Numbers." *Chemical and Engineering News.* January 25, 1993, p. 60.

Reitter, Chuck. "Bar-Code Benefits Outlined for NPCA Panel." *American Paint & Coatings Journal.* March 22, 1993, p. 13.

"Remote Control: Retail Technology." *Economist.* May 29, 1993, p. 90.

Rice, Judy. "Two-Dimensional Data Matrix Symbology . . . A Future Alternative to Bar Coding?" *Food Processing.* June, 1992, p. 55.

Sadhwani, Arjan T., and Thomas Tyson. "Does Your Firm Need Bar Coding?" *Management Accounting (USA).* April, 1990, p. 45.

Safi, Quabidur B. "MaxiLAN Bar-Code Reader." *PC Week.* July 5, 1993, p. 76.

"Scanners Eliminate Need for Tokens." *American City & County.* May, 1992, p. 70.

Schwartz, Evan I. "Bits and Bytes." *Business Week.* September 28, 1992, p. 122.

Seideman, Tony. "BC Labels Turn High-Tech." *Distribution.* January, 1993, p. 83.

Sharp, Kevin R. "Packing a Page of Info into Two Inches: Two-Dimensional Bar Codes Are Emerging as a Way to Get More Data into a Small Space." *Computerworld.* May 25, 1992, p. 83.

Shukovsky, Sam. "Bar-Code Scanners Help Post Office Automate." *PC Week.* January 13, 1992, p. 25.

Snell, Ned. "Bar Codes Break Out: Once You Learn What Bar Codes Do Today, You May Find Uses You Never Thought of Before." *Datamation.* April 1, 1992, p. 71.

Speitel, Thomas W. "Bar Code Your Classroom." *Science Teacher.* October, 1992, p. 18.

Stamper, Bonney. "Are You Monitoring Your Bar-Code Quality?" *Packaging Digest.* October, 1992, p. 103.

"Symbol Technologies, Inc.'s LS 5000 POS Bar-Code Scanners and DM-802 Data Collection Terminals." *Industrial Engineering.* October, 1993, p. 34.

Teitelbaum, Richard S. "Zebra Technologies." *Fortune.* January 25, 1993, p. 105.

Tucker, Tracey. "Nashville's 1st American Using Bar-Code System." *American Banker.* February 3, 1994, p. 18.

"Two-D Bar Codes: Better Known But Not Widely Used—Yet." *Modern Materials Handling.* March, 1994, p. 12.

Verity, John W. "Goodbye, Bar Codes, Hello, Buttons." *Business Week.* May 18, 1992, p. 130E.

BARTERING

Bartering is the exchange of goods and services without the use of currency. The technique has been used in commercial transactions since ancient times. More recently, U.S.-based multinational companies have used a form of bartering called **countertrade** when selling large-value items, such as jet aircraft, overseas. Bartering allows a company to dispose of excess inventory, use surplus production capacity, and obtain necessary raw materials when a cash shortage exists. In addition, the technique also enables firms to gain access to new production channels and customers, resulting in increased sales volume.

INTERNATIONAL BARTER ARRANGEMENTS

Countertrade refers to foreign trade arrangements that are adaptations on the idea of barter. The technique became popular in the 1960s and 1970s as a method for communist nations to finance their international trade. Countertrade involves an exchange of goods between two countries without the involvement of currency. Barter terms are typically established between two countries on the basis of a bilateral trading agreement under which an exporter in one country and an importer in another country exchange goods.

Payments for exports to Eastern Bloc countries are often made through clearing units that balance sales with purchases from other countries. The clearing unit attempts to identify the goods each country will trade and to set overall trade limits. The objective of this type of countertrade, known as switch trading, is to eliminate the imbalance in barter trade between two countries.

One of the countries, however, often fails to sell sufficient goods to its trading partner, and a shortage in clearing funds will develop for the deficit country. Hence, one of the countries becomes a debtor, and the bilateral trading agreement tends to break down.

Counterpurchase is a form of countertrade that usually occurs between a Western industrial country and an Eastern Bloc or Third World country. It includes a standard hard-currency export, but the seller agrees to return purchases with a minimum quantity of specified goods from the buyer. In a compensation (buy-back) agreement, the initial seller receives compensation in products that arise out of the original sale. Buy-back transactions typically involve large capital expenditures and a long time frame. Thus, these arrangements are viewed as an alternative to foreign **direct investment**.

BARTERING IN THE UNITED STATES

The uses of commercial barter in the United States were initiated in Los Angeles in 1960, and grew rapidly during the 1960s. The reputation of barter exchanges, however, was sullied in the mid-1970s when some exchange owners inflated their currencies in a bid to draw extra business. The situation began to change in 1979 with the establishment of the International Reciprocal Trade Association (IRTA). Formed to foster the interests of the barter industry, the IRTA works to establish professional standards concerning exchange operations. The association offers recommendations on establishing exchanges, and it produces programs that teach exchange owners how to administer and market their businesses.

The industry also received beneficial publicity because of the widespread use of bartering during the 1984 Summer Olympics in Los Angeles. The Olympics relied on barter to exchange licensing rights for $116 million worth of goods and services from 30 major corporations, including Buick, Fuji Film, and United Airlines. The success of the Olympic bartering activity led to increased interest in this technique.

In recent years, barter has increasingly become a viable alternative to cash transactions for small and medium-sized businesses. According to the IRTA, more than 220,000 American companies conducted $5.3 billion worth of barter in 1990 compared with 140,000 companies that exchanged $3.3 billion worth of goods and services in 1985.

HOW BARTER EXCHANGES OPERATE

There are currently an estimated 450 barter exchanges operating nationwide. These exchanges generally operate on a local or regional level, although many have reciprocal trade agreements with other exchanges. Barter exchanges usually consist of several hundred members who swap goods and services among themselves. Almost all individuals and businesses with a product or service to sell are eligible to join a barter exchange. Barter exchanges typically charge one-time cash membership fees—generally about $500—and also charge a commission equal to 10 percent of the transaction value.

Barter exchanges use the sophisticated data processing systems common in financial markets. Through the use of large, computerized databases, exchange brokers are able to precisely match the needs of their corporate clients. The exchange sets up a system of **trade credits** that operate like currency. Customers establish accounts and are given exchange checks. Exchange members use the trade credits instead of hard currency to purchase a variety of goods and services. The exchange sends members monthly statements summarizing their transactions.

[Robert T. Kleiman]

FURTHER READING:

Kim, Suk H., and Seung H. Kim. *Global Corporate Finance: Text and Cases*. 2nd ed., Miami, FL: Kolb Publishing, 1993.

BENCHMARKING

Benchmarking is the practice of identifying another business that is the best, or one of the better practices, in its class and learning as much as possible from it. The term was popularized in the 1980s by Xerox's Robert Camp, who wrote the first major book on the subject, *Benchmarking: The Search for Industry Best Practices that Lead to Superior Performance.*

Benchmarking is a business strategy that is used primarily by manufacturers, although it is applicable to other business activities as well. While it may involve learning from one's competitors, benchmarking is more focused and narrowly defined than competitive analysis. Competitive analysis can be used in conjunction with benchmarking to identify gaps and provide strategic direction, however, benchmarking itself measures specific performance gaps between a company and its competitors.

Benchmarking is used when there is a clearly defined gap between a company and its competitors that must be overcome in order to remain competitive. For example, the Xerox Corporation benchmarked Japanese manufacturers who were able to sell a copier for the same amount it cost Xerox to build one. Benchmarking may focus on products, manufacturing processes, management practices, and/or overall corporate direction. It is often focused on learning from one's direct competitors. Benchmarking can also lead to improved performance by studying general business practices that are not industry specific (generic benchmarking), specific business or manufacturing functions (functional benchmarking), general industry characteristics (industry benchmarking), strategies in general (tactical benchmarking), or the numerical characteristics of specific products or processes (performance benchmarking). As a result of its benchmarking in Japan, Xerox eventually developed a completely new copying process by creatively improving on the concepts it had learned from its chief competitors.

Benchmarking involves some measure of cooperation between two companies who become benchmarking partners. Xerox has pioneered benchmarking and often serves as a benchmarking partner for other companies interested in learning from it. After a company chooses a competitor to study, information is exchanged between the two companies through a series of on-site visits by teams representing each partner. These cross-functional benchmarking teams contain representatives from different functional areas of each company, including management. At the on-site visits, teams representing the two partners determine such issues as the focus for discussion, proprietary issues, the agenda, and who the participants will be.

Once the period of study and information exchange is completed, the benchmarking team issues an action plan and presents it to management for approval. The study and plan provide evidence that a top company is doing things in a better way and that the benchmarking company can implement similar changes to become more competitive. The action plan sets objectives and provides a roadmap for achieving those goals. It also spells out the necessary capital investment.

In the 1990s benchmarking was still relatively new to most companies. Xerox established the International Benchmarking Clearinghouse in Houston to help educate other companies to its benefits. Small companies as well as large corporations can use benchmarking techniques to improve their performance by learning from other companies in their field.

SEE ALSO: Competition

[David P. Bianco]

FURTHER READING:

Camp, Robert. *Benchmarking: The Search for Industry Best Practices that Lead to Superior Performance.* Quality Resources, 1989.

BENELUX

The Benelux Economic Union (BEU) was established in principle in 1944 by three signatories: Belgium, the Netherlands, and Luxembourg. The Union did not become fully effective until 1958, however. The term Benelux is derived from the first letters in the name of each country. Like other economic unions, the goal of BEU is to promote economic integration and cooperation between its members. This effort takes the form of coordinated planning and subsequent action in foreign trade, monetary policy, finance, transportation, and tourism. Ultimately BEU is striving towards full integration of its members, economies.

The historic roots of BEU go back to 1912 when Luxembourg and Belgium signed an agreement at the Convention of Brussels that created the Belgium-Luxembourg Economic Union. The purpose of this union was to equalize customs tariffs and move towards a single balance of payments. In 1932 the Belgium-Luxembourg Economic Union and the Netherlands ended the Convention of Ouchy with agreements on stabilizing customs duties, lowering import duties, and easing other restrictions and hindrances on commerce.

During World War II the three governments-in-exile periodically met in London to solidify their postwar economic plans. In 1944 the Dutch-Belgium-Luxembourg Customs Convention was signed but did not go into effect until 1948 when the war-ravaged economies began to stabilize. In 1953 the governments categorized their economic and social policies and in 1958 the Benelux Treaty of Economic Union was signed at The Hague. The signing and formalization of the union was hastened by other European countries moving towards the creation of the European Common Market now known as the European Economic Community.

BEU seeks to achieve its goals through a broad range of activities, both economic and social. BEU allows the free movement of agricultural and finished goods, labor, and capital across its members' borders. There is coordination in foreign trade resulting in consistent customs **duties** on imported goods from non-member countries and the dissolution of import duties and import quotas among members.

In areas of social reforms the Union has done away with passport restrictions and labor permits. Discrimination in terms of working conditions, benefits, and professional employment is also prohibited.

In 1987 BEU members began coordinating efforts to upgrade their respective infrastructures, especially in terms of communications, sewage handling, and disposal and fire and police control. Environmental enhancements were also put in place in an effort to reduce noise, air, and water pollution.

BEU is a signatory of the *Schengen Accord* along with France and the former Federal Republic of Germany (West Germany). This accord eases border restrictions and enhances internal security of the signatories. Revisions in the accord in 1990, however, addressed members' concerns over the joining of East and West Germany, immigration control, and restrictions and problems of political asylum. Italy, Portugal, Greece, and Spain all signed the accord by the early 1990s. With the dissolution of the Soviet Union and the opening of markets in eastern Europe, BEU is coordinating efforts for trade with members of the former Soviet bloc. Especially attractive are the Baltic States and the more open market economies of central Europe.

BEU is governed by its Committee of Ministers which is comprised of at least three ministers from each member country. Usually represented on the Committee are countries' ministers of foreign affairs and other officials responsible for foreign trade, economic affairs, or finances. The Committee meets quarterly and is responsible for seeing that BEU activities fall within the aims and goals of the 1958 treaty. All decisions made by the Committee are unanimous.

The Benelux Interparliamentary Consultative Council was established by convention on November 5, 1955, prior to the Union becoming fully active. The Council has 49 members, 21 from the Netherlands and Belgium and seven from Luxembourg. Member countries' parliaments choose the Council's representatives. The Council makes policy recommendations to the Committee of Ministres only on resolutions the Council has bassed by two-thirds majority; other decisions need only have a simple majority.

The Council of the European Union, which is comprised of senior officials from the various members' governments, is responsible for making recommendations to, and implementing decisions made by, the Committee of Ministers. It also coordinates inter-Union activities, such as committee, special committee and task force assignments, and serves as a liaison between these groups and the Committee of Ministers.

The Economic and Social Advisory Council submits proposals on various matters to the Committee of Ministers and, when asked, makes advisory proposals to the Committee.

The College of Arbitration settles inter-Union disputes, and the Court of Justice, which is made up of senior judges from each member country, advises and, under certain circumstances, rules on inter-Union legal matters and problems.

BEU is one of the world's oldest economic unions. Its philosophy and guiding principles operate within a democratic framework and have served as a model for other economic unions, especially the European Economic Community. BEU seeks to integrate not only the economies of its three member countries but also an impressive array of social, legal, and environmental activities.

[Michael Knes]

FURTHER READING:

Riley, R. C. *Benelux: An Economic Geography of Belgium, the Netherlands & Luxembourg.* New York: Holmes & Meier, 1975.

Soloveytchik, George. *Benelux.* Toronto: Canadian Institute of International Affairs, 1957.

BERNE CONVENTION

The Berne Convention, formally known as the International Convention for the Protection of Literary and Artistic Works, is an international **copyright** agreement originally signed in Berne, Switzerland in 1886. Since then, the agreement has been updated and revised numerous times.

The Berne Convention's central feature is the automatic copyright protection extended to all citizens of member nations. If a country is a signatory to the Berne Convention it must extend to nationals of other member nations the same copyright protection and copyright restrictions afforded to its own citizens. If the person responsible for the intellectual content of a work is not a citizen of a Berne Convention signatory, however, and his or her work is published or used commercially in a Berne Convention member country, that person's work is only protected to the extent covered by the copyright laws in its country of origin.

The Berne Convention of 1886 is the wellspring of most other national and international copyright regulations. European movements for international copyright protection were well under way by middle 1800s. These regional movements and other cooperative agreements between publishers, authors, and national governments solidified the need for an international copyright agreement and led to the signing of the Berne Convention accord in 1886. The original signers were Belgium, Germany, Spain, Switzerland, France, Italy, Great Britain, Tunis, and Haiti. The rules of the Convention were extended to the colonial holdings of the signing nations, giving the accord global influence.

The Berne Convention sorted out two views of copyright law. Continental Europe generally held that the interests of the author were preeminent. In the United States and Great Britain, however, it was generally felt that to a great extent public interest superceded the author's claim to the work, especially works of foreign authors. The treatment of both foreign and national authors within each member country was equalized by the Berne Convention. Thus the accord stayed true to its preamble which states in part "... to protect, in as effective and uniform a manner as possible, the rights of authors in their literary and artistic works."

Rapidly advancing technology through the 20th century has produced new formats for expressing ideas and providing entertainment. Technical innovations such as sound recordings, photography, and cinematic developments present new challenges to existing copyright laws. Technical advances in communication were matched by the pervasiveness of worldwide mass media. To meet these changes, the Berne Convention underwent revisions in Berlin in 1908 and Rome in 1928.

Under the Berlin Act of 1908 copyright protection was extended to photography, sound recordings, and cinematography. Literary works reproduced as sound recordings were covered, and protection was extended to cinematographers and those authors whose original works were brought to the movie screen. The concept of authorized or assigned usage of a work, particularly of sound recordings, emerged as a result of the Berlin revisions as well.

The Rome Act of 1928 addressed the moral rights of the author and broadcasters' access to works of literature, music, and sound recordings. Moral rights are the right of an author to object to changes in his or her work after the copyright had been transferred, especially if the changes could be deemed denigrating to the work or to the reputation of the author. The Rome Act determined that the moral right or moral claim would extend throughout the life of the author.

The Rome Act also dealt with broadcasting and broadcasters' rights. Radio broadcasting was becoming widespread throughout Europe. Some countries, especially those on the continent, gave clear copyright protection regardless of the means of reproduction. In other countries, most notably Great Britain, copyright law as it related to broadcasting was muddled at best. At the Rome meeting some countries wanted copyright restrictions on works transmitted over the air waves. Other countries viewed radio primarily as an educational tool that should not have copyright infringements or other legal restrictions placed on it. The meeting compromised by allowing the author the right to control his or her work through authorization procedures but also granted to the legislative bodies of the Berne Convention signatories power to "... regulate the conditions for the exercise of the right. ..."

The Berne Convention also underwent revisions in 1948, 1967, and 1971. The Brussels Act of 1948 covered enforcement of regulations within member countries. The Stockholm Acts of 1967 and 1971 addressed technological innovations and copyright law as it affected developing countries.

Until 1988 the United States was not a signatory to the Berne Convention. Instead the United States had its own internal copyright legislation and was a signatory to the Universal Copyright Convention of 1952 which was sponsored by the United Nations Educational, Scientific and Cultural Organization (UNESCO). The Universal Copyright Convention was less stringent than the Berne Convention on automatic copyright protection, did not prescribe minimum levels of protection for works produced outside of member nations, and allowed tighter internal control over copyright applications. The United States also had technical differences with Berne Convention regulations concerning notice, registration, and the legal relations between domestic manufacturers and copyright protection. In 1976 the United States revised and updated its 1909 copyright legislation with the Copyright Act of 1976, but by 1988 the United States began considering membership in the Berne Convention. The reasons for this move were largely political. The United States wanted to strengthen copyright relations with the 24 nations that belonged to the Berne Convention but had no formal copyright agreements with the United States. Joining the Berne Convention promised to strengthen United States trade relations and further normalize and legitimize global copyright law. Thus, on October 20, 1988, the United States Senate ratified the Berne Convention Implementation Act and became the 77th nation to join.

Berne regulations are administered by the World Intellectual Property Organization (WIPO). This organization was founded in 1967 in Stockholm and works closely with the United Nations. WIPO responsibilities encompass worldwide copyright protection of **intellectual property** including industrial property (inventions, trademarks, industrial designs etc.) and copyright property (literature, music, film, photographs, etc.).

[Michael Knes]

FURTHER READING:

Porter, Vincent. *Beyond the Berne Convention: Copyright, Broadcasting and the Single European Market*. John Libbey, 1991.

United States Congress Committee on Foreign Relations. *Berne Convention: Report to Accompany Treaty Doc. 99-27*. Washington, D.C.: GPO, 1988.

BETTER BUSINESS BUREAU (BBB)

"Call the Better Business Bureau!" has been the rallying cry of disgruntled consumers for several decades. This private, nonprofit organization is synonymous with fair business practice and buyer protection.

But even if the "BBB" is a virtual brand name in the consumer-protection field, its functions and history remain vague in the minds of most Americans. A popular belief, for instance, is that a BBB crackdown will force a disreputable retailer out of business. That's false; the Better Business Bureau has no policing powers. Neither does it give legal advice or assist in breaking legal contracts, make collections or give credit information.

Among other duties, what the organization *does* do—under the leadership of the Council of Better Business Bureaus—is collect and disseminate information about companies based on unanswered questions or unsettled complaints. In this respect, the BBB depends on input and feedback from the same consumers it serves daily. The bureau also provides buyer/seller mediation and arbitration services and monitors advertising and selling practices.

The advertising-watchdog aspect of the Better Business Bureau reaches back to the very beginning of the organization. Even before the BBB got its name, various advertising self-regulatory groups had been establishing the purpose of the organization. As far back as 1915, a BBB prototype group, the National Vigilante Commission, issued a report that stated in part: "There is a threefold responsibility for eliminating objectionable advertising. First, the advertiser; second, the writer of the advertising (especially the agencies); and third, the medium which disseminates the advertising. There must be cooperation between the three. The media are rapidly realizing that it is to their own selfish interest to have public confidence in their advertising pages."

In other words, even in 1915 some advertisers were trying to get away with bigger claims than their products or services could support. To say that conditions have changed little since then only makes it clearer the need for a Better Business Bureau. By the early 1920s, the Associated Advertising Clubs of the World took a major step toward the development of the modern BBB with its book *Truth in Advertising— The Better Business Bureau Movement to Protect Reader Confidence*. Back then, there were 32 BBB offices operating from coast to coast. Today, the bureaus number about 175, with dues-paying members in all walks of business handling some 11 million consumer questions yearly.

But that could change. In one city—Hartford, Connecticut—a declining economy is forcing businesses to re-examine their expenses, and many in the Hartford area and elsewhere have been canceling their memberships in associations, including the Better Business Bureau, as the *Hartford Courant* reported. Ironically, the cutbacks come at a time when consumers are calling for the bureau's help more than ever.

When bureau cutbacks occur, the article continues, "several things happen. Consumers who want to deal only with bureau members have less choice. The bureaus have less clout because they have less control over non-members. There are fewer businesses participating in the bureau-run arbitration programs. And the bureaus have less revenue with which to provide service."

According to BBB statistics, the highest number of business-related consumer complaints are in the category of home improvement services, with general service and ordered-product businesses running second and third. Complaints against vehicle dealers and auto-repair shops round out the top five. In a separate category, the BBB also keeps an eye on charitable organizations and other groups that seek donations. It is with the BBB's help that well-publicized reports of misuse of charitable funds was made available in recent years, leading to widespread reform efforts.

When a consumer calls a local BBB office to complain, the member in charge asks for a written version of the problem for bureau records. The bureau then presents a formal complaint to the company involved. "Because most business firms care about satisfying their customers," notes a BBB publication, "complaints are generally resolved and the matter is closed." But on those occasions when the offending company doesn't respond to BBB contact, mediation, or arbitration, a file is set up, which then may be transferred to a law enforcement agency.

Acknowledging the BBB's role in consumer protection, a San Antonio (Tex.) member told *Express News:* "Something I heard a long time ago . . . is that the Better Business Bureau has no teeth. But I say the BBB has a big mouth. Just because we don't bite all the bad guys in town, we have a mouth where we can tell all the people about the bad guys."

[Susan Salter]

FURTHER READING:

"BBB History and Traditions" and "What Is a Better Business Bureau?" Better Business Bureau Consumer Information Series.

Giorgianni, Anthony. "Consumer Helpers Hit by Hard Times," *Hartford Courant.* May 26, 1991.

Lambeth, Laura. "Better Business Bureau Strives to Settle Disputes," *Express News.* June 28, 1992.

BLACK MARKET (TRADING)

Goods that are not manufactured by or under the authority of trademark, copyright, or patent owners are known as black market goods. The sale of these goods as well other illegally produced or stolen goods is referred to as black market trading. The importation of black market goods into the United States is prohibited by state and federal trademark laws. The U.S. Customs Service is responsible for halting and impounding black market goods and in some cases for subjecting violaters to civil and criminal penalties. In many developing countries, black markets are an integral part of the economy and little is done to protect trademark owners. For example, in 1995 the United States considered imposing punitive trade sanctions on China for allowing the production and sale of counterfeit computer software, compacts discs, and other products for which U.S. citizens had trademark and copyright ownership.

Gray market goods are distinguished from black market goods in that gray market goods are legitimately produced but are sold outside authorized distribution channels. A 1984 ruling by the U.S. International Trade Commission in *In re Certain Alkaline Batteries* distinguished between gray and black market goods by identifying the former "genuine" and the latter as not. The ruling defined "genuine" as follows: "Genuine goods are goods produced or selected by the owner of a trademark, to which the owner of that trademark affixes the trademark or in connection with which the owner of the trademark uses the trademark" (as in advertising).

The phrase simply serves to distinguish the goods so produced and marked from goods marked with a trademark by someone not authorized to use the mark (i.e., someone other than the owner or licensee of the owner). Unlike black market goods, the legality of the trade of gray market goods was ambiguous, and a large number of legal cases in the 1980s and 1990s addressed this issue.

Black markets exist for a wide range of products. The early-1990s saw the rapid growth of a black market in stolen integrated circuit chips and a number of violent robberies involving these chips. The growth of the black market was facilitated by the fact that manufacturers did not imprint their chips with serial numbers. To combat this, the Intel Corp. announced in 1993 that it would put serial numbers on its 486 and Pentium chips and maintain a database enabling each chip to be tracked.

In the wake of the Cold War, the United States and the former Soviet Union dismantled nearly 40,000 warheads. The nuclear cores of these weapons were not destroyed, however, creating concern that a black market in nuclear weapons could develop. The problem was heightened by the political and economic instability in many of the countries that made up the Soviet Union.

The production of chlorofluorocarbons (CFCs), used as refrigerants, is scheduled to be phased out by 1996. As the deadline grows nearer, large quantities of the material, as much as 20 million pounds a year, were illegally imported into the United States, resulting in $100 million in lost tax revenues. Importers claimed the CFCs were used or recycled but were newly produced. The importation of black market CFCs was said to compromise the transition to non-ozone depleting refrigerants.

Other products for which there are significant black markets in the United States include computer software (with an estimated $1.5 billion in annual value), anabolic steroids (an estimated $500 million in annual value), and food products stolen and re-sold by supermarket employees.

[David C. Kucera]

FURTHER READING:

Dunn, Darrell. "Crime Fuels Black Market." *Electronic Buyers' News*, March 11, 1991.

Lipner, Seth E. *The Legal and Economic Aspects of Gray Market Goods*. Quorum Books, 1990.

Plumtre, A.F.W. "Theory of the Black Market." *Canadian Journal of Economics and Political Science*. 1947.

Ray, S.K. *Economics of the Black Market*. Westview Press, 1981.

BOARD OF DIRECTORS

Although the shareholders of a corporation own the firm, they do not manage it. Instead they elect a board of directors, which in turn, selects senior management. Therefore, unless altered by a special agreement, the board of directors has the authority to make all decisions in the regular course of business. Theoretically, the board is the representative of shareholders, and is supposed to ensure that management is acting in the best interests of the stockholders. Directors' duties must be discharged in good faith, with the care a prudent person in a similar position would exercise under similar circumstances, and in a manner the director believes to be in the best interests of the corporation.

The functions of the board of directors include: (1) selecting, evaluating, and—where appropriate—dismissing the **chief executive officer** (CEO); (2) reviewing and approving the corporation's financial objectives and **strategy**; (3) providing advice and counsel to senior management; (4) selecting and recommending to shareholders for election a slate of candidates for the board of directors; and (5) reviewing the adequacy of systems to conform with applicable laws and regulations.

Most companies have the following board committees: nominating, compensation, audit, finance, and executive. The nominating committee selects candidates for the board of directors. The compensation committee determines executive pay. The audit committee reviews the reports of the independent external auditor and oversees the internal audit function. The finance committee oversees the **capital** investment decisions of the firm and the raising of sources of capital. Finally, the executive committee approves important decisions between full board meetings.

The most common type of director is a senior executive of another company. Approximately one-quarter of Standard & Poor's 500 firms had a former CEO as a board member. More than 80 percent of board vacancies are filled via the recommendation of the chairman. Many directors serve on more than one board, in addition to holding a full-time job. Accordingly, directors have been criticized for being unable to contribute sufficient time to their duties.

THE CHANGING ROLE OF THE BOARD

In a time of hostile takeover battles and forced replacements of senior executives, the role of the corporate board of directors is rapidly evolving. In the early 1990s, outside directors began taking a more active stance in reacting to poor performance on the part of the management reporting to them. The new activism on the part of corporate directors rose in 1993 to include replacing the chief executive officers for such major corporations as American Express Co., Eastman Kodak Co., General Motors Corp., and IBM.

During the era of hostile **takeovers** in the late 1980s, companies began to nominate directors for three staggered sets of three-year terms as a protective device. For an acquirer to gain control, he or she would have to run a dissident slate three years in a row to gain control of the board.

As a result of the financial difficulties encountered by many companies during the 1980s and early 1990s, some **labor unions** were given the authority to designate one or more members of the firm's board of directors as part of an overall package that contained reductions from the usual wage increases and often outright cuts in labor compensation. In 1980, Chrysler Corp. became the first major company in the United States to elect a union leader to its board. As part of its bankruptcy reorganization, TWA gave its employees a 45 percent ownership of the company plus four board seats.

Another trend that has been noticeable over the last decade has been the ascent of independent outside directors. Independent outside directors have no connection to the company other than serving on the board of directors. Therefore, this category of directors excludes full-time employees, family members, and the company's lawyers and financial advisers. The prevalence of dependent outside directors (those who also provide services to the company) has diminished. In the 1970s, the average board included a commercial banker and/or an attorney. That is true in only a small minority of instances in the 1990s.

Recent studies also indicate that boards are slightly smaller today, reflecting in part the reduced role of inside directors, i.e., directors who are senior managers in the company. A broader diversity of backgrounds is evident in the type of people serving on corporate boards. Increased numbers of directors have public service, academic, and scientific experience, and there has been a dramatic rise in the representation of minorities and women. Finally, the frequency of board meetings has also declined somewhat.

COMPENSATION OF DIRECTORS

In most large companies, compensation committees evaluate the performance of top executives and determine the terms and conditions of their employment. These committees are composed largely or entirely of outside directors.

A director for a major corporation will generally receive a retainer of $20,000 to $30,000 per annum, with an additional stipend of about $6,000 for attending full board and committee meetings. Approximately one-quarter of large publicly traded firms also provide stock grants in addition to retainers.

Recruiting directors has become more difficult. Although the functions and the compensation of directors have helped make board service more attractive, these positive factors are offset by a change in the narrow area of directors' liability. In recent years, courts have narrowed the scope of the business judgment rule, which provides broad discretion to board members in carrying out their functions. The resulting increase in lawsuits against corporate boards has raised the costs of liability insurance. This has led to a appreciable decline in the willingness of insurance carriers to write directors' and officers' liability insurance policies.

CRITICISMS OF THE BOARD

A number of major criticisms have been leveled at corporate boards of directors in recent years. The most common criticism is that it is largely ceremonial, and simply rubber stamps the decisions of management. As a result of management's control of the proxy voting system, it is more likely for management to select directors than vice versa. Accordingly, the role of directors is largely advisory and does not involve significant **decision making**. Furthermore, it is argued that the "old boy" network that dominates some boards makes it undesirable for directors to question the performance of their peers.

A related criticism is that the board's discussions are dominated by the CEO, who typically also serves as chairman of the board. When the same person controls the agenda of boardroom proceedings as well as the day-to-day performance of the company, the power of the individual director may be diminished. Many directors act as partners of senior management, rather than as monitors able and willing to reward and penalize management's performance.

Corporate directors also are criticized for conflicts of interest and for showing greater concern for the welfare of other companies. Many outside directors of corporations do business with the companies on whose board they serve. An analysis of 286 banks that failed in 1990 and 1991 revealed that, in 25 percent of the cases, the main cause of failure was fraud and other abuses by directors and officers, such as receiving loans at very low rates. The board's compensation committee is typically a group dominated by outside directors. Frequently, those outside directors are senior executives of other firms, who are supportive of proposals for increased compensation of their counterparts. Other independent outside directors may represent another set of special interests—those of the local community. Another concern is the relationship of the inside directors to the chairman/CEO since he or she is their day-to-day supervisor and possesses the effective authority to change the directors' role in the company.

The National Association of Corporate Directors recommended certain reform proposals in 1995. First, the association suggested that companies should pay directors mainly with stock rather than cash. Directors who have a significant equity investment in a firm are more likely to take an active interest in the company's well being. Second, the trade group advocated setting a substantial target for director stock ownership and a time frame to meet it. Finally, the association urged companies to enact a prohibition against the hiring of a director's firm to provide professional services to the corporation.

[Robert T. Kleiman]

FURTHER READING:

Mace, Myles L. *Directors: Myth and Reality*. Boston: Harvard University, Graduate School of Business Administration, 1971.

Malott, Robert H. "Directors: Step Up to Your Responsibilities." *Directors & Boards*. Summer, 1992, pp. 69-72.

Weidenbaum, Murray. "The Evolving Corporate Board." *Contemporary Issues*. Series 65. St. Louis: Washington University, Center for the Study of American Business, 1994.

BONDS

Bonds are debt instruments issued by corporations and a variety of government entities to raise money to purchase **assets** and finance deficits. In effect the bond issuer borrows money from the bond purchaser and agrees to pay interest at an established rate over a fixed period of time. The "loan," or face value of the bond, is repaid at the end of the bond's term when it matures. The bond serves as a contract between the two parties, with stipulations regarding the obligations of the bond issuer to the bondholder. While shareholders are considered owners of a corporation, bondholders are among its creditors. A company's stock is part of its **equity**, while bonds are part of its **debt**. If the bond issuer is a corporation, bondholders have a prior claim against the corporation's assets and earnings to that of the corporation's shareholders.

There are many classifications of bonds. Within the United States there are government or civil bonds that are issued by the federal government, individual states, and municipalities, and corporate bonds that are issued by corporations. The international bond market includes bonds issued by international bodies, governments of other countries, and companies based in other countries.

Bonds may also be classified according to the reason for issuing them, such as school bonds, airport bonds, equipment bonds, or general improvement bonds. Bonds may be secured or unsecured, which refers to whether or not the bondholder has a specific claim against the assets of the bond issuer. Bonds also vary in terms of prinicipal and interest payments, and they may be registered or unregistered. Unregistered bonds are also known as bearer bonds.

Regardless of classification, all bonds share certain features. Bonds are a form of contract, and the rights of investors as well as the obligations of the issuer are usually set forth in what is known as a bond indenture. Most bonds are issued for a specified length of time, usually from one to 30 years, and are called term bonds. At the end of the term the bond reaches maturity, and all liabilities that have not been paid off before maturity must be paid to the bondholder. Bonds are usually categorized as short-term (one to 5 years), intermediate-term (five to 12 years), and long-term (more than 12 years). Short-term bonds are often referred to as notes, while those with terms of less than 12 months are called money market instruments.

All bonds pay interest to their holders. The nominal or coupon interest rate is the rate shown on the bond that the issuer has agreed to pay. If the bond has been sold or purchased for more than the face amount, then it is said to have been sold at a premium and the effective interest rate becomes less than the coupon rate. That is, the bond purchaser will actually earn less than the coupon rate because more than the face amount was paid for the bond. Similarly, if the bond is sold for less than the face amount, it is sold at a discount and the effective interest rate is more than the coupon rate.

Bond interest is usually paid twice a year, but there are several variations as to how bond interest is paid. Zero coupon bonds pay all of the interest at maturity, for example. The interest a bond pays may be fixed or floating. That is, it may yield a specified interest rate for its entire term, or the interest rate may be adjusted periodically.

Bonds that are callable are those that can be called in, or redeemed, by the bond issuer. Since bond issuers typically call in such bonds when **interest rates** are lower than the bond is paying, callable bonds usually yield higher rates of return than bonds that are not callable. On the other hand, convertible bonds are usually issued at lower rates of return. A convertible bond is one that gives the bondholder the option of converting the bond into another type of investment, usually some form of stock in the company.

Domestic corporate and government bonds are assigned credit ratings by five agencies recognized by the **Securities and Exchange Commission**, with Standard & Poor's and Moody's Investor Service being the two dominant rating agencies. Other agencies provide similar ratings for bonds in other countries. Bond ratings are based on such factors as the creditworthiness of the issuer, the issuer's past record of interest and/or **dividends** payments, and the nature of the assets or **revenues** that will be applied to repayment. Bond ratings range from AAA, the highest rating, to C. A D rating indicates the issuer is already in default. Bonds with lower ratings carry a higher risk of default and consequently usually pay a higher interest rate. Bonds with low ratings are also known as junk bonds.

[David P. Bianco]

BOOKKEEPING

Bookkeeping is that aspect of **accounting** that is concerned with the mechanics of keeping accounts, ledgers, and journals, including posting entries and taking trial balances. Bookkeeping provides the necessary support for such accounting matters as the preparation of financial statements, cost reports, and tax returns.

Bookkeeping involves keeping track of a business's financial transactions and making entries to specific accounts using the debit and credit system. Each entry represents a different business transaction. Every accounting system has a chart of accounts that lists actual accounts as well as account categories. There is usually at least one account for every item on a company's **balance sheet** and income statement. In theory there is no limit to the number of accounts that can be created, although the total number of accounts is usually determined by management's need for information.

The process of bookkeeping involves four basic steps: (1) analyzing financial transactions and assigning them to specific accounts; (2) writing original journal entries that credit and debit the appropriate accounts; (3) posting entries to ledger accounts; and (4) adjusting entries at the end of each accounting period. Bookkeeping is based on two basic principles. One is that every debit must have an equal credit. The second, that all accounts must balance, follows from the first.

Bookkeeping entries are made in a journal, which is a chronological record of all transactions. Journal entries are typically made into a computer from paper documents that contain information about the transaction to be recorded. Journal entries can be made from invoices, purchase orders, sales receipts, and similar documents, which are usually kept on file for a specified length of time.

Journal entries assign each transaction to a specific account and record changes in those accounts using debits and credits. Information contained in the journal entries is posted to ledger accounts. Posting is the process by which account balances in the appropriate ledger are changed. While account balances may be recorded and computed periodically, the only time account balances are changed in the ledger is when a journal entry indicates such a change is necessary. Information that appears chronologically in the journal becomes reclassified and summarized in the ledger on an account-by-account basis.

Bookkeepers may take trial balances occasionally to ensure that the journal entries have been posted accurately to every account. A trial balance simply means that totals are taken of all of the debit balances and credit balances in the ledger accounts. The debit and credit balances should match; if they don't match, then one or more errors have been made and must be found.

Other aspects of bookkeeping include making adjusting entries that modify account balances so they more accurately reflect the actual situation at the end of an accounting period. Adjusting entries usually involves unrecorded costs and revenues associated with continuous transactions, or costs and revenues that must be apportioned among two or more accounting periods.

Another bookkeeping procedure involves closing accounts. Most companies have temporary revenue and expense accounts that are used to provide information for the company's income statement. These accounts are periodically closed to owners' equity to determine the profit or loss of all revenue and expense transactions. An account called Income Summary (or Profit and Loss) is created to show the net income or loss for a particular accounting period. Closing entries means reducing the balance of the temporary accounts to zero, while debiting or crediting the income summary account.

A ledger is a collection of related accounts and may be called an Accounts Payable Ledger, Accounts Receivable Ledger, or General Ledger, for example. Prior to computer-based bookkeeping, ledgers were actual bound books. In computer-based accounting systems ledgers refer to collections of related accounts, with the general ledger containing all of the accounts.

[David P. Bianco]

BOYCOTTS

Consumer boycotts are organized efforts to abstain from using or purchasing a product. Boycotts may also take the form of strikes on the part of labor against an employer. International boycotts occur when a country refuses to purchase or even use the products of another country. International boycotts have also taken the form of abstention from a conference or sporting event (the most notable being the U.S. boycott of the 1980 Olympics, and the U.S.S.R.'s 1984 boycott of the same).

The majority of boycotts in history have been directed against employers. However, employers themselves, also have engaged in boycotts. For example, in the nineteenth and early twentieth centuries, employers created blacklists, refusing to hire workers who were unionized, and whose names appeared on the list. British landowners in late nineteenth-century Ireland began boycotting the goods and services of local Irish merchants who sided with the Irish Land League.

Boycotts are a powerful means of economic (and in the case of international boycotts, political) coercion. It is non-violent coercion, however, with the ultimate goal of forcing change through isolation and ostracism.

The word "boycott" is of much more recent origin than the act of boycotting. Many British absentee landowners in late nineteenth century Ireland took advantage of famine conditions in Ireland to evict tenants from their property and to lower wages for field work. One of the worst offenders was Captain Charles Boycott (1832-1897), estate manager of the Irish lands of the British Third Earl of Erne. In 1880, Boycott evicted undesirable tenants from the Earl's estates and paid laborers only half the day wage for field work. An American journalist in Ireland and an Irish priest came up with a fitting word to describe the Irish Land League's tactic of encouraging the peasantry to stop working and producing for oppressive landlords, coining the term "boycotting." Irish peasants "boycotted" the estates of absentee Earl of Erne, forcing Charles Boycott to harvest the crops. The boycott was extended further: no merchant would service the Boycott family, and their servants disappeared. This collective social and economic ostracism forced Boycott to stop his abusive tactics.

The example of the Irish Land League and the rise of organized labor in the United States encouraged the use of boycotts as never before. Hitherto the most famous "boycott" in the U.S., before the word was invented, was in 1765, to protest the Stamp Act. As a result, Parliament repealed the Act.

In 1885 alone, nearly 200 boycotts in the United States were carried out by organized labor groups against employers. Although the practice was suppressed by law, it was used successfully once again by labor in the Pullman Strike in 1894. Farmers in the West frequently resorted to boycotts to protest high freight charges. These actions encouraged the legalization of boycotts in most states by the turn of the century.

By the eve of World War I, boycotting had proliferated to all walks of life. Housewives used boycotts to protest high prices of meat and butter (usually the least effective kind of boycott), while labor advocacy groups maintained "white lists" of shopkeepers and department store owners who used fair labor practices towards their employees, urging the public to boycott stores that were not on the list.

The idea also caught on internationally, perhaps because of improvements in transportation and communication. In 1905, the Chinese government boycotted American goods to protest U.S. immigration policies against the Chinese. In 1935, the League of Nations instituted economic **sanctions** against Italy for its invasion of Ethiopia. Unlike a trade **embargo** (in which one country merely prohibits exports to another country), sanctions were meant to stop all commerce between members of the League and Italy.

The United Nations, successor to the League, adopted this form of boycott against Rhodesia in 1965, and more recently, against Iraq.

Boycotts continue to remain a popular and peaceful form of protest. The American civil rights movement used them to its advantage in the 1950s, and hundreds of consumer boycotts of products and services of "offending" companies take place annually. Most recently, boycotts to protest violence on television and in motion pictures have been waged, with mixed results, by the National Coalition On Television Violence, and by fundamentalist religious groups. Tobacco companies continue to be targets of boycotts, again with mixed results.

The tactic of isolating and ostracizing an employer, company, or nation is often enough to pressure the offending party to change. Boycotts are most successful when they are highly focused on one product (such as the seven year grape boycott) or on one or a handful of companies, such as tuna manufacturers, to protest the killing of dolphins. Least successful are economic sanctions, although the political fallout from sanctions usually outweighs the economic damage intended.

[Sina Dubovoy]

FURTHER READING:

Bertram, Anton Sir. *The Economic Weapon as a Form of Peaceful Pressure.* London, 1932.

Fahey, Patrick M. "Advocacy Group Boycotting of Network Television Advertisers and its Effects on Programming Content," *University of Pennsylvania Law Review.* Dec.1, 1991, p. 647.

Gewirtz, Sharon. "Anglo-Jewish Responses to Nazi Germany 1933-1939: The Anti-Nazi Boycott and the Board of Deputies of British Jews," *Journal of Contemporary History.* April, 1991, p. 255.

Glennon, Robert Jerome. "The Role of Law in the Civil Rights Movement: The Montgomery Bus Boycott, 1955-1957," *Law and History Review.* Spring, 1991, p. 59.

Laidler, Harry Wellington. *Boycotts and the Labor Struggle; Economic and Legal Aspects.* New York: Russell & Russell, 1968.

Marlow, Joyce. *Captain Boycott and the Irish.* New York: Saturday Review Press, 1973.

BRANDS AND BRAND NAMES

A brand is a name, symbol, or other feature that distinguishes a seller's goods or services in the marketplace. More than 500,000 brands are registered globally with pertinent regulatory bodies in different countries.

Brands serve their owners by allowing them to cultivate customer loyalty for, and recognition of, their offerings. Brands also serve the consumer; they supply information pertaining to factors such as the quality, origin, and value of goods and services. Without brands to guide buying decisions, the free market would become a confusing, faceless crowd of consumables. Among other detriments, the efficiencies of a self-service economy would be nixed. A brand is often the most valuable asset a company possesses.

Brands have been used since ancient times, to mark livestock for example—singular designs were, and in some places still are, burned into animals' skin to identify the owner. Egyptian brick makers used brands to identify their own bricks, and brands were later utilized to identify craftsmen's wares. A potter, for example, would mark his pots by putting his thumbprint or some other personal tag on the wet clay at the bottom of a vase or pot. Likewise, silversmiths would brand their pieces with marks or initials. The value of craftsmen's wares soon became associated with their brands, as consumers quickly learned to associate varying degrees of quality with the marked goods. At least one source traces the roots of present branding techniques to 16th century whiskey distillers, who burned their names into the top of their whiskey barrels.

It is only since the second half of the nineteenth century that branding evolved into an advanced marketing tool. The industrial revolution and new communications systems made it easier for companies to advertise brands over larger regions. Most impor tantly, improved modes of transporting goods emerged. Manufacturers transported merchandise primarily by ship prior to the late 1800s. As a result, large scale commercial branding was generally limited to regions served by particular ports and companies near to those shipping points. The development of the railroad system during the late 1800s, both in the United States and in other parts of the industrialized world, gradually diminished the transportation constraint.

As manufacturers gained access to national markets, numerous brand names were born that would achieve legendary U.S. and global status. Proctor and Gamble, Kraft, Heinz, Coca-Cola, Kodak, and Sears & Roebuck were a few of the initial brands that would become common household names by the mid-1900s. At least four important evolutionary changes occurred to cast those brands, and the entire branding concept for that matter, into the forefront of modern advertising strategy: (1) the internal combustion engine made possible the distribution of products into more remote areas; (2) branding became a tool used to distinguish nearly homogenous goods, such as eggs or bananas; (3) legal systems were devised to recognize and protect brand names; and (4) branding strategies were extended to encompass services, such as car repair.

An exemplary illustration of the evolution of branding is Guinness, an English beer. Started in 1750 by Arthur Guinness (1725-1803), the beer gained only local favor in a small region of the United Kingdom before the 20th century. Improved shipping and distribution technologies allowed Guinness to become one of the most recognized and successful brands in the world by the 1980s, with distribution and manufacturing operations throughout the globe. A more popular early example of branding in the United States is Coca-Cola, which dates back to the 1880s. As a result of the technological factors discussed above, Coke achieved unsurpassed brand recognition through its name and the (legally protected) shape of its soft drink bottle.

THE BRAND CONCEPT

A brand is backed by an intangible agreement between a consumer and the company selling the products or services under the brand name. A consumer that prefers a particular brand basically agrees to select that brand over others based primarily on the brand's reputation. He (or she) may stray from the brand occasionally because of price, accessibility, or other determinants, but some degree of allegiance will exist until a different brand gains acceptance by, and then preference with, the buyer. Until that time, however, he will reward the brand owner with dollars, almost assuring future cash flows to the company. The buyer may even pay a higher price for, or seek out, the goods or services because of his commitment, or passive agreement, to buy the brand.

In return for his brand loyalty, the company essentially assures the buyer that the product he purchases will confer benefits associated with, and expected from, the brand. Those numerous benefits may be both explicit and subtle. For example, the buyer of a Mercedes-Benz automobile may expect extremely high quality, durability, and performance. But he will also likely expect to receive emotional benefits related to public perception of his wealth or social status. If Mercedes licenses its nameplate to a manufacturer of cheap economy cars or supplies an automobile that begins deteriorating after only a few years, the buyer will probably assume that the agreement has been breached. The expectations and therefore the value of the brand, Mercedes-Benz, will be reduced in the mind of that buyer and possibly others who become aware of the breach.

Two major categories of brands are manufacturer and dealer. Manufacturer brands, such as Ford, are owned by the producer or service provider. Those brands typically are held by large corporations that sell multiple products or services affiliated with the brand. Dealer brands, like Die-Hard batteries, are usually owned by a middleman, such as a wholesaler or retailer. They often are applied to the products of smaller manufacturers. In summary, manufacturers or service providers may sell their offerings under their own brands, a dealer brand, or as a combination of the two types, which is called a mixed brand. Under the latter arrangement, part of the goods are sold under the manufacturer's brand and another portion is sold under the dealer brand.

BRAND STRATEGY

A company that wants to benefit from the consumer relationship allowed by branding must painstakingly strive to achieve even a small degree of brand loyalty. First, the company must gain name recognition for its product, get the consumer to actually try its brand, and then convince him that the brand is acceptable. Only after those triumphs can the company hope to secure some degree of preference for its brand. Indeed, name awareness is the most critical factor in achieving success. Companies may spend vast sums of money and effort just to attain recognition of a new brand. To penetrate a market with established brands, moreover, they may resort to giving a branded product away for free just to get people to try it. Even if the product outperforms its competitors, however, consumers may adhere to their traditional buying patterns for intangible or emotional reasons.

An easier way to quickly establish a brand is to be the first company to offer a product or service. But there are also simpler methods of penetrating existing niches, namely product line extension and brand franchise extension. Product line extension entails the use of an established brand name on a new, related product. For example, the Wonder Bread name could be applied to a whole-wheat bread to penetrate that market. Similarly, brand franchise extension refers to the application of an old brand to a completely new product line. For example, Coca-Cola could elect to apply its name to a line of candy products. One of the risks of brand and product extensions is that the name will be diluted or damaged by the new product. An example of a less-than-successful extension was Cadbury (chocolate), which was extended to include several food items. The diversified goods were eventually jettisoned in an effort to revive Cadbury's strength in the chocolate industry.

Besides offering ways to enter new markets, product line and brand franchise extension are two ways in which a company can capitalize on a brand's "equity," or its intangible value. Three major uses of brand equity include family branding, individual branding, and combination branding. Family branding entails using a brand for an entire product mix. The Kraft brand, for example, is used on a large number of dairy products and other food items. Individual branding occurs when the name is applied to a single product, such as Crest toothpaste or Budweiser beer. Combination branding means that individual brand names are associated with a company name; General Motors (GM), for example, markets a variety of brands associated with the GM name.

Once a company establishes brand loyalty, it must constantly work to maintain its presence with consistent quality and through competitive responses to new market entrants and existing competitors. This art and science of sustaining and increasing brand loyalty and maximizing brand equity is called "brand management." Companies often hire brand managers whose sole purpose is to foster and promote the name. During the 1980s and early 1990s, advanced research and statistical analysis techniques were developed to assist brand managers and their staffs in their goal.

LEADING BRANDS

Of the top ten brands in the world in the early 1990s, as ranked by Interbrand Group, plc. of London, seven were American. Of the top 50 brands, in fact, the large majority were American. They included renowned names such as Walt Disney, American Express, Wrigley's, Apple, International Business Machines Corp. (IBM) and Pepsi-Cola. The most popular foreign brands included Mercedes-Benz, Heineken, Sony, Porsche, and Rolls-Royce.

In the early 1990s, the best-known brand in the world was Coca-Cola, which achieved its status through years of savvy and aggressive global marketing. The Coke brand demonstrates the power of branding for products which are relatively homogenous. Although the Coca-Cola Company competes with numerous brands that taste very similar to Coke, it was able to mold public opinion and cultivate a preference for the taste of its drink by associating both tangible and intangible attributes, such as fun and tradition, to Coke.

Kellogg's, Interbrand's second-ranked global brand, also attained its strength through innovative, long-term marketing prowess. It provides the best case study of family branding. Consumers who purchase Kellogg's cereals expect to get extremely high quality and good taste, even for completely new cereal products. Kellogg's Corn Flakes has remained a part of many Americans' diets for decades. Its brand acceptance and preference is so great that it has sustained an immovable market leadership position throughout much of the 20th century.

The third leading brand, McDonald's, shows how quickly a brand can become popular if it creates a new market. Founded in 1955, McDonald's was the first restaurant chain to introduce the fast-food concept on a large scale. Because its name became associated with quality, value, good taste, and convenience, the McDonald's name became hugely popular and was known throughout the world within a few decades. Kodak, the number four international brand, also created its own market and bolted to fame during the 20th century. Founded in 1887, Kodak dominated the market for camera film and was practically unchallenged until the 1980s.

The success of the Marlboro brand, the fifth leading global trademark, demonstrates the importance of image and intangible attributes regarding branding. Marlboro was initiated in 1924 as a cigarette for women with the slogan, "a cherry tip for your ruby lips"—the cigarette had a red filter. The concept met with limited success. Marlboro was reintroduced in 1955 with the Marlboro man, a symbol of rugged individualism and freedom. The brand achieved massive success, delivering to its customers an emotional benefit unparalleled by any other cigarette on the market. The brand was successfully extended internationally, becoming the most recognized international cigarette brand.

LEGAL ASPECTS

A brand is a trademark (or service mark for brands associated with services), by legal definition. Trademarks may be protected by virtue of their original use. Most U.S. trademarks are registered with the federal government through the Patent and Trademark Office of the U.S. Department of Commerce. Federal trademark registration helps to secure protection related to exclusive use, although additional measures may be necessary to achieve complete exclusivity. The Lanham Trademark Act of 1946 established U.S. regulations for registering brand names and marks, which are protected for 20 years from the date of registration. Various international agreements protect trademarks from abuse in foreign countries.

Trademarks have suffered from infringement and counterfeiting since their inception. The U.S. government, in fact, does not police trademark infringement, but leaves that task to registrants. In the late 1980s approximately $7 billion worth of "gray market" goods, or imported branded goods that bypass the brand owner, were shipped into the United States annually. In addition, the trade of brand-counterfeited goods, such as falsely branded automobile parts, is a major hurdle for many brand owners.

[Dave Mote]

FURTHER READING:

Buzzell, Robert D. and John A. Quelch. *Multinational Marketing Management.* Addison-Wesley Publishing Company, 1988.

Hehman, Raymond D. *Product Management; Marketing in a Changing Environment.* Dow Jones-Irwin, 1984.

Schoell, William F., and Joseph P. Guiltinan. *Marketing: Contemporary Concepts and Practices*, 5th ed. Allyn and Bacon, 1992.

World's Greatest Brands; An International Review by Interbrand. John Wiley & Sons, Inc., 1992.

BREAK-EVEN ANALYSIS

Break-even analysis is used in **cost accounting** and **capital budgeting** to evaluate projects or product lines in terms of their volume and profitability relationship. At its simplest, the tool is used as its name suggests: to determine the volume at which a company's costs will exactly equal its revenues, therefore resulting in net income of zero, or "break-even." Perhaps more useful than this simple determination, however, is the understanding gained through such analysis of the variable and fixed nature of certain costs. Break-even analysis forces the analyst to research, quantify and categorize an entity's costs into fixed and variable groups.

The formula for break-even analysis is as follows:

$$BEQ = FC / (P - VC)$$

Where;

BEQ = Break-even quantity
FC = Fixed costs
P = Price per unit, and
VC = Variable costs per unit

A key component of break-even analysis is the contribution margin, which can be defined as the product's or service's price (P) minus variable costs (VC). This is the amount of net income the entity realizes from the last unit sold, considering the price obtained and the variable costs incurred, but ignoring, for the moment, fixed (or "sunk") costs. The contribution margin concept is grounded in incremental or marginal analysis; its focus is the extra revenue and costs that will be incurred with the next additional unit.

Break-even analysis can be used in several ways depending on which variable of the equation is being solved while the others are given. For example, to determine the quantity at which the operation nets zero profit, the variables of price, fixed costs, and variable costs are given. Alternatively, if given an assumed volume, price level, and variable cost structure, the maximum amount of fixed costs can be calculated. Or, at given quantities, and fixed and variable cost levels, the necessary selling price will become apparent. Finally, at an assumed volume, fixed cost level, and price, the allowable variable cost level can be quantified. Some examples are illustrative:

Company management is skeptical of the marketing department's projection for sales of 150,000 units of a new product, and wants to know what minimum quantity of units must be sold to avoid losing money, assuming a selling price of $25, fixed costs of $1 million and variable costs (generally materials, direct labor, shipping and other direct costs that are incurred incrementally with each additional unit) of $15. The equation tells us that these parameters will require a break-even volume of 100,000 units; fewer than that level yields losses, more than that level yields profits. This perspective of analysis may be employed where the analyst is highly confident of his estimates for price and costs, but feels less certain about the assessment of market demand. In this case, management might be interested in how low sales could fall below the marketing department's forecast without causing an embarrassment at year-end reporting time.

Another scenario may involve the question of how to manufacture a product, in terms of the nature of operations and how they will affect fixed costs. Here, management may have a good handle on the quantity expected, the likely selling price and the variable costs involved, but be undecided about how to structure the new operation. If the volume is expected to be one million units, at a selling price of $5 and variable costs of $3.50, the break-even equation tells us that fixed costs can be no greater than $1,500,000.

[Christopher Barry]

BRIBERY

It is not a legal violation to offer money to a low-level foreign government official to, for instance, expedite the processing of goods through customs. It is a legal violation to offer money to a foreign government or business official to secure a contract.

These seemingly contradictory statements are both true, illustrating how the issue of bribery is a sometimes complex one, made more complex by the increase of international trade. While the U.S. government prohibits the bribery of government personnel in any country, these regulations only apply within the U.S.'s jurisdiction. When dealing with other foreign nations it is quite possible that those nations (generally nonindustrialized, developing nations) do not have laws prohibiting bribery in the attainment of contracts. Obviously, this discrepancy results in an unlevel playing field for countries involved in international trade.

Bribery can be defined as a payment, in the form of money or gifts, offered in exchange for some positive consideration. That consideration could take the form of purchase contracts, overlooking illegal or unethical acts, or the processing of governmental paperwork. Bribery has been a factor in business transactions for many hundreds of years.

More than 1500 years ago St. Augustine wrote about the practice of ''mordida,'' a form of bribery in Mexico that is still an accepted practice. During the fifteenth century, Nigerians engaged in a practice called ''paying the dash'' in their contracts with the Portuguese.

Cases involving bribery continue to proliferate in the twentieth century. In the 1970s, Lockheed was involved in the payment of an estimated $25 million to Japanese officials to secure the sale of its Tristar L-1011 aircraft. The act resulted in the resignation, and eventual criminal conviction, of Japanese Prime Minister Kukeo Tanaka. Japan was not the only country involved. Lockheed admitted to making payments to secure sales in 15 countries, including Holland, Italy, and Turkey.

In the late 1980s, Young & Rubicam Inc., an international advertising firm, was indicted under the **Foreign Corrupt Practices Act (FCPA)** because the company had reason to know that one of its agents in Jamaica was paying off the minister of tourism to obtain advertising business. The case was settled when the company paid a penalty of $500,000 to avoid further litigation.

Today the practice of bribery continues to take place throughout the world. In many countries, however, bribery does not carry negative connotations. Nonindustrialized nations such as Nigeria and Thailand are widely known for having government officials who can be easily swayed through bribes. The practice proliferates because officials are lowpaid and the culture tolerates these actions.

These practices hamper the development of international trade by restricting free and open markets, destroying competition, and increasing the cost of doing business. The practice of bribery also destroys public confidence in political leaders and institutions.

While virtually all industrialized nations have laws and rules against bribery and corruption, those laws generally apply only to acts actually committed in that country. Only the United States and Sweden have laws that cover acts committed in other nations.

Studies have indicated that by 1988, 85 percent of the 2,000-largest American companies had a written, internal code of ethics that provided managers with ethical guidelines and, in many cases, ethics training.

American awareness of the implications of illegal acts came to a head in the 1970s, during the Nixon administration. In 1976 ''Guidelines for Multinational Enterprises'' were developed, urging firms to refrain from bribery in their business dealings, regardless of with which country they were dealing. The guidelines

identified and listed existing bribery and corruption provisions in national legislation. In addition, the tax treatment of bribes was reviewed, indicating that the majority of OECD (**Organization for Economic Cooperation and Development**) countries did not specifically include regulations regarding illicit payment. Rather, these payments were treated like any other taxable or deductible sources.

In 1977, following the Watergate scandal, the International Chamber of Commerce (ICC) adopted a code of behavior to combat extortion and bribery in business transactions. A group was established that had responsibility for interpreting, promoting, and applying the code. This year also saw the introduction of the Foreign Corrupt Practices Act (FCPA)—an amendment to the **Securities Exchange Act of 1934** that defines appropriate ethical and legal behavior. The FCPA contains three main provisions:

1. An antibribery section, prohibiting executives of U.S. companies from paying bribes to obtain contracts in foreign countries.

2. An accounting/record-keeping section that requires firms to set up internal accounting controls to provide assurance that transactions are executed in accordance with management's general or specific authorization.

3. A penalty section that holds business firms liable for a fine of up to $1 million for each violation; individual liability includes fines of up to $10,000 and up to five years in jail. The U.S. Supreme Court has also held that violation of the antibribery provisions of the FCPA can result in a private cause of action.

The FCPA outlaws both variance and outright purchase bribes. Variance bribes are payments made to secure a variance from an existing law or regulation—for instance, a payment made to an official to overlook an act that violates local pollution laws. Outright purchase bribes are payments or gifts made to officials to obtain government contracts.

The FCPA has been strengthened by case law that has allowed businesses to sue competitors for lost business if they can prove that bribery played a significant role in decisions made.

While, originally, the FCPA held U.S. companies liable if they knew, or had reason to know, that a payment was made on their behalf to a government official, the Omnibus Trade Act of 1988 modified this so that a company could only be held criminally liable if it could be proven that the company had actual knowledge of an illegal payment. In addition, under the Omnibus Trade Act, some forms of bribery are considered acceptable such as transaction bribes— payments made to speed the completion of a routine, clerical-type function such as the processing of papers, moving goods through customs, etc.

The OECD, a membership organization that includes 26 industrialized nations, adopted a ''Recommendation on Bribery in International Business Transactions'' in 1994. While not legally binding, the recommendation encourages countries to review their own criminal, civil, and administrative laws and regulations and to take ''concrete and meaningful'' steps to adopt measures to implement measures of surveillance and follow-up.

Additional guidance on the issue of bribery—what is and is not permissible—is available from the U.S. Department of Justice through its Foreign Corrupt Practices Act Opinion Procedures.

[Lin Grensing-Pophal]

FURTHER READING:

''Battling International Bribery.'' *OECD Observer*. February-March, 1995, pp. 16-17.

''Ganging Up on the Bosses.'' *The Economist*. July 24, 1993, p. 78.

Kimelman, John. ''The Lonely Boy Scout.'' *Business Ethics*. Auguts 16, 1994, pp. 50-51.

Pitman, Glenn A., and James P. Sanford. ''The Foreign Corrupt Practices Act Revisited: Attempting to Regulate 'Ethical Bribes' in Global Business.'' *International Journal of Purchasing and Materials Management*. Summer, 1994, pp. 15-20.

''Waging the War on Bribery.'' *Traffic Management*. April, 1993, pp. 29-30.

''Why Overseas Bribery Won't Last.'' *Management Review*. June, 1994, pp. 20-24.

BUDGETING

The major concern of any commercial enterprise is to be profitable and to build wealth. To do this a company strives to use its limited financial and human resources in a manner which best exploits existing business opportunities. A company engages in *budgeting*, an estimation of probable expenditures and income for a specific period, to determine the most efficient and effective strategies for making money and expanding its asset base.

Intelligent budgeting incorporates good business judgment in the review and analysis of past trends and data pertinent to the business enterprise. This information assists a company in determining the type of business organization needed, the amount of money to be invested, the type and number of employees to hire, and the marketing strategies required. In budgeting, a company devises both long-term and short-term plans to help implement its strategies and to conduct ongoing performance evaluations.

A HISTORICAL PERSPECTIVE

Budgeting is not a new concept. In ancient times individuals and societies engaged in processes of planning their economic activities, evaluating the annual outcomes, and revising when necessary. Through observation and experimentation, agrarian peoples discovered, invented, and standardized various practices to increase the quality and quantity of their yields.

The desire for excess supplies to sell for profits, and for storage as wealth, led to the discovery and use of crop rotation, fertilizers, fences, scarecrows, and irrigation. While having few devices against the vagaries of the weather, ancient peoples used their profits and hard labor to protect their fields by deploying armies, building walls, planting in remote locations, and paying tribute to powerful neighbors. Similarly, modern peoples employ various strategies to use their accumulated wealth to generate new profits and to continually expand their wealth. The fact that modern budgeting generally consists of a series of 12-month periods may reflect these agrarian origins.

PLANNING FOR PROFIT AND WEALTH

To engage in any profitable commercial enterprise, a company employs its resources to exploit various business opportunities. If the profits are consistent, a company may purchase more assets and, therefore, expand its base of wealth. To do this effectively, a company undertakes the budgeting process to assess the business opportunities available to it, the keys to successfully exploiting these opportunities, the strategies the historical data support as most likely to succeed, and the goals and objectives the company must establish. The company must also plan long-term strategies which define the overall effort in building market share, increasing revenues, and decreasing costs; short-term strategies to increase profits, control costs, and invest for the future; control mechanisms incorporating performance evaluations and good business judgment; and control mechanisms for making modifications in the above strategies when and where necessary.

Although opportunities initially find their impetus in the business judgment of company leaders, a company expresses its assessment of them and formulates its strategies in quantifiable terms, such as: the volume of units which the company expects it can sell, the percentage of market share the volume of units represents, the dollars of revenues it will receive from these sales, and the dollars of profit it will earn. Likewise, a company outlines its long-term goals and specifies its short-range plans in quantifiable terms which detail how it expects to accomplish its goals: the dollars the company will spend in selling the units; the dollar costs of producing the units; the dollar costs of administering the company's operations; the dollars the company will invest in expanding and upgrading facilities and equipment; the flow of dollars into the company coffers; and the financial position, expressed in dollars, at specific points in the future.

To be successful, the budgeting process establishes criteria and control mechanisms for the systematic evaluation of the company's ability to effectively implement its plans. These controls are often detailed and complex. Therefore, the company includes in the budgeting process employees from each organizational level and from each department. The company marshals these resources in a coordinated effort in the following functions.

PLANNING. The company establishes long-term financial goals and operational objectives as to the future size and activities of the company. These include products, product mix, services, markets, market share, volume of sales, quality of sales, level of debt and capitalization, number of employees, degree of horizontal and vertical integration, **research and development**, public or private ownership, advertising campaigns, training and development, and benefit packages.

STAFFING. The company clearly defines and assigns responsibility for the budgeting process itself, along with the level of detail required to formulate the business plan. The treasurer's office generally organizes and coordinates the budgetary process through a budget director, controller, or chief accountant. Budgeting hinges on accurate accounting of all activities including machine use, manpower needs, employee turnover, inventory levels, supplier pricing, sales discounts, benefit costs, production schedules, selling costs, and the like. Therefore, the accounting staff plays a central role in collecting, analyzing, and processing the needed data.

ORGANIZING. In planning for profits the staff needs to organize for action. They provide standardized reporting directives. The staff distributes familiar and ''user-friendly'' forms for collecting, organizing, evaluating, and disseminating information. They propose procedures to form a comprehensive plan for each activity and for the company as a whole.

DIRECTING. The budgetary process establishes lines of reporting and accountability for the execution of the plan. Besides spelling out the various responsibilities of the managers, it also sets limits to their authority. The budgeting process involves all levels of managerial responsibility: office, department, division, corporation. To maximize the benefits of the budgeting process, managers must not only be responsible and accountable, but also need to be in agreement with overall goals and objectives.

CONTROLLING. The budgetary process sets up the reporting procedures and techniques for evaluating both short-term and long-term outcomes. Since the budget program is an instrument of organizational control, a company's accounting and its chart of accounts will reflect clear lines of functional responsibility. However, not all control activity emanates from the accounting office. Line supervisors and individual employees keep their own logs. Consequently, the accounting/budgeting staff sets up schedules for the collection, processing, and analysis of data and its subsequent distribution to the appropriate managers. The managers use this information to evaluate their own performance with an eye toward making modifications where necessary.

THE FINANCIAL FORECAST AND THE BUDGET

The end product of this process is the creation of the *financial forecast*. It projects where the company wants to be in three, five, or ten years. The financial forecast quantifies future sales, expenses, and earnings according to certain assumptions adopted by the company. The company then considers how changes in the business climate would affect the outcomes projected. It presents this analysis in the **pro forma statement** which displays, over a time continuum, a comparison of the financial plan to ''best case'' and ''worst case'' scenarios. The pro forma statement acts as a guide for meeting goals and objectives, as well as an evaluative tool for assessing progress and profitability.

Through **forecasting** a company attempts to determine whether and to what degree its long-range plans are feasible. This discipline incorporates two interrelated functions: long-term planning based on realistic goals and objectives and a prognosis of the various conditions that possibly will affect these goals and objectives; and short-term planning and budgeting which provide details about the distribution of income and expenses and a control mechanism for evaluating performance. Forecasting is a process for maximizing the profitable use of business assets in relation to: the analyses of all the latest relevant information by tested and logically sound statistical and econometric techniques; the interpretation and application of these analyses into future scenarios; and the calculation of reasonable probabilities based on sound business judgment.

Future projections for extended periods, although necessary and prudent, suffer from a multitude of unknowns: inflation, supply fluctuations, demand variations, credit shortages, employee qualifications, regulatory changes, management turnover, and the like. To increase control over operations, a company narrows its focus to forecasting attainable results over the short-term. These short-term forecasts, called *bud-*

gets, are formal, comprehensive plans, using quantitative terms to described the expected operations of the organization over some specified future period. While a company may make few modifications to its forecast, for instance, in the first three years, the company constructs individual budgets for each year.

A budget describes the expected month-to-month route a company will take in achieving its goals. It summarizes the expected outcomes of production and marketing efforts, and provides management benchmarks against which to compare actual outcomes. A budget acts as a control mechanism by pointing out soft spots in the planning process and/or in the execution of the plans. Consequently, a budget, used as an evaluative tool, augments a company's ability to more quickly react and make necessary alterations.

PRINCIPLES AND PROCEDURES FOR SUCCESSFUL BUDGETING

REALISTIC AND QUANTIFIABLE. In a world of limited resources, a company must ration its own resources by setting goals and objectives which are reasonably attainable. Realism engenders loyalty and commitment among employees, motivating them to their highest performance. In addition, wide discrepancies, caused by unrealistic projections, have a negative effect on the credit worthiness of a company and may dissuade lenders.

A company evaluates each potential activity to determine those that will result in the most appropriate resource allocation. A company accomplishes this through the quantification of the costs and benefits of the activities.

HISTORICAL. The budget reflects a clear understanding of past results and a keen sense of expected future changes. While past results cannot be a perfect predictor, they flag important events and benchmarks.

PERIOD SPECIFIC. The budget period must be of reasonable length. The shorter the period, the greater the need for detail and control mechanisms. The length of the budget period dictates the time limitations for introducing effective modifications. Although plans and projects differ in length and scope, a company formulates each of its budgets on a 12-month basis.

STANDARDIZED. To facilitate the budget process, managers should use standardized forms, formulas and research techniques. This increases the efficiency and consistency of the input and the quality of the planning. Computer-aided accounting, analyzing, and reporting not only furnish managers with comprehensive, current "real time" results, but also afford them the flexibility to test new models, and to include relevant and high-powered charts and tables with relatively little effort.

INCLUSIVE. Efficient companies decentralize the budget process down to the smallest, logical level of responsibility, i.e., the *responsibility center*. Those responsible for the results take part in the development of their budgets, and learn how their activities are interrelated with the other segments of the company. Each has a hand in creating a budget and setting its goals. Participants from the various organizational segments meet to exchange ideas and objectives, to discover new ideas, and to minimize redundancies and counterproductive programs. In this way, those accountable buy into the process, cooperate more, work harder, and, therefore, have more potential for success.

SUCCESSIVELY REVIEWED. Decentralization does not exclude the thorough review of budget proposals at successive management levels. Management review assures a proper fit within the overall "master budget."

FORMALLY ADOPTED AND DISSEMINATED. Top management formally adopts the budgets and communicates their decisions to the responsible personnel. When top management has assembled the master budget and formally accepted it as the operating plan for the company, it distributes it in a timely manner.

FREQUENTLY EVALUATED. Responsible parties use the master budget and their responsibility center budgets for information and guidance. On a regular basis, according to a schedule and in a standardized manner, they compare actual results with their budgets. For an annual budget, managers usually report monthly, quarterly, and semi-annually. Since considerable detail is needed, the accountant plays a vital role in the reporting function.

A company uses a well-designed budget program as an effective mechanism for forecasting realizable results over a specific period, planning and coordinating its various operations, and controlling the implementation of the budget plans.

FUNCTIONS AND BENEFITS OF THE BUDGETING PROGRAM

Budgeting has two primary functions: planning and control. The planning process expresses all the ideas and plans in quantifiable terms. Careful planning in the initial stages creates the framework for control, which a company initiates when it includes each responsibility center in the budgeting process, standardizes procedures, defines lines of responsibility, establishes performance criteria, and sets up timetables.

The careful planning and control of a budget benefit a company in many ways, including:

ENHANCING MANAGERIAL PERSPECTIVE. In recent years the pace and complexity of business have outpaced the ability to manage by "the seat of one's pants.'' On a day-to-day basis, most managers focus their attention on routine problems. However, in preparing the budget, managers are compelled to consider all aspects of a company's internal activities. The act of making estimates about future economic conditions and about the company's ability to respond to them, forces managers to synthesize the external economic environment with their internal goals and objectives.

FLAGGING POTENTIAL PROBLEMS. Because the budget is a blueprint and road map, it alerts managers to variations from expectations which are a cause for concern. When a flag is raised, managers can revise their immediate plans to change a product mix, revamp an advertising campaign, or borrow money to cover cash shortfalls.

COORDINATING ACTIVITIES. Preparation of a budget assumes the inclusion and coordination of the activities of the various segments within a business. The budgeting process demonstrates to managers the interconnectedness of their activities.

EVALUATING PERFORMANCE. Budgets provide management with established criteria for quick and easy performance evaluations. Managers may increase activities in one area where results are well beyond exceptions. In other instances, managers may need to reorganize activities whose outcomes demonstrate a consistent pattern of inefficiency.

REFINING THE HISTORICAL VIEW. The importance of clear and detailed historical data cannot be over stated. Yet, the budgeting process cannot allow the historical perspective to become crystallized. Managers need to distill the lessons of the most current results and filter them through their historical perspective. The need for a flexible and relevant historical perspective warrants its vigilant revision and expansion as conditions and experience warrant.

THE MASTER BUDGET, A PROFIT PLAN

The master budget aggregates all business activities into one comprehensive plan. It is not a single document, but the compilation of many interrelated budgets which together summarize an organization's business activities for the coming year. To achieve the maximum results, budgets must be tailor-made to fit the particular needs of a business. Standardization of the process facilitates comparison and aggregation even of mixed industries, for example, financial services (General Motors Credit Corporation) and manufacturing (General Motors Corp.).

In the following discussion the term production includes the manufacture of goods expressed by their dollar value and number of units, and the provision of services expressed in labor-hours and in dollar value.

Table A presents an overview of the master budget. The budgeting process is sequential in nature, i.e., each budget hinges on a previous budget, such that no budget can be constructed without the data from the preceding budget. In addition, each line budget is comprised of a number of smaller responsibility center budgets. Responsibility budgets are an important element of an effective accounting system.

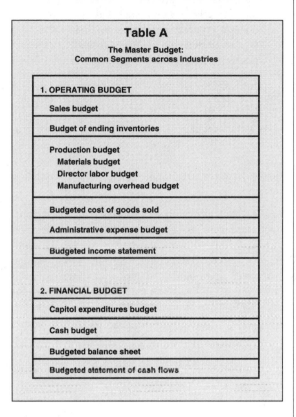

Table A

The Master Budget:
Common Segments across Industries

1. OPERATING BUDGET

Sales budget

Budget of ending inventories

Production budget
   Materials budget
   Director labor budget
   Manufacturing overhead budget

Budgeted cost of goods sold

Administrative expense budget

Budgeted income statement

2. FINANCIAL BUDGET

Capitol expenditures budget

Cash budget

Budgeted balance sheet

Budgeted statement of cash flows

CLASSIFICATIONS AND TYPES OF BUDGETS

Budgets may be broadly classified according to how a company makes and uses its money. Different budgets may be used for different applications. Some budgets deal with sources of income from sales, interest, dividend income, and other sources. Others detail the sources of expenditures such as labor, materials, interest payments, taxes, and insurance. Additional types of budgets are concerned with investing funds for capital expenditures such as plant and equipment; and some budgets predict the amounts of funds a company will have at the end of a period.

A company cannot use only one type of budget to accommodate all its operations. Therefore, it chooses from among the following budget types.

The fixed budget, often called a static budget, is not subject to change or alteration during the budget period. A company ''fixes'' budgets in at least two circumstances.

1. The cost of a budgeted activity shows little or no change when the volume of production fluctuates within an expected range of values. For example, a ten percent increase in production has little or no impact on administrative expenses.

2. The volume of production remains steady or follows a tight, pre-set schedule during the budget period. A company may fix its production volume in response to an all inclusive contract; or, it may produce stock goods.

The *variable* or flexible budget is also called a dynamic budget. It is an effective evaluative tool for a company which frequently experiences variations in sales volume which strongly affect the level of production. In these circumstances a company initially constructs a series of budgets for a range of production volumes which it can reasonably and profitably meet.

After careful analysis of each element of the production process, managers are able to determine overhead costs that will not change (*fixed*) within the anticipated range, overhead costs that will change (*variable*) as volume changes, and those overhead costs which vary to some extent, but not proportionately (*semi-variable*) within the predicted range.

The *combination budget* recognizes that most production activities combine both fixed and variable budgets within its master budget. For example, an increase in the volume of sales may have no impact on sales expenses while it will increase production costs.

The continuous budget adds a new period (month) to the budget as the current period comes to a close. Under the fiscal year approach, the budget year becomes shorter as the year progresses. However, the continuous method forces managers to review and assess the budget estimates for a never-ending 12-month cycle.

THE BUDGET PERIOD

As a general rule, a company adopts budgets covering a period long enough to show the effects of managerial policies, but short enough in which to make estimates with reasonable accuracy. Although planned activities differ in the length of operation, budgets describe only what a company expects to accomplish in the upcoming 12 months.

Capital expenditures for major investments in plant and equipment, are long-term by nature. A company constructing new facilities, laying pipelines, or paving roads may design projects encompassing periods of five to ten years. However, a company details the ongoing expenses on an annual basis.

Most operating and financial budgets (Table A) cover a period of one fiscal year, comprised of 12 months arranged in quarters (segments of three months) and semiannual periods (segments of six months).

THE OPERATING BUDGET

The operating budget gathers the projected results of the operating decisions made by a company to exploit available business opportunities. In the end analysis the operating budget presents a projected (*pro forma*) income statement which displays how much money the company expects to make. This net income demonstrates the degree to which management is able to respond to the market in supplying the right product at an attractive price, with a profit to the company.

The operating budget consists of a number of parts which detail the company's plans on how to capture revenues, provide adequate supply, control costs, and organize the labor force. These parts are: sales budget, production budget, direct materials budget, direct labor budget, factory overhead budget, selling and administrative expense budget, and *pro forma* income statement.

PREPARATION OF THE MASTER BUDGET

Preparation of the master budget is a sequential process which starts with the sales budget. The sales budget predicts the number of units a company expects to sell. From this information, a company determines how many units it must produce. Subsequently, it calculates how much it will spend to produce the required number of units. Finally, it aggregates the foregoing to estimate its profitability.

From the level of projected profits, the company decides whether to reinvest the funds in the business or in alternative investments. The company summarizes the predicted results of its plans in a **balance sheet** which demonstrates how profits will have affected the company's assets (wealth).

Robert F. Meigs and Walter B. Meigs in *Accounting: The Basis for Business Decisions* note the five major, sequential steps to preparing a master budget.

1. Preparation of the sales forecast. How many units can be sold? How many units *will* be sold? How much will it cost to sell these units? How much net revenue will these sales generate?

2. Preparation of the production and operating costs. How much will it cost to produce the units? How can production be more effi-

cient? How much will administrative expenses run?

3. Preparation of a budgeted income statement. What will be the net income? How much will be cash? Credit? Noncollectible? How much will be available for capital investments? How much will remain as cash for financing daily operations (liquidity)?

4. Preparation of a cash budget. Will cash flow be adequate? Will receipts be evenly or erratically distributed? Will third party financing be needed? How are excess funds to be invested? How much of the funds will be needed for capital expenditures?

5. Preparation of a budgeted balance sheet. How will the period's performance change the level of assets and liabilities? How will the profit position of the company change? How will the company's wealth be affected?

THE SALES FORECAST AND BUDGET

The sales organization has the primary responsibility of preparing the sales forecast. Since the sales forecast is the starting point in constructing the sales budget, the input and involvement of most other managers is important. First, those responsible for directing the overall effort of budgeting and planning contribute leadership, coordination, and legitimacy to the resulting forecast. Second, in order to introduce new products or to repackage existing lines, the sales managers need to elicit the cooperation of the production and the design departments. Finally, the sales team must get the support of the top executives for their plan.

The sales forecast is prerequisite to devising the sales budget on which a company can reasonably schedule production, and to budgeting revenues and variable costs. The *sales budget*, also called the *revenue budget*, is the preliminary step in preparing the master budget. After a company has estimated the range of sales it may experience, it calculates projected revenues by multiplying the number of units by their sales price.

The sales budget includes items such as: sales expressed in both the number of units and the dollars of revenue; adjustments to sales revenues for allowances made and goods returned; salaries and benefits of the sales force; delivery and setup costs; supplies and other expenses supporting sales; advertising costs; and the distribution of receipt of payments for goods sold. Included in the sales budget is a projection of the distribution of payments for goods sold. **Management** forecasts the timing of receipts based on a number of considerations: the ability of the sales force to encourage customers to pay on time; the impact of credit sales which stretch the collection period; delays

in payment due to deteriorating economic and market conditions; the ability of the company to make deliveries on time; and the quality of the service and technical staffs.

THE ENDING INVENTORY BUDGET

The *ending inventory budget* presents the dollar value and the number of units a company wishes to have in inventory at the end of the period. From this budget, a company computes its cost of goods sold for the budgeted income statement. It also projects the dollar value of the ending materials and finished-goods inventory, which eventually will appear on the budgeted balance sheet. Since inventories comprise a major portion of current assets, the ending inventory budget is essential for the construction of the budgeted financial statement.

THE PRODUCTION BUDGET

After it budgets sales, a company examines how many units it has on hand and how many it wants at year-end. From this it calculates the number of units needed to be produced during the upcoming period. The company adjusts the level of production to account for the difference between total projected sales and the number of units: currently in inventory, the *beginning inventory*; in the process of being finished, *work (goods, services) in process inventory*; and finished goods in the *ending inventory*.

To calculate total production requirements, a company adds projected sales to ending inventory and subtracts the beginning inventory from that sum.

Total Units to Be Produced — [Budgeted Sales
+ Desired Ending Inventory] — Beginning Inventory

BEGINNING INVENTORY BUDGET

The products completed and available for sale at the start of the period make up the *beginning inventory budget*. A company determines the value of the beginning inventory by: counting all products on hand, multiplying this quantify by the cost per unit, and aggregating the costs of the various products.

WORK IN PROCESS BUDGET

The *work in process budget* enumerates those units currently in the production phase. There will inevitably be some work in process at every point in the budget period. Therefore, a company needs to determine the number and value of the beginning and ending work in process inventories. Because the items are in different stages of production and finishing, these computations present a problem. Although computer technology has made great strides in simplifying the accounting process, predictive accuracy is contingent on the experience of line supervisors who feed the data to the accountants.

THE DIRECT-MATERIALS BUDGET

With the estimated level of production in hand, the company constructs a direct-materials budget to determine the amount of additional materials needed to meet the projected production levels. A company displays this information in two tables. The first table presents the number of units to be purchased and the dollar cost for these purchases. The second table is a schedule of the expected cash distributions to suppliers of materials.

Purchases are contingent on the expected usage of materials and current inventory levels. The formula for the calculation for materials purchases is:

Materials to Be Purchased for Production =
Units of Materials to Be Used
+ Units Desired in Ending Inventory
− Units of Material in Beginning Inventory

Purchase costs are simply calculated:

Materials Purchase Costs = Unit of Materials to Be Purchased × Unit Price

A company uses the planning of a direct-materials budget to determine the adequacy of their storage space, to institute or refine just-in-time inventory systems, to review the ability of vendors to supply materials in the quantities desired, and to schedule material purchases concomitant with the **flow of funds** into the company.

THE DIRECT-LABOR BUDGET

Once a company has determined the number of units of production, it calculates the number of direct-labor hours needed. A company states this budget in the number of units and the total number of dollar costs. A company may sort and display labor-hours using these parameters:

TYPE OF OPERATION. A company segregates employees according to the type of work they do regardless of the products. For example, a company will add up the costs for all assemblers even though they assemble different products.

DIRECT LABOR CLASSIFICATIONS. This method sorts labor by the production process. It focuses on the different types of employees working on one product. For example, a company constructs a budget showing the labor costs for all employees working on the same product, regardless of their role.

LABOR STATUS. This method classifies employees by seniority, level of skill, union affiliation, and the like. A company uses this information to better understand the relationships between labor, skills, experi-

ence, and production costs. This information assists management to more efficiently organize the labor force.

COST CENTERS. A company distributes direct-labor hours by the various organizational units against which operating costs are normally measured. This method encompasses the total production facility.

THE PRODUCTION OVERHEAD BUDGET

A company generally includes all costs, other than materials and direct labor, in the production overhead budget. Because of the diverse and complex nature of business, production overhead contains numerous items. Meigs and Meigs in *Accounting* list some of the more common ones:

1. Indirect materials—factory supplies which are used in the process but are not an integral part of the final product, such as parts for machines and safety devices for the workers; materials which are an integral part of the final product but are difficult to assign to specific products, for example, adhesives, wire, and nails.

2. Indirect labor costs—supervisors' salaries and salaries of maintenance, medical, and security personnel.

3. Plant occupancy costs—rent or depreciation on buildings, insurance on buildings, property taxes on land and buildings, maintenance and repairs on buildings, and utilities.

4. Machinery and equipment costs—rent or depreciation on machinery, insurance and property taxes on machinery, and maintenance and repairs on machinery.

5. Cost of compliance with federal, state, and local regulations—meeting safety requirements, disposal of hazardous waste materials, and control over factory emissions (meeting class air standards).

If any one cost traverses the various budgets listed in Table-A, the company would apportion that cost to reflect the benefits derived by the participating budgets.

BUDGET OF COST OF GOODS SOLD

At this point the company has projected the number of units it expects to sell and has calculated all the costs associated with the production of those units. The company will sell some units from the preceding period's inventory, others will be goods previously in process, and the remainder will be produced. After deciding the most likely mix of units, the company constructs the budget of the *cost of goods sold* by multiplying the number of units by their production costs.

ADMINISTRATIVE EXPENSE BUDGET

In the *administrative expense budget* the company presents how much it expects to spend in support of the production and sales efforts. The major expenses accounted for in the administrative budget are: officers' salaries; office salaries; employee benefits for administrative employees; payroll taxes for administrative employees; office supplies and other office expenses supporting administration; losses from uncollectible accounts; **research and development**; mortgage payments, bond interest and property taxes; and consulting and professional services.

Generally, these expenses vary little or not at all for changes in the production volume which fall within the budgeted range. Therefore, the administrative budget is a fixed budget. However, there are some expenses which can be adjusted during the period in response to changing market conditions.

A company may easily adjust some costs, such as consulting services, R&D, and **advertising**, because they are *discretionary costs*. Discretionary costs are partially or fully avoidable if their impact on sales and production is minimal. A company cannot avoid such costs as mortgage payments, bond interest, and property taxes if it wishes to stay in production into the next period. These *committed costs* are contractual obligations to third parties who have an interest in the company's success. Finally, a company has *variable costs* which it adjusts in light of cash flow and sales demand. These costs include such items as supplies, utilities, and the purchase of office equipment.

BUDGETED INCOME STATEMENT

A *budgeted income statement* combines all the preceding budgets to show expected revenues and expenses. To arrive at the *net income* for the period, the company includes estimates of sales returns and allowances, interest income, bond interest expense, the required provision for income taxes, and a number of nonoperating income and expenses, such as dividends received, interest earned, nonoperating property rental income, and other such items. Net income is a key figure in the profit plan for it reflects how a company commits the majority of its talent, time, and resources.

FINANCIAL BUDGET

The *financial budget* contains projections for cash and other balance sheet items—assets and liabilities. It also includes the *capital expenditure budget* (see Table A). It presents a company's plans for financing its operating and capital investment activities.

The capital expenditure budget relates to purchases of plant, property, or equipment with a useful life of more than one year. On the other hand, the cash budget, the budgeted balance sheet, and the budgeted statement of cash flows, deal with activities expected to end within the 12-month budget period.

CAPITAL EXPENDITURES BUDGET

A company engages in capital budgeting to identify, evaluate, plan, and finance major investment projects through which it converts cash (short-term assets) into long-term assets. A company uses these new assets, such as computers, robotics, and modern production facilities, to increase productivity, increase market share, and bolster profits. A company purchases these new assets as alternatives to holding cash because it believes that, over the long-term, these assets will increase the wealth of the business more rapidly than cash balances. Therefore, the capital expenditures budget is crucial to the overall budget process.

Capital budgeting seeks to make decisions in the present which determine, to a large degree, how successful a company will be in achieving its goals and objectives in the years ahead. Capital budgeting differs from the other financial budgets in that:

- Capital expenditures require relatively large commitments of resources whose dollar value may exceed annual net income.

- Capital expenditures extend beyond the 12-month planning horizon of the other financial budgets. To replace equipment may take 18 months. To build a new plant could involve years of planning and construction.

- Capital expenditures involve greater operating risks. A company encounters more difficulties in the long-term projecting of revenues, expenses, and cost savings. In addition, capital projects divert employee energies away from daily operations.

- Capital expenditures increase the financial risks by adding long-term liabilities. A company's short-term liabilities, in the form of mortgage or bond interest, increases long before the project becomes an earning asset.

- Capital expenditures require clear policy decisions that are in full agreement with the company's goals since a company has less flexibility to modify or cancel a project in mid-stream without serious potential consequences.

For the most part, a company makes its decisions about investments by the profits it can expect and by the amount of funds available for capital outlays. A company assesses each project according to its necessity and potential profitability. Using a variety of analytical methods, a company makes investment decisions based on criteria and within parameters such as:

- The correlation to company goals and objectives based on mathematical indexes which quantify the business judgment of the planners.

- The expected earning power of cash investments compared to the earning power of each project.

- The annual commitment of each project as a percentage of projected annual income during the development phase.

- The impact a project may have on a company's good will.

- The degree to which a company can control or influence the many factors involved.

- Projected productivity increases.

- The ability to manage the operating risks of displacing time and talent away from daily operations.

- The potential financial risks resulting from increased liability during the development stage of each project.

- The degree to which employees buy into, identify with, and cooperate in the development and implementation of each project.

- The costs of employee training and re-deployment needed to successfully implement each project.

A company uses several different approaches to capital budgeting. One approach is the payback period—a company evaluates alternative investments according to the length of time necessary to recover the entire costs of each investment from the resulting annual cash flow, generally stated as:

$$\frac{\text{Amount to be invested}}{\text{Estimated annual net cash flow}} = \frac{\text{Number}}{\text{of years}}$$

A company prefers a shorter payback period so that it can reinvest the funds as soon as possible. Furthermore, a shorter payback period reduces operating and financial risks. However, the payback period method has severe limitations when comparing competing investments.

The payback method merely determines which investment has the shorter payback. It says nothing of their total profit potential since this method ignores profits after the payback period. For example, a project having a payback period of four years and a useful life of eight years cannot earn as much profit as a similar project with a payback of five years and a life of 15 years. Although the first investment has a shorter pay back, the second project has a longer, more profitable life.

Another approach to capital budgeting is the *return on average investment method*. A company may also compare investments based on their average income over the life of an investment. This method is fairly simple for projects depreciated by the straight-line method.

First, a company calculates its average *carry cost* over the life of the investment. The carrying cost is equal to the investment outlay minus the accumulated depreciation. Since depreciation is a mechanism for recouping some of the costs of an investment, it reduces the carrying costs.

To compare the competing investments, a company completes the following calculations:

- *Average net income.* Calculate net income by including all expenses and depreciation. Aggregate projected net income and divide by the number of years of the useful life for each investment.

- *Average investment.* Add projected carrying costs to salvage value and divide by two. This method works only for straight-line depreciation where the carrying values decrease uniformly over the useful life.

- *Rate of return on average investment.* Divide the average net income by the average investment, and express as a percent.

A company compares the resulting percentages to determine which investment has the greatest rate of return. However, this method has shortcomings. It does not take into account the timing of the release of funds in payment for each project, nor the beginning of future cash receipts to a company. A company may reduce its cost of capital by making payments by installment rather than up front. In addition, a company will give a higher ranking to a project which throws off earnings earlier than its alternatives.

Discounted cash flow analysis is one more possible method of capital budgeting. To resolve this dilemma about the timing of cash flows, a company employs a method of analysis which incorporates time and earning power. In this way the company is able to compare investments which have different payback periods, useful lives, and rates of return. To arrive at a level playing field, the company adjusts the future stream of earnings by a factor which removes or *discounts* the rate of return for the number of years of useful life.

For example, a company assesses competing investments. For a cost of $10,000, a company expects to earn ten percent annually, or $5,000, over the next five years. Or, the company may invest $15,000 and earn 12 percent annually, or $7,200 over the next four years. The company discounts the cash flows to ease the comparison. Using the formula

$$\text{Present value} = 1/(1+i)^n$$

where i is the rate of return or interest rate and n is the number of years, the company multiplies $5,000 by 0.62 to arrive at a present value of $3,100, or 31 percent of the original investment. Alternatively, the company multiplies $7,200 by 0.63 for a present value of $4,536, or 30.2 percent of the original investment.

The company engages in a method of assessing which of the investments is most beneficial. Essentially, the company seeks a more advantageous use for its excess cash balances by asking itself a series of questions implicit in the calculations: Over the specified period how much interest could cash earn? Over the specified period what would be the total return (net income plus salvage value) of each of the competing capital investments? Which of the competing capital investments would provide the highest return? Over the specified period, do any of the capital investments clearly outperform the total return for cash investments? If so, is the difference between cash and the best capital projects sufficient to justify the risks inherent in a long-term capital project?

To calculate the earning power of cash, a company simply projects the earnings accumulated over a specified time by anticipated interest rates. If the company is pleased with the results, it will invest a certain sum of money in the *present* to earn all that interest in the future.

A company explores the feasibility of an alternative investment by *discounting the future cash flow* to determine if it outperforms a straight cash investment. The steps in this process are:

- Calculate the total stream of earnings over the life of the investment.

- Discount the earnings by a factor which compensates for inflation, financial and operating risks, and for lost revenues from the cash investment.

- Determine the salvage value of the investments and discount it.

- Add the discounted values for the earnings and for the salvage value.

- Subtract from this amount the original cost of the investment.

- The remainder is the *net present value* of the proposed investment.

THE CASH BUDGET

In the *cash budget* a company estimates all expected cash flows for the budget period by: stating the cash available at the beginning of the period; adding cash from sales and other earned income to arrive at the total cash available; and subtracting the projected disbursements for payables, prepayments, interest and notes payable, income tax, etc.

The cash budget is an indication of the company's liquidity, and, therefore, is a very useful tool for effective management. Although profits drive liquidity, they do not necessarily have a high correlation. Often when profits increase, collectibles increase at a greater rate. As a result, liquidity may increase very little or not at all, making the financing of expansion difficult, and the need for short-term credit necessary.

Managers optimize cash balances by having adequate cash to meet liquidity needs, and by investing the excess until needed. Since liquidity is of paramount importance, a company prepares and revises the cash budget with greater frequency than other budgets. For example, weekly cash budgets are common in an era of tight money, slow growth, or high interest rates.

THE BUDGETED BALANCE SHEET

A company derives the *budgeted balance sheet*, often referred to as the *budgeted statement of financial position*, from the budgeted balance sheet at the beginning of the budget period and the expected changes in the account balances reflected in the operating, capital expenditure, and cash budgets. (Since a company prepares the budgeted balance sheet before the end of the current period, it uses an estimated beginning balance sheet.)

The budgeted balance sheet is a statement of the assets and liabilities the company expects at the end of the period. The budgeted balance sheet is more than a collection of residual balances resulting from the foregoing budget estimates. During the budgeting process, management ascertains the desirability of projected balances and account relationships. The outcomes of this level of review may require management to reconsider plans which seemed reasonable earlier in the process.

BUDGETED STATEMENT OF CASH FLOWS

The final phase of the master plan is the *budgeted statement of cash flows*. This statement anticipates the timing of the flow of cash revenues into the business from all resources, and the outflow of cash in the form of payables, interest expense, tax liabilities, dividends, capital expenditures, and the like.

The statement of cash flows includes:

- The amount of cash the company will receive from all sources, including nonoperating items, creditors, and the sale of stocks and assets. The company includes only those credit sales for which it expects to receive at least partial payment.

- The amount of cash the company will pay out for all activities, including dividend payments, taxes, and bond interest expense.

- The amount of cash the company will *net* from its operating activities and investments.

The net amount is a clear measure of the ability of the business to generate funds in excess of cash outflows for the period. If anticipated cash is less than projected expenses, management may decide to increase credit lines or to revise its plans. Note that net cash flow is not the same as net income or profit. Net income and profit factor in depreciation and nonoperating gains and losses which are not cash generating items.

SUMMARY

Budgeting is the process of planning and controlling the utilization of assets in business activities. It is a formal, comprehensive process which covers every detail of sales, operations, and finance, thereby providing management with performance guidelines. Through budgeting, management determines the most profitable use of limited resources. Used wisely, the budgeting process increases management's ability to more efficiently and effectively deploy resources, and to introduce modifications to the plan in a timely manner.

SEE ALSO: Capital Budget; Profit & Loss Statement; Sales Forecasting

[Roger J. AbiNader]

FURTHER READING:

Ameiss, Albert P., and Nicholas A. Kargas. *Accountant's Desk Handbook*. Prentice-Hall, 1980.

Brock, Horace R., Charles E. Palmer, and Billie M. Cunningham. *Accounting Principles and Applications*. 5th ed. McGraw-Hill, Gregg Division, 1986.

Livingstone, John Leslie. *The Portable MBA in Finance and Accounting*. John Wiley & Sons, Inc., 1992.

Meigs, Robert F., and Walter B. Meigs. *Accounting: The Basis for Business Decisions*. 8th ed. McGraw-Hill, 1990.

BULLETIN BOARD SYSTEMS (BBS)

A bulletin board system (BBS), also known as a computer bulletin board, is a versatile method of electronic telecommunications that is becoming increasingly common in the business world. A BBS consists of at least one personal computer (PC) left running and connected to a telephone line through a modem for answering the phone automatically. Electronic messages can be posted and read by multiple, remote users, who access the system through their own personal computers and modems connected to phone lines and by dialing the BBS telephone number. The host computer runs a special kind of BBS software that permits callers to perform certain commands from remote computers. The term BBS also has been stretched to include any multi-user computer message and file exchange service that may be part of a larger, mainframe computer-based online information service. The following discussion deals with only the strict PC-based definition.

Common features of a BBS include the ability of callers to read announcements and brief messages, participate in conferences of string messages on a related subject, send electronic mail to specific addresses, download files, chat in real-time with other users who dialed in simultaneously to a multi-line BBS, and attain access through "doors" to specialized programs external to the BBS software, such as for searching large databases or for using retail sales systems which register credit card orders.

BBSs arose from the leisure-time activity of computer hobbyists by offering a forum for discussion on common topics and a means of exchanging shareware or other non-licensed computer software. The first BBS is considered to be the one created by

Ward Christensen and Randy Suess in 1978, just after Hayes introduced the first personal computer modem and about a year after personal computers were first commercially available. Many public BBSs around the country are still hobbies of their operators, but a number have become profit-making enterprises by charging users a fee.

Although the use of BBSs by hobbyists continues to be the better known application, business usage has in recent years become dominant. The number of corporate bulletin boards is several times that of the estimated 30,000 publicly accessible boards. In 1992 BBS software vendors reported that 80-85 percent of their sales were to business customers. The rapid spread of BBSs for business, beginning in the late 1980s, was due to the increasing base of installed modems in offices and homes. The trend continued to accelerate in the early 1990s with the introduction of modems with both faster speeds and cheaper prices. The main categories of business applications for BBSs are:

- Conducting business by companies that specialize in information services;

- Disseminating information by government agencies, trade associations, or other non-profit organizations of interest to business;

- Networking among business professionals;

- Facilitating information exchange between a company and its clients, vendors, and employees.

Small information service enterprises have emerged that provide their information principally or exclusively through a fee-charging BBS. Examples include companies that offer access to databases, software and graphics files, weather information, stock quotes, job listings and other classified advertisements. A number of periodical publishers also have introduced information service BBSs, which may offer select published articles and unpublished articles, forums for discussing topics in the news, classified advertisements, and a means of accepting letters to the editor.

Businesses can also be on the receiving end of BBS services. Many local, state and federal government agencies operate public-access BBSs, which provide valuable information for the business community. They may provide information on laws and regulations that affect business in general or certain industries. Economic and demographic statistics, which companies may utilize in their marketing plans, are also made available. An example is the Economic Bulletin Board run by the U.S. Department of Commerce. It provides daily quotes of Treasury notes for the Federal Reserve in New York and collections of qualified export leads compiled by the U.S. Foreign and Commercial Service. The **U.S. Small Business Administration** operates a BBS which provides information on SBA loan programs, government procurement services, and publications. Non-profit organizations have similarly established public information BBSs. A number of trade associations have set up BBSs to provide industry-related information for the specific needs of their members.

Some BBSs, both profit and non-profit, are set up specifically to serve professional business people as a source of networking. Issues of business management and marketing are discussed, and new contacts are made. This is an especially valuable resource for small businesses and the self-employed. BBSs are a suitable means of communication within a given geographic area where only a local telephone call is needed.

Most significantly, companies are increasingly setting up their own BBSs to facilitate communication and information exchange with their clients, vendors and their own employees. The first companies to utilize BBSs in their businesses were computer hardware and software companies, especially those that sold communications software and modems. They used BBSs in customer support services, since their customers were already computer literate. BBSs are also

a practical means of distributing software because they permit the transmission of computer programs and not merely text messages. Later, companies of all kinds realized the benefits of BBSs, as personal computers and modems became more widespread among their clients or potential clients.

CORPORATE USES OF BULLETIN BOARD SYSTEMS

Customer Support and Other Customer Relations. Customers dial into a BBS to have their problems addressed while saving the time of waiting on hold on customer support lines and saving companies costs from lengthy 800-number calls. Customers can submit their questions during non-business hours when it is both cheaper to call and often more convenient. Answers to frequently asked questions are made available, so a direct response from a customer service representative is often not even needed. Thus, BBSs are a more cost-effective means of customer service, because fewer employees are needed to handle incoming requests. For example, IBM's product support BBS has only two full-time staff personnel overseeing 20,000 calls per month.

Other customer relations services include conferences on a company's products and services, including suggestions for product use and announcements of new products or services. The possibilities for customer feedback are also enhanced with a BBS. Customers may explain their opinions at length without being restricted to the space on response forms, they feel less intimidated than speaking on the phone, and the posted comments often solicit additional comments from other customers who log on. Online polls and surveys can be made of clients for marketing research. The BBS itself may add to a company's reputation by being promoted as an additional service.

AUTOMATIC MAIL-ORDER SALES. A catalog of product descriptions and prices can be put on-line. Using software to validate customer credit card numbers, orders can be taken automatically. Such BBSs permit customers to shop at their convenience off-hours or during peak business hours without having to wait for the availability of a sales representative. They are most suitable for items such as music CDs, where the buyer need not see the product. A BBS is especially practical in selling software, which can be delivered electronically through the same system.

Business to business electronic mail correspondence Electronic mail eliminates the problem of telephone tag and provides a written record of correspondence. While the nation-wide commercial electronic mail services, such as MCI-Mail, SprintMail, AT&T's EasyLink, and CompuServe, are heavily used in business communications, they are only useful when both parties subscribe to one of the services.

When a company sets up its own BBS, anyone with merely a modem and computer can interact with it.

FILE TRANSFER. BBSs are used for the transfer of formatted files, such as financial data in spreadsheet programs or publishable documentation in a layout program, between an office and its affiliates or vendors. Available electronic-mail software or services may only permit the transfer of straight text messages.

REAL-TIME REMOTE MEETINGS. Multiple call-in BBSs permit teleconferencing among participants simultaneously logged in. This has the advantage over conference calls of providing a transcript and ensuring clarity.

IN-HOUSE COMMUNICATIONS. A BBS is often the most practical solution for a company of multiple locations for which a local area computer network would not suffice but a wide area network would be too expensive. BBSs are used for postings of inventory updates, policy statements, technical data, meeting minutes, memos for comment and other internal publications.

JOB POSTINGS. Companies reach qualified potential employees who are currently employed elsewhere and thus unable to visit a company in person to read through job descriptions. The potential applicants reading BBS postings can also be assumed to be computer literate.

COORDINATING REMOTE EMPLOYEES. Communications and file transfer is conducted with salespeople in the field or on the road, employees who work at home, and free-lance contractors.

The extent to which companies utilize BBSs in their business varies tremendously. For some it is merely an additional means of customer relations; for others, such as mail order companies, it may be the principle means of doing business. The owner of a BBS may also control its access, leaving it open to all callers or restricting it by the issuance of passwords. Different levels of access, such as the ability to read but not post messages, may similarly be controlled. Certain message conferencing areas may also be restricted. Thus, a BBS may be used for internal, vendor, and client communications at the same time with the confidentiality of messages maintained.

Each company tailors its BBS to its individual needs and may have devised creative applications not envisioned by the BBS software developers. Examples:

- Citibank's audit department uses a BBS to exchange audit reports in spreadsheet program formats among its auditors around the world.

- A Blue Cross Blue Shield subsidiary runs a BBS to collect health insurance claims from doctors and hospitals, whereby physicians' existing filing systems can be used to automatically submit claims. Claims are paid in as little as two days instead of two to four weeks.

- Coca-Cola Foods in Houston, Texas, has used a BBS since 1985 to facilitate communication between regional sales offices. Lotus 1-2-3 spreadsheets are transmitted to regional offices, which fill them out and return them via the BBS.

- WordPerfect Corp. uses an internal BBS to exchange pieces of WordPerfect software code, translated into foreign languages, among its overseas offices. It has found this as a more cost-effective means than mailing disks.

- Seagate Technology Inc. offers users of its BBS the ability to download entire product manuals. In 1992 its BBS received 8,000 calls per day through 11 lines.

Small companies also make use of BBSs for their specialized services. For example, a television program listings service uses a BBS to permit newspaper publishers to dial in and download the latest schedules in time to put them in print. A building service company collects building permit listings and offers them to construction suppliers on a subscription basis. Translation agencies send documents to be translated and receive translated versions from their free-lance translators while ensuring that special foreign language characters are preserved.

The startup costs for a BBS are very low. It requires dedicating at least one personal computer, which need not be powerful, a BBS software program (often less than $100 for a one- or two-line system), and a modem, which may cost around $100. Leading commercial BBS software packages include PCBoard, TBBS (The Bread Board System), Wildcat and Major BBS. Multiple calls coming in at once can be supported by either a network of multiple personal computers or the use of a single PC with multi-port serial cards and multitasking software. Up to 250 calls can be handled at once on a complex, networked system. At least one person, who is known as the systems operator, needs to be responsible for overseeing the flow of information on the system, posting new information and answering questions. For small BBSs, however, this need not be a full-time activity.

Companies have several options for starting a BBS. They can set one up themselves if they have a computer-savvy employee, hire a consultant to install one for them, or contract with an outside BBS service bureau to run the service on that bureau's computer. Companies with small needs often opt for the latter service, whereby they pay a flat annual subscription fee for a restricted-access message area on the BBS.

Although more sophisticated electronic telecommunications systems exist, the relatively simple BBS is destined to grow into a standard means of business communications, precisely because no standards are needed. Organizations with different computers and software have no difficulty in communicating through a BBS. Furthermore, even though brands of BBS software vary, the differences are not that great, and only three or four make up the bulk of the usage. Thus, it becomes easy for one familiar with BBSs to navigate in an unfamiliar BBS for the first time. Once a BBS is up and running successfully, a company may be able to convince more of its clients, vendors and remote workers to invest in modems and communications software if they do not already have them.

Enhancements in BBS software have also aided growth in their use. These include gateways providing links to local area network communications services, computer virus scanning, and full-screen editing capabilities for those typing online.

[Heather Behn Hedden]

FURTHER READING:

Balas, Janet L. "Bulletin Board Systems: A Nostalgic Look Back," *Computer In Libraries*. May 1993, pp. 24-26.

Brinker, Scott, J. "Corporate Bulletin Board systems: Customer Support and More in the 1990s," *Telecommunications*. November 1991, pp. 33-36.

Harrer, Jim. "Bulletin Board Systems are Beginning to Emerge in Business Applications," *Telecommunications*. March 1993, pp. 58-59.

"How Seagate, Seiko Instruments use BBS for Business," *Communications News*. August 1992, pp. 24 25.

Musgrave, Bill. "Bulletin Boards and Business," *Datamation*. January 15, 1987, pp. 61-62.

Wood, Lamont and Dana Blankenhorn. *Bulletin Board Systems for Business*. John Wiley & Sons, Inc., 1992.

Wood, Lamont. "Business Profits From Bulletin Boards," *Datamation*. May 1, 1993, pp. 45-48.

BUREAUCRACY

SEE: Organization Theory

BUSINESS BROKERS

Business brokers act as intermediaries between buyers and sellers of a business. They may represent either party in the transaction, and do not take possession of goods or property, or deal on their own account. Brokers differ from dealers in that the latter transact on their own account and may have a vested interest in the transaction. Brokers fill the important marketing function of bringing buyers and sellers together and helping them negotiate mutually beneficial agreements. In addition, they facilitate transactions by providing expertise and advice.

Indeed, brokers supply numerous benefits to both buyers and sellers. For example, sellers benefit because they do not have to spend time and money searching for buyers. Qualified brokers have access to people that are in the market to purchase a company, or they know how to find legitimate prospects much more quickly than typical business owners. The broker may also be able to help the seller place an accurate value on his enterprise, devise a strategy to transfer ownership over time, and overcome legal hurdles related to taxes.

The buyer also benefits from the brokers access to business buying and selling channels. A buyer that goes to a broker may be able to find a business that suits his abilities, wants, and financial constraints much more quickly than he would working independently. The broker can help him determine what he can afford and, importantly, can help arrange financing from a lender or the company owner to purchase the business. He may even go to bat for the buyer at a bank or other lending institution, or walk the buyer through the details of the financing process. Finally, it is the broker's duty to ensure that the interests of the buyer (and the seller) are protected by any contracts or agreements relating to the sale.

For their services, brokers typically receive in compensation a percentage of the total value of the transaction. The fee may be paid by the buyer, seller, or both parties, depending on the nature of the transaction. Commissions vary widely, usually depending on the size of the transaction and the amount of service provided by the broker.

THE BROKERAGE PROCESS

Although it is a broker's chief function, bringing buyer and seller together is often the easiest part of his/her job. Indeed, actually closing the transaction is usually much more complicated than buying or selling a car, or even a house. The process is usually compounded by a number of factors that are unique to each situation. For instance, the seller of a business often views the enterprise as his "baby." Therefore, the value which he places on it may be greater than its actual worth. Likewise, a buyer may fail to appreciate the amount of work involved in building a business to a certain point. Other major factors that differentiate business brokering from other large transactions is financing, which can become very complicated, and problems related to employees and clients of the business being sold.

Once a business broker brings an interested buyer and seller together, the succeeding brokerage process can be broken down into a five-step process (Garai and Pravda, *Mergers & Acquisitions*, March/April 1994). In the first stage of the process the broker attempts to set a target for completion of the transaction. This is usually accomplished by means of a letter of intent in which the buyer and seller agree to move toward a deal. The importance of the letter of intent is that it puts the deal into words and serves as a framework around which to structure negotiations. The letter also reduces ambiguity and misunderstanding, and ensures that both parties are serious about pursuing the transaction. Finally, establishing a deadline through a letter of intent helps to keep the buyer and seller focused on the big issues, rather than on minor details that can drag the deal out for months on end or kill the sale.

After setting a target, the broker must close price gaps that inevitably arise during the negotiation. A price gap is the difference between what the seller wants and what the buyer is willing to pay. Even after the buyer and seller agree on a price, discrepancies are likely to emerge when they sit down and begin working out the details of the plan. Differences of opinion may arise about the value of inventory or accounts receivables, for example, or one party may simply change his mind about the agreed upon price. Often times, tax issues come to light that change the way that each party views the deal. In such cases it is the broker's job to suggest a structure for the deal that will minimize tax burdens.

The third stage in the brokerage process involves overcoming "seller's remorse." Seller's remorse commonly occurs during the latter stages of negotiations when the seller suddenly realizes that he/she is relinquishing control of the company in which he has invested part of his life. The seller may wonder what he will do the day after the sale without an office to go to and subordinates to direct and assist. Or, he may be concerned the buyer will run the company into the ground, thus destroying the company he built. Seller's remorse can kill the deal if the broker fails to confront it early in the negotiations by assuaging the seller's particular fears or concerns. This can often be accomplished through acts as small as allowing the owner to keep a company car or country club membership, or by offering to retain him as a consultant for certain projects, etc.

The fourth phase of the business brokering process is due diligence, whereby various legal technicalities are identified and addressed which could thwart or obsolete an otherwise legal agreements. For example, the buyer of a valve manufacturing firm might want to ensure that he was procuring the legal rights to all patents held by the firm, and that all of the patents were valid. Or, the potential owner would want to make sure that there were no "ticking bombs" of which he is unaware, such as hazardous waste sites that the company has been required by law to remedy. It is the broker's job to facilitate due diligence to protect parties on both sides of the deal.

During the fifth stage, the purchase/sale agreement, the broker helps the buyer and seller iron out and sign a final contract. This stage is the one most likely to entail the use of attorneys on both sides, even for smaller transactions. The best way for the broker to reduce the chance that the deal will fail at this critical juncture is to try to address all questions and concerns in the letter of intent and due diligence stages. Despite his best efforts, one or both parties may employ brinkmanship tactics that threaten to scrap the entire deal, such as significantly raising the asking price or demanding that some new contingency be added to the agreement. At this point, the broker's expertise as mediator and peacemaker is key.

SEE ALSO: Acquisitions & Mergers

[Dave Mote]

FURTHER READING:

Bianchi, Alessandra. "The American Dream Revisited: Why You Won't Sell Your Business," *Inc.*, August 1992.

Chapman, Cornelius. "Corporate Finance: Surviving the Credit Crunch," *Small Business Reports*, September 1992.

Farrett, Joseph. "A New Paradigm for Lenders," *Mortgage Banking*, May 1989.

Garai, Gabor and Susan Pravda. "The Critical Line Between Dealmakers and Deal Breakers," *Mergers and Acquisitions*, March/April 1994.

Standard & Poor's Industry Surveys. New York: Standard & Poor's Corporation, December 31, 1993.

BUSINESS COMMUNICATIONS

SEE: Business Literature; Business Press

BUSINESS CONDITIONS

The economic, political, environmental, and regulatory circumstances in which a business operates combine to form the prevailing business conditions. Logically, the success or failure of an individual business is highly sensitive to these conditions. Events taking place at all levels of government—from decisions made by local legislators to global agreements outlining international policies—can greatly affect existing business conditions and, thus, corporate stability. While global agreements often affect the basic nature of an industry, business conditions at the city, state, and national level are highly sensitive to the economic realities of the area. Aside from the economy, political realities, environmental conditions, and regulatory policies—such as a government's stability, its environmental policies, and its general attitude toward industry—greatly affect prevailing business conditions. Thus, for an individual firm to survive, it must base its business decisions on reliable information about all of the factors composing existing business conditions at local, state, national, and global levels.

ECONOMIC INDICATORS

For those who are unfamiliar with economic indicators and their definitions, an introductory publication such as *Guide to Economic Indicators*, 2nd ed., 1994 by Norman Frumkin will be of help. From a business point of view, it is important to find the actual data for the various economic indicators. Generally data on economic indicators are available by country and within a country by state or cities. The guide mentioned above discusses about 48 different indicators. Depending on the circumstances, all the indicators may not be equally relevant. The main indicators are: labor force, employment and unemployment, wages, personal disposable income and savings, consumer price index, gross domestic product, housing starts, retail sales, manufacturing shipments, mineral production, and business bankruptcies. Statistical data on these economic indicators are generally collected and published by the statistical organization of the national government of a country.

As an example, the U.S. Bureau of the Census in the U.S. Department of Commerce annually publishes the *Statistical Abstract of the United States*. The U.S. Bureau of Economic Analysis in the same department publishes the monthly *Survey of Current Business*, which provides statistical data on a more frequent basis. Most countries in the world have similar governmental agencies that publish statistical data pertaining to their country. Any major public library or university library with a good collection of government documents would have such statistical publications from a number of different countries. International governmental agencies such as the **United Nations** or the **Organization for Economic Cooperation and Development** also publish statistical data for their member countries. Examples are the *Statistical Yearbook* of the United Nations and the *Main Economic Indicators* published monthly by the OECD. The **International Monetary Fund (IMF)**, a sister organization of the United Nations, also publishes a monthly, *International Financial Statistics*.

Many of the international governmental agencies and national governments have statistical data available in electronic formats such as online databases, floppy discs, and CD-ROMs. These tend to have the most current information. *International Financial Statistics* for example is available in a CD-ROM version and a computer tape version. The U.S. Bureau of the Census has an online database, called CENDATA that is updated daily. A publication such as the *Gale Directory of Databases* will help in identifying databases containing international and country statistics. It should be pointed out that there are several private institutions that create their own databases from data supplied by governments and international bodies, often combining and enriching that data with information generated within their organizations. Examples of such databases are Citibase, DRI(McGraw-Hill), and D&B-Donnelley Demographics.

The statistical information sources in printed and electronic form provide data on economic indicators, and economic indicators in turn are a good measurement of business conditions. In interpreting economic indicators and in using that information in business decisions, care should be taken to reach a balanced judgement. By placing too much emphasis on some factors, business decisions can get distorted. For example, a manufacturer that supplies electrical components to one of the three automobile giants in North America moved its factory from Canada to the southern United States to escape high wages and unionized labor. The quality of manufacture then suffered, resulting in high rejection rates by the automaker. When the automaker threatened to not buy from the parts manufacturer, the company was forced to return to its former location in Canada and rely on the skilled labor available there. Thus, lower wages and nonunionized labor force might have looked attractive in terms of economic indicators, but if the company could not sell its products, the data was misleading. Qualitative or subjective considerations are not reflected in economic indicators.

There are a number of business services that provide analytical information on business conditions in various countries. The Economist Intelligence Unit based in London and New York produces quarterly *Country Reports* and annual *Country Profiles* for most countries in the world. *Exporters' Encyclopedia* published by Dun and Bradstreet International is an annual with updating bulletins that give concise and informative reports on all aspects of doing business in each country. *Reference Book for World Traders* is a loose leaf service that provides practical background information on the business conditions in every country. International accounting firms such as Price Waterhouse publish booklets on doing business in a wide number of countries. These are excellent sources for companies to obtain an overview of the business conditions in countries they deal with. The only shortcoming is that these booklets are not updated very frequently. *Overseas Business Reports* issued by the U.S. Department of Commerce's International Trade Administration (ITA) is another source emphasizing business opportunities in a number of countries. International governmental agencies such as the OECD and the **World Bank** have annual country studies or surveys which are more substantive in their contents. There are weekly newsletters which monitor the business conditions in a region of the world or in a specific country. The Economist Intelligence Unit is one of the publishers of such newsletters.

POLITICAL AND ENVIRONMENTAL FACTORS

Business conditions are very much influenced by the political situation in a country. Government policies determine the framework in which a business operates. Some of the publications discussed in the previous section that provide a profile of a country often analyze the political situation in that country from a business point of view. The weekly newsletters referred to above also monitor political and policy changes. Business newspapers such as the *Wall Street Journal*, the *Asian Wall Street Journal Weekly*, the *Nikkei Weekly* and the *Financial Times* of London are the best sources to keep abreast of fast changing political situations. The political stability of a country and its government policies and regulations are factors that determine how hospitable the business climate is in that country. *Political Risk Yearbook* is an annual publication that provides a competent analysis of the political situation as well as a forecast for the coming five years in different regions of the world.

The **infrastructure** under which businesses operate in a country is largely determined by the history of government policies. The infrastructure includes such factors as communication, transportation, energy supply, and basic industries. Intangible factors such as a fair judicial system, strong environmental regulations, and a good social safety net are also important in the long run to nonvolatile business conditions. In a free market economy, **environmental law** and regulations and legislation providing an adequate social safety net are often seen as an economic burden making business conditions less competitive. If maximization of profit is the only consideration, this may be true in many cases. On the other hand, if the social cost of environmental clean up or the productivity loss due to stress, ill health, or economic insecurity are taken into consideration, the legislation and regulations are seen as economically sound. The cost of preventing problems is far less than the cost of remedying them.

Many industrially advanced countries have laws for environmental protection that in some cases may add to the cost of doing business in those countries. The wages and benefit costs also tend to be high. All of these factors have a bearing on the business conditions in these countries in that they create higher costs of doing business. The quality and the productivity of the workforce and savings in the cost of environmental clean up more than compensate for the higher costs involved in the short run. Newspapers and magazines periodically report country rankings based on the quality of life. This information can be retrieved through either printed indexes/abstracts or through electronic databases that often also provide the full text of articles. United Nations Development Programme (UNDP) publishes the annual *Human Development Report*, which ranks countries according to their human development index. Educational level of the population is an important element in this human development index. The quality of the human resource, which largely depends on education, is one of the most valuable criteria affecting business conditions. The Economist Intelligence Unit also publishes a ranking by cities around the world mainly based on the living costs.

OTHER FACTORS

Apart from the main economic indicators there are other economic factors that determine business conditions. Reliable capital sources, secure energy supply, good communication facilities, expansive transportation networks, and, in some instances, availability of raw materials are all factors to look for in assessing business conditions. Efficient distribution channels are also important for some businesses.

Governments at various levels offer investment incentives in the form of tax holidays, leasing of land at discounted rates, or low interest rates on capital loans. Such incentives make conditions of doing business very favorable. By simplifying and relaxing the regulatory environment in which businesses have to operate, governments can attract more businesses to their jurisdiction. Taxation is perhaps the most important regulatory concern. The degree to which businesses are taxed and the degree of simplicity in the taxation system determine favorable business conditions to a large extent. A loose-leaf reference service, *Foreign Tax and Trade Briefs*, published by Matthew Bender, describes the tax environment of different countries and monitors the changes.

The labor relations system of a country has a major influence on business conditions. If the system encourages speedy and amicable resolution of conflicts, it is a positive factor in the business conditions of that place. Labor unions can be either a positive or negative force depending on how they function. Unions can lend stability to the work situation or they can create considerable disruption. Closely related to the labor relations factor is the premise of social security. As noted earlier, strong social security provisions contribute to efficiency and productivity in spite of some increased initial cost. Often these social factors are as important as the economic factors in creating favorable business conditions.

Generally applicable components of business conditions have been discussed in this article as well as how to evaluate the conditions in a balanced manner. Sources of information on the different indicators have been provided. It should be pointed out that the sources mentioned are only examples of the types of information available. They are by no means a complete list. For specific countries, regions, and places, more in-depth sources in the same categories can be found.

SEE ALSO: Business Cycles

[Divakara K. (Dik) Varma]

BUSINESS CYCLES

In most basic terms, business cycles refer to fluctuations in the economic growth of a nation's economy. Sometimes, business cycles are simply referred to as ups and downs in the economy. The U.S. economy has experienced economic fluctuations almost throughout its history. For example, while the U.S. income has grown more than six-fold during the last 70 years, the U.S. economy has also experienced many economic downturns, some of which were very severe. The Great Depression (1929-33) was the worst downturn of this century. More recently, a fairly deep downturn was experienced during the Reagan administration (1981-82) and a mild downturn during the Bush administration (1990-92). Economists, over time, have studied the causes, consequences, and possible cures for the recurrent business cycles. Business cycles, however, have not been conquered to the fullest extent. After all, the most recent downturn ended only in 1992, and the next one might be around the corner. Nevertheless, the severity of economic downturns has been mitigated to a considerable degree. It is now widely believed that business cycles are here to coexist, at least in a mild form, with every economy that is based on capitalism. In what follows, common characteristics of business cycles are discussed in detail.

BUSINESS CYCLES AND FLUCTUATIONS IN OUTPUT AND EMPLOYMENT

Usually, when one talks about business or economic fluctuations, the person is using some notion of the aggregate economic output or income. The most commonly used measure of the national output is called **gross national product**, or GNP (the government has recently started using a related measure of output known as **gross domestic product**, or GDP).

GNP, in turn, measures the aggregate output by simply evaluating all *final* goods and services produced in the economy during a year at their market prices. When an economist examines fluctuations in gross national product, he or she uses the GNP measure that is adjusted for **inflation**. The inflation adjusted measure is called *real* GNP, or gross national product in *constant dollars*. It makes sense to use only the real GNP in studying business fluctuations, as we are interested in real fluctuations in economic activity.

While business cycles are expressed in terms of fluctuations in real gross national product, they are usually accompanied by fluctuations in the **unemployment rate** of labor as well. When the nation's output of goods and services falls, the unemployment rate typically rises—a direct consequence of the fact that fewer workers are needed to produce the reduced volume of output. It is important not to forget the employment (or unemployment) dimension of an economic downturn, as the higher unemployment rate leads to a number of economic and social costs that can have political repercussions. The unemployment rate during the depth of economic downturn during the Great Depression rose above 25 percent. The unemployment rate during the economic downturn under the Bush administration remained below 8 percent, peaking at 7.7 percent. Despite the fact that this downturn was a mild one, Bush lost his bid for the second term, a sign of increased expectations of the federal government on part of the public.

FOUR PHASES OF THE BUSINESS CYCLES

While economic fluctuations are often simply referred to as ups and down in the economy, these fluctuations follow a broad path—each business cycle displays all phases of a cycle, but its characteristics differ from one cycle to another. In other words, business cycles are not *regular* or consistent. This will become clearer as the discussion proceeds.

Each business cycle can be divided into four phases. As the economic downturn continues, the output level reaches a bottom, called a trough. A trough is basically a turning point—the real output stops declining any further and starts to increase after hitting the trough. The phase when the economy's real output is rising from the trough is termed expansion. The expansion continues to a peak where it achieves the highest output level for this particular business cycle. When output starts declining from the level achieved at the peak, a recession or contraction is said to have set in. The four phases—trough, expansion, peak, and recession—constitute a business cycle.

SOME NOTABLE PERIODS OF EXPANSION AND CONTRACTIONS. Duration and force of expansion and contractions vary from cycle to cycle. A particularly severe recession is called a depression. The Great

Depression of the 1930s has since been unparalleled in terms of severity. In October of 1929, the stock market witnessed a drastic decline, often referred to as the great stock market crash of 1929. After the stock market crash, the economy started declining at a staggering pace. The real gross national product declined by about one-third between 1929 and 1933. At the peak of the Depression in 1933, the unemployment rate rose above 25 percent of the labor force, resulting in inordinate hardship for a large number of Americans.

In the post World War II period, recessions have been generally mild, relative to the Great Depression. In recent years, recessions of 1974-75 (due, in part, to a great increase in oil prices) and 1981-82 have been fairly severe. However, even these recessions are considered quite tame relative to the Great Depression—the unemployment rate rose to only 8.5 percent in 1975, and to 9.7 percent in 1982 during the 1981-82 recession.

A particularly robust period of expansion is often called prosperity. The United States economy experienced an unprecedented period of prosperity during and after World War II. In fact, the effects of the Great Depression lingered on in the U.S. economy until the outbreak of World War II. The increase in government spending necessitated by the war provided an enormous expansionary force—the real U.S. gross national product increased by about 75 percent between 1939 and 1945. Prosperous periods of somewhat lower magnitudes were experienced during the Korean and Vietnam wars. Because the economy tends to operate at or near full capacity during periods of prosperity, such periods are also generally accompanied by inflationary pressures.

CAUSES OF BUSINESS FLUCTUATIONS

There are a multitude of factors that are considered responsible for causing business cycles. In a theoretical sense, though, they can be broadly characterized as belonging either to the demand side (the aggregate demand from all sections—consumers, investors, government, and foreign—for the economy's goods and services) or the supply side (which pertains to factors relevant to supply of goods and services, such as changes in input costs, technological advances, etc.).

THE THEORETICAL (GENERIC) REASON FOR BUSINESS FLUCTUATIONS

To understand why economic activities fluctuate at all, one needs to understand a little bit of **macroeconomics** theory. Basically, this theory explains how the equilibrium level of output is determined in the economy. The equilibrium output also determines the asso-

ciated equilibrium price level. Aggregate demand for and aggregate supply of goods and services ultimately determine the equilibrium output (and thus the price level). These concepts are briefly explained below.

AGGREGATE DEMAND. An aggregate demand schedule specifies the amount of goods and services demanded by all sectors of the economy at each price level. It is common sense that the quantity of goods and services demanded will be lower at higher prices and vice versa. In other words, price level and aggregate demand are inversely related—they move in the opposite directions. Economists formalize this relationship by saying that the aggregate demand curve (the graphical device that illustrates the relationship between the aggregate demand and price) slopes downward to the right. Now, what constitutes the aggregate demand? As alluded to above, it is made up of demands from all sectors of the economy. These sectors are primarily put under four headings—consumption spending, investment spending, government spending, and net exports.

Consumption spending is an important component of the aggregate demand. Private consumption expenditures constitute roughly 69 percent of the aggregate demand in the United States economy. Private consumption expenditures are further subdivided into expenditures on consumer durables (such as a washer, dryer, or an automobile), consumer nondurables (such as a shirt or a bag of groceries) and services (such as a hair cut or manicure).

Investment spending is a much smaller part of the aggregate demand in the economy—gross domestic private investment currently accounts for roughly 14 percent of total real gross domestic product. Investment is influenced by a number of tangible and nontangible factors. The cost of borrowing (the long-term interest rate is the main basis for determining the cost of borrowing) and expected profit rates (on proposed projects) are considered the major determinants of investment spending. However, investment is susceptible to a number of economic and psychological factors, including businessmen's confidence regarding the future of the economy.

As of 1994, government spending in the United States constituted a fairly sizable portion of the aggregate demand in the economy—estimated to be about 18 percent of the total spending in the economy. During wars or periods of international tensions, government spending tends to rise to meet the actual or perceived threat. However, during normal times, it is hard to pin down the factors that determine the level of government spending. In general, there exists a strong political inertia in changing spending.

The fourth component of the aggregate demand, the net foreign demand (measured by the difference between what the U.S. is **exporting** to other countries and what it imports from them) is not a significant component for the American economy. Actually, the United States imports more than it exports. As a result, the net foreign demand for the United States is negative. However, this negative amount is not a large percentage of the total gross domestic product for the United States. One can reasonably assume that the net foreign demand for U.S. products is not significant in aggregate demand.

Variations in the aggregate demand can occur due to variations in any component of the aggregate demand described above.

AGGREGATE SUPPLY. An aggregate supply schedule specifies the amount of goods and services supplied (produced) by all producers of goods and services in the economy at each price level. It is reasonable to expect that the quantity of goods and services supplied will be higher at higher prices and vice versa. In other words, price level and aggregate supply are positively related—they move in the same direction. Economists formalize this relationship by saying that the aggregate supply curve (the graphical device that illustrates the relationship between the aggregate supply and price) slopes upward to the right. Why do producers charge higher prices to supply greater output? This is explained in terms of the cost of producing increased output. In general, the average cost (cost per unit) of producing output rises due to increasing input prices—increased competition among producers for the given raw materials and labor raises their prices. As costs of production increase, so do prices of commodities produced.

The supply curve can shift for a number of reasons. Suppose, there is sudden increase in the price of a necessary input—say, oil. This will shift the supply curve to the left. In other words, prices of goods produced will rise in general, due to the increased input price.

FLUCTUATIONS IN THE ECONOMY

Business cycles or fluctuations in the economy result from shifts in the aggregate demand curve, the aggregate supply curve or both. A rightward shift in the aggregate demand curve leads to an expansion (putting, in general, an upward pressure on the price level) and a leftward shift leads to an opposite effect. Similarly, a rightward shift in the aggregate supply curve leads to an expansion (putting, in general, a downward pressure on the price level) and a leftward shift has the opposite effect. In what follows, we discuss a number of key factors that lead to business fluctuations, without specifically separating them under demand or supply categories.

VOLATILITY OF INVESTMENT SPENDING. Variations in investment spending is one of the important causes of business cycles. Investment spending is considered the most volatile component of the aggregate demand—it varies much more from year to year than the largest component of the aggregate demand, the consumption spending. Empirical studies by economists have revealed that the volatility of the investment component is an important factor in explaining business cycles in the United States. As explained above, increases in investment shift the aggregate demand to the right, leading to an economic expansion. Decreases in investment have the opposite effect. According to popular belief, the Great Depression was caused by a collapse in investment spending in the aftermath of the stock market crash of 1929. Similarly, prosperity of the late 1950s was attributed to a capital goods boom.

There are several reasons for the volatility in the investment spending. One generic reason is the pace at which investment accelerates in response to changes in sales—this linkage is termed as the acceleration principle by economists. This can be briefly explained as follows. Suppose, a firm is operating at full capacity. When sales increase, output will have to be increased by increasing plant capacity through further investment. However, because of the nature of investment goods, many dollars worth of investment must be made to meet the increased sales worth one dollar—investment goods are expensive, but they are worthwhile as they will continue to generate additional output for a long period. As a result, changes in sales result in magnified percentage changes in investment expenditures. This accelerates the pace of economic expansion, which generates greater income in the economy, leading to further increases in sales. Thus, once the expansion starts, the pace of investment spending accelerates. In more concrete terms, the response of the investment spending is related to the *rate* at which sales are increasing. In general, if an increase in sales is expanding, investment spending rises, and if an increase in sales has peaked and is beginning to slow, investment spending falls. Thus, the pace of investment spending is influenced by changes in the rate of sales, which vary greatly over time, this leads to business cycles.

Another reason for variations in investment is the timing of technological innovations. Technological innovations may relate to production and use of a new product or producing an existing product using a new process. The video imaging and personal computer industries have undergone immense technological innovations in recent years. When a new product is invented, large amounts of investment are needed to produce and market the product. Personal computers are now a commonplace item, available not only in most offices, but also in many homes. Large investments were made in the personal computer industry to bring it to its current level of product prices and competition in the market. As explained earlier, investment augments the aggregate demand and leads to an economic expansion. However, technological innovations, and consequent increases in investment, take place at irregular intervals. Fluctuating investments, due to variations in the pace of technological innovations, lead to business fluctuations in the economy.

There are many reasons why the pace of technological innovations varies. Major innovations do not occur every day. Nor do they take place at a constant rate. Chance factors greatly influence the timing of major innovations, as well as the number of innovations in a particular year. Economists consider the variations in technological innovations as random (with no systematic pattern). Thus, irregularity in the pace of innovations in new products or processes becomes a source of business fluctuations.

VARIATIONS IN INVENTORIES. Variations in inventories—expansion and contraction in the level of inventories of goods—also generate business cycles. Inventories are the stocks of goods firms keep on hand to meet unexpected demand for their products. How do variations in the level of inventories lead to business cycles. Usually, during a business downturn, firms let their inventories decline. As inventories are cut down considerably, businesses ultimately find themselves short of inventories. As a result, they start increasing inventory levels by producing output greater than sales, leading to an economic expansion. This expansion continues as long as the rate of increase in sales holds up and producers continue to increase inventories at the preceding rate. However, as the rate of increase in sales slows, firms begin to cut back on their inventory accumulation. The subsequent reduction in inventory investment dampens the economic expansion, and eventually causes an economic downturn. The process then repeats all over again. It should be noted that while variations in inventory levels produce business cycles, the resulting business cycles are not really long. The business cycles generated by fluctuations in inventories are called *minor* or *short* business cycles. They usually last about two to four years, and they are sometimes also called inventory cycles.

FLUCTUATIONS IN GOVERNMENT SPENDING. Variations in government spending are yet another source of business fluctuations. This may appear to be an unlikely source, as the government is widely considered to be a stabilizing force in the economy, not a source of economic fluctuations or instability. Nevertheless, government spending has been a major destabilizing force at several occasions, especially during and after wars. Government spending increased by an enormous amount during World War II, leading to an economic expansion that continued for several years after the war. Government spending also increased, though to a smaller extent compared to World War II, during the Korean and Vietnam wars. These also led to economic expansions. However, government spending not only contributes to economic expansions, but economic contractions as well. In fact, the recession of 1953-54 was caused by the reduction in government spending after the Korean war ended. More recently, the end of the Cold War has resulted in a reduction in defense spending by the United States. While this did not injure the U.S. economy as a whole, the California economy (heavily dependent on defense spending) came to a grinding halt as a result of the defense cuts.

POLITICALLY GENERATED BUSINESS CYCLES. Many economists have hypothesized that business cycles are the result of the politically motivated use of macroeconomic policies (monetary and fiscal policies) that are designed to serve the interest of politicians running for re-election. Political business cycles can be explained as follows. Usually a year or two before an election, the incumbent president, congress persons and/or senators engineer an expansionary macroeconomic policies. Use of fiscal policy, that is—increased government spending and/or tax cuts—is the most common way of boosting aggregate demand, causing an economic expansion. However, the president may also induce the use of monetary policy to aid in the economic expansion. Technically, the **Federal Reserve Bank** that conducts the monetary policy is independent of the president and the Congress; its independence is created, in part, by the long 14-year terms granted to the regular members of the Board of Governors of the Federal Reserve. Nevertheless, in reality, it is hard for the Federal Reserve to completely ignore the pressure put on it by the president and the Congress. Because of expansionary macroeconomic policies, economic growth picks up before the elections and the labor unemployment rate declines, making people feel good about the state of the economy. People find is easier to land jobs and their money incomes rise, putting them in an upbeat mood to re-elect incumbents to their offices.

Once the elections are over, the inflationary effects of expansionary macroeconomics policies start to become evident. The closer the economy was to the full employment level before the elections, the greater the inflationary pressure. To curb the inflationary tendencies in the economy, the president and the Congress turn to anti-inflationary measures, such as reducing government spending and increasing taxes. The Federal Reserve is likely to further aid these efforts by increasing interest rates. The net effect of these anti-inflationary fiscal and monetary policies is that there is a downward pressure on the aggregate demand and the economy, as a result, slows down. At times, the slowdown may actually result in a recession—a period of negative, not just slower, economic growth. Once again, before the next election, the economy will need to be stimulated to put the people in an upbeat mood. These fluctuations are often called political business cycles.

FLUCTUATIONS IN EXPORTS AND IMPORTS. As mentioned earlier, the difference between exports and imports is the net foreign demand for goods and services, also called net exports. Because net exports are a component of the aggregate demand in the economy, variations in exports and imports can lead to business fluctuations as well. There are many reasons for variations in exports and imports over time. Growth in the gross domestic product of an economy is the most important determinant of its demand for imported goods—as people's incomes grow, they want more goods and services, including goods produced abroad. The opposite holds when foreign economies are growing—growth in incomes in foreign countries also leads to an increased demand for imported goods by the residents of these countries. This, in turn, causes U.S. exports to grow. The United States economy is quite huge. The net foreign demand for the U.S. goods and services has been negative for some years. Because of the size of the U.S. economy, the net foreign demand is not considered a major source of business cycles. However, this is quite often a source of business cycles in export-dependent smaller economies.

VARIATIONS IN THE MONEY SUPPLY. We have alluded to the role monetary policy plays in business fluctuations in the context of political business cycles. However, many economists consider variations in the nation's money supply, independent of changes induced by political pressures, as an important source of business cycles. The Federal Reserve has been entrusted by Congress with the power to use monetary policy to stabilize the economy around full employment (with low and stable **inflation**). It is argued that the Federal Reserve, in its attempt to stabilize the economy, manipulates the money supply. However, the Federal Reserve, due in part to inadequate knowledge, is unable to successfully fine tune the economy. Policy mistakes ultimately become a major source of business fluctuations in the economy. Both the inflationary pressures of the 1970s and the recession of 1981-82 are attributed to variations in money supply.

CAN BUSINESS CYCLES BE ELIMINATED?

As mentioned at the beginning of this essay, business cycles have been a part of the U.S. economy for a long time. After the Great Depression of the 1930s, it was realized that the government should conduct macroeconomic policies to manipulate the level of aggregate demand and to stabilize the economy around full employment with price stability. One of the two macro-

economic policy instruments, fiscal policy, is conducted by Congress and the president. The conduct of the other instrument, monetary policy, is left to the independent federal institution, the Federal Reserve Bank. The U.S. experience has shown that the burden of stabilizing the economy has fallen disproportionately on the Federal Reserve—fiscal policy is said to be slow to respond and less decisive due to political conflicts among policy makers. Despite many shortcomings and imperfections of monetary and fiscal policies, the evidence seems to suggest that they had an effect on moderating business cycles. While business fluctuations continue to exist in the U.S. economy, recessions in the post-Depression period have been relatively modest. While not all economists subscribe to the conclusion that macroeconomic policies have moderated business cycles, these policies continue to be used to this day for stabilizing the economy.

[Anandi P. Sahu]

FURTHER READING:

Gordon, Robert J. *Macroeconomics*; 6th ed. HarperCollins College Publishers, 1993.

Mansfield, Edwin. *Principles of Macroeconomics*; 7th ed. W.W. Norton & Company, 1992.

BUSINESS EDUCATION

Business education is a term that encompasses a number of methods used to teach students the fundamentals of business practices. These methods range from formal educational degree programs such as Master of Business Administration (MBA) to school-to-work opportunity systems or cooperative education.

PURPOSE OF BUSINESS EDUCATION

Business education programs are designed to instill in students the basic theories of management and production. The goals of business education programs are to teach the processes of **decision making**; the philosophy, theory, and psychology of **management**; and practical applications; and business start up and operational procedures.

BUSINESS EDUCATION PROGRAMS

Traditional academic business education programs include college courses that teach students the fundamentals of management, marketing, ethics, accounting, and other relevant topics. Students can earn degrees ranging from an Associate to a Ph.D (Doctor of Philosophy). Some programs may consist of classwork only while others, such as tech-prep and cooperative education programs, **internships**, and school-to work opportunities, combine academics with on-the-job training.

A tech-prep program is a four-year planned sequence of study for a technical field which students begin in their junior year of high school. The program extends through either two years of college in occupational education, or a minimum two-year apprenticeship. Students who complete the program earn either certificates or Associate degrees. Nationally, there are over 800 partnerships between high schools and two-year postsecondary high schools that offer tech-prep programs.

Cooperative education (co-op) is a program which offers students a combination of college courses and work experience related to their majors. Co-op programs are available in a wide range of business disciplines, e.g., information systems, accounting, and sales. Participants enroll in a postsecondary educational program while employed in a related job. Most co-op participants are paid by their employers. The co-op program provides students with the work experience they need to obtain full-time employment after graduation. More than 1,000 postsecondary educational institutions and 50,000 employers participate in co-op programs throughout the United States.

Internships are related closely to co-op programs. The main difference, however, is that those who participate in internship programs are not paid, as internships are designed specifically to provide participants with work experience. Often, interns will complete the program separately from their academic setting, rather than combining the two.

School-to-work opportunity programs focus on career awareness for students. They provide participants with work mastery certificates and furnish them with links to technical colleges. In these programs, all participants have jobs, apprenticeships, or further schooling after finishing high school.

Career academies are occupationally-focused high schools that contain "schools within schools." Primarily, they train high school juniors and seniors in such areas as environmental technology, applied electrical science, horticulture, and engineering. In addition to these schools, there are also privately operated business schools that grant certificates to students who complete their programs.

RESULTS

Business education programs provide participants with career paths for high-skill technical and professional occupations by formally linking secondary and postsecondary education, and by integrating academic and occupational learning. Students who complete such programs gain an advantage over people who concentrate solely on the academic part of business education. Whichever route students use to acquire a basic knowledge of business skills and principles, there exist ample opportunities to prepare them for business careers.

FOCUS ON BUSINESS EDUCATION

There is a growing focus on business education programs in the United States. This new emphasis reflects the fact that the United States is one of the few industrialized nations without an organized, comprehensive system to help young people prepare for careers and enter the workforce. Due to the increasing demands of a highly competitive global economy, employers have had difficulty finding workers with the academic, analytical, and technical skills they require. In recognition of this fact, the United States government has attempted to promote business education across the educational spectrum.

In 1993, the federal government passed the School-to-Work Opportunities Act to establish a national framework for broadening the educational, career, and economic opportunities for youth through partnerships among businesses, schools, community-based organizations, and state and local governments. In 1994, the government provided $100 million to fund the included programs. At least $90 million of the money was used for grants to states and local communities, including grants to partnerships in urban and rural high poverty areas. President Clinton requested $300 million for fiscal year 1995, at least 90 percent of which was earmarked for grants. The new emphasis on business education in the United States will place the nation's business owners in a stronger competitive position in the global economy, which will benefit the entire country in the long run.

[Arthur G. Sharp]

FURTHER READING:

Lynton, Ernest A. *The Missing Connection Between Business and the Universities*. New York: Collier Macmillan Publishers, 1984.

Rion, Michael. *The Responsible Manager*. San Francisco: Harper & Row, 1989.

Ryder, Kenneth G., James W. Wilson, and Associates, *Cooperative Education in a New Era*. San Francisco: Jossey-Bass Publishers, 1987.

Sharp, Arthur G. and Elizabeth O. Sharp. *The Business-Education Partnership*. Morrisville, PA: International Information Associates, 1992.

BUSINESS ENTERTAINING

SEE: Expense Accounts

BUSINESS ETHICS

Ethics are values that give individuals the ability to decide between right and wrong. Business ethics, in an academic sense, are generally concerned with analyzing and promoting ethics in commercial enterprise, both at the individual and the organizational level. The relationship between ethics and business is ambiguous; numerous routes have been taken to analyze the subject. Two common methods of investigating business ethics in the academic arena are: (1) to study the (often conflicting) views of famous philosophers, and (2) to examine case studies that shed light on ethical dilemmas. The first of these two approaches is emphasized here.

The concept of business ethics is relatively new, having become an issue and an organized field of study only since the 1970s. Although numerous factors have contributed to the increased interest in business ethics, a chief influence has been a shift in societal values that underlie the business system. The change in American values has been characterized, in general, by a move away from traditional Judeo/Christian ethics toward pluralism, relativism, and self-fulfillment. The end result has been a diminished base of universal moral norms and a subsequent interest in, and concern about, resolving ethical conflict. Understanding the evolution of morality in the United States is crucial to the study of business ethics.

THE PROTESTANT WORK ETHIC'S RISE AND DECLINE

The Protestant work ethic that was imported from Europe to North America during the seventeenth, eighteenth, and early nineteenth centuries was a set of beliefs that encompassed secular asceticism—the disciplined suppression of gratification in favor of ceaseless work in a worldly calling according to God's will. It included the concepts of hard work, self-reliance, frugality, rational planning, and delayed gratification that formed the foundation of modern capitalism and allowed American and European societies to accumulate economic capital. The Protestant work ethic dominated white American society through the 1800s.

This ethic aided in the emergence of an upwardly mobile bourgeois class—comprised of successful farmers, industrialists, and craftsmen—that was preoccupied with social conformity and materialism. At the same time, a much clearer definition of success and failure, developed that was wrapped up in material terms; this definition would play a major role in the societal evolution of the western world.

A significant factor that contributed to the decline of the Protestant work ethic was the accumulation of wealth, which gradually diminished the religious basis of the ethic. By the late 1800s, in fact, those religious roots were sustained primarily by independent farmers and small business owners in rural areas and small towns. In the growing cities, by contrast, the religious component, which included frugality, was jettisoned in favor of the conspicuous consumption of a consumer society. The devotion to work and creation of wealth remained intact, but even the concept of self-reliance was eventually watered down in the twentieth century by bureaucratization (the development of large corporations and big government).

As the original Protestant work ethic gave way to a ''success ethic,'' other factors contributed to a change in moral norms during the latter half of the twentieth century. The demographic makeup of the United States changed as large numbers of non-Protestants immigrated and joined the work force. They brought with them different value systems and confronted the society's Protestant bias. In addition, many Americans rebelled against what they viewed as suppressive social norms that had carried over from Protestant asceticism. Those norms were replaced by a belief in individualism and relativism—which holds that any individual's or group's values are as good as any other's. As a result, a societal bias against universal norms of behavior developed. Such beliefs carried over into views about business-related conduct.

The new morality underlying business behavior in the United States was characterized by an emphasis on salary and status, self-fulfillment, entitlement, impatience, and consumption, and an attitude that the ends justify the means, (or it is all right to break the law to achieve your goal as long as you do not get caught). Proponents of the new morality point out that it has resulted in the most productive economy and living standard in the history of the world. Critics argue that the lack of moral norms has created havoc in the business world (and society) that threatens long-term economic stability. They cite destructive business behavior, such as the dumping of hazardous wastes and the exploits of corrupt financiers.

THE ETHICAL DILEMMA

In addition to ethical issues arising out of changing norms and contrasting social theories, ethical dilemmas plague everyone, even individuals who are honest and confident in their moral stance. Conflicts result from day-to-day business decisions that are intrinsically influenced by factors such as loyalty. For example, in choosing a course of action, individuals must ask themselves whom they are serving with their decisions: society, the corporation, their God, themselves, their family, or some other entity. Saul W. Gellerman, in his essay ''Why 'Good' Managers Make Bad Choices'' in *The Business of Ethics and the*

Ethics of Business, identified four common rationalizations that lead to unethical business behavior by well-intentioned managers.

One reason often cited for engaging in immoral behavior is that the activity seemed to fall within reasonably acceptable moral bounds; because everybody else was doing it, it was not "really" illegal or unethical. A second rationalization was that the unethical act was performed in the interest of the corporation; perhaps the company even expected or ordered the violator to perform the act, possibly with the threat of reprisal for inaction. A third reason was that the offender believed that the conduct was safe because it would never be discovered—because the risk of getting caught was so low, it was okay to commit the act. Fourthly, offenses are carried out because the company condones the behavior, minimizes its impropriety, and assures protection for those who engage in it.

In fact, employees often do have a motivation to engage in technically unethical behavior for their corporations. Studies have indicated that whistle-blowing, or divulging unethical corporate behavior, is generally frowned upon by American society. Pressure from fellow employees, managers, and even the local community can cause an employee to continue even highly unethical behavior, in the interest of being a team player and not being labeled a tattletale.

CONTRASTING PHILOSOPHIES

The intensified interest in business ethics, particularly during the 1980s and early 1990s, was partly the result of diverging moral norms and a perceived decay of self-regulation and honesty. Paradoxically, however, it is the accompanying bias against moral norms that makes the study of business ethics so imprecise. Because all philosophies relating to ethics are generally assumed to have merit (i.e., none is right or wrong), most treatises and educational programs on the subject do not advocate a philosophy. Instead, they offer contrasting views for contemplation, such as those outlined below.

ALBERT CARR. The twentieth-century thinker Albert Carr believes that ethics do not necessarily belong in business; they are a personal matter. The business world might contain a set of rules for participants to follow, but those have nothing to do with the morals of nonbusiness life. Business, Carr asserts, is really more like a poker game, the purpose of which is to win within the context of the rules. Cunning, deception, distrust, concealment of strengths and strategies—these are all parts of the game. Business people cease to be citizens when they are at work. Furthermore, no one should criticize the rules of the game simply because they differ from societal morals.

Carr's basic views on ethics in business are recognized for the insight they provide into the dynamics of a free and competitive market. Critics point out that he views business ethics very narrowly, simply as a set of rules created by the government and the courts that must be obeyed. He assumes that one's role as a businessperson takes precedence over one's other societal roles. But, if one's personal morals conflict with business rules, should one have to compromise one's personal beliefs?

Further study of Carr's views reveals a bent toward ethical relativism, which supports his view that we should not criticize rules of business, even if they conflict with our personal ethics. A positive aspect of relativism is that it cultivates tolerance of other people and groups (after all, who is qualified to determine what the social norms should be for everyone?). But it also raises questions about ethical conduct. For example, is it okay to accept a bribe to award a contract in a country where that practice is accepted? Were the Nazis correct in their beliefs simply because others did not have a right to judge them?

MILTON FRIEDMAN. Friedman advocates the classical theory of business, which essentially holds that businesses should be solely devoted to increasing profits as long as they engage in open and free competition devoid of fraud. Managers and employees, then, have a responsibility to serve the company they work for by striving to make money for it. The very act of seeking profits is, according to Friedman, a moral act. An extreme example relates his point: If a person invested all of his or her savings into a venture and then the company gave away the money to the homeless, would that be ethical? No, proffers the classical theory, because the investor gave the money to the company in good faith for the purpose of earning a profit.

ADAM SMITH. Friedman's views generally support those of Adam Smith, who held that the best economic system for society would be one that recognized individual self-interest. That concept seems to conflict with the classical theory of business ethics. In his renowned *Inquiry into the Nature and Causes of the Wealth of Nations* (1776), however, Smith stated that society is best served when each person pursues his own best interests; an "invisible" hand will ensure that self-interested behavior serves the common social good. The competition that would result between individuals would be played out within the confines of government regulations.

Smith's invisible hand concept is based on the theory of psychological egoism, which holds that individuals will do a better job of looking after their own interests than those of others. A tenet of that theory is that enlightened egoists will recognize that socially responsible behavior will benefit them.

Both psychological egoism and the classical theory can be defended by the utilitarian argument. **Utilitarianism** maintains that any action or system is good if it results in the greatest good for the greatest number of people. In summary, if, as Smith contended, self-interest is a chief motivator and the invisible hand really works, then as companies seek to maximize profits, the greatest public good will result for the greatest number.

Critics of Smith's and Friedman's theories contend that they neglect the need for cooperation and teamwork in society, and that chaos can only be avoided with heavy policing of self-interested behavior. Proponents of the invisible hand counter that individuals will usually pursue cooperation and self-regulation because it is in their own interest.

JOHN LOCKE. Although perhaps best known for his advocacy of life, liberty, and property during the seventeenth century, John Locke is credited with outlining the system of free enterprise and incorporation that has become the legal basis for American business. His philosophy was founded on a belief in property rights, which are earned through work and can be transferred to other people only at the will of the owner. Under Locke's theory, which now seems intuitive because of its commonality, workers agree by their own will to work for a company for a wage. Shareholders receive the profits because they have risked their property. Thus, it is the responsibility of the company's workers to pursue profits.

Opponents of Locke's system, particularly proponents of **socialism**, argue that property rights are not inalienable. For that reason, Locke-style capitalism is morally unacceptable because it prohibits the public from benefiting from property that actually belongs to everyone. Indeed, according to socialists, the right to profits is not assumed because the profits emanate from the surplus value created by the work of the entrepreneur and laborer. In fact, property ownership itself is unethical. It is merely an attempt by powerful owners to keep control of their property and to exploit other people.

To their credit, socialist and Marxist systems do lead to less inequality. Utilitarianists, however, would counter that those more equitable systems do not produce the greatest good for the greatest number.

IMMANUEL KANT. The German philosopher Immanuel Kant believed that morality in all spheres of human life should be grounded in reason. His renowned ''categorical imperative'' held that: (1) people should only act according to maxims that they would be willing to see become universal norms (i.e., the Golden Rule); and (2) people should never treat another human as a means to an end. The categorical imperative is easily demonstrated: It would be unethical for a person to break into a long line at a theater, because if everyone did the same thing anarchy would result. Similarly, it would be immoral for a person to have a friend buy him or her a ticket under the agreement that he or she would reimburse the friend, but and then fail to pay the friend back.

Kant's theory implied the necessity of trust, adherence to rules, and keeping promises (e.g., contracts). When people elect to deviate from the categorical imperative, they risk being punished by the business community or by government enforcement of laws. More importantly, Kant suggested that certain moral norms are ingrained in humans that allow them to rise above purely animalistic behavior: People have the capacity to forgo personal gain when it is achieved at the expense of others, and they can make a choice as to whether they will or will not follow universal norms.

CASE STUDIES

Ethical violations at the Manville Corporation (formerly called Johns Manville) a manufacturer of asbestos, reflect the many dynamics that influence immoral behavior in large organizations. In the 1940s the company's medical department began to receive information that indicated that asbestos inhalation was the potential cause of a debilitating lung disease. Manville's managers suppressed further research and elected to conceal the information from at-risk employees, even going so far as refusing to allow them to view chest x-rays. The company's medical staff also participated in the coverup.

After more than 40 years of suppressing this secret, Manville was exposed and was forced to turn over 80 percent of its equity to a trust that would pay benefits to affected workers and their families. An important point of the case is that many employees—mostly ordinary men and women—participated in the cover-up, with reasons ranging from company loyalty to fear of job loss. Rather than hurt the company or damage their career, executives and managers chose to remain silent and conceal data.

A similar incident occurred in the 1980s at E.F. Hutton & Company, a brokerage company that pleaded guilty to more than 2,000 counts of mail and wire fraud. The company stole money from 400 of its banks by drawing against uncollected funds or nonexistent sums. It would return the money into the accounts after it had used it—interest free. Like Manville's coverup, the E. F. Hutton conspiracy involved many managers over a period of several months. The company encouraged its branch managers to illegally borrow from the accounts, suggesting to them that the practice was savvy business rather than a violation of law or ethics. In some instances, Hutton even rewarded managers for their skill at utilizing the funds. The managers were likely influenced by the perception that everyone else was doing it and that the company would protect them in the unlikely event that they were caught. In the end, several managers were fired and/or indicted. E. F. Hutton agreed to pay between $3 million and $11 million in damages, and its reputation in the financial community was damaged.

An ongoing ethical dilemma in the business world involves the tobacco industry. Critics of cigarette companies argue that, despite abundant evidence that smoking is a health hazard responsible for millions of deaths, manufacturers continue to produce and sell the deadly goods. The cigarette manufacturers counter that their product embodies a heritage of smoking that dates back several centuries. They also argue that data linking smoking to cancer and other ailments is lacking. Cigarette makers continue to advertise their products using positive, alluring images, and to play down the potential health risks of smoking. As with most business ethics dilemmas, rationalization and the lack of a clear-cut solution cloud the issue.

[Dave Mote]

FURTHER READING:

Bowie, Norman E., and Ronald F. Duska. *Business Ethics*; 2nd ed. Englewood Cliffs, NJ: Prentice Hall, Inc., 1990.

Braybrooke, David. *Ethics in the World of Business*. Totowa, NJ: Rowman & Allanhead, 1983.

Cavanaugh, Gerald F., and Arthur F. McGovern. *Ethical Dilemmas in the Modern Corporation*; Englewood Cliffs, NJ: Prentice Hall, Inc., 1988.

Freeman, Edward R., ed. *Business Ethics: The State of the Art*. New York: Oxford University Press, Inc., 1991.

Harvard Business Review, The Business of Ethics and the Ethics of Business; Boston: Harvard College, 1986.

BUSINESS FAILURE

It is safe to say no one goes into business expecting to fail. But in a free market the stakes are high and the odds of success even higher. One business fails every hour of every day in the United States. And with the failure of a business comes psychological, emotional, and even physical ramifications.

Indeed, as Harlan D. Platt pointed out in his book *Why Companies Fail*, the end of a business "is remarkably similar to death. The most obvious similarity is that when a company fails, its operations cease; however, unlike natural death, a failed company can be revived."

What are the symptoms of a failing business? Platt named several indicators, including: the company announces that it has acquired a new accounting firm; management disputes surface in a public forum; members of the board suddenly resign; or company executives sell stock.

Rare is the business failure that derives from one fell swoop of bad luck. More commonly, a lack of foresight and market understanding, combined with what Platt called "a series of ill-conceived choices," chip away at a company's success margin. There are two categories of business failure.

First comes economic failure, characterized by the fading of opportunities, minimal earnings, then finally negative profits (money loss). "Economic failure on a grand scale occurs when the business loses money," noted Platt. "The cash drain can continue as long as the owners continue to contribute capital." If economic failure is not stemmed, it is followed by financial failure, characterized by technical insolvency (debt obligations cannot be met), then bankruptcy (the company has little or no real worth in its current form).

BANKRUPTCY HISTORY AND BACKGROUND

Bankruptcy—the very word is associated with failure. But the reality of bankruptcy can belie those images. Indeed, many companies both large and small employ bankruptcy creditor-protection laws to work to their advantage.

Bankruptcy as a concept dates back to the Old Testament of the Bible: "At the end of every seven years you shall grant a release and this is the manner of the release: every creditor shall release what he has lent to his neighbor . . ." According to author Jeff A. Schnepper, the word bankruptcy means "broken bench": "In common-law England, when a merchant or craftsman was unable to pay his debts, the custom in the community was to break his work bench. This publicly established that the craftsman was no longer in business."

The modern concept of bankruptcy—which establishes equitable treatment for creditors and a second chance for the business owner-is found in the U.S. Constitution, which gives Congress the power to establish "uniform laws on the subject of bankruptcies throughout the United States." The first bankruptcy laws were enacted in 1800. Today, through revisions and reorganizations, bankruptcy standards are defined through the Bankruptcy Code, which is divided into four Titles. Under Title I, eight odd-numbered chapters cover various aspects of business failure. Such phrases as Chapter 7, Chapter 11, and Chapter 13 have entered the public consciousness.

CHAPTER 7 BANKRUPTCY

Chapter 7 bankruptcy is thought of as "traditional" bankruptcy. "This is where you either pay for, or give up, your property for secured debts," as Edward A. Haman wrote in his guide, How to File Your Own Bankruptcy. "You will surrender any non-exempt property in order to pay off as much of your other debt as possible. You will keep all of your other exempt property, and will be forever released from any obligation to repay the remaining debt."

The "secured" debts Haman described refers to one of two kinds of debt—secured and unsecured. A secured debt covers a certain piece of property. "The most common examples are home mortgages and car loans," Haman noted. "The papers you signed when you borrowed the money specifically state that if you don't pay, the lender may take the property." An unsecured debt is not covered by any property (e.g., the payments on a credit card).

According to Schnepper, "the liquidation provisions of Chapter 7 are perhaps the most important to the individual debtor." A Chapter 7 filing can be voluntary (initiated by the debtor) or involuntary (initiated by the creditors). In an involuntary filing, the creditor must establish that (1) the debtor is generally not paying debts as they become due; and (2) a custodian was not appointed within 120 days preceding the petition.

During liquidation proceedings, the debtor's property "is normally reduced to money as expeditiously as is compatible with the best interests of the concerned parties," as Schnepper wrote. "This property is then first distributed among priority claimants. . . . Next, distribution is made to general unsecured creditors."

The debtor does retain certain rights under Chapter 7. For instance, the government may not deny or refuse the renewal of a license, permit, or similar status (that is, a licensed plumber who files for Chapter 7 is no less a plumber). Nor may a public utility discriminate against a debtor "solely because the debt owed to the utility by the debtor for service rendered before the bankruptcy case was filed was not paid for when due, if the debtor, within twenty days after the case was filed, furnishes adequate assurance of payment."

CHAPTER 11 BANKRUPTCY

Chapter 11 reorganization differs from Chapter 7 liquidation in that, under reorganization, the purpose "is to restructure a business's finances so that it may continue to operate, pay its creditors, provide employment, and produce a return for its shareholders," according to Schnepper. "Given a successful implementation of this plan, the debtor will come out of the case as a newly organized company."

As Schnepper viewed it, Chapter 11 exists to provide reorganization opportunity for both voluntary and involuntary filings. And if the allegations in an involuntary case are not proven, the author continued, "then the petition will be dismissed and the court may grant the debtor costs, attorney's fees, and, if a trustee was appointed and took possession of the debtor's property, damages. A trustee may be appointed by the court to operate the business on behalf of the party filing an involuntary petition. If a trustee is not appointed, the debtor may continue to operate the business and to 'use, acquire, or dispose' of property as if the bankruptcy case had not commenced."

In a Chapter 11 proceeding, the trustee relationship will develop outside of the court's jurisdiction. This is to prevent any potential conflict of administrative matters "and not to involve the judge in situations where evidence will be heard outside the context of a dispute that he or she must decide." The debtor will "appear and submit to examination under oath at the meeting of the creditors," Schnepper continued. "The scope of the examination will be broad, including inquiry into the liabilities and the financial condition of the debtor, the operation of the debtor's business, the desirability of the continuance thereof, and other matters relevant to the case."

In return, the trustee must prove several points, including that he or she is not a creditor, an equity security holder, or an insider; is not and was not an investment banker for any outstanding security of the debtors; and has no interest adverse to the interest of the estate. The trustee will be responsible for all property received; file schedules, investigate the assets, liabilities and financial condition of the debtor's business; furnish tax information; and so on.

CHAPTER 13 BANKRUPTCY

Chapter 13 was formerly known as the wage earner's code; the debtor must be an individual, not a partnership or corporation. The law provides that a debtor who owns and operates a business may continue to do so throughout the Chapter 13 proceedings—anywhere from three to five years, typically. The debtor will negotiate a payment plan to his or her creditors while receiving protection against foreclosure due to outstanding debt. Payments are sent through a trustee, who then pays the creditors according to the plan.

But Chapter 13 payments, noted author Kenneth Doran, "cover only past debts. The petitioner continues to pay most current expenses directly. These include such things as utilities, medical expenses or insurance, . . . food and clothing, and car repairs."

Under the new Bankruptcy Code a Chapter 13 filer has the right to convert a case to a Chapter 7 liquidation or to a Chapter 11 business reorganization plan any time before confirmation of the Chapter 13 plan.

[Susan Salter]

FURTHER READING:

Delaney, Kevin J. *Strategic Bankruptcy: How Corporations and Creditors Use Chapter 11 to Their Advantage.* University of California Press, 1992.

Doran, Kenneth. *Personal Bankruptcy and Debt Adjustment.* Random House, 1991.

Haman, Edward A. *How to File Your Own Bankruptcy (Or How to Avoid It).* Sphinx International, 1990.

Platt, Harlan D. *Why Companies Fail: Strategies for Detecting, Avoiding, and Profiting from Bankruptcy*; Lexington Books, 1985.

Schnepper, Jeff A. *The New Bankruptcy Law: A Professional's Handbook*; Addison-Wesley, 1981.

Stein, Sol. *A Feast for Lawyers: Inside Chapter 11, an Expose.* Evans, 1989.

BUSINESS INFORMATION

For as long as there has been business, there has been business information. It pervades society, providing everything from up-to-the-minute stock listings to long-range market forecasts. As Michael R. Lavin put it in his book *Business Information: How to Find It, How to Use It*, such data have "two valuable applications: problem solving and strategic planning." As he continued: "Information can be used to evaluate the marketplace by surveying changing tastes and needs, monitoring buyers' intentions and attitudes, and assessing the characteristics of the market. Information is critical in keeping tabs on the competition by watching new product developments, shifts in market share, individual company performance, and overall industry trends. Intelligence helps managers anticipate legal and political changes, and monitor economic conditions in the United States and abroad. In short, intelligence can provide answers to two key business questions: How am I doing? and Where am I headed?"

There are two primary sources of business information: external (documentation made available to the public) and internal (data created for the sole use of the company that produces it, such as personnel files, trade secrets, and minutes of board meetings). External information, comes in a variety of forms— from printed material to broadcast reports to on-line dissemination. Following are examples of two major sources of external information: print (the oldest form

of mass communication) and on-line services (the newest form).

PRINT INFORMATION

The category of print covers not only a vast array of books and periodicals, but also government reports (the U.S. Government Printing Office, according to Lavin, "is the largest publisher in the free world; its products can be purchased by mail, telephone or through GPO bookstores in major cities"), microfilm and microfiche, newsletters, and other subcategories.

Perhaps the most accessible documents in the print category are books and periodicals. Public and private libraries house an array of reference books; hundreds of trade journals are published yearly; nearly every newspaper prints a daily or weekly business section; and titles such as *The Wall Street Journal* are synonymous with breaking business news.

There is print for every level of expertise or interest. "General magazines such as *Business Week* contain well-written articles on all aspects of business," Lavin reported. "Magazines like *Forbes*, *Fortune*, and *Inc.* carry detailed stories profiling individual companies and executives."

Then there are the trade journals, an enormous subsection of print aimed at a very select audience. David Owen, in his book *The Man Who Invented Saturday Morning*, noted that a typical trade journal such as *Milling and Baking News* "has a tiny circulation . . . [but] its influence derives not from the number of people who read it but from who those people are. About a fifth of the magazine's readers are the chief executives of milling or baking companies."

Another subcategory of the specialized print category is the material published through business information services, such as Commerce Clearing House, the U.S. Bureau of National Affairs, and Dun & Bradstreet. These materials are sent to subscribers as "slender publications, often containing only 10 or 12 pages per issue," as Lavin noted. The thousands of newsletter-type publications include Lavin's examples of "indispensable" newsletters, *Platt's Oilgram News* and *Scrip World Pharmaceutical News*.

ON-LINE INFORMATION

The phenomenon of on-line information is burgeoning as much as **computers** are themselves. "The power of the computer to store, organize and disseminate vast amounts of information has truly revolutionized business publishing," noted Lavin.

The first on-line services emerged around the early 1970s, used primarily by "professors, scientists, programmers and librarians who rarely thought to initiate non-specialists into their secret," as Doran

Howitt wrote. The author of the book *Databasics*, Howitt went on to say that the computer has become the modern equivalent of the old "grapevine"—able to deliver breaking news with a speed that traditional print just cannot match.

Basic on-line equipment is relatively simple. The initial investment consists of a computer, a modem (a device that links computers via telephone lines), and a subscription with an on-line vendor such as America Online or DIALOG. To Lavin, an advantage to on-line vendors' services is that "large online systems can help overcome the incredible fragmentation of published information. Many online vendors offer global search capabilities, allowing access to the contents of dozens of databases simultaneously, the equivalent of reading dozens of different reference books at the same time." Access to **Internet** on-line resources have also become popular as an alternative to more expensive services offered by on-line vendors.

For business applications, the Internet contains subcategories of news groups and servers. Robert Fabian reported in *CMA* magazine that "many colleges, universities, libraries, research groups, and public bodies make information freely available to anyone with an Internet connection. Often, the motivation is to make information available to people within the institution. But it can be less costly to provide general access than to screen access." There are risks along the Information Superhighway, of course. **Electronic mail**, for instance, is notoriously unclassified, and virtually anything a user writes can end up on the screen of anyone who asks for it. But such caveats have not deterred the millions of business users who count on the Internet daily.

On-line systems are made for user convenience. Command languages allow a user to find information based on the subtlest cross-references. Common commands, as Lavin described them, invoke Boolean—or logical—operators. The user employs the words "AND," "OR" and "NOT" to cull and edit from a vast array of concepts, while field searching "permits the user to specify the portion (or field) of a record where the information must appear. Searchers can then limit the search to words appearing in the title of the article, the lead paragraph, the company name field, or elsewhere."

CD-ROM INFORMATION

CD-ROM (compact disc read only memory) is a popular alternative to online services. As the name implies, CD-ROM is not so much an interactive system; in usage it is close to traditional print. In fact, CD-ROM versions of such print staples as the *Oxford English Dictionary* are now commonly available. Business applications for CD-ROM include corporate

directories such as Dun & Bradstreet's *Million Dollar Disk* and demographic statistics such as Slater Hall Information Products' *Population Statistics*. An advantages of CD-ROM over on-line services is the amount of data that can be stored. Drawbacks include less timely updates and more effort on the user's part to reach the range of data available on-line.

[Susan Salter]

FURTHER READING:

Daniells, Lorna M. *Business Information Sources.* Berkeley: Univ. of California Press, 1993.

Fabian, Robert. "Business Information and the Internet," *CMA—The Management Accounting Magazine*. November 1994, p. 9.

Howitt, Doran. *Databasics: Your Guide to Online Business Information*. Garland, 1984.

Lavin, Michael. *Business Information: How to Find It, How to Use It*. 2nd ed., Oryx Press, 1992.

Owen, David. *The Man Who Invented Saturday Morning: And Other Adventures in American Enterprise*. Villard, 1988.

BUSINESS LAW

SEE: Commercial Law

BUSINESS LITERATURE

Business literature is a term that means many things to many people. For some, there will be a debate as to what actually constitutes business literature; others taking a broad view will claim that business literature dates back to the 17th century and earlier to include treatises about the development of agriculture and trade, as well as works about the discovery and use of natural resources; and finally others will take a more narrow view and say that business literature is really quite new and clearly a product of the 20th century.

BUSINESS LITERATURE PRIOR TO 1906

The first problem that has to be resolved is differentiating between business literature and economic literature. This may seem reasonably straight-forward today, but if one takes a 17th century perspective on this issue, business literature and economic literature are virtually synonymous. For example, John Reynolds's *Perfect Directions for all English gold now currant in this Kingdome* (London, 1633) was both an economic treatise on money and a manual on bookkeeping. While the development of separate business and economic literatures didn't really begin until the 19th century, we find other titles from the 17th century that could have come off last week's best seller list: *A Way to Get Wealth* (1625), *The Way to be Rich* (1662), and *The Pleasant Art of Honey Catching* (1684).

Included in the pre-19th century business literature are chronicles of early explorations of Africa, Asia, and the Americas; discussions of a variety of occupations such as accounting, banking, and retail trade; explanations of inventions and discoveries and their commercial potential; and last but not least the works of Adam Smith (1723-1790), Thomas Robert Malthus (1766-1834), David Ricardo (1772-1823), and others. Some of this early literature has reached the status of "classic" and is still valid today. Some of the literature of that time was important for a limited duration and now has only historical value, while other writings from this time period weren't even valid at the time they were written. Other kinds of business literature began to appear that had a more utilitarian purpose. For example, as the pace of business accelerated (circa the 18th century) price lists—or more accurately prices-current lists—began to appear on a regular basis to help regulate commercial transactions. This can be seen as an early form of the kind of business literature published to answer very specific information needs. However, all of this literature, taken as a whole, prepared the business community for having written information available to help them conduct their businesses. And the roots of today's business literature in the United States and elsewhere spring from them.

From a strictly American perspective, business literature developed slowly until the 20th century. While the *Wall Street Journal* got its start in 1889, our three most-read business magazines—*Forbes*, *Business Week*, and *Fortune*—got started in 1917, 1929, and 1930 respectively. While many business book publishers trace their origins back to the 18th or 19th centuries, the number of business titles actually published was never very large until the latter half of the 20th century. One of the contributing factors in this "late" development of a business press in the United States is the lack of formal educational programs for business. The first U.S. business school, the Wharton School of Finance and Economy, was established at the University of Pennsylvania in 1881. Only two other programs, one at the University of California, Berkeley and the other at the University of Chicago, were begun before the end of the 19th century. Harvard's Graduate School of Business did not begin until 1908. With the development of these university programs came the need for textbooks and other works to support the educational process. This introduction of formal business education also helped lead to the professionalization of business and the begin-

ning of a clear delineation between blue-collar and white-collar workers. This lead further to the establishment of a variety of professional associations representing the sub-divisions of the business world. One of the major roles for most of these groups was (and still is) to contribute to their body of professional literature by publishing newsletters, journals, and/or books. Slowly the amount of available business literature began to grow.

BUSINESS LITERATURE SINCE 1900

If the first half of the 20th century can be characterized by slow, steady growth, the second half of the century has been more of a stampede. The outpouring of written information has been tremendous in all fields, and business ranks right up there with the leaders. By the early 1980s 52 percent of the magazines tracked by Folio (the trade publication of the magazine industry) were business titles. Furthermore, 40 percent of the 400 largest revenue producing titles were specialized business publications. Book production has also increased. Fewer than 200 business titles were published in 1950; in 1993 that number was over 1100. Business books also have begun to sell more copies. While some business-related titles had reached "best seller" status before, the first to make it to the number one spot on the *New York Times*best seller list was Norman Darcey's *How to Avoid Probate*, which topped that list for 17 weeks in 1966. (This is no small feat, for example the *One-Minute Manager* was one of the top 25 non-fiction titles of the 1980s, however, it never spent a week in the top spot.) In the 25 years between 1966 and 1991, business titles topped the non-fiction list in all but nine of those years, and some years saw two different business titles make it to the top position. Business publishers today take a very broad view of the definition of publishing, as business literature is available in print, electronic, audio, and video formats. One indication of this is that titles available in CD-ROM format tripled in two years from 24 titles in 1991 to 73 titles in 1993.

There are primarily four types of business publishers in the United States. The first are commercial publishers such as McGraw-Hill, Commerce Clearing House, Forbes, Inc., and many others who produce various kinds of business literature, from textbooks to newsletters, in hopes of making a profit. Some of these publishers produce only business-related material, while some cover other subject areas in addition to business. The other three types of business publishers can all be considered non-profit publishers, although their publications are not free. The first group of non-profit publishers includes professional and trade associations, who produce specific literature of interest to their members and/or about the field represented by the association. One of the best examples of this type of publisher is the American Management

Association (AMA), which produces multiple book and periodical titles annually. The second of the non-profit publishers are university presses. This group primarily produces scholarly works that take a more quantitative approach to some aspect of business. *The Harvard Business Review* is perhaps the most recognizable business title published by the university press group and one of the most widely read because it is not as quantitative as other academic titles. University presses are also more likely to publish literature that is mostly historical in content or has more of a regional focus or interest. The last type of business publisher is also the largest—government publications. The amount of business-related material produced by the federal government is tremendous. Similar publications from state, regional, and municipal jurisdictions in the United States alone make this source of business literature overwhelming. Government publications are outstanding sources of statistical information for areas like industrial production, employment, foreign trade, and the like. One of the biggest problems in using this kind of information, especially at the federal level, had been the time lag from when the data were compiled to when the publication was available. Use of CD-ROMs and other methods of electronic publishing have helped enhance the timeliness of this information.

The big question facing all types of business publishers in the mid-1990s is, "How will they respond to the challenges of electronic information?" For many publishers the trend has been to make their publications available in many different formats to increase use and revenue from that use. As the pace of the business environment continues to speed up, and as information technology develops to bring all kinds of information to one's desktop or laptop, the demand for electronic access to business publications will grow. This could restrict access to information for some, usually small and/or new businesses which may not have either the financial or personnel resources to support the technological infrastructure needed to remain competitive. No clear-cut resolution to this problem has been found. What is known is that business literature is very important now and will continue to be important well into the future.

SEE ALSO: Business Press

[William Fisher]

FURTHER READING:

1994 Bowker Annual; Library and Book Trade Almanac, 39th ed. R.R. Bowker, 1994.

American Library Annual for 1956-1957. R.R. Bowker, 1957.

Bear, John. *The #1 New York Times Bestseller*. Ten Speed Press, 1992.

Cole, Arthur H. *The Historical Development of Economic and Business Literature*. Baker Library, Harvard Graduate School of Business Administration, 1957.

Fisher, William, ed. *Business Journals of the United States*. Greenwood Press, 1991.

Forsyth, David P. *The Business Press in America, 1750-1865*. Chilton Books, 1964.

Gussow, Don. *The New Business Journalism; An Insider's Look at the Workings of America's Business Press*. Harcourt Brace Jovanovich Publishers, 1984.

Hirsch, Donald. *Financial and Economic Journalism; Analysis, Interpretation, and Reporting*. New York University Press, 1978.

BUSINESS LOGISTICS

Business logistics refers to a group of related activities all involved in the movement and storage of products and information—from the sources of raw materials through to final consumers and beyond to recycling and disposal. Business logistics is a relatively new term and concept in modern business vocabulary; its origins can be traced back to World War II when the ability to mobilize personnel and matériel was critical to the outcome of the war. The first university level courses and textbooks dealing with business logistics appeared in the United States in the 1960s.

The relatively recent development of business logistics has led, as it has evolved, to the use of a variety of terms to refer to it. In the 1960s and 1970s the terms **physical distribution**, distribution, materials management, and physical supply were common. Physical distribution and distribution refer to the outbound flow of goods from the end of the production process to the consumer; physical supply and materials management refer to the inbound flow of material to the production process. As the importance of coordinating the entire flow of material from the raw materials to the end consumer became recognized, the term business logistics became widely used to reflect the broadening of the concept. Today, the term **supply chain management** is coming into use to reflect the importance of forming alliances and partnerships to streamline the flow of materials. Business logistics remains the dominant, all-encompassing term for this important concept at this time.

The most widely used definition of business logistics is that of the Council of Logistics Management (CLM) of Oak Brook, Illinois, the largest and best known of the professional logistics organizations. The CLM definition is: "Logistics is the process of planning, implementing and controlling the efficient, effective flow and storage of raw materials, in-process inventory, finished goods, services, and related information from point of origin to point of consumption (including inbound, outbound, internal, and external movements) for the purpose of conforming to customer requirements.''

For many people, what is often referred to as the ''seven rights'' provides a good working definition of logistics. The ''seven rights'' state that the logistician's job is to ensure the availability of the right product at the right time in the right quantity in the right condition at the right place for the right customer at the right cost.

Although these definitions refer primarily to managing the flow of goods, business logistics is also important in service organizations. It is important to recognize that all firms produce both goods and services, some more of one than the other, that all firms purchase supplies; and that all must meet or exceed customer expectations. In service organizations the logistician's job is to ensure the provision of all required inputs, including materials and information, at the point of service delivery.

The importance of business logistics to the economy is significant. According to estimates made by Robert V. Delaney of Cass Logistics, Inc., business logistics accounted for approximately 11 percent or $600 billion of the **gross national product** of the United States in 1991. Of the $600 billion, Delaney estimated that approximately $352 billion was spent on freight transportation; $221 billion on warehousing, storage and inventory carrying costs; and $27 billion for communication and management of logistical systems.

To the organization, business logistics is important in several ways. First, business logistics provides an opportunity for the firm to create a sustainable competitive advantage for itself by designing a system which fulfills customers needs better than the competition. For example, the firm could offer faster, more accurate, and more consistent order filling and delivery than competitors are capable of providing. Secondly, due to its complexity, a superior logistics system is a proprietary asset that cannot be easily duplicated. Many firms have begun to view business logistics as an effective competitive weapon.

HISTORY AND BACKGROUND

The activities which make up business logistics, such as transportation and storage, are as old as trade itself. The concept of grouping them together and managing them as a system, however, is quite new.

Traditionally, the responsibility for logistical activities have been scattered throughout the organization. For example, transportation might be under manufacturing, with finished goods inventory and warehousing under marketing and sales. Where management of the logistics system is uncoordinated, diseconomies will be found. For example, manufacturing

may choose to reduce transportation and manufacturing costs by producing and shipping in very large quantities—and in so doing greatly increase the costs of storage and the investment in inventory well beyond the amount saved in transportation costs. With proper coordination, transportation, manufacturing, storage, and inventory investment costs could be balanced so that the firm's total cost would be minimized. The initial development of business logistics began in the 1950s with an understanding of the potential for cost savings if the management of the logistical activities was coordinated.

There were a number of factors present in the 1950s which encouraged attempts to coordinate the management of logistical functions. In general, these attempts focused on cost savings and on the physical distribution or outbound part of the system.

An important factor present in many organizations were managers with military logistics experience from World War II. Not only did they have an understanding of the interrelationships found in logistics systems, but some of them also had used management science techniques developed during the war— such as linear programming and simulation, which are well suited to analyzing logistics problems.

Another factor which proved to be important in focusing management attention on logistics was the economic recession of 1958. Cost cutting was brought on by the recession and many firms targeted logistics because it was believed to have more potential than manufacturing and marketing. Manufacturing had been studied by industrial engineers for many years and it was believed that most of the excess costs had already been squeezed out. Marketing, although costly, was not understood well enough to intelligently cut costs. For example, most firms were probably spending more than was optimal on advertising but the relationship between sales and advertising was not known well enough to tell which advertising costs to cut. In addition, marketing costs are often difficult to quantify whereas logistics costs can be quantified—because tangible things are being moved and stored they can be tracked.

Two other developments in the business environment which began during this period and persist to the present are the proliferation of products and the shift of power to retailers from large manufacturers of national brands. The proliferation of new products and variations on existing products is the outcome of the application of the marketing concept and market segmentation. Marketers, attempting to satisfy their customers' increasing interest in fashion and their changing lifestyles, have offered more and more products to smaller and smaller segments of the market. Examples abound on retailer shelves. Consider such products as large appliances originally available only in white, or plastic trash bags, cereals, frozen prepared foods, athletic shoes, office furniture, cosmetics, and so on. Not only are more and more products available but the life cycles of the products are shortening. To remain competitive manufacturers must offer a continuous stream of new products.

Product proliferation and shorter product life cycles force logisticians to deal with growing complexity. Each time a new product or product variation is offered it increases the number of products to be manufactured, stored, transported, and generally kept track of. At the retail level the problem is compounded. A manufacturer may add a new color of a product thereby increasing its product line by one, but if all four of the manufacturer's competitors also add the new color, the retailer will be faced with five new products.

As retailers such as Wal-Mart and Kmart continue to grow in size and as their knowledge of the market becomes more and more sophisticated, their power relative to manufacturers also grows. As retailers expand to serve national (and more recently international) markets, they control access to larger and larger segments of the market. In addition, with the use of point-of-sale computerized information systems, retailers have much better and more timely information about customers than manufacturers.

Initially retailers used their newfound clout to push inventory back onto manufacturers. They reduced the storage space in stores and required smaller and more frequent deliveries to stores, thus increasing both transportation and inventory costs for manufacturers. More recently retailers such as Wal-Mart have used their size and information systems to forge partnerships with manufacturers and to design streamlined logistics systems that are more economical and result in fewer empty spaces on retail shelves. For example, sales information may be fed directly from the point of sale to the factory where production schedules are developed based on actual demand; and the product is then shipped directly to the retailer, bypassing several previously used storage facilities.

All of these factors caused many organizations to focus on their logistics systems in a way that was different than any time in the past. The recession, combined with more products to manufacture, move, and store as well as retailers forcing inventory back on them, caused manufacturers to focus on the large potential cost savings available from managing logistics as a system.

Another factor whose importance to the development of business logistics cannot be underestimated is the evolution of **computers and computer systems**. To realize the full potential of business logistics management requires the timely processing and analysis of tremendous amounts of data. It is not uncommon for a firm to have thousands of customers ordering thousands of products—resulting in tens of thousands of transactions and shipments, hundreds of suppliers shipping thousands of parts and components, and multiple factory and warehouse locations each with inventories to be tracked, and all of this occurring across several countries and continents.

Needless to say manual analysis and day-to-day control of all of this is not possible. It is probably not an overstatement to say that the computer has allowed the business logistics concept to be implemented. The computer is essential to process the thousands of transactions and record changes that occur daily. Computers are needed to analyze the logistics system to make plans concerning such things as where best to locate warehouses, the amount of inventory to have on hand at the various warehouses throughout the system, the efficient scheduling and routing of trucks, the scheduling of factories to make the products demanded by customers, and many other decisions which must be made to manage a logistics system.

During the 1950s and 1960s logisticians concentrated on reducing costs primarily in the physical distribution or outbound side of the system. In the 1970s attention shifted to the materials management or inbound side of the logistics system and to improving customer service along with reducing costs. The shift in focus to materials management was largely the result of the OPEC oil embargo which severely limited supplies of petroleum and related products such as plastics. Many firms began to place emphasis on using the logistics system to improve customer service as the pace of competition quickened in the United States, especially from firms located overseas. The net result was that many firms began to look for ways to integrate materials management and physical distribution and thus to adopt the concept of business logistics. In addition, many firms began to view business logistics as a way to strengthen their relations with customers through improved customer service.

The 1970s were also a time of relatively high inflation and **interest rates**. The high interest rates prompted many firms to reconsider their investments in inventories and to look for ways to reduce them.

The 1980s began with the federal deregulation of transportation in the United States. The changes in transportation regulation resulted in a much more competitive and flexible transportation system. Freight rates fell and transportation companies were allowed to tailor their service to the needs of individual customers. Many companies were also able to reduce inventory levels by using fast, responsive transportation service to deliver to customers from centrally located inventories, rather than having products stored close to customers.

The 1980s also saw the full development of truly global companies. These are companies that source parts and components in different countries for assembly in another country into products destined for markets in several others. The scope and complexity of the logistics systems of these firms far exceed those of a purely domestic company. The success or failure of such firms is even more dependent on an effective logistics system.

A third development of the 1980s which has had profound effects upon the concept of business logistics was the introduction of just-in-time (JIT) production from Japan to the rest of the world. The idea of producing only what is required at the time it is required has revolutionized repetitive manufacturing. Small quantities are delivered frequently on very stringent schedules in JIT manufacturing. Such systems are very dependent upon the logistics system to perform nearly flawlessly—not only in terms of meeting schedules but also in terms of doing so economically. It is necessary to combine several small shipments together in order to maintain transportation economies. Such systems require a great deal of planning and coordination across organizations to perform properly.

During the 1990s the major factors affecting logistics are the developments in communications technology, such as **electronic data interchange (EDI)** and global positioning systems, the growth of third-party logistics organizations and strategic alliances and partnerships, and the tendency to view logistics as an important component in the firm's overall strategy.

Electronic data interchange (EDI), which is simply the passage of business information electronically between organizations, such as computer-to-computer ordering and invoicing, allows for the rapid transfer of information between the various organizations involved in the supply chain. For example, a manufacturer's computer calls a supplier's computer to place an order to be delivered at a specific time. The supplier's computer places the order in the production schedule and arranges for transportation by placing an order with a trucking company. The supplier's computer also keeps the manufacturer informed of the status of the order and when the trucking company picked it up. The trucking company's computer advises the manufacturer of the shipment's expected time of arrival at the manufacturer's factory. If something goes wrong, such as the truck is delayed by an accident, all parties will be informed and can formulate a contingency plan.

Global positioning systems (GPS) make possible the precise tracking and monitoring of transportation equipment. A truck outfitted with a transponder can transmit a signal to a satellite which then signals a home base with the truck's location. In this way the truck and its contents can be followed. The trucking company's computer would keep track of the progress of the trip and either advise the manufacturer or the manufacturer could track its progress by asking the trucking company's computer for updates. Some systems even have the capability to monitor such things as the truck's engine temperature, oil pressure, and brake systems. The type of capability made possible with technology such as EDI and GPS make JIT systems possible and allow firms to operate with leaner inventories across many countries and continents.

Third-party or **contracts** logistics companies began to grow very rapidly in the 1990s. These companies allow a firm to spinoff all or part of the management and operation of its logistics system to an outside expert, thus freeing up assets and management attention for the firm's core business. Modern communications technology such as EDI allows firms to spinoff important logistics activities to third parties and still closely monitor and control the logistics system. The relationship of the manufacturer and the third-party logistics firm is often a long-term strategic alliance or partnership where the manufacturer entrusts the operation of an important part of its business to the third party and the third party makes a major commitment of its own assets to the manufacturer.

Another development has been the recognition by a growing number of organizations of the strategic benefits of a well-run logistics system which is structured to enhance the overall strategy of the firm. Wal-Mart is a good example of this. Wal-Mart's basic strategy is to be the low-cost/low-priced retailer of general merchandise. Like others who have this same basic strategy, Wal-Mart manages its stores efficiently and buys in volume at low prices. Where it excels and beats the competition, however, is in the management of its logistics system. Through the use of a very sophisticated communication system and strategically located distribution centers, Wal-Mart is able to supply its stores with proportionately fewer assets tied up in inventory and less money spent on transportation than its competitors. Wal-Mart's logistics system is estimated to give it a 2 to 3 percent overall cost advantage over rival Kmart.

LOGISTICAL ACTIVITIES

Logistical activities are the basic functions that have to be performed in any logistics system. They are the components of the system. It is important to recognize that they comprise the parts of a true system in that they are all interrelated and that very often a change in one will create a ripple effect of change through one or all of the others.

The basic logistics system can be described very simply. The process anbegins with a customer placing an order with the organization. A product is then either produced or shipped from an inventory to the customer. As more products are sold, more raw materials must be acquired from suppliers and more products produced to fill demand or replenish inventories. The way that the parts of this system are configured will determine how and when the customer receives the order. Thus, the output of the logistics system is customer service and the job of the logistician is to design a system that delivers a desired level of customer service at the lowest total cost.

Customer service can be defined and measured in many ways and, in fact, in most firms multiple measures will be used. For example, customer service could be defined as the percent of times a customer order can be filled from inventory (product availability), or the length of time it takes to get the ordered product to the customer (order-cycle time), or the percent of orders for which the correct product is sent to the correct destination, or the percent of orders the customer receives undamaged. The consistency or variability of the length of time it takes to get orders to customers has been found to be very important to customers, in fact more important than the average length of time to fill an order. Most customers if forced to choose would take consistency over speed. In other words, an average order cycle of 10 days with no variability would be preferable to one which averages 4 days but could take up to 14.

The starting point for the design of a logistics system is the determination of customer service levels that will give the firm a strategic advantage over competitors. The logistician must learn which elements are important to customers, how well competitors perform them, and how well the logistician's organization is perceived to perform them. The logistics system must then be designed to deliver the required level of service at the least possible cost. Determining customer service levels is an ongoing, never-ending task because customer needs are constantly changing and evolving—presenting challenges and opportunities to the firm and its competitors alike.

Transportation is a very important element in most logistics systems. It is often the most expensive element. Transportation is composed of five modes (air, truck, rail, water, and pipeline) and the individual companies or carriers within each mode, such as Union Pacific Railroad or Roadway Express. The logisticians' job is to select the modes and carriers which will deliver the desired level of service at the lowest cost.

Each mode is different in terms of its speed, reliability, cost, route flexibility, and the products it can practically carry. For example, air transport is often the fastest, but it is also the most expensive and is not usually practical for transporting large bulky commodities. Also, for short distances a direct truck delivery is usually faster than air. Truck deliveries account for at least a portion of most freight movements because they have the greatest route flexibility, are relatively fast, have moderate cost, and can carry a wide range of products. Railroads are usually used to carry large quantities over long distances (over 500 miles). Pipeline and water are relatively slow and inexpensive. Pipeline has the least route and product flexibility and water is susceptible to weather problems such as droughts, flooding, and storms.

Intermodal transportation is when two or more modes are combined to take advantage of the strengths of each. For example, the most popular form of intermodal transportation is the combination of trucks' route flexibility with the inexpensive long-haul capabilities of rail. In one version of truck/rail intermodal transportation called piggyback, a truck trailer is placed on a railroad flatcar. The pickup and delivery is performed by truck, and the long-haul terminal to terminal transportation is performed by rail, thereby capitalizing on the different characteristics of each mode.

Individual transportation companies or carriers also have varying characteristics. For example, the prices or rates they charge, the condition and age of their equipment, the points they serve, the length of time it takes them to get a shipment to a particular place, and the likelihood of the shipment being damaged may all vary from one carrier to another. In general, for both modes and carriers, the faster and more reliable they are, the more expensive they will be.

The logistics manager also has a choice as to whether the carrier to be used will be a common carrier, a contract carrier, or if the organization should buy its own trucks and set up its own do-it-yourself transportation company—called a private carrier. A common carrier is a transportation company—which offers its services to the general public on a for-hire, as-needed basis. A contract carrier is a carrier with which the organization establishes a longer contractual arrangement. Often the contract carrier will dedicate equipment to its customer and tailor its service to that customer, whereas a common carrier will offer mostly the same service to everyone on a first-come first-served basis. Many organizations set up their own private transportation operation especially if they have unique service requirements which cannot be met by common carriers. The disadvantage of having a private carriage operation is the investment in equipment, facilities, and people to operate and manage it. Contract carriage is often a good compromise.

The logistician has many choices to make in designing the transportation component of the system. Inventory is a very important part of a system and is found in many places throughout the logistics system.

On the inbound side inventories of raw materials or parts and components are kept in anticipation of their use in manufacturing. Within manufacturing, work-in-process inventory is found between the various stages of production and in production. Finished goods inventories may be kept in anticipation of demand by customers and may be found at plants or in warehouses in the field close to customers.

There are several very good reasons for having inventory in the logistics system. One of the most obvious is for customer service. Products are produced in advance of customer orders so customers do not have to wait for them to be manufactured. Customers are served directly from stock. Inventories may be held because suppliers offer cheaper prices if purchases are in large volumes. In addition, the cost of transporting them is lower if they are moved in large volumes. Inventories may also be held to achieve manufacturing economies. By producing in large lots that exceed immediate levels of demand, the costs of manufacturing may be reduced. Seasonality of products or seasonality of customer demand may also lead to inventories in the system. For example, tomatoes may be harvested in August and canned and stored to fill demand in the winter months. Or, seasonal products, such as lawn furniture may be manufactured year-round but only sold in the spring and summer. During the fall and winter an inventory is built to satisfy demand in the warmer months. Finally, some products may require aging or ripening, such as meat and bananas.

Although there are very good reasons for carrying inventory, there are always costs associated with it. The largest cost of carrying inventory is the cost of capital tied up in the inventory. In other words, if the firm did not have its money invested in inventory, it would be able to use that money elsewhere to increase its productive capacity or at the very least it could put it in an interest-bearing savings account. The capital cost of carrying inventory is an opportunity cost. If the money had not been tied up in inventory it could have been used to produce income. The income not produced is the opportunity cost. Other costs of carrying inventory include the danger that the product may become obsolete before it is ever sold or that it will be damaged or stolen while in storage. In addition, taxes may have to be paid on the value of the inventory, insurance may have to be bought to protect against loss or damage, and the space occupied by the inventory may have to be paid for. Holding inventory can be a rather expensive undertaking.

While the costs of carrying inventory may be a deterrent to keeping inventory, there are several other reasons for not carrying it which may be even more important than the cost. Inventory can be used to cover up problems rather than finding solutions. For example, an inventory of parts may be used to cover up quality problems with a supplier. When a defective part is found, it is just put aside and a replacement is found in the inventory rather than going to the supplier and correcting the cause of the defective part. Another example could be late, inconsistent deliveries from a supplier. An inventory of parts kept on hand to be used when deliveries are late rather than correcting the cause of the problem is obviously inefficient and wasteful.

Another problem caused by carrying too much inventory is that it reduces the firm's flexibility to meet changing customer preferences. A company with large stocks of current products and parts on hand must use up the inventory in the system before a new product can be introduced. In fast-changing markets competitors with lean inventories are able to adjust more quickly to changing customer needs.

Logisticians must continuously search for ways to acquire materials and operate factories efficiently while satisfying customers and carrying as little inventory as possible. Warehouses and distribution centers (DC) are where much of the inventory is kept. They are used to improve customer service by moving goods closer to the market and to reduce transportation costs by allowing goods to be shipped in large, economical loads to the DC, rather than from the plant in small, expensive shipments. Customers can be served more quickly from stock located in a nearby DC than from a remote stocking location.

Logisticians can choose between renting or leasing space in a public warehouse or building and operating the company's own private warehouse. A private warehouse or DC may be attractive if the firm's products require special handling, care or equipment, or if the facility can be used intensively. Public warehouses are attractive to firms that have seasonal sales patterns that would prevent them from fully utilizing the facility, or for firms that value the flexibility of being able to withdraw on short notice from a particular market. The logistician must decide how many warehouses and DCs to use, whether they should be private or public, and where they should be located to provide the desired level of service at the lowest possible cost.

The materials handling system is the equipment within the warehouse which consists of such things as cranes, forklift trucks, racks, and shelving which is used to move and store the inventory. The materials handling system is designed to handle a certain volume of goods of various dimensions and weights, and the warehouse is designed to enclose the materials handling system.

Logisticians are also concerned with protective **packaging** of the firm's products. The package should be strong enough to protect the product from all of the threats it is likely to encounter throughout the logistics system, yet be economical. The package will have a significant effect on the design of the materials handling system. For example, the dimensions and weight of the package and its stackability will influence the type of materials handling equipment which is suitable.

The materials management side of the logistics system is designed to support the production schedule which will determine where the firm's products will be produced, the quantities to be produced, and the timing of that production. The acquisition and procurement of raw materials, parts, and supplies are designed to feed the production schedule. The location of the source of inbound materials and their destinations, the quantities to be shipped and the timing of the deliveries all have serious implications for transportation, inventory levels, production schedules, and ultimately customer service. For example, companies using just-in-time production want small quantities of inbound materials shipped frequently to arrive on rigid time schedules and preferably from nearby suppliers.

In addition to the major logistical functions discussed above, many logistics managers are involved with related issues such as demand forecasting, salvage and scrap disposal, return goods handling, parts and service support, and plant location.

[George C. Jackson]

FURTHER READING:

Coyle, John J., Edward J. Bardi and C. John Langley. *The Management of Business Logistics*. St. Paul: West Publishing Co., Inc., 1992.

Lambert, Douglas M., and James R. Stock. *Strategic Logistics Management*. Homewood, IL: Richard D. Irwin, Inc., 1993.

BUSINESS PLANNING

Business planning is a management-directed process meant to design a desired future state for a business entity, and to define overall strategies for accomplishing the desired state. Through planning, **management** decides what objectives to pursue during a future period, and what actions to undertake to achieve those objectives. Successful business planning requires concentrated time and effort in a systematic approach which answers three basic questions:

1. Where is the business enterprise today?

2. Where does management want to be in the future?

3. How can the business accomplish this?

In answering the first question management assesses the present situation. The second question anticipates future profitability and market conditions, and leads management to determine the desired objectives and goals. Finally, management outlines a course of action and analyzes the financial implications of these actions. From an array of alternatives, management distills a broad set of interrelated choices to form its long-term strategy. It is in the annual **budgeting** process that management develops detailed, short-term plans that guide the day-to-day activities meant to attain the objectives and goals.

Through planning, management concerns itself with the future implications of current decisions it is about to make, and considers how these decisions limit the scope of future actions.

PURPOSE AND FUNCTION OF PLANNING

Planning enables management to affect rather than accept the future. Management sets objectives and charts a course of action so as to be ''proactive'' rather than ''reactive'' to the dynamics of the business environment. Management believes that through its continuous guidance it can enhance the future state of the business.

PLANNING CONCEPTS

Business planning is a systematic and formalized approach for accomplishing the planning, coordinating, and control responsibilities of management. It involves the development and application of: long-range objectives for the enterprise; specific goals to be attained; long-range profits plans stated in broad terms; adequate directions for the formulation of annual, detailed budgets, defining responsibility centers, and control mechanisms; and evaluative methods and procedures for making changes when necessary.

Implicit in the process are the following concepts:

- The process must be realistic, flexible, and continuous.

- Management plays a critical role in the long-term success of a business.

- Management must have vision and good business judgment in order to plan for, manipulate, and control, in large measure, the relevant variables that dominate the business.

- The process must follow the basic scientific principles of investigation, analysis, and systematic **decision making**.

- Profit-planning and control principles and procedures are applied to all phases of the operations of the business.

- Planning is a total systems approach, integrating all the functional and operational aspects of the business.

- Wide participation of all levels of management is fundamental to effective planning.

- Planning has a unique relationship to **accounting** which collects, books, analyzes, and distributes data necessary for the process.

- Planning is a broad concept that includes the integration of numerous managerial approaches and techniques such as **sales forecasting**, **capital budgeting**, cash flow analysis, inventory control, and time and motion studies.

A **business plan**, then, incorporates management by objectives, effective communications, participative management, dynamic control, continuous feedback, responsibility accounting, management by exception, and managerial flexibility.

BENEFITS OF PLANNING

Planning provides a means for actively involving personnel from all areas of the business enterprise in the management of the organization. Company-wide participation improves the quality of the plans.

Employee involvement enhances their overall understanding of the organization's objectives and goals. The employees' knowledge of the broad plan and awareness of the expected outcomes for their responsibility centers minimizes friction between departments, sections, and individuals. Involvement in planning fosters a greater personal commitment to the plan and to the organization. These positive attitudes improve overall organizational morale and loyalty.

Managerial performance also benefits from planning. Planning focuses the energies and activities of managers in the utilization of scarce resources in a competitive and demanding marketplace. Able to clearly identify goals and objectives, managers perform better, are more productive, and their operations are more profitable. In addition, planning is a mental exercise from which managers attain experience and knowledge. It prepares them for the rigors of the marketplace by forcing them to think in a future- and contingency-oriented manner.

HISTORICAL PERSPECTIVE

Planning has been a part of economic history for almost 5,000 years. Evidence suggests that in an agrarian economy most economic activity was governed by changing seasons and ran in short-term cycles of less than one year. Long-range planning of more than one year, although notable, was conducted by a few institutions and individuals. Extant records indicate the extensive use of plans in empire building, road paving, war waging, temple construction, and the like. Not until the Industrial Revolution in the United States, thought to have begun about 1860, did the scope and style of economic activity dramatically change.

The first major industrial expansion began with factories in the northeast and the canals throughout the middle-Atlantic states. Owners and developers employed long-term plans for the construction of their enterprises, but not necessarily for their operation. For the most part, they made decisions without the benefit of research and analysis. Since these businesses served regional markets, on-the-spot decisions sufficed as a highly expanding market masked poor business planning. With the subsequent development of a national rail system, economic activity became both more urban and national in scope. The rapid growth of the economy and the complex business systems it spawned called for new and sophisticated management techniques.

John Stevens (1749-1838) kicked off the boom in railroads in 1830. Track mileage expanded from about 6,000 miles in 1848 to over 30,000 miles by 1860. The surveying of lands, the engineering designs, and laying of track involved enormous amounts of long-range planning and implementation. The mere territorial expanse of the railroad required long-term financing and control of operations. The complexities of scheduling over long distances, the coordination of routes, and the maintenance of stations became overly complicated. With no historic model from which to develop paradigms, rail company managers eagerly sought solutions. The lack of speedy travel and communications did not bode well.

With Samuel F. B. Morse's (1791-1872) invention of the telegraph in 1844, managers gained the ability to coordinate and to communicate with unprecedented speed and efficiency. The era of the railroad hastened industrial development so that, by the last quarter of the nineteenth century, manufacturing replaced agriculture as the dominant national industry.

American business fell under the leadership of the ''captains of industry'' such as John D. Rockefeller (1834-1937) in oil, James B. Duke (1856-1925) in tobacco, Andrew Carnegie (1835-1919) in steel, and Cornelius Vanderbilt (1794-1877) in steamships and railroads. These men represented a burgeoning capitalist entrepreneur pursuing profit and self-interest above other national and cultural concerns. Their giant companies were characterized by new forms of organizations and new marketing methods. They formed distributing and marketing organizations on a national, rather than regional, basis. By 1890 previous management methods no longer applied to U.S. industry, and the study of business activities began in earnest. The corporate giant required new methods of decision making since on-the-spot decisions no longer served the interests of the long-term viability of the enterprise.

With the onset of the Great Depression, companies recognized the need for professional managers who applied scientific principles in the planning and control of an enterprise. Business planning, however, as it is known today, was not popular in the United States until after World War II. A limited survey conducted in 1929 found that about half of the respondents made plans in some detail up to one year in advance. Fewer than 15 percent, however, made plans for as long as five years. A 1956 survey found that 75 percent of responding organizations planned more than one year ahead. A more comprehensive survey in 1973 found that 84 percent did some type of long-range planning of up to three years. Little change was found in follow-up surveys conducted in 1979 and 1984.

The increase in the use of formal long-range plans reflects a number of significant factors:

- Competitors engage in long-range planning.

- Global economic expansion is a long-range effort.

- Taxing authorities and investors require more detailed reports about future prospects and annual performance.

- Investors assess risk/reward according to long-range plans and expectations.

- Availability of computers and sophisticated mathematical models add to the potential and precision of long-range planning.

- Expenditures for **research and development** increased dramatically, resulting in the need for longer planning horizons and huge investments in capital equipment.

- The postwar economy has suffered few cataclysmic events. Steady economic growth has made longer-term planning more realistic.

THE PARTICIPANTS

Planning is essentially a managerial function. Although the top executives initiate and direct the planning process, they involve as many key employees and decision makers as needed. Often, outside consultants assist the following personnel in the planning process:

The **board of directors** defines the purposes and direction of the business entity; the executive managers formulate objectives and goals; the **chief executive officer** gives direction and sets standards; the **chief financial** officer coordinates financial and accounting information with the **treasurer**, **controller**, and budget officer assisting; the chief operating officer provides production information; counsel provides a legal interpretation to proposed activities; also assisting are sales and marketing executives, department and division managers, line supervisors, and other employees who clarify the realities of the day-to-day routines.

Planning is an inclusive, coordinated, synchronized process undertaken to attain objectives and goals.

THE PLANNING HORIZON

Basically, there are two types of plans. The first is long range, extending beyond one year and, normally, less than five or ten years. Often called the strategic plan or investment plan, it establishes the objectives and goals from which short-range plans are made. Long-range plans support the organizational purpose by providing clear statements of where the organization is going.

The second is short range, covering a period of up to one year. Short-range plans are derived from an in-depth evaluation of the long-range plan. The annual budget is a quantified expression of the enterprise's plans for the **fiscal year**. It generally is divided into quarters, and is used to guide and control day-to-day activities. It is often called the tactical plan because it sets priorities, in the near term, for the long-range plans through the allocation of resources to specific activities. See Figure 1 for more detail.

FUNCTIONAL PLANS. Plans are often classified by the business function they provide. All functional plans emanate from the strategic plan and define themselves in the tactical plans. Four common functional plans are:

1. Sales and marketing: for developing new products and services, and for devising marketing plans to sell in the present and in the future.

2. Production: for producing the desired product and services within the plan period.

3. Financial: for meeting the financing needs and providing for capital expenditures.

4. Personnel: for organizing and training human resources.

Each functional plan is interrelated and interdependent. For example, the financial plan deals with moneys resulting from production and sales. Well-

Figure 1

CHARACTERISTICS OF THE PLANNING HORIZON

CHARACTERISTICS	SHORT-RANGE Up to One Year	LONG-RANGE More Than One Year
Objectives, goals, guidelines, and policies	Annual, quarterly, monthly budgets projecting profits, sales, costs and financing.	Strategic plan envisioning growth, repositioning, and capital/debt financing
Capital expenditures	Implementation activities within the annual budget period.	Basic capacity and functionality of equipment, buildings, infrastructure, and land.
Sales	Detail on sales departments and persons, products, customers, current markets, advertising and marketing campaigns in fiscal period.	Macro-view of potential markets, niche-markets, and intra-industry and global opportunities.
Personnel	Day-to-day operational and administrative concerns, labor-hour needs, training and organization.	Grooming and placement of supervisory, middle and top management.
R&D, design	Developing commercial applications to fit customer needs.	Basic research, new product development, and items of high capital cost which add to future viability.

trained and efficient personnel meet production schedules. Motivated salespersons successfully market products.

STRATEGIC AND TACTICAL PLANNING. Strategic plans cover a relatively long period and affect every part of the organization by defining its purposes and objectives and the means of attaining them.

Tactical plans focus on the functional strategies through the annual budget. The annual budget is a compilation of many smaller budgets of the individual responsibility centers. Therefore, tactical plans deal with the micro-organizational aspects, while strategic plans take a macro-view.

STEPS IN THE PLANNING PROCESS

The planning process is directly related to organizational considerations, management style, maturity of the organization, and employee professionalism. These factors vary among industries and even among similar companies. Yet all management, when applying a scientific method to planning, perform similar steps. The time spent on each step will vary by company. Completion of each step, however, is prerequisite to successful planning. The main steps are:

- Conducting a self-audit to determine capabilities and unique qualities

- Evaluating the business environment for possible risks and rewards

- Setting objectives that give direction

- Establishing goals that quantify objectives and time-frames

- Forecasting market conditions that affect goals and objectives

- Stating actions and resources needed to accomplish goals

- Evaluating proposed actions and selecting the most appropriate

- Instituting procedures to control the implementation and execution of the plan.

THE SELF-AUDIT. Management must first know the functional qualities of the organization, and what business opportunities it has the ability to exploit. Management conducts a self-audit to evaluate all factors relevant to the organization's internal workings and structure. A functional audit explores such factors as:

1. Sales and marketing: competitive position, market share and position, quality and service

2. Production: operational strategies, **productivity**, use and condition of equipment and facilities, maintenance costs

3. Financial: **capital structure**, financial resources, credit facilities, investments, cash

flow, **working capital**, net worth, profitability, debt service

4. Personnel: quantity and quality of employees, organizational structure, decision making policies and procedures.

THE BUSINESS ENVIRONMENT. Management surveys the factors that exist independently of the enterprise but which it must consider for profitable advantage. Management also evaluates the relationships among departments in order to coordinate their activities. Some general areas of the external environment considered by management are:

1. Demographic changes: sex, age, absolute numbers, location, movement, ethnicity

2. Economic conditions: employment level, regional performance, sex, age, wage levels, spending patterns, consumer debt

3. Government fiscal policy and regulations: level of spending and entitlements, war and peace, tax policies, environmental regulations

4. Labor supply: age, sex, education, cultural factors, work ethics, training

5. **Competition**: market penetration and position, market share, **commodities** or niche product

6. Vendors: financial soundness, quality and quantity of product, research and development capabilities, alternatives, foreign, domestic, just-in-time capabilities.

SETTING OBJECTIVES AND ESTABLISHING GOALS. The setting of objectives is a decision making process that reflects the aims of the entire organization. Generally, it begins at the top with a clear statement of the organization's purpose. If well communicated and clearly defined down through the hierarchy, this statement becomes the basis for short-range objectives in the annual budget.

Management articulates the overall goals to and throughout the organization in order to coordinate all business activities efficiently and effectively. It does this by:

1. Formulating and distributing a clear, concise statement of the central purpose of the business

2. Leading in the formulating of long-range organizational goals

3. Coordinating the activities of each department and division in developing derivative objectives

4. Ensuring that each subdivision participates in the budget process

5. Directing the establishment of short-term objectives through constructing the annual budget

6. Evaluating actual results on the basis of the plans.

The organization must know why it exists and how its current business can be profitable in the future. Successful businesses define themselves according to customer needs and satisfaction with products and services.

Management identifies the customers, their buying preferences, product sophistication, geographical locations, and market level. Analyzing this data in relation to the expected business environment, management determines the future market potential, the economic variables affecting this market, potential changes in buying habits, and unmet needs existing now and those to groom in the future.

In order to synchronize interdepartmental planning with overall plans, management reviews each department's objectives to ensure that they are subordinate to the objectives of the next higher level.

Management quantifies objectives by establishing goals that are: specific and concrete, measurable, time-specific, realistic and attainable, open to modification, and flexible in their adaptation.

Because goals are objective-oriented, management generally lists them together. For example:

1. Profitability. Profit objectives state performance in terms of profits, earnings, return on investments, etc. A goal might call for an annual increase in profits of 15 percent for each of the next five years.

2. Human resources. This broad topic includes training, deployment, benefits, work issues, and qualifications. In an architectural consulting firm, management might have a goal of in-house CAD training for a specified number of hours in order to reach a certain level of competence.

3. Customer service. Management can look at improvements in customer service by stating the number of hours or the percentage of complaints it seeks to reduce. The cost or cost savings are stated in dollar terms. If the business sells service contracts for its products, sales goals can be calculated in percentage and dollar increases by type and level of contract.

4. Social responsibility. Management may desire to increase volunteerism or contributions to community efforts. It would calculate the number of hours or dollars within a given time frame.

FORECASTING MARKET CONDITIONS. Forecasting methods and levels of sophistication vary greatly. Each portends to assess future events or situations that will affect either positively or negatively on the business's efforts. Managers prepare forecasts to determine the type and level of demand for products currently produced or that can be produced. Management analyzes a broad spectrum of economic, demographic, political, and financial data for indications of growing and profitable markets.

Forecasting involves the collection and analysis of hard data, and their interpretation by managers with proven business judgment.

Individual departments such as sales, and divisions such as manufacturing, also engage in forecasting. Sales forecasting is essential to setting production volume. Production forecasting determines the materials, labor, and machines needed.

STATING ACTIONS AND RESOURCES REQUIRED. With the objectives and forecasts in place, management decides what actions and resources are necessary in order to bring the forecast in line with the objectives. The basic steps management plans to take in order to reach an objective are its strategies.

Strategies exist at different levels in an organization and are classified according to the level at which they allocate resources. The overall strategy, often refer to as the grand strategy, outlines how to pursue objectives in light of the expected business environment and the business's own capabilities. From the overall strategy, managers develop a number of more specific strategies.

- Corporate strategies address what business(es) an organization will conduct and how it will allocate its aggregate resources, such as finances, personnel, and capital assets. These are long-term in nature.

- Growth strategies describe how management plans to expand sales, product line, employees, capacity, and so forth. Especially necessary for dynamic markets where product life cycles are short, growth strategies can be (a) in the expansion of the current business line, (b) in vertical integration of suppliers and end-users, and (c) in diversifying into a different line of business.

- Stability strategies reflect a management satisfied with the present course of action and determined to maintain the status quo. Successful in environments changing very slowly this strategy does not preclude working toward operational efficiencies and productivity increases.

- Defensive strategies, or retrenchment, are necessary to reduce overall exposure and

activity. Defensive strategies are used: to reverse negative trends in profitability by decreasing costs and turning around the business operations; to divest part or all of a business to raise cash; and to liquidate an entire company for an acceptable profit.

- Business strategies focus on sales and production schemes designed to enhance competition and increase profits.

- Functional strategies deal with finance, marketing, personnel, organization, etc. These are expressed in the annual budget and address day-to-day operations.

EVALUATING PROPOSED PLANS. Management undertakes a complete review and evaluation of the proposed strategies to determine their feasibility and desirability. Some evaluations call for the application of good judgment—the use of common sense. Others use sophisticated and complex mathematical models.

Prior to directing the development of a profit budget for the upcoming annual period, management resolves issues related to the internal workings of the organization from a behavioral point of view. For example:

- Ensuring managerial sophistication in the application of the plans

- Developing a realistic profit plan, and assigning adequate responsibility and control

- Establishing appropriate standards and objectives

- Communicating the attitudes, policies, and guidelines to operational and administrative personnel

- Attaining managerial flexibility in the execution of the plans

- Evaluating and updating the system to harmonize with the changing operational and business environments.

ASSESSING ALTERNATIVE STRATEGIC PLANS. Because of the financial implications inherent in the allocation of resources, management approaches the evaluation of strategic alternatives and plans using comprehensive profit planning and control. Management quantifies the relevant strategies in **pro forma statements** that demonstrate the possible future financial impact of the various courses of action available. Some examples of pro forma statements are: budgets, income statements, **balance sheet**s, and **cash flow statement**s.

The competing strategic long-range plans constitute simulation models that are quite useful in evaluating the financial effects of the different alternatives under consideration. Based on different sets of assumptions regarding the interaction of the entity with the outside world, these plans propose various scenarios of sales, production costs, profitability, and viability. Generally categorized as normal (expected results), above normal (best case), and below normal (worst case), the competing plans project possible outcomes at input/output levels within specified operating ranges attainable within the fiscal year.

In developing and using planning and control programs, management benefits from the realization that:

- Profit plans do not replace management and administration, but are tools for managers with which to keep business activities on track.

- Vigilance and consistent review are necessary because the plans are made in the present about future events and outcomes. Management's plans are highly dependent on the quality of its estimates and judgment. Therefore, it must be flexible in utilizing the results of models and in interpreting the actual results.

- Dynamic management continuously adapts plans to a changing environment, seeks improvements, and educates the organization.

- Profit plans do not implement themselves. Management must direct, coordinate, and control relevant actions. Management must have a sophisticated understanding of the plans, be convinced of their importance, and meaningfully participate in their implementation.

Management bases its choices on the overall return on investment (ROI) objective, the growth objective, and other dominant objectives. Management selects courses of action relative to pricing policy, advertising campaigns, capital expenditure programs, available financing, R&D, and so forth.

In choosing between alternative plans, management considers:

- the volume of sales likely attainable
- the volume of production currently sustainable
- the size and abilities of the sales forces
- the quality and quantity of distribution channels
- competitors' activities and products
- the pace and likelihood of technological advances
- changes in consumer demand
- the costs and time horizon of implementing changes
- capital required by the plan

- the ability of current employees to execute proposed plans.

CONTROLLING THE PLAN THROUGH THE ANNUAL BUDGET

Control of the business entity is essentially a managerial and supervisory function. Control consists of those actions necessary to assure that the entity's resources and operations are focused on attaining established objectives, goals, and plans. Control compares actual performance to predetermined standards and takes action when necessary to correct variances from the standards.

Control, exercised continuously, flags potential problems so that crises may be prevented. It also standardizes the quality and quantity of output, and provides managers with objective information about employee performance.

In recent years some of these functions have been assigned to the point of action, the lowest level at which decisions are made. This is possible because management carefully grooms and motivates employees through all levels to accept the organization's way of conducting business.

The planning process provides for two types of control mechanisms:

1. Feedforward: providing a basis for control at the point of action (the decision point); and

2. Feedback: providing a basis for measuring the effectiveness of control after implementation.

Management's role is to feedforward a futuristic vision of where the company is going and how it is to get there, and to make purposive decisions coordinating and directing employee activities. Effective management control results from leading people by force of personality and through persuasion; providing and maintaining proper training, planning, and resources; and improving quality and results through evaluation and feedback.

Effective management means goal attainment. In a profit-making business or any income generating endeavor, success is measured in dollars and dollar-derivative percentages. The comparison of actual results to budget expectations becomes a formalized, routine process that:

- measures performance against predetermined objectives, plans and standards
- communicates results to appropriate personnel
- analyzes variations from the plans in order to determine the underlying causes
- corrects deficiencies and maximizes successes

- chooses and implements the most promising alternatives

- implements follow-up to appraise the effectiveness of corrective actions

- solicits and encourages feedback to improve on-going and future operations.

THE ROLE OF ACCOUNTING

Accounting plays a key role in all planning and control because it: provides data necessary for use in preparing estimates; analyzes and interprets these data; designs and operates the budgeting and control procedures; and consolidates and reviews budgetary proposals.

DATA COLLECTION. Accounting is at the heart of control since it compiles records of the costs and benefits of the company's activities in considerable detail, establishes a historical basis upon which to base forecasts, and calculates performance measures.

DATA ANALYSIS. Accounting's specialty is in the control function, yet their analysis is indispensable to the planning process. Accounting adjusts and interprets the data to allow for changes in company-specific, industry-specific, and economy-wide conditions.

BUDGET AND CONTROL ADMINISTRATION. Accountants play a key role in designing and securing support for the procedural aspects of the planning process. In addition, they design and distribute forms for the collection and booking of detailed data on all aspects of the business.

CONSOLIDATION AND REVIEW. Although operating managers have the main responsibility of planning, accounting compiles and coordinates the elements. Accountants subject proposed budgets to feasibility and profitability analyses to determine conformity with accepted standards and practices.

SUMMARY

Business planning is more than simply forecasting future events and activities. Planning is a rigorous, formal, intellectual, and standardized process. Planning is a dynamic, complex decision-making process where management evaluates its ability to manipulate controllable factors and to respond to uncontrollable factors in an environment of uncertainty.

Management evaluates and compares different possible courses of action it believes will be profitable. It employs a number of analytical tools and personnel, especially in accounting, to prepare the appropriate data, make forecasts, construct plans, evaluate competing plans, make revisions, choose a course of action, and implement that course of action.

After implementation managerial control consists of efforts to prevent unwanted variances from planned outcomes, to record events and their results, and to take action in response to this information.

SEE ALSO: Break-Even Analysis, Business Conditions

[Roger J. AbiNader]

FURTHER READING:

Black, Homer A., John E. Champion, and Gibbes U. Miller. *Accounting in Business Decisions: Theory, Method, and Use.* 3rd ed. Prentice Hall, 1973.

Ewing, David W. *Long-Range Planning for Management.* Harper & Row, 1972.

Shillinglaw, Gordon, and Philip E. Meyer. *Accounting: A Management Approach.* Irwin, 1983.

Welsch, Glenn A. *Budgeting: Profit Planning and Control.* Prentice Hall, 1976.

BUSINESS PLANS

A company's business plan is one of its most important documents. It can serve many purposes. It can be used by corporate or business managers and executives for internal planning. It can be used as the basis for loan applications from **banks** and other lenders. It can be used to persuade investors that a company is a good investment. For start-up ventures, the process of preparing a business plan serves as a road map to the future by making entrepreneurs and business owners think through their strategies, evaluate their basic business concepts, recognize their business's limitations, and avoid a variety of mistakes.

Virtually every business needs a business plan. Lack of proper planning is one of the most often cited reasons for business failures. Business plans help companies identify their goals and objectives and provide them with tactics and strategies to reach those goals. Business plans are not historical documents; rather, they embody a set of management decisions about necessary steps for the business to reach its objectives and perform in accordance with its capabilities.

SITUATIONS THAT REQUIRE A BUSINESS PLAN

Business plans have several major uses. These include internal planning and **forecasting**, obtaining funding for ongoing operations or expansion, planned **mergers and acquisitions**, divestiture and **spin-offs**, and restructuring or reorganizing. While business plans have elements common to all uses, most business plans are tailored according to their specific use and intended audience.

When used for internal planning, business plans can provide a blueprint for the operation of an entire company as well as specific divisions and departments. A company's performance and progress can be measured against planned goals involving sales, expenditures, time frame, and strategic direction. Business plans also help management identify and focus on potential internal and external problem areas. Proposed solutions and contingency plans are incorporated into the business plan. Business plans also cover such areas as marketing opportunities and future financing requirements that require management attention. By mapping out a business's future, business plans can be used to persuade management and others outside the company of its promising future.

Ideally, everyone in the company, from the upper to lower echelons, will use the information contained in the company's business plan. At the upper levels of **management**, the business plan is used to set performance targets for overall and divisional operations. At the divisional or departmental level, managers use the business plan to guide their **decision making** with regard to ongoing operations. They also assess personnel performance in terms of the objectives set forth in the business plan. Workers who are informed about the business plan can evaluate and adjust their own performance in terms of company objectives and expectations.

Another internal use of business plans is in the restructuring or reorganization of the business. In such cases, business plans describe actions that need to be taken in order to restore profitability or reach other goals. Necessary operational changes are identified in the plan, along with corresponding reductions in expenses. Desired performance and operational objectives are delineated, often with corresponding changes in production equipment, **work force**, and certain products and/or services.

Banks and other lenders use business plans to evaluate a company's ability to handle more **debt** and, in some cases, **equity** financing. The business plan documents the company's cash flow requirements and provides a detailed description of its **assets**, capitalization, and projected financial performance. It provides potential lenders and investors with verifiable facts about a company's performance so that risks can be accurately identified and evaluated.

The business plan is the primary source of information for potential purchasers of a company or one of its divisions or product lines. As with outside lenders and investors, business plans prepared for potential buyers provide them with verifiable facts and projections about the company's performance. The business plan must communicate the basic business premise or concept of the company, present its stengths as well as weaknesses, and provide indica-

tions of the company's long-term viability. When a company is attempting to sell off a division or product line, the business plan defines the new business entity.

PREPARING THE BUSINESS PLAN

The process of preparing and developing a business plan is an interactive one that involves every functional area of a company. Successful business plans are usually the result of team effort. Functional managers, with help from their work force, provide input based on their special areas of expertise and technical skill. Top management provides overall support for the planning process as well as general guidelines and feedback on the plan as it is being developed.

Some companies make the planning process an ongoing one. In other cases, such as for a business acquisition, it may be necessary to prepare a business plan on short notice. The process can be expedited by determining what information is needed from each participant. Then, participants can meet to complete only those plan components that are needed immediately. During the planning process, it is usually desirable to encourage teamwork, especially across functional lines. Different functional managers may work together to collect and analyze data prior to a formal planning session, thereby helping diverse managers reach consistent objectives.

A few basic steps can be identified in the planning process. The first step is to organize the process by identifying who will be involved, determining the basic scope of the plan, and establishing a time frame within which the plan is to be completed. Upper management not only communicates its support of the planning process, it also defines the responsibilities of each party involved. Work plans that supplement the general timetable are helpful in meeting deadlines associated with the planning process.

Once the planning process has been fully organized, participants can begin the process of assessment. Internal and external evaluations are based on extensive information gathering. Strengths and weaknesses are identified in every functional area of the business. In addition, the overall management structure of the company is evaluated. It is useful to assess and evaluate such external factors as the general economy, **competition**, relevant technologies, trends, and other circumstances outside the control of the company that can affect or be affected by it.

Setting goals and defining strategies are the next key steps in the planning process. Using the assessment and evaluation of internal and external factors, fundamental goals for the business are developed. Pertinent areas are the way it decides to compete, its market focus, and its customer service philosophy.

Specific performance and operational strategies are then established, based on these goals.

After strategies and goals have been defined, they are translated into specific plans and programs. These plans and programs determine how a company's resources will be managed in order to implement its strategies and achieve its goals. Specific areas that require their own plans and programs include the overall organization of the company, sales and marketing, products and production, and **finance**. Finally, these specific plans are assembled into the completed business plan.

ELEMENTS OF A BUSINESS PLAN

Business plans must include authoritative, factual data, usually obtained from a wide range of sources. The plans must be written in a consistent and realistic manner. Contradictions or inconsistencies within a business plan create doubts in the minds of its readers. Problems and risks associated with the business should be described rather than avoided, then used as the basis for presenting well thought out solutions and contingency plans. Business plans can be tailored to the needs and interests of specific audiences by emphasizing or presenting differently certain categories of information in different versions of the plan.

Business plans contain a number of specific elements as well as certain general characteristics. These include a general description of the company and its products or services, an executive summary, management and organizational charts, sales and **marketing** plans, financial plans, and production plans. They describe the general direction of a company in terms of its underlying philosophy, goals, and objectives. Business plans explain specific steps and actions that will be taken as well as their rationale. That is, they not only tell how a company will achieve its strategic objectives, they also tell why specific decisions have been made. Anticipated problems and the company's response to them are usually included. In effect, business plans are a set of management decisions about how the company will proceed along a specified course of action, with justifications for those decisions. Listed below are brief descriptions of the major elements found in business plans.

EXECUTIVE SUMMARY. This is usually a two- to five-page summary of the entire business plan. It is an important part of the plan, in that it is designed to capture the reader's attention and create an interest in the company. It usually includes the company's mission statement and summarizes its competitive advantages, sales and profit projections, financial requirements, plans to repay lenders or investors, and the amount of financing requested.

DESCRIPTION OF BUSINESS. The business description includes not only a profile of the company, but also a picture of the industry in which the company operates. Every business operates within a specific context that affects its growth potential. The description of a company's operating environment may cover new products and developments in the industry, trends and outlook for the industry, and overall economic trends.

The intent of the company's profile is to provide readers with unique features that give the company a competitive edge. A brief history reveals how specific products and services were developed. Contracts and agreements affecting the business may be mentioned (and also included in an appendix to the business plan). Other topics covered include operational procedures and research and development.

DESCRIPTION OF PRODUCTS AND/OR SERVICES. The goal of this section is to differentiate a company's products or services from those of the competition. It describes specific customer needs that are uniquely met by the firm's products or services. Product features are translated into customer benefits. Product life cycles and their effects on sales and marketing can be described. The company's plans for a new generation of products or services may be included.

DESCRIPTION OF MANAGEMENT AND ORGANIZATIONAL STRUCTURE. The quality of a company's management **team** can be the most important aspect of a business plan. This section presents the strengths of the company's management team by highlighting relevant experience, achievements, and past performance. Key areas include management's ability to provide planning, organizational skills, control, and **leadership**. This section also contains information about the company's ownership and work force. It may present an existing or planned organizational structure that will accomplish the goals set forth in the business plan. Specific management and control systems are often described.

MARKET ANALYSIS. A thorough market analysis serves as the basis for a company's sales and marketing plans. The analysis generally covers the company's competition, customers, products, and market acceptance. The competitive analysis details the competition's strengths and weaknesses, providing a basis for discovering market opportunities. A customer analysis provides a picture of who buys and uses the company's products or services. This section of the business plan highlights how the company's products or services satisfy previously unfulfilled market needs. It also includes evidence of market acceptance of the company's unique products or services.

SALES AND MARKETING PLAN. The marketing plan delineates the methods and activities that will be employed to reach the company's revenue goals. Different revenue outcomes may be presented to allow for contingency planning in the areas of finance and production. This section describes the company's customer base, products or services, and marketing and sales programs. The latter is supported by conclusions drawn from the market analysis.

PRODUCTION PLAN. A production plan is usually included if the business is involved in **manufacturing** a product. Based on the sales and marketing plan, the production plan covers production options that are available to produce a desired mix of products. The production plan contains information that allows for budgeting (e.g., for labor and materials). In non-manufacturing companies, this section would cover new service development.

FINANCIAL PLAN. This section covers the financing and cash flow requirements implicit in other areas of the business plan. It contains projections of **income**, **balance sheet** items, and cash flow. The company's method of budgeting and its financial controls are described. Financial projections must be supported by verifiable facts, such as sales figures or **market research**. Monthly figures are generally given for the first two years, followed by annual figures for the next three to eight years. If the business plan is written for investors or lenders, the amount of financing required may be included here or in a separate section.

IMPLEMENTATION SCHEDULE. This section provides key dates pertaining to finance, marketing, and production. It indicates when specific financing is needed, when specific aspects of the marketing campaign will take place, and delivery dates based on production schedules.

CONTINGENCY PLANS. This section defines problems and challenges that the company may face and outlines contingency plans for overcoming those problems and meeting the challenges. Specific topics that may be explored are competitive responses, areas of weakness or vulnerability of the company, legal constraints, staffing, and continuity of leadership.

OTHER DETAILS. Most business plans include a table of contents and a cover sheet containing basic information about the company. An appendix may include a variety of documentation that supports different sections of the business plan. Among the items that may be found in an appendix are footnotes from the main plan, biographies, graphs and charts, copies of **contracts** and agreements, and references.

TAILORING THE BUSINESS PLAN TO SPECIFIC AUDIENCES

Business plans are organized to address major concerns and interests of their intended audience.

They are commonly tailored to a specific audience by emphasizing aspects that directly relate to the interests of the reader. For example, a business plan written to obtain a loan for ongoing operations would address the major concerns of potential lenders.

BANKS, INVESTORS, AND OTHER SOURCES OF FUNDING. Business plans are frequently written to obtain additional funding. Start-up capital may be needed for a new venture. The company may require additional working capital for ongoing operations. New capital may be needed to acquire assets for expansion. Equity financing may be needed to support a company's long-range growth. Potential lenders of debt or equity financing are usually concerned with minimizing their risks and maximizing the return on their investment.

Business plans written for this audience generally have a strong financial presentation and good documentation of projected sales and cash flow. Areas to be stressed in the business plan include the predictability of the company's cash flow, how well cash flow will cover debt servicing, the reasons additional funding is needed, strengths of the company's financial management, assets used to collateralize debt, and the capital and ownership structure of the company. In addition, business plans written to obtain funding for expansion provide details on the overall scope of the market and profit potential. Such plans typically enumerate the return on investment for equity investors.

POTENTIAL BUYERS. Potential buyers are generally interested in such factors as the basic business concept underlying the company, its long-term viability, and its strategic position within its industry. They also look for strengths and weaknesses in the company's basic functional components and its management team. Business plans written for this audience stress the company's strengths and include contingency plans designed to overcome weaknesses, challenges, and other possible developments.

Other factors that might be emphasized in a business plan written for potential buyers are the company's ability to improve profitability and market share, the company's competitive edge, the company's potential to take advantage of opportunities in related industries, managerial and technical skills within the company, and the company's financial capacity.

PARTIES INTERESTED IN REORGANIZATION OR RESTRUCTURING. Business plans written for a company reorganization may be tailored for a variety of readers, including internal management, outside creditors, or new owners. Such a plan sets forth the necessary action designed to reorganize or restructure the company to achieve greater profitability or production capacity. The business plan identifies operational changes that need to be made in different functional areas of the company. It establishes performance and operational measures against which the functional areas of the company are evaluated.

The audience for this type of business plan is interested in such factors as the timing and sequence of specific changes, the operational impact of such changes, and how those changes will affect costs, production, and cash flow. The business plan provides details on the new functional organization, as well as key personnel and their responsibilities. Transitional plans are typically furnished, and operating and financial goals are defined.

INTERNAL USERS. Business plans written primarily for use within the company generally stress the benefits that will result from the plan. These may include improved and more consistent performance, improved coordination and consistency among management, greater ability to measure performance, **empowerment** of the work force, and a better motivated and educated work force. The plan provides a comprehensive framework and direction for ongoing operations.

Business plans written for internal use typically identify the company's strengths and weaknesses, potential problems, and emerging issues. They set forth performance standards on which expectations will be based. Goals and objectives are clearly stated to allow for coordination and better communication between the company's functional areas. Desired outcomes are evaluated in terms of what can feasibly be achieved.

BUSINESS PLANS AS PLANNING DOCUMENTS

Business plans are not historical documents about a company's past performance. Rather, they are planning documents that provide information to decision-makers who can help the company achieve its goals and objectives. These decision-makers may be the company's own managers and executives, or they may be sources of capital or potential buyers. Regardless of the intended audience, all business plans address the fundamental strategic issues facing a business. They provide verifiable data and projections covering marketing and sales; production, service, and quality; product development; organization and management structure; and financial requirements.

[David Bianco]

FURTHER READING:

Covello, Joseph A., and Brian J. Hazelgren. *The Complete Book of Business Plans.* Sourcebooks Trade, 1994.

Kravitt, Gregory I. *Creating a Winning Business Plan.* Probus, 1993.

Massarella, Gregory J. et al. *How to Prepare a Results-Driven Business Plan.* AMACOM, 1993.

The business press is a major source of news about governmental regulation, corporate taxes, job leads, industry sales, even investment leads, since the business press frequently writes about emerging business trends before they are noticed by the general mass media press. The business press provides in-depth news features about individual companies and the issues facing different industries. It examines how business really operates and how it should operate. While business management books can take years to move from idea to research to the book store, the business press tackles the same issues on a monthly, sometimes weekly, basis.

The business press can be defined to cover a variety of disparate media. It can include the business section of the daily newspaper and the weekly business tabloid found in most cities. It also includes national daily, weekly and monthly general business newspapers and magazines like the *Wall Street Journal, Business Week, Fortune* and *Forbes*.

Trade magazines make up the biggest category of the business press. Each industry has at least one magazine covering it. There are literally thousands of magazines dealing with the day-to-day business intricacies of nearly every conceivable business. It is safe to say that no matter how small or new an industry is, there is—or soon will be—a trade magazine or newsletter that covers it.

Besides its importance for helping company owners and managers keep abreast of what is happening in their industry, the business press also offers many marketing and public relations opportunities. Many businesses selling only to other businesses use the trade press to promote their products and services through advertising and news exposure. While the mass media is busy selling deodorant and gasoline over the TV, the business press is selling industry-specific products through advertising that is usually more detailed and informative.

This focus also allows companies to get more detailed news coverage than they could expect from newspapers written for the average consumer and taxpayer. The trade press focuses on industry issues, new technology and how to use it, and new products. What newspapers may consider mundane information coming from a local company could be big product news worthy of extensive coverage in the trade press.

There can be no set "history" to the business press as it is one of the most diverse in all of publishing. Most early coastal colonial newspapers covered business news regularly by printing the arrival days and cargo manifests of ships docking at the wharves. As businesses and the nation grew, newspapers began to publish separate business sections. By the late 1800s when formerly small businesses were becoming national "industries," the first trade magazines came on the scene. National business press publications came along in this century to cover the country's emerging economic power. Today's business press has expanded to the point that business news junkies can watch cable TV programs reporting live on what is happening in the stock market.

TYPES OF BUSINESS PRESS

Two types of business publications are found on a local level in most medium to large cities. There is the local daily newspaper's business section plus a weekly business tabloid covering the companies in that locale. Besides general news concentrating on the major employers in the city, both publications usually feature local business columnists, management level new hires and promotions, times of meetings of business clubs, and coverage of how local company stocks are doing. The tabloids—usually owned either by a chain specializing in this type of publication or by a newspaper syndicate—will run special sections focusing editorial and advertising on special topics such as the environment or health care. These business tabloids offer good opportunities for business people to get local coverage through public relations efforts if they can demonstrate how their companies are having an impact on the community.

Many states also have at least one magazine covering the companies based in that state. Frequently owned by a larger news organization, the state business magazine concentrates on features and regular in-depth articles on the state's economy. Most publish an annual "economic outlook" for the state, a subject too big and of little interest to local newspapers and regional tabloids. Because the numbers of companies to cover are so large, PR opportunities are usually limited to "pitching" editors on the reasons why the magazine should run even a small feature on a particular business.

National business publications usually take in the big picture, looking at the largest and most innovative companies. One exception is the *Wall Street Journal*'s front page feature that focuses on quirky, sometimes small, business efforts or unusual social trends. *Inc.* is a national monthly magazine that tries to accomplish two tasks, report on medium-sized businesses, and help readers build their businesses by following the suggestions of the magazine. PR opportunities on the national level are tough since editors are inundated with requests to feature "unique" companies that rarely are all that different from each other.

TRADE PUBLICATIONS ARE LARGEST BUSINESS PRESS CATEGORY

The best PR opportunities and sources for information on running a better business are found in the trade press. Thousands of trade magazines, and an even larger number of subscription-only newsletters, cover only news pertinent to their industries. New product sections sometimes offer color photographs and detailed tests of the products by the magazine's staff. New hire sections and classified ads show where job openings are all over the nation. Many trade magazines have a legislative action section that covers state and national regulatory news that would never be carried in the local newspaper because of its specialization. Most trade publications feature detailed, researched "how to do it better" stories or interviews with industry experts.

The trade press can be very receptive to PR pitches if the news is important in the industry and if the company making the pitch is willing to cooperate with the magazine's editors and writers. The company seeking the publicity must be as open as possible with the magazine and go beyond the press release that probably started the media contact. While trade magazines have more respect for the press release than most newspapers or national business magazines, few trades will print a release announcing "an amazing new discovery" without any investigation.

SEE ALSO: Business Literature

[Clint Johnson]

FURTHER READING:

Gale Directory of Publications and Broadcast Media. Gale Research Inc. 1994.

BUSINESS AND SOCIETY

There was a time in United States history, particularly during the late 1800s, when business owners' view of society was summed up in the immortal words of William Henry Vanderbilt, who said, "the public be damned." Vanderbilt, the president of the New York Central Railroad at the time, allegedly made the statement to reporters in an October 8, 1882, interview. Afterwards, he denied he said it, but the fact is that, until recently, business owners and society were two completely different entities, with little interest in one another's activities—as long as businesses made money and provided jobs for people.

In the eyes of business owners during the nineteenth century and the first half of the twentieth, their role was to produce goods and services and make as much money as possible for themselves and shareholders. The public's duty was to buy the goods and services. It was not until the 1960s that the traditional roles changed and "stakeholders," i. e., anyone who has a vested interest in any action a company takes, began to play an important role in the relationship between business and society. Today, that relationship continues to evolve into a symbiotic partnership aimed at providing a safe, environmentally sound atmosphere for producers and consumers alike. Also, added to the mix is the government, whose role has changed considerably in the public policy arena.

Today, public policy is best defined as the mutual cooperation among business, society, and government required to make the world a safer, more productive place in which to live for every segment of the population. Government at all levels has taken an increasingly active role in shaping public policy. Federal, state, and local government agencies have enacted a complex battery of laws defining what businesses can and cannot do in such diverse areas as production techniques, workplace and product safety, hiring practices, contributions to political campaigns, conduct in foreign dealings ... the list goes on. The resulting legislation has reshaped the way business operates and has affected dramatically its bottom line in some cases. It marks A radical departure from the early days of the business-society relationship, which was shaped primarily by the interests of business.

THE EARLY DAYS

Industry in the United States operated on a small scale prior to the Civil War (1861-65). The majority of manufacturers in the United States were located in the North. The war spurred those manufacturers to improve production techniques in order to provide the goods required by the Union armies. Once the war ended, entrepreneurs sought new ways to mass produce the goods that the country's growing population demanded.

Advances in mass production techniques facilitated by the war made possible an abundance of goods and services for the public. Need to operate in-plant machinery and to transport goodsled to a reliance on petroleum products. The so-called "Captains of Industry," men like Andrew Carnegie, Andrew Mellon, John D. Rockefeller, J. Pierpont Morgan, and George Pullman, took advantage of the demands to provide the capital, transportation, oil, and other goods and services required to make the country grow and prosper. Few people gave any thought to what impact industry would have on the environment or society. All industrialists cared about was profits. They had the federal government on their side, too.

The government did not want to involve itself in the affairs of business during the late 1800s. It discouraged **labor unions** and in general gave business owners carte blanche in running their companies as they saw fit. After all, the public did not seem dissatisfied with the way business ran its affairs. That began to change, however, in the late 1880s.

Several monopolies existed in the United States toward the end of the nineteenth century. Industrial combinations controlled such **commodities** as whisky, oil, transportation, sugar, lead, and beef. Individual states, particularly those in the South and West, passed **antitrust laws** to regulate monopoly activities. However, they could not impact industries that crossed state lines. Thus, there grew a demand from the public to enact federal legislation to control interstate commerce.

The federal government was reluctant at first to involve itself in direct affairs of business. Slowly, though, it acceded to public demands. For example, in 1887 the House and Senate passed the Interstate Commerce Act, which created the first regulatory commission in U.S. history, the **Interstate Commerce Commission (ICC)**. Three years later, the Sherman Antitrust Act of 1890 became law. It stated that "every contract, combination in the form of trust or otherwise, or conspiracy, in restraint of trade or commerce among the several states, or with foreign nations, is hereby declared to be illegal." The ambiguously worded act was hard to enforce, but it at least served notice that the federal government was taking an interest in business activities.

There followed a succession of legislation in the first half of the twentieth century that curbed business' power and strengthened unions. The government tried to adopt a neutral stance in business affairs. However, government officials were too busy coping with a series of wars (e.g., World Wars I and II and Korea) to concentrate on business activities. That ended in the 1960s, however.

THE NEW ERA OF SOCIAL RESPONSIBILITY

Business executives, government officials, educators, and the public all took a new look at the relationship between business and society in the 1960s. The decade marked a new era in social awareness concerning virtually every aspect of life. People became more concerned with the environment, **corporate profits**, and a wide range of social issues. Educators implemented innovative courses defining the relationship between business and society and outlining business's social responsibilities. As a result, a new "contract" between business and society, based on the latest definition of public policy, fell into place.

Under the terms of the old "contract," a business' success or failure was based on how much money it made and how many jobs it produced. People in the 1960's developed a new awareness of the environment and the effects manufacturing had on air, water, etc. They realized for the first time that there sometimes existed an adverse relationship between economic growth and social progress. Critics of the "business at any cost" policy pointed to a number of problems that had been ignored or overlooked for years unsafe workplaces, urban decay, **discrimination** in the workforce, and the increasing use of toxic substances in the production process. To combat these problems, activists pushed for a higher level of social awareness on the part of business and among the population in general. They advocated a reduction in the social cost of doing business. Their goal was not to negate the old contract. They recognized that businesses had to make profits in order to survive. What they promoted was simply the addition of new policies to the old contract. Their ideas created considerable debate over the concept of social responsibility.

THE DIFFERING VIEWS OF BUSINESS' SOCIAL RESPONSIBILITY

Proponents of the new contract argued that it was in business' best interest to become conscientious "corporate citizens." They claimed that since business contributed to social problems, it should help resolve them. Doing so would give business a better image in the public's eye and benefit it in the long run. More importantly, it would help business avoid government regulation and provide business opportunities. After all, the proponents said, business has useful resources that it could employ to solve or alleviate social problems.

Opponents did not fully agree, they suggested that it was not business's responsibility to solve social problems, particularly from a free enterprise standpoint. In their viewpoint, honoring social responsibilities would put American businesses at a competitive disadvantage in the rapidly emerging international competitive arena and water down their responsibilities to shareholders. Second, they argued, corporations are not moral agents. Third, they claimed the very definition of social responsibility was so vague no one could state exactly what business's role in it would be. Finally, they stated that business simply did not have the skills or incentives to handle social problems. In effect, the opponents said, business would be shooting itself in the foot if it assumed a role as a watchdog of societal problems.

Both sides presented viable arguments, and they did agree on one central issue: that the concept of social responsibility did not include clear guidelines regulating managerial behavior. Nor did it consider the competitive arena in which businesses functioned. For example, if an individual firm implemented its own social responsibility program, that resulted in extra costs and reduced shareholders' profits, the company would be adversely affecting its ability to compete. Thus, individual companies were not willing to act unilaterally in meeting social responsibilities. As a result, business in general dragged its heels in formulating a united approach to social responsibility. Consequently, it was inevitable that the government would step in to set guidelines.

"UNCLE SAM" STEPS IN

Federal, state, and local government agencies concentrated on enacting and enforcing myriad regulations aimed at regulating business and social entities. Sometimes they acted individually; at other times they combined forces. As a result, business owners complained that government was driving them out of business and destroying the traditional capitalistic American economic system. The critics who complained that bureaucratic interference became too pervasive and comprehensive in the 1970s had a legitimate complaint. Government regulation of business literally became a growth industry of its own during that period.

Between 1970 and 1980, the number of federal employees engaged in social regulation increased dramatically. For example, according to figures presented by Melinda Warren and Kenneth Chilton, the number of government workers employed in consumer safety and health regulation rose 31 percent during that time. That was low compared to the employee increases in job safety and other working conditions regulatory agencies (144 percent) and environment and energy (298 percent). There were similar jumps in economic regulation agencies, although they were considerably smaller.

Warren and Chilton also revealed a 56 percent increase in finance and banking regulation employees, 21 percent in industry specific, and 33 percent in general business. Overall, there was a 62 percent increase. The rapid increase bewildered business owners, who simply could not keep up with the numbers of new laws and regulatory agencies with which they had to deal.

The federal government involved itself in several types of regulation simultaneously. Basically, there were four categories: competitive behavior, industry regulation, social regulation, and labor-management relations. The first two were not new. Government regulation in these categories dated back to the advent of the ICC and the Sherman Antitrust Act of 1890. Aditionally, The federal government had begun regulating **labor-management relations** seriously as early as the 1930's as an outgrowth of the Great Depression years. Two laws in particular had a bearing on these relations were the Wagner Act and the

Taft-Harley Act, which regulated unfair labor and union practices.

A look at a few of the agencies created by the federal government in the 1960s, through the 1980s attests to the effect social legislation had on labor and management. For example, the Occupational Safety and Health Act of 1970, which created the **Occupational Safety and Health Administration** (OSHA), had a major impact on working conditions in virtually every area of business. No longer did labor and management have to negotiate working conditions. OSHA oversaw conditions and had the power to levy heavy fines on businesses found to be in noncompliance with the agency's regulations. This had a potential major impact on companies' bottom lines, which was one of the reasons many business leaders objected to the new business-society contract.

Another federal agency that had a far-reaching impact on business operations was the **Environmental Protection Agency (EPA)**. The EPA became an official arm of the federal government on July 9, 1979, when President Nixon ordered that several existing agencies dealing with the environment be combined into one new, independent agency. The EPA's single purpose was to protect and enhance the physical environment. As the agency grew, its responsibility expanded to include the enforcement of several acts. Among them were:

- Water Quality Improvement Act (1970)

- Clear Air Act Amendments of 1970

- Federal Water Pollution Control Act Amendments of 1972

- Federal Insecticide, Fungicide and Rodenticide Act (1972)

- Noise Control Act (1972)

- Safe Drinking Water Act (1974)

- Toxic Substances Control Act (1976)

The variety of areas for which the EPA was responsible made real one of business' biggest fears: extensive federal regulation of its activities.

Perhaps the most ambitious act implemented by the federal government was the Comprehensive Environmental Response, Compensation, and Liability Act (CERCLA) of 1980 (Superfund). CERCLA provided the EPA with the money it needed to oversee the cleanup of old and abandoned waste sites that posed a threat to public health or the environment. The law had two purposes: to provide the funds to clean inactive waste sites for which responsible parties either could not be found or were unwilling to do the cleanup themselves, and to create liabilities for parties associated with waste sites. Under the law, responsible parties could either perform the cleanup themselves or reimburse the EPA for the cost of the process. The government did not bear the entire burden. The chemical industry had to pay $300 million per year in special taxes as its share of the financial burden.

The Superfund bill expired on May 31, 1986, well before all of the sites in need of cleanup were completed. Five months later, then President Reagan signed a new law, called the Superfund Amendments and Reauthorization Act (SARA), which allocated $9 billion more for cleanup projects—and set more stringent guidelines. Again, business had to provide matching funds. For example, petroleum taxes rose to $2.75 billion and a $1.4 billion tax was placed on chemical feedstocks. These were but two of many forms of taxation.

Not all government policy was aimed at cleaning up toxic waste sites. For instance, one agency created during the 1970's was the Consumer Product Safety Commission (CPSC), which was established on October 27, 1972. Its purpose was to protect the public against unreasonable risks of injury associated with consumer products. This was but one more attempt by the government to protect the public from possible harm.

One prominent example of such a policy was the National Highway Traffic Safety Administration's (NHTSA) 1969 mandate that required the installation of air bags in all vehicles manufactured in the United States. The mandate did not set well with the automobile manufacturing industry, which managed to delay the law's implementation for over 20 years. In the end, though, it was a losing battle. The government and the public wanted laws to protect citizens from virtually every imaginable danger. That explains why agencies such as the CPSC were having such a dramatic impact on public policy.

The CPSC was given responsibility to enforce a variety of laws, e.g., the Flammable Fabrics Act, the Refrigerator Safety Act of 1956, the Hazardous Substances Act of 1960, and the Poison Prevention Packaging Act of 1970. The agency's charter gave it sweeping regulatory powers over any article or component part produced or distributed for sale to a consumer or for the personal use, consumption, or enjoyment of a consumer. About the only exceptions were tobacco and tobacco products, motor vehicles and motor vehicle equipment, drugs, food, aircraft and aircraft components, and certain boats and certain other items. These were all covered by other federal agencies, such as the Food and Drug Administration (FDA), created in 1931, and the NHTSA, established in 1966.

The federal government did not restrict itself to regulating public safety, the environment, working conditions, etc. It also became involved in enforcing laws aimed at assuring equal rights for everyone regardless of race, creed, religion, etc. A series of acts aimed at equal opportunity were enacted in the 1960s and 1970s. Actually, many of them were offshoots of President Franklin D. Roosevelt's Executive Order 8802, issued in 1941. The order promoted equal opportunity as a matter of public policy.

Twenty years later, President John F. Kennedy issued Executive Order 10925, which established the President's Commission on Equal Employment Opportunity. It granted the commission the power to investigate complaints by employees and enforce a ban on discrimination by federal contractors. The order marked the first time the words "**affirmative action**" appeared in a public policy document.

A series of similar legislation ensued. Title VII of the Civil Rights Act of 1964 forbade discrimination in employment by an employer, employment agency, or labor union on the bases of race, color, sex, religion, or national origin in any term, condition, or privilege of employment. This act departed radically from Roosevelt's and Kennedy's executive orders, which applied strictly to employers working on federal contracts. It also established the **Equal Employment Opportunity Commission (EEOC)**—which had no enforcement powers. The government rectified that problem eight years later with the passage of the Equal Employment Opportunity Act of 1972.

The 1972 act broadened the EEOC's coverage and provided its power to bring enforcement action to the courts. It also allowed employees and job applicants to file discrimination charges on their own behalf. Moreover, it allowed for organizations to file discrimination charges on behalf of aggrieved individuals. As comprehensive as the amendment was, there were still a few groups exempted. For example, the EEOC did not have jurisdiction over private businesses with fewer than 15 employees, bona fide tax-exempt clubs, or local, national, and international **labor unions** with under 15 members.

A series of similar laws followed. These included the Pregnancy Discrimination Act of 1978, the Equal Pay Act of 1963, the Age Discrimination in Employment Act of 1967, the Vocational Rehabilitation Act of 1973, and the Vietnam Era Veterans' Readjustment Assistance Act of 1974. Some of these acts applied only to businesses working under federal contracts. Regardless, there were very few people in the United States who did not fall under the protection of at least one of the public policy acts.

It should be noted that at the same time the federal government was passing act after act, state governments also became involved in business regulation. New York was the first state in the union to pass a fair employment practice (FEP) act. It did so in 1945. Other states followed. Virtually every state now has FEP's on the books. The states also enacted their own EPA-type laws. In some cases, their laws duplicated federal legislation. In others, they superseded federal laws. In any case, they placed a more restrictive burden on business operators. However well meaning the legislation regulatory agencies were, the fact that the government was attempting to legislate morality and business ethics disturbed many people.

Critics contended that many of the new public policy laws interfered with the basic missionof business—to make as much money as possible for owners and shareholders. Wave after wave of reform affected business operations. There cane in rapid succession the civil rights movement, the feminist movement, the onset of societal concerns about pollution, the war on poverty, and a rebirth of consumerism. There was also a new emphasis on workplace safety and ethical concerns over foreign practices and operations. Each wave led to new legislation. There was so much legislation, in fact, that business operators could not keep up with it. They had little choice but to react to it, though. Government intervention and societal activism forced companies to change the way they did business. The change had a profound effect on business's bottom line—and on society in general.

THE NADER EFFECT

The changes in public policy prompted business leaders to take a close look at the way their companies were structured and governed. Outside groups such as Ralph Nader's Center for the Study of Responsive Law tried to become part of General Motors' governance process, for example. Nader quickly became a thorn in GM's side—and became a symbol for outside involvement in corporate affairs.

Ralph Nader had set the stage for public awareness of corporate activities in his 1965 book, Unsafe at Any Speed, which labeled the General Motors-produced Corvair as a poorly made, dangerous automobile. GM executives took exception and ordered an investigation of Nader. He, in turn, sued General Motors Corp. for invasion of privacy. The two settled out of court for $425,000. Nader used part of the money to establish the Center for the Study of Responsive Law.

Nader's attack on GM distrubed the company's leadership, which was used to the traditional model of corporate governance in which shareholders controlled the corporation and were the major factor in the governance process. The old saying went, "As General Motors goes, so goes the nation." In this instance, GM had to adopt a new approach to business and its role in an increasingly complex society, once GM made this change in approach, other leading companies followed.

To protect itself from Nader, GM founded a nominating committee to select members for its board of directors. Such strategies did not sway Nader and his fellow activists, however. They were more interested in bypassing traditional power sources and establishing a stakeholder form of governance, not only at GM, but in businesses in general, something most executives did not want to see happen.

R. Edward Freeman, in his book, *Strategic Management: A Stakeholder Approach*, defined the stakeholder model as "any group or individual who can affect, or is affected by, the achievement of a corporation's purpose. Stakeholders include employees, customers, suppliers, stockholders, banks, environmentalists, government and other groups who can help or hurt the corporation." The fact that so many disparate groups had an interest in business operations caused business leaders to sit up and take notice. They realized that they had to come to grips with a new approach to doing business. They embarked on a program of reform.

REFORM BECOMES A KEY ISSUE FOR MANAGEMENT

Business executives adopted a series of new strategies to adapt to the demands of public policy. For example, many companies instituted public responsibility committees at the **board of directors** level. The committees had several responsibilities, chief of which was to show employees and the public that the companies they served were indeed committed to becoming upstanding corporate citizens. They dealt with a diverse array of issues, including, but not limited to, affirmative action, workplace safety, government relations, pollution, and product quality and safety. Their role was important to the companies they served, since they acted as watchdogs in the vital area of public policy.

Companies also redefined the role of the **chief executive officer** (CEO). In some cases, the CEO became more of a specialist in government affairs than the hands-on leader of the company. The CEO also became the one person who defined the level of the company's commitment to public policy issues. The public measured just how serious individual companies were about public policy based on the CEO's actions, rather than rhetoric. The CEO's attitude filtered down through the workforce and influenced changes at the different levels of management.

Management throughout the business world underwent substantial changes. A new breed of specialists emerged in the **management** ranks. Companies developed affirmative action specialists, environmental control managers, workplace safety engineers . . . in short, a cadre of people trained to respond to the public policy demands of the late twentieth century.

Companies also paid a lot more attention to the legal aspects of their operations. In the early days of American business, lawsuits filed against businesses by government agencies or consumers were few and far between. However, as the public became more aware of environmental, product safety, and other concerns, and the government enacted more public policy laws, lawsuits became more common. The new laws provided for stiff financial penalties against public policy offenders and opened the door for more private citizens and agencies to sue corporations. Thus, companies had to protect themselves against possible heavy financial losses while acting socially responsible. The possibility of monetary losses definitely influenced business' strategic planning.

For the first time, business executives were forced to include in their strategic plans issues such as how to dispose of hazardous waste, ensure product safety, eliminate unsafe work conditions, and establish and enforce affirmative action plans. These issues meant a possible reduction in funds previously allocated for **research and development**, capital expenditures—and profits. Businesses had to balance their finances carefully to satisfy the public policy watchdogs and ensure profits. In order to do this, they had to be able to measure their performance. There came into play a new emphasis on a process called the social audit.

THE SOCIAL AUDIT

The social audit is nothing more than an internal management tool designed to ascertain whether a company's resources are being used effectively in dealing with public policy issues. It can be used to measure the performances of individual managers, report to the board of directors and stakeholders on a company's progress and provide an overall picture of the company as a responsible corporate citizen. The social audit process is by no means scientific, however.

The social audit is a generalized tool used by businesses to give them a broad idea of how they are performing. The measurements they use are subject to interpretation by government agencies and private citizens. Government officials and the general public have become more aware of the need for concrete proof that businesses are acting in a socially responsible manner.

THE GENERAL PUBLIC BECOMES MORE ACTIVE

One consequence of the increased emphasis on social responsibility has been the growth of many organizations aimed at protecting the public from pollution, poorly made products, unsafe workplaces, and the host of other problems, that affected citizens. These organizations have placed businesses in the proverbial "fishbowl," where they are under the scrutiny of an ever-watchful public.

Environmental organizations such as Greenpeace, the Sierra Club, and the National Wildlife Federation take an active role in monitoring the environment and forcing businesses to pay careful attention to public policy. Such private interest groups hire their own lawyers, scientists, and other public interest professionals who provide the expertise necessary to conduct research, litigation, and advocacy on the complex issues involved in public policy. These nonprofit, nonpartisan advocacy groups investigate problems, educate the public about solutions, and lobby locally, statewide, and nationally for reforms aimed at preserving the environment and protecting consumers. Often, they work in conjunction with government agencies to oversee business activities, which has caused them to incur the wrath of industry leaders and has led to costly, prolonged battles over the use and fate of certain products.

For example, in February 1994, the Environmental Protection Agency (EPA) suggested that an addition be made to the nation's **Clean Water Act** mandating a strategy for "substituting, reducing or prohibiting the use of chlorine and chlorinated compounds." The Chemical Manufacturers Association (CMA), an industry trade group, expressed outrage at the suggestion. The EPA backed down once the CMA flexed its muscles. Instead of an outright ban, it modified its stance to include only a study and a pledge to work with the industry on the issue. That did not mollify private advocacy groups.

Greenpeace, the National Wildlife Federation, the Sierra Club, and others pushed for an outright ban on chlorine in all forms. They squared off against industry specialists. The battle was reminiscent of other fights over controversial products. The issues were always the same: environmentalists suggested they were harmful to wildlife, the atmosphere, and life in general, while manufacturers insisted that the products were safe when used in moderation. The government often stood somewhere in the middle, but occasionally initiated the squabbles through legislation.

THE FUTURE OF BUSINESS, SOCIETY, AND PUBLIC POLICY

There is no doubt that the overall emphasis on the quality of the environment will create a continuing need for new laws and strategic planning to eliminate pollution, hazardous products, and workplace equality. Businesses, governments, and society in general all have a responsibility to ensure that the world in which they function is as close to ideal as possible. Through mutual cooperation and vigorous

attention to societal obligations, all three entities will create a safe, clean environment—and perpetuate the most livable conditions in which business and society can coexist.

[Arthur G. Sharp]

FURTHER READING:

Freeman, R. Edward. *Strategic Management: A Stakeholder Approach*. Marshfield, Massachusetts: Pitman, 1984.

Nader, Ralph. *Unsafe at Any Speed: The Designed-in Dangers of the American Automobile*. New York: Grossman Publishers, 1972.

Walton, Clarence C., ed. *Business and Social Progress*. New York: Praeger Publishers, 1970.

Warren, Melinda, and Kenneth Chilton. *The Regulatory Legacy of the Reagan Revolution: An Analysis of 1990 Federal Regulatory Budgets and Staffing*. St. Louis, Missouri: Washington University Center for the Study of American Business, 1989.

BUSINESS TRAVEL

The dawning of the twenty-first century signals a new era in international business travel both in terms of the number of businesspeople who are increasingly pursuing new ventures abroad and in the volume of business they generate. When combined, the **income** generated by the travel industry worldwide totals over $2 trillion per year, making it one of the ten largest industries. The competitive nature of hotels, airlines, cruise lines, incentive travel, and related businesses has led to several interesting trends in recent years.

First, the laws that govern business travel have become dramatically less rigid in the wake of the collapse of communism. Today, Americans can travel virtually unrestricted to most countries as long as they have a valid passport (good for ten years) and—for some countries—a visa (obtained through the embassy of the destination country, sometimes for a small fee). The United States has a reciprocal arrangement with most countries so that just as Americans can travel freely to other countries, their nationals can also travel here for business or recreation without bureaucratic delays.

The **European Economic Union** has further reduced the problems associated with business travel by providing a single passport for citizens of all member states so that travel between the more than 14 member nations is virtually unrestricted. Further enhancements of this nature are expected throughout Asia and in Africa in the years to come.

Business travel is one of the most important aspects of commerce today because with an international economy that is interdependent, businesses are sending sales and **marketing** personnel, scientists, and executives to learn about research, products, and production techniques both in their own country and abroad. An entire industry serves business travel clientele; two of the largest players are American Express Travel Services and Rosenbluth, both of which have offices in most major cities.

The impact of business travel is profound; cities throughout the world have collectively spent over a billion dollars since 1980 to enhance their convention and tourism facilities, including Paris, Philadelphia, Boston, Tokyo, Seoul, and Beijing. Visitor and convention bureaus are especially important to business travel; these quasi-public agencies seek to attract major industrial conventions and trade shows to their cities. The resulting economic profit to hotels, restaurants, and other businesses is estimated to grow at about 17 percent in the coming years in the United States and about 4 percent internationally.

According to a study at Penn State University, the number of Americans traveling to the Pacific Rim on business will increase 14 percent by the year 2000, while the number of Pacific Rim residents traveling to the United States will increase by almost 27 percent. Similar numbers exist in Latin America. Due to lower petroleum costs (that guide airfare prices in particular), the actual costs of business travel have been kept reasonable.

Business travel poses as many problems as benefits. Crime against business tourists has increased in recent years, primarily in urban areas. Although the business travel industry is working with law enforcement officials, rental car agencies, and other industry players to reduce the severity and number of crimes against business travelers, security awareness throughout the industry is often high only after a major incident. Many business travel corporations are rushing to sponsor training seminars on how to protect hotel and motel guests, convention attendees, and other business travelers. Other business travel hazards include potential outbreaks of food poisoning at major banquets.

Although one would assume that the rise in teleconferencing, **electronic mail**, and faxes has diminished the need for business travel, the meteoric rise of the Pacific Rim and parts of Latin America have actually counterbalanced any negative impact from new technologies. Indeed, the costs of business travel often outweigh any other factor. It is not uncommon throughout Asia to have entire departments of leading manufacturers travel to the United States or Canada for a major business tour; often a reciprocal arrangement will follow so that American colleagues will then have the opportunity to visit plants in Asia. Out of such exchanges new partnerships and joint ventures frequently emerge.

[Larry Barton]

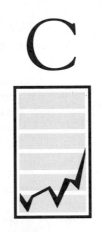

C

CALL AND PUT OPTIONS

An option is a financial instrument which gives its holder the choice of purchasing (call option) or selling (put option) an underlying security at a predetermined price. Most **options** are for limited periods of time, so the choice must be exercised before the option expires.

The security on which the option is written is known as the underlying security. The price which the option purchaser must pay to exercise the option is known as the exercise price or striking price. The expiration date is the last date on which the option may be exercised. An American option may be exercised at any time up to and including the expiration date. A European option can be exercised only at the expiration date.

An option is said to be "in-the-money" if by exercising the option it would produce a gain. Call options are in-the-money when the market price of the underlying security is greater than the exercise price. Put options are in-the-money when the market price of the underlying security is less than the exercise price. Call options are said to be "out-of-the-money" when the exercise price is more than the market price of underlying security. Puts are out-of-the-money when the market price of the underlying security is more than the exercise price.

The remainder of the discussion of options will use a call option as the example. However, everything stated also holds for puts—the reader should keep in mind that the transaction is reversed.

A typical call option may be written to give its buyer the option to purchase 100 shares of the PDQ Corporation at a price of $60 per share before a stated expiration date. The writer (i.e., seller) of the option will receive a premium for writing the option. The per share premium is the option price divided by the number of shares in the option. The purchaser of a call option hopes that either (1) the price of the underlying security will increase beyond the exercise price plus the cost of the option, thereby making exercise profitable, or (2) the premium on the option increases, thereby making sale of the option profitable.

Both buying and selling options offer profit opportunities. Buyers of call options have the following advantages:

- They know in advance the price they are going to pay (i.e., the exercise price).

- They know in advance the maximum loss they can sustain on the option (i.e., the cost of the option).

- They have the opportunity to benefit from the extreme amount of **leverage** implicit in most options.

Advantages to the seller include an opportunity to increase income from the underlying security in the option. For example, assume a portfolio contains some stock, the price of which is drifting around a certain market price. The investor could write an option against that stock and generate a profit, to the extent of the premium in the option, thereby gaining even though the stock's price has not moved.

Sellers who write options against securities held in their portfolios are said to be selling covered options. Options written without the underlying security in the writer's portfolio are known as naked options. A writer of naked option must have adequate funds on deposit with their broker to cover the option, should it be exercised.

The premium related to the option is pivotal to options trading. The lower the premium, the more favorable the option is to the purchaser for two reasons: (1) the purchaser can hope to subsequently sell the option at a higher premium, or (2) if the market price of the underlying security rises above the exercise price of the option, the purchaser can always exercise the option, thereby acquiring the security from the option writer at below the security's current market value.

For example, assume an option for 100 shares is purchased for $200 (premium of $2 per share) while a stock is selling at $30 per share and the exercise price is $35. If the price of the stock rises to $38, the option price should rise to at least $3 ($38-$35), and more likely will rise close to $5 [($38-$35) + $2]. If the price of this option rises to $3, the holder can either sell the option and realize a profit of $100 (a 50 percent profit margin) or the holder can exercise the option, purchasing the shares for $3,500 instead of $3,800.

FACTORS AFFECTING OPTION PRICE

There are several factors which affect the amount of an option's premium. The premium will be a reflection of demand and supply. During periods of rising stock market prices, there is an increased interest in purchasing options. Conversely, individuals owning securities would be less interested in writing options, opting to hold their stock for further price appreciation. The combination of these two typically raises the level of option premiums. When stock prices are declining, there is greater interest in writing call options but less in buying them; premiums thus tend to decline.

In addition, there are at least four other factors that interact to influence the level, and movement, of call option premiums:

1. The current market price of the stock. Whenever the option is in-the-money, the option price will rise if the price of the stock continues to rise, since the option has value in addition to the time-lock inherent in every option.

2. Time. Everything else remaining equal, the more time remaining until the option's expiration date, the higher its premium will be. This only makes sense, since the longer an option has to run, the less risk there is to the option holder that the exercise price will not rise to a level to make the option profitable.

As the option approaches its expiration date, its time value declines and near expiration, its only value will be the excess, if any, of the underlying security's market price over the exercise price.

It is because of the time value that it is likely an option will still have market value even though its exercise price plus premium is below the market value of the underlying security.

3. Volatility. If the price of the underlying security fluctuates substantially, the option is likely to command a heftier premium than the option for a security which normally trades in a narrow price range. As a general rule, call option premiums neither increase nor decrease point for point with the price of the underlying security. That is, a one point increase in the underlying security price commonly results in less than a one point increase in the call option premium. Reasons for this include:

- Rising premiums reduce the leverage inherent in the option. For example, if the price of a stock is $100 and the option is $10, the buyer's leverage is 10:1. But if a $1 increase in the stock price were to raise the option premium by the same amount, the leverage would be reduced.

- A rise in the stock price increases the buyer's capital outlay and risk. For example, an increase in stock price from $50 to $51 is only 2 percent, but a rise in option premium from $5 to $6 is a 20 percent increase.

- Assuming the underlying security has been in an upward trend, the option will have less time value, decreasing its attractiveness.

4. The risk-free rate of return.

As a result of the interaction of these variables, an in-the-money call option's price will be at least equal to the difference between the market price and the exercise price of the underlying security. If the underlying security's market price is near zero, it is conceivable that the option will be worthless. Therefore, the minimum price of an option is zero. Its maximum price will equal this difference plus the algebraic sum of the value of the above factors, limited by the market price of the security. An out-of-the-money call option's price will be a function of just the above factors. Note that as the expiration date of the option nears, the effects of these other factors are significantly diminished. Figure 1 illustrates these relationships.

In recent years, most analysts have been using the Black-Scholes model for the valuation of options. This model is designed for European options and is

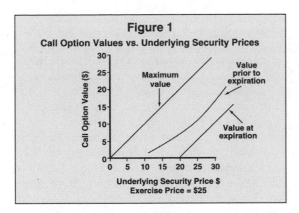

Figure 1
Call Option Values vs. Underlying Security Prices

Maximum value

Value prior to expiration

Value at expiration

Underlying Security Price $
Exercise Price = $25

mathematically complex. However, several **software** packages have been developed which makes its application considerably easier. As a result, it has gained widespread acceptance.

BUYER'S STRATEGIES

One of the main advantages of purchasing a call option is to have a security with mega-leverage. For example, going back to the earlier case, assume an option is written for a stock selling at $30. The option's exercise price is $35 and the option is selling for $2. Consider two investors with $3,000 to invest:

- Investor A purchases 100 shares of stock and investor B purchases 1500 options. If the price of the stock rises to $38, the investor in the stock will have a profit of $800 ($3800 − $3000), or 26.7 percent. Assuming the options rise in price to $3 ($38 − $35), and, it is likely the price will be higher, Investor B realizes a profit of $1500 ($4500 − $3000) or a 50 percent.

The call option purchaser also has the benefit of limited risk. Should the price of the underlying security decline, the option holder's maximum loss is always the price paid for the option (i.e., his total investment in the option).

A holder of a call option can always exercise the option before the expiration date. This is done only when the market value of the underlying security is above the exercise price of the option. However, because the commissions to sell an option are less than the commissions to both buy and sell the underlying security, most option holders prefer to simply sell the option rather than exercise it.

Another strategy for call options, assuming the holder believes there will be a rising market and wishes to purchase the underlying security in the future, is to lock in the price of the underlying security. This is especially useful if the investor anticipates cash flow in the future to pay for the purchase.

A final strategy for which call options are used is to **hedge** against a short sale since the option establishes the maximum price that will have to be paid for a security in order to satisfy the obligation of a short sale.

SELLERS' STRATEGIES

Assume an owner of 100 shares of stock which cost $50 a share can write an option at a premium of $5 per share. The stock would be deposited with the writer's broker and his account would be credited for $500. Note that the $500 belongs to the writer whether or not the option is exercised. It is erroneous, therefore, to think of the premium as a "down payment."

If the exercise price is below the market value of the security as the expiration date is approached, option writers can reasonably assume an option will be exercised and they will have to deliver the underlying security. Note that a writer can always terminate his obligation to deliver the security by simply purchasing an identical option at the current premium, thereby liquidating his position.

[Ronald M. Horwitz]

FURTHER READING:

Brealey, Richard A. and Stewart C. Myers. *Principles of Corporate Finance*, 4th ed. New York: McGraw-Hill, Inc., 1991.

Brigham, Eugene F. and Louis C. Gapenski. *Financial Management: Theory and Practice*, 6th ed. Fort Worth: The Dryden Press, 1991.

Chicago Board Options Exchange. *Understanding Options*. September, 1975.

Cox, J. and M. Rubenstein. *Option Markets*. Englewood Cliffs, NJ: Prentice-Hall, Inc., 1985.

Hull, J. *Options, Futures, and Other Derivative Securities*. Englewood Cliffs, NJ: Prentice-Hall, Inc., 1989.

Wilson, Thomas E., Larry D. Guin, Suzanne Pinac Ward, and Dan R. Ward. "Valuing Stock Options: A Cost Effective Spreadsheet Template," *The CPA Journal*. March 1995, p. 50.

CANADA, DOING BUSINESS IN

Canada is the second largest country in the world, located north of the United States of America. Among the free market economies, it is one of the leading industrialized countries and is part of the G7 group of economic powers. Along with the United States of America and Mexico, it is a partner in the **North American Free Trade Agreement**. The trade between Canada and the United States amounts to over twenty billion dollars a year. These two countries are the world's foremost trading partners; the trade between no other two countries amounts to this volume. The economies of the two countries are closely linked in terms of companies, industries, and general economic conditions. Canada is rich in natural resources, and Canadians enjoy one of the highest standards of living. Its economic climate is conducive to commerce.

The population of this vast country is only a little over twenty seven million, according to the 1991 census. The majority of this population lives in a narrow belt just above the northern boundaries of the United States of America. The three metropolitan areas of Montreal, Toronto and Vancouver account for one-third of the total population of Canada. The vastness of the country, the pattern of its population concentration, and plentiful natural resources are factors that contribute to Canada's business environment.

Starting with fur trade in the seventeenth century and continuing to the present time, the Canadian business scene has been dominated by resource-based industries. As business becomes global and as resource based industries lose their importance and profitability, the Canadian economy is turning to service and high technology industries. With a highly skilled work force, Canada is hoping to bring about a structural change in its economy.

Another aspect of Canadian business history is protectionism. Early in the nineteenth century, Canada's manufacturing industries and banking services developed. The abundance of natural resources and the sprawling underpopulated nature of the country contributed to the formation of markets that are thin and dispersed. Such an environment necessitated a certain amount of protection for industries to grow. The Canadian government enacted tariffs to protect manufacturing and trade. Two consequences of this policy were the growth of Canadian-owned enterprises and the establishment of branch plants by foreign businesses, mostly American. In the long run, Canada's protectionism lead to its products being uncompetitive in the world market and to an economy being over dependant on the export of resource products such as timber and minerals. In principle, Canada's membership in the North American Free Trade Agreement and in the **General Agreement on Tariffs and Trade (GATT)** is a corrective measure to make the Canadian economy competitive in the emerging global economy. In the short term, the structural changes necessary to move from a protectionist environment to a free market economy is causing dislocation in the manufacturing sector, and human hardship. At the same time, it is also a period of business opportunities. With its highly trained labor pool and well developed research and development facilities, Canada is ideally suited for entrepreneurial ventures in high technology and communications.

POLITICAL AND ECONOMIC STRUCTURES

The Canadian government is modeled on British traditions. It is a parliamentary system as opposed to the presidential system in the United States. The English queen, or crown, is the head of state. The governor general of Canada represents the crown and is appointed on the recommendation of the Canadian prime minister, who is the leader of the majority party in Parliament. Real political power is in the hands of the prime minister and the cabinet, who have collective responsibility and accountability to the legislature. The Canadian Parliament has two chambers, namely the House of Commons and the Senate. Unlike the American Senate, the Canadian Senate is not a directly elected body. Senators are appointed by the prime minister in consultation with the provincial governments. The Senate can delay legislation and suggest amendments but ultimately cannot stop legislation that is proposed and passed by the House of Commons. Although there are parliamentary committees taking a detailed look at issues of concern, there is no process comparable to senate hearings in the United States. Another difference is the lack of organized and structured lobbying as is prevalent in the United States.

Canada is comprised of ten provinces and two territories. Like the federal government, each province is headed by an appointed lieutenant governor who is the crown's representative in the province. The political power rests with the leader of the majority party in the provincial legislature, known as the premier. Within each province there are municipalities, which form the third tier of government. All three levels of government provide various incentives to businesses.

The legal system in Canada is based on British common law, except in the province of Quebec, where in civil matters, the French system prevails. Unlike the United States, where the **Securities and Exchange Commission** regulates trading in public companies' stocks in Canada, each province has its own regulatory body. In practical terms, since the Toronto Stock Exchange is the most important and popular trading place in Canada, the Ontario Securities Commission is the institution most similar to the SEC. Business corporations can be incorporated federally or provincially.

Economically, Canada is closely linked to the United States. Even minor changes in U.S. interest rates or stock exchange indexes usually have repercussions in Canada. As Canada's interest rates must be competitive with the U.S. to attract foreign capital. This limits the extent to which Canada can pursue an independent economic policy.

The main features of the Canadian economy are similar to that of the United States. Major corporations, such as GM, Ford, and Procter and Gamble, are the same in both countries and are closely linked. One major difference between the countries is in health care, where Canada provides more comprehensive coverage for its sick and disadvantaged than does the United States. The high business overhead costs required to maintain such a system are neutralized by a healthy and secure work force—even though such intangibles generally are not taken into account when financial decisions are made. Consistent with the high standard of living are high wages. Canada's productivity in comparison to other industrialized countries is high and is continuously improving. About 30 percent of the labor force is unionized (1992). Many unions are international, representing workers in both Canada and the United States. Industrial relations in Canada are relatively strife-free and stable.

[Divakara K. Varma]

FURTHER READING:

Hollohan, Brian. ''The Budget Meets the Target.'' *Canadian Outlook*. Spring 1995, pp. 1-7.

Myatt, Anthony et. al. ''Atlantic Canada: Performance and Prospects.'' *Canadian Business Economics*. April-June 1995, pp. 29-41.

''Performance 500.'' *Canadian Business*. June 1995, pp. 89-130.

''The Top Software and Professional Service Companies in Canada.'' *The Financial Post Magazine*. March 1995, pp. 37-62.

CAPITAL ASSET PRICING MODEL

The capital asset pricing model (CAPM) is one of the most important contributions of financial economics. It is the first model to fully describe the relationship between risk and return in a rational, equilibrium market. The CAPM has been employed in applications ranging from corporate capital budgeting to setting public utility rates (by specifying their ''natural'' rate of return). Additionally, the CAPM provides much of the justification for the trend toward passive investing in large index mutual funds.

The CAPM was simultaneously and independently discovered by William Sharpe, John Lintner, and Jan Mossin. Their research appeared in three different, highly respected journals during the period 1964-66. The investment community viewed the new model with suspicion, since it seemed to indicate that professional investment management was largely a waste of time. It was nearly a decade before invest-ment professionals began to view the CAPM as an important tool in helping people understand risk.

The key element of the model is that it separates the risk affecting an asset's return into two categories. The first risk is called unsystematic, or firm-specific, risk. The long-term average return for this kind of risk should be zero. The second kind of risk, called systematic risk, is due to general economic uncertainty. The CAPM states that the return to **assets** should, on average, equal the yield to a risk-free bond held over that time plus a premium proportional to the amount of systematic risk the stock possesses.

RISK IN THE CAPM

The treatment of risk in the CAPM refines the notions of systematic and unsystematic risk developed by Harry M. Markowitz in the 1950s. Unsystematic risk is the risk to an asset's value caused by factors or people specific to that company. For example, specific employees may make good or bad decisions, or the same type of manufacturing equipment may have different reliabilities at two different sites. In general, unsystematic risk derives from the fact that every company is endowed with a specific collection of assets, ideas, personnel, etc., which on any given day may work well or poorly.

A fundamental principle of all modern portfolio theory standard is that this kind of risk can be diversified away. That is, by holding many different assets, random fluctuations in the value of one will be neutralized by opposite fluctuations in another. For example, if one fast food company makes a bad policy decision, its lost customers will go to a different establishment. The investor in both companies will find that the losses in the former investment are balanced by gains in the latter.

Systematic risk is risk that cannot be removed by diversification. This risk represents the variation in an asset's value caused by unpredictable economic movements. This risk type represents the necessary risk that owners of a firm must accept when launching an enterprise. Regardless of product quality or executive ability, sometimes the economy is in a better state and the profits are higher than at other times.

In the capital asset priceing model, the relative amount of systematic risk an asset contains is measured by the market β. The returns to an asset with $\beta = 1$ will, on average, move equally with the returns of the overall market. Assets with $\beta < 1$ will experience average movements in return less extreme than the overall market, while those with $\beta > 1$ will on average have return fluctuations greater than the overall market. β is defined as the covariance of an asset's returns with the market divided by the variance of the market's return. The market's return is most often determined by using the return to a large equity index such as the Standard and Poor's 500 (S&P 500) or the Wilshire 5000.

The preceding paragraphs may be summarized by writing the risk equation for assets as follows:

$$\sigma_i^2 = \beta_{im}^2 \sigma_m^2 + \sigma_e^2$$

where:

- σ_i^2 is the variance of asset i's return, called the total risk of asset i

- $\beta_{im}^2 \sigma_m^2$ is the part of an asset's return variance caused by the market, called the systematic risk

- σ_e is the part of asset's return variance caused by firm-specific events, called the unsystematic risk.

RETURN IN THE CAPM

The CAPM models return to an asset by the following three guidelines. First, all assets must have an expected return of at least the return to a risk-free bond (except for rare assets with $\beta < 0$, which will be discussed below). The rationale is that any risky asset must be expected to return at least as much as one without risk or there would be no incentive for anyone to hold the risky asset.

Second, there is no expected return to taking unsystematic risk since it may easily be avoided. Diversification is simple, does not affect the economics of the assets being held, and only helps the people holding the assets. Therefore, there is no compensation inherent in the model for accepting this needless risk by choosing to hold an asset in isolation.

Finally, assets that contain systematic risk are expected to receive a return higher than the risk-free rate by an amount proportional to the amount of this risk present in the asset. This risk cannot be diversified away and must be borne by someone if the assets are to be financed and employed productively. The higher the amount of this risk, the higher the return to the asset if the market goes up and the lower the return to the asset if the market goes down. Therefore, the higher the systematic risk the higher the average long-term return must be for people to accept the risk.

The market risk premium is reported by R. Ibbotsen and R. Sinquefield to average about 6.1 percent. This amount is modified by the β which scales it up or down depending on the sensitivity to market movements the asset possesses. Interestingly, some assets have a negative premium. This is because their β is less than zero, meaning the assets' expected return is less than the risk-free rate. Assets with negative β are those that actually hedge against general

economic risk, doing well when the economy performs poorly. Examples of this type of asset are precious metals.

The preceding discussion may be summarized by the security market line (SML) which has the equation

$$E[R_i] = R_f + \beta_{im} E[R_m - R_f]$$

where:

- $E[R_i]$ is the expected return to asset i

- R_f is the risk free rate of return

- β_{im} is asset i's market beta

- $E[R_m - R_f]$ is the expected market risk premium

Graphically, the SML may be represented by the graph in Figure 1.

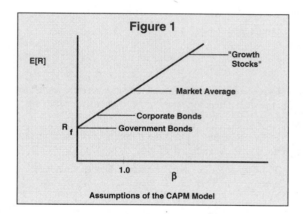

ASSUMPTIONS OF THE CAPM

The CAPM uses many assumptions to obtain its conclusions. Some are essential for the model to work, others cause only minor changes if they are untrue. Much research into the plausibility and effects of violations in these assumptions has been conducted since the early 1970s. The assumptions that form the basis for the CAPM are:

1. People measure asset risk by the variance of its return over the next period. All other measures of risk are unimportant.

2. People always desire more return to less, and they are risk averse; that is they will avoid risk if all else is equal.

3. There are no restrictions on the borrowing and lending of money at the risk-free rate of interest.

4. All possible investments are traded in the market which is available to everyone, the

assets are infinitely devisable, and there are no restrictions on short selling.

5. The market is perfectly efficient. That is, everyone perceives the same information, processes accurately, and trades costlessly. Moreover, taxes do not affect any person's decisions.

EMPIRICAL TESTS OF THE CAPM

Two of the first tests of the CAPM reported that the CAPM seemed to hold except that the SML intercept was estimated to be approximately 3 to 4 percent higher than the risk-free rate. This is consistent with a CAPM model where money cannot actually be borrowed at the risk-free rate.

R. Roll wrote a famous article in which he argued that tests of the CAPM are inherently impossible. The article isquite technical, but its basic point is the following. Since noone can observe the true market portfolio, only a proxy index, and since no one can actually observe expected returns, only average realized ones, it is impossible to know whether the correct relationship is actually being tested.

More recent tests of the CAPM show that there are many apparent violations of a strict interpretation in the model. Examples include unusually high returns for small companies in January, and different average returns on Friday and Monday than the rest of the week. Some analysts have argued that stock returns are more closely related to total variability and book value of the stock than a beta calculated using the market index.

Others argue that many apparent inconsistencies can arise in the CAPM because a capital-weighted index (such as the S&P 500) may not be an appropriate proxy for the market portfolio if both assumptions about short selling of assets and borrowing of risk-free assets are violated.

EXTENSIONS TO THE CAPM

In 1976, S. Ross published a model, named the arbitrage pricing theory (APT), which avoids the need for specifying a market portfolio, and has generally been found to be more powerful. Unfortunately, the model is less intuitive and is more difficult to implement. In the APT, an asset's return is related to multiple economic factors instead of the market portfolio. The APT equation may be written as:

$$E[R_i] = R_f + \beta_{1i}\lambda_1 + \cdots + \beta_{ni}\lambda_n$$

where β_{1i} is now a beta of asset i with respect to economic factor j, and each λ_1 is the risk premium for accepting the economic risk that factor j represents.

Another attempt to modify the CAPM involves making it intertemporal in nature. With intertemporal modeling, people consider the consequences of decisions over multiple periods, instead of over the next period only as the CAPM assumes. The resulting consumption capital asset pricing model (CCAPM) is much more complex than its nonintertemporal counterpart. Nevertheless, it has been shown to work successfully in situations where the normal CAPM has failed, most notably for forward exchange rates and for futures markets.

Many other adaptations of the CAPM are in use, from allowing for different tax rates among individuals, to allowing for people who look at both variance and skewness in assessing risk. It is a tribute to the widespread application of the CAPM that so many individuals have improved, transformed, or modified it to fit specific situations.

APPLYING THE CAPM

Despite limitations, the capital asset pricing model remains the best general description of long-term trade-offs between risk and return in the financial markets. Although very few people actually use the CAPM without modifications, its general principles are extremely important to understand, and may be sufficient for the average long-term investor to make investment decisions. These principles may be stated as:

1. Be diversified (there is no compensation for unsystematic risk)

2. Hold long term (do not worry about timing when to get in or out of the market).

3. To get a higher return, take more systematic risk (the more stocks one holds that are sensitive to the business cycle the more average return the portfolio will receive).

For shorter term, or more sophisticated investing, other models have been developed. Nevertheless, unless the model is based on market inefficiencies, or obtaining superior information, it will still have the CAPM's basic principles at its center.

[Rick A. Cooper]

FURTHER READING:

Bernstein, P. *Capital Ideas, the Improbable Origins of Modern Wall Street*. New York: Free Press, 1992.

Black, F., M. C. Jensen, and M. Scholes. "The Capital Asset Pricing Model: Some Empirical Tests." In *Studies in the Theory of Capital Markets*, edited by Jensen. New York: Praeger, 1972.

Fama, E., and K. French. "The Cross-Section of Expected Stock Returns." *Journal of Finance* 47. 1992, pp. 427-466.

Fama, E., and J. MacBeth. "Risk, Return, and Equilibrium: Empirical Tests." *Journal of Political Economy* 71. 1973, pp. 607-636.

Haugen, R. *Modern Investment Theory*. 3rd ed. Englewood Cliffs, NJ: Prentice Hall, 1993.

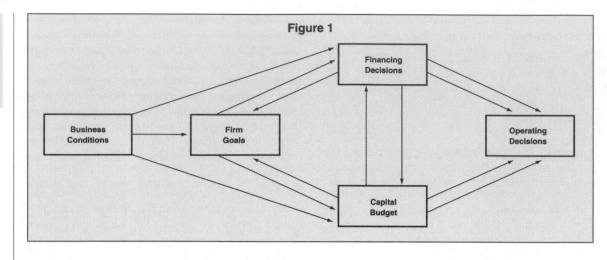

Figure 1

Ibbotsen, R., and R. Sinquefield. "Stocks, Bonds, Bills, and Inflation: Year-by-Year Historical Returns (1926-1974)." *Journal of Business* 49. 1976, pp. 11-43.

Keim, D., and R. Stambaugh. "A Further Investigation of the Weekend Effect in Stock Returns." *Journal of Finance* 39. 1984, pp. 819-835.

Lintner, J. "The Valuation of Risk Assets and the Selection of Risky Investments in Stock Portfolios and Capital Budgets." *Review of Economics and Statistics* 47. 1965, pp. 13-37.

Markowitz, H. "Portfolio Selection." *Journal of Finance* 7 1952, pp. 77-91.

Mossin, J. "Equilibrium in a Capital Asset Market" *Econometrica* 34. 1966, pp. 768-83.

Roll, R. "A Critique of the Asset Pricing Theory's Tests; Part I: On Past and Potential Testability of the Theory." *Journal of Financial Economics* 4. 1977, pp. 129-176.

Ross, S. "The Arbitrage Theory of Capital Asset Pricing." *Journal of Economic Theory* 13. 1976, pp. 341-360.

Schwert, G. "Size and Returns, and other Empirical Regularities." *Journal of Financial Economics* 12. 1983, pp. 3-12.

Sharpe, W. "Capital Asset Prices: A Theory of Market Equilibrium Under Conditions of Risk." *Journal of Finance* 19. 1964.

CAPITAL BUDGET

Capital expenditures are the allocation of resources to large, long-term projects. These projects are in essence the strategy chosen by the firm to reach it's goals. The capital budget is a statement of the planned capital expenditures. It is more than a simple listing, however, and is not a "budget" in the usual sense. Given the nature of capital expenditures, the capital budget is best thought of as an expression of the goals and strategy of the firm. Creation of the capital budget is a central task which affects, and is affected by, all others areas of **decision making**. The "capital budgeting process" can be envisioned as in Figure 1. Present and anticipated business conditions

are the environment within which the goals of the firm are developed. The goals drive the strategic decisions of capital budget and financing, but feasibility and consistency with the interdependent financing and capital budget decisions must be considered in setting the goals. Operating decisions may be thought of as the tactical choices driven by strategy, but again feasibility and consistency must be considered in setting strategy. The process is in actuality part simultaneous, part iterative. Given the interdependency of goals, strategy, and tactics in a changing environment, the capital budget is properly considered as a planning document, rather than a fixed conclusion.

From a narrow economic viewpoint creating the capital budget is relatively simple: a project should be accepted if the return is greater than the cost. Projects are listed in order of decreasing return, and investment should continue until the marginal return (roughly, the return to the next dollar expended) is greater than marginal cost (roughly, the required rate of return on the next dollar). This simple, elegant statement of the problem masks a number of complications. In the simple formulation, projects are considered homogeneous in risk, so that the cost (required rate of return) is solely a function of the size of the capital budget. Under more realistic conditions, projects may have different risk. Other problems include mutually exclusive projects, interdependency of projects, different project lives, and complicated and uncertain cash flows.

CAPITAL BUDGETING TECHNIQUES

Various techniques have been developed for application to individual projects. The simplest individual technique is the payback period, the time required for total cash inflows to equal total cash outflows. Projects are ranked according to payback period, and accepted if the payback period is below some maximum. While simple to compute, the maximum acceptable period is arbitrary, the technique does not consider the time value of money, and cash flows past the payback period are ignored. An alternative is the accounting rate of return, the average change in accounting earnings due to the project expressed as a percent of the initial cost. This technique also has no definite cutoff rate and fails to consider the time value of money, and is based on accounting earnings rather than on actual cash flows.

Discounted cash flow (DCF) techniques are preferable because they consider the time value of money, are based on actual cash flows rather than accounting profits, and have a definite standard. The present value of a series of cash flows is the amount required to just recreate the cash flows at a given rate of return. The present value of a project is the amount which, if invested at the rate of return required by the project, could produce the same cash flows as the project. The net present value (NPV) is computed as the difference between the present value of the project, and the cost of the project. It can be thought of as the value to the firm of undertaking the project. If NPV is negative, the present value of the cash flows is less than the cost of the project. Since the cash flows could be created more cheaply by investing at the required rate, the rate of return on the project is below the required rate, and the project is rejected. Where NPV is positive, the project return is greater than the required return and should be accepted. An alternate DCF technique is the internal rate of return (IRR). This is the rate of return which would be required to exactly recreate the cash flows from an investment equal to the cost of the project. If the IRR is greater than the required rate of return, the project should be accepted.

The rule of accepting projects until marginal return no longer exceeds marginal cost assumes unlimited funds. This assumption is theoretically justified on the basis that if marginal return exceeds the marginal cost, increasing the capital budget will return more than it costs. There are, however, a number of other reasons for limiting the size of the capital budget. Estimation of NPV or IRR proceeds on a project basis, but performance will be degraded if the firm accepts too many projects in a short space of time. Externally, lenders or investors may be unwilling to provide funds or may require added return or limitations on management past a certain point. Where funds are limited and not all otherwise acceptable projects can be implemented, a ranking technique is necessary.

While IRR and NPV will always give the same accept/reject decision, the ranking of projects on IRR may differ from the ranking on NPV. This difference in ranking arises because of differences in the implicit assumptions about the rate of return on cash flows from the project. The NPV technique implicitly assumes reinvestment of cash flows at the required rate of return, while the IRR implicitly assumes reinvest-

ment of cash flows at the IRR. The required rate is usually close to the actual reinvestment rate. The IRR, on the other hand, may depart widely from the actual reinvestment rate. Since NPV has the more accurate assumption, it is considered superior. Additionally, where net cash inflows are required at some point during the life of the project, IRR becomes ambiguous. Where information about the actual reinvestment rate is obtainable, however, both NPV and IRR can be modified to reflect this rate. This is accomplished by compounding all cash flows forward until the end of the project, and recomputing the IRR or the NPV based on the final amount. Finally, NPV provides a definite estimate of the value of the project, and can more easily be used to compare projects of differing length.

REQUIRED RATE OF RETURN

Determination of the required rate of return (sometimes called the ''hurdle rate'') is integral to evaluating projects and setting the capital budget. The controlling concept is that of opportunity cost. Opportunity cost reflects the idea that the relevant cost of using a resource is the rate of return on the competing alternative use of the resource. For projects which are extensions of or similar to the normal operations of the firm, and so have a similar risk profile, a readily available comparable use of funds is reinvesting in the firm itself. For these projects, the opportunity cost/required rate of return/hurdle rate can be approximated by the firm's weighted average cost of capital (WACC). WACC is computed by first estimating the rate of return required to meet the obligations for each source of capital. These obligations would include interest or **dividends**, flotation costs, and other similar expenses. The costs are then weighted according to the target **capital structure** of the firm to obtain the overall rate of return required to meet the combined obligations—the WACC. This is the return which could be obtained by reinvesting within the firm (downsizing).

Where the project is outside the normal operations of the firm or has a different risk profile, the weighted average cost of capital is not a good estimate of the required rate of return on the project. The required rate of return may be estimated by using the WACC for firms similar in nature to the project, or based on the systematic risk. These comparison-based estimates are satisfactory for projects of standardized technology which does not require that the firm develop new expertise. Where the project is nonstandard or innovative, or requires developing new expertise, such comparison my underestimate the risk. In such cases the required return on the new project must be arrived at by ad hoc adjustment. Decision tree, Monte Carlo, or other risk analysis tools are helpful.

LIMITATIONS OF QUANTITATIVE TECHNIQUES

An accept or reject indication on the above criteria does not mean that a project should be automatically accepted or rejected. First, the criteria are based on estimated cash flows and an estimated required rate. The estimates are themselves subject to uncertainty and this may lead to an increase or safety factor in the "hurdle." Second, as noted, the estimates proceed on a project basis, and their may be an interaction between projects. Third, and perhaps most important, the criteria consider only cash flows, and some factors cannot be reduced to a monetary basis. It must be remembered that a capital budget is in reality the strategy chosen to reach the goals of the firm. The indications of the quantitative economic analysis are only a part of the strategic planning process and are subsidiary to overall strategic considerations. Unless a project is compatible with the goals of the firm, it will not be accepted. Conversely, if a project has non-monetary benefits or interaction with other projects, it may be accepted despite a negative indication. Again, the capital budget is a planning document, and the greatest contribution of the capital **budgeting** exercise is not the indicated decision, but the heuristic benefits of greater understanding.

Finally, ethical standards are a vital part of the strategic considerations. An otherwise acceptable project may be unacceptable on ethical grounds. The social impact of projects has become increasingly important. It is necessary to consider the **externalities**—the effects of the project which are not felt by the firm. Externalities include such items as environmental impact and required increase in **infrastructure**.

[David Upton]

FURTHER READING:

Petty, J. William, Arthur J. Keown, David F. Scott, Jr., and John D. Martin. *Basic Financial Management, 6th ed.* Prentice Hall.

Pinches, George E. *Essentials of Financial Management.* HarperCollins Publishers.

Levy, Haim, and Marshall Sarnat. *Capital Investment & Financial Decisions.* Prentice Hall.

CAPITAL GAIN/LOSS

A capital gain or loss results from the sale, trade, or exchange of a capital asset. Simply stated, when the resulting transaction nets an amount lower than the value of the capital asset according to the basis, a capital loss occurs. When the resulting transaction nets an amount greater than the basis, a capital gain occurs. Capital gain/loss can either be short-term (transaction completed within one year) or long-term (transaction completed in more than one year). The factors relevant to capital gain/loss are the capital asset, the transactional event, and time.

The subject of capital gain/loss causes much debate in government and economic circles. The current philosophy rests on the principle of the benefits and efficiencies of capital accumulation and utilization. To encourage capital formation and investment, the federal tax codes tax capital gains at lower rates than ordinary income. In 1994, the maximum income tax rates were 31 percent, 36 percent, and 39.6 percent. The maximum tax rate on capital gain was 28 percent.

CAPITAL ASSETS

Everything one owns for personal use, pleasure, or investment is a capital asset. These include: securities, a residence, household furnishings, a personal car, coin and stamp collections, gems and jewelry, and precious metals.

PROPERTY HELD FOR PERSONAL USE. The property one holds for personal use is a capital asset. The sale or exchange of that property above the basis results in a capital gain, and is taxable. If one incurs a loss on that property from a sale or exchange, however, the person may not deduct the loss unless the loss resulted from a personal casualty loss, such as fire, flood, and hurricane.

INVESTMENT PROPERTY, COLLECTIBLES, PRECIOUS METALS, AND GEMS. All investment property is a capital asset. Therefore, any gain or loss is generally a capital gain or loss, but only when it is realized, that is, upon completion of the transactional event. For example, the public is familiar with the vagaries of the stock market where investors often claim substantial gain/loss in their positions. For a gain/loss to be realized, investors must actually sell shares at a market price higher or lower than their original purchase price.

The federal revenue code (Section 1244) treats losses on certain small business stock differently. If a loss is realized, one can deduct the loss as an ordinary loss. The individual, however, if holding the stock, will report gains as capital gain.

SALE OF A HOME. The sale of a personal residence enjoys special tax treatment in order to minimize the impact of long-term inflation, and to accommodate the changing lifestyle needs of persons 55 and over.

The residence, for most, is the largest asset an individual owns. While some appreciation is expected, residences are not primarily investment vehicles. Inflation may cause the value of a home to increase substantially while the constant-dollar value may increase very little. In addition, the growth in family size may encourage a family to step up to a larger home. To minimize the impact of inflation and to subsidize the new purchase, the tax code does not require reporting a capital gain if the individual purchases a more expensive house within two years.

For individuals 55 and over who are downsizing (perhaps due to the ''empty nest''), the code allows a once-in-a-lifetime exclusion of $125,000 of realized gain if the owners lived in that home three years of the last five.

SHORT-TERM AND LONG-TERM

Any capital gain or loss on investment property held for one year or less is a short-term capital gain or loss. Capital gain or loss on property held for more than one year is long-term. The period is determined from the day after acquisition to the day of disposal. This also applies to securities purchased on established markets irrespective of the settlement dates.

BASIS

Capital gain/loss is calculated on the cost basis which is the amount of cash and debt obligation used to pay for a property, and the fair market value of other property or services the purchaser provided in the transaction. The purchase of a property may include these charges and fees which are added to the basis to arrive at the adjusted basis:

1. Sales tax.

2. Freight charges.

3. Installment and testing fees.

4. Excise taxes.

5. Legal and accounting fees that are capitalized rather than expensed.

6. Revenue stamps.

7. Recording fees.

8. Real estate taxes where applicable.

9. Settlement fees in real estate transactions.

The basis may be increased by the value of capital improvements, assessments for site improvements (such as the public **infrastructure**), and the restoration of damaged property.

A basis is reduced by transactional events that recoup part of the original purchase price through tax savings, tax credits, and other transactions. These include **depreciation**, nontaxable corporate distributions, various environmental and energy credits, reimbursed casualty or theft losses, and the sale of an easement.

After adjusting the basis for these various factors, the individual subtracts the adjusted basis from the net proceeds of the sale to determine gain/loss.

NET GAIN OR LOSS

To calculate the net gain/loss, the individual first determines the long-term gain/loss and short-term gain/loss separately. The net short-term gain/loss is the difference between short-term gains and short-term losses. Likewise, this difference on a long-term basis is the net long-term gain/loss.

If the individual's total capital gain is more than the total capital loss, the excess is taxable generally at the same rate as the ordinary income. However, the part of the capital gain which is the same amount as the net capital gain is taxed only at the capital gains tax rate, maximum 28 percent.

If the individual's capital losses are more than the total capital gains, the excess is deductible up to $3,000 per year from ordinary income. The remaining loss is carried forward and deducted at a rate up to $3,000 until the entire capital loss is written off.

SEE ALSO: Capital; Taxes and Taxation

[Roger J. AbiNader]

FURTHER READING:

U.S. Treasury Depratment. Internal Revenue Service. *Tax Guide for Small Business*. Washington, D.C.: GPO, 1995.

CAPITAL MARKETS

Financial markets are defined as the institutions and procedures that facilitate transactions in financial securities. Financial markets can be categorized as either money markets or capital markets. The money market is the market for debt instruments with a maturity of one year or less at the time of issuance. Major examples of money market instruments include: **treasury bills**, commercial paper, and Eurodollar deposits. On the other hand, the capital market consists of those institutions and procedures that provide for transactions in long-term financial instruments with a maturity of more than one year. Thus, capital markets include the bond and **stock markets**.

The U.S. bond market can be categorized into three major issuers; the U.S. government, corporations, and municipalities. Corporate bonds constitute a smaller amount of long-term borrowing than either mortgages or municipal bonds.

The initial distribution of securities takes place in the primary market. The secondary market is a market for existing securities. Secondary markets may be established in the form of an organized exchange or as an over-the-counter (OTC) securities market. The predominant organized market is the New York Stock Exchange, but increasing attention is being directed to other markets. Although bonds dwarf stocks by a ratio of almost five to one in the primary market, secondary stock market volume is much greater than secondary bond market volume.

ORGANIZATION OF THE STOCK MARKET

A stock exchange is a voluntary organization formed by a group of individuals to provide an institutional setting in which **common stock**, and other financial securities, can be purchased and sold. Members of stock exchanges own seats on the exchange, and only members or their representatives are allowed to trade on the exchange. Each stock exchange allows trading only during approved trading hours on the floor of the exchange, which is an actual physical location. The New York Stock Exchange (NYSE) is the largest of the world's organized exchanges. Only firms meeting certain minimum requirements regarding financial strength and number of shareholders are eligible for listing. These requirements mean that only larger firms qualify for NYSE listing.

Trading on the OTC market has been growing faster than trading on organized exchanges, and advances in computer technology are expected to benefit the OTC market more than the organized exchanges. In the OTC market, there is no central trading location, but electronic communications systems are used to link participants. Firms traded OTC tend to be quite smaller than NYSE firms. The OTC market consists of about 15,000 securities, although many of these have only a local market. The most important stocks on the OTC market are listed on the National Market System, and transactions for these securities are reported more rapidly and more completely than for the less important stocks.

PRIVATE PLACEMENTS VERSUS PUBLIC OFFERINGS

In a **public offering**, the security is offered to the public, giving any investor the right to purchase part of the new issue. The issuing process is governed by the **Securities Act of 1933**. In private placements, the entire issue is sold to a single buyer, or a small consortium of buyers, without the issue ever being made available to the public.

Issuers may prefer private placements because they do not have to disclose information about the firm or its strategies in registration documents. Privately placed securities cannot be sold, since they have never undergone the process of scrutiny required for a public offering. Because these securities cannot

be resold, they carry a higher yield. The issuer, however, saves on flotation costs. Thus, the buyer of a privately placed issue forgoes liquidity in order to obtain the higher return paid on privately placed securities.

THE ROLE OF THE INVESTMENT BANKER

Investment bankers assist companies and government entities in issuing securities by acting as consultants, forming distribution networks, and bearing risk. Investment bankers often advise on the timing and pricing of securities. The ideal time to issue common stock is near stock market peaks; for bonds, the ideal time occurs when **interest rates** are low. The objective in pricing an issue is to set the highest price that will allow all of the issue to be sold in a short period.

Usually one investment bank is the lead bank for the issue. It has the primary responsibility for the issuance of a security. The syndicate members are other investment banking firms that assist in the offering of a given security. In addition, a selling group consisting of those investment houses that are participating to a smaller degree in the distribution process is also involved. The investment banker generally acts as an underwriter, and buys the securities from the issuing firm and then attempts to resell them to the public at a profit. Alternatively, the investment banker may distribute the issue on a best efforts basis whereby the bank promises to sell the securities at the best price it can obtain.

The costs of issuing securities are termed flotation costs. Flotation costs include the spread which is the difference between the price paid by the final investor and the amount the issuing firm receives from the sale of the security. Spreads are generally lower for debt issues than for issues of common stock. Furthermore, the spread, as a percentage of the proceeds, is smaller the larger the size of the issue.

SEE ALSO: Debt

[Robert T. Kleiman]

FURTHER READING:

Kidwell, David S., and Richard L. Peterson. *Financial Institutions, Markets, and Money*, 4th ed. Hinsdale, IL: Dryden Press, 1990.

Livingston, Miles. *Money and Capital Markets*. Miami, FL: Kolb Publishing, 1992.

CAPITAL STRUCTURE

Capital structure describes how a corporation has organized its capital—how it deploys the financial resources with which it operates its business. As shown on its **balance sheet**, a company's capitalization is constructed from three basic blocks:

1. Long-term **debt**: By standard **accounting** definition, obligations that are not due to be repaid within the next 12 months. Such debt consists mostly of **bonds** or similar obligations, including a great variety of notes, capital lease obligations, and mortgage issues.

2. **Preferred stock**: This represents an equity (ownership) interest in the corporation, but one with claims ahead of the common stock, and normally with no rights to share in the increased worth of a company if it grows.

3. Common stockholders' equity: This represents the underlying ownership. On the corporation's books, it is made up of: (1) the nominal par or stated value assigned to the shares of outstanding stock; (2) the capital surplus or the amount above par value paid the company whenever it issues stock; and (3) the earned surplus (also called retained earnings) which consists of the portion of earnings a company retains, after paying out **dividends** and similar distributions. Arrived at another way, common stock equity is the residual figure after all the **liabilities** (including long-term debt), as well as any preferred stock, are deducted from the total **assets** shown on the balance sheet. For investment analysis purposes, security analysts may use the company's market capitalization—the current market price times the number of common shares outstanding—as a measure of common stock equity. They consider this market-based figure a more realistic valuation.

It should be noted that companies may operate without funded debt or, more frequently, without any preferred stock. By the very nature of corporate structure, however, they must have common stock and the related stockholders' equity account—though, when the company fares badly, the equity can be a negative amount.

In arranging a company's financial structure, **management** normally aims for the lowest feasible cost of capital; whereas an investor seeks the greatest possible return. While these desires can conflict, they are not necessarily incompatible, especially with equity investors. The cost of capital can be kept low and the opportunity for return on common stockholders' equity can be enhanced through leverage—a high percentage of debt relative to common equity. But increased leverage carries with it increased risk. This is the inescapable trade off both management and investors must factor into their respective decisions.

The leverage provided by debt financing is further enhanced because the interest that corporations pay is a tax-deductible expense, whereas dividends to both preferred and common stockholders must be paid with after-tax dollars. Thus, it is argued, the lower net cost of bond interest helps accrue more value for the common.

But, of course, increased debt brings with it higher fixed costs that must be paid in good times and bad, and can severely limit a company's flexibility. The *Financial Handbook*, spells out four problems that tend to increase as leverage escalates: (1) a growing risk of bankruptcy; (2) lack of access to the capital markets during times of **credit** crunch; (3) the need for management to concentrate on finances and raising additional capital, at the expense of focusing on operations; (4) higher costs for whatever additional debt and preferred stock capital the company is able to raise. Aside from the unpleasantness involved, it is noted that each of these factors also entails tangible monetary costs.

The "optimal" capital structure is the one that minimizes the total cost of a corporation's capital. While complex mathematical formulas abound for devising varying capital structures and projecting potential returns under a vast number of scenarios, there is no proven way to arrive at an optimal structure except, to some extent, by hindsight. In practice, there are no fixed rules on what represents an ideal capitalization. In any case, an appropriate capitalization must depend greatly on the nature of the business, prevailing economic and financial conditions, and sundry other shifting factors.

Regulated utilities represent a special case. Agencies and organizations acting as consumer advocates regularly argue that utilities should be held to an optimal capitalization standard—optimal invariably meaning a heavy layer of debt so as to permit a higher percentage of profits to flow to the common, thus reducing the need for rate increases. Utility management in its turn warns of the danger of too much debt and the need for a stronger equity cushion—a structure that will require more **revenues** (i.e., higher rates) for the utility to earn its authorized rate of return.

In earlier days, a debt-free structure was often considered a sign of strength and many industrial companies that were able to finance their growth with an all-common capitalization prided themselves on their "clean balance sheet." Especially in the rapid expansion after World War II, however, the vast demand for capital and low interest rates—made even lower because of tax deductibility—made debt financing increasingly attractive. Not only was the immediate demand on income relatively modest but since the interest requirement remained fixed, all future income growth financed by this debt capital would flow straight through to the common.

Benjamin Graham and David Dodd, often considered the fathers of modern security analysis and noted for their advocacy of prudent investing, long ago pointed to the advantages of a "sound" but not "excessive" amount of debt in the corporate structure. In confronting the "debt-free is best" argument, they shrewdly asked how could you advise a conservative investor to buy good-quality bonds, if the very act of issuing bonds implied that "the company had taken a dangerous and unwise step?" Graham and Dodd recommended: "In most enterprises, a bond component no more than—[but] not too far below—the amount that careful financial institutions would be ready to lend . . . would probably be in the interest of the owners."

The **leveraged buyouts (LBO)** stampede of the 1980s brought a new twist to the capitalization issue. Large corporations with conservative capitalizations became especially vulnerable to capture. Corporate raiders with limited financial resources, had the ability to raise huge amounts of noninvestment-grade ("junk") debt to swing the deals. The captured companies could then be dismembered and stripped of cash holdings so the raiders could pay down their borrowings; in short, the prey's own assets were used to pay for its capture.

As a **takeover** defense, many potential targets began to assume heavy debt themselves, often to **finance** an internal buyout by its own management. Again, success would often depend on the successful sale of major assets.

The raiders make no apology for such actions. As described by Harvard professor Michael C. Jensen, they can purposely leverage the firm so highly (at times with current **income** insufficient to meet current interest requirements) so the company cannot continue to exist in its old form. But, he argued, this "generates benefits. It creates the crisis to motivate cuts in [low-return] expansion programs and the sale of those divisions which are more valuable outside the firm."

The problem with this theory, to some observers, is that it assumes any value tucked away by existing management is automatically fair game for distribution to stockholders—including those who move in for just that purpose—and makes no allowance for the company's long-term needs. As applied, the theory also made little distinction between good and bad management, but tended to brand the management of any targeted company as either inept or feathering-its-own-nest or, mostly, both.

Whatever the merits of the opposing arguments, the flood of LBOs brought with it an essentially new type of security—the **junk bond**, a bond rated as noninvestment grade or speculative.

The position of junk bonds in a capital structure, from a legal and accounting standpoint, is clearly that of debt. It is usually subordinated to the claims of many other lenders, but ranks ahead of any equity holders. From the investor's standpoint, if the bond portion of the portfolio is intended to represent a relatively safe anchor, with a dependable return on well-protected principal, it is important to stick to investment grade issues. For those willing to assume (and able to recognize) the increased risk, a holding of junk bonds, preferably a well-diversified selection, can be justified as part of the more speculative part of the portfolio.

Overall, in assessing a corporation's capital structure, it is important to reiterate not only that is there no single ideal structure, but also that a company's capital needs change constantly and evolve during its operating life. When new long-term financing is needed, it must decide what kind of debt or equity issue is most feasible at that time.

[Henry R. Hecht]

FURTHER READING:

Altman, Edward I., ed. *Financial Handbook.* 5th ed. New York: John Wiley & Sons, 1981.

Cottle, Sidney, Roger F. Murray, and Frank E. Block. *Graham and Dodd's Security Analysis.* New York: McGraw-Hill, 1988.

Fridson, Martin S. "What Went Wrong with the Highly Leveraged Deals." *Journal of Applied Corporate Finance.* Fall, 1991, pp. 57-67.

CAPITALISM

Capitalism is best described as a philosophy of social interaction rather than a strictly mechanical system of economic organization. It reflects the aggregate motivation of an entire population to improve its standard of living through an almost purely self-interested accumulation of wealth. As a result, it is an ultimately complex matrix of individual considerations and judgements.

Many economists have attempted, with limited success, to develop formulas and rules that can adequately explain how "free markets" behave as they do. The human elements inherent in capitalism have created a dearth of understanding that has deprived economists of the ability to accurately predict how the market in a capitalist society will behave in anything but the immediate term; there are simply too many variables for long-term forecasting. Economic analysis has thus been reduced from a scientific endeavor with predictive capabilities to a mere record of observation of the flow and growth of assets in society (although proponents of **econometrics** would debate this viewpoint).

Few people living in modern capitalist societies can offer an accurate description of the social order in which they live. This is largely due to the politicization of capitalism during the 20th century, when it became the centerpiece of western-style representative democratic institutions and a bulwark against domination by the political tyranny of Soviet-style socialism.

Thus capitalism was understood not as a system unto itself, but rather was judged in contrast to societies where markets were under state direction and political structures frustrated personal liberties, including the pursuit of personal wealth. Capitalism became synonymous with the American ideal of self-determination, leading many to believe that government played only a minuscule role in the administration of a capitalist economy.

In fact, the modern capitalist society is not free from government Empire intervention. State institutions govern the volume of money in circulation, manage growth in the economy and, through taxation and regulation, redistribute wealth. Capitalist societies carry the burden of just as much, if not more, direction by the public sector as a socialist economy.

Further complicating matters, economics textbooks define capitalism principally in terms of economic organization, ignoring its societal implications. Capitalism is described as a system in which the factors of production in both large and small industries are privately owned and managed.

By contrast, socialism is said to be a system in which the major factors of production and larger industries are state-owned or controlled, while smaller businesses remain under private control. And communism is described as a system in which all factors of production and all enterprises are state-owned, and market decisions are commanded by a central authority.

By this simple definition, no society is purely capitalist or communist. Postal services, rail transportation, federal banks, and other industries are run by the government in most capitalist societies, while private farms have been encouraged by communist governments.

Capitalism may not, therefore, be defined along purely economic lines, nor is it a necessarily integral feature of Western representative democracy.

THE DEVELOPMENT OF CAPITALISM

Capitalism emerged gradually from an evolution of feudal social values as individuals abandoned traditional forms of servitude in favor of self-employment and acquisition of personal property. This evolution occurred most rapidly in Europe after the collapse of the Roman Empire, during the social revolts in the 15th century that produced the Renaissance.

During this time, many thousands of people won autonomy from religious orders or escaped the control of warlords, landlords, and princedoms to engage in new commercial activities. A new secular merchant class evolved with tremendous capabilities to generate and accumulate personal wealth. Commercial transactions superseded other forms of social interaction, providing new forms of autonomy from established political orders.

Within this realm, merchants developed better production skills and cultivated privileged trading information to maintain sales margins, or profits. These margins were a significant motivating factor that provided the merchant capital with which to purchase food and other necessities as well as luxury items. Profits served as a personal reward for transactions that were now based on economic factors, rather than feudalistic command.

The commercial merchant invested in a raw material, added value by fashioning it into a salable item, and sold it at a premium over the cost of the original raw material. This circuit is described as M-C-M′, where money (M) is invested into a commodity (C), which is then finished and marketed for a larger sum of money (M′).

This marked an evolution of trade not for consumption value, but for exchange value. For example, a potter couldn't trade a thousand clay pots for a horse—but he could sell his pots to others for gold, and then use the gold to buy a horse.

The first scientist to describe this system of wealth accumulation was the world's first true economist, the English professor Adam Smith. In his seminal work *The Wealth of Nations*, published in 1776, Smith described how a merchant may realize production efficiencies by concentrating on making only one product. These items were produced not for his own use, but specifically for sale.

Smith described this as the commodity form of wealth accumulation. It made the best use of the merchant's time and skills relative to the costs of production, and yielded the greatest surplus value for his activity.

But what would the merchant do with his surplus value? In the example of the potter, he could buy a horse, and with that horse transport his wares to new markets that would enable him to increase sales volume. This produced even greater surplus value which might allow him to invest in a larger kiln and hire assistants. And with this increased output he became richer yet.

But this raised another question—why get rich? Merchants are surely motivated to accumulate wealth to improve their standard of living. Beyond that, wealth may afford someone great influence and power, but what continues to drive a rich man to even greater wealth when all his worldly desires are satisfied?

It is possible that such a person may consider wealth as an avenue to immortality or provide insurance against future hardship—or perhaps making money is simply an enjoyable intellectual exercise. In any case, the answer has no bearing on the indisputable fact that almost all people are driven to accumulate personal wealth. Smith called these the "animal spirits" that are inherent in all men.

But capitalism, as it emerged in Europe during the 17th and 18th centuries, involved more than the simple accumulation of personal wealth. It had every bit as much to do with deprivation as it did enrichment.

By definition, the use of personal property may be withheld from others by its owners. This has the effect of limiting supply to yield higher profit margins. For example, the owner of a toll bridge may refuse passage to all but those willing to pay the highest price. Anyone unable or unwilling to pay may not use the bridge.

At the most basic level, all able-bodied people possess personal property, or capital, in the form of their labor. They may enter the market with the option of withholding their services from any employer unwilling to meet their price.

By selling his labor to another person, a worker engages in a "wage-labor" contract. The worker profits from his labor and may use his earnings to buy food, shelter, and other necessities. The employer, however, also realizes a profit from the worker's labor. For instance, he may hire the worker to build a wheel and then sell the wheel for a price that covers both the wage and materials, but also provides a small profit. Thus, through the wage-labor contract a net portion of the worker's surplus value becomes the property of the employer.

During the late 1800s, the German communist Karl Marx argued that this system alienated workers from the surplus value of their labor. The employer controlled the employment of labor—in effect, the capitals necessary to add value to a raw material or service. Marx maintained that laborers were no better off than in feudal societies because of the inherently extractive nature of the relationship between an employer and his workers; social surpluses continued to flow to a superior class. Marx was awed by the ability of this economic order to generate great personal wealth, but it remained a system based on social domination rather than rational exchange.

Because the owner of an enterprise controlled the employment of capitals, including labor, this system was described as *capitalism*. The system works by exposing individuals to a series of costs in the course of daily living. Each individual strives to recoup these costs by making investments in time and capital (including labor) to generate profit. Ideally, these profits not only satisfy the demands of sustenance and cover the cost of the investments, but also provide a surplus.

Profits generally flow from three sources: differences in economic position (affecting the ability to invest), inequalities in skill and market knowledge (affecting costs and market prices), and margins from employed labor.

But the capitalist must also compete for profits in the marketplace. For example, the bridgeman who charges high tolls may invite a challenge to his monopoly on passage by a competitor who sets up a ferry service. By the same token, laborers with high wage demands may lose their jobs to workers willing to work for less.

Over time, competitive pressures force an employer to cut costs. Wages can be lowered only so far before laborers find it advantageous to seek employment elsewhere. Therefore, employers endeavor to introduce more efficient production methods and, wherever possible, substitute labor with cheaper capital—to replace five workers with a single worker and a machine. All along, the capitalist strives to achieve the highest possible average profit by managing production—that is, producing only enough to yield a marginal profit, but no more.

The competition for profits provides market economies with an excellent ability to allocate. Because it is based strictly on demand, products naturally flow to whichever markets offer the highest price.

The price mechanism inherent in capitalism defines public demand for a product and, therefore, the supply of that product. If, for instance, a population is inundated with snow, the public will compete for the supply of shovels by bidding up their price. This will encourage manufacturers to produce more shovels in order to take advantage of the greater profit provided by the higher price. The greater supply of shovels then reduces public demand for them and the price falls.

Capitalism provides every individual with an opportunity to participate in the market and employ whatever personal capitals are available to generate a profit. Thus social orders based on commercial relationships have supplanted established political systems, and the generation of profits has gained widespread moral acceptance.

Adam Smith and two of his contemporaries, Thomas Robert Malthus and David Ricardo, as well as Marx, described capitalism as a mere "stage," suggesting that the cycle of accumulation inherent in capitalism could only proceed so far. Smith failed to envision a stage beyond capitalism. Malthus suggested that capitalism was doomed to failure because population growth was exponential, while increases in food production were merely arithmetical——the world was doomed to starvation.

Ricardo's views were only slightly less gloomy, but it was Marx who provided the best description of capitalism as a necessary but temporary stage in the evolution of society. Capitalism, Marx declared, would generate its own destruction. Occasionally during the accumulation process, economies would falter in systemic "crises." These spasms yielded social upheavals in which capitals were reorganized and economies were prepared for subsequent cycles of accumulation in which wealth was concentrated into the hands of ever more privileged classes.

Marx argued that these crises would become more serious over time and eventually would inspire a revolution in which the laborers who were alienated from the profits of their effort would seize wealth from the higher classes and establish a society in which all property was communally owned and deprivation was eliminated—or, at least, averaged.

While Marx is regarded as the father of modern communism, he devoted nearly all his writings to the demise of capitalism rather than the creation of a communist society. Marx's analysis of capitalism was brilliant for the late 1800s, but he could not foresee the growing intervention of governments, the rise of powerful labor unions, nor the influence of new technologies. These developments relieved the pressures that Marx said would produce political revolution, rendering his ideas all but obsolete.

Nevertheless, the cycles of glut, financial panic, and economic recession, most notably in 1907 and 1929, forced the intervention of governments in free market economies specifically to maintain order. The public sector took a greater role in managing the economy—driving expansionary forces away from the ruinous cycle of crises Marx described.

The role of central **banks** was expanded to afford government greater control over the money supply, interest rates, investment, and economic expansion. Laws and regulations were established to govern the activities of corporations and other owners of capital, and massive state programs were initiated to stimulate employment, savings, and growth. The best example of the growing role of government in the economy was the New Deal policies of the 1933 Roosevelt Administration.

The creation of "state capitalism" has preserved expansionary cycles in a free market system, allowing certain risks, abuses, and forms of deprivational or monopolistic behavior to be eliminated. State-managed free market societies feature large public sectors, whose primary function is regulation, administration, and coordination of the economy. The result has been

greater control over the occasional crises, or "recessions," in the business cycle.

This involvement ensures that wealth is more evenly distributed throughout the population, breaking down the "class consciousness" Marx described and eliminating the conflicts that could cause political revolution.

Another feature of modern capitalist states is the presence of powerful and well-organized labor unions. Unions play an important role in allowing the workers to enforce demands upon employers under the threat of legal strikes. Thus the lowest-skilled worker—the "proletariat" Marx described—is capable of winning demands for better compensation by bargaining as a united workforce. Alienation from capital is no longer a severely socially divisive issue.

Malthus's depressing scenario of population growth and starvation has been made moot by technology. Production methods have been established that more than quadruple the yield of crops and other food sources. But more so, technology has raised the standard of living for the entire population, as products expand to other of markets, further obscuring the class consciousness that defined Marx's time.

Numerous other social scientists have contributed to the study of free market capitalism, including Max Weber, Thorstein Veblen, and John Stuart Mill. Each provided criticisms of the ability of a capitalist society to allocate wealth to an underclass.

One of the most important economists of the 20th century was John Maynard Keynes, who in 1936 argued in favor of government intervention in free market economies during recessionary cycles. His theories formed much of the justification for the programs launched by Roosevelt.

State capitalism, as it has become known, has been attacked by political conservatives in England and the United States who argued that it is socialist in nature. It restricts personal freedoms to pursue the accumulation of wealth and eliminates incentives to compete.

The battle between noninterventionism (described as neo-classicism) and limited intervention (Keynesianism) rages on within the political realm as conservative and liberal administrations trade positions of leadership in democracies.

The politicization of economic systems was especially pronounced after World War II, when capitalist western nations faced a competition for resources, political influence, and wealth with the communist Soviet Union. Economic philosophy thus became an instrument of geopolitical competition.

The United States, having emerged from the war as the most formidable military power in the world, exercised an unrivalled capability to project cultural and economic influence. This provided the United States and its allied economies with access to raw materials and new markets, fueling technological development and economic growth.

Socialist governments, namely in the Soviet Bloc, lost this competition in the early 1990s and were forced to abandon the cause of communism. Democratic governments in the former Soviet sphere have adopted capitalist mechanisms to drive the accumulation of national wealth. The establishment of free markets provides every individual with an opportunity to achieve a higher standard of living through participation in the market and efficient employment of personal capitals.

As Smith, Marx, and others imagined, a stage after capitalism has in fact emerged. But it is merely a system derivative of capitalism, rather than a radically new form of socioeconomic interaction.

In summation, capitalism is an historically developed ideology of social organization that evolved from the natural instincts of self-interest that are inherent in all humans. It is an order of social interaction, accumulation, and production that provides direct rewards to every person for the employment of his own capitals.

The engine of capitalism is private property and its primary motivational factor is profit. People are inspired to employ their personal capitals to recoup their investment—and perpetuate the cycle of production—and also generate profit. The profit thus becomes a reward for the activity, as it may be used to purchase items that raise the person's standard of living.

[John Simley]

FURTHER READING:

Albrecht, Wm. P., Jr. *Economics*, 4th ed. Englewood Cliffs, NJ: Prentice-Hall, 1986.

Baumol, Wm. J. and Alan S. Blinder. *Economics, Principles and Policy*, 2nd ed. New York: Harcourt Brace Jovanovich, 1982.

Cairncross, Sir Alec and Peter Sinclair. *Introduction to Economics*, 6th ed. London: Butterworth, 1982, pp. 135-137.

Eatwell, J., Ed. *The New Palgrave Dictionary of Economics*. London: Macmillan, 1987, pp. 347-353.

Fischer, Stanley and Rudiger Hornbusch. *Economics*. New York: McGraw-Hill, 1983.

CAPITALIZATION RATE

A capitalization rate (''cap rate'') is the rate at which earnings, **dividends**, or cash flows are converted into value or **equity**. (The root word of capital-

ize is capital, meaning equity interest.) A confusing aspect of the term cap rate is that some people use it to mean a whole number to multiply against the earnings measure, whereas others interpret it as a fraction by which the earnings figure is divided. Mechanically, the conversion of earnings to capital is done by either dividing or multiplying the selected earnings figure by the appropriate cap rate under the circumstances. The conversion formula will be one of the following:

$$\text{Capital Value} = \text{Earnings} / \text{Cap Rate}$$
(Where cap rate is stated as a fraction)

or

$$\text{Capital Value} = \text{Earnings} * \text{Cap Rate}$$
(Where cap rate is stated as a multiple)

Since the more common use of the term is as a fraction to be divided into an earnings figure, the remainder of this section will use cap rate in that context. To think of it in the reverse, simply take the reciprocal.

Another confusion about cap rates is that they are occasionally used interchangeably with discount rates. They are distinguished by the fact that the **discount rate** is applied to a series of adjusted future earnings figures, whereas cap rates are applied to a static measure of earnings.

The cap rate is a function of riskiness of the subject earnings, considering volatility, the time horizon, and the size of the entity involved. The higher the risk, the higher the cap rate will be, thus the lower the capitalized value, and vice-versa. This is because given identical cash flows or earnings, investors will place a lower value on those whose future receipt is perceived as more risky; that is, they will be more deeply discounted. Low-risk ventures, on the other hand, will have their earnings discounted only mildly, as there is less uncertainty about the return to the investor.

Probably the most common example to illustrate the cap rate concept is the stock market's price to earnings multiple (the ''P/E ratio''): the reciprocal of this multiple is the market's cap rate for that equity issue. As an example, if a company's stock is trading at $40 per share and its **earnings per share** (EPS) are forecast at $2.50, the P/E ratio is 16. Since the cap rate we have defined is the reciprocal of the P/E ratio, it equals 1/16, or .0625 (6.25 percent).

Care must be exercised when applying cap rates to make sure that factors such as **inflation**, growth rates, and maturity are understood and properly taken into consideration. For example, cap rates calculated by reference to market rates of return are usually stated in nominal terms and therefore include an element representing inflation. Since the amount of earnings or cash flow being capitalized is static, it is stated in real terms, which means that it does not include escalation for future inflation. In this case, the cap rate has to be converted into a real basis by subtracting an estimate of inflation from the observed nominal rate.

Another situation to be wary of is when the cap rate is determined by reference to comparable companies, such taking the reciprocal of the **stock market** P/E ratio. The stock market impounds into its determination of market price expectations about future earnings, including the forecast rate of growth in earnings. P/E ratios will often be significantly impacted by the market's expectation of future growth rate of earnings. For example, two companies with similar earnings and similar risk characteristics may have vastly different growth prospects, due to some outside factor such as management skill or favorable contractual arrangements. The company with the faster growth prospects will have a lower cap rate to divide into its earnings, therefore, other things being equal, will have a higher value.

[Christopher Barry]

CAPITALIZED COSTS

Capitalized costs are those expenses that are incurred in building or financing a fixed asset. Examples of capitalized costs include labor expenses incurred in building a fixed asset or interest expenses incurred as a result of financing the construction of a fixed asset. For accounting purposes, those expenses are capitalized, or added to the cost of the asset. They are not deducted from revenue in the period in which they were incurred. Instead, capitalized costs are deducted from revenues over a period of time through **depreciation**, depletion, or **amortization**.

The way an expense is categorized for accounting purposes affects a company's reported net income. Current net income is obtained by deducting current expenses from current revenues and taking other factors into account. Since capitalized costs are added to the cost of a fixed asset, they contribute to the basis value of the asset upon which depreciation, depletion, and amortization are calculated. Rather than being treated as a current expense and deducted from current revenues, capitalized costs affect net income over several reporting periods through depreciation, depletion, and amortization expenses associated with the fixed asset.

Fixed assets that qualify for such accounting treatment include facilities and other assets that a company constructs for its own use. Also covered are assets that a company constructs as a separate project

and intends to sell or lease, such as a real estate development, a large office building, or a ship. Capitalized costs include certain financing and construction expenses associated with building such assets.

By capitalizing such expenses, or adding them to the cost basis of the asset, a truer accounting picture emerges of the acquisition cost that more accurately reflects the company's investment in the asset. Since the asset will be generating revenue over future periods of time, it is more accurate to deduct the capitalized costs associated with the asset from revenues over those future accounting periods. Adding capitalized costs to the cost basis of a fixed asset follows the standard accounting practice of matching expenses with revenues in the periods in which revenues are earned.

[David P. Bianco]

CAREER AND FAMILY

Balancing the demands of the workplace and the demands of the family is the core of the definition of the term career and family. The joining of the two words, "career," and "family" into a single term came about in the last quarter of the twentieth century as a more complete image of the worker emerged. The worker is not separate from family at work, nor is he or she separate from work when with the family. The joining of the two words reflects the social recognition that the worlds of work and family overlap, influence one another greatly, and policies that affect one, affect the other.

Before the Industrial Revolution, "work" was done in the home or out of the home in a seamless relationship with family life. Often sons (and even daughters) took up the career or work of the parent. The Industrial Revolution saw the beginning of workers leaving the family business to work in the business of someone else. Work became separate from family life. Careers, work in which one gained personal fulfillment as well as financial stability, were restricted to a few professions.

The family unit usually refers to husband/father, wife/mother, and their natural and adopted children. The use of the word "career" and the words "job" or "work" are generally interchangeable today. The use of career, however, implies a commitment to the job market that goes beyond the earning of money and into a work atmosphere that provides satisfaction and with a source of self-esteem. The U.S. Department of Labor reports on many aspects of career and family, using the term "work and family," thus avoiding the normative implications of the word career.

Before the mid-twentieth century women worked primarily within the home. If a woman did have a job outside of the home, generally she stopped working when she became married and/or had children. Especially in the early years of a child's life, a mother's job was in the home and the father's was outside of the home. Variations in this pattern came when a father's income was not sufficient to support the family without the mother also working outside of the home. Women whose husbands were not present in the home or whose husbands had died also found it necessary to work outside of the home. Few married women worked outside of the home at that time, although many women were responsible for the production of many of the family's staples, and some women took in piecework that contributed to the family's income.

Through the early part of the twentieth century many children also worked to support the family, often leaving school at an early age or not attending at all. During the time when the United States was largely rural, this meant that children helped on the family farm. But as the early twentieth century brought more and more people from farms and from distant shores into America's cities, child labor meant children working in factories or mines. Child labor laws were passed in the early twentieth century to promote the sending of children to school rather than into the workplace.

During World War II as men left jobs and went to serve in the military, women were encouraged to enter the **workforce** to replace the men. When the war ended and the men returned, the women were forced out of the jobs and back into the home.

After World War II, higher education became open to more people and many chose to delay entering the workforce and instead continued their schooling. Many who went on to college believed that university training did not prepare one just for a job, but for a career. In the fifties and early sixties more and more women continued their education and then entered the workplace.

At first the workplace reacted by not allowing women in management positions and by implementing policies that made it difficult for women to remain in the workforce after marriage. Antinepotism policies for instance, did not permit married couples to work in the same firm. But as more and more women, married and unmarried, entered the workplace, first the legal and then the corporate cultural and general cultural taboos against women in the workplace began to fall. Beginning with a series of laws in the 1960s, federal legal standards demanded equal treatment and equal pay for men and women of all races. The law demanded that there be no discrimination in hiring.

Another factor which entered the equation was the ability of women to hold nontraditional and managerial jobs that had once been the preserve of men. Once women established their right to enter and remain in the workplace in jobs of their choice, they began to do just that. In the sixties and seventies, women often interrupted their careers when children were born, sometimes waiting until their children started school before reentering the workforce. Some mothers abandoned their careers altogether. This trend began to shift in the 1990s when more and more women with young children remained in the work force.

The U.S. Department of Labor predicts that women will account for 62 percent of its projected 26 million person increase in the civilian work force between 1990 and 2005. Even more startling will be the numbers of women who will be working while their children are still young. Although many mothers have the option of job sharing, flex time, telecommuting, or working part-time, the U.S. Department of Labor predicted in June 1994 that married mothers in the 1990s were more than twice as likely to work full time than were their counterparts in the 1970s. This large number of women in the workplace impelled a reevaluation of the role of outside-the-family **child care** and its relationship to the workplace. The role of the wife/mother as caretaker for elderly family members also underwent a change in the latter quarter of the twentieth century. With the wife/mother working outside of the home the question of who would care for the elderly arose. The corporate culture began to look for new ways to promote the family and meet the new demands for inclusion of women in the workplace. The issues of child care, care for elderly adults, **family leave** for the care of ill family members, and leave for maternity and adoption became paramount in the late 1980s and early 1990s.

Slowly the workplace has begun to respond. The U.S. Department of Labor's Women's Bureau has conducted a number of studies on the issues of women in the workplace and on the impact of work on the family. The workplace has responded with new flexible policies that allow men and women to better meet the demands of home and family. Laws such as the Family and Medical Leave Act of 1993 safeguard the right to maternity leave and the ability to take off time to care for a sick child or an elderly relative without having to fear the loss of one's job.

Some women found that they could not balance the needs of their families and the demands of their careers within the confines of a traditional work arrangement and schedule, so they often left their jobs. Rather than continue to lose the expertise of their women workers, companies began to change their policies and procedures. Many companies now sponsor or help their workers find day care and offer flexible work arrangements for either parent. The U.S. Department of Labor's Women's Bureau publishes resources for managers and women on implementing and executing workplace policies that promote the goals of both career and family simultaneously.

In *Best Companies for Women* Baila Zeitz and Lorraine Dusky report that in 1980 17 percent of all companies surveyed did not allow couples to work in the same company; by 1986 that figure was down to 2 percent. Surveys by Zeitz in 1980-81 and 1986-87 showed a significant increase in the number of companies that offered flexible working hours, maternity care, on-site child care, referrals for child care, and part-time work for professional employees. For instance, in 1980-81 only 37 percent of the companies surveyed had flexible work hours, but by the later survey, that number had risen to 59 percent.

The Family and Medical Leave Act of 1993 (FMLA) allows entitled employees up to 12 weeks of unpaid leave per year for the birth or adoption of a child, or to care for an immediate family member with a serious health condition. Congress's purpose in passing the FMLA was, according to the bill itself, to allow people to have a healthier balance between family obligations and their work lives, and to ensure that family development and cohesiveness are encouraged by our nation's public policy.

SEE ALSO: Women in Business

[Joan Leotta]

FURTHER READING:

Brazelton, T. Berry. *Working and Caring*. New York: Addison Wesley, 1983.

Friedman, Dana, and Ellen Galinsky. *Work and Family Trends*. New York: Families and Work Institute, 1991.

Hayghe, Howard V., and Suzanne M. Bianchi. "Married Mothers' Work Patterns: The Job-Family Compromise." *Monthly Labor Review*. June, 1994, pp. 244.

Scharlach, A., et al. *Eldercare and the Work Force: Blueprint for Action*. Lexington, MA: Lexington Books, 1991.

Zeitz, Baila, and Lorraine Dusky. *The Best Companies for women*. New York: Simon and Schuster, 1988.

CAREER PLANNING AND CHANGING

The average worker will change careers three times in his or her life. He or she will change jobs six times. Sometimes the changes will be voluntary. At other times, they will be forced due to the disappearance of outmoded industries, the emergence of new technologies, shifting demographics, new approaches to **production** and **management** . . . the list goes on. Therefore, it is in workers' best interests to maintain an awareness of both career planning and the need for occasional changes in career paths (also known as re-careering) throughout their business lives. That lesson

was made painfully clear to many workers who lost their jobs during the downsizing trend in the late 1980s and early 1990s.

CAREER CHANGES CAN ARISE AT UNEXPECTED TIMES

Career change (or transition) can arise in a variety of situations. For instance, some people may simply grow tired of their current careers because they have plateaued (reached their highest promotional level), they have acquired new skills, or technology renders certain occupations obsolete. Other people may be making a transition from military to civilian life. Retired people may feel a desire to start a new career, whether it is starting their own business or going into an entirely new field. Regardless of what prompts career changes, there is one common thread among the reasons: people planning changes must be serious about the planning process—and so should anyone preparing to enter the workforce.

THE NEED FOR CAREER PLANNING

Career planning requires that individuals never stop learning and acquiring new employment- and nonemployment-related skills that will enhance their chances of business success. Workers whose career aspirations include nothing more than getting a job— any job—do themselves a disservice. Employers are looking for candidates who are goal oriented and well-rounded. They seek well-prepared people who know exactly what they want in a career and who are willing and able to participate in nonwork activities designed to support an organization's position as a solid corporate citizen. Thus, the career-oriented decisions people make early in their lives may well have a significant impact on their futures—and may make the difference between success and failure in achieving their goals.

People who are looking for more than "just a job" engage in career planning, i.e., a systematic approach to entering a career field which will best match their goals, personal traits, educational backgrounds, and work experience. Career planning involves the continuous development of skills relevant to employment. In effect, career planning is a never-ending process.

THE CAREER PLANNING PROCESS

The career planning process comprises four stages: self-assessment, career exploration, job search, and maintenance. The steps *must* be completed in sequence if people are to benefit from the entire process.

SELF-ASSESSMENT. In the self-assessment stage, individuals perform audits of their emotional, physical, intellectual, and personality characteristics. They may do this on their own or in combination with qualified career counselors. In either case, people must identify their strengths and weaknesses and analyze whether they possess the traits necessary to function in their chosen career field. They must be brutally honest with themselves throughout the process. If they are not, they may set themselves up for failure once they enter the business world.

Self-assessment is in effect a reality check. In this stage, individuals begin their goal setting process. They establish exactly the career fields for which they are best qualified. To do so, they weed out those fields that do not match their personal characteristics. The weeding-out process involves a careful match of an individual's emotional, physical, intellectual, and personality traits and the specifications and responsibilities involved in the career fields. This matching process is completed through a combination of self-evaluation and career tests and inventories such as the Myers-Briggs Type Indicator, which are generally administered and interpreted by career counselors.

Personal honesty is crucial in the self-assessment stage. For example, 5'4, 145-pound individuals who aspire to become National Football League quarterbacks must recognize that their physical characteristics are definite barriers to achieving their goals. Likewise, introverted people may not be the best candidates for sales positions. People who do not recognize—or simply overlook—such limitations are dishonest with themselves, and are setting themselves up for failure.

Certainly, not all limitations should discourage people from pursuing careers they favor. There are some qualifications and characteristics that can be acquired or enhanced through education and experience. The purpose of the self-assessment stage, then, is to identify individual strengths and weaknesses and select career paths accordingly as a first step in the career development process.

Career development is a complex process. There exist many aspects of the process that some people either do not recognize or do not deem important. These aspects should be developed initially in the self-assessment stage. They fall into both personal and occupational categories. The occupational category, for example, includes topics like developing managerial skills, acquiring knowledge about organizational cultures and politics, learning foreign languages, and refining frequently overlooked skills like negotiating and networking. Another aspect of career development that is often not addressed in the self-assessment stage is the ability to recognize and take steps to overcome barriers to advancement such as stereotyping, gender and racial bias, etc.

Personal facets of career development and change include the development of ethics and work values, hobbies, outside interests, and non-work related skills. Many people looking for entry into the career field that best matches their qualifications and skills overlook the importance of the above categories. Yet, people who develop skills through hobbies and outside interests forget that what they have learned may be transferrable to their jobs. At the same time, these skills enhance well-roundedness, one of the most desired traits an employee can offer an employer. One of the advantages of career development and preparing for change is an acquired ability to recognize and capitalize on such categories and turn them into an advantage. This process should begin in the self-assessment stage.

CAREER EXPLORATION. The purpose of career exploration is to eliminate career paths that are not compatible with individuals' goals and characteristics and identify those which are. The idea at this stage is to perform a general study of career paths, rather than to concentrate on specific companies and positions. Career exploration is a complex and daunting task, since there are over 5,000 different career fields available to workers today. Moreover, some disappear and others emerge continuously.

In the career exploration stage, people look at factors in the job search such as supply/demand relationships, employment projections, and work settings. There are many sources from which to obtain relevant data concerning virtually any aspect of employment.

Publications such as the *Occupational Outlook Handbook*, published and updated by the U.S. Bureau of Labor Statistics, and the *Dictionary of Occupational Titles*, published by the U.S. Employment Service, are helpful in identifying which career fields hold the most promise for aspiring employees. They include such information as the number of jobs that will be available in the field in the future, promotional opportunities, educational requirements, salary ranges, and benefits. These bits of information are vital to anyone researching career possibilities.

Other publications such as the *Standard & Poor's Register of Corporations, Directors and Executives* are also very helpful. Magazines such as *U.S. News & World Report* often publish special issues identifying the career fields that are most promising. These publications facilitate the career exploration process, but they are by no means the only source of information.

People involved in career exploration should also talk to individuals currently employed in the workplace and career counselors. They can also access publications germane to specific fields, and investigate work opportunities such as **internships** and cooperative education that might provide hands-on experience. Once these steps are completed, the next phase is to apply for specific jobs with carefully selected potential employers.

THE JOB SEARCH. The job search stage is when individuals focus on specific employers and positions in order to obtain the jobs for which they are best qualified. In this stage, job seekers put together their application package: a cover letter, a **resume**, and a follow-up letter. The application package is a sales tool through which jobseekers market themselves. The goal of the package is to earn a selection interview and an offer of employment.

The cover letter is a one-page letter that identifies *exactly* what position is being sought and where the applicant heard about the job. Applicants include in the letter their most significant accomplishments and skills that qualify them for the job. They also request an interview. In effect, the cover letter is a summation of the resume, which, in itself, is a synopsis of an applicant's personal and work experience.

The resume is a document, generally one or two pages in length, that capsulizes an applicant's skills and qualifications for a job. There is no set format or style of presentation. Applicants can arrange their information functionally, chronologically, or in a hybrid style in virtually any acceptable format. The resume includes basic information about applicants' work experience, education, military service, foreign language skills, special skills, awards, certificates, and other relevant items. Different categories of information are pertinent to different jobs. Therefore, applicants should submit tailored resumes which apply to the one job for which they are applying at any given time, rather than providing generic resumes.

It is important to note that people should update their resumes continually. That is crucial in the career development process. Every time applicants earn a new degree, complete relevant certificate or training programs, acquire new skills, receive **patents**, or do anything that will lead to better employment opportunities, either within or outside their companies, they should update their resumes accordingly. After all, career planning and change is based on upgrading and acquiring skills, without which no one can hope to succeed in a business career. Thus, up-to-date resumes and correlating cover letters are keys in the career planning and change process—and in being invited for selection interviews.

Selection interviews can be highly informative and can dictate to some extent in which direction an individual's career may go. The key to the interview is that it is a two-way process. Applicants are trying to learn as much about the company as the company wants to learn about the applicants. The interview is an ideal opportunity for applicants to learn more about the company, the specific position being sought, and whether the job is exactly what they are seeking. With that in mind, applicants should arrive at the interview with two lists, written or mental, one of answers to questions they might be asked and the other of questions they might want to ask about the company. The exchange of information will be beneficial to both sides.

If applicants have diligently carried out their personal audit and job search phases, the interviews can be rewarding. Not all interviews result in job offers, however. And, not all interviewees want to accept jobs if they are offered. Those who do, however, are well-advised to write follow-up letters, which can make the difference in getting the jobs they want or being rejected.

The follow-up letter is a one-page informal note directed to the interviewer(s) shortly after the interview is completed. It can be submitted anywhere from one to five days interest in the job and thank the interviewer(s) for their time. Few applicants use the follow-up letter, although it is simply a matter of common courtesy. Whether it is used or not, there can only be two results to the jobseeking process: a position with the company or rejection. In either case, the career planning and change process continues. For the unsuccessful applicant, it means a renewed job search based on the first two stages. For the successful one, it is an entree to the final stage: maintenance.

MAINTENANCE. The philosophy that best describes the maintenance stage is this: earning a job is not the final step in the career planning process—it is the first. Successful job candidates will continue to upgrade their skills and educational backgrounds in preparation for the inevitable job changes. They will participate in **training and development** programs designed through individual efforts or jointly with supervisors or managers. Continual training and development are essential for individuals who want to stay aware of the ever-changing business environment and its effects on their career paths.

PLANNING FOR SUCCESS

Workers must always be looking forward to the next step in the employment ladder. For example, entry-level workers should begin preparing themselves for supervisory or managerial positions as quickly as possible. They can do this in a number of ways.

One step to success is constant education. Workers should take advantage of every relevant course, workshop, seminar, etc., available to them. The courses may be taken through adult education programs, formal degree granting programs at colleges and universities, or company-sponsored programs. Some companies, like Dana Corp. and Motorola, Inc., operate educational programs that rival those of colleges and universities. Opportunities to upgrade skills and expand knowledge bases are plentiful. Workers can acquire new skills and knowledge as a logical step in the career planning process. All they need is common sense and initiative to take advantage of the opportunities—which are two of the most common ingredients in the recipe for career success.

One of the most essential steps in the career planning process is to identify future employment trends, not only for today but well into the next century. The same tools available in the initial stages of the process can be utilized to prepare for changes in the local, national, and global work environment. The implications of changing trends in the business world can have profound implications on individuals, often when they do not expect them.

For example, in the late 1980's, thousands of workers in the United States and other industrialized countries lost their jobs due to massive downsizing projects carried out by companies large and small. The companies involved were trying to cut expenses and maximize **profits**. As a result, they eliminated jobs by the thousands. Many of the employees who lost their jobs were unprepared to find new ones or retrain for other positions. This was because they had not planned on the downsizing trend. Constant career planning and change can help some workers avoid similar fates.

STAYING CURRENT WITH TRENDS AND CHANGES

Young people who are involved in career planning can prepare for future employment through dual-tracking. If they are pursuing college degrees, they might want to earn a double major in diverse areas, e.g., music and **accounting** or history and **marketing**. Thus, if the number of jobs in their chosen field has shrunk, they might have the qualifications to enter another field. Or, non-college bound students might want to enroll in **apprenticeship programs** that allow them to acquire the necessary skills and experience to assume positions that utilize the latest technology and equipment. Rapid technological changes in business and industry make it mandatory that individuals upgrade their skills and increase their knowledge bases as a matter of survival.

Another area on which people should concentrate in order to keep abreast of changing trends is government legislation. New laws can have a major impact on entire career fields. Consider, for example, the effects of a series of environmental acts passed and amended by the United States government in recent

years, e.g., the Federal Water Pollution Control Act (FWPCA), the Water Quality Improvement Act of 1970, and the Clean Air Act. The acts were designed to monitor and limit the amount of pollutants spilled in the nation's waterways, air, and ground. They have done that, but they have also led to the dramatic creation or expansion of jobs and career paths that have opened new opportunities for well-trained workers.

For example, Oceaneering Techologies of East Amherst, New York—which is hundreds of miles away from the nearest ocean—has expanded from 23 to 40 employees, many of whom are divers. They inspect, repair, and build submerged structures like dams, bridges, and oil rigs. Much of the work they do is the result of the **Clean Water Act** of 1972 and other environmental regulations. It is common in the business world for new companies and technologies to form in response to legislation. Often, they need employees who are familiar with the most recent technologies, managerial theories, etc., to fill their ranks. That means opportunities for people who are prepared to enter emerging careers or to change careers completely. Either approach is predicated on constant attention to the process outlined above.

Not coincidentally, two of the fastest growing career paths in the late 1990s and early 21st century are change management consulting and environmental management. According to the October 31, 1994, issue of *U.S. News & World Report*, ''The transformation of the workplace by technology and **global competition** has business frantic to stay current—witness the whirlwind pace of downsizings and re-engineering. To yield lasting benefits, change must be carefully managed.'' Hence, the need for change management consultants.

Similarly, the magazine said that in 1994 alone, government and industry spent about $139 billion on environmental affairs, mainly for cleanup and compliance with regulations. It predicted the figure would hit $162 billion by 1998. The massive effort to clean the environment created a need for environmental managers, who could earn salaries ranging from $30,000 to $120,000 annually. There was an associated demand for environmental engineers and attorneys and ecotourism and pollution prevention specialists. Salaries for these positions ranged from $45,000 to $160,000 annually for lawyers and $21,000 to $36,000 annually for lab or field technicians. These salaries and positions are indicative of changes in the field of employment. More importantly, they indicate the need for constant career planning for individuals looking to change careers or upgrade their current skills.

THE IMPORTANCE OF CAREER PLANNING

The ability to plan for first careers and career changes is a skill in itself. It is one of the most important skills an individual can develop. Planning is the best tool available to people seeking success in their careers—and one that they must utilize constantly to its maximum throughout their working lifetimes.

SEE ALSO: Continuing Education

[Arthur G. Sharp]

FURTHER READING:

Breidenbach, Monica E. *Career Development.* Englewood Cliffs, NJ: Prentice Hall, 1989.

Kastre, Michael F. et al. *The Minority Career Guide.* Princeton, NJ: Peterson's, 1993.

Krannich, Ronald L. *Careering and Re-Careering.* Manassas, VA: Impact Publications, 1989.

Morgan, John S. *Getting A Job After 50.* Princeton, NJ: Petrocelli Books, 1987.

Powell, C. Randall. *Career Planning Today.* Dubuque, IA: Kendall/Hunt Publishing Co., 1990.

Rinella, Richard J., and Claire C. Robbins. *Career Power!* New York: AMACOM, 1980.

CARIBBEAN COMMUNITY AND COMMON MARKET (CARICOM)

The Caribbean Community and Common Market (CARICOM) was organized in 1973 as a result of the Treaty of Chaguaramas (Trinidad) and replaced the Caribbean Free Trade Association. CARICOM seeks to strengthen the integration of its member nations in both economic and non-economic spheres of activity. In 1993, members of CARICOM included: Antigua and Barbuda, Bahamas (belongs to the Community but not the Common Market), Barbados, Belize, Dominica, Grenada, Guyana, Jamaica, Montserrat, St. Kitts-Nevis, St. Lucia, St. Vincent, and Trinidad and Tobago. The British Virgin Islands and the Turks and Caicos Islands are associate members. There are also ten countries having observer status: Anguilla, Bermuda, Cayman Islands, Dominican Republic, Haiti, Mexico, Netherlands Antilles, Puerto Rico, Suriname, and Venezuela.

Many of these island states of the Caribbean achieved independence in the 1960s and 1970s. Although they obtained political freedom, their economies were shackled with single crop agricultural practices, undiversified production, economic dependence on foreign industrial powers, an imbalance of raw material exports and finished product imports, and weak regional ties. It became apparent to the regional states that the Caribbean Free Trade Association needed to be replaced by an organization that embraced a common market and economic integration philosophy. Incentive for the new organization came from Barbados, Guyana, Jamaica, and Trinidad. By 1974 all previous Caribbean Free Trade Association members had joined CARICOM.

The goal of CARICOM is to enhance the economies, sovereignty, and self-determination of member states through economic integration and cooperation in many non-economic activities. Economic integration is achieved through market integration, coordinated production plans, coordinated trade outside of the Caribbean region, and special programs to aid those CARICOM countries officially designated as "Less Developed Countries." Specific economic polices used to accomplish integration include the establishment of a common external tariff, common protective trade policies, fiscal incentives, similar economic policies among member states, and economic development projects. Non-economic areas of interest help stabilize other areas of society. Some of the areas of concentration include health programs, educational upgrading, and enhanced transportation systems.

Economic events of the mid-1970s, including the oil crisis and subsequent increases in the price of energy as well as the decrease in commodity prices, caused the stagnation of CARICOM initiatives and regional economic growth. Many members, in an effort to shore up their foreign exchange earnings, enacted trade restrictions on their extra-regional and intra-regional trading partners. Their actions led to subsequent retaliation, furthering the recession of the early 1980s.

Faced with these problems, the group adopted the CARICOM 1984 Nassau Agreement that called for various plans and measures to dismantle regional trade restrictions. The plans to revitalize trade failed, however, as several member nations kept their unilateral protectionist policies in place. In 1987 the Eighth Conference of CARICOM Heads of Government convened to create a West Indian Commission to advance CARICOM goals, address extra-regional sugar and textile export concerns, and voice concern about the military takeover in Haiti. The leaders also reviewed their pledge for a barrier-free regional common market. The plan was thwarted, however, by a coalition of Less Developed Countries who claimed their economies could not withstand free trade competition.

A 1990 summit again called for a common external tariff and free movement of skilled, professional, and contract labor between member nations. In 1991 the leaders proposed a single currency common market by 1994 and created a $50 million CARICOM Investment Fund for regional products, but again they postponed implementing a common external tariff.

World opinion has criticized CARICOM for its inability to implement long term goals such as the common external tariff, but has lauded the organization for creating an infrastructure capable of directing regional cooperation and economic development.

HOW CARICOM WORKS

The CARICOM Heads of Government Conference, comprised of one member from each signatory, decides policy at annual meetings. The chair of the Conference rotates annually and decisions are reached by unanimous vote.

A Common Market Council deals with market problems. Day-to-day operations of CARICOM are handled by the five departments of the Secretariat: Sectoral Policy and Planning, Legal (includes trade, economics and statistics), Functional Cooperation, General Services, and Administration. There are also standing committees on education, industry, labor, foreign affairs, finance, agriculture and mines.

CARICOM also has nine associate institutions created by the 1973 treaty. They are the Caribbean Development Bank, Caribbean Examinations Council, Caribbean Investment Corp., Caribbean Meteorological Council, Council of Legal Education, Organization of Eastern Caribbean States, Regional Shipping Council, University of Guyana, and the University of the West Indies.

[Michael Knes]

FURTHER READING:

The Commonwealth Caribbean—Planning for Stability. Centre for Security and Conflict Studies, 1989.

Erisman, H. Michael. *Pursuing Postdependency Politics: South-South Relations in the Caribbean.* L. Rienner, 1992.

Gomez, Maria. *The Caribbean Common Market: Complications for U.S. Business.* Washington, D.C.: U.S. Department of Commerce, GPO, 1981.

Ramsaran, Ramesh. *The Commonwealth Caribbean in the World Economy.* Macmillan, 1989.

CARIBBEAN, DOING BUSINESS IN THE

The Caribbean region refers to all the islands within the Caribbean Sea, and technically includes the countries in Central Central America and South America that border it, such as Costa Rica, Panama, Venezuela and Colombia. Dictionary definition aside, the Caribbean region popularly is considered to be the many island states that lie within the Caribbean Sea: Cuba, the islands of the Bahamas, and the island chains of the Greater and Lesser Antilles. The region is a very heterogeneous expanse of islands scattered about the Caribbean, many of which are just a speck in the sea, such as the Cayman Islands, or at most, moderately sized, such as Puerto Rico.

The Caribbean region is the United States' backyard, and until the early 1990s, American businesses tended to overlook the potential of these islands, and concentrate on Europe and the Far East. The sheer diversity of the Caribbean region, with its many different languages and cultures, the small size of its population (hovering around 35 million) and widespread poverty and political instability discouraged American businesses from investigating the possibilities of this area. History and geography seemed to condemn this region to poverty, political fragmentation, and instability.

The white man came to this region for the first time in the person of Christopher Columbus. The Spanish conquerors were followed over the next few hundred years by the Dutch, the French, the British, and even the Danes, all of whom carved out colonies for exploitation by their home countries. The Spanish introduced forced labor and Christianity, and slavery continued to be the major means of production on all the islands until the nineteenth century. Because of the tropical climate, most of the islands were ideally suited to the cultivation of sugar. The focus on sugar production continued well into the twentieth century, even after slavery ended on all of the islands by the mid-1850s.

Haiti was the first Caribbean colony to rebel against the mother country in a bloody revolution that resulted in independence in 1804. Plantation agriculture there gave way to small peasant subsistence farming; a rapacious native elite, however, replaced the French. Lacking France or some other big power as a mentor (as in Martinique and Guadeloupe), and governed by a tragic succession of dictatorships, Haiti remains without a viable infrastructure, and its exploited people live in poverty.

Puerto Rico and Cuba fared much better. Becoming wards of the United States after the Spanish American War in 1898, they attracted American investment and modern sugar refining technology. As a commonwealth of the United States, Puerto Rico as well as the U.S. Virgin Islands (acquired in 1917 from Denmark) became the most prosperous of the Caribbean island states. As to their less fortunate neighbors, the focus on one crop cultivation, to the neglect of diversification and industry, retarded their development and the building of infrastructures, even after most of the islands achieved their independence. The end of slavery was followed by the emigration to the Caribbean islands of nearly one million natives from Africa, British India, and even China as contract labor, adding to the cultural and ethnic diversity of the region, but perhaps also to its lack of cohesion and political disunity.

After the World War II, the Cold War encouraged the United States to pour millions into the pockets of right wing dictators professing anti-Communism. The Soviet Union in turn poured its millions into destabilizing already fragile regimes, encouraging anti-Americanism and discouraging free market reforms. With the fall of communism in Europe and Russia, even Cuba has been forced to experiment with free market alternatives to its faltering state-owned economy.

Only with the end of the Cold War has the Caribbean region been able to revitalize. In the process, Caribbean island states have been discovering a shared heritage of European colonialism but also of Christianity, of mutual dependence on international markets, and a regional rather than a national approach to solving their economic problems. Cultural diversity and a fascinating European heritage have become assets in attracting the growing numbers of tourists from all over the world to this scenic tropical area.

The fall of communism, the end of the Cold War, and the demise of racial apartheid in South Africa, have resulted all over the world in the subordination of cultural and linguistic differences for greater regional economic clout. This is evident in North America in NAFTA (**North American Free Trade Agreement**), and in Europe in the formation of a European superstate. In the hitherto politically and geographically fragmented Caribbean states, there is an unmistakable regional consciousness arising also, embodied in such entities as CARICOM (**Caribbean Common Market**), the Eastern Caribbean Common Market, and the Caribbean-Canada Free Trade Agreement (CARIBCAN). In one country after another in Latin America and in the Caribbean, one man or one party dictatorships have given way to democracy, and free market economics for traditional protectionism and high tariffs.

During the Bush administration, programs such as the Caribbean Basin Initiative (CBI) were strengthened, and drug trafficking was successfully curbed and even eliminated, as on the Turks and Caicos Islands.

With growing stability and economic liberalization evident even in Cuba, the Caribbean region, with the exception of Haiti, is becoming increasingly attractive to American business. American multinational corporations have gravitated to Puerto Rico and the U.S. Virgin Islands in particular, while small American companies, just beginning to venture into

the international market, prefer smaller islands that are tax havens, with little competition from multinationals. In some cases, as in the French islands of Martinique and Guadeloupe, or the Dutch island of Curacao, these small islands offer a toehold into the European Common Market that would be difficult for a small company to attain in Europe. Added attractions, as many American companies have discovered, are a large, underemployed and very inexpensive labor force in most of the Caribbean islands, and improving infrastructures that, for the time being, outrival South Asia or most African states. Education and health standards also have risen dramatically in all the Caribbean island states, except Haiti.

Taking advantage of the sizable tax breaks and financial incentives, the vast majority of U.S. business in the Caribbean produces goods for export to the American market, within easy reach of the Caribbean region's excellent sea and air transportation facilities. With few exceptions, labor is inexpensive, abundant, and desperate for employment. Unemployment in the Dominican Republic alone stands at 30 percent, and in Jamaica, at a still sizable 16 percent. Even in Puerto Rico (with unemployment over ten percent), where wages are among the highest in the Caribbean region, they are still 50 percent lower than on the mainland United States. The labor pool in the Caribbean, thanks to greatly improved educational standards, is by no means uniformly untrained. For that very reason, sophisticated industries such as data processing and satellite telecommunication services are being established by American companies throughout the Caribbean.

Even for the direct investor, the Caribbean market can be a lucrative one, especially for the small sized company which can profitably produce for a small market (since Cuba is still off limits to U.S. business, the population of the remaining Caribbean islands hovers around 25 million, including Haiti). There is a need throughout the Caribbean for foodstuffs, almost all of which are imported; on the Virgin Islands, even seafood is imported because of overfishing of local waters. The burgeoning tourist industry in the Caribbean region imports everything. Hence there is a constant need for building materials and refrigeration/cooling units, hotel and restaurant supplies, computers and software. In addition, there is a demand on all the islands for pharmaceuticals, medical and diagnostic equipment, and electronic products. Nowadays virtually anyone opening a used car lot on the U.S. Virgin Islands can grow rich, since used cars are at an absolute premium. As of this writing, there are no quick print shops on the Virgin Islands, either. There is also a perpetual demand on most islands for spare parts for cars and other transportation vehicles. While there is still endemic poverty in the Caribbean, this has been giving way to growing economic revitalization and economic power. Moreover, except for the

French islands of the Caribbean, English is the preferred business language everywhere. Local markets are easily accessible; free trade zones are abundant, and competition as yet is minimal, except for the U.S. Virgin Islands and Puerto Rico.

The inception of the Caribbean Basin Initiative (CBI), which Congress passed in 1983 (as part of the Caribbean Basin Economic Recovery Act), began to turn American business in the direction of the Caribbean island states. CBI has dramatically promoted economic reform and liberalization in the Caribbean region. Highlights of CBI are duty free entrance into the United States of 94 product categories manufactured in the Caribbean; the establishment in the Caribbean of development banks, chambers of commerce, and free trade zones; the funding of job training and self-help programs; and very importantly, providing U.S. companies doing business in the Caribbean with financial assistance on easy terms.

However, those islands which are not part of the CBI program, such as the French islands of Guadeloupe and Martinique and the British owned Cayman Islands and Turk and Caicos Islands, still have attractive business features that make it worthwhile to do business there. For instance, these islands belong to the European **Common Market** and can initiate an American company lacking foreign trade experience into the international marketplace arena. This is also possible in the Virgin Islands, a U.S. territory, which enjoys favored nation status with Denmark. On the Cayman Islands, there are no taxes whatever, and all profits earned can be deposited in dollar accounts or transferred to the United States; the government of the Turks and Caicos Islands will issue, upon request, a written guarantee of no taxes. In addition, these islands have highly developed infrastructures with well established port and air facilities, and populations that have very American consumer tastes.

The U.S. government also offers special incentives for doing business in Puerto Rico and the U.S. Virgin Islands, known as the Section 936 program. A company that does a major portion of its business in Puerto Rico or the Virgin Islands can qualify for Section 936 of the Internal Revenue Code, which exempts it from federal income tax on earnings that are derived from its Caribbean business. In addition, American businesses interested in the U.S. Virgin Islands have special government incentives embodied in the General Headnote 3(a)(iv) of the Harmonized Tariff Schedule, granting duty free status to any item on the CBI list, produced in the Virgin Islands and exported to the United States. These benefits and privileges are just the tip of the iceberg.

Besides U.S. incentives to doing business, there are also the benefits that the individual Caribbean states offer, and collectively, those offered by the Caribbean Common Market, or CARICOM (currently consisting of the thirteen English speaking Caribbean island states, among them the Bahamas, Jamaica, Trinidad and Tobago, Barbados, and St. Kitts-Nevis). There is also the Organization of Eastern Caribbean States (OECS), or Eastern Caribbean Common Market, consisting of the tiniest Caribbean island states, namely, the British Virgin Islands, St. Kitts-Nevis, Antigua and Barbuda, Dominica, Grenada, St. Lucia, among other, also English speaking islands. OECS members offer excellent incentives to foreign businesses in the form of free trade zones and no taxes. CARICOM members, some of whom also belong to OECS, have a common external tariff, simplifying business for foreign investors; CARICOM also sponsors the Eastern Caribbean Association of Commerce and Industry to advance outside investment. The Dominican Republic, not a member of CARICOM, nonetheless is aggressively seeking foreign investment and already boasts the best free trade zone setup in the world.

In addition, many institutions, including the British Commonwealth Development Bank (CDC) and the Overseas Private Investment Corporation, as well as the U.S. Eximbank, provide financial assistance to businesses wishing to invest on these islands. Once again, Section 936 program for Puerto Rico and the U.S. Virgin Islands applies to these Caribbean states.

In short, there are many bonuses and benefits for companies that are willing to invest directly or indirectly in most of the Caribbean island states, except Haiti and Cuba. Nonetheless, setting up shop in the Caribbean is no guarantee of an easy ride. After determining the kind of business you want to establish there, the next step should be to thoroughly arm yourself with information about the locale you choose, and to find out the shortcomings as well as benefits of doing your business there.

For openers, start with the U.S. Department of Commerce's publication, *Caribbean Basin Financing Opportunities: A Guide to Financing Trade and Investment in Central America and the Caribbean*, which can be had by mail or via one of the 68 district offices of the U.S. Department of Commerce, each of which has abundant information and offers assistance in doing business abroad. Another source of assistance is the Latin America/Caribbean Business Development Center in Washington, D.C., which offers many publications to the public, as well as one-on-one counseling. In addition, there is the Overseas Development Council in Washington; the "Export Development Program" office of the Caribbean Common Market located in St. Michael, Barbados, that offers counseling and information; and other Caribbean based offices (and Caribbean business offices in the United States), a list of which can be obtained through the U.S. Department of Commerce.

Whatever your preference as to type of business and Caribbean locale, you will have to have exhaustive knowledge about transportation costs of your product or products, repatriation of your profits, and which banks take American dollar deposits (not all of them do). This will necessitate either a personal investigative business trip of your own or a local contact. It is advisable in any case to have a native lawyer or accountant with whom you can consult.

For many American businesses, doing business in the Caribbean is their first serious venture abroad. A safe bet for a beginning business strategy is to work within the main trading blocs in the Caribbean, such as CARICOM or the OECS. There are many different cultures within the Caribbean, moreover, and sensitivity to local culture and customs is a must. In Puerto Rico, for instance, advertising and marketing announcements or brochures must be in both Spanish and English, or they will not be read. In the Dominican Republic, the business community is extremely close knit, and an outsider will be excluded from doing business there unless he is well acquainted with an insider from this group. On the English speaking island of Jamaica, having a native contact person, preferably a lawyer, to deal with the top heavy bureaucracy, is a must. In the French Islands of Martinique and Guadeloupe, though English is widely used and understood, proficiency in French also is a must. Lastly, doing business in both the French speaking islands and the Netherlands Antilles (Curacao, Bonaire, Sint Maarten, etc.) must be regarded as doing business with the mother countries, since these islands are regarded as extensions of the home country. This has the advantage of giving an American company, with little chance of competing in western Europe, a toehold in the European Common Market. The disadvantage is competition from a multitude of companies from the home country.

The Caribbean states are not just appealing to the small American company, inexperienced in foreign trade and not exceptionally well off financially. Certainly the big American multinationals are predominating in Puerto Rico, the U.S. Virgin Islands and increasingly, in Jamaica. However, the Caribbean will always be a niche for the small investor, because of the small and scattered markets that prevail on the islands, which rely almost totally on imports.

The Caribbean region, however, is by no means closed to Europeans and Asians who also wish to take advantage of the best tax incentives in the world. If American businesses fail to invest in their own backyard in favor of distant markets, they risk becoming latecomers, outcompeted by very strong foreign competitors.

[Sina Dubovoy]

FURTHER READING:

Auerbach, Stuart. "U.S. Caribbean Nations Sign Trade Agreement (U.S.-Caribbean Community Trade and Investment Council Established)," *The Washington Post*. July 23, 1991, p. D3.

Breitenecker, Rudiger L. "The Caribbean Basin Initiative—An Effective U.S. Trade Policy Facilitating Economic Liberalization in the Region: the Costa Rican Example," *Law & Policy in International Business*. Summer, 1992, pp. 913-949.

Caribbean Basin Business Information Starter Kit. Washington, D.C.: U.S. Department of Commerce, GPO, 1984.

Cavusgil, S. Tamer. *Doing Business in Developing Countries: Negotiations and Entry Strategies*. Routledge, 1990.

Dunn, Peter. "Money in the Sun—If You're Careful (Doing Business in the Caribbean)," *Electronic News*. March 30, 1992, p. 6.

Puckerin, Karen. "Jamaica Bank Aims Mutual Funds at U.S.," *American Banker*. July 2, 1992, p. 6.

Tuller, Lawrence W. *Doing Business in Latin America and the Caribbean*. Amacom, 1993.

"U.S. Extends Caribbean Loan Effort," *New York Times*. May 6, 1992, p. C16(N), D22(L).

Wilde, Thomas E., Jr. "U.S. Agribusiness Trade and Investment Rise in Latin America and the Caribbean," *Business America*. March 23, 1992, p. 4.

Ward, J.R. *Poverty and Progress in the Caribbean, 1800-1960*. Macmillan, 1985.

CARTEL

A cartel is formed when a group of independently owned businesses agrees not to compete with each other in areas such as prices, territories, and production. A cartel agreement is considered a collusive agreement in that the different parties agree not to allow market forces to determine their pricing, production, and other business practices. Rather, the members of the cartel agree on such matters as what price to charge, how much to produce, and which markets to serve. Well-known examples of cartels include the **Organization of Petroleum Exporting Countries** (OPEC), the Swiss banking cartel, and the International Tin Council. Cartels are particularly widespread in Japan and play a major role in many different industries there.

Such collusive agreements are illegal in the United States under **antitrust laws** contained in the Sherman Antitrust Act of 1890, the Clayton Act of 1914, and the **Federal Trade Commission** Act of 1914. This body of legislation, known as the antitrust laws, made illegal such practices as restraint of trade, price discrimination, tie-in contracts, acquisition of competitors, and interlocking directorates. These practices were declared illegal only "where their effect may be to substantially lessen competition or tend to create a monopoly."

Historically, cartels have been formed in markets characterized by excess production capacity. At one time or another international cartels have attempted to control the world market in commodities such as steel, oil, rubber, tin, and aluminum, and in chemical products such as linoleum and rayon involving patents. In the early part of the 20th century the world aluminum industry was effectively controlled by a cartel consisting of four companies from the United States, France, Germany, and Great Britain. At the start of World War II it was estimated that more than 30 percent of international trade was controlled by international cartels.

More recently a large number of cartels appeared in Third World countries following the short-lived success of OPEC in the 1970s. These Third World cartels were formed in order to establish market prices for raw materials that they produced. By the mid-1980s most of these cartels had collapsed. Disagreements among cartel members, lack of real power to enforce agreements and production quotas, and a glut of raw materials were among the factors contributing to their demise.

The collapse of international cartels usually follows a familiar pattern. Cartels generally begin by establishing a price for their raw materials or other commodities that is somewhat above their free-market value. In response to such price-setting, consumers cut back on their purchases and an oversupply of raw materials results. Soon supply exceeds demand, especially when cartel members fail to agree to cut back production accordingly. As it becomes clear the cartel has lost the power to enforce production quotas, it loses control and prices fall drastically. Such a scenario occurred in the mid-1980s as oil prices plunged, greatly reducing the power of OPEC.

In Japan formal and informal national cartels are accepted as part of doing business there. Operating under a system of managed competition with a great deal of government guidance and intervention, Japanese cartels enjoy acceptance in industries ranging from agriculture and banking to beer manufacturing and barbering. One example is Nokyo, a national umbrella group under which a huge agricultural cartel operates. Because of Nokyo, Japanese consumers pay a much higher price for home-grown rice, for example, than it sells for on the world market. Nokyo serves to keep out imports, not only in rice but also in farm equipment and supplies. In Japan, cartels are permitted by law, and many of them are supervised by the government.

[David Bianco]

CASH COW

An enterprise with a small but stable market share in a growing market is referred to as a cash cow. Such an entity, whether a company or a division of a company, is in a highly competitive position as long as it can take advantage of growing **economies of scale**.

As long as a cash cow has the capacity to expand its shipments and sales, its margins—and therefore its profitability—are in a strong growth position. These profits may be reinvested in the operation to build out additional capacity to further fuel growth in market share.

The term "cash cow" has its origin with a matrix developed by the Boston Consulting Group, in which enterprises are classified as having positions in either a growing or shrinking market, and with either a growing or shrinking total market share. An operation with a large market share in a growing market is called a "star," while an operation with a small market share in a growing market is called a "question mark" (or sometimes a "problem child").

While the cash cow has a large market share in a stagnant or shrinking market, a company with low market share in a declining market is called a "dog."

Question marks generally require high investment to achieve a more favorable position and become a star (hence they are sometimes referred to as "cash hogs." If they can manage the transition to star, they will, over time, be subjected to intense competition. As the market matures, stars become cash cows. If a cash cow's competitive position is allowed to deteriorate, it becomes a dog.

Dogs are enterprises that generally can never operate in high-growth markets because those markets have matured. The investment needed to turn them into cash cows is, in many cases, prohibitive. As a result, dogs are either divested by sale to a competitor or, especially if they are losing money, are closed down and liquidated to prevent further losses.

Because the cash cow has a high market share in a stable or slowly growing market, it is generally able to maintain a profitable position, hence the name "cash cow"—the operation may be "milked" for profit as long as its margins and market share can be maintained.

Additional investment in the cash cow's products, representing technological improvements that yield new applications, can sometimes result in its transformation into a star. Because it is profitable, the cash cow can often provide its own investment capital.

More often, however, the cash cow is milked for capital to fund the development of question marks into stars because it is easier to build market share in a growing market than to revive an entire market that has matured.

[John Simley]

FURTHER READING:

Bartol, Kathryn M., and David C. Martin. *Management*. McGraw-Hill, 1991

Donnelly, James H. Jr., James L. Gibson, and John M. Ivancevich. *Fundamentals of Management*. 6th ed. Plano, Tx: Business Publications, 1987.

CASH FLOW STATEMENT

A cash flow statement is a financial report that tells the reader the source of a company's cash and how it was spent over a specified time period. Because of the varied accrual accounting methods companies may employ, it is possible for a company to show profits while not having enough cash to sustain operations. A cash flow statement neutralizes the impact of the accrual entries. It also categorizes the sources and uses of cash to provide the reader with an understanding of the amount of cash a company generates and uses in its operations, as opposed to the amount of cash provided by sources outside the company, such as borrowed funds or funds from stockholders. The cash flow statement also tells the reader how much money was spent for items that do not appear on the income statement, such as loan repayments, long-term asset purchases, and payment of cash dividends.

In November 1987, the **Financial Accounting Standards Board (FASB)** adopted Statement of Financial Accounting Standards No. 95—Statement of Cash Flows. FASB 95 requires that a full set of financial statements includes a cash flow statement as the fourth required financial statement (along with a **balance sheet**, **income statement**, and statement of retained earnings). This statement established standards for cash flow reporting, and superseded APB Opinion No. 19, Reporting Changes in Financial Position (*Journal of Accountancy*, Feb. 1988).

APB Opinion No. 19, adopted in March 1971, had permitted but did not require enterprises to report cash flow information in a statement of changes in financial position. There was no required format for the statement. The statement referred to changes in funds, but there were problems with the ambiguity of terms such as funds. Some firms used cash, some used cash and short-term investments, some used quick assets, and some used working capital. There was a lack of comparability arising from diversity in the focus of the statement.

While it was widely recognized that the statement provided valuable and relevant information, the lack of consistency in format and focus from one firm to another was part of the reason that the FASB issued a Discussion Memorandum in December 1980, Reporting Funds Flows, Liquidity, and Financial Flexibility. The Board received 190 letters of comment in response to the Discussion Memorandum, and in May 1981, a public hearing was held to discuss the issues.

In late 1981, the Financial Executives Institute (FEI) encouraged its members to change to a focus on cash and short-term investments in their funds statements. In 1984, the Financial Executives Research Foundation of the FEI published *The Funds Statement: Structure and Use*, a research study on funds statements that solicited views of both preparers and users.

In April 1985, the FASB added a cash flow reporting project to its agenda, and in May 1985, board staff organized a Task Force on Cash Flow Reporting. This was followed by many discussions with advisory groups and other committees.

In July 1986, the FASB issued another Exposure Draft, Statement of Cash Flows. It proposed standards for cash flow reporting to require a statement of cash flows as part of a full set of financial statements of all business enterprises in place of a statement of changes in financial position.

The board received more than 450 comment letters in response to the Exposure Draft. Throughout the remainder of 1986 and 1987, the FASB staff met with many groups and members of the task force to discuss comments received on the Exposure Draft.

In November 1987, the seven members of the Financial Accounting Standards Board voted to adopt Statement of Financial Accounting Standards No. 95—Statement of Cash Flows. The statement was adopted with affirmative votes from four members of the board and three members dissenting. A discussion of the dissenting points of view is included in the Official Release of the Statement, which was published in the *Journal of Accountancy* in February 1988.

FORMATS AND REQUIREMENTS FOR THE CASH FLOW STATEMENT

Statement No. 95 requires that a statement of cash flows classify cash receipts and payments according to whether they stem from operating, investing, or financing activities. It also provides that the statement of cash flows may be prepared under either the direct or indirect method, and provides illustrative examples for the preparation of statements of cash flows under both the direct and the indirect methods.

CLASSIFICATIONS OF CASH RECEIPTS AND PAYMENTS

Think about the life cycle of a company. A person or group of people come up with a marvelous idea for a new company. The next question is, where to get the money? The initial money comes from the owners, or could be borrowed. This is how the company is "financed." Basically, the money owners put into the company, or money the company borrows, is classified as a financing activity. Generally, any item that would be classified on the balance sheet as either a long-term liability or an equity would be a candidate for classification as a financing activity.

What happens to this money? The owners or managers of the business use it to buy equipment or other assets they need to run the business. In other words, they invest it. The purchase of property, plant, equipment, and other productive assets is classified as an investing activity. Sometimes a company has enough cash of its own that it can lend money to another enterprise. This, too, would be classified as an investing activity. Generally, any item that would be classified on the balance sheet as a long-term asset would be a candidate for classification as an investing activity.

Now the company can start doing business. It has procured the funds and purchased the equipment and other assets it needs to operate. It starts to sell merchandise or services and making payments for rent, supplies, taxes, and all of the other costs of doing business. Generally, all of the cash inflows and outflows associated with doing the work for which the company was established would be classified as an operating activity. In general, if an activity would appear on the company's income statement, it would be a candidate for the operating section of the cash flow statement. (A complete discussion of investing, financing, and operating activities is provided in paragraphs 15 through 24 of FASB Statement No. 95.)

Revenues that were earned during an accounting period may not have been collected during that period, and appear on the balance sheet as accounts receivable. Some of the collections of that period may have been from sales made in prior periods. Cash may have been collected in a period prior to the services rendered or goods delivered, resulting in deferred recognition of the revenue. This would appear on the balance sheet as unearned revenue.

Sometimes goods or services are paid for prior to the period in which the benefit is matched to revenue (recognized). This results in a deferred expense, or a prepaid. Items such as insurance premiums that are paid in advance of the coverage period are classified as prepaid. Sometimes goods or services are received and used by the company before they are paid for, such as telephone service or merchandise inventory. These items are called accrued expenses, or payables, and are recognized on the income statement as an expense before the cash flow occurs.

When buildings or equipment are purchased for cash, the cash flow precedes the recognition of the expense by many years. The expense is recognized over the life of the asset as **depreciation**.

Generally accepted accounting principles (GAAP) require that financial statements are prepared on the accrual basis. The cash flow statement removes the effect of any accruals or deferrals.

METHODS OF PREPARING THE CASH FLOW STATEMENT

FASB Statement No. 95 allows the preparer a choice of the direct or the indirect method of cash flow statement presentation. The operating section of a cash flow statement prepared using either method converts the income statement from the accrual to the cash basis, and reclassifies any activity not directly associated with the basic business activity of the firm. The difference lies in the presentation of the information.

Companies that use the direct method are required, at a minimum, to report separately the following classes of operating cash receipts and payments:

Receipts:

1. Cash collected from customers

2. Interest and dividends received

3. Other operating cash receipts, if any

Payments:

1. Cash paid to employees and suppliers of goods or services (including suppliers of insurance, advertising, etc.)

2. Interest paid

3. Income taxes paid

4. Other operating cash payments, if any

Companies are encouraged to provide further breakdown of operating cash receipts and payments that they consider meaningful (Kieso and Weygandt, 1992).

Companies using either method to prepare the statement are required to disclose separately changes in inventory, receivables, and payables to reconcile net income to net cash flow from operating activities. In addition, interest paid (net of amount capitalized) and income taxes paid must be disclosed elsewhere in the financial statements or accompanying notes. An acceptable alternative presentation of the indirect method is to report net cash flow from operating activities as a single line item in the statement of cash flows and to present the reconciliation details elsewhere in the financial statements (Kieso and Weygandt, 1992).

The reconciliation of the operating section of a cash flow statement using the indirect method always begins with net income or loss, and is followed by a section entitled Adjustments to reconcile net income to net cash provided by operating activities.

Regardless of whether the direct or the indirect method is used, the operating section of the cash flow statement ends with net cash provided (used) by operating activities. This is the most important line item on the cash flow statement. A company has to generate enough cash from operations to sustain its business activity. If a company continually needs to borrow or obtain additional investor capitalization to survive, the company's long-term existence is in jeopardy.

The presentation of the investing and financing sections is the same regardless of the whether the statement is prepared using the direct or indirect method.

The final section of the cash flow statement is always a reconciliation of the net increase or decrease in cash for the period for which the statement is prepared with the beginning and ending balances in cash for the period.

ANALYZING AND CLASSIFYING COMMON TRANSACTIONS

Every balance sheet account reflects specific activity. There are only a few distinctive transactions that affect each account. Following are examples of some of the common transactions affecting balance sheet items.

Accounts receivable increases when the company sells merchandise or does a service on credit, and decreases when the customer pays its bill. Accounts receivable is associated with the income statement account Sales or Revenue. The change in accounts receivable or the cash collected from customers is classified as an operating activity.

Inventory increases when the company buys merchandise for resale or use in its manufacturing process, and decreases when the merchandise is sold. Inventory is associated with the income statement account Cost of goods sold. The change in inventory or the cash paid for inventory purchases is classified as an operating activity.

Prepaid insurance increases when the company pays insurance premiums covering future periods and decreases when the time period of coverage expires.

Prepaid insurance is associated with the income statement account Insurance Expense. The change in prepaids or the amount paid for insurance is classified as an operating activity.

The Land, Building, and Equipment accounts increase when the company purchases additional assets and decrease when the assets are sold. The only time the income statement is affected is when the asset is sold at a price higher or lower than book value, at which time a gain or loss on sale of assets appears on the income statement. The amount of cash used or received from the purchase or sale of such assets is classified as an investing activity. The gain or loss is classified as an adjustment in the operating section on a cash flow statement prepared using the indirect method.

Accumulated depreciation increases as the building and equipment depreciates and decreases when building and equipment is sold. Accumulated depreciation is associated with depreciation expense on the income statement. Depreciation expense does not appear on a cash flow statement presented using the direct method. Depreciation expense is added back to net income on a cash flow statement presented using the indirect method, since the depreciation caused net income to decrease during the period but did not affect cash.

Goodwill increases when the parent company acquires a subsidiary for more than the fair market value of its net assets. Goodwill amortizes over a time period not to exceed 40 years. Goodwill is associated with amortization expense on the income statement. Amortization expense appears in the operating section of a cash flow statement prepared using the indirect method. Amortization expense does not appear on a cash flow statement prepared using the direct method.

Notes payable increases when the company borrows money, and decreases when the company repays the funds borrowed. Since only the principal appears on the balance sheet, there is no impact on the income statement for repaying the principal component of the note. Notes payable appear in the financing section of a cash flow section.

Premiums and discounts on bonds are amortized through bond interest expense. There is no cash flow associated with the amortization of bond discounts or premiums. Therefore, there will always be an adjustment in the operating section of the cash flow statement prepared using the indirect method for premium or discount amortization. Premium or discount amortization will not appear on a cash flow statement prepared using the direct method.

Common stock and preferred stock with their associated paid in capital accounts increase when additional stock is sold to investors, and decrease when stock is retired. There is no income statement impact for stock transactions. The cash flow associated with stock sales and repurchases appears in the financing section.

Retained earnings increases when the company earns profit and decreases when the company suffers a loss or declares dividends. The profit or loss appears as the first line of the operating section of the cash flow statement. The dividends appear in the financing section when they are paid.

CASH INFLOWS OR RECEIPTS

When preparing the cash flow statement using the direct method, the cash collected from customers may be found by analyzing accounts receivable, as follows: Beginning balance of accounts receivable, plus sales for the period (from the income statement), less ending balance of accounts receivable, equals cash received from customers. This is an extremely simplified formula, and does not take into account written off receivables or other noncash adjustments to customer accounts.

If there is no accounts receivable on the balance sheet, the company does a cash business and cash collected from customers will equal sales or revenue on the income statement.

If the cash flow statement is prepared using the indirect method, the adjustment to net income may be found in a similar manner. If the cash received from customers is more than the sales shown on the income statement, causing accounts receivable to decrease, the difference is added to net income. If cash received from customers is less than the sales shown on the income statement, causing accounts receivable to increase, the difference is subtracted from net income.

The amounts borrowed during the period may be found by analyzing the Liability Accounts. The amounts received from investors during the period may be found by doing a similar analysis on the Equity Accounts. Both of these types of transactions will be classified as financing activities.

If any land, buildings, or equipment were sold during the period, the information will be found in the Land, Building, and Equipment Accounts and their associated accumulated depreciation. One simple way to properly categorize the transaction is to reconstruct the journal entry.

Assume that equipment that had cost $8,000 and had accumulated depreciation of $6,000 was sold during the period for $2,500. The journal entry for this transaction would have been:

Cash	2,500
Accumulated depreciation	6,000
Equipment	8,000
Gain on sale of equipment	500

The cash received from the sale of the equipment is classified as an investing activity. If the statement is prepared using the direct method, no other part of the journal entry is used. If the statement is prepared using the indirect method, the gain on sale of equipment is subtracted from net income. When the gain was recorded, net income increased. However, since the company is not in the business of buying and selling equipment, the gain needs to be subtracted from net income to arrive at the adjusted total related only to the proceeds from the company's direct business activities. If the sale had resulted in a loss, the loss is added back to net income.

CASH PAYMENTS

Cash payments are found using similar methods to those used for finding cash received. Cash payments for the purchase of inventory are found by analyzing accounts payable. The following formula can be used to find the cash paid for inventory purchases: beginning balance of accounts payable, plus inventory purchases during the period, less ending balance of accounts payable, equals payments made for inventory during the period.

This is a simplified formula and does not take into account any noncash adjustments.

If the cash paid for inventory is greater than the inventory purchased during the period, the difference between the amount purchased and the amount paid is deducted from net income if preparing the cash flow statement using the indirect method. If cash paid for inventory is less than the inventory purchased during the period, the difference between the amount purchased and the amount paid is added to net income if preparing the cash flow statement using the indirect method.

Cash payments for land, building, and equipment purchases, repayments of loans, purchases of treasury stock, and payment of dividends may be found by performing similar analysis on the appropriate accounts.

SIGNIFICANT NONCASH TRANSACTIONS

Noncash transactions are not to be incorporated in the statement of cash flows. Examples of these types of transactions include conversion of bonds to stock and the acquisition of assets by assuming liabilities. If there are only a few such transactions, it may be convenient to include them on the same page as the statement of cash flows, in a separate schedule at the bottom of the statement. Otherwise, the transactions may be reported elsewhere in the financial statements, clearly referenced to the statement of cash flows (*Journal of Accountancy*, Feb. 1988).

Other events that are generally not reported in conjunction with the statement of cash include stock dividends, stock splits, and appropriation of retained earnings. These items are generally reported in conjunction with the statement of retained earnings or schedules and notes pertaining to changes in capital accounts (Kieso and Weygandt, 1992).

[Susan M. Kasuba]

FURTHER READING:

Kieso & Weygandt. *Intermediate Accounting.* 7th ed. New York: John Wiley & Sons, 1992.

"Official Releases, Statement of Financial Accounting Standards No. 95—Statement of Cash Flows." *Journal of Accountancy.* February, 1988: pp. 139, 147.

CASH MANAGEMENT

Cash management is a broad area having to do with the collection, concentration, and disbursement of cash including measuring the level of liquidity, managing the cash balance, and short term investments.

If at any time a corporation fails to pay an obligation when it is due because of the lack of cash it is insolvent. Insolvency is the primary reason firms go bankrupt. Obviously, the prospect of such a dire consequence compels companies to manage their cash with care. Moreover, efficient cash management means more than just preventing bankruptcy. It improves the profitability and reduces the risk the firm is exposed to.

Cash collection systems aim to reduce the time it takes to collect the cash that is owed to the firm (for example, from its customers). The time delays are categorized as mail float, processing float, and bank float. Obviously, an envelope mailed by a customer containing payment to a supplier firm does not arrive at its destination instantly. Likewise, the moment the firm receives payment it is not deposited in its bank account. And finally when the payment is deposited in the bank account often times the bank does not give immediate availability to the funds. These three "floats" are time delays that add up quickly, requiring the firm in the mean time to fund cash elsewhere to pay its bills. Cash management attempts to decrease the time delays in collection at the lowest cost. A collection receipt point closer to the customer, with an outside third party vendor, such as a lock box, to receive, process, and deposit the payment (check) will speed up the collection. For example, if a firm collects $10 million each day and can permanently speed up collections by five days, at 6% interest rates, then annual before tax profits would increase by $3

million. The techniques to analyze this case would utilize data involving where the customers were; how much and how often they pay; the bank they remit checks from; the collection sites the firm has (their own or a third party vendor); the costs of processing payments; the time delays involved for mail, processing, and banking; and the prevailing interest rate that can be earned on excess funds.

Once the money has been collected most firms then proceed to concentrate the cash into one center. The rationale for such a move is to have complete control of the cash and to provide greater investment opportunities with larger sums of money available as surplus. There are numerous mechanisms that can be employed to concentrate the cash, such as wire transfers, automated clearinghouse (ACH) transfers, and checks. The tradeoff is between cost and time.

Disbursement is the opposite of collection. Here, the firm strives to slow down payments. It wants to increase mail delays and bank delays, and it has no control over processing delay.

Another aspect of cash management is knowing the optimal cash balance. There are a number of methods that try to determine the magical cash balance, which should be targeted so that costs are minimized and yet adequate liquidity exists to ensure bills are paid on time (hopefully with something left over for emergency purposes). One of the first steps in managing the cash balance is measuring liquidity. There are numerous ways to measure this, including: Cash to Total Assets ratio, Current ratio (Current Assets divided by Current Liabilities), Quick ratio (Current Assets less Inventory, divided by Current Liabilities) and the Net Liquid Balance (Cash plus Marketable Securities less Short Term Notes Payable, divided by Total Assets). The higher the number generated by the liquidity measure, the greater the liquidity and vice versa. However, there is a trade off between liquidity and profitability which discourages firms from having excessive liquidity.

To help manage cash on a day-to-day basis in actual dollars and cents, there are a number of cash management models exist. These include the Baumol Model, Miller-Orr Model and the Stone Model.

The Baumol Model is similar to the Economic Order Quantity (EOQ) Model. Mathematically it is:

$$C = ((2FS)/i)^{1/2}$$

where C is the optimal amount of cash to be acquired when reaching a threshold balance, F is the fixed cost of acquiring the cash (C) amount, S is the amount of cash spent during a time interval, and i is the interest rate expressed in the same time interval as S.

One shortcoming of this model is that it only accommodates a net cash outflow situation as opposed to both inflows and outflows. Also, the cash outflow is at a constant rate, with no variation.

The Miller-Orr Model rectifies some of the deficiencies of the Baumol Model by accommodating a fluctuating cash flow stream that can be either inflow or outflow. The Miller-Orr Model has an upper limit (U) and lower limit (L).

When there is too much cash and U is reached, cash is taken out (to buy short term securities to earn interest) such that the cash balance goes to a return (R) point. Otherwise, if there is too little cash and L is reached, cash is deposited (from the short term investments) to replenish the balance to R. The equations of the Miller-Orr Model are:

$$R = ((3fs^2)/(4i))^{1/3}$$

$$U = 3R$$

where R is the return point, f is the fixed cost for each transaction to withdraw or deposit cash, s^2 is the variance of the cash flows, i is the interest rate per same time period as s^2, and U is the upper limit. L is determined by other means, for example, compensating balance requirement, minimum balance to avoid bank service charges on checking account, or zero.

The Stone Model is somewhat similar to the Miller-Orr Model insofar as it uses control limits. However, it incorporates a look-ahead forecast of cash flows when an upper or lower limit is hit to take into account the possibility that the surplus or deficit of cash may naturally correct itself. If the upper control limit is reached but is to be followed by cash outflow days that would bring the cash balance down to an acceptable level, then nothing is done. If instead the surplus cash would substantially remain that way, then cash is withdrawn to get the cash balance to a predetermined return point. Of course, if cash was in short supply and the lower control limit was reached, the opposite would apply. In this way the stone Model takes into consideration the cash flow forecast.

The goals of these models are to ensure adequate amounts of cash on hand for bill payments and to minimize transaction costs in acquiring cash when deficiencies exist and disposing of cash when a surplus arises. These models assume some cash flow pattern as a given, leaving the task of cash collection, concentration, and disbursement to other methods.

A key cash management problem becomes which money market instruments to select to place the temporary excess funds (including how much money and for how long). This short term investment decision necessitates the analysis of return (need to annualize returns in order to compare) and liquidity. Only short term investments meet the liquidity test, as long duration instruments expose the investor to too much interest rate risk. In addition, federal government obligations are popular due to the absence of default risk and ease of resale in the secondary market. Nonetheless, there are numerous money market securities available with varying characteristics from many types of issuers.

[Raymond A.K. Cox]

FURTHER READING:

Emery, Gary W. ''Measuring Short-Term Liquidity,'' *Journal of Cash Management*. July/August, 1984, pp. 25-32.

Hill, Ned C. and William L. Sartoris, *Short-Term Financial Management*. MacMillan Publishing Co., 1992.

Shulman, Joel S. and Raymond A.K. Cox. ''An Integrative Approach to Working Capital Management,'' *Journal of Cash Management*. November/December 1985, pp. 64-67.

CATALOG MARKETING

Catalog marketing is a specialized branch of **direct marketing**. The two disciplines share many of the same characteristics. Like direct marketing, catalog marketing is based on interactivity, or one-to-one communication between the marketer and the prospect or customer. Catalogs always include response devices, and catalogers are able to measure the response to any and every mailing they make. It is safe to say that most at-home shopping takes place through catalogs.

Catalogs offer consumers a wide range of products of either a generalized or specialized nature. In this respect they share some of the characteristics of retailers. Like retailers, catalogers employ buyers to select merchandise. Catalog buyers attend the same trade shows as retail buyers. The layout of a catalog is planned in a way that is analogous to the layout of a retail store: space is at a premium in both locations, and merchandise is arranged so as to maximize sales.

THE ORIGINS OF CATALOG MARKETING

Catalogs represent some of the earliest examples of direct marketing and **mail order** businesses. Many of today's large retailers, notably Sears, Roebuck and Company and Montgomery Ward, began as mail order businesses. Interestingly, that trend continues today as successful specialized catalogers have opened their own retail outlets.

How old is catalog marketing? Garden and seed catalogs were known to be distributed in the American colonies before the Revolutionary War. Catalog shopping in the area of consumer goods entered a period of growth in the 1880s, when mail-order houses began to fiercely compete with local stores. Their marketing contest centered on three major issues—price, inventory, and assurances—the very factors which made mail order houses successful.

Aaron Montgomery Ward (1843-1913), regarded as the first of the consumer goods catalogers, started his catalog business in 1872, while Richard Warren Sears (1863-1914) mailed his first flyers in the 1880s. These catalogs had a liberating effect on nineteenth century consumers. They were no longer captive to their local stores, which had limited inventories and charged higher prices because they weren't big enough to receive large volume discounts from their suppliers. With the advent of mail order, consumers could get attractive goods and prices whether they lived in the middle of Manhattan or in a remote rural setting.

The postal system allowed direct-mail companies to operate on a national basis. With economies of scale working in their favor, mail order houses could undercut the pricing of local stores. In 1897, bicycles were selling for $75 to $100 and more, until Sears started offering them for $5 to $20 in its catalog. Sears could offer those low prices because it sold thousands of bicycles every week.

The large volume of business also allowed catalogers to offer a wider variety of goods. Consumers not only wanted low prices, they also wanted variety—twenty kinds of dresses rather than two. In 1897 Sears, Roebuck and Company mailed a 700-page catalog that listed 6,000 products. Here again, the enormous volume generated by leading mail order houses made huge inventories not only possible but also practicable. By 1906 Sears catalogs were generating in excess of $50 million in sales annually.

But price and variety, while important, have only limited value if the goods themselves are shoddy or poorly-made. So the mail-order firms protected consumers with powerful guarantees. Montgomery Ward was one of the first companies to offer a money-back guarantee, and the Sears Roebuck pledge of "satisfaction guaranteed or your money back" is one of the best-known commitments in American business.

Another successful cataloger, L.L. Bean of Freeport, Maine, began in 1913 when Mr. Leon Leonwood Bean mailed his first single-sheet flyer advertising his Maine hunting boots. Perhaps he got the idea of using **direct mail** from his brother Guy Bean, who was the Freeport postmaster. Bean targeted his mailing to individuals who had hunting licenses. He soon added more products and began mailing catalogs.

THE GROWTH OF CATALOG MARKETING

According to the Direct Marketing Association (DMA), catalog and other direct mail sales of goods to consumers represented about 3 percent of all retail sales in the late 1980s, a figure that is expected to remain in that range. In 1994 the DMA announced the results of a study of the catalog industry that it had commissioned from the WEFA Group, an econometric modeling and forecasting firm. The study covered a seven-year period from 1987 through 1993 and provided estimates for 1994 through 1997.

According to the WEFA Group study, catalog revenue reached $53.4 billion in sales in 1993, an average growth of nearly 7% per year from $35.7 billion in sales in 1987. **Gross Domestic Product** (GDP) linked to the catalog industry grew from $28.6 billion to $43.2 billion during the period from 1987 to 1993. In 1993 it was estimated that the catalog industry produced 0.68% of the nation's total GDP.

The same study forecast that catalog sales would grow by an average of nearly 6.8% annually to reach $69.5 billion by 1997. Employment in the catalog industry was forecast to grow at an annual rate of nearly 7.7%, somewhat below the projected growth rate of 9.5% for total employment in the U.S. economy. Catalog-related GDP was expected to reach $53.8 billion in 1997.

The same elements that have fueled the growth of direct marketing since the 1960s have contributed to the growth of catalog marketing. From the many factors contributing to the growth of direct marketing and mail order catalogs, direct marketing expert Jim Kobs selected five as the most important.

1) Changing lifestyles were an important factor in the acceptance of catalogs and direct marketing among consumers. The number of women working outside the home jumped from 42 to 58 percent between 1980 and 1990. This was a trend that began at least a decade earlier and contributed to the growth of at-home shopping. After all, isn't it logical that when you have less time to go shopping, it's more convenient to select and examine merchandise in your own home, at your own convenience? In this regard catalogs must compete with other direct mail offers, home shopping programs and networks available on television, and interactive online shopping services.

2) The growth of business-to-business catalog marketing was related to the increased cost associated with personal sales calls. By the end of the 1970s, the average cost of a single sales call was estimated to be about $137.

By the end of the 1980s, the cost had risen to more than $250 per call. An interesting application of catalog marketing in business-to-business selling is to use catalogs to make personal selling more cost-effective by generating qualified leads that can then be followed up by a personal sales call.

3) Technological growth in general, and computer-based technologies in particular, have played an important role in many areas of direct marketing. New computer technologies have allowed direct marketers to be more precise in the analysis of results, in the targeting of messages based on more complex psychographics and demographics, in developing more sophisticated customer and prospect databases, and even in the creative execution of direct mail packages.

4) The growth in the number of available products and services has made direct marketing more attractive than mass marketing when a larger number of goods and services are being offered to a smaller group of prospects. In addition, consumers have proven receptive to purchasing a wide range of products from catalogs, including everything from automobiles to food to collectibles.

5) Increased consumer acceptance of the telephone as a way to place orders has also helped direct marketing achieve phenomenal growth. Coupled with telephone-based ordering are faster order fulfillment and the elimination of delays previously associated with mail order. Today, placing an order by phone offers almost the same ''instant gratification'' as picking up a piece of merchandise at the store.

Other socioeconomic factors contributing to the growth and acceptance of direct marketing include a population growing older, rising discretionary income, more single households, more double income households, and the growth of the ''me'' generation. External factors include the rising cost of gasoline (at-home shoppers use less gasoline and reduce environmental pollution), the availability of **toll-free telephone numbers**, the expanded use of credit cards, the low cost of data processing, and the widespread availability of mailing lists.

DIFFERENT TYPES OF CATALOGS

The three major categories of catalogs are business-to-business catalogs, consumer catalogs, and catalog showrooms. Business-to-business catalogs are those which provide merchandise to be used in the course of business, including everything from office supplies to computers. In industrial settings business-to-business catalogs are used to sell everything from heavy machinery to hand tools. Business-to-business catalogs are mailed to individuals at their place of business, with most purchases being made on behalf of the business rather than the individual.

Consumer catalogs are mailed to consumers at home. Katie Muldoon in her book, *Catalog Marketing,* identified eight types of consumer catalogs. Unaffiliated catalogs are stand-alone ventures whose primary purpose is to sell merchandise by mail. These independent catalogers are not affiliated with any retailer or manufacturer. While the stores of unaffiliated catalogers were originally designed only to sell remaindered and unsold merchandise, some successful independent catalogers have opened their own retail outlets to take advantage of the consumer recognition their catalogs had built.

Consumers are also quite familiar with retail catalogs, of which Muldoon identified three types: traffic generators, independent profit centers, and a combination of the two. Catalogs that retailers produce as traffic generators are designed to build store traffic rather than to generate mail order sales. On the other hand, a retail catalog that is set up as an independent direct mail operation is expected to produce a profit on the basis of the mail order sales it is able to generate. Hybrids that are designed to generate store traffic as well as mail order sales combine the best of both worlds.

A noteworthy trend in retailers' catalogs is the disappearance of the large general catalog in favor of more specialized and targeted catalogs. In the 1970s the five major general catalogers were Sears, Roebuck and Company, Montgomery Ward, Spiegel, J.C. Penney, and Alden's. Alden's has since ceased operations. Montgomery Ward abandoned the general catalog for a while, only to bring it back using outside companies to produce the catalogs and supply the merchandise. Sears stopped mailing its general catalog in favor of a series of specialty catalogs, as did Spiegel. Penney's large catalog, begun in 1962, has remained successful. In the ever-changing world of catalog marketing, no one is bound to stick to formulas that worked in the past. Only what's working today counts.

A third type of consumer catalog is the manufacturer-supported catalog. These may be designed to generate mail order sales, build store traffic, or simply create an image. Incentive catalogs offer consumers discounted name-brand merchandise with some type of proof of purchase of a particular product or use of a particular credit card. The once-popular incentive catalogs of the trading stamp companies have largely disappeared, but they have been replaced by incentive catalogs issued by credit card companies and others.

Consumer catalogs issued by nonprofit organizations represent yet another type of consumer catalog. Museums have successfully used catalogs to increase sales of gift shop items. Co-op catalogs are used to highlight merchandise from a variety of companies. Co-op catalogs are relatively cheap to produce and are often found in non-traditional distribution channels such as bookstores and newstands.

Syndicated consumer catalogs carry the name of a particular company, usually one that is well known and prestigious. However, the company whose name is on the catalog is not involved in its production and does not carry the merchandise listed in the catalog. The syndicator pays a commission to the company for use of its name and handles all of the aspects of the catalog business.

Another category of consumer catalog is the international catalog. These may originate in Europe or elsewhere. With improved telephone service, it is possible to order by telephone or fax from virtually anywhere in the world.

Catalog showrooms are a category of consumer catalogers that combine retail marketing with catalog marketing. A catalog showroom is essentially a retail outlet. The catalog, usually quite large, serves primarily to build traffic in the showroom. The trend in catalog showrooms has been to de-emphasize the mail order aspect of the catalog and present the showroom as a retail outlet with the added benefit of being able to place catalog orders from the showroom.

ELEMENTS OF CATALOG MARKETING

A successful catalog operation is built on several key elements, including the right personnel, merchandise, catalog design and format, sales promotion, mailing lists, and order processing and fulfillment.

CATALOG PERSONNEL. Many of the functions necessary to maintain a catalog operation can be fulfilled either by employees or outside services. Within the company individual employees can be assigned to handle more than one function. Key functional areas include merchandising, catalog design, marketing and production, office services and data processing, warehouse operations, customer service, and administrative areas covering office operations, personnel, legal affairs, and finance. In addition most operations require some type of administrative support personnel.

MERCHANDISE. Merchandising involves selecting the appropriate items for the catalog. In the case of unaffiliated catalogers, merchandise is selected by buyers from a variety of trade shows and from merchandise centers such as New York City, Chicago, Dallas, and Atlanta where there are many showrooms to choose from. A wide range of publications also offer merchandise that is selected by catalog buyers.

Catalogs affiliated with retailers or manufacturers typically include merchandise that is also sold by the retailer or manufacturer through a store or other channels. However, affiliated buyers may be able to select additional merchandise for inclusion in the catalog. Catalog sales of such merchandise are then monitored to see if the items also should be offered through other channels.

CATALOG DESIGN AND FORMAT. Once the merchandise has been selected, it is necessary to determine how it will be presented in the catalog. Catalogs come in a variety of sizes, shapes, and overall general appearances. A cataloger must select a design concept for its catalog that is appropriate for its company. A catalog carrying discounted merchandise should look like a sale catalog. A catalog carrying high-end merchandise should have a quality look and feel about it. In the hands of a consumer it is the catalog that presents the image of the company.

Keys areas that catalog marketers focus their attention on when designing a catalog include page layout and design, space allocation for various products, the front cover, the back cover, sales copy, headlines, and the sales letter. The inside and outside of both covers as well as the center of a catalog are considered ''hot spots'' that have a disproportionally large influence on sales generation and how the prospect responds to the catalog.

SALES PROMOTION. The order device is also an important ''hot spot'' in any catalog. Sales can be won or lost with the order form, so most catalog marketers regard it as an important sales tool. The key to a successful order form is making it easy to use. Whether the order is placed by mail or a toll-free telephone call, a well-designed order form can facilitate the sale.

In addition the order form usually carries other information that is designed to overcome any reservations that prospects might have about ordering merchandise through the mail or over the telephone. Customers usually look to the order device or pages surrounding the order form to include information about guarantees and warranties, customer service, and any promotional incentives that might be offered.

MAILING LISTS AND DATABASES. As with all types of direct marketing, a key factor in a successful catalog marketing campaign is being able to reach the right audience. Catalog marketers acquire customers by renting mailing lists, then they build in-house databases based on customer histories. The two basic types of lists are response lists and compiled lists. Response lists contain the names of prospects who have responded to the same offer. These typically contain individuals who share a common interest. Response lists are not usually rented; rather, they are an in-house list compiled by a particular business. Most list rentals involve compiled lists, including mass consumer, specialized consumer, and business lists.

Direct marketing databases are similar to mailing lists in that they contain names and addresses, but they are much more. They are the repository of a wide range of customer information and may also contain psychographic, demographic, and census data compiled from external sources. They form the basis of direct marketing programs whereby companies establish closer ties and build relationships with their customers.

As with mailing lists, there are two basic types of marketing databases, customer databases and external databases. Customer databases are compiled internally and contain information about a company's customers taken from the relationship-building process. External databases are collections of specific individuals and their characteristics. These external databases may be mass-compiled from public data sources; they may contain financial data based on confidential credit files; they may be compiled from questionnaires; or they may be a combination of all three sources.

ORDER PROCESSING AND FULFILLMENT. Catalogers that seek to build relationships with their existing customers and acquire new customers must have an efficient system of fulfilling orders in a timely and accurate manner. Nothing turns a customer off more than receiving the wrong merchandise or receiving it too late for the purpose for which it was originally ordered. In some cases catalogers may have their own warehousing operation that is involved in picking, packing, and shipping orders. In other cases merchandise may be drop-shipped from another location, or the entire order fulfillment process may be handled by an outside service bureau.

In addition to efficiently fulfilling orders, catalogers capture order information to build their in-house customer databases. Such databases typically contain information concerning the amount of the purchase, what items have been purchased, and the dates purchases were made. Armed with this data, catalog marketers can more effectively target future mailings to customers based on when, what, and how much they have ordered in the past.

The success of a catalog marketing program depends on the same factors that determine a successful direct marketing program. The catalog must deliver the right offer at the right time to the right person in the right way. The target audience must be correctly identified. The offer must be made in the best possible way, and the catalog must employ the most effective creative execution to present the merchandise offered for sale. At its most effective, catalog marketing is an ongoing process of communication to maintain relationships with existing customers and build relationships with new ones.

[David Bianco]

FURTHER READING:

Kobs, Jim. *Profitable Direct Marketing,* 2nd ed. NTC Business Books, 1992.

Muldoon, Katie. *Catalog Marketing,* 2nd ed. American Management Association, 1988.

Simon, Julian L. *How to Start and Operate a Mail-Order Business,* 5th ed. McGraw-Hill, 1993.

Sroge, Maxwell. *Best in Catalogs,* Volumes 1 and 2. NTC Business Books, 1987.

Sroge, Maxwell. *Inside the Leading Mail Order Houses,* 3rd ed. NTC Business Books, 1989.

CENSUS DATA

''Census data'' most often is associated in the public mind with population. The U.S. census enters America's consciousness every ten years, usually in the form of a long, detailed mail-in questionnaire, quickly forgotten when it's mailed back. It would surprise many to learn that census data are used in a multitude of different ways. While the decennial population count is by far the biggest census that the U.S. Bureau of the Census undertakes, the Bureau also does thousands of different censuses, some annually, others monthly, while the U.S. Economic Census comes out every five years. The data results of all the censuses are awaited eagerly by members of Congress, federal and state agencies, and businesses throughout the United States.

As to the biggest and oldest census, the population count, there is almost no resemblance between the census of today and the first official one tabulated over two hundred years ago. The Articles of Confederation made no provision for a national census. The issue only arose when a federal constitution was debated in 1789. When delegates to the constitutional convention finally agreed to accept population as the principle of representation in the House, it became a problem to decide whom to include in the population. Delegates from southern states wanted slaves to be counted equally with white men and women, while northerners, fearing overrepresentation of southern whites in Congress, insisted that three slaves equaled only one white person. Native Americans would not be included at all. Finally, the Constitution mandated a national population census every ten years.

In 1880, Congress decided to do something about streamlining the census process, hence mandating the establishment of a separate Census Office in the U.S.

Department of the Interior, which would hire professionals to do the census. Special punch card tabulating machines were introduced, while women were hired for the first time as enumerators. In 1904, the Census Bureau was made a permanent part of the newly created U.S. Department of Commerce.

A new and rather daring departure from the traditional human census counter occurred in 1910, when the Census Bureau decided to introduce the census questionnaire by mail. Either because the public was insufficiently educated on the importance of the census or because few people had private telephones for follow-up reminders, most discarded the census form with its prying questions, necessitating the return of the census counter.

Conceived by Bureau mathematicians in 1943, the sample survey queried only a small percentage of the population to produce results reflective of the population at large. The sample survey opened the door for a multitude of different, and more detailed, surveys in the future, and is still used today.

To tabulate all of this data would have been a gargantuan task for a human enumerator. The computer and its improved successors arrived just in time to handle the 1950 census, however, the biggest population survey ever previously attempted.

The Census Bureau has been compiling ever greater numbers of censuses since it was first established by Congress in 1880. Every conceivable aspect of business, industry and commerce is documented either monthly, annually, biannually or quinquennially in the form of census surveys and polls, averaging two thousand a year. Some of the census data are published in the form of one or two page reports; others are compiled annually into the thousand pages of the *Statistical Abstract of the United States*. A recent innovation has been the Census Bureau's geographic database, TIGER (Topologically Integrated Geographic Encoding and Referencing), which provides a block by block population survey of the United States, including every bridge, stream, road and tunnel. TIGER is available on CD-ROM as well as on major internet networks, and many local libraries make it available to the general public.

In short, billions of facts are churned out by the Census Bureau annually. Approximately 40,000 different federal, state and local government agencies and business entities rely on these facts. The President is mandated to present the decennial census results before Congress by January 1 of the year following the taking of the population census, which is the signal to begin reapportionment of seats in the House. Several months later, on April 1, every state must have received a detailed population count from the Census Bureau to begin reapportionment of its legislature (which also includes county and municipal legislatures). Major cit-

ies also are vitally interested in the census data, since the population figures determine the amount of federal aid they receive. Anyone interested in ascertaining the amount of spending by state and local governments can also find this in the census data.

Virtually every business, industry and service uses (or could benefit from using) census data. Private entrepreneurs, from barbershop owners to the self-employed, can turn to the Census Bureau's popular publication, *Taking Care of Business: A Guide to Census Bureau Data for Small Businesses*. For example, a restaurant in Los Angeles was able to contact the Census Bureau to find out the number of residents from the Deep South residing in the city, in order to determine how many ham hocks the restaurant should order. For a business catering to an ethnic minority, the census provides the population figure, location, and incomes for that ethnic group, and much more data besides. Certain companies can plot their future marketing strategies more effectively when they discover that the 1990 census indicates that by 2050, America's elderly—over 85 years of age—will have increased sixfold. Census data can tell a utility business the percentage of homes that use gas for heating and cooking. In addition, many businesses and manufacturers rely heavily on the five year U.S. Economic Survey, which is the result of questionnaires sent to three and a half million companies. This can help them evaluate business opportunities, consumer preferences, market share, and the competition, as well as enable them to locate the best sites for new business and distribution routes for their products. It can provide strong clues as to how to advertise their products or where to target their direct mail. It is unfortunate that the Economic Survey has become so detailed and complex that the Bureau issues a special reference book to guide the researcher through the data. Lastly, the Census Bureau cooperates with the **U.S. Small Business Administration** to provide statistics for a range of publications and helps organize pre-business seminars and workshops throughout the country.

In the past 200 years the census and the Census Bureau have evolved into useful and profitable tools. Numerous private research firms offer their own census data "packages," complete with a user-friendly electronic format and their own projections. Whenever newspapers and magazines cite social or economic data on the United States, they often pick up these facts from current Census Bureau surveys.

Despite the utility and profit derived from using or marketing census data, there have nearly always been controversies surrounding the Census Bureau and the data it gives out. Because census data are vital in determining the amount of federal aid to cities, and whether or not to expand low income housing and other social programs, the Census Bureau has faced dozens of lawsuits alleging undercounting of minorities. The Bureau in fact has had to admit that it has undercounted minorities in the past: in the 1970 census, the population was underestimated by around five million, the vast majority of whom were members of minority groups. Better census methods have resulted in the smallest undercount of any census for the 1990 population count. In that census, the Hispanic population was underestimated by only 5.2 percent, African-Americans by 4.8 percent, Native Americans by 5 percent, and Asian and Pacific Islanders by 3.1 percent. Undercounting minorities can have severe consequences for cities who rely on federal grants. It also angers minority groups who feel left out of reapportionment and whose poor are underserved. Businesses, which, for most of this century, ignored the ethnic market, are transforming their marketing strategies to target minority groups in particular and can be harmed by sizable undercounts.

Besides the criticisms the Census Bureau has had to face regarding population undercounts, there is also the matter of privacy that has continually perplexed census efforts. While the postwar decades have escalated the pressure on the Bureau to provide increasingly detailed information, there is resistance to the ''prying'' nature of census questionnaires on the part of the public, from businesses to private individuals. The well known fear of illegal immigrants of filling out the census questionnaires is partly the reason for the undercount of the Hispanic population, for which the Bureau gets blamed. Since 1929, the Bureau has been especially mandated to keep all of its information confidential. Nonetheless, the computerization of government has cast public doubt on the ''leakproof'' nature of census information.

The public's, as well as government's, demands for more diversified data have been another problem for the Census Bureau. In the 1950s and 1960s, in response to these pressures, census data became ever more detailed, covering smaller and smaller geographic areas. This has enormously expanded the mandate of the Census Bureau from what it was initially called upon to do and increased sizably the budget of the Bureau. To the dismay of many small businesses, the Census Bureau is planning to scale back its survey activities, especially those involving small geographic areas. There are indications that even the ten-year population count will change significantly in the 21st century, possibly involving only a sample survey to a small percentage of the population, obviating the need, for instance, to tabulate 90 million household questionnaires. This indicates that census data and many other surveys may be conducted increasingly by the private sector, especially universities and research firms.

[Sina Dubovoy]

FURTHER READING:

Anderson, Margo. *The American Census: A Social History.* Yale University Press, 1988.

Dodd, Don. *Historical Statistics of the States of the United States: Two Centuries of the Census, 1790-1990.* Greenwood Press, 1993.

Halacy, D.S. *Census: 190 Years of Counting America.* Elsevier/ Nelson Books, 1980.

Myers, Dowell. *Analysis with Local Census Data: Portraits of Change.* Academic Press, 1992.

CENTRAL AMERICA, DOING BUSINESS IN

Central America consists of seven small republics, bounded on one side by the Caribbean Sea, and on the other, by the Pacific Ocean. The population is small, totalling about 30 million. All but one of the Central American nation states uses Spanish as its official language (although a great many Indian dialects prevail in the countryside). The exception in language and culture in this region is the little known country of Belize, formerly British Honduras, which became independent of British rule in 1981. Belize is the only country in Central America which belongs to the **Caribbean Common Market** (CARICOM); it has not joined with neighboring states in the **Central American Common Market** (CACM). The members of CACM are Costa Rica, Honduras, Guatemala, Nicaragua, and El Salvador. Like Belize, Panama also has not become a member of CACM.

Despite the cultural, linguistic, and even ethnic homogeneity of most of Central America, there has been almost continued discord and disunity among the states. When Spanish colonial rule ended in 1821, all seven Central American nations attempted to join together politically; this effort ended in dissolution in the 1830s. Thereafter, they went their separate ways. Belize succumbed to British colonialism in 1862. Costa Rica, where land was most equitably distributed of all the Central American nations, became the most stable state in the region, and consequently, the most prosperous and advanced. The same could not be said of El Salvador, Guatemala, Honduras, Nicaragua, and Panama, which were ruled by a succession of military dictatorships until well into the 20th century.

Because of the tropical climate, bananas, sugar and coffee production prospered in these countries, becoming the predominant crops of a small, wealthy landed elite. The wealthy leaders in turn became officers in the armed forces and exercised despotic control over the rest of the populace in their respective states. The result has been a long legacy of political oppression and dire poverty in this region, with the exception of democratic Costa Rica and sparsely populated, minuscule Belize.

COLD WAR INSTABILITY

Frequent military intervention in this area on the part of the United States did more to hinder than to help the people of Central America. The onset of the Cold War after the conclusion of World War II aggravated American and Soviet interventionism, and soon Central America and the Caribbean region became a pawn in the ideological rivalry between the United States and the Soviet Union. The consequences of Cold War rivalry in these areas wreaked havoc on several Central American countries, notably El Salvador, Nicaragua, and Guatemala, and intensified the historical disunity and tensions among the Central American states. Honduras, Costa Rica, and Belize suffered from the influx of hundreds of thousands of refugees fleeing civil war in El Salvador and Nicaragua, and the Guatemalan military's war against its Indian population in the 1980s. In addition, Honduras became a training ground for the Nicaraguan Contra army. The strife in those countries cost the lives of tens of thousands of civilians and damaged their economies and infrastructures for years to come.

POST-COLD WAR CLIMATE

Accordingly, most American businesses have been skeptical about doing business in this unstable region despite its proximity to the United States. However, the fall of communism in the U.S.S.R. and the end of the Cold War have triggered a dramatic transformation in Central America. Guatemala has gone from one of the most repressive military dictatorships in Latin America to a fragile democracy in which Nobel Peace Prize winner and military critic, Ramiro de Leon Carpio, became head of state in 1993. In 1992, the guerrillas in El Salvador handed over their Soviet made weapons to United Nations' peacekeepers, bringing the 12 year civil war to an end. The Sandinistas in Nicaragua conceded after electoral defeat in 1990. Guatemala and Belize have settled a serious but little known border dispute that has decreased tensions between them and increased economic cooperation. Finally, five central American nations have revived the defunct Central American Common Market and made it an instrument of economic empowerment. Free market reforms and economic liberalization are evident in every Central American nation.

As in so many regions of the world, the late 1990s is witnessing an unusual trend—away from military rivalry towards aggressive economic competition. To win in the economic sphere, hitherto disparate nations have downplayed their national differences in favor of regional economic cooperation. In the Western Hemisphere, the **North American Free Trade Agreement** (NAFTA) has been approved, and 21 Latin American nations have vowed to forge a similar economic pact in the future. In the Caribbean, the Caribbean Common Market has been revived; in Central America, the Central American Common Market.

ADVANTAGES OF DOING BUSINESS IN CENTRAL AMERICA

Hence the disadvantages of Americans doing business in Central America, with its recent unstable and bloody past, must be weighed against the advantages, and against the increasing economic presence of Asians and Europeans in the economies of Central America.

A powerful attraction to doing business in this area is the high unemployment rate in every Central American country except Costa Rica, which translates into a cheap pool of labor that drastically reduces the cost to manufacture. Most American business in Central America produces for the U.S. market, rather than for the meager domestic markets. However, a small company, that can manage to make a profit from shipping small quantities of products can do a lucrative business in regional markets, provided it finds the right niche. All Central American countries, including relatively affluent Costa Rica, have a constant need for construction material of all kinds, cooling and refrigeration units, computers and software, and medical and diagnostic equipment. Tourism is also a booming industry in Central America. The Central American infrastructure, even within a poverty stricken country such as Honduras, is superior at this point in time to that found in most parts of South Asia and Africa.

While Belize is not a member of the Central American Common Market, it does belong to its Caribbean counterpart, CARICOM. An advantage of doing business in Belize for the small company is the possibility of having a trade link with the European Common Market, which is a difficult one to establish for a small firm that lacks international marketing experience. CARICOM has created the Caribbean Council for Europe, which enables any company doing business with a CARICOM member to avail itself of a private pipeline to the Western European market.

While there still is endemic poverty in Central America, this is giving way to a growth in the GDP (Gross Domestic Product) in all seven states, and to a genuine economic revitalization. English is widely used in business, and American investment is warmly welcomed everywhere, in contrast to Cold War days.

The inception of the Caribbean Basin Initiative (CBI), which Congress passed in 1983 (as part of the

Caribbean Basin Economic Recovery Act), is beginning to turn American business in the direction of the Caribbean region and Central America, which borders the Caribbean. Most recently, Nicaragua was made eligible to become a recipient of the benefits of the CBI. The CBI has dramatically promoted economic reform and liberalization in the Caribbean/Central American region. Highlights of CBI are duty free entrance into the United States of 94 product categories manufactured in the Caribbean and Central America; the establishment in this area of development banks, chambers of commerce, and **free trade zones**; the funding of job training and self-help programs; and very importantly, the provision of easy-term financial assistance to U.S. companies doing business in the region. There are many government agencies involved in the promotion of trade and the development of the Central American economies, a list of which can be obtained from the U.S. Department of Commerce.

The U.S. government also offers special incentives for doing business in this region via the Section 936 program. A company that does a major portion of its business in the Caribbean/Central American area can qualify for Section 936 of the Internal Revenue Code, which exempts it from federal income tax on earnings that are derived from its business in this region. In addition, such institutions as the Overseas Private Investment Corporation, as well as the United States' Eximbank, provide financial assistance to businesses wishing to invest in Central America.

THE CENTRAL AMERICAN COMMON MARKET

With the end of the Cold War and spread of regional peace, five of the Central American states (Costa Rica, El Salvador, Honduras, Guatemala and Nicaragua) have revived and strengthened the Central American Common Market. CACM has eliminated trade barriers within the five member states and is working on developing a common foreign trade policy. Individually, the member states have designated free trade zones (including Panama, which does not belong to CACM) that offer foreign companies establishing their businesses there exemptions from import and export taxes, and in some cases (as in Costa Rica), elimination of income taxes for a certain number of years. There are at least 130 companies operating in Costa Rica, a Central American country with a relatively advanced economy, an educated work force, and excellent infrastructure, including superior port facilities. In neighboring Honduras, where government red tape is complicated and bureaucracy difficult to penetrate, an American company willing to endure the initial hardships of doing business there will discover that there is little competition.

Certainly the potential for making a profit in a country as poverty stricken as Honduras is growing, and opportunities for financing one's businesses in that country are many (primarily through the Overseas Private Investment Corporation and USAID). For small but important projects, there are even government aid programs. The Honduran Consulate General in New York City is the best place to turn to for information.

El Salvador and Nicaragua would appear to be poor business investment risks, despite the end of fratricidal war and the recent defeat of communism. The coming of peace has not solved many of the endemic social and political ills of these countries. To the surprise of many, then, the economic recovery of both nations has proceeded rapidly, thanks in large part to U.S. and European assistance. Prior to the Sandinista takeover of the Nicaraguan government in 1979, that country's textile industry was thriving and modern; since the defeat of the Sandinistas, it is rapidly getting back on its feet, thanks in part to the Caribbean Basin Initiative. Nicaragua's port is second to none in the region, and the Nicaraguan government is encouraging foreign investment in every branch of the economy. Privatization also is well under way in both countries, and purchasing a former state owned enterprise can present a profitable business option. Both Nicaragua and El Salvador have large labor pools who desire work, another advantage to doing business in these countries. Both Nicaragua and El Salvador boast successful free trade zones, and offer many tax exemptions to foreign businesses.

Guatemala's emergence as a fragile parliamentary democracy and free market economy have been so recent that it is hard to ignore the unpredictabilities of doing business there. Despite signs of progress in the country, government bureaucracy in Guatemala is still very corrupt, and drug trafficking is a serious problem. Nonetheless, with Guatemala City being the second most polluted city in the world next to Mexico City, any environmental business is sure to thrive in this country. Moreover, the government strongly encourages foreign trade as a way of earning foreign exchange, and with little competition and guaranteed repatriation of profits, business opportunities in this country are diverse and real.

In short, there are many bonuses and benefits for businesses that are willing to invest directly or indirectly in Central America. Nonetheless, setting up shop in this area is no guarantee of an easy ride. Anyone wishing to establish a business there, must be sure that there is a viable niche for that business in the chosen country. This means locating information about the chosen locale to find out the shortcomings as well as benefits of doing business there.

A good Place to start is the Department of Commerce publication, *Caribbean Basin Financing Opportunities: A Guide to Financing Trade and Investment in Central America and the Caribbean*, which can be obtained by mail or at one of the 68 district offices of the Department of Commerce, each of which has abundant information and offers assistance in doing business abroad. Another source of assistance is the Latin America/Caribbean Business Development Center in Washington, D.C., which offers many publications to the public, as well as one-on-one counseling. In addition, there is the Overseas Development Council in Washington, the trade sections of the embassies of each of the Central American states, and other Central American-based offices (and Central American business offices in the United States), a list of which can be obtained through the Department of Commerce.

Whatever type of business and Central American locale that is selected, exhaustive knowledge about transportation costs, repatriation of profits, and which banks take American dollar deposits (not all of them do) is crutial. This will necessitate a personal investigative business trip and a local contact. It is imperative to have a native lawyer (or law firm) or accountant who can steer through the maze found in most Central American bureaucracies. Business in Central America still proceeds via personal contacts, unless it is the tourist industry.

A recommended first step in getting started in business in Central America is to set up a joint venture with a native based industry, which knows the ropes and can initiate further business opportunities. The trade section of the embassy (or consulate) of each Central American country can establish contacts with representatives or firms. The need for marketing and advertising also will be minimal, since most new products are introduced in the numerous trade fairs held annually in the region.

The business potential of Central America is real, and growing.To ignore it because of difficulties with the bureaucracy or because of other unpredictable factors is to ignore the fact that other areas of the world also present thorny problems. If American businesses fail to invest in their own backyard in favor of distant markets, they risk becoming latecomers who fall behind very strong foreign competitors in the future.

[Sina Dubovoy]

FURTHER READING:

Arana, Ana. "The Dogs of War Make Way for the Pigs of Peace (Letter from El Salvador)," *Business Week*. April 13, 1992.

Baker, Stephen. "Back to Nature in Belize," *Business Week*. Feb.3, 1992, p. 86.

Breitenecker, Rudiger L. "The Caribbean Basin Initiative—An Effective U.S. Trade Policy Facilitating Economic Liberaliza-tion in the Region: the Costa Rican Example." *Law & Policy in International Business*, Summer, 1992, pp.913-949.

Cavusgil, S. Tamer. *Doing Business in Developing Countries: Negotiations and Entry Strategies.* New York: Routledge, 1990.

Chasteen, John Charles, ed. *The Contemporary History of Latin America.* Durham and London: Duke University Press, 1993.

"Costa Rica: Paradise Opens its Doors," *South Florida Business Journal.* March 19, 1993, p.18A.

"El Salvador," *Latin Finance.* September, 1993, p. TF91.

Holman, Richard L. "Honduras Sets Privatization," *The Wall Street Journal.* March 4, 1994, p.A7(W), p. A4(E).

Howell, Alvaro R. Castellanos. "Guatemala: Right On Track," *LatinFinance.* October, 1993, p. 69.

James, Canute. "Central America, Caribbean Back NAFTA Parity Bill," *Journal of Commerce and Commercial.* June 8, 1993, p. 3A.

Lee, Helen D. "Reforms and Integration Spur Growth of Market (Central American Common Market)," *Business America.* April 19, 1993, p. 10.

Lordan, Betsy. "Consulate to Lure Florida Investors to Belize," *South Florida Business Journal.* Oct.5, 1992, p. 13.

Milman, Joel. "Bienvenidos, Tigers: Modern Capitalism is Coming to Central America and Who is Bringing It? Koreans and Chinese," *Forbes.* May 27, 1991, p. 190.

Tuller, Lawrence W. *Doing Business in Latin America and the Caribbean.* Amacom, 1993.

Welch, Tom. "Economic Policies Make Headway for U.S. Business in Honduras," *Business America.* March 23, 1992, p. 11.

Wilde, Thomas E., Jr. "U.S. Agribusiness Trade and Investment Rise in Latin America and the Caribbean." *Business America,* March 23, 1992, p. 4.

CENTRAL AMERICAN COMMON MARKET

The Central American Common Market (CACM) was established in 1960 with the signing of the General Treaty of Central American Economic Integration at Managua, Nicaragua. The original signatories of the treaty, which became effective June 3, 1961, were El Salvador, Guatemala, Honduras, and Nicaragua. Costa Rica joined the market in 1962. These nations banned together under CACM to establish a common market for advancing the economic development of member nations through coordinated promotion of industrial growth, economic diversification, and the dismantling of trade barriers.

THE EARLY YEARS

The CACM had its beginnings with the Committee for Economic Cooperation of the Central American Isthmus which formulated the Central American Economic Integration Program of 1952. This economic coalition led to a series of agreements including: the Agreement on the Regime for Central American Integration Industries (1958), the Multilateral Treaty of Central American Free Trade/Economic Integration (1958), the Central American Agreement on the Equalization of Import Duties and Charges (1959) and the Protocol on Central American Preferential Tariff (1959). The tenets of these agreements were folded into the CACM treaty of 1960.

INFIGHTING HAMPERS DEVELOPMENT

Almost from its inception there were military, political and economic problems plaguing CACM. A number of ill-fated plans were initially enacted to deal with these problems and promote economic integration. Among the plans were the 1961 Central American Clearing House and the 1964 Central American Monetary Council. The Monetary Council integrated many operations of the central banks of CACM members and established the peso centroamericano as a standard unit of exchange. The Central American Clearing House ultimately failed to reach its goal of coordinating the domestic economy of CACM members and was unable to control the movement of capital between member countries. The peso centroamericano was never accepted as a unit of exchange on the world market. Internally the standard existed only as a yardstick of exchange rates. By 1966 any economic progress being made by the market countries came to a halt as severe balance of payment problems hindered CACM growth. All CACM members were in debt to one another and behind in their payments because of declining exports and reductions in import revenues. By 1967 the CACM nations were posting record deficits. Many members reacted by taking unilateral protective measures which led to further long term balance of payment problems.

In 1969 Honduras withdrew unofficially from CACM during its war with El Salvador. In 1970, Honduras began imposing tariffs on imports from CACM member nations. This continued until the peace treaty of 1980 between Honduras and El Salvador was signed, bringing with it pledges from Honduras to resume full membership and cooperation. In 1979 Nicaragua and El Salvador underwent internal political upheavals, and strained relations between Costa Rica and Nicaragua caused frequent border closings.

These political, economic, and military problems soon halted what little progress was being made towards CACM goals of establishing a common external tariff on goods imported from non-member countries and dismantling internal tariffs on intra-regional CACM trade. In the 1970s and 1980s intra-regional CACM trade declined. By 1981 worldwide recessional forces were adversely affecting CACM members and extra-regional exports began to decline as well. In 1982 the gross domestic product of all CACM countries fell as a result of budget deficits and inflation.

ASSOCIATION WITH EUROPEAN ECONOMIC COMMUNITY

A 1985 economic agreement with the European Community failed to spark an anticipated economic revitalization of CACM countries, but it did provide an impetus for the formation of the Central American Parliament in 1986. This body is modeled after the European Parliament which serves as a consultative body to the European Community. The two parliaments have formed cooperative economic ties between the European Community and CACM.

RETURN TO ORIGINAL GOALS

Summit meetings in the early 1990s began refocusing on economic integration by emphasizing the organizations original mission: lower tariffs, infrastructure improvements, and the dismantling of various technical trade barriers. In 1992 the System of Central American Integration was created to foster greater cooperation on political and economic matters. Other discussions focused on trading with common markets outside of the region and establishing various free trade zones. Suggested solutions to CACM economic stagnation include increasing extra-regional exports, restructuring foreign debts, stabilizing exchange rates, and implementing a common external tariff.

CACM policy is made by the Central American Economic Council. The council meets quarterly and is comprised of the financial ministers from member nations. Day-to-day operations are overseen by an Executive Council which also elects a Secretary General. For further information write: Central American Common Market, Apart Postal 1237, 4a Avenida 10-25, Zona 14, 01901 Guatemala City, Guatemala.

[Michael Knes]

FURTHER READING:

Irvin, George. *Central America: The Future of Economic Integration*. Westview Press, 1989.

Shaw, Royce Q. *Central America: Regional Integration and National Political Development*. Westview Press, 1978.

CENTRAL BANKS

A central bank is a financial institution established by a national government and is primarily responsible for regulating the monetary policies of that country. Responsibilities of central banks include:

holding the reserves of the reserves of commercial banks, controlling a country's monetary reserves, regulating a country's **money supply**, check collection, establishing **interest rates**, issuing legal tender, holding foreign currency reserves and monitoring exchange rates, and regulating governmental credit policies and government loans and borrowing. Although most countries have a central bank, the banks' specific functions, responsibilities, and administrative structures vary from country to country. With few exceptions (most notably France and Australia) central banks do not deal directly with the public sector—rather they deal with appropriate governmental agencies and other banking institutions. Because of this, central banks are often referred to as ''banker's banks'' or as a ''lender of last resort.'' Central banks are usually of the European model which is typified by centralized operations and government control, or the American model which is more decentralized and more independent of outside political control.

Some of the earliest central or government-sponsored banks are the Riksbank of Sweden which was founded in 1668 and the Bank of England which began in 1694. These early banks were extensions of their founding governments and were established for the convenience of those governments. Political favoritism was often involved in their operations which were usually mutually advantageous often at the expense of private commercial banks. Central banks were also founded for specific purposes such as restoring faith in a country's currency following a devastating upheaval such as a war or to bring order to currency issues. The nineteenth century saw the establishment of many central banks in Europe including the Bank of France in 1800, the Bank of the Netherlands in 1814, and the Bank of Belgium in 1835. It was not until the twentieth century, however, that these government-sponsored institutions began taking on the activities and responsibilities which characterize their operations today.

The United States was one of the last contemporary economic powers to found a central bank. The central banking authority in the United States is known as the Federal Reserve System. The **Federal Reserve System** followed, however, the establishment of two different government banks. The First Bank of the United States was a creation of Alexander Hamilton (1757-1804) acting in his role as the first Secretary of the Treasury. Although opposed by Thomas Jefferson, the bank was nevertheless established in 1791 and continued to operate until 1811 when its charter was allowed to lapse. Although the First Bank operated successfully, there was much political opposition to its existence from those who felt it was monopolistic, those who felt it was unconstitutional, and those who felt its operations impeded the development of state banks. In 1816 Congress chartered the Second Bank of the United States. Opposition soon mounted especially from various coalitions of entrepreneurs, industrialists, and agrarians. They largely felt that the bank's fiscal responsibilities, which were exercised as financial restraints on their activities, were overly oppressive. Constitutional issues soon arose over the bank's creation and operations and Andrew Jackson who was elected president in 1828 became a focal leader for those who opposed the bank. In 1832 Congress voted to renew the bank's charter which was due to expire in 1836. Jackson however vetoed the congressional act and moved federal deposits out of the Second Bank and into various state-chartered banks, effectively signaling the Second Bank's end. The United States did not have a central bank again until President Woodrow Wilson signed the Federal Reserve Act of 1913 which established the Federal Reserve System as of November 1914. Impetus for the creation of a central bank for the United States was based on a need for an agency to regulate and supervise the banking industry and manage the money supply of the United States.

The Federal Reserve Act mandated that the United States be divided into Federal Reserve Districts each with its own Federal Reserve bank. There must be no fewer than eight districts nor more than the present maximum of 12. Each Federal Reserve bank is named after the city in which it is located. In addition to the 12 banks there are 25 Federal Reserve branches. All national commercial banks in the United States must be members of the Federal Reserve System. State-chartered banks have optional membership in the Federal Reserve System but are nonetheless subject to regulation by the ''Fed.'' The Federal Reserve System is administered by the Federal Open Market Committee and a board of governors from which one member is nominated by the president of United States to serve as chairman.

[Michael Knes]

FURTHER READING:

deKock, M. H. *Central Banking*. Crosby Lockwood Staples, 1974.

Goodhart, C. A. E. *Evolution of Central Banks*. MIT Press, 1988.

CENTRALLY PLANNED ECONOMY

Central planning of an economy is most often associated with the system of economic direction and control in the Soviet Union and other communist states because it was developed most extensively in these economies. But while central planning comprised the basic form of economic administration in these countries, it is by no means limited to nor synonymous with **communism**. In fact, the concept of central planning predates—and now has outlived—the Soviet Union, and has been used from time to time by governments regardless of their social philosophy to achieve overriding national goals.

A centrally planned economy is one in which the employment of a nation's entire resources—land, labor, and capital—is determined by state authorities. This authority determines by decree what should be produced, the quantities of these products, where they will be sold and at what price. Simply put, the government planning authority controls supply and demand for all products, to the exclusion of market mechanisms.

This system of economic management has been widely criticized, almost to the point of being completely discredited as a viable approach to sustainable economic planning and growth. However, it is brutally efficient at channeling resources for economic imperatives and making greater utilization of underemployed **assets**.

As a result, central planning is ideally suited for emergency conditions, most notably a general state of war. Standard market mechanisms are ill-suited to cope with these conditions because under state direction, the market becomes a monopsony, excess profits are inefficient, and, in the case of war, armaments technically have no economic value.

Central planning, which occurs under a command economy, is effective only as long as the supply of products remains reasonably close to demand. If demand for a certain product sufficiently exceeds supply, an alternative market outside the realm of central planning will invariably form. This secondary economy, or "black market," provides the necessary mechanism to satisfy excess demand, but it also may frustrate the goals of central planning by diverting needed assets to "nonproductive" uses.

For example, nylon was essential for making parachutes during World War II. Because supplies of the fabric were limited, government planners requisitioned all available nylon for making parachutes. This eliminated future supplies of nylon hosiery, whose only utility—beautifying a woman's legs—had no military value. But because people were willing to pay dearly for nylon hosiery, a black market formed that satisfied some demand, albeit at the cost of more parachutes.

This example of **competition** for scarce resources illustrates a primary feature of central planning: subordination of the price mechanism. The fact that 5000 pairs of nylon hosiery could generate $50,000 in revenue, or produce a single $25 parachute, is irrelevant to the planning authority.

This is because the planning authority has determined supply on the basis of the government's own needs and imperatives. Demand, manifested in offering prices, has no bearing on the supply quotas established by the government.

[John Simley]

FURTHER READING:

Baumol, Wm. J., and Alan S. Blinder. *Economics, Principles and Policy.* 2nd ed. New York: Harcourt Brace Jovanovich, 1982.

Eatwell, J., ed. *The New Palgrave Dictionary of Economics*, London: Macmillan, 1987.

Fischer, Stanley, and Rudiger Hornbusch. *Economics*. New York: McGraw-Hill, 1983.

Tinbergen, Jan. *Central Planning*. New Haven, CT: Yale University Press, 1964.

CEO

SEE: Chief Executive Officer

CERTIFICATE OF ORIGIN

A certificate of origin is a document attesting to the country from which a product or good is imported or the source country of any and all parts or materials that went into the completion of the product. Certificates of origin may be issued by various responsible organizations or institutions including chambers of commerce and national consulates. A certificate of origin is required of all goods imported into the United States.

Many countries require a certificate of origin for all imported goods while other countries may require such a document only on specified goods. A certificate of origin may be required for a variety of reasons including statistical records or tariff schedules which may be part of a treaty such as the **United States-Canada Free Trade Agreement**. Certificates of origin also have political ends and may be employed during **boycotts** such as the one imposed on the Union of South Africa during the 1980s and early 1990s.

The certificate of origin document is usually a standard or generic form usually available from a country's consulate. Some importing countries however require their own specific forms. After completion, a form is then certified, usually by a **chamber of commerce** and returned to the respective consulate to be officially stamped and signed. There may or may not be small fees imposed for these various services.

Certificates of origin are generally lengthy and require information on the following: exporter and importer; any intermediate agents such as customs brokers; freight forwarder; invoice and purchase order number; bill of lading or air waybill number; country of origin; **export** date and export references; port of embarkation; carrier and planned route; physical description, including number of packages, gross and net weight, description of merchandise, description of package markings; and the exporter's and chamber of commerce's certification.

A certificate of value and origin also includes the value of the merchandise. A negative certificate of origin states that goods, final products, or any parts thereof did not originate in a particular country.

[Michael Knes]

FURTHER READING:

"The Certificate of Origin," *Traffic Management.* August, 1990, pp. 86a-87a.

CERTIFICATION

SEE: Licensing and Certification, Occupational

CERTIFIED PUBLIC ACCOUNTANTS (CPAS)

Accounting is a profession designed to provide financial information about a business or an individual. Accountants—individuals who practice in this profession—perform the function of preparing and analyzing financial records and reports. Anyone can be an accountant as long as he or she follows the rules and regulations established for the proper preparation of financial reports and documents. Not everyone, however, can claim the title of Certified Public Accountant, or CPA.

A CPA represents a position at the top of the accounting profession. It is a position gained through the successful completion of the Uniform CPA Examination, prepared by the Board of Examiners of the American Institute of Certified Public Accountants and granted by the individual's state board of accountancy.

While being a CPA is not a requirement to practice accounting, the possession of this distinction is regarded as an indication of advanced knowledge and professionalism. The CPA exam is an extensive, 2½-day examination. It is the same in every state and consists of:

- Accounting Practice, Part I 4.5 hours
- Auditing 3.5 hours
- Accounting Practice, Part II 4.5 hours
- Business Law 3.5 hours
- Accounting Theory 3.5 hours

The exam consists of both multiple-choice and essay or problem-type questions—60 percent multiple-choice and 40 percent essay. The test is designed to measure both the technical knowledge of CPA candidates and their conceptual knowledge of the accounting field and use of sound judgment in response to the questions.

While the exam itself is consistent across all states, the District of Columbia, Guam, Puerto Rico, and the Virgin Islands, the requirements for taking the test and receiving a license to practice varies among jurisdictions. Most territories, but not all, require that the candidate possess a bachelor's degree. In addition, candidates may need to meet certain experience qualifications. Also, in most areas, candidates may take and pass individual parts of the test before proceeding to the next part. The American Institute of Certified Public Accountants (AICPA) recommends a four-year college course with an accounting major as the minimum educational requirement for becoming a CPA. Accounting is the only profession where all states and territories have been able to reach agreement on the use of one, standard examination.

The successful completion of the CPA exam allows the individual to use the designation of "certified public accountant" or "CPA." To maintain that distinction, 48 states require ongoing continuing education courses.

In preparation for the exam many candidates take advantage of intensive review courses and self-study programs. The AICPA also provides information and sample tests to aid in the preparation process.

Applications for taking the CPA examination can be obtained from the board of accountancy in the territory where the candidate is seeking the CPA certificate. Exams are held twice a year, in May and November. A summary of examination and licensing requirements is available in two publications: *Digest of States Accountancy Laws and State Board Regulations*, available through the AICPA; and *Accountancy Law Reports*, published by Commerce Clearing House.

[Lin Grensing-Pophal]

FURTHER READING:

Rosenberg, Martin. *Opportunities in Accounting Careers.* Chicago: NTC Publishing Group, 1991.

Rosenthal, Lawrence. *Exploring Careers in Accounting.* New York: Rosen Publishing Group, 1993.

SEE: Chief Financial Officer

CHAMBER OF COMMERCE

A chamber of commerce is a voluntary association whose membership is comprised of companies, civic leaders, and individual business people. Its members seek to promote the interests of business, typically in a broad-based way. Chambers of commerce exist on municipal, state, regional, national, and even international levels.

Chambers of commerce evolved from the merchant guilds that arose during the Middle Ages. The first association to call itself a chamber of commerce was established in 1599 in Marseille, France. Subsequently, other chambers of commerce were formed, with widespread proliferation occurring during the 18th and 19th centuries, most notably in France, Britain, and the United States. Today, chambers of commerce—sometimes called boards of trade or commercial associations—can be found in most of the world's industrialized countries.

In the United States, the first chamber of commerce was created in 1768 in New York City. Its stated objectives encompassed "encouraging commerce, supporting industry, adjusting disputes relative to trade and navigation, and producing such laws and regulations as may be found necessary for the benefit of trade in general." Soon other chambers of commerce formed—in Charleston, SC, for example, and in other major seaboard cities. Arising in quick succession during the 19th century, chambers of commerce spread throughout the land and today number in the thousands.

At the local level, chambers of commerce strive to develop and publicize business opportunities in their community, as well as work for the betterment of local schools and other community institutions. To their members, local chambers of commerce offer a range of programs and services, including information and advice on timely business matters, opportunities for networking, and sundry publications. Local chambers of commerce also provide their members with varied forums—task forces, committees, special events, and so on—in which individual members can express their specific views and concerns, whether pertaining to the challenges facing small businesses or to the issues surrounding international commerce. Depending on their geographic setting, local chambers of commerce can be small or large in terms of

their membership and scope of activities. The Greater Boston Chamber of Commerce, for instance, has 2,000 members, 80 percent of which are small businesses.

At the national level, chambers of commerce function as a unified voice for their affiliates. The Chamber of Commerce of the U.S., counts some 185,000 companies, affiliate chambers of commerce, and **professional and trade associations** among its members and, through them, represents five million business organizations and individuals. This body, founded as a national federation in 1912 and headquartered in Washington, D.C., was instrumental in persuading the federal government to institute a national budget and in gaining passage of the Federal Reserve Act. Its chief aims are: to promote economy in government, cut taxes, and devise an equitable tax system; improve labor relations; increase production, develop new markets, and provide more jobs; raise educational levels; build better cities; and keep organized business strong and increasingly effective. To carry out its mission the national chamber maintains a staff of 1,500 and engages in a broad spectrum of activities, ranging from informing and counseling its members on key government developments to conducting policy studies and issuing reports, bulletins, booklets, and the monthly magazine *Nation's Business*. In addition, the national chamber maintains a vigorous stance in making its policies and members' viewpoints known to federal agency personnel, members of Congress, and other public officials. Augmenting the national chamber are four regional offices and 50 foreign-based American chambers of commerce.

At the global level is the International Chamber of Commerce, founded in 1920. This organization constitutes an international federation of business organizations and individuals and as such serves as a powerful voice for business interests worldwide. It holds the highest-ranking status afforded to organizations the United Nations calls on in a consultative capacity. It also operates a prominent court of arbitration to settle international business disputes; utilizes teams of experts to formulate solutions to problems in such areas as communications, law, and financial relations; and issues a quarterly publication entitled *World Trade*. Headquartered in Paris, the International Chamber of Commerce functions as a vital mechanism for articulating global business concerns to world opinion leaders and the public at large.

Junior chambers of commerce, or the Jaycees, originated in the 1920s. These associations, evolving from the larger chamber of commerce movement, are composed of businesspeople in their twenties and thirties. Prevalent throughout the United States and in many other countries as well, junior chambers of commerce principally devote their energies to projects of community improvement.

For further information on the Chamber of Commerce of the United States, write the organization at 1615 H Street NW, Washington, DC 20062.

[Roberta H. Winston]

CHANNELS OF DISTRIBUTION

Channels of distribution move products and services from businesses to consumers and to other businesses. Also known as marketing channels, channels of distribution consist of a set of interdependent organizations involved in making a product or service available for use or consumption. Channel members are assigned a set of distribution tasks by those responsible for channel management.

For many products and services, their manufacturers or providers use multiple channels of distribution. Personal **computers**, for example, might be bought directly from the manufacturer, either over the telephone or via **direct mail**, or through several kinds of retailers, including independent computer stores, franchised computer stores, and department stores. In addition, large and small businesses may make their purchases through other outlets.

Channel structures range from two to five levels. The simplest is a two-level structure in which goods and services move directly from the manufacturer or provider to the consumer. Two-level structures occur in some industries where consumers are able to order products directly from the manufacturer and the manufacturer fulfills those orders through its own physical distribution system.

In a three-level channel structure retailers serve as intermediaries between consumers and manufacturers. Retailers order products directly from the manufacturer, then sell those products directly to the consumer. A fourth level is added when manufacturers sell to wholesalers rather than to retailers. In a four-level structure retailers order goods from wholesalers rather than manufacturers. Finally, a manufacturer's agent can serve as an intermediary between the manufacturer and its wholesalers, making a five-level channel structure consisting of the manufacturer, agent, wholesale, retail, and consumer levels. A five-level channel structure might also consist of the manufacturer, wholesale, jobber, retail, and consumer levels, whereby jobbers service smaller retailers not covered by the large wholesalers in the industry.

BENEFITS OF INTERMEDIARIES IN CHANNELS OF DISTRIBUTION

If selling directly from the manufacturer to the consumer were always the most efficient way, there would be no need for channels of distribution. Intermediaries, however, provide several benefits to both manufacturers and consumers: improved efficiency, a better assortment of products, routinization of transactions, and easier searching for goods as well as customers.

The improved efficiency that results from adding intermediaries in the channels of distribution can easily be grasped with the help of a few examples. In the first example there are five manufacturers and 20 retailers. If each manufacturer sells directly to each retailer, there are 100 contact lines—one line from each manufacturer to each retailer. The complexity of this distribution arrangement can be reduced by adding wholesalers as intermediaries between manufacturers and retailers. If a single wholesaler serves as the intermediary, the number of contacts is reduced from 100 to 25: five contact lines between the manufacturers and the wholesaler, and 20 contact lines between the wholesaler and the retailers. Reducing the number of necessary contacts brings more efficiency into the distribution system by eliminating duplicate efforts in ordering, processing, shipping, etc.

In terms of efficiency there is an effect of diminishing returns as more intermediaries are added to the channels of distribution. If, in the example above, there were three wholesalers instead of only one, the number of essential contacts increases to 75: 15 contacts between five manufacturers and three wholesalers, plus 60 contacts between three wholesalers and 20 retailers. Of course this example assumes that each retailer would order from each wholesaler and that each manufacturer would supply each wholesaler. In fact geographic and other constraints might eliminate some lines of contact, making the channels of distribution more efficient.

Intermediaries provide a second benefit by bridging the gap between the assortment of goods and services generated by producers and those in demand from consumers. Manufacturers typically produce many similar products, while consumers want small quantities of many different products. In order to smooth the flow of goods and services, intermediaries perform such functions as sorting, accumulation, allocation, and creating assortments. In sorting, intermediaries take a supply of different items and sort them into similar groupings, as exemplified by graded agricultural products. Accumulation means that intermediaries bring together items from a number of different sources to create a larger supply for their customers. Intermediaries allocate products by breaking down a homogeneous supply into smaller units for resale. Finally, they build up an assortment of products to give their customers a wider selection.

A third benefit provided by intermediaries is that they help reduce the cost of distribution by making transactions routine. Exchange relationships can be standardized in terms of lot size, frequency of delivery and payment, and communications. Seller and buyer no longer have to bargain over every transaction. As transactions become more routine, the **costs** associated with those transactions are reduced.

The use of intermediaries also aids the search processes of both buyers and sellers. Producers are searching to determine their customers' needs, while customers are searching for certain products and services. A degree of uncertainty in both search processes can be reduced by using channels of distribution. For example, consumers are more likely to find what they are looking for when they shop at wholesale or retail institutions organized by separate lines of trade, such as grocery, hardware, and clothing stores. In addition producers can make some of their commonly used products more widely available by placing them in many different retail outlets, so that consumers are more likely to find them at the right time.

WHAT FLOWS THROUGH THE CHANNELS OF DISTRIBUTION

Members of channels of distribution typically buy, sell, and transfer title to goods. There are, however, many other flows between channel members in addition to physical possession and ownership of goods. These include promotion flows, negotiation flows, financing, assuming risk, ordering, and payment. In some cases the flow is in one direction, from the manufacturer to the consumer. Physical possession, ownership, and promotion flow in one direction through the channels of distribution from the manufacturer to the consumer. In other cases there is a two-way flow. Negotiation, financing, and the assumption of risk flow in both directions between the manufacturer and the consumer. Ordering and payment are channel flows that go in one direction from the consumer to the manufacturer.

There are also a number of support functions that help channel members perform their distribution tasks. Transportation, storage, insurance, financing, and **advertising** are tasks that can be performed by facilitating agencies that may or may not be considered part of the marketing channel. From a channel **management** point of view, it may be more effective to consider only those institutions and agencies that are involved in the transfer of title as channel members. The other agencies involved in supporting tasks can then be described as an ancillary or support structure. The rationale for separating these two types of

organizations is that they each require different types of management decisions and have different levels of involvement in channel membership.

Effective management of the channels of distribution involves forging better relationships among channel members. With respect to the task of distribution, all of the channel members are interdependent. Relationships between channel members can be influenced by how the channels are structured. Improved performance of the overall distribution system is achieved through managing such variables as channel structure and channel flows.

SEE ALSO: Physical Distribution Management; Retail Trade; Wholesaling

[David Bianco]

FURTHER READING:

Rosenbloom, Bert. *Marketing Channels*, 4th ed. Dryden, 1991.

Stern, Louis W., and Adel I. El-Ansary. *Marketing Channels*. 3rd ed. Prentice-Hall, 1988.

CHAPTER 11

SEE: Business Failure

CHAPTER 7

SEE: Business Failure

CHIEF EXECUTIVE OFFICER (CEO)

The Chief Executive Officer (CEO) is the leading executive officer of a corporation charged with principal responsibility of the organization and accountable only to the owners, directors, and/or stockholders. As the principal corporate officer, the CEO's basic function is to provide overall leadership to a corporation by establishing direction and tone, overseeing internal management, and functioning as the company's primary representative with outside groups and organizations. The emergence of the CEO is closely related to the growth of businesses during the Industrial Age. As businesses became too large to be managed by individual owners, professional managers slowly assumed responsibility for the company's operations. In addition, the development of public companies with thousands of stockholders has made the likelihood of a primary owner nearly impossible. Although the stockholders are represented by a **board of directors**, the board cannot oversee the daily operations of the organization thus requiring a CEO. In fact, the cumulative responsibilities of the CEO have become so immense that many corporations have established Chief Executive Offices, in which responsibilities are divided among a Chairperson of the board, a CEO, and a President.

In providing direction for the company, the CEO will set important goals and objectives, formulate corporate strategy, and establish standards and guidelines by which the company will conduct its business. Although a CEO may require approval from the board of directors to do so, the CEO is primarily responsible for the formulation of the company's overall direction. In order to communicate the direction of the company to employees, the CEO will set goals and objectives. While employees might well understand these goals, they are typically unable to achieve them of their own accord. To provide a means towards reaching these goals, the CEO must formulate strategies providing short and long-term plans. Furthermore, in implementing these plans and strategies, the CEO must function as a salesperson and cheerleader. Plans and strategies must not only be understood, but accepted. A successful CEO will instill enthusiasm for his plans among employees. In addition, a CEO will define the character of the company by establishing and employing acceptable standards of behavior in conducting business. Finally, based on the direction and priorities of the company, a CEO must allocate the resources of the company in a manner that will maximize its ability to reach its goals.

As primary manager of the corporation, the CEO is charged with the creation of an organizational structure, the management of business units and divisions, the development of executive personnel, overseeing acquisitions and mergers, and the responsibility for any decisions that will have a major impact on the company's welfare. By creating an organizational structure, the CEO establishes an internal management structure in which major functions and responsibilities are defined in order to establish a clear mission for each unit, as well as provide accountability among these units. In reaching long-term corporate strategies and goals, a CEO will direct individual business units towards these goals by establishing short-term objectives and strategies for each unit. Finally, the CEO will continually review the status of each unit to ensure that goals are being met and that the company's financial outlook is favorable.

As the principal executive, the CEO is responsible to the corporation's board of directors and acts as the primary interface between the board and the corporation. The CEO continually reports to the board on the company's activities and situation, gains approval for any major goals, policies, or strategies and executes any mandates of the board. In addition, the CEO participates in the board's activities by being involved in the selection of new directors.

Finally, the CEO is the primary external interface for the corporation acting as its primary representative with outside individuals, groups, and organizations by monitoring outside conditions, improving public relations, and acting as a personal liaison. In order to understand and anticipate the effects of outside factors, the CEO must monitor the social, economic, and political conditions as they relate to the corporation. As the company's primary agent, the CEO must work to maintain and improve public relations by effectively communicating the company's desires and strategies to the outside public. The CEO must maintain individual relationships with important business and civic leaders on behalf of the company. As corporations struggle to maintain their position in an increasingly competitive and global market, the ability of a corporation to change will be fundamental to its success, and such change must begin with its leaders. If that is the case, the role of the CEO will continue to grow and change, taking on new responsibilities and initiatives as the marketplace evolves.

[Bradley T. Bernatek]

FURTHER READING:

Fallon, William K., ed. *AMA Management Handbook.* 2nd ed. AMACOM, 1983.

Rock, Robert H. *The Chief Executive Officer: Managing the Human Resources of the Large, Diversified, Industrial Company.* Lexington Books, 1977.

Stieglitz, Harold. *Chief Executives View Their Jobs: Today and Tomorrow.* The National Industrial Conference Board, 1985.

CHIEF FINANCIAL OFFICER (CFO)

The Chief Financial Officer (CFO) is the primary executive officer responsible for the financial management of a corporation. Depending upon the company's size, structure, and diversification, the role of the CFO may encompass a wide variety of responsibilities and functions which include the management and administration of financial, internal control, and **accounting** issues, in addition to acting as an external interface to the investment community and various governmental agencies. CFO is a generic term describing a variety of titles and offices such as vice president-finance, vice president and treasurer, executive vice president, and controller.

In managing the corporation's financial interests, the CFO is primarily responsible for the management and protection of corporate assets. To assure the continual growth and prosperity of the corporation, the CFO participates in the development of short and long-term planning strategies along with other senior executives to provide them with an understanding of the company's financial outlook, as well as an analysis of regional, national, and global economic conditions that will affect the company's position. Afterwards, the CFO will oversee the creation of budgets and business plans based upon these long-term strategies.

Asset management includes the investment of surplus profits, as well as the acquisition of funding from external sources for those companies that lack sufficient internal resources. In investing corporate assets, the CFO ensures that capital is invested in areas that are not exceedingly risky, and yet provide a yield that is competitive. In order to support new initiatives, research and development, and sustained growth, the acquisition of additional capital may be accomplished through the sale of stock and the acquisition of loans from banking institutions. At the same time, the CFO must develop an acceptable debt to equity ratio in order to ensure that the company does not become over-extended.

Another important function is the development of standard accounting policies, procedures, reporting methods, and internal controls, as well as effective data management systems and strategies. Because the company's financial data forms the basis for nearly every decision made by a **CEO**, the CFO must ensure that standards are in place that allow for the consistent manipulation, accounting, and reporting of financial data. The CFO must develop and maintain effective data management systems that facilitate the storage and manipulation of the data. In addition to providing the company with a thorough and accurate picture of its financial conditions, the CFO must establish internal control methods to ensure that accounting policies are being followed to minimize the company's exposure to fraudulent activities. As well as providing internal management, the CFO may act as an interface for various external groups, organizations, and agencies by maintaining and improving the company's standing in the investment community, maintaining a market for the company's stock, and fostering good relations with both the investment community in general and with the company's own investors.

In recent years, the role of CFO has grown in size and stature due to greater financial reporting demands placed on corporations by government agencies and the investment community. Furthermore, the increasing complexity and uncertainty of **economic conditions** due to periods of high **inflation** and the increasing severity of the economic cycle has made corporate management increasingly dependent upon the expertise and advise of the CFO securing its place at the very highest levels of management.

[Bradley T. Bernatek]

FURTHER READING:

Bacon, Jeremy and Francis J. Walsh. *Duties and Problems of Chief Financial Executives*. The National Industrial Conference Board, 1968.

Fallon, William K., ed. *AMA Management Handbook*. 2nd ed. AMACOM, 1983.

CHIEF INFORMATION OFFICER

The Chief Information Officer (CIO) is the executive officer of a business or organization who is responsible for managing the data, systems, and personnel involved with information systems (IS). This person must not only be able to understand complex **computers** and information systems but also find and apply new technologies and equipment as they are developed. In addition the CIO must act as a liaison between the IS department and the other executive officers.

The position of CIO is a fairly new development, coming of age in recent decades as the use of computer technology has grown in the work place. In the 1960s and 1970s when information systems were just beginning to be a major part of business, the CIO was usually a technologically trained executive who had risen from the ranks of the information systems department. He or she held a strictly technical expertise and other officers and managers relied on his or her expertise when it came to MIS decisions and questions.

In the 1980s the CIO was expected to have evolved into a more strategic business partner. The ideal CIO was thought to be someone who understood the business thoroughly, had a big-picture attitude, and could easily communicate to his or her peers. This meant that in some cases a CIO had little or no IS experience.

In the 1990s, the CIO position has evolved even more and the **chief executive officer** now often looks for a person that can assimilate the best of both worlds—that is, a person with a firm technical IS background and strong managerial and strategic skills as well. According to Bud Mathaisel, director of Ernst & Young's Center for Information Technology and Strategy, in an article for *Datamation*, "CIOs today must play several new roles concurrently. Among them are:

• R&D director, scouting new technologies that can be applied to emerging business needs . . .

• Infrastructure builder, creating standard base technologies

- Technologist, discovering how new technologies . . . can be applied to existing businesses

- Change agent, using his or her company wide perspective . . . to lead or guide the redesign of business processes."

Finding managers who can fill all these roles successfully is not easy. There is no formal training for CIOs. No colleges or universities offer classes to prepare future CIOs. Hopeful future CIOs should start with a strong IS technical and managerial background. In addition, they should prepare for a CIO position by broadening their general business skills through classes, reading, and seminars.

The path to becoming a CIO is not a clear one, and, once attained, a CIO position is not an easy one to maintain. The rewards, however, are great for those who do achieve CIO positions. According to a survey done in 1993 by the management compensation consulting firm of Edward Perlin Associates of New York, average annual CIO cash compensation has increased by 156 percent in the past ten years to more than $407,000.

Chief information officers are relative newcomers to the executive officer ranks. Not surprisingly, this position has grown quickly as the use of computers has expanded in the business world. No doubt the position will continue to evolve well into the twenty-first century, as the use of computers continues to revolutionize the way we do business.

[Judith A. Zimmerman]

FURTHER READING:

Goff, Leslie. "Climbing the CIO Ladder." *Computerworld.* October 18, 1994, p. 20.

Hopper, Max D. "Seeking CIO: Technical Experience OK." *Computerworld.* June 6, 1994, p. 35.

Moad, Jeff. "Wanted: The Multithreaded CIO." *Datamation.* April 15, 1994, pp. 34–38.

CHILD CARE/ELDER CARE

"America has become a society in which everyone is expected to work—including women with young children. But many of society's institutions were designed during an era of male breadwinners and female homemakers. What is needed is a . . . reform of the institutions and policies that govern the workplace to ensure that women can participate fully in the economy and that men and women have the time and resources to invest in their children." (Source: Women's Bureau, "Work and Family Resource Kit," 1993, from a study entitled Workforce 2000 performed by the Hudson Institute for the U.S. Department of Labor).

Workforce data confirm that the quote could be extended to include time and resources to also care for sick or elderly relatives. As more and more people live longer, the middle-aged person becomes "sandwiched" between two ends of intense care demands—that of a young child or children and that of an elderly person. In the past, women not in the labor force provided this care. As more and more women participate in the the labor force, however, new options must be found.

The U.S. Department of Labor predicts that by the year 2000 more than 50 percent of all women will be in the workforce. The U.S. Department of Labor's 1990 figures showed that of women already in the workforce, over 50 percent had children under six. At the same time, a study by Travelers' Insurance Company found that 28 percent of its employees were providing care for a friend or relative aged 55 or older. The U.S. Department of Labor figures show that about 32 percent of all employees, male and female, are parents.

This dual responsibility for people in the workforce is expected to continue and to increase. If workers are to perform effectively in the workplace, then, according to the U.S. Department of Labor, it would be beneficial to employers to recognize and assist employees in taking on these two tasks—child care and elder care.

The Women's Bureau "Work and Family Resource Kit" suggests many options for employers and employees from flextime to flexplace to long term care insurance, setting up child and elder care centers, voluntary reduced time, and job sharing.

Employers who have set up day care centers for children and who have had these centers operating for a long period of time are more numerous than employers who have set up care options for the elderly, a more recent phenomenon. Because day care centers have been in place for some time, several groups have studied the impact of employer assistance in this area. One such study was published in 1984 by the National Employer Supported Child Care Project and reported by the U.S. Department of Labor in the "Work and Family Resource Kit." This study reported the results of a review of 178 companies. Of those, 90 percent said that morale improved as a result of instituting a care center. Recruiting was affected positively in 85 percent of the companies, and that same percentage reported an increase in positive public relations.

The need for employers to work with employees in search of ways to deal with child care and elder care was formally recognized by the passage of the Family Medical Care and Leave Act of 1993.

[Joan Leotta]

FURTHER READING:

"Work and Family Resource Kit," Women's Bureau, Office of the Secretary, U.S. Department of Labor. Washington, DC, Government Printing Office.

CHILD LABOR

Many of the sepia photos of the early twentieth century reveal scruffy, dirt covered children, grinning for the camera. But their background is not the playground. These children have not been making merry, they have been hard at work in the mines and factories, laying the foundation of the industrial age in America. Their presence attested to the need for large amounts of unskilled, cheap labor, and to the awkward translation of farm life, where everyone—even the youngest—worked, to the city, where the factories replaced the field.

As the twenties waned and the depression loomed, more and more children entered the workplace—and more and more children were injured in the workplace, calling the attention of the public to the conditions in the factories. Many states began to pass laws against the employment of young children in dangerous places. Finally, as a part of the Fair Labor Standards Act of 1938 (FLSA), the federal government entered the reform effort. A part of the FLSA are its child labor provisions, which set standards regarding the employment of children under the age of 16 in industry and in agriculture. The administration and enforcement of these provisions is the responsibility of the U.S. Department of Labor, Employment Standards Administration, Wage-Hour Division. All States have their own child labor laws and compulsory school attendance laws. Where a local law is more stringent than the Federal, the more stringent standard must be observed.

The essence of the law is that work should not interfere with the schooling, health, and well-being of a child. The law applies to migrant children as well as local residents in any area.

The minimum age for industrial employment is 16 during school hours and 14 after school hours. There are also restrictions on night time work, with the exception of certain occupations (including mining) which are considered hazardous. Hazardous occupations are closed to persons under the age of 18.

Children 12 and 13, with written parental consent, may work in non-hazardous non-agricultural occupations. Certain exemptions also exist for children working in a family-owned business, newspaper delivery persons, actors, and homeworkers.

In agriculture, minors under 16 years of age may not be employed during school hours unless it is by their parent or guardian and may not operate hazardous machinery as set out in the law. Certain exceptions are made for student-learners and 4-H extension service training programs.

Unless otherwise exempt or a part of a specific training wage plan approved by the U.S. Department of Labor, even child laborers must be paid according to the minimum wage and overtime standards of the FLSA. Farm workers are not subject to the overtime provisions of the FLSA nor to certain other wage provisions.

Penalties for the violation of the child labor laws include $1,000 for violations of each provision and up to $10,000 in fines for each willful violation. They may include prison for repeated willful offenses.

To protect oneself against accidental violation of the standards, an employer should first contact the U.S. Department of Labor Wage and Hour Office about the position being offered, and one's state department of labor to ensure that the offering meets the expectations of the law. Employers should keep on file an employment or age certificate for each minor they employ to show that every minor meets age requirements. Every employer, except a parent, should maintain records that show the child's name in full, address, date of birth, evidence of parental permission (if needed), and a detailed record of the hours worked, including the times.

An explanation of those federal provisions is available in WH 1295 (Bulletin 102) and WH 1330 (Bulletin 101). Single copies of these bulletins may be obtained free of charge by writing to the Wage-Hour Division, U.S. Department of Labor, 200 Constitution Ave. NW, Washington, D.C. 20250. Inquiries about the FLSA and the Child Labor provisions may be directed to that office or can be answered by mail, telephone, or in person at any office of the Wage and Hour Division. Local offices of the Wage and Hour Division are listed in the telephone directory under U.S. Department of Labor, among the other U.S. Government listings.

[Joan Leotta]

CHINA, DOING BUSINESS IN

China is a country in the East Asia land mass, slightly larger than the United States at 3,695,500 square miles, and lying at about the same latitudes. It has borders with Russia, Mongolia, North Korea, Afghanistan, Tajikistan, Kirghistan, Kazakhstan, Pakistan, India, Nepal, Bhutan, Myanmar, Laos, and Vietnam. To the east is the Yellow Sea and the East China Sea, and to the south is the South China Sea and the peninsulas of Macao and Kowloon (across from the island Hong Kong). Both peninsulas will revert to China (in 1999 and 1997 respectively).

Over two-thirds of China is mountainous terrain, and the northwest includes the huge Gobi desert. The rugged western territories are difficult to access and are sparsely populated; 95 percent of the people of China live in the hills and plains of the east and south. Although China's cities are huge, nearly two-thirds of China's immense population of approximately 1.2 billion inhabit the countryside. Only 11 percent of the land is arable.

For administrative purposes, China is divided into six regions: the northwest, the northeast, the southwest, the south, the central, and the east. China has 23 provinces, including Taiwan, and five autonomous regions. Three large municipalities are included in the list of provinces. They are Beijing, Tianjin, and Shanghai.

GENERAL BUSINESS CLIMATE

China was closed to private business from the mid-1950s to the mid-1980s. However, the climate has been growing more friendly towards foreign investors since the watershed declaration in 1979 that opened China's door to the rest of the world. Now thousands of foreign-owned companies and joint ventures are operating in China. With the de-linking of human rights in China to trade with the United States, even greater activity is expected. Some of the considerations foreigners must face are: (1) the regionally-centered distribution systems; (2) the limitations of transportation and communication infrastructures; (3) the structure of Chinese industry and commerce; (4) expectations (which vary with region) of foreigners' abilities to pay for unofficial as well as official services with numerous—sometimes unannounced—fees; (5) currency conversion; (6) tax breaks; (7) and the importance of being well-connected. In general, it is much easier to buy from China than sell to China.

BRIEF HISTORY OF CHINA

China's culture is at least 6000 years old, and the earliest kingdom is said to be the Xia dating from around 2700 B.C. Trade and War. Trade for Chinese silk was already known before 200 B.C., in the late Han dynasty. The Chinese kept the secret of silk production to themselves and foreign consumers did not guess the prized fabric came from a worm. Trade with central and western Asia, and ultimately Europe, continued for many centuries. Silk was not the only commodity foreigners sought from China. Luxury items such as semiprecious stones and hand-crafted items such as carved

ivory also found their way to the Middle East, Europe, and South Asia. By the eighteenth century porcelain and tea became major exports.

Portuguese traders were the first in China in 1516. They were followed by Spanish (1557), Dutch (1606), and English (1637) traders. The foreign Qing dynasty, anxious to prevent social unrest and challenges to their rule, initially refused European traders entry into the country and limited them to trading ports on the coast. The European powers pressed for more trade, with limited success. By 1839 the English, anxious to outdo the other European trading powers and to balance their trade deficit with China, sent gunboats to force China to open to trade. The commodity the English wanted to sell was opium from India; the armed conflict became known as the Opium War (1839-1842). China lost, and the result was the Treaty of Nanjing (1842), which was the first of the "unequal treaties" that gave foreign powers autonomous areas or concessions in major Chinese ports and gave Hong Kong to Britain. Large trading companies opened in Hong Kong, which greatly enriched their foreign owners. The privileges for foreigners became known as the Treaty System; in 1917 there were 92 treaty ports, containing foreign-governed and armed areas. The Germans, French, Russians, and Japanese were the most active. Thus the Chinese experience with foreign traders was one of war, destruction, exploitation, and humiliation.

A final military attempt to expel foreigners took place in 1900. The Society of Harmonious Fists was a secret society that the West called the Boxers because their martial training involved physical movements that looked to Westerners like shadow boxing. They killed foreign missionaries and attacked the trade delegations in Beijing. Foreign forces put down the Boxer Rebellion, destroyed much of Beijing, and extracted a heavy indemnity. China was demoralized. During the Russo-Japanese war of 1904-1905, China was helpless to prevent fighting within its borders.

The Qing dynasty, weakened by the military and political losses, finally lost the "mandate of Heaven" to rule, and in 1911 was overthrown. The Republic of China was born.

FOREIGN INFLUENCES IN THE REPUBLIC OF CHINA

Sun Yat Sen, the revolutionary who inspired the overthrow of imperial rule, was a Methodist Christian educated in Hawaii and Hong Kong. He traveled widely outside China to generate support for his new, European-model government. Internal disorder plagued the young republic, however, and rival claims to the presidency gave way to a warlord era that lasted until 1927.

During the political upheaval following World War I, the Chinese Communist Party (CCP) was born in 1921, based on ideology from two non-Chinese, Marx and Lenin. The small party included Mao Zedong and Chinese students who had formed a communist party in Paris, among them Zhou Enlai. Communism was the most sweeping foreign ideology to impact China since Buddhism 1700 years earlier. Sun's Nationalist Party (Guomindang) had tried to cooperate with the communists, but his successor, Jiang Jieshi (Chiang Kaishek) was determined to wipe them out. The communists were hunted down from 1929 to 1935, but never fully destroyed.

In 1937 Japan invaded China; Japan had been nibbling at China's northern borders since the late 1890s and had conquered all of Manchuria in 1931. In 1937 full-scale war erupted and China suffered heavily in the brutal invasion. The Guomindang was demoralized by the Japanese attack, but the CCP grew stronger by taking the countryside between the cities held by the Japanese. By the end of the war, the CCP was unified and strong, the Guomindang weak and corrupt. After a four-year civil war, the communists established a government in 1949 that has continued to rule to the present. Chiang Kaishek and the Nationalist Party retreated to Taiwan.

During the early years of Communist rule the USSR viewed China as an ally and helped the regime launch its first five-year plan. This assistance, which primarily involved the establishment of industry, began to dissolve in the late 1950s. By, 1960, all Soviet advisors had left China. Until 1970, China was essentially closed to the outside world. This begun to change when first Canada, and then the United States, began to establish relations. In 1972, U.S. President Richard Nixon visited China; the Republic of China then replaced Taiwan on the United Nations Security Council.

Despite these improving relations, Mao Zedong's power in China was still absolute and often brutal. In 1958, the "Great Leap Forward" established 26,000 communes across the country. These communes were characterized by corruption and inefficient labor practices that killed an estimated 30 million people.

In 1966, Mao launched another disastrous campaign-the Great Proletariat Cultural Revolution. Led by young communists, the Revolution targeted established party members who Mao believed had become soft and lost sight of party goals. Massive numbers of people were killed, more than 500,000 temples were razed, and cultural artifacts were destroyed. The damage caused by the Cultural Revolution included a general breakdown of law and order, a slump in productivity, a stagnation of food prices, an undermining of the incentive system, a crisis of confidence in the Communist Party and Mao, disruption in education and government, and tremendous personal suffering.

In 1970 Premier Zhou Enlai, with Mao's concurrence, began the "Four Modernizations" program for economic renewal, targeting industry, agriculture, science and technology, and the military. Population control was addressed seriously, although not until 1979 was the one-family, one-child policy established. Zhou died early in 1976, as did Mao in September of the same year. Mao's wife and three associates, the notorious "Gang of Four," were arrested and tried for their crimes, bringing the Cultural Revolution to an end.

AFTER THE CULTURAL REVOLUTION

A new order began with Deng Xiaoping's rise to the position of Premier, and two major reforms since his rehabilitation in 1977 have made foreign investment possible. The most important was launched in 1979 at the third plenary session of the 11th congress of the Central Committee of the CCP (called "Third Central" for short). Deng pronounced a policy of openness to the outside and flexibility internally, ushering in an era of economic development that still exists.

In 1982 China adopted a new Constitution that restored the office of head of state and protected the rights of citizens. Millions of people who had been criticized, condemned, or purged during the Cultural Revolution were rehabilitated. Serious opposition to the Communist government and its policies was still not tolerated. Expressing critical opinions about the government has alternately been encouraged and repressed by Beijing.

In the late 1980s a policy was implemented to open up land use; this policy has accelerated foreign investment in China. Before this policy, land was not available as a commodity. It was owned by the proletariat and could neither be bought nor sold. However, the government came to see land use as a source of economic revenue and began allowing Chinese organizations, often with foreign partners, to lease the *use* of the land. Chinese experiments with home ownership began in 1988, and now large numbers of government workers own their homes.

In 1989 a student-fueled demonstration took place in the large Tiananmen Square in Beijing. Thousands of students gathered when Hu Yaobang died. He had been forced to resign as party chief in 1987 following his support of increased democracy. The gathering became a pro-democracy movement in which students called for freedom of information and more direct access to government leaders. They wanted reform within the communist government, not a change of government. Their movement was finally put down when the government of Beijing called in the military. More than 3000 civilians are said to have been killed when soldiers opened fire.

POLITICAL AND ECONOMIC STRUCTURES

China, according to its constitution, is "a socialist state under the people's democratic dictatorship led by the working class and based on the alliance of workers and peasants." The Chinese Communist Party (CCP) holds political power. The CCP makes policies and the government carries them out.

The National People's Congress (NPC) is an elected body of 3000 representatives who are CCP members. It meets once every March to approve what the State Council and the Central Committee of the Party have planned. The cabinet of the government is the State Council, an executive arm of the NPC, directed by the Premier. The NPC appoints and removes the Premier and members of the State Council, on advice from the CCP. The Premier, four Vice-Premiers, 10 state councilors, the ministers in charge of ministries and commissions, the auditor-general, and the secretary-general make up the State Council.

Below the central government are 22 provincial governments, five autonomous region governments, and municipal governments of large cities (Beijing, Shanghai, and Tianjin). Below them are county, township, and village governments.

POLITICAL PARTIES. The Chinese Communist Party is the party in power in China, although there are 14 other political parties protected by the constitution. At the top of the CCP is the Secretary-General. Below him (it has always been a male) is the Politburo Standing Committee, consisting of five people. They in turn give direction to the Politburo, which has an additional 12 members for a total of 17. The Politburo is the superior body to the four-member Secretariat and to the CCP Central Committee, which is the main party organ; its 210 members are elected by the National People's Congress every five years. The Central Committee represents and directs the party committees in the provinces, and they in turn direct the party members who make up about four percent of the population. The Politburo directs the Central Military Council as well as the Central Committee, and it in turn has power over the People's Liberation Army.

The dual organizational-party hierarchical structure occurs in all government industries, agencies, and bureaus. The Director or President follows the lead of the party secretary for that organization; the party secretary may also hold the title of deputy director or vice president. At each level throughout the organization, a parallel party structure exists; the party members are usually employees of the organization at the same time. Their membership in the CCP gives them upward mobility in their work organization. All personnel decisions (hiring, promoting, rewarding) are made in consultation with the party hierarchy in the organization. Typically, as people move to higher ranks in the CCP they also assume positions of greater responsibility in their organization.

ECONOMIC STRUCTURES. By traditional measures, China's economy is the 10th largest in the world. But studies by the **International Monetary Fund (IMF)** and the **World Bank** that compare consumers' purchase power find China's economy is the third largest, after Japan and the United States. China's economy in the mid-90s has growth rates that lead all other nations: 14.5 percent in 1993. The gross domestic product was about $2.35 trillion in 1993, the same as Japan's according to the IMF, and is predicted to grow by 11.5 percent in 1994. **Inflation** in Beijing for the first quarter of 1994 was 24 percent.

This represents fairly sudden change—10 years ago China was just beginning to achieve growth. Twenty years ago, city-dwellers could buy chicken for their dinner tables only twice a year. Now chicken along with a huge range of other consumer goods is available daily. The change has resulted from enormous growth in exports, an effort to make domestic production accountable for profitability, and more flexibility toward private enterprise. In the mid-1980s the government condoned the slogan, "To get rich is glorious!" and entrepreneurial individuals and organizations began to grow successful businesses of all sizes.

China's socialist economy means industry is largely government-owned and economic planning is centralized. Until the 1990s, workers expected lifetime employment with one organization that also supplied social services and housing—the unbreakable "iron rice bowl." Workers had few incentives and their productivity was low. If an employee went to work for another company, the employee's former company could change large sums of money for benefits it had provided. As a result, workers rarely changed employers. Consumption kept pace with production, as the population grew in the decades after the Revolution, and little capital investment was made in machinery, railways, factories, and energy sources. Even now, a third of the state run enterprises operate at a deficit of close to $3.5 billion (29.2 billion yuan).

However, state enterprises are being urged to become competitive and labor protection laws are being introduced. In the 1990s, the government has introduced measures for fiscal accountability in the manufacturing, agricultural, energy, and military sectors. The government is experimenting with allowing workers to buy their own homes, thus freeing the company (or enterprise) from the responsibility of housing employees. As market forces are given more power, an increasing percentage of commodity goods—about 80 percent in 1993—are distributed through market channels at prices set by the market. This coincides with greater decision-making on local levels. The government moved in 1992 to decentralize implementation of economic policies and informal capital markets developed. Local bonds and shares were issued to finance local projects. As incentives, local officials are allowed to retain some of the benefits of development.

The rampant growth of the early 1990s has also spurred inflation: retail prices rose 17.5 percent in 1993. In response, the People's Bank of China raised interest rates and introduced temporary austerity measures, especially against unauthorized loans, to cool the economy. Tax reform was introduced in late 1993. At the same time, China is trying to attract foreign investors with preferential tax treatment and eased restrictions on converting the Chinese yuan (unit of currency), in order to expatriate profits. Foreign investment has increased, to approximately $11 billion in 1992. Entrepreneurial activity has also grown, including firms trading in securities and real estate companies which by 1994 numbered over 4000. A Company Law was enacted at the end of 1993 that attempts to regulate activity in limited liability and joint stock limited companies. In 1992, imports to China from the United States totaled $7.5 billion but imports to the United States from China totaled $25.7 billion. In 1993 the United States' trade deficit was about $24 billion. The United States is China's biggest market.

The central government in Beijing still faces the challenges of keeping inflation under control, trimming the overstaffed government enterprises, regulating the unevenness of the economic growth that has benefitted the cities and coastal areas more than the poor interior, eliminating bureaucratic waste and corruption, and building a legal system. The unevenness of growth is evident in the need for issuing farmers "green money" or IOUs, because funds have been channeled into more profitable ventures, usually in cities.

HOW TO DO BUSINESS IN CHINA

Foreign **manufacturing** business in China falls into one of three categories: foreign equity joint ventures, foreign cooperative joint ventures, and solely-owned foreign investment enterprises. To these foreign investments are added direct investment in bonds or shares. Selling is done through a joint venture partner whose business license allows sales within China. Sourcing in China—to be successful—involves a contract agreement with a Chinese partner in order to guarantee quality control and product availability.

Direct investment in China may be supplying **equity** for joint venture projects, buying stocks in a joint stock limited company, and buying bonds that are floated for large infrastructure projects, for example. The rate of return on bond investments can be between 15 percent and 17 percent for a 15-year period; however, the investment is not returned.

The first step in entering China for business is to identify one's own company's needs. China is not the right environment for every kind of foreign business. Foreign companies also need to identify goals: (1) to sell to China; (2) to buy from China, (3) to manufacture in China for export only; or (4) to manufacture for domestic markets.

The next step, if the goal is buying, selling, or forming a joint venture, is to identify a partner. The choice of a partner is extremely important and can be accomplished several ways. Chinese consulates and embassies can offer information about potential partners. Consulting firms in China and abroad can also identify potential partners. Chinese government commissions that approve foreign investment, such as the Shanghai Foreign Investment Commission, can provide lists of partners. Delegates from China may travel to a foreign firm's head office and initiate talks about partnership. These projects usually already have official blessing and therefore stand a good chance of being approved.

The third step is to find out about these potential partners, usually by having one's own representatives meet with the Chinese in China. Good research is important. Key factors are the Chinese company's experience with foreign joint ventures, relationship with the government body that will approve the business license, and capability in the business. Foreign firms do not usually have more than one partner for each project.

The fourth step involves three major documents. The first is a Letter of Intent that establishes the agreement reached between partners to work together to accomplish the goals of both sides in this partnership. This is recommended for the linkage between foreign buyers from China with an import-export agent that will oversee the buying, as well as for joint venture partners for marketing and manufacturing. When the partners plan a joint venture company they will next have Articles of Association or a Charter drawn up, detailing how the new company entity will be structured. This leads to a joint venture contract. It may have appendices that specify other specific contract agreements, such as **intellectual property** rights, patent rights, and export numbers. The documentation is often prepared for foreign companies by foreign law firms operating in China or Hong Kong.

The fifth step in a joint venture is a feasibility study. This document, approximately 20 pages long, follows a specific format and is really a joint justification study, signed by both partners. The feasibility study must be performed by a Chinese-approved organization, usually a consulting firm in China. In some cases, an environmental impact study is part of this step.

The final step is approval resulting in the business license. Businesses must operate strictly within the scope specified in the business license. It is renewed every year.

Within each industry there are specific requirements for the business license as well. Of course, once authority is given for the joint venture to exist, the company has to implement the approvals. This usually results in further negotiations between partners.

CHINESE LAW. Foreign businesses will find an atmosphere of enthusiasm for entrepreneurial activity in China with few legal constraints. China's legal system is slowly beginning to develop, but is still in the early stages. The new Company Law, effective July 1, 1994, is the first of its kind since the establishment of the People's Republic of China in 1949. Previously, foreign investors had to rely on vague rules cited by officials and on hearsay from other foreign firms' experiences, now they can base their decisions on this law, adopted at the Fifth Session of the Standing Committee of the 8th National People's Congress. The Company Law governs all limited liability and joint stock companies, including those with foreign investment. Earlier legislation governing joint ventures takes precedence where provisions differ.

ACCOUNTING. Accounting practices are not universal in China; the kind of organization—equity joint venture, cooperative joint venture or solely foreign investment enterprise—will determine how accounts are kept. Foreign-investment manufacturing firms are not subject to import duty if their products are exported. Duty-free havens exist to encourage manufacture-for-export by foreign-investment enterprises. Auditing is in infancy.

MARKETING. Marketing inside China is very difficult for foreign firms unless they are joint venture partners of Chinese firms already involved in domestic marketing. Distribution channels usually coincide with the governmental administrative regions. Transportation and telecommunication infrastructures limit development also. Nevertheless, the market is so enormous that even one region is enough to sustain a business. Consumer demand for commodities and services is great. Manufacturers can sell with very little promotion, but at the same time name recognition is very important for the appeal to status that is a characteristic of Chinese culture. Billboard advertising is effective, along with television commercials.

FINANCING. Financing of foreign business in China may take several forms. Wholly foreign investment enterprises usually export to a subsidiary or trading company in another country. The total investment in joint ventures is registered capital (equity) plus circulating funds (**debt**). Debt-equity ratios are published and conform to levels set by China. The equity often comes from the foreign partner and working capital from the Bank of China. In large projects, companies can go public. Some enterprises in China float **bonds**; in 1993 convertible bonds appeared, convertible into common shares. One successful example is the Shanghai Pinkerton Float Glass plant.

Equity joint venture operations allow either partner to bring anything into China without duty. Labor is not equity; when the contract is being negotiated, each side inflates its contribution. In a cooperative joint venture, only things used specifically for production are duty free.

Another issue that is subject to negotiation is land use. Formerly Chinese negotiators claimed land as equity. Now that use is leased, negotiations address three ways land is acquired: land is allocated by a government; land is equity rom an earlier joint venture and now is subject to a renewal fee; or land use is granted for a specific number of years at a rate set by the local land bureau in a land grant fee. The first two are not transferrable. The third, the land grant, is transferrable under the new land use laws. Land is "cooked"—with infrastructure (gas, sewage, water, electricity) in place—or "raw."

MANAGEMENT. Until recently, the CCP had considerable authority over management decisions regarding sourcing, planning, production scheduling, directing personnel, and other management tasks in industry and government. In the 1990s market factors are playing a larger role in decision-making, but the decision-makers remain CCP members who work within the enterprises and institutions. Recently the Chinese government introduced the notion of a "socialist free market" system, making manufacturing enterprises accountable for profit and loss. The CCP is still firmly in control. Party leaders are the managers, directors, and heads, and management in Chinese organizations is very closely aligned with CCP affiliation.

In foreign joint venture operations, party leaders simply move over from the Chinese partner firm to occupy positions of responsibility in the new joint venture enterprise. Typically, the Chinese side prefers to hold senior positions in human resources—since they do the hiring for the most part—and act as liaison with local authorities. The foreign side usually prefers to manage production and accounting functions, for quality and cost controls. Foreign firms discover that incentives encourage workers to perform well, but care must be taken when decisions are made to fire or lay off workers. In solely foreign-owned manufacturing firms, investors find they often have to provide benefits and services to employees that are unfamiliar. In the Special Economic Zone of Shenzhen, for example, where many employees come from other provinces, firms must provide housing and meals for employees, among other benefits.

Chinese white-collar government workers are all ranked into 26 levels; one being the highest level. Certain privileges are granted to people according to their level and access to information is based on level. Foreign joint venture enterprises do not need to hire by level, but should be aware of the system.

INTERCULTURAL COMMUNICATION. While language is an obvious communication hurdle, culture can present more obstacles to understanding. Successful management requires awareness of, and some accommodation to, Chinese cultural priorities. Chinese culture is collectivist—group membership is long-term—and group consensus is important when decisions are made.

Communication is often indirect, rather than to the point, in order to prevent someone from losing face. Indirectness is especially preferred when bad news has to be communicated. Because status is important, however, subordinates may be directed by superiors in a straightforward communication style. Compliments give face.

Chinese make direct eye contact when listening, and do not sustain eye contact when they are speaking. This can be disconcerting to Westerners, who usually do the opposite. The Chinese respect age and with age comes seniority in the hierarchy of an organization. Hierarchy is preserved by a strong preference for harmony in communication among coworkers. Dissenting views are couched in careful and respectful language, when they are aired at all. Communication with seniors is always respectful and never confrontational. A certain degree of form and courtesy characterizes Chinese communication with foreigners. Visitors are treated with hospitality and the Chinese host can lose face seriously if visitors complain about their treatment or criticize China. Women often hold important positions, but a woman by herself does not meet with males unless in a public place.

Chinese joint venture partners may ask for favors beyond the contract document; this partly comes from the Chinese view that being in the other party's debt shows a willingness to enter into a relationship.

Tasks are often performed simultaneously, rather than sequentially as in the West, and task completion may be viewed as independent from the clock. An important goal at work is establishing and nurturing good relationships with people, specifically those in

power. This means people take time to drink tea and talk with colleagues and it is not seen as a disruption to a tightly planned schedule. The work week is generally 11 days every two weeks; in other words, people work every other Saturday. There are few national holidays; October 1 (National Day), New Year's Day (January 1), Labor Day (May 1), and the three-day Spring Festival (January-February). The Chinese observe no religious holidays, but many Chinese follow religious practices.

SEE ALSO: Socialism & Communism

[Linda Beamer]

FURTHER READING:

Books

China Yearbook Taipei, Taiwan: China Pub. Co., Annual.

Engholm, Christopher. *The China Venture.* Glenview, IL: Scott, Foresman and Company, 1989.

Fairbank, John K. and Craig Reinschauer. *East Asia: Tradition and Transformation.* New York: Houghton-Mifflin, 1989.

Fairbank, John and Denis Twitchett, eds. *The Cambridge History of China.* 15 vols. New York: Cambridge University Press, 1978.

McLeod, Roderick. *China Inc.: Doing Business with the Chinese.* New York: Bantam, 1988.

Moise, Edwin.E. *Modern China.* New York: Longman, 1986.

''China.'' *Academic American Encyclopedia.* Danbury, CT: Grolier Inc., 1995.

''Hearing of the Joint Economic Committee: China's Economy.'' *Federal News Service.* July 30, 1993.

Ho, David. ''China's New Company Law: Something Concrete to Go By.'' *East Asian Executive Reports.* February 15, 1994, pp. 9 ff.

Imai, Hiroyuki. ''China's Business Cycles.'' *The China Business Review.* January 1994, pp. 14 ff.

Sommer, Jeff. ''An Open Door: Foreign Companies are Settling Down in China for the Long Term.'' *Newsday*, May 3, 1994, Section A, p. 17.

''The Issues Behind Accommodation: Out of House and Home.'' *Business China.* December 13, 1993.

Thomson, Robert. ''Survey of China.'' *The Financial Times,* November 18, 1993, pg. XI.

CIO

SEE: Chief Information Officer

CIVIL RIGHTS ACT OF 1991

The Civil Rights Act of 1991, enacted into law on November 21, is the most comprehensive civil rights legislation to pass Congress since the Civil Rights Act of 1964. Like its predecessor, the 1991 Act prohibits all discrimination in employment based on race, gender, color, religious, or ethnic considerations. This recent law, however, strengthens the preceding law, especially in the realm of employer liability and the burden of proof.

The factors leading to the eventual passage of the Civil Rights Act of 1991 were as controversial and complex as the Act itself. Prior to 1964, the only major civil rights legislation to emanate from Congress was the post-Civil War law, Title 42 of United States Code, Section 1981, which was often quoted and cited in the debates surrounding the 1991 act. The 1866 law applied only to black employees, giving them the right to sue their employers for punitive and compensatory damages in cases of employment discrimination. In addition, the law permitted jury trials in such cases. These features are part of the present 1991 law but were not included in the 1964 Civil Rights Act.

The 1964 Act had been the most comprehensive civil rights legislation since the Civil War. It not only outlawed discrimination in employment against blacks but against all minority groups and women as well. The 1964 Act, however, did not include jury trials for people seeking redress, as did the law of 1866 (which applied only to racial discrimination). In addition, the "burden of proof" in the 1964 law lay with the employee rather than the employer. This made it relatively easy for the employer to prove that a specific hiring or employment practice was necessitated by business and was not discriminatory. Lastly, the Civil Rights Act of 1964 did not allow damages or compensation for the injured party.

The passage of the 1964 Civil Rights Act, whose weaknesses would necessitate another even more sweeping legislative act 27 years later, did have one major consequence: the birth of **affirmative action** programs in businesses and institutions to encourage the hiring of women and minority persons. This encouragement in some businesses took the form of employment tests where scores were adjusted in favor of disadvantaged minorities. The subsequent charges of "reverse discrimination" and hiring "quotas" resulting from affirmative action were a factor in President George Bush's veto of the civil rights bill of 1990.

The purpose of the 1990 civil rights bill was not only to strengthen the 1964 Civil Rights Act but to counter the rigid, narrow interpretation of the 1964 Act by a conservative Supreme Court. For instance, in *Wards Cove Packing Company v. Antonio* (1989), the Supreme Court ruled that an employer merely had to produce a business justification for an employment practice, while the burden of proving that it was discriminatory lay entirely with the employee. In another

1989 Supreme Court case, *Price Waterhouse v. Hopkins*, a female accountant sued her former employer for sexual discrimination because she was bypassed for a promotion. She was denied redress because the accounting firm was able to claim that gender was only one of several factors in its decision not to promote her, and that had the plaintiff been a man, those other factors would have disqualified him also. In another case, the court strictly interpreted the old civil rights employment law, Section 1981, as applying only to discriminatory hiring practices and not to actual employment practices.

By February 1990, civil rights groups were determined to strengthen the provisions of the Civil Rights Act of 1964, and they applied pressure on Congress. A comprehensive civil rights bill, introduced by Representative Hawkins and Senator Kennedy, was subjected to endless debate until its death by veto in the fall of 1990.

President Bush, who had opposed the Civil Rights Act in 1964, strenuously objected to a Democratically initiated bill that he and other Republicans feared would lead to racial hiring quotas. This fear stemmed from the 1990 bill's provision that allowed hefty punitive and compensatory damages to employees in cases of proven discrimination, which conservatives thought would encourage firms to establish hiring quotas to avoid being sued. Opponents of affirmative action also decried the retroactive clause, which allowed the bill, if turned into law, to be applied to cases of discrimination that were either pending or had happened years earlier. Strangely enough, a vocal minority of civil rights activists also opposed the bill on grounds that it favored well-educated, well-heeled middle-class minority men and women and did nothing for the poor underclass.

These factors contributed to President Bush's vetoing of the 1990 Civil Rights Act. However, sensitive to the rising number of sexual harassment suits in the country as well as to the unpopularity of his action, he sent to the House a Republican-sponsored civil rights bill that resembled the 1990 version in almost all respects.

In this "newer" version, President Bush included the provision that shifted the burden of proof in discrimination cases to the employer rather than to the employee. However, he ommited the retroactivity clause from the new bill. Nonetheless, because the two bills were so similar, Republicans criticized their own version of the civil rights bill as much as they had the Democratic version. President Bush, whom the media dubbed the "veto President," vowed to veto the bill again. What ultimately restrained him from doing so was the extremely negative political impact of the widely publicized Anita Hill/Clarence Thomas hearings that took place in the fall of 1991. A veto was unthinkable when public opinion from coast to coast was denouncing sexual harassment in the workplace. As a result, President Bush signed the 1991 Civil Rights Act, but not before White House counsel C. Boyden Gray directed federal departments and private businesses with federal contracts to end affirmative action programs. The reason for this unusual action was a clause Democrats inserted into the final version of the 1991 civil rights bill that strictly prohibited employers from considering race, gender, or ethnic/religious minority status in an employment practice. Republican opponents interpreted this—the heart of the Civil Rights Act of 1991—as mandating the dismantling of all affirmative action programs, at least in the federal government. But this was far from the intent of Democratic supporters of the bill, who countered by inserting a "saving clause" that affirmed the legality of affirmative action as long as it did not violate the Civil Rights Act, which some critics claimed saved very little indeed, since affirmative action has never been defined.

In essence, the new Act reiterated the Civil Rights Act of 1964 in making employment discrimination on the basis of color, race, gender, and religious creed illegal. It also incorporated the same features of the old 1866 civil rights employment law by granting punitive and compensatory damages to the injured party, as well as allowing the employee to sue an employer in a jury trial and by placing the "burden of proof" in employment discrimination suits on the employer. In addition, for the first time, the law covered American employees working for American firms abroad. The Civil Rights Act of 1991, however, does not apply to businesses that employ fewer than fifteen workers, nor does it cover employment discrimination based on sexual preference. Americans covered by the 1967 Age Discrimination in Employment Act can now sue for damages and have jury trials in cases of discriminatory seniority practices; disabled Americans, protected from employment discrimination on the basis of the 1990 **Americans with Disabilities Act**, are entitled to the same.

The Civil Rights Act of 1991, in short, is an employment law that threatened businesses with huge costs if discrimination could be proven. There is a ceiling on the amount of damages and compensatory claims, currently standing at $300,000 for a business that employs 500 or more, and $50,000 maximum for one that employs between 15 and 100. However, the maximum amount for punitive and compensatory damages applies to each person suing, so if five people sue a company for employment discrimination and win, that amount increases fivefold. The maximum amounts also do not include expert witness fees, attorney fees, or back pay. In addition, there is no ceiling at all on damages awarded in cases of racial discrimination. Any employee suing for punitive and compensa-

tory damages is entitled to a jury trial rather than, as under the Civil Rights Act of 1964, to a judge's decision. Juries are considered to be more sympathetic to employee grievances than judges.

IMPACT OF THE ACT ON BUSINESS

The severe penalties for employment discrimination as set out in the Civil Rights Act of 1991 sent shock waves throughout the business community and satisfied those civil rights groups and feminists who wanted to put "teeth" into the 1964 Civil Rights Act. The most controversial part of the new Act, however, was the "burden of proof," which in the 1964 Act was left up to the employee. Under the 1964 Act, gender or race could be a factor in an employment decision as long as the employer could prove that other factors besides race, color, gender, or religious creed had been considered. In other words, employers had to provide only a business justification for their employment action. With the 1991 Act, however, none of these factors was permissible, even if no overt or conscious intent to discriminate had existed on the part of the employer. For example, a bodyguard firm that stipulated certain height and weight criteria that effectively barred Hispanics and women from consideration could be sued for damages, even if the firm could prove that it had had no intent to discriminate because the effects of the employment criteria are discriminatory.

Many considered the new Civil Rights Act to be expressed in unambiguous language and to be free of loopholes. If the provisions of the Act appeared to be lucid, that might have been because certain important terms were left undefined or omitted entirely. For instance, many also consider that a major injustice resulted after the passage of the new Act because retroactivity was omitted from the provisions. Cases of employment discrimination that were pending at the time of the passage of the Act were not covered by it; it would take another two and a half years before the Supreme Court ruled that the Civil Rights Act was not retroactive, even though civil rights activists, lawyers, and law professors argued that that had been the intent of the law.

While affirmative action programs heavily favor such factors as gender and race and are protected in the "saving clause" of the Civil Rights Act of 1991, the advocates of retroactivity have criticized the new Act for failing to define affirmative action. In the absence of a definition, affirmative action programs are as vulnerable to attack as though there had been no saving clause. The Civil Rights Act specifically prohibited such factors as gender, race, color, ethnic origin, or religious persuasion from being used as criteria by employers or employment agencies. Far from protecting women and minorities from discrimination in employment, the new Act could well have the ironic consequence that fewer women and minorities are hired. (Title II of the Civil Rights Act of 1991, however, does provide for a "Glass Ceiling" Commission to study the problem of employment of women and minorities.) By virtue of awarding damages in discrimination cases, the new act may encourage "reverse discrimination" suits. With the passage of the Civil Rights Act, businesses began to discard employment tests whose scores were "adjusted" to favor disadvantaged minority persons.

Another major vagueness of the new act concerns sexual (gender) discrimination. Because "sexual harassment" is not defined or even mentioned in the new act, women who sue employers on the basis of sexual harassment will not necessarily win their cases. A wealthy corporation's team of lawyers could take issue with the term and define it in the company's favor.

While the Act does punish with severe penalties those employers who discriminate, many discrimination cases are not as clear cut as the notorious *Jenson v. Eveleth Taconite Co.* In this 1991 case, three female employees of the Taconite mining company sued on the basis of blatant sexual harassment. The Taconite mining firm did not promote women to managerial positions and did nothing to put an end to the unwanted sexual advances of the male miners and their blatant displays of pornographic material. Most employment discrimination cases, however, are "dual motive" or "mixed motive" cases, in which an employee may sue an employer for discrimination on the basis that gender was a factor in a discriminatory employment action. Even if an employer can cite other motivating factors besides gender, he would still lose the suit, but the jury may not award full damages to the employee. Such "mixed motive" cases, in which an employer can cite other factors that would have led to the same employment decision, are common.

Finally, the 1991 Act, which for the first time protects U.S. employees who work for an American firm abroad, does not extend that protection if the host country has its own explicit employment laws.

ACCOMPLISHMENTS OF THE ACT

The Civil Rights Act of 1991 is certainly perceived by the public and especially by businesses as strongly protective of the rights of women and minorities. This perception has resulted in businesses from coast to coast, large and small, either reexamining their hiring and other employment policies, or in the absence of clearcut policies formulating them. It has led to the imposition of "education" policies so that male employees will recognize entrenched female stereotypes, and it has put an end to blatant sexual harassment in the workplace. Cases in which women

and minorities have sued successfully and won large damages have caused businesses to review their employment procedures and hire more minorities and women. Such settlements also lead to finding ways to counter "subconscious stereotypes" of women and minorities.

The perception of the Civil Rights Act of 1991 therefore has demonstrated the intent of lawmakers and has not, thus far, resulted in worst case scenarios, such as dismantling of affirmative action programs and across-the-board racial hiring quotas. By the same token, the predicted increase in litigation against businesses, encouraged by financial incentives, also has failed to materialize. Nevertheless the threat of such litigation, coupled with the fact that employment discrimination is not covered by business liability insurance, appears to be sufficient incentive to comply with the intended purpose of the Civil Rights Act.

In sum, the Civil Rights Act of 1991 has had dramatic, even sweeping, effects on small businesses and corporations. Small businesses are perhaps most affected by the new regulations, because they have the most to lose if sued, and many are without detailed employment guidelines. The net effect of the Civil Rights Act has been positive and has outweighed possible negative side effects from vagueness in the wording or outright omission of important clauses defining affirmative action or sexual harassment, and specifying retroactivity. These omissions and definitions have become the responsibility of the Supreme Court, the ultimate interpreter of the Civil Rights Act. The court already has made its pronouncement on retroactivity in favor of business. It is expected to rule on the constitutionality of the damages awarded and may eventually define sexual harassment and affirmative action.

[Sina Dubovoy]

FURTHER READING:

"Bush: Civil Rights and Wrongs," *Black Enterprise*. March, 1992, p. 25.

Barnes, Fred. "Last Laugh (White House Watch—Manipulation of the Meaning of the New Civil Rights Act of 1991)," *The New Republic*. Dec. 16, 1991, p. 9.

Biskupic, Joan. "1991 Civil Rights Law Not Retroactive, Court Rules," *Washington Post*. April 27, 1994, p. A8.

Brown, Peter A. "Ms. Quota: White Women and the Civil Rights Act (New 1991 House Legislation Politically Unwise)," *The New Republic*. April 15, 1991.

Feltes, Patricia, et al. "American Female Expatriates and the Civil Rights Act of 1991: Balancing Legal and Business Interests (Women in Business)," *Business Horizons*. March-April, 1993, p. 82.

Kurtz, Janell, et al. "The Civil Rights Act of 1991: What Every Small Business Needs to Know," *Journal of Small Business Management*. July, 1993, p. 103.

Lans, Maxine S. "Civil Rights Act of 1991 May Give Discrimination Victims More Rights (Marketing and the Law)," *Marketing News*. Nov. 23, 1992, p. 12.

McElveen, Mary. "How to Avoid Discrimination Suits (Compliance With Civil Rights Act of 1991)," *Nation's Business*. March, 1992, p. 46.

Mishkind, Charles S., et al. *The New Civil Rights Act of 1991 and Employment Discrimination*. Prentice Hall Law and Business, 1992.

Naidoff, Caren E.I. "Understanding the Civil Rights Act of 1991," *Management Review*. April, 1992, p. 58.

Perritt, Jr., Henry H. *Civil Rights Act of 1991 Special Report*. John Wiley & Sons, Inc., 1992.

Sandroff, Ronni. "Sexual Harassment," *Working Woman*. June, 1992, p. 47.

CLEAN AIR ACT

Clean Air Acts expressing concern for the hazards of air pollution were enacted by the U.S. Congress in 1955, 1963, 1965 and 1967. The most common usage of this term, however, is in reference to the Clean Air Act Amendment of 1970, 1977, and 1990. These three pieces of legislation set standards for environmental air quality, established enforcement protocols and in some cases, dictated the means by which these standards were to be achieved.

The 1970 Act charged the Environmental Protection Agency (EPA) with the establishment of two kinds of air quality standards, ambient air quality standards and emissions standards. The National Ambient Air Quality Standards (NAAQS) govern the maximal allowable concentrations of several priority pollutants: carbon monoxide, sulfur dioxide, nitrogen oxides, ozone, and particulate matter. Lead was added to this list in 1978. Primary standards are grounded in concerns for human health, and are set so as to protect the most sensitive members of human society, e.g. infants and the elderly. Secondary standards, ostensibly stricter, are intended to protect human welfare by preventing injury to crops, livestock, wildlife, buildings, and visibility. In practice, secondary standards have frequently been set at the same level as primary standards.

The National Emission Standards for Hazardous Air Pollutants (NESHAP) regulate emissions from industrial sources and motor vehicles. NESHAPs have been established for inorganic arsenic, asbestos, benzene, mercury, beryllium, vinyl chloride, coke oven emissions, and radionuclides. The application of these standards depends upon the location of the source. Areas already meeting the NAAQS are called attainment areas and are subject to prevention of significant deterioration requirements. Non-attainment areas must implement programs designed to bring them into attainment. Among the latter are new source performance standards, providing for the review of new major sources or major modifications with significant emissions. These are technology-oriented standards mandating use of the best available technology to control pollutant emissions.

States are responsible for enforcement of the NAAQS and NESHAPs via State Implementation Programs (SIPs). Emissions limits, monitoring requirements, permitting procedures, and enforcement provisions must all be specified by the relevant state agency. States failing to implement acceptable SIPs are subject to sanctions and the imposition of more stringent standards.

Pollution from mobile sources is addressed by the Motor Vehicle and Aircraft Emissions Standards. The 1970 Clean Air Act prescribed a 90% reduction in the amount of hydrocarbons, carbon monoxide, and nitrogen oxides emitted from automobiles, which was to be achieved by the mid-1970s. The standards were not met on time, and the 1977 Amendments postponed their achievement even further. (They were reached in the 1990s.) Reduction of automobile source air pollution continues to be a priority under the 1990 Amendments.

The Clean Air Act of 1990 reauthorized the existing Clean Air Act and added substantial changes addressing problems caused by automobile emissions, urban smog, toxic air pollutants, depletion of the ozone layer, and acid rain. Title V of the act requires comprehensive federal permits for all "major sources," similar to those required under the Clean Water Act, stating all of a source's obligations under the Act and SIPs. Permitted sources must monitor compliance and self-report violations.

The 1990 Act reduces permissible emission rates of hydrocarbons and nitrogen oxides from automobiles and requires cleaner fuel and more durable pollution control equipment. Additional limitations are placed on urban ozone concentrations, a critical component of smog. The EPA is required to set standards for 189 hazardous air pollutants, with the goal of reducing toxic emissions by 90% by 2003. Ozone-depleting chemicals (e.g. chlorofluorocarbons) are to be phased out by the beginning of the century.

The acid rain program applies to large utility units and caps total sulfur dioxide (SO_2) emissions at pre-1980 levels. It allows for trading of a gradually decreasing number of emission allowances which may be used to offset SO_2 emissions, a key component in the formation of acid rain. During Phase I, a fixed number of allowances are issued to existing generators based on historical production figures. In Phase II, beginning in 2000, emissions are to be monitored continuously and sources must surrender one allowance for every one ton of SO_2 emitted the previous year. Utilities likely to have emissions beyond their stock of allowances may choose to repower units, use cleaner fuel, install scrubbers, reduce the amount of electricity generated, or purchase additional allowances from "cleaner" utilities. The plan's proponents stress its flexibility and efficient allocation of economic resources, while critics claim it will result in disproportionate environmental hardship among the poor.

[Mark A. White]

CLEAN WATER ACT

In the late 1960s and early 1970s, the U.S. government passed a series of pollution control acts designed to clean up and protect the nation's environment. The lawmakers' intent was to reduce the impact of conventional pollutants in the air and on surface waters. Later, lawmakers recognized that toxic pollutants discharged into the water were also dangerous. They took steps to control these, too. One of the results of their concern was the Clean Water Act (CWA) of 1977, which drew—and continues to draw—a considerable amount of opposition from some manufacturers, many of whom have been assessed large fines for violating it. The law survives today in a strengthened form, even though President Reagan attempted to eliminate it during his term of office.

BACKGROUND OF THE CLEAN WATER ACT

Any discussion of the CWA must be prefaced with a history of water pollution control laws, particularly the relationship between the Federal Water Pollution Control Act (FWPCA) Amendments of 1972 and the CWA. Anti-water pollution laws in the United States are by no means new. The Rivers and Harbors Act of 1899, which prohibited the discharge of pollutants or refuse into or on the banks of navigable waters without a permit, set the standard. Twenty-five years later the government passed the Oil Pollution Act of 1924, which prohibited the discharge of refuse and oil into or upon coastal or navigable waters of the United States. After World War II came the Water Pollution Control Act of 1948, which declared that water pollution was a local problem. It charged individual states with coordinating research activities into water pollution problems, with the assistance of the U.S. Public Health Service. Two more acts followed in the next 13 years.

The Water Pollution Act of 1956 contained enforcement provisions that provided for federal abatement suits at the request of state pollution control agencies. The act was amended in 1961 to broaden federal jurisdiction. More importantly, it shortened the enforcement process by stating that where health was being endangered, the federal government did not need permission from affected states to become involved. The federal government continued to expand its powers in the regulation of water pollution through the next two decades.

The Water Quality Act of 1965 set water quality standards enforceable by state and federal governments. The act became the basis for interstate water quality standards. It also created the Water Pollution Control Administration within the U.S. Department of Health, Education, and Welfare. Next came the Clean Water Restoration Act of 1966, which imposed a fine of $100 per day on any polluter who failed to submit reports required by the law.

Four years later, the federal government passed the Water Quality Improvement Act of 1970, which prohibited the discharge of harmful quantities of oil into or upon the navigable waters of the United States or its shores. The act applied to both offshore and onshore facilities and vessels. It also provided for regulation of sewage disposal from vessels. All of these acts combined still left gaps open in the overall regulatory system. So, the government enacted the Federal Water Pollution Control Act (FWPCA) Amendments of 1972, which mandated a powerful federal-state campaign to prevent, reduce, and eliminate water pollution. This was by far the most sweeping of the federal anti-water pollution laws.

THE GOALS OF THE FEDERAL WATER POLLUTION CONTROL ACT AMENDMENTS

The amendments to the FWPCA had two aims: to reduce the pollution of free-flowing surface waters and protect their uses and to maintain the quality of drinking water. The need to protect the nation's drinking water grew from the realization in the mid-1970s that over half of the country's drinking water was being threatened by contamination from such sources as underground storage tanks, fertilizers and pesticides used in farming, and the ever-growing number of hazardous waste sites. It was only a matter of time before experts connected the problems affecting the nation's drinking and surface waters. Thus, the government turned its attention to regulating the quality of surface waters, too.

The federal government set fairly specific calendar deadlines by which changes in water pollution should be effected. According to the amendments, by July 1, 1983, water across the nation should be clean enough for swimming and other recreational uses— and for the protection and propagation of fish, shellfish, and wildlife. By 1985, the government hoped to eliminate the discharges of pollutants into U.S. waters. The second deadline proved elusive. Businesses of all types are still discharging pollutants into water, sometimes deliberately and sometimes inadvertently. Nonetheless, the government has made significant headway into preventing the discharge of pollutants from water and eliminating those that do enter it. That is due in part to the stringent demands of the FWPCA amendments.

The amendments established a national pollutant discharge elimination system (NPDES), which required permits for *all* point sources of pollution—i.e., those which are evident, confined, discrete places through which pollutants enter the water—thus providing the first major direct enforcement procedure against polluters. The system mandated that it is illegal for any industry to discharge any pollutant into the nation's waters, unless it has an NPDES permit. The amendments also made abundantly clear what constituted a pollutant and what was excluded.

Pollutants covered under the permit included solid waste; incinerator residue; sewage; garbage; sewage sludge; munitions; chemical wastes; biological materials; radioactive materials; heat; wrecked or discarded equipment; rock; sand; cellar dirt; and industrial, municipal, and agricultural wastes discharged into water. Among the pollutants not included under the permits were discharges of sewage from vessels; water, gas, or other material injected into oil or gas wells; and dredged or fill material. All exclusions were covered by other pollution control regulations. The federal government took seriously its responsibility to control pollution. So did the individual states.

By 1988, 39 states were issuing permits under the NPDES structure. The **Environmental Protection Agency (EPA)**, formed in 1972 from 15 separate components of 5 executive departments and independent agencies, issued permits in the other states and on Native-American reservations. Occasionally, there arose conflicts between the EPA and state regulations, which confused and infuriated some businesspeople, but they were ordinarily resolved on a case-by-case basis. The permit system laid out exactly what any industry could or could not discharge into water.

The permits issued regulated what could be discharged. Furthermore, the EPA mandated that industries must monitor their waste and report on discharges and comply with all applicable national effluent limits and with state and local requirements that may be imposed. For facilities that could not comply immediately, the permit allowed for a firm schedule of dates by which they had to reduce or eliminate pollutants. Many business leaders saw these mandates as an unnecessary intrusion of government on private rights. Eventually, some members of government, notably President Ronald Reagan, agreed. But, that disagreement did not come until the late 1980s. In the meantime, the federal government continued to closely scrutinize the surface water pollution problem in an effort to eliminate it as quickly as possible.

THE PROBLEMS AFFECTING SURFACE WATER

Ordinarily, water is capable of cleansing itself of impurities through the use of its oxygen. It cannot complete the task, however, when the quantity of wastes exceeds its capacity to assimilate the pollutants. In such cases, the oxygen simply cannot break down the organic pollutants. In other cases, excessive nutrients from agricultural activities and municipal sewage can cause entropication, a state of ecological imbalance in which algae growth occurs at the expense of other forms of aquatic life. This chemical imbalance can be devastating to the environment.

Abundant algae formations on the surface of water deplete available oxygen and inhibit sunlight from reaching submerged vegetation. That hampers photosynthesis, the process by which chlorophyll-containing cells in green plants convert light to chemical energy and synthesize organic compounds from inorganic compounds, especially carbohydrates from carbon dioxide and water, with the simultaneous release of oxygen. If left unchecked, conditions such as excessive organic pollutants and entropication can choke bodies of water and create serious societal problems. In order to avoid such situations, the federal government took a leading role in passing anti-water pollution laws, especially those pertaining to surface water.

THE CAUSES OF SURFACE WATER POLLUTION

There are basically six sources of surface water pollution: organic wastes from urban sewage, farms, and industries; sediments from logging, agriculture, and construction; biological nutrients, e.g., phosphates in detergents and nitrogen in fertilizers; toxic substances from industry and synthetic chemicals, e.g., those found in plastics, pesticides, and detergents; acid and mineral drainage from open-pit and deep-shaft mining; and runoff containing harmful chemicals and sediment drained from streets and parking lots. These pollutants can come from point and nonpoint sources.

Point sources include such things as sewer pipes, culverts, and tunnels. Generally, point sources are those that come from industrial facilities and municipal sewage systems. Nonpoint sources, on the other hand, are those which wash off, run off, or seep from broad areas of land. They cannot be identified with much precision. Small amounts of nonpoint sources are generally not harmful to surface water. However, the cumulative effects of all the pollutants that empty from large land areas into single watersheds can be extremely harmful. (A watershed can be either a ridge of high land dividing two areas that are drained by different water systems or the region draining into a river, river system, or body of water.) Perhaps the most common nonpoint sources are acid rain; sediment eroded from soil exposed during construction of buildings, roads, etc.; and pesticides washed off cropland by rainwater. Combined, point and nonpoint sources were having a devastating effect on the nation's environment. The government's concern gave rise to the FWPCA Amendments, but even they were not enough. The federal government amended the 1972 act through the Clean Water Act of 1977, which made over 50 changes in the Federal Water Pollution Act. The CWA had an immediate impact on cleaning the nation's waterways.

THE CLEAN WATER ACT OF 1977

The most significant change provided by the CWA from a business standpoint was in the classification system of industrial pollutants and the establishment of new deadlines. The changes placed a greater emphasis on the control of toxic pollution, which had become an increasing problem in the United States.

Toxic substances such as heavy metals and synthetic chemicals posed a serious threat to the nation's water. Their proliferation led to a steady decline in water quality. The amendments paid particular attention to this problem. The CWA of 1977 added several new categories of pollutants to the federal guidelines. Among them were conventional, toxic, and nonconventional pollutants.

Conventional pollutants include biological oxygen demand, suspended solids, fecal coliforms, acidity, and other pollutants designated by the EPA. According to the CWA, industries had to install the best conventional technology available as quickly as possible to control these pollutants.

Toxic pollutants included an "initial list" of toxic substances which the EPA could add to or subtract from at its discretion. To control these pollutants, the EPA allowed industries to install the best available technology not later than three years after a substance is placed on the toxic pollutant list to control toxic substances.

The category that drew the most opposition from industry leaders was nonconventional pollutants, which was a catch-all category. It included "all other" pollutants, i.e., those not classified by the EPA as either conventional or toxic. According to the law,

the treatment for pollutants in this category was the installation of "the 'best available' technology as expeditiously as possible or within three years of the date the EPA established effluent limitations." The EPA did allow a modification of these requirements under certain circumstances. Modifications aside, the CWA has had a positive effect on surface water pollution.

By 1992, there were an estimated 48,400 industrial facilities and 15,300 municipal facilities that had NPDES permits. The EPA estimated that at least ten percent were out of compliance with their permit conditions. Therefore, they are subject to federal and state enforcement action, which can range from informal telephone calls to formal judicial proceedings and heavy fines. Despite the EPA's success in bringing businesses into compliance with the CWA and its threats to induce companies in noncompliance to comply, there is still considerable opposition to its activities.

OPPOSITION TO THE CLEAN WATER ACT

Opposition to the CWA mounted early in the 1980s and continues today. For example, executives claim that there are too many bureaucratic levels enforcing the act's mandates. There are federal and state mandates, the U.S. Army Corps of Engineers' involvement, and outside groups that interfere in the affairs of business. Thus, compliance is difficult.

Under Section 404 of the CWA, for instance, the Corps of Engineers is authorized to issue dredge and fill permits. The EPA then reviews these permits to ensure that unacceptable adverse impacts do not occur. The EPA may veto a permit, although that is not a frequent occurrence. For example, the EPA has only vetoed six permits in the southeastern section of the United States since 1972. Yet, the possibility does exist, and that, business leaders argue, can lead to excessive costs for companies to satisfy EPA requirements.

Crown Butte Mines Incorporated spent $35 million to explore a new mine site in Montana near Yellowstone National Park and to obtain the necessary EPA permits. Still, a coalition of nine Montana and Wyoming environmental groups initiated a lawsuit against the company to stop the project. Such lawsuits cost companies millions of dollars to defend, with no guarantees that the necessary permits will eventually be provided. That is one example of why so many business leaders complain about excessive bureaucracy in the compliance process.

There is also concern among business leaders that excessive CWA regulations adversely affect profits and eliminate or curb the creation of jobs. That is manifested in the effects of EPA requirements on the printing industry around Memphis, Tennessee. There, job growth has been hindered because the EPA listed the region as a non-attainment area, i.e., one in which water quality does not meet national standards. Companies looking to relocate or expand are reluctant to do so in such areas, which has a negative impact on the local economy. It is estimated that for every 100 jobs created in **manufacturing**, 64 more service or administrative positions are created. Excessive EPA mandates can curb such growth. They also place entire industries in jeopardy.

In 1994, President Clinton established his administration's intention to phase out the industrial use of chlorine, a plan that could dramatically reduce pollution in the nation's waters. Such a plan, however, if implemented, would have a drastic financial impact on certain industries, particularly paper production. Needless to say, the plan did not sit well with industry representatives.

The plan was based in part on growing evidence that chlorine and chlorine-based chemicals cause cancer and damage to humans' neurological, reproductive, developmental, and immunological systems. Eliminating chlorine and chlorine-related pollutants from the nation's waters, the EPA suggested, would cut down on such health problems. Paper-making industry spokespeople, however, claimed that the process would cost the industry billions of dollars in plant conversions and drive some companies out of business.

They suggested that the EPA was overreacting to the presence of chlorine and chlorine-related products in the nation's waters. Environmentalists entered the argument on the EPA's side. This was one more example of the ongoing debate over the EPA's regulatory powers and the costs to the economy in terms of dollars and jobs. Arguments aside, the EPA believed it was acting judiciously in enforcing the act. In its eyes, there was a crying need for such regulation in the United States in view of the damage occurring to the nation's water supply. That has long been the EPA's view. In fact, the EPA, through its regulatory power over clean water violations, has even been able to withstand assaults from high-ranking federal government officials—including one president of the United States.

In 1987, Congress approved additional amendments to the CWA by passing a $20 billion bill over President Reagan's veto. The new bill authorized $9.6 billion in grants and $8.4 billion in revolving construction projects for wastewater treatment plants. It also provided for as much as $2 billion to clean up specific lakes, rivers, and estuaries; $400 million in grants to help states plan ways to reduce the toxic runoff from farms and city streets; and funds to eliminate "hot spots" of toxic chemicals in waterways. The money was helpful, but the question was whether it was enough.

THE EFFECTS OF THE CLEAN WATER ACT

Despite the government's efforts over the years to control water pollution, problems still remain. For example, nonpoint sources of pollution, which are regulated by Section 208 of the CWA, are still hard to pinpoint and control. For the most part, they cannot be collected and treated because of their abundance. A partial list of nonpoint sources demonstrates the difficulty involved in controlling them.

Major nonpoint sources include urban storm water; water running off buildings and streets, carrying with it oil, grease, trash, etc.; agricultural, forestry, and construction runoff; and acid runoff from mines. Some of these sources simply cannot be controlled. In fact, there is no technology available that can control nonpoint water pollution, although it accounts for as much as 79 percent of all nitrates and 92 percent of all suspended solids that get into surface waters. The best way to handle the problem is to reduce nonpoint pollutants through careful **management** of water and land resources. Nonetheless, the CWA mandates under Section 208 that states and localities establish programs to control nonpoint source pollution.

The states are responsible simply because soil conditions, climate, and topography vary throughout the country. Therefore, it falls on the shoulders of state and local authorities to identify the significant nonpoint pollutants endemic to their jurisdictions and develop programs to control them. That is a large task, and one which poses a major challenge to state and local officials in the coming years.

ENFORCEMENT POWERS UNDER THE CLEAN WATER ACT

The EPA has significant enforcement powers under the terms of the CWA. It has the authority to assess fines and seek arrests of individuals found guilty of entering pollutants into water supplies. For example, in April 1994 Beech Aircraft, based in Wichita, Kansas, agreed to pay $521,000 in fines for pouring wastewater contaminated with heavy metals down its sewer system in violation of the CWA. Such fines are not unusual.

An Indianapolis battery recycling company was cited in August 1994 by the EPA on an 11-count federal indictment charging criminal violations of the CWA. The company was accused of discharging toxic materials into the city's sewer system and a tiny creek. An assistant U.S. attorney suggested that the corporation could be fined from $5,000 to $50,000 for *each* of the 11 charges. Each individual involved could face up to ten years in jail for each of the 11 charges and a fine up to $250,000. That would certainly be a high price to pay for violating EPA guidelines.

Sometimes the EPA will resort to lawsuits to deal with violations—or alleged violations—of the CWA. For example, the village of Oconomowac Lake, Wisconsin, initiated a lawsuit against the Dayton Hudson Corporation. The village alleged that Dayton Hudson had failed to obtain all the permits required under the CWA before it built a $63 million Target Stores distribution center in Oconomowac. A federal judge dismissed the suit on the basis that the company had obtained the necessary permits. Going one step farther, the judge said the village could not sue in federal court under the CWA because any ground-water pollution that could be attributed to the center would not be discharged directly into navigable waters. The village persisted and appealed the decision.

At that point, the EPA tried to join the suit on the village's behalf. The judge, however, disallowed the EPA's intervention. That did not deter the EPA, which was involved in several other similar lawsuits in other states. EPA officials stated that they would possibly join any other lawsuit filed by village officials against Dayton Hudson. For the EPA, joining such lawsuits has become standard procedure, along with the imposition of fines and criminal enforcement as a means of upholding the CWA.

SIDE EFFECTS OF THE CLEAN WATER ACT

The CWA has had some unpredicted side effects. For instance, it has spurred business for testing and **consulting** companies. **Revenues** for commercial environmental laboratories were about $1 billion in 1990 and were expected to reach $2.5 billion by 1999. Energy Laboratories, of Casper, Wyoming, planned to invest $250,000 in new analyzing equipment in 1994 because more and more businesses are utilizing its services to ensure they comply with the provisions of the CWA. The investment came after Energy Laboratories had a record year for sales in 1993. On the other hand, some companies have been forced out of business or moved due to what they consider extremely harsh federal regulations.

Caribe Tuna, one of Puerto Rico's three remaining tuna processors, threatened to leave the island for the Far East because of overly strict CWA mandates. Allegedly, the company, owned by Mitsubishi Foods, has violated the terms of its NPDES permit with the EPA. The EPA alleged in a July 1991 lawsuit brought against the company that 332 times between December 1986 and July 1990 Caribe dumped wastewater into Ponce Bay that exceeded federal CWA limits for lead, chromium hexavelent, mercury, copper, zinc,

and fecal coliforms. As a result, the company faced huge fines and other penalties which could conceivably drive it out of the United States. There exist several other cases of this type in other states.

THE FUTURE OF THE CWA

There is no doubt the CWA will continue to have an effect on the nation's industries. Companies will be forced to pay close attention to how they treat the environment before embarking on major projects. There are large numbers of watchdog agencies which oversee industries and work in conjunction with the EPA to enforce the CWA mandates.

For example, in March 1994 Indiana's Governor Evan Bayh signed legislation allowing Amoco Corp. to discharge saltwater into Lake Michigan. Immediately, several environmental groups announced plans to institute legal action to ensure that Amoco adhered to the CWA. They contended that Amoco engaged in economic blackmail by threatening to close the refinery in question and eliminate jobs. This is a typical case in which environmentalists and businesspeople are pitted against one another in the battle to keep U.S. waters clean. There will no doubt be more such cases in the future as more provisions of the CWA come into play.

There exist plans among government officials to strengthen the mandates of the CWA in keeping with the ultimate goal of the act: to rid the nation's waterways of pollution. It is safe to say, then, that the CWA will continue undergoing revisions in the near future, just as it has in the past.

[Arthur G. Sharp]

FURTHER READING:

Berger, John J. *Restoring the Earth: How Americans Are Working to Restore Our Damaged Environment*. New York: Doubleday, 1987.

Dix, H. M. *Environmental Pollution: Atmosphere, Land, Water, and Noise*. New York: John Wiley & Sons, 1980.

Freedman, Warren. *Federal Studies on Environmental Protection: Regulation in the Public Interest*. New York: Greenwood, 1987.

Freeman, A. Myrick. *Air and Water Pollution Control: A Benefit Cost Assessment*. New York: John Wiley & Sons, 1982.

Sandbach, Francis. *Principles of Pollution Control*. White Plains, New York: Longman Publishing Group, 1982.

CLOSED ECONOMY

A closed economy is an economic unit which has no business or trading relations with anyone outside of that unit. Usually referring to a nation or area of common currency (but that can, in general, refer to any system of self reliance), the relatively closed system would be characterized by a small amount of exposure to the world market, as opposed to the relatively **open economy**. The latter allows large movements of goods and services, financial **capital**, and **foreign exchange** across its borders. Policy tools such as restrictions on imports and import quotas, monetary or **fiscal policy**, exchange rate controls, and controls on capital are some of the means whereby a national government might try to influence the degree of openness of its economy.

In developing some aspects of economic theory, it has been advantageous in some cases to assume that the economy is "self-sufficient" (or what is sometimes referred to as an autarkic position). The theory then, having been worked out under these simplified conditions, can be expanded to take into account the effects of international transactions. Openness then, depending on one's theoretical perspective, may (or may not) alter many of the established policy precepts of a closed economic system. Much of what is generally referred to as **macroeconomics** has been primarily focused on the study of "closed" systems while international economics studies what happens when closed economies are opened up to international **competition**.

In recent years the distinction between open and closed economies has become blurred as world capitalist production, distribution, and exchange have become increasingly integrated along international and interregional lines. Some notable phenomena include: the absorption of the former eastern bloc nations into the world economic order; the movement toward the economic integration of Western Europe into one common currency; and the ongoing discussions of the **General Agreement on Trade and Tariffs (GATT)** which addresses trade, tariffs, and patent issues (among other issues) worldwide. Recent debates around the **North American Free Trade Agreement (NAFTA)** and the **U.S.-Canada Free Trade Agreement (FTA)** center around the effects of allowing the free movement of capital across Canada, the United States, and Mexico, with the relative openness or closedness (and, perhaps, political independence itself) of these geographic economic units at stake. In any case, the degree of self reliance (or closedness) depends on the unit of analysis. For example, NAFTA will create a continental economic trading block.

While the vast majority of the economics profession advocates openness or "free trade," (removal of tariffs, taxes, **subsidies**, exchange rate controls, capital controls) as most beneficial to all who participate, the historical record of uneven development—poor nations, and poor regions within wealthy nations—indicates that openness hardly guarantees fairness. In any case, notwithstanding the debates over "**free trade**," clearly the national economy as a closed economy does not provide the setting for analyzing the political economy of development. While no economy is completely closed or completely open, any thoughtful analysis must take into account the larger framework of the global economy and, therefore, economic issues must be analyzed within the context of an open economy.

In the post World War II period it was possible, until very recently, to make a meaningful analytical distinction between open and closed economy in the case of the United States. Foreign trade made up only a small portion of U.S. Gross National Product (GNP). But from 1960 to 1990, exports and imports as a percentage of GNP rose from around 5% to over 15.5%, indicating that the United States could no longer be analyzed as if it were a closed system. In dollar volume, exports and imports increased by over 24 times while GNP increased only ten-fold.

The percent of foreign trade, however, does not capture the full flavor of the forces that dominate international economic linkages. A more adequate measure of the openness or closedness of an economy might be the percentage of tradeable goods (goods that are subject to competition on the world market) versus nontradable goods (goods that must be bought and sold in local markets) produced in a nation. Nontradable goods might arise for a variety of reasons—restrictions such as protection, tariffs, high transport costs, or simply because of their nature. For example, certain types of services might be provided far more cheaply locally. For the United States, 37% of U.S. **Gross Domestic Product** was considered to be tradable goods, while for India the figure is 63%. A further indication of increased openness, in general, is the fact that financial markets that provide the foreign currency (and speculation) that finances international transactions operate 24 hours a day—so that financial investment may move continuously in search of a higher rate of return in response to real flows of investment.

[John A. Sarich]

FURTHER READING:

Edwards, Chris. *The Fragmented World: Competing Perspectives on Trade, Money and Crisis.* Methuen & Co. Ltd., 1985.

Peterson, Wallace C., and Paul S. Estenson. *Income, Employment, and Economic Growth.* 2nd ed. W.W. Norton & Company, 1992.

Rivera-Batiz, Francisco L. and Luis. *International Finance and Open Economy Macroeconomics.* Macmillan, 1985.

Shaikh, Anwar. "Free Trade, Unemployment, and Economic Policy," *Unemployment in the 1990s.* M.E. Sharp Inc., 1995.

CLOSELY HELD CORPORATIONS

Closely held firms are those in which a small group of shareholders control the operating and managerial policies of the firm. These firms differ from most publicly traded firms in which ownership is widely disbursed and the firm is administered by professional managers. Most closely held firms are also family businesses.

Family businesses may be defined as those companies where the link between the family and the business has a mutual influence on company policy and on the interests and objectives of the family. Over 90 percent of all businesses in the United States are closely held. Furthermore, family businesses account for the majority of jobs and produce almost half of the **gross national product** in the United States. Families control the operating policies at many large, publicly traded companies. In many of these firms, families remain dominant by holding senior management positions, seats on the board, and preferential voting privileges even though their shareholdings are significantly less than 50 percent.

Family businesses contain two complexities that make them quite different from other businesses. First, people involved in family firms must understand how family relationships affect the business and how business ownership affects that family, and keep those relationships in balance. Second, intricate succession planning is required.

Different people in the closely held firm will see the same issues in different ways, depending on their position in the family-business system. Family businesses have to contends with such problems as generational disputes and sibling rivalries in addition to standard business concerns.

The **chief executive officer** (CEO) in a family controlled enterprise must consider three perspectives simultaneously. The CEO must be a caring family member, a capable executive, and a fiduciary and steward of family assets. In addition, the business's strategic plan, the leadership succession plan, and the owners' retirement and financial-security plan all depend on one another.

An active, effective board of outside directors can assist the CEO in the development of strategy and the resolution of family conflicts. Boards also provide a knowledgeable, objective, and understanding perspective, which helps family members reach consensus on important issues. An outside board should be composed of three or four currently active chief executives who have business and personal experience relevant to the key issues the family business faces and

who have no personal stake in the family's business decisions.

Family business units provide two major advantages: (1) a unified management shareholder group since managers and shareholders are typically one in the same and (2) continuity in management policies and operating focus. Yet, less than 30 percent of these business entities will survive into the second generation.

MANAGEMENT SUCCESSION

Management succession is especially critical in a closely held business. Founders may be unwilling to engage in succession planning due to the fear of retirement. Personal financial security is also a powerful motivator to keep control of the business. For many founders who build successful enterprises, their business is their identity. Insecurities relating to their declining prowess generate interpersonal conflicts that may sabotage succession planning or even the performance of potential successors.

Founders often do not make good teachers. They are usually ill-suited for a teaching role because they tend to be impatient, action-oriented people who like to retain control. On the other hand, teaching requires patience and relinquishing of control.

Families contemplating the involvement of a new generation in the family firm need to decide how much nepotism should be allowed. It is helpful to define rules for the employment of offspring in the business. Three standards are recommended: (1) education appropriate for the job sought; (2) three to five years of outside work experience; and (3) entry into an existing, needed job, with precedents for pay and performance expectations. Outside experience is good for both the business and the new generation.

Veteran members of family businesses should respect the newcomer. It is important to clearly define responsibilities. Finally, sibling rivalries should not be allowed to determine company rules.

ESTATE FREEZES

The founding generation in a closely held firm desires to transfer ownership of the firm to the succeeding generation with as few tax consequences as possible. One method of accomplishing this is through the use of a technique known as an estate freeze. Without the freeze, the tax cost of transferring a family business from parents to children is often prohibitively high. In a classic estate freeze, the family business owner would plan to lower the taxable estate by transferring appreciating assets to other family members, consequently freezing the value of the estate (and the potential estate tax) by removing the appreciation potential. Congress enacted Internal

Revenue Code Section 2036(c) to curb perceived abusive freezes. As part of the Revenue Reconciliation Act of 1990, Congress retroactively repealed the Section 2036(c) estate tax rules and replaced them with a new set of rules known as Chapter 14.

The new rules aimed to ensure that the parties realistically value transferred and retained interests. They modify the valuation of retained rights in both corporations and partnerships and the valuation of retained interests in property. In addition, the new rules address the effect of buy-sell agreements and options on valuation and the transfer tax consequences of lapsing rights.

The new rules apply to situations where a family member transfers an interest in a partnership or corporation that is controlled by the family to another family member, while retaining either a right to a distribution based on stock ownership or a liquidation, put, call, or conversion right that would affect the value of the transferred interest. Control is defined as 50 percent of the voting power or value of the stock or 50 percent of the capital or profit interest in the partnership.

The new rules concentrate on accurately valuing the retained interest in anticipation of expected events. The new approach to valuing the transferred interest on which gift tax is paid is to subtract the value of the interest retained from the value of the entire entity in order to determine the value of the gift. The new law assigns a zero value to the retained interest unless the retained interest is entitled to qualified payments or is a qualified interest. To be classified as a qualified interest, dividends will have to be paid on the preferred stock retained by the older generation. The new rules, however, do not restrict the employment of older generation family members or the leasing of property from older family members by the corporation or partnership.

BUY/SELL AGREEMENTS

It is important to have detailed plans and procedures for the sale or transfer of stock at the time of the death, disability, or retirement of a shareholder in a closely held firm. Without such procedures, the departure of one major shareholder could also signal the end of a business. Buy/sell agreements spell out the terms governing sale of company stock to an outsider and thus protect control of the company. These agreements allow co-owners to buy out heirs in the event of death or disability. In order to be considered valid for estate tax purposes, a stock buy-sell agreement must meet several conditions, including a "full and adequate consideration" provision. Life insurance is generally used to provide the funds to purchase the shares of a closely held company if one of the owners dies.

There are two basic types of buy-sell agreements: cross-purchase agreements and redemption agreements. With a cross-purchases agreement, the owner separately purchase a policy on the other owner. With a redemption agreement, if any of the business owners die, the corporation is obligated to redeem the stock at a price set in the agreement. Typically, the buy/sell agreements are funded with life insurance; the life insurance proceeds provide the necessary funds for the purchase of the business.

The prolonged disability of a principal can also present serious difficulties for closely held firms. A long-term disability buy-sell agreement can provide a cushion to protect the disabled principal's interests during recovery. The first step in implementing such an agreement is to determine how long the company should be without the disabled partner's services before a buyout is activated. It is recommended that an actual buyout of ownership interest be postponed at least 12 months but not more than 24 months after the infirmity occurs.

VALUATION ISSUES

One of the major concerns associated with closely held firms is the determination of their value. The shares of a closely held business are owned by a small number of stockholders, often by members of a family. Because there is no established market for the shares, it is difficult to establish the value of the shares in an estate or gift tax situation.

In preparing a valuation report, the major guidelines to be followed are contained in Internal Revenue Service Revenue Ruling 59-60. According to this ruling, the proper estimate of value should be based on the price at which a property would change hands between a willing buyer and a willing seller, with neither party under any compulsion to buy or sell and with all relevant facts available to both parties (the fair market value standard). Revenue Ruling 59-60 provides valuation criteria for closely held businesses that are generally accepted by appraisers and the courts. The criteria include: the history of the business, economic outlook, book value, earning capacity, dividend-paying capacity, goodwill and other intangibles, past sales of company stock, and stock of comparable businesses.

Without a marketplace that reflects the price arrived at by both buyer and seller, the security prices of a closely held firm must be set by calculation, comparison, and the use of financial ratios. **Valuation** techniques that have evolved fall into three principal categories: (1) market (price-earnings) methods, (2) cash flow methods, and (3) book value (balance sheet) methods. Another area of concern when addressing valuation issues is the notion of discounts for minority interests and lack of marketability.

SEE ALSO: Family-Owned Business Enterprises; Publicly Held Company

[Robert T. Kleiman]

FURTHER READING:

Klaris, Raynor J. "Valuing the Family Business." *Trusts & Estates*; February, 1990, pp. 18-29.

Owens, Thomas. "Buy-Sell Agreements." *Small Business Reports*. January, 1991, pp. 57-61.

Szabo, Joan C. "Congress Thaws the Estate Freeze." *Nation's Business*. February, 1991, pp. 23-25.

Ward, John L., and Craig E. Aronoff. "Two 'Laws' for Family Businesses." *Nation's Business*. February, 1993, pp. 52-53.

COMMERCIAL ATTACHÉ

A commercial attaché is a person posted to a foreign embassy to promote the economic interests of his or her home country. The terms commercial attaché and commercial officer are often used interchangeably; in the United States, however, both job titles occur as part of a hierarchical ranking system. Traditionally attachés differed from career diplomats in that they did not represent their country's foreign ministry (in the case of the United States the U.S. Department of State). Rather, they represented the governmental agencies responsible for their field of endeavor: agriculture, military, or commerce for instance. Present day foreign missions, however, especially foreign missions to large countries, often require groups of specialists. These specialists may function in the manner of traditional attachés or their assignment may be as secretaries on the diplomatic staff.

Generally a foreign embassy will have an economic/commercial section. This section is headed by an experienced senior officer who supervises his or her staff of specialists, a clerical staff, and nationals of the host country. The commercial half of the section is concerned with facilitating exports to, and investments in, the host country. The economic part of the section deals with economic relations at a government-to-government level and provides economic information and analysis to its home government. Commercial attachés representing the United States are employees of the U.S. Foreign and Commercial Service which is part of the International Trade Administration (ITA). The ITA is part of the U.S. Department of Commerce and was established in January of 1980. Its purpose is to promote world trade and especially U.S. international trade and investment. The ITA is administered by three assistant secretaries who are responsible for the agency's main areas of operations, the Assistant Secreaty for International Economic Policy, the Assis-

tant Secretary for Import Administration, and the Assistant Secretary for Trade Development.

The United States and Foreign Commercial Service is headed by an Assistant Secretary and Director General who oversees foreign postings and operations (132 posts in 68 countries), 47 district offices, and 21 branch offices in the United States. Through these operations and postings, the U.S. Foreign and Commercial Service (USFCS) supports the commercial activities of American exporters and the American international business community. The USFCS has three levels of commercial officers. The highest are the Senior Commercial Officers followed by the Commercial Attachés and the Commercial Officers.

Commercial attachés are involved in many diverse activities in the course of their work. These include supervising embassy employees assigned to them, meeting with businessmen from both their own country and their host country, and attending trade fairs and expositions. Upon beginning an assignment at a new post, a commercial attaché generally initiates some form of basic country survey. This survey familiarizes the new officer with the internal workings of the host country's business community and government offices. The new officer also compiles sources of information needed to accomplish his or her commercial objectives. Sources of information and contacts would include the country's central bank, import and export trade associations, chambers of commerce and of course the host country's media. Attachés can be assigned to a single foreign post for as long as five years. If the posting is to a major trading partner, he or she may be part of a staff of between 35 and 45 personnel.

[Michael Knes]

FURTHER READING:

Barrows, Leland. *Commercial Diplomacy: Government Representation in Support of U.S. Exporters*. Center for Strategic and International Studies. 1974.

"Commercial Representatives: Getting to Know Your Territory." *International Trade Forum*. January/March 1988.

Exporters' Encyclopedia. Dun and Bradstreet Publications Corp.

COMMERCIAL LAW

Commercial law refers to the body of law that pertains to commercial transactions. Its wide-ranging scope includes many different areas that affect businesses and individuals who enter into commercial transactions. **Contracts**, agency, bailments, carriers, sales, **product liability**, partnerships, corporations, unfair **competition**, secured transactions, property, **commercial paper**, insurance, and bankruptcy are all governed by commercial law.

Modern commercial law in the United States evolved from a system of mercantile courts in England that administered a law known as *lex mercatoria*, or ''law merchant.'' The law was based on the customs of merchants and served to resolve disputes between merchants or between merchants and their customers. The ''law merchant'' was incorporated into common law tradition in the eighteenth century, and thus became part of American law.

In the United States a large part of commercial law has been codified in the **Uniform Commercial Code** (UCC). All 50 states, the District of Columbia, and the Virgin Islands have adopted the UCC as law, although Louisiana has only adopted Articles 1 (General Provisions), 3 (Commercial Paper), 4 (Bank Deposits and Collections), and 5 (Letters of Credit).

The original impetus for codification of commercial laws in the United States came in the nineteenth century from the National Conference of Commissioners on Uniform State Laws, which drafted uniform statutes covering commercial laws and recommended that individual states adopt them as law. Among the statutes they drafted were the Negotiable Instruments Act, approved in 1896, the Uniform Sales Act (1906), the Uniform Warehouse Receipts Act (1906), the Uniform Stock Transfer Act (1909), and the Uniform Bills of Lading Act (1909). When states adopted the UCC, these laws were repealed.

Work on drafting the UCC began in 1942 under the joint sponsorship and direction of the National Conference of Commissioners on State Laws and the American Law Institute. They were assisted by hundreds of practicing lawyers, judges, teachers, bankers, and business people. In 1952, a finished draft was submitted to the states for approval. Pennsylvania became the first state to enact the UCC on April 6, 1953, effective July 1, 1954. The UCC editorial board issued a new code in 1957, and by 1966 48 states had enacted the code. A permanent editorial board monitors changes in business practices and reviews the applicability of the UCC.

While the UCC covers a broad scope of commercial activity, there are areas of commercial law that are untouched by the code. As with all other laws, the UCC is subject to interpretation in the courts. In common law, the doctrine of *stare decisis* means that decisions that are reached in specific cases serve as precedents for determining future controversies. In the United States *stare decisis* is a flexible doctrine that serves as a guiding, but not binding, principle that

provides stability and a certain measure of certainty, predictability, and reliability to the legal system. In general, then, trial court decisions are not binding upon reviewing courts or any other trial courts.

In addition to the UCC, businesses are governed by numerous federal and state regulations. State laws cover such areas as how to set up a business, how to qualify for and obtain a business license, what types of insurance coverage are needed, and what taxes must be paid. State laws that do not fall within the scope of the UCC vary widely from state to state. Those laws that are based on the UCC, on the other hand, have the advantage of uniformity from state to state, making it easier for businesses and individuals to seek remedies and resolve disputes in different states.

Federal regulations cover interstate commerce and other matters that cannot be covered by individual state laws. Other commercial areas that are covered by federal law include product development, which can be protected by trade secret, patent, trademark, and **copyright** laws, and product quality, which must comply with product liability law, government regulation of certain types of products, and **packaging** and labeling regulations. Federal antitrust laws govern business practices relating to acquisitions and mergers as well as pricing and distribution channels. Business advertising must comply with Federal Trade Commission rules and regulations concerning deceptive acts or practices.

Commercial law can be distinguished from the maze of federal and state regulations that govern business conduct. Federal and state laws and regulations provide businesses with rules of conduct. Businesses that violate state or federal laws are guilty of misconduct. Commercial law, on the other hand, serves to effectively resolve disputes and provide remedies that arise from commercial transactions. Commercial law is designed to safeguard the rights of all parties engaged in commercial transactions. Since business is based on transactions, a uniform body of commercial law serves to enhance our ability to enter into transactions and conduct business.

[David Bianco]

COMMERCIAL LOAN

Loans from commercial banks are an important source of negotiated short-term financing. Bank loans may be secured by **assets** or may be unsecured. Such loans usually appear as notes payable on the **balance sheet**.

In granting loans, the bank must balance the benefit of the additional interest income generated against the cost of increasing bad debts. To estimate the probability that a borrower will pay, banks gather information on their potential customers. Banks often use credit scoring models that predict future payment performance on the basis of financial and non-financial factors. Generally, the financial institution group these factors into the five Cs: capacity, capital, character, collateral, and conditions. Capacity refers to the borrower's ability to meet credit obligations out of the business's cash flow. Capital refers to the customer's financial reserves. In analyzing character, the bank attempts to evaluate the borrower's willingness to meet credit obligations. Collateral is an asset pledged by the borrower in case of default. Finally, the bank must also analyze the general economic conditions and the borrower's line of business.

LENDING AGREEMENTS

Bank **credit** is commonly available under three different arrangements: single loans, lines of credit, and revolving credit agreements. Single loans are usually arranged for specific financing needs. The **interest rates** charged on single loans are usually related to the **prime rate**.

A line of credit is an agreement which permits the firm to borrow up to a predetermined credit limit at any time during the life of the agreement. A line of credit is usually negotiated for a 1-year period, and the interest rate is usually stated in terms of the prime rate and varies as the prime rate changes during the year. A line of credit usually requires that the firm have no loans outstanding under the agreement for a portion of the year, known as the clean-up period. This type of lending agreement does not guarantee that the bank will lend the requested funds since the bank is not legally obligated to make loans if the firm's financial position has deteriorated.

Revolving credit agreements legally commit the bank to making loans up to the credit limit specified in the agreement. Revolving credit agreements are usually secured, and generally require the firm to pay a commitment fee on the unused portion of the funds.

TYPES OF BANK LOANS

Most commercial loans are amortized loans. With an amortized loan, the borrower is required to make equal periodic payments. As payment are made, a portion of charges for the period, and is based on the outstanding balance at the time of the payment. The remainder of the payment is then applied to the principal balance. Since the principal balance declines with each payment, the interest portion of the payment decreases and the principal repayment portion of the payment increases over time. With a discounted loan, the lender receives payment of all the interest at the time the loan is granted. Since the interest is prepaid, the borrower must only repay the principal, usually in equal payments. In an add-on loan, the total interest for the loan is calculated and added to the principal. The sum of the principal and interest is then divided by the number of periods to calculate the constant periodic payment. The effective interest rate on discounted and add-on loans may differ significantly from the stated rate.

TYPES OF COLLATERAL

Accounts receivable are one of the most common forms of collateral for secured short-term borrowing. When accounts receivable are pledged, the firm retains title to them and continues to carry them on its balance sheet. The borrower sends copies of invoices to the lender who determines the amount that will be advanced depending on the credit-worthiness of the receivable. **Factoring** receivables involves the outright sale of the receivables to a financial institution, called a factor. When receivables are factored, title passes to the factor and they no longer appear on the balance sheet of the firm. Therefore, the factor assumes the risk of default.

The inventory constitutes another common source of collateral for secured loans. Three basic arrangements exist with regard to possession of the collateral by the borrower or by a third party. A floating lien is a general claim on all the firm's inventory. These arrangements offer little security to the lender and are used for large-volume, small-value, high-turnover inventory held by the borrower. A trust receipt is another type of loan in which the inventory is held by the borrower. As the inventory is sold, the proceeds are forwarded to the lender along with notification of the goods sold. Trust receipts require specifically identifiable units of inventory, and are frequently used for automobiles and appliances. With a terminal warehouse plan, the inventory is held in a bonded warehouse operated by a public warehouse company. As the loan is paid off, the lender authorizes the warehouse to release the inventory.

[Robert T. Kleiman]

FURTHER READING:

Sinkey, Joseph F., Jr., *Commercial Bank Financial Management.* 4th ed. New York: Macmillan Publishing Co., 1992.

COMMISSION OF THE EUROPEAN COMMUNITIES

The Commission of the European Communities (CEC) is a constituent part of the European Community. The European Community is a term which collectively describes the merging in 1967 (under provisions of a 1965 treaty) of the executive agencies of three European organizations formed after World War II. These three organizations are the European Economic Community, the European Coal and Steel Community (ECSC), and the European Atomic Energy Community. The 1967 treaty did not formally merge the three into a single organization but rather created the CEC which acts as an administrative organ common to the three organizations. The purpose of the European Community and thus the CEC is to promote European economic integration among its members. The original member states were Belgium, France, Luxembourg, the Netherlands, Italy, and West Germany. Denmark, Ireland, and Great Britain joined in 1973, Greece in 1981, and Spain and Portugal in 1983.

The CEC functions by setting policy for the European Community, mediating differences that may arise between member governments and monitoring member activity for compliance with European Community rules, regulations and treaty provisions. The CEC has the authority to bring member governments before the European Court of Justice (also an organ of the European Community) for breaches of European Community laws. The CEC also administers various economic programs including the European Regional Development Fund, the Social Fund, and the Agricultural Guidance and Guarantee Fund. International agreements are ultimately decided on by the European Community's Council of Ministers, but the agreements are initially negotiated by the CEC.

The CEC policy is set by its seventeen commissioners who meet collectively as the College of Commissioners. France, Germany, Italy, Spain, and the United Kingdom each have two nationals on the Commission while the seven ''smaller'' countries have one each. Every four years a new commission is appointed although previous commissioners may be re-appointed. The commissioners are appointed by the governments of member nations who also choose one commissioner to be President. The European Court of Justice has the authority to remove commissioners for not fulfilling the conditions of their appointment or for committing a serious offense. The Council of Ministers and the Commission also have the authority to petition the Court to suspend commission members for the above mentioned offenses.

Policy decisions of the CEC are carried out by its 23 Directorates-General and the Special Units and Services. Examples of the various Directorates-General include:

External Relations, Economic and Financial Affairs, Agriculture, Transport, Energy, Credit and Investments, Science, Research and Development, Telecommunications, Informational Industry and In-

novation, Regional Policies, and Fisheries. Special Units and Services encompass such departments as: the Translation Service, the Consumer Policy Service, the Joint Research Centre, Security Service, the Legal Service, and the Statistics Service.

The College of Commissioners meets weekly where unanimous votes on policy matters are sought, but where a majority vote often suffices. Commissioners are assigned specific areas of responsibility and are thus responsible for policy leadership concerning these areas. A Director General (who heads each Directorate-General) for the same area of responsibility reports to the appropriate Commissioner. Beneath the Directors General are Directors and beneath them in the administrative hierarchy are heads of division. The College of Commissioners policy decisions are carried out by the approximately 12,000 (1991) employees of the CEC.

[Michael Knes]

FURTHER READING:

Budd, Stanley A. *The European Community: A Guide to the Maze*. Kogan Page, 1991.

Ludlow, Peter. *The European Commission in a Changing European Community*. Centre for European Policy Studies, 1990.

Nugent, Neill. *The Government and Politics of the European Community*. Macmillan, 1991.

COMMODITIES

The word ''commodity'' encompasses several products, and instruments among them precious metals (including gold, silver, copper, and palladium), agricultural items (such as sugar, coffee, soybeans, corn, wheat, and pork bellies), energy (for example, crude oil and heating oil), foreign currencies (Japanese yen, French franc, British pound sterling, among others), interest rates (including U.S. Treasury bills, U.S. Treasury bonds, and Government National Mortgage Association (GNMA) certificates), and equity indexes (Standard and Poor's 500 is one example). Commodity products or instruments are known by many names, among them **futures contracts**, leverage contracts, options on futures contracts, options on physicals, managed accounts, commodity pools, funds, limited risk forward accounts, deferred delivery contracts, bank financed forward accounts, gold or silver bullion contracts, and long-term forward accounts.

Futures markets exist only in relation to cash markets, which are the underlying primary markets in which actual physical commodities are bought and sold. In many basic commodities, price volatility is inherent and that volatility is a source of significant financial risk for those who produce, market, process, or ultimately consume these commodities and any products which are derived from them.

The first organized **commodity exchanges** in the United States date back to the 1800s; the Chicago Board of Trade (CBOT), founded in 1848, is the oldest existing U.S. futures exchange. When it was first established, the CBOT was a centralized cash market, formed in response to the need for a central marketplace that would bring together large numbers of buyers and sellers, thus providing liquidity, as well as providing a place with rules for ethical trading practices and reliable standards of weights and measures. Soon after the founding of the exchange, grain brokers began trading in "cash forward contracts," in order to assure buyers a source of supply and sellers the opportunity to sell 12 months a year. As the use of the cash forward contracts escalated, the futures contract, as it is known today, evolved. Futures contracts differed from cash forward contracts in that they specified the price at the time the contract was made, as well as the quantity, quality, and delivery time.

Two types of futures contracts exist: those that provide for the physical delivery of a particular commodity or item and those which call for a cash settlement. Even though delivery on futures contracts is the exception rather than the rule, the delivery provision exists because it affords buyers and sellers the opportunity to take or make delivery of the physical commodity. Also, the fact that delivery can actually take place helps to ensure that futures prices accurately reflect the cash market value at the time the futures contract expires.

If delivery of delivery-type futures contracts does take place, it takes the form of a **negotiable instrument**, such as a warehouse receipt, that proves the holder's ownership of the commodity at some designated location. Cash settlement futures contracts are settled in cash rather than by delivery and are based on a given index number times a specified dollar multiple.

Delivery-type futures contracts stipulate the specifications of the commodity to be delivered, such as one soybean contract is equivalent to 5,000 bushels of soybeans, or one contract of gold is equivalent to 100 troy ounces of gold. Foreign currency futures provide for delivery of a specified number of Deutsche marks, French francs, or British pounds. U.S. Treasury obligation futures are stated in terms of instruments having a stated face value (such as $100,000 or $1 million) at maturity.

Competitive price discovery is a major economic function and benefit of futures trading. The trading floor of a commodity exchange is where available information about the future value of a commodity or item is translated into the language of price. Commodity prices are volatile because they are subject to many factors, among them: weather, strikes, inflation, foreign or international exchange rates, new technology, politics, transportation, and storage factors.

Futures prices are usually quoted the same way that prices are quoted in the cash market, when a cash market exists. This means dollars, cents, and often fractions of a cent, per bushel, pound, or ounce. For foreign currency futures, prices are quoted in dollars, cents, and increments of a cent. For financial instrument futures, prices are quoted in points and percentages of a point. Cash settlement futures contract prices are quoted in terms of an index number, usually stated to two decimal points.

Commodity exchanges establish the minimum amount that the price can fluctuate upward or downward. This minimum amount is known as the tick. The exchanges also establish daily price limits, which are stated in terms of the previous trading day's closing price, plus and minus a specified amount per trading unit. Once a futures contract price has increased or declined by its daily trading limit, trading cannot take place at prices beyond this limit. For some contracts, daily price limits are not imposed during the month in which the contract expires.

SEE ALSO: Inflation; International Exchange Rate; Options/Options Contracts.

[Susan Bard Hall]

FURTHER READING:

Commodity Futures Trading Commission. *Before Trading/Get the Facts*. Washington, D.C., March 1993, pp. 1-3.

Futures Industry Association. *An Introduction to the Futures Markets*. Washington, D.C., 1982, pp. 40-41.

Chicago Board of Trade. *Speculating in Futures*. Chicago, 1990, pp. 1.

National Futures Association. *Understanding Opportunities and Risks in Futures Trading*. Chicago, 1990, pp. 8-10, 33-35.

COMMODITY EXCHANGES

Commodity exchanges or **futures** exchanges, like **stock** exchanges, are membership organizations. Their mission is to provide a suitable place where members can trade **commodities** (futures) and/or options on futures in a controlled, orderly manner. The exchange itself is not a principal to any futures transaction, nor does it trade for its own account. Except for developing, publishing, and enforcing trading rules, including the establishment of daily price limits to ensure fair and equal treatment for all market participants, the exchange does nothing to determine prevailing prices in the market.

The first organized commodity exchange in the United States was the Chicago Board of Trade (CBOT), founded on April 3, 1848. When first established, the CBOT was a centralized cash market formed in response to the need for a central marketplace that would bring together large numbers of buyers and sellers; thus providing liquidity, as well as bringing traders together in a place that provided rules for ethical trading practices and reliable standards of weights and measures. Soon after the founding of the exchange, grain brokers began trading in ''cash forward contracts'' in order to assure buyers a source of supply and sellers the opportunity to sell twelve months a year. As use of the cash forward contracts escalated, the futures contracts, as it is known today, evolved.

Generally, membership in an exchange is individual, and only members may buy and sell futures contracts and/or options on futures contracts on the exchange trading floor. Administration of the day-to-day operations of the exchange are handled by a paid staff. Members make the ultimate decisions, first by committee approval, then by passage of the **board of directors** or board of trustees. Administrative decisions are subject to full membership vote.

The heart of the exchange is the exchange trading floor, where a specific area, known as a pit or ring, is designated for the trading of each commodity. Bids (offers to buy a specific quantity of a commodity at a stated price) and offers (an indication of willingness to sell a specific quantity of a commodity at a stated price) are made by open outcry. As each transaction is completed in the pit, a pit reporter records it; this information is immediately displayed on the trading floor quotation board, and also appears on computer screens in brokerage offices and trading centers worldwide. Each trade is also recorded by the participating member on trading cards; each entry shows the amount bought or sold, with whom the trade was made, the price, and the trading bracket (time period) in which the trade was made. These cards enable each member to recheck his trades, as every trade must be resolved before the start of trading the following day.

Worldwide commodity exchanges (futures and **options** exchanges) are listed in alphabetical order by country, city, and date established:

Argentina: Mercado de Futuros y Opciones S.A. (MERFOX) Buenos Aires July 3, 1991.

Australia: The Australian Options Market, Sydney, 1976 (calls only; puts introduced in 1982); Sydney Futures Exchange (SFE), Sydney, 1960.

Austria: Austrian Futures and Options Exchange, Vienna, October 4, 1991.

Belgium: Belgian Futures and Options Exchange (BELFOX), Brussels, 1990.

Brazil: Bolsa de Mercadorias & Futuros (BM&F), Sao Paulo, May 9, 1991, a merger of Bolsa Mercantil & de Futuros (BM&F) and Bolsa de Mercadorias de Sao Paulo (BMSP).

Canada: Montreal Exchange (ME), Montreal, 1874. Toronto Futures Exchange (TFE), Toronto, May, 1983; Toronto Stock Exchange, Toronto, October 25, 1861. Vancouver Stock Exchange (VSE), Vancouver, 1907; Winnipeg Commodity Exchange (WCE), Winnipeg, July, 1887.

Denmark: FUTOP Market—Copenhagen Stock Exchange and Guarantee Fund for Danish Options and Futures, Copenhagen, July, 1987.

Finland: Finnish Options Exchange, Ltd., Helsinki. Finnish Options Market, Helsinki, 1987.

France: Marche a Terme International de France (MATIF), Paris, February, 1986; Marche des Options Negociables de Paris (MONEP), Paris, March 1987.

Germany: Deutsche Terminboerse (DTB), Frankfurt. August, 1988.

Hong Kong: Hong Kong Futures Exchange Ltd. (HKFE), Hong Kong. December, 1976.

Ireland: Irish Futures & Options Exchange (FOX), Dublin, May, 1988.

Israel: Tel Aviv Stock Exchange Ltd. (TASE), Tel Aviv, 1953.

Japan: Kobe Raw Silk Exchange, Kobe. Kobe Rubber Exchange (KRE) Kobe, December, 1951; Nagoya Stock ExchangeNaka-ku, March, 1986; Nagoya Textile Exchange, Nagoy, February 21, 1951; Osaka Grain Exchange (OGE), Osaka, October 6, 1952; Osaka Securities Exchange, Osaka, April, 1949; Osaka Sugar Exchange, Osaka, April, 1952; Osaka Textile Exchange, Osaka. October, 1984; Tokyo Commodity Exchange (TOCOM), Tokyo, November 1, 1984; Tokyo Grain Exchange (TGE), Tokyo. September, 1952; Tokyo International Financial Futures Exchange (TIFFE), Tokyo, June 30, 1989; Tokyo Stock Exchange (TSE), Tokyo, April, 1949; Tokyo Sugar Exchange, Tokyo, May 7, 1952.

Malaysia: Kuala Lumpur Commodity Exchange, Kuala Lumpur, July, 1980.

Netherlands: European Options Exchange (EOE-Optiebeurs), Amsterdam, April, 1978; Financiele Termijnmarkt Amsterdam N.V. (FTA), Amsterdam, June 19,1987.

New Zealand: New Zealand Futures & Options Exchange Ltd. (NZFOE), Auckland, 1984.

Norway: Oslo Stock Exchange, Oslo, 1819 (options trading began May 22, 1990).

Philippines: Manila International Futures Exchange Inc. (MIFE), Makati, 1984.

Singapore: RAS Commodity Exchange, Singapore, 1991; Singapore International Monetary Exchange Ltd. (SIMEX), Singapore, September 1984.

South Africa: South African Futures Exchange (SAFEX), Johannesburg, September 30, 1988.

Spain: Mercado de Opciones Y Futuros Financieros (MEFF RENTA FIJA), Barcelona, March 16, 1990; MEFF RENTA VARIABLE, Madrid, December 1988.

Sweden: OM Stockholm AS, Stockholm, 1985.

Switzerland: Swiss Options and Financial Futures Exchange (SOFFEX), Dietikon, 1986.

United Kingdom: London Futures and Options Exchange, London, July 1987 (merged with Baltic Futures Exchange and BIFFEX in January 1991). International Petroleum Exchange of London Ltd. (IPE), London, April 1981. London International Financial Futures and Options Exchange (LIFFE), London, September 1982 (merged in March 1992 with the London Traded Options Market). London Metal Exchange (LME), London, December 1876. OM London Ltd. (OML), London, December 1989.

United States: American Stock Exchange (AMEX), New York, 1908; Chicago Board Options Exchange (CBOE), Chicago, April 26,1973. Chicago Board of Trade (CBOT), Chicago, 1848. Mid America Commodity Exchange (MidAm, an affiliate of the CBOT), Chicago, 1880 (affiliated with the CBOT In 1987). Chicago Mercantile Exchange (CME), Chicago, 1919 (as the successor to the Butter and Egg Board, created in 1898). International Monetary Market (IMM) division of the CME, Chicago, 1972. Index and Option Market (IOM) division of the CME, Chicago, 1982. GLOBEX, Chicago, London, New York Paris and Tokyo, June 25,1992. Coffee, Sugar, and Cocoa Exchange, Inc. (CSCE), New York 1882 (began as the Coffee Exchange of the City of New York, merged with the New York Cocoa Exchange in 1979 to form current exchange). Commodity Exchange, Inc. (COMEX), New York July 5,1933. Kansas City Board of Trade (KCBT), Kansas City, 1856. Minneapolis Grain Exchange (MGE), Minneapolis, 1881. New York Cotton Exchange (NYCE), New York 1870 (also includes the Citrus Associates of the New York Cotton Exchange and FINEX). New York Futures Exchange (NYFE), New York, August 7,1980. New York Mercantile Exchange (NYMEX), New York, 1872. New York Stock Exchange (NYSE) Options, New York 1983. Pacific Stock Exchange (PSE), San Francisco, September 18, 1882. Philadelphia Stock Exchange (PHLX) Philadelphia Board of Trade (PBOT), Philadelphia, April 2, 1790 (the oldest U.S. securities exchange.).

[Susan Bard Hall]

FURTHER READING:

Futures Magazine's 1993 Source Book. Cedar Falls, IA: Oster Communications Inc., pp. 76-113.

An Introduction to the Futures Market. Washington, D.C.: Futures Industry Association, pp. 2,3, and 6.

COMMODITY FUTURES-SPREADS

Commodity futures-spreads or **futures** spreads are one of several, basic trading strategies that futures traders use to make a profit in the commodity futures markets. In its simplest form, a spread takes place when a trader buys one futures contract while simultaneously selling another futures contract, in hopes of making a profit when the price difference becomes wider or narrower. Spread trading differs from outright trading, where a trader buys a futures contract in anticipation of higher prices, or sells a futures contract when lower prices are expected.

Spreads are often considered to be less risky than an outright trade (buy and take a long position or sell and take a short position). Therefore, the margin requirements or funds needed to initiate a spread position are less than what is required for an outright trade. Since each side—or "leg"—of the spread may be negatively affected by fundamental or technical factors that affect the market(s), the widening or narrowing of the spread may exceed the up or down movement of the market.

Spreads between different delivery months for the same commodity (for example, buying and selling wheat) are known as intramarket spreads. Spreads between two different futures markets (buying wheat and selling corn) are known as intermarket spreads.

In example of an intramarket spread, a trader anticipates that over time, the price difference between the March and May wheat futures contracts will widen. When there is no anticipated shortfall in supply, the deferred (in this example, the May contract) tends to gain in price relative to the nearby contract (in this example, the March contract).

In this example, March wheat is trading at $3.50 per bushel, while May wheat is trading at $3.55 per bushel, for a price difference of five cents per bushel. In anticipation of this market move, the trader sells the lower price contract or one March wheat futures contract (5,000 bushels) and buys the higher price contract or one May wheat futures contract (also 5,000 bushels). A few months later, the March contract has risen to $3.60 per bushel while the May contract has climbed to $3.75 per bushel. The difference between these contracts is now 15 cents. The spread did widen by 10 cents, which translates into a $500 profit since each one-cent-move on a 5,000-bushel contract equates to $50. Examining each leg of the spread also verifies the 10-cent-profit in this trade. Selling the March wheat contract at $3.50 and buying it back a few months later at $3.60 created a 10-cent loss. However, buying the May wheat contract at $3.55 and later selling it at $3.75 created a 20-cent profit. The 10-cent loss coupled with the 20-cent gain creates a net gain of 10 cents or $500 per contract.

Two other examples of spreads are the gold/silver spread and the municipal over bond (MOB) spread. The gold/silver spread involves selling a gold futures contract and buying a silver futures contract. Traders use this strategy when the gold/silver ratio is historically high (the gold/silver ratio is calculated by dividing the price of gold by the price of silver; if gold is trading for $400 per ounce and silver for $5 per ounce, the ratio would be 80:1 or 80). When the ratio is at the lower end of the scale, the strategy is to buy gold futures and sell silver futures. The MOB spread is defined as the price difference between a municipal bond futures contract and a U.S. Treasury bond futures contract.

SEE ALSO: Commodities; Commodity Exchanges; Commodity Futures Trading Commission; Futures/Futures Contracts

[Susan Bard Hall]

FURTHER READING:

Chicago Board of Trade. *Commodity Trading Manual*. Chicago: Chicago Board of Trade.

Chicago Board of Trade. *Gold/Silver Ratio Spread*. Chicago: Chicago Board of Trade, 1994.

Chicago Board of Trade. *Speculating Workbook*. Chicago: Chicago Board of Trade, 1990, pp. 11, 13.

Chicago Board of Trade. *Understanding The MOB Spread: A Reprise*. Chicago: Chicago Board of Trade, 1991, pp. 1.

National Futures Association. *Understanding Opportunities and Risks in Futures Trading*. National Futures Association, Chicago: 1990, pp. 19, 39, 40.

COMMODITY FUTURES TRADING COMMISSION (CFTC)

Created by the Congress of the United States in 1974, the Commodity Futures Trading Commission (CFTC) is the federal regulator and overseer of the trading of commodity **futures** and **options** on commodity futures contracts in the United States. As an independent agency, the CFTC's mission is to protect customers who use these futures and options on fu-

tures markets and to monitor the markets to detect and prevent distortions in the price of **commodities** and market manipulations.

Signed into law by President Gerald Ford, the bill creating the CFTC completely overhauled the Commodity Exchange Act (CEA) which, as part of the U.S. Department of Agriculture, had regulated trading in domestic agricultural commodities since its inception in 1936. The Commodity Futures Trading Commission (CFTC) was created as an independent agency with the mandate to regulate the commodity futures and options on commodity futures markets in the United States. The agency's mandate was renewed and expanded in 1978, 1982, 1986, and 1992.

The CFTC is responsible for ensuring the economic utility of futures and options on futures markets by encouraging their competitiveness and efficiency, ensuring their financial and market integrity, and protecting market participants against manipulation, abusive trade practices and fraud.

The Commodity Futures Trading Commission Act of 1974 provides for five CFTC commissioners who collectively comprise the commission. Each commissioner serves a five-year term and the terms are staggered, so turnover is regular. These five commissioners are appointed by the President of the United States with the advice and consent of the U.S. Senate. The President designates one of the five commissioners to serve as CFTC Chairman. It is the chairman's role to preside over commission meetings and to oversee the management of the agency. As a general rule, commission meetings are open to the public. It requires a majority vote of the commissioners to approve major policy decisions and actions, such as approval of contract market designations, adoption of agency rules and regulations, and the authorization of enforcement actions.

The CFTC is headquartered in Washington, D.C. and maintains regional or subregional offices in cities where there is a U.S. futures exchange, including Chicago, Kansas City, Minneapolis, and New York. Although there is no futures exchange located in Los Angeles, the CFTC also has an office in that city.

The CFTC has six major operating units: the Division of Economic Analysis; the Division of Market Review and Development; the Division of Financial and Intermediary Affairs; the Division of Enforcement; the Office of the General Counsel; and the Office of the Executive Director.

The Division of Economic Analysis: 1) reviews proposed futures contracts and options on futures contracts to determine whether they would serve a valid economic purpose and conform with cash market practices; 2) analyzes the economic ramifications of CFTC policies and regulations; 3) monitors trading on all contract markets to detect actual or potential for manipulation, congestion, and price distortion; and 4) conducts or sponsors long-term research on the functioning of futures and options on futures markets. During fiscal year 1993, the Market Analysis Section of the Division of Economic Analysis completed economic review of 21 applications for new futures contracts; 27 applications for new options on futures contracts; and 113 rule amendment packages for existing futures and options on futures contracts. A total of 48 new contracts were approved in fiscal year 1993, the highest total for any single fiscal year to date.

The Division of Market Review and Development is involved with: 1) international issues; 2) rule-making to implement market reforms; 3) exchange oversight (including exchange trading floor surveillance and rule enforcement reviews); and 4) regulatory analysis of contracts, screen-based trading systems, and other innovative systems.

The Division of Financial and Intermediary Affairs is responsible for: 1) managed fund issues and regulatory development affecting financial intermediaries; 2) financial and risk assessment rules, including interpretations and exemptions; 3) audit and review of futures commission merchants (individuals, associations, partnerships, corporations, and trusts that solicit or accept orders for the purchase or sale of any commodity for future delivery on or subject to the rules of any contract market and that accept payment from or extend credit to those whose orders are accepted), clearinghouses (an adjunct to, or division of, a commodity exchange through which transactions that are executed on the floor of the exchange are settled), and sales practices; and 4) oversight of the National Futures Association (the commodity industry's first self-regulatory organization) and exchange financial and sales practice surveillance programs.

The Division of Enforcement investigates alleged violations of the CEA and CFTC regulations. When it finds violations, it may, at the commission's direction, file complaints in the CFTC's administrative courts or in the U.S. District Court. Alleged criminal violations of the CEA or violations of other federal laws involving commodity futures trading also may be referred to the U.S. Department of Justice. In fiscal year 1993, the commission instituted 11 injunctive actions, 27 administrative proceedings, and 18 statutory disqualification actions.

The Office of the General Counsel acts as legal advisor to the commission and represents the CFTC before the U.S. Circuit Court of Appeals; along with the Solicitor General, the Office of the General Counsel represents the commission before the U.S. Supreme Court in cases involving review of remedial sanctions ordered by the CFTC as a result of its own administrative proceedings and in appeals from District Court decisions involving the CFTC's injunctive and subpoena enforcement actions. The Office of the General Counsel also defends the CFTC, its members, and staff acting in their official capacities in suits brought in district courts to challenge CFTC regulations or to enjoin commission investigative or other regulatory activities. This office also acts as commission counsel in resulting appeals.

The Office of the Executive Director is responsible for overseeing the administration of commission programs. It develops an agency budget for commission consideration, provides necessary agency services, supplies and equipment, and handles personnel matters.

SEE ALSO: Commodity Exchanges

[Susan Bard Hall]

FURTHER READING:

"Commodity Futures Trading Commission Annual Report 1993." Commodity Futures Trading Commission, 1994, pp. 13, 14, 31, and 45.

"The CFTC." Commodity Futures Trading Commission, March 1993, pp. 1, 3, 4, and 5.

"Glossary," Commodity Futures Trading Commission, March 1993, pp. 11, 28, and 41.

"An Introduction to the Futures Markets." Futures Industry Association, 1982, pp. 46.

"From Beans to Bonds: A Brief Look at the Chicago Board of Trade." Chicago Board of Trade, 1992, pp. 18.

COMMON MARKET (EUROPEAN COMMUNITY)

What started off in 1957 as the European Economic Community (EEC, popularly called the Common Market) has evolved swiftly over the years into the European Community (EC), a change that implies a social as well as an economic entity. By 1999, the latest date set for the adoption of a single currency, the European Community will have given way fully to the European Union—a step along the way towards a United States of Europe.

While the dream of a united Europe is an ancient one, few in the 20th century would have thought that it could happen in their century. Never were there more compelling reasons for Europeans to establish a permanent peace as there were after World War II. However, even after the establishment of the Common Market, which did not take place until 1957, few would have foreseen the dizzying pace of European integration thereafter. Moreover, the Common Market initially consisted only of six European states (one of which was Luxembourg), not including one of the most important, Great Britain, which vowed never to join.

Indeed, the first hesitant steps towards establishing economic integration might have been delayed even longer had it not been for the United States and the Cold War. With western Europe battered and bleeding at the end of World War II, the United States came forth with its multi-billion dollar Marshall Plan aid package. The U.S. government imposed one condition on this plan, namely, that it was to be administered by Europeans in some form of joint organization. In due course arose the Organization for European Economic Cooperation (OEEC), in which Europeans formulated a common economic policy and sowed the seeds of the much more elaborate future Common Market.

The Cold War provided the impetus for the establishment of an actual framework for economic integration. Western Europe needed a common defense against Soviet aggression. There was NATO, but this did little to calm French fears, one in particular, a rearmed Germany. The West German government, on the other hand, wanted nothing more than to build trust with its wary neighbors. To remove for all time the danger of another European war, the governments of West Germany, France, Italy, Luxembourg, Belgium and the Netherlands at last agreed to integrate their coal, iron and steel industries—indispensable in war—to create the European Coal & Steel Community (ECSC), in 1952. A Council of Ministers made up of representatives from the six nations would be the decision making body, while a democratic assembly, or parliament, would review these decisions, and a European Court of Justice would settle any legal disputes.

Advocates within the ECSC of a united Europe were far from satisfied with this arrangement but worked to broaden the ECSC even further. The result was the birth of the European Economic Community, or ''Common Market.'' This came about when the respective prime ministers and foreign ministers of the six members of the ECSC signed the Treaty of Rome, establishing the EEC, in 1957. The Common Market, as it was popularly called, got its name from the pre-war French statesman Aristide Briand (1862-1932), who in 1929 introduced a scheme for a European ''common market'' before the League of Nations, the predecessor to the **United Nations**. While nothing came of it, his plan was resurrected and formed the basis of the later EEC.

Two notable features of the Treaty of Rome was its tacit acceptance of the idea of eventual political union, and the irrevocable nature of the Common Market—once a member, always a member—no nation had a right to ''secede.'' In addition, the institutions of the ECSC were adopted by the new EEC. The Treaty of Rome also set up the European Atomic Energy Community (EURATOM), to which the six nations belonged. The ECSC did not disappear, but merged with the EEC in 1969, as did EURATOM.

Headquarters of the new EEC would be located mainly in Brussels, but also in Luxembourg, as well as in Strasbourg, France. The French insisted that a condition of French membership would be the location of at least some EEC institutions in France.

The Common Market was unique in the annals of European history, and unduplicated anywhere else. The member states yielded some of their sovereignty to a collective leadership (and not the other way around) for the sake of harmony in Europe and greater prosperity. Its goals were to eliminate trade barriers among its members, to endow their citizens with equal rights, which included the elimination of internal tariffs (fully achieved in 1968) and complete freedom of movement, and to provide free transfer of their goods and funds.

While only one third of the nations of Western Europe were included initially in the Common Market, there was a procedure in place for voting in new members. The criteria for acceptance of a prospective member were (and still are): that its government be democratic (this excluded any communist or fascist form of government), and that it have a viable economy that would not constitute a strain on the economies of the other member states. The Common Market functioned smoothly at first primarily because of the still recent memories of the horrors of war. However, a crack in its outward harmony did occur in the early 1960s when the British government decided to apply for membership. Surprisingly, the application took years to approve, even though five of the six member nations were eager to strengthen the Common Market by the addition of this valuable neighbor. Great Britain's admission was stalled by France's President Charles DeGaulle (1890-1970), who was convinced that British membership would pave the way for overwhelming American influence in Europe. Only in 1970 did the French government come to regard the British as a counterweight to the economic clout of the West Germans.

Great Britain (designated as the ''United Kingdom'' in the Common Market) finally was accepted by the original six in that year. Ireland and Denmark also became new members in 1970. A decade later Greece joined, followed in 1986 by Spain and Portugal. In fewer than 20 years since the signing of the Treaty of Rome, the Common Market had doubled in size.

What the new members were joining was a complex organization that, increasingly, was being criticized as bureaucratic and inefficient. By the 1970s, the Common Market employed close to 20,000 people, and each of its tens of thousands of documents had to be translated into its nine official languages.

The basic structure of the Common Market (and of the current European Community) consists of a

European Parliament, a European Commission, the Council of Ministers, and the Court of Justice. Essentially decisions (policy) are made by the European Commission and the Council. The Commission is made up of two representatives from each large state and one from each small state. Commissioners serve four year terms. These Commissioners, in a sense, represent ''Europe,'' and owe their loyalty strictly to the Common Market (now the EC). The Council represents the individual states and usually is composed of their foreign ministers. Because ministers come and go, another entity, the Committee of Permanent Representatives (COREPER), supports and advises the Council and is made up of permanent civil servants of the Common Market.

Decisions made by these institutions are sent to the European Parliament (or ''Assembly,'' as it is designated in the Treaty of Rome), whose members are directly chosen by the electorate of each member state. In 1990, there were 518 members of the European Parliament, elected proportionally (hence, Germany has more MEPs than Luxembourg). The parliament serves only a consultative function, and can neither make laws nor raise taxes. Far from being a rubber stamp, however, it is an important forum for discussion and debate (the Commissioners appear regularly before the parliament) and has the ultimate power to dismiss the Commission or to veto the EC's budget. In addition to parliament, the Economic and Social Committee advises parliament as well as the Commission and Council. It is one third the size of parliament and consists of representatives of unions, employers, and others in the workforce.

Once parliament has been consulted and has given its advice, the decision returns to the Commission for execution. When the Common Market consisted of only six members, decisions had to be unanimous. After 1986, when the EC had enlarged to twelve members, this was changed to majority voting on most matters, except for decisions on revenues.

The Common Market's (and EC's) budget is largely derived from a tax, levied on citizens of the EC and collected by their governments, called a VAT (Value Added Tax). This tax is progressive insofar as it accords with the individual state's ability to pay. (For example Portugal would be subject to less tax than Italy).

Finally, the permanent European Court of Justice in Luxembourg is the arbiter of disputes between institutions as well as the enforcer of EC laws. Laws are based on decisions of the Commission and Council, on the major treaties signed among the member states, on international conventions and treaties, and the special agreements made when a new member is accepted into the ranks of the EC.

In 1979, the EMS or **European Monetary System** was created to establish stable exchange rates among its members. The basic unit of exchange among Common Market members was the ECU, or European Currency Unit (ECU), whose value is based on the average value of the currencies of the members of EMS.

The scope of the Common Market clearly reached beyond the elimination of **trade barriers** and open borders. There are common policies on a variety of issues that lie outside the strictly economic realm—the environment, energy, social and health issues, patents, and external (foreign) policy. In the case of relations of the Common Market to foreign (non-European) countries, these range from trade treaties to foreign assistance. By 1990, approximately 130 nations had formal diplomatic ties with the EC.

As one analyst of the European Community has observed, without the Common Market, hundreds of products would disappear from store shelves, there would be long lines at border crossings, and Europeans once again, as before World War II, would be madly competing against one another. Under the Common Market, prosperity, especially for Europe's traditionally poor countries such as Spain, Portugal, and Greece, surged remarkably, as did industrial productivity. Lastly, the Common Market brought Europeans closer together, especially the Germans and French.

Yet the Common Market, meant to usher in a single internal market, with free movement of **capital**, goods, services and people, seemed to many to fall far short of that ideal. Besides, there was no uniformity in technical and educational standards. A manufacturer of TV sets in Great Britain would have to make slightly different versions of the same TV to accommodate different voltages and meet other technical requirements, and citizens of one country desiring educational or vocational training could not automatically transfer their credits to schools outside of their country. Environment and product safety laws differed from country to country as well, and neither were all financial transactions transferable. The slowness in realizing the Treaty of Rome's single market goal led cynics to discount the future viability of the Common Market.

Others were more sanguine. Italian statesman Altiero Spinelli worked out a plan in the 1970s for a single European Community plan that was the model for the one eventually adopted in 1986. The Single Market Act became law that year after government leaders of the majority of Common Market states had sent the European Commission a proposal to speed up the attainment of a single internal market. The plan, which called for the completion of a single internal market by January 1, 1993, would make tiny western

Europe the largest and richest free trade zone in the world. From 1986 onwards, the Common Market gave way, more precisely, to the European Community, the ultimate goal of the Treaty of Rome.

The institutions would remain the same. By 1993, however, it was expected that there would be full freedom of movement of goods, people, and products and complete transferability of financial transactions within the twelve EC states. Meanwhile, communism had fallen in eastern Europe and Russia, and eastern Germany had swiftly united with its western half. This opened the possibility of broadening the EC beyond its twelve members: Finland no longer would be compelled to stay out because of Soviet objections, while Austria did not have to adhere to its Soviet imposed policy of official neutrality. It also raised the prospect—almost unimaginable to many—that eastern Europe might join a European community as well. As strange as this appeared, the Common Market itself had taken root in a prosperous Europe only a dozen years after that continent's most catastrophic war.

In fact, the most stable of the eastern European states—the Czech republic, Slovakia, Poland, and Hungary—lost little time in signaling to the EC that they would begin to transform themselves into a free trade zone as a first step in their eventual goal of inclusion in the EC. Consequently, in December, 1992, they signed the Central European Free Trade Agreement (CEFTA), which created a semblance of a common market in eastern Europe (without the institutional trappings).

This dramatic happening was already being overshadowed by yet another milestone, perhaps the biggest, in the history of the EC: the **Maastricht Treaty** on European Union. This came about as a result of a summit held in the Dutch city of Maastricht in December, 1991.

With the goal of a free internal market just two years away from being realized, Chancellor Helmut Kohl of Germany and President Francois Mitterand of France took the initiative to propose laying the groundwork for a union that would go far beyond full economic integration.

The European Union that the Maastricht Treaty envisaged was not yet a political union, but only the framework for one. At the heart of the treaty was an article making ''subsidiarity'' a principle of the new Union: namely, member states would voluntarily yield to a central authority those functions which they could not perform as well on their own. This would entail a uniform monetary policy, a common currency (the ECU), a common foreign policy, as well as common policies on most police and justice matters.

These radical changes required getting used to the idea of a central bank and to an enhanced central authority, although this authority would reside in the collective entities of the European Commission and the Council. To calm fears of some menacing new government gaining control over sovereign states, the Maastricht Treaty extended the powers of the European Parliament.

Although all of these changes were foreseen as far back as the 1957 Rome Treaty, they were so radical, and followed so closely on the heels of Europe's full economic integration, that the Maastricht Treaty would engender much rancorous debate and friction each time it was put before the voters of an EC state. In those countries that accepted the Treaty, the European Union would go into effect on November 1, 1993. A common European currency would take longer to implement, however. The date would fall one month short of the establishment of the long awaited single internal market called for by the act of 1986.

By October 29, 1992, one day before the formal emergence of the European Union, it was decided to locate the future European Monetary Institute in Frankfurt, Germany, presaging Europe's adoption of a single currency. When this is in place, scheduled to occur no later than 1999, it will make western Europe the wealthiest area on earth, with an annual gross domestic product that will be in the neighborhood of $7 trillion. Unwilling to have the full European Union catch it unprepared, the United States intensified its efforts to create a regional trade block that could compete meaningfully with the European giant. The result was the signing of the **North American Free Trade Agreement (NAFTA)**, ushering in the largest free trade zone in the world in 1994, a few years short of the date for the consummation of the Maastricht Treaty.

There was much controversy and opposition to the Maastricht Treaty, in Great Britain; Denmark rejected it the first time around but relented the second time after special concessions were made; and Switzerland soundly defeated it. Despite all this, a total of sixteen European nations have ratified the Treaty: the 12 EC members as well as Austria, Finland, Norway, and Sweden. Nowadays, no one is surprised any longer that a nation, such as economically depressed Bulgaria, is planning to apply for membership one day. It is taken for granted that CEFTA will join in the early 21st century. Even the prospect of Russia becoming a member, however long that may take, is not even so remote.

If the United States of Europe does take place, it will be a greater achievement than the creation of the U.S.A., given the multitude of languages and cultures and their disparate and mutually hostile histories. Economic necessity is only one factor explaining the phenomenon of a previously divisive Europe forming a political union. Rather, it is clear that fear of future war has become, as it were, inbred, and hence, the desire for permanent peace is being passed down from generation to generation.

[Sina Dubovoy]

FURTHER READING:

Goodman, S.F. *The European Community*. St.Martin's Press, 1990.

van Ham, Peter. *The European Community, Eastern Europe and European Unity: Discord, Collaboration, and Integration Since 1947*. St. Martin's Press, 1993.

The Origins and Development of the European Community. Leicester University, 1992. Distributed in the U.S. by St. Martin's Press, 1992.

Urwin, Derek W. *The Community of Europe: A History of European Integration Since 1945*. 2nd ed. Longman, 1995.

Williams, Allan M. *The European Community: The Contradictions of Integration*. B. Blackwell, 1991.

COMMON STOCK

Common stock represents basic ownership of a corporation, whether a small privately owned company with a few shares held by a single owner and perhaps a few associates, or a giant publicly-traded corporation with hundreds of thousands of stockholders.

The holders of common stock rank behind all creditors (bondholders, **banks**, other lenders) as well as any holders of **preferred stock** in their claims on the current income of the company and, in case of liquidation, to whatever resources remain. In essence, these senior holders must be paid their due before the common stockholders are entitled to anything. By the same token, once these senior claims are met, the entire income and increase in the value of the company accrues for the benefit of the common stockholders.

Common stock is divided into shares, each representing a proportionate part of the total common stock ownership. The corporate charter or bylaws fixes the number of shares that are authorized for issue. The issued shares are those that have actually been sold to stockholders or otherwise distributed in return for value—for acquisitions, options or grants to employees, stock dividends to stockholders, etc. Outstanding shares are those currently in the hands of stockholders. The difference between the number of issued and outstanding shares is usually accounted for by treasury stock—shares reacquired by the company through market purchases or special solicitations and held in the company's treasury. This stock is then available for reissue in employee stock plans, acquisitions, conversion of convertible **bonds** or preferred stocks, or other corporate operations. While in the treasury, such stock is not entitled to dividends, has no voting rights, and is not counted in the computation of earnings per share. For practical purposes, when looking at a company's capitalization, what counts is the number of outstanding shares.

Sometimes the common stock is divided into separate classes. Usually one class has greater (or even exclusive) voting power, often with the aim of keeping control within a founding family. In return, some companies may grant their non-voting common stockholders the right to receive larger dividends.

Stocks have a par value (or, if the company chooses to issue no-par stock, a stated value). In modern times, this is strictly an **accounting** formality (accountants need a dollar amount at which each share is entered on the company's books) and has no relation whatever to the actual value of the stock.

Since the common stock, as a class, has claim to all a company's resources after senior claims are met, stockholders' **equity** (the value allocated to the stockholdings on the company's books) consists of the total **assets** shown on the company's **balance sheet**, less all the lliabilities. This equity may be shown in the financial statement as the sum of the par value of the stock, capital surplus (the amount paid for newly issued stock above that nominal par value), and retained earnings (sometimes called earned surplus). The total stockholders' equity is divided by the number of shares outstanding to arrive at the book value per share—the theoretical value of the net assets behind each share on the books of the company.

While book value can be one useful guide in assessing a company's shares, it is by no means a reliable measure of a stock's investment worth, and may bear little relation to the stock's price on the stock market. The assets used in the book value calculations may be worth more or less in the company's operations than the value on the books (e.g., a property may be worth far more than its ancient acquisition price or a plant may be obsolete), and in any case it's the company's future profitability that is most important in establishing investor value. And besides, investors (including expert financial analysts) may be wrong in their expectations of the future. From a practical standpoint, a stock at any point in time is worth what a buyer in the marketplace is willing to pay for it.

Because, by their nature, common shares carry all the risks as well as potential rewards of ownership, they tend to fluctuate considerably more than other investment instruments such as good-quality bonds and preferred stocks. However, a large number of investment studies show that over the long run common stocks as a whole offer a higher investment return than other investment categories and have demonstrated the greatest ability to outpace **inflation** over the decades. Thus, most experts agree that any long-term investment plan (especially for **retirement**) should rely heavily, but not exclusively, on common stocks.

[Henry R. Hecht]

FURTHER READING:

Engel, Louis and Henry Hecht. *How to Buy Stocks*. Little Brown & Co.

Teweles, Richard and Edward Bradley. *The Stock Market*. John Wiley & Sons.

COMMUNICATION SYSTEMS

Communication systems can be defined here as the process, both formal and informal, by which information is passed up, down, and across the network of managers and employees in a business. Information will be defined as any sort of communication, written or verbal, which has an impact on the way business is conducted.

There is no formal history of business communication systems. It has existed in some form since the first business owner hired the first employees and issued the first instructions. Those instructions were the first official "employee communications," an action taken by management to make sure the employee knew what management expected of him or her. Once the business owner hired enough employees to create a staff, they reacted to those management mandates by creating the first form of informal company communications, "the grapevine."

This informal grapevine between and among top management, middle management, line management, and employees has always been, and no doubt always will be, part of the process of doing business.

COMMUNICATIONS AS A FUNCTION OF MANAGEMENT

During the early part of the history of corporate America, which stretches back little more than 150 years, American management operated as strict "top down communications" companies. Whatever the majority owners of the company said was the law. If the company had a senior management committee, strategies for doing everything from selling product to dealing with employees would be discussed behind closed doors. Once those decisions were made by managers, lower levels of management were asked to put those decisions into effect. Employees had little input. They did as they were told or found work elsewhere.

Such management attitudes, particularly when they applied to worker safety issues in such places as coal and steel mines, led to the growth of **labor unions**. If nothing else, unions had the power in many cases to slow or shut down production until management at least listened to demands.

In reaction to union demands, corporations eventually set up communication systems where rank and file members could speak their minds through union representatives. While forced to create the systems by unions, corporate managers have realized over the past 20-30 years that employees are not the mindless drones that the managers of the early part of this century believed them to be. When presented the opportunity to help the company solve problems, many employees have jumped at the chance. This is called "bottom-up communication."

Most corporations now encourage employees to take an active part in their company. Employees who notice ways to improve production lines are encouraged, and usually rewarded, for passing those ideas on to managers. Employees who submit ideas that withstand intense study can be rewarded with a percentage of the savings to the company. Employees who are harassed on the job are strongly encouraged to report such harassment as far up the chain of management as necessary to stop it. Regular employee meetings are held where the lowest level employee can stand up and ask the **CEO** a direct question with the full expectation that a direct answer will be offered in return.

Top management also has a method of monitoring how the company is running while meeting employees and managers halfway. Sometimes called "management by walking around," this method of communication and management calls for top managers to get out and see what is happening at the level where work is done. Instead of reading reports from subordinates, the CEO visits the factories or service centers, observes line managers' employees on the job, and asks their opinions. Although the practice seems to be both praised and denigrated regularly by business management experts, this form of communications keeps the boss in touch.

FORMS OF CORPORATE COMMUNICATIONS

Although the content of corporate communications within the organization has remained fairly constant through the years, technology has improved the way management and employees keep in touch with each other.

Almost all companies of any size have some regular method of keeping in touch with employees through bulletin boards, newsletters, or magazines. Larger, more technically proficient and geographically spread out companies may also use corporate produced television shows, or copy-only messages transmitted by closed circuit television. Some companies distribute **electronic mail** (E-mail) newsletters or messages, which can be instantly transmitted and placed in all the **computers** wired into the company's network.

These forms of communications always get the approval of top management. Many newsletters, magazines and television shows leave no doubt about this by including a ''message from the president'' column near the front of the publication or with an early appearance.

Bulletin boards are the oldest form of corporate communications. In the early days of businesses, bulletin boards were frequently the only communication that management might have with employees. Everything from longer hours demands to the announcement of new plant openings would be announced on the boards. Today, bulletin boards are not always found in businesses. Some companies use them for nothing more important than posting legal requirements such as wage and hour rates. Other companies try to make bulletin boards a force for employee recognition and information. The challenge all companies have with bulletin boards is that they fade in the consciousness of employees who get used to seeing them every day. Unless the boards' information is changed regularly and presented in an attractive way, employees can ignore it.

Newsletters and magazines try to address the inability of management to speak to each employee. Written communication explains management policies, announces new products, answers questions, and provides each employee with a reminder of what the company is all about. The downside of written communication is that it is a slow and cumbersome process.

That is one of the reasons why closed-circuit, satellite, and videotape-based television have become popular with some corporations. Employees are used to watching television. Some corporations have spent millions of dollars in developing a television presence that would be difficult to distinguish from the quality produced by regular television networks, an approach that can quickly grab the attention of employees. Television is also immediate. A CEO who has to make an emergency announcement to employees can do so within minutes' notice while a newsletter or magazine takes weeks to produce.

The latest and fastest growing method of corporate communications is electronic mail. E-mail is instantaneous and is available to anyone with a computer terminal. An employee who has a great idea, but who is afraid a superior may take credit for it, can send the CEO a message on the corporation's computer system. There is no guarantee that the CEO has not set up a program to filter out such E-mail messages from employees, but most report that they have not. Some corporations even encourage their computer-literate customers to E-mail comments and complaints directly to the people at the top.

Memos and reports are the life blood of many corporations. They frequently are the only way some business gets done. The boss either approves or disapproves something based on what a sheaf of memos and stack of reports recommend. Live presentations are sometimes conducted to put life in what the reports have concluded.

The key to making memos and reports effective is to make them both readable and pertinent to the entire company. A memo from the head of **accounting** outlining procedure changes may be useless to the CEO who has a **marketing** background unless the memo plainly spells out why accounting changes will improve the company's operations.

Bureaucratic language, pompous phrasing, technical jargon, departmental protection, and incorrect conclusions all contribute to unclear communication within the corporation. One management book author estimates that up to 70 percent of business communications between managers misses the mark.

Informal methods of communication, such as rumors and ''the company grapevine,'' can be out of the company's control. The grapevine is a bottom-up form of communication as employees try to understand what is happening around them when there is no official word from management. When management is silent, employees fill the void with verbal guesses about what is happening. It may start when the graveyard shift's loading-dock workers are laid off because better production scheduling eliminates their jobs. The second shift loaders may interpret the loss of that shift's jobs as an economic signal that the company is in trouble. A telephone receptionist who fields calls for senior managers from competitors might conclude that the company is negotiating to buy out, or be bought out. She passes the word that something big is up. Junior managers who notice out of town consultants nosing around may smell ''restructuring'' in the wind.

There is no way the grapevine can be stopped. It can only be influenced. When dealing with questions that cannot, or should not, be answered, senior managers should take the initiative before negative rumors get started. If it is true and obvious to employees that the company will soon undergo major changes, tell them it will. Do not lie. Do not threaten people to stop the rumors. Tell the employees that management recognizes they have legitimate concerns, which will be addressed when possible. If official talk would damage the company, make that clear to the employees. Let them know that damaging the company by loose talk is not in anyone's interest.

ROADBLOCKS TO COMMUNICATIONS

Various writers on management topics have addressed the problems of communicating within an organization. What follows is a short compilation of obstacles frequently encountered.

EXPECTATIONS AND PERCEPTIONS. Old school managers of employees sometimes do not believe that employees can contribute anything useful to the operation of a company other than their unquestioning labor. These managers separate "**management**" from "employees" with the idea that they will tell employees what to do. They don't want any questioning or backtalk. Employees, operating from the same circumstances, usually see little stake for themselves in a company in which they are not personally involved.

SELECTIVITY. Most people pick and choose what they actually retain when someone is talking. Any number of factors can cause this, ranging from the respect a person has for the speaker to what the speaker is saying and how it relates to what the employee is doing. For example, line employees might not pay too much attention to a hated supervisor who stands up in a general meeting to address quality problems of components that are delivered to the line. They may listen more attentively to a respected supervisor who urges them to shut down the line and remove the bad parts before they are installed so a poor quality product does not reflect on them.

DISTRACTIONS. Ringing phones, scheduled meetings, and unfinished reports all contribute to the problem of hurried and sometimes misunderstood communications. Careful listening and understanding takes dedication. Time must be put aside for communication.

KEYS TO GOOD COMMUNICATIONS

All forms of communication, even the lack of it, can have an impact. A stiffly-worded, lawyerly-sounding memo to employees telling them not to talk to the press about impending litigation could be interpreted as admitting that the company did something wrong. Management's repeated "no comments" to employees and the press on rumored merger talks may launch dozens of brush fire discussions about company suitors, how much the company will sell for, and how many employees will be laid off.

Communicate all the time. Think twice before eliminating the company newsletter as a cost saving measure. Keep the bulletin board up-to-date. Keep holding meetings in which employees can ask questions of management.

Make communication easy and understandable. Management terms and jargon, stiff or flowery language may contribute to the impression among employees that management is talking down to them.

Obtain and analyze feedback. What do employees think of management's communications efforts? Do they believe what managementt says? Do they want more information? Are some methods more effective than others? How quickly can management adjust its efforts to make the communication better?

Corporate communications systems are nothing new. In the final analysis, they can be reduced to two elements: explanation and reaction to that explanation.

[Clint Johnson]

FURTHER READING:

Townsend, Robert. *Up the Organization.* Alfred E. Knopf, 1984.

COMMUNISM

SEE: Socialism & Communism

COMPARABLE WORTH

Comparable worth is an extremely controversial type of employment d1iscrimination claim, a claim which has been argued in many cases but which has been accepted by few courts. The rationale behind comparable worth claims is an assumption that the continuing disparity between men's wages and women's wages in the job market is the result of an illegal and discriminatory view of the value of any work traditionally done by females.

Women began filing comparable worth lawsuits as early as the 1970s, claiming that unequal wage structures between similar male-dominated and female-dominated positions were a violation of Title VII of the Civil Rights Act of 1964. Courts were reluctant to accept this new theory and many decided that, like the Equal Pay Act of 1963 passed by Congress in 1963, Title VII only allowed a claim if the jobs with unequal pay scales required absolutely equal skill, effort, and responsibility, and were performed under similar working conditions.

In 1981, the Supreme Court in *County of Washington, Oregon v. Gunther* decided the issue of whether the Equal Pay Act and Title VII necessarily covered the same type of situation. The highest court found that the "equal" restriction of the Equal Pay Act was not necessarily a requirement in a Title VII claim. It stated in the *Gunther* case that employees could be successful in a lawsuit alleging unequal pay between men and women at the same place of employment if they could prove that the disparity was the result of illegal discrimination, even if the jobs were not considered "equal."

The employer in the *Gunther* case had already done its own comparable worth survey and had found that the two positions at issue were similar, yet it had set the pay scale for female guards in the female section of the county jail lower than that of the male guards in the male section. The survey had also concluded that there was no differentiation warranted by outside market forces or the worth of the jobs. Therefore, the women claimed in the *Gunther* case that the only reason for the lower pay was a biased view by the county that women should be paid less than men. This, they contended, was illegal gender discrimination in violation of Title VII's requirement that there be no compensation differences based on sex.

The U.S. Supreme Court agreed with the female guards that Title VII allowed a lawsuit in their situation where jobs which were similar were paid on disparate pay scales, but it also specifically stated this case should be differentiated from a comparable worth claim. In *Gunther*, the employer had already evaluated the worth of the positions, and the court was not being asked to "make its own subjective assessment of the value of the male and female guard jobs, or to attempt by statistical technique or other method to quantify the effect of sex discrimination on the wage rates."

Comparable worth claims, in fact, do require a court to make a subjective assessment of the worth of a job to an employer. Because this is a difficult determination and also because of the many potential defenses to an unequal pay scale, even if jobs are judged "comparable," most courts will not uphold a comparable worth claim.

The *Gunther* opinion continues to be debated. Some claim that the opinion merely allowed a lawsuit in a case where the jobs at issue did not fit the Equal Pay Act's definition of "equal." Proponents of the theory of comparable worth continue to claim that even though *Gunther* was not a comparable worth claim itself, it opened the door to such suits by allowing Title VII to cover more situations than the Equal Pay Act.

One of the major proponents of a comparable worth theory of discrimination is the highly controversial commentator Ruth Blumrosen. As one court summarized her theory:

> "[J]ob segregation and wage discrimination are intimately related; whenever there is job segregation, the same forces that determine that certain jobs will be reserved for women or minorities determine that the economic value of such jobs is low; studies undertaken in the fields of history, anthropology, economics, and sociology demonstrate that the

valuation of segregated jobs has been influenced by the fact that these jobs are held by disfavored groups; therefore in a lawsuit, minorities or women who can demonstrate that they occupy traditionally segregated jobs will have made a prima facie showing that the wage rates for those jobs are discriminatorily depressed, so that the burden is on the defendant employer to demonstrate or articulate the reasons why the rate is not influenced by discriminatory factors."

In short, Ms. Blumrosen argues that the historically-documented devaluation of the worth of any work done by women should be adequate evidence to make out a Title VII case of discrimination if women in jobs traditionally done by women prove that they earn less than the men at a place of employment. It would then be up to the employer to prove that discriminatory practices did not cause the difference in wages. This, of course, represents a very wide view of comparable worth claims, one which courts, to date, merely quote and then reject.

Most comparable worth claims do not rely on the theory as articulated by Ms. Blumrosen but rather involve the presentation of extensive evidence that the jobs being compared are substantially "similar," although not "equal." The women bringing these lawsuits show comparisons between their predominantly female-held jobs and a comparable male-dominated position. This comparison usually includes an analysis of the skills required for the jobs, responsibilities of the employees in each of the two positions, effort required to succeed in the jobs, and the relative working conditions. This evidence is used to prove that the only reason which can be deduced for the difference in pay is that discrimination is occurring because of the gender of the employees in the lower paying positions. This, the parties bringing the lawsuit contend, violates Title VII.

Courts are very reluctant to determine whether skills, responsibility, effort, and working conditions are similar in two jobs, because it is a decision which can be seen, in part, as somewhat subjective. This subjectivity, according to some judges, requires policy choices, which they contend is the responsibility of legislatures, not courts. In addition, even if there is a finding that all four criteria *are* similar, there are many other factors which courts accept as legal rationales for disparate pay structures. A real-case example of a comparable worth lawsuit helps in understanding what is involved in comparisons, what the potential defenses are, and why courts are reluctant to get involved.

In *Briggs v. City of Madison*, a group of public health nurses filed a comparable worth lawsuit. This suit claimed that the nurses pay structure violated Title VII because they were being paid substantially less than sanitarians who also worked for the City of Madison, Wisconsin Department of Public Health. The public health nurses performed a variety of nursing, education, and enforcement duties and had extensive responsibilities related to health problems in the City of Madison. The sanitarians were largely involved in waste removal programs, including inspections, responding to complaints, and reviewing of commercial plans. The nurses presented a great deal of evidence which they claimed showed that the two jobs were substantially similar, yet the pay in their female-dominated position averaged 85.64 percent of the male-dominated sanitarians' salary.

The judge in the *Briggs* case reviewed the evidence presented by the nurses and agreed that the two jobs were similar under the criteria usually used to evaluate positions. The pre-hiring requirements were slightly higher for the nurses than for the sanitarians. Both jobs required a college degree, although the nursing position required specialized training. In addition, nurses had to be certified, while sanitarians did not. People in both positions were exposed to a variety of similar work assignments. Nurses were somewhat more involved in education programs than were sanitarians. The court concluded that both positions required a great deal of tact and an ability to relate well to the public, although sanitarians had more coercive power than the public health nurses. Nurses also had the additional problem of often dealing with people they did not know who had difficulty communicating due to language, cultural, mental, or emotional impediments. Nurses often supervised interns, which was not a requirement for the sanitarians, but both positions allowed workers to work regular daytime hours, with little required overtime. In addition, reporting requirements, assessment procedures, time spent walking and standing, and travel requirements were all substantially similar for both jobs. In short, the court concluded that these were jobs of comparable worth, yet the nurses still lost the lawsuit.

The public health nurses in the *Briggs* case lost because the city presented one of the many rationales which courts allow to discredit an otherwise meritorious comparable worth claim. The City of Madison Department of Public Health claimed that the sanitarians were paid more because the market value of these positions was higher; i.e., all employers paid sanitarians more than public health nurses. Thus, it was market forces which set the job pay rates and, as a consequence, higher pay was needed to attract and recruit people to the sanitarian job. Such an incentive was not required in the public health nurse position, and the market reflected this by uniformly paying nurses less.

This market defense has been argued and used extensively in comparable worth situations. Employers claim that their pay scales are the result of the market and are, thus, not illegal. Most courts agree with this rationale, but there continue to be critics of this defense. These critics claim that the market merely reflects the biases and stereotypes of the value of women's work and, thus, it should not be allowed as an excuse for paying lesser wages to women performing similar jobs to men. In fact, they note that the defense has been rejected in Equal Pay Act cases and that Title VII was specifically designed to eliminate practices which cause a discriminatory effect. Basing pay on market trends does, in fact, have a discriminatory effect. In addition, the critics also argue that many discriminatory practices, while arguably more efficient than non-discriminatory actions, are not allowed by Title VII. Equality, not efficiency, is required by the federal law.

While some courts may agree that the market does reflect stereotyping and the devaluation of women's work, they still do not readily accept that it should not be allowed as a defense to a comparable worth claim. The judges almost unanimously agree that Title VII was designed to deal with discrimination by employers, not socially discriminatory situations and, if the law is to be expanded to cover such problems, it must be done by a legislature. Legislatures traditionally make policy choices in our system of government, the judges argue, and a requirement that employers not use market trends to set wages would be a policy decision.

Several other rationales are also put forward for the disparity in women's wages which are usually accepted as defenses in comparable worth cases. One of these, closely related to the market defense, is a rationale known as "occupational crowding." For every position in a female-dominated field there are far more women available than are males for most jobs in male-dominated fields. Men, in fact, have traditionally had more career choices than women and, even today, women gravitate toward certain types of jobs more than others. Thus, the rationale continues, the scarcity of men is what sets the job pay rates, not the mere fact that men are traditionally in these positions. Critics argue that women, historically and even today, are channeled into fewer careers than men by social pressures, educational biases, male-dominated workplaces which are not conducive to women's success, harassment when they do enter male strongholds, and other discriminatory practices. Thus, the claim is made that the fact that women, realistically, have fewer choices for career options, should not be allowed as a rationale for paying them less in the positions which they do hold.

Other rationales have also been forwarded by businesses for the disparate pay between women, rationales which the companies claim are not discriminatory. Because women still usually find themselves having the primary responsibility for children and home work, they can not devote the same time and effort to advancing in the workplace and succeeding to higher levels and pay scales. These dual roles, according to some who defend the lower pay rates, is the reason for discrepancies, not a bias against women or women's work. In addition, some claim that women leave the work world for varying amounts of time during childbearing years which results in breaks in their career path and, thus, lesser pay scales than the men of the same age.

While most comparable worth claims have been rejected by the courts, women and women's groups continue to bring intermittent claims under Title VII, asking judges to find that the pay rates at certain places of employment are discriminatory. Those that are currently successful are ones in which the employer, having done a comparable worth study of its own, did not adhere to the findings of the study in setting the pay scales. Cases which require the court to undertake a comparable worth analysis are not currently very successful but, with the law constantly changing and differing views being offered as to the role of anti-discrimination laws, it is not inconceivable that the future might change this situation. The U.S. Supreme Court has not specifically rejected comparable worth as a viable cause of action and, until they do, claims will continue to be filed.

SEE ALSO: Civil Rights Act of 1991; Equal Employment Opportunity Commission (EEOC)

[Anne Levy]

FURTHER READING:

Levin, Michael. "Comparable Worth: The Feminist Road to Socialism," *Commentary*. September, 1984.

"Equal Pay, Comparable Work, and Job Evaluation," 90 *Yale Law Journal* 657. 1981.

Nelson, Opton & Wilson. "Wage Discrimination and the 'Comparable Worth' Theory in Perspective," 13 *University of Michigan Journal of Law Reform* 231. 1980.

Blumrosen, Ruth. "Wage Discrimination, Job Segregation and Title VII of the Civil Rights Act of 1964," 12 *University of Michigan Journal of Law Reform* 397. 1979.

COMPENSATION ADMINISTRATION

Compensation administration is a segment of **human resource management** focusing on planning, organizing, and controlling the direct and indirect payments made to employees for the work they perform or the services they render. The ultimate objectives of compensation administration are: efficient maintenance of a productive workforce; equitable pay; and compliance with federal state, and local regulations.

On its surface, compensation administration appears a rather simple proposition: employees work, employers pay them. While this facile equation was used for centuries of pay relationships, the social, economic, and political forces that came to bear on twentieth century businesses impelled the evolution of an entire profession. Management of pay has virtually come full-circle over the course of its relatively brief history. It started in the early twentieth century as the very subjective, internal purview of business owners and managers. The field was professionalized and highly standardized during the mid-twentieth century. Economic and social pressures of the 1980s and 1990s have since driven a less formulaic, more multidisciplinary approach to compensation management.

HISTORY

Rudimentary pay management has existed as long as there have been employers and employees. Owners of typically small, pre-industrial businesses commonly weighed their ability to pay against employee responsibilities and contributions to determine compensation. The rapid development of corporations, multiplication of administrative hierarchies, and specialization of jobs in the twentieth century removed owners from the day-to-day evaluation of jobs. Unionization brought a measure of standardization to wage labor, but neither the private sector nor the federal government began to study systematic job evaluation until after World War I. The federal government spearheaded the development of formal compensation administration with the passage of the Federal Classification Act of 1923, which ranked government jobs and set salary levels accordingly.

Milton L. Rock, author of *The Compensation Handbook*, has credited human resource professional Edward N. Hay with "laying the foundation for the modern era of salary administration." Hay began his work in the late 1930s, when his employer, a bank, asked him to create a system of pay "blind to interpersonal relations, race, creed, or gender." He embarked on the assignment by analyzing jobs—their duties, responsibilities, skills, education levels, etc.—and composing descriptions based on his findings. Hay operated on the theory that "something that can be measured has value while something that can't be measured has none." Accordingly, this pioneer devised guide charts that systematically evaluated and ranked jobs according to several variables: know-how, accountability, working conditions, physical effort, and problem solving. The guide charts that bore his name would become the world's single most widely used job evaluation technique. By 1943, when Hay founded his trendsetting consulting practice, organizations throughout America (including the federal government) had acknowledged the need for a consistent salary-administration system that would facilitate job evaluation, ranking, and pricing.

During the period between the world wars, the American Management Association began to compile descriptions of non union (especially clerical and blue-collar) jobs. Beginning in the mid-1930s, the federal government's Employment Service enlisted its field offices throughout the country to describe and codify jobs. The first edition of the resulting *Dictionary of Occupational Titles* (DOT), published in 1939, contained about 17,500 summary definitions presented alphabetically by title. Blocks of jobs were assigned 5- or 6-digit codes that classified them in one of 550 occupational groups and indicated whether the positions were skilled, semi skilled, or unskilled. This erratically published compendium became the ''bible'' of the emerging compensation profession. It provided a foundation for systematic pay plans by promoting internal classifications of jobs and later, external comparisons of jobs across industries.

Mobilization of the domestic economy for World War II significantly advanced the compensation discipline, both indirectly and directly. The war's technological advances helped add 3500 new occupations in the plastics, paper and pulp, and radio manufacturing industries to the economy, and to the second edition of the *Dictionary of Occupational Titles*. The war era also saw the imposition of governmental wage and price controls and guidelines. During the ''freeze,'' only companies with rational job evaluation plans could justify upward pay and benefit adjustments. This requirement helped coerce some recalcitrant corporations into formulating systematic pay plans. Since the controls on wages were more stringent than those on benefits, unions lobbied for increased benefits and employers gladly capitulated. At the time, generous packages of benefits were non taxable and cost-effective to employers. Now common benefits like **pension plans**, supplementary **unemployment**, extended vacations, and guaranteed wages were added to the roster of statutory benefits that had included Social Security (federal), **workers' compensation**, and **unemployment compensation**. Over the years, aggressive unions negotiated an astonishing array of benefits, the administration of which fell to compensation managers.

Most companies limited their pay analysis efforts internally until after the war. During the 1950s, Hay and other human resource professionals joined the federal government in broader examinations of compensation. The introduction of computers quickly and continuously simplified and advanced the data collection, quantification, and storage processes. The resulting databases have enabled survey analysts to thoroughly study relationships within and among corporations, industries, and geographic regions.

Sunshine laws ratified in the 1970s combined with equal pay for equal work initiatives began to usher in a new era for the compensation profession, as employees demanded explanations of the rationale behind job assignments, remuneration, and opportunities, as well as employers' overall capacity to pay. Over the course of the decade, pay administration evolved into a thoroughly scientific and bureaucratic method, with its own technologies and rationalization methods.

The profession grew so systematized, in fact, that its precepts were considered nearly as inviolate as natural law until the early 1990s. At that time, corporate downsizing, global competition, and new management schemes compelled compensation managers to be more adaptive to the changing needs of employers and employees. These shifts went to the heart of wage and salary administration: job descriptions. As companies asked their employees to use their competencies and skills to contribute to results in several ways, rather than just one easily described way, the compensation administrator's tasks of job description and comparison have grown more difficult and variable. One observer of these changes has characterized compensation managers in this environment as ''engineers'' who apply established techniques as situationally warranted. The basics of the discipline still apply, but they are adapted to each corporate culture.

BASIC PRINCIPLES

Given the fact that labor costs are a significant part of operating expense of any American business, compensation management is a vital segment of overall corporate management and strategy. The discipline reflects and sometimes shapes the economic, social, and political environments in which businesses operate.

Compensation must reinforce the organization's strategic conditions. Intensifying competition in many industries has brought about shifts in overall corporate strategies and effected changes in compensation. In the 1990s, Ford Motor Co. decided to emphasize customer service as part of its marketing strategy. In order to encourage dealerships to shift their focus as well, Ford had to change its incentive program. Whereas incentives had previously been based strictly on sales, they began to relate to more customer-service oriented goals.

Environmental and regulatory factors have also become very practical considerations of compensation management. The increasing diversity of the workforce, for example, is one significant trend. Compensation managers at E.I. du Pont de Nemours & Co., for example, have promoted **child care**, flexible work schedules, career breaks, and other progressive benefits in response to the needs of increasing numbers of women in its workforce. Compensation management has been strongly influenced by regulatory pressures. From state and local payroll taxes, to minimum wage legislation, workers' compensation, **child labor** laws, **equal opportunity** mandates, and unemployment and social security requirements, pay administrators wrangle with a daunting array of legal pressures. In all likelihood, the litany of regulations will continue to grow. In the early 1990s, for example, outrage over excessive executive pay at publicly owned companies prompted the Securities and Exchange Commission to require that businesses disclose total executive pay and how that compensation relates to performance.

Writing for *HR Focus* in 1992, Mircea Manicatide noted that "An organization's approach to compensation needs to be flexible enough to reflect the different needs of the individual and the organization; joint investments in ongoing training; the ebb and flow of an employee's contributions without creating expectations of permanence, and each employee's changing needs over time."

The compensation professional uses an impressive (and sometimes abstract) array of tools and techniques to relate these real world concerns to pay.

MODERN COMPENSATION ADMINISTRATION

Modern compensation administration encompasses the creation and management of a pay system designed to meet three basic, interrelated objectives: internal consistency, external competitiveness, and individual employee equity. Compensation professionals balance these goals according to individual corporations' needs, keeping in mind the ultimate objectives of compensation administration—efficiency, equity, and compliance.

INTERNAL CONSISTENCY. Compensation managers seek to achieve internal equity and consistency—rationalizing pay within a single organization from the **chief executive officer** on down—through the analysis, description, evaluation, and structure of jobs. Job analysis examines the discrete functions in an operation, then describes each one. The resulting narrative job description lists duties and responsibilities and the requisite training and knowledge.

The *Dictionary of Occupational Titles* is essentially a compendium of standardized, codified job descriptions. The series has grown evermore scientific over the course of the three volumes and several supplements published since 1950. By 1991, each of its over 25,000 entries was composed of seven parts: occupational code, number occupational title, industry designation, alternate titles (if applicable), narrative definition, undefined related titles, and definition trailer. Each entry's unique nine-digit occupational code number is a shorthand classification made up three sets of numbers.

The first three digits refer to a particular occupational group. The second set of numerals indicates worker functions and/or skills. The last three numbers in an occupational code distinguish a particular occupation from all others, thereby facilitating computer analysis. The occupational title is the name most commonly used to describe a given function. The industry designation distinguishes between two or more occupations with identical titles but industry-specific duties. Some jobs receive the self-explanatory designation "any industry." Alternate titles assist users with cross-referencing. The narrative description of an occupation succinctly summarizes the entire job. It is followed by a list of titles related to the job, but not described in the DOT. The definition trailer codifies particular attributes and "auxiliary profile data."

Compensation managers use descriptions such as those in the *DOT* to evaluate or compare jobs within an organization, then rank the occupations to create a job structure. There are four primary methods of job (not employee) evaluation. Job ranking and job classification are subjective, nonquantitative techniques commonly used by civil employers and small companies. Quantitative methods such as the point system and the factor comparison system are considered more scientific, but in practice often arrive at the same conclusions as the former two methods. Ranking merely orders job descriptions from highest to lowest based on their value or contribution. Two types of ranking are commonly used: alternation ranking and paired comparison. Alternation ranking begins with determination of the most and least valuable jobs, then proceeds to the next most valued and next least valued, in turn, until all the jobs have been organized. The paired comparison technique compares all possible pairs of jobs under study, usually using a **matrix**. Each job is compared to all the rest in turn. A job's overall ranking depends on the total number of times it is deemed higher in each pairing. The classification method involves categorizing job descriptions into a series of classes or grades that encompass the total range of functions. The federal government's Office of Personnel Management uses an 18-grade classification system known as the "General Schedule." **Ranking** and classification are relatively simple to understand and inexpensive to initiate, but can be more difficult to justify and defend than the quantitative systems.

Though more complicated and costly to set up, the quantitative point system is the most widely-used method of job analysis, because once established, it is easy to administer. It analyzes weighted factors such as skills, effort, responsibility, and working conditions, assigns numerical values appropriate to each individual job, then adds up each position's score. The resulting value can then be used to rank each job. The factor comparison system is similar, in that it evaluates jobs according to five factors: mental requirements, skills, physical requirements, responsibilities, and working conditions. The factor system, however, selects "key" or **benchmark jobs**, then compares and ranks all other jobs in relation to the benchmarks.

Job evaluation has grown increasingly complicated in the waning decades of the twentieth century. The use of **teams**, for example, has made the process exponentially more complicated. As employers ask their employees to perform a variety of tasks that were previously part of separate job descriptions, compensation managers must rationalize both the tasks and the worker's flexibility with appropriate pay.

The job structure is the product of these job evaluations. It is one factor utilized to formulate pay structure—the pay for each job relative to other jobs within a single company. From the 1930s until the 1950s, internal equity and ability to pay were the primary determinants of compensation. In the last half of the twentieth century, human resource professionals began to systematically compare pay across companies and industries. This concern for external competitiveness has evolved into an important aspect of compensation management.

EXTERNAL COMPETITIVENESS. Achieving external competitiveness in the area of compensation means balancing the need to keep operating costs (including labor costs) low with the need to attract and retain quality workers. Milkovitch and Newman rank "the policies and practices related to external competitiveness ... among the most critical in compensation management."

Compensation managers achieve external competitiveness, or **equity**, by determining comparable labor markets, examining competitive pay levels, and establishing their own pay level accordingly. In general, companies can set their pay level to lead, match, or follow competitors' pay practices. Contemporary compensation policies include "variable pay," where pay levels reflect the fluctuation of the firms' success or decline, and positioning as "employer of choice." "Employer of choice" emphasizes the total compensation package, and may include employment security, educational opportunities, and the promise of intellectual challenges or latitude. In practice, some employers use different policies for different units and/or job groups.

Comparative surveys help compensation administrators correlate jobs and salaries across a given industry and/or the entire economy. The U. S. Bureau of Labor Statistics (BLS, an office of the U.S. Labor Department) conducts and publishes three types of annual occupational wage surveys as well as a *Monthly Labor Review*. The BLS's *Area Wage Surveys* examine occupations common to a broad variety of industries in hundreds of Standard Metropolitan Statistical Areas, providing a geographical basis for comparison. The agency's industry wage surveys analyze nearly 100 manufacturing and service sector industries individually. The BLS's National Survey of Professional, Administrative, Technical and Clerical Pay (PATC), which has been conducted since 1959, examines specific positions, including accountants, auditors, attorneys, buyers, job analysts, directors of personnel, chemists, engineers, engineering technicians, draftsmen, and clerical posts.

Job surveys have also been developed by professional human resource groups over the decades. New York-based American Management Association's "Executive Compensation Service" has compiled and published information on compensation and related subjects since 1950. Its purpose is "to provide an orderly basis for measuring a company's compensation practices against those of other companies of comparable size within their own industry as well as in industry in general."

Establishing the pay level balances a company's profit requirements with competition for competent employees. Factors determining pay level include: competition in the labor market, financial characteristics of a given firm and its industry, and organizational characteristics. Weighing all these considerations, firms can choose to pay more than the industry average, and therefore favor attracting and retaining quality employees, or pay less than their competitors' average in order to keep labor costs comparatively low. A competitive pay level—one that balances all considerations—can help contain labor costs, enlarge the pool of qualified applicants, increase quality and experience, reduce voluntary turnover, discourage unionization, and abate pay-related work stoppages.

Once a company has determined its pay level relative to its competitors, compensation managers must ascertain the compensation mix—the combination of direct and indirect pay—for each occupation. Most employers apply a combination of direct and indirect pay in what is known as a total compensation package.

COMPENSATION MIX. Pay packages are used to attract, retain, and motivate employees. The compensation mix consists of both direct and indirect forms of financial returns, services, and benefits. Direct pay includes base pay: the cash that an employer pays for the work performed. This base pay can be further delineated as either a wage or a salary. Wages are hourly rates of pay regulated by the **Fair Labor Standards Act of 1938**. This federal legislation formed the foundation of minimum wage, overtime pay, **child labor**, gender equality, and record keeping requirements for American businesses. Employees who are subject to the Fair Labor Standards Act are known in compensation management parlance as "nonexempt." Salaries, which are usually paid to managers and professionals, are annual or monthly calculations of pay that usually have less relation to hours worked. Most (but not all) salaried workers are "exempt" from the Fair Labor Standards Act of 1938. Direct pay also includes merit and seniority increases, incentive and variable pay, and cost-of-living adjustments (or COLAs). Merit and seniority increases, as well as incentives and variable pay, are used to recognize the performance of individual employees. COLAs are usually across-the-board contractual increases tied to an economic indicator like the Consumer Price Index.

Indirect pay includes employee services and benefits. George T. Milkovich and Jerry M. Newman called benefits "the most volatile area in the compensation field" in their 1990 text titled simply *Compensation*. Social Security, workers' compensation, and unemployment compensation are three legally required benefits. Since its initial passage in 1935, The Social Security Act has been amended and expanded to protect workers and their families from losses due to **retirement**, disability, and/or death. Employers, employees, and the self-employed make contributions to the Social Security fund over the course of their careers. In the past, the fund has been more than sufficient to subsidize retirees, but warnings that it may begin to fall short after the turn of the century have been well publicized in the 1990s. Workers' compensation benefits have evolved from the early 1900s, when rising industrial accident rates prompted state legislatures to action. All 50 states have enacted laws designed to compensate victims, minimize accident-related litigation, reduce on-the-job accidents, and provide treatment and/or rehabilitation where applicable. Unemployment insurance is designed to help workers through the unexpected loss of a job. Employers pay the premiums for unemployment insurance in the form of variable federal and state taxes. Workers who become unemployed and meet pre-set eligibility requirements receive weekly benefits.

Benefits may also come in the form of protection programs, such as life and health insurance and pensions and retirement plans. Group life insurance is one of the most widely-offered benefits because of its cost-effectiveness. Most employers shoulder the premiums for employees (and sometimes retirees), but end coverage at employee termination. Group health insurance has also become an expected component of benefits plans. Employers typically choose between five prevalent systems: community-based, commercial insurance, self-insurance, health maintenance organization, or preferred provider. Each of these systems has advantages and drawbacks, and in an era of skyrocketing medical costs and impending federal and/or state supervision of the health care industry, this aspect of compensation management has become evermore complex.

Pension and retirement plans include defined benefit plans and defined contribution plans. As many as 80 percent of pension plan participants are the beneficiaries of defined benefit plans. In such a program, the employer promises a fixed pension level, either in terms of a dollar amount or a percentage of earnings scaled to seniority. Defined contribution plans specify the amount an employer will set aside in an investment fund for the benefit of each employee. These plans have grown increasingly popular in the 1980s and 1990s because employers know their costs up front, employees can also contribute, and the funds can accumulate in a tax shelter. **Employee Stock Ownership Plans (ESOP)** and **401(K) plans** are the most popular **defined contribution plans**. 401(k)s allow employers and employees to defer a maximum amount of annual compensation to a tax sheltered "savings account" that can then be invested on the employees behalf. ESOPs are allocations of company-donated stock that can be used as retirement or incentive funds. Upon retirement, a worker receives cash based on the value of the stock and seniority.

Credit for time not worked, including vacations, sick time, and parental leave, is also considered indirect pay. Some companies also offer employee services, such as **financial planning**, **vocational training**, and **child care**, and perquisites like a company car or luxury office as part of a package of indirect compensation. Some experts assert that promotions and recognition of accomplishments should not be overlooked as powerful forms of indirect compensation.

EMPLOYEE EQUITY. Companies regularly recognize individual employees for their unique contributions by measuring performance and compensating them accordingly. In this way, firms give their employees a measure of control over their compensation. While the human resources jury is still out on whether (and if so, how) pay strategies affect (or effect) performance, incentives like seniority (which rewards longevity) and merit pay (which rewards achievement) are distributed on the basis of employee evaluations.

A performance evaluation may include objective and/or subjective measurements. Although objective assessments (such as number of pieces produced per hour, number of words typed per minute) are clearly reliable and easily established, they often do not encompass the sum of an employee's contribution. Still, some objective methods of compensation for performance have become very popular incentives in the late twentieth century. Perhaps the most common examples are sales commissions and piecework, but creative additions to these staples have been added recently. Gain-sharing programs tie incentives to increased productivity, quality improvements, and or cost savings. **Profit-sharing** links pay to increases in company profits, and Employee Stock Option Plans base increased compensation on a company's stock performance. These programs are geared toward making each employee's vested interest in the company clearer and more immediate through his or her paycheck. These concepts also help control labor costs, because employees do not receive the rewards unless the company performs well.

Six subjective evaluation methods are most prevalent: essay, **ranking**, adjective checklist, standard rating scale, behaviorally anchored rating scale, and management by objectives. Perhaps most subjective, the essay evaluation is a narrative assessment of performance as interpreted by the evaluator. **Ranking** (employees, not occupations, this time) can be accomplished any of four ways: a straight, top-down ranking of performance; alternate ranking; paired comparison; or forced distribution. A straight ranking is self-explanatory. Alternate and paired ordering apply the same concepts as in job analysis. A forced distribution compels the evaluator to rank individuals' performances in a given proportion—a bell curve, for example. Adjective checklists are a predetermined list of positive and negative descriptors. Evaluators compare an employee's performance to the list, then score the employee according to the number of positive descriptors. Standard rating scales use weighted attributes. The appraiser rates an employee's achievement of each attribute, then calculates the total score. Although similar, behaviorally anchored rating scales (BARS) use job-specific attributes. The rater characterizes how well each employee could be expected to react to a given situation, and the employee's score is calculated according to the number of good decisions he or she could be expected to make. A relatively new method, management by objectives (MBO) combines planning, development, and appraisal by setting performance goals in consultation with employees, then evaluating according to the agreed-upon standards. This process is becoming increasingly popular, especially as it applies to team-oriented work environments. Companies may use different evaluation systems for particular groups of employees and/or distinct aspects of employee performance. The standard rating scale and MBO were the most popular evaluation programs in the late 1980s and early 1990s.

SEE ALSO: Employee Performance; Performance Appraisal & Standards

[April Dougal Gasbarre]

FURTHER READING:

Manicatide, Mircea, and Virginia Pennell. "Key Developments in Compensation Management," *HR Focus*. v.69, October 1992, pp. 3-4.

Milkovich, George T., and Jerry M. Newman. *Compensation*, 3rd ed. Boston: BPI/Irwin, 1990.

Rock, Milton L., and Lance A. Berger. *The Compensation Handbook: a State-of-the-Art Guide to Compensation Strategy and Design*, 3rd ed. New York: McGraw-Hill, c.1991.

Shafritz, Jay M. *Dictionary of Personnel Management and Labor Relations*. Oak Park, IL: Moore Publishing Company, Inc., 1980.

U.S. Department of Labor, U.S. Employment Service *Dictionary of Occupational Titles, Fourth Ed.* Washington, D.C.: GPO, 1991.

COMPETITION

The notion of competition is very widely used in economics in general and in microeconomics in particular. Competition is also considered the basis for capitalist or free market economies. In the ordinary usage of the term, competition may also imply certain virtues. Markets are the heart and soul of a capitalist economy, and varying degrees of competition lead to different market structures, with differing implications for the outcomes of the market place. We will discuss the following market structures that result from the successively declining degrees of competition in the market for a particular commodity: (1) Perfect Competition, (2) Monopolistic Competition, (3) Oligopoly, and (4) Monopoly. Based on the differing outcomes of different market structures, economists consider some market structures more desirable, from the point of view of the society, than others.

CHARACTERISTICS OF A MARKET STRUCTURE

Each of the above mentioned market structures describes a particular organization of a market in which certain key characteristics differ. The characteristics are: (a) number of firms in the market, (b) control over the price of the relevant product, (c) type of the product sold in the market, (d) barriers to new firms entering the market, and (e) existence of nonprice competition in the market. Each of these characteristics is briefly discussed below.

NUMBER OF FIRMS IN THE MARKET. The number of firms in the market supplying the particular product under consideration forms an important basis for classifying market structures. The number of firms in an industry, according to economists, determines the extent of competition in the industry. Both in perfect competition and monopolistic competition, there are large numbers of firms or suppliers. Each of these firms supplies only a small portion of the total output for the industry. In oligopoly, there are only a few (presumably more than two) suppliers of the product. When there are only two sellers of the product, the market structure is often called duopoly. Monopoly is the extreme case where there is only one seller of the product in the market.

CONTROL OVER PRICE OF THE PRODUCT. The extent to which an individual firm exercises control over the price of the product it sells is another important characteristic of a market structure. Under perfect competition, an individual firm has no control over the price of the product it sells. A firm under monopolistic competition or oligopoly has some control over the price of the product it sells. Finally, a monopoly firm is deemed to have considerable control over the price of its product.

TYPE OF THE PRODUCT SOLD IN THE MARKET. The extent to which products of different firms in the industry can be differentiated is also a characteristic that is used in classifying market structures. Under perfect competition, all firms in the industry sell identical products. In other words, no firm can differentiate its product from those of other firms in the industry. There is some product differentiation under monopolistic competition—the firms in the industry are assumed to produce somewhat different products. Under an oligopolistic market structure, firms may produce differentiated or identical products. Finally, in the case of a monopoly, product differentiation is not quite relevant, as there is only one firm—there are no other firms from whom it should differentiate its product.

BARRIERS TO NEW FIRMS ENTERING THE MARKET. The difficulty or ease with which new firms can enter the market for a product is also a characteristic of market structures. New firms can enter market structures classified as perfect competition or monopolistic competition relatively easily. In these cases, barriers to entry are considered low, as only a small investment may be required to enter the market. In oligopoly, barriers to entry is considered very high—huge amounts of investments, determined by the very nature of the product and the production process, are needed to enter these markets. Once again, monopoly constitutes the extreme case where the entry of new firms is blocked, usually by law. If for whatever reasons, new firms are allowed to enter a monopolistic market structure, it then no longer is a monopoly.

EXISTENCE OF NON-PRICE COMPETITION. Market structures also differ to the extent that firms in industry compete with each other on the basis of non-price factors, such as, differences in product characteristics and advertising. There is no non-price competition under perfect competition. Firms under monopolistic competition make considerable use of instruments of non-price competition. Oligopolistic firms also make heavy use of non-price competition. Finally, while a monopolist also utilizes instruments of non-price competition, such as advertising, these are not designed to compete with other firms, as there are no other firms in the monopolist's industry.

We now turn to discussing each of the four market forms mentioned at the beginning, in light of the preceding characteristics used to classify market structures. The discussion that follows also provides additional details about the four market structures.

PERFECT COMPETITION

Perfect competition is an idealized version of market structure that provides a foundation for understanding how markets work in a capitalist economy. The other market structures can also be understood better when perfect competition is used as a standard of reference. Even so, perfect competition is not ordinarily well understood by the general public. For example, when business people speak of intense competition in the market for their product, they are, in all likelihood, referring to their rival suppliers, about whom they have quite a bit of information. However, when economists refer to perfect competition, they are particularly referring to the *impersonal* nature of this market structure. The impersonality of into the market organization is due to the existence of a large number of suppliers of the product—there are so many suppliers in the industry that no firm views another supplier as a competitor. Thus, the competition under perfect competition is impersonal.

To understand the nature of competition under the perfectly competitive market form, one should briefly examine the three conditions that are necessary before a market structure is considered perfectly competitive. These are: homogeneity of the product sold in the industry, existence of many buyers and sellers, and perfect mobility of resources or factors of production. Homogeneity of product means that the product sold by any one seller in the market is identical to the product sold by any other supplier. The homogeneity of product has an important implication for the market: if products of different sellers are identical, buyers do not care who they buy from, so long as the price is also the same. While the first condition of a perfect market sounds extreme, it is, in fact, met in markets for many products. Wheat and corn are good examples. Wheat and corn produced by different farmers is essentially the same, and can thus be considered identical. The second condition, existence of many buyers and sellers, again leads to an important outcome. When there is a large number of buyers or sellers, each individual buyer or seller is so small relative to the entire market that he or she does not have any power to influence the price of the product under consideration. As a result, whether a person is a buyer or a seller, he or she must accept the market price. All buyers and sellers in the market are effectively price takers, not price makers. The market price for the product is established by the entire market, and individual buyers or sellers simply decide how much to buy or sell at the given market price. The third condition, perfect mobility of resources, requires that all factors of production (resources used in the production process) can be readily switched from one use to another. Furthermore, it is required that all buyers, sellers, and owners of resources have full knowledge of all relevant technological and economic data. The implication of the third condition is that resources move to the most profitable industry.

No industry in the world (now or in the past) satisfies all three conditions stipulated above fully. Thus, no industry in the world can be considered perfectly competitive in the strictest sense of the term. However, there are token examples of industries that come quite close to being a perfectly competitive market. Some markets for agricultural commodities, while not meeting all three conditions, come reasonably close to being characterized as perfectly competitive markets. The market for wheat, for example, can be considered a reasonable approximation. The wheat market is characterized by an almost homogenous product, and it has a large number of buyers and sellers. It thus satisfies the first two conditions fairly well. However, it is difficult to assert that resources employed in the wheat industry are perfectly mobile.

Despite the fact that no industry is truly perfectly competitive, it is still worthwhile to study perfect competition as a market structure. Conclusions derived from the study of the idealized version of perfect competition are often helpful in explaining behavior in the real world.

THE ECONOMICS OF PERFECT COMPETITION. The study of the idealized version of perfect competition leads to some important conclusions regarding solutions to key economic problems, such as quantity of the relevant product produced, price charged, the mechanism of adjustment in the industry.

As mentioned earlier, under perfect competition, an individual supplier of the product has to take the market price as given. Given this price, the supplier determines how much to produce and sell. The quantity he or she decides to produce is the quantity that maximizes profit for the firm (more technically, where marginal cost of producing the product equals the market price of the product). The total of production of all firms in the industry determines the market supply of the product under consideration. This market supply of the product, in conjunction with the total demand for the product by all consumers, determines the market price. Thus, while an individual buyer or seller is a price taker, their collective decisions affect the market price. Since the consumers of the product receive a price that is equal to the cost of production (on the margin), it is argued that consumers are treated fairly under perfect competition.

In addition, the total output produced under perfect competition is larger than, for example, under monopoly. To understand this, we should look at the mechanics of maximizing profit, the guiding force behind a supplier's output decision. In order to maxi-

mize profits, a supplier has to look at cost and revenue. Usually, it is assumed that a supplier's marginal cost (the cost of producing an additional unit of the product under consideration) rises ultimately. The producer then, in making the output decision, must compare the cost of producing an additional unit of the product with the revenue the sale of that additional unit (called the marginal revenue) brings to the firm. So long as the marginal revenue from the sale exceeds the marginal cost, there is a gain from producing that additional unit—the unit adds more to revenue (proceeds) than to costs. The supplier will continue producing while the process is profitable (i.e., it increases profits or reduces loss). The firm will stop production where marginal revenue equals marginal cost—this output level maximizes profits (or minimizes loss). In the case of a perfectly competitive firm, the market price for the product is also the marginal revenue. Since the firm is a price taker and supplies an insignificant portion of the total market supply of the product, it can sell as many units of the product as it desires at the going price. We will later show that this is not the case with a monopolist, for example. A monopolist stops production of the product before reaching the point where marginal cost of the product equals the market price of the product.

THE DESIRABILITY OF PERFECT COMPETITION. Perfect competition is considered desirable for society for at least two reasons. First, the price charged to individuals equals the marginal cost of production to each firm. In other words, one can say sellers charge buyers a reasonable or fair price. Second, in general, output produced under a perfectly competitive market structure is larger than other market organizations. Thus, perfect competition becomes desirable also for the amount of the product supplied to consumers as a whole.

These are two reasons why a capitalist society adores the virtues of perfect competition. In fact, to maintain a reasonable amount of competition in a market is generally considered a goal of government regulatory policies. Nhat no single firm dominates the market under perfect competition; this parallels the status of an individual citizen in a democracy, a widely practiced form of government in capitalist countries.

MONOPOLISTIC COMPETITION

As pointed out above, industries in the real world rarely satisfy the stringent conditions necessary to qualify as perfectly competitive market structures. The world in which we live is invariably characterized by competition of lesser degrees than stipulated by perfect competition. Many industries that we often deal with have market structures that are monopolistic competition or oligopoly. Apparel retail stores (with many stores and differentiated products) provide an example of monopolistic competition.

MAJOR CHARACTERISTICS OF MONOPOLISTIC COMPETITION. As in the case of perfect competition, monopolistic competition is characterized by the existence of many sellers. Usually, if an industry has 50 or more firms (producing products that are close substitutes of each other), it is said to have a large number of firms. However, the number of firms must be large enough that each firm in the industry can expect its actions go unnoticed by rival firms.

Unlike perfect competition, the sellers under monopolistic competition differentiate their product. In other words, the products of these firms are not considered identical. It is, in fact, immaterial whether these products are actually different or simply perceived to be so. So long as consumers treat them as different products, they satisfy one of the characteristics of monopolistic competition. The *product differentiation* is considered a key attribute of monopolistic competition. In many U.S. markets, producers practice product differentiation by altering their physical composition, using special packaging, or simply claiming to have superior products based on their brand images and/or advertising. Toothpastes and toilet papers are examples of differentiated products.

In addition to the existence of a large number of firms and product differentiation, relative ease of entry into the industry is considered another important requirement of a monopolistically competitive market organization. Also, there should be no collusion among firms in the industry, like price fixing or agreements regarding the market shares of individual companies. With the large number of firms that monopolistic competion requires, collusion is generally difficult, though not impossible.

The above mentioned characteristics of monopolistic competition basically yield a market form that is very competitive, but probably not to the extent of perfect competition.

THE ECONOMICS OF MONOPOLISTIC COMPETITION. As in the case of perfect competition, a firm under monopolistic competition decides about the quantity of the product produced on the basis of the profit maximization principle—it produces the quantity that maximizes the firm's profit. Also, conditions of profit maximization remain the same—the firm stops production where marginal revenue equals marginal cost of production. But unlike perfect competition, a firm under monopolistic competition has a bit of control over the price it charges, as the firm differentiates its products from those of others. However, this price making power of a monopolistically competitive firm is rather small, since there are a large number of other firms in the industry with somewhat similar products. Remember that a perfectly competitive firm has no price making power—each firm is a price taker, as it produces a product identical to those produced by a large number of other firms in the industry.

An important consequence of the price making power of a monopolistically competitive firm is that when such a firm reduces price, it can attract customers buying other "brands" of the product. The opposite is also true when the firm increases the price it charges for its product. Because of this, price charged for a product is different from the marginal revenue for the product (marginal revenue refers to the increase in total revenue as a result of selling one more unit of the product under consideration). To understand this, consider, for example, that a firm reduces the price for its product. The firm must now sell all units at this lower price. Because the lower price applies to all units sold, not just the last or the marginal unit, price for the product is higher than the marginal revenue at each level of sale. It should be noted that as there are a large number of firms under monopolistic competition, individual firms in the industry are not appreciably affected by a particular firm's behavior.

As mentioned above, a monopolistically competitive firm stops production where marginal revenue equals marginal cost of production—the output level that maximizes its profits (often called the equilibrium output for the firm).

THE DESIRABILITY OF MONOPOLISTIC COMPETITION. Aforementioned profit maximizing behavior of a monopolistically competitive firm implies that now the price associated with the product (at the equilibrium or the profit maximizing output) is higher than marginal cost (which equals marginal revenue). Thus, the production under monopolistic competition does not take place to the point where price equals marginal cost of production. Remember that, with increased production, price charged (which is higher than marginal revenue at every level of output) is successively falling while the marginal cost of production is rising. Therefore, if a monopolistically competitive firm were to stop production where price is equal to marginal cost (a condition met under a perfectly competitive market structure), output produced would be greater than when it stops production where marginal revenue equals marginal cost (its profit maximizing output). The net result of the profit maximizing decisions of monopolistically competitive firms is that price charged under monopolistic competition is higher than under perfect competition. In addition, quantity of the commodity produced under monopolistic competition is simultaneously lower. Thus, both on the basis of price charged and output produced, monopolistic competition is less socially desirable than perfect competition.

OLIGOPOLY

Oligopoly is a fairly common market organization. In the United States, both the steel and auto industries (with three or so large firms) provide good examples of oligopolistic market structures.

MAJOR CHARACTERISTICS OF OLIGOPOLY. An important characteristic of an oligopolistic market structure is the interdependence of firms in the industry. The interdependence, actual or perceived, arises from the small number of firms in the industry. However, unlike monopolistic competition, if an oligopolistic firm changes its price or output, it has perceptible effects on the sales and profits of its competitors in the industry. Thus, an oligopolist firm always considers the reactions of its rivals in formulating its pricing or output decisions.

There are huge, though not insurmountable, barriers to entering an oligopolistic market. These barriers can involve large financial requirements, availability of raw materials, access to the relevant technology, or simply patent rights of the firms currently in the industry. Several industries in the United States provide good examples of oligopolistic market structures with obvious barriers to entry. The U.S. auto industry provides an example of a market where financial barriers to entry exist. In order to efficiently operate an automobile plant, one needs upward of half a billion dollars of initial investment. The steel industry in the United States, on the other hand, provides an example of an oligopoly where barriers to entry have been created by the ownership of raw materials needed for producing the product. In this industry, a few huge firms own most of the available iron ore, a necessary raw material for steel production.

An oligopolistic industry is also typically characterized by **economies of scale**. Economies of scale in production imply that as the level of production rises the cost per unit of product falls for the use of any plant (generally, up to a point). Thus, economies of scale lead to an obvious advantage for a large producer. Once again, the automobile industry provides an example of a market structure where firms experience economies of scale. It should be noted that there may exist economies of scale in promotion just as there exist economies of scale in production. In the automobile industry, the promotion cost per unit of product falls as sales increase since promotion costs rise less than proportionately to sales.

ECONOMICS AND DESIRABILITY OF OLIGOPOLY. There is no single theoretical framework that provides answers to output and pricing decisions under an oligopolistic market structure. Analyses exist only for special sets of circumstances. For example, if an oligopolistic firm cuts its price, it is met with price reductions by competing firms; however, if it raises the price of its product, rivals do not match the price increase. For this reason, prices may remain stable in an oligopolistic industry for a prolonged period of time.

It is hard to make concrete statements regarding price charged and quantity produced under oligopoly. However, from the point of view of the society, one can say that an oligopolistic market structure provides a fair degree of competition in the market place if the oligopolists in the market do not collude. *Collusion* occurs if firms in the industry agree to set price and/or quantity. In the United States, there are laws that make collusion illegal.

MONOPOLY

Monopoly can be considered the opposite of perfect competition. It is a market form in which there is only one seller. While at first glance a monopoly may appear to be a rare market structure, it is not so. Several industries in the United State have monopolies. Your local electricity company provides an example of a monopolist.

CAUSES AND CHARACTERISTICS OF MONOPOLY. There are many factors that give rise to a monopoly. For example, in the United States the inventor of an item has the exclusive right to produce that product for 17 years. Thus, a monopoly can exist in an industry because a patent was obtained for a product by its inventor. The United Shoe Machinery Company held such a monopoly in certain important shoe making equipment until 1954, when the monopoly was broken under the **antitrust laws**. A monopoly can also arise if a company owns the entire supply of a necessary material needed to produce a product. The Aluminum Company of America exercised such power until 1945, when its monopoly was also broken under provisions of the antitrust laws. A monopoly can be legally created by a government agency when it sells a market franchise a particular product or service. Often a monopoly so established is also regulated by the appropriate government agency. Provision of local telephone service in the United States provides an example of such a monopoly. Finally, a monopoly may arise due to declining cost of production for a particular product. In such a case the average cost of production falls and reaches a minimum at an output level that is sufficient to satisfy the entire market. In such an industry, rival firms will be eliminated until only the strongest firm (now the monopolist) is left in the market. This is often called a case of *natural monopoly*. A good example of a natural monopoly is the electricity industry. The electric power industry reaps benefits of economies of scale and yields decreasing average cost. A natural monopoly is usually regulated by the government.

THE ECONOMICS OF MONOPOLY. Generally speaking, price and output decisions of a monopolist are similar to those of a monopolistically competitive firm, with the major distinction of a large number of firms under monopolistic competition and only one firm under monopoly. Thus, one may technically say that there is no competition under monopoly. This is not strictly true, as even a monopolist is threatened by indirect and potential competition. Like monopolistic competition, a monopolistic firm also maximizes its profits by producing up to the point where marginal revenue equals marginal cost. As the monopolist is a price maker and can increase the amount of sales by lowering the price, a monopolist does not lure consumers away from rivals, rather he or she induces them to buy more. Nevertheless, at any output level, the price charged by a monopolist is higher than the marginal revenue. As a result, a monopolist also does not produce to the point where price equals marginal cost (a condition met under a perfectly competitive market structure).

DESIRABILITY OF MONOPOLY. An industry characterized by a monopolistic market structure produces less output and charges higher prices than under perfect competition (and presumably under monopolistic competition). Thus, on the basis of price charged and quantity produced, a monopoly is less desirable socially. However, a natural monopoly is generally considered desirable if the monopolist's price behavior can be regulated.

SUMMARY

Industry in the real world is rarely characterized by perfect competition. In certain circumstances, society has to tolerate monopoly (say, the case of a natural monopoly or a monopoly due to patent rights). However, the idea of competition is very deeply ingrained in society. So long as there is a reasonable degree of competition (as in the case of monopolistic competition or oligopoly), society feels reasonably secure with respect to the working of its markets.

[Anandi P. Sahu]

FURTHER READING:

Mansfield, Edwin. *Principles of Microeconomics*, 7th ed. W.W. Norton & Company, 1992.

Taylor, John B. *Economics*, 1st ed. Houghton Mifflin Company, 1995.

COMPLIANCE AUDITING

The process of compliance auditing determines whether an organizational unit or function is, or is not, following particular rules or expectations. Such rules or expectations can originate internally or externally and can include one or more of the following: organizational policies; performance plans; established procedures; required authorizations; applicable external regulations; relevant contractual provisions; and federal, state, and local laws. Characteristic of compliance audits is the yes/no aspect of the evaluation. For each transaction or event examined, either it follows the rules or does not. Compliance auditing is considered the most objective of the various types of audits because transactions or events are evaluated against predetermined criteria. Also, methods used to judge results are usually decided prior to performing any audit tests.

Compliance auditing usually requires only a quick preliminary survey at the onset because this type of audit focuses on the specifics of particular activities rather than the overall organizational environment. Once the requirements that will be audited have been defined and understood, detailed testing of conditions can begin. For each event or transaction being examined, the auditor evaluates the evidence from audit tests. If established rules have been followed, the event is judged to be in compliance. If an event or transaction has violated the rules, it is deemed not in compliance. The auditor considers the number of events or transactions found to be in compliance, and the number which were not and makes an overall assessment of the organization's level of compliance or noncompliance with respect to the activities that were audited. The auditor will typically report the implications and risks of noncompliance and suggest corrective action whenever noncompliance is found. The auditor may also report reasons for noncompliance, if known.

Compliance auditing is expedited and most credible when established standards or expectations to be audited have been written with great precision. This is not always the case. Many organizational directives, and even some governmental regulations, have been stated more generally—allowing for some flexibility in application. Under these circumstances, compliance auditing tends to become more subjective. When expectations and requirements are not documented and are not widely accepted, the compliance audit process may not be valid. In cases where requirements and expectation are imposed arbitrarily, compliance auditing produces little value beyond pointing out that the standards have not been applied consistently.

Compliance auditors must understand how to apply large bodies of information. They must learn how to research issues effectively using authoritative materials. They must also be able to comprehend and explain how an organizations should operate with respect to specific criteria and standards. Compliance auditors must motivate organizations to implement procedures and achieve compliance, even when the changes might be an inconvenience.

HISTORY AND BACKGROUND

The growth of compliance auditing is fundamentally a twentieth-century phenomena. Its emergence as a distinct type of auditing coincided with the rapid growth of business after the Industrial Revolution, and the concurrent growth in efforts by organizations and governments to direct and control business practices.

Regulations, policies, and procedures were implemented to provide direction and control. It became the responsibility of auditors to verify that the rules were indeed being followed. Three distinct groups of auditors emerged and grew: external auditors in public accounting firms, internal auditors employed within organizations, and governmental auditors serving state, local, or federal jurisdictions. Each group performed compliance audits within their own domains.

Perhaps the growth in the number of federal audit agencies has been the most visible. Federal auditors perform a variety of audit services, but compliance auditing has always played a key role. Federal audit divisions include the General Accounting Office (GAO), the Internal Revenue Service (IRS), Defense Contract Audit Agency (DCAA), and the Office of the Inspector General (OIG). According to public law 95-452, 61 individual offices of the Inspectors General had been established as of mid-1995. (There is an Office of Inspector General for each federal department including Agriculture, Commerce, Defense, Education, Energy, Equal Employment Opportunity Commission, Federal Emergency Management Agency, Health and Human Services, Housing and Urban Development, Interior, Justice, Labor, State, Transportation, Agency for International Development, Environmental Protection Agency, General Services Administration, National Aeronautics and Space Administration, National Science Foundation, Small Business Administration, and Veterans Administration.) In addition, several federal regulatory agencies perform their own audits. These agencies include the **Securities and Exchange Commission**, Federal Energy Regulatory Commission, **Federal Communications Commission**, Federal Maritime Commission, **Federal Trade Commission**, and the **Interstate Commerce Commission (ICC)**.

Despite the seemingly large number of governmental audit units, governmental resources to audit compliance with the growing number laws and regulations have not kept pace. More and more regulatory compliance audits are being performed by the private sector. In response, public accounting firms have significantly expanded their compliance audit services. That expansion has been further stimulated by legisla-

tion requiring that organizations pay external auditors to perform compliance audits to be submitted to the government. That requirement for an external compliance audit frequently becomes a condition for receiving funds. Organizations should be aware that under these circumstances the external auditor serves the interests of the regulator and acts as their agent, even though the organization is paying the audit fee.

TOPICS FOR COMPLIANCE AUDITS

The expectations and requirements that serve as criteria in a compliance audit can be established internally by the organization or imposed by some external authority. Owners, directors, and managers communicate expectations in the form of mandates, policies, procedures, performance measures, or product specifications. External directives from creditors, customers, and outside funding sources take the form of contracts, covenants, program guidelines, or grants. Laws and regulations issued by federal, state, county, and city governments are expected to be integrated into day-to-day operations. Consequently, a broad range of topics for compliance audits has been created by the policies and rules that exist in virtually every private, public, and nonprofit organization.

WHO PERFORMS COMPLIANCE AUDITS AND WHO REQUESTS THEM?

Compliance audits can be performed by employees of the organization, public accountants hired by the organization, or governmental auditors directed by a regulatory agency to audit certain activities within the organization. Auditors are not the only group of practitioners in the field of compliance auditing. More attorneys have joined in performing these audits as legal aspects of compliance issues increase with respect to real estate, employment, pension, environmental, occupational health, and safety practices. The auditor's responsibility in any case is the same; that is, providing independent assurance as to the level of compliance to the person or entity requesting the audit.

Compliance audits are most often requested by the same person or entity that initially established the expectations and requirements for the organization. It is natural for them to verify that their directives have been followed. External regulators often require periodic compliance audits especially when major programs or significant amounts of funding are involved. External authorities levying taxes verify periodically that they are collecting what is due. Owners and directors may request compliance audits, and also incorporate them into a long-range audit plan, when they perceive noncompliance could become a significant risk to the organization. Managers may request internal auditors to examine activities in advance of an external compliance audit so that any potential problems can be detected and corrected. When internal auditors have already audited activities and management has taken action to correct noncompliance, external examiners may request that documentation as evidence of the organization's good-faith effort to correct noncompliance. Such a proactive approach to achieve compliance can potentially prevent legal sanctions, penalties, and fines. When outside legal counsel, public accountants, or external examiners perceive sloppiness or a cavalier attitude with respect to compliance, they may take more time than usual with their investigations. This most likely occurs at the organization's expense.

The following examples illustrate some of the varied combinations of compliance audit sponsors, audit practitioners, and audit topics that are possible. The **board of directors** of an organization asks the internal auditors to examine the company's investment portfolio to assess whether maximum maturities, foreign investments, degree of diversification, and credit ratings of issuers conform to board-mandated investment policies. A lender requires that a municipality provide annual certification, prepared by a public accounting firm, that debt covenants have not been violated. A federal agency sends auditors to a defense contractor to determine whether cost accounting practices meet federal standards. The **chief information officer** requests internal auditors to verify that system access protocols have been followed by security administrators. Having included a right-to-audit clause in its agreement with the organization, an outside sponsor requests audit access to verify that terms of its contract with the organization are being met. The human resources manager requests that a staff attorney review the employee hiring process to decide whether practices conform to employment regulations. The Internal Revenue Service (IRS) sends auditors to evaluate whether the company is properly withholding and remitting income, social security, and Medicare taxes.

THE COMPLIANCE AUDIT PROCESS

The person or entity requesting the compliance audit plays the key role in determining the content and conduct of the compliance audit. This audit sponsor defines the specific requirements and expectations to be examined, as well as the period to be reviewed. The sponsor determines which auditor—internal, external, or governmental—will do the work. Some compliance audit sponsors may further control the audit process by prescribing detailed procedures for the conduct of the audit and methods for judging audit results.

Before beginning the compliance audit, the auditor must have a clear understanding of the requirements being tested, how to recognize when a devia-

tion has occurred, and how to evaluate evidence obtained through audit tests. This means that the auditor must figure out, for each event to be tested, just what evidence signifies compliance and what evidence signifies noncompliance. In addition, it is important for the auditor to find out the degree of deviation from standards that is considered tolerable by the audit sponsor. Detailed information about key compliance audit questions often exists in the form of independently published compliance audit guidelines and generally accepted auditing standards. Otherwise, the auditor should make sure that key questions and issues are clarified with the audit sponsor.

Assessing compliance may be simple, requiring a brief inspection to find out whether rules were followed or not. At the other extreme, making a judgment may require extensive research of regulatory requirements, interpretations, and technical materials before a valid conclusion about one event or a single transaction can be made. If the auditor is not sufficiently experienced in very specialized compliance topics, then the opinions of an expert should be sought.

The auditor will usually choose a sample of events or transactions for testing when it is not practical to examine every one that falls within the scope of the audit. Compliance audit tests can incorporate statistical sampling techniques and measure sampling risk when the following conditions can be reasonably assumed: the population is large enough to permit the mathematical laws of statistics to operate; errors are distributed randomly throughout the population; and evidence of such randomness exists. More often than not such assumptions cannot be made and a nonstatistical sampling approach is used. Estimates of sampling risk are not valid with nonstatistical sampling.

At the conclusion of testing, the auditor evaluates evidence from audit tests as a whole. If testing evidence indicates, within tolerable limits, that rules have been followed and prohibitions have not been violated, the organization is deemed to be in compliance with respect to the activities audited. If incidents of noncompliance exceed tolerable limits, the frequency and severity of deviations are studied. Penalties and sanctions may be imposed in serious cases of noncompliance. Identification of corrective measures that could be applied to bring activities back into compliance becomes important.

Compliance audit reports must communicate in a fashion that is relevant to the person or entity sponsoring the audit. Reports issued to federal regulators must often follow guidelines prescribing form and content. Reports usually describe the objectives of the compliance audit, the number of conditions examined during the period considered, the frequency of events conforming to conditions, and the number of exceptions. When a sample of events has been tested and it is statistically valid results from the sample may be used to predict the level of compliance for all events or transactions within the scope of the audit. Compliance audit reports often indicate reasons for deviations from standards, describe implications of those deviations, and recommend actions to strengthen control procedures for assuring compliance.

SEE ALSO: Audits and Auditoring; Internal Auditing

[Aldona Cytraus]

FURTHER READING:

American Institute of Certified Public Accountants. ''Statement on Auditing Standards No. 68. Compliance Auditing Applicable to Governmental Entities and Other Recipients of Governmental Financial Assistance.'' In *Codification of Statements on Auditing Standards Numbers 1 to 71*. Chicago: Commerce Clearing House, 1993.

American Institute of Certified Public Accountants Statistical Sampling Subcommittee. *Audit Sampling*. New York: American Institute of Certified Public Accountants, 1983.

Feldesman, James L., Jacqueline C. Leifer, and Michael B. Glomb. *Federal Auditing Information Service for Higher Education*. Washington, DC: National Association of College and University Business Officers, 1992.

Resource Guide to Federal Program Compliance Audits. Washington, DC: Thompson Publishing Group, 1994.

Willson, James D., and Steven J. Root. *Internal Auditing Manual*. Boston: Warren, Gorham, & Lamont, 1989.

COMPREHENSIVE ENVIRONMENTAL RESPONSE, COMPENSATION & LIABILITY ACT (CERCLA) OF 1980 (SUPERFUND)

In December of 1980, Congress passed the Comprehensive Environmental Response, Compensation, and Liability Act of 1980 (CERCLA), which is commonly called ''Superfund.'' Superfund was passed in response to public concern about chemical contamination such as that revealed in connection with the Love Canal disaster in the state of New York, where health effects—including unusually high rates of cancer, miscarriages for pregnant women, and birth defects in babies—were traced to chemical wastes from an abandoned chemical dumpsite. The 1980 Superfund law created a $1.6 billion fund to be used to identify and clean up hazardous waste sites over a period of five years. The program is administered by the federal **Environmental Protection Agency (EPA)**, which often acts in cooperation with its state counterparts. Major amendments to Superfund were passed in 1986 in the Superfund Amendments and Reauthorization Act (SARA). Pursuant to SARA, the Superfund program was extended for five years and additional funding of $8.5 billion was provided for the period from 1986 to 1991. In the 1991 Superfund Amendments and Reauthorization Act, the Superfund program and

provisions for taxes supporting it were extended for four more years but there were no significant changes made in the program. Funding for the program and liability for those parties who have been required to pay for cleanup actions have been sources of great controversy throughout Superfund's history. It is expected that Superfund will be reauthorized with amendments during 1995.

IMPETUS FOR CREATION OF SUPERFUND

The Love Canal disaster near Niagara Falls, New York and similar crises in Times Beach, Missouri and Woburn, Massachussetts were brought to the attention of U.S. citizens through extensive news media coverage during the late 1970s. At Love Canal, an emergency declaration by the federal government condemned a school and two hundred houses. In the wake of that action, Congress passed CERCLA as a means of identifying and cleaning up such hazardous waste dumps. CERCLA was signed into law in December of 1980 by President Carter.

STRUCTURE OF CERCLA AND ADMINISTRATION OF SUPERFUND

CERCLA has four parts. First, it establishes a system to identify chemical dump sites and develop priorities for clean up actions. Second, it grants authority to the EPA to engage in ''removal'' actions to respond to emergency situations involving hazardous substances and to engage in ''remedial'' actions to clean up hazardous waste sites. Third, CERCLA creates a Hazardous Substances Trust Fund to pay for removal of hazardous wastes and for remediation actions at hazardous waste sites. Fourth, the Act places liability for clean up costs upon ''responsible parties'' who contributed wastes to the site being cleaned up.

''Removal'' actions include clean up of hazardous materials in emergency situations such as chemical spills resulting from a train wreck or collision of motor vehicles or where polluted waters threaten to overflow. Removal actions are usually handled by state or local officials, but the EPA assists in particularly difficult situations. Removal actions in which the EPA participates are limited by statute to one year and $2 million in costs.

''Remediation actions,'' in contrast, are longterm and involve such activities as groundwater treatment, removal or incineration of wastes, and treatment or removal of soil. State governments work with the federal EPA's ''remedial action'' division of the EPA's Superfund Office to identify the most dangerous hazardous waste sites throughout the United States. After a state ''nominates'' a site for consideration, a ''paper'' analysis is done to select sites to be visited. When a site is visited by EPA inspectors, air, soil, and water samples are taken to assess the nature and degree of contamination of the site. The worst sites are placed on the EPA's National Priority List (NPL). As of 1994, there were over 1,200 sites on the NPL, but that figure is expected to eventually rise to about 3,000. The EPA's current inventory of hazardous waste sites is about 37,000, of which 12,000 are in various stages of evaluation to be considered for inclusion on the NPL. (The EPA has determined that approximately 24,000 sites listed on the inventory are not so severely contaminated that they belong on the NPL.)

Once a site is placed on the NPL, more intensive testing is done at the site to further assess the extent of contamination at the site, and a feasibility study is done to identify potential remedies such as incinerating the waste, **recycling** it, treating it, or removing it from the site for containment elsewhere. Then a design study is conducted. Finally, when a site is ready for action, the EPA relies on the Army Corps of Engineers to draw up plans and specifications and obtain competitive bids for the work to be done.

Clean up operations at Superfund sites have progressed slowly. By the end of fiscal year 1992, only forty of the 1,200 NPL sites had been "delisted" by the EPA. (Delisting means that remediation goals for the site have been achieved.) Another 109 of these sites had been "cleaned up" but had not been delisted because long-term treatment was continuing or the site was in the process of being "delisted." One of the most controversial aspects of Superfund has been and continues to be the question of who pays. Industry argues that a company should not be liable for the clean up of hazardous wastes dumped in the past if no laws were violated at the time the wastes were dumped. However, Congress has, thus far, not accepted that argument and has relied on the principle of "polluter pays" with respect to at least part of the funding for clean up actions.

Pursuant to CERCLA, companies identified as "responsible parties" for the dumping at a site can be compelled by the federal EPA to clean it up, or, in the alternative, the EPA can clean up the site with Superfund money and then seek reimbursement from the responsible party (or parties) through court action. There are four broad categories of "responsible parties:" (1) present owners or operators of the site; (2) those who owned or operated the site at the time hazardous substances were disposed of on the site; (3) generators of the waste that ended up at the site; and (4) the who transported the waste to the site. The categories have created a great deal of controversy because they have been interpreted broadly by the courts. For example, in *U.S. v. Fleet Factors Corp.*, a 1990 opinion of the Eleventh Circuit United States Court of Appeals, it was held that a secured creditor may be held liable as a responsible party if it participates in financial management of a facility in a way that shows that it could influence the facility's decisions regarding handling of hazardous waste.

The EPA can use an "enforcement first" action and seek an administrative order to force one or more potentially responsible parties (PRPs) to clean up a site. A court order can be pursued if a party contests the administrative order. Failure to comply with an administrative order or court order for such clean up can result in fines of $25,000 per day against a party.

In the alternative, the EPA itself may pursue remediation of the NPL site and later try to recover all or part of the costs from PRPs. The EPA is particularly likely to pursue this route when there are many PRPs, where it is difficult to identify PRPs, or where PRPs are "judgment proof" because they are out of business or are in precarious financial condition. Such clean ups are financed through the Hazardous Substances Trust Fund, except that clean up of land used by the U.S. Department of Defense and the U.S. Department of Energy is paid for through separate, direct federal budget appropriations for that purpose. It should also be noted that states are required by federal law to pay for a portion (usually 10 percent to 50 percent) of clean up costs for any site within their boundaries. In addition, the EPA has the authority to delegate the responsibility for leading clean up of a specific site to the state in which that site is located. Thus, businesses often find themselves dealing with a state counterpart to the EPA rather than the EPA itself.

Pursuant to the 1980 Superfund law, the Hazardous Substances Trust Fund received monies from taxes on certain basic chemicals referred to as "feed stock" chemicals, taxes on crude oil and imported petroleum products, and general federal tax revenues. Pursuant to the 1986 amendments to Superfund, those sources of monies were renewed, and a surtax was imposed on all U.S. businesses with an annual income of more than $2 million as an additional source of revenues.

NEW PROGRAMS ADDED PURSUANT TO SARA IN 1986

In addition to reauthorizing and providing additional funding for the Hazardous Substances Trust Fund, the 1986 Superfund Amendments and Reauthorization Act (SARA) included the Emergency Planning and Community Right-to-Know Act (EPCRA), also known as Title III. EPCRA established important new programs designed to extend "Right to Know" protections to communities and to plan for dealing with emergencies created by chemical leaks or spills. EPCRA was enacted in response to public concerns arising from a disaster in Bhopal, India in 1986. In

Bhopal, an accidental release of methyl isocyanate, a poisonous gas, from a Union Carbide plant killed over 2,000 people. Most people residing near the plant had not known that toxic chemicals were used there. Further, there were no advance plans for dealing with such a chemical emergency. U.S. citizens were concerned that similar accidents could occur here.

EPCRA has two sets of provisions. First, communities are required to establish plans for dealing with chemical leaks or spills. Second, businesses must convey to the public the same kinds of information about chemical hazards that they have been required to convey to their workers pursuant to the "right to know" provisions of the Occupational Safety and Health Administration (OSHA)'s Hazard Communication Standard. EPCRA is viewed as an important step away from crisis-by-crisis kinds of environmental protection and toward a proactive, preventative approach. Pursuant to EPCRA, the governor of each state has established a State Emergency Planning Response Commission. In turn, each state commission has established various emergency planning districts and has appointed a Local Emergency Planning Committee (LEPC) for each. Each LEPC is required to prepare plans for potential chemical emergencies within its communities. Plans must include the identities of business facilities with hazardous chemicals on their premises, the procedures to be followed in the event of a chemical release, the identities of community emergency coordinators, and the identity of a facility coordinator for each business facility covered by EPCRA.

A business facility is covered by EPCRA if it has a substance in a quantity meeting or exceeding a quantity specified on a list of about 400 extremely hazardous substances published by the EPA. In addition, after public notice and comment, the State Emergency Planning Response Commission or the state governor may designate additional facilities to be covered.

In the event of an accidental release of a hazardous substance, the covered facility must report that release immediately and provide follow up notices and information to the Community Coordinator of its LEPC. Hazardous substances which trigger such a report include those on the EPA's extremely hazardous substance list and those which are so classified under CERCLA.

The second major set of EPCRA's provisions provides for a community right to know program. The program requires businesses to prepare two sets of **annual reports**: the Hazardous Chemical Inventory and Toxic Chemicals Release Inventories (TRI's), also known as Chemical Release Forms.

For the Hazardous Chemical Inventory, each covered business facility must obtain or prepare a Material Safety Data Sheet (MSDS) for each chemical on its premises meeting or exceeding the threshold quantity. These forms are submitted to the LEPC, the local fire department, and the State Emergency Planning Response Commission. In addition, for each chemical in the inventory, the business must file a Chemical Inventory Report each year.

The Toxic Chemicals Release Inventory is a second set of reports which must be filed annually. In the TRI, releases made by the facility into air or water or onto land during the preceding 12 months are listed and totalled. Those releases reported on the form must include even those made legally pursuant to permits issued by the EPA or its state counterparts. The TRI must be filed by any company with ten or more employees if that company manufactures, imports, stores, or otherwise uses designated toxic chemicals at or above threshold levels.

Information submitted pursuant to both the emergency planning and the community right to know provisions of EPCRA is available to the general public upon request to the LEPC. In addition, health professionals may obtain access to specific chemical identities in order to treat or protect individuals who may have been exposed to the chemicals. Such access by health professionals is available even if the information is claimed to be a trade secret by the business facility.

Congress has provided stiff penalties for noncompliance with EPCRA. A business failing to comply with reporting requirements may be assessed up to $25,000 per day for a first violation and up to $75,000 per day for a second violation. Private citizens have the right to sue companies that fail to report. Enforcement by the government can include criminal prosecution and can result in imprisonment of managers of businesses that fail to report.

PUBLIC REACTION TO EPCRA AND SUPERFUND

Studies reveal that EPCRA has had far-reaching effects on businesses, prompting many to implement new waste reduction programs or adapt their existing programs. Other companies have developed safety audit procedures, reduced their chemical inventories, and changed their operations to substitute less hazardous chemicals for those they were using previously. In addition, various industry groups, such as the Chemical Manufacturers Association, have conducted workshops and prepared educational materials to assist their members in communicating risk EPCRA information and risk information in general to their communities. EPCRA is not an unqualified success, however. It is criticized for being less effective in conveying information to the public than it should be. One problem is lack of funding for the program. For example, LEPCs depend on unpaid, volunteer members. Also, information conveyed in MSDS is not in a language or a format that is easily understood by most laypeople.

In its administration of the Superfund program, the EPA has received extensive criticism. During the first six years of Superfund, not only did the EPA fail to act aggressively to implement and enforce the program, but there were charges of mishandling of funds, illegal favorable treatment of industries identified as Potentially Responsible Parties (PRPs), and manipulation of the Superfund for political purposes. A scandal dubbed "Sewergate" by the newsmedia ensued. As a result of a Congressional investigation, Ann Burford Gorsuch, chief administrator of the EPA, and twenty other EPA officials resigned from their positions. Among those resigning was Rita LaVelle, head of the Superfund program, who went to prison after being convicted of perjury in her testimony on the affair before Congress.

Since 1986, the credibility of the EPA has been rebuilt, in part, because EPA administrators following Ann Burford Gorsuch have been chosen carefully by our U.S. presidents to assure that each has demonstrated an appreciation for the cause of environmental protection. However, criticism of the Superfund program continues to come from diverse sources including businesses, the financial community, environmental groups, practicing attorneys, and legal scholars. Studies criticizing Superfund have come from a variety of organizations including, but not limited to, Congressional Committees, the **General Accounting Office (GAO)**, the Center for the Study of American Business, and the Rand Institute for Civil Justice.

Such groups have issued reports evaluating the implementation and effectiveness of the Superfund program, and they have been highly critical for a variety of reasons. Those reasons include those already described in this article such as the EPA's lack of progress in cleaning up and delisting sites; the enormous compliance costs imposed on companies identified as responsible parties; the broad sweep of Superfund's definitions of "responsible parties," which has extended liability even to financial institutions which have acquired the ability to engage in management decisions; and at least four other major sets of criticisms, which are described below.

First, Superfund's liability scheme is criticized, because it has resulted in a plethora of lawsuits. The EPA sues polluters to recovers costs; polluters sue their insurance companies and each other. Litigation with respect to a site in Glenwood Landing, New York presents an extreme example of this phenomenon. There, the EPA identified 257 PRPs who hired over 130 law firms to represent them; 442 insurance companies were sued, and the insurance companies hired 72 law firms for their defense.

Second, Superfund's retroactivity is harshly criticized. Companies pay for clean up of wastes placed at sites before Superfund's passage in 1980 regardless of whether the practices were legal at the time of disposal and even if disposal methods followed what was common industrial practice at the time.

Third, U.S. businesses allege that Superfund places them at a competitive disadvantage in the developing global economy. They say that Superfund imposes more stringent regulations on them than those placed on manufacturing firms operating in other countries.

Fourth, it is alleged that EPA has pursued levels of clean-up that are unrealistic and not cost-effective. Critics of Superfund say that individual communities insist on "gold-plated" clean ups even where such a level is not warranted. "How clean is clean?" is a major, complicated issue facing the EPA, and the issue will be before Congress as it considers renewal of or amendments to Superfund.

THE EFFECTS AND THE FUTURE OF SUPERFUND

Superfund has changed the way business is done in this country. EPCRA, added to Superfund in 1986, requires record keeping and reporting that affect businesses in their every day operations and in their dealings with the public. Since its initial implementation in 1980, Superfund has changed the way land and facilities are bought and sold in the United States. Environmental audits have become a standard step of the process of buying and selling commercial or industrial real property in this country, and most lending institutions require such audits as a precondition to issuance of any kind of mortgage on business property. One unfortunate result of Superfund is that it appears to encourage businesses to purchase and develop previously unused property rather than risk the potential Superfund liability which might arise with respect to land previously used for industrial purposes.

As Congress debates reauthorization of Superfund in 1994 and 1995, it is being asked to make fundamental changes in Superfund's provision. The range of proposals includes plans to reform its liability scheme; proposals for new, broad-based taxes to fund clean ups; and mechanisms to develop more flexible ways to deal with the question of "How clean is clean?" Debate in the public arena and before Congress promises to be heated and vigorous.

[Paulette L. Stenzel]

FURTHER READING:

Lis, James and Melinda Warren. *Reforming Superfund.* Center for the Study of American Business, Policy Study #118, Feb. 1994.

Kelly, Cynthia C. and Leah B. Benedict. "Superfund: What Every Manager Should Know," *Public Manager.* Aug., 1990, p. 11.

Findley, Roger W. and Daniel A. Farber. *Environmental Law in a Nutshell*, 2nd ed. West Publishing Company, 1988, pp. 169-191.

"Waste Not, Pay Anyway: Most Firms Foot Cleanup Bill," *Nation.* Nov. 17, 1986, pp. 18-19.

Stenzel, Paulette L. "Small Business and the Emergency Planning and Community Right-to-Know Act," *Michigan Bar Journal.* 1980, pp. 181-183.

COMPUTER-AIDED DESIGN (CAD) AND COMPUTER-AIDED MANUFACTURING (CAM)

Computer-aided design (CAD) involves creating computer models defined by geometrical parameters. These models typically appear on a computer monitor as a three-dimensional representation of a part or a system of parts, which can be readily altered by changing relevant parameters. CAD systems enable designers to view objects under a wide variety of representations and to test these objects by simulating real-world conditions.

Computer-aided manufacture (CAM) uses geometrical design data to control automated machinery. CAM systems are associated with computer numerical control (CNC) or direct numerical control (DNC), systems. These systems differ from older forms of numerical control (NC) in that geometrical data is encoded mechanically. Since both CAD and CAM use computer-based methods for encoding geometrical data, it is possible for the processes of design and manufacture to be highly integrated. Computer-aided design and manufacture are commonly referred to as CAD/CAM.

THE ORIGINS OF CAD/CAM

CAD had its origins in three separate sources, which also serve to highlight the basic operations that CAD systems provide. The first of these sources resulted from attempts to automate the drafting process. These developments were pioneered by the General Motors Research Laboratories in the early-1960s. One of the important time-saving advantages of computer modeling over traditional drafting methods is that the former can be quickly corrected or manipulated by changing a model's parameters. The second source of CAD's origins was in the testing of designs by simulation. The use of computer modelling to test products was pioneered by high-tech industries like aerospace and semiconductors. The third source of CAD development resulted from efforts to facilitate the flow from the design process to the manufacturing process using numerical control (NC) technologies, the use of which was widespread in many applications by the mid-1960s. It was this source that resulted in the linkage between CAD and CAM. One of the most important trends in CAD/CAM technologies is the ever-tighter integration between the design and manufacturing stages of CAD/CAM-based production processes.

Numerical Control (NC) of automated machinery was developed in the early-1950s and thus preceded the use of computerized control by several years. Like CAM, NC technologies made use of codified geometrical data to control the operations of a machine. The data was encoded by punch holes on a paper tape that was fed through a reader, essentially the same mechanism as that on a player piano. Once the control tape was produced, it offered a reliable means to replace the skilled machinists that had previously operated such machines. From the firm's point of view, the drawback of the old NC technologies was the difficulty in converting the design for a three-dimensional object into holes on a tape. This required the services of a tape encoding specialist. Since this specialist was required to work without any significant visual feedback, work was essentially trial and error and could only be tested in the actual production process. The tape encoder had to account for a large number of variables, including optimal feed rates and cutting speeds, the angle at which the tool should contact the part, and so on. Given the considerable time and expense involved in NC technologies, it was only economically viable when a large number of parts were to be produced.

The development of CAD and CAM and particularly the linkage between the two overcame these problems by enabling the design and manufacture of a part to be undertaken using the same system of encoding geometrical data. This eliminated the need for a tape encoding specialist and greatly shortened the time between design and manufacture. CAD/CAM thus greatly expanded the scope of production processes with which automated machinery could be economically used. Just as important, CAD/CAM gave the designer much more direct control over the production process, creating the possibility of completely integrated design and manufacturing processes.

The rapid growth in the use of CAD/CAM technologies after the early-1970s was made possible by the development of mass-produced silicon chips and the microprocessor, resulting in more readily affordable computers. As the price of computers continued to decline and their processing power improved, the use of CAD/CAM broadened from large firms using large-scale mass production techniques (the automobile industry, for instance) to firms of all sizes. The scope of operations to which CAD/CAM was applied broadened as well. In addition to parts-shaping by traditional machine tool processes such as stamping, drilling, milling, and grinding, CAD/CAM has come to be used by firms involved in producing consumer electronics, electronic components, and molded plastics. Computers are also used to control a number of manufacturing processes that are not defined as CAM because the control data are not based on geometrical parameters. An example of this would be at a chemical processing plant.

Using CAD, it is possible to simulate in three dimensions the movement of a part through a production process. This process can simulate feed rates, angles and speeds of machine tools, the position of part-holding clamps, as well as range and other constraints limiting the operations of a machine. The continuing development of the simulation of various manufacturing processes is one of the key means by which CAD and CAM systems are becoming increasingly tightly integrated. CAD/CAM systems also facilitate communication among those involved in design, manufacturing, and other processes. This is of particular importance when one firm contracts another to either design or produce a component.

ADVANTAGES AND DISADVANTAGES

Modeling with CAD systems offer a number of advantages over traditional drafting methods, that use rulers, squares, and compasses. Designs can be altered without erasing and redrawing. CAD systems offer "zoom" features analogous to a camera lens whereby a designer can magnify certain elements of a model to facilitate inspection. Computer models are typically three dimensional and can be rotated on any axis, much as one could rotate an actual three dimensional model in one's hand, enabling the designer to gain a fuller sense of the object. CAD systems also lend themselves to modeling cutaway drawings, in which the internal shape of a part is revealed, and to illustrating the spatial relationships among a system of parts.

To understand CAD it is also useful to understand what CAD cannot do. CAD systems have no means of comprehending real-world concepts, such as the nature of the object being designed or the function that object will serve. CAD systems function by their capacity to codify geometrical concepts. Thus the design process using CAD involves transferring a designer's idea into a formal geometrical model. In this sense, existing CAD systems cannot actually design anything.

In their 1993 volume *CADCAM: From Principles to Practice*, McMahon and Browne summarize limitations of existing CAD/CAM systems as follows: "There is a widespread view that CAD is not yet adequate as an *aid* to the designer in generating a design. CAD is considered to concentrate rather too much on providing means of representing the final form of the design, whereas designers also need a continual stream of advice and information to assist in decision making.... The tasks of CAD systems of the future are therefore to represent a wider variety of a design's properties, in terms that are familiar to engineers, and of a company's organization and equipment, that influence design." Some of these limitations of CAD were addressed by the development of the Parametric Technology Corporation's Pro/ENGINEER software, which provides the designer with a number of geometrical building blocks on which to base designs. The firm's software packages have been extremely successful, with sales increasing by 88 percent in fiscal year 1993, to $161 million.

Other limitations to CAD are being addressed by research and development in the field of **expert systems**. This field derived from research done on **artificial intelligence**. One example of an expert system involves incorporating information about the nature of materials—their weight, tensile strength, flexibility and so on—into CAD software. By including this and other information, the CAD system could then "know" what an expert engineer knows when that engineer creates a design. The system could then mimic the engineer's thought pattern and actually "create" a design. Expert systems might involve the implementation of more abstract principles, such as the nature of gravity and friction or the function and relation of commonly used parts, such as levers or nuts and bolts. Expert systems might also come to change the way data is stored and retrieved in CAD/CAM systems, supplanting the hierarchical system with one that offers greater flexibility.

One of the key areas of development in CAD technologies is the simulation of performance. Among the most common types of simulation are testing for response to stress and modeling the process by which a part might be manufactured or the dynamic relationships among a system of parts. In stress tests, model surfaces are shown by a grid or mesh, that distort as the part comes under simulated physical or thermal stress. Dynamics tests function as a complement or substitute for building working prototypes. The ease with which a part's specifications can be changed facilitates the development of optimal dynamic efficiencies both as regards the functioning of a system of parts and the manufacture of any given part. Simulation is also used in electronic design automation, in which simulated flow of current through a circuit enables the rapid testing of various component configurations.

The processes of design and manufacture are, in some sense, conceptually separable. Yet the design process must be undertaken with an understanding of the nature of the production process. It is necessary, for example, for a designer to know the properties of the materials with which the part might be built, the various techniques by which the part might be shaped, and the scale of production that is economically viable. The conceptual overlap between design and manufacture is suggestive of the potential benefits of CAD and CAM and the reason they are generally considered together as a system.

AN EXAMPLE OF THE USE OF CAD/CAM

The Boeing Corporation's development of the 757 airplane illustrates the benefits of CAD/CAM technologies. The 757 was the first plane Boeing produced that was completely designed by CAD systems. Designing the 757 took longer than the 747, its predecessor. This occurred in part because the use of CAD incorporated a broader scope of considerations into the design process. The benefits of CAD/CAM were seen most clearly in the post-design phases of production. The 757 was made from parts, produced by over 50 different firms. CAD/CAM enabled the more precise fit of parts, the result being that the first 757 required only six shims, compared to several hundred for the first 747. Additionally, Boeing engineers had scheduled ten days for the assembly of the fuselage and wing spars of the first 757, but actual assembly took only two days. Boeing estimated that the use of CAD throughout the design process lowered overall person-hours for assembly by one-third. Last, the analysis functions of CAD enabled the number of working prototypes to be reduced to three, down from twelve for the 747.

The integration of CAD and CAM systems with the broader aspects of a firm's operations is referred to as simultaneous or concurrent engineering. Concurrent engineering was adopted by the Ford Motor Co.'s Engine Division, B.F. Goodrich, and Cannondale in the early-1990s. Ford's Engine Division was moving to integrate all production and design systems into a single database that could be accessed from workstations, Macintoshes and IBM-compatible personal computers alike, enabling a large number of groups to comment on engine designs. This enabled not only engineers and designers but also buying agents to make comments. In its production of wheels and carbon braking systems for Boeing's new 777, B.F. Goodrich developed a system that linked all relevant departments, including planning, purchasing, design, manufacturing, quality control and marketing. Cannondale claimed that CAD/CAM technologies enabled it to produce five times as many bicycles per year with the same floor space. CAD/CAM also enabled the firm to redesign 90 to 95 percent of its 37 models each year.

THE FUTURE OF CAD/CAM

Recent technical developments have addressed all aspects of CAD/CAM systems. The use of personal computers and the Microsoft Corp.'s Windows software emerged as an alternative to older mainframe- and workstation-based systems. The greater viability of personal computers for CAD/CAM applications results from their ever-increasing processing power. An important trend is toward the standardization of software, so that different packages can readily share data. Standards have been established for some time regarding data exchange and graphics, and the X Windows System and Microsoft's Windows are becoming established as industry standards for user interfaces. An increasing number of software producers based their products on Windows in the mid-1990s. For electronic design automation software, the trend toward standardization was facilitated by the standards put forth by Computer Framework Initiative Inc. in the early-1990s. Other improvements in software include greater sophistication of visual representation, such as the replacement of three dimensional by solid modeling, in which objects are represented in a more fully defined manner. Improvements have also been made in the greater integration of modeling and testing applications.

[David Kucera]

FURTHER READING:

''All Together Now,'' *Automotive Industries*. December 1992, p. 73.

Bedworth, D.D., M.R. Henderson and P.M. Wolfe. *Computer-Integrated Design and Manufacture*. McGraw-Hill, 1991.

''B.F. Goodrich Says'Bravo' to Concurrent Engineering,'' *Design News*. November 23, 1992, p. 36.

''CAD/CAM Spells Big Market,'' *Computing Canada*. October 13, 1992, p. 23.

''Cannondale Pedals its Way to the Top,'' *U.S. News and World Report*. January 10, 1994, p. 53.

''Leaders of the Pack,'' *Machine Design*. February 21, 1994, p. 52.

McMahon, Chris and Jimmie Browne. *CADCAM: From Principles to Practice*. Addison-Wesley Publishing Co., 1993.

Medland, A.J. and Piers Burnett. *CAD/CAM in Practice: A Manager's Guide to Understanding and Using CAD/CAM*. John Wiley & Sons, 1986.

Mortenson, M.E. *Geometric Modelling*. John Wiley & Sons, 1985.

''1993 CAD/CAM Buyer's Guide,'' *Automotive Industries*. November 1992, p. 61.

Oshuga, S. ''Toward Intelligent CAD Systems,'' *Computer-Aided Design*. 21(5), pp. 315-37.

Taylor, D.L. *Computer-Aided Design*. Addison-Wesley Publishing Co., 1992.

''Technology of the Year: Parametric Technology Corp; Changing the Way Products Are Designed,'' *Industry Week*. December 20, 1993, p. 28.

''The CAD/CAM Claims Come True After All,'' *Machine Design*. October 22, 1992, p. 126.

COMPUTER CONFERENCING

Computer conferencing systems (CCS) automate the structure, storage, and processing of information among a group of people. In a CCS, computers, communications, and people combine to foster exchange without regard to geographic or time barriers. Known alternately as groupware, **electronic mail**, or computer mediated communication (CMC), computer conferencing systems integrate processors and participants. **Computer networking** creates the framework of electric signals, transmission, and topology. These networking capabilities enable the physical relay of information. Human participants create the essence of a CCS. Individual participants control the pace and content of a CCs, allowing large groups to perform without sacrificing individual participation rates. The group members of a computer conference determine content and discussion parameters. A CCS tailors digital communication features to support information exchange. Specific options frequently include the ability to send electronic mail, read categorized information files, work in subgroups and create common interest groups. Structurally, three specific types of computer conferencing exist: one to one, one to many, and many to many participants. Affected by factors like medium of exchange, size and structure of group, space and time constraints, participation rates, common memory, and speed, computer conferencing provides unique capabilities in communications. Social and psychological factors also influence the effectiveness of electronic communication systems. The user interface constitutes the primary interactive platform between the human user and the microcomputer. Group characteristics and access rights, skill, usage, and training affect conferencing effectiveness. Issues like privacy, **computer security**, and telecommuting represent the convergence and conflict of digital information with individual rights. Companies may obtain conferencing systems from other vendors or develop in-house capabilities.

THE DEVELOPMENT OF CCS

One of the first widely publicized conferencing systems, EMISARI, served as the foundation for the Emergency Management Information System. At the same time in the early 1970's, researchers at the University of Michigan developed the CONFER system. Other early systems frequently relied on the manipulations of the UNIX operating system to allow copying of files from one computer to another, or UUCP (Unix to Unix Copying Program). In 1979, a computer based bulletin board software released into the public domain by Ward Christensen set the stage for further developments in computer conferencing. By 1980, a software program called Usenet appeared to maintain a set of publicly accessible message files on geographically dispersed computers. Advances in speed and cost of networked microcomputers and the advent of the network of networks, the Internet, combined to foster the growth and popularity of computer conferencing. Current technologies support full motion video and audio conferencing although cost is high and performance inconsistent.

COMPONENTS

At a minimum, a computer conference consists of an input device, a computer processor, an output device and a linkage to other computers. The computer input device appears most often as a keyboard but can also be audio and/or video, as well. The computer processor, the master set of instructions and minimum number of electrical pathways, directs the flow of information between user and computer and computer and other systems. Output devices frequently include a computer display screen but can also include audio output. Connections to other computers, networking cables, and complex software complete the necessary equipment package.

NETWORKING FOUNDATIONS

Computers exchange information based on the binary coding system. The presence or absence of an electric signal indicates whether or not a 1 or a 0 is transmitted or received. Called a bit of information, these 1's and 0's combine into an 8 bit pattern to make a byte. The American Standard Code of Information Interchange (ASCII) set represents most alphanumeric information in bytes. Analog and digital signals present two opposite types of computer exchange. Analog signals are transmitted over a continually varying or real time connection. Digital signals, conversely, are stop and go signals that relay from one point to the next. The two types of signals must converge when computer conferencing relies on telephone transmission since both analog and digital signals are involved.

Modem is an acronym for modulator-demodulator. A modem smooths a pulsing digital signal into a phase (curved and continuous) signal by using amplitude and frequency modulation. By exaggerating the signal and increasing its occurrence, a modem translates the mere presence or absence of a signal into a continuous transmission. As a result, digital signals may be sent and received using a computer, modem, and active phone line.

Transmission speed and media represent two different aspects of networking. Bandwidth refers to the difference between the highest and lowest cycle per second (hertz) capacity of the transmission media.

When bandwidth is limited, text based transmissions relay quickly while larger graphic image and sound files require greater transmission times. Twisted copper telephone lines, coaxial cable, and fiber optic wires are three common carrier materials for networked communications. Each limits bandwidth according to its transmission capabilities with fiber optic providing the greatest bandwidth. Wireless communications, the transmission of information over radio or microwaves, increasingly interests business operations that require mobility and remote servicing.

The physical arrangement of participating computers defines a network topology. The topology of a computer network falls into one of four categories; bus, ring, star, or tree. A simple bus topology chains together any number of computers beginning to end. When beginning and end both connect, a ring topology forms. Star networks employ one central and stronger computer with individual nodes. A tree network combines branching and central processing microcomputer to form complex paths. Client-server technology is one variant of a star network. Normally, a faster and more powerful server maintains information and responds to requests for information. The client machine formats requests and displays results.

INDIVIDUAL PARTICIPATION

Individual efforts and participation greatly influence a computer conference by virtue of a primal interaction with the system. Computer interface refers to the mechanism of interaction between human user and computer generated information. Usually, interfaces are generalizable, offer guidance or help, and embody flexibility in design. Graphical user interfaces (GUI) are increasingly popular, with the Windows software program dominating business use. Computers equipped with video or audio devices use natural human interaction as an interface. The user interface influences individual participation based on its effectiveness, ease of use, and special features. Another influence on the type and frequency of individual participation, degree of formality, depends on the individual members, task, and position within the organization.

Optional features that enhance participation among most popular conferencing systems include messages, conferences, notebooks, and bulletins. Messages are synchronous information packets. Shorter than normal electronic mail, messages signal immediacy and more limited scope of distribution. Conferences run in real time or asynchronous modes. Many different people at different locations discuss issues and decisions in a conference. Notebooks constitute private workspace and may include electronic filing space and digital work areas. Bulletins create public viewing information and contain general purpose data and announcements. Companies like Citibank routinely use bulletin board systems to coordinate the exchange of auditing information.

STRUCTURES

Computer conferencing relies on three basic structures to exchange information; one to one, one to many and many to many. One to one correspondences, or **electronic mail**, are not technically considered conferencing systems. Paralleling the spoken or visual interaction, electronic mail records the textual equivalent. When electronic mail is gathered and sorted among a group of people, it becomes a form of text based conferencing. The basic one to many model forms the backbone of the listserv conference. A listserver is an automated software package for subscription to a text based conferencing system. Messages posted appear in each subscribers electronic mailbox through a redistribution subroutine. Such an application serves as a reminder and public announcement system as well. In the many to many model, informational materials are posted for individual access. The bulletin board system and Usenet, a giant global bulletin board of groups, are two examples of many to many conferencing structures. Groupware is another computer conferencing structure that relies on the many to many model of communication. Groupware programs, like calendars and project management, provide sharing of information resources, message management, conferencing, scheduling, and work flow management for many members of a group. Generally, groupware programs transcend conferencing and include other features like automated project management.

CONFERENCE FACTORS

Several factors determin the nature of a computer conferencing system. First, is the medium of exchange. Conferencing systems exchange data using audio, video, and typed input. Typed exchange of information is more common and cheaper while full motion desktop video carries a much higher price tag. Second is the size and structure of a group. Large group disadvantages of decreased participation are overcome by individually determined participation levels. And, special project or interest groups easily form and disband. Structurally, electronic conferences negate the effects of time and space simultaneously. Travelling on the impulse of an electric signal, connected to a worldwide network of networks, conferencing systems join the distant members of a group quickly and efficiently. Finally, common memory of group interaction exists in human minds and computer storage. messages or exchanges retrieved from computer memory augment individual knowledge. Additionally, group memory provides a solid history and past for social cohesion. At Electric Power Research Institute (EPRI), a computer conference called EPRINet formed in 1984. With ten year group memory, vast informational resources are available to its members.

HUMAN FACTORS

People communicate to exchange information. Electronic communication, both individually and group, provides for special and common interest interactions. Quick response, expert knowledge, enjoyable discourse, and problem solving are all examples of human motivations for using a conferencing system. Key factors in participation levels include training, ongoing usage, and skill level. Conferencing systems that rely on keyboard input are particularly affected by participant typing abilities. Biases and prejudices based on race, sex, and physical disability disappear in text based conferencing systems when visual cues are not provided.

Conferences create opportunities for collaborative work. Forums for heated and sometimes irrational discourse are also available. Flaming defines a computer conferencing phenomenon that occurs when members perceive they are anonymous and respond with more overt hostility than they would in face-to-face communications. Combined with lack of visual cues and ease of immediate transmission, flaming presents a unique social byproduct of computer conferencing.

PRIVACY, ACCESS, AND SECURITY

The digital transmission of information is fast and reliable but often vulnerable to hijack or destruction. Issues with privacy include violation of messaging privacy, monitoring, matching or redesigning personal data for other than intended uses, caller identification, and other personal indignities like **computer fraud**. Accuracy of digital information arises as an issue when credit and financial decisions rely on automated credit ratings. Access to information and intellectual property laws and copyright conflict with rights of individual access. Recent encryption schemes, or coded information, seem to infringe on fair use doctrine and remain unresolved. **Computer security** issues involve protecting both hardware and software. Intellectual properties, eavesdropping, and fraudulent use are all examples of security issues raised within a computer conference. Other examples include trading of illegally copied software and pornography on conferencing systems.

ACQUISITION

Several advantages and disadvantages exist for both out sourcing or in-house development of CCS.

Generally, buying available commercial conferencing services provides advantages based on experimentation, support, quality, connectivity, and accessibility. Because commercial services already exist, companies may preview or experiment with systems before purchase. Support contracts and maintenance activities can be arranged to minimize on-site system and personnel expense. Quality of commercial service is high and accompanied by built-in features. For companies with wide spread operations, well connected commercial services provide instant connectivity. Additionally, because commercial services support almost all computer models, advantages are great for companies with a diverse hardware support base. Cost and customizability of a commercial system are the disadvantages. Commercial systems require upfront expenditures and may not be sufficiently alterable for special business uses. When a company is small and cannot afford to buy a commercial system, or when special features are necessary but unavailable, in-house development offers an advantageous option. Investment in programming personnel and lengthy development time are the disadvantages of in-house development of a CCS.

[Tona Henderson]

FURTHER READING:

"Communications, Computers, and Networks." *Scientific American.* September 1991.

"EPRINet—How Innovation Can Take Place." *Business Communications Review.* August, 1993, p. 8.

Arnold, David O. *Computers and Society: Impact!* McGraw-Hill, 1991.

Cronin, Mary J. *Doing Business on the Internet: How the Electronic Highway is Transforming American Companies.* Von Nostrand Reinhold, 1994.

Halhed, Basil R. "Desktop Video Begins Edging Into The Picture." *Business Communications Review.* January 1992, pp. 30-34.

Hiltz, Starr Roseanne and Murray Turoff, eds. *The Network Nation: Human Communication via Computer.* MIT Press, 1993.

Kobielus, James. "The Time Is Ripe To Pick Groupware." *Network World.* August 1993, pp. 47-53

Martin, E. Wainright et al. *Managing Information Technology: What Managers Need to Know.* MacMillan, 1991.

Morrison, Joline and Olivia R. Liu Sheng. "Communication Technologies and Collaborative Systems: Common Domains, Problems and Solutions." *Information & Management.* August 1992, pp. 93-112.

Quartermain, John. "What Can Businesses Get Out Of The Internet." *Computerworld.* February 22, 1994, pp. 81-83.

Rapaport, Matthew. "Groupware vs. CCS: Comparing Benefits and Functionality." *Telecommunications.* November 1991, pp. 37-40.

Rapaport, Matthew. *Computer Mediated Communications.* Wiley and Sons, 1991.

Senn, James A. *Information Systems in Management.* Wadsworth, 1990.

Shieh, Jackie and Rhea Ballard. "E-Mail Privacy." *Educom Review*. March-April 1994, p. 59.

Stevens, Tim. "The Smart Office." *Industry Week*. January 17, 1994, pp. 31-34.

Whaley, Carlos C. "New Electronic Technologies (NET) Emerge in the Brokerage Distribution System." *Broker World*. August 1993, pp. 46-50.

Wood, Lamont. "Business Profits From Bulletin Boards." *Datamation*, May, 1993. pp. 45-48.

COMPUTER CRIMES

SEE: Computer Security

COMPUTER FRAUD

The advent of **computers** revolutionized the business world and simplified life for many people. Unfortunately, computers also contributed to an increase in fraud, which results in severe financial losses for businesses and individuals alike. Estimates suggest that computer thefts in the United States amount to $3 to $5 billion per year. Computer thieves are not content to steal small amounts of money at a time, either. The typical bank robber averages about $5,000 a heist; electronic thieves average about $500,000 per incident.

As long as there is money to be stolen via computers, thieves will find a way to steal it. There does not appear to be any end to the number of computer fraud schemes devised to bilk people and companies. Computer fraud is a growing problem throughout the world, and one which must be taken seriously by everyone from executives to government officials and law enforcement personnel.

WHAT IS COMPUTER FRAUD?

There is no clear-cut definition of computer fraud. It can best be described as any activity perpetrated via use of a computer to steal money or services. Ironically, the computer can either be the tool of crime or the target. Computer criminals are adept at using their knowledge of technology to commit any number and variety of crimes to enrich themselves at others' expense.

Unfortunately, computer crimes are often very difficult to detect; often criminals need only to destroy their computers or programs to escape being caught. Experts, however, are developing more sophisticated weapons in their fight against computer fraud. The trick for them is to stay one step ahead of the criminals, which is not always an easy task, but they do not shy away from the challenge.

WHY COMPUTER CRIME IS DIFFERENT THAN OTHER TYPES

Computer crime creates special problems for investigators. Generally, computer criminals possess more intelligence than criminals in other fields. The most salient characteristics that set them apart are their aggressiveness and technological expertise. Many computer criminals see their activities as a challenge, not only against their victims, but against the computers themselves. They relish attempts to create programs that will enable them to siphon money from unsuspecting victims or to unravel the sophisticated programs installed by security personnel to thwart their criminal efforts. Consequently, they are not afraid to challenge any type of organization, including powerful government agencies such as the **Internal Revenue Service (IRS)**. In fact, criminals defraud the IRS out of as much as $5 billion dollars annually—one percent of the amount the IRS collects from individual taxpayers in a single year.

In a case in Texas in the early 1990s, 24 people, primarily West African nationals, electronically filed 800 false tax returns using valid Social Security numbers they had obtained deceptively from taxpayers. The IRS handed out more than $1 million in refunds based on the fraudulent returns before detecting the scheme. But, the IRS has nothing about which to be ashamed. Corporations and individuals often fall prey to computer crooks, too. Often, society simply does not care.

SOCIETY'S REACTIONS TO COMPUTER FRAUD

Society has not always reacted strongly to computer fraud. Courts have often been reluctant to punish criminals who indulge in computer crimes because they view such infractions as somewhat harmless compared to street crime. According to a study conducted in Washington, D.C., of 82 people convicted of **white-collar crimes**, only 50 percent received suspended sentences or probation. About eight percent received sentences ranging from one week to six months in prison. Approximately ten percent received sentences ranging from six months to three years in prison. Only about 20 percent received sentences exceeding three years in prison. One of the first things that must happen if computer crime is to be taken seriously is to change judges' and juries' attitudes about its importance.

One of the problems in dealing with computer criminals is that, until recently, the people charged with detecting their activities, apprehending them, and ultimately trying them in court have not been capable of dealing with the technological aspects of the crimes. That is partly because computer crime is a relatively new phenomenon. Major cases of computer crime date back only to 1971 or so.

One of the first major cases allegedly involving computer tampering was reported by the New York-Penn Central Railroad. Officials disclosed that more than 200 of the company's freight cars had been rerouted from Philadelphia to an obscure yard in Chicago. The original markings on the cars were painted out and changed. The same thing happened to another 200 more or so cars, which were also reported missing. Each lost car cost the railroad an average of $60,000.

The chief of the Federal Organized Crime Strike Force at the time suggested that someone may have gained unauthorized access to the railroad's computer and changed program instructions to misroute the cars to other locations. Since that case, and another highly publicized case in California a year later in which an engineering student stole more than $1 million worth of electronic equipment from the state's largest telephone company, computer crime has drawn more attention from business, law enforcement, and judicial officials. It has also become a focus of home computer owners, many of whom have fallen prey to computer fraud.

HOME COMPUTERS AND FRAUD

The great increase in the number of personal computers in people's homes has spawned a new era of crime. Investment scam artists in particular are busy defrauding individuals of millions of dollars a year through sophisticated scams. Often, scam artists operate across state lines in perpetrating their schemes. While this presents them with larger audiences of potential victims, it also opens the door for federal officials to hunt and prosecute them. That does not faze a lot of computer criminals, however. If they are brazen enough to steal from the IRS, other government agencies certainly are not going to prevent them from committing crimes. Besides, the spurt in membership in on-line computer networks is too good an opportunity for computer crooks to pass up.

In recent years, the number of people who subscribe to large commercial on-line services such as Prodigy, CompuServe, and America Online has risen to around 5,000,000. Criminal computer users are making serious efforts to bilk as many of these subscribers as they can. For example, computer crooks might masquerade as money **management** specialists or stock brokers trying to promote worthless penny **stocks**. They try to entice prospective victims into joining pyramid schemes, in which participants must enlist others in order to make promised profits, or investing in lucrative-sounding international deals and fuel-drilling ventures. They may be acting on their own or as representatives of shady businesses. These crooks approach unsuspecting victims through computer **bulletin board systems**—computer files where users may leave messages, make comments, and carry on electronic conversations with other users.

In one Missouri case, an unlicensed stockbroker offered his services to unsuspecting victims. He made dubious claims about stocks which were not licensed for sale in the state. He suggested fallaciously that Donald Trump was a major investor in a small cruise line whose seldom-traded stock the unlicensed stockbroker was promoting. Fortunately, state regulators uncovered his scheme before he could bilk state residents out of large sums of money. Not all criminals are detected so quickly, though.

In another scam, in New Jersey, computer criminals pushed the stock of a Canadian modular housing firm whose shares jumped from 42 cents a share to $1.30 early in 1994. As a result, activity in the stock among computer users rose quickly. The daily trading volume reached 600,000 shares—for a stock which had an activity level of only 175,000 shares in all of December 1993! The stock price dropped quickly from $1.30 to only 60 cents a share, which meant a lot of people lost money on the deal. That did not include the criminals, however. They walked away with a healthy profit.

Another popular activity of computer criminals is pyramid schemes. In these, people are encouraged to send sums of money ranging from $1 to $2,000 each to the top five names on an **electronic mail** chain list. After they send the money, their names go on the bottom of the list. Eventually, they are led to believe, they will rise to the top of the list and will receive sums as high as $600,000 from people on the lower rungs. Needless to say, more people lose their few dollars than gain $600,000—or even recoup their original investments. Pyramid schemes are invented solely for the benefit of the criminals who run them, and computers facilitate the process.

THE EFFECTS OF COMPUTER FRAUD IN THE BUSINESS WORLD

Companies of all sizes have begun using computers for more and more purposes in recent years. Consequently, their exposure to fraud has increased exponentially. And, computer theft is often internal in origin. One classic example involved the transfer of $54 million from the London office of the Union Bank of Switzerland to another Swiss bank. Fortunately, one of the computers broke down at an opportune time. The malfunction alerted auditors to the attempted theft.

HOW COMPANIES CONTROL COMPUTER FRAUD

Businesses have implemented a wide variety of techniques to forestall computer fraud. They have, for example, created **internal auditing** systems that will detect illegal activities as quickly as possible and erase them when found. Companies have limited access to their computers to people who must know constantly changing passwords to gain entry. They have upgraded backup systems so they can quickly restore files and alleviate the damage created by any hackers who do manage to gain access to computers. Nevertheless, computer fraud will continue. The primary goal of business executives in fighting computer crime is to reduce its impact as much as possible and uncover fraud quickly. They are being aided in this respect by law enforcement officials and government agencies.

THE LAW ENFORCEMENT RESPONSE TO COMPUTER FRAUD

Police departments are becoming more sophisticated in their approach to fighting computer crime. They are adding more computers to their arsenals and establishing partnerships with local businesses. For example, representatives of the Lake Worth, Florida, Police Department meet monthly with a coalition of people from the city's private businesses, **banking** and **financial institutions**, other law enforcement agencies, and government organizations. Other departments are adopting similar partnership approaches.

A growing number of the police departments in the United States today have added people to their staffs who specialize in the investigation of computer-related crimes. In fact, 80 percent of the departments polled by *Law and Order Magazine* for an article in its July 1994 issue reported that they had such specialists on their staffs. This is an indication that police departments are becoming more active in their investigations into computer crimes—and more proficient besides. In fact, the federal government is encouraging enhanced police involvement in detecting computer-related crimes. In Title XXI of its 1994Crime Act , the federal government set aside $122 million for the operation of state and local courts and to improve police use of computers and other advanced technological equipment. Also, in Title XXIX, the government identified the types of unauthorized entry into computer systems and networks that constitute federal crimes. Basically, it says, any unauthorized entry into a computer or computer network that causes any damage to the system is illegal and subject to federal prosecution. These inclusions in the bill are indicative of the growing law enforcement interest in computer crime—which is matched in other sectors of society.

SOCIETY AND COMPUTER CRIME

There are many people who are neither law enforcement administrators nor government officials who are becoming active in fighting computer fraud. For example, the state of Maryland publishes *Tips for Tough Times*, which is distributed statewide through more than 340 businesses, community associations, churches, unions, agencies, and service groups. The publication provides tips to consumers on how to recognize signs of fraud *before* they lose money to unscrupulous criminals. Securities regulators in several states have launched attacks to root out promoters of computer scams of all types. Their chief message to computer users is simply: ''Use common sense.'' This is also the message preached by government spokespeople.

The IRS announced in 1994 new procedures designed to crack down on computer fraud. The procedures, detailed in a 47-page regulation, included steps such as requiring tax preparers with access to computers to be at least 21 years of age and either U.S. citizens or permanent resident aliens. The IRS detected 21,000 electronic fraud cases during the first four months of 1994. Unfortunately, it only turned up two-thirds of them in time to stop refund checks. The fact that it is uncovering as many cases as it is, however, is encouraging and indicative of the gains in the overall fight against computer fraud.

THE FUTURE OF COMPUTER FRAUD

Computer fraud will probably never be eradicated completely. In fact, it is likely to increase as more and more computers are introduced into businesses and homes. As computer crooks become more active, law enforcement administrators, business people, and government officials will need to develop more sophisticated systems to detect fraud.

[Arthur G. Sharp]

FURTHER READING:

Bequai, August. *Computer Crime*. Lexington, MA: D. C. Heath and Company, 1978.

Krauss, Leonard I. *Computer Fraud and Countermeasures*. Englewood, NJ: Prentice-Hall, 1979.

Tien, James M. *Electronic Fund Transfer Systems Fraud*. Washington, D.C.: U.S. Department of Justice, 1985.

Wagner, Charles R. *The CPA and Computer Fraud*. Lexington, MA: Lexington Books, 1979.

Whiteside, Thomas. *Computer Capers*. New York: Thomas Y. Crowell Company, 1978.

COMPUTER NETWORKS

A computer network consists of two or more computing devices connected by a medium allowing the exchange of electronic information. These computing devices can be mainframes or PCs; they can also be connected to a variety of peripherals, including printers, modems, and CD-ROM drives.

Research facilities sponsored by the US Department of Defense were among the first to develop computer networks. Perhaps the most famous example of such a network is the Internet, which began in 1969 as part of a project to link computers at four research sites. More and more universities connected to the Internet until it became an international giant—in 1993 it had 15 million daily users in 50 countries, and was connected to 10,000 separate networks.

By the mid-1990s, networks in their many manifestations had become commonplace. In order to reach this stage, many technological challenges had to be met; the most daunting involved enabling communications between hardware and software made by many different manufacturers.

A network can allow information to be shared among many different users very quickly. This information can include programs, data, backups, voice, or video. Networks can also be connected to other networks or to mainframes. The concept of the paperless office made possible by networking has other advantages, reducing paperwork by recording memos in **electronic mail** and making large directories and inventory lists accessible without distributing large numbers of printed copies. Electronic mail, or "e-mail," can greatly facilitate communication among users, whether they are housed in the same building or not. Through e-mail, updates can be automatically distributed at specified times; memos and personal messages can be transmitted instantaneously.

Networks can also allow businesses to reduce expenses by sharing common equipment, such as printers, among many different computers. While printers can be shared in other ways, such as by carrying information on floppy disks from one PC to another, or using manual or electronic data switches, networks have the capacity to accommodate more users with less frustration. The power of mainframes or minicomputers can be used in harmony with personal computers. The larger machines can process larger and more complex jobs, such as maintaining the millions of records needed by a national company, while individual PCs manned by individual users handle smaller jobs such as word processing. And older equipment can be rotated to less demanding jobs as workstations are upgraded. Many software pro-

grams also offer **license agreements** for networks, which can be more cost effective than purchasing individual copies for each machine. The costs of implementing a network depend on issues of performance, compatibility, and whether value must be added to a turnkey system through additional programming or the addition of special components.

Through coordinating all data and applications through a single network, backup copies of data for all systems can be made more consistently than could be expected if left to individual users. Additional, updated software for all machines on a network can be installed through a single PC. A centralized system simplifies other aspects of administration, too. With the proper software, computer security can also be implemented more effectively in a network than among many individual hard drives. Access to files can be restricted to password holders or it can be limited to inquiry-only access for public users. Generally, security measures are more vulnerable at machines with single user operating systems than those with network security precautions.

The types of machines that can be connected to a network include PCs, intelligent workstations, dumb terminals, host computers, clients, and file and other types of servers. File servers control network activity such as printing and data sharing, as well as controlling security. Important factors to consider in selecting a PC for a file server include its speed, processor performance, memory, hard drive capacity, and most importantly, its compatibility with network software.

File servers can be run in either a dedicated or a nondedicated mode. Nondedicated file servers can be used as a work station as well, although workstation functions can take up much of the processor's capacity, resulting in delays for network users. Also, if a workstation program causes the file server to lock up, the entire network may be affected and suffer a possible corruption of data. One compromise for a small office is to use a nondedicated file server as a workstation for a light user. A disk subsystem can increase the performance of a file server in large network applications.

Individual users access the file server using workstations, also referred to as data terminal equipment (DTEs). Some type of monitor is included in the typical workstation setup.

Networks are usually differentiated between local area networks (LANs) and wide area networks (WANs) based on differences in distance and technology. LANs are usually located within a single building, while WANs are not, often using leased or dial-up telephone lines as a medium.

Some type of media is required in order to connect network components. Various types of cables exist for this purpose; as with most hardware, their price is related to their performance. Two PCs can be connected quite simply and cheaply by using a null modem cable. At the upper end of the spectrum, wireless and even satellite connections are used by large corporations and the military.

The earliest cable to become widely used is coaxial cable (nicknamed "coax"). As it is shielded and resistant to electrical noise, it has proven useful in factory situations. Twisted-pair cable, also called UTP (unshielded twisted pair), has replaced coax in most applications, as it is cost effective. Similar to telephone wire, noise problems prevented it from being accepted more quickly. Underwriters Laboratories rates UTP cable from Levels I through V based on performance. Levels I and II are only suitable for low grade or slower applications.

Fiber optic is the most expensive and the fastest of the cables. For these reasons, it is frequently used for high-volume backbones connecting network segments. Another benefit of fiber optic cable is that it is immune to electrical interference.

In addition, companies such as NCR and Motorola, Inc. have introduced wireless systems for connecting workstations with the file server. Microwave dishes are among the oldest means of connecting computers over long distances, though they are limited to line-of-sight transmissions and can be affected by weather conditions. Depending upon frequency, microwave equipment can transmit up to 30 miles. Other options include using cellular telephone systems or satellites (provided by such companies as AT&T and GTE) as media. The latter have been used to transmit price changes among stores in national retail chains.

Other network hardware includes the connectors that interface computing devices with the connecting media. While mainframes usually have connectors built in, most PCs require the addition of a network interface card. Larger, more powerful computers require more expensive connections due to the cost of their high-performance microprocessors and support circuitry. Such devices often implement the protocol to which electronic messages on the network must conform. Connecting devices such as bridges, routers, and gateways are used to subdivide networks both physically and logically, to extend the range of cabling, and to connect dissimilar networks.

More sophisticated protocols generally require greater performance systems and therefore more expensive components, connections, and cabling. Protocol is either generated by network hardware or the nodes themselves, or both. Various standards exist; Open Systems Interconnect (OSI) is among the most widely accepted.

Network software is needed to perform network functions. In a LAN, some type of network software is typically installed in each computer on the network. In some environments, such as bulletin board systems, workstations need only a simple communications program (and a modem) to interface with the file server. Functions of network software include file transfer and real-time messaging, automatic formatting of e-mail, and creating directories and unique addresses for each node. Management utilities such as problem detection, performance analysis, configuration assistance, usage and accounting management (billing), and network security are usually included in network software packages.

It is the often complicated job of the network manager to ensure that all the hardware and software work together. An important aspect of the job is fault management, or the detection, isolation, and resolution of problems in the network. Performance management ensures that data exchange proceeds at an acceptable rate, a factor influenced by workload and the configuration of the network. Other duties include accounting management, monitoring user activity on the network, and security management, limiting access of certain files or the network itself to authorized users.

The topology, or the physical layout, of the network is the concern of configuration management. The three main arrangements are the bus, ring, and star. In the bus configuration, each node is connected to a common cable and detects messages addressed to it. Because it is reliable and uses the least amount of cabling, this layout is often used in offices. However, fiber optic systems cannot usually be arranged this way.

In the ring layout, packets of information are retransmitted along adjacent nodes. It has the possibility of greater transmission distances and fiber optic systems can use this layout. However, the components necessary are more expensive.

In the star arrangement, all traffic is routed through one central node. It offers the advantages of simplified monitoring and security. Also, unlike the other layouts, the failure of one node, unless it is the central one, does not cause the entire network to fail. This drawback is addressed in the clustered star layout, in which a number of star networks are linked together.

While topology refers to the physical layout of the network, architecture refers to the design of the rules computers must follow in order to communicate. The specific procedures that must be followed are called protocols. Architectures can be classified as either centralized or decentralized. The former is useful when many users need the same information; less maintenance is required to update the network. However, distributed processing via decentralized networks is becoming the standard as it allows work to be spread out, taking advantage of the capabilities of the ubiquitous and increasingly powerful PC.

The introduction of standards has reduced the cost of networking dissimilar products. Standardization organizations, government or industry-sponsored, reference standards in profiles or abstract models that leave some parameters open for software and hardware developers. For example, one thing that has not been defined in operating standards for modems is what to do if transmission speed must be reduced due to a drop in line quality. Individual manufacturers have been left to solve this problem, resulting in the possibility of different makes of modems being unable to communicate in such a situation.

The OSI model of network families is becoming the predominant standard. Like the TCP/IP (Transmission Control Protocol/Internet Protocol) standard that came before it, OSI is based on layered architectures; i.e., different layers in the software and hardware are devoted to different network functions. The lower layers exchange information between directly connected nodes and are concerned with electronic signal characteristics such as voltage. The middle layers are usually involved in detecting and correcting transmission errors and providing end-to-end connectivity. The upper layers are devoted to such higher level functions as e-mail capability. The X.25 protocol, used for high performance communications over telephone lines in wide area networks and other network families, is one of the first to be based on the OSI model.

Connecting devices can be used extend the range of cabling or to subdivide networks into segments, which is useful for isolating faults. However, repeaters merely extend distance of cable by receiving and retransmitting information packets. They do not provide isolation between the components they join. Connecting devices are classified according to the functional layer at which they operate.

Bridges operate at layer two (also known as the datalink layer). They are used to isolate segments from a network backbone, to connect two networks with identical lower layers, and to convert one lower level technology into another. They can be configured to transmit only appropriate messages (filtering).

Routers operate at layer three (network layer). They can also be used to isolate network segments from a backbone, but unlike bridges, they can connect segments with different lower-layer protocols. Software exists which can perform this function, though not usually as fast. "Brouters" are a hybrid between bridges and routes that operate at layers two or three.

Gateways operate at layers four (transport layer) or higher. They are required for minicomputer or mainframe access from PCs and are much more complex and costly than other connecting devices. They are capable of converting data for use between dissimilar networks.

[Frederick C. Ingram]

FURTHER READING:

Black, Uyless D. *Data Networks: Concepts, Theory, and Practice*. Englewood Cliffs, NJ: Prentice Hall, 1989.

Chorafas, Dimitris N. *The Handbook of Data Communications and Computer Networks*. 2nd ed., Blue Ridge Summit, PA: TAB Books, 1991.

Crowe, Elizabeth Powell. *The Electronic Traveller: Exploring Alternative Online Systems*. Blue Ridge Summit, PA: TAB Books, 1993.

Glossbrenner, Alfred. *The Complete Handbook of Personal Computer: Everything You Need to Go Online With the World*, 2nd ed., New York: St. Martin's Press, 1985.

Niedermiller-Chaffins, Debra. *Inside Novell NetWare, Special Edition*. Indianapolis, IN: New Riders Publishing, 1993.

Schatt, Stanley. *Understanding Network Management: Strategies and Solutions*. Blue Ridge Summit, PA: TAB Books, 1993.

Welch, Frank. *Integrated Computer Network Systems*. New York: Marcel Dekker, Inc., 1992.

COMPUTER SECURITY

Computer security is concerned with preventing information stored in or used by computers from being altered, stolen, or used to commit crimes. The field includes the protection of electronic funds transfers and other communications, as well as the prevention of computer viruses.

The power of the electronic digital computer to enable humans to handle mathematical and cryptological problems on an unprecedented scale has prompted governments to keep their use subject to the tightest security from the very beginning. In fact, details of the first operational electronic digital computer, the Colossus, were not made public until 1975. Until this time, the UNIVAC I, developed at the University of Pennsylvania and operational in 1946, was thought to have been the first one.

The Colossus was first put into service by the British government in 1943. It was used in cryptanalysis (the breaking of codes), and was used specifically, against the German Enigma communication codes. So sensitive was the information handled by the Colossus that mere knowledge of the machine's existence was limited to a few individuals. The computer was kept in a sealed room and was not connected to other computers or to any phone lines.

CRIMINAL THREATS AND HACKING

The post-war use of computers for business produced two important developments: timesharing and remote connections. Economies of scale required that early computers, which were very costly, be kept running as much as possible. One way to do this was to allow users access at different times, facilitated by the use of either dedicated lines or public telephone lines connecting the computer to remote users. However, the security vulnerabilities these measures produced would be exploited by a new breed of bandit, the ''hacker.''

Early use of the term ''hacker'' was applied to computer hobbyists who spent their spare time creating video games and other basic computer programs. However, this term acquired a pejorative connotation as certain of these amateurs created a scare by violating important databanks in the 1980s through ''hacking.'' Databases at the Los Alamos National Laboratory (a center of nuclear weapons research) and the Sloan-Kettering Cancer Center in New York City were among their targets. The introduction of relatively inexpensive personal computers and modems helped make this pastime affordable; the use of regular telephone lines as accessways made it possible. Automatic dialing programs, used to call all numbers in an exchange and to determine which are answered by computers, were among many tools hackers used to simplify their work. The designation ''hacker'' has also been given to programmers and disseminators of computer viruses. The military and some corporations have used ''tiger teams'' employing some of the same tactics as hackers to test the security of their networks.

Even more serious threats exist than the highly publicized hackers. The vital information kept in computers have made them a target of government and corporate espionage , as well as fraud and embezzlement. Computer hardware itself has been a target of vandalism by disgruntled employees and even terrorists.

Security has been defined as ''the protection of assets.'' Assets that can be stored or transmitted by computers include **electronic fund transfers** between **banks**. Proprietary information, such as product designs and databases containing information about clients, as well as other data files and computer programs themselves, must also be protected; they can be easily destroyed by computer viruses or unauthorized hacking. It can be difficult to place a dollar value on these assets, especially when such factors as potential loss of reputation or liability issues are considered. In some cases (e.g., military and hospital applications) there is a potential for loss of life due to misplaced or destroyed data; this cannot be adequately conveyed by risk analysis formulas. The question most users face is not whether to practice computer security measures, but how much time and effort to invest. Larger firms must incorporate procedures and policies for dealing with computer security issues; however, some basic principles apply to most applications regardless of scale.

Information is vulnerable to theft or misappropriation whether it is stored in memory or transmitted over cables. It must also be guarded once it reaches peripherals such as printers; one woman was able to print 200 paychecks for herself by simply pressing the repeat button on a printer. Data has also been gleaned from printouts found in trash baskets. This was one of many ways a teenager stole information from a telephone company in southern California in the 1970s and used it in a scheme to order supplies using the company's account, much like using a stolen credit card. The criminal merely picked up the merchandise at the company's loading dock, taking advantage of the premise's lack of security controls.

The thief, while searching for damaged electrical components to resell, searched the telephone company's disposal bins and obtained instructions for using the company's automated ordering system. Other vital information was gained by touring the company while posing as a journalist and through telephone calls made under false pretexts. In the final stages of the scam, the company was actually buying its own equipment back from the criminal's electronic parts business.

Law enforcement agencies have developed specialized techniques for prosecuting crimes specific to computers. Since 1976, computer crime-fighting techniques have been part of standard Federal Bureau of Investigation training. The Computer Fraud and Abuse Act of 1986, passed 10 years after the first federally prosecuted case involving criminal use of a computer, attempts to address this type of crime; most states have adopted similar statutes.

Physical access to computers can be limited in various ways, including power-on passwords; magnetic card readers; and biometrics, which verifies the user's identity through matching patterns in hand geometry, signature or keystroke dynamics, neural networks (the pattern of nerves in the face), DNA fingerprinting, retinal imaging, or voice recognition. More traditional site control methods such as sign-in logs and security badges can also be useful.

OTHER SECURITY THREATS

Not all threats to computer security are from parties with criminal intent, however. Computer supplies and hardware must also be protected from both environmental forces, such as power surges, floods, fires, etc., and simple operator incompetence, such as the careless handling of floppy disks.

The fundamentals of any computer security program begin with the environmental conditions the computer requires to operate properly. Adequate power must first be provided. Due to the distances electricity must travel, its nominal voltage may drop

10 percent by the time it reaches the computer. In addition, drops in voltage or blackouts can occur due to utility switching problems or to lightning strikes at the utility company. Besides the potential for loss of unsaved data, there exists the possibility of ''disk crashes,'' or damage to the disk due to contact with the read/write heads. Also dangerous are ''spikes,'' sharp increases in voltage that can seriously damage hardware. A variety of voltage regulators, surge protectors, grounding techniques, and filters exist to combat these problems. In the 1990s, intense activity centered on the development of uninterruptible power systems that use storage batteries to ensure a smooth transition between power sources in the event of power failure. Local area networks as well as individual computers can be protected by these devices.

Fire is another important threat to computer systems. Their susceptibility to fire damage is exacerbated by the flammability of paper supplies likely to be stored in close proximity. Plastics used in the manufacture of computers can produce explosive gases when exposed to high temperatures. A common safety measure, water sprinklers, can further damage computers, especially if the computers are under active power. The use of fire-resistant construction materials, fire walls, vent closure systems, etc., are standard ways to mitigate the threat of fire. Special attention should be given to fire detection and personnel should be trained in the use of hand extinguishers. Carbon dioxide and Halon 1211 gas extinguishers are suited for use near electronic equipment because they do not leave a residue.

Other physical security concerns include protection against excessive heat, humidity, and water, which can be introduced by flooding, burst pipes, or ''operator error'' (spilled beverages, etc.). Electronics equipment can also be damaged by airborne particles and cigarette smoke; smoking is also a potential fire hazard. Plastic covers can protect the machines somewhat from dust particles and falling water. Organizations vitally dependent on data processing facilities should prepare contingency plans for disasters such as hurricanes, earthquakes, or blizzards. Ideally, backup facilities should be located far enough away to be spared the disaster, but not too far to be reached quickly.

VIRUSES AND OTHER THREATS

The next level of security involves protecting software from viruses, ''logic bombs,'' and ''Trojan horses,'' all of which have the capacity to disable computer systems by infecting software. A computer virus is a program that is self-replicating, attaches itself to other programs, and generally performs some sort of function. An early virus demanded a ''cookie;'' after the word was typed it would disappear for a time. A later virus caused all the characters on the screen to fall to the bottom. Originally a hobby of programmers (an experimental virus was demonstrated as far back as 1974), viruses eventually appeared with sinister missions. The Pakistani Brain is one that can drastically affect a computer system.

This virus was developed in 1986 by two brothers from Pakistan as an experiment in preventing use of unauthorized copies of **software**. The original strain changes the volume name of disks to ''(c) BRAIN'' once it has infected them; however, mutations have been produced that are not as forthcoming about their identity. The virus inserts its code into the boot sector of a disk, making it the first data loaded into the computer upon startup, before any anti-viral programs can be executed. The original version spread through bootable floppy disks; however, variations have been written that can affect hard drives. Its code is difficult to locate because of measures it uses to counteract standard anti-viral programs and its method of recording parts of its code in disk sectors marked ''bad.''

Another type of insidious program is the ''Trojan horse,'' which performs an intended function but also a covert one. Computers users have become more savvy and cautious about sharing software; however, these types of programs continue to exist. Examples include a program ostensibly to increase monitor performance that instead erases the entire hard drive. True Trojans horses typically operate in the background of a valid program, such as a video game. Trojan horses have also been used for ''salami'' techniques—banking programs that compile the results of rounding errors in a large number of computations and add them to the perpetrator's account.

''Logic bombs'' are viruses that are programmed to perform a task once a particular set of conditions is met; the most famous are ''time bombs'' set to go off on a significant date, e.g. the ''Friday the 13th'' virus and the ''Michelangelo'' virus. These viruses activate at a given date or time. Logic bombs have been set by programmers to cause damage if their names are ever deleted from payroll records. The Pakistani Brain contained a logic bomb that searched for the names of unauthorized duplicates of programs written by the authors of the virus.

''Worms'' spread through networks and replicate themselves but do not affect programs. They were invented in 1980 by two Xerox Corporation researchers to perform useful network chores—such as searching for computer malfunctions or idle computers. Worms disseminate themselves throughout networks. Though considered relatively benign, worms can tie up memory and bring networks to a standstill.

PREVENTING AND RECOVERING FROM VIRUSES

Many steps can be taken to prevent or recover from virus infections. Having a source of clean (i.e., uninfected by viruses) backup copies for data files and programs is as important as it is elementary. Ideally, alternating sets of backup media should be used to increase the chances of having a clean original. The manufacturer's original diskettes for programs should be kept in a safe place and the write-protect tabs should be set to prevent their erasure in case they are unknowingly installed on an infected system.

Users should be wary of sources of software, particularly pirated copies of software, which may contain Trojan horses. "Swapping disks" has been compared to swapping hypodermic needles in terms of virus infection. Disks used by employees on their home computers can transmit viruses. Also, the size of critical files such as COMMAND.COM on DOS systems should be noted, as increases are a giveaway for virus infection.

Once a system is confirmed to be infected, it should not share disks or communication lines with other computers. Disks that could have perpetuated the virus should not be used unless they are certain to contain only data files and the virus is known not to attack the boot sector. All other disks should be reformatted or destroyed.

The computer itself should be shut down and rebooted with the original operating system disk, and the operating system files should be restored. If application programs have been infected, the hard disk should be reformatted. Data files may be backed up and recopied after the disk has been formatted.

The capacity of both local and wide area **networks** to share information can be used to unwittingly disseminate viruses. If networks are to be useable, they, like disks, must be secured against viruses, Trojan horses, and unintended information transfer. Most networks employ some means of verifying a user's identity, such as passwords. One creative way hackers have bypassed password access controls is by using spell-checking dictionaries from word processing programs to supply possible passwords. Other sources of passwords include information known about network users. Smart cards have been developed to overcome these weaknesses. With these, a variation on the "call-back" system, hardware at the remote site must confirm that the correct user is calling the system from the correct terminal location. More sophisticated smart cards contain microchips within them that transmit an **algorithm** recognized by the network server, making their misuse even more difficult.

Within an organization, multi-level password systems can insure that individuals are granted access only to the information required for their jobs. When correctly implemented, they can prevent Trojan horse routines from using the operating system to help copy confidential information.

Encryption systems are a way to secure information as it travels over phone lines or network cables. However, these usually slow down the network, and the encryption keys must be distributed in a secure way, a daunting task for large networks. For each user, double-key systems provide a public key, available to anyone wanting to communicate with its owner, and a private key, known only to the owner.

A controversial encryption standard, the Key Escrow chip—a.k.a. the "Clipper Chip"—was adopted by the U.S. government in 1994 against much opposition from the technical community. The Clipper system was installed on a silicon chip, not on software that could be rapidly applied throughout a network. It was incompatible with the existing Data Encryption Standard (DES) and RSA encryption. The most controversial aspect of the Clipper chip was the fact that the federal government would hold a key to the system. This is similar to what occurred when the National Security Agency persuaded IBM to limit the length of the key used in the DES, making it resistant to decoding by commercial cryptanalysis but susceptible to the larger, more powerful government resources.

The "firewall" is a tactic many corporations began to use in the mid-1990s to secure communications on large public access networks such as the Internet. Firewalls can be made using intermediate computers that monitor and screen information being sent from the private corporate network to the public one, and vice versa.

A computer isn't entirely secure even if it is not connected to any networks. Sophisticated electronic surveillance techniques have been known to recover data from the radio emissions generated by CPUs, peripheral cables, etc. The level of shielding available ranges from FCC Class A (commercial) to Class B (residential) to the federal government's Tempest standard for military contractors.

A strong potential for abuse also exists with improperly destroyed or recycled media. Shredders can be used to destroy various types of media, particularly paper printouts. A variety of different models are available, each a compromise between price, capacity, speed, and the thoroughness of destruction. Not all shredders can cut into diskettes. Specialized types of shredders include "pulpers" which wet the paper and "disintigrators" which repeatedly cut the documents until their particles fall through a fine screen.

The information stored on magnetic media can be destroyed by overwriting. This is a more involved process than merely "erasing" files from a disk, which merely changes the disk's directory. Overwriting changes each bit of binary information to either 1 or 0. Precautions must be taken to ensure that all the medium is overwritten, to destroy erased information not currently listed in directories. Even this does not complete the process, however. Just as a faint whisper of previously-recorded material can be audible in audiocassettes that have been reused, so can bits of overwritten information still exist. Bits that remain the same after the overwriting may be recorded at a slightly higher level of saturation than those that do not change; hence, most overwriting methods repeat the process, alternating between 1's and 0's each time.

The information on magnetic media can also be destroyed more quickly by degaussing, or driving the media through a strong magnetic field until saturation is reached. Diskettes, tapes, and other formats can be erased in bulk in less time than with overwriting.

Burning is perhaps the most thorough method of destroying information recorded on paper, diskettes, punched cards, and semiconductors. Disadvantages are that the materials cannot be reused and that there is a possibility of data recovery from incomplete burning; i.e., from intact paper ash, for which techniques exist to recover printed information.

The most important aspect of computer security involves personnel. Not only are inside jobs the greatest threat of computer crime, but if personnel are lax, security measures may be improperly and ineffectively implemented. Therefore, any computer security program should include efforts to adequately screen new employees, and a system of accounting and administrative controls to detect and deter criminal activity should be in place.

[Frederick C. Ingram]

FURTHER READING:

Avolio, Frederick M. "Building Internet Firewalls," *Business Communications Review*. January, 1994, pp. 15-20.

Baker, Richard H. *Computer Security Handbook*. McGraw-Hill.

Belsie, Laurent. "Firewalls Help Protect Internet From Attack of the Hackers," *Christian Science Monitor*. April 29, 1994, p. 4.

Bottoms, David T. "Solution Presents a Problem: Is Encryption Policy'Putting Potholes' in the Information Highway?" *Industry Week*. March 21, 1994, p. 61.

"Business Code," *Banker*. December, 1993, p. 69.

Cooper, James Arlin. *Computer and Communications Security*. McGraw-Hill.

Del Nibletto, Paolo. "Anti-Piracy Forces Find Ally in Soft-Cop," *Info Canada*. March, 1994, pp. 1, 34.

DeMaio, Harry B. *Information Protection and Other Unnatural Acts*. AMACOM.

Fites, Philip E., Martin P.J. Kratz, and Alan F. Brebner. *Control and Security of Computer Information Systems*. Computer Science Press.

Fites, Philip, Peter Johnston, and Martin Kratz. *The Computer Virus Crisis*. Van Nostrand Reinhold.

Gallery, Shari Mendelson, ed. *Computer Security: Readings from Security Management Magazine*. Butterworth Publishers.

Johnson, Johna Till. "The Internet: Corporations Worldwide Make the Connection," *Data Communications*. April 1994, pp.66-78.

Merrick, Bill. "Electronic Funds Transfer: Biometrics, Neural Networks Poised to Fight Fraud," *Credit Union Magazine*. November, 1993, pp. 33-34.

Roberts, Ralph and Pamela Kane, eds. *Compute!'s Computer Security*. Compute! Books.

Shain, Michael. "Security Issues with Enterprise Multimedia," *Computers & Security*. February, 1994, pp. 15-22.

Steffora, Ann and Martin Cheek. "Hacking Goes Legit," *Industry Week*. February 7, 1994, pp. 43-46.

"Toll Fraud: Ways to Reduce Your Business' Vulnerability," *Managing Office Technology*. February, 1994, p. 56.

COMPUTERS AND COMPUTER SYSTEMS

A computer is a programmable device that can automatically perform a sequence of calculations or other operations on data without human aid. It can store, retrieve, and process data according to internal instructions.

A computer may be either digital, analog, or hybrid, although most today are digital. Digital computers express variables as numbers, usually in the binary system. They are used for general purposes, whereas analog computers are built for specific tasks, typically scientific or technical. The term "computer" is usually synonymous with digital computer, and computers for business are exclusively digital.

The core, computing part of a computer is its central processing unit (CPU), or processor. It comprises an arithmetic-logic unit to carry out calculations, main memory to temporarily store data for processing, and a control unit to control the transfer of data between memory, input and output sources, and the arithmetic-logic unit.

A computer as such is not fully functional without various peripheral devices. These are typically connected to a computer through cables, although some may be built into the same unit with the CPU. These include devices for the input of data, such as keyboards, mice, trackballs, scanners, light pens, modems, magnetic strip card readers, and microphones—and for the output of data such as monitors, printers, plotters, loudspeakers, earphones, and modems. In addition to these input/output devices, other types of peripherals include computer data storage devices for auxiliary memory storage, where data is saved even when the computer is turned off. These devices most often are magnetic tape drives, magnetic disk drives, or optical disk drives.

Finally, for a digital computer to function automatically, it requires programs, or sets of instructions written in computer-readable code. To be distinguished from the physical or hardware components of a computer, programs are collectively referred to as **software**.

A computer *system*, therefore, is a computer combined with peripheral equipment and software so that it can perform desired functions. Often the terms "computer" and "computer system" are used interchangeably, especially when peripheral devices are built into the same unit as the computer or when a system is sold and installed as a package. The term "computer system," however, may also refer to a configuration of hardware and software designed for a specific purpose, such as a manufacturing control system, a library automation system, or an accounting system. Or it may refer to a network of multiple computers linked together so that they can share software, data, and peripheral equipment.

Computers tend to be categorized by size and power, although advancements in computers' processing power have blurred the distinctions between traditional categories. Power and speed are influenced by the size of a computer's internal storage units, called words, which determine the amount of data it can process at once and is measured in bits (binary digits). Computer speed is also determined by its clock speed, which is measured in megahertz. Additionally, the amount of main memory a computer has, which is measured in bytes (or more precisely, kilobytes, megabytes, or gigabytes of RAM (random access memory), plays a role in determining how much data it can process. The amount of memory that auxiliary storage devices can hold also determines the capabilities of a computer system.

HISTORICAL BACKGROUND

EARLY HISTORY. Precursors to computers include the abacus, the slide rule, and the punched-card tabulating machine. The concept of a programmable computing machine was invented by the British mathematician Charles Babbage (1792-1871) in the mid-1800s. He took the idea of using punched cards to store programs from the automatic loom devised by Joseph-Marie Jacquard (1752-1834). He worked on developing a machine that could perform any kind of analytical computation, not merely arithmetic. Automatic data processing was introduced in the late 1800s by statistician Herman Hollerith (1860-1929) who developed the electric tabulating machine which processed data by sorting punched cards. The Hollerith machine was used by the U.S. Census Bureau to efficiently process the 1890 census.

The first operational electronic digital computer, the ENIAC (electronic numerical integrator and computer), was completed in 1946 by John W. Mauchly (1907-80) and J. Presper Eckart, Jr. (1919-) at the University of Pennsylvania. It was based on designs for an unfinished special-purpose computer made a few years earlier by Iowa State University physics professor John V. Atanasoff. The ENIAC, funded by the U.S. Army to compute artillery shell trajectories, could perform an unprecedented 5,000 additions or 300 multiplications per second. Electronic processing took place in 18,000 vacuum tubes, and the device was programmed by plugging wires into three walls of plug-boards containing over 6,000 switches. The tendency of the vacuum tubes to burn out, however, made the computer rather unreliable.

THE FIRST THREE GENERATIONS OF COMPUTERS. The first commercially successful computer was the UNIVAC I (Universal Automatic Computer), introduced by Remington Rand in 1951. It was based on the EDVAC (Electronic Discrete Variable Automatic Computer)—Mauchly and Eckart's second computer—the technology rights to which were sold to Remington Rand. EDVAC used instruction cards developed by mathematician John von Neumann, (1903-57) and thus became the first computer with stored programs. UNIVAC and other first-generation computers continued to use vacuum tubes as their primary switching components, and memories were made of thin tubes of liquid mercury and magnetic drums.

Due to their high costs, the first computers were aimed at government and research markets, rather than business and industry. This changed once International Business Machines Corp. (IBM) entered the computer industry, for the company already had an established sales force and a commercial clientele through its business of leasing electric punched-card tabulating machines. The IBM 650 computer, introduced in 1954, used existing IBM tabulating machine punched-card readers, punches, and printers, which its clients already had, and it was also made affordable through IBM's established leasing programs. The first business enterprises to rely on computers were those that needed to process large volumes of data, such as banks, insurance companies, and large retail operations. The 650 became the most widely used computer in the world by the end of the 1950s, with 1,800 systems installed, making IBM the world's leading computer manufacturer.

The invention of the transistor in 1947 provided a substitute for vacuum tubes in the second generation of computers. Consequently, computer system size was reduced and reliability was significantly improved. Transistorized computers were not shipped in large quantities until 1959, however. Computers of this period all used magnetic core storage systems for main memory. Some used magnetic drums or disks in addition to magnetic tape for auxiliary memory. Examples include the IBM 410 and the Honeywell 800.

The third generation of computers, from the mid-1960s to the mid-1970s, used integrated circuits and large-scale integration, in which large numbers of transistors were put on a single wafer of silicon. They were also the first to use operating systems and database management systems. On-line systems were developed, although most processing was still done in batch mode. Examples of computers from this period include the IBM 360 and 370, the Control Data 6000 series, the Burroughs 5500, and the Honeywell 200.

Until the 1960s, all computers were of the category called mainframes. The term mainframe refers to the cabinet which houses the CPU. Separate multiple cabinets contain the tape drives and disk drives, and a mainframe computer system typically takes up the space of an entire room. Mainframe computers tend to have 32- or 64-bit processors, and by the beginning of the 1990s, mainframes often had hundreds of megabytes of main memory and hundreds of gigabytes of storage space.

THE MINICOMPUTER. A new class of computers, the minicomputer, was introduced in December 1959 with the launch of the PDP-1 by Digital Equipment Corp. (DEC), although the term ''minicomputer'' itself was not used until the introduction of the PDP-5 in 1963. The computers were smaller and cheaper than mainframes and were also programmed to be used interactively, in ''real-time,'' instead of in batch mode. Soon after, Hewlett-Packard and Data General also introduced minicomputers, and eventually Wang, Tandem, Datapoint, Prime, and IBM followed suit.

Generally, minicomputers can perform the same functions as mainframes but have less storage capacity, processing power, and speed. Traditionally, minicomputers had 16-bit processors, but later ones were 32-bit. Minicomputers may be small enough to sit on a desktop, but typically are the size of a small cabinet and stand on the floor. Minicomputer systems range in size from single-user units to those which can support several hundred terminals, and their prices range between $15,000 and $250,000. The class of minicomputers having the fastest processing speeds, similar to those of small-scale mainframes, are called superminis.

Minicomputers became predominant in the 1970s, by serving a broad range of businesses. The most widely used minicomputer line in the 1980s was the DEC VAX, starting with the VAX-11/780 in 1977, a 32-bit computer which runs DEC's proprietary VMS operating system. The IBM AS/400, introduced in 1988, was one of the more popular minicomputers for small business in the early 1990s. Recently, the term ''midrange'' has begun to replace that of minicomputer, to differentiate the medium-sized computer from the even smaller, microcomputer.

THE MICROCOMPUTER. The development of the microprocessor, a CPU on a single integrated-circuit chip, enabled the development of affordable single-user microcomputers for the first time. The slow processing power of the early microcomputers, however, made them attractive only to hobbyists and not to the business market. The first microprocessor, introduced by Intel Corp. in 1970, could handle only 4 bits at a time. Later Intel introduced the 8000 series of 8-bit microprocessors. (The Altair 8800 was introduced in 1974 and was the first commercially successful microcomputer, although in keeping with the interests of the electronics hobbyist market, it was actually a kit.) In 1977 the personal computer industry got under way with the introduction of off-the-shelf home computers from three separate manufacturers: Commodore Business Machines, Inc. (Commodore PET), Apple Computer, Inc. (Apple II), and Tandy Corp. (TRS-80). These were each 8-bit computers that had a maximum of 64 kilobytes of memory and used only floppy disks, instead of an internal hard disk, for data storage. Popular home computers at the beginning of the 1980s included the Commodore 64 and Commodore 128, the Apple II, and the Atari 500. CP/M was the dominant operating system of microcomputers in the early 1980s.

The term ''personal computer'' (PC) was coined by IBM with the launch of its PC in 1981, which became an instant success and set the standards for the microcomputer industry. Hence the term PC is often used specifically to designate microcomputers that are ''compatible'' with the IBM PC line, although it may also be synonymous with any microcomputer. Actually, an ''IBM-compatible PC'' means a microcomputer that has a chip compatible with the Intel 80x86 chip and is capable of running the DOS operating system and therefore can run the same applications software. By the late 1980s, DOS had overtaken CP/M as the dominant operating system for personal computers of any manufacturer.

Apple's Macintosh line, introduced in 1984, is the leading personal computer make that does not use DOS; it instead uses Apple's own proprietary operating system, MacOS. MacOS made the Macintosh very popular because of its excellent graphical user interface. However, Apple did not begin licensing MacOS to other computer manufacturers until 1994. Beginning with Windows 3.0, the graphical user interface that Microsoft Corp. developed for the PC, increasing numbers of software applications were written for the DOS/Windows platform. Thus DOS continued to hold the largest share of the personal computer operating system market into the 1990s. The Macintosh, meanwhile, remained dominant in desktop publishing and graphics applications.

In addition to IBM and Apple, leading manufacturers of personal computers include Compaq, AST

Research, NEC, and Dell. Personal computers range in price from $300 to $10,000. The entire computer system usually fits on top of a desk. Since they are designed for single users, personal computers typically come with at least a monitor, keyboard, and disk or tape drive. Hard disks for auxiliary data storage only became standard on personal computers in the later 1980s.

By the early 1990s personal computers, which by then were either 16-bit or 32-bit, had become the fastest-growing category of computers. This was largely due to the adoption of their use in businesses of all sizes. The availability of these small, inexpensive computers brought computer technology to even the smallest of enterprises.

Although personal computers opened up a whole new market for computers, minicomputers or midranges still remained widely used in business in the 1990s. Nevertheless, by the beginning of that decade, new sales of midranges had shifted to a significant extent to UNIX workstations. Workstations are a class of microcomputers that combine the processing power and speeds of lower-end midranges with the size of personal computers.

The workstation was first introduced by Apollo Computer in 1980. However, it was Sun Microsystems, founded only in 1982, that soon dominated the new industry segment by producing affordable computers from standard off-the-shelf parts and using a form of the versatile, commonly used operating system, UNIX. Workstation performance was further enhanced with the adoption of a microprocessor based on reduced instruction set computing (RISC), first developed by IBM in 1986. Sun introduced its first workstation based on RISC, called the SPARCstation, in 1989. Soon, other workstation manufacturers, such as Hewlett-Packard, were also providing computers which had RISC-based microprocessors and ran UNIX. Thus, it was not only the increased power at a low price that made workstations more attractive than midranges, but also the greater compatibility among the computers of different workstation manufacturers.

Workstations are used most often in graphic design, engineering, or manufacturing operations, where the processing power to handle sophisticated **computer aided design** and **manufacturing** software and graphics is needed, yet individual engineers or designers require their own computers instead of sharing a midrange. By the early 1990s networked workstations began to replace midranges to a certain extent in general business usage as well.

The latest category of microcomputers to enter the business world are portable computers—including laptops, notebooks, and personal digital assistants—that are small and light enough to be carried and can run on AC power or batteries. Laptop computers have the same power as desktop personal computers, but are built more compactly and use flat screen monitors, usually using liquid crystal display, that fold down to form a slim unit that fits in a brief case and usually weigh under 15 pounds. A notebook computer is one that weighs under 6 pounds and may or may not have a full-size keyboard. A pocket computer is a hand held calculator-size computer. A personal digital assistant is a pocket computer that uses a pen and tablet for input, has a fax/modem card, and is combined with the capabilities of a cellular telephone for remote data communications. Portable computers are increasingly popular among businesspeople who travel, such as executives or sales representatives.

BUSINESS USAGE OF COMPUTERS

Computers are used in government, industry, nonprofit and nongovernmental organizations, and in the home, but their impact has been greatest in business and industry. The competitive nature of business has created demands spurring continuous advancements in computer technology and systems design. Meanwhile, the declining prices of computer systems and their increasing power has led more and more enterprises to invest in computer systems for increasingly more of their business functions. Computers are used to process data in all aspects of a business enterprise: product design and development, manufacturing, inventory control and distribution, quality control, sales and marketing, service data, **accounting**, and personnel management. They are also used in businesses of all sizes and in all industry segments: manufacturing, wholesale, retail, services, mining, agriculture, transportation, and communications.

Although small companies may use mainframes (or at least smaller mainframes), and large companies use personal computers, the various sizes and capabilities of entire computer systems tend to match the size of a company. A single personal computerpersonal computer, its software, and its printer, suitable for the self-employed individual's home office is a type of computer system. A small business of several employees typically has a computer system comprising multiple personal computers, printers, and other peripherals such as a scanner or a CD-ROM drive, linked together in a network. Slightly larger companies may use a midrange with multiple terminals and printers, while others may use a network of personal computers or workstations. Many large corporations use several independent computer systems for different functions or departments. Midranges are often connected to mainframe computers to perform subsidiary functions. Mainframes may also have numerous other smaller computers, such as personal computers, attached to them.

Computer systems may be designed for a specific industry usage, including all the necessary software, and as such are called "turnkey" systems. Vendors that provide integrated computer systems and not merely computers, may either be the original equipment manufacturers (OEMs), or they may be value-added resellers (VARs). VARs, as wholesalers, buy computers, software, and peripherals from separate manufacturers and configure them into new systems. Alternatively, a business may have its computer system custom-designed by a computer service firm. Increasingly, however, businesses are purchasing their computers and other system components separately and installing their own computer systems. This trend emerged in the late 1980s as more computer hardware manufacturers designed their computers to run standard operating systems software, and software applications became available in multiple versions for different operating systems.

The most common business uses of a computer system are for database management, financial management and **accounting**, and word processing. Companies use **database management systems** to keep track of changing information in databases on such subjects as clients, vendors, employees, inventory, supplies, product orders, and service requests. Financial and accounting systems are used for a variety of mathematical calculations on large volumes of numeric data, whether in the basic functions of financial service companies or in the accounting activities of any firms. Using either spreadsheet or database management software, computers are used by accounts payable, accounts receivable, and payroll departments. In addition to merely processing and tabulating financial data, companies use computers to quickly analyze their cash flow situations. Finally, word processing is ubiquitous and is used to create the simplest memos to lengthy reports for external distribution.

Databases, however, may also be used to help make strategic decisions through the use of software based on artificial intelligence, or the use of logic. A database system may include—in addition to records and statistics of products, services, clients, etc.—a database of information about past human experience within a specific field with solutions to past problems. This is referred to as a knowledge base. Knowledge-based systems, also called **expert systems**, therefore, can help a company automatically come up with solutions for current problems based on past information or knowledge, which would normally require a human expert. Examples of expert system usage include business activities that require predictions, such as investment analysis, financial planning, insurance underwriting, and fraud risk prediction. Expert systems are also used for the instant solutions needed for regulatory compliance, contract bidding, complex production control, customer support, and training.

Computer systems are increasingly being used also in **telecommunications**. Computers can transmit data over regular telephone lines, whereby a device called a modem is needed to convert a computer's digital signals into the analog signals used by telephone lines. Digital signals may also be transmitted without modems by using dedicated data lines, which an organization may lease or own. Using the telephone lines, data can be transmitted from one computer system to another or between a computer and a fax machine anywhere in the world. Certain telecommunications companies, computer service bureaus, and on-line information services have set up "host" computers dedicated to communications services by storing the files and messages electronically exchanged by third party computer system users or providing databases to be remotely searched. Some organizations and companies have even set up their own electronic **bulletin board systems** on computers where files and messages are exchanged either internally or among clients or other outside users. Similarly, in the mid-1990s businesses began to make files available on the Internet, a global network of computers.

RECENT TRENDS IN COMPUTER SYSTEMS

OPEN SYSTEMS. The most significant trend in computer systems, as opposed to the capabilities of the computers themselves, has been the compatibility of computer hardware and software from different manufacturers. In the past, all components of a computer system originated from the same manufacturer. There were no industry-wide standards, and therefore peripherals,—such as printers or monitors—from one manufacturer would not operate with the computer of another. More significantly, software could only run on the specific computer brand for which it was designed. The key to software compatibility and the operation of various peripherals is the computer's operating system software, but the computer's CPU also has to be designed to support a given operating system. Although a level of compatibility has existed among personal computers since early on, the trend came later to the more powerful workstations and midranges. "Open systems" is a term often used to refer to such computer systems, whose components are independent of a single vendor and whose standards are set by agreement among multiple vendors.

The use of open systems in business has the advantages of allowing an enterprise to upgrade or expand its computer system more easily and cheaply, avoid the expenses of employee retraining on new systems, share computer files with outside clients or vendors more easily, and even integrate its computer system with that of another company following an acquisition or merger.

NETWORKING. Another major trend in computer systems is the networking of multiple computers so that they can share data and peripherals. Computers on a network are physically linked by cables and use network software in conjunction with the operating system software. Depending on the hardware and software used, different types of computers may be put on the same network. This may involve computers of different sizes—such as mainframes, midranges, and microcomputers—or computers and peripherals of different manufacturers, which the trend toward open systems has facilitated. **Local area networks (LANs)** link computers within a limited geographical areas, such as the same building or facility. Wide area networks (WANs), using another type of cable, connect computers in different geographic regions, such as in different states. Networks may have various architectures, or designs of their communications systems, which determine whether computers on the network can act independently or are controlled by one another. A commonly used architecture is client-server, whereby a server computer is designated as the one storing and processing data and is accessed by multiple users each at a client computer.

LANs have transformed how employees within an organization use computers. In organizations where employees formerly accessed midrange computer through "dumb" terminals, these employees now typically have more capabilities, since they have their own personal computer at their desks while still being able to access needed data from a midrange or other server through the network. In very small companies that can afford only personal computers, employees can now automatically share data, which previously either had to be printed out or transferred by floppy disks. WANs are often used by companies with multiple, geographically-dispersed facilities. Thus, a company's databases can be accessed at headquarters in one city, at a manufacturing plant in other city, and at sales offices in other locations.

CD-ROM. A relatively new form of data storage medium that is beginning to make an impact on business computer systems is CD-ROM (compact disc read-only memory). CD-ROMs store data optically instead of magnetically and therefore can hold over 600 megabytes of data, instead of the 1.44 megabytes held by the typical high-density 3½-inch floppy diskette. A corresponding peripheral device, a CD-ROM drive, is required for a computer to read CD-ROMs.

Due to their capacity to hold large volumes of data, one of the most practical applications of CD-ROMs has been the publishing of indexes or directories on a single disc that would otherwise require multiple volumes of printed text; the data can then be searched by a database management program. For business applications, this may involve directories of companies, products, or patents and indexes to business literature.

Although a CD-ROM can only have data read from it and not written onto it in normal usage, in the early 1990s desktop computer peripheral devices for the writing of optical disks were introduced. Optical disk drives can write data onto a disk and then read the data from the disk later. Some optical drives and their disks may be designed for only one-time writing, known as write-once read-many (WORM) technology, while others permit repeated writing and erasing, as with magnetic disks. Some companies have begun using such devices to archive large amounts of internal documentation or huge graphics files which would not fit on single magnetic diskettes. The newest optical drives can write 1.3 gigabytes (1,300 megabytes) onto a single disk. Another device, a CD-recorder, is used to create CD-ROMs that can be read in regular CD-ROM drives. The introduction of the desktop CD-recorder allows CD-ROM publishers to handle production in-house, which used to have to be done in clean-room facilities.

An emerging business application of CD-ROM production is in the marketing of software, since a single CD-ROM can hold dozens of software packages. Full software packages are made available on the CD-ROM, but they are encrypted and only demonstration versions are immediately available to the prospective client.

MULTIMEDIA. Closely associated with the trend toward CD-ROM use, are multimedia computer systems, which emerged at the beginning of the 1990s. A multimedia system has a user interface that produces more than merely text and simple graphics on the monitor, but also sound through loudspeakers or earphones and high-quality color animation though the monitor, and often video images as well. Sound, graphics, and video data require a great deal of data storage space, and hence such multimedia software is stored on CD-ROMs. A multimedia computer system, therefore, requires a CD-ROM drive, circuit boards for sound, graphics, and possibly video, a super VGA monitor, and speakers or earphones. Multimedia systems, like the personal computers upon which they are usually based, gained their initial popularity in the consumer market, in which they are used for entertainment and games software. Businesses, however, are beginning to implement multimedia technology, such as in training and in marketing.

SEE ALSO: Computer Networks

[Heather Behn Hedden]

FURTHER READING:

Anderson, Ronald E., and David R. Sullivan. *The World of Computing*. Boston: Houghton Mifflin Company, 1988.

Codkind, Alan. "Automating The Business Process." *CMA—The Management Accounting Magazine*. October, 1993, pp. 29-30.

DeLamarter, Richard Thomas. *Big Blue: IBM's Use and Abuse of Power*. New York: Dodd, Mead and Company, 1986.

Freedman, Alan. *The Computer Glossary: The Complete Illustrated Desk Reference*, 5th ed. New York: AMACOM, 1991.

Hall, Mark. *Sunburst: The Ascent of Sun Microsystems*. Chicago: Contemporary Books, 1990.

Ichbiah, Daniel. *The Making of Microsoft: How Bill Gates and his Team Created the World's Most Successful Software Company*. Rocklin, CA: Prima Publishers, 1991.

"Is It New? Or Is It Hype?" *Nation's Business*. August, 1993, p. 42.

Killen, Michael. *IBM: The Making of the Common View*. Boston: Harcourt Brace Jovanovich, 1988.

Olsen, Kenneth H. *Digital Equipment Corporation, The First Twenty-Five Years*. New York: Newcomen Society in North America, 1983.

"Small Firm's Usage Patterns." *Nation's Business*. August, 1993, pp. 39-40.

CONFIDENCE INTERVAL

The confidence interval is a tool of probability that is used to estimate mean values for a population given sample means. It enables statisticians to make indicative statements about a population with a certain degree of confidence, with the caveat that the estimate has a small but significant chance of being wrong.

For example, political pollsters may find it impossible to query every adult in the United States about whether or not they approve of the performance of the president. This would require asking more than 200 million people for their opinion: is the president doing well in his job or is he doing poorly?

Instead, pollsters may sample only a small number of people, typically 5000 people, and draw statistical inferences for the entire population based on the results of that sample. As long as the sample population is chosen at random and the number is significant (more than 30 people), one may be reasonably assured that the opinions expressed by the sample population will be normally distributed and therefore usefully indicative of the opinions of the entire population.

Assume that a telephone poll is conducted in which 5000 randomly selected people are asked to express approval, disapproval, neutrality or no opinion about the performance of the president. The sample reveals that 2000, or 40 percent, approve of the president's performance, while 2250, or 45 percent, disapprove. Meanwhile, 450, or nine percent, are neutral, and the remaining 300, or six percent, have no opinion about how the president is doing.

The figures are 100 percent accurate only for the sample population because every one of the 5000 has been asked. But in attempting to draw an inference for the entire population based on this sample data, one cannot be absolutely sure the proportions will remain accurate.

Instead, one would hope to express a likelihood that these numbers are accurate for the entire population. This likelihood is expressed by the confidence interval; it enables the pollster or statistician to estimate the parameters of a population mean based on a sample mean. As a result, presidential approval ratings are commonly expressed with degrees of accuracy which are reflections of the confidence interval. The results always include an indication of the error (plus or minus a percentage) that may exist in the poll.

It is logistically very difficult to measure values for entire populations. Rather than attempting to find the correct value for an entire population, the statistician may attempt only to find the *most correct* value for the population using only a sample of the population, and use the confidence interval to determine whether or not that value is absolutely correct.

To use a somewhat different example from the presidential opinion poll, assume that an automobile manufacturer has developed a new car and must provide an estimate of the mileage that drivers can expect from this model. A sample of 100 cars is taken from the assembly line and given test runs on a closed track. The worst performing car among the sample gets 38 miles per gallon, while the best gets 49 miles per gallon. The sample mean of the entire population (the total mileage of all the cars divided by 100) is 44 miles per gallon.

The results can be expressed as

$$\text{Mileage} = 38 < \bar{x} < 49$$

which indicates that the sample mean $\bar{x}$ lies between 38 and 49 miles per gallon. Can one be more assured that the true mean μ falls between 35 and 53, and less certain that it falls between 41 and 47? Yes, and there is also a 100 percent certainty that the true mean falls between 0 and ∞. But, conversely, how confident can one be that the true mean μ for the entire population equals the sample mean $\bar{x}$, or 44?

The interval estimate must include a specification of limits or boundary values for the interval, and a probability that the interval of values contains the population parameter. The interval of values is the *confidence interval*, and its boundaries of values are called *confidence limits* of the interval.

The confidence interval expresses the probability that the interval contains the population parameter. As a measure of probability, it is usually expressed as a

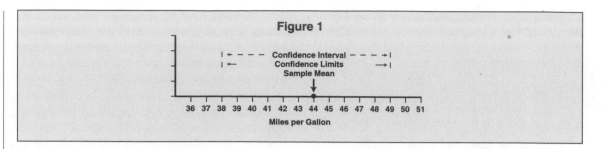

Figure 1

```
        | ← – – – Confidence Interval – – – → |
        | ←          Confidence Limits          → |
                      Sample Mean
                          ↓
                          ●
   36  37  38  39  40  41  42  43  44  45  46  47  48  49  50  51
                      Miles per Gallon
```

percentage. The confidence interval, confidence limits and mean may be diagrammed as in Figure 1.

The width of the confidence interval is determined by the degree of confidence. A 95 percent confidence interval will be narrower than a 99 percent confidence interval, indicating that one may be more certain that the true mean lies within a wider confidence interval.

The difference between the sample statistic $\bar{x}$ and the true mean μ is attributable to an unknown variable degree of error ϵ. This relationship may be expressed as

$$\mu = \bar{x} \pm \epsilon$$

The error ϵ is essential to defining a confidence interval for the mean μ. But while the error ϵ for the sample mean $\bar{x}$ is unknown, we can make assumptions about the size of the errors if one know the mean, standard deviation and shape of the distribution of those errors.

SAMPLING PROBLEMS

One problem associated with sampling is that samples often are not randomly selected. For instance, in the presidential opinion poll referred to earlier, the sample consists only of individuals who have telephones. It includes only those who bothered to answer the pollster's question.

In addition, the sample includes only those who happened to be home at the time the pollster called. If the pollster's callers only placed calls between 1:00 pm and 5:00 pm, the sample would reflect only those with telephones who took the time to answer who happened to be at home (and perhaps not at work).

For these reasons, the poll may be suspect because its respondents are not truly and absolutely randomly selected members of the population. The poll excludes busy people, people without telephones, and people who are not at their telephones between 1:00 and 5:00 in the afternoon.

Similarly, the Nielsen Ratings, which are used to measure the television viewing preferences of the population, do not use completely randomly selected subjects. They consist only of households selected to be Nielsen subjects. "Nielsen families" may be aware of their ability to influence the poll and, knowing that their preferences are being watched, take their viewing habits more seriously.

"Sweeps week" is another distortion of random selection. During these brief periods, television stations run unusually attractive programming with the specific intent of achieving high ratings. Sensational blockbuster shows with high production values yield abnormally large audiences. Because they are not indicative of the regular programming schedule, these shows cannot provide an accurate indication of a station's popularity during periods outside the occasional "sweeps week."

[John Simley]

FURTHER READING:

Johnson, Robert. *Elementary Statistics*, 3rd ed. North Scituate, MA: Duxbury Press, 1980.

Kachiga, Sam Kash. *Statistical Analysis*. New York: Radius Press, 1986.

Kazmier, Leonard J. *Basic Statistics for Business and Economics*. New York: McGraw-Hill, 1990.

CONFLICT OF INTEREST

Conditions that create a conflict of interest for individuals and organizations are likely to occur as the result of the multitude of transactions and relationships that occur in politics, government, industry, commerce, research, education, and the professions. A person cannot commit or perform a conflict of interest. Conflicts are arrangements or relationships, not actions.

In determining whether a given situation creates a conflict of interest, it is important to analyze first whether a conflict of interest exists, by definition. If a conflict does exist, the concerned parties can then determine whether the conflict of interest is acceptable or troublesome according to prevailing cultural and ethical standards. Without such clear staging through the analytical process, preconceptions can prevent objective recognition of conflicts when they are actually present and confuse an examination with valuative judgements. Social and cultural beliefs have a profound influence in determining the existence of conflict-of-interest situations.

Black's Law Dictionary describes conflict of interest in connection with "public officials and fiduciaries and their relationship to matters of private interest or gain to them" in situations where regard for one duty tends to lead to disregard of another. John R. Boatright's definition extends beyond the realm of public officials and fiduciaries. In his essay entitled "Conflict of Interest: An Agency Analysis," he stated that a conflict of interest arises when one party's (A's) personal interests interfere with that party (A's) actions so as to promote the interest of another party (B) when the other party (A) has an obligation to act in the other party's (B's) best interest. Personal interest in this definition is not limited to direct financial reward. It can be a any tangible benefit accruing to the person with a conflict of interest or his or her associates or family members. Such benefits include special appointments to a position, free promotions and publicity, or the awarding of exclusive or "no-bid" contracts. The second type of conflict of interest occurs when a person has a dual obligation to act in the interest of two different parties, and the obligations conflict with each other.

PERTINENT ASSUMPTIONS

One's obligation to a principal, the presence of an agency relationship, is a necessary element for both types of conflict of interest. If no obligations or duty to a principal are present, then differing interests within a particular situation are simply competing interests, not a conflict of interest.

Boatright's definition is not limited to individuals, but includes organizations acting as agents or principals. Consequently, this definition is flexible and widely adaptable for evaluating potential conflicts of interest in a variety of settings. In a corporation, the agent is the employee with a duty to the company, which is the principal. In state, local, or federal governments, employees and officials are the agents of the government. In professional practices, the agent is an individual or firm engaged to provide service to a client, who is the principal and who can also be an individual or a firm.

All that is required for a conflict of interest to exist is that conflicting interests have the *potential* to interfere with the duty; actual interference need not occur. Moreover, the conflicting interest does not need to directly affect the principal. Use of position or use of confidential information for personal advantage brings about a conflict of interest without having any affect on the principal. For example, an insider trading securities and profiting based on privileged informa-

tion does not harm the company whose securities are being traded. In Boatright's words, "to exploit an agency relation for personal gain is to violate the bond of trust that is an essential part of the relation."

The conflict of interest inherent in an act of **bribery** has been deemed unacceptable conduct by society throughout history. In Babylonia during the eighteenth century B.C. the Code of Hammurabi punished judges who altered judgements for a bribes. Plato suggested that public servants convicted in court for accepting bribes be executed. Roman law contained many penalties against bribery of public officials and judges. In medieval England both the briber and the officers accepting the bribes were subject to fines and imprisonment.

The Constitution of the United States prohibited bribery of officials and prohibited the receipt of titles (Article I, section 9, clause 8). An act prohibiting congressmen and federal officials from accepting bribes passed in 1853. During the same time period, legislatures of state and local governments were full of scandals resulting from bribery and other conflicts, such as free railroads passes for legislators, purchases of U.S. Senate seats. Common law provisions prohibiting those practices existed in some states at the time, but were rarely enforced.

Situations creating conflicts of interest other than bribery did not receive major attention until recently. The need for capital presumably overrode any such concerns. Between 1850 and 1900, railroad executives created construction companies through which they personally profited by steering business from the railroads to their own companies. These practices of self dealing attracted attention after several railroad bankruptcies. Executives and financiers condemned such conflicts. By the 1880's such practices had diminished.

In the early twentieth century two government investigations highlighted some conflicts of interest that affected several economic groups. The Armstrong life insurance investigation in New York unearthed a variety of practices between 1904 and 1906 that were damaging to both corporations and policy holders. Some insurance companies incurred losses as they participated in investment syndicates by purchasing securities that could not be sold elsewhere by the investment bankers. Other insurance company directors were found controlling subsidiary trust companies whose funds were used for personal loans and personal stock purchases. The Armstrong investigation ultimately led to new laws and regulations for the industry. Laws passed in New York that prohibited the underwriting of securities issues by life insurance companies and self-dealing by company officials were soon copied by other states.

A similar problem was investigated in 1912 and 1913 by the Pugo Committee, a subcommittee of the House Banking and Currency Committee. The committee investigated conflicting interests and concentrations of monetary power in the large investment-banking houses. The Pugo committee's report influenced legislation which produced the Clayton Act of 1914, which outlawed interlocking directorate among large banks and trust companies.

Despite the investigations and legislation, corporate misuse of conflict of interest situations did not end. During the 1920s, the officers of a number of majors banks were using bank funds to create speculative gains for themselves, often at the expense of the bank. One of the most blatant cases involved National City Bank president, Charles E. Mitchell, who through the use of an affiliate, the National City Company, drove the price of the stock with a book value of $70 to a price of $2,925 before it crashed. The public lost $650 million in market value. Without the stockholders' knowledge, Mitchell also received over $3 million in management funds in addition to his regular salary. Mitchell's actions and similar activities by an officer Albert Wiggins of Chase Manhattan Bank were major reasons for the passage of the Glass Steagal Act of 1933, which separated commercial banking from investment banking.

From 1934 to 1941, the **Securities and Exchange Commission (SEC)** made efforts to control conflict of interest in the securities markets. However, efforts to curb conflicts of interest by separating dealers from brokers, as was the practice in great Britain, were severely criticized. Broker-dealer firms were buying and selling for their own accounts as well as those of customers. The members of the stock exchange wanted to continue their practices; the SEC retreated. Later, a major **embezzlement** scandal involving an exchange member did bring about a program of self-regulation by the Association of Security Dealers. Conflict of interest as it affected securities markets attracted less attention during World War II.

Significant concerns about conflicts of interest did not surface again until the 1970's. A study financed by The Twentieth Century Fund entitled *Abuse on Wall Street: Conflict of Interest in the Securities Market* reviewed conflicts in the sale of securities, and conflicts in administration of commercial bank trust departments, real estate investment trusts, pension fund management, investment banking firms, broker-dealer firms, and nonprofit institutions. The study did not conclude that all conflicts be eliminated; some conflicts were inescapable. It did call for the industry to voluntarily self-regulate in advance of legislation, and strongly advocated disclosure processes to deter illegal or unethical conduct. The Twentieth Century Fund report also pointed out that legislators should consider the dangers of conflict of interest

when drafting legislation and avoid features that would invite abuse, as they did for real estate investment trusts. It further asserted that Congress encouraged conflicts when it broadened savings and loan activities without increasing regulations. Further, the report recommended that a sufficient number of directors independent of the corporation be appointed to the boards of both for-profit and not-for-profit corporations and that trustees of not-for-profit corporations avoid exploiting their appointments by securing accounts for banks, brokers, or investment managers.

Despite studies, investigations, and new legislation, conflict of interest abuses continued. During the 1980s and 1990s, a large percentage of savings and loan failures resulted from officers making risky loans to friends and affiliates, contrary to the interest of the institutions such officers were managing. Insider trading scandals abounded, resulting from the numerous **leveraged buyouts** and mergers prevalent at the time. Judicial attitudes tightened, investigations were launched, and enforcement of the Securities and Exchange Acts became more strict. The frequency and ease with which conflict of interest situations were exploited, in some cases by graduates of prestigious business schools, alarmed many. This led to a call in the 1990s for institutions to provide more education and training in ethical conduct and proper business practices.

REGULATIONS AND CODES OF CONDUCT

Bribery, graft, and conflict of interest affecting the United States government is addressed in *United States Code, Title 18, Part 1, Chapter 11*, which applies to public officials, officers, members of congress, federal judges, employees in the executive, legislative, or judicial branch, or any federal agency. The Code also covers proceedings in which the United States is a party or has a direct interest. Similar directives on ethical problems connected with conflicts of interest have been addressed in many state and local jurisdictions with the United States.

Other federal agencies, in addition the SEC, also regulate conflict of interest that falls within their domain. For example, heavy excise taxes are imposed by the **Internal Revenue Service (IRS)** on private foundations for engaging in prohibited acts of self-dealing between the foundation and its substantial contributors, managers, owners, or business affiliates. The **Employee Retirement Income Security Act of 1974 (ERISA)** requires the fiduciaries of employee benefit plans managers and administrators from engaging in certain transactions with parties in interest, such as the employer, the union, officers, or persons providing services to the plan. Specifically, a fiduciary is prohibited from using the income or assets of a plan for his own account, or receiving consideration for his personal account from a person dealing with income or assets of the plan (i.e., a kickback).

Outside the United States, conflict-of-interest regulations vary widely. A bribe paid to a government official is an act that creates a conflict of interest for the official, by definition. However, in many countries it continues to be viewed as an acceptable business practice. Other countries strictly forbid bribery of, but allow ''gifts'' to, public officials, which in some cases becomes necessary if the *public* is to be *served* at all.

Insider trading is still an acceptable practice in many securities markets outside of the United States. However, requirements for disclosures of conflict of interest are stricter in Western Europe than they are in the United States. France requires that administrators disclose conflicts to a board of administrators who in turn report the matter to stockholders and auditors. Auditors and stockholders can disapprove the situation. In England, directors must disclose all potential conflicts and must refrain from voting on matters involving those conflicts. In Germany, transactions between a corporation and any board members can be made only with a supervisory committee providing oversight.

Independent of legal statues and regulations, many ethical issues connected with conflicts of interest are recognized by business organizations, firms providing professional services, and institutions. Organizations expect their employees to act with loyalty and promote the organization's objectives and interests. Many organizations establish and enforce conduct codes addressing conflict-of-issue situations. Such policies often contain a general definition of conflict of interest, followed by general expectations stating that an employee will not engage in activities that will impede, impair or conflict with their duties as an employee, and will not use the organization's property, products, facilities, confidential information, and other resources for personal benefit or for the benefit of another organization. Provisions for periodic disclosures of potential conflicts is a common practice. The codes and policies may further define how conflicts of interest will be managed when they do occur.

Those conflicts of interest which arise in the course of businesses providing services to clients are recognized and dealt with using the various codes of conduct for those professions. For example, actual or potential conflicts of interest that arise between attorney and client are governed by *The Code of Professional Responsibility* and *Model Rules of Professional Conduct*. **Certified Public Accountants** must avoid conflict of interest in engagements where they provide an opinion used by a third party. They are required by the American institute of Certified Public Accountant's *AICPA Professional Standards, AU Section 220* to be ''free from any interest or obligation to or interest in the client, its management, or its owners.'' Chartered Financial Analysts providing investment management services that encounter any issues of conflict of interest are guided by the Association for Investment Management and Research's *AIMR Standards of Practice Handbook*.

As research and technological advances have accelerated, collaborative relationships between government, industry, laboratories, research hospitals, and universities have grown. At the same time, the potential for developing conflicts of interest has also expanded. When researchers discover applications with commercial potential, often with the assistance of outside funding, some degree of conflict of interest becomes inevitable. Not surprisingly, the researcher also expects some personal reward. The issue for researchers, institutions, and sponsors becomes finding the means to support the growth of new technology while managing conflicts of interest. In response, universities, industries, and research institutions have intensified their reviews and strengthened their policies to manage their unique set of conflicts.

[Aldona Cytraus]

FURTHER READING:

Benson, George C.S. ''Conflict of Interest.'' In *Business Ethics and Common Sense*. Westport: Quorom Books, 1992.

Boatright, John R. ''Conflict of Interest: An Agency Analysis'' In *Ethics and Agency Theory*. New York: Oxford Press, 1992.

Association of American Universities. *Framework Document on Managing Financial Conflicts of Interest*. Washington: Association of American Universities, 1993.

U.S. Department of Health and Human Services. Public Health Service. ''Objectivity in Research Financial Disclosure Policy.'' *Federal Register*. July 11, 1995, pp. 35810-19.

National Science Foundation. ''Investigator Financial Disclosure Policy''.

Federal Register, July 11, 1995 (Volume 60, Number 132), 35820-35823.

Twentieth Century Fund. *Abuse on Wall Street: Conflict of Interest in the Securities Market*. Westport: Quorom Books, 1980.

CONFLICT MANAGEMENT

Conflict **management** is the application of strategies to resolve incompatible objectives in a positive manner. Traditionally, conflict was seen as negative. ''In recent years, however,'' as Deborah Borisoff and David Victor observe, ''we have come to recognize and to acknowledge the benefits dealing with conflict affords. Because of our differences, we communicate, we are challenged, we are driven to find creative solutions to problems.''

THE DEVELOPMENT OF CONFLICT MANAGEMENT STRATEGIES

Until the early 1960s, virtually all conflict was perceived as negative. Resolution of conflict had one basic strategy: a win-lose scenario. Since the loser in the win-lose scenario inevitably felt resentment, the typical managerial technique for dealing with conflict was to avoid it. Avoidance, in turn, tended to make the avoided parties feel neglected. Moreover, avoidance rarely resolved the underlying incompatible objectives at the heart of the conflict so that the source of the conflict remained, awaiting only for another situation to surface. Thus, these strategies did not prove particularly valuable in interpersonal work settings.

In the early 1960s, R.R. Blake and J.S. Mouton developed a managerial grid for identifying conflict-handling strategies. The grid illustrated how strategies for handling conflict fell into differing levels of assertiveness and cooperation.

Blake and Mouton identified five modes of handling conflict: (1) smoothing; (2) forcing; (3) withdrawal; (4) compromising; and (5) problem-solving.

Smoothing involved the loser of the win-lose configuration and represented high cooperation with the needs of others along with low assertiveness of one's own needs. The winner of the win-lose model undertook forcing, which included low cooperation and high assertiveness. Traditional conflict avoidance (withdrawal) was seen as low in both assertiveness and cooperation. Compromise was seen as the center of the grid; that is, moderate in both assertiveness and cooperation. Compromise was simultaneously winning and losing, a situation in which neither party was completely satisfied nor dissatisfied. In their last mode, problem-solving, Blake and Mouton suggested a new approach altogether. Problem-solving created a win-win option combining both high assertiveness of one's own needs coupled with high cooperation in solving the needs of others.

The first four conflict-handling modes represented variations of win-lose scenarios, but with the identification of how each could be a strategic decision for handling a particular conflict situation. For example, in conflict for market share between two companies fighting for survival, one might choose a forcing strategy with a winner and loser since the goal would be to eliminate the loser. Such a technique would not work very well within interpersonal conflict in an office environment, however, since both parties would continue to need to work together. Smoothing or intentionally losing could even be useful in conflicts over issues one did not feel particularly strongly about when used to help out a fellow worker who faced stress from other areas. Even conflict avoidance could be seen as useful in an attempt to avoid broaching a subject with a person under temporary emotional duress. Compromise could be useful when the issue was too small to justify the time and effort needed to solve the problem at the heart of the conflict.

Conflict as a problem-solving technique, however, represented an ideal mode for all types of conflict management. In such cases, conflict can be seen as a managerial tool pointing out to the parties involved the underlying problems faced by the organization. Through collaborative behavior, the parties combine their efforts to find creative solutions to old problems.

The other four conflict-handling modes (as variations of the win-lose model) represent only conflict interventions. Problem-solving as a conflict-handling mode, by contrast, represents an attempt to harness conflict as a positive force and to use conflict as a managerial tool to resolve otherwise incompatible objectives within the organization. The problem-solving mode of handling conflict, therefore, can be seen less as a conflict intervention than true conflict management.

CONFLICT MANAGEMENT AS A COMMUNICATION PROCESS

Conflict management as a problem-solving device is an ongoing procedure. In its most effective form, it involves continual communication and supervision. As Borisoff and Victor note, ''conflict-handling behavior is not a static procedure; rather it is a process that requires flexibility and constant evaluation to truly be productive and effective.''

PSEUDOCONFLICT

Within this process, one can identify various barriers based on spoken strategies, writing styles, and nonverbal communication styles that can cloud the communication needed to reach creative solutions to conflict. These barriers are often further distorted by differences in communication based on gender and cultural background. When these barriers impede communication, they often result in misreading by the parties involved. This misreading, in turn, may easily lead one to perceive conflict based on misunderstood behavior where no conflict actually exists. Miller and Steinberg call this misreading ''pseudoconflict,'' that is, perceived conflict rather than true conflict. Much of what is thought to be an actual conflict is the product of such pseudoconflict.

CONFLICT MANAGEMENT TECHNIQUES

Victor and Borisoff identified five steps in the conflict management process: assessment, acknowledgement, attitude, action, and analysis. They assert that these five steps allow for a continual process of problem-solving conflict management.

In the assessment step, the parties gather appropriate information regarding the problem. They select which of the conflict-handling modes would be most appropriate for the situation. They determine what is and what is not at the heart of the problem, what they might be willing to compromise on, and what each party actually wants.

The acknowledgement step is one in which each party attempts to hear out the other. Acknowledgement allows both parties to build the empathy needed for the motivation of a synergistic solution to the problem.

The attitude step attempts to eliminate sources of pseudoconflict. Prejudices regarding cultural differences or gender-linked communication styles are recognized. Differences in communication styles—written, nonverbal or spoken—are examined with the attempt to remain objective to both parties' concerns simultaneously.

The action step is the implementation of the conflict-handling mode selected. If that is the problem-solving mode, one communicates the possibilities for a solution building on trust and continually getting feedback on positions reached. At the same time, one must read cues in the other party to anticipate concerns while at the same time remaining conscious of one's own communicative behavior and seeking productive solutions.

Finally, in the analysis step, decisions are reached, summarized, and then reviewed to establish that the needs of all parties have been met (if possible). Additionally, the analysis step sets the process side of conflict management into motion as something that is ongoing by attempting to anticipate and check for short-term and long-term effects from the solution reached.

Though traditional approaches to conflict may still be employed in special circumstances, the currently preferred approach in most workplace conflicts treats conflict management as an ongoing process through which opposed interests are resolved. This problem-solving conflict management process can be used as an effective technique for problem-solving in a win-win scenario.

[David A. Victor]

FURTHER READING:

Blake, R.R. and J.S. Mouton. "The Intergroup Dynamics of Win-Lose Conflict and Problem-Solving Collaboration in Union-Management Relations." *Intergroup Relations and Leadership* (M. Sherif, ed.). Wiley, 1962. pp. 94-142.

Blake, R.R. and J.S. Mouton. *The Managerial Grid*. Gulf Publishing, 1964.

Borisoff, Deborah and David A. Victor. *Conflict Management: A Communication Skills Approach*. Prentice Hall, 1989.

Miller, Gerald R. and M. Steinberg. *Between People: A New Analysis of Interpersonal Communication*. Science Research Associates, 1975.

CONSIGNMENT

Goods that are offered for sale on consignment have been shipped to the seller by the owner, with the seller acting as agent for the owner. Generally the owner, known as the consignor, retains title to the goods and authorizes the seller, known as the consignee, to sell them. For example, an art gallery selling original art is usually a consignee for the art works, while the artist is the consignor who retains ownership of the art until it is sold.

For the rights of the consignor to be fully protected under the **Uniform Commercial Code**(UCC), it is necessary that the person making delivery meet one of the following conditions: (1) The consignor must comply with an applicable law providing for a consignor's interest or the like to be evidenced by a sign; (2) It must be established that the consignee is generally known to be engaged in selling the goods of others; or (3) The consignor complies with the filing provisions of Article Nine of the UCC covering secured transactions.

If none of the above conditions is met, then the goods in possession of the consignee are considered to have been delivered for resale and are subject to the claim's of the consignee's creditors, provided that the consignee maintains a place of business where such goods are normally sold. The consignee's creditor's claims take precedence over those of the consignor, even if such goods are delivered under an agreement purporting to be "on consignment" or "on memorandum." In this way the UCC differentiates between goods shipped on consignment and those shipped for resale in the normal course of doing business.

When a consignee accepts merchandise for resale, he or she is obligated to exercise due diligence in caring for the goods and in selling them. Although the consignee does not have any money at risk in the consigned goods, the UCC provides remedies for consignors if their goods are damaged through the negligence of the consignee.

Delivering and selling goods on consignment allows the consignee to carry inventory without having to raise adequate working capital to cover the cost of such inventory. Until the consigned merchandise is sold, it is carried on the books of the consignor. Typically the consignee provides the consignor with sales reports accounting for merchandise received and sold, expenses incurred relating to the consignment, and cash remitted. When the goods have been sold, the consignor recognizes the revenue and removes the inventory from the books.

Exporting goods on consignment is a common way to finance such exports. The exporter ships merchandise to an importer on consignment, with the exporter retaining title to the goods and carrying the goods on its books as inventory. The importer does not pay the exporter for the goods until they are sold, at which time title is transferred to the buyer. Once the goods are sold, the importer is paid, and payment is made to the exporter. In these types of transactions it is common practice for the importer's bank to act as trustee for the consigned goods, with payments to the importer and exporter made through the importer's bank.

[David Bianco]

CONSULTANTS AND CONSULTING

Consultants are professionals with expertise in a particular field who offer advice related to their experience. Consulting, then, is the business of providing advice to clients in order to solve a particular problem or range of problems within a particular area of business. The majority of consultants have gained their expertise from former employment. A former stock broker might become a financial consultant; computer scientists would become computer consultants; a former employee in a non-profit organization might begin a business as a fund-raising consultant; an accountant might become a tax consultant. All of these professionals are problem solvers and most of them are, or tend to work as, independent contractors.

Expertise alone, however, does not make you a consultant, at least not a full time one. To be a consultant, you must be able to apply your expertise to practical problem solving. Consulting, moreover, is a business, and hence, you must have marketing skills and the ability to reach out and establish job contacts. Personality also plays a role in consulting success: generally the kind of people who can put the needs and interests of clients before their own, who are not condescending, and who are unfailingly courteous and patient have a chance at success.

As an outgrowth of the "information revolution" of the late 1970s, the consulting profession is rela-

tively new. The advent of computers has made a vast amount of information available and has changed the way we do business. Using their expertise, consultants find information, and "package" it for their clients. A small minority of consultants work as internal consultants; they work for one firm only, usually a very large one. The majority, however, work independently and with no partners, often from their own homes, or they run their own consulting firm.

Both consultants and consulting firms have mushroomed in recent years. Even after the recession of 1991-1992 officially ended, large and small companies continued to "downsize," many of them finding it less expensive to hire a former employee as a consultant than to keep him or her on a full time payroll. Consultants constitute a growing number (as yet undetermined since there are no licensing requirements for consultants) of the self-employed, who in 1990 made up 13 percent of the work force. According to the American Consultants League, between 1993-1994, the consulting field grew by over 400,000 men and women, approximately 150,000 of whom had lost their jobs. The vast majority of these new entrepreneurs were found to be between the ages of 35-55, many of them former mid-level managers.

According to the American Consultants League, the failure rate for first time consulting businesses is extremely high, 91 percent in the first year. Those who do succeed, however, usually earn as much if not more than their former employment. Reasons for failure are often a combination of such factors as poor initial planning, careless marketing of one's business, and intense competition. The successful consultants, however, are those who find a market niche for themselves. This is not just a matter of luck, but of prior research, intensive marketing, and, at times, of locale. Charging the right fee and avoiding falling into the trap of "free" consulting (for instance, the client whose contract with you has ended but who still desires additional "feedback" or "follow up" on the work you did) requires business sense. Consulting fees can vary from almost nothing to several thousand dollars per assignment, depending on the assignment, market conditions, and the minimal rate for that type of work.

Since the vast majority of consultants are self-employed professional business people, consulting typically is a business that requires long hours and is done under much pressure. One's field of expertise must be studied continuously to keep abreast of developments. To the millions who enter the consulting profession, the attraction and the challenge of creative, independent work, done in a comfortable environment, often in a small office or in the home outweigh the difficulties. And while competition is great, the number of large firms that dominate this profession are few. Thanks to the advent of home computers, consulting as a business has "downsized" increasingly since the 1980s. While some consulting fields have become saturated—such as for computer and the environmental fields—there are always new trends emerging. For instance, with the unexpected fall of communism, the demand for east European specialists and "free market" consultants skyrocketed. Hence the need for information keeps escalating, and the demand for consultants keeps growing.

[Sina Dubovoy]

FURTHER READING:

Karlson, David. *Marketing Your Consulting or Professional Services*. Crisp Publications, 1988.

Kelley, Robert E. *Consulting, The Complete Guide to a Profitable Career*. Charles Scribner's Sons, 1986.

Weiss, Alan. *Million Dollar Consulting: The Professional's Guide to Growing a Practice*. McGraw-Hill, 1992.

CONSUMER ADVOCACY

Consumer advocacy refers to actions taken by individuals or groups to promote and protect the interests of the buying public. Historically, consumer advocates have assumed a somewhat adversarial role in exposing unfair business practices or unsafe products that threaten the welfare of the general public. Consumer advocates use tactics like publicity, **boycotts**, letter-writing campaigns, and lawsuits to raise awareness of issues affecting consumers and to counteract the financial and political power of the organizations they target. Periods of vocal consumer advocacy around the turn of the twentieth century and in the late 1960s have left a legacy of federal legislation and agencies intended to protect consumers in the United States. The rights of consumers have expanded to include **product safety**, the legitimacy of advertising claims, the satisfactory resolution of grievances, and voice in government decisions.

The role of consumers in the world of business has evolved over time. In the early days of industry, companies could afford to ignore consumers' wishes because there was so much demand for their goods and services. As a result, they were often able to command high prices for products of poor quality. The earliest consumer advocates to point out such abuses were called "muckrakers." These turn-of-the-century journalists, novelists, and social critics—including Lincoln Steffens, Ida Tarbell, and Upton Sinclair—investigated and publicized harmful business practices and government corruption. One famous expose that uncovered the unsanitary conditions at meat-packing plants led to the passage of the Pure Food and Drug Act in 1906. Federal legislation and agencies created during the first half of the twentieth century helped to address some of the most serious abuses. At the same time, increased competition began to provide consumers with more choices among a variety of products of higher quality. Still, some notable cases of corporations neglecting the public welfare for their own gain continued. Large businesses maintained a great deal of influence in the government through campaign contributions and lobbying efforts. This allowed certain industries to resist the passage of laws mandating the use of expensive safety or pollution-prevention equipment.

This situation led to the consumer movement of the 1960s. One of the country's most outspoken and controversial consumer advocates, lawyer Ralph Nader, came to the forefront during this time. Nader attacked the powerful automobile industry in his 1965 book *Unsafe at Any Speed*, which alleged that some car models contained correctable design flaws that caused the deaths of thousands of Americans each year. Nader argued that the auto industry used its political influence to postpone the implementation of safety standards. He initiated class-action lawsuits and promoted product recalls, two tactics he felt elevated consumers' complaints to a financial level where companies could no longer ignore them. Rather than simply learning to live with unsafe products and their consequences, Nader encouraged average citizens to work together to "give the institutions of society something to fear from their victims," according to Robert F. Buckhorn's biography. Some of Nader's notable successes included establishing safety standards for cars, children's toys and clothing, and a wide range of household products. He also founded the Center for the Study of Responsive Law, the Center for Auto Safety, Public Interest Research Groups (PIRG) on college campuses, and the fundraising vehicle Public Citizen.

The efforts of Nader and other activists led to the formation of several federal agencies designed to protect consumer interests. The U.S. Office of Consumer Affairs, created in 1971, investigates and resolves consumer complaints, conducts consumer surveys, and disseminates product information to the public. The Consumer Product Safety Commission, formed in 1973, sets national standards for product safety and testing procedures, coordinates product recalls, and ensures that companies respond to valid consumer complaints. Other agencies that benefit consumers include the **Better Business Bureau** and state consumer agencies. The Consumer Federation of America is the largest consumer advocacy group in the United States, consisting of about 220 member organizations. The International Organization of Consumers Unions, based in the Netherlands, actively promotes consumer interests on a global scale. In the 1990s, the widespread use of home **computers** advanced consumer advocacy by making it easier for citizens to gather information and make their views known. Some hot issues affecting consumers in the United States included airline fares, loan-fee scams, and lawsuit reform.

[Laurie Collier Hillstrom]

FURTHER READING:

Buckhorn, Robert F. *Nader: The People's Lawyer.* Englewood Cliffs, NJ: Prentice-Hall, 1972.

"A Consumer Warning on New Ripoffs," *Money.* March 1992, p. 34.

Cook, Gareth G. "The Case for (Some) Regulation," *Washington Monthly.* March 1995, p. 34.

Hamburg, Joan. "From Refunds to Ripoffs: Your Consumer Problems Solved," *Family Circle.* February 1, 1994, p. 134.

"How to Use Your Computer to Effect Change," *Compute.* March 1993, p. S7.

"Is Lawsuit Reform Good for Consumers?," *Consumer Reports.* May 1995, p. 312.

Kemper, Vicki. "A Citizen for All Seasons," *Common Cause Magazine.* Spring 1995, p. 12.

Mayer, Robert N. *The Consumer Movement: Guardians of the Marketplace.* Boston: Twayne, 1989.

Stingley, Ruth Nauss. "It Pays to Complain," *Reader's Digest.* October 1993, p. 116.

CONSUMER PRICE INDEX (CPI)

The Consumer Price Index (CPI), sometimes called the cost-of-living **index**, measures the average change in prices that typical American wage earners pay for basic goods and services, such as food, clothing, shelter, transportation, and medical care. It is expressed as a percentage of the cost of the same goods and services in a base period. For example, using the years 1982 to 1984 as a base period with a value of 100, the CPI for April 1995 was 151.9, meaning that prices had increased by an average of 51.9 percent over time. The CPI is often used to measure **inflation**, so it is closely monitored by government policymakers and by individuals whose wages vary with the **purchasing power** of money. The practice of indexing wages to the CPI is known as a cost of living adjustment (COLA). The term "cost of living" is often applied to the numerical result of the CPI. Loosely defined, it refers to the average cost to an individual of purchasing the various goods and services needed to maintain a reasonable living standard.

The U.S. Bureau of Labor Statistics (BLS) began calculating the CPI in 1917, and over the years it has become an important economic statistic. The CPI is calculated monthly and is usually reported within the first two weeks of the following month. In order to calculate the CPI, the BLS surveys about 24,000 households to find out where families shop regularly and what types of goods and services they purchase. It then contacts about 21,000 retail businesses in 85 major metropolitan areas to obtain prices for 90,000 items. All of this information is combined in the CPI, which represents the average price of a "market basket" of goods and services. The BLS tries to incorporate any new developments in the market by changing 20 percent of the retail outlets and items in its survey every year on a rotating basis.

A separate CPI is calculated for different income levels, geographical areas, and types of goods and services. For example, the CPI-U is calculated for all urban households, which includes about 80 percent of the U.S. population. In contrast, the CPI-W measures average price increases for the 32 percent of Americans who derive their primary income as wage earners or clerical workers. The BLS also publishes a CPI for each of seven major categories of items: food and beverages, housing, apparel, transportation, medical care, entertainment, and other goods and services. In addition, it compiles individual indexes for 200 different items and combined indexes for 120 smaller categories of items. Separate CPI measurements are also released for four major geographical regions of the United States—Northeast, North Central, South, and West—as well as 29 large metropolitan areas.

The CPI influences the American economy in several ways. A high annual percentage increase in the CPI reflects a high rate of inflation. The Federal Reserve Board, which controls the nation's money supply, often reacts to such increases by raising **interest rates**. This makes it more expensive for individuals and businesses to borrow money, which usually slows spending, encourages saving, and helps to curb inflation in the economy. The CPI also determines the percentage of annual increase or decrease in income for many Americans. For example, COLA formulas based on the CPI are built into many **employment contracts**. The federal government also uses the CPI to adjust Social Security and disability benefits, to determine the income level at which people become eligible for assistance, and to establish tax brackets. In addition, the CPI is often used to compare prices for certain goods within a set of years, and to calculate constant dollar values for two points in time.

Some economists believe that the CPI overstates actual increases in the cost of living by 1 percent or more annually. They generally attribute the discrepancy to some combination of the following four factors: improvements in the quality of goods; the introduction of new goods; substitution by consumers of different goods or retail outlets; and the difficulty of measuring the prices consumers actually pay for goods. The annual increase in the CPI from April 1994 to April 1995 was 3.1 percent.

[Laurie Collier Hillstrom]

FURTHER READING:

"Cost-of-Living Lesson," *American Demographics.* December 1994, p. 6.

Darnay, Arsen J., ed. *American Cost of Living Survey.* Chicago: American Marketing Association, 1994.

Epstein, Gene. "Economic Beat: Increases in Consumer Prices May Be Less Than Meet the Eye," *Barron's.* September 19, 1994, pp. 45-46.

Money Income of Households, Families, and Persons in the United States. Washington, D.C.: U.S. Bureau of the Census, 1994.

Reinsdorf, Marshall. "The Effect of Price Dispersion on Cost of Living Indexes," *International Economic Review.* February 1994, pp. 137-149.

Wynne, Mark A., and Fiona D. Sigalla. "The Consumer Price Index," *Economic Review* (Federal Reserve Bank of Dallas). Second Quarter 1994, pp. 1-22.

CONSUMER PRODUCT SAFETY COMMISSION

The Consumer Product Safety Commission (CPSC) was established in 1972 with the passage of the Consumer Product Safety Act. The primary responsibility of the CPSC is to protect the public from unreasonable risks of injury that could occur during the use of consumer products. The CPSC also promotes the evaluation of consumer products for potential hazards, establishes uniform safety standards for consumer products, eases conflicting state and local regulations concerned with consumer safety, works to recall hazardous products from the marketplace, and selectively conducts research on potentially hazardous products. The CPSC promotes the development of voluntary safety standards and under certain circumstances has the authority to issue and enforce standards and ban unsafe products. In all its activities the CPSC strives to work closely with private consumer groups, industry, the media, and agencies of various state and local governments.

Although the CPSC is an independent federal regulatory agency it does not have jurisdiction over all consumer products. Safety standards for trucks, automobiles, and motorcycles are set by the U.S. Department of Transportation; drugs and cosmetics are handled by the U.S. Food and Drug Administration; (FDA) and alcohol, tobacco, and firearms fall under the authority of the U.S. Department of the Treasury. Nevertheless, approximately 15,000 types of consumer products are regulated by the CPSC.

Early federal consumer safety legislation dealt primarily with foods, drugs, and cosmetics. The Federal Food and Drugs Act of 1906 (also known as the Wiley Pure Food and Drug Act) forbade the adulteration and fraudulent misbranding of foods and drugs sold through interstate commerce. Other early consumer legislation included the Meat Inspection Act of 1907 (amended in 1967 by the Wholesome Meat Act). In 1933 legislation was introduced to strengthen the Federal Food and Drugs Act of 1906. This legislation mandated the standardized labeling of food products, required that manufacturers prove drugs are safe for the purpose for which they are sold, and established a pre-market clearance procedure for new drug products. Many drug companies opposed this bill, as did much of the media fearful of potential lost **advertising** revenue. After a five-year battle in Congress the bill was passed in 1938 as the Food, Drug, and Cosmetic Act. Amendments to the bill in 1962 established biennial factory inspections, disclosure through labeling of dangerous side effects, FDA approval of all new drugs, FDA power to remove dangerous drugs from the market, and the requirement that a manufacturer prove that drug is not only safe but also effective for its stated purpose.

The scope of federal consumer safety legislation broadened throughout the 1950s and 1960s. The Flammable Fabrics Act, enacted in the early '50s, established safety standards for fabrics used in clothing. The Refrigerator Safety Act of 1956 required that refrigerator doors have inside release mechanisms. The 1962 National Traffic and Motor Vehicle Safety Act established federal jurisdiction over motor vehicle safety, while the 1965 Federal Cigarette Labeling and Advertising Act required the infamous "Caution: Cigarette Smoking May Be Hazardous to Your Health" label. Other pre-1972 consumer product safety legislation included the Radiation Control for Health and Safety Act of 1968 which dealt with radiation emission levels of electronic products and the Poison Prevention Packaging Act of 1970 which established packaging standards to protect children from potentially hazardous substances.

In 1967 the National Commission on Product Safety was established. It was believed that federal consumer safety legislation was not effective enough because it took a piecemeal approach by targeting specific types of products for regulation. What was needed was legislative authority over broad categories of potentially hazardous goods and products. The National Commission on Product Safety was charged with identifying these broad categories of potentially hazardous goods and evaluating existing legal and voluntary methods for securing consumer product safety. The commission found that ". . . the exposure of consumers to unreasonable product hazards is excessive by any standards of measurement." The commission also asserted that even though consumers must take some responsibility for their own safety, industry must also assume responsibility for the design and manufacturing of safe consumer products and in this regard they had been lax.

On the basis of their inquiry the commission recommended the creation of an independent federal regulatory agency and a presidential appointee to the commission to serve as a consumer advocate before the new agency. The commission also recommended that the new agency have the authority to issue safety regulations and standards. Subsequently, the Consumer Product Safety Commission was created in 1972.

The CPSC consists of five commissioners each appointed by the president with the advice and consent of the Senate. One of the commissioners is appointed chairman. The CPSC is headquartered in Bethesda, Maryland, with regional offices in Chicago, New York, and San Francisco and field offices in various cities across the country. The CPSC also maintains a toll-free Consumer Product Safety Hotline (1-800-638-CPSC).

For further information: Office of Information and Public Affairs, Consumer Product Safety Commission, East West Towers, 4340 EAST WEST Hwy., Bethesda, Maryland 20814, (301)504-0580.

[Michael Knes]

FURTHER READING:

Kimble, William. *Federal Consumer Product Safety Act.* West Publishing Co., 1975.

Lemov, Michael R. *Consumer Product Safety Commission.* Shepard's/McGraw-Hill, 1981.

CONSUMERISM

The term "consumerism" has been historically, and still is associated both positively and pejoratively with acquiring and using consumer goods or services. In the 1960s "consumerism" broadened its scope to be identified with consumer activism—the protection and advocacy of the rights of consumers. In the 1980s the definition of "consumerism" was extended to include consumer groups who had learned to use their economic clout to further specific economic and political goals.

The use of "consumerism" as a term to describe the consumer movement began in the sixties, but the movement itself for legal and social protection of consumers has roots that delve far back into history. The Bible advises a merchant to have fair standards. Hammurabi's code included merchant standards, and while ancient Rome also had laws to protect the consumer, *caveat emptor*, "let the buyer beware" or at least be wary, was as good advice then as now.

In simpler times, the way in which buyers most often assured themselves of the quality of goods, in addition to inspecting those goods before buying, was to know and trust the seller. In the United States, these personal relationships between buyer and seller began to break down as American industry mushroomed during and just after the Civil War. Instead of buying an item made by Joe in the village, the item needed might be made by Company X, hundreds of miles away. The direct relationship between the buyer and the seller was severed. The seller could make all sorts of claims about the goods, knowing that the consumer was too far away to do much about it when the product did not live up to the claims. The shoddy nature of mass-produced goods at this time attests to this phenomenon.

To restore the sense of reliance on the "good name" of the seller, many companies during the 1870s and 1880s began to attach the founder's name to the product. Ketchup was no longer just generic ketchup, there was "Heinz" ketchup. Buyers began to trust that each bottle was of good quality and as good as the one bought before because they trusted **brand names**.

The need for laws to supplement this private sector effort to protect the consumer was first raised in the United States by Dr. Harvey W. Wiley (1844-1930) in 1883 over the issue of food additives. Wiley, who was head of the U.S. Department of Agriculture's chemistry division, was particularly concerned with the wild claims of a number of "patent" medicines then on the market. In 1903 he established a "poison squad" of young male volunteers who ingested small amounts of chemical preservatives; Wiley garnered a lot of media coverage for his efforts.

In 1889 the national Consumers Union was founded and in 1906 Upton Sinclair's novel, *The Jungle* was published. Sinclair had meant to highlight the unsanitary conditions of the meatpacking workers, but the public fastened its attention instead on the unsanitary conditions of the meatpacking industry. In June 1906 the Pure Food and Drug Act was passed, followed in 1915 by the creation of the Federal Trade Commission, which among its other duties, monitors advertising claims.

In 1936 the Consumers Union split off from Consumer's Research and the union broadened its base to include the conditions of the worker as well as a code of quality for goods and services. The magazine *Consumer Reports* began and is still one of the most reliable sources of information on goods and services available to the modern consumer.

After World War II the U.S. economy took off and a new era of emphasis on goods and services began. Again, advertising became the issue that galvanized the consumer movement, but this time it was not claims made for products, but the subtle ways in which ads induced one to buy the product. Vance Packard's book about advertising, *The Hidden Persuaders* was published in 1957. Not long after, in *The Silent Spring* published in 1962, Rachel Carson called upon America to look at how the modern consumerist society was affecting the environment. In 1965, Ralph Nader published *Unsafe at any Speed*, his scathing attack on the Corvair automobile and the automobile industry.

In 1962, President John F. Kennedy introduced the Consumer Bill of Rights, and began the revitalization of Progressive era (1900-1914) federal programs designed to protect the consumer. The Consumer Bill of Rights included a "Truth in Lending" law and a "Truth in Packaging" law; it held that consumers had the right to be safe, to be informed, to choose, and to be heard.

President Johnson led the way for consumer efforts around the country by appointing Esther Peterson (1906-) as the first special presidential assistant for consumer affairs. The Consumer Product Safety Commission was created in 1973 and one of its primary missions is to protect the public from the risk of injury caused by consumer products. The idea of fair play and open and aboveboard treatment of consumers was extended into the financial realm with the passage of the 1974 Fair Credit Reporting Act and the Equal Credit Opportunity Act. In rapid succession each state and the District of Columbia established offices of consumer protection to deal with consumer problems on the state level.

Consumerism is not limited to legislation and the public sector. Private-sector merchants and manufacturers have long taken steps to assure the quality and reliability of their goods and services. The number of customer relations representatives in firms grew from a few "complaint department employees" in large firms into a specialty that has its own nationwide 3,000 member professional organization. Many manufacturers offer **toll-free telephone numbers** (800 numbers) for consumers to use for inquiries or complaints about products.

The consumer movement is not a phenomenon restricted to the United States. Many countries, especially in Western Europe, regulate **advertising** and keep an eye on the interest of the consumer. Robert N. Mayer in *The Consumer Movement* found that consumerism in the United States is distinctive in its development and use of legal remedies such as the class action suit, "lemon laws" (a set of laws designed to enforce warranties and make it easier to return and be reimbursed for a "bad" product), and the doctrine of strict liability (beginning in 1963 a manufacturer could be found guilty of product liability without any evidence of negligence).

Each of these legal or self-imposed restraints adds a cost for the consumer of the good or service. The opponents of the growth of consumerism hold that the cost has been too high, and believe that regulatory measures and restrictions imposed by government have become a restraint on free enterprise. Consumer advocates believe that deregulation will leave consumers unprotected and cite as evidence the unwillingness of industry to deal with issues such as the flammability of children's sleepwear and safer toys and cars until pressure was applied through the law.

In the last decades of the twentieth century the consumer movement progressed beyond simple protection of consumers into harnessing those consumers into a political force. The lettuce boycott of the seventies to support the formation of a migrant workers union was one of the first nationwide attempts to use consumer power to advance political goals. Consumer associations began to be formed for the purpose of affecting public policy on certain issues, often those dealing with the environment. Special directories are published to enable people to "vote with their consumer power" by purchasing goods and services from those who contribute to causes that the consumer supports. Advertising campaigns on television urge consumers to buy products made in the United States to protect the jobs of U.S. workers; other ads encourage consumers to "look for the union label," to further worker protection by supporting firms that hire unionized labor.

Consumerism is likely to continue into the twentieth century; the role of the consumer, using purchasing power to support political causes, is likely to continue to expand as well. Whether or not movements to streamline government result in federal deregulation, the legal precedents in place and general structure of citizen-run organizations guarantee the consumer a strong voice well into the next century.

SEE ALSO: Credit Approval; Customer Relations

[Joan Leotta]

FURTHER READING:

Aaker, David A., and George S. Day, eds. *Consumerism: Search for Consumer Interest*. New York: Free Press, 1984.

Lesko, Matthew. *The Great American Gripe Book*. Kensington, Md.: Information USA, 1991.

Mayer, Robert N. *The Consumer Movement: Guardians of the Marketplace*. Boston, MA: Twayne Publishers, 1989.

Mitford, Jessica. *The American Way of Death*. New York: Simon and Schuster, 1963.

Nader, Ralph. *Unsafe at Any Speed*. New York: Grossman, 1965.

Peduzzi, Kelli. *Ralph Nader*. Milwaukee: Gareth Stephens Books, 1990.

Silmer, Norman. *Test and Protest.* New York: Holmes and Meier, 1983.

The Smart Consumer's Directory. Nashville: Thomas Nelson Publishers, 1993.

Tasaday, Lawrence. *Shopping for a Better Environment.* Deephaven, MN: Meadowbrook Press, 1991.

USA Foundation. *Made in USA.* Washington, D.C.: National Press Books, 1992.

Vance, Packard. *The Hidden Persuaders.* New York: David MacKay, 1957.

CONSUMPTION TAX

A consumption tax is a broad category of tax that is levied on the consumption value of goods and services. Examples of consumption taxes include the retail **sales tax**, **excise taxes, value added taxes** (VATs), use taxes, taxes on gross business receipts (also known as business transfer taxes), and import **duties**. Consumption taxes are paid for by consumers rather than businesses, even though they may originally be paid by a business that passes the tax along to the consumer in the selling price. Consumption taxes are generally not collected by the government directly from consumers. Rather, they are collected by vendors at the retail level, who then pay the national or state taxing authority.

While the United States has no national consumption tax, many nations of the world have some form of national consumption tax. Value-added taxes are a common form of national consumption tax in effect in most European countries, Canada, and elsewhere in the world. A value-added tax (VAT) is one that is levied on the "value added" to goods or services produced by businesses. Such a tax is collected in stages from each business that contributes to the final market value of goods and services. While the VAT is collected by the state from businesses, the actual tax burden is passed along to consumers as part of the final selling price. Thus, the VAT is considered a consumption tax even though it is initially paid by businesses.

Similarly, import duties are considered consumption taxes, because the duty that is collected from the importer is passed along to the consumer as part of the final selling price. An import duty is charged on goods entering a country. It is usually either calculated as a percentage of the value of the goods being imported or exported (an *ad valorem* duty), or as a specific duty, which is based on the quantity, weight, or volume of the goods being imported.

An excise tax is another example of a consumption tax that is initially paid by a manufacturer who includes the cost of the tax in the selling price to the consumer. An excise tax is applied to a specific commodity or type of goods, such as cigarettes, gasoline, or alcoholic beverages. Excise taxes that are designed to discourage consumption of a particular commodity for the benefit of society are known as sumptuary taxes, or more commonly as "sin taxes." Other excise taxes can be justified as a user charge on the basis of the benefit principle. In the case of gasoline taxes, it is reasoned that only those individuals who benefit from road and highway construction and maintenance have to pay the gasoline excise tax.

While consumption taxes such as excise taxes, import duties, and VATs are hidden from the consumer, the retail sales tax is a more visible consumption tax. The tax base for sales taxes was originally confined to merchandise or tangible goods. More recently, sales taxes have been applied to services as well, thus making them more of a consumption tax rather than a tangible goods tax.

Like other consumption taxes, the retail sales tax is considered a regressive tax. That is, individuals and families with lower incomes pay a greater proportion of their income for sales taxes than people with higher incomes. By exempting food and other necessities from the sales tax, it can be argued, some of its regressive nature can be mitigated.

The effects of a consumption tax are somewhat different from those of a production tax or income tax. A consumption tax tends to encourage savings and investment and discourage consumption. Excise taxes in particular are often used to regulate the consumption of certain goods, including luxury items, cigarettes, and alcoholic beverages. Those who put forth the argument for a national consumption tax in the United States point to it as a revenue source that could be used to reduce the national deficit and improve the nation's trade balance.

[David Bianco]

CONTINUING EDUCATION

Continuing education is a synonym for success in the business world. Workers at all levels, ranging from entry-level to senior management, cannot achieve success without constantly upgrading their skills. Nor can businesses continue operating without well-trained employees. Hence, continuing education has become an extremely important and highly popular tool for business people and individual companies in recent years.

Continuing education includes formal and informal training. Workers may earn college degrees through formal programs, concentrate on professional development courses aimed at personal enrichment in informal surroundings, or combine the two. Generally, the skills people develop for personal enrichment can be applied to their work lives. As a result of continuing education, people get the feeling that they have control over their own destinies. That is one of the primary reasons continuing education is becoming so important today.

THE GOALS OF CONTINUING EDUCATION

Continuing education is designed to benefit both businesses and individuals. Corporations which encourage the process develop work forces highly capable of functioning in the rapidly changing global economy. Individuals learn to hone their business, **decision making**, and analytical skills, which prepares them for promotions in their chosen career paths. More importantly, continuing education enhances companies' abilities to maintain their competitive advantages in the international environment and improves learners' chances of being selected over less-prepared workers for the shrinking number of **management** positions.

Courses are available through a variety of channels. Schools at all levels, from high schools to community colleges to universities, offer continuing education programs. Some offer night courses; others run weekend-only programs that allow access to college classes for learners who work traditional Monday through Friday schedules. Often, schools team with businesses to operate programs jointly. Many companies run their own continuing education programs, ranging from workshops and seminars to full-fledged college credit curriculums. Courses may be conducted on or off site.

For example, Associated Spring, in Bristol, CT, a division of the Barnes Group, co-sponsors an on-site training program for employees on a voluntary basis that allows participants to earn credits toward associate degrees. The classes are run by instructors from Tunxis Community-Technical College in nearby Farmington. Classes range from basic subjects such as English Composition to advanced managerial courses, e.g., **Organizational Behavior**, Business and Society (the study of Public Policy), and Labor Relations. Funding such courses provides students with a broader knowledge and skill base and ensures the company of a steady supply of qualified managers.

Not all continuing education courses are aimed at professionals. Some schools offer training facilities and programs for tradespeople such as plumbers and carpenters. Classes in such programs are designed to teach these learners not only how to build houses and drain pipes, but also how to start and manage their own businesses. The result, whether the programs are geared toward professionals or tradespeople, is partnerships that benefit companies and employees alike.

THE BENEFITS OF CONTINUING EDUCATION

People who pursue continuing education can benefit immeasurably. They learn the most recent theories, philosophies, and psychologies extant in the business environment and how to apply them practically. Expanded knowledge of theory, philosophy, psychology and practical application is critical to workers in the light of the rapid technological and management changes occurring in the global market.

A major benefit to continuing education is that it provides learners with relevant information and skills that they can use immediately in their jobs. Training facilities often contain state-of-the-art equipment such as computer labs that utilize the latest technological **software** and hardware features. The **computers** also facilitate interactive training through satellite information. Thus, learners have instant access to experts in virtually every business discipline as well as arts and humanities, sciences, and other academic fields.

THE VARIETY OF COURSES

There is no limit to the types of courses available to learners. Courses, workshops, seminars, etc., are run on topics such as **sexual harassment**, OSHA regulations, public speaking, supervisory skills, **International management** . . . the list goes on. Course developers are generally able to stay abreast of the never-ending changes occurring in the business world and develop or adapt classes to respond to emerging trends. Significantly, the courses can be customized to fit individual companies' needs, which is one of the more appealing aspects of continuing education. For instance, as the economy switches from a **manufacturing** to a service base, continuing education courses provide the training necessary for workers to make the transition. Often, the courses can be developed quickly through partnerships among schools, businesses, government agencies, and other interested participants. The resulting programs keep workers' skills upgraded, and facilitate their abilities to change jobs and careers as conditions warrant.

Continuing education is almost mandatory if contemporary workers and companies are to survive in today's increasingly competitive and complex business environment. Visionary executives striving to make their companies the best in their fields look to continuing education as the vehicles to remain competitive and up-to-date. Individuals utilize continuing education as the best way to acquire and maintain the skills necessary to succeed in the business world. Companies and businesses alike must make commitments to continuing education today. Without that commitment, neither can survive in today's business competition.

[Arthur G. Sharp]

FURTHER READING:

Brookfield, Stephen. *Developing Critical Thinkers: Challenging Adults to Explore Alternative Ways of Thinking and Acting.* San Francisco, CA: Jossey-Boss, 1987.

Evans, Norman. *Post-Education Society: Recognizing Adults as Learners.* London, England: Croom Helm, 1985.

Lamdin, Lois. *Earn College Credit for What You Know*, 2nd. Ed., Chicago, IL: CAEL, The Council for Adult & Experiential Living, 1992.

Mandell, Alan and Elana Michelson. *Portfolio Development & Adult Learning*, Chicago, IL: CAEL, The Council for Adult & Experiential Living, 1990.

Smith, Peter. *Your Hidden Credentials*, Washington D.C.: Acropolis Books Ltd., 1986.

CONTRACTORS

As companies seek ways of keeping expenses down, one option that has become increasingly more attractive is the use of contract labor. Concern over a recessionary economy as well as seasonal shifts in productivity and a growing desire among workers to have more control over their work and free time are all factors that have contributed to an upswing in the use of contract labor. Now, rather than "staffing up" to handle peak times, companies can avoid the additional cost of training, housing, and paying full-time employees, by employing workers as they need them.

Companies also choose to work with contractors when the service provided is not part of the core business. For instance, Southern Pacific Rail Corporation has contracted with an IBM unit to handle its computing needs. In fact, computer services represent a large percentage of contracted services. According to the Yankee Group, a market research firm in Boston, 40 percent of the Fortune 25 have contracted out their computer systems.

A company working with independent contractors rather than employees benefits from not being required to provide benefits, not being held to minimum wage laws, not being required to pay overtime, and avoiding the payment of payroll taxes. These benefits accrue, however, only to those companies that are, indeed, working with employees who can legitimately be classified as independent contractors. The **Internal Revenue Service (IRS)** has a vested interest in assuring that companies do not incorrectly assume these benefits when they are, in fact, dealing with individuals that should be classified as employees.

Because of these concerns, the IRS has increased its efforts to identify companies that are misclassifying employees as independent contractors when they are actually employees and are subject to Social Security and unemployment taxes.

IRS Revenue Ruling 87-41 outlines 20 factors used to determine whether a person is an independent contractor or an employee. These factors generally involve the issue of how much control the company exercises over the contractor. For instance, when working with an independent contractor, a company cannot control where the individual works, the equipment used, the hours worked, or whether the individual subcontracts. The company should not be providing the tools, work space, or materials required to perform the job.

A company should consider the following factors when making a determination of whether a company is working with a contractor or an employee:

1. The contractor must assume the risk of profit or loss from the association.

2. A relationship with a contractor represents a limited time frame marked by the completion of a project, while employees are hired for an ongoing time.

3. A contractor controls where and how the work is performed.

4. Contractors are not trained by the company that purchases their services.

5. Contractors may delegate aspects of the work they are doing to others, while employees are required to do the work themselves.

6. Contracted services are not an integral part of the company's operation. For Southern Pacific Rail Corporation, computer services are not an integral part of their business—transportation.

7. Contractors control the hiring, firing, and supervision of any assistants with which they might work.

8. The outside contractor's hours of work are not dictated by the organization.

9. There are no full-time work requirements.

10. The contractor is not required to work at the employer's business location.

11. The sequence in which the work is performed is not dictated by the organization.

12. Contractors are less likely than employees to be required to complete and submit regular reports to management.

13. Contractors are paid based on a project or commission basis, not on an hourly, weekly, or monthly basis.

14. The contractor is responsible for the payment of work-related business or travel expenses.

15. Independent contractors provide their own work tools and supplies.

16. Contractors have a significant investment in the facilities they use for work.

17. Contractors are able to work for more than one company at any given time.

18. The contractor regularly makes his/her services available to the public.

19. Independent contractors cannot be "fired." The relationship can, however, be terminated if the contract agreement is violated or the work is not performed as outlined in the contract specifications.

20. Employees are free to sever their relationship with a company at any time; independent contractors may be liable for breach of contract if they do not complete the work they have been contracted to do.

Companies working with independent contractors are responsible for filing the appropriate forms with the IRS. Form 1099-Misc (Statement for Recipients of Miscellaneous Income) must be sent to every independent contractor whose fee was $600 or more for the year. A copy of this form is also sent to the IRS, along with Form 1096 (Annual Summary and Transmittal of U.S. Information Returns). The forms require simply the contractor's Social Security number and the amount paid to the contractor for the year. They serve the purpose of notifying the IRS that the contractor is liable for income tax payments. Failure to file the forms can result in penalties for the business.

The IRS estimates an annual loss of $1.6 billion each year associated with improper classification of independent contractors and has stepped up actions to identify misclassification by companies. If the IRS finds that an independent contractor has been incorrectly classified, and should be an employee, it can assess back Social Security taxes and employment taxes. The employee who has been incorrectly classified may also file a claim against the company for the payment of any benefits that he or she would have been entitled to as an employee of the company.

[Lin Grensing-Pophal]

FURTHER READING:

"Bull's Eye." *Executive Female.* March/April, 1991, p. 12.

Faegre & Benson. *Workplace Law Notes.* Summer, 1989.

"Independent Contractor or Employee?" *Bureau of National Affairs.* 1990, p. 54.

Lee, Louise. "Hiring Outside Firms to Run Computers Isn't Always a Bargain." *Wall Street Journal.* May 18, 1995, p. 1.

"Payroll Manager's Letter." *Prentice-Hall Professional Newsletters.* February 2, 1987.

Pouliot, Janine S. "The Outsiders." *Entrepreneurial Woman.* April, 1991, pp. 12-15.

Shenson, Howard L. "Payment for Performance." *Nation's Business.* April, 1991, p. 52R.

CONTRACTS

A contract is a legally enforceable promise. Contracts are vital to society because they facilitate cooperation and trust. Rather than relying on fear of reprisal or the hope of reciprocity to get others to meet their obligations, people can enlist other people to pursue common purposes by submitting to contracts that are backed by impartial authority. Without contracts and their supporting institutions, promises would be much more vulnerable to ill will, misunderstanding, forgetfulness, and other human flaws. Indeed, contracts allow people that have never even met to reach agreements, such as lending/borrowing money to buy a house, that they would never consider making outside of a legal framework.

Discussed below are characteristics and types of contracts and the **Uniform Commercial Code** (UCC), which governs most commercial contracts in the United States.

BACKGROUND

Contracts have been used since ancient times to ensure the performance of different parties in all types of promises. Contract law had reached a relatively sophisticated state by the 15th century in England. Then, during the Industrial Revolution in the 1800s, the increasing complexity of contracts, combined with new ideas about free market economies, forced a new type of contract law. It was based on the "freedom of contract" concept, which basically held that individuals should be free to create their own agreements free of outside intervention. The role of the courts was only to enforce the promises and not to determine the rightness or wrongness of the agreement.

Contract law during the 19th and early 20th century was characterized by strict interpretation. If two parties entered an agreement voluntarily, the courts were not concerned with complaints of perceived unfairness, such as illegal bargaining power. However, as business dealing became more geographically diverse and larger in volume, many types of contracts became standardized. Companies and individuals often used the same forms, or contracts, to handle numerous similar transactions. As a result, many contracts were not specifically tailored to the agreements that they represented, and the party to which the terms were dictated usually did not have a complete understanding of the promise. A corollary of that development was that contracts were often used to take advantage of less powerful, or less informed, parties.

Contracts continued to become more standardized and less representative of individual agreements during the middle and late 1900s. Consider how few people draft a truly singular contract (or even carefully read a standard contract) when they buy a car, assume a mortgage, take a job, or enter into other important agreements. Because of that trend, courts have gradually shucked the strict, technical interpretation of contracts in favor of a "fairness" approach based on criteria such as good faith, reasonableness, and justice. For instance, a plaintiff might successfully argue in court that he is not obligated to execute an agreement because the contract did not reflect his true intent.

The move toward more ambiguous criteria and greater intervention in the contract process by the courts has resulted in greater protection of weaker parties and a more realistic interpretation of agreements. The drawback, however, has been a dilution of the strength of contracts. Because the rules governing contracts have become more vague, agreements no longer supply the same predictability and social stability that they once afforded. Furthermore, individuals and companies are less able to craft agreements that will ensure the performance of both parties. Contract law and theory continues to evolve, though, in response to societal pressures and needs.

CONTRACT ELEMENTS

By its most basic definition, a contract is a legally enforceable promise. It differs from a simple verbal promise in that either party may ask the state to force the other party to honor its promise. To distinguish contracts from other types of promises and agreements, courts have established basic elements that are necessary for a contract to exist. A contract may be legally defined as a voluntary, legal, written agreement made by persons with the proper capacity. It should include: 1) an offer; 2) an acceptance; and 3) consideration, or an exchange of value. There are legal exceptions to most of these conditions, and all of them are subject to interpretation in the courts. Furthermore, some contracts do not meet these requirements, such as implied contracts and those created under promissory estoppel, both of which are discussed later.

Contracts not entered into voluntarily are voidable. For example, if a banker threatens to kill a client if he does not refinance his mortgage at a higher interest rate, the client would not be required to submit to the contract. Although that case is extreme, agreements made under any duress are generally not enforceable. For example, a company might tell a supplier that it was considering ending their business relationship if, within the next ten minutes, the supplier didn't sign a contract to provide materials at a certain cost. If the supplier signed the agreement, it might be able to convince the courts that it did so under duress or undue influence, and therefore was not bound by its terms. In general, contracts created under duress, undue influences, fraud, and misrepresentation are voidable by the injured party.

Contracts are also void if they involve a promise that is illegal or violates public policy. For instance, a contract regarding the sale of illegal drugs is unenforceable. Likewise, contracts that are legal but are not in the public interest may be null. For example, a contract in which a company requires a customer to pay an extremely high rate of interest on borrowed funds could be deemed invalid by the courts. Or, suppose a company contracts with a customer to sell supplies to him that he uses to grow marijuana. If the company also tells him how to grow the illegal substance, the contract would become unenforceable because the agreement promoted the violation of a statute. As another illustration, a retail company that required an employee to sign an agreement that he would never work for another retailer would likely not be able to enforce the contract because it had unreasonable restrictions or imposed undue hardship on the worker.

Contracts do not have to be written to be enforceable in court. In fact, most oral contracts are legally enforceable. However, they are obviously much more difficult to prove. Furthermore, most states have adopted "statutes of frauds," which specify certain types of contracts which must be in writing. Examples of contracts that typically fall under the statues of frauds include agreements related to the sale of real estate, contracts for the sale of goods above $500, and contracts in which one person agrees to perform the obligation of another person. Even those contracts do not have to exist in stereotypical fashion. In fact, a simple memo or receipt may suffice. Furthermore, their are several exceptions to the statutes of frauds. For instance, when one party will suffer serious losses as a result of reliance on an oral agreement, the statute of frauds may be waived (see promissory estoppel below).

Even if the contract is voluntary, legal, and written, it is void if the person that makes the agreement does not have the mental and legal capacity to do so. Obviously, a mentally retarded individual or a child could not be bound by a contract. But a person without the authority to make an agreement may also void a contract. For instance, suppose that an overly zealous salesman representing a ball bearing company signed an agreement with a buyer to supply one billion ball bearings to be delivered in 24 hours. The contract could be worthless if the salesman was acting outside of his authority to commit the company to that agreement. Or, suppose that a person signed a contract between her former employer and one of its customers. The agreement would likely be null because she did not have the capacity to act on the company's behalf.

In addition to being voluntary, legal, written, and made by persons with proper capacity, contracts usually must possess three basic components: an offer, an acceptance, and consideration. An offer is a promise to perform an act conditioned on a return promise of performance by another party. It is recognized by a specific proposal communicated to another party. Once a legal offer has been made, the offeror is bound to its terms if the other party accepts. Therefore, the offeror must clearly indicate whether the proposal is an offer or some other communique, such as an invitation to negotiate. The offeror may stipulate certain terms of acceptance, such as time limits, and even withdraw the offer before the other party accepts.

Acceptance, the second basic requirement for the existence of a contract, is legally defined as "a manifestation of asset to the terms [of the offer] made by the offeree in the manner invited or required by the offer." As with offers and offerors, the courts look for an intent to contract on the part of the acceptor. The difference is that the offeror may stipulate terms of acceptance with which the other party must comply. If the offeree attempts to change the terms of the offer in any way, a rejection is implied and the response is considered a counteroffer, which the original offeror may reject or counter. As with most rules regarding contracts, exceptions exist. For example, the Uniform Commercial Code includes a "Battle of the Forms" provision whereby an offeree may imply acceptance under certain circumstances even if it changes or alters the offer.

Even if an offer is accepted, it must be consummated by consideration for a legally enforceable contract to exist. Consideration entails doing something that you were not previously bound to do outside of the agreement. In other words, promisees must pay the price (consideration) that they agreed to pay the promisor in order to gain the right to enforce the promisor's obligation.

The requirement of consideration serves an important purpose. It protects the promisor from being liable for granting, or relying on, gratuitous promises. For example, suppose that a person told her roommate that she would always pay the entire rent for their apartment. If she later changed her mind, she could not be held liable for the rent because she had neither asked for, nor received, anything in exchange for the promise. Had the other roommate promised to clean the apartment in exchange for the roommate's promise to pay the rent, an enforceable contract would exist (assuming other requirements were met).

CONTRACT TYPES

The two primary categories of contracts are "unilateral" and "bilateral." In a unilateral contract only one party promises something. For instance, if a car dealer tells a customer, "I will give you that car if you give me $15,000," he has made an offer for a unilateral contract—the contract will only be created if the customer accepts the offer by paying the $15,000. If the dealer says "I will promise to give you the car if you promise to pay me $15,000," a bilateral contract has been proposed because both parties must make a promise. The concept of unilateral contracts is important because it has been used by courts to hold a party liable for a promise even when consideration was not given by the other party. For instance, an employer may be liable for providing pension benefits that it promised to an employee, even if the worker gave no promise and did nothing in return.

Contracts may also be classified as "express" or "implied." Express contracts are those in which both parties have explicitly stated the terms of their bargain, either orally or in writing, at the time that the contract was created. In contrast, implied contracts result from surrounding facts and circumstances that suggest an agreement. For instance, when a person takes a car to a repair shop he expects the shop to exercise reasonable care and good faith in fixing the car and charging for repairs. Likewise, the shop expects the customer to pay for its services. Although no formal agreement is created, an implied contract exists.

In addition to express and implied contracts are "quasi-contracts," which arise from unique circumstances. Quasi-contracts are obligations imposed by law to avoid injustice. For instance, suppose that a man hires a woman to paint his house. By accident, she paints the wrong house. The owner of the house knows that she is painting it by mistake but, happy to have a free paint job, says nothing. The painter would likely be able to collect something from the homeowner because he knowingly was "unjustly enriched" at her expense. Had she painted his house while he was on vacation he would be under no obligation to her.

Contracts may also be categorized as valid, unenforceable, voidable, and void. Valid contracts are simply those that meet all legal requirements. Unenforceable contracts are those that meet the basic requirements but fail to fulfill some other law. For instance, if a state has special requirements for contracts related to lending money, failure to comply could make the contract unenforceable. Voidable contracts occur when one or both parties have a legal right to cancel their obligation(s). A contract entered into under duress, for example, would be voidable at the request of the injured party. Void contracts are those that fail to meet basic criteria, and are therefore not contracts at all. An illegal contract, for example, is void.

A separate type of contract, and one which overtly exemplifies the trend away from strict interpretation and toward fairness, is created by promissory estoppel. Under the theory of promissory estoppel, a party can rely on a promise made by another party despite the nonexistence of a formal, or even implied, contract. Promissory estoppel can be evoked if allowing a promisor to claim freedom from liability because of a lack of consideration (or some other contractual element) would result in injustice. Suppose that a business owner promised an employee that he would eventually give him the business if he worked there until he (the owner) retired. Then, after 20 years of faithful service by the employee, the owner decides to give the business to his son-in-law. The owner could be "estopped" from claiming in court that a true contract did not exist, because the worker relied on the owner's promise.

UNIFORM COMMERCIAL CODE

The Uniform Commercial Code (UCC) was established by the American Law Institute and the National Conference of Commissioners on Uniform State Laws. Adopted by 49 states, the UCC is a set of rules that governs commercial transactions. Although total uniformity of application has not been achieved, the UCC is considered a standard for fair dealing in everyday commercial transactions related to the sale of goods. Article two (of nine) deals with contract law. It reflects the tendency toward fairness, rather than technical interpretation of contracts, and is more likely to reward legitimate expectations than are traditional contract laws.

Three basic assumptions on which Article Two is founded are: duty of good faith; recognition of unconscionable contracts; and merchant duties. The duty of good faith assumption implies that all parties in a contract are expected to observe "reasonable commercial standards of fair dealing" as defined by the UCC. The concept of unconscionable contract implies that a grossly unfair or one-sided contract can be corrected by the courts. Finally, the UCC recognizes that merchants are held to a higher standard in contracts than are nonmerchants because merchants are naturally more knowledgeable and better able to protect themselves.

The UCC only covers what it classifies as "goods," which includes most movable, tangible property. It does not cover contracts and transactions related to services, real estate, stocks and bonds, or other intangibles. The UCC is generally used by courts for cases in which "goods" are predominant in the contract. Where no specific UCC rules exist, the courts usually revert to common law.

[Dave Mote]

FURTHER READING:

Business Law and the Regulatory Environment. 8th ed. Irwin, 1992.

Fried, Charles. *Contract as Promise: A Theory of Contractual Obligation.* Harvard University Press, 1981.

Goldberg, Victor P., ed. *Readings in the Economics of Contract Law.* Cambridge University Press. 1989.

Metzger, Michael B., et al. *Business Law and the Regulatory Environment: Concepts and Cases.* Irwin, 1992.

Rubin, Paul H. *Managing Business Transactions: Controlling the Cost of Coordinating, Communicating and Decision Making.* The Free Press, 1990.

Wincor, Richard. *Contracts in Plain English.* McGraw-Hill Book Co., 1976.

CONTROLLER

A controller, also known as a comptroller, is the chief accounting officer of a company or organization. The controller is usually responsible for analyzing, interpreting, and controlling the organization's accounting and financial records. As the chief accounting executive, the controller's duties cover all of the **accounting** functions in the organization. These may include general accounting, cost accounting, **budgeting** and **forecasting**, accounting methods and procedures, taxes, and **internal auditing**.

The top finance and accounting positions in an organization are usually the vice president of finance, also known as the **chief financial officer**, the controller, and the **treasurer**. Whereas the controller is concerned with accounting matters, the treasurer is usually responsible for financial matters, such as handling corporate investments, managing relations with creditors, and meeting capital needs. The treasurer may be responsible for handling the company's funds, following procedures established by the controller. In smaller organizations the chief financial officer may assume the duties of controller and treasurer.

The controller is responsible for reports to management on the financial operations of the company. These may include regular reports on the firm's performance in terms of sales and revenue. The controller may prepare special reports on specific operational areas undergoing change or targeted for reorganization. Operational areas suspected of inefficiences or malfunctions may also be investigated by the controller.

Management reports issued by the controller typically compare actual performance with planned performance. It is the controller's duty to establish, coordinate, and administer a plan for the control of operations. The plan is usually based on budgets and forecasts received from operational managers in the company. The controller's plan may include budgets and forecasts for the entire company and its component operations, programs for capital investing and financing, cost standards, profit planning, and other factors relating to measuring the financial results of the company's operations.

As part of the management team, the controller evaluates and consults with other managers. The controller's special area of interest is meeting the objectives of the company's operating plan. Other managers may consult with the controller regarding such matters as plan objectives, operating policies and procedures, and organizational structure.

In addition to providing internal accounting reports, the controller is also responsible for reporting the financial results of operations to the appropriate government agencies. The controller makes sure that the company's accounting system provides the necessary information for the preparation of all tax returns. Outside financial reports and tax returns are usually prepared in consultation with a public accountant.

Other duties typically handled by the controller include protecting the company's assets through internal control and auditing. The controller may be responsible for proper insurance coverage. In addition the controller may be responsible for keeping track of relevant government regulations and outside economic and social forces that may affect the company's operations.

SEE ALSO: Operations Management

[David Bianco]

COOPERATIVES

According to *The McGraw-Hill Dictionary of Modern Economics*, a cooperative is "A voluntary organization engaged in an economic activity which is established, owned, and operated by those persons who together will share the total benefit." Over the years the cooperative form has extended to **credit unions**, wholesale and/or retail consumer groups, res-

idential organizations, producer enterprises, and marketing associations. Certain broadly defined economic advantages accompany each specific cooperative type. For example members of a consumer cooperative are entitled to receive a patronage dividend. Distributed from net earnings, the amount of current dividend received per member is determined by how much members spent on the cooperative's products since the last period's payout. Moreover, members working within the cooperative can qualify for substantial in-store merchandize discounts. For members of a residential cooperative, property-owning members function as stockholders and receive benefits from the cooperative nature of incurring maintenance and interest costs.

Much of the modern day cooperative research and historical literature has been dominated by the category of producer cooperatives, even though consumer cooperatives have been in existence since the 1840s. For the most part, this one-sided treatment is historically related to the rise of the capitalist factory system. To many workers experiencing the harsh routines of the factory systems' exacting discipline for the first time, producer cooperatives held out the promise of a more humanistic, alternative form of economic organization.

The International Cooperative Alliance (ICA), to which a majority of nationally-based producers cooperatives are members, classifies cooperatives according to more precisely defined conditions. A firm's inclusion requires internal governance procedures such as free and voluntary membership and one member-one vote. In particular, qualification requires adherence to a set of worker control parameters. These cover participation in firm decision making (including management appointments), **profit sharing**, and employee ownership. Excluded from the ICA's definition are firms that incorporate some but not all of the above characteristics. For instance firms that have employee stock ownership plans (ESOP) and/or profit sharing programs without allowing for worker decision-making rights fail to qualify as cooperatives.

Advocates of producer cooperatives claim numerous comparative advantages over what is generally referred to as a classical firm (CF). The proposed advantages extend to a host of theoretical issues. Many overlap the separate disciplines of labor economics, industrial management and **organizational theory**, investment and finance, and property rights theory. Issues about which a significant amount of comparative economic analysis as well as empirical research have been devoted include: the absence of "shirking" by workers in producer cooperatives; superior productivity rates that result from the extension of democratic principles into the cooperative workplace; the lack of unnecessary supervision due to the "horizontal monitoring" performed by cooperative members; and the pursuit of cooperative employment and output strategies that are less sensitive to business cycle fluctuations.

Still other cooperative advocates simply emphasize the overall influence exerted by the set of worker control parameters. These are thought to have a transformational quality that convert adversarial relationships common to most CFs into an atmosphere of cooperation. The logic of cooperative theory unfolds thusly—once worker members begin to identify their individual and collective efforts with their firm's enhanced performance, an atmosphere of cooperative problem solving takes root. As a result of this more communicative workplace, improvements in production methods result from an upward or horizontal flow of information originating from the shop floor. With heightened satisfaction spreading throughout its membership, lower worker turnover and **absenteeism** result, facilitating the accumulation of firm task-specific member expertise.

Compared to CFs, producer cooperatives suffer from two interrelated investment disadvantages. Both are readily acknowledged by most cooperative proponents. The first concerns the problem of intra-firm finance or underinvestment. This tendency arises when the disparity between a worker member's expected profit share of income and what they could earn by investing outside the firm, say at a bank rate of interest, becomes significant. A second, and related, underinvestment point concerns the apprehension of nonmember financiers to lend to cooperatives. Since they must risk their funds within an organizational form where they have little control, outside financiers are reluctant to lend except on terms unfavorable to cooperatives. At the same time cooperative members are reluctant to borrow on terms exceeding the going interest rate and wary of relinquishing management control to outside parties who might not share a similar commitment to cooperative forms of organization.

THE NATURE OF COOPERATIVES

Although certain internal rules and policies of producer cooperatives resist easy generalization, adherence to the ICA's basic membership criteria is mandatory. As a proportion of the total labor force, cooperatives tend to attract greater numbers of unskilled blue-collar workers and fewer white-collar and managerial workers than CFs. In terms of income distribution, a percentage of the firms residual revenue (i.e. revenue that exceeds costs, including contractual wage payments set to approximate trade-union-agreed rates) is required by an individual cooperative's bylaws or statutes. Accordingly, this amount might be a fixed percentage or may vary and is distributed to workers as a "bonus" payment. Comparative data on wages for unskilled workers employed in coopera-

tives versus CFs indicate no significant difference. However, once bonus payments are factored in, earnings for blue-collar cooperative workers exceed their CF counterparts (in many instances, this is simply the result of working longer hours).

Income distribution within producer cooperatives is structured along egalitarian principles. Either peer pressure or cooperative bylaws see to it that, depending on their skill-level, members receive equal pay for equal work while differences in the number of hours worked are minimized. Most cooperatives institute income differential constraints. In terms of voting weight, and unlike a CF, the principal of one-person one-vote applies independent of member's percentage share of ownership.

Most producer cooperatives face the thorny problem of hiring nonmember workers. In most cases nonmember workers receive bonus payments, but since they do not own shares in the firm they are excluded from its participatory process, including distribution of profit shares. Unless accounted for in the bylaws, there are built-in incentives for cooperatives to increase the ratio of hired workers to share-owning members. Assuming that nonmember labor of equivalent quality can be hired as either an additional worker or to replace a departing member, then profit share paid out to all remaining members increases even when the new worker receives a bonus payment. Over time such behavior can lead to a cooperative's de facto transformation into a classical share-member/owner firm.

THE SPREAD OF COOPERATIVE IDEAS

Interestingly enough, by the late 20th century many, but not all, of the ideas and workplace advantages inherent in cooperative firms began to take root in CF workplaces. Indeed, these same ideas and organizational structures formed the substance guiding a majority consensus emergent within the industrial relations field. Though referred to as "labor-management cooperation," the term carried within it the essentials of cooperative thought. Under this rubric an attempt was made at transplanting the cooperatives' nonadversarial work environment into the CF workplace. Management found the cooperatives lack of "rigid" job assignments and pay according to group or individual effort and not just seniority appealing. General Motors Corp. and the United Auto Wokers had been operationg under a form of labor-management cooperation since 1982.

At the close of the 20th century the general insertion of labor-management cooperation clauses into contractual agreements of organized labor appeared imminent. According to the prevailing wisdom, the institutionalization of labor-management cooperation schemes represented nothing less than the central industrial strategy through which the competitiveness and productivity of U.S. firms could be restored. A potential legal roadblock existed, however, in Section 8(a)(2) of the NLRA which prohibited "employer dominanted" labor organizations. A minority of union activists have argued that labor-management cooperation schemes were little more than a new form of old business unionism.

[Daniel E. King]

FURTHER READING:

Bonin, John P., Derek C. Jones and Louis Putterman. "Theoretical and Empirical Studies of Producer Cooperatives: Will Ever the Twain Meet?" *Journal of Economic Literature*. September, 1993, pp. 1290-1320.

Craig, Ben and John Pencavel. "The Behavior of Worker Cooperatives: The Plywood Companies of the Pacific Northwest," *American Economic Review*. December, 1992, 82(5), pp. 1083-1105.

Curl, John. *History of Work Cooperation in America*. Howard Press, 1980.

Ellerman, David P. *The Democratic Worker-Owned Firm*. Unwin-Hyman, Inc., 1990.

The McGraw-Hill Dictionary of Modern Economics: A Handbook of Terms and Organizations, 3rd ed. McGraw-Hill Book Company, 1983.

Thomas, H.B. and C. Logan. *Mondragon: An Economic Analysis*. Allen and Unwin, 1982.

Vanek, Jaroslav. *The General Theory of Labor-Managed Market Economies*. Cornell University Press, 1970.

Ward, Benjamin. "The Firm in Illyria: Market Syndicalism," *American Economic Review*. September, 1958 48(4) pp. 566-89.

COORDINATING COMMITTEE FOR MULTILATERAL EXPORT CONTROLS

The Coordinating Committee for Multilateral Export Controls (COCOM) was established in 1949 for the purpose of preventing western companies and countries from selling strategic goods to Eastern bloc countries. Any goods or materials having military applications were considered to be strategic, but until its demise in 1994 COCOM concentrated largely on electronic and computer hardware. COCOM was based in Paris and was also known as the Coordinating Committee on Export Controls. The founding members of COCOM were the United States, Belgium, France, Italy, the Netherlands, Luxembourg, and the United Kingdom. Countries joining COCOM at later dates included: Spain, Canada, Australia, Denmark, Germany, Greece, Italy, Norway, Portugal, and Turkey. There is a similar organization identified as CHINCOM that concerns itself with the export of strategic goods to the People's Republic of China.

Exports from the United States to other countries is regulated by the U.S. Bureau of Export Administra-

tion which is part of the U.S. Department of Commerce. Legislative authority controlling exports includes:

1. The Export Control Act of 1949, which was related to the establishment of COCOM.

2. The Battle Act of 1951, which stopped countries exporting strategic goods to Eastern bloc nations from receiving U.S. foreign aid.

3. The Export Administration Act of 1969, which dealt with the export of goods having both strategic and non strategic applications. This act was amended in 1979, 1981, and 1985.

4. In 1987, the U.S. Bureau of Export Administration was created as part of the U.S. Department of Commerce. The purpose of the newly created bureau was to coordinate and control United States' export policy.

The U.S. Bureau of Export Administration functioned under three policy guidelines: work hand-in-hand with the American business community, prevent violations of American export legislation by close scrutiny of license applications, and when necessary initiate criminal and administrative sanctions as proscribed by the Export Administration Act.

COCOM members met annually at the Paris headquarters to review, and if necessary, update its International List. This was a list of embargoed strategic commodities, which, if exported, could be used to strengthen the military capabilities of Eastern bloc nations. COCOM had the unenviable task of preventing strategic goods from entering these countries while at the same time encouraging non strategic trade and growth in home industries. This was particularly difficult with so called dual purpose goods, which had both strategic and non strategic applications.

While the United States considered its export policies to be in compliance with COCOM regulations, other western countries were often lax. Violations were frequent because of poor enforcement, a lack of stiff penalties, inadequate personnel, and because of the high profits that could be made when non member countries "transfered" strategic goods from COCOM members to Eastern bloc nations, often with the surreptitious knowledge of the COCOM member.

On March 30, 1994, the United States announced it would greatly ease the restrictions it had placed on the sale of computer and telecommunications equipment to countries that had comprised the Eastern bloc. With the fall of the communist regimes in the former Soviet Union and many eastern European nations, the military and political threat that had fueled the creation of COCOM had largely dissipated. Export controls on certain radio and encryption technologies however remained in effect. On March 31, 1994, COCOM was formally dissolved. Former members could not reach agreement on a successor organization, leaving each country free to unilaterally determine its export policies. The members did agree to keep the spirit of COCOM intact, especially in regard to the export of strategic goods to such countries as North Korea, Libya, Iraq, and Iran. Other multilateral agreements that are still viable and affect export controls on strategic technology include the Nuclear Non-Proliferation Treaty, the Missile Technology Control Regime, and the Australia Group which deals with chemical weaponry.

[Michael Knes]

FURTHER READING:

''America's Domestic and International Role in Protecting the Free World's High Technology.'' *Business America* 109. Jan. 18, 1988, pp. 7-9.

COPYRIGHT

Copyright protection provides the author of an original work in any tangible medium of expression with certain rights to use and to authorize the use of the work. Copyright law provides the copyright holder with several effective remedies when there is copyright infringement. The copyright holder may obtain an injunction to restrain the infringer from using the copyrighted material. In addition, the holder has the right to impound and destroy any reproductions of the copyrighted work that were made in violation of the copyright. The copyright holder may also seek to recover damages and attorney's fees involved in the case.

Article I, Section 8, of the Constitution gives Congress the power to enact copyright laws ''to promote the progress of science and useful arts, by securing for limited times to authors and inventors the exclusive right to their respective writings and discoveries.'' The creations of inventors are protected by patents. Manufactured goods and other tangibles may be protected through trademarks. When Congress passed the Copyright Act of 1790, it granted copyright protection to ''the authors and proprietors'' of maps, charts, and books. Subsequent acts and revisions have taken technological advances into account and expanded copyright protection to include musical and dramatic compositions, computer programs and software, sound recordings, and paintings and drawings, among other items.

The copyright laws of the United States are contained in Title 17 of the United States Code Annotated (USCA). The most recent major revision of U.S. copyright law became effective January 1, 1978. It was the first major revision since 1909, although the 1909 act was enacted into positive law in 1947. Among other things, the 1909 act established the office of Register of Copyrights as part of the Library of Congress. During the twentieth century, international copyright protection has been afforded by countries that were signees to the Berne Convention for the Protection of Literary and Artistic Works (1886) and the UNESCO Universal Copyright Convention (1952).

Like other laws, copyright laws are subject to interpretation by the courts. Copyright protection does not give the copyright owner complete control over all possible uses of the copyrighted work. Rather, it provides five specific rights, which the holder may exercise or authorize others to exercise. These are the right to reproduce the copyrighted work, the right to prepare derivative works based on the copyrighted work, the right to distribute copies of the copyrighted work (or, in the case of dramatic, audiovisual, and similar works, the right to perform the copyrighted work publicly), and the right to display the copyrighted work publicly.

Not all uses of copyrighted material are subject to copyright protection. The doctrine of fair use allows individuals to reproduce a copyrighted work for a ''fair use.'' The notion of fair use is subject to a variety of interpretations, however, and often involves legal proceedings to determine if a particular use is in fact ''fair.'' The most recent copyright revision identified four factors to be considered when determining fair use. These are the purpose and character of the use, the nature of the copyrighted work, the amount and substantiality of the portion used, and the effect of the use on the potential market or value of the copyrighted work.

Not all original works are subject to copyright protection. For example, ''useful articles'' are not copyrightable under copyright law. In the case of a work that combines artistic and useful features, it may be necessary to obtain a court judgment to determine if the article may be copyrighted. There is also a category of works that are said to be in the public domain; these are not copyrightable. An example of a work in the public domain might be a book that was never copyrighted or whose copyright had expired, or a traditional song whose composer is unknown. Facts cannot be copyrighted, although compilations of factual material can be. Ideas cannot be copyrighted, nor can titles of books or songs.

Copyright law provides that where a work was made for hire, the copyright belongs to the employer rather than to the creator. This is the single major exception to copyright ownership vesting in the author or creator of the work. There are two major sets of circumstances where a work is said to be made for hire. One is when the work is prepared by an employee within the scope of his or her employment. The other is when the work is specially ordered or commissioned, and there is an express written agreement between the parties that the work shall be considerd a work made for hire.

In order to enforce one's copyright against infringers, it is necessary to register the work with the Register of Copyrights at the Library of Congress before a suit may be filed. A work need not be registered to have copyright protection, but it must carry a notice of copyright that includes the copyright symbol, the year, and the name of the copyright holder. Copyright notice is essential to obtain copyright protection unless one of the following conditions exists:

1. The notice was omitted in violation of an express written agreement.

2. The notice was omitted from only a few publicly distributed copies.

3. The owner registered the work within five years after publication without notice and made every reasonable attempt to add the notice to all publicly distributed copies after discovering the omission.

SEE ALSO: Intellectual Property, Licensing Agreements

[David Bianco]

CORPORATE CONTROL

The term "corporate control" refers to the authority to make the decisions of a corporation regarding operations and strategic planning, including capital allocations, **acquisitions** and **divestments**, top personnel decisions, and major marketing, production, and financial decisions.

Partnerships involving an owner responsible merely for providing capital and a manager responsible for running the business have been traced back to the twelfth century. During the Industrial Revolution, however, a class of managers who hold ultimate decision-making power in their companies—even though they own a relatively negligible amount of stock evolved. This concept of managerial control, made possible through a scattered and diverse ownership, had been established by the end of the nineteenth century, and was epitomized by railroad promoters who managed to control enterprises while putting up very little, if any, capital of their own. The ordinary stockholder is relatively powerless in this situation, thus, corporate control is quite distinct from corporate ownership.

The power to make decisions regarding a firm's operations and policies can be based on legal authority—i.e., ownership—or the power of one's position in the company. The government, competition, **banks**, and societal forces limit this power but do not make the decisions, except in industries that are regulated by the government or that are under the control of a financial institution.

Whether managers in a position of control act to further their interests or those of the owners is a point of potential conflict. The interests of owners are usually simply defined in terms of profit maximization. Those of management have been variously categorized on one hand as altruistic, i.e., desiring the freedom to carry out policies that better serve the good of society than purely profit-seeking activities would, and on the other, pure self-interest in lavish pensions, compensation, perquisites, and other "expense preferences" that are not related to firm performance. A bias towards growth over profits has also been speculated, figuring that with a larger organization, executives will be able to justify larger salaries. Also, there has been a justified perception of larger corporations as being less vulnerable to **takeover**, although the **leveraged buyouts** and takeovers of the 1980s have proven that the Goliaths among corporations are not invincible.

At the same time, studies have found managers whose compensation is not as incentive-based more cautious in borrowing money for development, perhaps because they do not want to place their firms under greater control by financial institutions, as well as jeopardize their stability and reputation. Also, the larger the managers' own corporate holdings, the more aggressively they tend to borrow.

Shareholders have the legal right to remove managers who are not carrying out their interests. A number of factors, however, e.g., **management** control of proxy machinery, make this very difficult in the case of large corporations; it is usually only attempted in times of severe crisis or mismanagement and even then it is unlikely to succeed. Nonetheless, a "market for corporate control" has arisen. If not responsible to the owners directly, inefficient managers are susceptible to takeover bids caused by reduction in stock value.

Corporations can pass from owner control to management control in various ways. The early growth of large corporations is typically a period in which they are dominated by an entrepreneur who owns a controlling interest in the company's stock. This was typical of large firms in the United States in the beginning of the twentieth century. In order to raise capital for expansion, the entrepreneur can sell off most of his holdings and use the authority of his position in the company to maintain control, as happened in many U.S. firms in the postwar years.

Firms can also be management-controlled from the beginning, such by issuing widely dispersed shares as those the railroad promoters succeeded in building in the nineteenth century. A company under the control of one group or family can also be taken over by management, as in the case of the retailer S. S. Kresge. The Kresge family owned a large minority (37 percent) of stock in 1964 and occupied several important positions. The company, however, expanded enormously under its hired managers, reducing the relative holdings of the family. By 1977, the management was able to win a symbolic vote to change the company's name to "Kmart."

One way management control is maintained is by controlling the composition of the **board of directors**, mostly composed of company officers, officers of important suppliers or financial institutions, or personal friends of management. The few outside directors, or directors who do not themselves hold offices in the corporation, are often unable to make informed decisions or suggest alternative courses of action due to their unfamiliarity with the company, or, in many cases, other responsibilities, such as serving on other boards, for example. Representatives of banks are often limited by legislation as to their involvement as directors.

To some observers in the 1990s, the contest for corporate control seemed poised on the brink of a new revolution in which corporate takeover battles would be more politicized. An example is Carl Icahn's hostile takeover of USX that ended with a negotiated solution involving input from many parties. Recognizing the increasing desire of investors to control corporate policy for short-term growth, some managements, such as at MCI Communications, for example, began to track stock ownership patterns with private detective firms in order to find sympathetic investors.

[Frederick C. Ingram]

FURTHER READING:

Alkhafaji, Abbass F. *A Stakeholder Approach to Corporate Governance.* Quorum Books.

Berle, Adolf A., and Gardiner C. Means. *The Modern Corporation and Private Property.* Rev. ed. Harcourt, Brace & World.

Bush, Janet. "Called to Account: Short Term, Long Term." *International Management.* July/August, 1993, pp. 40-41.

Davis, Gerald F., and Suzanne K. Stout. "Organization Theory and the Market for Corporate Control: A Dynamic Analysis of the Characteristics of Large Takeover Targets, 1980-1990." *Administrative Science Quarterly.* December, 1992, pp. 605-633.

Fligstein, Neil. *The Transformation of Corporate Control.* Harvard University Press.

Gage, Theodore Justin. "To Counter Activists, Firms are Buying Shareholder Data." *Corporate Cashflow.* December, 1993, pp. 11-12.

Galloway, Duncan, and Peter Jackson. "The Keys to Control." *CA Magazine.* May, 1993, pp. 22-29.

Herman, Edward S. *Corporate Control, Corporate Power.* Cambridge University Press.

Hogler, Raymond L., and Herbert G. Hunt, III. "Accounting and Conceptions of Control in the American Corporation." *British Journal of Management.* September, 1993, pp. 177-190.

Lasserre, Philippe. "The Management of Large Groups: Asia and Europe Compared." *European Management Journal.* June, 1992, pp. 157-162.

Mehran, Hamid. "Executive Incentive Plans, Corporate Control, and Capital Structure." *Journal of Financial and Quantitative Analysis.* December, 1992, pp. 539-560.

Pound, John. "Beyond Takeovers: Politics Comes to Corporate Control." *Harvard Business Review.* March/April, 1992, pp. 83-93.

Santerre, Rexford E. and Stephen P. Neun. "Corporate Control and Performance in the 1930s." *Economic Inquiry.* July, 1993, pp. 466-480.

Walsh, James P., and Rita D. Kosnik. "Corporate Raiders and Their Disciplinary Role in the Market for Corporate Control." *Academy of Management Journal.* August, 1993, pp. 671-700.

Williamson, Oliver E. *Corporate Control and Business Behavior.* Prentice-Hall.

Zantout, Zaher. "External Capital Market Control, Corporate Restructuring, and Firm Performance during the 1980s." *Journal of Business Accounting.* January, 1994, pp. 37-64.

CORPORATE CULTURE

Corporate culture refers to the shared values, attitudes, standards, codes, and behaviors that characterize members of an organization and define its nature as a socioeconomic unit. Corporate culture is rooted in an organization's goals, strategies, structure, and approaches to labor. The term "culture audit" refers to the process of analyzing, evaluating, and determining areas for change in a corporate culture.

HISTORY AND BACKGROUND

Since the 1980s, several factors have led American businesses to evaluate corporate culture alongside such traditional "hard" measures of corporate health as assets, revenues, profits, and shareholder return. One such factor is the transition from a manufacturing-based to a service-based economy, with the corresponding shift in emphasis from the quality of a material product to the quality of business relationships. Another factor is the need for American businesses to compete in a global marketplace against international rivals whose corporate cultures are distinct but demonstrably effective. A related factor is the need for creative adaption to technological advances in the marketplace; conservative, complacent organizational cultures have been blamed for the slow response of the American automobile industry to competition from Japanese manufacturers and of IBM to the personal computer revolution. The rash of **acquisitions and mergers** associated with the 1980s also drew attention to the often intractable aspects of organizational culture that facilitate or impede corporate assimilation.

CORPORATE CITIZENSHIP AND HUMAN RESOURCE MANAGEMENT

One broad area of corporate culture involves corporate citizenship, the company's relationship to the larger environment. Are business ethics an inherent and articulated corporate concern? What is the company's attitude toward public service, and how is this attitude formalized? Has the company responded to the "green" movement, with its emphasis on eliminating or minimizing environmentally-damaging practices?

A second broad area of corporate culture involves **human resource management**. Is the company highly stratified, or does it promote participatory management, with egalitarian and flexible interaction among managers and employees? Does the company stress individual effort, or teamwork and collectivism? Does the company promote standardization through norms such as dress codes, or does it foster individuality and creativity? Corporate culture is also reflected in human resource issues such as flextime and telecommuting policies, safety and training programs, and employee access to medical care, counseling services, and health and recreation facilities.

Responsiveness to diversity in the workplace is a component of corporate culture that spans the areas of corporate citizenship and human resource management. Does the company accommodate the specific concerns of women, minorities, gays and lesbians, older employees, and employees with young children?

In a smoothly-functioning organization, all such policies and practices foster an internally consistent corporate culture.

SEE ALSO: Diversity Culture

[David Sprinkle]

FURTHER READING:

Hindle, Tim. *Field Guide to Strategy.* Boston: Harvard Business/The Economist Reference Series, 1994.

CORPORATE DEBT

Debt represents borrowed funds in which the borrower promises to make regular interest payments and to repay the principal. Along with equity (**common stock**), debt represents one of the two major sources of capital for business enterprises.

The primary raisers of funds in the debt market are the U.S. Treasury Department, federally sponsored credit agencies, state and local governments, and corporations. Historically, the amount of new, long-term debt financing issued in the United States greatly exceeds the volume of equity financing. Corporate **bonds** constitute a smaller amount of long-term borrowing than either federal government and agency issues or the issues of state and local governments.

GENERAL CHARACTERISTICS OF CORPORATE BONDS

When a corporation issues a bond, it promises to make a series of payments of a certain amount on pre-specified dates. Hence, bonds are referred to as fixed income instruments. To assist bond investors in making their assessment about the likelihood of future payments on a particular bond, bond issues are rated by rating agencies, the two most prominent of which are Moody's Investors Service and Standard & Poor's. These ratings attempt to measure default risk—the chance that one or more payments on the bond will be deferred or missed altogether. The ratings range from AAA to D, and determine the required yield to sell the security in the market. Although there are no firm rules to determine a rating, strong attention is paid to such factors as cash flow and earnings in relation to interest and other obligations (coverage ratios) as well as to the amount of debt in relation to stockholders' equity and total **assets** in the issuing firm's capital structure. In addition to financial-ratio analysis, other factors of importance including the nature of the industry, the relative position of the firm within the industry, and the overall quality of **management**.

The bond indenture, or bond contract, is a legal document stating the promises made by the issuer of a bond and the rights of the bondholders. For all bonds issued by firms involved in interstate commerce with an issue size exceeding $5 million, the Trust Indentures Act requires that an independent trustee be named to protect the interests of the bondholders and insure that the terms of the indenture are fulfilled. The bond indenture also contains numerous protective covenants. Some covenants define the security that the issuer is offering for the bond and others protect the bondholders by restricting the behavior of the issuer.

Mortgage bonds have specific **real estate** assets pledged as collateral. First mortgage bonds have the first claim on the assets, while second mortgage bonds have the next claim. Collateral trust bonds are secured by financial assets and equipment trust certificates are secured by equipment, such as railroad cars or airplanes. Debentures, on the other hand, have no specific security pledged. Subordinated debentures are unsecured bonds that have an inferior claim to other outstanding debentures and are paid only after straight debentures, which were offered to the public at an earlier time.

Investors evaluate corporate debt on a variety of factors, including yield, maturity, and security provisions. The greater the protection and privileges granted the bondholder, the lower the yield. Thus, U.S. Treasury securities generally provide a lower yield than corporate bond issues because of the lower likelihood of default. For the 1926-1993 period, high-quality, long-term corporate bonds offered an annual rate of about 5.5 percent, which translated into a real return of slightly more than 2 percent.

The bond market is reasonably efficient in terms of incorporating new information into the price of existing issues. Some researchers have suggested that the bond market may be slightly less efficient than the stock market in pricing outstanding issues because of the lack of a highly active secondary market for certain issues. Institutional investors, such as pension funds, and bank trust departments are not normally active traders in their bond portfolios.

TYPES OF CORPORATE DEBT

The money market is the market for debt instruments with a maturity of one year or less at the time of issuance. The primary example of a corporate money market instrument is commercial paper. Commercial paper represents short-term pure discount obligations issued by the largest and most credit-worthy industrial and financial firms.

A pure discount bond promises to make a single payment at a specified time in the future, but its selling price is less. The promised future payment is the par value or face value of the bond, whereas the difference between the par value and the selling price is the bond discount. Coupon bonds make regularly scheduled payments, termed **coupons**, between the issuance and the maturity date. These bonds also have a par value that is paid to the owner of the bond at a specified time in the future. Most bonds have semi-annual cash flows; that is, they pay interest twice a year.

Typically, bond issues are originally sold at a price approximating the face value. If the market price equals the face value, the bond is a par bond. Subsequently, they may trade at prices above or below par value. When the market price exceeds the face value, the bond is a premium bond. When the price is less than the face value, the bond is termed a discount bond. For most bonds, the bond price does not reflect the actual price that an investor must pay. Instead, the investor must pay the stated price plus the accrued interest, which reflects the portion of the following coupon payment that has been earned by the bondholder.

In some bonds, the individual interest coupons from the bond are separated, and each payment is treated as a separate security through a process known as coupon stripping. The resulting securities are zero coupon bonds, and each instrument represents a single payment due on a particular date. The purchaser pays less than the par value for zero coupon bonds, and redeems them for face value at maturity.

The high-yield corporate bond market gained increased prominence in the 1980s. High-yield bonds are those bonds which are rated below investment grade, and are commonly referred to as **junk bonds**. The majority of issuers do not qualify for investment grade ratings, and many junk bonds were issued to finance **mergers and acquisitions**. If junk bonds have higher default rates than investment grade issues, they also earn sufficiently high return to compensate for the greater default risk.

A term loan is defined as any debt obligation having an initial maturity between one and thirty years. Term loans have a number of advantages over public debt issuances of debt including speed, flexibility, and lower issuance costs. The key provisions of term loans are negotiated between the lender and borrower, and therefore can be worked out more quickly or modified more easily than the terms of public debt issues. Term loans are available from banks, insurance companies, pension funds, small business investment companies, government agencies and equipment suppliers. These instruments are often used for financing small additions to plant and equipment where the cash flows from the investment cover the requirements of the debt, and can also be used to finance increases in working capital if the length of the loan approximately matches the time the working capital will be needed. Term loans usually require that the principal be amortized over the life of the loan.

RETIREMENT OF BONDS

With callable bonds, the issuer has the right to call the bonds in prior to maturity and pay them off at a certain price. The call price is stipulated in the bond contract, but callable bonds are not usually called unless they can be refunded by issuing new bonds at a lower interest rate. The call price usually gives a premium over the par value to the bondholder equivalent to one year's interest.

Many bonds also have a **sinking fund** which provides for the orderly retirement of the bond issue over its life. One method of satisfying the sinking fund requirement is to purchase the required amount of bonds in the open market each year. Alternatively, the firm may randomly call the bonds.

Sometimes bonds are scheduled for retirement with a certain portion of the principal amount becoming due at predetermined dates. These bonds are called serial bonds.

Another method of retiring bonds is through conversion. Convertible bonds are bonds that give the bondholder the option of converting the bond into a specified number of shares of common stock. The conversion ratio determines the number of shares received for each bond. The conversion price is the market price of the bond divided by the conversion ratio. The conversion premium is the additional amount per share of stock that the investor would pay to obtain the stock by converting the bond rather than by purchasing buying the shares in the open market.

INTERNATIONAL DEBT INSTRUMENTS

One of the primary forms of credit in the international debt market is a form of bank lending called a syndicated loan, which is a loan made by a consortium of banks to a single borrower. Syndicated loans are priced as a spread above the London Interbank Offered Rate (LIBOR). LIBOR is the rate that banks participating in the international debt market charge each other for short-term loans. Euro-commercial paper is commercial paper traded in the international market, usually denominated in dollars. Note issuance facilities are a form of medium-term lending through an assortment of instruments, usually floating rate notes.

International bonds can be either **Eurobonds** or foreign bonds. A Eurodollar bond or Eurobond is a bond issued by a borrower in one country, denominated in the borrower's currency, and sold outside the country of the borrower. If a U.S. firm issues a bond denominated in a foreign currency for sale solely in the country of the foreign currency, the bond is a foreign bond.

International bonds can also be classified as straight bonds, floating rate notes, and equity-related bonds. A straight bond is a bond with a fixed payment schedule with no special characteristics, such as convertibility into stock or a variable interest rate. A floating rate note is a bond that pays a different coupon rate over time as the general level of **interest rates** changes. Thus, the coupon rate is tied to an index rate, typically LIBOR. Equity-related bonds include both convertible bonds and bonds with equity warrants. An equity warrant is a security that gives the holder the right to acquire newly issued share of common stock from a company for the payment of a stipulated price. The majority of new international bond issues are straight bonds with floating rate notes being relatively scarce.

PRINCIPLES OF BOND VALUATION

The price of a bond is computed by summing the present value of future interest payments plus the repayment of principal at maturity. There is an inverse relationship between bond prices and market interest rates. As interest rates go up, bond prices go down, and vice-versa. Long-term bond prices are more sensitive than shorter maturities for a given change in interest rates. Furthermore, zero-coupon bonds are more price sensitive than coupon bonds to a change in interest rates. An investor who wishes to capture maximum gains from an anticipated interest-rate decline should maximize the length of his portfolio while investing in low-coupon, interest-sensitive securities.

Duration is the number of years, on a present-value basis, that it takes to recover an initial investment in a bond. In calculating duration, each year is weighted by the present value of the cash flow as a proportion to the present value of the bond, and is then summed. The greater the duration, the more sensitive the bond price is to a change in interest rates. Duration captures the three variables—maturity, coupon rate, and market rate of interest—to indicate the price sensitivities of different bonds. Bond duration increases as both coupon rates and market interest rates decrease. On the other hand, duration increases as the maturity of the debt instrument goes up.

The true return on a bond investment may be measured by yield to maturity or the yield to call. The yield to maturity is the yield that will be realized if the promised payments are made and the investor holds the bond to maturity. The yield to maturity is the interest rate that equates the present value of the interest and principal payments with the initial market price of the bond. For bonds likely to be called, the yield to maturity is inappropriate. In this case, the yield to call is a better calculation. This measure is the promised return on a bond from the present to the date that the bond is likely to be called.

Another important valuation concept has to do with the reinvestment of interest at rates other than the coupon rate. The technique used to explain the effect on the total return is terminal wealth analysis. This method assumes that the investment is held to maturity, and all proceeds over the life of the bond are reinvested at the reinvestment rate. In general, the longer the maturity, the more the total annualized return approaches the reinvestment rate. If the reinvestment rate is significantly different from the coupon rate, the annualized return and the coupon rate can substantially differ.

The **term structure of interest rates** depicts the relationship between term to maturity and yield to maturity over a long time horizon for bonds similar in all respects except maturity. The slope of the curve gives some indication as to future movements, with an upward sloping pattern generally followed by higher interest rates and a descending pattern associated with a possible decline in the future.

Management of a bond portfolio will also include a consideration of the yield spread or risk premium between low- and high-quality issues. The risk structure of interest rates analyzes the differences in risk among different classes of bonds. The yield spread between long-term U.S. government bonds and corporate Baa's increases during a **recession** and decreases during periods of strong economic growth. When interest rates are high, risk premiums tend to be large. In addition, the evidence tends to suggest that longer maturities lead to higher yield spreads. Finally, there is evidence that the marketability of the bond issue has an effect on the risk premium with lower marketability leading to higher yield spreads.

BOND PORTFOLIO STRATEGIES

A laddered portfolio strategy spreads bonds out across the entire maturity spectrum. The laddered strategy technique makes it relatively easy to maintain the chosen maturity distribution of bonds but difficult to change the maturity of the portfolio significantly without making many trades. The dumbbell strategy places bonds only in very short and very long maturities, making it easy to shift the average maturity of the portfolio.

A number of studies have examined interest rate **forecasting** models. The tests indicate that sophisticated forecasting models have generally not been able to outperform naive forecasts of no change. Given the lack of success of models or experts in predicting interest rates, some managers have taken a passive approach to bond **portfolio management**. Passive management strategies do not seek active trading possibilities in an attempt to outperform the market.

Immunization strategies attempt to create portfolios whose investment returns are not affected by increases or decreases in interest rates. Thus, immunized portfolios are managed passively once the immunization is in effect. By careful management of its **liabilities** and assets, a bank can achieve immunization by setting the asset and liability portfolios to the same duration. With identical durations, the value of both portfolios will rise and fall by the same amount for a given change in interest rates. Under planning period immunization, the duration of the bond portfolio is set equal to the number of years in the planning period. When duration equals planning period, a change in interest rates will have a reinvestment rate effect that almost exactly offsets the capital gain or loss, which is also caused by the change in **interest** rates. Under contingent immunization, the manager is permitted to manage the portfolio as long as its value is large enough to cover the minimum

guaranteed return. However, the manager agrees to implement immunization once the portfolio's value falls below the trigger point, the value necessary to guarantee the minimum return. The investor risks earning a return less than that which could be achieved on a portfolio immunized throughout its life in exchange for the possibility that the initial pursuit of an active strategy will generate higher returns.

[Robert T. Kleiman]

FURTHER READING:

Jones, Charles P. *Investments: Analysis and Management*, 4th ed. New York: John Wiley and Sons, 1994.

Sears, R. Stephen, and Gary L. Trennepohl. *Investment Management*. Fort Worth, Texas: The Dryden Press, 1993.

CORPORATE DIVESTITURE

Divestiture involves the disposal of an **ownership** interest in a company or subsidiary in exchange for other forms of assets. Divestiture may be a voluntary act effected to raise money, stem operating losses, or reorganize a corporation. It also may be compulsory, where a government or regulator demands a divestment to achieve a public policy goal under the threat of legal action.

Companies usually divest themselves of subsidiary business units because the capital invested in that operation could be more wisely employed somewhere else. These disposals are frequently carried out under the authority of a **board of directors**, and usually do not require the express consent of shareholders.

Where the owner is not a corporation, but an investment trust, the investor may elect to divest the trust of a certain asset because that asset is performing poorly or is engaged in activities which are opposed by the investor. Divestiture allows the owner to undertake a more beneficial employment of assets by making them transferable.

Corporate laws and regulations provide few barriers for divestment, except when it is related to fraudulent or anticompetitive activity. The ability to convert an investment into a transferable asset benefits owners tremendously by allowing their capital to be employed with optimal efficiency.

BASIC PRINCIPLES

The basic concept of divestiture is as old as trade itself, but the principle of corporate divestiture has a relatively brief history because the procedures involved developed out of modern forms of legal incorporation. Any company endowed with a certain asset maintained an ownership right that entitled it to employ that asset any way it chose, including financial disposal, or divestment.

For example, a railroad line might purchase a coal mining company to provide a direct source of fuel for its fleet of locomotives. But with development of more efficient diesel engines, the value of the coal mine is seriously eroded. As the railroad replaces its steam engines with diesels, it has no use for its coal, other than to sell it to someone else. Thus, it faces a crucial decision of whether to sell the mine or hold on to it and enter the coal supply business.

If the company decided that it could not compete effectively with other coal producers, and should remain *only* a railroad, it might choose to divest itself of the mine. If this were the case, the railroad would begin negotiations with a potential buyer.

As an operating subsidiary of the railroad, the mine would be worth $2 million. But one potential buyer, another coal company, offers $2.5 million for the mine. A second buyer, a steel mill, offers $2.8 million. This illustrates a necessary motivation for divestment: a difference in **valuation** among the parties. In this case, the steel mill wins the **competition** and agrees to take over the railroad's mine for payment of $2.8 million.

A somewhat more complex scenario arises if the coal company offers only $1.5 million for the mine, and the steel company's top bid is $1.8 million. Again, there is a difference in valuation, but the railroad would incur a loss from the sale.

Under these circumstances, it might choose to go ahead with the sale anyway, because it could employ the $1.8 million offered by the steel mill to increase its profitability in other ways. It could use the proceeds of the sale to upgrade its facilities and purchase new diesel engines. This might enable the railroad to derive additional efficiencies from its existing operation that might be valued at $1 million. Despite the loss of $200,000 on the sale of its mine, the railroad stands to gain a net profit of $800,000.

These examples demonstrate the most common reasoning behind the divestiture of certain assets where a justification lies in increased economies of scale and scope. The steel mill clearly could make better use of the coal mine in its own operations than could the railroad, and this is reflected in the valuation.

Divestiture may result from instances where anticipated synergies do not result. Although related to the concept of economies of scale, synergistic combinations attempt to translate product-specific technologies to entirely different markets.

For example, a manufacturer of military aircraft may purchase a loss-making company whose primary business is building business jets and other civilian aircraft. The justification for such an acquisition is that the company's engineering expertise from building fighter jets could be applied to design better, and therefore more profitable, airplanes for the private market.

But in practice, the company discovers that its primary strengths with military aircraft, such as high-speed maneuverability and radar-evading designs, provide no marketable benefit to private aircraft. As a result, the company is unable to apply the benefits from its most valuable military technologies to the civilian aircraft market.

In this case, the company's military and civilian aircraft enterprises remain divorced, each with distinctly separate engineering requirements, cost structures, and markets. Since no benefit can be derived from the combination, the company may elect to divest the civilian aircraft operation. With the proceeds, it might purchase another company that will benefit more from an association with the core business.

Divestiture also may be advantageous where **business cycles** are involved. For example, a paper and lumber company gradually diversified its operations to include certain types of specialty chemicals. This sideline provided the company with a valuable source of income from an operation that was well-insulated from the business cycles in the paper and lumber markets. When paper and lumber were unprofitable, the successful chemicals enterprise provided earnings stability, and by the time chemicals declined, paper and lumber had recovered to take its place.

But two dissimilar business cycles will not always coincide so conveniently. At one point, assume chemical operations became unprofitable well before demand for paper and lumber could recover. The company might decide to divest the chemical operations to stem its financial losses and even provide capital to pay off whatever debt it may have incurred to keep the company solvent.

If the company simply cannot afford to run the division any longer, its only option is to divest quickly. The paper company would be forced to sell the chemicals division at a substantial loss, because the chemicals market is at the low point of its cycle.

As a result, the purchaser of the chemical division can assume control of it at a very low cost. Eventually, the demand for chemicals will recover and the division will become profitable again. Accordingly, the value of the operation increases. If the valuation continues to grow, the new owner may elect to sell the operation, if only to realize a profit before the cycle turns down again.

Both instances illustrate the motivation behind a divestment due to circumstances solely attributable to business cycles. The same dynamic also applies to the cycles that govern individual products and product lines.

In some cases, a company may choose to divest itself of completely unrelated divisions because the parent company's management believes it can no longer administer them efficiently.

For example, a manufacturer of aluminum diversifies into a variety of final products, including outdoor structures, automotive assemblies, household appliances, and missiles. The only thing that each of the four divisions has in common is that its products are constructed of the parent company's aluminum. As a result, each division builds unique administrative organizations and cultures based on their different markets. In effect, they function as completely different enterprises.

These differences would be amplified if the parent company were to lose its competitive advantage in aluminum production. In this instance each of its units would be better off purchasing aluminum from competitors. If the parent company were to exit the aluminum business, it would remain in charge of four functionally disparate companies.

Management at this point might ask whether this represents an appropriate distribution of its assets. It might identify one or two business units for divestment, based on which unit would provide the lowest earnings, relative to its worth. The company then could use the proceeds of the sales to make additional investments in the remaining businesses it felt it could operate best.

Divestment, coupled with acquisition, provides an effective means for a company to discover unanticipated economies and synergies through trial and error. A company whose core skills lie in financial control and administrative consolidation might strive to assemble a fully diversified conglomerate.

In this case, the company's mission is to assemble unrelated businesses, in the hope that their profitability can be restored through restructuring or that their combination might provide some unforeseen benefit. When a division fails to deliver such benefits, its parent company might choose to divest itself of the operation and try again with another type of company.

Some companies may resist divestiture of underperforming divisions because there is inadequate pressure from the company's owners to maximize the company's profitability. The primary motivating factor in this resistance lies in the financially irrational concept of empire building, where sheer size and diversification feeds the egos of management.

This situation usually persists until a group of activist shareholders can persuade the company's management to consider divestiture of these assets, usually through proxy battles.

The award of substantial stock options to managers serves to more closely align the interests of management with interests of shareholders. In addition to merely drawing a salary from the company, these managers would become significant shareholders who would benefit from the greater profitability that a divestiture might create.

During the 1980s, the concept of **leveraged buyouts (LBO)**, was propelled by the potential value of divesting undervalued operations. Several corporations progressed to a point where each of their operating units were unable to compete efficiently in their respective markets. This depressed the value of these corporations and made them targets of "raiders" who financed, or "leveraged," their bids for these companies with the companies themselves as collateral.

These raiders understood that such companies were comprised of several divisions that, if sold separately to others—even their own competitors—could exact a total selling price well in excess of the total company's **market value**. By divesting certain operations, the raiders could raise funds to pay off the often substantial loans that were needed to launch the LBO in the first place.

For example, an underperforming company with 10 divisions might be acquired for $500 million, financed by **banks** or other investors. Six of these divisions are sold for $350 million. These funds are immediately transferred to the lenders, reducing the **debt** to $150 million, and cutting the amount of payments on the company's debt by 70 percent.

However, the remaining four divisions have a market value of $300 million. The raider can sell the company at this amount and take a $150 million profit, or use the profits from its remaining operations to pay down its debt over a period of, say, three years. At the end of that term, the company might be sold for $300 million, all of which would be profit.

Often the managers of potential takeover targets recognize the precarious position their companies are in and initiate divestments to raise the market value of their companies. This, it is hoped, would discourage others from launching LBOs that could cost them their jobs. They do exactly what a raider would do, but they do it before losing control of their company to a raider. In both instances, the owner benefits, whether the owner is a corporate raider or a group of shareholders.

Because managers often are in the best position to understand the state of their company, they themselves may opt to purchase the company from shareholders, in effect, launching their own LBO. These management buy-outs take many forms: they may involve the entire company, or just a single division of it.

To illustrate this, assume a group of managers arranges financing to offer shareholders $600 million for the same underperforming 10-division company. At this price, shareholders may realize an immediate 20 percent premium on the market value of their shares. If the shareholders can be convinced to sell at this price, the managers would take control of the company and initiate the same divestments described earlier. Again, the managers are acting the same way as a raider, only it is they, as owners, who benefit from the divestiture.

But if a group of managers within one of the company's 10 divisions believes it can administer the operation more efficiently than the parent company, they might arrange financing to purchase only that division from the parent company. If the managers can offer a price for the division that is greater than the company's valuation of it, the company may elect to divest the operation.

TYPES OF DIVESTITURES

Divestitures take several distinct forms, based on the nature of the exchange of assets and the relationship between the buyer and seller. Because these forms have subtle differences, the terms used to describe them are frequently used incorrectly.

The most common term, used to describe the most common form of divestiture, is the sell-off. Here a company agrees to sell one of its divisions, as an individual enterprise, to another company. The defense industry has provided several examples of sell-offs in recent years.

General Dynamics, a maker of nuclear submarines, battle tanks, and aircraft, decided to exit the military aircraft portion of its business in 1993. This operation was centered at a single plant, the Convair works in Fort Worth. It found a buyer in Lockheed, a military aircraft manufacturer that was better structured to profitably operate the Fort Worth facility. In exchange for the plant, Lockheed paid a single amount in cash to General Dynamics.

A second type of divestiture is the **spin-off**. Here, a company divests itself of a part of its operations by replacing its existing shares with two or more classes of shares, representing the new, independent operations.

Morton Thiokol, a manufacturer of chemicals, salt, and rocket motors, executed a spin-off when it divided its operations into two companies in 1990. Shareholders exchanged their shares in Morton Thiokol for an equivalent value of shares in the two new companies, Morton International and Thiokol, Inc.

The most celebrated spin-off occurred in 1984 when, under antitrust pressure from the Justice Department, AT&T was forced to divest its 22 local Bell operating companies. Shareholders were issued new shares in AT&T, which retained its long distance, manufacturing, and research divisions, and shares in seven new companies—Ameritech, Bell Atlantic, BellSouth, Pacific Telesis, Nynex, Southwestern Bell, and US West.

In both examples, there were no buyers and sellers. Shareholders were compensated with new shares, and no money changed hands.

In some cases, a company may choose to create a divestment by offering partial equity in its **subsidiaries**. For example, General Motors Corp. offers three classes of stock shares—Class A for its core automotive operations, Class E for its EDS subsidiary, and Class H for its GM Hughes Electronics group.

The company maintained a majority stake in EDS and GM Hughes, but allowed a minority of those shares to trade independently of General Motors Corp. Class A. If at some point, for example, GM elected to divest most or all of its interest in EDS, it could merely sell its shares in that company to a buyer or to the general population of shareholders. The exchange would be made between GM and the buyer on the basis of money for shares.

Another form of divestment, described earlier, is the **management buy-out**. Union Carbide, a diversified manufacturer of industrial chemicals and plastics, operated a small consumer products group. In 1989, Union Carbide announced its intention to sell the consumer group in order to focus on improving the performance of its core operations. A group of managers organized financing, some of which was provided by Union Carbide, to make the division an independent company, now called First Brands Corp.

In this instance, the buyer was a group of managers, and the company was compensated with both cash and shares. Union Carbide gradually reduced its equity interest in First Brands by later selling its shares in the company.

Asset trades constitute a fifth form of divestment. Telephone companies have been known to divest of certain service territories with asset trades. For example, a company that's operations are centered in Louisiana, but which operates telephone **franchises** in Ohio, might benefit from trading its operations in Ohio to a company whose business is stronger in that state. In return, the Ohio telephone company offers operations it has in Louisiana as payment.

In this case, both companies are buyers as well as sellers. Payment is in the form of **barter**, where each company's divestment is the other's acquisition.

The final form of divestment involves total liquidation, where all of a company's divisions are sold off or its operations are wound down and the assets sold for cash. In 1990, Eastern Airlines fell into such a deep financial morass that it was forced to close down.

The company's debts far outnumbered its assets. A court ordered liquidation of the company to provide at least partial settlement for its **liabilities**.

The company's aircraft, facilities, routes, and even its venerable name were divested. A shell corporation remained in place only to administer the divestiture of assets. In this case, there were many buyers, and payment was strictly in cash.

Regardless of the form or the specific motivations behind it, a divestiture is almost always undertaken to do one thing: maximize the value of invested capital. It provides an exit mechanism to convert invested capital back into a negotiable form of assets, usually cash, shares, or some other debt instrument. These assets, freed of their previous application, can then be applied to some new form of investment.

[John Simley]

SEE ALSO: Divestment

FURTHER READING:

Baumol, Wm. J., and Alan S. Blinder. *Economics, Principles and Policy*; 2nd Ed., New York: Harcourt Brace Jovanovich, 1982.

Derdak, Thomas, Ed. *International Directory of Company Histories, Vol. I and V*. Chicago: St. James Press, 1990.

Eatwell, J., ed. *The New Palgrave Dictionary of Economics*. London: Macmillan, 1987.

General Dynamics Forth Worth Division. *Continuing the Tradition, 50 Years of Building the Best*. Fort Worth: General Dynamics, 1992.

"Morton Thiokol Completes Spinoff," *Journal of Commerce*. July 6, 1989.

"A High-Stakes Bet that Paid Off," *Fortune*. June 15, 1992, pp. 121-122.

"First Brands: Anatomy of an LBO that Worked," *Business Week*. December 4, 1989, p. 104.

CORPORATE DOWNSIZING

The rapid advancement of technologies related to new product development and design, engineering, manufacturing, marketing, and distribution has caused many companies to gain new competitive advantages over competitors with regard to the efficiency of providing products and services. Conversely, companies that have failed to incorporate these advancements have lost the ability to compete effectively, resulting in losses in market share and profit margin. These companies have resorted to basic reengineering of business processes—reinvention those processes—to lower costs, speed production and reaction to changing consumer demands, lower cycle times, and raise quality.

This process often involves a general restructuring of the existing enterprise. Noncore businesses, defined as less profitable or lower-growth sideline operations that share few synergies with the principal business, are sold or closed down, with the proceeds used to invest in improvements in the core business.

These improvements commonly involve increased automation and better-organized logistical processes, often resulting in the elimination of jobs. The combination of spinning off noncore businesses and reducing employment is referred to as "downsizing," or "right-sizing." In fact, the operative factor is really more a matter of improved skill matching, where outmoded job skills are replaced by skill sets that are better matched to new business processes. This is typically synonymous with workforce reductions as new, more efficient processes allow consolidation of job functions. During the 1980s, many companies in service and manufacturing sectors restructured in response to increased competition, both from within the domestic economy and from foreign competitors able to enter new markets because of the progressive removal of trade barriers.

SERVICE INDUSTRY RESTRUCTURING: AMERITECH CORPORATION

One example of restructuring within the service industry is provided by the Ameritech Corporation, a provider of local telecommunications services serving five states in the Midwest. Established in 1984 as the result of the divestiture of AT&T, Ameritech operated for ten years as the amalgamation of five Bell companies. A regulated entity prevented from entering the long-distance, manufacturing, and information services industries by judicial decree, Ameritech retained essentially the same operational model established decades earlier by AT&T.

Largely precluded from expansion into new markets, Ameritech's earnings were strictly regulated. State authorities mandated that Ameritech was entitled to a return on equity of about 12 percent. As a result, Ameritech was a "cost-plus" type of business; as long as it could maintain certain levels of service performance, regulatory authorities allowed it to maintain employment levels to support those service levels. The costs of operation were supported by service rates, while also providing a guaranteed return of about 12 percent.

In the early 1990s, Ameritech began to experience competition from alternative service providers, in the form of local network providers and long-distance companies (including AT&T). These competitors were unburdened by the regulatory restraints on Ameritech and were capable of generating much higher returns than Ameritech.

In response, Ameritech and other "Baby Bells" facing similar conditions launched an effort to replace the regulatory regimes under which they operated with new systems that promised better service levels, lower rates, and higher earnings. In effect, Ameritech lobbied for the elimination of costly regulatory burdens that were not in the public economic interest.

In anticipation of gradual deregulation, Ameritech launched a transformation of its structure to improve its cost competitiveness compared to its emerging rivals. It eliminated its geographically defined operating companies in favor of business units defined by market types, such as large business, small business, consumer, information industry, and cellular.

By incorporating more efficient business processes, Ameritech found it possible to consolidate or eliminate entire job functions, resulting in **workforce** reductions. And as deregulation enabled it to enter new businesses, it gained a need for employees possessing new skill sets. In effect, its workforce declined in some areas, but grew in others.

Similar restructurings occurred at British Airways, Bank of America, Citicorp, GTE, and AT&T.

MANUFACTURING INDUSTRY RESTRUCTURING: ZENITH ELECTRONICS

An example of restructuring in manufacturing is provided by the Zenith Electronics Corporation, a manufacturer of color television sets, cathode-ray tubes, and products for the cable TV industry. Zenith began operations in 1920 manufacturing radios, but by the 1980s was principally a manufacturer of color televisions and computers.

During the 1970s and 1980s, competition from Asian companies who had access to cheap labor, collaborative research and larger markets, effectively caused the failure of American consumer electronics companies such as RCA, Magnavox, and Motorola/Quasar—all of which were acquired by foreign parent companies. Zenith, however, remained independent and in business.

Its competitiveness eroded, however, and Zenith soon began to lose money. By the late 1980s, its only hope of maintaining solvency was in massive restructuring. The company sold its money-losing computer operations in 1989 and successively sold or closed down every operation not related to its core television business.

In 1994, Zenith launched a companywide reengineering of its business, investing heavily in product development, manufacturing, and distribution process improvements. These improvements led to the elimination of outmoded job functions and the consolidation of others. The result was that Zenith reduced its cycle times and production and distribution costs,

helping it to maintain a strong competitive position, despite losses throughout the industry.

Similar restructurings occurred at General Electric, Motorola, Inc., Lockheed Martin, IBM, and LTV.

THE RESTRUCTURING PROCESS

Restructuring generally refers to the reorganization of corporate operations to achieve higher levels of operating efficiency. This can involve the elimination of noncore businesses and business processes, the consolidation of related operations and business functions and, to a great extent, reengineering of existing processes.

A company reengineers its operations first by viewing its markets and evaluating its strengths with regard to those markets. It then determines how it would operate under ideal conditions. In other words, if it were entering the business from scratch, how would it operate?

The process of reengineering lies in establishing a detailed strategy to transform the operation as it exists today into the ideal operation it has defined. This process must be performed carefully to ensure that projects bearing the greatest benefit are pursued first, and that each project will have a minimum adverse effect on the operation and the transformation strategy.

SEE ALSO: Spin-offs

[John Simley]

FURTHER READING:

Bartol, Kathryn M., and David C. Martin. *Management*, New York: McGraw-Hill, 1991.

Donnelly, James H., Jr., James L. Gibson, and John M. Ivancevich. *Fundamentals of Management*. 6th ed. Plano, TX: Business Publications, 1987.

Griffin, Ricky W., and Ronald J. Ebert. *Business*. 2nd ed. Englewood Cliffs, NJ: Prentice Hall, 1991.

CORPORATE FINANCE

Corporate finance pertains to the acquisition and allocation of a company's resources to maximize shareholder wealth. More simply, it is the process of obtaining funds and investing them in a manner that will cause the firm's stock price to rise.

Resource acquisition and allocation is typically carried out by a finance department headed by a financial manager(s). It is the financial manager's responsibility to conduct both functions in a manner that maximizes shareholder wealth, or stock price. If the firm performs better than other companies, its stock price will (in theory) rise and it will be able to raise additional funds at a lower cost, among other benefits. In pursuing shareholder wealth, the manager is forced to balance the interests of: owners, or shareholders; creditors, including **banks** and bondholders; and other parties, such as employees, suppliers, and customers.

Resource acquisition, the first corporate finance function, refers to the generation of funds from both internal and external sources at the lowest possible cost to the corporation. Two main categories of resources are liabilities and equities. Examples of **liabilities** include accounts payable, **debt**, leases, and other types of primarily fixed-rate commitments. Examples of **equity** are proceeds from the sale of stock—**common stock** and **preferred stock**—and retained earnings.

Resource allocation, the second corporate finance function, is the investment of funds with the intent of increasing shareholder wealth over time. Two main categories of investments are current assets and fixed assets. The former includes cash, inventory, securities, and accounts receivables. Examples of fixed assets are **real estate**, buildings, and equipment. Resource allocation decisions have a profound effect on the value of the firm (i.e., the market value of the firm's securities) which, in turn, affects the firm's future cost of capital.

A pharmaceutical firm may choose to invest a large portion of its resources in a risky biotechnology venture in an effort to offer its shareholders the potential for large profits. A likely result of that decision is that the risky investments will reduce the market's perceived security of the company's bonds, thus decreasing their value and increasing the rate of interest that the firm must pay to borrow money in the future. Conversely, the company may elect to conservatively direct its resources into improving established operations. Such a decision might strengthen the company's debt rating but fail to maximize the value of its equity.

Thus, it is through the objective of maximizing shareholder wealth that the discipline of financial markets is implemented. In other words, if management decisions consistently fail to maximize shareholder wealth, the market price of the common stock may fall to a level which makes the firm an attractive takeover target.

[Dave Mote]

FURTHER READING:

Shapiro, Alan C. *Modern Corporate Finance*. New York: Macmillan Publishing Company, 1990.

Swanson, Mary Stewart. *FLS Financial Writing Guide*. Minnetonka, MN: Financial Learning Systems, 1982.

Weston, Fred J., and Eugene F. Brigham. *Essentials of Managerial Finance*. New York: Dryden Press, 1982.

CORPORATE GOVERNANCE

Corporate governance involves the relationship among the various participants involved in determining the **strategy** and performance of corporations. The major participants include the firm's shareholders (including large institutions), the management team, and the **board of directors**. Corporate governance encompasses: corporate performance, succession/nomination, relations between the board and the **chief executive officer** (CEO), and relations with shareholders and stakeholders.

THE ROLE OF THE BOARD OF DIRECTORS

The ultimate control of the corporation rests with the shareholders. The shareholders elect the members of the board of directors, who set overall policy for the corporation, and appoint the officers. The directors elect a chairperson. The board also designates the CEO, who manages the day-to-day affairs of the corporation. Being a director is a part-time position that provides compensation in the form of an annual stipend or a fee for meetings attended.

Most large corporations have boards which are composed of notable corporate executives of other major firms. The directors are typically not aware of the company's daily workings and rely on management to provide this information. They provide, however, an overall direction to the corporation and deliberate on major decisions and proposed changes. Increasingly, boards are viewed as proactive, and are becoming more involved in replacing executives of under-performing corporations.

Board of directors generally consist of both inside members and outside members. Inside members consist of the corporation's senior management, whereas outside directors do not have direct managerial responsibilities over the firm's day-to-day activities. Boards of public companies consist of approximately 13 members, 9 of whom are outside directors.

Many issues, such as attempts at **takeovers**, are usually required to be brought up before the board of directors. The board determines requirements and may recommend that the issue be taken to a shareholder vote. The compensation of the senior executive officers of the corporation is also set by the board of directors. The directors usually appoint a compensation committee that is charged with recommending executive compensation to the board as a whole.

INCREASED PRESENCE OF INSTITUTIONAL INVESTORS

In 1950, institutional investors held less than 3 percent of the publicly trade stock of U.S. corporations. By 1991, however, they controlled 53 percent. As a result, institutional investors now have the power to directly influence managerial decisions in many corporations.

The collapse of the takeover market in the early 1990s led institutional investors to seek other means of protecting their investment interests. They began introducing shareholder resolutions at annual meetings. Critics of this trend express concern that institutional investors will pressure management to support or increase stock prices, preventing management from undertaking long-term strategic initiatives that will make U.S. corporations competitive in the global marketplace.

In October 1992 the **Securities and Exchange Commission** adopted rules which reformed the proxy solicitation process. The new amendments made it easier for institutional stockholders to communicate with each other. Previously, shareholders who desired to communicate with more than ten other shareholders were required to have their comments approved by the SEC before the comments could be circulated. Under the new rules, the SEC no longer serves as editor/ sponsor of the material; the only requirement is that the materials be filed with the SEC.

The increased activity of institutional investors has in turn led to a greater emphasis on shareholder value creation. Management now places greater priority on the impact of decisions on corporate shareholders rather than on other stakeholders such as bondholders, employees, customers, and communities. In addition, companies are actively attempting to communicate important corporate developments to the Wall Street community (and institutional shareholders) through press releases and meetings with Wall Street security analysts and institutional shareholders.

RELATIONSHIP INVESTING

Senior managers are beginning to embrace key equity investors through a process known as relationship investing. Relationship investing consists of an established committed link between a company and one or more shareholders. Under this model, large investors will have greater knowledge about the portfolio companies and play a more significant role in corporate governance and oversight. Accordingly, relationship investing should better align the interests of shareholders and corporations, and increase the probability that the firm will realize the benefits associated with independent oversight of corporate affairs.

In the relationship investing model, representatives of large shareholder groups meet with the company's board of directors on a regular basis to discuss the company's long-term strategy to gain market share and profits and press for change when needed. Armed with greater knowledge, these investors are more likely to work with management and invest for the long-term rather than seeking short-term trading profits. Advocates of the relationship investing concept contend that it would bring the corporate governance process in the United States closer to the models employed in Germany and Japan.

Relationship investing comes in two major forms—negotiated and nonnegotiated transactions. In nonnegotiated investments, large institutional shareholders—typically pension funds—offer suggestions about corporate policy to the firm's senior managers. This usually occurs when the investor has held a stock in his or her portfolio that has declined in value, and resolves to take corrective action. In negotiated transactions, the investor makes a large, long-term financial commitment to a company in return for a voice in the way it is managed.

Relationship investing is not without its pitfalls. Investors with sizable stakes may demand constant updates on major corporate decisions, irrespective of their skill levels or ability to effectively manage the corporation. Thus, a CEO could potentially spend all of his or her time communicating with a relationship investor, and not enough time managing the corporation. Moreover, the constant scrutiny of a powerful investor might force a CEO to become more risk averse.

Critics of relationship investing also suggest that nothing fundamentally changes with the firm. In fact, they argue that the extended evaluation period, often stretching from one year to three years, ties up capital longer, and drives up the required rate of return. The strategy of taking small, minority stakes in companies makes the funds more vulnerable to poor managerial decisions than funds that take control of investee companies. In addition, relationship investing may not allow funds the ability to take immediate corrective action if an investment deteriorates, nor determine the timing of the exit strategy for their investments.

CORPORATE GOVERNANCE OVERSEAS

The corporate governance systems in Japan and Germany differ quite markedly from those in practice in the United States. In Japan and Germany, companies benefit from the long-term holdings of banks and other financial institutions, and are less subject to short-term performance pressures.

The boards of Japan's major corporations represent the collective interests of the company and its employees rather than the interests of the firms' shareholders. Almost all directors are senior executives or former employees of the company. Most companies have no outside board members. In large corporations, the outside directors are typically major bank lenders.

Japanese shareholders are passive owners. In Japan, there are overlapping boards of directors, and companies maintain close formal and informal ties with shareholders, customers, suppliers, and employees. These constituent groups overlap in Japan whereas in the United States they are generally independent of one another.

The members of the Japanese *kereitsu* are usually organized around the leadership of a major financial institution. The shares held by business partners and institutional investors are rarely sold, thus forming blocks of friendly and stable shareholders. This all but prevents the possibility of a hostile takeover attempt being successful in Japan.

Companies in Germany have two boards: a supervisory board and an executive board. The supervisory board typically includes professional advisers to the company, such as lawyers, accountants, and bankers. In turn, the supervisory board appoints the executive board. The most important decisions of the executive board have to be ratified by the supervisory board. In addition, plants with more than five employees are required to have a **works council**, which must be consulted prior to changes in work practices and dismissals.

In Germany, only a small number of multinational firms have a diversified share ownership. Institutions exert relatively little influence over board policy. As in Japan, corporate cross share holdings are common. Also, the major universal **banks** exert substantial control over companies.

[Robert T. Kleiman]

FURTHER READING:

Kleiman, Robert T., Kevin Nathan, and Joel M. Shulman. ''Are There Payoffs for Patient Corporate Investors.'' *Mergers and Acquisitions.* March/April, 1994, pp. 34-41.

Monks, Robert A. G., and Nell Minnow. *Corporate Governance.* Cambridge, MA: Blackwell Business, 1995.

CORPORATE GROWTH

Corporate growth can be defined in numerous ways and be achieved in several strategic forms. In general, the matter of whether—and at what rate—a company is growing can be highly ambiguous. A company can experience strong sales growth, but simultaneously be losing market share and experiencing financial losses. In such a case, the company's volume is rising, but that of its competitors is rising even faster. And, on the bottom line, sales growth means little when the company can not turn a profit.

The same company may be gaining market share, but losing sales volume and money. This suggests that volume is falling throughout the industry, but only less so for this company. In any case, it still loses money on its operations.

Consider a third case, where a company's earnings are rising, but its losing sales volume and market share. This is quite possibly the only favorable scenario, because it suggests that the company is cutting marginal operations to concentrate on what it does best—in effect, becoming smaller but more profitable.

While these criteria can provide some insight into the true nature of the firm—whether it really is growing or not—they also can provide some indication of what type of firm the company is: a dog, a question mark, a **cash cow** or a star.

A dog is a company with low or declining market share and low or declining market growth, typically a description of a dying firm. A company with low or declining market share but a high rate of sales growth is a question mark because its success depends on whether it can outperform competitors in terms of sales growth and eventually gain market share.

Alternatively, a company with low or declining sales growth but high or increasing market share is a cash cow because its position in the market is secure even though the industry in which it operates has matured. Such a company is typically overrun by successful question marks and becomes a dog. In the meantime, however, it generates a healthy income. A company with high or growing market share and high or growing sales volume is called a star because it is outperforming its competitors. Dogs typically lose—or will lose—money, while stars typically make—or will make—money.

Whether in terms of market share or sales volume, growth may be pursued in one of three ways. In a high-growth company, either or both market share and sales volume growth are pursued vigorously, even at the expense of short-term profitability. This is a risky **strategy** because the company risks going bankrupt before it can achieve commanding positions in terms of market share and/or sales volume.

A slow-growth company concentrates on maintaining profitability while pursuing incremental gains in market share and/or sales volume. The slow-growth strategy emphasizes financial longevity.

The third growth strategy is based on negative growth, or retrenchment. A company in retrenchment is purposely sacrificing market share and sales growth with the singular goal of emphasizing short-term profitability. In other words, the company is abandoning operations in markets where it has the fewest advantages, vis a vis competitors.

When the retrenchment has run its course, the company is left with a core business in which it enjoys solid advantages over competitors, and may take advantage of its superior profitability to pursue either a high- or slow-growth strategy. In effect, retrenchment strategies establish bases for the other growth strategies.

[John Simley]

FURTHER READING:

Baumol, William J., and Alan S. Blinder. *Economics, Principles and Policy*. 2nd ed. New York: Harcourt Brace Jovanovich, 1982.

Fischer, Stanley, and Rudiger Hornbusch. *Economics*. New York: McGraw-Hill, 1983.

Griffin, Ricky W., and Ronald J. Ebert. *Business*, 2nd ed. Englewood Cliffs, NJ: Prentice Hall, 1991.

CORPORATE IMAGE

The management of a corporation's image increasingly is being viewed by senior executives as vital to the success of their companies. Although the origins of corporate image are uncertain, the basic concept has been around since the earliest firms started using specific marks or logos to differentiate their products or companies from competitors. By the 1970s, a robust consulting industry had emerged that specialized in helping companies improve their image through visual articulation or graphic design. More recently, in response to the dynamics of the business environment, many of these design **consultants** have broadened their focus to embrace a strategic view of communicating corporate image.

IMPORTANCE OF CORPORATE IMAGE

The growing significance of managing corporate image, or corporate identity as it is being called with increasing frequency, is underscored by a 1989 survey in Britain by Market Opinion Research International (MORI). This study found that 77 percent of the leading industrialists questioned believed that the importance their firms attached to developing and promoting their corporate image would increase in the near future. Research a year later by CBI and Fitch Consultants corroborated this finding.

The overriding reason for the burgeoning concern for corporate image is abundantly clear. We live in a time of immense environmental complexity and change, and consequently corporations have been forced to significantly alter their strategies to better compete and survive. Mergers, acquisitions, and divestitures represent a major dimension of corporate change over the past several decades. Consider the extreme example of the Greyhound Corporation. For most of this century, Greyhound was the largest busing company in North America. However, in the 1970s the company initiated an aggressive acquisition/diversification strategy and by the late 1980s was competing in five different industries (it even sold off most of its busing operations). To signal this metamorphosis to its external audiences, the company belatedly (in 1990) changed its name to the Dial Corporation and completely revamped its corporate communications.

The acceleration of product life cycles is another vital dimension of the turbulent business environment. Nowhere is this more evident than in the electronics industry. Personal computers can become outmoded in the period of a year. In the audio segment of the market, tapes replaced records and, in turn, were replaced by compact discs, which may in the future be superseded by digital audio tapes. Companies with strong corporate images, such as Sony Corporation and JVC, obviously have an advantage in such fluid markets because their name adds value to their products by reducing uncertainty in the eyes of distributors, retailers, and consumers.

Deregulation has been a critical factor in many industries. For instance, as a result of the court-ordered breakup, AT&T has had to develop a new strategy and a more aggressive marketing-oriented culture to adjust to its new realities. Concurrently, the telecommunications giant adopted a new logo and initiated a communication program to help convey its new identity. In another example, deregulation of the financial services industry has allowed savings and loans to expand their services and compete with banks. Consequently, institutions such as Glendale Federal Savings and Loan Association and California Federal Savings and Loan Association have changed their charters to become savings banks. Their new names are Glendale Federal Bank F.S.B. and California Federal Bank, a Federal Savings Bank; they have fittingly redirected their corporate communication programs.

Globalization has been still another catalyst in the rise of corporate image programs. To illustrate, American Express Co. originally was a freight company in the North American market. As the company matured into a global credit card, banking, and travel organization, it wisely developed a corporate communication program aimed at projecting its new identity. American Express understood that a strong and positive global image can be a powerful weapon for firms expanding internationally. IBM, McDonald's and Baskin and Robbins are examples of other companies that have been able to expand to all areas of the world with relative ease because of their global prominence.

A related factor is that as a corporation expands its operation internationally, or even domestically, through acquisitions, there is a danger that its geographically dispersed business units will project dissimilar or contrary images to the detriment of corporate synergy. British-based Courtaulds has a globally dispersed organization but until its latest corporate image review allowed its operating companies to use their traditional names. As a consequence of this policy, there was little cooperation among these units and no cohesive corporate identity. Courtaulds remedied this situation by instituting a common naming policy and a correlated corporate communication program.

A final factor stimulating the current interest in corporate image is society's growing expectation that corporations be socially responsible. One salient manifestation of this trend is that many of today's consumers consider the environmental and social image of firms in making their purchasing decisions. Companies such as Ben and Jerry's and The Body Shop have built their strategies around this idea and consequently have grown very rapidly. Another manifestation of the trend is the rise of socially responsible investment funds.

THEORY OF CORPORATE IMAGE

Theory always underlies good practice. Theory identifies and defines the key variables in the process under consideration and explains the interrelationship among them. In the process for managing corporate image, the fundamental variables are corporate identity, corporate communication, and corporate image. Corporate identity is the reality of the corporation. It is the unique, individual personality of the company that differentiates it from other companies. To use a marketing metaphor, it is the corporate brand. Corporate communication is the aggregate of sources, messages, and media by which the corporation conveys its uniqueness or brand to its various audiences. Corporate image is in the eye of the beholder. It is the impression of the overall corporation held by its several audiences.

The interrelationship among the three variables is shown diagrammatically in Figure 1. The objective in managing corporate image is to communicate the company's identity to those audiences or constituencies that are important to the firm in a manner that is both positive and accurate. This process involves fashioning a positive identity and communicating this identity to significant audiences in such a way that they have a favorable view of the company. The feedback loops in the model indicate that an unsatisfactory image can be improved by modifying corporate communication or re-shaping the corporate identity or both. The principal issues relating to the four components of the model—identity, image, communication, and feedback—will now be examined in greater detail.

CORPORATE IDENTITY

Corporate identity, as explained above, is the reality and uniqueness of the organization. It may be broken down into its component parts: corporate strategy, **corporate culture**, organizational design, and operations. **Strategy** is the overall plan that circumscribes the company's product/market scope and the policies and programs which it chooses to compete in its chosen markets. For example, Southwest Airlines is a regional carrier competing in the airline industry through strategies that result in low costs and low fares.

Corporate culture is the shared values and beliefs that the organization's members hold in common as they relate to each other, their jobs, and the organization. It defines what the firm's personnel believe is important and unimportant, and explains to a large degree why the organization behaves the way it does. Southwest Airlines has a strong corporate culture that highly prizes company loyalty, internal cooperation, and service to the customer. Southwest's culture supports the company's strategy and is a salient component of its identity.

Organizational design refers to the fundamental choices top managers have in developing the pattern of organizational relationships. It encompasses issues such as whether basic departmentation should be by function or product division, the overall configuration (tall vs. flat), the degree of decentralization, the number of staff personnel, the design of jobs, and the internal systems and procedures. All of these factors

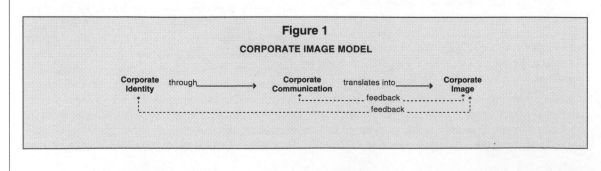

Figure 1

CORPORATE IMAGE MODEL

can affect, to some degree, corporate identity. However, from the perspective of the firm's external constituents, the corporate/product relationship normally is the most critical element of organizational design.

The corporate/product relationship refers to the deliberate approach a firm follows in structuring the relationship of its products to one another and to the corporate entity. Corporate/product relationships may be categorized as single entity, brand-dominance, equal-dominance, mixed-dominance, or corporate-dominance.

Single entity companies offer one product line or set of services; consequently, the image of the company and the image of the product tend to be one and the same. Southwest Airlines is an obvious example of a single entity company; it is 100 percent involved in the airline business. Identity/image problems typically arise for single entity firms such as Southwest Airlines if they expand into areas and activities not immediately related to their current strategy. The corporate planners must carefully consider the corporate identity they desire to have and the concomitant image they wish to project.

Under the brand-dominant approach, the decision has been made not to relate the product brand and corporate names. This approach is followed by many consumer products companies. For instance, Marlboro and Merit cigarettes, Post cereals, Jell-O, Kraft cheeses, and Oscar Mayer meats are all well-known products but few consumers realize that they are all marketed by the Philip Morris Companies, Inc.

General Motors Corp., historically, has exemplified the equal-dominance approach. The principal General Motors' automobile divisions—Chevrolet, Pontiac, Oldsmobile, Buick, and Cadillac—maintained separate identities, but each was also closely associated with the corporation. Neither the corporate nor the individual brand was predominant.

In mixed-dominance companies, sometimes the brand name is dominant, sometimes the corporate name is dominant, and in some cases they are used together with equal emphasis. The German firm Robert Bosch GMBH follows this approach. Bosch identifies some of the products it manufactures (for example, its spark plugs) with the corporate name, but chooses to allow other brands such as Blaupunkt radios to stand independently.

IBM, Hewlett-Packard, Xerox Corporation, and Gerber Products Co. are exemplars of the corporate-dominance strategy. In these companies, the corporate image is paramount and all implementation decisions are aimed at reinforcing this image.

Two examples will illustrate the identity considerations involved in corporate/product relationship decisions. A number of years ago, Pillsbury developed a franchised restaurant chain called Bennigan's Tavern. The company had to decide if it wanted to create an identity for Bennigan's that linked the restaurant to Pillsbury or create a separate identity for it. A crucial question was whether a corporation known for its traditional kitchen products such as flour and cake mixes should associate its name with an institution serving beer. Prudently, Pillsbury chose the brand-dominant approach.

The classic example of the Transamerica Corporation illustrates an equally logical but very different outcome. Transamerica was a conglomerate with divisions in such diverse fields as air travel, business forms, entertainment, and insurance. For many years the company followed a brand-dominant (or more precisely, a subsidiary-dominant) approach in which the relationships between the subsidiaries and the parent were de-emphasized. In the late 1960s, however, company executives decided to take advantage of the synergies that a unified corporate identity could render. As part of the implementation program, Transamerica created the "T" logo as a unifying symbol to connect the various subsidiaries to the parent and to each other. Each subsidiary retained the company name under which its reputation had been built, and the corporate relationship was communicated through a linking phrase such as, "Entertainment from the Transamerica Corporation."

Operations, the fourth and final component of corporate identity, is the aggregate of activities the firm engages in to effect its strategy. These activities become part of the reality of the corporation and can influence its identity in a wide variety of ways. Several examples will highlight the range of possibilities. First, the cleanliness of Disney Corporation's theme parks, together with the efficiency and helpfulness of their employees, has become a significant and very positive dimension of the corporation's identity. At the other end of the spectrum, Sears Roebuck & Co.'s systematic overcharging of auto repair customers has become an unwanted facet of its identity, as has the now infamous Exxon Valdez oil spill for the Exxon Corporation.

CORPORATE IMAGE

As stated earlier, corporate image is the reputation of the firm with the various audiences that are important to it. In academic parlance, these significant audiences are called stakeholders. They are groups that have a stake in the company. Stakeholders are affected by the actions of the company and, in turn, their actions can affect the company. Consequently, its image in the eyes of its stakeholders is important to the company. The principal stakeholders with which most large corporations must be concerned are:

- Customers
- distributors and retailers
- financial institutions and analysts
- shareholders
- government regulatory agencies
- social action organizations
- the general public
- employees

The image that these groups have of the company will influence their willingness to either provide or withhold support. Thus, if its customers develop a negative perception of the company or its products, its sales and profits assuredly will decline. American Stores learned this truth the hard way. In the mid-1980s, American Stores acquired the southern California chain Sav-on Drugs, and proceeded to operate it under the combined name of Osco Sav-on with the expectation that the Sav-on name would eventually be dropped. Since American Stores was already operating the nation's largest chain of super-drugstores in 27 states under the Osco designation, the move seemed logical. In short order, however, Osco Sav-on's sales and profits began to wane. It was determined that one reason for the turnabout was that merchandising responsibility for the southern California stores had shifted to Osco's buying offices in Chicago, and consequently regional tastes were no longer being adequately addressed. Moreover, it was also discovered that Osco was pronounced exactly like the Spanish word "asco" which means sickening—hardly the positive image a drugstore would like to project in an area with a large Hispanic population. In 1989, the company reverted to the Sav-on name for its southern California stores and, subsequently, sales improved tellingly.

The impact of corporate image in the financial community was dramatically illustrated by the changing fortunes of United Airlines. This company, which had been strictly an airline during most of its existence, diversified during the 1980s into hotels and the car rental business, and renamed itself Allegis to reflect its new identity. Financial analysts, however, seriously questioned the new strategy, and subsequently the price of the company's stock dropped to well below what the individual parts of the company were worth separately. Eventually, the diversified businesses were sold off, and the firm reverted to its original strategy, renaming itself United Airlines, Inc.

The company's shareholders are another critical stakeholder group because they ultimately give or withhold their approval of management's decisions through their proxies. Moreover, as illustrated by the United Airlines example, their "buy" and "sell" decisions influence the corporation's stock price.

Government regulatory agencies, another important set of stakeholders, are required by law to monitor and regulate firms for specific, publicly defined purposes. Nevertheless, these agencies have considerable discretion in how they interpret and apply the law. Where they have a positive perception of the firm, they are likely to be much less censorious.

Social action organizations represent still another set of stakeholders. To the extent a corporation projects a negative image in the particular area of concern of a social action group, it likely will be targeted for criticism and harassment by that group. For example, the Labor/Community Strategy Center has organized a boycott of Texaco stations and products in an effort to influence the company to reduce the air pollution emanating from its refinery in Wilmington, California. Although there are many refineries in the Wilmington area, the environmental group selected Texaco for its boycott because of a recent much publicized explosion at the company's refinery.

A strong positive image with the general public can be beneficial to the firm. Research suggests that a superior corporate image is a consequential factor in attracting a high quality workforce. Merck & Co., Inc. and Hewlett-Packard, for instance, have traditionally attracted top-notch job applicants because of their sterling reputations.

Current employees represent the internal constituency that a firm must consider when communicating corporate identity. It is widely believed that a positive image in the eyes of employees is a prime causal factor of high morale and productivity. This condition is frequently cited as a fundamental reason for the success of Japanese firms. Additionally, it should be noted that employees play a large role in representing the company to its external stakeholders.

Obviously, each of the various stakeholder groups is likely to have a somewhat different perception of the corporation because each is concerned primarily with a different facet of its operation. Thus, consumers are principally interested in the price, quality, and reliability of the company's products and services. Financial institutions are concerned with financial structure and performance. Employees are mainly concerned with wages, working conditions, and personnel policies. Logically, then, a company should tailor its communication to each stakeholder group individually to engage the special concerns of that group.

A consistent image among the several stakeholder groups, however, is also vital. Although it is prudent to stress different facets of the firm's identity to its various publics, the firm should avoid projecting an inconsistent image. There are two key reasons for this admonition. First, some of the concerns of the several stakeholders overlap. For instance, the financial community and the shareholders would have many of the same financial and strategic concerns about the company. In fact, many shareholders rely heavily on the advice of experts from financial institutions. Both employees and the general public have an interest in the overall prestige of the firm and the reputation of its products. A social action group's criticism, as in the case of the Texaco boycott, whether economically effective or not, is bound to influence some customers and affect the company's public reputation. Of course, a regulatory agency such as OSHA would focus narrowly on the firm's safety record and policies but the company's employees and their labor unions also have a stake in these matters.

The second and related reason for avoiding an inconsistent image is that the sundry stakeholders are not separate, discrete entities. Membership overlaps. Consider the example of a typical public utility. Almost all of its employees are also customers and a significant number may also be shareholders. Furthermore, it is not unlikely that some of its employees will be active in environmental or consumer rights groups that challenge the company on specific issues. It is also probable that some of the company's bankers and regulators will be among its customers.

CORPORATE COMMUNICATION

Corporate communication is the link between corporate identity and corporate image. It should be defined in the broadest possible sense because companies communicate identities in many different ways. It includes almost everything the company does from the way telephones are answered to the involvement of company employees in community affairs. A description of the principal communication sources is presented below.

NOMENCLATURE. The primary concerns in this category are the names used to identify the corporation, its divisions, and its products. In recent years, many firms have changed their corporate names to communicate a major change in identity. To illustrate, International Harvester changed its name to Navistar to signal its exit from the agricultural equipment industry. More recently, Carter Hawley Hale Stores has decided to change its name to Broadway Stores to identify more closely with its store operations and accentuate its revitalization since emerging from Chapter 11 bankruptcy in 1992.

GRAPHICS. Graphics, which were the original focus of image consultants, are concerned with the overall visual presentation of the organization. The graphics system should dictate the design style of the company's literature, signs, and stationery. It involves coordinating the style of the typeface, photography, illustrations, layout, and coloring in all the company's graphics. The key question here, as with the nomen-

clature issue, is whether the company's visual presentation is appropriately communicating its identity. Consider the example of Alitalia Airline. Although Alitalia was one of the largest transatlantic carriers, it projected an image of a relatively small, casual, inefficient "Italian" airline. To counter this negative image, Alitalia, following the lead of Olivetti and Ferrari, developed a graphics program stressing superior design and high technology. All forms of corporate communication such as aircraft insignias, uniforms, baggage tags, and promotional materials were redesigned to consistently project and reinforce this positive image. Today Alitalia is regarded by the flying public as a major global carrier.

The logo is the heart of the corporate graphics design system. Unlike nomenclature, logos can be changed subtly over time to reflect the evolving corporate identity. For example, Shell has varied its graphics system many times over the past century. Through all its changes, the company retained, for the sake of continuity, some version of its basic sea shell logo. In contrast, Transamerica Corporation abruptly replaced its recognizable "T" logo with the "Transamerica Pyramid" (a well-known San Francisco landmark) to signal its metamorphosis from a conglomerate to a focused financial services company.

FORMAL STATEMENTS This category includes mission statements, credos, codes of ethics, annual reports, advertising copy, and company slogans. Company slogans can be a particularly potent means of communicating to stakeholders. Avis' "We Try Harder," for instance, has been remarkably effective in conveying the company's identity. Other examples include Prudential's "Own a Piece of the Rock," which communicates the company's financial stability, and E.I. Du Pont de Nemours & Co.'s "Better Living through Chemistry," which underscores the firm's science-driven culture.

ARCHITECTURE. The design of corporate buildings and the interior layout of offices and factories also can reveal much about a company. A series of closed offices suggests a very different culture from a large open room with desks in full sight of each other. The "Transamerica Pyramid" as a symbol of financial services illustrates the potential for communicating through architecture. Smith Kline Beecham (the resultant company from the merger of the pharmaceutical firms Beecham and Smith Kline Beckman) specifically selected a corporate headquarters complex in London that projects a culture that it hopes will evolve at the merged company.

INTERACTIONS AND EVENTS. This is a catch-all category, but a critical one, because every interaction a company employee has with a stakeholder and every event related to a company, communicates something of the firm's identity. This means, for one thing, that employees should be trained and motivated to project a positive image of the company. The increased popularity of training employees on answering telephones shows that many firms understand the criticality of this communication source.

Unexpected events also can conspicuously communicate corporate identity. As mentioned above, the Exxon Valdez oil spill became a dimension of the Exxon Corporation's identity, but it also immediately imparted a negative image to most, if not all, of the company's stakeholders. In similar fashion, the catastrophe at its Bhopol plant projected a negative image of Union Carbide as did the controversy over breast implants for Dow Corning Inc. A company's reaction to such events, however, also can play a prominent role in its projected image. The failure of Chairman Rawls to travel to the site of the oil spill further compounded Exxon's image problems. Conversely, Johnson and Johnson's prompt nationwide recall of Tylenol bottles after Chicago area deaths were attributed to a few poisoned Tylenol capsules significantly reduced the negative impact of these tragedies on the company. In fact, many observers believe that Johnson and Johnson's image has emerged stronger than ever.

FEEDBACK

Feedback is essential to the management of corporate image. Without it, company executives are "flying blind." They need accurate information on stakeholder perceptions if they are to make sound decisions. Ideally, feedback should be continuous. As a practical matter, continuous feedback can be elicited from salespeople, public relations executives, finance managers, and other employees who routinely interact with stakeholders. Based on such input, modifications may be made in the company's communication methods or, if warranted, a formal study of the corporate image initiated. In addition to systematically utilizing internal sources, it is prudent to conduct formal studies of the corporate image on a regular basis, say every five years. Formal studies are typically performed by identity/image consultants using in-depth, one-on-one and group interviews as their chief research tools. This type of comprehensive outside review would normally include an analysis of the corporate identity, an appraisal of the firm's image in the eyes of its stakeholders, and an evaluation of the efficacy of its corporate communications. The consultant's recommendations might run from making slight alterations in the corporate communication program to a re-shaping of the company's identity.

Two examples will illustrate the importance of feedback and taking appropriate remedial measures based on the feedback. In the first example, Consolidated Foods found that it had a deficient and inaccurate image in the financial community. Specifically, it learned that its rather bland sounding name translated into a bland image in the eyes of financial analysts. The company also discovered that not only was its name bland, but it also was inappropriate because its organization was decentralized and encompassed a variety of business units; therefore, it could not be accurately described as "consolidated." To remedy the situation, the company re-named itself Sara Lee after its most prestigious product line. Subsequent research showed that awareness of the company among financial analysts increased significantly.

In the second example, Jaguar, in the days prior to privatization, learned from research that it had a terrible reputation among customers for quality and reliability. To correct this image, Jaguar initiated a rigorous quality program which has helped the firm regain its earlier reputation for quality vehicles.

CONCLUSION

In the past, corporate image was seen almost universally as the narrow, peripheral function of graphic design. Today, however, as a consequence of the epochal, often abrupt changes occurring throughout the business world, and the resultant danger of corporate images becoming outmoded and erroneous, the issue of managing the corporate image has been elevated to a level of strategic importance in executive circles.

The modern concept of corporate image/identity has a broad sweep. Concisely stated, the objective of any serious corporate image program is to communicate an accurate and positive image of a company to its stakeholders. To accomplish this goal, senior management must discern, through valid feedback, the image being projected to its stakeholders. These executives must also comprehend the true corporate identity along with the efficacy and potential of the company's system of communication with the stakeholders. The concept is simple but its implementation can be profoundly challenging. The firms that master this challenge, in all likelihood, will be the ones that will survive and prosper in our dynamic business environment.

[Edmund R. Gray]

FURTHER READING:

Balmer, John M.T. "Building Societies: Change, Strategy and Corporate Identity," *Journal of General Management*. Winter, 1991, pp. 20-33.

Balmer, John M.T. "The BBC's Corporate Identity: Myth, Paradox, and Reality," *Journal of General Management*. Spring, 1994, pp. 33-49.

Garbett, Thomas. *How to Build a Corporation's Identity and Project Its Image.* Lexington, MA: Lexington Books, 1988.

Gray, Edmund R., and Larry R. Smeltzer. "Corporate Image—An Integral Part of Strategy." *Sloan Management Review*. Summer, 1985, pp. 73-78.

Gray, Edmund R., and Larry R. Smeltzer. ''Planning a Face-Lift: Implementing a Corporate Image Program.'' *Journal of Business Strategy*. Summer, 1987, pp. 4-10.

Ind, Nicholas. *Corporate Image*. London: Kogan Page, Ltd, 1992.

Margulies, W.P. ''Make the Most of Your Corporate Identity.'' *Harvard Business Review*. July–August 1977, pp. 66-72.

Olins, Wally. *Corporate Identity: Making Business Strategy Visible through Design*. Boston, MA: Harvard Business School Press, 1990.

CORPORATE OWNERSHIP

Corporate ownership is one of three broad categories of legal ownership of a business, the other two being sole proprietorship and partnership. In a sole proprietorship, the owner is personally liable for his or her business's debts and losses, there is no distinction made between personal and business income, and the business terminates upon the death of the owner (unless some specific arrangement is made for someone to inherit the business). A partnership is merely joint ownership, and hence, in terms of personal liability, it is similar in every way to a sole proprietorship. Both categories of business ownership are simple arrangements that can be entered into and dissolved easily, without even a written contract, in some cases, merely by shaking hands.

Corporate ownership, on the other hand, is much more complex, because it involves the creation of a legal ''person.'' While an individual may own all the shares of a corporation, he or she is not the owner of the corporation, and hence, is not personally responsible for it. That is because a corporation is, strictly defined, a legal entity that is ''immortal'' (does not terminate upon the owner's death), which can enter into and dissolve contracts, incur debts, sue or be sued, own property and sell it, as any individual may do.

The corporation is rooted in medieval European history. Long before there were viable urban centers in Western Europe, monastic orders existed independently of their membership. All assets belonged to the order, rather than to the individual member. Monastic orders and eventually, universities and towns, became the earliest forms of corporations. By the High Middle Ages, corporations had become so widespread that their status needed legal definition. In the fifteenth century, English high courts elaborated a legal principle inherent in all corporations: limited liability. Henceforth, creditors of a bankrupt corporation could not sue individual owners of corporate stock for the recovery of debt, the corporation being solely responsible for losses. Hundreds of years later, the U.S. Supreme Court refined the status of corporations still further. In *Santa Clara County vs. Southern Pacific Railroad* in 1886, the Court ruled for the first time that a corporation was a legal person, with the same rights, privileges, and responsibilities.

Corporate ownership has evolved over the centuries to the point where, by the twentieth century, there are several major types. Private, for-profit corporate ownership characterizes the majority of present-day corporations. Most of these are general business or C corporations. These can determine whether corporate profits are paid out to stockholders (or, as the case may be, to the sole stockholder), or remain with the corporation. Many artists and other professional people, however, prefer to file for **S corporation** status, whereby profits go entirely to the individual shareholders (or sole shareholder) as personal income, and are taxed as such. These are among the smallest corporations.

Other major categories of corporate ownership are public, quasi-public, nonprofit, and foreign. A public corporation is created solely for government purposes, as, for example, a school district. Quasi-public corporations are not established with the sole purpose of carrying out government objectives, but they do serve the same clientele, namely, the general public. Utility companies are the most prevalent type of quasi-government corporation. A nonprofit corporation (i.e., ''eleemosynary'') is established for charitable purposes, rather than for the purpose of making a profit or serving a public need. Hence while private nonprofit corporations can and often do generate profits, these profits are not taxed and are reinvested in the corporation, distributed back to the membership, or donated to other charities. Foreign corporations usually are private and operate as general business corporations, with no significant differences with their American counterparts.

Because all categories of corporations enjoy limited liability—stockholders can never lose more than they have invested in the corporation, and they are not liable for any of the corporation's debts—they have become the most prevalent business organization in the United States, Europe, and Japan. For the self-employed person in the United States, a compelling reason for turning a sole proprietorship into a corporation has been the opportunity to qualify for **workers' compensation**, and to obtain full health coverage (the entire cost of which can be claimed as a business expense). In all countries where corporate ownership is legal, corporate taxes are significantly lower (30 percent-50 percent) than for a sole proprietorship. Similarly, complete exemption from federal, state, and local taxes is the prime incentive for establishing a nonprofit corporation.

The process of incorporation, either for a sole proprietor or a group of people, is an uncomplicated one. It begins by choosing a corporate name that is not duplicated by any other corporation, and complying with a state's filing requirements. Every state requires a corporate seal, a set of corporate records, and corporate stationery. All states require an employer identification number, and the filing of articles of incorporation, which may vary from state to state. The articles of incorporation request the company's name, the purpose of forming the company, the number and amount of the company's authorized stocks, the resident agent's name and address, and the name and address of any other corporate officer. Most but not all states require that the filer show evidence of an organizational meeting (such as a copy of the minutes). Only after the articles of incorporation are filed with the appropriate state, do corporations acquire legal "existence." All former and future business assets and liabilities henceforth become the property of the new corporate "person."

Virtually all states levy corporate income taxes, as well as sales and other taxes. In addition, there is a federal corporate income tax, which is usually a flat-rate amount instead of a graduated tax. The exception is the **excess profits tax**, which is graduated and based on the amount of invested capital rather than on earned profits. Since 1981, federal tax legislation affecting corporations has been passed annually.

[Sina Dubovoy]

FURTHER READING:

Kirk, John. *Incorporating Your Business*. Chicago: Contemporary Books, 1994.

Mancuso, Anthony. *How to Form a Nonprofit Corporation*. 2nd ed. Berkeley: Nolo Press, 1994.

McQuown, Judith H. *Inc. Yourself*. 7th ed. New York: Harper Business, 1992.

CORPORATE PHILANTHROPY

Corporate philanthropy is the giving of a certain amount of pretax profit (up to 5 percent) to charity on the part of a corporate foundation, or by the corporation outright. In 1993, charitable donations by companies in the United States (not all of them American-owned companies) amounted to $5.8 billion dollars. Of this sum 15 percent consisted of nonmonetary contributions (goods and services). Despite this impressive outpouring of philanthropy, this figure represents a decline of 2 percent from 1992. Overall corporate philanthropy has been declining since it peaked in 1990. Nonetheless, the fact is that even foreign-owned multinationals quickly embrace American style corporate philanthropy when they establish offices in this country, while American-owned companies abroad engage in "global grantmaking." This indicates that corporate giving has become a firmly rooted tradition, one that nonprofit organizations and charities cannot afford to overlook.

Philanthropy on the part of major companies, at least, has come to be expected, yet corporate giving is a relatively recent phenomenon of the twentieth century. It began to spread after World War II, showing especially striking growth between 1975 and 1985. Corporate giving in that time rose from just under one billion dollars to five billion, peaking at six billion dollars in 1990.

Of the tens of thousands of companies in the United States, only one in three even make charitable contributions. However, the percentage of companies that give has grown over the years: in 1984, 1000 companies made charitable contributions in money and/or in goods and services; four years later, this figure climbed to more than 4000. Some companies, such as oil corporation ARCO, have large corporate giving foundations in place. ARCO Foundation has a staff of 15 and donates millions of dollars annually. Other prominent corporate foundations are Eastman Kodak Co. in Rochester, NY and the retail concern, Dayton Hudson Corporation, in Minneapolis, MN, which have perhaps the oldest established corporate giving programs in the country. In a largely one industry community such as Detroit, prominent auto makers Ford Motor Co., General Motors Corp. and Chrysler Corp. combine to donate tens of millions of dollars annually to local nonprofit institutions and charities (in 1992, GM alone donated $62 million). Corporate giving definitely is tied to the amount of profit a company makes and to what the shareholders are willing to approve, and usually, only after elaborate justification.

Only 25 percent of corporate donations are made through corresponding foundations. A corporate foundation is considered a tax-exempt, private organization, even though it began with a grant from the parent company, and periodically the foundation's funds are replenished with infusions of cash from the company's pretax profit. The company **CEO** and other executives usually sit on the foundation's **board of directors** and exercise great influence on charitable **decision making**. A company's executive officers, in turn, are members of boards of many community or private foundations. Officially, foundation and non-foundation (direct) corporate giving constitutes 5 percent of charitable donations in this country. Private foundations contribute another 5 percent, while individual giving makes up by far the largest share of American philanthropy.

While the number of companies that give to charity grew significantly in the 1970s and 1980s, only one out of three gives at all. Corporate philanthropy does have its detractors. The Renowned conservative economist, Milton Friedman, maintains that the business of business should be business, with no charity of any kind. However, Friedman is in a minority. Most business schools in this country teach social responsibility in business, and advocate giving. Philanthropy, however, is always tied to profit, and very often to shareholders' concerns, which would explain why only the biggest and most wealthy companies give at all.

An important factor in corporate giving is self-interest. A 1991 **marketing** survey indicated that over 58 percent of consumers would prefer to buy from a company that gives to charity or that supports worthy causes. A 1993 survey of 163 company managers indicated that the majority of them believed that market share was higher for those companies that gave. In some cases, charitable giving can turn around a company's bad reputation, as with an oil company's environmental record or a pharmaceutical company's ill-fated newest drug. In other words, charitable giving can be profitable in more than one respect for the company that can afford it.

In order to make the most of this wisdom, some of the largest corporations with the most well-developed charitable foundations have embarked on "cause related marketing," or CRM. Starting in 1981 with AT&T, which inaugurated a campaign to restore the Statue of Liberty and Ellis Island, many companies have linked themselves with suitable nonprofit organizations and causes to enhance or rehabilitate their image, and to increase their market share. CRM is usually a short-lived but (from a company's perspective) worthwhile philanthropic and marketing **strategy**. For the first time in the history of corporate giving, there are corporations—usually the largest ones—that actively seek out causes rather than wait for the causes to come to them.

The dominant trend for most companies is still to give over the long term, and most often, to consistently fund the same nonprofit institutions or organizations year after year. More often than not, this involves "strategic" or "targeted" philanthropy, with objectives similar to those of CRM. Strategic marketing requires prior **cost/benefit analyses** on the company's part in order to plan the best match between its marketing goals and a charity that would most likely advance these goals. A 1991 survey of corporations with strategic marketing programs and their corresponding charities revealed that while the charitable concerns were aware of the risk of being used to further a company's objectives, the benefits outweighed the risks. Strategic philanthropy, inaugurated in 1990, has increasingly supplanted traditional company philanthropy and demands more of the charitable concern than traditional giving—namely, the

charity more often than not is expected to produce some conspicuous results.

These newer and, to some critics, more self-interested modes of corporate giving differ from traditional company philanthropy that involves giving outright grants of money to a charity, primarily because it is located in the same geographic area. However, corporations must vindicate their charitable outlays before shareholders, boards of directors, and CEOs, and in some cases, even employees (particularly when companies are undergoing "downsizing"). Therefore, from the corporate fundraiser's perspective, it makes practical business sense to present charitable giving as an investment, rather than as charity. Only the wealthiest, biggest corporations give nationally or globally. The percentage of companies in this category is minuscule. The great majority of corporate giving continues to occur at the community level, and while traditional corporate philanthropy is less directly conscious of furthering a company's objectives than CRM or strategic philanthropy it is by no means overlooked. In the 1950s as in the 1990s, the most popular philanthropic corporate cause continues to be education. Companies that donate to education have a stake in it and always fund educational activities that are related to the company's interests. In addition, companies have always avoided controversial causes. For instance, few if any religious causes or institutions attract corporate charity. However, some traditional causes and charities—sports and the arts—are becoming increasingly less favored. In general, however, the passage of time has merely refined the traditional kind of "interested" giving.

Corporate giving has slowed markedly since 1990, an indication that corporate philanthropy has reached its saturation point. The inauguration of CRM and strategic philanthropy have clearly left some worthy causes underfunded. This has become especially true of the arts, for which corporate support is declining everywhere in this country except in major metropolitan centers. Identified increasingly with "elitism," the arts find it ever more difficult to attract corporate dollars, which tend to go toward funding pragmatic, general causes. Along with the overall decline in corporate giving since 1990, corporate funding for the arts has dropped nearly 20 percent.

During the Reagan administration, corporations were expected to take up the slack left by government. In fact, government spending on social concerns dropped $34 billion during President Reagan's first two years in office alone. While corporate giving did indeed rise greatly during those years, it never exceeded $6 billion; moreover, businesses resented the implication that they should take up responsibilities that seemed to belong more properly to the government. With the advent of strategic philanthropy in the 1990s, even less in the way of funding for social concerns can be expected of corporations across the board.

Since most corporate giving still is targeted to the community in which the company is located, a problem arises when the company relocates, restructures, or significantly downsizes. These are all trends of the late twentieth century, and in the era of global trade and **international competition**, these trends probably will continue. They will even take their toll on the nonprofit organizations and causes still favored by corporate givers.

A similar phenomenon was experienced by charitable causes after World War II, when many of the old privately wealthy families in major cities (the traditional donors to charity) began to die out and not be replaced. Increasingly charities turned to businesses to make up for the slack in funding, and to a large extent, corporate philanthropy took up this slack to the point where, by 1988, IBM was donating as much as the wealthiest and biggest private foundations. It remains to be seen how the decline in corporate philanthropy since 1990 will be offset in the twenty-first century.

While the new era of strategic philanthropy and CRM will make it even more difficult for some worthy causes and concerns to attract the corporate dollar, others will benefit. Proposals from nonprofit groups and causes are most likely to be considered if they are geographically close to the corporation. Every business has a stake in its locale, and it is in the company's interest to improve the community and enhance its local image (also, only the wealthiest companies that donate money nationally).

Another criterion for considering a proposal is the potential of a nonprofit organization to achieve goals and to attract other sources of funding: a convenient yardstick for determining whether a charity is "worthwhile." Moreover, when distributing corporate funding most companies try to avoid being the sole source of charitable dollars. Lastly, a charity must demonstrate its uniqueness and innovativeness.

The five most frequently funded philanthropies (funded by at least 75 percent of corporate givers) are educational institutions, "united" charitable funds such as United Way, organizations for youth, health projects and institutions, and museums. The task of obtaining funding for those causes and concerns outside of these preferred areas definitely will become more complex in the future. For those that do fall within the preferred fields, more will be demanded of them.

If present trends are any indication, the struggle for the corporate dollar will intensify in the next century. Since only one out of three companies donates, there is hope that more will. Since the remaining two-thirds are the less wealthy firms, overall corporate funding may not increase dramatically. However, since companies almost always prefer to contribute locally, this may be beneficial for many charities. Getting more companies to donate, however, may not help the very expensive, "elitist" causes and organizations such as the arts and sports. Many of these may have to find innovative ways of raising money on their own, including—opening up gift shops in strategic locations and developing memberships that offer special benefits and "exclusive" programs.

One thing is certain: corporate philanthropy is ill-suited to taking up the slack left by budget conscious federal and state governments. Self-interest will guide corporate philanthropy in the next century, and important causes, especially education, youth, and health (which are fortunate to cater to a corporation's self-interest), will continue to flourish, albeit in a more insecure, unstable, and demanding funding environment.

[Sina Dubovoy]

FURTHER READING:

Bonavoglia, Angela. "Making a Difference: The Impact of Women in Philanthropy." New York: Women & Foundations/ Corporate Philanthropy, 1991.

Dickerson, Ralph, Jr. "The Good and Bad of Targeted Charity." *The New York Times.*(December 26, 1993): F9(N)(L).

Fairchild, D.G.,et al. "Stop the Slide in Corporate Philanthropy." *Los Angeles Times.* (August 15, 1994): B7.

Logan, David. *U.S. Corporate Grantmaking in a Global Age.*Washington, D.C.: Council on Foundations, 1989.

Works, Gabriel. *Effective Corporate Philanthropy, Building a Giving Program with Impact.* Grand Rapids, MI: Issue Network Group, 1991.

CORPORATE PROFITS

Corporate profits refers to the amount of revenue remaining from a corporate enterprise after all expenses—including labor, materials, and taxes—have been paid. Corporate profit is also known as return on capital, or earnings. A company can only register a profit if its revenue from goods sold and/or services rendered is greater than the amount of expenses that the firm has incurred in conducting business. Another measure that is often used to measure corporate worth is cash flow, which refers to the cash receipts or net income of a business—after **taxes** and other costs—from one or more assets for a given period of time.

Measurement of an establishment's earnings can be determined via a number of **accounting** methods. Most individuals and many businesses—especially those involved in service industries—use the cash method of accounting, while most corporations use the accrual method. The **Internal Revenue Service** (IRS) requires that the accounting method used be implemented fairly and in a way that reflects actual income.

ACCOUNTING METHODS

Under the cash method, also known as the cash receipts and disbursements method, a company or individual determines taxable income solely on the basis of transactions that have been completed. **Income** is included in the taxpayer's gross income in the year in which it is received, even if the income was not earned that year. Similarly, the expenses of users of the cash method are deductible only in the year in which payment is actually made (even if the funds are borrowed); a mere obligation to make payment at a future time is not deductible. The cash method is popular because it often allows the company to choose the year in which it claims the deduction; it can either postpone or accelerate payments of expenses in accordance with its business **strategy**. Historical users of the cash method have included C corporation service providers with average annual gross receipts of less than $5 million, partnerships owned by individuals, S corporations, and certain personal service corporations.

The accrual method of accounting is used by businesses if they purchase or sell merchandise. Under the accrual method, an establishment figures its gross income for the year by including all payments earned and deductions earned during that year, regardless of when the income is actually received. Income and deductions may be counted under the accrual method if 1) the company has adequately completed all tasks for which it was to receive payment, and 2) the amount due can be determined fairly accurately.

A third method of determining earnings is also available. Known as the hybrid method, it incorporates elements of both the cash and accrual methods. As with the other accounting methods, the Internal Revenue Service (IRS) has imposed limitations on its use. An establishment may change its method of accounting if it gains the permission of the IRS.

In recent years, "the IRS has increasingly challenged the use of the cash receipts and disbursements method of accounting by taxpayers in service businesses," noted Carol Conjura and Jay Kalis in *Tax Advisor* in June 1995, because "the cash method of accounting fails to clearly reflect income." Several tax court decisions have favored the IRS in this matter, but Conjura and Kalis observed that in one 1995 case "the court found that the Service's determination was an abuse of discretion." The magazine speculated that the decision "may help to forestall and resolve some of the recent challenges taxpayers have faced on examination" of their chosen accounting method.

CORPORATE PROFITS IN THE UNITED STATES

The U.S. Bureau of Economic Analysis reported that U.S. corporations registered nearly $394 billion in worldwide profits in 1992, after factoring in the value of inventory and capital consumption adjustments. Nearly $330 billion of the total came from domestic business, while another $64 billion was attributed to international earnings. **Financial institutions** reported $56 billion in corporate profits in 1992, while **manufacturing** industries accounted for more than $113 billion. The U.S. transportation industry reported nearly $45 billion in earnings, a little less than wholesale and retail trade establishments, which registered $47 billion. Service and other nonfinancial industries accounted for the single largest block of corporate profits in the United States, with $243 billion.

In the mid-1990s—a period in which U.S. companies in a wide range of industries registered significant growth and increased fiscal health, only 81 percent of corporate income went to wages, salaries, and benefits, the lowest level since 1969, reported Michael J. Mandel in *Business Week* in early 1995. "And wages and salaries alone are now less than 67 percent of income, a post war low, as downsizing, job cuts, and wage restraint continue to dominate business strategies." Some of the United States' largest companies have been trendsetters in this area. General Motors Corp., for instance, spent 26 percent of its gross revenue on employees (via wages, salaries, and benefits) in 1989; by 1993 the percentage of revenue that the company spent on labor costs had dwindled to 22 percent.

Fortune contributor Vivian Brownstein and other analysts attributed much of the increase in corporate earnings to cost-cutting measures introduced in the latter part of the 1980s and the early 1990s. "Many U.S. manufacturers and some retailers are . . . starting to rake in the payoff from earlier efforts aimed at reducing costs and improving productivity—the slashed employment as well as the investment in **automation**, inventory-monitoring equipment and the like." Corporate efforts to cut or hold the line on operating costs, coupled with rising sales, gradually translated into higher corporate profits. Government figures indicate that operating profits rose to over 15 percent of national income in the corporate sector in the mid-1990s, their highest level in almost 20 years, according to Mandel.

Economists are heartened by such statistics. As university economist Fred Moseley stated in *Business Week*, "profitability is the most important determinant of the health of the economy." Analysts reason that high profits spur increased investment, which contributes to **productivity** gains. At the same time, however, inflationary pressures are lowered because of already sizable profit margins. Investors in the nation's stock markets keep a close eye on corporate earnings as well. "Indeed," commented Mandel, "the market is far more responsive to the profit share than it is to the overall growth of the economy."

[Laurie Collier Hillstrom]

FURTHER READING:

Brownstein, Vivian. "The Profit Drought is Over," *Fortune*. June 15, 1992, pp. 37-8.

Conjura, Carol, and Jay Kalis. "When Does the Cash Method Clearly Reflect Income?" *Tax Advisor*. June 1995, pp. 336-37.

Hoffman, Jr., William H., and Eugene Willis, eds. *West's Federal Taxation: 1988*. St. Paul, MN: West Publishing Co., 1987.

Mandel, Michael J. "Plumper Profits, Skimpier Paychecks," *Business Week*. January 30, 1995, pp. 86-7.

O'Connor, Eileen J. "Using the Cash Method of Accounting," *Tax Advisor*. February 1995, pp. 89-90.

CORPORATE SPONSORSHIP

Corporate sponsorship is the blending of **advertising** and promotion into a third type of **marketing** in which a corporation pays an independent party a fee in exchange for public recognition by that party. The short definition of sponsorship is that corporations pick up the bills for public events or products in exchange for the rights to associate their corporate names, images and advertising with those events or products.

Sponsorships like The Blockbuster Bowl (the marriage of college football and a videotape rental company), United Center (Chicago's sports arena supported by an airline), and the Budweiser Thunderbird (proving that auto racing and beer can carefully mix if no one complains too loudly about the implications), are new arrangements in an old business practice. Corporations associating themselves with events in some form can be traced back more than 100 years. For example, tobacco companies first created baseball trading cards. In the 1920s football teams were owned and cross-promoted by everything from starch companies (Decatur Staleys, which became the Chicago Bears) to meat packers (Green Bay Packers).

Corporate ownership of sports teams still is common, but in recent years the tie-ins have been more subtle with few fans thinking twice about Turner Broadcasting owning the Atlanta Hawks and Braves, or the Chicago Tribune Co. Inc. owning the Cubs. That is changing. The Disney Corporation owns a professional hockey team called the Mighty Ducks, named after two Disney movies about a kids' hockey team of the same name. Blockbuster Entertainment's founder, who owns several professional sports teams, is also planning a south Florida amusement park. He envisions an entertainment empire of cross-promotions and discount tickets that would send consumers from one entertainment venue to another.

Individual sponsorship by corporations is more likely than actual team ownership or renaming an arena. Sponsorships can take such forms as an auto racing series (the IndyCar series sponsored by PPG Industries Inc.), a specific race (The Daytona 500 by STP), a major golf tournament (The Vantage on the Seniors Tour named after a cigarette manufactured by R.J. Reynolds Tobacco Company), or women's tennis series (Virginia Slims, another cigarette).

According to companies that monitor corporate sponsorship like International Events Group in Chicago, the trend to attach a company's name to an event or a particular person associated with a popular event is growing. In 1989 corporations spent $1.4 billion for sponsorships. By 1992 it had grown to $2.2 billion. In 1994 IEG estimates that more than 4,500 corporations are spending nearly $4 billion each year on some sort of sponsorship. By the 1996 Olympics in Atlanta, sponsorship expenditures will be even higher. Sports events already account for almost two-thirds of the sponsorships followed by music concerts, festivals and fairs, "cause marketing" (corporate donations of profit portions to save the rain forests, help the homeless, etc.), and the arts.

Another market research study has found that spending on corporate sponsorships has been increasing at 17% a year at a time when most other forms of marketing such as print and broadcast advertising have leveled off or are growing at much smaller rates. There is a lot of growth potential left in sponsorships. American companies spend nearly $250 billion a year in sales and marketing-related activities, so the $4 billion spent this year on corporate sponsorship represents only 1.6% of total marketing efforts.

The reason for the growth of sponsorship can be attributed to companies looking for alternatives to advertising. Ad messages are always competing to "cut through the clutter" of all the other advertising messages. At the same time consumers report through surveys that they are becoming increasingly annoyed with advertising. As one enthusiastic sponsorship user puts it, advertising is designed to intrude on a person's life to make them pay attention to the sales message. Sponsorships try to establish a relationship with that person to become part of the lifestyle rather than interrupt it.

THE MODERN SPONSORSHIP ERA

Aside from sports team ownership, corporate sponsorship of events not directly owned by the companies was not very common until recently. Then in 1971 the modern era of corporate sponsorship was born. A stock car race team owner and former driver named Junior Johnson approached R.J. Reynolds Tobacco Company with the request that the company sponsor his race car on the National Association of Stock Car Auto Racing (NASCAR) circuit. The cost would be under $100,000, but big money in those days. RJR thought about individual sponsorship, looked at the demographics of the people who attended stock car races, then plunged into sponsoring the whole racing series. Over the past 25 years, what used to be called NASCAR's Grand National championship has been transformed into the Winston Cup Championship. Each year RJR pumps millions of dollars into the Winston Cup's 30 races, and at least 3,000 other smaller racing events all over the country. Sources say RJR has spent at least $200 million over 24 years in prize money, advertising, banners, signs, ''gimme'' giveaways such as baseball caps emblazoned with the Winston logo, entertainment, and hospitality.

Corporations generally refuse to reveal how effective such sponsorships are in increasing sales, but it must work. RJR has been joined in NASCAR's sponsorship ranks by over 100 corporations. The largest companies spend up to $4 million just to put their corporate name on a car, They spend a matching amount or more in off-track dollars for public relations, hospitality events for distributors, sales force and customers, and special race-related versions of the products. Some firms, such as Miller Brewing Co. or Hanes Cos. Inc., may sponsor individual races on the circuit for close to $1 million. In exchange for that cash, all advertising, directional/promotional signs, sports page mentions, and radio/TV announcer dialog will revolve around the ''Hanes 500'' mile race.

MEASURING CORPORATE SPONSORSHIP EFFECTIVENESS

While auto companies like Ford Motor Co. and General Motors Corp. coined the phrase ''Win on Sunday; Sell on Monday,'' any evidence that that philosophy ex ists is hard to find. As of 1994 no market research company had developed a way of determining if people buying cases of Miller Genuine Draft beer on Monday were inspired by watching race driver Rusty Wallace in the Miller Genuine Draft Ford Thunderbird win the previous day.

One of the ways companies do justify sponsorships is by converting sponsorship ''views'' or ''mentions'' during a racing radio and TV broadcast into something that can be measured: the dollars such notice would have cost had it been purchased as advertising. Sponsors hire companies to watch TV and listen to radio coverage of races in order to calculate how much air time they get. Once a total air time is established, most companies multiply that by several times the actual sponsorship cost. The multiplication is done in the belief that simple exposure to a company logo is not as valuable as a coherent, factual advertising message selling the product. If the multiplied value is more than actual sponsorship cost, most sponsors are happy.

Other companies rely on consumer surveys to prove that sponsorships are working. NASCAR fans are repeatedly surveyed to find out if they buy sponsors' products. These surveys have been remarkably consistent. As many as 70% of NASCAR fans ''always'' or ''frequently'' buy products from companies that sponsor race cars or the races themselves. Market researchers, racing officials, team owners, drivers and fans all agree that the reason for this high degree of loyalty to racing sponsors (only 36% of NFL fans say they buy sponsors' products) is that the fans know how expensive racing is. They know that without the millions of dollars sponsors bring to the sport, ticket prices would be much higher and the caliber of racing would be much lower. Fans seem to go out of their way to remember sponsors. In one telephone survey of 1,000 fans, more than 200 companies were correctly mentioned as racing sponsors, though only about 50 companies are primary sponsors of race cars. (The primary sponsor gets the official mention such as ''Mark Martin driving the 'Valvoline' Ford Thunderbird.'')

Other evidence of loyalties can be proven by anecdotes that do not cost sponsors a penny. Several years ago, a couple painted their washer and dryer to look like boxes of Tide detergent. They loaded the appliances on the back of a pickup and drove to a race. An alert marketing executive persuaded Darrell Waltrip, then a Tide-sponsored driver, to meet the couple and autograph the appliances as they drove in the gate.

MAKING SPONSORSHIPS WORK

Effective sponsorships involve more than spending several million dollars in exchange for being named ''official sponsor'' of the event or putting a logo on a car that may or may not be seen on television.

Sponsorships can be squandered, or simply lost in the shuffle as consumers struggle to remember exactly who sponsored what. A survey taken after the 1992 Winter Olympics found that 30 percent of consumers said that American Express Co. was an official sponsor, which came as a surprise to Visa USA Inc., which had paid more than $20 million for that title at both the Winter and Summer Olympics.

According to marketing experts, failed sponsorships result from two mistakes: assuming that sponsorship visibility at the event results in sales, and treating the event as a short-term media buying opportunity rather than the start of a long term connection between product, consumer, and event.

Putting the logo on a car and erecting a giant balloon in the shape of the product do not necessarily generate sales. Again pointing to racing for proven successes, most of the top sponsored teams use a variety of marketing opportunities that only start with the race car on the track. Most teams have a "show car," a car outfitted and painted the same as the real race car. The show car visits shopping centers so fans can see and touch it. The driver sometimes accompanies it so fans can get autographs. Some teams develop specialty products tied to the racing. Countrytime Lemonade, which fields a NASCAR team, developed a series of canned lemonade mixes featuring the pictures of race drivers. These products became collectibles, as did the Kellogg's Corn Flakes box featuring its NASCAR driver.

Sponsor PR people work to get local press interested in profiling team members, particularly drivers. Sponsors may stage special contests such as pitting consumers against drivers. In 1994 the winner of the Daytona 500 competed in a lawnmower race against a grandmother. Somehow, the professional driver lost the race but the lawnmower company's products were seen on TV.

A growing number of companies are using sponsorships to entertain customers and sales forces. At every major event from golf to racing there will be sections set aside for tents where VIPs are treated to food and a place to get out of the sun. Some companies carry the incentives to another level, using the chance at perks to boost sales. John Hancock Mutual Life Insurance Co. boosted its 1994 quota for its sales staff by 20%. The prize for anyone making it was a free trip to the Winter Olympics in Lillehammer, Norway, where the company, an official sponsor, would fete them.

CAUSE MARKETING

The newest form of corporate sponsorship is cause marketing, building a sales campaign around identified public interests that benefit from corporate donations if the campaign is successful. Cause marketing first got widespread corporate attention in the 1980's when American Express headed a drive to restore the Statue of Liberty. According to research, corporations spent nearly $1 billion on cause marketing in 1993, up 24% over 1992 and 151% from 1990. Campaigns can be whatever captures the corporation's attention and could have nothing to do with product. Sears Roebuck & Co. has sponsored Phil Collins in a concert tour to raise money for the homeless. Kraft General Foods Inc. has issued coupons

good for money off on Stove Top Stuffing with a portion of the profits' going to college scholarships for African-Americans.

Consumers are not so sure if they really support cause marketing. A Roper Starch Worldwide survey in 1993 found 66 percent of people surveyed said they would switch brands if the purchase supported a cause that concerned them. On the downside, the same survey also found 58 percent of the people said cause marketing is just a way to improve the corporation's image. Only 12 percent said a cause was the most important factor in purchasing decisions. The most important factors in making a purchase were the same ones that have always been important: experience with the brand (71 percent), price (62 percent), company's reputation for quality (56 percent), and word of mouth recommendations (31 percent).

THE KEYS TO SUCCESSFUL SPONSORSHIPS

The following tips are offered by corporate marketers as being necessary to generate sales from corporate sponsorships.

The company must be able to afford to go beyond the entry fee of sponsorship. Count on spending up to three dollars in marketing support for every dollar spent in direct sponsorship.

Company products must be compatible with the image of the event being sponsored. Hanes, which makes sweat clothes, is not likely to sponsor a Harley Davidson rally where leather is the clothing of choice.

The people who come to the event must be the right target market. A company that makes male hair coloring with a target market of well-to-to older men concerned with their appearance could not find a more targeted market than the fans of the Seniors Golf Championship. The Seniors tour does not even allow professional golfers to compete until they are over the age of 50. Lowe's Home Centers, which tell men and women they can undertake most home projects themselves, could not ask for a more perfect, captured market than the six million middle-aged, middle-income people who attended NASCAR events in 1994.

Sponsorships should not be short-term handouts of money. They have to be long term relationships that build each year so the public begins to associate sponsor with event. It is a "background association" that transcends advertising. Only long term race fans even remember NASCAR's old "Grand National" championship. "Winston Cup" championship sounds natural.

Sponsorships should generate news coverage and publicity. Sponsoring the CEO's passion for a tournament for stud poker will not generate the same attention from television and the sports pages as being the sponsor for a major auto race.

New business opportunities should be a consideration. The McDonald's sponsors race cars on both the NASCAR and National Hot Rod Association circuits. One wonders if corporate officials have possibly asked sanctioning officials about the future possibilities of selling hamburgers to the millions of race fans who attend those events each year.

Employees should feel connected to the sponsorship. They cannot view the sponsorship as just another management perk that does not benefit them. Some companies send their employees to sponsored events as sales and service incentives.

Consider whether line managers support the sponsorship. It does no good to buy millions of dollars worth of sponsorship if the sales force is not out selling the tie-in to customers.

How far can sponsorships go? Corporate sponsors may one day find out by pushing the envelope. Led by CBS Inc., which was stung by losing NFL football to the Fox network, a number of companies spent 1993 investigating the idea of starting an advertiser-owned league of its own. Individual advertisers would own football teams, which would play in advertising-bedecked stadiums with only advertiser/owner commercials being allowed during the game. The team uniforms would feature decals promoting their corporate owners and may even adopt team names of the sponsors. Imagine, for example, The McDonald Big Macs versus The Coca Cola Bottlers in the Sears SuperGame playing in the Sony Surround-Sound Bowl.

[Clint Johnson]

FURTHER READING:

Barr, John. "Maximizing The Value of Sponsorships," *Public Relations Journal*. April 1993, pp. 30-31.

Brynes, Nanette. "Rolling Billboards," *FW*. April 12, 1994, pp. 47-56.

Kate, Nancy Ten. "Make It An Event," *American Demographics*. November 1992, pp. 40-44.

CORPORATE WELFARE

Corporate welfare is an unofficial term used to describe government **subsidies** and tax breaks that support American businesses and industries. The term, which is usually used in a derogatory manner, implies that these subsidies are equivalent to the government assistance, or welfare, provided to poor persons. It is also sometimes called "corporate pork." According to a report released by the Cato Institute and quoted in the *New York Times*, 127 separate government programs existed to give subsidies to particular companies or industries in 1994. These programs were expected to provide $86.2 billion in subsidies in 1995, while tax breaks were anticipated to raise the total to over $100 billion—a figure equivalent to half of the federal budget deficit.

Some programs currently termed corporate welfare were initiated to address a specific societal need. For example, the Rural Electrification Administration (REA) began receiving federal funds in 1949 to provide electricity and telephone services to the nation's rural farmers. However, loopholes, oversights, intense lobbying efforts, and corporate greed turned some of the programs into expensive and embarrassing examples of government waste. The REA program has come under fire in recent years for using $2 billion in government-subsidized loans to enable large, wealthy companies to provide the electricity for such things as lighting the strip in Las Vegas or running the ski lifts in Aspen. By 1995, analysts across the political spectrum—from liberal Democrat Labor Secretary Robert Reich to conservative Republican leaders of Congress-had identified corporate welfare as the last large source of funds available for federal budget cuts. "Lawmakers just about have to clip corporate goodies if they're serious about balancing the budget," Howard Gleckman explained in an editorial for *Business Week*. Adding to the urgency of the situation was a growing sense of moral outrage among many American citizens. Just as lawmakers cut funding for a variety of social programs that benefitted taxpayers, the media publicized numerous examples of wealthy corporations using taxpayer money for their own benefit.

Most outlays considered to be corporate welfare can be classified into six major categories. Agricultural programs received $31.3 billion in subsidies and an additional $2.9 billion in tax breaks in 1994. The largest portion of these payments took the form of price supports for various crops. Energy programs received $15.3 billion in subsidies and $21.1 billion in tax breaks. A special deduction for **capital costs** accounted for a major segment of these figures. Another $30.6 billion in subsidies went to transportation programs, with the largest portion supporting airline user fees. Aerospace and other high-technology industries received $16.7 billion in subsidies, with efforts to build a space station accounting for a big chunk of payments. Construction programs received $17.4 billion in tax breaks, largely due to an allowance for rapid **depreciation** of rental properties. Finally, miscellaneous programs—which included financial services and natural resources programs—received $42.3 billion in subsidies along with $60.4 billion in tax breaks. The largest portions of this category of corporate welfare went toward tax exemptions for companies operating in Puerto Rico and tax deductions for **advertising**.

CORPORATE WELFARE STIRS PUBLIC OUTRAGE

Supporters of federal aid to industry—mostly business leaders, lobbyists, and politicians representing industrial regions—argue that government support for certain strategic industries helps ensure the health of the American economy. They also claim that it protects high-paying jobs and keeps American industry competitive on a global scale. Others—ranging from taxpayers' and environmental groups to free-market economists and politicians intent on reducing the federal budget deficit—believe that much of this government aid has turned into corporate welfare. For example, opponents claim that federal aid often leads industries to become dependent and lose their competitive edge. According to *Reader's Digest,* corporate welfare also tends to corrupt the political process, since "some industries become trapped in a system where success is achieved not by ability to produce but by skill at political manipulation." Opponents also argue that corporate welfare increases final costs to consumers and diverts government resources from other, potentially more productive uses.

Another prominent argument against corporate welfare is that it tends to favor large, influential businesses over small, innovative competitors. For example, the U.S. government spends $100 million annually to support Sematech, a consortium of the 14 largest American producers of semiconductors. Sematech was originally formed when Japanese companies dominated the global semiconductor industry and many American firms had begun to flounder. Since chip technology was considered vital to national interests, the consortium was formed to facilitate technology exchange and help U.S. companies become more competitive in overseas markets. In recent years, however, Sematech has benefitted only the largest firms and has discouraged smaller ones, which may possess innovative new technologies, from entering the industry—thus threatening future U.S. competitiveness. As Gleckman stated, "Such government interference distorts markets and promotes established businesses over more creative start-ups with fewer political connections."

A similar example involves the $110 million annually that goes toward advertising certain American agricultural products overseas. The program was originally intended to help U.S. producers overcome trade barriers to entering foreign markets. As of 1990, however, producers no longer had to prove that they faced unfair trade practices in another country in order to use federal subsidies to advertise there. Furthermore, the funds were distributed unevenly and went almost exclusively to large companies. As Stephen Moore explained in a *New York Times* editorial, "tens of thousands of businesses export products abroad;

perhaps one percent receive federal assistance." Two further arguments against corporate welfare are that the government has a relatively poor record in identifying and supporting the important companies and industries of the future, and that subsidies may actually be harmful to the economy because they often disguise significant problems in troubled companies.

In the mid-1990s, as lawmakers continue to pare social programs in an attempt to get the budget deficit under control, the business and popular press has abounded with stories detailing abuses of corporate welfare. This publicity has centered around the ability and willingness of many large businesses to manipulate the system and use taxpayer money for their own gain. For example, environmental groups have focused on reducing the money the government spends ($140 million in 1994) to build roads in national forests to make it easier for forest products companies to cut down and remove trees, as well as subsidies to large farm owners for using water for irrigation or for grazing animals on public lands. Taxpayers' groups have targeted the $33 million in annual price supports on **commodities** like sugar. The government restricts sugar imports in order to keep the prices artificially high for U.S. producers, which opponents argue acts like a regressive tax and harms poor people the most. Others have objected to the $19.7 billion in tax breaks that companies, including many large pharmaceutical manufacturers, receive for operating in Puerto Rico. As public pressure mounts, lawmakers have proposed various plans for capping outlays or significantly reducing payments in several categories of aid that have been termed corporate welfare.

[Laurie Collier Hillstrom]

FURTHER READING:

Dennis, Richard J. "Privilege and Poverty," *Reason.* April 1993, p. 29.

Donlan, Thomas G. "The Big Handouts: Corporate Welfare Impoverishes the Productive Economy," *Barron's.* March 27, 1995, p. 50.

Gleckman, Howard. "Welfare Cuts: Now, It's Corporate America's Turn," *Business Week.* April 10, 1995, p. 37.

Hershey, Robert D., Jr. "A Hard Look at Corporate 'Welfare,'" *New York Times.* March 7, 1995, p. C1.

Ingersoll, Bruce, Carolyn Lochhead, Charles McCoy, and Doug Turetsky. "Do We Really Need Corporate Welfare?," *Reader's Digest.* March 1992, p. 70.

Moore, Stephen. "How to Slash Corporate Welfare," *New York Times.* April 5, 1995, p. A25.

COST ACCOUNTING

Cost accounting is a subset of **accounting** that develops detailed information about costs as they re-

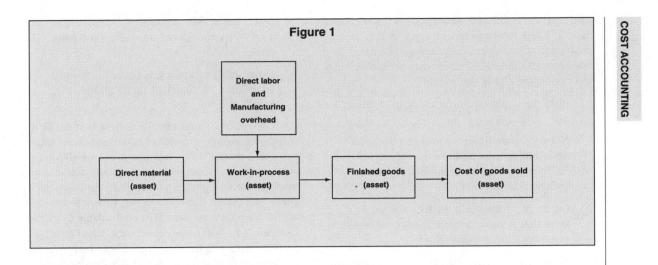

Figure 1

Direct labor and Manufacturing overhead

Direct material (asset) → Work-in-process (asset) → Finished goods (asset) → Cost of goods sold (asset)

late to units of output and to departments, primarily for purposes of providing inventory valuation (product costing) for **financial statements**, control, and **decision making**.

Manufacturing costs flow through three basic responsibility centers: the raw materials storeroom, the factory, and the finished good storeroom. These inventory accounts are usually provided to accumulate costs as they relate to the three responsibility centers: raw material inventory, work-in-process inventory, and finished good inventory. When goods are sold, costs are transferred from the finished goods inventory account to the cost of goods sold account. The flow of costs through the manufacturing process is illustrated in Figure 1.

TYPES OF COST SYSTEMS

Either job-order cost system or a process cost system is used to assign costs to manufactured products for purposes of controlling costs and costing products. A job-order cost system accumulates costs of material, labor, and manufacturing overhead by specific orders, jobs, batches, or lots. Job-order cost systems are widely used in construction, furniture, aircraft, printing, and similar industries where the costs of a specific job depend on the particular order specification.

A process cost system accumulates costs by processes or departments over a period of time. Process cost systems are used by firms that manufacture products through continuous-flow systems or on a mass-production basis. Industries that use process cost systems include chemicals, petroleum products, textiles, cement, glass, mining, and many others. In a process cost system, costs for a department or process are accumulated. Per-unit costs are obtained by dividing the total departmental costs by the quantity produced during a given period in the department or process.

MANUFACTURING COSTS

Manufacturing costs include direct material, direct labor, and manufacturing overhead costs. Direct material and direct labor costs can usually be traced directly to particular units manufactured. Manufacturing overhead costs incurred during a period are usually allocated to units manufactured based on a predetermined overhead rate. This overhead rate is based on the budgeted overhead costs for the period and the estimated level of activity (for example, units produced, direct labor hours, direct labor costs). The predetermined factory overhead rate per direct labor hour would be computed as shown below (using assumed data):

$$\frac{\text{Predetermined}}{\text{Overhead rate}} = \frac{\text{Estimated overhead for the year}}{\text{Estimated direct labor hours for the year}}$$
$$= \frac{\$500,000}{100,000}$$
$$= \$5 \text{ per direct labor hour}$$

If 400 direct labor hours were worked on a particular job, $2,000 (400 × $5) in overhead costs would be assigned to that job. Any difference between the total overhead costs actually incurred during a year and the total amount assigned to units in production can be charged to cost of goods sold for the year if the amount is not material. If material, the variance can be distributed among the work-in-process inventory, finished goods inventory, and cost of goods sold.

STANDARD COSTS SYSTEMS

Standard cost systems are widely used for **budgeting** and performance evaluation purposes in both job-order and process cost systems. Standard costs are predetermined target costs, and are used to assist in the budget process, identify trouble areas, and evaluate performance. In a standard cost system, product costing is achieved by using predetermined standard costs for material, direct labor, and overhead. Standard costs are developed on the basis of historical cost data adjusted for expected changes in the product, production techniques, engineering estimates, and other considerations. Standards may be established at any one of the following levels:

1. Ideal standards are set for the level of maximum efficiency.

2. Normal standards are set to reflect the conditions that are expected to exist over a period sufficient to take into consideration seasonal and cyclical fluctuations.

3. Currently attainable standards are set at a level that represents anticipated conditions assuming efficient operations.

Because predetermined standards usually differ from actual costs incurred, a variance typically exists. An unfavorable variance results when actual cost exceeds standard cost; a favorable variance results when standard cost exceeds actual cost. The usual approach followed in standard cost analysis is to separate price factors from efficiency factors. When the actual amount paid differs from the standard amount, the variance is referred to as a price, rate, or spending variance. When the actual input quantity (e.g., tons, labor hours) differs from the standard input quantity, the variance is referred to as a quantity, volume, or yield variance. The relationships between actual and standard price/quantity are illustrated in the diagram in Figure 2. The diagram shows two types of prices and quantities: actual and standard. A price variance is conceptualized as the difference between quadrant 1 and 2. A quantity variance is reflected in the difference between quadrants 2 and 4.

Figure 2

	ACTUAL PRICE	STANDARD PRICE
Actual Quantity	Actual quantity at actual price *Quadrant 1*	Actual quantity at standard price *Quadrant 2*
Standard Quantity	Standard quantity at actual price *Quadrant 3*	Standard quantity at standard price *Quadrant 4*

The formulas for typical direct material and direct labor variances include the following:

1. Direct material price variance = Actual quantities purchased × (Actual price − Standard price).

2. Material quantity (usage, efficiency) variance = (Actual quantity used − Standard quantity allowed) × Standard price.

3. Direct labor rate variance = Actual hours used × (Actual labor rate − Standard labor rate).

4. Direct labor efficiency variance = (Actual hours used − Standard hours allowed) × Standard labor rate.

Controlling overhead costs is usually more difficult than controlling direct material and direct labor costs because it is difficult to assign responsibility for overhead costs incurred. A general approach to controlling overhead costs involves computing two variances: the controllable overhead variance and the overhead volume variance. The controllable overhead variance is the difference between the actual overhead costs incurred and the factory overhead budgeted for the level of production achieved. This variance measures the difference between the overhead costs actually incurred and the costs that should have been incurred at the level of output attained. The overhead volume (or usage) variance is the difference between the factor overhead budgeted for the level of production achieved and the overhead applied to production using the standard overhead rate. A volume variance arises if more or less plant capacity than normal is actually used. When the expected capacity usage is exceeded, the overhead volume variance is favorable.

Variances should be analyzed if the cost of doing so does not exceed the benefits that can be expected from the analysis. If the variances are to be analyzed, they should be examined to find their causes. At this point, it should be determined what action should be taken, if any.

JUST-IN-TIME COSTING

Just-in-time costing is used in manufacturing whereby each unit of product is produced only upon request or requisition. This can result in the maintenance of minimal inventory levels of finished goods, work-in-process, and raw material. When JIT costing is used as a costing system, material cost and work-in-process costs are combined into a single "resources in process" account. Direct labor and overhead are also combined into a conversion cost account.

ACTIVITY-BASED COSTING

Activity-based costing (ABC) is a recent development in cost accounting. Under ABC, overhead costs are allocated to products on the basis of the resources consumed in each activity relating to the design, production, and distribution of particular products. Costs are assigned to homogeneous cost pools that represent specific activities. The allocation of these costs to products is accomplished through appropriate cost drivers. Cost drivers are transaction-related and volume-related, which represent the causes of costs incurred in specific activities. This is illustrated in this table.

Activity-Based Costing

Activity	Cost driver
Repairs, maintenance	Repair hours or machine hours
Cafeteria	Number of employees
Material handling	Pounds of material moved
	Number of materials moved
Personnel management	Number of employees served
Warehouse activities	Pounds or crates handled
Delivery of products	Miles driven
	Number of products
Order entry	Orders processed
	Number of customers
	Number of products
Billings	Lines typed or bills processed
Selling costs	Units sold or sales in dollars
Administrative costs	Units sold or sales in dollars
Receiving department	Number of shipments received
Disbursing	Number of checks issued
Machining	Number of machine hours
Purchase of material	Number of purchase transactions

JOINT PRODUCTS AND BY PRODUCTS

Joint costs are costs of simultaneously producing or acquiring two or more products that are produced or acquired together. Joint products resulting from the single-production process usually require further processing. Typically, none of the joint products have a relative value of such a size that it can be designated a major product. Joint products have common costs incurred before the split-off point. The split-off point is the point of production when the joint products can be identified and removed from the common process.

By-products are those products emerging at the split-off point that have minor sales value as compared with those of the major products. In many operations, by-products are the same as scrap. By-products frequently are not allocated to any of the total joint costs incurred in the process. If additional costs incurred after the split-off to further process the by-products, these costs are usually assigned to the by-product.

COST OF GOODS MANUFACTURED STATEMENT

A cost of goods manufactured statement summarizes the manufacturing activities of a period. The statement is illustrated in Figure 3.

COSTS

Costs are expenditures (decreases in assets or increases in liabilities) made to obtain economic benefit, usually resources that can produce revenues. Cost can also be defined as sacrifices made to acquire a good or service. Used in this sense, a cost represents an asset. An expense is a cost that has been used by the company in the process of obtaining revenue, i.e., the benefits associated with the good or service have expired. Costs can be classified in many ways including:

1. Direct and indirect costs:
   - Direct costs are outlays that can be identified with a specific product, department, or activity. For example, the cost of material and labor that are identifiable with a particular physical product are direct costs for the product.
   - Indirect costs are those outlays that cannot be identified with a specific product, department, or activity. Taxes, insurance, and telephone expense are common examples of indirect costs.

2. Product and period costs:
   - Product costs are outlays that can be associated with production. For example, the direct costs of materials and labor used in the production of an item are product costs.
   - Period costs are expenditures that are not directly associated with production, but are associated with the passage of a time period. The president's salary, advertising expense, interest, and rent expenses are examples of period costs.

3. Fixed, variable, and mixed costs:
   - Fixed costs are costs that remain constant in total (not per unit) regardless of the volume of production or sales, over a relevant range of production or sales. Rent and **depreciation** are typically fixed costs.
   - Variable costs are costs that fluctuate in total (not per unit) as volume of production or sales fluctuates. Direct labor and direct material costs used in production and sales commissions are examples of variable costs.
   - Mixed costs are costs that fluctuate with production or sale, but not directly in pro-

XYZ Company
Cost of Goods Manufactured Statement
Year Ended December 31, 19x

Direct material		$500,000
Direct labor		75,000
Factory overhead:		
Indirect labor	$15,000	
Supplies	5,000	
Utilities	20,000	
Depreciation	25,000	
Other	5,000	70,000
Manufacturing costs incurred, 19x		645,000
Add work-in-process inventory, Jan1		55,000
Manufacturing costs to account for		700,000
Deduct work-in-process inventory, Dec 31		10,000
Cost of goods manufactured (completed)		$690,000

Figure 3

portion to production or sales. Mixed costs contain elements of fixed and variable costs. Costs of supervision and inspection are usually mixed costs.

4. Controllable and uncontrollable costs:

- Controllable costs are costs that are identified as a responsibility of an individual or department, and that can be regulated within a given period. Office supplies would ordinarily be considered controllable costs for an office manager.

- Uncontrollable costs are those costs that cannot be regulated by an individual or department within a given period. For example, rent expense is an uncontrollable cost for the factory manager.

5. Out-of-pocket costs and sunk costs:

- Out-of-pocket costs are costs that require the use of current economic resources. Taxes and insurance are out-of-pocket costs.

- Sunk costs are outlays or commitments that have already been incurred. The cost of equipment already purchased is a sunk cost.

6. Incremental, opportunity, and imputed costs:

- Incremental cost (or differential cost) cost is the difference in total costs between alternatives.

- Opportunity cost is the maximum alternative benefit that could be obtained if economic resources were applied to an alternative use.

- Imputed costs are costs that can be associated with an economic event when no exchange transaction has occurred.

7. Relevant cost is an expected future cost and a cost that represents difference in costs among alternatives.

[Charles Woelfel]

FURTHER READING:

Polimeni, Ralph S. *Cost Accounting: Concepts and Managerial Applications.* New York: McGraw-Hill, Inc., 1991.

Horngren, C. T., and G. Foster. *Cost Accounting: A Managerial Emphasis.* 8th ed. Englewood Cliffs, NJ: Prentice-Hall, 1994.

COST BENEFIT ANALYSIS

Cost benefit analysis is, as its name suggests, the exercise of evaluating an action's consequences whereby the pluses are weighed against the minuses. It is the fundamental assessment behind virtually every business decision, and stems from the simple fact that business managers do not spend money unless the resulting benefits are expected to exceed the cost. Managers are generally rational decision makers, and the net economic outcome of a decision is a critical element considered.

Although its name seems deceptively simple, there is often a degree of complexity, and subjectivity, to the actual implementation of cost benefit analysis. This is because not all costs or benefits are obvious at first. Take for example the situation where a company is trying to decide if it should make or buy a certain subcomponent of a larger assembly it manufactures. A quick review of the cost accounting numbers may suggest that the cost to manufacture of $5 per piece can easily be beat by an outside vendor who will sell it to the company for only $4; apparently an easy decision. Other factors that need to be considered and quantified (if possible) include:

1. When a subcomponent's **manufacturing** is contracted to an outside vendor, the company's own factory will become less utilized, and therefore its fixed overhead costs have less components over which to be spread. As a result, other parts it continues to manufacture may show an increase in costs, consuming some or possibly all of the apparent gain. (Note: one way to avoid this particular problem is to derive the internal cost of manufacturing on an incremental basis; that way no fixed cost effect will be caused by the change in factory utilization.)

2. The labor force may be concerned about outsourcing of work to which they feel an entitlement. Resulting morale problems and labor unrest could quickly cost the company far more than it expected to save.

3. Loss of control must be weighed. Once the part is out-sourced, the company no longer has direct control over the quality, timeliness, or **reliability** of the product delivered.

4. Unforeseen benefits may be attained. For example, the newly freed factory space may be deployed in a more productive manner, making more of the main assembly or even another product altogether.

This list is not meant to be comprehensive, but rather illustrative of the ripple effect that occurs in real business decision settings. The cost benefit analyst needs to be cognizant of the subtle interactions of other events with the action under consideration in order to fully evaluate the impact.

Capital budgeting has at its core the tool of cost benefit analysis; it merely extends the basic form into a multi-period analysis, with consideration of the time value of money. In this context, a new product, venture, or investment is evaluated on a start-to-finish basis, with care taken to capture all the impacts on both the cost and benefits. When these inputs and outputs are quantified, by year, they can then be dis-

counted to present value to determine the net present value at the time of the decision.

[Christopher Barry]

FURTHER READING:

Brealey, Richard A. and Stewart C. Myers. *Principles of Corporate Finance*, 4th ed. McGraw-Hill, 1991.

Horngren, Charles T. and Gary L. Sundem. *Introduction to Management Accounting*. Prentice-Hall, 1990.

COST CONTROL

A complex business requires frequent information about operations in order to plan for the future, to control present activities, and to evaluate the past performance of managers, employees, and related business segments. To be successful, management guides the activities of its people in the operations of the business according to pre-established goals and objectives. Management's guidance takes two forms of control: 1) the management and supervision of behavior, and 2) the evaluation of performance.

Behavioral management deals with the attitudes and actions of employees. While employee behavior ultimately impacts on success, behavioral management involves certain issues and assumptions not applicable to accounting's control function. On the other hand, performance evaluation measures outcomes of employee's actions by comparing the actual results of business outcomes to pre-determined standards of success. In this way management identifies the strengths it needs to maximize, and its weaknesses which it seeks to rectify. This process of evaluation and remedy is called *cost control*.

Cost control is a continuous process that begins with the proposed annual budget. The budget helps to: a) organize and to coordinate production, and the selling, distribution, service, and administrative functions, and b) to take maximum advantage of available opportunities. As the fiscal year progresses, management compares actual results to those projected in the budget and incorporates into the new plan the lessons learned from its evaluation of current operations.

Control refers to management's effort to influence the actions of individuals who are responsible for performing tasks, incurring costs, and generating revenues. Management is a two-phased process in that *planning* refers to the way that management plans and wants people to perform, while *control* refers to the procedures employed to determine whether actual performance complies with these plans. Through the budget process and accounting control, management establishes overall company objectives, defines the centers of responsibility, determines specific objectives for each responsibility center, and designs procedures and standards for reporting and evaluation.

A budget segments the business into its components or centers where the responsible party initiates and controls action. *Responsibility centers* represent applicable organizational units, functions, departments, and divisions. Generally a single individual heads the responsibility center exercising substantial, if not complete, control over the activities of people or processes within the center and controlling the results of their activity. *Cost centers* are accountable only for expenses. *Revenue centers* primarily generate revenues. *Profit centers* accept responsibility for both revenue and expenses. The use of responsibility centers allows management to design control reports to pinpoint accountability, thus aiding in profit planning.

A budget also sets standards to indicate the level of activity expected from each responsible person or decision unit, and the amount of resources that a responsible party should use in achieving that level of activity. A budget establishes the responsibility center, delegates the concomitant responsibilities, and determines the decision points within an organization.

The planning process, then, provides for two types of control mechanisms:

Feedforward: providing a basis for control at the point of action (the decision point); and

Feedback: providing a basis for measuring the effectiveness of control after implementation.

Management's role is to *feedforward* a futuristic vision of where the company is going and how it is to get there, and to make clear decisions coordinating and directing employee activities. Management also oversees the development of procedures to collect, record, and evaluate *feedback*. Therefore, effective management controls results from leading people by force of personality and through persuasion; providing and maintaining proper training, planning, and resources; and improving quality and results through evaluation and feedback.

CONTROL REPORTS

Control reports are informational reports that tell management about an entity's activities. Management requests control reports only for internal use, and, therefore, directs the accounting department to develop tailor-made reporting formats. Accounting provides management with a format designed to detect variations that need investigating. In addition, management also refers to conventional reports such as the income statement and funds statement, and external reports on the general economy and the specific industry.

Control reports, then, need to provide an adequate amount of information so that management may determine the reasons for any cost variances from the original budget. A good control report highlights significant information by focusing management's attention on those items in which actual performance significantly differs from the standard.

Because key success factors shift in type and number, accounting revises control reports when necessary. Accounting also varies the control period covered by the control report to encompass a period in which management can take useful remedial action. In addition, accounting disseminates control reports in a timely fashion to give management adequate time to act before the issuance of the next report.

Managers perform effectively when they attain the goals and objectives set by the budget. With respect to profits, managers succeed by the degree to which revenues continually exceed expenses. In applying the following simple formula,

$$\text{Net Profit} = \text{Revenue} - \text{Expenses}$$

managers, especially those in operations, realize that they exercise more control over expenses than they do over revenue. While they cannot predict the timing and volume of actual sales, they can determine the utilization rate of most of their resources, that is, they can influence the cost side. Hence, the evaluation of management's performance and its operations is cost control.

STANDARDS

For cost control purposes, a budget provides standard costs. As management constructs budgets, it lays out a road map to guide its efforts. It states a number of assumptions about the relationships and interaction among the economy, market dynamics, the abilities of its sales force, and its capacity to provide the proper quantity and quality of products demanded.

An examination of the details of the budget calculations and assumptions indicates that management expects the sales force to spend only so much in pursuit of the sales forecast. The details also reveal that management expects operations to produce the required amount of units within a certain cost range. Management bases its expectations and projections on the best historical and current information, as well as its best business judgment.

When calculating budget expenses, management's review of the historic and current data might strongly suggest that the production of 1,000 units of a certain luxury item will cost $100,000, or $100 per unit. In addition, management also determines that the sales force will expend about $80,000 to sell the 1,000 units. This is a sales expenditure of $80. With total

Table 1
Comparison of Actual and Standard Costs

	Projected		Actual		
	Total	Per Unit	Units Sold	Month	Projected —Actual
Units	1,000	1.00	100.00	100.00	0.00
Gross Revenues	$500,00	$500	$50,000	$50,000	0
Expenses	$180,000	$180	$18,000	$19,000	-1,000
Sales Expense	$80,000	$80	$8,000	$7,000	1,000
Production Expense	$1000,000	$100	$100,00	$12,000	-2000.00
					Total Variance = -2000

expenditures of $180, management sets the selling price of $500 for this luxury item.

At the close of a month, management compares the actual results of that month to the standard costs to determine the degree and direction of any variance. The purpose for analyzing variances is to identify areas where costs need containment.

In Table 1 above, accounting indicates to management that the sales force sold 100 units for a gross revenue of $50,000. Accounting's data also shows that the sales force spent $7,000 that month, and that production incurred $12,000 in expenses. Table 1 summarizes, in a simple format, the data that management reviews to identify variances. While revenue was on target, actual sales expense came in less than the projected, with a per unit cost of $70. This is a *favorable* variance. Production expenses registered an *unfavorable* variance since actual expenditures exceeded the projected. The company produced units at $120 per item, $20 more than projected. This variance of 20% significantly differs from the standard costs of $100 and would call management to action if the variance exceeded acceptable levels (levels that were established before manufacturing began).

THE ROLE OF ACCOUNTING

Accounting plays a key role in all planning and control. It does this in four key areas:

DATA COLLECTION. Accounting is at the heart of control because it compiles records of the costs and benefits of the company's activities in considerable detail, establishes a historical basis upon which to base forecasts, and calculates performance measures.

DATA ANALYSIS. Accounting's specialty is in the control function, yet its analysis is indispensable to the planning process. Accounting adjusts and interprets the data to allow for changes in company specific, industry specific, and economy-wide conditions.

BUDGET AND CONTROL ADMINISTRATION. The accountants play a key role in designing and securing support for the procedural aspects of the planning process. In addition, they design and distribute forms for the collection and booking of detailed data on all aspects of the business.

CONSOLIDATION AND REVIEW. Although operating managers have the main responsibility of planning, accounting compiles and coordinates the elements. Accountants subject proposed budgets to feasibility and profitability analyses to determine conformity to accepted standards and practices.

SUMMARY

Control of the business entity, then, is essentially a managerial and supervisory function. Control consists of those actions necessary to assure that the entity's resources and operations are focused on attaining established objectives, goals and plans. Control, exercised continuously, flags potential problems so that crises may be prevented. It also standardizes the quality and quantity of output, and provides managers with objective information about employee performance. Management compares actual performance to predetermined standards and takes action when necessary to correct variances from the standards.

SEE ALSO: Costs; Cost Accounting; Managerial Accounting

[Roger J. AbiNader]

FURTHER READING:

Ameiss, Albert P., and Nicholas A. Kargas, *Accountant's Desk Handbook*. Prentice-Hall, Inc., 1977.

Dopuch, Nicholas, Jacob G. Birnberg, and Joel Demski. *Cost Accounting: Accounting Data for Management's Decisions*. Harcourt Brace Jovanovich, Inc., 1974.

Meigs, Robert F., and Walter B. Meigs, *Accounting: The Basis for Business Decisions*, 8th ed. McGraw-Hill Publishing Company, 1990.

Neuner, John J., and Edward B. Deakin, *Cost Accounting: Principles and Practices*. Richard D. Irwin, Inc., 1977.

COSTING METHODS (MANUFACTURING)

Accounting methods are comprised of a set of procedures and guidelines for recording, classifying, and reporting the financial results of a business entity. Costing methods are often referred to as **cost**s or managerial accounting and focus primarily on activities within a firm's production facilities. One of the central concerns of costing methods is the determination of cost and profitability in response to changing levels of production. Costing methods thus enable firms to determine the comparative efficiency of their various plants and operations and also to estimate profitability based on projected sales.

HISTORY OF COSTING METHODS

Double-entry **bookkeeping**, developed in Northern Italy in the fourteenth and fifteenth centuries, was the predecessor to modern accounting methods. Modern methods were developed in the United States in the 1850s and 1860s by accountants in the railroad industry. These methods were just one of several innovations originating with the railroads that marked the transition from traditional to modern business enterprise. Most important were the developments of J. Edgar Thomson and his cohorts at the Pennsylvania Railroad. The work of these and other pioneering accountants in the railroad industry was the subject of widespread public discussion and numerous articles in the new financial journals of the day.

Cost accounting was one of three interrelated types of accounting developed at the time, the others being financial and capital accounting. Financial accounting addressed issues relating to a firm's daily financial transactions as well as overall profitability. For example, railroads began deriving operating ratios

in the late-1850s, which for the first time related absolute quantities of profit and loss to business volume. Capital accounting addressed issues relating to the **valuation** of a firm's capital goods. This was particularly important in the railroad industry given the unprecedented quantities of capital involved and the problem of how to account for the repair and renewal of capital.

Innovations in cost accounting followed those in financial and capital accounting. Cost accounting involved the determination and comparison of costs among a firm's divisions or operations. Thus the historical development of cost accounting accommodated the development of the multidivisional firm towards the end of the nineteenth century. There was necessarily a considerable amount of overlap among financial, capital, and cost accounting. For example, to accurately determine unit costs, it was necessary to relate overhead costs and capital depreciation to the volume of production. At the same time, unit costs were typically used to determine prices, which in turn affected financial accounts. The separation of these types of accounting followed their historical institutional separation. That is, until the innovations of E.I. Du Pont de Nemours & Co. in the twentieth century, financial, capital, and cost accounting operations were carried out in relative autonomy within firms.

Cost accounting was first used by the Louisville & Nashville Railroad in the late-1860s. This enabled the company to determine such measures as comparative cost per ton-mile among its branches, and it was by these measures, rather than earnings or net **income**, that the company evaluated the performance of its managers. The accounting methods developed by the railroads were adopted by the first large **manufacturing** firms in the United States upon their formation in the last quarter of the nineteenthth century.

The largest U.S. manufacturing firms in the 1870s were textile producers. Because these years were a period of hardship for the industry, textile producers began to devote more attention to the determination and control of costs. By 1886, Lyman Mills, one of the country's largest textile producers, began to determine unit costs for its various products, though it did not use this information to make pricing or investment decisions. The Standard Oil Trust, formed in 1882, also began to determine the comparative costs of their different refineries in the 1880s and on this basis opted to concentrate production in their largest units. However, the enterprise did not accurately account for overhead or capital **depreciation** in its determination of costs.

The firm with the most detailed and sophisticated costing methods in the 1880s was the Carnegie Company, a steel producer. In this case, the connection between costing methods in the railroad and manufacturing industries was direct, as Andrew Carnegie patterned the organization of his firm after the Pennsylvania Railroad, where he had been an executive. Carnegie's costing method was referred to as the voucher system of accounting. In this system, each of the company's departments kept track of the quantity and price of materials and labor for each order. These data were aggregated into cost sheets that the company's accountants were able to produce on a daily basis. Though the Carnegie Company made extensive use of its cost sheets to determine prices, it focused on prime rather than overhead and depreciation costs.

It was in the early-1900s that firms came to systematically relate overhead costs to variations in the quantity of goods produced. Accountants began determining standard costs, based on a standard level of capacity utilization. The greater unit costs of running below standard capacity were defined as unabsorbed burden, whereas the lesser unit costs of running above standard capacity were defined as over-absorbed burden. Such methods of accounting for overhead were widely discussed in trade journals at the time.

It was not until later that modern methods of accounting for capital depreciation came into widespread use. Until then, manufacturing firms continued to use the renewal accounting methods borrowed from the railroads. That is, the repair and renewal of capital goods was charged to operating expenses and profits were determined as the difference between earnings and expenses. Firms did not determine changes in the value of capital resulting from depreciation, repair, and renewal, and thus profitability could not be determined as the ratio of profits to the value of capital.

Chemical producer Du Pont was among the first firms to integrate cost, capital, and financial accounting. This resulted in part from Du Pont's rejection of traditional renewal capital accounting in which profitability rates were typically determined in relation to sales or costs. Du Pont's accountants established careful records of changes in fixed capital, made up of plant and equipment, and **working capital**, made up of inventories, financial assets, and accounts receivable. By doing so, Du Pont was able to derive monthly reports on profitability as a return on capital invested. In his 1977 volume, *The Visible Hand*, Chandler described the critical role of Du Pont manager Donaldson Brown in accounting for stock turnover and thus contemporary calculations of profitability. He wrote: ''Brown . . . related turnover to earnings as a percentage of sales (still the standard definition of profit in American industry). He did this by multiplying turnover by profit so defined, which gave a rate of return that reflected the intensity with which the enterprise's resources were being used. This formula devised by Brown is still the method employed by the Du Pont Company and most other American business enterprises to define rate of return.''

THE BASICS OF COSTING METHODS

In cost accounting terminology, costs are distinguished from expenses. Costs refer to the valuation of assets used to purchase other assets; expenses refer to the valuation of assets used to generate revenues. In a cycle of manufacture and **marketing**, costs typically precede expenses. That is, today's labor and material costs used in the manufacture of a commodity become tomorrow's expenses upon the sale of that commodity. In other cases, such as the purchase of office supplies for a manufacturer's marketing operations on an as-needed basis, the temporal relation of costs and expenses is nearly simultaneous. Costs that do not eventually generate revenues are accounted for as losses, and only in such a case do costs not become expenses. Costing methods focus on costs rather than expenses.

One of the key issues in costing methods is distinguishing among types of costs. A basic distinction is made between fixed and variable costs. Fixed costs are those costs that are invariant with respect to changes in output and would accrue even if no output were produced. Such costs might include interest payments on the purchase of plant and equipment, rent, property taxes, and executive salaries. The notion of fixed costs is restricted within a certain time frame, since over the long run fixed costs can vary. For example, a manufacturer may decide to expand capacity in the face of increased demand for its product, requiring a higher level of expenditure on plant and equipment.

Variable costs change proportionately to the level of output. For manufacturers, a key variable cost is the cost of materials. In terms of total costs at increasing output levels, fixed costs are constant and variable costs increasing at a constant rate. In terms of unit costs at increasing output levels, fixed costs are declining, and variable costs constant. Manufacturers are vitally interested in unit costs with respect to changes in output levels, since this determines profit per unit of output at any given price level. The characteristics of fixed and variable costs indicates that as output increases, unit costs will decline, since there is constant variable cost and lesser fixed cost embodied in each unit. These costing methods thus suggest that it is in manufacturers' interest to run, within the limits of plant design, at high capacity levels.

Costing methods distinguish between the direct and indirect costs of any costed object. Direct costs are those costs readily traceable to the costed object whereas indirect costs are less-readily traceable. Direct costs typically include the major components of any manufactured good and the labor directly required to produce that good. Direct costs are often subdivided into direct material costs and direct labor costs. Direct costs are also referred to as prime costs.

Indirect costs include plant-wide costs such as those resulting from the use of energy and fixed capital, but indirect costs may also include the costs of minor components such as solder or glue. While all costs are conceivably traceable to a costed object, the determination of whether to do so depends on the cost-effectiveness with which this can be done. Indirect costs of all kinds are sometimes referred to as overhead, and in this sense prime costs can be distinguished from overhead costs.

ESTIMATING TOTAL COSTS

Several methods are used in manufacturing to estimate total cost equations, in which total costs are determined as a function of fixed costs per time period, variable costs per unit of output, and the level of output. These methods include account analysis, the engineering approach, the high-low approach, and linear regression analysis. In all these methods, the central issue is how total costs change in relation to changes in output.

In account analysis, all costs are classified as either strictly fixed or variable. This has the advantage of ease of computation. However, some costs may be semivariable costs or step costs. Utility bills are typically semivariable in that they contain fixed and variable components. Step costs increase in discrete jumps as the level of output increases. In account analysis, such costs are typically categorized as either fixed or variable depending what element predominates. Thus the accuracy of account analysis depends in large part on the proportion of costs that are not strictly fixed or variable. For many manufacturing firms, account analysis provides a sufficiently accurate estimation of total costs over a range of output levels.

The engineering approach infers costs from the specifications of a product. The approach works best for determining direct material costs and less well for direct labor costs and overhead costs. The advantage of the engineering approach is that it enables manufacturers to estimate what a product would cost without having previously produced that product, whereas the other methods are based on the costs of production that has already occurred.

In the high-low approach, a firm must know its total costs for previous high and low levels of output. Graphing total costs against output, total costs over a range of output are estimated by fitting a straight line through total cost points at high and low levels of output. If changes in total costs can be accurately described as a linear function of output, then the slope of the line indicates changes in variable costs. The problem with the high-low approach is that the two data points may not, for whatever reasons, accurately represent the underlying total cost-output relationship. That is, if additional total cost-output points were

plotted, they might lay significantly wide of the line connecting the two initial high-low points.

Linear regression analysis addresses the shortcomings of the high-low approach by fitting a line through all total cost-output points. The line is fitted to minimize the sum of squared differences between total cost-output points and the line itself, in standard linear regression fashion. The drawback of this approach is that it requires more data points than the other approaches.

STANDARD COSTS

The relation of total costs to output levels is combined in the idea of standard costs. Standard costs are estimates of unit costs at targeted output levels, including direct materials costs, direct labor costs, and indirect costs. Standard costs are used to prepare budgets for planned production and to assess production that has occurred. The estimation of standard costs requires the separate estimation of standards for direct materials, direct labor, and overhead.

Direct material standards are the easiest to estimate. Costs are determined from the prices of all necessary material inputs into the product, plus sales tax, shipping, and other related costs. Unanticipated price changes complicate this otherwise straightforward process. Since standard costs are a measure of unit costs, it is also necessary to determine the quantity of materials per unit. This can be done using an engineering approach.

Direct labor standards are somewhat more difficult to estimate. The determination of costs must account for wages, though if workers in a production process are earning different wages, it is necessary to estimate a weighted average of wage costs. The cost of benefits, **employment**-related taxes, and overtime pay must also be accounted for. As with direct material standards, the quantity of direct labor required to produce a unit of output can be estimated with an engineering approach. Average set-up time and downtime must also be included in the estimation. Many union **contracts** codify labor time standards, which can make **budgeting** easier.

Overhead standards are the most difficult to estimate, and they are typically accounted for in an approximate manner. The problem of accounting for overhead costs per unit of output was noted above—it is often difficult to trace indirect costs to a particular product. The problem is made more complicated if these costs are highly centralized within a plant and if multiple products are produced within a plant. Overhead standards are typically estimated by taking total overhead costs and relating them to a more readily-knowable measure, such as direct labor hours, direct labor costs, or machine hours used. Direct labor hours was traditionally the most widely-used measure for determining overhead standards, but the growth of automated plants resulted in a shift to machine hours used.

DETERMINING PROFITABILITY THROUGH CVP ANALYSIS

Cost equations are combined with revenue equations to determine profitability at different levels of output. This is referred to as cost volume profit (CVP) analysis. That is, *net income* equals total revenue minus total cost; *total cost*, as noted above, equals average variable cost times the quantity of output plus fixed cost; and *total revenue* equals price times the quantity of output sold. Combining cost and revenue equations reveals that *net income* equals price times quantity of output sold minus average variable cost times the quantity of output minus fixed costs. That is: *net income* = [(P*Q) − (AVC*Q) − FC], where P = price, Q = quantity of output, AVC = average variable cost, and FC = fixed costs. This is referred to as the cost-volume-profit equation, and is one of the most widely-used of cost accounting tools.

CVP analysis allows a firm to determine a break-even point, the level of output at which total revenue equals total cost. That total cost and total revenue functions will be equal at some nonzero level of output is assured by the fact that at zero units of output, total costs will be positive as a result of fixed costs and total revenues will be zero. This is based on the assumption that the unit price for which a product can be sold is greater than the unit cost, so that total revenue increases faster than total cost as output increases. In addition to estimating profitability across a range of output levels, firms use CVP analysis to determine whether projected sales are sufficiently beyond the breakeven point to warrant production.

Economic theory also concerns itself with changing costs as a function of changing output within a given plant. This is an analog to the slope of an accountant's cost function curve and is referred to as marginal cost. In his essay, "Economic Concepts in Cost Accounting," Shillinglaw describes the relationship between mainstream economic theory and cost accounting as follows: "Cost accounting springs mainly from the needs of managers and others to make decisions affecting the allocation of economic resources. This might suggest that cost accounting is based directly on a fairly well-defined set of concepts drawn from economic theory. The truth is something else.... The uneasy and ambiguous relationship between cost accounting and economics is nowhere more apparent than in the application of the concept of short-run marginal cost." In mainstream economic theory, marginal costs are generally assumed to be decreasing at lower levels of output, more or less flat over medium levels, and increasing at an accelerating rate at higher levels. As noted above, cost accountants generally base their calculations on the assumption that costs change at a constant rate with respect to output.

[David Kucera]

FURTHER READING:

Bartenstein, Edwin. "Different Costs for Different Purposes." *Management Accounting*. August 1978.

Bryant, Murray, and Mary Mahaney. "The Politics of Standard Setting." *Management Accounting*, March 1981.

Chandler, Alfred Jr. *The Visible Hand: The Managerial Revolution in American Business.* Belknap Press, 1977.

Dean, Joel. *Statistical Cost Estimation.* Indiana University Press, 1976.

Estes, Ralph. *Dictionary of Accounting.* The MIT Press, 1981.

Johnson, H. Thomas. "Toward a New Understanding of Nineteenth-Century Cost Accounting." *The Accounting Review.* July 1981.

Moriarity, Shane and Carl Allen. *Cost Accounting.* Harper & Row Publishers, 1987.

Parker, L.D. "Management Accounting and the Corporate Environment." *Management Accounting.* February, 1978.

Shillinglaw, Gordon. "Economic Concepts in Cost Accounting," in Sidney Davidson and Roman Weil (eds.), *Handbook of Cost Accounting.* McGraw-Hill Book Company, 1978.

Wiener, Julius. "Separation of Fixed and Variable Costs." *The Accounting Review.* October 1960.

COSTS

Costs are an integral part of doing business. Every factor of production has a cost associated with it: labor, fixed assets, and capital, for example. The cost of labor used in the production of goods and services is measured in terms of wages. The cost of a fixed asset used in production is measured in terms of depreciation. The cost of capital used to purchase fixed assets is measured in terms of a percentage equal to the interest expense associated with raising the capital needed to purchase the asset.

Businesses are vitally interested in measuring their costs. Many types of costs are observable and easily quantifiable. In such cases there is a direct relationship between cost of input and quantity of output. Other types of costs must be estimated or allocated. That is, the relationship between costs of input and units of output may not be directly observable or quantifiable. In the delivery of professional services, for example, the quality of the output is usually more significant that the quantity, and output cannot simply be measured in terms of the number of patients treated or students taught. In such instances where qualitative factors play an important role in measuring output, there is no direct relationship between costs incurred and output achieved.

DIFFERENT WAYS TO CATEGORIZE COSTS

Costs can have different relationships to output. Costs also are used in different business applications, such as financial accounting, cost accounting, budgeting, capital budgeting, and valuation. Consequently, there are different ways of categorizing costs according to their relationship to output as well as according to the context in which they are used. Following this summary of the different types of costs are some examples of how costs are used in different business applications.

FIXED AND VARIABLE COSTS. The two basic types of costs are fixed and variable. Fixed costs do not vary with output, while variable costs do. Fixed costs are sometimes called overhead costs. They are incurred whether a firm manufactures 100 widgets or 1,000 widgets. In preparing a budget, fixed costs may include rent, depreciation, and supervisors' salaries. Manufacturing overhead may include such items as property taxes and insurance. These fixed costs remain constant in spite of changes in output.

Variable costs, on the other hand, fluctuate in direct proportion to changes in output. Labor and material costs are typical variable costs that increase as the volume of production increases. It takes more labor and material to produce more output, so the cost of labor and material varies in direct proportion to the volume of output. The direct proportionality of variable costs to level of output may break down with very small and very large production runs.

In addition, some costs are considered mixed costs. That is, they contain elements of fixed and variable costs. In some cases the cost of supervision and inspection are considered mixed costs.

DIRECT AND INDIRECT COSTS. Direct costs are similar to variable costs. They can be directly attributed to the production of output. The system of valuing inventories called direct costing is also known as variable costing. Under this accounting system only those costs that vary directly with the volume of production are charged to products as they are manufactured. The value of inventory is the sum of direct material, direct labor, and all variable manufacturing costs.

Indirect costs, on the other hand, are similar to fixed costs. They are not directly related to the volume of output. Indirect costs in a manufacturing plant may include supervisors' salaries, indirect labor, factory supplies used, taxes, utilities, depreciation on building and equipment, factory rent, tools expense, and patent expense. These indirect costs are sometimes referred to as manufacturing overhead.

Under the accounting system known as full costing or absorption costing, all of the indirect costs in manufacturing overhead as well as direct costs are included in determining the cost of inventory. They are considered part of the cost of the products being manufactured.

PRODUCT AND PERIOD COSTS. The concepts of product and period costs are similar to direct and indirect costs. Product costs are those that the firm's accounting system associates directly with output and that are used to value inventory. Under a direct or variable costing accounting system, only direct or variable costs are charged to production. Indirect costs such as property taxes, insurance, depreciation on plant and equipment, and salaries of supervisors are considered period costs. Period costs are charged as expenses to the current period. Under direct costing, period costs are not viewed as costs of the products being manufactured, so they are not associated with valuing inventories.

If the firm uses a full costing accounting system, however, then all manufacturing costs—including fixed manufacturing overhead costs and variable costs—become product costs. They are considered part of the cost of manufacturing and are charged against inventory.

OTHER TYPES OF COSTS. These are the basic types of costs as they are used in different accounting systems. In addition other types of costs are used in different business contexts. In budgeting it is useful to identify controllable and uncontrollable costs. These simply mean that managers with budgetary responsibility should not be held accountable for costs they cannot control.

Financial managers often use the concepts of out-of-pocket costs and sunk costs when evaluating the financial merits of specific proposals. Out-of-pocket costs are those that require the use of current resources, usually cash. Sunk costs have already been incurred. In evaluating whether or not to increase production, for example, financial managers may take into account the sunk costs associated with tools and machinery as well as the out-of-pocket costs associated with adding more material and labor.

Financial planning also utilizes the concepts of incremental, opportunity, and imputed costs. Incremental costs are those associated with switching from one level of activity or course of action to another. Incremental costs represent the difference between two alternatives.

The sacrifice that is made when the means of production are used for one task rather than another, or when capital is used for one investment rather than another represents an opportunity costopportunity cost. Nothing can be produced or invested without incurring such a cost. By making one investment or production decision using limited resources, one necessarily forgoes the opportunity to use those resources for a different purpose. Consequently, opportunity costs are not usually factored into investment and production decisions involving resource allocation.

Imputed costs are costs that are not actually incurred, but are associated with internal transactions. When work in process is transferred from one department to another within an organization, a method of **transfer pricing** may be needed for budgetary reasons. Although there is no actual purchase or sale of goods and materials, the receiving department may be charged with imputed costs for the work it has received. When a company rents itself a building that is could have rented to an outside party, the rent may be considered an imputed cost.

BUSINESS APPLICATIONS USE DIFFERENT TYPES OF COSTS

Costs as a business concept are useful in measuring performance and determining profitability. What follows are brief discussions of some business applications in which costs play an important role.

FINANCIAL ACCOUNTING. One of the major objectives of financial accounting is to determine the periodic income of the business. In manufacturing firms a major component of the income statement is the cost of goods sold (COGS). COGS is that part of the cost of inventory that can be considered an expense of the period because the goods were sold. It appears as an expense on the firm's periodic income statement. COGS is calculated as beginning inventory plus net purchases minus ending inventory.

Depreciation is another cost that becomes a periodic expense on the income statement. Every asset is initially valued at its cost. Accountants charge the cost of the asset to depreciation expense over the useful life of the asset. This cost allocation approach attempts to match costs with revenues and is more reliable than attempting to periodically determine the fair market value of the asset.

In financial accounting, costs represent assets rather than expenses. Costs only become expenses when they are charged against current income. Costs may be allocated as expenses against income over time, as in the case of depreciation, or they may be charged as expenses when revenues are generated, as in the case of COGS.

COST ACCOUNTING. Cost accounting, also sometime known as management accounting, provides appropriate cost information for budgeting systems and management decision making. Using the principles of general accounting, cost accounting records and determines costs associated with various functions of the business. This data is used by management to improve operations and make them more efficient, economical, and profitable.

Two major systems can be used to record the costs of manufactured products. They are know as job costing and process costing. A job cost system, or job order cost system, collects costs for each physically identifiable job or batch of work as it moves through the manufacturing facility and disregards the accounting period in which the work is done. With a process cost system, on the other hand, costs are collected for all of the products worked on during a specific accounting period. Unit costs are then determined by dividing the total costs by the number of units worked on during the period. Process cost systems are most appropriate for continuous operations, when like products are produced, or when several departments cooperate and participate in one or more operations. Job costing, on the other hand, is used when labor is a chief element of cost, when diversified lines or unlike products are manufactured, or products are built to customer specifications.

When costs are easily observable and quantifiable, cost standards are usually developed. Also known as engineered standards, they are developed for each physical input at each step of the production process. At that point an engineered cost per unit of production can be determined. By documenting variable costs and fairly allocating fixed costs to different departments, a **cost accounting** system can provide management with the accountability and cost controls it needs to improve operations.

BUDGETING SYSTEMS. Budgeting systems rely on accurate cost accounting systems. Using cost data collected by the business's cost accounting system, budgets can be developed for each department at different levels of output. Different units within the business can be designated cost centers, profit centers, or departments. Budgets are then used as a management tool to measure performance, among other things. Performance is measured by the extent to which actual figures deviate from budgeted amounts.

In using budgets as measures of performance, it is important to distinguish between controllable and uncontrollable costs. Managers should not be held accountable for costs they cannot control. In the short run fixed costs can rarely be controlled. Consequently, a typical budget statement will show sales revenue as forecast and the associated variable costs with that level of production. The difference between sales revenue and variable costs is the contribution margin. Fixed costs are then deducted from the contribution margin to obtain a figure for operating income. Managers and departments are then evaluated on the basis of costs and those elements of production they are expected to control.

COST OF CAPITAL. Capital budgeting and other business decisions such as lease-buy decisions, bond refunding, and working capital policies require estimates of a company's cost of capital. Capital budgeting decisions revolve around deciding whether or not to purchase a particular capital asset. Such decisions are based on an estimate of the net present value of future revenues that would be generated by a particular capital asset. An important factor in such decisions is the company's cost of capital.

Cost of capital is a percentage that represents the interest rate the company would pay for the funds being raised. Each capital component—**debt**, **equity**, and retained earnings—has its own cost. Each type of debt or equity also has a different cost. While a particular purchase or project may be funded by only one kind of capital, companies are likely to use a weighted average cost of capital when making financial decisions. Such practice takes into account the fact that the company is an ongoing concern that will need to raise capital at different rates in the future as well as at the present rate.

OTHER APPLICATIONS. Costs are sometimes used in the valuation of assets that are being bought or sold. Buyers and sellers may agree that the value of an asset can be determined by estimating the costs associated with building or creating an asset that could perform similar functions and provide similar benefits as the existing asset. Using the cost approach to value an asset contrasts with the income approach, which attempts to identify the present value of the revenues the asset is expected to generate.

Finally, costs are used in making pricing decisions. Manufacturing firms refer to the ratio between prices and costs as their markup, which represents the difference between the selling price and the direct cost of the goods being sold. For retailers and wholesalers, the gross margin is the difference between their invoice cost and their selling price. While costs form the basis for pricing decisions, they are only a starting point, with market conditions and other factors usually determining the most profitable price.

[David Bianco]

COUNSELING

SEE: Employee Assistance Programs (EAPs)

COUNTERTRADING

Countertrading refers to a category of international trade in which an exporter agrees to accept payment in the form of goods or services. There are many forms of countertrading, ranging from simple **barter** agreements to complex offset deals that involve the exporter agreeing to compensatory practices with respect to the buyer. Countertrading commonly takes place between private companies in developed nations and the governments of developing countries, although countertrading also occurs between developed nations. It has become popular as a means of financing international trade to reduce risks or overcome problems associated with various national currencies.

TYPES OF COUNTERTRADE TRANSACTIONS

Barter involves the exchange of goods or services of equal value without the use of currency. If the exchange does not take place simultaneously, then some financing is usually involved. Although bartering is the oldest and simplest form of countertrading, it is not often used in modern corporate countertrading. It is difficult to structure and inefficient, because it requires matching needs between buyers and sellers. In some cases a barter may be accepted by an exporter as substitute payment when financing arrangements fall through. The exporter may use the services of a trading company to find a market for the bartered goods, if it has no need for them.

Variations on the simple barter include the closed-end barter, which involves finding a third party who will purchase the goods as part of the agreement. In a deferred barter, there is a delay between the two shipments of goods or performances of services. When barters do occur, they are usually for one-time, spot transactions and are covered under one contract. They typically include some form of financing to cover delays in shipments and differences in the value of the goods or services being exchanged. Countries that are attempting to increase their hard currency earnings may impose restrictions, such as higher export tariffs, designed to reduce barters and other countertrading in marketable commodities.

Buy-backs are a more complicated form of countertrading that involve two separate contracts. Buy-backs typically take place between a private corporation from a developed country and the government (or government agency) of a developing nation. Under the first contract of a buy-back arrangement, the exporting private corporation agrees to provide a production facility or other type of capital goods to the developing nation. Then, under the second contract, the developing nation repays the exporting private corporation with output produced at the facility or derived from the originally exported capital goods. The exporter, in effect, buys back the output of the facility it has constructed.

Buy-backs are used to finance direct investment in developing countries. They are popular because they meet the needs and objectives of both parties. From the developing country's viewpoint, buy-backs expand the country's export base, provide employment, and help it meet its goals for industrialization and development. From the point of view of a private corporation, the buyback may help it gain a market presence in the country and provide it with a source of products it can use or sell. If the particular output of the facility is not needed by the corporation, it can involve a third party to help it meet its countertrade obligations.

Buy-back agreements often extend beyond the simple exchange of capital goods or production facilities and their related output. In order to win the contract for a specific facility, the private corporation may agree to provide the developing nation with a variety of other types of assistance, including **loans**, **technology transfer**, personnel training, plant operation, and joint ventures. Such arrangements can be attractive to corporations for a variety of strategic and marketing reasons.

A compensation trade is one in which an exporter and importer agree to make reciprocal purchases of specific goods. The exchange is covered under a single contract. It may or may not take place simultaneously. Each delivery is invoiced in an agreed currency, with payments going either to the supplier or to a clearing account. A third party may be involved to fulfill the purchase commitment of one of the parties.

Two countries that enter into a cooperation contract agree to continuous purchases of goods and services from each other. The master agreement may include a series of buy-back subcontracts, under which the exporter is paid with products derived from the original export. Another variation of a cooperation contract involves the sale of technical expertise to a **joint venture** by the exporter, who is then repaid by sales from the joint venture.

A counterpurchase involves two linked transactions that are covered by two separate contracts. Under one of the contracts, the sale of goods between an exporter and importer is negotiated and paid for in a specified currency. The second contract obligates the exporter to purchase goods from the importer at a specified value over a period of time. Unlike buy-backs, counterpurchases involve hard currency.

The primary contract usually takes the form of a standard export contract without making reference to any counterpurchase obligations. The secondary contract then binds the exporter to counterpurchase goods from the importer and usually contains provisions designed to protect the exporter. These provisions may allow the exporter to transfer its counterpurchase obligations to a third party. The secondary contract also would typically contain a clause that specifies if the primary sale is cancelled, then the exporter is freed from any counterpurchase obligations. A side agreement called a protocol typically links the two contracts.

Offsets originally referred to compensatory transactions involving military equipment and aircraft. Offsets may also involve large civilian transactions. They are a common form of countertrade between two industrialized nations. Offsets may involve a range of compensatory practices that the exporter of military equipment must perform in order to realize the sale of the goods involved.

There are two types of offset deals, direct and indirect. Under a direct offset, the exporter agrees to perform compensatory practices directly related to the product being exported. These practices may include the coproduction or subcontracting of all or part of the goods in the buyer's country. Licensed production is another compensatory practice that involves the overseas production of goods based on the transfer of technical information under arrangements made between a U.S. manufacturer and a foreign government or producer. **Technology transfer** may also be a part of the offset agreement, taking a variety of forms ranging from research and development conducted abroad to technical assistance provided to a subsidiary or joint venture in the buyer country.

With an indirect offset agreement, the compensatory practices required of the exporter are not related to the goods originally sold abroad. Indirect offsets may involve counterpurchases or buy-backs involving unrelated products. They may require the exporter to use or promote the buyer country's services in other areas, such as tourism and travel.

Offset agreements are used by buyer nations to increase employment. Such arrangements also help them achieve their goals in the areas of industrial and export development. Offset trade typically occurs between two governments or between a private corporation and a government.

Switch trade (also known as a switch deal) involves a third party to a countertrade agreement who agrees to assume the countertrade obligations of one of the parties. For example, an exporter may have agreed to counterpurchase goods for which it has no use, simply for the sake of completing the original sale. The exporter may switch its obligation to pay the importer to a third party, who is known as a switch trader, who then acquires the goods from the importer at a discount. The switch trader then sells the goods for hard currency, which is used to meet the exporter's payment obligation to the original importer. Under such agreements the size of the switch trader's discount depends on the importer's need for hard currency.

HISTORY OF MODERN COUNTERTRADING

Throughout history countertrading and barter occurred whenever there was a shortage of money, or before money even existed. In modern times, countertrading arose as a means of conducting international trade when money was scarce, currencies couldn't be converted, or they were subject to inflationary and deflationary swings in value. In Germany between the two World Wars and after World War II, money was scarce, and countertrading and barter became a way of conducting international trade. Eastern European countries followed Germany's lead and employed countertrading to overcome the problems of its own nonconvertible currencies. It was a practice that was favored by the centrally planned Eastern European economies. In the 1990s Eastern Europe and the countries of the former Soviet Union began countertrading with Western nations to overcome difficulties associated with their currencies.

Countertrading became more important in international trade in the 1970s as a result of the oil price increases. It expanded greatly in the 1980s and by the middle of the decade had spread to nearly every country of the world. In the United States military offsets were the most common form of countertrading, accounting for an estimated 80% of all U.S. countertrade in 1984. It is difficult to estimate how much international trade is accounted for by countertrading, because many deals are made confidentially or in secret. In 1985 it may have accounted for ten percent of all international trade. During the second half of the decade, interest in countertrading softened as oil prices fell and the international business climate improved. At that time oil was the most countertraded of all the **commodities**.

OUTLOOK FOR THE 1990S

Countertrading is firmly established as a method of financing international trade. For developing countries that have hard currency shortages or whose national currencies are not readily convertible to other types of foreign exchange, countertrading offers a means of financing imports. By marketing their import potential to companies in developed nations, developing countries also benefit by finding new export markets.

Suppliers in developed countries who are willing to countertrade have found that it provides them with a competitive edge. By being flexible in the type of payment they are willing to receive, companies that are willing and able to countertrade have a stronger position in competitive bidding for projects involving emerging markets in developing countries. Many such companies are anxious to find outlets for their products in emerging markets such as China and Mexico.

Emerging markets in developing countries typically experience swings in the values of their currencies, and they often have strict currency and import controls. Such countries often have to allocate their foreign exchange resources according to a prioritized list of projects and products they wish to import. Countertrading provides a way around such controls. In the case of low-priority imports, suppliers are more likely to win a contract if they are willing to accept some form of countertrade instead of hard currency. Countertrading can also protect supplier corporations from swings in currency values.

In the case of Eastern Europe and the countries of the former Soviet Union, countertrading is likely to play an important role in their international trade in the 1990s. Many of these countries have inconvertible currencies, making it difficult to conduct international trade without some form of countertrading. In Russia, for example, the country's banking system has been unable to provide traditional export financing. The most popular form of countertrade with Russia has been buy-backs, in which exporters have accepted payment in the form of products derived from the original export.

While the United States government does not officially promote countertrading, official interest in countertrading has grown in the 1990s. The Financial Services and Countertrade Division at the U.S. Department of Commerce provides advice to business firms interested in countertrading. The Business Information Service for the Newly Independent States at the U.S. Department of Commerce is a source of information on countertrading with the countries of the former Soviet Union.

Historically, countertrading has expanded when international economies have been sluggish. As international economic growth has increased, there has been a reduction in the volume of countertrading. Since countertrading offers unique benefits to emerging markets in developing countries as well as to supplier corporations from industrialized countries, it is likely to be an area that will be exploited as private corporations and economic developers seek to find practical solutions to their common concerns.

[David Bianco]

FURTHER READING:

Alexandrides, Costas. *Countertrade: Practices, Strategies, and Tactics.* Wiley, 1987.

Francis, Dick. *The Countertrade Handbook.* Woodhead-Faulkner, 1987.

Liesch, Peter. *Government Mandated Countertrade.* Avebury and Gower, 1991.

Schaffer, Matt. *Winning the Countertrade War.* Wiley, 1989.

COUPONS

Coupons are certificates with a stated value that consumers can redeem with retailers or manufacturers when they make appropriate purchases. They are offered mainly by retailers and manufacturers as **sales promotion** tools to accomplish specific sales and **marketing** goals. In the early 1990s coupon distribution rose to more than three billion annually in the United States. Consumers are attracted to coupons because they offer immediate value and savings. With the growth of coupon distribution, problems such as coupon clutter have resulted in falling redemption rates. Only an estimated 1.8 percent of all coupons distributed in the United States in 1993 were redeemed by consumers.

Like other sales promotion tools, coupons have their advantages as well as their problems. On the plus side, they have the advantage of passing along savings directly to consumers, as opposed to trade allowances given to retailers by producers. Consumers perceive coupons as a temporary special offer rather than a price reduction, so the withdrawal of coupons usually doesn't have an adverse effect on sales. Coupons create traffic for retailers, who can double or triple the value of manufacturers' coupons at their own expense to create even more store traffic.

The two main problems with using coupons as a sales promotion tool are coupon clutter and the question of whether coupons actually generate incremental business from new users. The increased quantity of distributed coupons has been paralleled by falling redemption rates. Excessive coupon distribution also increases the likelihood of fraud and misredemption. Coupons that are issued for established brands tend to be redeemed primarily by loyal users who would have purchased the product without a coupon.

Coupons may be issued to serve many different strategic marketing objectives. These include issuing coupons for trial and awareness; coupons appear to be fairly efficient at getting consumers to try new products by reducing the risk of trying something new. Coupons are also issued to convert trial users into regular customers, such as when a product sample includes a cents-off coupon. Coupons can be used to manipulate consumers into making larger purchases or buying a particular size, flavor, or form of a product.

Other objectives served by issuing coupons include building retail distribution and support, moving out-of-balance inventories, targeting different markets, cushioning price increases, and enhancing other promotional efforts with coupon add-ons. Coupons are frequently used by manufacturers because of competitive pressure. When used offensively against the **competition**, coupons are issued to get users of a competitive product to try a new brand. When used defensively, manufacturers provide coupons to current users to keep them from purchasing a competing brand.

There are five basic ways that coupons are distributed: direct mail, in-store or central location, print media, in-pack and on-pack, and through retailer **advertising**. Because of its targeted distribution, coupons sent by direct mail offer higher redemption rates than coupons distributed by print media—an estimated 4.3 percent in 1991. Freestanding inserts (FSIs) in newspapers accounted for approximately 77 percent of all coupon distribution in 1991 and as much as 88 percent by 1993. Coupons distributed through FSIs were redeemed at a 2.4 percent rate in 1991 and 1.8 percent in 1993.

A recent innovation in coupon distribution in grocery stores has been the issuance of computer-generated coupons at grocery checkout counters. This has become a reality largely through the efforts of a St. Petersburg, Florida-based company called Catalina Marketing, which had installed electronic coupon printers at some 80,000 checkout counters in 8,400 supermarkets in the United States, Mexico, the United Kingdom, France, and Belgium by mid-1994. The overall redemption rate for these coupons reached nine percent in 1994. The company sells four-week blocks to manufacturers, during which time their coupons can be distributed to shoppers. Through computerization and the use of **bar codes**, Catalina's printers can be programmed to issue specific coupons based on the products consumers have purchased.

Companies that issue coupons use them to make an offer to consumers. While the most common such offer is a cents-off coupon, there are many other types of offers that can be conveyed through couponing. For example, a free product may be given upon redemption of a coupon. Coupons may carry a "buy one, get one free" offer. Several coupons can be positioned together with different expiration dates to get consumers to make purchases over a length of time. Coupons may specify that more than one unit of a product must be purchased. Coupons known as "self-destructs" are printed over each other in an overlap manner, so that one coupon is destroyed when the other is redeemed. Other varieties of coupons include personalized coupons that can only be redeemed at a specific store or location, cross-ruff coupons that offer one product to purchasers of another related product, and sweepstakes entry coupons.

[David Bianco]

CREATIVITY

SEE: Innovation; Organizational Behavior

CREDIT

Credit is a transaction between two parties in which one, acting as creditor or lender, supplies the other (the debtor or borrower) with money, goods, services, or securities in return for the promise of future payment. In modern economies the use of credit is pervasive and the volume enormous. Electronic transfer technology moves vast amounts of capital instantaneously around the globe irrespective of geopolitical demarcations. The monetization of **loans** in units of currency, such as yen, marks, pounds, and dollars, facilitates the pricing, booking, exchange, and sale of credit and credit instruments. As a financial transaction, credit is the purchase of the present use of money with the promise to pay in the future according to a pre-arranged schedule and at a specified cost defined by the interest rate.

HISTORICAL PERSPECTIVE

Although credit derives from the Latin *creditum* (a loan), and *credere* (to trust, to believe, to have faith in), credit existed in Persia at least 3,000 years before the founding of Rome. Credit became necessary with the rise of private property and international trade. Almost all credit came from individuals or singular institutions that had excess reserves of money or a desired commodity.

In **bartering** economies, commodities of value to the trading parties constituted commodity money. However, the transportation **costs** of commodity money hampered trade. This led to the use of bills of exchange in which one party would promise to pay the holder of the bill a certain amount of a commodity. Traders used bills of exchange as credit money in a manner similar to modern paper currency. The person demanding settlement of the bill most likely was not the original recipient.

The almost universal minting of coins gave rise to money changers and a small banking system in Greece by the late fifth century BC. **Banks** functioned primarily to settle bills of exchange and make credit money loans. With the fall of the Roman Empire in 476 AD, a feudal system arose in Europe that had little need for money and credit. However, by the eleventh and twelfth centuries, **privatization** and trade exploded. The need for credit drained the available reserves of traditional lenders. To fill the gap, money traders and lenders developed new sources of funds. They accepted deposits entrusted to them for safe keeping and for interest. From these funds they, in turn, made loans. Thus, **banking** spread over Europe.

The overextension of credit and poor business practices repeatedly brought down banks all over Europe. By 1300, the first laws concerning bankruptcy and fraud were enacted. The principality of Catalonia, Spain, instituted a municipal bank that systematized and centralized banking activities and regulation.

Chronic cash shortages, excessive **interest rates**, and bank failures forced governments to enact legislation and form their own banking systems to regulate private banking. In 1694, the Bank of England was formed to provide the government with loans to finance its war with France. The government chartered only the Bank of England with the power to issue notes (credit money) acceptable to the government for taxes and other **debts**. By the mid-1800s, the Bank of England had a virtual monopoly on banking. As a result, the Bank of England became the central bank, accepting reserve deposits from other banks and savings from the citizenry. Modern banking had begun.

CREDIT IN THE CAPITALIST ECONOMY

In a capitalist economy credit money is the ''normal'' form of money. Although governments had standardized credit money in units of their national currencies prior to the Industrial Revolution, it is that revolution that led to the modern financial system.

The drive to accumulate wealth is the single most important element in defining the types of investments capitalists undertake, whether for conducting a business enterprise or offering labor for wages. To accumulate wealth and expand **purchasing power**, business and labor must be ''profitable.''

In a production economy, credit bridges the time gap between the commencement of production and the final sale of goods in the marketplace. In order to pay labor and secure materials from vendors, the production capitalist secures a constant source of credit to fund production expenses, i.e., **working capital**. The promise or expectation of continued economic growth motivates the production capitalist to expand production facilities, increase labor, and purchase additional materials. These create a need for long-term financing.

To accumulate adequate reserves from which to lend large sums of money, banks and insurance companies act as intermediaries between those with excess reserves and those in need of financing. These institutions collect excess money (short term assets) through deposits and redirect it through loans into capital (long term) assets.

REASONS FOR PURCHASING CREDIT

In a production economy, credit is widely available and extensively used. Because credit includes a promise to pay, the credit purchaser accepts a certain amount of financial and personal risk. With profit theory in the background, three strategies summarize the reasons for purchasing credit.

1. The lack of liquidity prevents profitable investments at advantageous times. The advantage may be objective or subjective, but it is temporarily unattainable without financing. The advantage may rest in a future income stream more than adequate to retire the **debt**.

2. Favorable borrowing costs make it less expensive to borrow in the present than in the future. Borrowers may have expectations of rising rates, tight credit supplies, growing **inflation**, and decreasing economic activity. Conversely, profit expectations may be sufficiently favorable to justify present investments that require financing.

3. Tax incentives, which expense or deduct some interestcosts, decrease the cost of borrowing and assist in **capital** formation. Borrowing extends one's purchasing power and ability to invest in capital assets to build wealth.

USES FOR CREDIT

A debtor accepts the risks of borrowing to secure something of value, whether perceived or real, profitable, or neutral. The determinants do not necessarily correlate with orthodox capitalist theory of production, profit, and capital accumulation. Credit may be necessitated by psychological and cultural factors as well.

ENJOYMENT. Credit has come to finance the enhancement of one's life style or quality of life through activities and purchases for enjoyment. Activities ''profitable'' to one's well being may translate into a more productive economic life. Enjoyment includes the financing of a boat, an education, a vacation, a health club membership, a retreat, etc.

UTILITARIAN CONSUMPTION. With the introduction of credit cards in the 1950s and the increase of home **equity** debt in the 1980s, the financing of daily consumption has greatly expanded. Consumer credit in 1990 was four times that of 1975, while that of consumer goods only doubled. Much of this debt was for convenience purchases, consumer goods and services with a life of less than one year.

PROFIT AND WEALTH BUILDING. The previous discussion outlined the important role the profit incentive plays in the accumulation of **capital assets** and in **wealth** building. It focused on the production capitalist who increases profits through the introduction of capital improvements that must be financed over the long-term. Home buyers come to similar conclusions when buying a house. They expect the purchase of a certain house in a certain location to be more ''profitable'' than renting or purchasing another house elsewhere. Although a home is not a factory, it is the production backdrop for the capitalist employee selling labor and services.

PROMISE TO PAY

The credit **contracts** define the terms of the agreement between lender and borrower. The terms of the contract delineate the borrower's obligation to repay the principal according to a schedule and at a specified cost or interest rate. The lender reserves the right to require collateral to secure a loan and to enforce payment through the courts.

The lender may levy a small charge for originating or participating in a loan placement. This charge, measured in percentage points, covers administrative costs. This immediate cash infusion decreases the costs of the loan to the lender, thereby, reducing the risk. The lender may also require the borrower to provide protection against nonpayment or default by securing insurance, by establishing a repayment fund, or by assigning collateral **assets**.

A promissory note is an unconditional written promise to pay money at a specified time or on demand. The maker of the note is primarily liable for settlement. No collateral is required. A lien agreement, however, holds property as security for payment of debt. A specific lien identifies a specific property, as in a mortgage. A general lien has no specific assignment.

CREDIT TERMS

The terms of the credit contract deal with the repayment schedule, interest rate, necessity of collateral, and debt retirement.

REPAYMENT SCHEDULES. Credit **contracts** vary in maturity. Short-term debt is from overnight to less than one year. Long-term debt is more than one year to 30 or 40 years. Payments may be required at the end of the contract or at set intervals, usually on a monthly basis. The payment is generally comprised of two parts: a portion of the outstanding principal and the interest costs. With the passage of time, the principal amount of the loan is amortized, repaid little by little, until completely retired. As the principal balance diminishes, the interest on the remaining balance also declines.

Interest on loans do not pay down the principal. The borrower pays interest on the principal loan amount and is expected to retire the principal at the end of the contract through a balloon payment or through **refinancing**.

Revolving credit has no fixed date for retirement. The lender provides a maximum line of credit and expects monthly payment according to an amortization schedule. The borrower decides the degree to which to use the line of credit. The borrower may increase debt at anytime the outstanding amount is below the maximum credit line. The borrower may retire the debt at will, or may continue a cycle of paying down and increasing the debt.

INTEREST RATES. Interest is the cost of purchasing the use of money, i.e., borrowing. The interest rate charged by lending institutions must be sufficient to cover operating costs, administrative costs, and an acceptable rate of return. **Interest rates** may be fixed for the term of the loan, or adjusted to reflect changing market conditions. A credit contract may adjust rates daily, annually, or at intervals of three, five, and ten years.

COLLATERAL. Assets pledged as security against loan loss are collateral. Credit backed by collateral is secured. The asset purchased by the loan often serves as the only collateral. In other cases the borrower puts other **assets**, including cash, aside as collateral. **Real estate** or land collateralizes mortgages.

Unsecured debt relies on the earning power of the borrower. A debenture is a written acknowledgment of a debt similar to a promissory note in that it is unsecured, relying only on the full faith and credit of the issuer. Corporations often issue debentures as **bonds**. With no collateral, these debentures are subordinate to mortgages.

A bond is a contract held in trust obligating a borrower to repay a sum of money. A debenture bond is unsecured. A mortgage bond holds specific property in lien. A bond may contain safety measures to provide for repayment. An indenture is a legal document specifying the terms of a bond issue including the principal, maturity, date, interest rates, any qualifications and duties of the trustees, and the rights and obligations of the issuers and holders. Corporations and government entities issue bonds in a form attractive to both public and private investors.

Overnight funds are lent among banks to temporarily lift their reserves to mandated levels.

A special commitment is a single purpose loan with a maturity of less than one year. Its purpose is to cover cash shortages resulting from a one time increase in current assets such as a special inventory purchase, an unexpected increase in accounts receivable, or a need for interim financing.

Trade credit is extended by a vendor who allows the purchaser up to three months to settle a bill. In the past it was common practice for vendors to discount trade bills by one or two percentage points as an incentive for quick payment.

A seasonal line of credit of less than one year is used to finance inventory purchases or production. The successful sale of inventory repays the line of credit.

A permanent working capital loan provides a business with financing from one to five years during times when cash flow from earnings does not coincide with the timing or volume of expenditures. Creditors expect future earnings to be sufficient to retire the loan.

Commercial papers are short-term, unsecured notes issued by corporations in a form that can be traded in the public money market. Commercial paper finances inventory and production needs.

A **letter of credit** (''l/c'') is a financing instrument that acts more like credit money than a loan. An l/c is used to facilitate a transaction, especially in trade, by guaranteeing payment at a future date. Unlike a loan, which invokes two primary parties, an l/c involves three: the bank, the customer, and the beneficiary. The bank issues, based on its own credibility, an l/c on behalf of its customer, promising to pay the beneficiary upon satisfactory completion of some predetermined conditions.

A bank's acceptance is another short-term trade financing vehicle. A bank issues a time draft promising to pay on or after a future date on behalf of its customer. The bank rests its guarantee on the expectation that its customer will collect payment for goods previously sold.

Term loans finance the purchase of furniture, fixtures, vehicles, and plant and office equipment. Maturity generally runs more than one year and less than five. A large equipment purchase may have longer terms, matched to its useful production life.

Mortgage loans are used to purchase **real estate** and are secured by the asset itself. Mortgages generally run 10 to 40 years. When creditors provide a mortgage to finance the purchase of a property without retiring an existing mortgage, they wrap the new mortgage around the existing debt. The interest payment of the wraparound mortgage pays the debt service of the underlying mortgage.

Treasury bills are short-term debt instruments of the U.S. government issued weekly and on a discounted basis with the full face value due on maturity. T-bill maturities range from 91 to 359 days and are issued in denominations of $10,000.

Treasury notes are intermediate-term debt instruments ranging in maturity from one to ten years. Issued at par, full face value, in denominations of $5,000 and $10,000, T-notes pay interest semiannually.

Treasury bonds are long-term debt instruments. Issued at par values of $1,000 and up, T-bonds pay interest semiannually, and may have call dates (retirement) prior to maturity.

CREDIT WORTHINESS

The granting of credit depends on the confidence the lender has in the borrower's credit worthiness. Generally defined as a debtor's ability to pay, credit worthiness is one of many factors defining a lender's credit policies.

Creditors and lenders utilize a number of financial tools to evaluate the credit worthiness of a potential borrower. Much of which relies on analyzing the **balance sheet**, **cash flow statement**s, inventory turnover rates, debt structure, management performance, and market conditions. Creditors favor borrowers who generate net earnings in excess of debt obligations and contingencies that may arise.

- Credit worthiness. A history of trustworthiness, a moral character, and expectations of continued performance demonstrate a debtor's ability to pay. Creditors give more favorable terms to those with high credit ratings via lower point structures and interest costs.

- Size of debt burden. Creditors seek borrowers whose earning power exceeds the demands of the payment schedule. The size of the debt is necessarily limited by the available resources. Creditors prefer to maintain a safe ratio of debt to capital.

- Loan size. Creditors prefer large loans because the administrative costs decrease proportionately to the size of the loan. However, legal and practical limitations recognize the need to spread the risk either by making a larger number of loans, or by having other lenders participate. Participating lenders must have adequate resources to entertain large loan applications. The borrower must have the capacity to ingest a large sum of money.

- Frequency of borrowing. Customers who are frequent borrowers establish a reputation which directly impacts on their ability to secure debt at advantageous terms.

- Length of commitment. Lenders accept additional risk as the time horizon increases.

To cover some of the risk, lenders charge higher interest rates for longer term loans.

- Social community considerations. Lenders may accept an unusual level of risk because of the social good resulting from the use of the loan. For example, banks participating in low income housing projects or business incubator programs.

INTEREST RATES AND RISK

Lenders use subjective and objective guidelines to evaluate risk and to establish (a) a general rate structure reflective of market conditions, and (b) borrower-specific terms based on individual credit analysis. To be profitable, lenders charge interest rates that cover perceived risks as well as the costs of doing business. The risks calculated into the interest rate are the following.

OPPORTUNITY COST RISK. The lender fixes interest costs at a level sufficient to justify making a loan in the present rather than waiting for more advantageous terms in the future. The lender focuses on a desired rate of return rather than the credit worthiness of the borrower.

CREDIT RISK OR REPAYMENT RISK. The borrower may not be able to make scheduled payments nor repay the debt at all. The greater the credit risk, the higher the interest rate. Creditors charge lower **interest rates** to those with the highest credit ratings, and who are the most able to pay. Those least able to pay find themselves paying the highest rates.

INTEREST RATE RISK AND PREPAYMENT RISK. There risks arise when the payment or prepayment of outstanding debt does not match the terms and pricing of current debt, thus exposing the lender to a "mismatch" in the costs of doing business and the terms of lending.

INFLATION RISK. Inflation decreases the purchasing power of money. Lenders anticipate these losses with higher interest rates.

CURRENCY RISK. International trade and money markets may devalue the currency, decreasing its purchasing power abroad even during times of low inflationary expectations at home. Since currency devaluation heightens inflationary expectations in a global economy, interest rates rise.

FINANCIAL INTERMEDIATION

Financial intermediation is the process of channeling funds from financial sectors with excesses to those with deficiencies. The primary suppliers of funds are households, businesses, and governments. They are also the primary borrowers. Financial intermediaries, such as banks, finance companies, and insurance companies, collect excess funds from these sectors and redistribute them in the form of credit. Financial intermediaries accumulate reserves of funds through investment and savings instruments.

Banks provide savings and checking accounts, certificates of deposit and other time accounts for customers willing to loan the bank their funds for the payment of interest. Insurance companies gather funds through various investments and through the collecting of premiums. Banks, finance, and insurance companies also raise cash by selling equity positions or borrowing money from private or public investors. Pension funds utilize available funds from participant contributions and from investment earnings. Federally sponsored credit intermediaries capitalize themselves in a manner similar to banks. For example, the **Federal National Mortgage Association**, sells securities in the national capital markets.

Financial intermediation provides an efficient and practical method of redistributing purchasing power to qualified borrowers. Banks aggregate many small deposits to finance a single family home mortgage. Finance companies break large pools of cash down to sizes appropriate for the purchase of an automobile. The pooling of funds from many sources and the distribution of credit to a large number of creditors spreads the risks. Managers of financial intermediaries also reduce risk by qualifying borrowers, thereby funneling funds into creditworthy situations. Furthermore, financial intermediation increases liquidity in the system, acting as a buffer against cash shortages resulting from unexpected increases in deposit withdrawals.

CREDIT SECURITIZATION

Credit securitization is one of the most recent and important developments in financing and capital formation. **Underwriters** of financial investments gather together a large number of outstanding credit instruments and other receivables, and repackage them in the form of securities which, to the layperson, are similar to closed-end mutual funds. Underwriters sort the credit instruments into homogeneous groups by maturity, purpose, interest rates, and so forth, and market participation in the cash Dow generated by the debt instruments backing these securities. Hence, the term "asset backed securities."

In many instances the underlying debt is mortgages, secured by real estate, and guaranteed by some agency or insurance company. For example, an underwriter may place into securitization only mortgages guaranteed by the Veterans Administration of maturities no less than 20 years, with interest rates of not less than 9 percent, and with a cumulative principal (face) value of $10 million. The underwriter sells

shares in this pool of mortgages to the public. Other credit instruments securitized are commercial mortgages, auto loans, credit card receivables, and trade receivables.

Credit securitization supports the viability of financial intermediaries by (a) spreading the risk over a broader range of investors who purchase the securities, and (b) increasing liquidity through an immediate cash infusion for the securitized debt. This process is also helpful to investors and borrowers alike. The large volume and efficiency of the system put downward pressure on interest rates. The pooling of loans into large, homogeneous securities facilitates the actuarial and financial analysis of their risks.

Investors may participate in a portion of the cash flow generated by the interest and/or principal payments made by borrowers of the underlying debt. Investor participation may be limited to the cash flow of a set number of years, or to a portion of the principal when the underlying debt is retired. Investors also choose to participate at a point suitable to their risk/reward ratio. Hence, investors have the opportunity to derive different benefits from one package of credit instruments.

SEE ALSO: Banking Act of 1933; Corporate Finance; Credit Approval; Factoring; Loans; Negotiable Instruments; Opportunity Costs

[Roger J. AbiNader]

FURTHER READING:

Board of Governors of the Federal Reserve System. *The Federal Reserve System: Purposes & Functions.* Washington, D.C., 1984.

Guttman, Robert. *How Credit-Money Shapes the Economy: The United States in a Global System.* M.E. Sharpe, 1994.

McNeil, Jane H., and Edward T. O'Leary. *Introduction to Commercial Lending.* American Institute of Banking, American Bankers Association, 1983.

Rosenthal, James A., and Juan M. Ocampo. *Securitization of Credit: Inside the New Technology of Finance.* John Wiley & Sons, Inc., 1988.

Wray, L. Randall. *Money and Credit in Capitalist Economies: The Endogenous Money Approach.* Edward Elgar Pub. Co., 1990.

CREDIT APPROVAL

Credit approval is the process a business or an individual undertakes to become eligible for a loan or pay for goods and services over an extended period. Granting credit approval depends on the willingness of the creditor to lend money in the current economy and that same lender's assessment of the ability and willingness of the borrower to return the money or pay for the goods obtained—plus interest—in a timely fashion. Typically, businesses seek approval to get loans and also grant approval for loans to their customers.

The term credit is derived from the Latin *credo* or I believe or trust. Credit implies a condition of trust between borrower and lender that the funds (or goods lent) will be repaid. In the past when the economy operated on a simpler scale, a person would lend money to a friend on trust. The success of this arrangement depended upon the assessment of the friend's creditworthiness, a situation summed up by Shakespeare as "Neither a borrower, nor a lender be." There were also people known as money lenders who specialized in the extending of money with the expectation of being repaid, ususally with interest. In the late Middle Ages and early Renaissance, the foundations of the modern banking system developed in Italy. The impersonalization of credit and the availability of investment capital have helped provide the large sums of money necessary for modern business expansion.

There are three general types of business loans, the short term loan, the long term loan, and equity funding. A short term loan is usually undertaken for a year or two and is often repaid by liquidation of assets or from earnings. Often such a loan is granted on a "signature" basis, that is, without collateral. In these cases, the credit history of the individual or firm making the application is enough to fix the bond of trust. A longer term loan is usually repaid from earnings over time and is usually undertaken for larger improvements. These loans, depending upon the amount, are at times secured, that is, guaranteed by the pledge of assets or other collateral; if repayment is missed then the person granting credit becomes the owner of whatever assets were pledged. In equity capital funding, money is raised by selling interest or shares in the company. The credit approval process used by potential investors to determine the value of the stock includes the ratio of the net worth of debt to the assets, the quarterly earnings of the company, the value and condition of any collateral, the borrower's management ability and character, and the future prospects of the company and the industry in the current and projected economic forecast. The selling of stock is a form of equity financing. The future of the business becomes the asset pledged.

To establish credentials for any credit approval process, from short term loans to equity funding, a firm needs to have a business plan and a good credit history. The company must be able to show that it can repay the loan at the established interest rate, as well as be prepared to establish that the outlook for business in general and for their type of business in particular supports their future projects and the reasons for their borrowing. The process of granting loans to businesses is regulated by the Federal Trade Commission (FTC) to ensure fairness and guarantee nondiscrimination and disclosure of all aspects of the process.

The **Small Business Administration (SBA)** publishes a series of pamphlets and other information designed to assist businesses in obtaining loans. These publications advise businesses on a range of credit approval topics including describing assets, preparing a business plan, and determining what questions to expect and how to prepare responses to those questions.

Credit approval is also something that a business issues for its customers. Many customers today use national credit cards, but many stores offer their own individual credit approval terms for purchases of goods and services. The process by which a store grants credit to individuals is governed by a series of laws administered by the **Federal Trade Commission** that guarantee nondiscrimination and other benefits. These laws include the Equal Credit Opportunity Act, Fair Credit Reporting Act, Truth in Lending Act, and Fair Debt Collection Practices Act.

To approve credit for a customer, a firm often requests credit references. In a shortened form of credit approval ("instant credit" in the retail trade), a client provides credit references in the form of a bank account number and another credit card. The fact that others grant credit and consider the client credit-worthy then becomes the basis for the business in question to extend credit for purchases up to a certain amount. The customer's Social Security Number is often used for identification purposes in this process.

It would be difficult for every business to investigate every aspect of the credit record of an individual customer in today's society. Many businesses and banks use the services of a credit bureau to assess the credit rating of applicants. Credit bureaus maintain a record of each and every request for credit a person makes as well as keep a record of timeliness in debt repayment. The Social Security number is a key element in obtaining information. Information on a person can be released only with that person's permission. The individual's rights are protected by the FTC.

[Joan Leotta]

FURTHER READING:

Hosmer, LaRue T. *A Venture Capital Primer for Small Business.* Washington, D.C.: U.S. Small Business Administration, Management Assistance, Support Services Section, 1982.

U.S. Federal Trade Commission. *A Guide to the Federal Trade Commission.* Washington, D.C.: U.S. Federal Trade Commission, 1992.

U.S. Small Business Administration. *The ABC's of Borrowing.* Washington, D.C.: U.S. Small Business Administration, 1989.

U.S. Federal Trade Commission. *A Guide to Building a Better Credit Record.* Washington, D.C.

CREDIT UNIONS

The term credit union implies a cooperative effort, which in fact is what a credit union is, a financial cooperative designed exclusively for the purposes of serving its members, the "owners" of the cooperative. The credit union is a non-profit financial institution and is generally as concerned with community involvement as with its profits. As reported in *Black Enterprise* magazine, "Not for profit, not for charity, but a service" is considered the credit union motto, especially as it relates to the fees that banks were charging their customers in the early 1990s. Typical higher bank fees were for such items as stop-payment orders, below minimum balances, and check bouncing. Whereas these fees help to increase the bottom line for banks, credit unions are typically more forgiving concerning these service fees.

Credit unions provide a lower cost, "friendly" savings investment option, while still maintaining competitive interest rates as well as a wide variety of financial services for their members. Whether an individual wants a car loan, personal loan, vacation, home-improvement, or education loan, a credit union can, and in most cases will, easily accommodate its members' needs. In addition to **loans**, credit unions also offer (depending upon size) **ATMs** (automated teller machines) access; direct-deposit bill payments and checking services; CD's (**certificates of deposit**); credit cards; money orders; **money market** accounts, and even individual retirement accounts (IRAs).

CREDIT UNION MEMBERSHIP

Membership in a credit union is limited; that is, it is not open for anyone to join. On the other hand, banks operate on an "open-enrollment" basis, provided one has the appropriate, pre-determined funds with which to open an account. Credit union membership is determined by its charter. Most members are from employee groups, associations, churches, or even residential communities. Because members of credit unions are "shareholders" (owners), they have a direct say in what the management practices of their credit union will be. Although membership in a credit union appears limited, a key objective of the credit union "industry" is to avoid exclusivity and try to extend its services to as many people as possible. This helps further the credit union community image.

There are a few basic practices credit unions try to adhere to when soliciting membership. While banks may reject potential customers whose main purpose for joining is to gain loan access, a credit union may actually desire a member (credit unions have members; banks have customers) such as this. According to Jack Dublin in his book, *Credit Unions, Theory and Practice*, nearly half of the world's credit union members joined a credit union with one intention, to secure a hassle-free loan. Many of these members became diligent savers and contributors to their respective credit union because of the pleasant loan experience they shared.

Another credit union membership principle, or practice, is to induce all members of a family to join, not just the main wage earners in the household (family members are automatically eligible). By encouraging the entire family to join, credit unions will not only enhance their assets, but may also have stumbled upon future leaders and high-wage earners. Credit unions also don't shy away from financial relationships with younger members (those below the age of 18). This practice not only is of great value to the youth of their respective community, it once again provides opportunity for asset growth to the credit union.

Membership in a credit union may also be granted to organizations (such as a church parish family), provided the organization is comprised of members who would otherwise be eligible for credit union membership on an individual basis.

SAVINGS, OWNERSHIP, AND INTEREST RATES

A credit union serves its members for two primary reasons: to provide a place for savings and to provide funds for its members to borrow in a time of need. Because credit unions operate democratically, they may tend to discourage potential members whose deposits would become so large that the credit union begins to rely on this member's deposits to keep business flowing. This potential member, as a shareholder of the credit union, may in fact attempt to influence credit union operations, thereby taking power away from the many and diverting to the few. Relative to "normal" day-to-day savings, a credit union will provide easy to follow savings plans designed to encourage its membership to save regularly. This practice enhances the credit union's portfolio, making it easier for members to obtain loans, receive favorable interest rates, and **dividends** distributions.

A credit union has advantages over most profit-seeking banks and lending institutions regarding guidelines on regular checking and savings accounts. For example, a bank may require a minimum balance of $300.00 for a checking account, charge fees for each check written, and assess penalties for the time one's balance dips below the minimum. On the other hand, a credit union is very likely to require no minimum balance, no fee accounts, thereby attracting much greater interest for this everyday banking service. Credit unions are very competitive with interest rates paid to members, and as a bonus, based on the shareholder relationship, many credit unions pay their members dividends, depending on financial performance for the year.

To learn more about credit unions, contact the National Credit Union Association (NCUA), headquartered in Madison, WI.

[Art DuRivage]

CRISIS MANAGEMENT

In the past two decades, crisis management has become one of the fastest emerging of the business sciences. The reason for this interest is that a single crisis—any unexpected, negative event that could impair an organization—could lead to a loss of life as well as injure the reputation and profitability of a business.

Hundreds of potential threats exist for every organization, ranging from a plant fire to loss of competitive secrets. To assess whether a particular company has a higher exposure than others to categories of crisis, a company may employ a risk or crisis manager who may prepare statistical models, review industry data, or work with consultants to understand how one or more crises could impact the organization. Once this process of risk is completed, many companies then design a Crisis Management Plan (CMP) to determine how negative events can be avoided or reduced in scope.

INTERNAL AND EXTERNAL THREATS

The list of corporate crises may include violence in the workplace, product defect and **product liability**, embezzlement and extortion, chemical spill, sabotage and terrorism, and natural disasters that can destroy corporate assets, such as earthquakes, hurricanes or floods. Any of these events—as well as numerous others—can cause an immediate and prolonged financial loss to a company, require an intensive communications effort directed to investors, employees, consumers and other publics, and may present a series of regulatory, community relations and competitive challenges.

Some examples of incidents that have required insight into crisis management include:

- the intentional tampering of products, like the poisoning of Tylenol capsules in 1982;

- considerable environmental damage caused by accidents, like the millions of gallons of oil dumped into Prince William Sound,

Alaska by the Exxon Valdez in 1989 and the death of 3,100 persons in Bhopal, India after a chemical leak at a Union Carbide processing plant in 1984;

- threats to executives, like the 1992 kidnapping and shooting of Exxon International president Sydney Reso by a former Exxon security guard;

- acts of terrorism that can impair a company, like the 900 businesses displaced after the bombing of the World Trade Center in New York in 1993;

- workplace violence, including the murder of several dozen supervisors at facilities of the U. S. Postal Service throughout the past decade and the murder of 23 patrons at a Luby's Cafeterias in Killeen, Texas in 1989.

Although none of these events could be predicted, the principles of crisis management suggest that several could have been reduced in their severity of impact if the organization had engaged in an intensive review of risk and crisis susceptibility. Various crisis management scholars have argued that signals exist prior to many crises emerging; these may include verbal or written threats made to a company, "near miss" accidents in which an employee was injured but not killed, customer complaints, or serious incidents that occur in competing firms.

DURING A CRISIS, A SINGLE VOICE

During and throughout a crisis, the challenges presented to a company can be overwhelming. Crisis management strategists typically suggest that an organization engage the services of one spokesperson to reduce the possibility of contradictory statements. For instance, when Perrier Group of America voluntarily recalled bottled water because of abnormally high levels of benzene in 1990, two news conferences were held—one in Europe and one in North America—and executives of the company made remarks that were embarrassingly contradictory. By contrast, Luby's Cafeterias Inc. president Ralph Erben served as the sole spokesperson for his company for three days in the aftermath of the Texas violence. As a result of his skill and comments, Luby's stock value did not fluctuate on the New York Stock Exchange—a rare success for a company under siege.

By contrast, Exxon chairman Lawrence Rawl was widely criticized by regulators, environmentalists, and consumers for not traveling to Alaska and speaking to the press to inspect damage caused by the Valdez until three weeks after that catastrophe. His decision was perceived by some as a lack of sensitivity to an incident in which the captain of the tanker admitted that he routinely drank vodka while on board and was drinking on the night of the incident. The absence of swift, professional response can cause lingering financial and reputational harm; hundreds of thousands of Exxon customers reportedly tore up their credit cards and mailed them to the company.

Although crisis management is practiced by many large and medium sized firms, the responsibility for assessing and preventing a disaster may be headquartered in a company's human resources, public relations, regulatory affairs or safety departments; there is no single model that applies across industries. Today, many companies are implementing CMP's; many others schedule simulations to test managerial response prior to an incident. A series of books, journals and conferences have emerged to guide managers through this high-profile process. This author's study found that 67 percent of the Fortune 500 and 39 percent of the Fortune 1000 has a CMP in place.

For example, British Petroleum Exploration in Anchorage, AK has prepared a CMP that details how different teams of managers would respond to any incident, ranging from an earthquake to an industrial accident. The plan also designates how business relationships will be managed, ranging from trade associations to vendors of the company. Every day of the year at least three BP managers are on call around-the-clock to assume leadership during any serious incident that could challenge the company internally or externally.

CRISIS MANAGEMENT AND PRODUCT LIABILITY

The process of insurance and risk management is as important to crisis management as is **public relations**. For instance, after more than twenty years of denying that their products posed any serious health threats to women, manufacturers of silicone breast implants acknowledged in 1994 that hundreds of thousands of patients had suffered from multiple, serious side effects. As a result, a $4.3 billion trust fund was established by firms that had previously competed feverishly against one another, constituting the single largest product liability case of its kind in history.

Up until a federal judge allowed the 1994 trust fund to disperse these funds to patients and their families, implant manufacturers such as Dow Corning Inc. had faced a crisis of unprecedented proportions: a former engineer with the company, Thomas Talcott, engaged in whistle blowing and frequently testified in court, producing documents suggesting that Dow Corning executives knew for more than 20 years that their product could cause serious harm.

Numerous women won major lawsuits against the implant manufacturers, including judgments that reached over $6 million in a single case. Insurers of these manufacturers were eager to see the trust fund established so that their exposure to thousands of potential, individual lawsuits could be avoided. Increasingly, insurance companies are urging both corporations and nonprofit organizations to design and implement a CMP so as to reduce their exposure to a crisis.

[Laurence Barton]

FURTHER READING:

Barton, Laurence. *Crisis In Organizations: Managing And Communicating In The Heat of Chaos.* SouthWestern Publishing, 1993.

CRITICAL PATH METHOD

Also known as critical path analysis, the critical path method (CPM) is one of the most useful methods of developing and displaying information necessary for scheduling and controlling time variables associated with large projects. It is a visual technique that gives managers the ability to more effectively plan, schedule, and analyze their projects; it is often used to help complete large manufacturing and construction projects.

Any time a manager is trying to determine the date by which a project will be completed, he or she needs to have a basic understanding of the time needed to complete each task that makes up the overall project. For small projects, managers are often able to remember and to coordinate all of the various tasks necessary for their completion. For larger projects, however, with numerous activities occurring simultaneously, remembering and coordinating these activities can prove much more difficult. CPM allows managers to determine which particular tasks within a project most affect the total time of the project and enables them to better schedule each task so that deadlines are met at the least possible cost.

HISTORY OF THE CRITICAL PATH METHOD

In the mid-1950s, people became increasingly interested in the efficiencies related to solving scheduling problems associated with large projects. One such effort was undertaken in Great Britain by the Operational Research Section of the Central Electricity Generating Board. The board examined problems associated with refurbishing a generating plant, a very complex project. By 1957, it had come up with a technique that identified the "longest irreductable sequence of events." (The technique was later renamed "major sequence" of events.) This technique was used in an experimental overhaul of a power plant; in the end, it reduced the time needed to complete the overhaul to 42 percent of the average time needed for completing the same types of projects. At the time, officials involved pointed out that, while delays in this major sequence would delay the project's completion, delays in other activities would not necessarily have an impact on the completion time.

While these events were occurring in Great Britain, similar work was being undertaken in the United States. At the onset of 1958, the U.S. Navy established a team to formulate a way to plan and control complicated projects. The investigation was referred to as the Programme Evaluation Research Task, the code name of which was PERT. By February of that year, Dr. C. E. Clark, a mathematician on the PERT investigation team, introduced the first arrow diagrams. Later known as the Programme Evaluation and Review Technique, PERT was applied to the Fleet Ballistic Missiles Programme in October 1958. For this project, PERT was credited with taking two years off the estimated time to develop the Polaris missile.

Simultaneously, similar work was being undertaken in the private sector. For example, E.I. Du Pont de Nemours & Co. devised a technique to control its large projects. Its technique, known as CPM, was credited with saving the company $1 million in the first year of its implementation. By 1959, Dr. Mauchly of the Du Pont effort established an organization to solve industrial problems using CPM. Since that time, a great deal of work has been completed to improve upon all of these related techniques, much of it by people in the computer industry.

THE BASICS OF THE CRITICAL PATH METHOD

For CPM to be used appropriately, a project should have three attributes. First, it must be comprised of tasks that are independent of each other, which managers can stop and start within the duration of the project. Second, the distinct tasks, upon completion, must result in the end of the project. Third, while some tasks can be performed simultaneously, others must be performed in a particular sequence.

If the above are characteristics of a project, CPM is appropriate. CPM consists of (1) planning, (2) analyzing and scheduling, and (3) controlling project tasks. To plan a project using this method, a diagram of each of the tasks comprising a project must be devised. The diagram can be constructed by, first, assigning a symbol (such as X, Y, or Z) to all of the tasks and listing them in the order that they are to be performed. The time estimated for each task to be completed should also be given. It should be mentioned that it will likely be possible to perform many of the tasks simultaneously.

Take, for example, a project involving the transportation of goods using three trucks from place W to place X. Two trucks go first to place Y, from there one truck (Truck A) goes to place X and the other (Truck B) goes to place Z and then to place X. The third truck (Truck C) goes directly from place W to place X. These events would be represented in the diagram below, which is not a true map of events, but only a figurative representation. (The estimated times needed to complete the individual segments of the trips are listed in the diagram.)

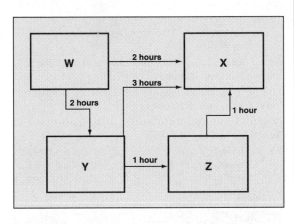

To analyze this scenario, the manager must figure out the shortest amount of time in which it is possible to complete the project, given that all of the individual tasks are necessary and take the previously defined amounts of time to complete. For the above example, the answer is 5 hours, the time needed for Truck A to leave place W, go to place Y, and reach place X. The other two trucks (B and C) take only four hours and two hours, respectively. Thus, Truck A traveling from W to Y to X is seen as the critical path. Anything delaying that truck will delay the project, while any delays experienced by the other two trucks would not be significant, unless they pushed the project beyond 5 hours.

Defining the critical path can allow the manager to concentrate his or her efforts appropriately and make optimal scheduling decisions. Thus, it follows that if the project manager can reduce the time it takes for Truck A to complete its path, the overall project will save time. He or she will not waste efforts on reducing the time spent by Trucks B and C. Furthermore, knowing that Trucks B and C have more time to complete their tasks, the manager can schedule them more conveniently. For instance, Truck C is unoccupied for three hours and could be used for other tasks during that time.

Finally, by using CPM, the manager can control the project as the tasks are being completed. Comparing the actual performance with the planned performance will let the manager know whether or not the project is on schedule. Thus, if Truck A is behind schedule going from place W to place Y, the truck's trip from point Y to point X will have to be expedited—that is, if the project is to be completed on time.

[Kathryn Snavely]

FURTHER READING:

Adrian, James J. *CM: The Construction Management Process.* Reston, VA: Reston Publishing Company, 1981.

Antill, James M., and Ronald W. Woodhead. *Critical Path Methods in Construction Practice,* 4th ed. New York: John Wiley & Sons, 1990.

Argenti, Paul A. *The Portable MBA Desk Reference.* New York: John Wiley & Sons, 1994.

Busch, Dennis H. *The New Critical Path Method.* Chicago, IL: Probus Publishing Company, 1991.

Lockyer, K. G. *An Introduction to Critical Path Analysis.* New York: Pitman Publishing Corporation, 1964.

O'Brien, James J. *CPM in Construction Management,* 4th ed. New York: McGraw-Hill, 1992.

Pierce, David Jr. *Project Planning and Control for Construction.* Kingston, MA: R. S. Means Company, 1988.

CROSS-CULTURAL/INTERNATIONAL COMMUNICATION

Business is not conducted in an identical fashion from culture to culture. Consequently, business relations are enhanced when managerial, sales, and technical personnel are trained to be aware of areas likely to create communication difficulties and conflict across cultures. Similarly, international communication is even further strengthened when businesspeople can anticipate areas of commonality. Finally, business in general is enhanced when people from different cultures find new approaches to old problems creating solutions by combining cultural perspectives and examining the problem at hand from each other's differing cultural perspectives.

ETHNOCENTRISM

Problems in business communication conducted across cultures often arise when participants from one culture are unable to understand culturally determined differences in communication practices, traditions, and thought processing. At the most fundamental level, problems may occur when one or more of the people involved clings to an ethnocentric view of how to conduct business. Ethnocentrism is the belief that one's own cultural group is somehow innately superior to others.

It is easy to say that ethnocentrism only affects the bigoted or those ignorant of other cultures, and so is unlikely to be a major factor in one's own business

communication. Yet difficulties due to a misunderstanding of elements in cross-cultural communication may affect even enlightened people. Ethnocentrism is deceptive precisely because members of any culture perceive their own behavior as logical, since that behavior works for them. People tend to accept the values of the culture around them as absolute values. Since each culture has its own set of values, often quite divergent from those values held in other cultures, the concept of proper and improper, foolish and wise, and even right and wrong become blurred. In international business, questions arise regarding what is proper by which culture's values, what is wise by which culture's view of the world, and what is right by whose standards.

Since no one individual is likely to recognize the subtle forms of ethnocentrism that shape who he or she is, international business practitioners must be especially careful in conducting business communication across cultures. It is necessary to try to rise above culturally imbued ways of viewing the world. To do this, one needs to understand *how* the perception of a given message changes depending on the culturally determined viewpoint of those communicating.

THE FACTORS AFFECTING CROSS-CULTURAL BUSINESS COMMUNICATION

Culture directly affects the communication process in an international business setting through seven variables:

1. language

2. environmental and technological considerations

3. social organization

4. contexting and face-saving

5. authority conception

6. nonverbal communication behavior

7. time conception

These seven items form the acronym LESCANT.

Most barriers when communicating across cultures derive from the communicator's misgauge of the LESCANT factors. By assessing in advance the roles these variables play in business communication, one can improve one's ability to convey those messages effectively to an audience from a different culture.

The seven LESCANT factors alone do not provide a thorough knowledge of another culture. Moreover, these seven dimensions of culture are not intended to represent the *only* cause of intercultural communication difficulties. Being aware of these factors does, however, provide an underlying foundation on which one can construct a framework for understanding the businesspeople from other cultures. In short, these seven factors represent an approach for asking the right questions needed to see the most significant cultural differences and similarities. The answers to those questions vary according to the individual experiences of those involved.

LANGUAGE

Among the most often cited barriers to conflict-free cross-cultural business communication is the use of different languages. It is difficult to underestimate the importance that an understanding of linguistic differences plays in international business communication. Difficulties with language fall basically into three categories: gross translation problems, the problems in conveying subtle distinctions from language to language, and culturally-based variations among speakers of the same language.

Gross translation errors, though frequent, may be less likely to cause conflict between parties than other language difficulties for two reasons. First, they are generally the easiest language difficulty to detect. Many gross translation errors are either ludicrous or make no sense at all. Only those errors that continue to be logical in both the original meaning and in the mistranslated version pose a serious concern. Nonetheless, even when easily detected, gross translation errors waste time and wear on the patience of the parties involved. Additionally, for some, such errors imply a form of disrespect for the party into whose language the message is translated.

The subtle shadings that are often crucial to business negotiations are also weakened when the parties do not share a similar control of the same language. In English, for example, the mild distinctions between the words ''misinterpret'' and ''misunderstand'' can prove significant in a sensitive situation. To a touchy negotiator, to say that he or she ''misunderstands'' may imply that he or she is dim-witted. To say that same negotiator ''misinterprets'' a concept, by contrast, allows the negotiator a way to save face since all interpretations are arguable. He or she has reached an understandable though inaccurate interpretation of the matter. In such a situation, the term applies more objectively to the matter at hand than to the specific negotiator. To a nonnative speaker with inadequate control of the language, however, such subtle distinctions might be lost. When other parties with full control over the language with whom the nonnative speaker communicates assume that knowledge of this distinction exists, conflict deriving from misunderstanding is likely.

Nor do such mistranslations need to actually cross languages in cross-cultural business situations. Dialectical differences within the same language often create gross errors. One frequently cited example of how variations within a single language can affect business occurred when a U.S. deodorant manufacturer sent a Spanish translation of its slogan to their Mexican operations. The slogan read ''if you use our deodorant, you won't be embarrassed.'' The translation, however, which the Mexican-based English-speaking employees saw no reason to avoid, used the term ''*embarazada*'' to mean ''embarrassed.'' This provided much amusement to the Mexican market, as ''*embarazada*'' means ''pregnant'' in Mexican Spanish.

Attitudes toward accents and dialects also create barriers in international business communication. The view that a particular accent suggests loyalty or familiarity to a nation or region is widespread in many languages. The use of Parisian French in Quebec, of Mexican Spanish in Spain, or subcontinental Indian English in the United States are all noticeable and may suggest a lack of familiarity even if the user is fluent. More importantly, regional ties or tensions in such nations as Italy, France, or Germany among others can be suggested by the dialect a native speaker uses.

Finally, national prejudices and class distinctions are often reinforced thorough sociolinguistics—the social patterning of language. For example, due to regional prejudice and racism certain accents in the United States associated with urban areas (e.g., a Bronx accent), with rural regions (e.g., an Appalachian accent), or race (e.g., black English) may reinforce negative stereotypes (usually erroneously) regarding business ability, education level, or acumen among certain U.S. subgroups. Similarly, some cultures use sociolinguistics to differentiate one economic class from another. Thus, in England, distinct accents are associated with the aristocracy and the middle and lower classes. These distinctions are often unknown by foreigners.

ENVIRONMENT AND TECHNOLOGY

The ways in which people use the resources available to them often shifts drastically from culture to culture. Culturally-engrained biases regarding the natural and technological environment can create communication barriers.

Most people are accustomed to ways of looking at the environment and the use of technology particular to their own culture. This, in turn, may make it difficult to accept or even to understand those views held by other cultures.

ISSUES OF ENVIRONMENT. Five major areas of attitudes toward a nation's physical characteristics and natural resources are likely to result in cultural environmental presuppositions. These are:

1. climate

2. topography

3. population size

4. population density

5. the relative availability of natural resources

These five sources of environmental differences surface when people communicate on a wide spectrum of business-related subjects. Notions of transportation and logistics, settlement, and territorial organization are affected by topography and climate. For example, transportation and logistics in one culture may seem patently absurd in another. The manager of a Canadian company doing business in South America might never think to ship goods from Chile to neighboring Argentina by the circuitous route of the Panama Canal. Because Canada is relatively flat and has an excellent network of railroads and highways, the Canadian manager might assume that the easiest way to transport goods for any short distance would be overland. This preference would be reinforced by the fact that many Canadian waterways freeze over due to its harsh climate. As a result, the Canadian might well assume or even specify a preference for overland transport in any relevant business communication. What the Canadian might not understand in such a situation is that the rugged physical environment of the Andean terrain and the related absence of cross-Andean railroads and freeways would make such an option unreasonably expensive or even impossible. By contrast, warm water ports and relatively easy access to the Panama Canal or other waterways would reinforce the option of water routes even for such relatively short overland distances.

Population size and the availability of natural resources influence each nation's view toward export or domestic markets. The United States and China, for example, both have gigantic domestic markets and are rich in natural resources. Both nations export out of choice, and have a tendency to internalize their views of foreign markets. Foreign markets in such countries may be culturally reinforced as being secondary markets as a result, with a cultural emphasis on domestic markets. By contrast, Switzerland, with neither a large domestic population nor abundant natural resources, is culturally oriented toward export with foreign markets viewed as their primary markets and the domestic Swiss market as a comparatively negligible secondary market.

Population density and space usage influence the development of different cultural perceptions of how space and materials are used. Thus, how people lay out or use office space, domestic housing, and buildings in general shifts from nation to nation. For example, in many nations the size, layout, and furnishings of a business office communicate a message. The message communicated, however, varies from nation to nation.

Such differences may be subtle or overt. For example, the distinctions between the U.S. and French upper-level executive's office may be quite subtle. In both France and the United States, the size of an office, plushness of its furnishings, and location in the building (corner office or top floor of the building) reflect the status of the office's owner. In France, however, the individual aesthetics of the office decor convey an important statement about the office owner while in the U.S. office the wall decorations and furnishings are often selected by a designer with little input from the office's occupant.

Much more overt is the contrast between the U.S. or French executive office and the "open system" offices of Japan. In the open system office, Japanese department heads have no individual offices at all. Instead, their desks are simply one of numerous other desks placed in a regularly patterned arrangement in a large open area. No partitions are used between the desks at all and no individual offices exist. Yet each person in this officeless open system is strategically placed in a way that communicates his or her rank and status just as surely as the U.S. or French individual office system. Thus, the department heads' desks are normally placed at a point farthest from the door where the department heads can view their whole department easily at a glance. Moreover, further status may be indicated by placement near a window. The messages communicated by such placement in a large open area may be entirely lost on the French or U.S. visitor unfamiliar with it.

ISSUES OF TECHNOLOGY. More seriously, the failure of businesspeople to modify their communication to accommodate environmental differences often derives from ethnocentric inflexibility toward culturally learned views of technology.

Generally, cultures may be divided into three approaches toward technology: (1) control; (2) subjugation, and (3) harmonization.

In control cultures such as those of northern Europe and North America, technology is customarily viewed as an innately positive means for controlling the environment. If a road approaches a mountain in a control culture, a tunnel is blasted through the mountain. If the tunnel collapses, the cultural view is that the technology was inadequate to the task and needs to be improved.

In subjugation cultures such as those of central Africa and southwestern Asia, the existing environment is viewed as innately positive and technology is viewed with some skepticism. If a road approaches a mountain, the road may simply stop at the mountain. If a tunnel is used and does collapse, the cultural view is that the very idea of going through the mountain was misguided, not that the technology was inadequate.

In harmonization cultures such as those common in many Native American cultures and some East Asian nations, a balance is attempted between the use of technology and the existing environment. In these cultures, neither technology nor the environment are innately good and members of such cultures see themselves as part of the environment in which they live being neither subject to it nor master of it.

One major communication stumbling block among those from control cultures is the belief that other cultures wish to be more like them. Control cultures tend to describe themselves as the "industrialized nations." Their members are often acculturated to believe that the way in which people in less industrialized nations use their resources results from inherently inferior technology. Arguably, in some cases this position may be defensible. Often, though, the reason people use the resources available to them in the manner that they do is because it makes good business sense to use them in that fashion within the context of their own cultural views.

SOCIAL ORGANIZATION

Social organization, as it affects the workplace, is often culturally determined. One must take care not to assume that the view held in one's own culture is universal on such issues reflecting the culture's social organization as **nepotism** and kinship ties, educational values, class structure and social mobility, job status and economic stratification, religious ties, political affiliation, gender differences, racism and other prejudices, attitudes toward work, and recreational or work institutions.

All of these areas have far-reaching implications for business practice. Choosing employees based on **resumes**, for example, is considered a primary means of selection in the United States, Canada, and much of northern Europe—all nations with comparatively weak concepts of familial relationships and kinship ties. In these cultures, nepotism is seen as subjective and likely to protect less qualified workers through familial intervention. By contrast, it would seem anywhere from mildly to highly inappropriate to suggest to members of many Arabic, central African, Latin American, or southern European cultures to skip over hiring relatives to hire a stranger. For people in these cultures, nepotism both fulfills personal obligations and ensures a predictable level of trust and accountability. The fact that a stranger appears to be better qualified based on a superior resume and a relatively brief interview would not, as it might for example in the United States or Sweden, affect that belief. Such a suggestion, depending on the situation at hand, could be made. To effectively suggest such a course of action, however, one would need to communicate this

in a manner adjusted to the way that employees would likely react to so distressing an order.

Similarly, the nature of praise and employee motivation can be socially determined. For example, a promotion of a single member of a traditional Japanese work group may cause the **productivity** and morale of both the group and the promoted employee to fall. A similar promotion in the United States, by contrast, might be seen as a reward for the promoted employee and might even be viewed as encouraging the remaining members of the group to work harder for a goal that they too might attain. Thus to communicate such a promotion openly may prove to be a poor policy in Japan but a good policy in the United States.

Finally, it is often difficult to rid business communication of a judgmental bias when social organization varies markedly. For example, those from the United States may find it difficult to remain neutral on class structures prevent upward mobility. For instance, the socially determined inferior role of women in much of the Islamic world, or of lower castes in India—to name just two—may prove particularly disturbing to those from the United States. Nevertheless, if the U.S. businessperson cannot eliminate the attendant condemnation from his or her business communication, then he or she cannot expect to function effectively in that society. An individual may personally believe that a country's social system is inefficient or incorrect. Nevertheless, in the way that individual conducts business on a daily basis, it is necessary to work within the restraints of that culture to succeed. One may choose *not* to do business with people from such a culture but one cannot easily impose one's own values on them and expect to do well.

CONTEXTING AND FACE-SAVING

Communication depends on the context in which the communication is set. The more information sender and receiver share in common, the higher the context of the communication and the less necessary to communicate through words or gestures. Communication, then, can be seen as being high or low in contexting.

In a highly contexted situation, much of what people choose *not* to say is essential to understanding the transmitted message. Even though a person may not have said anything directly, others are still expected to understand the unspoken message.

Edward T. Hall was the first person to coin the term "contexting." Hall observed:

> The matter of contexting requires a decision concerning how much information the other person can be expected to possess on a given

subject. It appears that all cultures arrange their members and relationships along the context scale, and one of the great communication strategies, whether addressing a single person or an entire group, is to ascertain the correct level of contexting of one's communication . . . the rules vary from culture to culture, so that to infer by the level of contexting that "they" do not understand may be an insult, even though your assumption is correct.

High context cultures include such nations as Japan, China, Mexico, Greece, the Arab countries, Brazil, and Korea. Mid-level contexted cultures include England, Finland, Italy, and France. Low context cultures include the United States, Denmark, Sweden, Norway, Germany, and the German-speaking portion of Switzerland. This set of examples is very limited and also fails to account for cultural and regional differences domestically. Thus, the Western Apaches of the southwestern United States may well be the most highly contexted of all cultures worldwide, although their numbers are insufficient to affect the general low context communication among the majority of people in the United States. Similarly, regional differences in Germany are apparent in the contrast between relatively higher contexted Bavarians and lower contexted north Germans although all are Germans and all would be lower contexted than the average Briton or Japanese.

Finally, no two cultures share the same level of contexting. Thus, in any cross-cultural exchange, one party will act as the higher contexted and one the lower contexted.

In high context cultures much of what is not actually said must be inferred through what may seem to be indirection. To people from lower context cultures, those in high context cultures may seem needlessly vague. Conversely, those from high context cultures may view their low context counterparts as impersonal and confusingly literal. As a communicator in an international business setting, it is important to assess the level of contexting inherent in the communication of the culture in which one conducts business to understand clearly what has been conveyed.

Since contexting represents a cross-cultural shift in the conception of explicit versus implicit communication, any area of business communication in which such distinctions play a part are significantly affected. Thus, in high context cultures, the emphasis on words chosen in general and on the written word in particular is relatively weak since words provide only one aspect of the context of the communication. As a result, how something is said matters more than what is actually said. By contrast, in low context cultures, the actual words matter more than the intended meaning. What

is actually said—and especially what is actually written—matters more than the context in which it was said.

The contexting implications of this variance in the emphasis on the actual word are far-reaching for business. In low context cultures, emphasis on explicit communication leads to a rigid adherence to law while in high context cultures the law is seen as flexible to accommodate different situations. In low context cultures written agreements are seen as binding while personal promises are viewed as nonbinding. In direct contrast, high context cultures are more likely to hold a flexible understanding of written agreements while holding personal promises to be more binding. High context cultures, as a result, find that their interpersonal behavior is governed by individual interpretation (that is, the context of the relationship) while low context cultures find that their relationships are dictated by external rules.

Finally, a correlation exists between face-saving and contexting. Cultures with high contexting are more concerned with face, that is, preserving prestige or outward dignity. Low context cultures are less concerned with face since words are more likely to be taken without underlying implied meaning. As a result, high context cultures tend to favor a business communication approach based on indirection and politeness; low context cultures follow more of a confrontation strategy and use a direct plan approach to business communication. High context cultures tend to interpret directness in communication as uncivil and rude; low context cultures tend to view directness as honest and inoffensive. As a corollary, high context cultures view indirectness as honest and showing consideration while low context cultures view indirectness as dishonest and offensive. Finally, high context cultures tend to prefer minimal amounts of verbal self-disclosure, preferring vagueness to stating the obvious. Low context cultures by contrast are intolerant of vagueness and demand a high amount of explicit verbal self-disclosure.

AUTHORITY CONCEPTION

Different cultures often view the distribution of authority in their society differently. Geert Hofstede, the Dutch international business researcher, has called this dimension of cultural variation "power distance" defining this as "the extent to which a society accepts the fact that power in institutions and organizations is distributed unequally."

The view of authority in a given society affects communication in the business environment significantly as it shapes the view of how a message will be received based on the relative status or rank of the message's sender to its receiver. Thus in a relatively decentralized business environment—as exists even in many highly centralized U.S. companies—people generally pay attention to a person based on how convincing an argument he or she puts forth, regardless of that person's rank or status within the organization or society at large. By contrast, in a highly centralized culture, a relatively high-ranking individual communicates is taken very seriously, even if one disagrees.

This, in turn, has far-reaching effects for the form managerial communication takes based on the relative authority conception of a given culture. In working with cultures such as Israel and Sweden, which have a relatively decentralized authority conception or small "power distance," one might anticipate at the outset more acceptance of a participative communication management model. Conversely, in working with cultures such as France and Belgium, one might anticipate at the outset relatively less use of participative management models and more concern with who has the relevant authority.

NONVERBAL BEHAVIOR

Among the most markedly varying dimensions of intercultural communication is nonverbal behavior. Knowledge of a culture conveyed through what a person says represents only a portion of what that person has communicated.

Much of nonverbal communication may be broken down into six areas: dress; kinesics, or body language; oculesics, or eye contact; haptics, or touching behavior; proxemics, or the use of body space; and paralanguage. Any one of these areas communicates significant information nonverbally in any given culture.

One of the most apparent differences is how dress is interpreted. The message given by polished shoes, for instance, could easily be lost on a culture in which sandals are the standard footwear. Similarly, a woman's decision to wear her best suit would be lost in a culture in which no women wear business suits.

Even when cultures share similar forms of dress, the message inherent in the choice of clothing is not always the same. For instance, the selection of a conservative tie for a formal negotiation might well be shared by several cultures, but exactly what a conservative tie is (even when all parties belong to cultures in which men generally wear ties) remains determined by the standards that prevail in that particular culture. Thus, what is a conservative tie in one culture may seem unconservative or flashy in another, giving a different message altogether.

Just as importantly, people often bring to a cross-cultural meeting ethnocentric prejudices regarding what they believe to be proper dress. Thus, a European or American may condemn as somehow less than civilized a Saudi or Iranian in traditional garb. Conversely, a Saudi or Iranian may well consider as flagrantly immoral the bare face, arms, and legs of a European or American woman in business attire.

Nonverbal behavioral differences in kinesics may be less obvious than dress differences. How people walk, gesture, bow, stand, or sit are all, to a large part, culturally determined. In many cases, a kinesic sign well understood in one culture is totally unknown in another culture. In Indonesia and in much of the Arab world, for example, it is offensive to show the soles of one's feet to another. This often clashes with behavior in the United States where foot-crossing is common with no attention to where one's sole points. In Japan, a relatively elaborate system of bowing is common but has no counterpart in the United States. This entire system of nonverbal communication is therefore generally lost on most U.S. business-people.

Some kinesic behavior may carry distinctly different meanings in more than one culture. In such cases, all parties recognize the gesture, but interpret it differently. During George Bush's visit to Australia while he was president, he held up two fingers in a V sign. In both countries the symbol is widely understood, but in the United States the "V" emblem is a sign of good will, victory, and solidarity, while in Australia it carries a lewd, sexual meaning.

Haptics or touching behavior also reflects cultural values. In a generally nonhaptic society such as Japan, touching another person in a business setting even with a handshake is traditionally considered foreign. While those Japanese familiar with U.S. handshaking may adapt to its use, one can expect that such cultural compromise would not easily extend to so haptic a response as a pat on the back.

The United States itself is a fairly nonhaptic society, particularly between men. In many cultures that behave more haptically, men often walk with arms interlinked or hold hands which to U.S. males might appear effeminate or overly intimate.

Oculesics or the use of eye contact also varies significantly depending on the culture involved. In several cultures, for example, it is considered disrespectful to prolong eye contact with those who are older or of higher status. In many cultures, it is considered improper for women to look men in the eye. By contrast, in the United States, studies have shown that eye contact has less to do with age or rank than with a person's credibility or sense of belonging. While fairly steady eye contact in the United States may indicate the listener's interest and attentiveness, intense eye contact may prove disconcerting.

Finally, proxemics or how far apart people stand when speaking or how far apart they sit in meetings carries significant information to people who share the same culture. Here, too, as with other nonverbal behavior, such information is likely to be garbled across cultures. Personal space is culturally determined. In the United States, for instance, people tend to feel most comfortable in business settings when speaking at approximately arm's length apart from each other.

In many Latin American, southern European, central African and Middle Eastern cultures, however, a comfortable conversational distance would be much closer. Indeed, in many parts of the world, friendly or serious conversations are conducted close enough to feel the breath of the speaker on one's face. The U.S. or northern European communicator unaware of this may face a very discomforting situation, with the speaker literally backing his or her U.S. or northern European counterpart into a corner as the speaker continues to move closer to the retreating listener. The result in a business situation could be disastrous. The speaker with the closer personal space conception would likely feel distrustful and even spurned by the listener with the larger space conception. Conversely, the person with larger personal space conception might feel the encroaching speaker to be pushy, overly aggressive, or rude.

TEMPORAL CONCEPTION

International business communication is also affected by cross-cultural differences in temporal conception or the understanding of time. Most U.S. and northern European businesspeople conceive of time as inflexible, a thing to be divided, used, or wasted. This is not, however, a universal view. How one uses time, consequently, may profoundly affect the way in which business is conducted in various parts of the world.

While it is dangerous to overgeneralize, most cultures fall with varying degrees into two types of temporal conception. The first type adheres to preset schedules in which the schedules take precedence over personal interaction or over the completion of the business at hand. Edward Hall coined the term ''monochronic'' to describe this system of temporal organization. By contrast, those who follow what Hall termed a ''polychronic'' temporal organization rank personal involvement and completion of existing transactions above the demands of preset schedules.

Admittedly, not all societies can be easily divided into monochronic and polychronic systems. Often certain subsets within a society will function monochronically, while others within the same culture will function polychronically. For example, most major corporations in the United States follow a strict monochronic system. Many doctors in the United States, however, follow a comparatively polychronic

system. Still on the whole, one might generalize that U.S. culture as a whole holds a monochronic conception of time.

Because people generally complete tasks at the expense of scheduling in polychronic societies, people in high authority may become easily overwhelmed with multiple tasks. To prevent overloading people in positions of high authority, those in polychronic societies often use subordinates to screen for them. Once a person can get past those screening, the person in authority will generally see the task through regardless of the relative importance of the task. Because a polychronic system encourages a one-on-one interaction, such cultural organization usually allows for highly personalized relationships to flourish between the person in authority and the task-bringer. The flow of information is open in both directions at all times. Indeed, for the system to work smoothly, it is to the advantage of both superior and subordinate to stay fully aware of all aspects—professional and personal—of each other's lives. This personal involvement makes it even harder for the person in authority to refuse once the task is presented. Thus, in such situations being able to break through those who screen for the person in authority is often the hardest part of having the person in authority assist in a task. No direct barriers exist between the leader and the subordinate; the superior will always welcome the subordinate. This develops a system in which influence and close circles of contacts among those screening for those higher up create an informal and unofficial business hierarchy.

In a monochronic system, personal feelings are rarely allowed to flourish on the job precisely because personal involvement must not be allowed to affect preset schedules if the system is to function smoothly. Personal relationships are determined by the terms of the job. Multiple tasks are handled one at a time in a prescheduled manner. People in authority are, in contrast to those in polychronic societies, available by scheduling appointments. In such a system, time screens tasks for the authority figure rather than the authority figure's subordinates or the personal relationship among the people involved.

The communication strategy for facing a generally polychronic system of time conception differs significantly from the strategy for facing a generally monochronic one. For example, in a polychronic system, one should be aware that people distinguish between insiders and those outside the existing personal relationships. One must therefore try to establish an inside connection to facilitate the effectiveness of a given message. By contrast, in a monochronic society, one needs only to schedule a meeting with the appropriate people. One should not expect people in a monochronic system to give preference to those they know over complete strangers. The outsider is treated in exactly the same fashion as the close associate.

The influence of temporal conception on communication is extensive. This is further complicated by the fact that no culture is exclusively polychronic or monochronic. Members of any culture lean to one direction or the other, although the cultures as a whole may organize their thoughts and conceive of time more one way or the other. The central issue here is to keep alert to communication differences that would indicate that one culture was more monochronic or polychronic in orientation, and to adapt one's communication strategies accordingly.

CONCLUSION

As business has turned more and more to an integrated world market to meet its needs, the difficulties of communicating at a global level have become increasingly widespread. Lack of understanding deriving from ethnocentrism or ignorance of culturally based assumptions erroneously believed to be universal can readily escalate to unproductive conflict among people of differing cultural orientation. Still, in an increasingly competitive world economy, it is harder for the successful business venture (than it may have been in the past) to conduct business exclusively within the safe confines of a single domestic business environment. Consequently, the need for dealing with intercultural differences and cross-cultural communication barriers has grown as well.

The cross-cultural issues suggested in this brief summary provide a framework for asking the right questions when preparing for business communication with those from other cultures. By asking the way in which each of these factors is likely to affect communication with people from that specific culture, many of the communication barriers between people of different cultures can be anticipated.

[David A. Victor]

FURTHER READING:

Hall, Edward T. *The Dance of Life: The Other Dimension of Time.* Garden City, NY: Anchor Press/Doubleday, 1984.

Hall, Edward T. *The Silent Language.* Greenwich, CT: Fawcett Publications, 1959, p. 10.

Hofstede, Geert. *Culture's Consequences: International Differences in Work-Related Values.* Beverly Hills, CA: SAGE Publications, 1984.

Hofstede, Geert. *Cultures and Organizations: Software of the Mind.* London: McGraw-Hill, 1991.

Ricks, David A. *Big Business Blunders: Mistakes in Multinational Marketing.* Homewood, IL: Dow-Jones Irwin, 1983.

Victor, David A. *International Business Communication.* New York: Harper Collins, 1992.

CUSTOMER RELATIONS

Customer relations describes the resources of a company—be it a store, manufacturer, or service industry—that are devoted to discerning and then serving the needs of customers. In earlier times, this was known as the complaint department, the part of the operation that dealt with negative client comments, returns, and other concerns. Renaming this function customer relations is more than a word game. It reflects the proactive nature of the department in modern industry and retailing. Customer service extends beyond sales and advertising to ensure that the company understands its customer base and what its customers really want. Customer relations works within the business to direct the quality of the product or service, its delivery, and the advertising strategy to meet that need. This part of a business operation responds to customer inquiries and complaints and resolves problems so as not to lose customers; at the same time, customer relations works with the marketing department to attract new customers.

The short answer to why so much attention should be paid to customer needs and dissatisfied customers is that such attention has been found to support long-term success. Some of the earliest such endeavors began with concern over product reputation—as far back as the early days of the Industrial Revolution in the 1890s. Placing one's own name on a product was considered to be a bond of trust between the customer and the merchant and/or manufacturer.

Over the years, many firms developed a policy of "the customer is always right," finding that it was more profitable to take a small loss and keep a good customer than to argue with customers about alleged defective products or problems that occurred with staff. Firms developed complaint departments to deal with customers who had bad experiences with products or services.

As consumer consciousness grew in the late twentieth century the focus of the industry shifted from dealing with dissatisfied customers as they complained, to a more active approach of reaching out to discover why the complaint was made, to ensure that the dissatisfied customers remain customers, and to study each case and improve the product or service and the way in which it was delivered to customers. In the 1960s the complaint department began to be known as the customer relations department. Customer relations departments still take on the complaints. The advent of **toll-free numbers** makes it easier for people to register complaints—and praise. Customers who phone in praise for or complaints about a product are often offered free coupons and recipes for that product.

Studies of the customer relations movement show that the shift to an aggressive policy of customer study is more than "nice," it is profitable for business. Resources expended in the customer service area are more than offset by savings from customers not lost. Goodwill toward all customers reaps tangible rewards in the form of increased profits for business.

In a study of service industries, Ron Zemke cited two studies by Technical Assistance Research Institute (TARP) in Washington, D.C., on consumer complaints. TARP found that one in four customers was upset enough about a product or service or both to seek an alternative business for that product or service. Of those unhappy customers, however, only five percent had bothered to complain. The other 95 percent just voted with their cash by switching. To reduce the loss of customers in the future, customer relations tries to analyze the five percent who complained in order to understand the ninety-five percent who did not complain yet were unhappy. Customer relations must anticipate the needs of each individual customer, up and down the social scale, across the vast racial and cultural lines that make up the American melting pot.

Zemke and others offer many strategies for building a good customer relations department. The best strategies involve learning as much as possible about the customer base and training staff well as to what customers want and the way they want it. Zemke and others show that a company with excellent service toward customers is one that understands the tie between employee relations and customer relations. A well-trained satisfied employee is better able to satisfy the needs of the customer.

An acknowledged leader in customer service in the retailing field is Nordstrom's department store. Nordstrom's stresses quality in every aspect of its service and merchandise down to the last detail. A 1994 *Washington Post* article about a survey of the quality of women's rest rooms in metro-D.C. stores and malls reported that the best overall was Nordstrom's. Nordstrom's was not seeking to highlight this area. When interviewed the Nordstrom local officials seemed not to understand the fuss. Maintaining their store rest rooms as one would maintain one's home bathroom for expected guests is just one small part of Nordstrom's total commitment to customer service. Nordstrom associates are encouraged to learn about their customers, to send thank-you notes, to send postcard reminders to customers when products they might like arrive and to give regular customers advance notification of Nordstrom's infrequent sales.

The conversion of complaint departments to customer relations departments became so widespread that in 1973 the Society of Consumer Affairs Professionals in Business was founded. Consisting of more than 3,000 members who are involved with the management of consumer affairs divisions of businesses, the society takes the cause of customer relations to a national level, promoting harmonious relationships between business, government, and consumers. The society works on ways to help businesses assess and compare their successes and failures in consumer relations and maintains a library and bookstore of materials on customer relations as well as publishing a magazine, *Mobius Quarterly*.

[Joan Leotta]

FURTHER READING:

Albrecht, K., and L. Brandford. *The Service Advantage*. Homewood, Ill.: Dow Jones Irwin, 1990.

Cannie, Joan Koob. *Turning Lost Customers into Gold*. Washington, D.C.: Amacon, 1994.

Connellan, Thomas and Ron Zemke. *Sustaining Knock-Your-Socks Off-Service*. New York: Amacon, 1993.

Desatnick, Robert L. *Keep the Customer!* Boston, New York: Houghton Mifflin, 1990.

Hanan, Mark and Peter Karpar. *Customer Satisfaction: How to Maximize Measure, & Market Your Company's "Ultimate Product."* New York: Amacon 1989.

Whitely, R. C. *The Customer-Driven Company*. Reading, Mass.: Addison Wesley, 1991.

Zemke, Ron and Dick Schaaf. *The Service Edge: 101 Companies That Profit from Customer Care*. New York: NAL Books, 1989.

CYCLE TIME

An important aspect in manufacturing is the cycle time. Cycle time is defined as the total time that a machine or a workstation takes to complete its different tasks or operations on a part or product. This is particularly useful in assembly lines, production lines, or manufacturing cell operations. Cycle time may be used for capacity planning and to determine the following quantities:

- Average production output or rate per period.

- Operating time per day for each machine or workstation.

- Number of machines or workstations required for production flow analysis.

Cycle time includes machine or operation time and idle time that the machine or machining center will experience. In other words:

Cycle time = machining or operation time + idle time

Suppose that the fabrication of a certain part requires the execution of six different operations or tasks as follows:

Task Number	Time Required
Task 1	1.0 minute
Task 2	21.2 minutes
Task 3	0.6 minutes
Task 4	0.8 minutes
Task 5	1.5 minutes
Task 6	0.9 minutes

For simplicity, let's assume that the idle time is negligible, which is not always the ideal case.

To compute the cycle time for this situation, the number and the nature of workstations need to be defined. For example, all tasks may be done on a single machine or a machining center. On the other hand, each task may be performed on a separate machine or in a different workstation. In other words, the determination of cycle time requires the definition of the manufacturing system that will be used to produce the part.

Let's consider these two situations. If all tasks will be done on a single machine or workstation, then the total time required to produce the part is simply the sum of all cycle time and the cycle time is determined to be 6.0 minutes. The processing of tasks in this case is said to be *sequential*.

If we assume that each task will be performed or executed on a different machine, then the cycle time will be the longest time among all tasks, which is 1.5 minutes. In this case, the different tasks are performed in *parallel*.

Once the cycle time has been determined, it is possible to determine the daily production output as follows:

$$\text{Daily Production Output} = \frac{\text{Daily Operating Time}}{\text{Cycle Time}}$$

As an example, Assume that there are two daily shifts, each shift is eight hours long, and the daily operating time is 16 hours or 960 minutes. For the sequential processing case, the daily production output will be:

$$\text{Daily Production Output} = 960/6 = 160 \text{ parts}$$

If the tasks are performed in parallel, the daily production output will be:

$$\text{Daily Production Output} = 960/1.5 = 640 \text{ parts}$$

Optimum cycle times can be determined using the line balancing techniques. Line balancing problems are mostly concerned with assembly line or production lines where optimum decisions are needed regarding the optimum number of work stations needed for a certain assembly or production line. Line balancing problems are also concerned with the determination of optimum cycle times for a given assembly or production line. In order to appropriately solve a line balancing problem, the following information may be needed: production quantity for each product item, operations performed on each item, sequence of operations, and operation times.

[Ahmad K. Elshennawy, Ph.D.]

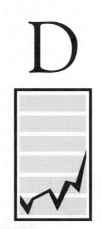

D

DATA SECURITY

Businesses have a wide range of data security concerns. With the widespread use of electronic data, new security measures have been developed to protect data from uninvited or unwanted intrusion, intentional malice, human error, and physical damage. In larger companies an entire department may be devoted to maintaining data security and establishing policies for employees to follow. In some cases firms may bring in data security consultants to develop systems and procedures to ensure their data is secure.

General information security management involves taking such steps as announcing and making periodic reminders to the staff about established security policies. Companies may make a registration list of all systems and directories and who has access to them. Data security personnel may work with regular security personnel to ensure that unauthorized personnel are prevented from entering the premises. These procedures help in a general way to prevent data theft or tampering.

Security measures involving mainframe **computer systems** can be classified into five general types. In some cases these measures can be adapted to personal computers and **local area networks (LANs)**. The first involves identification and authentication. Through the use of assigned passwords, companies can limit access and identify who the system's users are. The second is known as discretionary access control. These types of security measures regulate who has access to specific applications, files, and servers. Companies can restrict users to specific directories of

network resources, for example, and take other restrictive measures to prevent unauthorized use and modification.

Audit control, the third security measure, makes it possible for system managers to keep track of all events on a company's computer network. While they may generate too much information, audit controls track what programs have been used, what files have been opened, and other aspects of network use. Another mainframe security measure is known as object reuse, which performs such tasks as clearing sensitive data from memory and hard disks and automatically disconnecting inactive computers and other network connections. Object reuse programs may also lock out a user who has left a workstation unattended for a certain length of time.

Secure communications, the final security measure, means protecting the network or system at the point where it meets the outside world. Techniques to secure communications include leasing private data lines instead of using public lines, using modem management programs to prevent unauthorized dial-ins over the telephone, and encrypting data before sending them over a public network or local area network.

Electronic data must also be made secure from physical as well as human threats. Power failures and surges, hardware failures, and fire and water damage are some of the physical threats against which companies must protect their data. Many companies back up their data on a daily basis and store it off-site to protect it from physical and natural disasters. A disaster recovery plan can help a company prepare for the unthinkable—a natural disaster that destroys all of its data.

The U.S. government is in the process of developing new computer security standards. For many years the existing standards were found in specifications of the U.S. Department of Defense's Orange Book, which was developed essentially for military applications. With the growing use of electronic data in business, industry, and government, a need arose for a commercial computer security standard. The National Institute of Standards and Technology is developing security standards that will address what a secure computer system is supposed to do (functional requirements) as well as how to determine that a system does what it is supposed to (assurance requirements).

SEE ALSO: Automated Office Security

[David Bianco]

DATABASE MANAGEMENT SYSTEMS

A database is collection of units of data (or facts) that are logically organized and can easily be searched for information. The term database typically refers to data in electronic form, which is stored on and can be searched by computer. A database may consists of one or multiple computer files.

A database management system (DBMS) is the category of computer **software** program used for creating, organizing, retrieving, analyzing, and sorting information in computer-based databases. Often such software is informally referred to as "database software." The database and the DBMS, however, are distinct, just as a text document is distinct from the word processing program used to create and modify it.

Companies have many uses for accurate, comprehensive databases. These include databases of clients, vendors, employees, inventory, supplies, product orders, and service requests. The design of a database to allow it to handle all the relevant attributes of a type of data and to provide the desired methods for analyzing the data is an important **management** task of an enterprise.

HISTORY

There are forms of databases that predate the computer age. During the first half of the twentieth century, companies kept large numeric databases on punched cards, and the data was retrieved and sorted by mechanical tabulating equipment. However, the term database—sometimes written as two words— did not come into usage until the 1960s, and today it is only used to refer to computer databases.

Computer databases predated true DBMS's, because in the 1960s most computers stored data sequentially on magnetic tape. This precluded quick access to data, which requires random access such as

that which is possible with a spinning computer disk. Early database systems, which were developed for mainframe computers, could handle only a single data file and were oriented toward specific data processing functions. For example, a certain DBMS would be used for maintaining **accounting** records and an entirely different DBMS program would be used for tracking inventory. Later, DBMS's were developed that could handle multiple functions and different files. Instead of being designed for a specific industry or task, subsequent generations of DBMS's have offered more flexibility for customization, including the ability to perform additional programming. DBMS's tailored to specific applications, however, continue to abound. Some of the more common general purpose DBMS's for the large and complex data processing needs of corporations include Oracle, INFORMIX, Ingres, and Sybase SQL-Server, all of which run on UNIX-based workstations and minicomputers, and DB2 for IBM mainframe computers.

DBMS's became commercially available for the personal computer in 1981 with the introduction of dBASE II, a program originally developed in 1976. This and subsequent versions, dBASE III and dBASE IV, were the most popular DBMS's for personal computers in the 1980s. By the 1990s, numerous DBMS's for DOS, Windows, and the Macintosh operating systems were competing on the market, but none dominated. Some of the more common programs are Paradox, FoxBASE and its successor FoxPro, Microsoft Access, FileMaker Pro, DataEase, and Lotus Approach. These software packages typically cost several hundred dollars.

DATABASE AND DBMS STRUCTURES

Units of data within a database are generally called "records." Each record is unique and is further broken down into a limited number of "fields," which describe attributes of the record. For example, in an employee database a record exists for each employee, and the fields within each record may be for employee name, title, salary, date of hire, telephone extension, supervisor's name, etc. The fields may or may not be unique to the record, but at least one must be unique for the record to be unique. The fields may contain fixed or variable information, and they may contain text or numbers. Figures in value- and date-type fields can be used for computations when the DBMS is used to analyze the data. Fields can even contain pictures, video clips, or sound if the DBMS and the computer hardware are capable of handling such multimedia forms of data. Records with the same set of field classifications are kept within one file. In a business database, sets of records often exist both for concrete things, such as clients or vendors, and for activities, such as orders, and payments. Examples of fields within records of an order file include purchase order number, date of order, part number, price, and customer identification number.

Except for DBMS's that are sold already tailored to specific industry applications, the user of the DBMS can also design the fields for the records and specify how fields, records, and files relate to each other. In companies or organizations that maintain complex databases, a database designer or database administrator is responsible for this task. Designing databases is also a major activity of computer **consulting** services.

Once a database is designed, records are created by performing data entry. Records can be added, deleted, or modified one at a time and at the very instant that a computer user types in the changes; or, when there are large volumes of records that need changing, they can by updated, or "processed," by a computer operating in batch mode at some specified time after multiple computer users have input the requests for changes. Such batch mode data processing typically takes place after the business day is over and typically is used to record the day's sales or shipments.

While all databases include records and fields in one form or another, DBMS's vary in how they treat the relationships between records and files. The two best known categories of DBMS structures or models are flat-file and relational. Flat-file systems treat the relationship between fields and records as a two-dimensional table with columns and rows for records and fields, and they are limited in their ability to analyze data from more than one file. Some of the simpler flat-file programs, usually called "file managers" instead of DBMS's, can only open and analyze records in one file at a time. Relational DBMS's, on the other hand, can analyze data from multiple files with complete flexibility of relationship between records of the multiple files. Other types of DBMS models that can relate data in more than one file but only in restricted relationships include hierarchical DBMS's, which relate records from different files in a one-way, many-to-one tree structure. Another type, network DBMS's, can relate records bidirectionally. The ability to relate records reduces the redundancy of data and makes it unnecessary to update multiple records when data in a single related record changes. A typical scenario of the relationship between data in two files would be the linking of a record in a purchase order file to the customer file based on a single unique field, such as a customer identification number. The latest model is the object-oriented database, in which units of data are treated as abstract objects. This model is most suited for databases containing a combination of media, such as text, sound, and pictures. By the early 1990s, relational DBMS's had become the most popular category for new DBMS purchases among businesses.

DBMS USAGE

Once a database is created, the DBMS can be used to select records that meet desired requirements based on the information contained in their fields. For example, in using an inventory database, the user can check the availability of a product that meets certain criteria—such as style, color, and presence of additional features—each of which are defined in the fields. A retrieval request may be made for a single, specific record or for multiple records. An example of a request for multiple records in a customer database would be for all those customers whose invoices are past due. This would be done by requesting records in which the difference between today's date and the date the invoice was sent, for which there is a field, is greater than 30 days and the date of payment receipt field is blank. Different DBMS's offer different methods of typing the commands or "queries" to retrieve information. The most common query command format is Structured Query Language (SQL). Some DBMS's offer the choice of query by command, through menus, or by example forms.

In addition to data retrieval, DBMS's allow the sorting of data in the fields by any criteria. This could involve all records in a database or, more practically, those that meet specified selection criteria. For example, records can be selected from a sales database of all salespeople who sold over a certain total dollar amount, and then this list can be sorted to rank the salespeople by amount sold.

Finally, DBMS software allows the generation of various printed reports from the selected data. One of the most common formats of a database report is a table based on a list of sorted records with selected fields displayed. Data from individual records can also be automatically merged into "templates" or empty fields of specific forms or form letters. Additionally, mailing labels can be created by printing data from name and address fields. Some DBMS's also incorporate additional software features, such as a **spreadsheet**, **word processor**, and communications functions, permitting further manipulation of information retrieved from the database.

Databases and DBMS's are used on all kinds of computer systems, many of which permit multiple users to access a database simultaneously. On mainframe and minicomputer systems, users access the database through multiple terminals. DBMS's are also increasingly being used on client-server **computer networks** of personal computers or workstations. The database and the DBMS server software reside on one computer that acts as the server, and other copies of the DBMS software are on each of the client computers linked to the server. Finally, there are distributed databases, in which a database is physically stored in two or more computers at different locations yet managed by a single DBMS through copies of the software at each location.

BUSINESS APPLICATIONS

Databases are used in all kinds of businesses for all types of functions: in sales to compile information about clients and potential clients and to keep track of client correspondence; in accounting to keep track of accounts payable and receivable; in purchasing to choose suppliers and their goods and place orders; in **manufacturing** to keep track of supplies of component or raw materials; in shipping and receiving to keep track of orders and shipments; and in **human resources** to maintain records of employees and match resumes of applicants to job openings. The same DBMS may be used to manage all such tasks in the same organization.

Customer databases are especially important to service industries that maintain ongoing customer relationships. Financial service institutions, such as **banks**, stock brokerages, and insurance companies, rely on DBMS's to keep track of customer financial accounts. Utilities, such as telephone and electric companies, also keep databases of customers, tracking usage of utility service, varied rates, and bills. Maintenance and repair services, such as those repairing office equipment or appliances, keep appliance service and repair records for each customer. A specialized DBMS called contact management software is popular for keeping track of clients or contacts.

For certain brokers or agents, database systems are especially crucial for selecting the goods or services to be sold. One of the first large-scale DBMS's for business was the Sabre airline reservation system introduced in 1964. It contains data on the flights and seats of most commercial airlines, permitting a coordination of reservations. Both airline booking departments and travel agents depend upon Sabre and other computer reservations systems, such as Apollo. Travel agents also use other computer reservation systems to book hotel rooms in major hotels. Other businesspeople who use databases in their business include real estate agents, who keep databases of properties for sale that can be searched by the attributes desired by individual customers. Car dealers and brokers also use databases for locating the various makes and models of cars and their accessories. **Real estate** agency or car dealer networks may use distributed databases to share information on the properties or cars each broker has locally.

Finally, for some companies, the production or management of a database *is* their business. They conduct their business by selling access to their databases to other companies or the public. The types of databases provided by database vendors include literature retrieval databases (citations and full text of articles or reports), numeric databases (such as stock quotes), individual credit histories, directories, client names, maps or other graphics, and employment listings. Some of the better known text information database vendors are DIALOG Information Services, Lexis/Nexis, Dow Jones News/Retrieval, ORBIT/Questel, and Chemical Abstracts Service. Corporations subscribe to these database services to research information about their market, competitors, or emerging technologies. For most subscription databases, the software used by the customer for searching the databases is not the same as the DBMS used by the company for creating and updating the database. The software used by the client only permits retrieval and possibly sorting and printing of the data, and it typically has an easy-to-use graphical user interface. Such database software is called "search software." The client may remotely access the vendor's database through telephone lines with the use of communications software and a modem, or the database vendor may distribute the database with search software on disk, typically a CD-ROM (compact disc-read only memory).

[Heather Behn Hedden]

FURTHER READING:

Awad, Elias M., and Malcolm H. Gotterer. *Database Management*. Danvers, Mass.: Boyd & Fraser Publishing Company, 1992.

Matheson, Ken. "Databases: More Than a Bunch of Numbers," *CMA - The Management Accounting Magazine*. June 1993, pp. 13-16.

Mattison, Robert M. *Understanding Database Management Systems: An Insider's Guide to Architectures, Products, and Design*. New York: McGraw-Hill, 1993.

Ullman, Jeffrey D. *Principles of Database and Knowledge-Base Systems*. Vol. 1, *Classical Database Systems*. Rockville, Maryland: Computer Science Press, 1988.

DATABASE MARKETING

Database Marketing (DBM) takes place when a computer is used to compile data on a customer, and this data is used to determine the customer's tastes, needs and desires. Once these are established, the attempt is made to sell the customer a product or service that is tailored to him or her, in the hope that the customer will remain a loyal one and keep buying from the goods or service producer. In short, DBM is customer tailored marketing. While the customer is a very important component of any marketing approach, in DBM, the customer, rather than the product or service one is trying to sell, is the focus. DBM is a form of **direct marketing**, but the two are not synonymous. It goes beyond the straightforward direct marketing approach of a regular mass mailing, which the customer often discards, or cold calling. Rather, DBM is a marketing tool involving sophisticated computer analysis in order to target the right customers and establish a long lasting relationship with them.

Establishing a relationship with customers is certainly an old concept. It used to be that the corner grocer or hardware store owner would see his customers regularly and be able to gauge mentally what their needs and tastes were; then he would try to tailor his merchandise to satisfy them. But the era of mass marketing, which is still with us today, has attracted many thousands of customers to a company, as in the case of airline or long distance phone firms. Mass marketing helped to reduce prices and make them affordable to all. However, what was missing was a relationship with the customer and the resulting high attrition rate of customers to competitors who offered still cheaper prices. Most companies cannot survive in the face of constant price reductions, as was the case with many airline companies. Moreover, many customers, especially the more affluent ones, value personalized service and quality as highly as cheap prices.

The advent of personal computers in the early 1980s and the resulting information explosion made it possible for some intrepid marketers to have an edge over the **competition**. Businesses in which competition was fiercest—banks (after deregulation in the 1980s), car dealerships, and retail stores—were turning to computers in creative ways to attract the right customers and, more importantly, to keep them coming back. Firms were becoming aware that hanging on to customers was more important than attracting new ones.

Examples of DBM strategies abound. A car dealership sells a vehicle to a customer and asks the customer to fill out a questionnaire in order to help the car dealer better understand what motivates a customer. Weeks later, the dealership mails the customer a ''free'' vehicle checkup. Weeks after that, the customer receives an invitation to a ''dealership picnic,'' followed by other social events. Several years later, the car dealership attempts to interest the customer in trading in the old vehicle for a new model. The customer meanwhile has ''bonded'' with the dealership and presumably would not be attracted to competing dealerships offering cheaper prices. In another example, a retail store might send a questionnaire to its customers, find out what service customers would like, and offer that service (such as free gift wrapping) in the hope that the customer will keep coming back.

The more a company knows about a customer or likely customer, the better able it is to attract and hold on to that customer. The requirements for a successful DBM strategy are a sophisticated understanding of the database—somebody who is a computer specialist—as well as a creative marketing person or staff who can generate and implement ideas that attract the right customers. Since DBM takes time to produce results, another requirement is long range persistence and patience.

Many companies have been reluctant to invest in DBM because the payoff is not immediate and the requirements are demanding. Numerous studies confirm the fact, however, that the company which shies away from DBM will eventually lose customers to the competitor that does employ this strategy. This is especially true in businesses in which competition is most intense, such as in retail or in non-profit organizations dependent on private donations.

DBM appears to cater to the affluent customer with lots of discretionary income. However, in 1993, Pizza Hut compiled a vast database on millions of customers who had phoned in pizza orders. From this list, Pizza Hut mailed coupons to all its phone-in customers, offering discounts on their particular favorite (which Pizza Hut could determine from the data). Most of these customers responded positively.

DBM, in which the right customer is targeted and remains a loyal customer, is the wave of the future. It is not without controversy. Often a great deal of personal information is required of the customer, and the issue of privacy is going to become more important as more organizations and businesses turn to this method of marketing. Data obtained by private industry and organizations is unregulated. Abuses of information have occurred. Surveys conducted in the early 1990s by private research firms such as Lou Harris, indicated a strong reluctance on a consumer's part to too great an invasion of privacy. How a firm handles the information it gathers will increasingly determine its future success or failure using DBM strategy.

[Sina Dubovoy]

FURTHER READING:

Hughes, Arthur M. *Strategic Database Marketing*. Probus Publishing Company, 1994.

The New Marketing Strategy: How to Implement a Profit-Driven Database Marketing Strategy. 1995.

DAY CARE

SEE: Child/Elder Care

DEBIT AND CREDIT SYSTEM

Debits and credits are the basis for the system of double-entry **accounting** that is accepted as standard accounting practice today. The system had its beginning in the Renaissance, when a 15th-century Franciscan monk, Luca Pacioli (1445?-1514?). described an accounting system whereby every financial transaction would have a debit amount and an equal and offsetting credit amount. One of the basic rules of accounting is that, for each recorded transaction, the debit amount must equal the credit amount.

A corresponding rule is that the sum of all debit balances must equal the sum of all credit balances. When bookkeepers run a trial balance, they are checking to make sure that the debit balances equal the credit balances. If they are not equal, an error has been made and must be found. Thus, the debit and credit system of accounting has a built-in means of checking for accuracy.

Accounts are usually set up as T-accounts, where the stem of the "T" serves to divide left and right sides of the account record. All debits are recorded on the left side, and credits on the right side. While such designations are arbitrary, they are nevertheless universally observed. In accounting, the words debit and credit have no other meaning and, unlike in common usage, have no positive or negative connotations. They are often abbreviated as Dr. and Cr.

Increases in asset accounts, such as cash, marketable securities, accounts receivable, or plant and equipment, are recorded in the debit side of the account. Increases in liability accounts, such as accounts payable or accrued expenses, and in owners' equity accounts, such as paid-in capital or capital stock, are recorded in the credit side of the account. Similar rules apply to revenue and expense accounts. Since an expense is a reduction in owners' equity, increases in expense accounts are recorded on the debit side. Increases in revenue accounts are recorded on the credit side, since revenues increase owners' equity. In this way account balances conform to the equation that states that a company's assets are equal to the sum of its liabilities and its owners' **equity**.

[David Bianco]

DEBT

Debt refers to promises made by the issuing firm to repay the original amount borrowed (the principal) when due and to make regularly scheduled interest payments on the unpaid balance. The person or firm making the loan is called the creditor or lender. The corporation borrowing the money is called the debtor or borrower.

Coupon bonds involve regularly scheduled payments, called coupons, between the original date of issue and the maturity date. They also have a par (or face) value that is paid to the owner of the bond at the maturity date. If the market price equals the face value, the bond is a par bond. Because market **interest rates** fluctuate daily, the contract interest rate will seldom equal the market interest rate on the date the bonds are sold. When the market price exceeds the face value, the bond is a premium bond. When the price is less than the face value, the bond is a discount bond.

Some **bonds** do not involve regular interest payments. These bonds, called zero coupons, or pure discount bonds, promise to pay a certain amount, once, at a specified time in the future and sell for less than face value.

In contrast to equity, debt is not an ownership interest in the firm. Creditors generally do not have voting power. The corporation's payment of interest is a fully tax-deductible cost of doing business. Unpaid debt is a liability of the issuer. If it not repaid, the creditors can legally seize the assets of the firm, which could result in either liquidation or reorganization. Thus, a major cost of issuing debt is the possibility of financial distress. This possibility does not arise when equity is issued.

The money market is the market for debt instruments with a maturity of one year or less at the time of issuance. Short-term debt is often referred to as unfunded debt. Major types of money market instruments include: **treasury bills**, commercial paper, and Eurodollar deposits. Long-term debt consists of fixed income securities with a maturity of more than one year.

The two major categories of long-term debt are public issues and private placements. In a public offering, the security is offered to the general public, giving any investor the right to purchase part of the new issue. The issuance process is governed by the regulations of the **Securities and Exchange Commission**. By contrast, **privately placed securities** are directly placed with an institutional investor and not offered to the public. In a private placement, the specific terms are negotiated between the parties involved. Issuers may prefer private placements because they do not have to disclose information about the firm or its plans in registration documents. Although this type of issue is more flexible, it generally carries a higher interest rate than a public offering.

THE DOMESTIC BOND MARKET

The primary raisers of funds in the domestic bond market are the U.S. Department of the Treasury, federally sponsored credit agencies, state and local governments (municipalities), and corporations. The amount of new, long-term debt financing in the United States significantly exceeds the volume of equity financing.

The largest issuer of securities in the world is the U.S. government. **Treasury notes** and bonds are long-term obligations of the federal government. These obligations are similar in the structure of their payment streams. Each is coupon bearing, but notes have an initial maturity of one to ten years, whereas bonds have an initial maturity of greater than 10 years, often 30 years.

Federal agencies—direct arms of the U.S. government—does not issue their own debt, but instead secure financing through federal financing bank issues. Federally sponsored agencies are privately owned entities, such as the Federal National Mortgage Association (Fannie Mae), and raise funds in the long-term debt markets. With the exception of Government National Mortgage Association (Ginnie Mae) securities, there is no federal guarantee of agency issues. Nevertheless, federal securities are perceived as low risk, and therefore have slightly higher yields than those of comparable Treasury issues.

The largest components of the federal agency debt market is the mortgage market. Through the process of securitization, it has become common to create a mortgage pool, and then create securities based on the mortgages in the pool. Thus, illiquid individual mortgage loans are transformed into more liquid, less risky securities backed by pools of mortgages. With these mortgage pass-through securities, the original lender continues to collect payments from the borrower and passes them through to the investors in the mortgage pool. Agency-guaranteed mortgage pass-throughs, issued by Ginnie Mae and Fannie Mae, provide an attractive means for investors to invest in safe residential mortgages with yields higher than those on Treasury issues.

State and local governments also issue vast quantities of securities, called municipal bonds. Interest on municipals is exempt from federal, and often state, taxes. Although the stated yields on municipals are lower than on other debt instruments, when one converts the stated yields to an equivalent before-tax return on a taxable investment, the returns may be attractive. Two basic types of municipal bonds are general obligation bonds, which are backed by the "full faith and credit" of the issuer, and revenue bonds, which are repaid from revenues generated by the project they were sold to finance (such as a toll road). The corporate sector is made up of industrials, public utilities, railroads, and transportation, as well as financial issues. The municipal bond market exceeds the size of the corporate bond market, but it is not very liquid.

THE INTERNATIONAL BOND MARKET

An international bond is a bond available for sale outside the country of its issuer. Thus, if a U.S. corporation issues a bond that is available for sale both in the United States and Great Britain, the issue is an international bond. If a U.S. firm issues a bond denominated in a foreign currency for sale exclusively in the country of the foreign currency, the bond is a foreign bond.

There are a number of different types of international bonds, including straight bonds, floating-rate bonds, equity related bonds, and Eurobonds. A straight bond is a bond with a fixed payment schedule with no special features, such as convertibility into stock or a floating interest rate. Thus, a straight bond is a conventional coupon-paying debt instrument. A floating-rate bond is a bond that pays a different coupon rate over time as the level of interest rates fluctuates. Equity-related bonds include both convertible bonds and bonds with equity warrants. A Eurobond is a bond issued by a borrower in one country, denominated in the borrower's currency, and sold by an international syndicate outside the borrower's country. Thus, if IBM were to issue securities denominated in U.S. dollars in Europe, the issue would be a Eurobond. In recent years, the significant majority of new international bond issues have been straight bonds. Equity-related bonds made up the next largest category, with floating-rate instruments being relatively scarce.

One of the dominant forms of short-term credit in the international market is a form of bank lending called a syndicated loan—a loan made by a consortium of banks to a single borrower. Syndicated loans are priced as a spread above the London interbank offering rate (LIBOR). LIBOR is the rate that banks participating in the international debt market charge each other for short-term loans.

EVALUATING DEBT SECURITIES

Debt securities are evaluated on the basis of a number of factors, including yield, maturity, method of repayment, security provisions, and tax treatment. Bonds may be either secured or unsecured. Unsecured bonds, which are termed debentures, carry a higher rate of interest than secured bonds. With a secured bond or mortgage bond, the issue is backed by some asset (the collateral). Accordingly, the risk to the investor is lower, and so is the yield.

The relationship between the interest rate on a bond and the time to maturity is called the yield curve or the structure of interest rates. Generally, the yield curve is upward sloping whereby longer maturity bond issues provide higher yields than shorter maturities. All else equal, the longer the time to maturity, the greater the fluctuation in bond prices for a given change in interest rates. Therefore, owners of longer maturity issues demand higher interest rates because of the greater price sensitivity of their bond holdings.

Bonds can be repaid at maturity, at which time the bondholder will receive the face value of the bond, or they may be repaid in part or in entirety prior to maturity. A **sinking fund** is an account managed by a bond trustee for the purpose of repaying the bonds. The issuer makes annual payments to the trustee, who then uses the funds to retire a portion of the debt. A call provision allows the issuer to repurchase, or call, a bond issue at stated prices over a specific period. The call price is generally higher than the bond's face value. The difference between the call price and the face value is termed the call premium. Rather than having the entire bond issue maturing at one date, some corporations issue bonds with staggered maturity dates, known as serial bonds.

Another method of retiring bonds is through conversion. A convertible bond is a bond that gives the bondholder the option of turning in the bond and receiving in return a specified number of shares of **common stock**, thereby converting the bond into stock.

A significant feature of a corporate bond issue is the rating received by Moody's Investors Service or Standard & Poor's. The bond ratings generally range from AAA to D and reflect the risk of default on the security. Bonds rated BBB or above are termed investment grades, whereas those rated BB or below are termed noninvestment grade (or junk bonds).

In determining a rating, much attention is paid to such factors as cash flow and earnings relative to interest and other obligations (coverage ratios) as well as to operating margins and returns on capital and total assets. Besides financial ratios, other important factors of importance include the nature of the industry, the relative position of the firm within the industry, and the overall quality of **management**.

SEE ALSO: Eurobond Market; Mortgages/Mortgage-Backed
     Securities

[Robert T. Kleiman]

FURTHER READING:

Fabozzi, Frank, J. *The Handbook of Fixed Income Securities*. 3rd ed. Homewood, IL: Business One Irwin, 1991.

Lederman, Jess, and Keith Park. *Global Bond Markets*. Chicago, IL: Probus Press, 1991.

DECISION MAKING

Decision making can be a process (with a decision the action) that allocates goods and values in the unit of resources which is the "system" (one's own time and assets, family or organizational wherewithal, or community and national resources). In a business context, the system is the business organization as the decision unit, with the manager or executive the decision maker.

All businesspersons recognize the painful necessity of choice. Furthermore, choice must be timely, because "not to decide to is to decide" (as the popular saying goes). Ultimately, what drives business success is the quality of decisions, and their implementation. Good decisions mean good business.

The concept of decision making has a long history; choosing among alternatives has always been a part of life. But sustained research attention to business decision making has developed only in recent years. Contemporary advances in the field include progress in such elements of decision making as the problem context; the processes of problem finding, problem solving, and legitimation; and procedural and technical aids.

THE ELEMENTS OF DECISION MAKING

THE PROBLEM CONTEXT. All decisions are about problems, and problems shape context at three levels. The macrocontext draws attention to global issues (exchange rates, for example), national concerns (the cultural orientations, toward decision processes of different countries), and provincial and state laws and cultures within nations. The mesocontext attends to organizational cultures and structure. For example, how does Ben and Jerry's Homemade Inc. approach decisions, as opposed to the Federal Reserve Board? How are universities different from governments, and how are these in turn different from Fortune 500 companies? The microcontext addresses the immediate decision environment—the organization's employees, board, or office.

Decision processes differ from company to company. But all companies need to take these three context levels into consideration when a decision episode begins. Fortunately, economical ways to obtain this information are available and keep the cost of preparing for decisions from becomimg prohibitive.

PROBLEM FINDING AND AGENDA SETTING. To be a problem, an issue must be identified as problematic and of consequence. An important difficulty in decision making is failure to act until one is too close to the decision point—when information and options are greatly limited. Organizations usually work in a "reactive" mode. Problems are "found" when there is a "whack on the side of the organizational head." Nevertheless, processes of environmental scanning and strategic planning are designed (though they do not often work well) to perform problem reconnaissance to alert business people to problems that will need attention. Proactivity can be a great strength in decision making, allowing less fateful experiments, prototypes, and research. Proactivity requires, however, a decision intelligence process that is missing from many organizations.

Even if problem finding works, a subsequent procedure of agenda setting is needed. Less is known about how potential problems get on the action agenda in companies. Too frequently, potential areas of difficulty are noticed, and even mentioned, but are neither heeded nor resolved.

As a problem is identified, information is needed about the problem and potential actions to be taken. One kind of information is purely factual—what is the problem? A complication is that the processes and procedures of gathering and packaging information—"editing"—often leaves business executives at the mercy of "editors." In 1958, J. G. March and H. Simon pointed to an important aspect of the editing process, one they called "uncertainty absorption." They suggest that since uncertain information may imply the editors (other staff in the organization) are inept, editors tend to edit out the uncertainty and present information to their superiors as more certain than it really is.

Another kind of information reflects the array and priority of solution preferences. These options are the "values" in the famous "fact and value in decision-making" idea. What is selected as possible or not possible, acceptable or unacceptable, negotiable or non-negotiable depends upon the culture of the firm itself and its environment, as in the statement "We here at J & J always look for victory."

A third area of information is the possible scope and impact that the problem and its consequent decision might have. Knowledge about impact may alter the decision preferences. To some extent, knowledge about scope dictates who will need to be involved in the decision process.

PROBLEM SOLVING. Problem solving (or problem managing) can be divided into two parts—process and decision.

The process of problem solving—what system does the organization actually have for making decisions about problems? In many organizations, there doesn't seem to be any system—what happens, happens. (2) The decision, or choice, itself. It is the moment when selection is made—someone gets the job, or someone gets promoted, while the others don't. This "point" is often elusive, even to those who are in the same room at the same time.

THE DECISION PROCESS. Several sets of elements need to be considered in looking at the decision process. One set refers to the rationales used for decisions. Others emphasize the setting, the scope and level of the decision, and the use of procedural and technical aids.

RATIONALES. One approach to process is optimizing, in which all decision possibilities are listed, explored, and prioritized. The rational decision maker proceeds, perhaps one-item-at-a-time, through the list and the "best" solution is found after a complete review. This is also called the rational-individual approach (Daft, 1992). The problem, of course, is that such a process in its pure form cannot really be accomplished, and it is time consuming and exhausting. Alternatively, one can decide on something which is acceptable for the matter at hand, though less than optimal. These approaches reflect the famous distinction made by Simon, and reported (later) in March and Simon (1958, pp. 141-142) between optimizing and "satisficing" in the solution of day-to-day organizational problems—the difference between finding the sharpest needle in the haystack and finding one sharp enough to sew with.

From a welfare economics perspective, the economist would list preferences, and similarly work through the list. This perspective focuses somewhat on system optimality, and questions might be raised about whether individual optimality should be replaced by system optimality (does the hidden hand really work?). Braybrook and Lindbloom (1961) present a good discussion of these problems.

They also introduce a new approach called disjointed incrementalism. Lindbloom has also called it "muddling through." Decisions are made "at the margin" or built, element by element (with an element being the smallest irreducible part of the decision matrix, a matrix which contains many such small parts), until the overall decision has been assembled. In this approach what we often call "decisions" might better be called a "decision mosaic"—a construction made of decisions about each element. (Once the mosaic has been constructed, one can use "decision sculpting" to look at the overall mosaic and make adjustments so that everything fits).

Timing and order can be crucial in the "disjointed incremental" approach. To be effective, decisions must be taken in a timely manner, such that the overall "construction project" can proceed. This just-in-time approach occurs at the appropriate moment, not the last possible moment. Sequence is also important. Dominant elements which influence later elements need to be completed first. While it is clear in construction that one does the basement first, then adds the other floors, such clarity is not always obvious in decision processes.

Sometimes events take over, in what Daft calls "nonprogrammed" decisions. A process of constraints and tradeoffs dominate, often simultaneously (Daft, 1992).

SETTINGS. In most cases, business decisions are made in collective settings called "meetings." Meetings, committees, and taskforces have taken on a pejorative meaning. Most meeting humor expresses a meeting's ineptitude, as in the examples, "A camel is a horse constructed in a meeting," and "A meeting is a group which takes minutes to waste hours!" Meetings can be improved, and made into effective information processing systems which have decisions as their outcome. Much work has been done to develop more effective meetings. Antony Jay's famous piece, "How to Run A Meeting" (1976) essentially became the script for the well-known meeting improvement video starring John Cleese, "Meetings, Bloody Meetings" (Video Arts). *Entrepreneurial Systems for the 1990s* (1989), also deals with the issues of executive group decision making. Meetings can be thought of as places where "coalitions" crystalize and ebb (Daft, 1992. p. 335). Coalitions are important in business organizations because of the myth of the individual decision maker. As discussed, organizational "editors" assemble information, making subdecisions along the way. But also, different perspectives are needed. The final decision mosaic is a construction of many hands, as often blessed as made by the decision maker. Our individualistic culture retains a fiction that individuals decide; more often they are components in a decision process. (The truth is even more stark—many times decisions are made, or not made, in the meeting situation without an actual decision maker; rather, there is a decision system/team which works well, or not).

SCOPE AND LEVEL. Finally, attention must be paid to problem scope and organizational level. Problems of large scope need to be dealt with by top levels of the organization. Similarly, problems of smaller scope can be handled by lower levels of the organization. Most organizations could improve on getting the right problems to the right decision groups. Typically, top level groups spend much too much time deciding low level, low impact problems, while at the same time avoiding problems of high importance and organizational impact.

In recent years, a number of procedural and technical aids have been developed to deal with effective group decision making in meetings (Tropman, 1985). Other such aids deal with the use of **computers** and computer based decisions. Decision assistance software, called groupware, is helpful. Groupware is a term used for computer based decision support systems, group writing programs, and group spreadsheet programs—programs which tally preferences in order to aid the business team in making high quality decisions (Johansen, 1988). For example, in "chauffeur driven" systems individuals respond over a set of keypads to questions. Overall preferences can be displayed anonymously without regard to race, gender, or power.

THE OUTCOMES. Whatever the process, there also needs to be an outcome. Many times there is uncertainty in business meetings about what has actually happened. In exit interviews the author has conducted, participants of decision making meetings were unclear about what happened, and in a considerable number of instances different participants thought different results had been achieved. Stepping away from a decision, or failing to nail it down, is a non-result which occurs for many reasons. One cause is stalling; opposing interests neutralize each other. Another cause is that decision making tears at group cohesion, something groups resist, especially when the same individuals defeated this morning are one's colleagues this afternoon. And there is sometimes honest confusion about what is up for decision, and which group (or person) should make it.

One should not confuse results with decisions. Keep the following equation in mind: $R = D + I$. RESULTS equals DECISION plus IMPLEMENTATION. Great decisions can be foiled by lousy implementation; great implementation can save awful decisions. The point is that decisions do not equal results; there is another step, or steps. (There is a story about the researcher who asked members of a multi-level organization: "If technology permitted, at what level could this place become automated?" Respondents from all 12 levels of the organization gave the same answer: "Below me!")

LEGITIMATION PROCESSES

Once made, or while being made, decisions need to be legitimated. Decisions are accepted by the losers, even if they do not like the outcome. Quinn, Rohrbaugh, and McGrath (1985) provide an excellent slant on decision legitimacy with four perspectives or orientations to decision making in organizations—consensual, empirical, rational, and political as in Table 1.

Readers will doubtless recognize their own styles, and may also sense that their business approaches different kinds of decisions with different perspectives. There may also be conflict over which perspective is appropriate. Two key points are important, and for high quality decisions, some of each of these perspectives is needed. First, if an executive or firm works only in one area, then there is vulnerability and exposure from the others. Secondly, one can supplement or buttress one's own style with that of others, in a "decision team." It's unlikely that any of us have the ability to work in all of these areas; we can build a decision ensemble that can.

Another approach to decision legitimacy is to look at decision rules, which are defined as "extragroup norms which make decisions ok." There are several decision rules, and they conflict with the other

Table 1
Four Perspectives on Decision Making and Their Central Concerns, Bases, and Results
(based on Quinn, Rohrbaugh, and McGrath, 1985)

Concerns/ Bases/ Results	Perspectives			
	Consensual	Empirical	Rational	Political
Chief Concern	Supportability	Accountability	Efficiency	Legitimacy
Key Base	Participation Base	Data Base	Goal Base	Adaptive (Interests) Base
Result/Outcome	Good Feelings Results	Numbers Add Up	Logic Is Flawless	Stakeholder Needs Met

(an outcome determined by any one of them would have a different distribution of winners and losers). So far, five rules seem prominent: the extensive rule (one person one vote); the intensive rule (what people who care or feel deeply about the issue want); the involvement rule (what those who might have to implement any decision prefer); the expert rule (what the "lawyers" or other experts think); and the power rule (what the boss wants). It appears these rules are brought into decision settings from the culture at large. Since they conflict, decisions tend to be sought which will address as many as possible. Three or more seems like the minimum acceptable number. In other words, managers who can frame decision options which can be seen to address at least three of these five at any one time are more likely to make decision progress than managers who can't (Tropman, 1991).

EVALUATING DECISIONS AND DECISION MAKING PATTERNS

Managers, executives, and business people attending to each of these areas still have more elements to take into consideration. One of them is the quality of the decision. In the press for action, groups not only avoid decisions, they make premature decisions (and exhibit other problems).

DEFINING THE QUALITY OF DECISIONS. Decisions are a product, and decision makers need to look at those products and ask if they are of high quality. One method is to sample the group's decisions (or your own, for that matter) and give them a grade: A B C D F. An A decision is one in which all stakeholders come out ahead, though they do not need to come out equally ahead. The B decisions involve winners and losers, but the final result is that the organization is better off. The C decision, a very common one, occurs when there is a shift in the winner/loser mix, but the organization is no better off than it was. The D is the opposite of the B; now there are some losses which mean that the organization is worse off. Finally there is the "nuclear war" decision, the F. In this decision, everyone winds up worse off than before.

This method relies on judgement, as a small group looks at each decision in the sample and gives it a grade. It certainly has no claim to superiority over other methods the business person might develop. The

important thing about decision analysis, however, is that some system be used so that a review can occur. Once decision making systems are aware that their decisions are being reviewed, greater attention will be paid, and they are likely to improve, for reasons of the measurement itself.

What happens after the "grading?" The executive can sit down with a staff or an operations group and review the results, seeking to find out, in the spirit of constant improvement, what—about problem finding, problem context, decision legitimation, or problem solving—could be improved. This "decision audit" can be helpful in pointing to specific problem areas, and in calling attention to the whole area of decision making in general. Care must be taken to avoid blame, and to avoid a "shooting the messenger" mentality, in these situations.

A further step one can take is the decision autopsy. Here, one takes an A and an F decision and takes each of them apart. One seeks to find out what went right, and continue it; and what went wrong, and stop it. For most companies, these are not the same things. Because most organizations are doing some things right and some things wrong at the same time (we all have many processes going on), they tend to assume that if they are doing things right then they are not doing things wrong. This error is a common one, because wrong things and right things are generally in different business behavioral repertoires. Consider Figure 2. It assumes that an organization has a mix of success decisions and failure decisions. Depending upon the mix or ratio of these, the organization can be in any quadrant. True excellence requires that one do lots right, and little wrong (the upper left quadrant). Executives should seek to have a decision pattern that can fit there. Doing lots right and lots wrong at the same time can lead to a shooting star organization, one that can "drop dead" at any moment (upper right quadrant). Many organizations don't make many right decisions, or many wrong ones—they don't do much at all. These organizations are "lingering", and may move into "organizational death" (from the lower right to the lower left quadrant).

Why do decisions go wrong? Given the great desire to do the right thing, decisionwise, one might wonder why things go wrong, so badly, so often. The

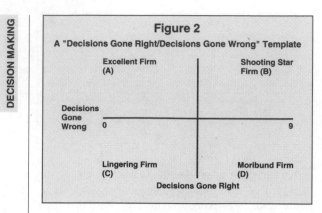

Figure 2

A "Decisions Gone Right/Decisions Gone Wrong" Template

Excellent Firm (A)　　　　Shooting Star Firm (B)

Decisions Gone Wrong　0　　　　　　　9

Lingering Firm (C)　　　　Moribund Firm (D)

Decisions Gone Right

reason is that there are important limitations in each of the five areas mentioned above, especially in the decision process.

The following list suggests some of the more common and perhaps inherent, process limitations: limited organizational capacity; limited information; the costliness of analysis; interdependencies between fact and value; the openness of the system(s) to be analyzed; the diversity of forms on which business decisions actually arise (adapted from Braybrook and Lindbloom, 1963). Problems of time insufficiency, distraction, low level of decision making skill, conflict over goals (and no way to resolve the conflict) are also important (Janis and Mann, 1977). While these cannot be completely controlled, executives can be alert to them.

A second category of difficulties is captured in a number of common pitfalls of the decision procedure. One such pitfall is "decision avoidance psychosis" which occurs when organizations put off making decisions that need to be made until the very last minute. One form of this is the "non-decision." It may appear a decision has been made, when in reality one has not. Things go along very much as they have. Over time this pattern of nondecision can lead to the boiled-frog phenomenon, as described by Tichy and Devanna (1986). This phenomenon takes its name from an experiment in which one puts a frog in a petri dish filled with water, and slowly heats the water over a burner. The frog boils to death. Why does it not leave? The answer seems to be that the barely perceptible difference in the temperature is never enough to cause action. This "just noticeable" difference phenomenon is an important source of nondecision in organizations. Members see things pretty much as they were, and thus wrongly conclude that there is no need to act.

A second problem is decision randomness. This process was outlined in the famous paper called "A Garbage Can Model of Organizational Choice" by Cohen, March and Olsen (1971). They argued that organizations have four roles or vectors within them: problem knowers (people who know the difficulties

the organization faces): solution providers (people who can provide solutions but do not know the problems); resource controllers (people who don't know problems and don't have solutions but control the allocation of people and money in the organization) and a group of "decision makers looking for work" (or decision opportunities). For effective decision making, all these elements must be in the same room at the same time. In reality, most organizations combine them at random, as if tossing them into a garbage can.

Decision drift, or the Abilene Paradox is another famous bad decision case (Harvey, 1974). A group of people were outside of Abilene, Texas with nothing to do. It was hot. Somehow they wound up going into town (many miles, dusty drive, no air conditioning) to have a very bad meal. On the way back, the "search for guilty parties" began. As they sought to find out whose idea this was, the troubling truth emerged that it was no individual's idea—each had thought the others wanted to do it; no one had questioned it. The Abilene Paradox has come to refer to group actions where there never really was a decision to take that action.

Decision coercion, also known as **groupthink**, is another very well known decision problem (Janis, 1983). In groupthink, decisions are actually coerced. It is a false agreement in the face of power. When the boss says, "We're all agreed then," most at the table say "Aye." Only later, in the hallway, when the real discussion occurs, do the problems surface.

Naming these common problems will not prevent them. However, because they are so common, executives can be more aware of them, and seek to prevent them.

IMPROVING DECISION MAKING

What can businesspersons do to improve the decision making progress at their firms? Six sets of possibilities are explored below.

1. Improve the setting. Organizing better meetings, with more focused agenda, clear questions, the right information and people are very helpful steps. Avoid the garbage can; get the relevant people in the same room at the same time. Pay attention to planning and seek closure.

2. Use Logical techniques. In the film "Meetings, Bloody Meetings," a five step discussion sequence is proposed: a) State the problem; b) present the evidence; c) argue about what the evidence proves; d) decide; e) act. And, the narrator says, "Keep people from jumping ahead or going over old ground." This technique is as good as any. The use of

the **Delphi technique**, in which group preferences are continually sought, tallied, and then fed back to the group, is another approach.

3. Enlist decision aids. Groupware and decision software might be helpful, as well as steps to improve one's meeting processes. Specific attention to the structure of the decision system might yield useful results.

4. Evaluate decisions and decision making patterns. Evaluation tends to focus the attention, and make individuals and teams more sensitive to what they are actually doing in their decision making tasks. Evaluation is especially helpful in today's business environment because of the interdependency of individuals in a decision matrix. No one person does it all, regardless of what she or he may think.

5. Be prepared to deal with poorly structured problems. The executive may still seek some answers to questions of what she or he could do to develop personally. This question is especially pertinent to a certain class of problems that require decision, but are poorly structured. The executive needs to develop his or her own approach to a point where it can be dealt with by others. McCaskey (1982) suggests skill areas that would help in dealing with such poorly structured problems.

6. Play the right game. Much emphasis here has been on business decision making. But what kinds of decisions might executives be looking for? Complaints about ''micromanaging'' and ''pie-in-the-sky'' are common enough that one might conclude executives have a substantial lack of clarity about the types of decisions they should be looking to make. Sayles and Chandler (1971) provide a useful list:

- Giving problems their proper weight and context

- Taking problems at the right time

- Taking problems in the right sequence

- Establishing and shifting decision criteria

- Acting as the coxswain (beating out the pace of decision action)

Decision making is at the heart of business operations. High quality decision making is essential for businesses to thrive and prosper. Unfortunately, the decision process is hard to pin down and understand and often receives far less attention than it deserves. The future of one's business is written in the decisions of today. Every effort to make those decisions of high quality will be rewarded.

SEE ALSO: Management Science; Operations Management

[John E. Tropman]

FURTHER READING:

Benedict, R. *The Crysthanthemum and the Sword.* Houghton Mifflin, 1946.

Braybrook, David, and Charles E. Linbloom. *A Strategy of Decision.* The Free Press, 1963.

Cohen, M. James, G. March, and J. Olsen. ''A Garbage Can Model of Organizational Choice.'' *Administrative Science Quarterly.* 17, 1. March, 1972, pp. 1-25.

Daft, Richard. *Organization Theory and Design.* 4th ed. West Publishing, 1992.

Edwards, Ward. *Decision Making: Psychological Aspects.* Cambridge University Press, 1993.

Harvey, Jerry B. ''The Abilene Paradox.'' *Organizational Dynamics.* Summer, 1974, pp. 63-80.

Janis, I., and L. Mann. *Decision Making: A Psychological Analysis of Conflict, Choice, and Commitment.* The Free Press, 1977.

Janis, I. *Crucial Decisions.* The Free Press, 1989.

Janis, I. *Groupthink: Psychological Studies of Policy Decisions and Fiascoes.* Houghton Mifflin, 1983.

Jay, Antony. ''How To Run A Meeting.'' *Harvard Business Review.* March/April, 1976, pp. 43-57.

Johansen, Robert. *Groupware: Computer Support for Business Teams.* The Free Press, 1988.

Kahneman, D., Paul Slovic, and A. Tversky. *Judgement Under Uncertainty: Heuristics and Biases.* Cambridge University Press, 1982.

March, J. G., and H. Simon. *Organizations.* Wiley, 1958.

McCaskey, Michael. *The Executive Challenge: Managing Change and Ambiguity.* Pitman. 1982.

Plous, S. *The Psychology of Judgement and Decision Making Temple.* University Press, 1993.

Quinn, Robert, J. Rohrbaugh, and M. R. McGrath. ''Automated Decision Conferencing.'' *Personnel.* November, 1985, pp. 49-58.

Simon, Herbert. *Administrative Behavior.* 2nd ed. Macmillan, 1960.

Thurow, Lester. *The Management Challenge.* MIT Press, 1986.

Tichy, Noel, and Mary Ann Devanna. *The Transformational Leader.* Wylie, 1986.

Tropman, John E., and Gersh Mornigstar. *Entrepreneurial Systems for the 1990s.* Quorum Books, 1989.

Tropman, John E. ''The Decision Group.'' *Human Systems Management.* 3 1982, pp. 107-118.

Tuchman, Barbara. *The March of Folly: From Troy to Vietnam.* Knopf, 1984.

DECISION SUPPORT SYSTEMS

From a very elementary viewpoint, decision support systems are a set of manual or computer-based tools that assist in some **decision making** activity. In order to discuss the support of decisions and what these tools can or should do, it is necessary to have a perspective on the nature of the decision process and thus what it means to support it. One way of looking at a decision is in terms of three areas or components. The first component is the data collected by a decision maker to be used in making the decision. The second component is the process selected by the decision maker to combine this data. Finally, there is an evaluation or learning component that compares decisions and examines them to see if there is a need to change either the data being used or the process that combines the data. These components of a decision interact with the characteristics of the decision that is being made. One approach to categorizing decisions is to consider the degree of structure in the decision making activity.

THE STRUCTURE OF DECISIONS

A structured decision is one in which all three components can be fairly well specified, i.e., the data, process, and evaluation are determined. Usually structured decisions are made regularly and therefore it makes sense to place a comparatively rigid framework around the decision and the people making it. An example of this type of decision may be the routine **credit** granting decision made by many businesses. It is probably the case that most firms collect rather similar sets of data for credit granting decision makers to use. In addition the way in which the data is combined is likely to be consistent. For instance, household debt must be less than 25 percent of gross income. Finally, this decision can also be evaluated in a very structured way (specifically when the marginal cost of relaxing credit requirements equals the marginal revenue obtained from additional sales). A system to support this type of decision may simply be a checklist or form to ensure that all necessary data is collected, i.e., the data gathering phase is supported by eliminating the problem of missing data. If the choice is also to support the procedural or process component of the decision, then it is quite possible to develop a program either as part of the checklist or form. In fact, for structured decisions it is also possible and desirable to develop computer programs that collect and combine the data, thus giving the process a high degree of consistency or structure. When there is a desire to make a decision more structured, the support system for that decision is designed to ensure consistency. Many firms that hire individuals without a great deal of experience provide them with detailed guidelines on their decision making activities and support them by giving them little flexibility. One interesting consequence of making a decision more structured is that the liability for inappropriate decisions (discriminatory credit practices) is shifted from individual decision makers to the firm.

At the other end of the continuum are unstructured decisions. These decisions have the same components as structured ones, however, there is little agreement on their nature. For instance, with these types of decisions, each decision maker may use different data and processes to reach a conclusion. In addition, because of the nature of the decision there may also be few people that are even qualified to evaluate the decision. These types of decisions are generally the domain of experts in a given field. This is why firms hire **consulting** engineers to assist their decision making activities in these areas. To support unstructured decisions requires an appreciation of individual approaches, and it may not be terribly beneficial to expend a great deal of effort to support them.

Generally, unstructured decisions are not made regularly or are made in situations in which the environment is not well understood. New product decisions may fit into this category for either of these reasons. To support a decision like this requires a system that begins by focusing on the individual or team that will make the decision. These decision makers are usually entrusted with decisions that are unstructured because of their experience or expertise, and therefore it is their individual ability that is of value. One approach to support systems in this area is to construct a program that simulates the process used by a particular individual. These systems have been called expert systems. It is probably not the case that an expert decision maker would be replaced by such a system, although it may offer support in terms of providing another perspective of the decision. Another approach is to monitor and document the process that was used so that the decision maker(s) can readily review what has already been examined and concluded. An even more novel approach used to support these decisions is to provide environments that are specially designed to give these decision makers an atmosphere that is conducive to their particular tastes. The key to support of unstructured decisions is to understand the role that individuals experience or expertise plays in the decision and to allow for individual approaches.

In the middle of the continuum are semi-structured decisions, and this is where most of what are considered to be true decision support systems are focused. Decisions of this type are characterized as having some agreement on the data, process, and/or evaluation to be used, but there is still a desire not to place too much structure on the decision and to let some human judgment be used. An initial step in analyzing which support system is required is to understand where the limitations of the decision maker may be manifested, i.e., will it be in the data acquisition portion, or in the process component, or possibly in the evaluation of outcomes. For instance, suppose an insurance executive is trying to decide whether to offer a new type of product to existing policyholders that will focus on families with two or more children that will be ready to attend college in six to nine years. The support required for this decision is essentially data oriented. The information required can be expressed in terms of the following query (question) on the insurance company's database: "Give me a list of all of our policyholders that have a college education and have more than two children and the ages of these children are between 10 and 12 years."

Of course this is not the decision but merely provides the decision maker with data that they consider relevant. To support this portion of the decision would require a query system attached to a database that contains all of the policyholders of this firm. The easier that this query system is to use for decision makers, the better it will be able to support the data acquisition phase of different decisions. There are an increasing number of on-line computer systems that are specifically designed to assist in the acquisition of data. These systems offer combinations of keyword and matching text type searches. Examples of this type of system are Infotrac, Lexis, and Nexis. Each of these systems has a large collection of references which can be searched for using different combinations of keyword and text searches. For example, using the Infotrac system, you could look for all journals articles published before 1989 that are about bankruptcy.

PROCESSING INFORMATION

Another limitation that decision makers confront has to do with combining or processing the information that they obtain. In many cases these limitations are due to the number of mathematical calculations required. For instance, the insurance executive that wanted to offer the new product now has to decide on a price for the product. In order to make this decision, the effect of different variables (including price) on demand for the product and the subsequent profit must be evaluated. The executive's perceptions of the demand for the product can be captured in a mathematical formula that portrays the relationship between profit, price, and other variables considered important. Once the relationships have been expressed, the decision maker may now want to change the values for different variables and see what the effect on profits would be. The ability to save mathematical relationships and then obtain results for different values is a feature of many decision support systems. This is called "what-if" analysis and spreadsheet packages such as Lotus 1-2-3 and Quattro Pro can support this decision making activity quite well.

When the decision maker obtains these profit figures, his choice probably still cannot be made without some additional mental processing. For instance,

the executive may have estimated what interest rates would be during the life of the contract. Certain probabilities could be assigned to different levels and used in the calculations, such as 10 percent probability that rates will go down 2 percent, 40 percent that they will rise 6 percent, and so on. There may also be certain aspects of the decision that can't be easily quantified, such as the policies of state and federal governments. So even though the calculations may indicate that a certain demand for the product will be achieved at a certain price, the decision maker must use his or her judgment in making the final decision. If the decision maker simply follows the output of a process model, then the decision is being moved toward the structured end of the continuum. In certain corporate environments, it may be easier for the decision maker to follow the prescriptions of the DSS; users of support systems are usually aware of the risks associated with certain choices. If decision makers feel that there is more risk associated with exercising judgment and opposing the suggestion of the DSS than there is in simply supporting the process, the DSS is moving the decision more toward the structured end of the spectrum. Therefore, the way in which a DSS will be used must be considered within the decision making environment.

Another problem with the use of support systems that perform calculations is that the user/decision maker may not be fully aware of the limitations or assumptions of the particular processing model. There may be instances in which the decision maker has an idea of the knowledge that is desired, but not necessarily the best way to get that knowledge. This problem may be seen in the use of statistical analysis to support a decision, that is, looking at data to uncover or verify that certain patterns exist. Most statistical packages provide a variety of tests and will perform them on whatever data is presented, regardless of whether or not it is appropriate. For instance, a credit manager may want to know what variables influence the degree to which a person is likely to default on their debt and may use **regression** to uncover this relationship. While this may be an appropriate technique to support the decision, the results may be misinterpreted simply due to a lack of understanding of the situations that may lead to erroneous results. This type of problem has been recognized by designers of support systems and has resulted in the development of DSS that support the choice of the type of analysis. The importance of this component in newer decision support systems can best be realized in the context of the decisions required before the data is acquired or the process is defined. In many decisions, the decision maker is faced with preliminary choices that must be made. Initially, he or she must decide what the real question or decision is, what other decisions must be made to arrive at the final decision, what data may be used for each decision, and so on. As computers gain processing capabilities it becomes possible to include more support for decisions that are part of the process.

Systems such as the Statistical Navigator go through a dialogue with the user to determine what the data's characteristics are and what questions are actually being asked of the data. Then the system suggests what techniques are most appropriate to use. This approach to supporting decision makers requires that the DSS possess a great deal more than database or processing capabilities—it should actually have understanding of the domain in which the system is being used. The Statistical Navigator has knowledge of statistical methods and the benefits, assumptions, and problems associated with each method. A future step would be a system that has an understanding of more processing options than just statistical methods. This might include linear programming or present value analysis. As DSSs start to include many different processing models in the library of choices, two possibilities exist.

One possibility is that the system will merely allow users to choose different methods within the same overall DSS. In this instance the user must still supply the knowledge of what is the most appropriate method and must be able to interpret the results. Another possibility is similar to the approach used in the Statistical Navigator, which would be to include a knowledge of the methods in the DSS and let it help the user select among many methods, not just statistical. Of course each approach does have its problems. There are **software** packages that allow users to select among different methods, but they do not offer a great deal of guidance on their use. Thus, as is the case with certain statistical analysis packages, the conclusions may not be correct because the method was applied incorrectly. The second possibility presents a very different problem, or perhaps challenge; that is, how much knowledge to build into the DSS. A single system with general knowledge of most processing methods would be very popular with most users. However, designers would be confronted with the problem of what to include in a support system or what decision activities should it support. Should it have simple knowledge of the processing methods, such as linear programming, statistical regression, and present value? Or should it have knowledge about decision areas, such as cash **budgeting**, locating a new plant, or pricing policies. This second approach may keep inappropriate data from being used, but then the questions about the role of the decision maker and how structured decisions may become must be addressed. Is the decision maker merely an information provider to a DSS that performs many functions, or should the role of the DSS be simply to make whatever analysis is desired as easy as possible. As software develops more

and more capabilities, designers and users of decision support systems will have to answer the question of what it actually means to support a decision.

[Graham Gal]

DECISION TREE

A decision tree is a diagram that a decision maker can create to help select the best of several alternative courses of action. The primary advantage of a decision tree is that it assigns exact values to the outcomes of different actions, thus minimizing the ambiguity of complicated decisions.

A decision tree represents a choice or an outcome with a fork, or branch. Several branches may extend from a single point, representing several different alternative choices or outcomes. There are two types of forks: 1) a decision fork is a branch where the decision maker can choose the outcome; and 2) a chance fork is a branch where the outcome is controlled by chance. By convention, a decision fork is designated in the diagram by a square, while a choice fork is usually represented by a circle.

A decision tree emanates from a decision fork at the left hand side of the diagram. At least one, if not all, of the alternative branches then lead to new decision forks or chance forks. The diagram may continue to branch as different options and chances are diagrammed. Each branch is assigned an outcome and a probability of occurrence. For example, the decision maker may determine that the chance of drilling an oil well that generates $100,000 (outcome) is 25 percent (probability of occurrence).

To solve the decision tree, the decision maker begins at the right hand side of the diagram and works toward the initial decision branch on the left. The value of different outcomes is derived by multiplying the probability by the expected outcome; in the example above, the value would be $25,000 (.25 × $100,000). The values of all the outcomes emanating from a chance fork are combined to arrive at a total value for the chance fork. By continuing to work backwards through the chance and decision forks, a value can eventually be assigned to each of the alternatives emanating from the initial decision fork.

In the rudimentary example below, a decision maker is trying to determine whether or not to drill an oil well. If the decision is made not to drill the well, no money will be made or lost. Therefore, the value of the decision not to drill can immediately be assigned a sum of zero dollars.

If the decision is to drill, there are several potential outcomes, including: a 10 percent chance of getting $300,000 in profits from the oil; a 20 percent chance of extracting $200,000 in profits; a 10 percent chance of wresting $100,000 in profits from the well; and a 60 percent chance that the well will be dry and post a loss of $100,000 in drilling costs. Multiplying the probability of each outcome by its dollar value, and then combing the results, assigns an expected value to the decision to drill of $20,000 in profits. Thus, the profit maximizing decision would be to drill the well.

For the purposes of demonstration, suppose that the chance of hitting no oil was increased from 60 percent to 70 percent, and the chance of gleaning $300,000 in profits was reduced from ten percent to zero. In that case, the dollar value of the decision to drill would fall to negative $20,000. A profit-maximizing decision maker would then elect to not drill the well.

Although decision trees are considered effective at simplifying complex decisions, their usefulness is limited by the uncertainty inherent in assigning probabilities to events that haven't occurred.

[Dave Mote]

FURTHER READING:

Chase, Richard B. *Production and Operations Management: A Life Cycle Approach*, 5th ed. Irwin, Inc., 1989.

Mansfield, Edwin. *Managerial Economics: Theory, Applications, and Cases*. W.W. Norton & Company, 1990.

DEFAULT

A default on a loan or bond issue occurs when the borrower fails to make the interest or principal payments when they are due. The default risk affects the interest rate charged on a **security**. The higher the default risk, the higher the interest rate charged by lenders. Federal governments do not declare bankruptcy, they simply print more money. Therefore, investors do not have to worry that the U.S. Treasury will default on its **bonds**. As a result, Treasury securities carry the lowest **interest rates** on taxable securities.

Default risk is a function of a number of different variables. The default risk of a particular bond is directly related to the firm's operations. An increase in the riskiness of a firm's operating cash flows will enhance the likelihood of default. On the other hand, a firm operating in a risky environment will be less likely to default if the debt service payments relative to its operating cash flows are modest. In addition, the longer the firm has been operating without creditors incurring losses, the lower the default risk. The longer the firm has sustained operations, the lower the default risk.

MEASURING DEFAULT RISK

The difference in the promised yield between a corporate bond and a government bond with the same coupon and maturity is called the default premium. The greater the chance that the company will experience financial distress, the higher the default premium required by investors. The default risk premium is typically measured by comparing the yield on a long-term Treasury bond with a long-term corporate security that is comparable to the Treasury security in all material respects. The difference in the two yields serves as a proxy for the default premium.

There is a cyclical nature to default premiums. In general, the yield spread narrows during periods of economic prosperity, and widens during economic downturns. A rationale for this phenomenon is that investors may be more willing to take on additional risk during times of prosperity, thus requiring less yield from lower-rated bonds. On the other hand, during economic downturns, investors are more interested in security, and thus require higher yields from riskier, lower-rated bonds.

Patterns in default rates reflect a firm's life cycle. Lower-rated issuers—which are smaller, younger, and more heavily leveraged—tend to have wider **credit** spreads that narrow with maturity. Higher-rated firms—which are more mature and stable—tend to have narrower credit spreads that widen with maturity.

DEFAULT AND BOND RATINGS

To assist bond investors in making their assessment about the future payment prospects of a particular bond issue, ratings services such as Standard & Poor's and Moody's Investors Services assess the quality of various bonds by measuring default risk. Bond ratings have provided a good guide in gauging the future risk of default. Default rates are very low for higher-rated bonds, and increase as the bond ratings decline. The higher the rating, the smaller the number of issues that subsequently default. With lower ratings, the default percentage increases dramatically. Thus, the default premium widens as the ratings decrease.

A number of studies have examined the relationship between bond ratings and the financial variables of firms. These studies have found higher debt ratings assigned to the bonds of firms that have lower **debt** ratios, higher interest coverage ratios, higher returns on **assets**, lower variability in **earnings per share** over time, and lower use of subordinated debt. Accordingly, the bonds of firms having these characteristics would be expected to have a lower risk of default.

Once a bond rating has been established, it can change because of either an improvement or deterioration in the company's fortunes. In recent years, the number of downgraded bond ratings has exceeded the number of upgradings. The inclination of a deterioration in credit quality reflects to a certain extent the greater use of financial leverage as a result of **leveraged buyouts** and restructurings.

Since 1971 there has been a prolonged deterioration in overall corporate credit quality. The default rates associated with different ratings over time have clearly increased since 1971. Since January 1971 the five-year cumulative default rate has increased within all ratings categories. For speculative grade classes, the default rate has increased by approximately three times; for investment grade issues, the increase has been less pronounced. Although the five-year default rates rose during the growth of the **junk bond** market, the deterioration in credit quality was common to both investment grade and speculative issues. The increase in default rates is also associated with the deterioration in leverage ratios within each rating class that started during the mid-1980s. The median earnings to fixed charge ratio decreased and the ratio of debt to assets increased for bonds in the BBB, BB, and B ratings classes.

The rating agencies do not intend their ratings to suggest the same default probabilities at all times. They are reluctant to make ratings changes based on cyclical considerations, although the occurrence of defaults within ratings categories clearly increases during recessions. Therefore, long-term default probabilities are assumed to exhibit relative stability for frequencies longer than the business cycle. Legislators and regulators of the financial markets presume such stability when they set specific ratings levels into law and regulation.

DEFAULT AND OPTION PRICING THEORY

Default has also been analyzed in an option pricing framework. Shareholders possess an option to default, which will be exercised only if the firm's **liabilities** are greater than the value of its assets. Due to shareholders' option to default, a corporate bond can be viewed as equivalent to the combination of a default free Treasury bond less the value of a corporate option to default. As the value of the firm increases, for a given amount of debt, the value of the option to default becomes smaller. If the market value of the firm declines or its assets become riskier, however, then the option to default increases in value.

There are three primary ways in which shareholders can increase the value of the option to default and therefore transfer wealth from bondholders to shareholders. First, a company can make an unexpectedly large **dividends** distribution to its shareholders resulting in an increase in the debt to equity ratio and less collateral to meet bondholders' claims. Second, by issuing more debt having equal or more senior priority, the company dilutes the amount of equity available to meet the claims of the old bondholders. Since the original bonds are now riskier, their price declines. Third, by increasing business risk through the adoption of high risk projects, the value of existing bonds drops.

DEFAULT EXPERIENCE

The rough consensus is that bond portfolios might lose one to two percent of their value each year through default. An analysis of all defaults on straight debt during the 1977-88 period reveals that annual default loss rates averaged 1.63 percent, with a principal loss of 42.7 percent. Low-grade (high-yield) bonds have historically had annual default rates of approximately 3 percent. The default experience for high-yield bonds, however, increased markedly during the 1989-90 period.

Financially distressed firms will attempt to fend off defaulting on their obligations and avoiding liquidation of the firm's assets. Two alternative out-of-court options are an extension and a composition. In an extension, creditors agree to accept delayed payments from the firm. In a composition, the creditors receive a pro-rata settlement (proportionate allocation) of their claims. An additional option is to undertake an exchange offer whereby a new package of securities—often including equity—is exchanged for the existing bond issue. Distressed exchange offers reduce the measured rate of bond defaults.

Empirical work indicates that default rates on low-grade bonds increase with the age of such a bond. Some studies, however, failed to account for the fact that default rates for all bonds, irrespective of age, depend critically on prevailing economic conditions. Further analysis indicates that a significant portion of the higher default rates attributed to the age of a bond might better be attributed to general **economic conditions** than to age itself. There are more defaults in some years than in others, irrespective of bond age. When this systematic variation in defaults is accounted for, the statistically significant relation between bond age and default rate is greatly diminished.

LOAN PORTFOLIOS AND DEFAULT RISK

Loan portfolio diversification to limit default risk—by borrower, type of loan, industry, or geography—is a major objective of bank **management**. By increasing the number and diversity of borrowers in a loan portfolio, bank management reduces the importance of any single borrower to the loan portfolio. This, in turn, decreases the potential impact of a loan loss from a single borrower on that portfolio. In addition, the likelihood of several borrowers defaulting at the same time decreases under diversification, which also increases the predictability of loan losses and reduces potential fluctuations in future bank earnings.

Diversification may result in a lower average credit quality of the loan portfolio. This normally will be offset by higher returns on the portfolio due to the direct relationship between risk and return. Undesirable side effects associated with loan portfolio diversification, however, include higher portfolio origination and servicing costs.

SEE ALSO: Interest Rate Risk

[Robert T. Kleiman]

FURTHER READING:

Altman, Edward, ''Measuring Corporate Bond Mortality and Performance,'' *Journal of Finance*, 44, September, 1989, pp. 909-922.

Blume, Marshall E., and Donald B. Keim, ''The Risk and Return of Low-Grade Bonds: An Update,'' *Financial Analysts Journal*, September/October, 1991, pp. 85-89.

Cantor, Richard, and Frank Packer. ''The Credit Rating Industry,'' *Federal Reserve Bank of New York Quarterly Review*, 19: 2, Summer-Fall, 1994, pp. 1-26.

Fons, Jerome S., ''Using Default Rates to Model the Term Structure of Credit Risk,'' *Financial Analysts Journal*, 50: 5, September/October, 1994, pp. 25-32.

DELEGATION

SEE: Organization Theory; Organizational Behavior

THE DELPHI TECHNIQUE

The Delphi technique is a group problem-solving method in which members never meet face to face. Originally, it was created as a **forecasting** tool. It was created around 1955 for the purpose of estimating the probable effects of a massive atomic bombing attack on the United States. In the mid-1960s, people began applying it to technological forecasting. Since then, its use has spread into other disciplines as a method of identifying and solving problems.

THE BEGINNINGS OF THE DELPHI TECHNIQUE

In the early 1950s, there existed considerable concern in the United States over possible atomic bomb attacks by Russia. Experts were interested in what would happen if such attacks did occur. Therefore, the Air Force, which was responsible for defending the nation's skies, decided to ascertain what damage would be incurred by the country if it were attacked via air. The Air Force commissioned the Rand Corporation to question experts regarding what would happen as a result of these theoretical bombing raids. Thus was born the Delphi technique.

Guessing at what would happen as the result of an atomic bomb raid was dependent on the collection and analysis of large amounts of data. Today, that would be considerably easier than it was in the 1950s. Computers were just coming into popular use then, and data collection techniques had not been refined. Even if large amounts of data were collected, project members would have had to rely heavily on subjectivity, since information on Soviet intelligence, military strength, economic policies, etc., was not readily available. Rand Corporation sought an alternative collection and analysis method.

THE PHILOSOPHY OF THE DELPHI TECHNIQUE

The founders of the Delphi technique based it in part on traditional philosophical premises. They looked to philosophers such as Gottfried Liebnitz, John Locke, Immanuel Kant, Georg Hegel, and Isaac Singer for the foundations of the techniques. They developed a basic set of questions on which to base the Delphi inquiry methods. Questions included:

- How can we independently of any empirical or personal considerations give a purely rational justification of the proposed proposition or assertion? (Leibnitz)

- What is the probability that we are right in our answers? (Locke)

- What alternative sets of propositions exist and which best satisfy our objectives and offer the strongest combination of data and model? (Kant)

- Since every set of propositions is a reflection of a more general theory or plan about the nature of the world as a whole system, does there exist some alternative sharply differing world view that would permit the serious consideration of a completely opposite set of propositions? Why is this opposing view not true or more desirable? (Hegel)

- Have we taken a broad enough perspective of the basic problem? Have we asked the right questions from the beginning? Have we focused on the right objectives? (Singer)

These were by no means all the questions the technique's founders asked, but they represented a start. They were simply looking to find all the strengths and weaknesses involved in their new technique. They applied the philosophical lessons to the realities involved in the method.

REALITY AS PART OF THE DELPHI TECHNIQUE

Delphi technique developers wanted to delineate sharply between theory and reality. Ultimately, what they wanted was for Delphi panel members to conceptualize in realistic terms the problems on which they were working, rather than in theoretical terms. Theoretical findings, after all, were of limited value unless they were matched to reality. Since no atom bomb raids had actually been conducted by the Russians, the Delphi practitioners had no reality on which to base their findings. Yet, they were expected to develop accurate results of a true bombing. The question, then, was how to arrive at those findings without relying too heavily on theory.

They perceived a step-by-step process through which the conceptual process could be carried out. Basically, it consisted of preparing the materials, interpreting the responses, integrating the insights, and presenting the results. The key was in repetition of these steps. For example, once the results of a round of questions were presented to Delphi members, they could reformulate their answers based on the new input. The founders believed that through the constant iterations of the questions based on new information, the answers the participants ultimately presented would be as realistic as possible.

THE DELPHI TECHNIQUE

The Delphi technique comprises several steps involving participants who do not meet face to face. The participants (or panel) might be employees of a specific company conducting a Delphi project or experts selected from the outside for their in-depth knowledge of a given academic discipline or **manufacturing** process. No matter who they were or what their specialties, they were to be kept isolated from one another.

The purposes of keeping them apart are to restrict undue influence that individuals may wield in group situations and protect participants' anonymity. The technique is designed so that the participants' physical presence in the process is unnecessary throughout the multi-step process.

The steps included in the Delphi technique are:

1. Identify a problem.

2. Ask participants to provide potential solutions through a series of carefully designed questionnaires. There may be a specific time horizon over which the solutions are to be based, e.g., for 50 years in cases of scientific breakthroughs.

3. Participants complete the first questionnaire anonymously and independently.

4. The results of the first questionnaire are tabulated at a central location, transcribed, reproduced, and forwarded to each participant.

5. After reviewing the initial results, members submit new solutions.

6. They may make new estimates, often based on a 50-50 probability, as to whether each breakthrough will occur earlier or later than predicted by the other participants. Or, they might suggest that the events predicted may not occur at all and explain why they feel that way. In any case, each round of results invariably triggers new resolutions.

7. The submission of new solutions based on reiterations of the questionnaire process is repeated until the participants reach a consensus.

Generally, three to four cycles of the process result in a consensus among the participants.

ADVANTAGES OF THE DELPHI TECHNIQUE

There are several advantages to the Delphi technique. One of the most significant is its versatility. The technique can be used in a wide range of environments, e.g., government planning, business and industry predictions, volunteer group decisions. Another important advantage lies in the area of expenses.

For example, the Delphi technique saves corporations money in travel expenses. They do not have to gather participants from several points of the globe in one place to resolve a problem or predict the future, yet they can still generate relevant ideas from the people best suited to offer their expertise. This is particularly beneficial to multinational corporations, whose executives and key personnel may be based in cities as far apart as Melbourne, New York, Tokyo, Buenos Aires, and London.

The technique also protects participants' anonymity. Thus, they feel better protected from criticism over their proposed solutions and from the pitfalls of ''groupthink'', i.e., the withholding by group members of different views in order to appear in agreement. On the other hand, the technique has its drawbacks.

THE DISADVANTAGES OF THE DELPHI TECHNIQUE

The Delphi technique is somewhat time consuming, which renders it ineffective when answers to problems are needed quickly. It might also be deficient in the degree of fully-thought-out resolutions. People acting together in a group setting benefit from others' ideas. Thus, there might be more insightful and pragmatic resolutions to problems offered by people in interactive settings, e.g., through the nominal group technique, in which participants are gathered in one place but operate independently of one another. However, in situations where time is not of the essence or group interaction is not important, these disadvantages diminish in importance.

VARIATION ON THE DELPHI TECHNIQUE

There exist variations of the original Delphi process, which was applied primarily to technical topics. For example, there is the Policy Delphi, which marked the first major deviation from the original technique.

In the original process, the goal was to seek a consensus among homogeneous groups of experts on a given topic. Several years after the Delphi technique came into use, proponents introduced the Policy Delphi, which was based on a somewhat different approach.

The Policy Delphi tries to generate the strongest possible opposing views on the potential resolutions to a problem. Policy Delphi is based on the premise that the person (or people) making the ultimate decision in the process does not want the group to generate the decision. Rather, the idea is to have an informed group present all the options and leave the ultimate resolution to the decision maker.

SITUATIONS IN WHICH THE DELPHI TECHNIQUE IS PRACTICAL

The Delphi technique is applicable in virtually any situation requiring group solutions to problems or prognostications on future events. For instance, government officials, medical specialists, and business executives have used the technique with considerable success in a variety of situations since its inception.

For example, in 1970, Professors Alan Sheldon of the Harvard Medical School and Curtis McLaughlin of the University of North Carolina Business School led a Delphi project on the future of medical care. The two applied a somewhat different approach in their project (which in itself is an indication of how flexible the Delphi technique can be).

They combined the events evaluated by the respondents into scenarios in the form of typical newspaper articles. They asked the respondents to propose additions or modifications to the scenarios and give their reactions to the scenarios as a whole. Inadvertently, they introduced a new way of conducting Delphi projects. Their concept of utilizing the vote on individual items to group events in scenarios classed by such things as likelihood and/or desirability became a standard technique in the project.

Bell Canada was one of the first businesses to adapt the Delphi technique to its forecasting activities. In the late 1960s, the company developed a study plan to evaluate future trends in the visual and computer communications fields. There existed a clear lack of qualitative data on future prospects for these fields as they pertained to Canada. Company leaders decided to use the Delphi technique to examine the future of these fields.

Bell Canada conducted a series of wide-ranging Delphi studies to determine the future course of technology and its applications in diverse areas of life. The company developed extensive questionnaires asking a variety of questions examining the future of technologically advanced applications from a user's point of view. The questions touched on social issues such as value changes in North American society and who would be most likely to use new communications products. Products included in the study included computerized library systems and computer-aided instruction systems for education, remote physiological monitoring and computer-assisted diagnosis for medicine, and terminals and data processing in the business environment. The study addressed questions such as evolutions in school design, trends in the medical profession, and changes in business procedures. Bell Canada derived an impressive amount of information from the studies.

The data Bell Canada derived resulted in a significant increase in the company's store of qualitative data used in the planning and forecasting processes. Perhaps more importantly, both for Bell Canada and other Delphi users, the studies led to widespread modifications from the original Rand Corporation approach, particularly in the emphasis on analyzing participants' comments and establishing threshold levels of acceptance. The studies set the tone for future Delphi projects and how the information derived could be used—and misused.

THE USE AND MISUSE OF DELPHI RESULTS

Information derived from Delphi studies can be highly valuable to businesses. For example, entities involved in Delphi projects can trade results with other interested parties, e.g., members of a trade association or competitors. They can furnish the results to specialists in their organizations, e.g., engineers or scientists, to stimulate **innovation**. Or, the results can be used as an educational tool for senior managers who are attempting to predict a company's future course via long-range planning.

Long-range forecasting is essential to any business that hopes to survive in the increasingly competitive global environment. While executives may not have enough time to gather data via Delphi for short and intermediate planning, they can use it for long-range forecasting. Delphi projects are ideal for such a purpose.

Many companies have utilized the Delphi technique as a forecasting tool. Among them are TRW, IBM, AT&T, Corning Glass Works, Goodyear Tire and Rubber Company, and the Alaska Department of Commerce and Economic Development, which used the Delphi technique in the early 1980s to assess the state's energy, economic, and resource development future. The billion-dollar company, Bharat Heavy Electricals, Ltd. (BHEL), India's largest heavy electrical equipment company, demonstrated the value of Delphi in long-range planning in the mid-1980s.

The company explored the future direction of power development in India, particularly in the fields of electric energy and electric transportation. BHEL's products create systems for electric power generation through thermal, nuclear, and hydro sources, and for power transmission to India's industrial and transportation processes. To forecast the company's needs in these areas, management solicited data from 286 employees in a variety of engineering disciplines.

In the first round, participants received an open-ended questionnaire. The purpose was to gather as much information as possible regarding major technological breakthroughs that conceivably could be developed over the next few decades. Participants were asked to estimate when these breakthroughs would occur.

The compiled list of ideas and predictions was returned to the participants in the second round. The respondents were asked to reassess their earlier estimates in view of the new information. They were also requested to assign a priority ranking for each projected technological development. Once they completed this round, a consensus began to emerge. In the third round, the participants submitted final estimates based on the results of the second round, along with their rationales for their ideas. The results were positive.

The process identified the likely development of 19 new energy sources. It also provided estimates as to when each of the new sources would be available. BHEL's management found these predictions extremely helpful in its long-range forecasting plans—

which is exactly what the Delphi technique is designed to do. However, data developed in Delphi projects can also be misused.

One of the most common misuses of Delphi-generated information is to assume that the results are to become official company policy. That is not the purpose of the Delphi technique. The information gathered is intended to be used simply as an aid in the problem-solving or forecasting process, not as the foundation of company policy.

Similarly, corporate **public relations** representatives sometimes treat the results of Delphi projects as information that is to be applied immediately to the production of goods and/or services. Hence, in their minds, what Delphi participants have projected to occur in 30 or 40 years is to be implemented immediately. They release the results to the world at large in order to tout their company's innovative philosophies and progressiveness, only to discover that the information is of no use in the present. In the process, they might inadvertently leak trade secrets to competitors and harm their own company's competitive advantage. Worst of all, they can damage their company's reputation.

One last misuse of Delphi results is in the interpretation of the findings. In many cases, results are fed into computers for analysis and verification. The computer programs that are used may be making "best guess" predictions regarding the data. For example, in the initial Rand study, any computerized analysis of the data analyzed by a computer could not have been based on actual events, since they never happened. Thus, any results of Delphi data analyzed by the computer would have been based on projection. It is easy, then, for people to misinterpret computer-generated analyses as events that will occur exactly as predicted. Mistakes such as this can render the results of Delphi projects unreliable and unusable. Despite the potential for misuse, Delphi procedures are still valuable tools for researchers.

THE FUTURE OF DELPHI

The Delphi technique has evolved dramatically since its first application in the 1950s. Researchers have expanded its uses and modified the procedures through which they gather information. The evolution of computers and their applications have simplified the decision-making part of the Delphi process. Computer models can now make more efficient use of the data gathered through basic techniques and generate highly realistic projections and results of future events. The modifications and enhanced computers have by no means banished Delphi to the scrap heap of forecasting history. Indeed, the opposite is true. There will continue to be a growing demand for long-range forecasting and for Delphi projects.

The Delphi technique will remain a viable technique in the business world for the foreseeable future. In fact, it will take on added importance as global competition expands and finite sources of raw resources diminish. Corporations will seek new replacements as resources such as oil, coal, and minerals reach extinction. They will look for more efficient production techniques that will enable them to improve their profitability ratios, e.g., their net **profit margins** and return on investment, in order to remain competitive with domestic competitors and manufacturers in emerging nations. It is not inconceivable that Delphi projects will be used to promote innovative ideas regarding the future of space travel, colonizing other planets, etc. That is simply because Delphi is a technique designed primarily to deal with long-range forecasting.

It is hard for people living today to envision what life will be like in the next 40-50 years. Yet, as the population of the earth expands and resources shrink, planners will have to learn as much as they can about the future and how the human race will adapt to it. Thus, planners in all phases of society, government, business, medicine, agriculture, etc., will rely on the Delphi technique to suggest solutions to long-range problems. It is a safe bet that Delphi will an important part of that process for a long time to come.

[Arthur G. Sharp]

FURTHER READING:

Drucker, Peter F. *Technology, Management and Society.* New York: McGraw-Hill, 1970.

Huber, George P. *Managed Decision Making.* Glenview, IL: Scott, Foresman, 1980.

Linstone, Harold A. and Murray Turoff, Editors. *The Delphi Method:* Techniques and Applications. Reading, MA: Addison-Wesley Publishing Company, 1975.

Wheelright, Steven C. and Spyros Makridakis. *Forecasting Methods for Management.* New York: John Wiley & Sons, 1985.

DEMOGRAPHICS

SEE: Organization Theory; Organizational Behavior

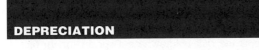

DEPRECIATION

The cost of assets that are totally consumed within an **accounting** period will be recognized as an expense within that period. When assets are not totally consumed within a single accounting period, the cost must be allocated as an expense over the periods in which the assets are consumed. Depreciation arises from this attempt to assign asset cost to the periods of asset consumption. The depreciation for an asset in a period is simply an estimate of the portion of the original cost to be assigned as an expense of the period. A similar concept which is applied to the extraction of natural resources is depletion, which is simply the recognition that a certain part of the natural resource has been consumed.

MISCONCEPTIONS ABOUT DEPRECIATION

Since depreciation is an allocation of cost over accounting periods, it is not directly connected to **market value.** The book value of an asset, computed as the actual cost minus the accumulated depreciation, is simply the unallocated cost of the item. The pattern of depreciation is fixed, and does not respond to changing market conditions.

Depreciation does not involve any cash flow. This is clearest in the simple case of an asset acquired entirely by cash payment. Although the initial purchase is a cash flow, the subsequent allocation of part of the cost as a period expense involves only a book entry. Depreciation is not intended as a mechanism to provide for replacement of the asset. There are no cash flows associated with depreciation, and there is no connection with any cash accumulated for replacement of the asset. The asset may or may not be replaced—this is a capital budgeting decision that is immaterial to the recognition of expense.

Because depreciation is an expense but has no associated cash flow, it is sometimes described as being "added back" to arrive at cash flow for the firm. This gives the impression that depreciation is somehow a source of cash flow. The "adding back," however, is simply a recognition that no cash flow occurred, and depreciation cannot supply cash.

METHODS OF DEPRECIATION

The concept and relevance of allocating the portion of the original cost of an asset "used up" in a period as an expense of the period is clear. In many practical cases, however, the proportion of cost to be allocated as an expense of a particular accounting period can only be estimated. Allocating cost as an expense requires estimation of the useful lifetime of the asset (which may be expressed in terms of time or in terms of units of production), and any residual or salvage value. These estimates must reflect obsolescence, and may be dependent on maintenance, rate of use, or other conditions. While some guidelines exist, they are in the form of suggested ranges, and the estimate may be strongly influenced by industry practice. The choice of depreciation parameters and methods is made by **management**. For a given type of asset, the estimates may differ widely among firms or industries.

In recognition of the difficulties of such estimation, generally accepted accounting principles (GAAP) allow wide discretion in the method used. Where the productive life of an asset can be expressed in terms of units of production, the units-of-production method can be applied. Under this approach, the amount of depreciation for an accounting period is the depreciable value of the asset (actual cost minus any residual value), divided by the (unit) lifetime, and multiplied by the units produced in the period; depreciation in a period will thus be a function of production in the period. Straight-line depreciation is the allocation of equal depreciation amounts to accounting periods over the life of the asset. The straight-line depreciation amount is the depreciable value divided by the lifetime in accounting periods. For example, for an asset with a four-year useful life yearly depreciation would be 25 percent of its depreciable value. An argument against this procedure is that obsolescence and other factors are not linear over time, but rather reduce the usefulness or productivity of an asset by larger amounts in early years. Accelerated depreciation methods recognize this nonlinear decrease in productivity by assigning more depreciation to early periods, and less depreciation to later periods. The double-declining balance accelerated method allocates depreciation as a constant percent equivalent to twice the straight-line rate, but applies this to the book value of the asset. For an asset with a four-year useful life, yearly depreciation would be two times 25 percent or 50 percent of book value. The final year of double-declining balance depreciation, however, is the amount necessary to equate book value to residual value. Sum-of-years' digits accelerated depreciation is computed by multiplying depreciable value by the remaining periods of useful life at the start of the period divided by the sum of the digits in the original useful life. For an asset with a four-year useful life, depreciation in the first year would be 4/(4 + 3 + 2 + 1) or 40 percent of depreciable value.

DEPRECIATION AND TAXES

Depreciation is an expense, and affects **taxes** by reducing taxable income. A firm may use different depreciation treatments for tax and **financial statements**. Typically, straight-line depreciation would be used for financial reporting because it produces more consistent earnings and is easily understood. An accelerated depreciation treatment would be chosen for tax accounting because the higher depreciation in early periods results in lower taxable income, and shifts tax payment to later periods when lower depreciation results in higher taxable income. This is solely

a timing advantage. The total amount of taxes paid is not reduced, but a portion of the payments is shifted to later periods.

The Tax Reform Act of 1986 created a modified accelerated cost recovery system (MACRS) that may be used for tax accounting purposes. This system groups assets into eight classes of estimated useful life, and most classes are depreciated using some form of double-declining balance (rental property, however, is depreciated using straight-line depreciation).

[David E. Upton]

FURTHER READING:

Bernstein, L. A. *Financial Statement Analysis: Theory, Application and Interpretation*. 4th ed. Homewood, IL: Irwin, 1989.

Harrison, Jr., W. T., and C.T. Horngren. *Financial Accounting*. 2nd ed. Englewood Cliffs, NJ: Prentice Hall, 1995.

Kieso, Donald E., and J. G. Weygandt. *Financial Accounting*. New York: John Wiley & Sons, 1995.

White, G. I., A. C. Sondhi, and D. Fried. *The Analysis and Use of Financial Statements*. New York: John Wiley & Sons, 1994.

DERIVATIVE SECURITIES

Derivative Securities is a term commonly used to encompass **option contracts**, **futures contracts**, forward contracts, swap agreements, stock **warrants**, and similar, more exotic assets. Additionally, some assets, such as convertible bonds, have features which are similar to one of the listed derivative securities. The name derivative security refers to the notion that these securities have market values directly related to, or derived from, another traded security. For example, the most important determinant of the price of a company's call options is the current price of the company's **stock**.

The primary purpose of derivative securities is that they establish a market for the risk of the underlying asset apart from the question of actual ownership. For example, suppose a farmer wishes to hold his corn crop until spring because prices tend to be higher than in the fall. However, he doesn't like the uncertainty that comes with waiting six months to know the value of the corn crop. Futures contracts allow the farmer to keep the corn until spring yet lock in the price today. The uncertainty is sold off in the market to someone willing to hold it. In this case the farmer is known as a hedger and the person who accepts the risk is known as a speculator. In fact, it was the need for exactly this type of transaction that spawned the first derivative security markets. Medieval Japan was known to have organized rice futures trading.

OPTIONS

Call options are securities that allow a person to buy a stock at a specified price, known as the exercise (or strike) price, on or before a certain date, known as the expiration date. For example, IBM April calls at 50 would refer to a security that allows the buyer to acquire a share of IBM stock for $50 any time on, or before, the Saturday following the third Friday in April—Saturday after the third Friday being the usual expiration date for exchange traded options. As long as the price of IBM is greater than $50, exercising the option would generate positive cash flow when the stock was re-sold. If IBM stock sells for less than $50 there is no obligation to exercise (and lose money), hence the name option. The amount of money paid up front to acquire the option is known as the option premium.

Put options are like call options except that they give the buyer the right to sell stock at a specific price instead of buying it. Following the same example as before, if IBM stock is below $50 then the buyer of the option could exercise the option and generate a positive cash flow. Here, the stock is purchased for less than $50 then immediately sold at the exercise value. Once gain, the buyer of the option is under no obligation to exercise.

On the opposite side of every option purchase, is someone who agrees to sell either the put or call. This person accepts the premium payment up front, and also accepts the risk that the buyer will later exercise the option, forcing them to pay the buyer whatever the amount of the positive cash flows exercising generates. The premium is determined in the open market as the value that equates buy orders with sell orders.

FUTURES AND FORWARD CONTRACTS

Futures contracts are an agreement to buy or sell an asset at some time in the future. The first futures markets were for agricultural commodities such as corn and wheat, but now financial futures such as treasury bond futures, **foreign exchange** futures, and **stock index** futures trade far higher volumes than do agricultural futures.

The unit of trade on the futures exchange is one contract, which varies in size with the commodity traded. For example, the September corn contract is an agreement to buy 5,000 bushels of corn in September at whatever the agreed price is, while the treasury bond contract requires delivery of $100,000 face value of treasury bonds. The futures price is the price that matches buyers of these contracts with sellers.

In theory, no money needs to change hands when the agreement is made since it is a future purchase, however, some earnest money, called a margin, must be deposited up front. Also, at the end of each day gains and losses from the movement of the futures price are charged to the investor for immediate payment. This process is called marking-to-market. For example, if the futures price of corn goes down $.10 then anyone holding a previously bought a contract will be asked to pay the extra $.10 × 5,000 = $500 to which they agreed, immediately. Those who sold the contact will receive the extra $500 over market price they were promised immediately.

Forward contracts work similarly to futures except they are not traded on formal exchanges, and they do not undergo marking to market. Gains and losses accrue until the contract's expiration date or until the holder of the contract reverses the position. Forward contracts are used mainly by large financial institutions to trade foreign exchange.

OTHER DERIVATIVE SECURITIES

Warrants are essentially call options given by a company for their own stock, usually as "sweetener" along with a bond issue. So the buyer of a bond with an attached warrant will actually get a bond and a call option with an expiration date of several years or more. Convertible bonds are very similar except that the bond actually get converted into stock if the holder exercises.

Interest rate swaps are agreements to trade fixed interest rate payments for floating **interest rate** payments in return for a premium. Currency swaps are agreements to exchange debt in two different currencies. Although these, and other derivatives, are complicated, they can generally be analyzed as extensions of either the basic options or basic futures contracts. In fact, the diversity of the derivatives markets is so great there are even options on futures contracts.

HEDGING

Almost all participants in derivative securities markets may be classified as hedgers, speculators, or arbitrageur. However, the same participant may fill different roles at different times.

A hedger refers to a market participant who is using the derivative market to change their risk exposure to an underlying asset or commitment to purchase an asset. Common examples of **hedging** are:

1. A food processor with commitments to buy grain at market price in the future will buy futures contracts now so that future increases in grain price will be offset by gains in the futures market (when the futures price goes up, people who bought futures contracts at lower prices get money immediately).

2. Large international pension funds will often sell currency forward contracts so that any losses in value of their foreign stock holdings due to currency movements will be offset by gains in the forward contract value;

3. Companies that plan to take over another company may buy stock index futures to protect themselves against a general market price increase during the time they are acquiring shares. If the company is going to hold a large position for a long time they may also use call options and put options to protect themselves from stock price swings. For example, buying puts will compensate for lost value if the stock price falls. Selling calls will allow them to pay for the puts, and if the stock price goes up, the loses on the calls are compensated for by the fact the stock itself is worth more.

In general, hedging with futures and forward contracts requires taking a position opposite to the position one holds in the primary (or spot) market. That is, if a trader owns an asset (called being long), to hedge he or she would sell futures or forward contracts (called being short). Conversely, if a trader plans to buy an asset in the future (called being short in the spot market) then he or she should buy futures or forward contracts (called being long). The rule is long spot-short futures, and vice-versa.

Options hedging, generally relies on buying puts or selling calls to protect against declines in the value of stock one owns. Other, more complicated variants also exist. For a more complete discussion of this section's topics, see the related article on HEDGING.

SPECULATION

Speculators are derivative securities market participants who do not hold the underlying assets. A speculator does not buy futures contracts because he or she plans to purchase corn later. A speculator buys futures contracts merely because he or she believes the price of corn is going up beyond the current futures price. If this happens the speculator makes money, without ever needing to buy an actual asset. The drawback is that should the futures price of corn fall the speculator will lose money, without ever actually owning anything. Needless to say, speculation is extremely risky and scrupulous brokers will only handle these transaction for sophisticated clients who thoroughly understand the risks involved.

Options speculation is similar, except that now traders who believe the stock is increasing in price buy calls and those who believe it is falling buy puts. Their are even far more complicated strategies, given fancy names such as the butterfly spread, and the straddle, but they all have the same purpose. Namely, this is to design a payoff structure such that the speculator makes money when the asset price moves in the proper direction. Once again, should the asset fail to move in the proper direction, the option premiums paid are lost without the receipt of any physical good.

It has long been debated among economists whether speculators are good for the market. Although some people still argue that speculation can be destabilizing, most agree that speculators are necessary participants in the market who help provide liquidity that hedgers need to trade.

ARBITRAGE

Arbitrageur attempt to identify inconsistent prices among markets and profit immediately from them. In the process, they help make markets more efficient. One tool of the arbitrageur is called **put-call parity** which states:

payoff to stock = payoff to put − payoff to call + payoff to bond.

Here the put and call are assumed to have exercise prices equal to the stock price, and the bond is assumed to have a face value equal to the stock price and maturity date same as expiration of the options. Also, in the real world the equation is not expected to hold exactly.

However, the equation does indicate that a put option, a call option, and a bond can be used to create a synthetic stock. This provides a second opinion of what the appropriate stock price should be and provides a stabilizing influence on the market. If for some reason a stock should behave unreasonably, the arbitrageur will create a synthetic stock, sell the expensive asset, buy the cheap asset, and make a riskless profit, driving the two prices back together in the process.

Other types of **arbitrage** help keep the relationship between different maturities of futures and options in line, and some even work across products. One of the more common approaches is to look at interest rates and currency futures for two different currencies. If it is more profitable to buy bonds in one country and guarantee conversion of the currency with futures than it is to invest in the other country directly, an arbitrage opportunity exists.

One popular strategy is called index arbitrage. Here, the trader calculates the price of borrowing money, buying a stock index, and accepting the **dividends**, and then hedging the future selling price of the index with futures (the index must be sold later to pay off the loan). If this calculation yields a profit arbitrage is possible since the futures price and the spot price are out of line. There is some risk to this strategy, however, because dividends must be forecast and cannot be guaranteed.

CONCLUSION

Derivative securities markets play an important role by allowing people who do not want the risk of holding an asset to transfer it to people who do. However, because they are markets for risk as opposed to physical asset markets they can be very dangerous places for unsophisticated investors. People who reduce their risk by entering a derivative market are called hedgers, and those who increase their risk are called speculators.

Derivative securities markets also play a fundamental role in market efficiency by linking together various markets. The people who exploit these links and attempt to profit from mispricing are called arbitrageur. Arbitrageur, through their actions drive the mispriced securities back into line. The derivative securities markets play a vital role in the modern financial systems, and without them many common business transactions would be rendered much riskier or practically impossible.

[Richard A. Cooper]

FURTHER READING:

Chance, Don M. *An Introduction to Derivatives. 3rd ed.* Dryden, 1994.

Hull, John C. *Options, Futures, and other Derivative Securities. 2nd ed.* Prentice Hall, Englewood Cliffs, NJ 1993.

Kolb, Robert W. *Options, An Introduction.* Miami, FL: Kolb Publishing, 1991.

Peck, A. E., ed. *Selected Writings on Futures Markets: Basic Research in Commodity Markets.* Chicago Board of Trade.

DESKTOP PUBLISHING

Desktop publishing is computer-generated publishing of text and graphics (in color, including photographs) by means of desktop or laptop personal computers, and a laser printer; ''graphics'' are understood to mean drawings, prints, or diagrams. What makes desktop publishing so popular is that it saves time, because **computers** have eliminated several tedious stages of publishing and design, and saves money, since one person can do the work formerly done by several. Best of all, the quality of desktop publishing can be indistinguishable from that of mainstream publishing. The most common examples of desktop publishing are simple business cards, stationery and newsletters—to complex graphics for a magazine or architectural journal. Some desktop publishing products, for instance, a self-published book, may not

involve any graphics. For other projects, graphics are all that matter.

The term ''desktop publishing'' was coined in 1985 by the Aldus Company, makers of the first desktop publishing program, called PageMaker. When desktop publishing first appeared in the mid-1980s, photographs could not be reproduced, to say nothing of color graphics. Scanners were just being developed, and inexpensive inkjet printers—capable of high quality printing, including complex graphics—were still in the future.

The advent of the versatile IBM micro or personal computer (small enough to fit on a desk) in 1981 enabled desktop publishing as we know it today to evolve. The popularity of the IBM desktop computer spurred intense competition. In the early 1980s, the Macintosh computer, brainchild of the Apple Computer, Inc., was unveiled for the first time. One of the radical differences between the Mac and the IBM was the computer screen, a ''high resolution'' screen that showed text in the exact type and size in which it would be printed. For the first time, the personal computer (pc) user could see text on the screen that was underlined or italicized or in bold. The Macintosh enabled the user to make changes right on the screen, knowing that what was printed out would be identical to what was on the screen. Moreover, the software was ''user-friendly'' and consisted of visual symbols that enabled virtually anyone to use it.

The appearance of the Macintosh computer did not immediately usher in desktop publishing. For that to happen, a high speed printer with typesetting qualities had to be developed. The dot matrix printer, while affordable for the individual, could not print ''publishable'' quality. The Apple Computer Company once again showed itself a pacesetter when it pioneered the development of the world's first laser printer, the LaserWriter, using a laser photographic technique similar to a photocopy machine. While the laser printers of the mid-1980s were expensive and beyond the price range of most individuals, small offices could afford them. Soon, laser printers in offices were as ubiquitous as computers, thanks in part to declining prices.

Hence, the hardware for desktop publishing was launched by 1985. What made it possible for the screen to depict the exact type and size of text was the software, called PageMaker, produced in that same year by the Aldus Company. This was the first desktop publishing software in existence, and it became an enormous success. Soon competition led to a proliferation of desktop publishing software programs for both the IBM and Macintosh, once again driving down prices and resulting in more error-free, exacting programs. By the early 1990s, even individuals of relatively modest means could afford a desktop publishing system. Moreover, almost anyone with a personal computer could learn desktop publishing, since most pc users are proficient in basic desktop publishing tasks, such as formatting text and adjusting type (bold, shadow, etc.).

For these reasons, there has been a boom in private desktop publishing in recent years, reaching out to the broader public: a writer who had little hope of getting a book published by a publishing house can now do most of the work on his or her own—composing, proofing, editing, and designing. A printer can bind the pages and make copies on demand; most churches and synagogues can produce professional-looking monthly newsletters; a one newspaper town may now have the opportunity to have two hometown newspapers, thanks to the efficiency of desktop publishing. Many large and small businesses have turned to desktop publishing because of the control they can exercise over their own printed manuscripts, and because of the fast turnaround time. Not surprisingly, desktop publishing has become big business.

COSTS, REQUIREMENTS, AND PROCESS

For under ten thousand dollars, it is possible to purchase all the requirements for major desktop publishing tasks. This would include hardware (a computer with a large hard drive, laser printer, scanner) and software (**word processing** and special page layout software). A scanner, however, can cost as much as a computer, requiring its own software, and is unnecessary for small print jobs; inkjet printers approach the laser printer in quality and versatility, and cost far less. A modem, either external or internal, is desirable for the electronic transfer of files.

Most desktop publishing software comes in ''packages'' designed to be used with other programs, particularly word processing. Macintosh no longer has a monopoly on ''windows'' software, with Microsoft Windows being currently the most popular for IBM computers. Among the most popular interface desktop publishing programs is the Aldus PageMaker, unique because it can operate on both IBM and Macintosh PC's. Other leading brands, for Macintosh, are QuarkXPress, Ventura for Macintosh (a bestseller when it came out in 1990), and DesignStudio; for the IBM, the IBM version of Ventura Publisher, Ventura Publisher Windows Edition, Finesse, and Legacy. Program packages that reproduce color still are in the process of refinement and are much more expensive than noncolor. Color imaging requires large amounts of computer memory and hard-drive space, and is still difficult to proof.

The major tools of any desktop publishing software (as opposed to word processing software, although some do incorporate many of these features) are graphics and text organizers. Graphics organizers include grids (which define the horizontal and vertical placement of type and artwork and which show up only on the computer screen), borders, boxes (to separate different parts of a publication), and columns. Text organizers are, in the main, headlines, subheadlines, mastheads, headers, and footers. Typology is very important in any desktop publishing software. This includes, for instance, serif type (vertical and horizontal strokes of different thicknesses), various type styles such as bold, italics, and roman, as well as tracking and kerning (referring to the space between letters), word spacing, tabs and indents, alignments, and stretching out or compressing type, known as distortion (to create special effects).

OPPORTUNITIES AND CAREERS

Desktop publishing has not only entered the mainstream, but is also changing rapidly, almost month by month. The future of desktop publishing will follow the course of computer development, which is becoming increasingly multimedia oriented, that is, combining not only text and graphics, but video and audio in a single system. The future meaning and possibilities of desktop publishing may change even more drastically than over the last ten years.

Courses on desktop publishing and design proliferate at two- and four-year colleges. Except for graphic art—a profession that requires design skill—and highly specialized engineering positions such as networking engineers or Windows programmers, most of the desktop publishing jobs on the market are technician-oriented ones that require great attention to detail (for instance, technical illustrators). Layout design, formerly done by hand, can now be done on a computer screen. This involves knowledge of electronics and computer engineering concepts that change rapidly, as computers evolve. Desktop publishing technicians work in print shops and publishing firms and often find themselves branching out eventually into sales and managerial positions.

[Sina Dubovoy]

FURTHER READING:

Angelo, Jean Marie. ''Desktop Changes Reshape Publishing Environment.'' *Folio: The Magazine for Magazine Management.* September 1, 1993, p. 55.

Bjelland, Harley. *Create Your Own Desktop Publishing System.* Blue Ridge Summit, PA: Windcrest/McGraw-Hill, 1994.

Cavuoto, James, and Stephen Beale. *Guide to Desktop Publishing.* Pittsburgh: Graphic Arts Technical Foundation, 1992.

Curtin, Dennis. *Desktop Publishing with WordPerfect 5.1.* Englewood Cliffs, NJ: Prentice Hall, 1992.

LaPlante, Alice. ''New Job Titles, Functions, Abound in Market (Computer Careers).'' *Computerworld.* May 4, 1992, p. 90.

Morgenstern, Steve. *No-Sweat Desktop Publishing.* New York: Amacom, 1992.

O'Brien, Timothy L. "A PC Revolution: Aided by Computers, Many of the Disabled Form Own Businesses." *The Wall Street Journal*, October 8, 1993, p. A1(W).

Parker, Lucy V. *How to Open and Operate a Home-Based Writing Business*. Old Saybrook, CT: Globe Pequot Press, 1994.

Rooney, Paula. "Macintosh Software Goes Beyond Word Processing." *PC Week*, February 15, 1993, p. 35.

Schiff, Kenny. *Opportunities in Desktop Publishing Careers*. Lincolnwood, IL: VGM Career Horizons, 1993.

Shandle, Jack. "Who Will Dominate the Desktop in the 90s? IBM and Apple Rev Their Technology Engines as the Multimedia Age Begins." *Electronics*. February, 1990, p. 48.

Wagner, Stephen. *A Guide to Successful Self-Publishing*. Englewood Cliffs, NJ: Prentice Hall, 1992.

Wilke, John R. "Powersoft Aims for PC Market with Database (Powerbuilder Desktop)." *Wall Street Journal*. February 14, 1994, p. B5.

Zachary, G. Pascal. "Big Bundles: Consolidation Sweeps the Software Industry." *Wall Street Journal*. March 23, 1994, p. A1.

DEVALUATION (MONEY)

Devaluation refers to a decline in the value of a currency in relation to another currency (or currencies), usually brought about by the actions of a central bank or monetary authority. If we define an exchange rate of, for example, the U.S. dollar in terms of the British pound as: e = dollars/pounds, where "e" is the exchange rate, then this specifies the number of dollars that will be exchanged for pounds or, put another way, the price of dollars in terms of British pounds. Thus, if the exchange rate (e) is increased, this means that the price of foreign currency, in terms of domestic currency, is increased, and the domestic currency is said to have been devalued (or depreciated). In addition, this devaluation of the dollar, by definition, also means that the value of the British pound has been *revalued* or *appreciated*. Of course, this calculation could be made for each currency bilaterally or against groups of currencies, and even against all other currencies. In fact, various currency values are calculated on a regular basis, as a summary of **foreign exchange** market activity, by the Federal Reserve Bank and the **International Monetary Fund**, among other organizations.

Often times the terms devaluation and revaluation are used interchangeably with the terms **depreciation** and appreciation, respectively. Whether one uses the term depreciation or devaluation to refer to the decline in the value of a currency, the outcome is the same—the amount of foreign currency that can be purchased with domestic currency is reduced (or, conversely, the amount of domestic currency that can be bought with the foreign currency is increased). The

difference is largely a terminological distinction associated with different exchange rate regimes. Devaluation of a currency is most often associated with fixed exchange rates and comes about merely through the central monetary authority announcing that the fixed standard will change. For example, in 1967, the British government devalued the pound by 14 percent versus the dollar.

Depreciation, on the other hand, is associated with flexible exchange rate regimes and is brought About by the workings of the foreign exchange markets. Here, though the government doesn't peg the exchange rate directly, it might nonetheless intervene by buying and selling currency reserves it holds in an attempt to influence the market value of the country's currency within some range; the result, of course, is much more uncertain. In late 1993, for example, the U.S. government loaned $6 billion to the Mexican government so that it could buy Mexican pesos (in the foreign exchange markets) in order to stave off the declining value of the peso. Thus, in the present day world of largely flexible exchange rates, the terms devaluation/depreciation and revaluation/appreciation can be used interchangeably—the results are the same, but the processes are different. In any case, monetary authorities, even in a flexible exchange rate system, wield considerable (albeit limited) power over the value of currencies. Many argue that it is the goal of foreign exchange policy to maintain a country's exchange rate within some range that reflects the competitive position of that nation's industries.

Whether brought about by decree or by manipulation of the market (through buying and selling of foreign exchange), a currency devaluation is usually justified when some determination is made that the domestic currency is overvalued relative to the rest of the world (or relative to one country's currency, etc.). Since a declining currency translates into relatively cheaper export products, devaluation is often used as a policy tool in attempts to correct for an unfavorable balance of trade and/or to enhance export development. Under a fixed exchange rate regime, a country with a persistent **trade deficit** must somehow finance that deficit (much like an individual must finance **credit** card **debt**). If a country is experiencing a chronic deficit on its current account (i.e., it is not paying for imported goods by **exporting** an equivalent value of exports), then this implies that domestic currency is leaving the country (to pay for the excess of imports over exports). The relative demand for foreign currency (to pay for the net imports) will be very strong and put downward pressure on the deficit country's currency value. In such instances, to alleviate these downward pressures on the currency, national governments usually run down their international reserves; that is, they sell foreign currency in order to raise the value of their own currency and thereby keep the currency pegged at the fixed level. This situation by itself, however, is an indication that the country's currency might be overvalued relative to the competitive position of its industries. Thus one can already see a barrier to the maintenance of fixed exchange rates in a country with a chronic trade deficit. More pointedly, since a country's international reserves are finite, a chronic ''trade deficit'' country might eventually be forced to devalue its currency to relieve pressure on its limited international reserves. In addition, since a devaluation (depreciation) means that less of the domestic currency is required to purchase that country's goods, foreigners have to pay relatively less for the devaluing country's goods, leading, in theory, to an expansion of the devaluing country's exports relative to imports and hence an improvement in the country's international trade position. So the textbook argument goes.

However, the use of currency devaluation is not a remedy without limits; its use as a policy instrument has been, historically, called into question at a number of levels, and, its use as a policy tool has been tarnished by controversies over its effects. For one thing, continued reliance on devaluation can lead to the complete loss of confidence in a country's currency, leading to a complete collapse, or, at the very least, to speculative pressures and wide fluctuations in the value of the currency. Further, it is far from certain whether a devaluation actually leads to the desired result of an improved **trade balance** without very strict conditions being met. And, of even more serious concern is the potential that a cycle of competitive devaluations (by the devaluating country's trading partners) might be set off, leading to a stagnation of world trade (as some have argued was the case during the Great Depression of the 1930s). In the end there appears to be little agreement about what determines exchange rates and how a country might use exchange rate policy to achieve national objectives such as low **unemployment** and a stable balance of payments. Whatever the case, the historical record has provided scant evidence that exchange rate policy, by itself, can achieve these stated goals of national economic policy.

According to the orthodox theory of international trade and **finance** (found in most textbooks), devaluation is not necessary (and is, in fact, disruptive since it distorts the hypothesized free flow of markets) as a policy tool since, in a free market unfettered by any regulations, any trade deficit will automatically be translated into a decline in the deficit country's relative price level (via the outflow of money that is assumed to reduce prices and in turn depreciate the country's *real* exchange rate). In turn, this would make that country's goods more competitive, expand its exports and lead the country toward trade balance—the opposite effects occurring in trade surplus countries. With flexible exchange rates, the exchange rate adjusts to push the trade balance towards zero. In any case, according to traditional theoretical doctrine, forces operating on the real exchange rate (the exchange rate adjusted for changes in relative national price levels) pushes international trade toward balance. By this logic then, the prescription for advancement of a nation's development is open and free trade—opening of trade is hypothesized to lead to convergence of regions and countries over time. The controversy however arises from the fact that it is highly questionable that this process is actually played out on the historical stage of the international economy (See e.g. Shaikh, 1994).

The prolonged study of the effects of devaluation has produced results that are theoretically indeterminate and empirically unconfirmed. First, depending on the responsiveness of the prices of exports and imports, a devaluation can theoretically lead to a *decline* in the devaluing country's trade balance. Second, at best, some studies show that the responsiveness of the trade balance is shaped like a ''J-curve''.

This curve indicates that the effects of a devaluation might actually worsen the trade balance in the short term and thus have a contractionary effect on the devaluing country's output and employment. The shape reflects the hypothesized initial deterioration of, but eventual improvement in, the trade balance in response to the devaluation of a country's currency. The explanation for this phenomenon lies in the famous Marshall-Lerner condition, which states that the sum of the price elasticities (the responsiveness of exports and imports to changes in prices) of exports and imports must be greater than 1.0 if the depreciation is to induce a shift to greater export **revenues** (and hence an improvement in the trade balance). Some empirical evidence supports the ''J-curve'' idea and indicates that these effects (that is, price elasticities) are small in the short run, but in the longer term, as producers and consumers adjust to the relative price changes, the Marshall-Lerner condition holds—the trade balance eventually improves. According to empirical estimates, however, the time lag can be substantial, depending on the country. Of course, with many forces operating simultaneously at the international level, the difficulties of separating out the precise effects of a currency depreciation are immense.

Other empirical studies that take into more careful account interdependence of national economies note that an improvement in the trade balance, if it increases a country's **gross national product** (through the expansion of exports), might also lead to an increase in that country's import demand (by virtue of its greater income). That, in turn, might lead to an expansion of foreign production (and foreign income) with the unintended consequence of an expansion of demand for the domestic country's products. Put more simply, one might argue that the initial devaluation could set off a virtuous cycle of expansion for both countries.

But the same initial devaluation could also, some have argued, lead to unintended negative repercussions. Even if the currency devaluation leads to an increase in domestic production (through an improvement in the domestic trade balance, say through the J-curve effect), an improvement in the devaluing country's position means (other factors held constant) a decrease in the trade balance of the rest of the world (since the sum of *all* of the world's countries' trade balances must equal zero). By the logic of this argument then, an improvement in one country's trade balance must be gained at the expense of declining trade balances for that country's trading partners. This is why devaluation is often referred to as a "beggar-thy-neighbor" policy since the increased domestic output (of the devaluating country) is bought at the expense of the output of the country's trading partners.

Whatever the case, history has shown that one cannot assume that other countries will remain passive in their policies in face of a revaluation of their own currencies. That is to say, the "foreign" country (or countries) in our discussion, by definition, experiences a currency *re*valuation with all of its effects (an increase in the demand for imported goods, a declining trade balance, and declining output and **employment**). In the face of such revaluation, trading partners might then respond by devaluing their own currency against the country that originally devalued in order to offset the original devaluation. This could then provoke further devaluation (the "competitive devaluation" mentioned above) as countries seek domestic expansion through export promotion at the expense of their trading partners. Nonetheless, the attractiveness of currency depreciation as a policy is its ease of implementation, and its use is far easier to swallow than a policy which tries to improve the trade balance by choking off demand for imports, that (in the absence of import quotas, tariffs, etc.) must be brought about by inducing a recession (reducing people's incomes).

To conclude, the uses and effectiveness of currency devaluation as a policy tool are clearly controversial. One thing is clear: chronic trade imbalances have existed historically and continue to exist in the present—witness the United States with its declining currency and chronic trade imbalance. In addition to fluctuating widely, the value of the U.S. dollar versus a number of other currencies (weighted by the volume of international trade) declined by about 28 percent from 1967 to 1992; the real value of the dollar (adjusted by consumer price levels) fell by about 14 percent (from 1973 to 1992); for example, 362 Japanese Yen could be exchanged against one dollar in 1967, while it took only 127 Yen to purchase one dollar in 1992, a decline in the value of the dollar of 65 percent; 3.99 German Marks equalled one dollar in 1967 compared with only 1.56 Marks in 1992.

Thus, the limits to devaluation/depreciation as a policy tool appear to be very real, and currency devaluations, used without addressing **costs** structures in a country's industries, are unlikely to "cure" a trade deficit. For countries with these types of structural problems, depreciation of the currency is most likely a superficial, temporary, and potentially dangerous solution. In this light, the secular decline of the dollar as the world's currency over the past two decades more likely reflects shifts in international competitive developments of key industries. In other words, despite desirable short term effects of a devalued currency (increased exports, etc.), no country can be happy with a collapsing currency over a long period. Thus, without addressing the more fundamental forces of international **competition** (especially in an open world of unregulated investment flows), a depreciating dollar is unlikely to lead the United States out of its downward slide in the world economy.

[John A. Sarich]

FURTHER READING:

Edwards, Chris. *The Fragmented World: Competing Perspectives on Trade, Money and Crisis.* Methuen & Co. Ltd., 1985.

Kubarych, Roger M. *Foreign Exchange Markets in the United States.* Federal Reserve Bank of New York, March, 1983.

Rivera-Batiz, Francisco L., and Luis Rivera-Batiz. *International Finance and Open Economy Macroeconomics.* Macmillan Publishing Company, 1985.

Shaikh, Anwar. "Free Trade, Unemployment, and Economic Policy." *In Unemployment in the 1990s.* M.E. Sharp Inc., 1994.

DEVELOPMENT BANKS

Development banks are commonly thought to be huge multibillion dollar entities, like the World Bank, which holds the title as the world's richest institution. Established after World War II, this bank is funded by the treasuries of its member nations and contributes only to governments, or their state run enterprises, in need of development capital. New ones, however, such as the North American Development Bank (NADBANK), are continually being established as the need arises. In the case of NADBANK, established in 1994, both the governments of Mexico and the United States have contributed equal amounts to the bank to fund environmental cleanup projects resulting from the implementation of the **North American Free Trade Agreement** (NAFTA).

A development bank, in short, does what most commercial banks cannot do: it funnels major amounts of capital into projects of dubious profitability. The vast majority of the world's development banks, however, have very little in common with their sprawling, multibillion dollar international counterparts, such as the World Bank. Rather, most development banks—and there are perhaps hundreds in this country—are geared toward grassroots economic assistance.

These development banks, most often referred to as community development banks, differ from commercial banks in salient ways. they are always located in depressed urban and rural areas, where there are very few if any banks or bank branches. While they offer such standard commercial services as checking and savings accounts and **loans**, they also have important non-bank functions, such as investing in low cost housing projects and in technical assistance programs. For these reasons, development banks, unlike commercial banks, have access to many private and government grant monies. Development banks also are more stringently regulated by the federal and state governments. Even lending services of development banks differ from commercial banks, since the former are mandated to provide loans as small as $500, which commercial banks would consider unprofitable. Development banks promote these enterprises by providing loans on easier terms, and often, for smaller sums than would be profitable for most commercial banks.

Development banks are by and large profit making institutions, with additional, non-profit functions. They are almost always established by individuals and organizations rooted in the community they wish to serve. They often evolve from a grassroots community development project. For example, a recent Newark, New Jersey housing association, initially financed by charities and government subsidies, is now a development bank. By injecting depressed urban and rural areas with much needed capital, these banks empower their communities to revitalize their neighborhoods and strengthen local businesses. A major reason for the endemic poverty of many urban and rural areas is the absence or near absence of financial institutions. Southeast San Diego, for instance, a depressed neighborhood of 250,000 residents, possessed only one branch bank until a development bank was founded.

Not all development banks are successful. The undertaking of such an enterprise is risky, because of factors often beyond the control of most banks of this kind: the prevalence of urban crime and the inexperience of many in the local community with even such basic banking services such as checking and savings accounts. The risks of lending to startup businesses in poor areas also are higher than in affluent areas. However, Chicago's South Shore Bank, a national model of a community development bank that was established in 1973, began with only $42 million in assets which, by 1994, had risen to $200 million. Because of the profitability of South Shore Bank and the resulting economic revival it has nurtured in Chicago's traditionally depressed south side, this bank has had many imitators.

President Bill Clinton's anti-poverty program, passed by Congress in 1994, aims to provide nearly $300 million dollars over a period of four years to the establishment of over one hundred community banks in depressed urban and rural areas throughout the United States. This amount is to be matched by private funds. A federal bank would distribute the funds and act as regulator for these new community banks. They are expected to generate a total of at least $2 billion in badly needed loans, mainly to small businesses and not-for-profit community services.

The development bank idea is not new. In fact, providing financial services to the entire community, including impoverished people, is what small banks used to do. Small banks and **credit unions**, however, are struggling for survival nowadays, especially since the banking industry was deregulated in the 1980s. As a result of the intensification of **competition** among banks, they are reluctant to establish branches in areas that entail unusually high risk and the expectation of low returns. Were it not for the federally mandated Community Reinvestment Act (CRA, passed in 1977), which stipulates that commercial banks must provide credit services to all segments of the community in which they are located, most banks would be unwilling to invest in community services or provide loans to non-profit institutions at the rate that they do. This still does not make them development banks, but it does mean that all banks since 1977 have some development functions. The future definitely will witness the rise of more development banks at the community level, an attractive and low cost means of empowering a local community to help itself.

[Sina Dubovoy]

FURTHER READING:

"Development Banking: Double Trouble," *Economist*, May 14, 1994, pp.81-84.

Evaluation of the Illinois Neighborhood Development Corporation. Woodstock Institute, 1982.

Kane, Kevin T. "Banking on Better Neighborhoods," *Mortgage Banking*. May, 1993, pp.58-69.

McCabe, James R. "Credit Where It's Due: Development Banking for Communities," *Growth & Change*, Summer, 1993, pp.428-431.

DIRECT INVESTMENT

Direct investment generally refers to situations in which a company has established manufacturing facilities in another country, either through a wholly owned subsidiary or as a joint venture partner with a partial ownership stake. Direct investments are governed by the laws of both the country in which the parent company is domiciled and the country in which the subsidiary does business. In cases where international trade sanctions have been imposed or the host country has appropriated the assets of the subsidiary, **international law** may pertain as well.

Interest in direct investments in foreign-based enterprises grew strongly in the late 1960s and early 1970s, as American companies sought to augment corporate growth through expansion into new markets. This created a basis for criticism in sociopolitical circles, as some studies indicated that such practices were extractive and exploitative.

Direct investment came under scrutiny again in the late 1980s as British and Japanese companies took aggressive actions to establish foreign **subsidiaries**, primarily in the United States. Far from being extractive, these enterprises boasted job creation and support of local economies. The driving force behind these enterprises, however, was circumvention of trade duties on imported goods.

There are several economic advantages provided by direct investment, which is why a foreign country would welcome the establishment of such a subsidiary within its borders.

First, direct investment by a foreign company facilitates the diffusion of superior technologies and managerial techniques into the country, generally enhancing the position of domestic manufacturers across all industries. Second, establishment of a subsidiary facilitates trade, allowing the host nation to more fully employ its own **assets**, whether through cheaper labor, access to raw materials, or employment of other companies. Third, the introduction of a foreign subsidiary can raise standards of efficiency for domestic firms, which must compete with the foreign subsidiary.

Disadvantages stem primarily from the ability of the foreign parent company to extract economic profits from the operations of its subsidiary and repatriate them out of the country. Another disadvantage may lie in the fact that the subsidiary may divert the employment of national assets, such as labor and capital, away from other activities that may be more beneficial to the economy.

A hypothetical illustration of forms of direct investment may be provided by the fictional Acme Electronics Company, an American manufacturer of television sets. In this example, assume that Acme's American market is growing at 2 percent annually in terms of volume, but that pricing pressure from competitors yields negative profit in that market. An analysis of foreign markets indicates demand for television sets is growing by 20 percent in Argentina and Brazil.

Acme funds the development of a wholly owned subsidiary in Brazil to produce television sets for that market. However, as part of an industrial policy to support the growth of domestic companies, Argentine law precludes the establishment of wholly owned subsidiaries. In Argentina, an Acme subsidiary must provide for at least 50 percent ownership by an Argentine company.

The Brazilian enterprise, capitalized at $400,000, is wholly owned by Acme. An identical plant in Argentina requires investments of $200,000 from Acme and $200,000 from an Argentine joint venture partner.

While both enterprises pay local taxes and other fees in each country, Acme may repatriate all the profits from its Brazilian operation, but is only entitled to repatriate half the profits from its Argentine business, commensurate with its ownership interest. The other half belongs to Acme's Argentine joint venture partner.

In addition to advantages from expansion into more profitable, higher-growth markets, direct investment may yield other important benefits to the parent company.

The parent company may enjoy numerous **economies of scale** and scope from foreign operations. In the case of Acme Electronics, the company already has the technology and managerial expertise to produce television sets in the United States, and merely extends those advantages to foreign markets through its subsidiaries. These may be considered "internal" economies, because they provide room for greater capacity without substantial additional investment.

In addition, Acme's competition in its foreign markets may not be as well developed. Therefore it enjoys a greater advantage over competing enterprises that may be realized in terms of greater market share and profitability.

[John Simley]

FURTHER READING:

Donnelly, James H., Jr., James L. Gibson, and John M. Ivancevich. *Fundamentals of Management*. 6th ed. Plano, TX: Business Publications, 1987.

Griffin, Ricky W., and Ronald J. Ebert. *Business*. 2nd ed. Englewood Cliffs, NJ: Prentice-Hall, 1991.

Newcomers to the field of direct mail often use the terms "direct mail," "**direct marketing**," and "mail order" interchangeably. Perhaps the best way to distinguish these three similar, yet different, terms is to remember that direct mail is simply an **advertising** medium like print or broadcast media. In print media, advertising messages are delivered through the printed word, usually in newspapers or magazines. In broadcast media, messages are delivered through the airwaves, on television or radio. In direct mail, advertising and other types of messages are delivered through the mail.

By way of contrast, mail order is simply a way of doing business, just as retail and personal selling are other ways of doing business. A **mail order business** delivers its products through the mail. It may also use direct mail to send out advertising messages, but many other businesses use direct mail without being in the mail order business.

Direct marketing is a broader term that refers to a type of marketing that utilizes a variety of advertising media. Direct marketing is distinct from other types of marketing in that it makes an offer and solicits a direct response. Direct mail is simply one advertising medium that direct marketers employ, although it is the one most frequently used.

USES OF DIRECT MAIL

Direct mail is the most heavily used direct marketing medium and the one direct marketers learn first. Despite postage increases, direct mail continues to grow. While most advertisers use third class mail, a significant number of mailings are sent first class, making it difficult to arrive at accurate statistics about the volume of advertising mail being sent. For fiscal year 1993, the U.S. Postal Service (USPS) reported that third class mail increased by 5.2% over 1992. In his book, *Profitable Direct Marketing,* Jim Kobs noted that 714,000 businesses have bulk mail permits and send out more than 63 billion pieces of advertising mail a year. The catalog industry, a specialized area of direct mail, generated $54.7 billion in sales via direct mail during 1993.

The primary application of direct mail is to reach consumers with offers of traditional goods and services. Some of the earliest examples of direct mail were seed catalogs sent to American colonists before the Revolutionary War. Aaron Montgomery Ward (1843-1913), regarded as the first of the consumer goods cataloguers, started his catalog business in 1872, while Richard Warren Sears (1863-1914) mailed his first flyers in the 1880s. L.L. Bean of Freeport, Maine, utilized direct mail to send out his first flyer advertising Maine hunting boots in 1913.

More recently, consumers have been sent direct mail packages offering a range of financial services, coupons offering discounts on packaged goods, and letters requesting donations to and offering memberships in a variety of nonprofit organizations.

Direct mail is also an effective medium in business-to-business marketing. Since business orders are usually larger than consumer purchases, it often takes more than one mailing to make a sale. Imaginative packages are often used to get through to hard-to-reach executives whose mail is screened by their secretaries. In addition to making sales, business-to-business direct mail can be used to generate sales leads and reinforce the personal selling effort.

ELEMENTS OF DIRECT MAIL

The direct marketing adage that says success depends on making the right offer to the right person at the right time in the right way touches on the three key elements of direct mail: the offer, lists and databases, and the direct mail package.

Making an offer is one element that distinguishes direct marketing from general advertising and other types of marketing. Offers are designed to motivate the reader to take action: place an order, request more information, etc. According to Kobs, "The offer is one of the simplest and most dramatic ways to improve results."

In *Successful Direct Marketing Methods,* Bob Stone gave this example of how the same offer can be presented in three different ways: 1) Half-price! 2) Buy one—get one free! 3) 50% off! All convey the same offer, but statement number two pulled 40% better than statement one or three. Stone wrote, "Consumers perceived statement number two to be the most attractive offer."

An offer can be structured around marketing's four P's: product, price, place (or distribution channel), and promotion. Some basic offers include optional features (product); introductory price or quantity discount (price); free trial or bill me later (price); order by mail, phone, or fax (place); premiums or sweepstakes (promotion); special conditions of sale and types of guarantees (promotion).

In direct mail the offer can be tailored to fit the characteristics of the individual recipients. Direct mail allows marketers to target individuals with known purchase histories or particular psychographic or demographic characteristics, thus affecting how an offer will be made. Even geographic considerations, based on zip codes or other criteria, may affect how direct marketers construct their offers.

Mailing lists and databases offer direct marketers the opportunity for more selectivity and personalization than any other advertising medium. According to Standard Rate & Data Services in *Direct Mail List Rates and Data*, there are more than 50,000 mailing lists to choose from, and that's not the only list of lists available. Jim Kobs estimated there are 5,500 consumer lists available for rental. Some 9 million businesses can also be reached via direct mail through compiled lists.

Lists can be categorized in different ways. Two basic types of lists are in-house lists and external lists. In-house lists are usually not available to competitors for rental and are based on responses to previous mailings; hence, they may be called response lists. External lists are typically compiled for rental by sources outside the company.

Compiled lists are either lists of consumers or businesses. Some examples of compiled consumer lists available for rental are buyers of certain vehicle models, different types of collectors, subscribers to various periodicals, organic gardeners, and golf enthusiasts. Business lists are typically categorized according to the **Standard Industrial Classification (SIC)** system, where various types of businesses are assigned two-, three-, or even four-digit codes, with two-digit codes for major business groups and four-digit codes for more specialized business types.

In direct mail, lists are rented from a list source for one-time use. When multiple lists are rented, a technique known as merge/purge is used to eliminate duplications. A list broker's job is to match his client, the list buyer, with the appropriate list. Although representing both the list buyer and the list owner, the list broker is usually paid by the list owner. While a list broker represents the buyer's interest in finding the right list, a list manager is more like an agent who represents one or more specific lists. The list manager handles the rental and billing procedures for the list owner. The list manager works with list brokers and list compilers as well as with heavy mailers to get them or their clients to use the list.

List costs tend to vary with specificity. That is, a list of subscribers to a particular magazine may rent for $50 per thousand (lists are typically rented on a "per thousand" basis). However, for a list of women subscribers who live in certain zip codes, the cost may increase to $100 per thousand.

Direct mailers employ a variety of selectivity techniques to better target their mailings. Traditional segmentation techniques look at past behavior, including time since most recent purchase, frequency of purchase, and amounts of purchases (known as the RFM formula, recency/frequency/monetary). More advanced segmentation techniques employ formulas that help predict future behavior.

One such technique is list enhancement, or the process of overlaying social, economic, demographic, or psychographic data obtained from other sources on a mailing list. Adding such data to an in-house list allows mailers to develop a customer profile based on such factors as age, gender, car ownership, dwelling type, and lifestyle factors. Once that process is undertaken, the in-house list becomes an in-house database, or collection of information about customers and prospects that can be used for marketing purposes. Modeling techniques can then be applied to the in-house database to help predict response rates from externally compiled lists whose individuals share some of the characteristics of the company's customer profile.

Direct mail packages come in all shapes and sizes, making it one of the most flexible of the direct marketing media. A standard direct mail package, which itself may be done in a variety of sizes, includes an envelope, a letter, a brochure, and a response device. A variation on the classic format is the multimailer, a package with a number of flyers each selling a different product. Another popular format is the self-mailer, any piece that is mailed without an outer envelope.

More complex direct mail packages are three-dimensional; that is, they include an object such as a gift or product sample. These three-dimensional mailings can be effective in reaching top executives whose mail is screened by a secretary, and they are practically guaranteed to be opened by consumers at home.

Catalogs ranging from six to more than 100 pages are used to sell a variety of goods. They are also used to sell services, such as seminars. A variation of the catalog is called a magalog, which combines a certain amount of editorial content along with sales content to give the catalog the appearance of a magazine. A specialized field of direct marketing, catalog marketing is a discipline unto itself and accounts for a significant part of all direct mail activity.

Looking more closely at the classic direct mail package, the envelope's job is to motivate the recipient to open the package. The recipient's decision whether to open, set aside, or discard the mailing piece takes just one or two seconds. Regardless of the volume of mail a person receives, whether at home or a place of business, the envelope must distinguish itself from other mail by its size, appearance, and any copy that might be written on it. Envelopes that take on the appearance of an invitation or telegram might grab someone's attention faster than a plain "#10" envelope. Other choices that are made concerning envelopes are color and texture, window or closed face, and whether to use a preprinted indicia or a postage stamp.

The letter is a sales letter and provides the opportunity to directly address the interests and concerns of the recipient. In a sense the letter replaces the salesperson in face-to-face selling. The letter typically spells out the benefits of the offer in detail. The more personal the sales letter, the more effective it generally is. The letter writer must be intimately familiar with not only the product or service and its benefits, he/she must know and understand to whom the letter is addressed.

While the letter tells the recipient about the benefits of the offer, the brochure illustrates them. Illustrated brochures are used to sell services as well as products. Brochures come in a range of sizes and different folds. While the use of color may increase response, the brochure's look should fit the product or service it is selling.

Finally, the package must include a response device, such as a business reply card or coupon, that the recipient can send back. Response rates are generally higher when the response device is separate from, rather than part of, the brochure or letter. Toll-free numbers are often prominently displayed to allow the recipient to respond via telephone. However, since some customers will not use the phone to place an order, a response device should be included in addition to a toll-free number. The key to a successful response device is to keep it simple and easy to fill out.

A "lift letter" is often added to the package to "lift" the response rate. The lift letter often carries the message, "Read this only if you've decided not to accept our offer," or something similar to grab the recipient's attention one more time.

Other enclosures that may be added to the direct mail package include gift or premium slips, article reprints, a business reply envelope, and a variety of involvement devices. Involvement devices such as stamps, stickers, pencils, and rub-off messages motivate the recipient to become involved with the response device and, hopefully, continue to take the action required to make a purchase.

TESTING DIRECT MAIL

Since large expenditures are involved in mailing lists in the tens of thousands or even millions, direct mailers take advantage of the medium's testing capabilities. Every element of direct mail—the offer, the list, and the package—can easily be tested to avoid committing major resources to unproductive mailings. In *Successful Direct Marketing Methods*, Bob Stone recommended testing in six major areas: products and services, media, propositions made, copy platforms, formats, and timing. The point is that tests should concentrate on meaningful components.

For products and services being sold by mail, pricing and payment options are often tested. A test may reveal that a higher price actually produces a better response. While the product and the price are considered the main offer, premiums and other incentives that enhance the offer are also subject to testing.

List testing is basic to direct mail. Experts recommend testing different segments of a particular list, preferably testing the best segment first. The appropriate size of a test sample is dependent on the anticipated response. The smaller the anticipated response rate, the larger the necessary list sample should be. A rule of thumb is that the list sample should be large enough to generate thirty to forty anticipated responses.

While list testing may clearly identify winners and losers, it will also reveal that some lists are marginal, or near break-even. In that case, the list may be discarded, or another test may be conducted using different selection criteria on the list to make it pay out better.

The direct mail package is subject to a variety of tests that usually focus on format and copy. If the mailer has established a control package, then one element at a time is tested to see if it lifts the response to the package. Another type of creative testing is sometimes called breakthrough testing, where an entirely new approach is developed to sell a product or service.

Lists, offers, and packages can all be tested in one mailing when done properly. A test matrix consisting of individual test cells is constructed. Each test cell contains a unique combination of elements being tested and makes up a portion of the overall mailing. After the entire mailing is dropped, responses from each test cell are tracked to determine the performance of the tested elements.

WHEN DIRECT MAIL WORKS BEST

Direct mail offers marketers several advantages over other advertising media. It provides a high degree of measurability, one of the hallmarks of direct marketing, that in turn allows for extensive testing. Of course, for direct mail to work well the direct marketer must be able to identify the target audience and be able to create or rent the appropriate mailing lists.

Direct mail gives direct marketers the opportunity to present one-on-one communications and motivate the recipient to act. Direct mail gives marketers greater control over the sales message and allows them to say a lot about a product or service in the sales letter and brochure. Repeat mailings can be done to take advantage of the product's or service's potential for repeat sales as well as to sell related goods and services to the same lists.

While direct marketing has grown over the years to employ a variety of advertising media as they became available, such as the telephone, broadcast media, and print media, it is direct mail that remains the most heavily used medium in direct marketing today.

SEE ALSO: Database Marketing

[David P. Bianco]

FURTHER READING:

Bly, Robert W. *Business-to-Business Direct Marketing*. NTC Business Books, 1993.

Direct Mail List Rates and Data. Standard Rate & Data Services, 1994.

Jones, Susan K. *Creative Strategy in Direct Marketing*. NTC Business Books, 1991.

Jutkins, "Rocket" Ray. *Direct Marketing: How You Can Really Do It Right*, 2nd ed. Rockingham*Jutkins*Marketing, 1990.

Kobs, Jim. *Profitable Direct Marketing*, 2nd ed. NTC Business Books, 1992.

Lewis, Herschell Gordon. *Direct Marketing Strategies and Tactics*. Dartnell, 1992.

Stone, Bob. *Successful Direct Marketing Methods*, 4th ed. NTC Business Books, 1989.

DIRECT MARKETING

According to the official definition of the Direct Marketing Association (DMA), direct marketing is an "interactive system of marketing which uses one or more advertising media to effect a measurable response and/or transaction at any location." While there are many other definitions of direct marketing, the DMA definition captures four basic concepts of direct marketing.

The notion of interactivity, or one-on-one communication between the marketer and the prospect or customer, distinguishes direct marketing from general **advertising** and other types of **marketing**. Direct marketing makes an offer and asks for a response. By developing a history of offers and responses, direct marketers acquire knowledge of their prospects and customers, resulting in more effective targeting.

Measurability sets direct marketing apart from general advertising and other forms of marketing. Direct marketers can measure the response to any offer. Measurability allows direct marketers to test a variety of lists, offers, media—virtually any aspect of a campaign—in order to allocate marketing resources to the most effective combination of elements.

Direct marketing uses a variety of media, including mail, magazine ads, newspaper ads, television and radio spots, **infomercials** (also television but longer format), free standing inserts (FSIs), and card decks. This flexibility allows direct marketing to provide interactivity and measurability and still be able to take advantage of new technologies. By being able to utilize virtually any media, direct marketing will lead marketers into the twenty-first century as interactive television, the information highway, and other new technologies become a reality.

In direct marketing, the transaction may take place at any location and is not limited to retail stores or fixed places of business. The transaction may take place in the consumer's home or office via mail, over the phone, or through interactive television. It may also occur away from the home or office, as at a kiosk for example.

In his book, *Profitable Direct Marketing,* Jim Kobs wrote: "Direct marketing gets your ad message to the customer or prospect to produce some type of immediate action. It usually involves creating a database of respondents." He also said, "Direct marketing is really the straightest line between you—the advertiser—and the action you want those who receive your message to take."

HISTORY AND BACKGROUND

The history of direct marketing starts with mail order shopping and **direct mail**, two traditional elements that still play a role in many direct marketing campaigns. It is necessary to distinguish direct marketing from direct mail or **mail order business**, although direct marketing encompasses those two concepts. A firm may spend millions of dollars on direct mail and not sell anything through the mail. Direct mail is an advertising medium, one of several media that direct marketers utilize. Mail order is a distribution channel; the other two distribution channels are retail and personal sales.

How old is direct marketing? Garden and seed catalogs were known to be distributed in the American colonies before the Revolutionary War. Mail order shopping of consumer goods entered a period of growth in the 1880s, when mail-order houses began to fiercely compete with local stores. Their marketing contest centered on three major issues—price, inventory, and assurances—the very factors that made mail order houses successful.

Aaron Montgomery Ward (1843-1913), regarded as the first of the consumer goods catalogers, started his catalog business in 1872, while Richard Warren Sears (1863-1914) mailed his first flyers in the 1880s. These catalogs had a liberating effect on 19th century consumers. Consumers were no longer captives of their local stores, which had limited inventories and charged higher prices because the stores weren't big enough to receive large volume discounts from their suppliers. With the advent of mail order, consumers could get attractive goods and prices whether they lived in the middle of Manhattan or a remote rural setting.

The postal system allowed direct-mail companies to operate on a national basis. With economies of scale working in their favor, mail order houses could undercut the pricing of local stores. In 1897, bicycles were selling for $75 to $100 and more, until Sears started offering them for $5 to $20 in its catalog. Sears could offer those low prices because it sold thousands of bicycles every week.

The large volume of business also allowed catalogers to offer a wider variety of goods. Consumers not only wanted low prices, they also wanted variety—20 kinds of dresses rather than two. Here again, the enormous volume generated by leading mail order houses made huge inventories not only possible but also practicable.

But price and variety, while important, have only limited value if the goods themselves are shoddy or poorly-made. So the mail-order firms protected consumers with powerful guarantees. Montgomery Ward was one of the first companies to offer a money-back guarantee, and the Sears Roebuck pledge of ''satisfaction guaranteed or your money back'' is one of the best-known commitments in American business.

Another successful cataloger, L.L. Bean of Freeport, Maine, began in 1913 when Mr. Leon Leonwood Bean mailed his first single-sheet flyer advertising his Maine hunting boots. Perhaps he got the idea of using direct mail from his brother Guy Bean, who was the Freeport postmaster. Bean targeted his mailing to individuals who had hunting licenses.

Another landmark in direct marketing occurred in 1926, when copywriter John Caples wrote a direct response advertisement for a music correspondence school using the headline, ''They Laughed When I Sat Down at the Piano . . . But Then I Started to Play!'' Today the Caples Award is a coveted prize among direct marketing copywriters.

GROWTH OF DIRECT MARKETING

Despite these and many other successes, direct marketing did not come into its own as a marketing discipline until the 1970s. It's interesting to note that the successful introduction of bank credit cards, including Visa and MasterCard, in the 1960s and 1970s was conducted using direct marketing methods to convince consumers, merchants, and banks to accept the cards. Why were consumers, merchants, and banks ready to embrace bank credit cards, and why was direct marketing the most effective way to present the message about credit cards?

The very elements that contributed to the increased effectiveness of direct marketing in the 1960s and 1970s have continued to fuel the discipline's growth in the 1980s and 1990s. From the many factors contributing to the growth of direct marketing and mail order catalogs, direct marketing expert Jim Kobs selected five as the most important.

Changing lifestyles were an important factor in the acceptance of direct marketing among consumers. The number of women working outside the home jumped from 42 percent to 58 percent between 1980 and 1990. This was a trend that began at least a decade earlier and contributed to the growth of direct marketing. After all, isn't it logical that when you have less time to go shopping, it's more convenient to select and examine merchandise in your own home, at your own convenience? Direct marketing extends this convenience beyond mail order shopping to consumers receiving all kinds of offers in the home, either via mail or commercial television, as is common today, or via home shopping networks and interactive television.

Another factor contributing to the growth of direct marketing was the increased cost associated with personal sales calls. By the end of the 1970s, the average cost of a single sales call was estimated to be about $137. By the end of the 1980s, the cost had risen to more than $250 per call. An interesting application of direct marketing now is to use direct marketing methods to make personal selling more cost-effective by generating qualified leads that can then be followed up by a personal sales call.

Technological growth in general, and computer-based technologies in particular, have played an important role in many areas of direct marketing. New computer technologies have allowed direct marketers to be more precise in the analysis of results, in the targeting of messages based on more complex psychographics and demographics, in developing more sophisticated customer and prospect databases, and even in the creative execution of direct mail packages.

The growth in the number of available products and services has made direct marketing more attractive than mass marketing when a larger number of goods and services are being offered to a smaller group of prospects.

Increased consumer acceptance of the telephone as a way to place orders has also helped direct marketing achieve phenomenal growth. Coupled with telephone-based ordering are faster order fulfillment and the elimination of delays previously associated with mail order. Today, placing an order by phone offers almost the same ''instant gratification'' as picking up a piece of merchandise at the store.

Other socioeconomic factors contributing to the growth and acceptance of direct marketing include a population growing older, rising discretionary income, more single households, and the growth of the "me" generation. External factors include the rising cost of gasoline (at-home shoppers use less gasoline and reduce environmental pollution), the availability of **toll-free telephone numbers**, the expanded use of credit cards, the low cost of data processing, and the widespread availability of mailing lists.

DIRECT MARKETING MEDIA

While many people associate direct marketing with direct mail, direct mail is only one of several advertising media utilized by direct marketers. Other major direct marketing media include the telephone, magazines, newspapers, television, and radio. Alternative media include card decks, package and bill inserts, and matchbooks. Within the major media, new technological developments are giving direct marketers a new range of choices from videocassettes (possibly advertised on television, requested by telephone or interactive computer, and delivered via mail or alternate delivery services) to home shopping networks and interactive television.

DIRECT MAIL. This is the most heavily used direct marketing medium and the one direct marketers learn first. Direct mail has been used to sell a wide variety of goods and services to consumers as well as businesses. Despite postage increases, direct mail continues to grow. According to Kobs, a recent count showed some 714,000 businesses have bulk mail permits that allow them to mail at lower, third class rates, and they send out more than 63 billion pieces of advertising mail a year. More recently, in 1993 third class mail increased by 5.2 percent over 1992.

Direct mail offers several advantages over other media. Perhaps the most important is selectivity and personalization. This doesn't necessarily mean addressing every individual by name, but it does allow targeting individuals with known purchase histories or particular psychographic or demographic characteristics that match the marketer's customer profile. Direct mail can be targeted to a specific geographic area based on zip codes or other geographic factors. Personalization in direct mail means not only addressing the envelope to a person or family by name, it can also mean including the recipient's name inside the envelope on a letter, for example, or elsewhere in the package.

Direct mail packages come in all shapes and sizes, making it one of the most flexible of the direct marketing media. A standard direct mail package includes an envelope, a letter, a brochure, and a response device. The envelope's job is to motivate the recipient to open the package. Regardless of the volume of mail a person receives, the envelope must distinguish itself from other mail by its size, appearance, and any copy that might be written on it.

The letter is a sales letter and provides the opportunity to directly address the interests and concerns of the recipient. The letter typically spells out the benefits of the offer in detail. The more personal the sales letter, the more effective it is generally. While the letter tells the recipient about the benefits of the offer, the brochure illustrates them. Illustrated brochures are used to sell services as well as products. Finally, the package must include a response device, such as a business reply card, that the recipient can send back. Response rates are generally higher when the response device is separate from, rather than part of, the brochure or letter. Toll-free numbers are often prominently displayed to allow the recipient to respond via telephone.

A "lift letter" is often added to the package to "lift" the response rate. The lift letter often carries the message, "Read this only if you've decided not to accept our offer," or something similar to grab the recipient's attention one more time.

More complex direct mail packages are three-dimensional; that is, they include an object such as a gift or product sample. These three-dimensional mailings can be effective in reaching top executives whose mail is screened by a secretary, and they are practically guaranteed to be opened by consumers at home.

Direct mail is the most easily tested advertising medium. Every factor in successful direct marketing—the right offer, the right person, the right format, and the right timing—can be tested in direct mail. In terms of selecting the right list, computer technologies have made it easier to select a randomized name sample from any list, so that mailers can run a test mailing to determine the response from a list before "rolling out," or mailing, the entire list. Different packages containing different offers can also be tested. Other media allow some degree of testing, but direct mail is the most sophisticated.

Direct mail is the most effective media for reaching a company's customer base, which is likely to provide the best sales opportunities, thereby maximizing the profit from a business's customer list. The only other advertising medium that allows a marketer to reach its customers without any waste is telephone-based selling.

In relation to the other direct marketing media, direct mail is considered to offer the most cost-effective way of achieving the highest possible response. Only **telemarketing** produces a higher response rate, but usually at a much higher cost per response.

TELEPHONE-BASED DIRECT MARKETING (TELEMARKETING). The use of the telephone in direct marketing has grown dramatically over the past two decades. Expenditures now may equal, or even surpass, those of direct mail. Telephone-based direct marketing may be outbound and/or inbound. Inbound telemarketing is also known as teleservicing and usually involves taking orders and responding to inquiries. Out-bound telemarketing for consumers may be used for one-step selling, lead generation, lead qualification or follow-up, and selling and servicing larger and more active customers. In business, telemarketing can be used to reach smaller accounts that don't warrant a personal sales call as well as to generate, qualify, and follow up leads.

Telemarketing has the advantage of being personal and interactive. It's an effective two-way communications medium that enables company representatives to listen to customers. Telephone sales people typically work from a script, but the medium allows the flexibility of revising the script as needed. It also allows up- and cross-selling. While the customer is on the phone it's possible to increase the size of their orders by offering them additional choices, something that tends to lead to confusion in other direct marketing media. Examples include offering ''telephone specials'' to callers or letting them know about clearance or discounted merchandise.

Telemarketing is more expensive than direct mail. It also lacks a permanent response device that the prospect can set aside or use later. It is not a visual medium at present, although the technology to make it one may be available in five years. Finally, it's perceived as intrusive, generating consumer complaints of ''invasion of privacy'' that have led to legislative actions to regulate the telemarketing industry.

MAGAZINES. Direct response print ads in magazines must ask the reader to do something by making a definite offer or request of the reader. Typically this means sending in a coupon or bound-in reply card, or calling a toll-free number. With well over 2000 consumer magazines now being published, magazine ads allow direct marketers to reach audiences with identifiable interests. In addition to advertising heavily in special interest magazines, direct marketers utilize mass consumer magazines and take advantage of regional advertising space to target specific audiences.

Unlike general advertisers, who measure the effectiveness of their print ads in terms of reach and frequency, direct marketers measure the effectiveness of their print ads in terms of cost effectiveness, either cost-per-inquiry or cost-per-order. Magazine ads offer the advantages of good color reproduction, a relatively long ad life (especially compared to daily newspapers), and a lower cost per thousand. Creative costs for magazine ads are also usually lower than for direct mail.

Direct marketers find magazines' long lead times, slower response, and scarcer space than direct mail to be disadvantages. In some cases magazine advertising is not as selective as direct mail or telemarketing.

NEWSPAPERS. While direct marketers advertise in magazines more than newspapers, newspapers have some distinct advantages over magazines, the more popular direct marketing medium. They include the variety of sections offered within a newspaper, shorter closing dates, an immediate response, and broad coverage of a large and diverse audience. Disadvantages include poor ad reproduction and the limited availability of color. Editorial content can also have more of an adverse effect on ad response than in magazines. In addition to advertising in the regular pages of a newspaper, direct marketers also advertise in free-standing inserts (FSIs) that are usually distributed with the Sunday editions of newspapers.

TELEVISION. Direct marketing on television is increasing. It has undergone an evolution from the early days when products for the home were sold on television by carnival-like pitchmen giving lengthy product demonstrations. Television viewers are also familiar with direct response advertisements for products like knives, garden tools, exercise equipment, records, and books, which ask them to call in and order a specific product.

More recent developments in direct response television advertising include a return to a lengthier format, evident today in **infomercials**, where a product or other offer is explained in some detail over a time period extending from several to 30 minutes or more. Advocates of this format point out that the lengthier format gives the advertiser the opportunity to build a relationship with the viewer and overcome initial viewer skepticism, and at the same time present a convincing story spelling out product features and benefits in greater detail.

Not all direct response television involves asking for an order. Long distance telephone companies and automobile manufacturers, among other advertisers, have included toll-free telephone numbers with their television ads to get viewers to call and request more information about their product or service. Any television ad that includes an 800 number is asking for a response and qualifies as a direct response advertisement.

With the prospect of interactive television looming on the horizon, together with developments in the delivery of more cable channels that offer audiences with identifiable interests and demographics, direct response television promises to be a dynamic area in the future of direct marketing.

DIRECT MARKETING LISTS AND DATABASES

Lists are commonly used in direct mail and telemarketing. The two basic types of lists are response lists and compiled lists.

Response lists contain the names of prospects who have responded to the same offer. These typically contain individuals who share a common interest. Names on a response list may include buyers, inquirers, subscribers, continuity club members, or sweepstakes entrants. They may have responded to an offer from one of several media, including direct mail, television, or a print ad. Response lists are not usually rented; rather, they are an in-house list compiled by a particular business. Compiled lists are often rented by direct marketers. Compiled mass consumer, specialized consumer, and business lists are available for a wide range of interests.

Direct marketing databases are similar to mailing lists in that they contain names and addresses, but they are much more. They are the repository of a wide range of customer information and may also contain psychographic, demographic, and census data compiled from external sources. They form the basis of direct marketing programs whereby companies establish closer ties and build relationships with their customers.

In the 1980s, **database marketing** became one of the prevalent buzzwords of the direct marketing industry. Whether it's called relationship marketing, relevance marketing, or bonding, the common theme of database marketing is strengthening relationships with existing customers and building relationships with new ones. Databases allow direct marketers to uncover a wealth of relevant information about individual consumers and apply that knowledge to increase the probability of a desired response or purchase.

As with mailing lists, there are two basic types of marketing databases, customer databases and external databases. Customer databases are compiled internally and contain information about a company's customers taken from the relationship-building process. External databases are collections of specific individuals and their characteristics. These external databases may be mass-compiled from public data sources; they may contain financial data based on confidential credit files; they may be compiled from questionnaires; or they may be a combination of all three sources.

Database marketing, and especially the prospect of using confidential information for marketing purposes, has made privacy an important issue in the direct marketing industry. Some states have passed legislation limiting access to previously public data or limiting the use of such data as automobile registrations, credit histories, and medical information. In order to avoid excessive government regulation, the direct marketing industry has attempted to be self-policing with regard to the use of sensitive data. However, the struggle between industry self-regulation and government regulation continues and will probably continue for some time.

DIRECT MARKETING SUCCESS FACTORS

There are certain situations where direct marketing is more likely to work than others. The direct marketer must be able to identify the target audience in terms of shared characteristics. Are they likely to read a particular magazine? Live in a certain geographic area? Have a certain minimum income? Be a certain age or gender? The more characteristics of the target audience that can be identified, the more likely a direct marketing campaign targeted to those individuals will work.

Since direct marketing relies on one-on-one communications and motivating the recipient to act, it is essential to be able to reach the target audience. It's no use identifying a target market if there's no mailing list or print or broadcast medium available to reach them.

Some other situations in which direct marketing works well are when there's a lot to say about a product or service; when the product or service has the potential for repeat sales; and when there's a need to have greater control over the sales message.

The success of a direct marketing program depends on delivering the right offer at the right time to the right person in the right way. Direct marketing is a complex discipline that requires expertise in several areas to achieve success. It involves identifying the target market correctly and selecting the appropriate media and/or lists to reach it. The offer must be presented in the best way, and direct marketers must use the most effective creative execution to successfully motivate customers and prospects. At its most effective, direct marketing is an ongoing process of communication to maintain relationships with existing customers and build relationships with new ones.

[David P. Bianco]

FURTHER READING:

Jutkins, ''Rocket'' Ray. *Direct Marketing: How You Can Really Do It Right*, 2nd ed. Rockingham*Jutkins*Marketing, 1990.

Kobs, Jim. *Profitable Direct Marketing*, 2nd ed. NTC Business Books, 1992.

Lewis, Herschell Gordon. *Direct Marketing Strategies and Tactics*. Dartnell, 1992.

Nash, Edward L., ed. *The Direct Marketing Handbook*, 2nd ed. McGraw-Hill, 1992.

David Shepard Associates. *The New Direct Marketing: How to Implement a Profit-Driven Database Marketing Strategy*. Business One Irwin, 1990.

Stone, Bob. *Successful Direct Marketing Methods*, 4th ed. NTC Business Books, 1989.

DIRECTORS

SEE: Board of Directors

DISCLOSURE LAWS AND REGULATIONS

Companies that are privately owned are not required by law to disclose detailed financial and operating information. They have a wide latitude in deciding what types of information to make available to the public. They can shield information from public knowledge and determine for themselves who needs to know specific types of information.

Companies that are publicly owned, on the other hand, are subject to detailed disclosure laws about their financial condition, operating results, management compensation, and other areas of their business. The current system of mandatory corporate disclosure began in the 1930s with the passage of the **Securities Act of 1933** and the **Securities Exchange Act of 1934**. These acts as well as subsequent legislation related to disclosure have been implemented by rules and regulations of the **Securities and Exchange Commission** (SEC).

Disclosure laws are designed to protect investors through the disclosure of business and financial information that could be considered relevant to making an investment decision. Since private companies do not raise money from the investing public, they are not subject to the same disclosure laws as public companies. Investors in private companies are considered to be sufficiently well informed about their investment decisions so as not to require the protection of disclosure laws.

Congress and the SEC balance a concern for investor safety with a concern for business's ability to raise capital. They recognize that disclosure laws should not be so burdensome on companies that they discourage capital formation through the offering of stock and other securities to the public. It is generally recognized that registration requirements for new securities issues and the ongoing reporting requirements for public companies are more burdensome on smaller businesses and stock issues than on big ones. Consequently Congress has over time raised the limit on the small issue exemption from $100,000 as it was in the original 1933 act to $300,000 in 1945, $500,000 in 1970, $1.5 million and then $2 million in 1978, and $5 million in 1982. That means that securities issues up to $5 million are not subject to the registration requirements of the SEC.

All of the SEC's disclosure requirements have statutory authority, and these rules and regulations, such as the small issue exemption, are subject to changes and amendments over time. Some changes are made as the result of new **accounting** rules adopted by the principal rule-making bodies of the accounting profession. In other cases changes in accounting rules follow changes in SEC guidelines. In any event SEC regulations have a direct impact on what are known as generally accepted accounting principles (GAAP). The rule-making bodies of the accounting profession, most notably the **Financial Accounting Standards Board (FASB)** and the American Institute of Certified Public Accountants (AICPA), must rely on "acceptance" of their statements. While FASB and AICPA statements do not have the force of law, they are widely accepted in the accounting profession and in some cases influence subsequent SEC rules on disclosure. In some cases, FASB statements on disclosure are modified after the reaction to them by the accounting profession has been determined.

DISCLOSURES REQUIRED BY THE SECURITIES AND EXCHANGE COMMISSION

SEC regulations require publicly owned companies to disclose certain types of business and financial data on a regular basis to the SEC and to the company's stockholders. The SEC also requires disclosure of relevant business and financial information to potential investors when new securities, such as **stocks** and **bonds**, are issued to the public (with exceptions for small issues and private placements).

The current system of mandatory corporate disclosure is known as the integrated disclosure system. By amending some of its regulations, the SEC has attempted to make this system less burdensome on corporations by standardizing various forms and eliminating some differences in reporting requirements to the SEC and to shareholders. The system integrates the different requirements of the 1933 and 1934 acts and those of shareholder reports.

REPORTING REQUIREMENTS. Publicly owned companies are in the habit of preparing two **annual reports,** one for the SEC and one for their shareholders. Form 10-K is the annual report made to the SEC, and its content and form are strictly governed by federal statutes. It contains detailed financial and operating information. In 10-K reports management typically provides a narrative response to specific questions about the company's operations, and public accountants prepare the detailed **financial statements**.

Historically, companies have had more leeway in what they include in their annual reports to stockholders. Over the years, however, the SEC has gained more influence over the content of such annual reports, primarily through its statutory power concerning proxy statements. By amending its rules covering proxy statements, the SEC has been able to increase its authority over the content of corporate annual reports. Since most companies mail annual reports along with their proxy statements, they must make their annual stockholder reports comply with SEC requirements.

SEC regulations require that annual reports to stockholders contain certified financial statements and other specific items. The certified financial statement must include a two-year audited **balance sheet** and a three-year audited statement of income and cash flows. In addition annual reports must contain five years of selected financial data, including net sales or operating revenues, income or loss from continuing operations, total assets, long-term obligations and redeemable **preferred stock**, and cash **dividends** declared per common share.

Annual reports to stockholders must also contain management's discussion and analysis of the firm's financial condition and results of operations. Following broad guidelines provided by the SEC, this section of the annual report should focus on the company's financial condition, changes in financial condition, and results of operations. Management's discussion and analysis should disclose or discuss the firm's liquidity, capital resources, results of operations, any favorable or unfavorable trends in the industry, and any significant events or uncertainties.

Other information to be included in annual reports to stockholders includes a brief description of the business covering such matters as main products and services, sources of materials, and status of new products. Directors and officers of the corporation must be identified. Specific market data on **common stock** must also be supplied.

One objective of the SEC's integrated disclosure system is to require that similar information be disclosed in SEC filings as in reports to shareholders. The basic information package that publicly owned companies must disclose includes audited financial statements, a summary of selected financial data, and management's description of the company's business and financial condition. As a result, annual reports to shareholders now contain more detailed financial information than before.

REGISTRATION OF NEW SECURITIES. Private companies that wish to become publicly owned or "go public," must comply with the registration requirements of the SEC. In addition companies floating new securities must follow similar disclosure requirements. The required disclosures are made in a two-part registration statement that consists of a prospectus as one part and a second part containing additional

information. The prospectus contains all of the information that is to be presented to potential investors. It should be noted that SEC rules and regulations governing registration statements are subject to change.

In order to meet the disclosure requirements of new issue registration, companies prepare a basic information package similar to that used by publicly owned companies for their annual reporting. The prospectus, which contains all information to be presented to potential investors, must include such items as audited financial statements, a summary of selected financial data, and management's description of the company's business and financial condition.

In effect a company seeking to go public must disclose its entire business plan. In addition to the basic data noted above, the registration statement must disclose the company's material business contracts and all forms of cash and noncash compensation given to the **chief executive officer** (CEO) and the top five officers making more than $100,000 a year. Compensation paid to all officers and directors as a group must also be disclosed.

An important part of the company's registration statement is management's description of the company's business and financial condition. In the prospectus management must cover such areas of the business as results of operations, liquidity, capital resources, and the impact of **inflation**. Management must also focus on events and uncertainties that might affect future operating results. Potential investors must be given an indication of the amounts and certainty of cash flows from operations and other sources.

SECURITIES INDUSTRY REGULATIONS. Additional disclosure laws apply to the securities industry and to the ownership of securities. Officers, directors, and principal stockholders (defined as holding 10 percent or more of the company's stock) of publicly owned companies must submit two reports to the SEC. These are Form 3 and Form 4. Form 3 is a personal statement of beneficial ownership of securities of their company. Form 4 records changes in such ownership. These reporting requirements also apply to the immediate families of the company's officers, directors, and principal stockholders. It is through these forms that insider trading is reported to the SEC and becomes public record.

Individuals who acquire 5 percent or more of the voting stock of a SEC-registered company must submit the appropriate form (either Form 13D or 13G) to the SEC. The form must be filed within ten days of reaching the reporting level of stock ownership.

Securities broker-dealers must provide their customers with a confirmation form as soon as possible after the execution of an order. These forms provide customers with minimum basic information required for every trade. Broker-dealers are also responsible for presenting the prospectus to each customer for new securities issues.

Members of the securities industry are also subject to reporting requirements of their own self-regulating organizations. These organizations include the New York and American Stock Exchanges for listed securities transactions, the National Association of Securities Dealers (NASD) for over-the-counter traded securities, and the Chicago Board of Exchange for all listed **equity**, **debt**, stock index, and other option activities.

One area of the securities industry in which new disclosure rules are being developed by the SEC is that of **mutual funds**. While mutual funds must issue a prospectus for potential investors, the prospectus does not have to disclose what stocks and bonds the fund owns. The language of some prospectuses as they are currently written also does not clearly indicate the risks and potential rewards of investing in the mutual fund. More information about the compensation paid to the fund's director and other fees may also be required, along with information about the effect of such fees and compensation on the performance of the fund.

DISCLOSURE RULES OF THE ACCOUNTING PROFESSION

Generally accepted accounting principles (GAAP) and specific rules of the accounting profession require that certain types of information be disclosed in a business's audited financial statements. As noted above these rules and principles do not have the same force of law as SEC rules and regulations. Once adopted, however, they are widely accepted and followed by the accounting profession.

It is a GAAP that any information must be disclosed in a financial statement if its nondisclosure would tend to mislead readers of the statement. That is, financial statements must disclose all significant information that would be of interest to a concerned investor or creditor. The relevant information may be disclosed in a footnote, a separate schedule, or another part of the financial statement. Among the types of information that accountants must disclose are accounting policies employed, litigation in progress, lease information, and details of pension plan funding. Generally, full disclosure is required when alternative accounting policies are available, as with inventory valuation, **depreciation**, and long-term contract accounting. In addition accounting practices applicable to a particular industry and other unusual applications of accounting principles are usually disclosed.

Certified financial statements contain a statement of opinion from an auditor, in which the auditor states that it is his or her opinion that the financial statements

were prepared in accordance with GAAP and that no material information was left undisclosed. If the auditor has any doubts, then a qualified or adverse opinion statement is written. Under AICPA Statement on Auditing Standards No. 32, auditors must issue a qualified or adverse opinion when they conclude that audited financial statements omit information required by GAAP.

Disclosures required by the rules and regulations of the accounting profession may exceed those required by the SEC. For example, FASB recently issued statement No. 119, ''Disclosure about Derivative Financial Instruments and Fair Value of Financial Instruments,'' which affected the 1994 financial statements of many companies. It called for more complete disclosures by businesses and nonprofit organizations about the derivative financial instruments they held. Derivatives are financial agreements, such as **futures** and options contracts, whose returns are linked to, or derived from, the performance of underlying assets. They are considered volatile investments, and the lack of specific disclosures about them was considered misleading to interested investors and creditors.

OTHER DISCLOSURE LAWS

Another area of business in which disclosure laws play a role is consumer lending. Under Federal Reserve Regulation Z, commonly known as the Truth in Lending Act, lenders must disclose certain types of information to borrowers. This regulation applies to anyone making loans to consumers, including **banks**, **savings and loan associations**, credit card issuers, hospitals, finance companies, and others. Among the types of information that must be disclosed are conditions under which a finance charge may be applied, when payments may be made without incurring a finance charge, method of determining finance charges, the periodic rate used and the corresponding annual percentage rate, the minimum periodic payment required, and similar information.

[David Bianco]

FURTHER READING:

Seligman, Joel. *The SEC and the Future of Finance*. Praeger, 1985.

Skousen, K. Fred. *An Introduction to the SEC*. 5th ed. South-Western Publishing Co., 1991.

DISCOUNT BROKER

One kind of brokerage firm, known as a discount broker or discount firm, does not provide its clients with extra services, such as research or investment advice; in exchange, this firm charges reduced or discounted commission rates for executing orders and clearing trades to every customer on every transaction.

For a number of years, the commission rates that stockbrokers charged their customers for buying and selling securities were established by a schedule of minimum rates set by national securities exchanges for their members, and most brokers adhered to this policy. Rates were "fixed" throughout the industry. In May 1975, the **Securities and Exchange Commission** (SEC) adopted a rule that abolished fixed commission rates. In today's trading environment, brokerage firms can compete with one another to offer their customers the best combination of commission rates and services.

Opening a trading account with a discount broker is one way a speculator, outside investor, or trader can participate in the stock and/or futures markets. Using risk capital, the speculator assumes risk in the hope of making a profit by correctly forecasting future price movement. Many traders prefer to do their own research and analysis and make their own decisions about what and when to buy and sell. In essence, they prefer and have chosen to manage their own futures or stock portfolios.

People who prefer to manage their own portfolios also may prefer to open a trading account with a discount firm because the firm offers reduced or discounted commission fees in exchange for limited services. When traders decide to manage their own portfolios, they should take into account their knowledge and previous experience, how much time and attention they can devote to the markets, and the amount of capital they are willing to risk as well as their temperament and tolerance for risk.

On the other hand, an inexperienced investor may want to utilize the services of a full-service broker who will provide research services and make investment recommendations based on the individual's situation and style. The broker will take into account the amount of money being invested, the type of investment (is it short-term or long-term?), as well as the risks and rewards.

All brokerage firms that conduct futures business with the public must be registered with the **Commodity Futures Trading Commission** (CFTC) as a Futures Commission Merchant (FCM) or Introducing Broker (IB), and must be members of the National Futures Association, the commodity industry's first self-regulatory association. The CFTC is the federal regulator and overseer of commodity futures and options on commodity futures contracts in the United States. FCM are individuals, associations, partnerships, corporations, and trusts that solicit or accept orders for the purchase or sale of any commodity for future delivery on or subject to the rules of any

contract market and that accept payment from or extend credit to those whose orders are accepted. An IB is any person, other than a person registered as an associated person of an FCM, who is engaged in soliciting or in accepting orders for the purchase or sale of any commodity for future delivery on an exchange that does not accept any money, securities, or property to margin, guarantee, or secure any trades or contracts that result therefrom.

All securities firms must be registered and conduct their business in accordance with the **Securities and Exchange Act of 1934** and the rules issued under that Act by the SEC. The SEC is an independent agency, established by the U.S. Congress in 1934, to administer the federal securities laws. The SEC's principal objectives are to ensure that the securities markets operate in a fair and orderly manner, that securities industry professionals deal fairly with their customers, and that corporations make public all relevant information about themselves so that investors can make informed investment decisions.

SEE ALSO: Commodities; Futures/Futures Contracts; Hedging; Options/Options Contracts; Stock Market.

[Susan Bard Hall]

FURTHER READING:

Glossary. Washington, D.C.: Commodity Futures Trading Commission, March, 1993.

Understanding Opportunities and Risks in Futures Trading. Chicago: National Futures Association, 1990.

U.S. Securities and Exchange Commission, Consumer Affairs and Information Services. *Information for Investors: Facts about Stockbroker's Commissions.* Washington, D.C.: GPO, 1994.

U.S. Securities and Exchange Commission, Consumer Affairs and Information Services. *Information for Investors: Selecting A Broker.* Washington, D.C.: GPO, 1994.

U.S. Securities and Exchange Commission, Consumer Affairs and Information Services. *What Every Investor Should Know: A Handbook from the U.S. Securities and Exchange Commission.* Washington, D.C.: GPO, 1992.

Veale, Stuart R., ed. *Stocks, Bonds, Options, Futures Investments & Their Markets.* New York: New York Institute of Finance, 1987.

DISCOUNT RATE

The term *discount rate* has different meanings depending on the context in which it is used. In one sense the discount rate may simply refer to the interest rate used in present value calculations. That is, the **discount rate** is the interest rate used to calculate the present value of money to be received in the future. In the context of economic and monetary policies, especially regarding banks and bank lending, the discount rate is the interest rate that Federal Reserve banks charge on loans to member banks. The Federal Reserve discount rate is the same throughout the **Federal Reserve System**. In the days before regional credit markets became a single national market, each of the 12 Federal Reserve banks could set its own discount rate to reflect regional banking and credit conditions.

The discount rate is one of the tools used by the Federal Reserve System to control bank lending and expansion. By raising or lowering the discount rate the Federal Reserve System can encourage or discourage member banks from borrowing from the Federal Reserve's discount window. If the discount rate is low in comparison to other **interest rates**, banks will be stimulated to borrow at the discount window. On the other hand, if the discount rate is high in comparison to other interest rates, banks will consider other sources of funds. Through such borrowing banks can increase their reserves and raise the overall expansion power of the banking system.

Over the years the Federal Reserve's control over the discount rate has proved to be an ineffective tool for controlling bank lending and expansion. The primary reason for this is that most banks are reluctant to go into debt with the Federal Reserve, even for a short time. In practice, then, lowering the discount rate has not effectively stimulated bank borrowing from the Federal Reserve's discount window. Banks continue to borrow from the Federal Reserve, but usually only when they unexpectedly have insufficient reserves to meet their legal requirements. The Federal Reserve views the use of the discount window as complementary to its more effective open-market operations, by which the Federal Reserve controls member bank reserves through the purchase and sale of U.S. government securities on the open market.

The Federal Reserve reviews the discount rate and adjusts it periodically to bring it in line with other **money market** rates. Changes in the discount rate may serve as a signal from the Federal Reserve of its future monetary policies. Changes in the discount rate can also affect other money market rates as well as investment strategies in stocks, **bonds**, and other securities.

[David Bianco]

DISCOUNTED CASH FLOW

Discounted cash flow (DCF) is the sum of a series of future cash transactions, on a **present value** basis. DCF analysis is a capital budgeting technique used to quantify and assess the receipts and disbursements from a particular activity, project, or business

venture in terms of constant dollars at the outset, considering risk-return relationships and timing of the cash flows.

The formula for calculating the present value of future cash flows is:

$$\text{Present Value} = CF1/(1 + i)^1 + CF2/(1 + i)^2 + \cdots + CFn/(1 + i)^n$$

Where CF1 to CFn = future cash flows,

i = the appropriate **discount rate**, and

n = the number of years over which cash flows occur

Each successive year's cash flow is discounted to a greater extent than the prior year, due to the fact that it is received further out in time. Using an example of $400 to be received in equal $100 installments at the end of each of the next four years, at a discount rate of 10%, the calculation is:

$$PV = 100/(1.10)^1 + 100/(1.10)^2 + 100/(1.10)^3 + 100/(1.10)^4$$
$$= 90.91 + 82.64 + 75.13 + 68.30$$
$$= 316.98$$

Many familiar examples exist of the application of DCF. A mortgage loan is probably the simplest and most common: assume a 15-year term and a cap on monthly payments of $1,500. Under a market interest rate of 8%, the bank will be willing to lend exactly $156,961. That amount represents the DCF, or present value, of the $1,500 monthly loan payments to be received over the next 180 months. An example with a single cash flow is the issuance of government savings bonds. With these instruments, the U.S. Treasury sells bonds for exactly half their face value. The maturity date is established based on the current rate of interest being paid: the higher the rate of interest, the shorter the required holding period will be. (If the interest rate is at about 6%, the maturity date will be about 12 years after the date of issuance; that is the length of time it takes to double an amount earning interest at 6% compounded annually.) Thus, the $100 to be repaid by the government at the maturity date has a DCF value, or purchase price, of $50.

One of the most useful applications of DCF analysis is for business valuation purposes. Here the analyst calculates the present value of the company's future cash flows. The most common form of this analysis involves using company-produced forecasts of the next five or so years' cash flows, plus a "steady state" cash flow for year six and beyond. The explicit period of the forecast is usually limited to five years since forecasting accuracy may lose reliability after that point. The analyst will calculate the present value of the first five years' cash flows, plus the present value of the capitalized residual value from the steady state cash flow. In this way all years of the company's future cash flows are impounded in the measure of value.

It is critical that the cash flows are reasonably estimated, with due care given to the various factors than can affect future results of operations. The analyst must work with knowledgeable company management, and gain a thorough understanding of the business, its competitors, and the marketplace in general. Collateral impacts of various decisions must be quantified and entered into the calculus of the overall cash flows.

Of similar importance is the determination of the proper **discount rate** to apply to bring the cash flows back to their present value. Entire books have been written, and courses taught, on the topic of discount rates. In very basic terms, the discount rate should be determined considering the following factors:

1. Riskiness of the business or project. The higher the risk, the higher the required rate of return, e.g. **junk bonds** pay much higher rates of interest than utility bonds.

2. Size of the company. Recent research has shown that returns are also related inversely to the size of the entity. That is, a larger company will provide lower rates of return than a smaller company of otherwise similar nature.

3. Time horizon. Generally, yield curves are upward sloping (longer term instruments command a higher interest rate, other things being equal), therefore cash flows to be received over longer periods may require a slight premium in interest, or discount, rate.

4. Debt/equity ratio. The leverage of the company drives the mix of debt and equity rates in the overall cost of capital equation. This matters since rates of return on debt and equity within a company can vary considerably (with the latter being higher).

5. Real or nominal basis. Market rates of interest or return are on a nominal basis. If the cash flow projections are done on a real basis (non-inflation adjusted), then the discount rate must be converted to real terms.

6. Income tax considerations. If the cash flows under consideration are on an after-tax basis, then the discount rate should be calculated using an after-tax cost of debt in the cost of capital equation.

The use of cash flows, as opposed to earnings, warrants comment. Because of differences in the timing of actual cash flows versus accrual-based accounting, the earnings of an entity will often vary from the cash flow. One obvious reason this can occur

is in the instance of a major fixed asset acquisition, such as a factory. Suppose a company pays cash for a building and equipment whose useful life is expected to last 30-years. The accounting convention of depreciation will properly spread the expense over the 30-year life, rather than showing it all in the year of acquisition. From an actual ''money in the bank'' perspective, however, the company has had a cash outflow early in time, with resulting cash inflows (from running the plant) expected over the next 30 years. When giving effect to the time value of money over such a long period, the present value of this company's cash flows will be significantly different than the present value of its earnings. There is an old adage that ''cash is king''; one reason is because the market values cash flows.

[Christopher Barry]

DISCRETIONARY INCOME

Discretionary income (also known as disposable income) is any income over and above one's necessary expenses. Knowing the pertinent facts about discretionary income is of vital importance to both business and government. For this reason, the Conference Board, the U.S. Department of Labor, and the U.S. Bureau of the Census have collaborated on ongoing studies of discretionary income. After the 1980 population census was completed, a study entitled *A Marketer's Guide to Discretionary Income* was released, presenting exhaustive statistics of discretionary income per U.S. household. A similar study of the 1990 census results is underway. Many private firms in the country undertake their own studies of discretionary income, but their analyses also are based on the publicly available (online as well as on CD-ROM) census data.

The basic definition of discretionary income does not specify the difference between ''necessary expenditure'' and ''luxury.'' For that reason, Census Bureau statisticians rank a certain number of households according to age, size, and geographic area of residence. They then determine how much money a household typically needs to maintain its standard of living.

Based on 1990 census data, approximately 26 million households in the U.S. were determined to have discretionary income. Since a household typically consists of more than one individual, this 26 million figure translates into the majority of the population having some kind of disposable income, totalling in the hundreds of billions of dollars. Such enormous sums of potential buying power make it worthwhile for business and industry to know as much as they can about discretionary income.

For instance, it is noteworthy that even during the worst recessions of the early 1980s and early 1990s, discretionary income not only was not affected, but even grew slightly. Discretionary incomes of people in certain age groups are of particular value to business and marketing specialists. Those over the age of fifty have 50 percent of the total amount of discretionary income in their control, making the 50-plus age category the wealthiest group in the nation. This group also corners three quarters of the bank deposits in the nation, and account for 80 percent of all savings accounts. In short, the ''over 50s'' have enormous financial clout.

The largest generation since the baby boomers—the 50 million 18-29 year olds—also has formidable discretionary spending power. In 1991, it totaled $130 billion, averaging out to $260 per month per person; this is a little less than the baby boomer average of $288 per month. But since the 18-29 year olds usually are single, while baby boomers are not, they tend to purchase more for themselves.

Even children (age 6 to 17), have noteworthy discretionary income, totalling over $33 billion in 1991. More surprising, perhaps, is the fact that many of the very poor—those earning under $10,000 per year—tend to have some amount of disposable income over and above basic necessities.

Discretionary income studies agree that the higher the level of education, the greater the amount of disposable income. Gays and lesbians in general have an unusually high level of education and a corresponding high level of income. A little more than half of gay couples have household incomes of at least $50,000 per year, a fact that translates into high discretionary income, all the more so since most of these couples often do not have children. This is a fact that many businesses are noticing.

Even though statistics point to the fact that most people meet their bills and have money left over, studies reveal that people with moderate discretionary income usually feel poor. This has to do with people's perceptions of their salaries (many feel they should or could earn more) or the material possessions which they still feel they lack.

There are a wide range of businesses that depend entirely on discretionary incomes: florists, arts and crafts shops, jewelry stores, gambling casinos, symphony orchestras, and many non-profit organizations. Knowing where the most discretionary income is located and who has most of it is important for these and many other businesses. When statistics revealed in the early 1990s that Long Island, New York, with its densely packed population of 2.7 million, had the highest discretionary income in the U.S., many new

stores decided to set up shop there. It is also important to know who has little disposable income. Just because a certain ethnic group has relatively little discretionary income does not mean it has none, and marketing decisions can be made based on what these consumers would most likely purchase.

[Sina Dubovoy]

FURTHER READING:

A Marketer's Guide to Discretionary Income: A Joint Study. Conference Board, 1983.

Russell, Cheryl. The Official Guide to American Incomes: A Comprehensive Look at How Much Americans Have to Spend: With a Special Section on Discretionary Income. New Strategist Publications and Consulting, 1993.

DISCRIMINANT ANALYSIS

Discriminant analysis is a statistical method that is used by researchers to help them understand the relationship between a *dependent variable* and one or more *independent variables*. A dependent variable is the variable that a researcher is trying to explain or predict from the values of the independent variables. Discriminant analysis is similar to **regression analysis** and analysis of variance (ANOVA). The principal difference between discriminant analysis and the other two methods is with regard to the nature of the dependent variable.

Discriminant analysis requires the researcher to have measures of the dependent variable and all of the independent variables for a large number of cases. In regression analysis and ANOVA, the dependent variable must be a *continuous variable*. A numeric variable indicates the degree to which a subject possesses some characteristic, so that the higher the value of the variable, the greater the level of the characteristic. A good example of a continuous variable would be a person's income.

In discriminant analysis, the dependent variable must be a *categorical variable.* The values of a categorical variable only serve to name groups and do not necessarily indicate the degree to which some characteristic is present. An example of a categorical variable would be a measure indicating to which one of several different market segments a customer belongs; another example would be a measure indicating whether or not a particular employee is a ''high potential'' worker. The categories must be mutually exclusive; that is, a subject can belong to one and only one of the groups indicated by the categorical variable. While a categorical variable must have at least two values (as in the ''high potential'' case, it may have numerous values (as in the case of the market segmentation measure). As the mathematical methods used in discriminant analysis are complex, they are only described here in general terms. We will do this by providing an example of a simple case in which he dependent variable has only two categories.

Discriminant analysis is most often used to help a researcher predict the group or category to which a subject belongs. For example, when individuals are interviewed for a job, managers will not know for sure how job candidates will perform on the job if hired. Suppose, however, that a human resource manager has a list of current employees that have been classified into two groups: ''high performers'' and ''low performers.'' These individuals have been working for the company for some time, have been evaluated by their supervisors, and are known to fall into one of these two, mutually exclusive categories. The manager also has information on the employees' backgrounds: educational attainment, prior work experience, participation in training programs, work attitude measures, personality characteristics, and so forth. This information was known at the time these employees were hired. The manager wants to be able to predict, with some confidence, which future job candidates are high performers and which are not. A researcher or consultant can use discriminant analysis, along with existing data, to help in this task.

There are two basic steps in discriminant analysis. The first involves estimating coefficients, or weighting factors, that can be applied to the known characteristics of job candidates (i.e., the independent variables) to calculate some measure of their tendency or propensity to become high performers. This measure is called a *discriminant function*. Second, this information can then be used to develop a decision rule that specifies some cut-off value for predicting which job candidates are likely to become high performers.

The tendency of an individual to become a high performer can be written as a linear equation. The values of the various predictors of high performer status (i.e., independent variables) are multiplied by *discriminant function coefficients* and these products are added together to obtain a predicted discriminant function score. This score is used in the second step to predict the job candidate's likelihood of becoming a high performer. Suppose that you were to use three different independent variables in the discriminant analysis. Then the discriminant function has the following form:

$$D = B_1X_1 + B_2X_2 + B_3X_3$$

where: D = discriminant function score; B_i = discriminant function coefficient relating independent variable i to the discriminant function score; X_i = value of independent variable i. The equation is quite similar to a regression equation. Conventional regression analysis should not be used in place of discriminant analysis. The dependent variable would have only two values (high performer and low performer) and would thus violate important assumptions of the regression model. Discriminant analysis does not have these limitations with respect to the dependent variable.

Estimation of the discriminant function coefficients requires a set of cases in which values of the independent variables and the dependent variables are known. In the case described above, the company has this information for a current group of employees. There are several different ways that can be used to estimate discriminant function coefficients, but all work on the same general principle: the values of the coefficients are selected so that differences between the groups defined by the dependent variable are maximized with regard to some *objective function*. One commonly used objective function is the F-ratio, which is defined as it is in ANOVA and regression problems. The coefficients are chosen to maximize the F-ratio when analysis of variance is performed on the resulting discriminant function, using the dependent variable (i.e., job performance) as the grouping variable. Most general statistical programs, such as the *Statistical Package for the Social Sciences* (SPSS), contain discriminant analysis modules.

There are various tests of significance that can be used in discriminant analysis. One widely used test statistic is based on Wilks lambda, which provides an assessment of the discriminating power of the function derived from the analysis. If this value is found to be statistically significant, then the set of independent variables can be assumed to differentiate between the groups of the categorical variable. This test, which is analogous to the F-ratio test in ANOVA and regression, is useful in evaluating the overall adequacy of the analysis.

Unfortunately, discriminant analysis does not generate estimates of the standard errors of the individual coefficients, as in regression, so it is not quite so simple to assess the statistical significance of each coefficient. For example, most discriminant analysis programs have a stepwise option. Independent variables are entered into the equation one at a time. Again, Wilks lambda can be used to assess the potential contribution of each variable to the explanatory power of the model. Variables from the set of independent variables are added to the equation until a point is reached for which additional items provide no statistically significant increment in explanatory power.

Once the analysis is completed, the discriminant function coefficients can be used to assess the contributions of the various independent variables to the

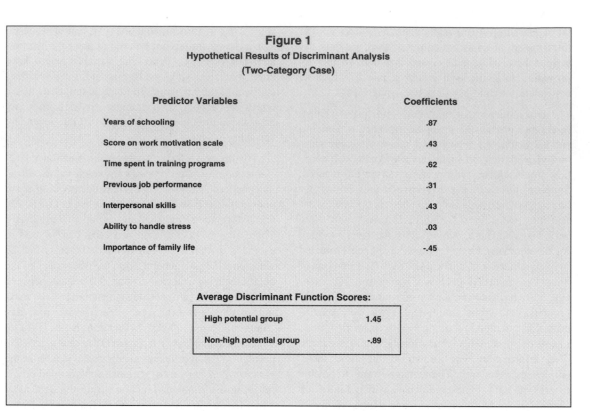

Figure 1
Hypothetical Results of Discriminant Analysis
(Two-Category Case)

Predictor Variables	Coefficients
Years of schooling	.87
Score on work motivation scale	.43
Time spent in training programs	.62
Previous job performance	.31
Interpersonal skills	.43
Ability to handle stress	.03
Importance of family life	-.45

Average Discriminant Function Scores:

High potential group	1.45
Non-high potential group	-.89

tendency of an employee to be a high performer. The discriminant function coefficients are analogous regression coefficients and they range between values of −1.0 and 1.0. The first part of Figure 1 provides hypothetical results of the discriminant analysis. The box provides the within-group averages for the discriminant function for the two categories of the dependent variable. Note that the high performers have an average score of 1.45 on the discriminant function, while the low performers have an average score of −.89. The discriminant function is treated as a standardized variable, so it has a mean of zero and a standard deviation of one. The average values of the discriminant function scores are only meaningful in that they help us interpret the coefficients. Since the high performers are at the upper end of the scale, all of the positive coefficients indicate that the greater the value of those variables, the greater the likelihood of a worker being a high performer (e.g., education, motivation). The magnitudes of the coefficients also tell us something about the relative contributions of the independent variables. The closer the value of a coefficient is to zero, the weaker it is as a predictor of the dependent variable. On the other hand, the closer the value of a coefficient is to either 1.0 or −1.0, the stronger it is as a predictor of the dependent variable. In this example, then, years of education and ability to handle stress both have positive coefficients, though the latter is quite weak. Finally, individuals who place high importance on family life are less likely to be high performers than those who do not.

The second step in discriminant analysis involves predicting to which group in the dependent variable a particular case belongs. A subject's discriminant score can be translated into a probability of being in a particular group by means of Bayes Rule. Separate probabilities are computed for each group and the subject is assigned to the group with the highest probability. Another test of the adequacy of a model is the degree to which known cases are correctly classified. As in other statistical procedures, it is generally preferable to test the model on a set of cases that were not used to estimate the model's parameters. This provides a more conservative test of the model. Thus, a set of cases should, if possible, be saved for this purpose. Having completed the analysis, the results can be used to predict the work potential of job candidates and hopefully serve to improve the selection process.

There are more complicated cases, in which the dependent variable has more than two categories. For example, workers might have been divided into three groups: high performers, average performers, low performers. Discriminant analysis allows for such a case, as well as many more categories. However, the interpretation of the discriminant function scores and coefficients becomes more complex. The readings included in the reference section explain in detail how to perform discriminant analysis with multiple categories and provide in-depth technical discussions.

[John Lawler]

FURTHER READING:

Klecka, William R. *Discriminant Analysis for Social Sciences.* Beverly Hills, CA: Sage Publications, 1980.

Lachenbruch, Peter A. *Discriminant Analysis.* New York: Hafner Press, 1975.

Norusis, Marija J. *SPSS for Windows: Professional Statistics (Release 6.0).* Chicago: SPSS, Inc., 1993.

Overall, John W., and C. James Klett. *Applied Multivariate Analysis.* New York: McGraw-Hill, 1972.

DISCRIMINATION

SEE: Affirmative Action; Age and Employment; AIDS in the Workplace; Americans with Disabilities Act (ADA); Civil Rights Act of 1991; Equal Employment Opportunity Commission (EEOC); Equal Opportunity; Sex Discrimination

DISTINCTIVE COMPETENCE

Distinctive competence is a set of unique capabilities that certain firms possess allowing them to make inroads into desired markets and to gain advantage over their competition; generally, it is an activity that a firm does better than its competition. To define a firm's distinctive competence, management must complete an assessment of both internal and external corporate environments. When management finds an internal strength that both meets market needs and gives the firm a comparative advantage in the marketplace, that strength is the firm's distinctive competence. Taking advantage of an existing distinctive competence is essential to business strategy development. Firms can possess distinctive competence in a wide variety of areas, including technology, marketing, and management. Whatever distinctive competence a firm possesses, it is valued for itself, rather than solely for the products or services it generates.

THEORETICAL ORIGINS

From 1949 to 1957, Philip Selznick studied vastly differing organizations, from the Communist Party to the Tennessee Valley Authority. He noticed that as these institutions developed, there was a gradual emergence of special strengths and weaknesses in each one of them. Thus, he first coined the term "distinctive competence" in 1957. Kenneth R. Andrews elaborated on this concept in 1971, when he noticed that distinctive competence was more than just the strengths of an organization. In his view, distinctive competence was the set of activities that an

organization could do especially well in relation to its competitors. In 1976, Howard H. Stevenson released a study that examined the strategic planning of six companies. He found that top managers had a wide variation in their perceptions of their own organization's strengths and weaknesses, and not surprisingly distinctive competences.

FORMULATING STRATEGY

Strategy can be defined as the tool managers use to adjust their firms to the ever-changing environmental conditions. Unless a firm produces only one type of merchandise or service, it must devise strategies at both the corporate and business levels. Corporate strategy defines the underlying businesses and determines the best methods of coordinating them. At the business level, strategy outlines the ways that a business will compete in a given market. Strategic planning is often closely tied to the development and use of distinctive competences, and having an area of distinctive competence can present a major strategic advantage to any firm.

To devise corporate strategy, firm managers must consider a host of influences in their surrounding environment which can affect their firm's ongoing operations as well as internal strengths and weaknesses that characterize their firm. When assessing the external business environment, management must analyze the given situation, forecast potential changes to it, and either try to change the situation or adapt to it. The assessment must include an evaluation of current and projected market needs and an evaluation of any existing comparative advantage over competitors.

Moreover, to determine the best strategy for their firm, managers must realistically assess their own firm's status. A firm's internal strengths and weaknesses make it better suited to pursue some strategic paths than others. When looking for a match between opportunities and capabilities, managers must try to build upon the strongest qualities of their firm and avoid activities that rely on more vulnerable areas or are adverse to the firm's existing **corporate culture**. Further, it is important for managers to account for potential problems involved in carrying out a strategy before they embark upon it. Thus, managers should examine potential strategies, while keeping in mind their firm's history, its culture and experiences, and its basic proficiencies. Once this assessment is complete, management must decide which opportunities in the business environment to pursue and which ones to pass up. Even if a firm does not have a distinctive competence, as is the case for many firms, it must devise its overall strategy to build upon its strengths and best use its resources.

Obviously, many successful business strategies are built around a determined distinctive competence. To truly succeed, a firm will have a competitive advantage over its rivals, giving it some sort of strategic advantage. Logically, strengthening a competitive position is made a great deal easier for a firm with one or more distinctive competences. Having a distinctive competence can allow a firm to follow a different path than rival firms, have a strategy difficult for them to imitate, and end up in a better position in the long term. If other firms in the marketplace do not have a similar or an countervailing competence, they will have a very difficult time remaining competitive.

DEFINING AND BUILDING DISTINCTIVE COMPETENCE

To define a company's distinctive competence, managers often follow a particular process. First, they identify the strengths and weaknesses of their firm. Next, they determine the strategic importance of these strengths and weaknesses in the given marketplace. Then, they analyze specific market needs and look for comparative advantages that they have over their competition. Importantly, while managers generally follow this process, they often undertake more than one step simultaneously.

Distinctive competence can be built in a number of ways. Firms can hire more qualified professionals than those employed by their competitors; they can find and exploit previously neglected market niches; and they can be especially innovative or can gain advantage over competitors through sheer strength of management. There are numerous areas in which a firm can have a distinctive competence. Some companies have distinctive competence because they manufacture a product with superior quality. Other firms excel in technological innovation, research and development, or new product introduction. Still other firms have advantages in low-cost production, customer support, or creative advertising. For example, McDonald's distinctive competence is its system of controls for operating its franchises, which gives the company an unusually high profit margin.

PREDICTING FUTURE DISTINCTIVE COMPETENCE

Since business environments and marketplaces are always changing, the challenge for strategists is to maintain the firm's distinctive competence. As defined earlier, distinctive competences are distinctive skills and capabilities firms can use to achieve an unusual market position or to gain an advantage over the competition. Thus, a firm's advantage comes largely from the fact that it has differentiated itself from its competition. It follows that if the environment changes such that numerous rivals have obtained competences identical to those characterizing a particular firm, the firm is in a very poor position and would do well to reconsider its strategy.

Future strategic success requires that firms keep their distinct advantages over their rivals. Thus, firms must continuously assess their surrounding environments. They must be aware of potential shifts in industrial standings and must realistically evaluate whether their distinctive competency continues to yield an advantage. They should also look to new markets and evaluate the potential use of their distinctive competences in those markets.

As business conditions and markets change, many of the strengths and weaknesses that characterize a firm will also change. Indeed, some vulnerabilities and strengths will be exaggerated, while others will be eliminated. Success in these changing conditions can only come from taking advantage of opportunities highlighted by close scrutiny of a firm's internal and external environment. The most successful firms will be those that are able to locate and use distinctive competences found in these assessments.

[Kathryn Snavely]

FURTHER READING:

Barnett, John H., and William D. Wilsted. *Strategic Management.*Boston, MA: PWS-Kent Publishing Company, 1988.

Burgelman, Robert A. ''Fading Memories: A Process Theory of Strategic Business Exit in Dynamic Environments.'' *Administrative Science Quarterly.* March, 1994, pp. 24-56.

Hitt, Michael A., and R. Duane Ireland. ''Corporate Distinctive Competence, Strategy, Industry and Performance.'' *Strategic Management Journal.* John Wiley & Sons: pp. 273-293, 1985

Meyer, Alan D. ''What Is Strategy's Distinctive Competence?'' *Journal of Management.* 17: 4. pp. 821-833, 1991.

Mintzberg, Henry. ''The Design School: Reconsidering the Basic Premises of Strategic Management.'' *Strategic Management Journal.* 11, pp. 171-195, 1990.

Mintzberg, Henry, and James Brian Quinn. *The Strategic Process—Concepts, Contexts, Cases.* 2nd ed. Englewood Cliffs, NJ: Prentice-Hall, 1991.

Snow, Charles C., and Lawrence G. Hrebiniak. ''Strategy, Distinctive Competence, and Organizational Performance.'' *In Strategic Management Concepts and Cases.* edited by Arthur A. Thompson, Jr. and A. J. Strickland III. 3rd ed. Plano, TX: Business Publications, 1984.

DISTRIBUTION SYSTEM

SEE: Channels of Distribution

DIVERSIFICATION IN INVESTMENTS

Diversification refers to the reduction in the overall risk of an investor's portfolio even when it is comprised of a number of highly risky individual investments. The risk in a group of investments may be lower than the risk associated with any individual element in the group. Diversification occurs because there are unique factors associated with individual securities that are not related across securities.

The concept of diversification of risk has a long history as evidenced by the adage "don't put all of your eggs in one basket." The mathematics of diversification were formalized by Harry M. Markowitz in 1952 and influence the practice of portfolio management on its most fundamental level.

The explanation for diversification can be either statistical or economic. From a statistical perspective, the volatility, or variance, of the price changes and cash flow associated with an individual security can be quite high. However, the actual changes in these amounts will not coincide perfectly for any two securities. More specifically, as the correlation of the returns generated by two securities weakens, the potential for significant diversification of risk increases for an investor holding both.

From an economic perspective, consider the simple example of an investor who buys **stock** in a firm that makes umbrellas and another that makes sunglasses. Clearly, each firm's fortunes are related to the weather, but in a very different way. In this example, the investor's portfolio will likely have lower risk than either of the individual elements because of the distinct response each has to the common factor. More specifically, any security's price is affected by unique factors that are very firm specific (e.g., strikes, departure of key employees, inaccurate forecasts of demand). But price is also affected by broad economic factors that influence all securities in a similar manner (e.g., changes in tax code, **inflation**, new regulations). Diversification occurs because an investor holding a large number of securities has essentially neutralized most of the impact of unique risk contributed by each one. The aggregate portfolio will behave more like the entire market since all securities are influenced in a similar manner by common factors. The diversifiable component of an individual security's risk is often referred to as unsystematic while the component that remains is labeled systematic risk.

There are a variety of methods to put this diversification effect into practice. First, naive diversification refers to the reduction in total risk that takes place when securities are randomly added to a portfolio. Studies have shown that approximately 75% of the total risk of a typical U.S. security is unsystematic. A portfolio containing 30 stocks chosen randomly effectively eliminates that risk component. If securities are selected from around the world, this same strategy will eliminate approximately 88% of the total risk exhibited by a typical security.

However, there are more effective methods of diversifying risk. Rather than selecting securities randomly, investors can purposely select securities from different industries, different countries, and at different stages in their growth cycles. By actively identifying sets of securities that have weakly correlated returns, the diversification effect can be accelerated. The ability to perceive and exploit the potential diversification of risk is important because individual securities will not reflect any compensation for bearing their unique, or unsystematic risk. This is because some investors will be able to diversify it away.

[Paul Bolster]

FURTHER READING:

Evans, John L., and Stephen N. Archer. "Diversification and the Reduction of Dispersion: An Empirical Analysis," *Journal of Finance.* December 1968, pp. 761-767.

Markowitz, Harry. "Portfolio Selection," *Journal of Finance.* March 1952, pp. 77-91.

Solnik, Bruno. *International Investments*, 2nd edition, Addison-Wesley, 1988.

DIVERSITY CULTURE

The term "diversity" refers to the way in which people differ from one another. Since such differences affect the way people interact in the work place, diversity management is a factor for most organizations. Taylor Cox, Jr. explains that "cultural diversity means the representation, in one social system, of people with distinctly different group affiliations of cultural significance." Differing group affiliations that are likely to affect the **work force** generally involve cultural or identity groups based on ethnicity, national origin, race, and religion.

Sensitivity to cross-cultural issues in values and communication styles is, however, only a beginning. As R. Roosevelt Thomas, Jr. indicates, it is still necessary in the work place to go beyond simple recognition of cultural diversity to active diversity management. Roosevelt indicates that, "Managing diversity is a comprehensive managerial process for developing an environment that works for all employees." Diversity management is an inclusive process since all employees belong to a culture, including those from the organization's traditionally dominant cultural group. Thomas indicates that diversity management must not be viewed as "an us/them kind of problem to be solved but as a resource to be managed."

Anthony Carnevale and Susan Carol Stone have emphasized that valuing diversity involves "recognizing that other people's standards and values are as valid as one's own."

They go on elsewhere to note that for most organizations, valuing and managing diversity requires nothing less than cultural transformation. This is a prodigious task, for it requires people—especially those of the dominant culture—to let go of their assumptions about the universal rightness of their own values and customary ways of doing things and to become receptive to other cultures.

In this regard, cultural diversity in the work place mirrors many of the same issues at play in the realm of international business. In international business interactions, people who have learned differing conceptions of normative behavior are forced to suspend judgment of one another. Cultural norms shift relative to language, technological expectations, social organization, face-saving, authority conception, nonverbal behavior and the perception of time.

While these areas of cultural difference are foreign in one's own culture, they remain normal within the confines of one's foreign counterpart. Thus, speaking Portuguese is culturally unusual or different in the United States but culturally expected in Brazil—and vice versa. The use of Portuguese or English in a U.S.-Brazilian joint venture, however, carries no normative expectation. While speaking Portuguese in the United States might be seen as undesirable or even wrong, international business effectiveness demands the suspension of such judgments. No culture is inherently "natural" or "normal." As a result, what is right in one culture is not necessarily right or wrong, only different.

By contrast, in an entirely domestic setting, the dominant culture has traditionally passed judgment as to right and wrong regarding cultural differences. The norms of the dominant culture take on the aura of right; behavior differing from such norms, accordingly, take on the aura of wrong.

Difficulty in accepting the judgments of the dominant culture in a society, however, is becoming more and more prevalent. In part, this results from the greater awareness of foreign cultures in an increasingly integrated world economy. Yet the matter is more complex than this. In many countries such as the United States, the demographic changes in the work force have reduced the size and influence of the historically dominant culture significantly. Large and important minority cultures live and work side by side with the historically dominant culture. It is no longer fully possible to speak of most countries in terms of a single culture. As James Clifford observed, it has become "increasingly hard to conceive of human diversity as inscribed in bounded independent cultures."

In other words, one can speak of a Brazilian or a U.S. culture—but to which of the many subcultural groups in those countries does one refer? It is difficult to indicate, in short, what constitutes a national cultural norm. Cultural diversity deals with how to manage those varying cultural norms within a single nation.

Cultural diversity as an issue in the workplace may deal with any differences among people who work together. A broad definition of diversity can have a positive or negative effect on how an organization approaches the issue.

Underscoring the inclusive nature of the term (all people, by definition, belong to some group) allows the organization to include people in ways that best refer to their needs. Diversity can refer to job-related functions. In a hospital, for instance, the presence of physicians, registered nurses, and hospital administrators may present diversity issues. Diversity can indicate differences in thought processing or personality. For example, the different outcomes of employees on psychological indicators (such as Myer-Briggs test scores) can be useful in establishing **management** teams. Diversity can also refer to historical groupings; these might include political party or work committees peculiar to the organization. For example, a bipartisan committee of council members would represent a specialized form of diversity on a city government task force.

On the negative side, as a term, "diversity"—is often the subject of debate. The term may be imbued with political meaning. Not all people in organizations value diversity. As a rule, people are most comfortable with those like themselves and emphasizing diversity may undermine that comfort level. Diversity tends to breed new approaches to old practices and long-standing problems. Individuals in organizations may find such change troubling. Moreover, individuals with strong prejudices against certain groups may find rapidly changing demographics in the work force threatening either because they find change itself disquieting or because they hold a position they feel they might not be able to maintain if groups historically excluded from their work place were allowed to compete in an unhindered way for their positions.

NON-CULTURAL IDENTITY GROUPS AND DIVERSITY

Cultural diversity as used here does not include diversity based on non-cultural identity groups. While, arguably, sexual orientation or differences in ability (such a case is often made for the deaf community, for example) may act as a cultural difference, they are not traditionally viewed as a culture per se and so exceed the scope of this discussion. Similarly, the marked increase in the number of women in the work force mirrors the large-scale increase in those of minority or immigrant backgrounds. Women, however, are not a cultural group but rather represent one half of every culture. While women may be treated differently from men in every culture, the way they are treated differently varies from culture to culture and so gender differences remain a subset of cultural diversity. Any comprehensive discussion of diversity in the U.S. work force, however, should include reference to those with different physical abilities and to women.

CULTURAL DIVERSITY AND THE CIVIL RIGHTS MOVEMENT

The United States has always been an immigrant culture. Aside from Native Americans, the entire population has immigrant origins. The traditional view toward immigrants was that they would wish to assimilate to the dominant Anglo-Saxon population of the nation's earliest colonial settlers. The assimilation process, according to the traditional view, however, was never expected to be total. Each group would add a distinguishing contribution to the overall national culture so that in time the myriad immigrant groups would alter the cultural norms of the rest of the nation in subtle ways. This philosophy was called the "American melting pot."

The difficulty with this notion was that the melting pot demanded assimilation of most major cultural factors. For example, individuals employing a language other than English, or those having markedly different conceptions of kinship ties, for example—faced significant pressure to conform to the dominant Anglo-Saxon norm. Thus, use of a non-English language in the workplace or favorable attitudes toward nepotism were actively discouraged. Such practices that differed from the dominant majority culture, in the melting pot philosophy, were viewed not as merely different but as innately wrong.

Additionally, certain groups were deemed—by the dominant culture—unable to assimilate. Some of these groups were considered "unassimilable" because of marked behavioral differences. For example, Jewish people, as a cultural group and a religious group, differed from the dominant norm. Other groups were considered to be relatively unassimilable simply due to physical appearance. Asian Americans and African Americans, for example, were frequently judged by physical appearance alone, even when their behavior was a mirror image of the dominant culture.

The Civil Rights movement of the 1960s had a direct effect on the assimilationist norm of the melting pot. It changed the view of the United States as a single culture welcoming those different from the dominant norm if they would only drop their ethnic or cultural distinctiveness. The double standard as applied to certain groups of Americans came under scrutiny; the belief in integration into a dominant norm was questioned.

Assuredly, such re-examination took place within the dominant native-born, white, non-Hispanic community. Still the most significant impact of the Civil Rights movement was that immigrants and distinctive native-born minority groups began, as Stephen Steinberg has argued, "to affirm their right to a separate identity within the framework of a pluralist nation."

The re-examination of the desirability of the domination of the work force by a culturally monolithic norm led to laws that placed a requirement on business to provide the chance for culturally diverse groups to enter the work place. Title VII of the Civil Rights Act of 1964, for example, made it unlawful to discriminate on the basis of race, color, national origin, or religion. **Equal opportunity** for employment, in turn, allowed for the entry into the American workforce of increasing numbers of individuals from cultural groups historically discriminated against. This, in turn, led groups that had attempted to assimilate to question their decision to subsume their own cultural values to the dominant norm. Thus, even within the historically favored white community, ethnic groups began to see benefits in returning to—or at least not hiding—their own cultural differences.

THE SIGNIFICANCE OF CULTURAL DIVERSITY

Demographic shifts based on population changes and immigration have led to the reassessment of native-born, non-Hispanic whites. This group no longer represents the dominant cultural norm whom all other groups are expected to mimic in attempts to assimilate. Increasingly, one can no longer accurately talk about some variety of mainstream American culture. The normative Anglo-Saxon culture that had been held forth as "the" American culture until the mid-1960s is now viewed as just one more group (albeit a still powerful and influential one) in a culturally diverse society. The United States can no longer be viewed as a single culture but rather of many cultures joined by a common set of laws. In so diverse a society, the work place itself may serve to be a unifying element, since those working at the same organization will have their work together as a point in common.

Even if an organization were to resist the demographic pressures of change, it is would be unlikely to succeed. If an organization were, for example, to limit itself to the hiring of non-immigrant white males with no strong ethnic ties—the norm for the 1950s, the number of people available to fill the requisite positions would be too small. Only 15 percent of the incoming labor force can be described as white male. This figure itself includes ethnically distinct groups such as Jewish, Italian, and other Americans with strong ethnic identities. To ensure hiring the best person for the job, so small a base would be impractical on a large scale.

On the other hand, the organization that attempts to sensitize itself to the cross-cultural issues of a diverse work force will likely benefit. Such an organization will have increased opportunity to identify and attract the best employees from culturally different groups. Additionally, the organization that remains cross-culturally sensitive to the needs of a diverse work force is likely to reduce absenteeism and employee turnover based on cross-cultural conflict. Absenteeism declines in an organization that is responsive to the needs of its employees. In today's diverse work force, responsiveness to employee needs will rest on understanding the cultural issues that affect people's beliefs as well as their work performance.

Perhaps the most promising benefit of cultural diversity in the U.S. work place is the opportunity it provides for cross-cultural synergy. Synergy—the result of a combination in which the whole is greater than the sum of its parts—has long been a side-benefit to global business involving multiple cultures. The same is likely to hold true with regard to domestic cultural diversity. Different cultural values and world-views, by their nature, provide for non-traditional solutions to long-standing problems.

The culturally heterogeneous work force has an obvious advantage in cross-cultural marketing and management. On the domestic level, changing demographic patterns allow for new areas of segmented ethnic marketing. This, in turn, represents new domestic markets for goods or services in mature markets that have little room for expansion in their traditional market share. Most ethnically identifiable markets, in addition, currently show potential for growth.

Finally, cross-cultural sensitivity associated with managing cultural diversity in the domestic work place provides an advantage that is valuable in competing in foreign markets. Domestic cross-cultural sensitivity increases the likelihood that U.S. companies will have an edge on cross-cultural issues abroad, areas in which competitors from more homogeneous nations would be well versed only after having entered the foreign market in question.

[David A. Victor]

FURTHER READING:

Amott, Teresa L. and Julie A. Matthaei. *Race, Gender, and Work.* Boston: South End Press, 1991.

Borisoff, Deborah and David A. Victor. *Conflict Management: A Communication Skills Approach.* Englewood Cliffs, New Jersey: Prentice-Hall, 1989.

Carnevale, Anthony Patrick and Susan Carol Stone. *The American Mosaic.* New York: McGraw-Hill, 1995.

Clifford, James. *The Predicament of Culture.* Cambridge, Massachusetts: Harvard University Press, 1988.

Cox, Taylor, Jr. *Cultural Diversity in Organizations.* San Francisco: Berrett-Koehler Publishers, 1993.

Faird, Elashmawia and Philip Harris. *Multicultural Management.* Houston, TX: Gulf Publishing Company, 1993.

Fernandez, John P. *Managing a Diverse Work Force.* Lexington, MA: Lexington Books, 1991.

Pollar, Odette and Rafael Gonzalez. *Dynamic of Diversity: Strategic Programs for your Organization.* Menlo Park, CA: Crisp Publications, 1994.

Simons, George, Philip Harris, and Carmen Vasquez. *Transcultural Leadership: Empowering the Diverse Workforce.* Houston, TX: Gulf Publishing Company, 1993.

Steinberg, Stephen. *The Ethnic Myth: Race, Ethnicity, and Class in America.* New York: Atheneum, 1981.

Thomas, R. Roosevelt, Jr. *Beyond Race and Gender.* New York: AMACOM, 1991.

Victor, David A. *International Business Communication.* New York: Harper Collins, 1992.

DIVESTITURE

SEE: Corporate Divestiture; Corporate Downsizing

DIVESTMENT

Divestment is closely related to the concept of divestiture. In fact, the two terms can be—and often are—used interchangeably. For purposes of this essay, however, the term divestment is used to describe actions taken to encourage or effect the dissolution of business enterprises owned by multinational corporations in foreign countries, particularly where those foreign countries operate under repressive regimes.

Divestment as a social demand may be traced as far back in history as the quasi-governmental British East India Company, which facilitated the trade of Indian opium into China during the eighteenth and nineteenth centuries as a way of offsetting a persistent British **trade deficit** with China. No less a figure than Queen Victoria (1819-1902) led demands that British commercial groups cease all trade in the addictive drug, due to the vicious hardship and misery opium consumption caused the Chinese.

Such demands made on social or moral grounds are directly related to the degree of freedom in a society. Opposition of this kind flourished in democracies such as Great Britain, France, the Netherlands, and the United States during the early twentieth century.

By the 1960s, the onus of action was shifted from governments to individual corporations. An excellent example is provided by the involvement of American corporations in South Africa.

The South African government was dominated by a minority of whites who used laws to disenfranchise the black majority. Policies of racial separation, and limits on personal mobility and ownership enriched the white minority at the expense of the black majority.

Groups within American society, particularly on college campuses, called upon American corporations to suspend or abandon commercial activity in South Africa as a way of pressuring social change in that country through economic pressure. Specifically, they called for corporations to divest South African operations entirely. These demands were based on the assertion that engagement in South Africa aided the white minority regime and its racial policies.

Companies whose South African operations were profitable generally resisted calls for divestment on the grounds that they were using engagement as a means to influence change in South Africa. While there is evidence that this engagement did have that effect, it is also true that engagement helped to perpetuate the status quo by providing the economy with additional capital and the government with tax revenue.

Opponents of engagement in South Africa mounted numerous campaigns to pressure corporations toward divestment. Some groups implored investors, including pension funds and banks, to sell their shares in companies involved in South Africa. Others adopted exactly the opposite strategy, using the rights associated with share ownership to query management, disrupt shareholder meetings, and sponsor shareholder resolutions.

Another strategy involved calls for worldwide **boycotts** of all products produced by companies involved in South Africa, coupled with damaging publicity campaigns.

Divestment, as a component of more general economic sanctions, was widely embraced by the South African opposition, led by Nelson Mandela (1918-). These sanctions caused economic difficulties in South Africa that led to a political backlash of the non-Boer white minority. This resulted in new government leadership which instituted policy changes that led to the abolition of racist laws.

SEE ALSO: Corporate Divestiture

[John Simley]

FURTHER READING:

Baumol, William. J., and Alan S. Blinder. *Economics, Principles and Policy.* 2nd ed. New York: Harcourt Brace Jovanovich, 1982.

Fischer, Stanley, and Rudiger Hornbusch. *Economics.* New York: McGraw-Hill, 1983.

Labadie, Barbara B. "Social Investing: Social Value and the Value of Money." *Pension World.* October, 1991, p. 32.

DIVIDEND RELEVANCE/SIGNALING

Dividend policy refers to the decision regarding the magnitude of the dividend payout, the percentage of earnings paid to the stockholders in the form of **dividends**. The central and—as yet unresolved—issue concerning dividend policy is whether changes affect firm value.

THE DIVIDEND IRRELEVANCE ARGUMENT

Consider a firm which has been financed entirely through sale of 100,000 shares of **stock**, will have a two-year life, and has a required rate of return of 10 percent. In order to consider only the effect of dividends, assume that the investment plans of the firm are fixed, and will provide profits of $100,000 in each of the two years. Will changing the amount of the first dividend affect the value of the firm? Consider first a dividend policy which pays out all profits as dividends—$1.00 per share at the end of each year. Since the value of a share is the present value of the future dividends, under this policy the value of a share is $1.7355:

$$PV = \$1.00/(1.10) + \$1.00/(1.10)^2 = \$1.7355$$

Now, suppose the first dividend is increased to $1.50, in the hope that this will increase the stock price. In order to accomplish this, the firm must acquire another $50,000. Assume for simplicity that the firm sells $50,000 of new stock (a more complicated example could include bonds). Since the $50,000 paid for the new stock is the present value of the dividend to be received (at the end of the second year) by the new shareholders, the amount paid to the new shareholders as year two dividends will be $50,000:

$$\text{Dividend to New Shareholders} = \$50,000 \times (1.10) = \$55,000$$

The original shareholders now receive $1.50 at the end of the first year, but as a result can only expect $0.45 per share at the end of the second year:

$$
\begin{aligned}
\text{Year Two Dividend} &= \left(\$100,000 - \begin{array}{c}\text{Amount paid to}\\ \text{New Stockholders}\end{array}\right) \Big/ 100,000 \\
&= (\$100,000 - \$55,000)/100,000 \\
&= \$0.45
\end{aligned}
$$

The value of a share under this modified dividend policy is now the present value of the modified dividends:

$$PV = \$1.50/(1.10) + \$0.45/(1.10)^2 = \$1.7355$$

The equivalence of share value under the two different dividend policies indicates that dividend policy may shift the timing of dividends, but does not alter the total value of the dividends, and stock value remains unchanged.

An alternative example is to note that the rate of return on a share of stock has two components: return from dividends equal to Dividend/Price, and return from growth in price G. If a firm has a rate of return on equity of K and retains all earnings, G = K. If the firm pays a portion of dividends b, however, g = K(1 − b). For example, a firm with a rate of return of 10 percent but paying half of earnings as dividends will grow at a rate of 5 percent. Now, consider a firm with a 10 percent rate of return which pays 50 percent of earnings out as dividends per share, which will be $1.00 this year. Using the Dividend Discount Model, the price of the stock is

$$P = D / (k - g) = \$1.00 / (0.10 - 0.05) = \$20.00$$

If the firm changes to a dividend payout policy of 75% of earnings, the price of the stock becomes:

$$P;PR = \$1.50 / (0.10 - 0.025) = \$20.00$$

Again, the sole effect of dividend policy has been to shift the timing of dividends but not alter the total value of the dividends.

F. Modigliani and M.H. Miller (1961) also argue that the investor need not passively accept the dividend policy of the firm. Instead, the stockholder can adjust the policy to the desired stream of payments. The stockholder can shift dividends to closer time periods by selling stock, producing a "home made" immediate dividend increase at the expense of later payments. Conversely, the stockholder can shift dividends to a later period by using dividends to purchase stock, increasing future payments. Again, this is a switch between dividend returns and **capital gains** returns.

The argument against dividend relevance is based on an idealized theoretical world of perfect markets. This approach ignores the possibility of a number of factors or "imperfections" which affect the conclusions.

FACTORS FAVORING A HIGHER DIVIDEND PAYOUT

AGENCY COSTS. Agency costs are differences between the interests of stockholders and the interests of **management**. Higher dividend payments are argued to require more acquisition of external capital, and subject management to greater scrutiny by the market.

BIRD-IN-HAND. The bird-in-hand argument holds that future earnings are less predictable and more uncertain than dividends. The greater uncertainty of future earnings should be reflected in a higher **discount rate**. This in turn would cause investors to prefer a more certain $1.00 of dividends over a less certain $1.00 of future earnings.

PROSPECT THEORY. The prospect theory argument suggests that investors have a different attitude toward capital gains than toward dividends. Capital gains become part of the investment base, whereas dividends are considered as current income. Creation of "homemade" dividends is thus viewed as reducing the investment base, and such dividends are less desirable than dividends paid by the firm.

FACTORS FAVORING A LOWER DIVIDEND PAYOUT

TAXES. Although both capital gains and dividends are taxed, the tax on capital gains will not be paid until the stock is sold. Payment of capital gains tax can be delayed. Investors attempting to undo a dividend payment by buying stock with dividends must pay **taxes** on the dividends, and cannot totally reverse the dividend. The investor will be better off if the firm retains the earnings and reinvests them to produce capital gains, since tax payment is deferred.

TRANSACTION COSTS. In addition to taxes, investors reinvesting dividends will also face various **transaction costs** such as brokerage fees. Conversely, a firm which pays dividends and then must turn to external sources also faces transactions costs such as the "flotation costs" of issuing new **securities**. If the firm retains the funds and reinvests directly, both types of cost are avoided.

Also worthy of consideration is the concept that a number of arguments are considered with the relative, rather than the absolute, level of dividends.

DIVIDENDS AS A RESIDUAL. The argument for dividend irrelevancy assumes that all investment takes place at the required rate of return for the firm. In actuality, it is likely that the firm faces a mix of risk/return possibilities. The firm should thus accept all projects with a positive net present value, and pay dividends only if it has more funds than are expected to be required for attractive projects. While attractive to academics, this approach is seldom used in practice because it results in uncertain dividends and a greater perception of risk by investors.

CLIENTELE EFFECT. The clientele effect notes that those investors preferring more certain dividends over uncertain future earnings, or having a preference for current income over capital gains, will tend to hold stocks with relatively high dividend payout, and vice versa (i.e., a stock will have a clientele attracted by its dividend policy). Under these conditions, it is not the dividend policy itself which is relevant, but the stability of the policy.

SIGNALING. The theoretical model assumes that information is freely available to all. It has been suggested that management access to inside information causes an "information asymmetry" between management and stockholders. Signaling refers to the use of dividends and dividend changes to convey information to investors. Similar to the clientele effect, it is not the absolute but rather the relative level of dividends which is important. Under this argument management will avoid increasing dividends unless it is highly likely that the higher level of dividends can be maintained. This implies that a dividend increase is a signal that the firm has reached a new level of profitability, and is a positive signal. A dividend decrease, on the other hand, indicates that profitability has decreased and the former dividend level cannot be supported, a negative signal. Note that under the residual argument, however, a dividend increase (decrease) signals a lack (abundance) of attractive projects and decreased (increased) future firm growth. Because of the potential for false signals, more costly signaling is considered more reliable.

DIVIDEND POLICY IN PRACTICE

It is clear that many investors consider dividends as a promise, and that signaling is an important consideration. The residual approach is also seen in the tendency of rapidly growing firms to have a lower payout than more mature firms. Retention and reinvestment of earnings to postpone taxes is apparent in smaller or **closely held firms**. It appears that there is not a single universal explanation of dividend decisions—all of the above factors and arguments have an impact which varies with the situation.

[David E. Upton]

FURTHER READING:

Black, F. "The Dividend Puzzle," *Journal of Portfolio Management*. Vol. 2, no. 2 (Winter, 1976), pp. 5-8.

Jaffe, J.F., S.A. Ross, and R.W. Westerfield. *Corporate Finance*. 3rd ed. Homewood, IL: Irwin, 1993.

Mann, S.V. "The Dividend Puzzle: A Progress Report," *Quarterly Journal of Business & Economics*. Vol. 28, no. 3 (Summer, 1989), pp. 3-35.

Miller, M.H., and F. Modigliani. "Dividend Policy, Growth, and the Valuation of Shares," *Journal of Business*. Vol. 24 (October, 1961), pp. 411-433.

Petty, J.W., A.J. Keown, D.F. Scott, and J.D. Martin. *Basic Financial Management*, 6th ed. Englewood Cliffs, NJ: Prentice Hall, 1993.

Pinches, G.E. *Essentials of Finance*. 4th ed. New York: HarperCollins, 1992.

DIVIDENDS

Dividends and stock repurchases are the two major ways that corporations can distribute cash to their shareholders. **Dividends** may also be distributed in the form of **stock** (stock dividends and stock splits), scrip (a promise to pay at a future date), or property (typically commodities or goods from inventory). By law dividends must be paid from profits; dividends may not be paid from a corporation's capital. This law is designed to protect the corporation's creditors and is known as the impairment of capital rule, which states that dividend payments may not exceed the corporation's retained earnings as shown on its **balance sheet**.

Companies usually pay dividends every quarter, or four times per year. When the company is about to pay a dividend, the company's **board of directors** makes a dividend announcement which indicates the amount of the dividend, the date of record, and the date of payment. The date the dividend announcement is made is known as the declaration date.

The date of record is significant for the company's shareholders. All shareholders on the date of record are entitled to receive the dividend. The ex-dividend date is the first day on which the stock is traded without the right to receive the declared dividend. All shares traded before the ex-dividend date are bought and sold with rights to receive the dividend, or cum dividend. Since it usually takes a few business days to settle a stock transaction, the ex-dividend date is usually a few business days before the record date. On the ex-dividend date the trading price of the stock usually falls to account for the fact that the seller rather than the purchaser is entitled to the declared dividend.

A company's dividend policy involves deciding whether to distribute a certain amount of earnings to the company's shareholders or to retain them for reinvestment. Dividend policy is influenced by a number of factors that include various legal constraints on declaring dividends (bond indentures, impairment of capital rule, availability of cash, and penalty tax on accumulated earnings) as well as the nature of the company's investment opportunities and the effect of dividend policy on the cost of capital of common stock. Most firms have chosen to follow a dividend policy of issuing a stable or continuously increasing dividend. Relatively few firms issue a low regular dividend and declare special dividends when annual earnings are sufficient.

The effect of a company's dividend policy on the value of the company is a field of ongoing investigation and study. In 1961 Modigliani and Miller published a classic study that demonstrated that a company's dividend policy has no effect on its value under a certain set of assumptions: there are no taxes on dividends or capital gains; there are no transaction costs associated with buying or selling securities; all investors have the same information as the managers of the firm; and the firm's investment policies are fixed and known by investors. With those assumptions the authors analyzed the dividend policies of various firms and concluded that investors could simply create their own dividends by selling shares of stock instead of holding them.

Subsequent research into dividend policies has focused on removing one or more of Modigliani and Miller's assumptions. In the real world, of course, there are taxes and transaction costs associated with buying and selling securities and receiving dividends or capital gains. It is also evident that financial managers and stock analysts appear to be concerned about dividends and their effect on stock prices. After more than 30 years of research and study, though, there is little or no agreement as to the effect of dividend policy on the value of the firm.

[David Bianco]

DOWNSIZING

SEE: Corporate Divestiture; Corporate Downsizing

DUE DILIGENCE

Generally, due diligence is the care that people with normal discretion employ in all of their dealings in order to avoid damage to others or themselves. In business, the term refers to the prudent inspection of anything intended for purchase.

Due diligence in business has evolved from the legal application of the concept which relates to the care that may be reasonably expected, depending on the relative facts of the "special case." This concept is also referred to as reasonable care, due care, and ordinary care.

Although the legal definition of due diligence allows for several degrees of care and is open to interpretation, the commercial application of the term corresponds more closely to the legal category "special diligence." Special diligence, involves the particular skill of a businessperson which must be done well and performed better than that of a nonspecialist or ordinary person. Therefore, due diligence in business

refers to the evaluation of the degree of risk involved in potential courses of action, especially investments.

In this application, due diligence is a process that echoes the Latin axiom caveat emptor: "Let the buyer beware." Due diligence can apply to virtually all business transactions and is sometimes legislatively required. For example, lenders maintain due diligence when they perform background checks for loans, whether they are mortgages or large-scale commercial finance packages. Individual investors investigate the soundness of stocks, bonds, and mutual funds by examining prospectuses, reading third-party reports in trade journals, and consulting investment rating services and surveys.

The term, however, has been used most frequently in reference to **acquisitions and mergers**. The concept and practice of due diligence lapsed during the 1980s, when acquisitions and mergers frenzy precluded prudence on the part of many acquirers. As Russ Banham cautioned in a December 1993 *Risk Management* piece, "What may appear to be a neatly wrapped corporate package becomes, upon buying, a Pandora's box of financial hardship." The consequences of these hasty purchases were sometimes painful, other times devastating. A February 1995 article in *Management Today* cited a Ferranti's 1987 acquisition of International Signal & Control as a "classic example of neglect in this matter." The acquirer's failure to detect its target's falsification of several important pending contracts led to "the demise, liquidation, and break-up of a once highly respected British company."

As the pace of deal making slowed and the likelihood of litigation increased in the early 1990s, acquirers grew evermore diligent. Acquirers began to pursue several categories of due diligence. Financial due diligence, a commonly-investigated factor, involves analysis of fiscal soundness through research on past performance, current economic health, and even management personnel. Commercial due diligence refers to the evaluation of a target's competitive position in its market. Legal due diligence, which determines the validity of the transaction, has grown increasingly important in light of globalization. Companies and investors accustomed to operating in one jurisdiction may need to make themselves aware of the legal limitations of another locale, as well as international trade laws. Environmental due diligence grew more pertinent in the wake of the 1986 federal Superfund Amendments Reauthorization Act (SARA), which extended the definition of parties responsible for environmental remediation to include lenders, creditors, and shareholders related to the property. Both legal and environmental due diligence were hot topics in the early 1990s, because either could uncover hidden, yet potentially expensive, aspects of a given transaction.

In the case of mergers or acquisitions, due diligence is often performed internally, by corporate attorneys and accountants. Experienced acquirers create detailed "due diligence checklists" enumerating pieces of information that should be obtained or verified before a transaction is completed. Both the proliferation of acquisitions and mergers and the increasing risk of incurring litigation have fueled the establishment of "strategic research consultancies," third-party organizations that investigate and subjectively analyze potential investments throughout the business world.

[April Dougal Gasbarre]

FURTHER READING:

Augenstein, Corey. "Look before You Leap." *Success*. January-February, 1993, p. 14.

Banham, Russ. "Risk Management and Pre-Acquisition Due Diligence." *Risk Management*. December, 1993, p. 17.

"Giving Diligence Its Due." *Management Today*. February, 1995, p. 9.

Hubbard, Graham, Shawn Lofstrom, and Richard Tully. "Diligence Checklists: Do They Get the Best Answers?" *Mergers & Acquisitions*. September-October, 1994, p. 33.

"M&A Due Diligence That Leaves Nothing to Chance." *Mergers & Acquisitions*. July-August, 1993, p. 11.

DUMPING

Dumping is a term that is used in financial markets as well as in international trade. In the context of buying and selling securities, dumping refers to the practice of selling large blocks of securities. More specifically, when dumping securities the seller is primarily interested in getting rid of the insecurities at any price. One simply dumps, or unloads, on the market with no regard to their selling price.

Dumping is also used in a commercial sense in the context of international trade. It refers to the practice of one country selling **commodities** or finished products in another country at below cost of fair market value. Predatory dumping occurs when one nation exports goods to another nation below **costs** of fair market value in order to obtain market share at the expense of domestic competitors. In many cases, predatory dumping drives out domestic **competition**. Then, having established a dominant **marketing** position in the industry, the predatory dumpers raise their prices well above previous levels.

Many nations, including the United States, have enacted antidumping laws that provide for the imposition of antidumping penalties or tariffs when a case of dumping can be proven. Following the Uruguay Round of Multilateral Trade Negotiations in 1993, the **General Agreement on Tariffs and Trade (GATT)** contained provisions to standardize antidumping measures by different nations. Antidumping measures affect not only the practice of dumping goods into the U.S. market, they also affect the ability of U.S. companies to export goods to other countries at competitive prices.

The enforcement of antidumping measures in the United States and elsewhere has not only caused friction among trading partners, it has also proven to be exceedingly complex at times. In foreign markets the use of antidumping laws has rapidly increased in the 1990s. In the past, U.S. firms have been subject to dumping decisions where it was not clear by what criteria the cases were decided.

In the United States dumping cases are investigated by the **U.S. International Trade Commission (ITC)** on the basis of industry complaints. Under GATT there must be more expressed support among domestic producers than expressed opposition to the initiation of an investigation. In addition, investigations are not to be initiated when imports from any one country constitute less than three percent of U.S. imports of the product in question, or if imports from all countries subject to a complaint are less than seven percent of total U.S. imports of the product.

Among the questions that are material to a dumping investigation are the pricing policies and **profit margins** of the exporter in its home market and in other export markets. The ITC must determine what constitutes unfair pricing. How does the ITC or an investigative body in another country determine that a product or commodity is being sold below cost or fair market value? How much above cost can an exporter sell its goods in the U.S. and still be accused of dumping? Using fairly complex rules and guidelines, the ITC compares the price of the goods in the U.S. market with those in the exporters' domestic market as well as its sales to other countries. Such price comparisons may be complicated by the fact that home market sales may be too small to make valid comparisons, the exporter may make occasional sales below cost in its home market, and other factors.

The object of the ITC investigation is to determine if an exporter's practices have injured or might pose the threat of an injury to an existing U.S. industry. If an industry complaint passes the ITC's preliminary investigation, it must then be confirmed by the U.S. Secretary of Commerce. The ITC then conducts a final investigation. Once the ITC determines that dumping has occurred, it is up to the nations involved to come to a corrective agreement, or else the president of the United States may impose antidumping measures in the form of higher tariffs and **duties** on the imported product or commodity.

In the case of the minivan controversy between the United States and Japan, the major U.S. automakers accused Japanese automakers of selling minivans in the United States at less than fair market value. In its preliminary investigation the ITC agreed with the U.S. automakers. The U.S. Department of Commerce then issued a ruling that Toyota and Mazda were in fact dumping minivans in the U.S. marketplace. When the ITC conducted its final investigation, however, it determined that the Big Three automakers—Ford, Chrysler Corp., and General Motors Corp.—had not been hurt by Japanese pricing practices in the U.S. minivan market. The Big 3 appealed, but a judge in the U.S. Court of International Trade upheld the ITC decision, and Toyota and Mazda were cleared of dumping charges.

[David Bianco]

DUN AND BRADSTREET REPORTS

Credit-reporting agencies, such as Dun & Bradstreet (D&B), collect credit information from individuals and business establishments and sell it to other companies and financial institutions for a fee. The major competitors of D&B—TRW, Equifax, and Trans Union—tend to focus on consumer credit information. Dun & Bradstreet, on the other hand, concentrates on commercial credit reports.

Although information can also be obtained from trade associations, banks, and other firms, the credit reporting agencies are the major source of credit data. Dun & Bradstreet, the largest of the credit agencies, maintains files on the creditworthiness of 9.5 million domestic and foreign firms. The company also offers an investigation service that can provide credit managers with information on almost any company. Controlling 90 percent of the commercial credit market, D&B data has a vital role in lending decisions and, in fact, many credit decisions are based almost entirely on the information in D&B credit reports.

A large amount of information is collected by D&B reporters who interview top officers of the subject company. Other D&B personnel examine documents filed with bankruptcy courts and public agencies. Another group of employees assembles the credit histories; these are based on interviews with trade references, information mailed in by creditors, or computer tapes of accounts provided by creditors.

Dun & Bradstreet reports include both qualitative and quantitative information. A standard "Business Information Report" includes a summary **balance sheet** and **income statement** as well as key financial ratios, with trend information. The Payments Re-

ported section shows data from the firm's suppliers stating whether it has been paying bills in a timely manner, the dollar amount of high credit extended, dollar amounts either currently owed or past due, selling terms, and the date of the last sale. The Banking section provides information on average balances, present balances, size of bank credit lines or loans outstanding, whether borrowing is secured or unsecured, and how these amounts will be repaid. Other information in the report includes a description of the physical condition of the company's operations as well as a description of the backgrounds of the firm's owners, including litigation, previous bankruptcies, divorce settlements, and the like.

D&B also furnishes a summary credit rating similar to those available on corporate bonds. The overall credit rating consists of two parts. The first part, the estimated financial strength, consists of a number and letter (or two letters), and is based on ratable net worth. The rating's second part—a number from one to four—represents D&B's composite credit appraisal of the enterprise. The second score is useful to credit managers for classifying the risk of the account. For example, a D&B rating of CB2 indicates that the company's estimated financial strength is between $125,000 and $199,999, with a "good" overall credit appraisal. The higher the rating, the greater the likelihood that the enterprise will pay its debts promptly.

[Robert T. Kleiman]

FURTHER READING:

Brigham, Eugene F., and Louis C. Gapenski. *Financial Management: Theory and Practice*; 6th ed. New York: Dryden Press, 1991.

Manness, Terry S., and John T. Zietlow. *Short-Term Financial Management: Text, Cases, and Readings*. Minneapolis/St. Paul: West Publishing Company, 1993.

DUOPOLY

A duopoly refers to a market where there are only two firms selling a particular product, service, or commodity. It is a special case of an **oligopoly**, which is a market condition where the production of identical or similar products is concentrated in a few large firms. Examples of oligopolies in the United States include the steel, aluminum, automobile, gypsum, petroleum, tire, and beer industries. While unregulated competition may result in oligopolies in certain industries, genuine duopolies in unregulated markets are quite rare.

Duopolies occur mainly as theoretical constructs that are useful in illustrating competitive behavior of business firms. As is the case with oligopolies, duopolies affect a company's competitive behavior.

In a competitive market situation that is not a duopoly or oligopoly, firms compete by acting for themselves to maximize profits without regard to the reactions of their competitors. In a duopoly, one firm must consider the effects of its actions on the other firm in the industry. The actions of one firm in the duopoly typically cause a reaction by the other firm in the industry.

Prices in oligopolistic industries tend to be unstable to the extent that companies will shade, or lower, their prices slightly to gain a competitive advantage. In duopolies it is more common for prices to be artificially high, at least to the extent that both companies can be profitable. It must be remembered that collusion between firms to fix prices is illegal under the United States' antitrust laws, so duopolies and oligopolies must reach industry agreements on pricing indirectly. Companies can signal their pricing intentions indirectly in a variety of ways, such as through press releases, speeches by industry leaders, or comments given in interviews. In some cases there is a recognized price leader with the other firm setting its prices according to that of the industry's price leader.

Until the end of 1994, rules of the Federal Communications Commission (FCC) allowed only two cellular phone companies in a market. Thus federal regulations created duopolies in each local market for cellular phone service. From 1985 to 1991, rates remained virtually unchanged in the nation's top 10 markets. When the FCC announced it would open local markets to greater competition by auctioning off new licenses, rates fell dramatically. Even though new cellular phone services were not yet operating, simply the threat of competition served to cause rates to fall.

The cellular phone situation illustrates how prices in duopolies can remain high without the threat of outside competition. With cellular phone duopolies, the two services competing in each market did not need to expand their customer base significantly by lowering prices. Once additional services entered the marketplace, however, additional subscribers were needed for the new services to be profitable. These new customers were attracted primarily by lowering the price of the service.

In the radio industry, which is also regulated by the FCC, duopolies refer to ownership of two radio stations in one market. Starting in 1992, the FCC changed its rules to allow a company to own two FM or two AM stations in one market. While such ownership is referred to as a duopoly, it is not a true duopoly in the sense of two firms providing a product or service in a market. Rather, the FCC rules had the effect of creating oligopolies, in that a few large firms could dominate certain markets by owning two FM or two AM stations.

[David Bianco]

DURABLE GOODS

Durable goods are those which are not consumed immediately, but gradually wear out over the period of time during which they are used. The U.S. Department of Commerce uses three years as the consumption period to distinguish durable from nondurable, or soft, goods. **Nondurable goods** consist mostly of food, clothing, and other items that are consumed within three years. Some soft goods, though, are expected to last longer than three years when purchased, such as an expensive suit or coat.

Within the economy, durable goods are made for consumers as well as producers. Examples of consumer durable goods include automobiles, furniture, appliances, jewelry, and books. Producer durable goods consist mainly of equipment and machinery. Structures such as houses, factories, dams, and highways are not considered durable goods and are categorized separately when calculating the **gross national product** (GNP) or **gross domestic product** (GDP).

The production of durable goods is a component of a country's GDP. As reported in the *Survey of Current Business* by the Bureau of Economic Analysis, durable goods that are sold to consumers appear under personal consumption expenditures. The other two categories of personal consumption expenditures are nondurable goods and services.

Consumer durable goods that are produced but not sold are reported as changes in business inventories. If more goods are produced than sold, then business inventories increase. On the other hand, when more goods are sold than are produced during a given time period, business inventories decline. The category of changes in business inventories is used as an economic indicator to gauge the direction of a country's economy. Increases in business inventories may signal a weakening of consumer demand or a strengthening of productive activity.

Changes in business inventories and the purchase of producer's durable equipment are reported under private domestic investment in the GDP. Fixed investment, including producer's durable equipment, and changes in business inventories are the two main categories of the gross private domestic investment component of the GDP. Finally, the production of durable goods also appears in the GDP as part of a nation's exports and as part of national, state, and local government purchases.

The category of personal consumption expenditures for durable goods is also used as an economic indicator. Since the purchase of consumer durable goods can be postponed, the level of consumer expenditures tends to fluctuate a great deal from year to year. During a recession consumer expenditures for durable goods tend to decline. Increases and decreases can be used as an indicator of consumer confidence and the direction of the economy. Increases in such consumer expenditures are usually interpreted as a sign of a recovering or strong economy. Similarly, businesses tend to put off buying new equipment under uncertain **economic conditions**. An increase in the purchase of producer's durable equipment may signal recovery from a recession or a period of expanding productivity.

The purchase of durable goods by consumers and producers represents a significant portion of the United States's GDP, although it is by no means the largest category of expenditures. Personal consumption expenditures in 1993, including durable goods, nondurable goods, and services, amounted to $4.39 trillion in 1993 out of a total GDP of $6.374 trillion, or 69 percent of GDP. Of that total, consumers spent $537.7 billion on durable goods (8.4 percent of GDP), $1.350 trillion on nondurable goods (21.2 percent of GDP), and $2.503 trillion on services (39.3 percent of GDP). Producers spent $444.4 billion on durable equipment in 1993 (seven percent of GDP). In addition, durable goods contributed to the GDP in the categories of exports and government purchases. Overall, the production of durable goods accounted for $1.048 trillion (16.4 percent of GDP) in 1993, of which $1.035 trillion were final sales and $13 billion were changes in business inventories.

[David Bianco]

DURATION

Duration is a measure of the price sensitivity of a fixed income security to changes in the interest rate. It was developed by Frederick R. Macaulay in 1938 to replace the inferior price sensitivity to interest rate change methods: term to maturity and weighted average term to maturity. Duration is a form of the weighted average term to maturity. The mathematical expression to define duration is:

$$\frac{\sum_{t=1}^{m} [C_{(t)} \times t]/(1 + i)^t}{\sum_{t=1}^{m} C_t/(1 + i)^t}$$

where

- C_t is the cash flow (interest or principal payment)

- t is the time of the cash flow

- m is the length of time to the final maturity of the fixed income security

- i is the interest rate (yield to maturity) of the fixed income security, expressed in decimal form

That is, duration is the sum of the present value of each cash flow multiplied by the time period when it occurs divided by the current price of the instrument.

For example, a bond has a 6% coupon interest rate (paid annually) with five years left to maturity when it repays the face value (principal) of $1,000. The current market interest rate (yield to maturity) is 8%. What is the duration? Table 1 on the next page illustrates this.

The importance of duration is that it tells us how much the price of a fixed income security will change by, given a change in **interest rates**. To be precise, the modified duration is used. The modified duration is the duration divided by the quantity one plus the interest rate (in decimal form).

Thus, the percentage change in price of a fixed income security equals the modified duration multiplied by the percentage change in interest rates. Of course, the price moves in opposite direction to the interest rate change.

That is, mathematically,

$$\Delta \% \text{ Price} = - \text{ (Modified Duration) } \Delta \% \text{ Interest Rate}$$

To illustrate, what would happen to the price of the $920.1457 bond if interest rates changed by 1%? The modified duration is 4.11 years (4.44/(1 + .08). Therefore, the bond price would decrease by 4.11% to a price of $882.33.

Other considerations impacting on the degree of duration include call or put clauses and other early retirement features as well as other means of altering the payment pattern.

Besides having a measure which tells us how much the price changes for an interest rate change, the investor can acquire a portfolio to take advantage of an interest rate forecast. For example, if interest rates were predicted to drop, a long duration bond portfolio would be ideal to maximize return. On the other hand, some investors desire to protect themselves against interest rate fluctuations. In this situation, the portfolio would want to be immunized against interest rate volatility. The use of duration would help to achieve the optimal bond strategy to prevent wealth losses that would occur in the face of increasing interest rates.

[Raymond A.K. Cox]

Table 1

TIME	CASH FLOW	PRESENT VALUE OF CASH FLOW	PRESENT VALUE OF CASH FLOW x TIME
1	$60	$55.5555	$55.5555
2	$60	$51.4403	$102.8806
3	$60	$47.6299	$142.8897
4	$60	$44.1018	$176.4072
5	$1060	$721.4182	$3607.0910
	TOTAL	$920.1457	$4084.8240

Price of bond	$920.1457
Duration in years	$4084.824/$920.1457
	= $4.44 years

FURTHER READING:

Cox, Raymond A.K. and Rose M. Prasad. "Strategies for Banks to Cope with Changing Interest Rates," *Review of Business*, Vol. 14, Summer/Fall 1992, pp. 14-18.

Hopewell, Michael H. and George C. Kaufman. "Bond Price Volatility and Term to Maturity: A Generalized Respecification," *American Economic Review*, Vol. 63, September 1973, pp. 749-753.

Macaulay, Frederick R. *Some Theoretical Problems Suggested by the Movement of Interest Rates, Bond Yields, and Stock Prices in the United States Since 1865*. National Bureau of Economic Research, 1938.

DUTY

A duty is a tax imposed by a government on exported or imported goods. The terms duty and tariff are often used synonymously, but a duty is the actual tax imposed on goods while a tariff is the schedule of duties. Contemporary duties are usually imposed on imported goods in an effort to protect home markets and stimulate home production and employment. However, duties can be imposed simply to generate revenue for a government, as was the case with some duties imposed by the United States during parts of the eighteenth and nineteenth centuries. **Exporting** duties are uncommon and are prohibited in the United States. Export tariffs can be used to generate revenue but are often used politically to punish or influence a country dependent on the duties goods.

There are many determinants affecting duty rates. A country may have treaties granting most favored nation status to other countries. In such a case the lowest duty imposed on any one country cannot be raised for other signatories of the treaty. Customs unions strive to eliminate all tariffs on goods traded between members of the union and mandate a common tariff on goods imported from nonmember coun-tries. A common market is similar to a customs union but economic cooperation is extended beyond the sphere of just trade. Free trade areas eliminate tariffs between member countries while leaving each member free to set duty rates with nonmember countries. Preferential tariffs may be granted to specific countries in order to reach certain political or economic goals. Tariffs are generally either specific or *ad valorem*. A specific tariff is a rate based on a physical measurement, such as charging a cents per pound rate on goods imported. An *ad valorem* tariff is a percentage of the calculated value of the item. A tariff may also be a combination of the two.

Tariffs existed in ancient Greece and Rome and throughout medieval Europe and were largely imposed to raise revenue. Export tariffs were also popular in medieval Europe in attempts to keep scarce commodities available for home markets. Through much of the sixteenth, seventeenth, and eighteenth centuries, however, import tariffs were seen as a way to guarantee the accumulation of gold and silver within one's borders. In the 1700s, in an effort to increase exports, many countries sought trade agreements that would bilaterally lower tariffs. However many of these countries were caught in a tariff dilemma when they sought to protect their own burgeoning industrialization efforts by imposing import duties on other countries.

In the United States, the Tariff Act of 1789 was meant to protect American industry, raise revenue, and force trading partners into more equitable tariff agreements. Tariffs gradually rose, creating conflict between those who wanted to protect home industries and those who wanted cheap imports. The conflict took on regional overtones with the industrial North favoring high tariffs and the agricultural South and West desiring cheaper and better made European imports. Henry Clay of Kentucky convinced western representatives that their region would likely prosper from high tariffs, and in 1824 and 1828 (to the further alienation of the agricultural South) tariffs were again raised. Duty rates see-sawed during the pre-Civil War years, depending on economic conditions. The high tariffs of 1824 and 1828 were lowered by the Compromise Tariff of 1833 and the Walker Tariff Act, which followed an 1846 recovery. Tariffs were again lowered following an economic resurgence in 1857.

However tariffs had been raised in 1842 and again in 1861 by the Morrill Tariff Act. Tariffs were raised during the Civil War and again with the McKinley Tariff Act of 1890. The Payne-Aldrich Tariff Act of 1909 and the Underwood Tariff Act of 1913 lowered tariffs, but in 1922 the Ford-McCumber Tariff Act raised duties again, as did the Smoot-Hawley Tariff Act of 1930. The Reciprocal Trade Agreements Act of 1934 allowed the President to reduce tariffs to specific nations and to set tariff rates on specific goods and products, a power previously held by Congress. Most recently the United States was one of 23 signatories to the **General Agreement on Trades and Tariff (GATT)**. GATT is a tariff reduction plan and contains provisions for settling trade disputes. With GATT becoming operational and having more than 100 signatories, many nations have substantially reduced their tariffs.

Tariffs remain controversial, with their advantages often being offset by negative side effects. Tariffs are meant to protect home markets, domestic employment, and new industries, while offsetting unfair trade practices such as dumping and lessening dependence on foreign goods. Tariffs however can also result in higher prices and a lessening of competition.

[*Michael Knes*]

FURTHER READING:

Ratner, Sidney. *The Tariff in American History*. D. Van Nostrand, 1972.

E

EARNINGS FORECASTS

The forecasting of a company's earnings is important to a firm, its creditors and its investors. The business usually prepares its annual earnings forecast as part of its budget process. The forecasting of earnings is extremely difficult since it is dependent on several variables.

In order to forecast a company's earnings, three major factors must be considered:

1. forecasted sales

2. the company's cost structure, and

3. the company's **capital structure**.

And, just to complicate matters, the numerical results of these considerations can be affected by the company's accounting policies.

SALES FORECASTS

The starting point in any forecast is sales. Forecasting sales is primary to earnings forecasts. Although **management** exerts some degree of control over expenditures, it has little ability to direct the buying habits of individuals; the level of sales depends of the vagaries of the market place. Yet, a sales forecast must attain a reasonable degree of reliability to be useful.

The analyst needs to know capacity utilization, unit cost of production, expected rate of **inflation**, general economic and business conditions, government rules and regulations, competitive forces, and social changes which would impact on the cost of **marketing** and sales, labor and raw materials, etc. The analyst will determine the impact of these variables on the industry and the specific company to project growth rates of sales. (See Sales Forecasting)

Since volume and selling price forecasts will differ by product or business segment, the ideal sales and related cost forecasts should be done for each major product or segment of the firm. This is particularly critical when products or segments have different **manufacturing** or distribution cost structures.

Sales volume in units and unit selling prices need to be projected. The level of sales for future periods is dependent on not only what the firm has done in the past, but also what it thinks it can do in the future. Some ancillary issues that may arise which will need to be resolved as part of the sales forecast. For example, if sales are projected to increase, will the firm be required to redesign its production process, purchase new equipment, raise for capital, hire more employees, purchase new types of materials? Increasing sales may cause bottlenecks and inefficiencies. Decreasing sales may assist the firm to reach an optimal production level. Statistical techniques or econometric forecasts are frequently used to assist in developing volume. Marketing personnel can be helpful in forecasting anticipated unit selling prices. Marketing executives can gather forecasts from each individual salesperson for a particular territory or product. The firm's sales forecast becomes the aggregate of the individual forecasts.

OTHER FACTORS IN FORECASTS

The next step in the forecast is to project the related costs. In order to complete this step a firm needs to have a handle on the related cost structures.

Exhibit 1

ABC Corporation
Forecasted Earnings
For The Year 199X
(In 000s)

	Segment (or product)			
	1	2	3	Total
Sales volume	1,000	700	2,000	
Unit selling price	$10	$12	$18	
Projected sales	$10,000	$8,400	$36,000	$54,400
Variable costs	$3,000	$3,360	8,000	$24,360
Direct fixed costs	5,000	3,000	8,000	16,000
General overhead				7,500
Total costs				$47,860
Operating income				$6,540
Interest expense				1,000
Earning before taxes				$5,540
Taxes (at 40%)				2,216
Preferred dividends				200
Net income				3,124
Earnings per share (1,000,000 shares outstanding)				$3.12

For each major element of cost, the firm needs to know the variable/fixed split. Again, some statistical analyses may be needed to determine this. The firm will also need to project the overhead costs common to all products or segments.

Once the related costs are determined, the forecast needs to reflect the interest charges or preferred dividend obligations inherent in its capital structure. The interest charges, since they are tax deductible, will need to be ascertained before income taxes for the year are projected.

The last step is to calculate forecasted earnings per share. To do this, divide earnings after any preferred dividend by the forecasted average number of common shares which will be outstanding during the forecast year.

A sample forecast is in Exhibit 1.

USERS AND USES OF EARNINGS FORECASTS

LENDERS. Financial institutions, especially those who are creditors, or potential creditors, of a company are acutely interested in the firm's earnings forecast. Before a loan is approved, many lenders ask potential borrowers for pro-forma **financial statements** which include earnings forecasts. Especially for longer-term loans, the lenders are eager to see if the borrowers will be generating sufficient cash flow through operations to retire the loan. Many lenders ask for forecasts just to see if potential borrowers know enough about their company to prepare a comprehensive forecast.

OWNERS AND SECURITY MARKETS. Owners of a company want to see earnings forecasts in order to determine if their capital will be generating a sufficient rate of return to warrant their continued investment. For publicly traded firms, security prices generally represent values based on the firm's future cash flows. Earnings forecasts supply data to enable investment analysts to determine the course of investing action (e.g., buy, hold, sell). Earnings forecasts for publicly held companies are typically updated quarterly. Actual earnings results are compared to forecasts and variations may affect the firm's security prices. (For example, it is not uncommon for a firm's **common stock** to drop in price when it misses its forecasted earnings by as little as one cent.)

MANAGEMENT. A very popular use of earnings forecasts is as benchmarks by management. Since the forecasted earnings are generally an outgrowth of the budget process, all components of the budget can be compared to actual to see how the firm is performing.

SEE ALSO: Budgeting; Business Conditions; Business Planning; Delphi Technique; Discriminant Analysis; Histograms; Regression Analysis; Time Series Analysis

[Ronald M. Horwitz]

FURTHER READING:

Baginski, Stephen P., Kenneth S. Lorek and G. Lee Willinger. "Economic Determinants of Quarterly Earnings Data," *The Quarterly Review of Economics and Finance*, volume 33, number 1, Spring 1993, pp. 87-100.

Cohen, William A. *The Practice of Marketing Management.* Macmillan Publishing Co., 1988.

Kang, Sok-Hyon, John O'Brien and S. Sivaramakrishnan. "Analysts' Interim Earnings Forecasts: Evidence on the Forecasting Process," *Journal of Accounting Research*, volume 32, number 1, Spring 1994, pp. 103-111.

Mueller, Dennis C. *Profits in the Long Run.* Cambridge University Press, 1986

Shim, Jae J. and Joel G. Siegel. *Handbook of Financial Analysis, Forecasting, and Modeling.* Prentice-Hall, 1988.

Welsch, Glenn A. *Budgeting: Profit Planning and Control.* Fourth Edition. Prentice-Hall, Inc., 1976.

EAST AFRICAN COMMUNITY (EAC)

The East African Community (EAC), an economic cooperative, was formed by the African countries of Kenya, Tanzania, and Uganda as a result of the Treaty of Kampala. Prior to gaining independence these three countries had been under British colonial rule. One of the purposes of the treaty was to keep intact cooperative regional trade mandated under British rule. There was a failed attempt in 1964 to form a cooperative East African Federation, but it failed because of strong nationalistic tendencies and diverging economic and political policies. By June 6, 1967, however, these differences were set aside and the Treaty for East African Cooperation was signed creating the East African Community. A long-term goal of the EAC was the establishment of an East African common market. The purpose of the EAC and the eventual common market was to promote, strengthen and regulate common industrial and commercial developments. This was to be accomplished by cooperative and regulated development and trade. The economic results of this policy would be shared equally by all member states. EAC headquarters were in Arusha, Tanzania.

EAC policy was governed by the East African Authority, which consisted of the President of each respective member country. Decisions were to be unanimous and each member nation appointed a Minister for East African Affairs who served in an advisory capacity to the East African Authority. The community also had five councils: Common Market Council, Communications Council, Economic Consultative and Planning Council, Finance Council, and the Research and Social Council. There was also an East African Legislative Assembly, a Common Market Tribunal, and a Court of Appeal.

In the hope of attaining a viable East African Common Market, the treaty called for regulations covering intra-community trade and trade with non-member states. The three nations had to retain a common customs tariff and could not establish privileged or unilateral trade agreements with non-members. The treaty also called for transfer taxes in lieu of internal tariffs; these taxes served to regulate intra-community trade. There were also coordinated investment programs and attempts to stabilize currency exchange rates. The community also created four corporations: the East African Railways Corporation, the East African Airways Corporation, the East African Harbors Corporation, and the East African Posts and Telecommunications Corporation. These corporations grew out of the largely intact, formerly British infrastructure which included roads, rail systems, airways, port facilities, a telegraph and postal system, and a common currency.

Although the existing infrastructure served as a framework for the EAC to build on, the Community was soon overwhelmed by political strife, ideological rifts and severe economic problems. In February 1971, General Idi Amin seized power in Uganda in a military coup d'état. The deposed Milton Obote of Uganda was granted political asylum in neighboring Tanzania. In 1976 Idi Amin claimed part of Kenya as rightfully belonging to Uganda before the 1902 British land transfer to the old British East Africa Protectorate. In the intervening years this area had become a focal point of Kenyan farming, transportation, and economic development. Kenya responded to Amin's threats by curtailing the movement of Ugandan goods across its borders.

There were also ideological differences between member countries. Kenya was developing a free market economy and much of its resources went towards capital improvements. Tanzania, however, was developing a planned socialist economy and much of its resources went towards welfare programs. Each country respectively felt it was bearing an unfair economic burden within the EAC. The problems between Tanzania and Kenya were intensified by Idi Amin's 1971 and 1972 nationalizing of the commercial assets of Uganda's mostly Asian merchants and entrepreneurs. The resulting Asian exodus to Tanzania and the subsequent decline in foreign investment exacerbated an already tense situation.

The three nations were also facing severe balance of payment problems due to the rising cost of energy and imported and finished goods. Trade throughout much of East Africa declined while nationalistic goals overshadowed economic integration efforts. By June of 1977 the three member nations could not agree on the EAC budget for the coming fiscal year, and the EAC for all intents and purposes ceased to function. Tanzania, Uganda, and Kenya claimed whatever EAC assets remained within their respective borders. It wasn't until 1983, however, that the three countries formally came to an agreement on the division of EAC assets and obligations. Kenya and Tanzania initially gained more at the breakup but now agreed to reimburse Uganda $191 million in goods, services, and cash. They also helped with Uganda's International Monetary Fund and World Bank debts. Simmering border problems between Kenya and Tanzania were also resolved by the agreement which was concluded at Arusha, Tanzania on November 16, 1983.

EAST AFRICAN DEVELOPMENT BANK

The Kampala Treaty of 1967 that created the East African Community also established the East African Development Bank (EADB). The EADB survived the dissolution of the East African Community because it did not rely on the EAC for funding. Headquartered at Kampala the bank was revitalized by a rare show of unity in 1977 when Kenya, Uganda, and Tanzania momentarily set their differences aside in an effort to bolster the bank's activities.

In 1984 the **International Monetary Fund (IMF)** agreed to provide further financial backing and by the latter part of the 1980s the African Development Bank, the European Investment Bank, and the Japanese government agreed to channel $56.4 million in credit through the EADB for regional projects. By 1990, however, the EADB had loaned $28 million to nineteen separate projects and many of these and other previous loans soon were in arrears. Many of the bank's problems were blamed on currency devaluations and various technical financial adjustments, but in 1993 the EADB agreed to a complete restructuring under the guidance of a new Director-General.

The EADB is administered by a Governing Council, an Advisory Panel, a board of Directors, and a Director-General. Originally the bank was created to enhance industrial development by providing funding for regional projects and technical assistance. The bank has since included agriculture, tourism promotion, and infrastructure improvement in its sphere of activities.

SEE ALSO: Doing Business in Africa

[Michael Knes]

FURTHER READING:

Cox, Thomas S. "Northern Actors in a South-South Setting: External Aid and East African Integration." *Journal of Common Market Studies.* March, 1983, pp. 283-312.

Hazlewood, Arthur. *Economic Integration: The East Africa Experience.* St. Martins Press, 1975.

Umbrichet, Victor H. *Multilateral Mediation: Practical Experiences and Lessons. Mediation Cases: The East African Community.* Dordrecht, Netherlands: Martinus Nijhoff, 1989.

EASTERN EUROPE, DOING BUSINESS IN

Not only are the economies and politics of Eastern European states still in flux, but what we understand by "Eastern Europe" also is changing. Some would include the Baltic states and Ukraine, newly independent of Soviet control. East Germany and Czechoslovakia, considered part of "Eastern Europe" for 40 and 76 years, respectively, have disappeared altogether from the map. "Yugoslavia" has shrunk dramatically to include only Serbia and Montenegro; Slovenia, Croatia and Macedonia, the Balkan states formerly part of Yugoslavia, have appeared on the map for the first time as independent nation states. For practical purposes and because it is still acceptable practice, the states of the former Soviet Union will be excluded from our definition of "Eastern Europe." Rather, Eastern Europe will include the major nations of east central Europe, namely Poland and Hungary, former Czechoslovakia (the republics of Slovakia and Czechia), and the Balkan states of former Yugoslavia, as well as Romania, Bulgaria, and Albania, an area that contains approximately 125 million inhabitants.

As far as focusing on *doing business* in Eastern Europe, one can only feasibly consider Poland, Hungary, the separate states of Slovakia and Czechia, Romania, and Bulgaria. The Yugoslav war, which continues to embroil most of former Yugoslavia and seriously threatens Macedonia and Albania, excludes former Yugoslavia from our consideration. It is simply not advisable to do business there, with U.N. sanctions in force, and trade on the Danube threatened by illegal arms shipments to Serbia.

The Yugoslav tragedy reflects only a small part of the turmoil in Eastern Europe resulting from the collapse of communism in the Soviet Union in the late 1980s. Almost all of Eastern Europe at that time, with the exception of Yugoslavia, overthrew their communist dictatorships, with Bulgarians the only ones reinstating the communists a year after toppling them. This scenario becomes more confusing with the ethnic disturbances in Bulgaria and Romania, and the division of Czechoslovakia into two separate political entities in 1993. Following these historic events, foreign investors found themselves facing a political situation which could easily have gotten out of control. Political, economic, and ethnic turmoil make Eastern Europe one of the most challenging regions in the world in which to do business.

What many in Western Europe and the United States perceived as a strong desire in Eastern Europe for democracy and free market economies was premature. The Balkan states of former Yugoslavia, as well as Bulgaria, Romania, and Albania, have all failed to implement serious free market reforms, including major privatization, and to elect strong democratic governments, unlike their neighbors in former Czechoslovakia, Hungary and Poland (all of which have serious problems of their own, especially huge foreign debts, insufficient foreign capital, and hyperinflation). Nonetheless, this did not prevent Americans, individuals as well as companies, from flocking eastward as though it were a new Eldorado. Only the hardiest of them lasted.

What kind of business can one best undertake in Eastern Europe? When the Iron Curtain came tumbling down, Eastern Europeans, with millions of dollars worth of **discretionary income** hoarded from communist days, went on a spending spree, indulging their pocketbooks for consumer goods long denied them. Electronic products of all kinds and computers topped their lists. By the early 1990s, this kind of discretionary income disappeared, unemployment set in, and the fluctuations of an unplanned economy undergoing privatization drove down the already low standard of living. Nowadays, few if any Eastern European governments welcome foreigners who come only to sell, despite countless shortages of goods and services. Doing business in Eastern Europe in the mid-1990s should involve some form of investment, preferably in the form of a partnership with a native firm. The best kinds of investments still remain any kind of pollution control equipment, construction equipment, medical equipment, computers and peripherals, tourism, telecommunications systems, and electronic products; customer services of all kinds, from the financial to the mundane—quick-copy shops, auto repair shops, used car dealerships, dry cleaners, and laundromats—can also be lucrative enterprises.

The American entrepreneurs who flocked to Eastern Europe in 1989 and 1990 were usually unprepared for the difficulties they encountered in doing business in there, difficulties which still plague those foreigners who have managed to survive. For instance, it is still impossible to do reliable market studies in order to find out if a niche exists for one's product or service. Statistics under the communist regimes often were falsified, if they were kept at all. In fact, any kind of business information is difficult to come by. The legalities of setting up a business in Eastern Europe—can be as formidable as the market scene. Foreign investment laws keep changing, and keeping up with the changes, can prove challenging.

American companies have had to deal with a dearth of reliable business managers in all Eastern European countries. There are just too few often, and the companies that penetrated Eastern Europe earliest snapped up the few good ones around. The explanation for the paucity of competent managers lies in the near absence of private business prior to the fall of communism. The communist regimes in Hungary and Czechoslovakia did allow very limited private ownership of business (up to four employees), but this did not produce a lot of first class business managers. Other countries, such as Romania and Bulgaria (to say nothing of Albania), had no private enterprise under communism.

Every Eastern European country also suffers from a lack of **foreign exchange**, without which neither foreign businesses nor foreign imports can be compensated. At times, large foreign companies do not mind being paid in barter (vodka or some other salable item in the West); but most, if not all, small business firms can do little with vodka or cans of sardines. The lack of foreign exchange can seriously discourage any business investment. In Bulgaria, a dearth of foreign exchange led to a precipitous 40 percent decline in foreign trade with the United States in 1992, despite Bulgaria's desperate need for U.S. exports. Unfortunately, for the lack of foreign exchange is largely caused by meager foreign investment in Eastern Europe (despite large financial aid packages from abroad). In 1992, all of Eastern Europe *including* the former Soviet Union received approximately the same amount of direct **foreign investment**, $4.5 billion, that Argentina received in that year. From the point of view of a foreign investor, however, Argentina does not face the enormous **privatization** and ownership problems that Eastern Europe faces, and has a far superior infrastructure, **telecommunications**, and banking network.

Finally, a problem of almost nightmarish proportions for many foreign investors wishing to do business in Eastern Europe is ownership of property. Until the fall of communism, all Eastern European countries had state-owned economies, that is, all industry was owned by the government (and in half of former communist Eastern Europe, agriculture also was government-owned). Never in modern history has there been such large-scale privatization as is now slowly occurring in Eastern Europe. (Before the fall of communism, Chile had the largest privatization program in history—over 500 industries were sold off to private investors between 1973 and the late 1980s. Chilie's program was much smaller than the thousands of industries to be sold off in a country such as Poland.) Foreign companies initially eager to purchase an Eastern European company on the auction block came face to face with the dilemma of ownership—who really owned the company in the first place? Many Eastern Europeans, whose families had owned a business which the communists confiscated after World War II, have been coming forward to reclaim the "family" firm. And frequently this has happened (and still is happening) after the government already has sold the firm off to an unwary foreign investor. In such cases, in lieu of demanding back the business (which the original owners have a legal right to do), they often demand financial recompense from the new owner, and it is given reluctantly. The difficult problem of original ownership is unlikely to be encountered in many regions other than Eastern Europe and the former Soviet Union.

If one is aware of this problem ahead of time and can thoroughly research the original ownership of the property one is interested in, the next and frequently encountered difficulty is the workers who come with the enterprise. In all of the industries that are being sold to private investors, the workers attached to the firm exercise the right to influence the government on whether or not to sell. Almost always there are too many workers attached to an enterprise, a factor that the prospective owner must know how to deal with tactfully.

These are but some of the obstacles faced by the intrepid foreign investor trekking to Eastern Europe in the hope of reaping large profits from goods-starved Poles, Bulgarians, and Hungarians. Large profits in fact have been reaped, only after foreign investors have thoroughly studied the problems of doing business in Eastern Europe, which is the first task of the aspiring investor. Fortunately, incentives for doing business in Eastern Europe as well as assistance and information are not lacking.

One of the incentives is the opportunity to obtain financing on easy terms from the U.S. government as well as from international financial institutions. As communism was falling in Eastern Europe in 1989, Congress passed SEED I, or the Support Eastern Europe Democracy Act, which provided millions of dollars for investment in Poland and Hungary for the small- and middle-sized American company. SEED I was supposed to be succeeded by other SEEDs, as more and more Eastern European countries turned to free market reforms.

This has set the stage for a plethora of other programs providing financing for private business development in Eastern Europe. More than a dozen government agencies and programs, provide loans on easy terms for small- and medium-sized American businesses. These include: Eximbank (Export-Import Bank of the United States), the Consortia of American Business in Eastern Europe, the Overseas Private Investment Corporation (which also provides insurance for "political risk" investments), the **World Bank** (MIGA, or the Multilateral Investment Guarantee Agency, also provides insurance for foreign investment), and the **Small Business Administration (SBA)**.

Finally, in terms of incentives to doing business in Eastern Europe, not to be overlooked are the ones that Eastern European countries themselves provide to attract foreign trade. In all of them, the currency has become convertible; 100 percent ownership of a business is allowed; all of them provide for repatriation of profits back to the United States; unlike many developing foreign countries, Eastern European governments have no restrictions or stipulations about hiring (i.e., requiring that a certain percentage of the work force be citizens of the country).

Undoubtedly the most desirable incentive to doing business in an Eastern European country is the fact that labor currently is cheaper in Eastern Europe (and in the former Soviet Union) than perhaps anywhere else on earth—and a whopping 90 percent lower than in Western Europe. Even Chinese and Indonesian workers earn more. Cheap labor has been one reason that American investment in Eastern Europe has been higher than that of any other foreign country, with the possible exception of Germany. Laborers are many, thanks to high unemployment, and are also very literate and highly skilled. Lastly, Eastern Europeans all possess consumer tastes similar to Western Europeans (an important factor if one is considering investing in a consumer goods enterprise).

Hungary, Poland, Slovakia, and Czechia are particularly attractive for foreign investors for several reasons. First they have fairly well-developed infrastructures and a minimum of red tape to deal with in setting up a business. Their locations are strategically close to Western Europe, and they are considered prime candidates for merger into the **European Union** in the near future, so it might be considered wise to establish business in these countries sooner rather than later.

Where are the best places to educate oneself about doing business in Eastern Europe? To find out about financial assistance programs as well as other information, one should start with the Eastern European Business Information Center (EEBIC) of the U.S. Department of Commerce. Its purpose is to help the prospective entrepreneur in Eastern Europe, and to this end, it offers one-on-one counseling assistance and a plethora of printed information. This information can be obtained by mail or from any of the Commerce Department's 68 district offices. In addition, the Commerce Department operates BISNIS, or Business Information Service for the Newly Independent States, with relevant publications, phone and fax numbers.

Aside from the Commerce Department, the would-be foreign investor can get assistance and information from the International Division of the U.S. Chamber of Commerce in Washington, D.C. and from chambers of commerce located in the Eastern European country of one's choice (the Commerce Department can supply you with their addresses and phone/fax numbers). The prospective entrepreneur should also contact the trade mission and/or consulate of the country in which one is interested in pursuing business.

There are many weekly and monthly newsletters that keep you abreast of economic developments in Eastern Europe: *Business Eastern Europe, Doing Business with Eastern Europe, Eastern Europe Business Bulletin*, and *PlanEcon Report* to name but the most significant ones, are invaluable.

In setting up a business in Eastern Europe, however, it will be important to immerse oneself in know-how and to obtain an Eastern European business partner. For one thing, a reliable Eastern European business partner knows the market better than an outsider and for another, he or she speaks the language (assuming you do not) and is better able to deal with the constantly changing laws and regulations concerning foreign business. Finally, one can avoid the pitfalls of the ownership problem if one has a partner. If one can afford it, engaging a native lawyer is also a good idea, once again, because of the fluctuating laws concerning foreign investment in a region that is still undergoing profound transition.

In recognition of the need for a business partner, the EEBIC of the U.S. Commerce Department has established a service called "Eastern Europe Looks for Partners." If the information provided by this program does not work, one should consider attending one of the many trade fairs in Eastern Europe (announced in all of the aforementioned newsletters) or getting in touch with an Eastern European lawyer or accountant who has the connections one lacks. Embassies and trade missions also are good places to meet a prospective partner. If all else fails, traveling to the country is a good place to start. The American embassy in each country has ways of assisting the prospective American business person.

If partnership is not the answer but selling a product is, then the difficulty one faces resides in doing business in an area perpetually short of foreign currency. In that case, one might want to investigate the many assistance programs to Eastern Europe that are fueling billions of dollars into development programs toward rebuilding the economies, in particular the infrastructures, of former communist Eastern Europe (the World Bank alone is footing a $10 billion aid package). Latching on to one of these programs (competition is stiff) can result in lucrative profits, especially if what one is selling has anything to do with pollution control or environmental cleanup.

In short, there are many opportunities for doing business in an area that is undergoing such rapid changeover to parliamentary democracy and free market enterprise. Thus far, competition is less keen than in the Far East. And if the obstacles to doing business in Eastern Europe appear to be daunting, they are no less so in China or the Middle East. Furthermore consumer tastes, attitudes, and habits of Eastern Europeans, are similar to our own. The location of Eastern Europe, in between giant Russia and the wealthy European Union, is also far more strategic.

[Sina Dubovoy]

FURTHER READING:

Dahl, Jonathan. "Eastern Europe Gains as Business Destination." *The Wall Street Journal.* March 19, 1993, pp. B1(W), pp.B1(E).

Engholm, Christopher. *The Other Europe, A Complete Guide to Business Opportunities in Eastern Europe.* New York: McGraw-Hill, Inc., 1994.

Goodrich, Monica M. "Construction Market Booms in Eastern Europe." *Business America.* September 6, 1993, p.11.

Farnsworth, Clyde H. "U.S. Seeks to Ease Technology Sales in Eastern Europe." *New York Times.* May 3, 1990, pp. A1(N), A1(L).

Fuerbringer, Jonathan. "Doing Business in Eastern Europe." *New York Times.* December 23, 1990, pp. F12(N), F12(L).

Gupta, Udayan. "Small U.S. Firms Find It Tough to Finance Their Deals in Eastern Europe." *Wall Street Journal.* April 18, 1994, pp. B2(W), B2(E).

"Here Come the Westerners: In Eastern Europe, Kmarts and Playboy." *New York Times.* September 7, 1993, pp. A16(N), A18(L).

Loiry, William S., editor. *U.S.-Eastern Europe Trade Sourcebook Reference for Doing Business in Poland, Hungary, Czechoslovakia, Yugoslavia, Bulgaria, Romania, and Albania.* Chicago: St. James Press, 1991.

Shipman, Alan. "Shock Therapy Has Yet to See Eastern Europe on the Way to Economic Recovery." *International Management.* March, 1994, p. 8.

Woodard, Colin. "Unspoiled Albania Promotes New Eco-Sensitive Tourism Industry." *The Christian Science Monitor.* April 27, 1994, p. 9.

ECOLOGY

SEE: Business and Society; Environmental Law and Business; Environmental Protection Agency

ECONOMETRICS

Econometrics is a science built on the unification of economic theory with statistical analysis and mathematics. It evolved out of a necessity to apply logical theories about economic relations to the real world, while enabling general economic laws to be constructed from organized data. It provides economists with analytical tools necessary to understand a broad range of primarily macroeconomic phenomena.

Within limits, econometric methodology enables economists to test their assumptions about given sectors of an economy. In addition, it affords the analyst opportunities to modify theoretical conclusions—or the theories themselves—over time, as new data become available. Therefore, statistical tests in econometrics may be used not just to test economic models, but to help build them.

Econometric analysis is every bit as much as an art as it is a science. It requires proper consideration of practical issues, the use of relevant economic theories, and correct application of valid statistical inputs. As a result, econometrics, despite being thoroughly rooted in the concrete natural sciences of statistics and mathematics, is deeply influenced by less concrete social considerations.

The numerical data used in econometric analysis is not static or stable, but the product of policies resulting from legal, legislative, and regulatory considerations, and individual demand characteristics. They are, therefore, skewed by factors that are difficult to predict or quantify.

In addition, econometrics has historically been applied to the phenomena of **macroeconomics**, where theories are notoriously underdeveloped and lacking firm **microeconomic** foundations. Specifically, for the sake of simplicity, theories tend to fumble around minute factors, latent variables, and time lags, either dealing with them inadequately or dismissing them altogether.

Increasingly, however, econometrics has recently been applied to a wide variety of analysis, including numerous microeconomic phenomena. This has helped to improve the reliability of econometric forecasts, which are used to evaluate the effect of housing starts and other general economic indicators on the economy in general. These "leading economic indicators" thus influence the behavior of the very factors they measure. This may be considered an example of how econometrics evaluates policies, but in doing so also helps to shape them.

THE DEVELOPMENT OF ECONOMETRICS

Although not taken seriously as a major economic science until this century, econometric concepts have a surprisingly long history. Economic historians credit the 16th-century school of political arithmeticians with providing the genesis of econometrics. Sir William Petty (1623-1687), Gregory King (1648-1712), and others focused on the statistical measurement of commodity prices and international trade on the **money supply** and **taxation**. These early economists were the first to use a quantitative approach to analyze government economic policies.

King used data on corn harvests and market prices to construct a highly accurate demand model, illustrating a formulaic relationship between supply and demand that, for the first time, offered astoundingly accurate predictive capabilities.

The political arithmeticians provided a scientific basis to economic policies, elevating them from the whimsical realm of politics to a valid natural science. Their goal was to demonstrate that economies were governed by natural laws that were as universal as physics.

At the heart of this analysis were statistical formulas and mathematical functions. But because these sciences were barely developed, they were unable to manage the immense complexities of economic systems, particularly as numerous variables changed over periods of time. As a result, theoretical assumptions frequently broke down, allowing critics to claim proof that such formulaic approaches were useless and that "economic laws" did not exist.

However, statistical and mathematical sciences evolved rapidly during the 19th century. One important discovery was the method of multiple regression, where several variables would comprise a single prediction. With adequate data, a statistician could provide a solution for an unknown variable.

In 1907, the Italian statistician Benini became the first to apply regression analysis to economics, providing viable demand characteristics for the coffee market. Benini's work was expanded upon a decade later by Henry Moore, who derived economic conclusions using statistical estimation. In doing so, Moore created "statistical economics," a school of thought that would provide a foundation for econometrics.

Palgrave's claims that Pawel Ciompa was the first economist to use the term "econometrics," publishing it in a paper in 1910. However, Ciompa probably didn't understand the emerging science as well as Ragnar Frisch, who must be credited with establishing an epistimological foundation for econometrics.

Frisch wrote that econometrics is not analogous to economic statistics, economic theory, or to applied mathematics. Instead, he wrote, "Each of these viewpoints is a necessary, but not by itself sufficient, condition for a real understanding of the quantitative relations in modern economic life. It is the *unification* of all three that is powerful." Econometrics provided the method for that unification.

When Frisch wrote these words in 1933, statistics and computing methods had evolved to a point where they could handle many of the complex mechanical variables facing the econometrician. However, sampling theory remained a weak area of this new science.

Critics maintained that, despite significance tests, errors were inherent in sampling methods. An observation of a sample of 5000 or so subjects could provide a telling view of the entire population, but only within certain degrees of accuracy. But sampling had never been applied to economics in such a way because the margins of error inherent in statistical methods exceeded the tolerances most economists were willing to accept. Sampling would permit the introduction of random errors into the analysis, providing a potential for wider corruption of data.

Econometrics was most vociferously denounced by John Maynard Keynes, whose 1936 *General Theory* established a new basis for the study of macroeconomics. Keynes' ideas were especially popular at the time because economists were struggling to gain some understanding of the factors that produced the Great Depression and yearned for a mathematical justification of this model.

But while Keynes provided a formidably logical theory about the relationships between macroeconomic phenomena, he lacked a mathematical proof to support it. Nonetheless, he criticized the application of statistical sampling methods to macroeconomic phenomena specifically because the data was, by definition, *not exactly correct*. The introduction of probabilities, he feared, would drive analysis away from greater accuracy, rather than toward it.

Haavelmo provided a powerful defense of statistical sampling of data by arguing that the product of such analysis could and should be expressed only in terms of probabilities. The data derived from sampling did not necessarily represent reality, it merely provided a hypothetical starting point from which analysis might proceed.

Haavelmo was interested in inference and estimation, not a single, solid correct answer. He maintained that the absolute accuracy of the data was irrelevant. Even with the inclusion of random errors, defensible statements about reality could be made with confidence factors that would allow an assumption that the data is "correct for practical purposes."

Furthermore, Haavelmo stated that sampling shouldn't be used specifically to test and summarily reject economic theories. Instead, it should be applied simply to provide a basis for the analysis of policies and to help judge the relative validity of general economic models.

The availability of better **time series** data and the development of computing capability and statistical methods permitted the application of econometrics to macroeconomic models, specifically Keynes' models. It is ironic, considering Keynes' earlier skepticism, that his own theories helped to legitimize econometrics.

Economists were elated with the prospect that econometric analysis could provide empirical basis for their hitherto vague and imperfect theories. Fortunately for econometricians, the 1950s and 1960s were relatively stable decades, providing few complications for the standard and somewhat simple Keynesian approach. There were no major disruptions that could cause time-delayed economic shockwaves that might trigger other shocks for years on end. Such externalities threatened to challenge basic Keynesian assumptions.

But this is exactly what happened during the 1970s, as a result of the Vietnam War, the OPEC oil embargo, and the suspension of the Bretton Woods agreements (A United Nations Monetary and Financial Conference held at Bretton Woods, N.H., in 1944, that established the **International Monetary Fund** and the **World Bank**. The monetary policy conceived at Bretton Woods commits every participating country to keepits currency within a percentage point or two of an agreed dollar value). Econometric analysis was overwhelmed by the combination, forcing Keynesian monetarism to abandon policy making by econometrics and concentrate on developing the micro-foundations it had always lacked.

Much of the weakness in macroeconomic policies was due to inherent weaknesses in the econometric methods that were used to justify them. The statistical methods of inference and estimation produced rigid linear regressions and quadratic functions. Dealing only in aggregates, macroeconomics operated only in terms of "representative households" and "representative firms." This approach, using averages, was ill-suited for explaining specific economic microcosms that were responsible for producing the deviations that so frustrated econometric analysis.

MODERN ECONOMETRICS

The work of Jan Tinbergen and Trygve Haavelmo provided a basis for econometric analysis of the Keynesian/monetarist approach of stabilizing the economy through monetary and fiscal policy.

Following Keynes' theory, econometricians analyzed the relationships between consumption, disposable income, and **gross national product** (GNP) to develop predictive capabilities about these factors. The functions they developed were highly complex, representing hundreds of economic variables deemed significant.

For illustrative purposes, these functions can be simply expressed in terms of consumption, disposable income, and gross national product. The consumption function is expressed as $C = a + bDI$, where C is consumption, a is the intercept, and b is the straight-line slope (the change in C from a one unit change DI) of DI, which is disposable income.

The disposable income function is expressed as $DI = Y - T$, where Y is gross nation product and T represents tax receipts. GNP, meanwhile, is expressed as $Y = C + I + G$, where again C is consumption, I is investment, and G represents government spending.

To demonstrate how the approach works, assume that government spending, tax receipts, and investment are not affected by the interrelationships in the formulas; they are *exogenous variables* whose values are determined outside the model. Consumption, disposable income, and GNP are *endogenous variables*, whose values are determined within the model.

The econometrician uses these assumptions to develop forecasts of the endogenous variables from forecasts of the exogenous variables simply by formulaic substitution.

An observation of consumption can be derived from a scatter diagram and least squares analysis. This will provide a simple regression with an intercept and slope. Assume the intercept is $200 billion and the slope is 0.8, yielding a consumption function where

$$C = 200 + (0.8)DI$$

This can be substituted into the GNP function as

$$Y = 200 + (0.8)DI + I + G$$

The formula for disposable income is then substituted, to give

$$Y = 200 + (0.8)(Y\text{-}T) + I + G$$

Expressed another way,

$$Y = 200 + (0.8)Y - (0.8)T + I + G$$

Subtracting (0.8)Y from both side of the equation leaves

$$(0.2)Y = 200 - (0.8)T + I + G$$

Dividing both sides by 0.2 leaves

$$Y = \frac{200 + I + G - (0.8)T}{0.2}$$

Solving the math is simple,

$$Y = 1000 + 5I + 5G - 4T$$

By adding in the values for the forecasted exogenous variables, the formula will produce a forecast for GNP. Assume investment to be $500 billion, government spending to be $300 billion and tax receipts to total $400 billion. The result is:

$$Y = \$1000 + \$2500 + \$1500 - \$1600$$

or

$$Y = \$3400 \ billion$$

Again, the actual inputs used to forecast GNP are substantially more complex than those in this simple model. Each exogenous input must be individually forecasted through additional statistical measurements, and corrections made over time.

An observation of the effects of each of these inputs over time will produce an indication of how they might affect other variables. It is in this realm that econometric data may be used to help shape policy. For instance, a change in taxation is likely to affect investment, disposable income, and consumption. But the question is, to what degree?

After the economic crises of the 1970s, government policy makers, particularly in the Thatcher and Reagan Administrations, abandoned Keynesian monetarism in favor of a neoclassical macroeconomic approach. However, econometrics remained an integral part of policy research. The economic theories embraced in the United States and the United Kingdom during the 1980s were guided by and modified with econometric data.

In the policy making realm, these advisors believed that a massive tax cut would stimulate investment, eliminate undercapacity, and create a supply driven demand. Instead, the shortfall in government revenues from lower taxes had to be covered with massive loans, and the ballooning debt overran whatever gains had been realized from the tax cut.

At the time, few economists believed such an approach would work, and econometric analysis of the strategy suggests that it did not. The fact that Reagan administration policy makers used econometric analysis to evaluate their theory says nothing about the validity of their theory. Econometrics merely applies an economic theory—and if its assumptions are wrong, the analysis will be wrong.

One of the major factors contributing to the longevity of the econometric approach is its thorough grounding in the natural sciences—and, some would argue, its aspiration to *become* a legitimate natural science. This grounding has become more firm, despite the occurrence of extremely disruptive events, through the perfection of method, the exponential growth in computing power, and greater accuracy of the data collected.

Furthermore, economic theories, upon which econometrics depends for its methodology, evolved significantly. Some of these changes occurred as a result of the shocks during the 1970s, providing opportunities for theories to be tested under extreme circumstances.

Econometric analysis is only as good as the instructions provided by the theory that drives it. It is not a separate science merely related to economics, but an application of economic theory. Thus, it may be considered a rather dry, purely computational science—except for the fact that it provides an indication of the validity of the theories applied to it.

Tinbergen himself innocently suggested that econometricians were not economic theorists, but a type of laboratory technician whose job was to take a theory, plug in numbers, and see if it worked.

[John Simley]

FURTHER READING:

Baumol, Wm. J. and Alan S. Blinder. *Economics, Principles and Policy*, 2nd ed., New York: Harcourt Brace Jovanovich, 1982.

Eatwell, J., Ed. *The New Palgrave Dictionary of Economics*. London: Macmillan, 1987.

Fischer, Stanley and Rudiger Hornbusch. *Economics*. New York: McGraw-Hill, 1983.

Johnson, Robert R. *Elementary Statistics*, 3rd ed., North Scituate, MA: Duxbury Press, 1980.

Trager, James. *The People's Chronology*, 2nd ed., New York: Henry Holt and Company, 1992.

ECONOMIC COMMUNITY OF WEST AFRICAN STATES (ECOWAS)

The Economic Community of West African States (ECOWAS) was established May 28, 1975 with the signing of the Treaty of Lagos in that Nigerian city. The community is headquartered in Lagos, Nigeria and has 16 members:

Benin, Burkina Faso, Cape Verde Islands, Ivory Coast, Gambia, Ghana, Guinea, Guinea-Bissau, Liberia, Mali, Mauritania, Niger, Nigeria, Senegal, Sierra Leone, and Togo. Cape Verde was not an original signer but joined ECOWAS in 1977. The purpose of the community is to promote economic cooperation and integration among members states with the goal of forming a West African economic union.

STRUCTURE OF ECOWAS

ECOWAS is governed by the authority of heads of states and government. Other ECOWAS executive authorities include the Chairman, the Council of Ministers, the Executive Secretary, and the Community Tribunal. Four commissions oversee specific spheres of economic activity: Trade, Customs, Immigration, Monetary and Payments; Industry, Agriculture and Natural Resources; Transport, Communications and Energy; and Social and Cultural Affairs. The community's official languages are French and English. In 1991 the organization had an annual operating budget of approximately 7 million U.S. dollars.

ECOWAS is divided between former French colonies and former British colonies because of their differing cultural and economic traditions. A third group of countries uses the U.S. dollar as their monetary standard. These differences in culture, heritage, demographics, and fiscal orientation have had a destabilizing influence on ECOWAS.

When it was founded, ECOWAS had numerous short term goals including elimination of customs duties, abolishment of trade restrictions, establishment of a common customs tariff, and coordination of economic, industrial, and **monetary policy**. There were also plans for allowing the free movement of labor, goods, and capital on an intra-community level; common **infrastructure** development projects; and broad plans for economic, political, and monetary integration. The long range ECOWAS calendar called for the removal of intra-community import duties by 1986. Planners also envisioned a full customs union and a common external tariff by 1991. Despite the threat of divisive problems, in November of 1976 enough governments had formally ratified the Treaty of Lagos to make it operational.

To further complicate matters, most ECOWAS nations had colonial economies based on producing and exporting primary **commodities**. Subsequently, they lacked impetus for intra-regional trade. A persistent destabilization of commodity prices and disparities in the economic development of member countries were other leftover problems of colonial rule. Also, the governments of ECOWAS member nations kept tariffs high because they were a major source of tax revenue.

In 1979 ECOWAS formulated an Industrial Policy and Programme that was a model for balanced and equitable industrial development. At a 1981 meeting a mutual defense pact was agreed upon in principle. Other summits throughout the 1980s stressed setting aside national considerations and developing a variety of economic and revitalization schemes as well as joint programs with other African and European economic unions. Very few of these plans were implemented, however, and by the 1990 summit, a general malaise had descended upon the community. Many countries did not attend this summit because of their own pressing internal problems, financial difficulties of ECOWAS, and the organization's failure to set and attain realistic goals. Those countries that did attend the 1990 summit, however, called for a single monetary zone by 1994 and a mediation board to settle intra-community disagreements.

LIBERIAN CRISIS

In late summer of 1990 a devastating civil war broke out in Liberia. ECOWAS became enmeshed in the fighting and eventually sent in 4,000 troops under its banner. The purpose of the peacekeeping force was to restore order, organize an interim government, and supervise national elections. Only five member countries committed troops, however, with other members remaining neutral or vigorously protesting what they regarded as ECOWAS's involvement in the internal affairs of a sovereign nation. By 1993 a tenuous peace was achieved due in large part to ECOWAS's military intervention. The signing of the peace accord brought about a healing of the rift among ECOWAS members, largely divided along francophone-anglophone lines. The achievement of peace in Liberia, no matter how tenuous, produced a revitalized ECOWAS at its 1993 mid-summer summit. In a spirit of cooperation unseen since its inception, ECOWAS members signed the Treaty of Cotonou which revised the founding Lagos treaty. The new treaty called for an enhanced decision making process and a special tax upon member countries to ensure ECOWAS funding.

COMPLICATIONS

ECOWAS has many intrinsic problems that the community has difficulty overcoming. Foremost is the diversity of the community especially along cultural, demographic, linguistic, and economic lines. The community, for instance, is divided between those countries with an English speaking heritage and those with a French orientation. This division became evident itself with the establishment of the Communuaté Economique de l'Afrique (CEA), an economic union separate from ECOWAS but formed by six francophone ECOWAS members. Ivory Coast, Senegal, Niger, Burkina Faso, Mali, and Mauritania formed CEA to counter-balance Nigerian influence in the west-African subregion. Because of other political and economic friction, two other competing economic unions, the Mano River Union and the Council of the Entente, were formed as well.

ECOWAS countries are also divided between agricultural and labor intensive economies and countries with far different stages of economic development. The ECOWAS accord also calls for the eventual free movement of labor within the community. If implemented, however, this policy would be a boon to poor countries with pools of cheap labor such as Ghana and Burkina Faso while harming relatively richer countries such as Nigeria and Ivory Coast. This dynamic was evident in 1982 when Nigeria expelled Ghanian workers. Nigeria felt the foreign workers were undercutting the wage structure of its citizens.

PROBLEM SOLVING

Short term solutions to ECOWAS's problems center on increased aid and more cooperation with other more viable economic unions, especially those in western Europe. To help attain this, ECOWAS actively seeks official development aid from the Euro-

pean Economic Community. Other goals are equitable intra-ECOWAS trade and stabilization of commodity prices and currency exchange rates.

SEE ALSO: Doing Business in Africa; East African Community (EOC)

[Michael Knes]

FURTHER READING:

Asante, S.K.B. *The Political Economy of Regionalism in Africa: A Decade of the Economic Community of West African States.* Praeger, 1986.

Ndebbio, John ''Science, technology and development in ECOWAS.'' *Journal of Asian and African Studies.* Jan.-Apr. 1992. pp. 114-23.

Okolo, Julias. *West African Regional Cooperation and Development.* Westview Press 1990.

ECONOMIC CONDITIONS

Economic conditions can be considered the economic characteristics that describe the state of an economy. Often, people comment that the economy is in terrible shape, that the economy is doing well, or that the economy is inherently sound. All such statements are based on certain characteristics of the economy that the issuer of the statement has in mind.

THE KEY CHARACTERISTICS OF AN ECONOMY

There are a large number of variables or characteristics that are used in gauging the health of an economy, with four of them usually referred to as the key macroeconomic variables in gauging the state or health of an economy: aggregate output or income, the **unemployment** rate, the inflation rate, and the interest rate. There are, however, numerous additional measures or variables that are collected and used to understand the behavior of an economy. In the United States, for example, additional measures include: the index of **leading economic indicators** (which gives an idea where the economy is headed in the near future); retail sales (which indicate the strength of consumer demand in the economy); factory orders, especially for big ticket items (which indicate the future growth in output, since the orders will have to be filled); housing starts (robust increase in housing starts are usually taken as a sign of good growth in the future); the consumer confidence index (which indicates how likely consumers are to make favorable decisions to buy both durable and nondurable goods, services, and homes). Other variables tracked are more innocuous than the ones included in the preceding list, such as: aluminum production, steel production, paper and paperboard production, industrial production, hourly earnings, weekly earnings, factory shipments, orders for durable goods, new factory orders, new-home sales, existing-home sales, business inventories, initial jobless claims, help-wanted advertising, purchasing manager's survey, and the foreign **trade deficit**.

OUTPUT/INCOME. An economy's overall economic activity is summarized by a measure of aggregate output. Since the production or output of goods and services generates **income**, any aggregate output measure is closely associated with an aggregate income measure. The United States uses an aggregate output concept known as the **gross domestic product** (GDP). The GDP is a measure of all currently produced goods and services valued at their market prices. One should notice several features of the GDP measure. First, only currently produced goods (produced during the relevant year) are included. This means that if you buy a 150-year old classic Tudor house, it does not count towards the GDP, but the service rendered by your real estate agent in the process of buying the house does. Secondly, only final goods and services are counted. In order to avoid double counting, intermediate goods used in the production of other goods and services, do not enter the GDP. For example, steel used in the production of automobiles is not valued separately. Finally, all goods and services included in the GDP are evaluated at their market prices. Thus, these prices reflect the prices consumers pay at the retail level, including indirect taxes such as local sales **taxes**.

A measure similar to GDP is the **gross national product** (GNP). Until recently, the government used the GNP as the main measure of the nation's economic activity. The difference between GNP and GDP is rather small. The GDP excludes incomes earned abroad by U.S. firms and residents and includes earnings of foreign firms and residents in the United States. Several other measures of output and income are derived from the GNP. These include the net national product or NNP (which subtracts from the GNP an allowance for wear and tear on plants and equipment, known as depreciation); the national income (which mainly subtracts indirect taxes from the NNP); the personal income (which measures the income received by persons from all sources and is arrived at by subtracting from the national income such items as corporate profit tax payments and social security contributions that individuals do not receive, and adding such items as transfer payments that individuals do receive but are not part of the national income); and the personal disposable income (which subtracts personal tax payments such as income taxes from the personal income measure). While all these measures move up and down in a related manner, it is personal disposable income that is intimately tied to

consumer demand for goods and services, the most dominant component of aggregate demand.

It should be noted that the aggregate income/output measures discussed above are usually quoted both in current prices (in "nominal" terms) and in constant dollars (in "real" terms). The latter are adjusted for inflation and are thus most widely used since they are not subject to distortions introduced by changes in prices.

When is the economy considered to be in good shape? Of course, zero growth in the real gross domestic product (a stagnant economy) or negative growth in the real GDP (a shrinking or a recessionary economy) is not a good reflection on the economy. Positive growth is considered desirable. Whether or not a given positive growth rate is good enough, however, depends on whether it can be sustained without generating serious inflationary pressures. Once an economy reaches full employment, a 3-percent growth in the real GDP is considered sustainable on a long-term basis—higher rates are considered inflationary. Nevertheless, when an economy is coming out of a **recession**, a growth rate of more than 3-percent may not generate a serious inflationary pressure due to unemployed resources. Thus, how well an economy is doing in terms of real GDP growth should be judged on the basis of the 3-percent benchmark, with appropriate upward adjustment for slack in the economy.

UNEMPLOYMENT. The level of **employment** is the next crucial macroeconomic variable. The employment level is often quoted in terms of the **unemployment** rate, defined as the fraction of labor force not working (but actively seeking employment). Contrary to what one may expect, the labor force does not consist of all able-bodied persons of working age. Instead, it is defined as consisting of those working and those not working but seeking work. Thus, the labor force as defined leaves out people who are not working but also not seeking work—termed by economists as being voluntarily unemployed. For purposes of government macroeconomic policies, only people who are involuntarily unemployed really matter.

For various reasons, it is not possible to bring down the unemployment rate to zero in the best of circumstances. Realistically, economists expect a fraction of the labor force to be unemployed at all times—this fraction for the U.S. labor market has been estimated to be 6 percent. The 6 percent unemployment rate is often referred to as the bench mark unemployment rate. In effect, at 6 percent unemployment, the economy is considered to be at full employment.

Whether or not the economy is doing well in terms of the unemployment rate depends on how far this rate is above the 6 percent benchmark. If the economy has an unemployment rate around 6 percent, it is said to be doing well. Higher unemployment rates reflect worse economic conditions. During the Bush recession, the unemployment rate peaked at 7.7 percent; during the Reagan recession, it peaked at 9.7 percent; and during the Great Depression, it reached more than 25 percent.

INFLATION RATE. The third key macroeconomic variable is inflation. The inflation rate is defined as the rate of change in the price level. Most economies face positive rates of inflation year after year. The price level, in turn, is measured by a **price index**, which measures the level of prices of goods and services at a point in time. The number of items included in a price index varies depending on the objective of the index. Government agencies periodically report three kinds of price indexes, each having their particular advantages and uses. The first index is called the consumer price index (CPI); it measures the average retail prices paid by consumers for goods and services bought by them. A couple thousand items, typically bought by average households, are included in this index.

A second price index used to measure the inflation rate is called the producer price index (PPI). It is a much broader measure than the consumer price index. The PPI measures the wholesale prices of approximately 3,000 items. The items included in this index are those that are typically used by producers (manufacturers and businesses) and thus include many raw materials and semifinished goods. The third measure of inflation is the called the implicit GDP price deflator. This index measures the prices of all goods and services included in the calculation of the current GDP. It is the broadest measure of price level.

The three measures of the inflation rate are most likely to move in the same direction, even though not to the same extent. Differences can arise due to the differing number of goods and services included in compiling the three indexes. In general, if one hears about the inflation rate in the popular media, it is most likely to be the one based on the CPI.

A zero percent inflation may appear ideal, but it is neither practical nor desirable. A moderate rate of inflation—1 to 2 percent—is considered desirable by a vast majority of economists. An inflation rate of up to 5 percent is tolerable. Double-digit inflation rates, however, are definitely considered undesirable by most economists.

THE INTEREST RATE. The concept of **interest rates** used by economists is the same as that used widely by other people. The interest rate is invariably quoted in nominal terms—that is, the rate is not adjusted for inflation. Thus, the commonly followed interest rate is actually the nominal interest rate. Nevertheless, there are literally hundreds of nominal interest rates, including: savings account rate, six-month certificate of deposit rate, 15-year mortgage rate, variable mortgage rate, 30-year Treasury bond rate, 10-year General Motors bond rate, and the commercial bank prime-lending rate. One can see from these examples that the nominal interest rate has two key attributes—the duration of lending/borrowing involved and the identity of the borrower.

Fortunately, while the hundreds of interest rates that one encounters may appear baffling, they are closely linked to each other. Two characteristics that account for this linkage are the risk worthiness of the borrower and the maturity of the loan involved. So, for example, the interest rate on a 6-month **Treasury bill** is related to that on a 30-year Treasury bond, as bonds/loans of different maturities command different rates. Also, a 30-year General Motors bond will carry a higher interest rate than a 30-year Treasury bond, as a General Motors bond is riskier than a Treasury bond.

Finally, one should note that the nominal interest rate does not represent the real cost of borrowing or the real return on lending. To understand the real cost or return, one must consider the inflation-adjusted nominal rate, called the real interest rate. Tax and other considerations also influence the real cost/return. But the real interest rate is a very important concept in understanding the main incentives behind borrowing or lending.

The desirable level of the nominal interest rate is linked to the desirable level of the inflation rate. If we consider that an inflation rate of 1 to 2 percent is desirable, then the short-term nominal interest rate will lie in the 4 to 5 percent range (assuming a real interest rate of 3 percent).

VARIABLES THAT PROJECT FUTURE ECONOMIC CONDITIONS

There are a number of economic variables that are used to project or forecast future economic conditions. There exist theoretical as well as empirical reasons why economists believe that certain variables are harbingers of future economic activities. Some of the variables often used by economists and policy makers to gauge future economic conditions are briefly described below.

HOUSING STARTS. Changes in the number of houses being built (simply called housing starts by economists) have an important implication for the direction in which the economy is headed. Notice first that houses are bulky items involving large sums of money—in fact, in the United States, a home is considered an individual's biggest investment. Thus, potentially, housing starts can either lead to a powerful expansion in the economy (by augmenting the aggregate demand) or a serious downturn (by reducing the aggregate demand), depending on the direction and the magnitude of the change in housing starts. Housing starts project the future state of the economy for two main reasons. First, once construction on a house starts it will, most likely, be completed. Thus, work on a ''started house'' will continue for several months. Second, once the new house is completed, the first occupant of the newly completed house may need to buy additional items (such as a refrigerator, washer, or dryer) to make the house comfortable. This provides a secondary (and, generally, quite large) push to the aggregate demand for goods and services in the economy. Because of these reasons, housing starts are routinely used by economists and participants in financial markets to gauge the future direction of the economy.

BUILDING PERMITS ISSUED. Building permits indicate the intention of builders to start building new homes and buildings. Thus, the number of building permits issued today tells us something about the number of housing starts in the near future, with the usual implications for changes in output and employment. If the number of building permits issued is rising, it bodes well for future economic growth. A falling number of building permits issued, on the other hand, has the opposite implication.

Building permits, by nature, can project future economic conditions even further than housing starts, since a building permit must be obtained before construction on a house begins. Nevertheless, one should notice that building permits are far less potent in projecting future growth than housing starts. Although houses started are normally completed, a building permit obtained does not imply that a house will necessarily be built—a change in circumstances can force the builders to defer or scrap their building plans.

NEW FACTORY ORDERS. New factory orders indicate new orders for goods by retail outlets or other businesses. An increase in these orders will generally lead manufacturers to increase production of the items ordered. Thus, an increase in new factory orders is a precursor to an increase in output and employment in the economy. A fall in factory orders will have the opposite effect.

While looking at new factory orders, economists particularly concentrate on big ticket items, items that involve relatively large sums of money. Big ticket items can be consumer goods, such as automobiles, washers, or dryers, or capital goods, such as machines and equipment. An increase in orders for big ticket items provides a big forward push to the economy not only because these items have to be produced, but also because they can generate secondary demands for raw materials. For example, an increase in automobile production would necessarily increase the demand for steel, causing steel production to go up as well.

BUSINESS INVENTORIES. Businesses maintain certain levels of inventories to meet unexpected demands for their products—economists often refer to businesses' usual inventory levels as normal levels of inventories. When firms stock up on inventories, output and employment rise. Rising or falling inventories serve to indicate the future direction of output and employment as well. This can be explained as follows. Suppose that business inventories rise far above the normal level because firms are unable to sell their current output of goods. Businesses have only one sure cure to trim the piling inventories—cut future. Thus, a rise in inventories can often be precursor to a decline in output and employment in the next period. The opposite is true when business inventories fall far below the normal level. To replenish inventories, manufacturers must increase production in the near future, spurring economic growth and lowering the unemployment rate.

THE CONSUMER CONFIDENCE INDEX. The consumer confidence index is an index that attempts to measure the level of consumer confidence. This index is based on a survey of consumers regarding their outlook. An increase in the consumer confidence index implies that consumers feel more confident about the economy and their own economic well-being. A rise in the consumer confidence index is most likely to lead to an increase in consumer spending, increasing the level of aggregate demand. This, in turn, implies that output and employment will increase in the near future. By contrast, decline in the consumer confidence index will most likely lead to a decline in output and employment.

INDEX OF LEADING INDICATORS. The index of leading indicators combines several factors that are considered useful in indicating the future course of the economy. In the United States, the index of **leading economic indicators** (often abbreviated as the **LEI**) is based on about a dozen economic series that are deemed capable of **forecasting** future economic activities. Some of the important leading variables included in the construction of the LEI are: new orders for durable goods, average workweek, building permits, stock prices, certain wholesale prices, and claims for unemployment insurance.

If the index of leading indicators keeps increasing, then economists take this as a sign that the economy will keep expanding (if it is already growing) or that it will start expanding (if the economy is in a recession or if it is experiencing stagnation). The opposite is the case if the index starts to decline. In that case, economists take this as a warning sign that the economy will slow down or even dip into a recession (if the economy is growing) or that the downturn will become worse (if the economy is facing a recession or stagnation).

While changes in the index of leading indicators have been successful in forecasting future economic activity, the LEI has failed several times in the past to live up to its predictions about the future of the U.S. economy.

THE MOST IMPORTANT VARIABLES

As is apparent from the preceding discussion, economists and financial observers use observations on numerous economic variables to understand the behavior of an economy. However, the four key macroeconomic variables—aggregate output measure, the unemployment rate, the inflation rate, and the interest rate—do summarize the most important characteristics of a macroeconomy. These four variables can be reduced to an even smaller group because they are related.

Notice that if the real gross domestic output goes up, employment will go up sooner or later. Producers may first request overtime from existing workers if they are not sure whether the increased level of output can be maintained in the future. But as soon as they feel reasonably sure that the increased output level is relatively permanent, they will hire additional permanent workers. This will raise the level of employment of the labor force in the economy and will, in general, reduce the unemployment rate. Thus, the aggregate output measure and the unemployment rate variable go hand in hand. Either will suffice to convey roughly the same information about economic conditions in the economy. Of the two, it is has been customary to use the unemployment rate because it is more readily understood than a measure of aggregate output such as GDP.

Similarly, the nominal interest rate and the inflation rate are linked. If the inflation rate goes up, so does the nominal interest rate. This is because people care about the real interest rate (the interest rate adjusted for the inflation rate). Thus, if the inflation rate goes up, the real value of a given nominal interest rate declines. As a result, savers require higher nominal interest rates in order to be compensated for the higher inflation rate. Usually, the difference between the nominal interest rate and the inflation rate is 3 percent—a level at which lenders feel comfortable lending. Thus, the nominal interest rate and the inflation rate also go hand in hand. Out of these two variables, it has been customary to use the inflation rate to describe economic conditions because the public readily understands it.

Thus, the minimum number of characteristics used to describe economic conditions are two: the unemployment rate and the inflation rate. They both have negative connotations—neither a higher unemployment rate nor a higher inflation rate is considered desirable. Even reporting information on these two variables gets a little complicated as it is widely believed that there is a trade-off between the unemployment rate and the inflation rate. That is, macroeconomic policy makers can follow an economic policy that may lower one rate while increasing the other. Thus, an expansionary monetary policy may reduce the unemployment rate by increasing the aggregate demand in the economy—due to a lower interest rate, consumers are able to finance additional spending through borrowing, and businesses are able to invest more as the cost of borrowing goes down. The upward pressure on aggregate demand, however, also places upward pressure on the price level, raising the inflation rate.

Because of the above mentioned trade-off, it is desirable to examine information on both the unemployment rate and the inflation rate to better understand the economic conditions in the economy. Sometimes, these two variables are combined, in an attempt to give a better picture than when unemployment and inflation rates are looked at separately. The sum of the unemployment rate and the inflation rate has been dubbed as the misery index. The adjective "misery" alludes to the negative connotations associated with the unemployment and inflation rates. Adding them together takes care of the trade-off—one rate may go up and the second may go down, but the misery index captures both. Thus, the higher the value of the misery index, the worse are the overall economic conditions. One must, however, realize that the use of a single broad concept such as the misery index is probably not adequate to describe economic conditions properly. At the bare minimum, one should use the unemployment rate and the inflation rate separately to summarize the economic conditions of an economy.

[Anandi P. Sahu]

FURTHER READING:

Froyen, Richard T. *Macroeconomics: Theories and Policies*, 4th ed. Macmillan Publishing Company, 1993.

Gordon, Robert J. *Macroeconomics*, 6th ed. HarperCollins College Publishers, 1993.

Sommers, Albert T. *U.S. Economy Demystified*. Lexington Books, 1985.

ECONOMIC DEVELOPMENT

The term "economic development" is widely used by the ordinary public and the popular media. The concept, however, is not quite as well understood as its frequent use may suggest. First one must realize that the term "economic development" in one form or an other keeps surfacing in the popular media. Instances of economic miracles (reflecting favorable effects of economic development) regularly make headlines. Japan was in ruins after World War II. Within 30 years, Japan emerged as an economic superpower and one of two main economic rivals of the United States (Germany being the other). Similarly, South Korea's economic situation was widely regarded as hopeless after the devastation of the Korean War, but it too Korea has turned into another Asian economic miracle—South Korea now challenges Japan for a share of the export markets in the United States and other countries. The economies of Taiwan and Hong Kong are in such great shape that even Mainland China (the country they were once part of) views them with great respect. Malaysia and Singapore are also cited as examples of economic success stories. Malaysia had only half of the per capita income of Chile as recently as 1963; only 25 years later Malaysia had caught up to Chile. While these success stories have grabbed public attention, one must also notice that many Asian, African, and Latin American economies continue to languish in utter poverty.

While referring to underdeveloped countries many different terms are used. The terms used are intended to describe the stage of development of these countries in comparison to more developed countries. As a result, the terms used are almost always in pairs. The most dramatic way of referring to the two sets of countries is to make a distinction between backward and advanced economies, or between traditional and modern economies. As the term "backward" carries a negative connotation, it is rarely used these days. It is much more popular to put all countries of the world on a continuum based on the degree of economic development. Using this criterion, several pairs of terms are employed in distinguishing countries with different degrees of economic development—developed and underdeveloped countries, more developed and less developed countries (the latter are often simply referred to as LDCs), developing and developed economies. As the terms "less developed countries" and "developing countries" embody a sense of optimism, their use has become commonplace. Developed countries are also referred to as industrialized countries. Countries that have recently developed are referred to as the newly industrialized economies.

The distinction among economies is also made based simply on income levels, where income is expressed in per capita terms. Based on the income criterion, countries have been classified into poor and rich economies. The **World Bank** has further refined this division by categorizing poorer countries into low income (less than $400 in per capita income in 1983) and middle income (per capita income between $400 and $6,900 in 1983). a third category consists of five developing countries (Oman, Libya, Saudi Arabia, Kuwait, and the United Arab Emirates) that have relatively high per capita income (in the $6,300 to $23,000 range in 1983), but have economies that are more traditional than industrialized. These economies are referred to by the World Bank as the "capital-surplus oil exporters." Finally, developed or industrialized economies themselves are subdivided into market economies (capitalist economies of the West) and non-market economies (Communist or centrally planned economies of Eastern Europe). The latter distinction is now largely irrelevant as Russia and countries in Eastern Europe are all following the capitalist route to economic development. These economies are referred to in the popular media as belonging to a new category called "emerging economies."

ECONOMIC DEVELOPMENT AND ECONOMIC GROWTH

As one can see, labels used to distinguish between economically developed and developing countries vary quite a bit. The terms used to describe the economic development process itself, however, are much more rigorously defined. For example, while the terms "economic growth" and "economic development" are often used interchangeably, there is an important distinction between these two terms. The term "economic growth" refers to an increase (or growth) in real national income or product expressed usually as per capita income. National income or product itself is commonly expressed in terms of a measure of the aggregate output of the economy called **gross national product**. Per capita income then is simply gross national product divided by the population of the country. When the GNP of a nation rises, whatever the means of achieving the outcome, economists refer to it as a rise in economic growth. The term "economic development," on the other hand, implies much more. This can best be illustrated with the help of an example. If we look at the developments in South Korea and Libya since 1960, we discover fundamentally different situations. Both these countries experienced a huge rise in the real per capita income, but the reasons for the increases are vastly different. Libya's increased per capita income resulted from the discovery of crude oil reserves—Libya harvested these oil resources with the help of foreign corporations that were largely staffed by foreign technicians. Libya thus produced a single product of great importance that was exported mainly to the United States and Western Europe. While Libyans (both the government and people) received large incomes from selling oil, they did not play a major role in producing that income—their income increased based on a windfall gain.

Economists do not usually consider Libya's increased per capita income as an instance of economic development. "Economic development" embodies a greater number of characteristics than a rise in per capita income alone—it implies certain fundamental changes in the structure of the national economy. South Korea provides an example of a country that has experienced economic development. The South Korean economy has also undergone a large increase in its per capita income. In addition, it has also witnessed some important structural changes. Two of the most important changes taking place in South Korea are: (1) A rising share of industry in the total national output (the real gross national product), and the accompanying falling share of the agricultural sector in GNP; (2) An increasing percentage of the total population of South Korea lives in cities rather than in the countryside. In addition to these two fundamental changes, a nation undergoing economic development goes through a number of additional changes. The demographic composition of the population (age groups that comprise the total population) changes as economic development progresses. Consumption patterns of individuals also change—people no longer have to spend most of their income on food and other necessities. Instead, they spend a small fraction of their income on necessities and the remaining large fraction on consumer durables and items that pertain to leisure activities

A key characteristic of economic development is that the people substantially participate in the development process and in changing the fundamental structure of the economy. While some foreign involvement is generally inevitable, for economic growth to be described as economic development, the people of the country must participate not only in the enjoyment of benefits from the rise in per capita income, but also in the production process itself. Moreover, economic growth must confer benefits on a broad group of individuals—if it benefits only a small minority, it is not deemed as economic development. It should be noted that while much more is implied by economic development than economic growth, there can be no economic development without economic growth (that is, a rise in the real per capita income).

THE ROLE OF SCIENCE AND INNOVATION IN ECONOMIC DEVELOPMENT

Perhaps the most important prerequisite of economic development is the aspiring nation's access to the discoveries of modern science and innovators to adapt these discoveries to the needs of marketplace. It would be impossible to imagine the mighty industrial economies of the twentieth century in the absence of the technological knowledge arising out of many fields such as physics, chemistry, and biology. A large majority of products used today did not exist before the advent of modern science. While modern science is considered absolutely crucial for the economic development of a nation, no country today is fully cut off from the main fruits of science. Even the poorest

developing economies have access to the scientific knowledge, while fruits of scientific discoveries are often embodied in many domestically produced goods (some of them exported to more advanced countries). While developing countries do not have to rediscover the basic laws of thermodynamics, they do have to convert the scientific discoveries into products and processes—successful conversions are called innovations. The latter task is often more difficult than discoveries of pure science. Thus, as an alternative to internal innovations, developing countries may be able to copy others' innovations or collaborate to learn from those that have succeeded in converting scientific discoveries into desirable products or processes. In fact, technology transfer has become an important aspect of the quest for development. As the latest technology also tends to be more efficient and productive, developing countries attempt to borrow these in some fashion. Many of the latest innovations come with patent rights, and thus the innovators of these products or processes must consent. As a consequence of this constraint, developing countries have resorted to use of the **joint venture**, in which a firm from a developing country collaborates with a firm from an advanced country in a production process involving advanced (and sometimes not so advanced) technology.

While scientific knowledge is important for economic development, most economists assume that most developing countries have access to basic scientific discoveries. Further, while most economists believe that a nation's failure to achieve economic development is mainly the result of economic forces within the country, both economic and non-economic barriers exist to economic development.

ECONOMIC BARRIERS TO DEVELOPMENT

Different models of economic growth and development reveal that capital formation is an important vehicle of economic development. Capital formation essentially refers to an accumulation of capital resources that are used in the process of production (such as machines, plants, equipments, buildings, etc.). Of course, capital assets will also embody technology. Sometimes, capital formation itself can be considered to have two components: non human and **human capital**. A machine or a factory shed is an example of non human capital. Human capital formation takes the form of education and training of individuals. Both human and non human capital formations are important as they both increase productivity and lead to economic growth. Moreover, a non human capital asset embodying an advanced technology also requires a better-trained human operator of the machine. The view that capital formation was central to economic growth, called capital fundamentalism, was reflected in the development strategies and plans of many countries over decades. Thus, the solution to the problem of economic development was viewed primarily as securing enough investment funds to generate a certain targeted rate of economic growth.

Capital formation is essentially based on two factors: generating the desired level of savings and converting them into investment in capital equipment (and/or human capital formation). When savings from domestic sources were deemed inadequate to generate the targeted rate of economic growth, foreign aid donors were approached. Foreign aid and developmental assistance from advanced industrialized countries in the 1950s and 1960s were justified by the need to fill the savings gap. During those days, capital shortage in developing countries was considered as the single most important barrier to economic growth and development. A heavy emphasis was put particularly on designing economic development plans that embodied this point of view. Pakistan's third five-year plan in the early 1960s, for example, showed a heavy initial requirement of capital and a consequent need for an inflow of foreign capital (in the form of foreign aid). It was believed that a large initial injection of foreign aid would spur additional domestic savings, ultimately reducing the foreign aid requirement in the long run.

It is now widely recognized that abundance of savings and capital formation are not adequate to guarantee an accelerated pace of economic development, in particular when capital is deployed in low-productivity projects. There are many examples of capital being employed in an improper manner. Examples include the large-scale showcase steel mills and thousands of small inefficient hydroelectric plants. Moreover, investment projects financed by foreign savings, even if highly productive, may have little effect on economic growth if the recipient country's policies are not well suited to capture a fair share of returns from these projects. Indeed, such was the experience of several natural-resources-rich countries before the mid-1960s. These countries had little to show at the end from major foreign investment projects.

The crucial role of savings and investments in generating economic growth has been well established in developed industrial economies. Based on one estimate, more than 50 percent of the growth in aggregate income of nine developed countries during 1960-1975 was due to an expansion in the physical capital inputs alone. Many now believe that the very low investment rate during the 1970s and early 1980s in the United States was the primary reason for the low U.S. per capita income growth since 1970, relative to the per capita income growth in Japan and Western Europe.

While capital formation is no longer viewed as the ultimate instrument of economic development in poorer countries, it is nevertheless recognized that

even a mildly robust pace of economic growth cannot be maintained over a long time until these countries invest a sizable fraction of their gross national product. At the very minimum the investment rate (the fraction of gross national product invested) should be 15 percent and in some cases it may be required to go as high as 25 percent. The 15 to 25 percentage interval provides a range of likely requirements—the actual investment rate would depend upon the environment in which capital formation takes place and the desired rate of economic growth. Of course, the desired growth rate is generally based on the development experience of other countries. Average rate of per capita income growth in middle-income countries from 1965 to 1983 was about 3.5 percent. If developing countries desire to match the per capita income growth experienced by the middle-income countries in the post-1965 period, their per capita income will have to grow at the rate of at least six percent per year—given that the average rate of population growth in less developed countries is about 2.5 percent.

EXPORT-LED ECONOMIC GROWTH

Many low-and middle-income countries have attempted to use foreign trade, rather than foreign aid, as a vehicle of economic growth. Favoring different types of exports and imports, however, lead to different outcomes for economic growth. One such strategy is to utilize exports of primary goods (agricultural products and raw materials) to spur economic growth, often called primary-export-led growth. Even now, exports of food and raw materials remain principal means by which many developing countries generate resources to import capital equipments and other necessary inputs that are essential for their development goals. However, dependence on primary exports as a vehicle of economic development is viewed as being fraught with many difficulties.

Many third-world leaders and some economists since the late 1950s have argued that primary exports (except petroleum) cannot be used as an effective vehicle of economic growth. This belief is based on several factors. First, markets for primary products grow very slowly and, as a result, exports of primary products also grow slowly. There is an intrinsic reason for the slow growth in markets for primary products— the elasticity of demand for foods is probably less than one-half. This implies that if there is a ten percent increase in income of an advanced nation, its food requirements grow by less than five percent. Thus, imports of foods (and other primary products) would lag behind income growth in industrialized countries. Second, prices received for primary exports are relatively unfavorable. This implies that prices received for these goods will fall on world markets, relative to prices paid for manufactured products imported from industrialized nations by developing countries. Finally, export earnings from primary exports are not stable. The fluctuations in export earnings may be due to an instability in demand for the product, supply of the product, or both.

For the preceding reasons, dependence on primary exports is not preferred by developing countries, as far as possible. More and more developing countries are attempting to export manufactured products to developed nations. In most cases, these manufactured products do not embody the highest level of technology. Efforts of China and India provide examples of this change in emphasis. It should be noted that manufactured big-ticket items (embodying high technology) are still exported by advanced countries. Thus, while China may export toys and Taiwan may export assembled televisions and radios, the United States still exports airplanes. Nevertheless, exporting manufactured products has spurred economic development in many developing countries, especially in smaller economies such as Singapore, Taiwan and South Korea. More and more nations are using an export-led approach to economic development.

NON-ECONOMIC BARRIERS TO ECONOMIC DEVELOPMENT

In eyes of most economists, there is no single economic barrier to development that can explain why so few countries were able to initiate economic growth prior to the twentieth century. While savings rates in many of these countries were too low to finance investments necessary to achieve economic development, the important question then remains as to why the savings rates were low. Poverty alone cannot account for low savings rates—some poor countries in the late nineteenth century, such as Japan, were able to generate large amounts of savings needed for growth. Japan's success in mobilizing large amounts of savings was partly due to a strong governmental structure that helped extract a surplus through taxation. Thus, economic explanations alone cannot account for why particular economic barriers exist and non-economic barriers need to be considered.

POLITICAL AND GOVERNMENTAL BARRIERS. Governments and political institutions play an important role in the economic development process even in capitalist countries. While early experiences with economic development, such as England's experience during the eighteenth century, did not involve a large role for government, the role played by the government has steadily increased in importance. At the current time, if a government is unable or unwilling to play an active role in the economic development process, then the government itself is considered an obstacle to economic development.

A government can foster economic development in many ways. First and foremost, governments must create and maintain a stable political environment and a climate of peace in which modern enterprises, private or public, can flourish. China's inability to initiate modern economic growth before 1949 is largely explained by prolonged instability connected with civil war and foreign invasions. After the creation of a stable political environment when Communists took power in 1949, economic growth began. Civil strife, tribal warfare, and political instability in several African countries have prevented them from embarking on a path of serious economic development.

A stable government in itself, however, is not enough. In most cases, colonial governments were able to provide political stability—often for a prolonged period. This was the case for India under British rule and Korea under Japanese rule. Nevertheless, very few European or Japanese colonies experienced significant economic development. The benefits of the stable environment under colonial rule mainly accrued to a small group of traders and investors from the colonizing nation. Moreover, ruling Colonial nations made no serious attempt at economic development through investment in training or through promotion of industries. Many colonial nations initiated economic development strategies after gaining independence. India provides such an example. After gaining independence from the British in 1947, the Indian government started planning to develop the country in an organized way. While India is still relatively poor, it is one of a small group of countries seven or so that possess space technology.

It should also be noted that political independence does not necessarily imply that a sovereign government would pursue an active policy to promote economic development. The decisions to pursue economic development involve trade-offs—some people may become better off following economic development while others may become worse off. If political power is in the hands of those who will become worse off, the country's leaders may impede efforts towards economic development. In some instances, nations have pursued social goals rather than economic development. In Cuba, during the 1960s much effort was expended to redistribute income to benefit the poor and to improve education, rather than promote economic development. Nevertheless, sooner or later, stable governments in developing countries are bound to pursue economic development.

SOCIAL BARRIERS. Economic development rides on the shoulders of entrepreneurs who venture to do things that benefit them and the society. Whether or not a society has a sufficient number of entrepreneurs to foster modern economic growth may depend on the society's values and structure. Many of the developed nations of today encouraged **entrepreneurship** who pursued dreams in search of reaping potential profits from innovations. What has prevented the development of entrepreneurship in underdeveloped economies? Some believe that certain individuals in a traditional society are blocked from becoming entrepreneurs, which normally implies more social prestige, power, and wealth. These blocked minorities attempt to rise through entrepreneurship. However, it is difficult to establish a clear causal relationship between the blocked minorities and entrepreneurship. Perhaps more important than this relationship are the factors other than minority status that induce people to become entrepreneurs. David McClelland, a Harvard University psychologist, believes that the need for achievement is a factor—certain societies produce a high number of individuals with strong desire to improve themselves financially or to be recognized by the society for their achievements. The experience of Malaya provides a historical example that illustrates McClelland's premise. Malaya was a country rich in resources, but natives of Malaya—primarily fishermen and farmers comfortable with their lives—did not become entrepreneurs until the middle of the twentieth century. Meanwhile, migrant Chinese mining workers who survived disease such as malaria became entrepreneurs in Malaya. One interpretation of this episode is that the Chinese possessed a strong desire to rise and the Malays did not.

GOVERNMENT POLICIES AIMED AT ECONOMIC DEVELOPMENT

Modern governments are playing an active role in promoting economic development, primarily within two categories. The first category includes communist and socialist governments that use a centralized planning process to promote growth. In a centrally planned economy, the government literally makes the consumption and savings decisions, channeling the surplus funds into investment to promote economic growth. The Soviet Union used such a centrally planned system after the Communists took power in 1917. While Russia no longer follows the central planning model, a few countries, such as China and Vietnam, still do.

The second category consists of governments that primarily believe in market economies, but play an active role in promoting economic development. These governments promote economic growth in many ways. One way of promoting growth is to make active use of monetary and **fiscal policy** to spur savings and investments. Fiscal policies are also used to provide tax incentives that are conducive to risk-taking and innovations. Some capitalist governments have an industrial policy in place—directly or indirectly the government supports a pattern of industrial development. Finally, a government may follow an active policy of promoting foreign trade.

[Andrew P. Sahu]

FURTHER READING:

Gillis, Malcolm, Dwight H. Perkins, Michael Roemer, and Donald R. Roemer, *Economics of Development*, 3rd ed., W. W. Norton & Company, 1992.

ECONOMIC FORECASTS

Economic forecasts are widely used at the firm, industry, and economy-wide level. For a firm, economic forecasts facilitate planning for future production, expansion, or contraction. For example, a retailing firm that has been in business for the last 25 years may be interested in **forecasting** the likely sales volume for the coming year. Similarly, the auto industry may want to know the total demand for vans in the coming model year. Both production plans and the extent of competition in the automobile industry may depend on the magnitude of the forecasted auto demand. At the economy-wide level, one may want to know the economic forecast for growth in the real gross domestic product. One may also be interested in other macroeconomic variables such as the projected inflation rate. There are numerous techniques that can be used to generate economic forecasts.

While the term "economic forecast" may appear to be rather technical, planning for the future is a critical aspect of managing any organization business, nonprofit, or other. In fact, the long-term success of any organization is closely tied to how well the management of the organization is able to foresee its future and to develop appropriate strategies to deal with likely future scenarios.

Intuition, good judgment, and an awareness of how well the economy is doing may give the manager of a business firm a rough idea (or "feeling") of what is likely to happen in the future. Nevertheless, it is not easy to convert a feeling about the future into a precise and useful number such as the next year's sales volume or the raw material cost per unit of output.

Suppose that a forecast expert has been asked to provide estimates of the sales volume for a particular product for the next four quarters. How should one go about preparing the quarterly sales volume forecasts? One will certainly want to review the actual sales data for the product in question for past periods. Suppose that the forecaster has access to actual sales data for each quarter over the 25-year period the firm has been in business. Using these historical data, the forecaster can identify the general level of sales. He or she can also determine whether there is a pattern or trend, such as an increase or decrease in sales volume over time. A further review of the data may reveal some type of seasonal pattern, such as peak sales occurring before a holiday. Thus by reviewing historical data over time, the forecaster can often develop a good understanding of the previous pattern of sales. Understanding such a pattern can often lead to better forecasts of future sales of the product. In addition, if the forecaster is able to identify the factors that influence sales, historical data on these factors (or variables) can also be used to generate forecasts of future sales volumes.

FORECASTING METHODS

There are many forecasting techniques available to assist in business planning. All forecasting methods can be divided into two broad categories: qualitative and quantitive. Many forecasting techniques use past or historical data in form of time series. A time series is simply a set of observations measured at successive points in time or over successive periods of time. Forecasts essentially provide future values of the time series on a specific variable such as sales volume. Division of forecasting methods into qualitative and quantitative categories is based on the availability of historical time series data.

When historical data are not available, qualitative forecasting techniques are used. Such techniques generally employ the judgment of experts in the appropriate field to generate forecasts. Quantitative forecasting methods are used when historical data on variables of interest are available—these methods are based on an analysis of historical data concerning the time series of the specific variable of interest and possibly other related time series.

There are two major categories of quantitative forecasting methods. The first type uses the past trend of a particular variable to base the future forecast of the variable. As this category of forecasting methods simply uses time series on past data of the variable that is being forecasted, these techniques are called time series methods. The second category of quantitative forecasting techniques also uses historical data. But in forecasting future values of a variable, the forecaster examines the cause-and-effect relationships of the variable with other relevant variables such as the level of consumer confidence, changes in consumers' disposable incomes, the interest rate at which consumers can finance their spending through borrowing, and the state of the economy represented, by such variables as the unemployment rate. Thus, this category of forecasting techniques uses past time series on many relevant variables to produce the forecast for the variable of interest. Forecasting techniques falling under this category are called causal methods, as the basis of such forecasting is the cause-and-effect relationship between the variable forecasted and other time series selected to help in generating the forecasts.

Some economic forecasts are generated using a hybrid of the above two methods.

[Anandi P. Sahu]

FURTHER READING:

Anderson, David P., Dennis J. Sweeney and Thomas A. Williams. *An Introduction to Management Science: Quantitative Approaches to Decision Making.* 7th ed. West Publishing Company, 1994.

Anderson, David P., Dennis J. Sweeney and Thomas A. Williams. *Statistics for Business and Economics.* 5th ed. West Publishing Company, 1993.

ECONOMIC POLICY

The term "economic policy" is used to refer to macroeconomic policies used by governments to stabilize the overall economy. Until the Great Depression of 1930s and the advent of Keynesian economics, there were no conscious attempts on the part of the U.S. government to stabilize the economy. Both economists and politicians believed in classical economics, which held that there was no need for economic policy at all. The classical economists had argued that the self-adjusting market mechanism would restore full employment in the economy, should the economy deviate from the full employment path for some reason. The experience of the Great Depression, however, showed that market forces did not work as well as the classical economists had believed. The unemployment rate in the United States rose to above 25 percent of the labor force. Hard working people were out in the street looking for nonexisting jobs. Wages fell quite substantially. But the lower wages did not reestablish full employment.

THE NEED FOR ECONOMIC POLICY

The English economist John Maynard Keynes (1883-1946) argued that self-adjusting market forces could take a long time to restore full employment. He predicted that an economy can be stuck at a high level of unemployment for a prolonged period, leading to untold miseries. Keynes explained that classical economics suffered from major flaws. Wages and prices are not as flexible as classical economists assumed—in fact, nominal wages tend toward the downward direction. Keynes further argued that classical economists had ignored a key factor that determined the level of output and employment in the economy—the *aggregate demand* for goods and services in the economy from all sources (consumers, businesses, government, and foreigners). Producers produce (and provide employment in the process) to meet the demand for their goods and services. If the level of aggregate demand is low, the economy would not create enough jobs and unemployment can result. In other words, the free working of the macroeconomy does not guarantee full employment—deficient aggregate demand can cause unemployment. Thus, if the aggregate private demand (i.e., the aggregate demand excluding government spending) falls short of the demand level needed to generate full employment, the government should step in to take up the slack.

The central issue underlying Keynesian thought was that those who have incomes demand goods and services and, in turn, help to create jobs. The government should thus find a way to increase aggregate demand.

MONETARY AND FISCAL POLICIES AS A WAY TO MANIPULATE AGGREGATE DEMAND

One direct way of increasing aggregate demand is to increase government spending. Increased spending on a government project such as reforestation will generate jobs and incomes for the persons employed on the project. This, in turn, would provide demand for goods and services from private producers and generate additional employment in the private sector. Keynesian economists thus recommend that the government should use **fiscal policy** (which includes decisions regarding both government spending and taxes) to make up for the shortfall in private aggregate demand and to create jobs in the private sector machine. Keynesian economists went so far as to recommend that it may be worthwhile for the government to employ people to dig holes and to fill them up.

The Roosevelt administration followed Keynesian recommendations, although reluctantly, and embarked on a variety of government programs aimed at boosting incomes and aggregate demand. As a result, the economy started improving. The really powerful push to the depressed U.S. economy, however, came when World War II broke out. The war generated such an enormous demand for U.S. military and civilian goods that factories in the United States operated multiple shifts. No serious unemployment was seen in the U.S. economy for a long time to come.

Modern Keynesians (also, known as neo-Keynesians) recommend **monetary policy**, in addition to fiscal policy, to manage the level of aggregate demand. Monetary policy essentially refers to the manipulation of the nation's money supply by the Federal Reserve Bank (the central bank of the United States) in order to influence the state of the economy. The Federal Reserve employs several methods to influence the level of money supply in the economy. The most favored and the frequently used method is called open market operations.

THE OPEN MARKET OPERATIONS. Open market operations is the instrument used most frequently by the Federal Reserve to manipulate the money supply. Through open market operations, the Federal Reserve manipulates the reserves in the banking system by buying or selling Treasury securities in the open market in which major commercial banks (known as the money center banks) participate. When the Federal Reserve sells Treasury bonds to banks, it receives cash in exchange—the excess reserves in the banking system go down and thus the money supply will, potentially, go down also. The opposite is the case when the Federal Reserve buys Treasury securities from the banking system. The Federal Reserve uses open market operations to manipulate the nation's money supply on a regular basis—it is considered the main instrument of monetary policy.

Monetary policy affects aggregate demand in the Keynesian system by influencing private investment and consumption demand. An increase in the money supply, for example, leads to a decrease in the interest rate. This lowers the cost of borrowing and thus increases private investment and consumption, boosting aggregate demand in the economy.

BALANCING EMPLOYMENT AND INFLATION. An increase in aggregate demand through the use of monetary and fiscal policies under the Keynesian system, however, not only generates higher employment but also leads to higher **inflation**. This causes a policy dilemma—how to strike a balance between employment and inflation. According to laws that were enacted following the Great Depression, the policy makers are expected to use monetary and fiscal policies to achieve high employment consistent with price stability.

SUPPLY-SIDE ECONOMICS

While monetary and fiscal policies attempt to stabilize the economy by manipulating the level of aggregate demand, supply-side economists, have advocated the manipulation of supply-side factors to promote growth in the economy.

While supply-side economics became popular during the Reagan era, it had been a part of the U.S. macroeconomic policies for some time. Supply-side theory was also rooted in classical economics, even though it accepted some Keynesian policies of demand management. Basically, supply-siders emphasize enhancing economic growth by augmenting the supply of factors of production (such as labor, and capital. This would be accomplished through increased incentives mainly in the form of reduced taxes and regulations. Reagan, for example, used a major tax cut as a part of his fiscal policy. The supply-siders, in general, want a greater role for the market forces and a reduced role for the government.

HAVE ECONOMIC POLICIES SUCCEEDED IN ELIMINATING BUSINESS CYCLES?

The main goal of monetary and fiscal policies was to stabilize the macroeconomy—reducing or eliminating economic fluctuations or business cycles (as they are commonly known). Business cycles, however, have not been conquered to the fullest extent. After all, the most recent downturn ended only in 1992.

Business cycles have been with the U.S. economy for a long time. After the Great Depression of the 1930s, it was realized that the government should use macroeconomic policies—monetary and fiscal policies—to manipulate the level of aggregate demand and to stabilize the economy around full employment with price stability. One of the two macroeconomic policy instruments, fiscal policy, is conducted by the Congress and the president. The conduct of monetary policy is left to the Federal Reserve Bank, an independent federal institution. The U.S. experience has shown that the burden of stabilizing the economy has fallen disproportionately on the Federal Reserve—fiscal policy is said to be slow to respond and less decisive due to political conflicts among policy makers. Despite many shortcomings and imperfections of monetary and fiscal policies, the evidence seems to suggest that they have had a moderating influence on business cycles. While business fluctuations continue to exist in the U.S. economy, recessions in the post-Depression period have been relatively modest. While not all economists subscribe to the conclusion that the macroeconomic policies have moderated business cycles, these policies continue to be used to stabilize the economy.

CONTROVERSY REGARDING MONETARY AND FISCAL POLICIES

While aggregate demand-based economic policies are widely used across the globe, economists disagree on the exact effects of monetary and fiscal policies on an economy. There are two major opposing schools of thought—**monetarism** and Keynesian economics.

Monetarists believe that fiscal policy does not have a significant effect on output and employment in the economy. According to them, when a government conducts fiscal policy through increasing government spending, financed by borrowing, it raises interest rates in the process. As a result, private expenditures (both consumption and investment) get crowded out. Thus, the increased government spending comes at the expense of private sector spending, offsetting the ultimate effects of the fiscal policy on the economy.

Monetarists believe that the effects of monetary policy (such as increasing the money supply) on real

variables, such as output and employment, are short-lived. They assert that an increase in the money supply only affects the price level in the long run. Monetarists also believe that the conduct of monetary policy by the Federal Reserve is the primary cause of instability and fluctuations in the economy. They are thus against manipulating the money supply to influence the levels of output and employment in the economy. Instead, they would like the money supply to grow at a low constant rate, so as to keep the price level relatively constant.

Keynesian economists, on the other hand, recommend using both fiscal and monetary policies to favorably influence output and employment, and to reduce inflation. They believe that market forces are slow to adjust. Therefore, if the economy is experiencing high unemployment, an expansionary monetary or fiscal policy can be used to increase the level of employment. An increase in the money supply implies greater resources available for lending, which reduces interest rates (the cost of borrowing). At lower interest rates, total demand (or aggregate demand) in the economy increases, as consumers and businesses spend more on consumption and investment, respectively. Increased demand for goods and services requires increased production, which in turn requires higher level of employment. The technique works, according to Keynesian economists, in the opposite direction in an inflationary environment. Reducing money supply and increasing the interest rate decrease the level of aggregate demand in the economy, which puts downward pressure on the price level. The basic Keynesian logic is: if we have a way to improve the economy, why not do it? According to Keynesians, fiscal policy expands or contracts demand even more directly. Thus, a tax cut would stimulate aggregate demand by increasing disposable income in the hands of consumers. Similarly, increased government spending would accomplish this by adding to the existing level of private demand.

Keynesian policy recommendations have been widely adopted throughout the world. Both monetary policy and fiscal policy (that use government spending and taxes to influence the level of aggregate demand) are used to improve economies (that is, to attempt to stabilize them at or near full employment with low inflation). In the United States, laws have been enacted that require the government to achieve full employment if it is considered desirable, given the economic circumstances.

[Anandi P. Sahu]

FURTHER READING:

Froyen, Richard T. *Macroeconomics: Theories and Policies;* 4th ed. Macmillan Publishing Company, 1993.

Gordon, Robert J. *Macroeconomics;* 6th ed. HarperCollins College Publishers, 1993.

Mansfield, Edwin. *Principles of Macroeconomics*; 7th ed. W. W. Norton & Company, 1992.

ECONOMIC THEORIES

Economic theories broadly fall under two categories: **microeconomics** and **macroeconomics**. In most basic terms, microeconomics deals with the economy at a smaller level or at a smaller scale, such as the market for a particular product (e.g., automobiles) or the behavior of an individual firm in a particular industry (e.g., decisions made by one of the Big Three in the U.S. automobile industry). Macroeconomics, on the other hand, studies the behavior of the overall economy (e.g., the U.S. economy as a whole), although, it sometimes also looks at economies of different regions that comprise the overall economy.

MICROECONOMIC THEORIES

Economics in general (and microeconomics in particular) is defined as the social science which deals with the problem of allocating limited resources to satisfy unlimited human wants. Solving this riddle is based on the price mechanism which, in turn, uses forces of demand and supply for different products. Price mechanism refers to an adjustment mechanism in which the price of a product serves as a signal to both buyers and sellers; it is often considered the centerpiece of microeconomic theory. Theories of demand, supply, and the price mechanism are briefly discussed in what follows.

THEORY OF DEMAND, SUPPLY, AND THE PRICE MECHANISM. The demand for a particular product by an individual consumer is based on three important factors. First, the price of the product determines how much of the product the consumer buys, given that all other factors remain unchanged. In general, the lower the price of the product the more a consumer buys. Second, the consumer's **income** also determines how much of the product the consumer is able to buy, given that all other factors remain constant. In general, the greater is his or her income, the more **commodities** a consumer will buy. Third, prices of related products are also important in determining the consumer's demand for the product. The total of all consumer demands yields the market demand for a particular commodity. The market demand curve shows quantities of the commodity demanded at different prices, given that all other factors remain constant; as price increases, the quantity demanded falls.

The amount supplied by an individual firm depends on profit and cost considerations. In general, a producer produces the profit by maximizing output.

The total of all individual company supplies yield the market supply for a particular commodity. The market supply curve shows quantities of the commodity supplied at different prices, given that all other factors remain constant; as price increases, the quantity supplied increases.

The interaction between market demand and supplies determines the equilibrium or market price (where demand equals supply). Shifts in the demand curve and/or the supply curve lead to changes in the equilibrium price. The market price and the price mechanism play crucial roles in the capitalist system—they send signals to both producers and consumers. The price mechanism is an integral part of the study of market structures that constitute the bulk of microeconomic theories.

Analyses of different market structures have yielded economic theories that dominate the study of microeconomics. Four such theories, associated with four kinds of market organizations, are discussed below: perfect competition, monopolistic competition, oligopoly, and monopoly. Based on the differing outcomes of different market structures, economists consider some market structures more desirable, from the point of view of the society, than others.

PERFECT COMPETITION MARKET STRUCTURE. Perfect **competition** is the idealized market structure that provides a foundation for understanding how markets work in a capitalist economy. The nature of competition under the perfectly competitive market form is based on three conditions that need to be satisfied before a market structure is considered perfectly competitive: homogeneity of the product sold in the industry, existence of many buyers and sellers, and perfect mobility of resources or factors of production. The first condition, the homogeneity of product, requires that the product sold by any one seller is identical with the product sold by any other supplier—if products of different sellers are identical, buyers do not care whom they buy from, so long as the price charged is also the same. The second condition, existence of many buyers and sellers, also leads to an important outcome—individual buyers or sellers are so small relative to the entire market that they do not have any power to influence the price of the product under consideration, and they simply decide how much to buy or sell at the given market price. The implication of the third condition, the perfect mobility of resources or factors of production, is that resources move to the most profitable industry.

There is no industry in the world that can be considered perfectly competitive in the strictest sense of the term. Token examples of industries, however, come quite close to having perfectly competitive markets. Some markets for agricultural commodities, while not meeting all three conditions, come reasonably close to being characterized as perfectly competitive markets. The market for wheat, for example, can be considered a reasonable approximation.

The study of the idealized version of perfect competition leads to some important conclusions regarding the solutions of key economic problems, such as the quantity of the relevant product produced, price charged, and the mechanism of adjustment in the industry. The total output produced under perfect competition is larger than, say, under monopoly. This follows from the mechanics of maximizing profit, the guiding force behind a supplier's output decision. In order to maximize profits, a supplier has to look at **costs** and revenues. The firm will stop production at the level where marginal revenue (the revenue that the sale of an additional unit generates) equals marginal cost (the cost of producing an additional unit of the product under consideration)—this output level maximizes profits (or minimizes loss). In the case of a perfectly competitive firm, the market price for the product is also the marginal revenue, as the firm can sell additional units at the going market price. This is not so for a monopolist. A monopolist must reduce price to increase sales—as a result, a monopolist's price is always higher than the marginal revenue. Thus, even though a monopolist also produces the profit-maximizing output, where marginal revenue equals marginal cost, it does not produce to the point where price equals marginal cost (as does a perfectly competitive firm). Perfect competition is therefore considered desirable from the point of the view of society for at least two reasons—in general, output produced under a perfectly competitive market structure is larger and the price charged is lower than under other market structures.

MONOPOLISTIC COMPETITION MARKET STRUCTURE. Many industries have market structures that are monopolistic competition or **oligopoly**. The apparel retail industry, which features stores and differentiated products, provides an example of monopolistic competition. As in the case of perfect competition, monopolistic competition is characterized by the existence of many sellers. Usually, if an industry has 50 or more firms (producing products that are close substitutes for each other), it is said to have a large number of firms. The sellers under monopolistic competition differentiate their product—unlike under perfect competition, products are not considered identical. This characteristic is often called the product differentiation. In addition, relative ease of entry into the industry is considered another important requirement of a monopolistically competitive market structure.

As in the case of perfect competition, a firm under monopolistic competition determines the quantity of the product produced on the basis of the profit maximization principle—it stops production when marginal revenue equals marginal cost of production.

One very important difference between perfect competition and monopolistic competition, however, is that firm under monopolistic competition has some control over the price it charges, since it differentiates its products from those of others. As a result, the price associated with the product (at the equilibrium or profit-maximizing output) is higher than the marginal cost (which equals marginal revenue). Thus, the production under monopolistic competition does not take place to the point where price equals marginal cost of production. The net result of the profit-maximizing decisions of monopolistically competitive firms is that the price charged is higher than under perfect competition and the quantity produced is simultaneously lower. Thus, both on the basis of price charged and output produced, monopolistic competition is less socially desirable than perfect competition.

OLIGOPOLY MARKET STRUCTURE. Oligopoly is a fairly **common market** organization. In the United States, both the steel and automobile industries (with about three large firms each) provide good examples of oligopolistic market structures.

The most important characteristic of an oligopolistic market structure is the interdependence of firms in the industry. The interdependence, actual or perceived, arises from the small number of firms in the industry. Unlike under monopolistic competition, if an oligopolistic firm changes its price or output, it has perceptible effects on the sales and profits of its competitors in the industry. Thus, an oligopolist always considers the reactions of its rivals in formulating its pricing or output decisions.

There are huge, though not insurmountable, barriers to entry into an oligopolistic market. These barriers can exist because of large financial requirements, availability of raw materials, access to the relevant technology, or simply existence of patent rights with the firms currently in the industry. Several industries in the United States provide good examples of oligopolistic market structures with obvious barriers to entry; for example, the U.S. automobile industry has financial barriers to entry.

An oligopolistic industry is also typically characterized by **economies of scale**. Economies of scale in production imply that as the level of production rises the cost per unit of product falls from the use of any plant (generally, up to a point). Thus, economies of scale are an obvious advantage to a large producer.

There is no single theoretical framework that provides answers to output and pricing decisions under an oligopolistic market structure. Analyses exist only for special sets of circumstances. One of these circumstances refers to an oligopoly in which there are asymmetric reactions from rivals when a particular firm formulates policies—if a certain oligopolistic firm cuts price, it is met with price reductions by competing firms; if it raises the price of its product, however, rivals do not match the price increase. For this reason, prices may remain stable in an oligopolistic industry for a prolonged period.

Due to theoretical difficulties, it is hard to make concrete statements regarding price charged and quantity produced under oligopoly. Nevertheless, from the point of view of the society, an oligopolistic market structure provides a fair degree of competition in the market place if the oligopolists in the market do not collude. Collusion occurs if firms in the industry agree to set price and/or quantity. In the United States, there are laws that make collusion illegal.

MONOPOLY MARKET STRUCTURE. Monopoly can be considered the polar opposite of perfect competition. It is a market form in which there is only one seller. While, at first glance, a monopolistic form may appear to be rare, several industries in the United State have monopolies. Local electricity companies are examples of monopolists.

There are many factors that give rise to a monopoly. **Patents** can lead to a monopoly situation, as can ownership of critical raw materials (to produce a good) by a single firm. A monopoly can also be legally created by a government agency when it sells a market franchise to sell a particular product or to provide a particular service. Often a monopoly so established is also regulated by an appropriate government agency. Provision of local telephone services in the United States provides an example of such a monopoly. Finally, a monopoly may arise due to the declining cost of production for a particular product. In such a case the average cost of production keeps on falling and reaches a minimum at an output level that is sufficient to satisfy the entire market. In such an industry, rival firms will be eliminated until only the strongest firm (now the monopolist) is left in the market. Such an industry is popularly dubbed natural monopoly. A good example of a natural monopoly is the electric power industry which reaps the benefits of economies of scale and yields decreasing average cost. Natural monopolies are usually regulated by the government.

Generally speaking price and output decisions of a monopolist are similar to a monopolistically competitive firm, with the major distinction that there are a large number of firms under monopolistic competition and only one firm under monopoly. Nevertheless, at any output level, the price charged by a monopolist is higher than the marginal revenue. As a result, a monopolist does not produce to the point where price equals marginal cost (a condition met under a perfectly competitive market structure).

An industry characterized by a monopolistic market structure produces less output and charges higher prices than under perfect competition (and presumably under monopolistic competition). Thus, on the basis of price charged and quantity produced a monopoly is less socially desirable. One must recognize, however, that a natural monopoly is generally considered desirable if the monopolist's price behavior can be regulated.

SUMMARY OF MARKET STRUCTURES. The real world is rarely characterized by perfect competition, and in certain circumstances, the society has to tolerate a monopoly (e.g., a natural monopoly or a monopoly due to patent rights). Nevertheless, the idea of competition is very deeply ingrained in the society. So long as there is a reasonable degree of competition (as in the case of monopolistic competition or oligopoly), the society feels reasonably secure with respect to the working of its markets.

MACROECONOMICS

Macroeconomics is a social science that studies an economy at the aggregate (or nationwide) level. Macroeconomic theories study an overall economy and prescribe policy recommendations based on the study of the behavior of key macroeconomic variables. While numerous additional measures or variables are used to understanding the behavior of an economy, the following four variables are considered to be the most important in gauging the state or health of an economy: aggregate output or income, the **unemployment** rate, the **inflation** rate, and the interest rate.

OUTPUT/INCOME. An economy's overall economic activity is summarized by a measure of aggregate output. As the production or output of goods and services generates income, any aggregate output measure is closely associated with an aggregate income measure. The United States now uses an aggregate output indicator known as the **gross domestic product** or GDP. The **GDP** is a measure of all currently produced goods and services valued at their market prices. Other related measures of output can be derived from the GDP measure.

UNEMPLOYMENT RATE. The level of **employment** is the next crucial macroeconomic variable. The employment level is often quoted in terms of the unemployment rate. The unemployment rate itself is defined as the fraction of the labor force not working but actively seeking employment. Labor force, in turn, is defined as consisting of those working and those not working but seeking work. Thus, the unemployment rate leaves out people who are not working but also not seeking work—termed by economists as voluntarily unemployed. For purposes of government macroeconomic policies, only people that are involuntarily unemployed really matter.

For various reasons, it is not possible to reduce the unemployment rate to zero even in the best of circumstances. Realistically, economists expect the labor force to always include an unemployed fraction—usually estimated at six percent for the U.S. labor market. The six percent unemployment rate is often referred to as the benchmark unemployment rate. In effect, if the unemployment level is at the six percent level, the economy is considered to be at full employment.

INFLATION RATE. Inflation is considered to be a macroeconomic variable of key concern. The inflation rate is defined as the rate of change in the price level. Most economies face positive rates of inflation year after year. The price level, in turn, is measured by a **price index** which measures the level of prices of goods and services at any point of time. The number of items included in a price index vary depending on the objective of the index. Usually three kinds of price **indexes** are periodically reported by government sources: the consumer price index or (CPI), which measures the average retail prices paid by consumers for goods and services typically bought by them; the producer price index or (PPI), which measures the wholesale prices of items that are typically used by producers; and the implicit GDP price deflator, which measures the prices of all goods and services included in the GDP. The inflation rate index most commonly reported in the popular media is the consumer price index.

INTEREST RATE. The concept of the interest rate used by economists is the same as the one commonly used. The interest rate is invariably quoted in nominal terms—that is, the rate is not adjusted for inflation. Thus, the commonly followed interest rate is actually the nominal interest rate. Nevertheless there are hundreds of nominal **interest rates**.

Fortunately, while the hundreds of interest rates that one encounters may appear baffling, they are closely linked to each other. Two characteristics that account for the linkage are—the risk worthiness of the borrower and the maturity date of the loan involved. So, for example, the interest rate on a six-month U.S. Treasury bill is related to that on a 30-year Treasury bond, just as bonds and loans of different maturities command different rates. Furthermore, a 30-year General Motors bond will carry a higher interest rate than a 30-year U.S. Treasury bond, since a General Motors bond is riskier than a U.S. Treasury bond.

THE MACROECONOMIC THEORIES AND RELATED POLICY RECOMMENDATIONS

The branch of social science called macroeconomics essentially examines the factors that lead to changes in the main characteristics of the economy—output, employment, inflation, and interest rates. A set of principles that describes how the key macroeconomic variables are determined is called a macroeconomic theory. Typically, every macroeconomic theory comes up with a set of policy recommendations that the proponents of the theory hope the government will follow. Since the 1930s, four macroeconomic theories have been proposed: Keynesian economics, **monetarism**, the new classical economics, and supply-side economics. All these theories are based, in varying degrees, on the classical economics that preceded the advent of Keynesian economics in the 1930s.

CLASSICAL ECONOMICS. The macroeconomic theory that dominated the capitalist economies prior to the advent of Keynesian economics in 1936 has been widely known as the classical macroeconomics. The classical economists believed in free markets and that the economy would always achieve full employment through forces of demand and supply. So, if there were more people seeking work than the number of jobs available, wages would fall until all those seeking work are employed. Thus, the full employment of workers was guaranteed by market forces. The level of full employment resulted in a fixed aggregate output/income. The price level (and thus the inflation rate) was determined by the supply of money in the economy. Since, the output level was fixed, a ten percent increase in money supply would lead to a ten percent increase in the price level—too many dollars chasing too few goods. The real interest rate (the nominal interest rate minus the inflation rate) was also determined by forces of demand and supply in the market: the demand and supply for lendable funds. The nominal interest rate was then simply the sum of the real interest rate and the prevailing inflation rate. The classical economists thus had an unwavering faith in a self-adjusting market mechanism. For the market mechanism to work, however, the market structure had to be that of perfect competition, and wages and prices had to be fully flexible.

The classical economists did not see any role for the government. As market forces led to a full employment equilibrium in the economy, there was no need for government intervention. Monetary policy (increasing or decreasing the money supply) would only affect prices—it did not affect the important factors of output and employment. Fiscal policy (using government spending or **taxes**), on the other hand, was perceived to be harmful. For example, if the government borrowed to finance its spending, it would simply reduce the funds available for private consumption and investment expenditures—a phenomenon popularly termed as crowding out. Similarly, if the government raised taxes to pay for increased spending, it would reduce private consumption in order to fund public consumption. Instead, if it financed the spending by an increase in the money supply, it would have the same effects as an expansionary monetary policy. Thus, the classical economists recommended use of neither monetary nor fiscal policy by the government. This hands-off policy recommendation is known as the **laissez-faire** policy.

THE KEYNESIAN ECONOMICS. Keynesian economics was born during the Great Depression of the 1930s. The classical economists had argued that the self-adjusting market mechanism would restore full employment in the economy, should the economy deviate from the full employment path for some reason. The experience of the Great Depression, however, showed that the market forces did not work as well as the classical economists had believed. The unemployment rate in the United States rose to above 25 percent of the labor force. Hard-working people were out in the street looking for nonexisting jobs. Wages fell substantially, but the lower wages did not reestablish full employment.

The English economist John Maynard Keynes (1883-1946) argued that the self-adjusting market forces would take a long time to restore full employment. He predicted that an economy can be stuck at a high level of unemployment for a prolonged period, leading to untold miseries. Keynes explained that the classical economics suffered from major flaws. Wages and prices are not as flexible as classical economists assumed, in fact, nominal wages tend toward the downward direction. Keynes further argued that classical economists had ignored a key factor that determined the level of output and employment in the economy—the aggregate demand for goods and services in the economy from all sources (consumers, businesses, government, and foreigners). Producers produce (and provide employment in the process) to meet the demand for their goods and services. If the level of aggregate demand is low, the economy would not create enough jobs and unemployment can result. In other words, the free working of the macroeconomy does not guarantee full employment—deficient aggregate demand can cause unemployment. Thus, if the aggregate private demand (i.e., the aggregate demand excluding government spending) falls short of the demand level needed to generate full employment, the government should step in to take up the slack.

The central issue underlying Keynesian thought was that those who have incomes demand goods and services and, in turn, help to create jobs. The government should thus find a way to increase aggregate demand. One direct way of doing so is to increase government spending. For example, increased spending on a government project will generate jobs and incomes for the persons employed on the project. This, in turn, would provide demand for goods and services from private producers and generate additional employment in the private sector. The early Keynesian economists thus recommended that the government should use fiscal policy (which includes decisions regarding both government spending and taxes) to make up for the shortfall in private aggregate demand and to create jobs in the private sector. Keynesian economists went so far as to recommend that it may be worthwhile for the government to employ people to dig holes and to fill them up.

The Roosevelt administration did followed the Keynesian recommendations, although reluctantly, and embarked on a variety of government programs aimed at boosting incomes and aggregate demand. As a result, the economy started improving. The really powerful push to the depressed U.S. economy, however, came when World War II broke out. The war generated such an enormous demand for U.S. military and civilian goods that factories in the United States operated multiple shifts. No serious unemployment was seen in the U.S. economy for a long time to come.

Modern Keynesians (also known as neo-Keynesians) recommend monetary policy, in addition to fiscal policy, to manage the level of aggregate demand. Monetary policy affects aggregate demand in the Keynesian system by affecting private investment and consumption demand. An increase in the money supply, for example, leads to a decrease in the interest rate. This lowers the cost of borrowing and thus increases private investment and consumption, boosting the aggregate demand in the economy.

An increase in aggregate demand under the Keynesian system, however, not only generates higher employment but also leads to higher inflation. This causes a policy dilemma how to strike a balance between employment and inflation. According to laws that were enacted following the Great Depression, policymakers are expected to use monetary and fiscal policies to achieve high employment consistent with price stability.

MONETARISM. Monetarism was an attempt by conservative economists to reestablish the wisdom of the classical laissez-faire recommendation. By 1950, Keynesian economics was well established. The birth of monetarism took place in the 1960s. The original proponent of monetarism was Milton Friedman (1912—), now a Nobel Laureate. The monetarists argued that while it is not possible to have full employment of the labor force all the time, it is better to leave the economy to market forces. Friedman contended that the government's use of active monetary and fiscal policies to stabilize the economy around full employment leads to greater instability in the economy. He argued that while the economy would not achieve a state of bliss in the absence of the government intervention, it would be far more tranquil.

Friedman modified some aspects of the classical theory to provide the rationale for his noninterventionist policy recommendation. In essence, monetarism contends that the use of fiscal policy is largely ineffective in altering output and employment. Moreover, it only leads to crowding out. On the other hand, while monetary policy, is effective, monetary authorities do not have suufficient knowledge to conduct a successful monetary policy—manipulating the money supply to stabilize the economy only leads to greater instability. Hence, monetarism advocates that neither monetary nor fiscal policy should be used in an attempt to stabilize the economy, and that the money supply should be allowed to grow at a constant rate. The monetarist policy recommendations are similar to those of the classical economists, even though the reasoning is somewhat different.

THE NEW CLASSICAL ECONOMICS. The 1970s saw a further push to revive the classical orthodoxy. The new classical economists (also known as proponents of rational expectations) provided a theoretical framework and empirical evidence to support the view that neither fiscal nor monetary policy can be effective in altering the output and employment levels in a systematic manner. The proponents of the new classical economics argued that if economic agents (consumers, businesses, and others) used rational expectations (i.e., all available information) regarding government policies, they would frustrate any anticipated policy action by the government by altering their own behavior. Thus, there was no point in conducting monetary and fiscal policies, since market forces are not amenable to such manipulations.

THE SUPPLY-SIDE ECONOMICS. While supply-side economics became popular during the Reagan era, it had been a part of the U.S. macroeconomic policies for some time. Supply-side theory was also rooted in classical economics, even though it accepted some Keynesian policies of demand **management**. Basically, supply-siders emphasized enhancing economic growth by augmenting the supply of factors of production such as labor and capital. This would be accomplished done through increased incentives mainly in the form of reduced taxes and regulations. Ronald Reagan, for example, used a major tax cut as a part of his fiscal policy. The supply-siders, in general, want a greater role for the market forces and a reduced role for the government.

THE DOMINANT MACROECONOMIC THEORY. While the existence of numerous macroeconomic theories is somewhat confusing, there is usually a dominant theory that the government follows. In the mid-1990s one can safely argue that the United States and many other capitalist countries largely follow Keynesian policy recommendations.

[Anandi P. Sahu]

FURTHER READING:

Froyen, Richard T. *Macroeconomics: Theories and Policies*. 4th ed. Macmillan Publishing Company, 1993.

Mansfield, Edwin. *Principles of Microeconomics*. 7th ed. W. W. Norton & Company, 1992.

ECONOMIC VALUE ADDED

Value-based strategic planning techniques, which tie business-level competitive strategies to the corporation's stock price, have achieved increasing recognition among financial managers. These models evaluate business strategies in terms of their ability to create value for the shareholders, and attempt to ensure that business-level competitive strategies are related to the fundamental objective of maximizing the return to the company's shareholders.

There are different variations on the concept of value-based strategic planning. Perhaps the best known technique is Economic Value Added (EVA), which was developed by the consulting firm Stern-Stewart & Co. According to the EVA approach, managers should be evaluated by the economic returns they generate for shareholders. Strategies that are expected to create the greatest sustainable competitive advantage are those that also generate the largest value for the firm's shareholders. Only investments providing positive economic returns should be undertaken. Positive economic returns are generated when the returns on an investment are greater than the market cost of capital. The market cost of **capital** reflects what the business could earn on an investment of similar risk.

DEFICIENCIES OF TRADITIONAL ACCOUNTING MEASURES

Traditionally, the most popular methods of evaluating company performance have been through accounting measures such as **earnings per share** (EPS) and return on equity (ROE). These measures, however, can be misleading in that they are often poor indicators of shareholder value creation.

Accounting numbers can be manipulated to the detriment of the interests of shareholders since **management** has flexibility in how it records transactions. For example, several different ways exist to record sales and costs. The method employed can have a significant impact on the recognition of revenues and expenses, and therefore, the net income of the firm.

Accountants do not measure economic profits. Generally accepted accounting principles (GAAP) deduct only the interest on debt, but not the cost of equity capital in arriving at net income. Nevertheless, the right of shareholders to receive an economic return on their investment is as legitimate as a creditor's right to receive interest.

Risk is of central importance in calculating the economic value of assets. Assets seldom offer both high returns and safety. Accounting measures, however, fail to consider the level of business and financial risk associated with generating a given level of earnings. Therefore, accounting-based measures can be inaccurate measures of the financial performance of a company.

Earnings calculations also ignore the time value of money. The economic value of an investment is the discounted (or present) value of the forecasted cash flows produced by the investment. The discount rate used in computing the economic value of an investment includes a premium for bearing risk as well as a premium for expected inflation.

Finally, earnings-based measures fail to incorporate the ongoing investment requirements of a firm. As the business grows, there generally will be an associated growth in both working capital and fixed investment. For a business to remain competitive, these incremental working and fixed capital expenditures must be funded in a timely manner.

In contrast to accounting-related measures, economic value added incorporates risk and considers the time value of money. Furthermore, the value-based technique considers the cost of equity capital, working capital, and capital expenditure investment requirements.

CALCULATION OF ECONOMIC VALUE ADDED

EVA recognizes that a business must not only break even on an accounting basis but also have sufficient earnings to cover the cost of the capital used in financing its operations. The business unit is earning an economic profit only if it is generating a return on its capital that is greater than the firm's total cost of capital. Thus, the economic break-even point exceeds the **accounting** break-even point which excludes capital costs.

EVA enables managers to look at the firm's business operations and determine whether they are becoming more or less valuable to their owners. EVA is computed by subtracting the total annual cost of capital (including both **debt** and **equity**) from after-tax operating profit [or EBIT (1-t)].

The capital in EVA represents the money invested in long-term fixed assets (such as equipment and **real estate**) plus working capital, which consists of cash, inventories, and receivables. In addition, the money spent on **research and development** and on employee training is also defined as capital investment even though accounting rules classify them as expenses.

Most firms employ two major sources of funds—debt capital and equity capital in financing their operations. Although the cost of borrowed funds or cost of debt capital shows up as interest expense in its income statement, the cost of equity capital typically does not appear in the firm's **financial statements**. This omission is significant, because equity capital is significantly more expensive than debt.

The cost of debt capital is the yield to maturity on a firm's debt, adjusted to reflect its tax deductibility. Managers, however, find it quite difficult to estimate the cost of equity capital. One calculating method is to sum the dividend yield and the growth rate in dividends per share where the dividend yield equals the current dividend divided by the share price.

An alternative method used by some managers that determines the cost of equity is the **capital asset pricing model** (CAPM). The CAPM is based on the assumption that the greater the risk in holding a stock the greater must be its required return in the form of **dividends** and capital appreciation. The calculation begins with the long-term, risk-free rate of return on a U.S. government bond. To this figure is added the risk premium that depends on factors related to economic growth, **inflation**, and investors' attitudes toward **stocks**. Historically this premium has run about 7 percent a year. This risk premium is adjusted for the risk of owning a specific stock, and is called the "beta" of that stock. It measures the stock's volatility compared with the rest of the market. To obtain the cost of equity, we multiply the market risk premium by the beta and add the result to the market's risk-free rate. According to the CAPM, business units that are riskier than the overall market would command a higher risk premium, whereas divisions of less than average risk would employ a lower risk premium.

Once a business unit has determined the cost of capital for both debt and equity, it then computes the weighted average cost of capital. The weighted average cost of capital is calculated by multiplying the after-tax cost of debt times the proportion of debt in the firm's capital structure and adding this figure to the cost of equity times the proportion of equity in the firm's capital structure. The proportions of debt and equity are based on the current market values of the firm's securities rather than the historical book values given in the firm's balance sheet.

To compute EVA, the dollar amount of capital is multiplied by the weighted average cost of capital to compute the total annual (dollar) cost of capital:

$$\text{EVA} = \text{EBIT} (1 - t) - \$ \text{Cost of Capital}$$

If EVA is positive, the business operation is earning more than its cost of capital and thus creating value. If it is negative, however, the operation is destroying value.

Most firms that calculate EVA also examine market value added (MVA). Market value added is the difference between the amount of capital investors have contributed to a company and the company's market capitalization. MVA indicates how well managers have increased the value of capital that investors have entrusted to them. If investors expect the business unit to continue to generate a positive EVA, the operation will have a positive MVA.

To compute MVA, first add up the book value of the firm's **liabilities** and shareholders' equity. Then examine how the capital market evaluates the company by determining the value of its **common stock** and adding its debt. Then, MVA is calculated as:

$$\text{MVA} = [(\text{Price Per Share}) \times (\text{\# of Common Shares Outstanding}) + \text{Market Value of Debt}] - (\text{Book Value of Liabilities} + \text{Shareholders' Equity})$$

If the company's market value is greater than the book value of all its capital, then it has a positive MVA. This means that the managers have created value. In some cases, however, the market value of a company is actually less than the contributed capital which indicates that the managers have destroyed wealth.

USING EVA IN PRACTICE

A firm can increase its EVA in four basic ways. First, the business can attempt to earn more profit without using more capital through increasing the operating profit margin. Second, the firm can use less capital by abandoning operations with operating profits less than the cost of capital. Third, the business can invest capital in projects yielding returns higher than the market cost of capital. Finally, companies reduce the cost of capital through the judicious use of financial leverage. Generally, the cost of debt is less than the cost of equity.

Studies indicate that EVA predicts MVA far more reliably than traditional accounting measures such as return on equity and earnings per share growth. The techniques are winning wide acceptance in corporate America. Firms that employ EVA—including AT&T, Briggs & Stratton, Coca-Cola, CSX, and Quaker Oats—have significantly increased their market values.

Successful implementation of EVA requires an explicit commitment on the part of senior executives to the goal of shareholder value creation. Business unit managers must be educated on the concepts of EVA and MVA. The focus on shareholder value creation must be communicated to all levels of the organization. Instead of hoarding information at top levels

of the organization and analyzing it sequentially, successful firms share information across the company. These companies decentralize **decision making** and ownership by providing incentives that link EVA and managerial compensation.

[Robert T. Kleiman]

FURTHER READING:

Rappaport, Alfred. *Creating Shareholder Value*. New York: Free Press, 1986.

Stewart, G. Bennett, III. *The Quest for Value*. New York: HarperBusiness, 1991.

ECONOMIES OF SCALE

Economies of scale is a concept that arises in the context of production of a good or service, and other similar activities undertaken by a business or nonbusiness organization. "Economies of scale" refer to economic efficiencies that result from carrying out a process (such as production or sales) on a larger and larger scale. The resulting economic efficiencies are usually measured in terms of the costs incurred as the scale of the relevant operation increases. Partly based on Edwin Mansfield's *Principles of Microeconomics*, important elements of economies of scale, necessary to gain a basic understanding of the concept, are briefly discussed in what follows.

PRODUCTION, INPUTS, COSTS, AND ECONOMIES OF SCALE

In order to gain a reasonable understanding of economies of scale, one needs to understand a few concepts, related to the production process. These are: the production function, fixed and variable inputs, and average costs.

PRODUCTION FUNCTION AND INPUTS. Production of a product (or a set of products) is generally based on a technological relationship—amounts of certain factors of production (inputs) are converted into a product based on some technological constraints. The technological relationship is termed by economists as the "production function." In more technical terms, the production function can be defined as the function that shows the most output that existing technology permits the manufacturing firm to extract from each quantity of inputs. The production function thus summarizes the characteristics of existing technology at a given time. This concept can be illustrated with the help of an example. Suppose, Better Steel Corporation decides to produce a certain quantity of steel. It can do so in many different ways. It can choose from among available technological choices: it can use open-hearth furnaces, basic oxygen furnaces, or electric furnaces. Similarly, Better Steel Corporation can choose from among various types of iron ore and coal. Given that Better Steel has decided to produce a certain quantity of steel, which production technique will it use (that is, what particular combination of inputs will it decide on)? An economist's answer to this question is: the one that minimizes the firm's costs and maximizes its profits.

Given that a technology has been chosen, in general, as inputs used in the production of a commodity increase the total output increases as well. It is useful to understand different kinds of inputs.

FIXED AND VARIABLE INPUTS. Primarily, there are two kinds of inputs—fixed and variable. A plant and a factory shed are examples of fixed inputs (or factors) of production. These inputs are called "fixed" inputs as the quantities needed of these inputs remain fixed, up to point, as the quantity produced of the product (the output) increases. Using the steel industry as an example, a blast furnace used in producing steel is considered a fixed input—Better Steel Corporation can produce more steel by using more raw materials, and get more production out of the existing blast furnace. It should be noted that a fixed input does remain fixed for all levels of output produced. As the scale of production increases, the existing plant may no longer suffice. Suppose that the blast furnace chosen by the steel firm can, at the very maximum, produce 100,000 tons of steel per day. If Better Steel Corporation needs to supply 150,000 tons of steel per day (on average), it has to add to capacity—that is, it has to install a new blast furnace. Thus, even a fixed input does not remain fixed forever. The period over which a fixed input remains fixed is called the "short run." Over the "long run," even a fixed input varies.

Inputs that vary even in the short run are called "variable" inputs. In the above steel manufacturing example, iron ore serves as a variable input. Given the fixed input (the blast furnace in this case), increasing the quantity of the variable input (iron ore) leads to higher levels of output (steel).

For the manufacturing firm, it is not very important as to what combination of fixed and variable inputs are used. As a firm is interested in maximizing profits, it would like to minimize costs for any given level of output produced. Thus, costs associated with inputs (both fixed and variable) are the main concern of the firm engaged in the production of a particular commodity.

TOTAL AND AVERAGE COSTS. A manufacturing firm, motivated by profit maximization, calculates the total cost of producing any given output level. The total cost is made up of total fixed cost (due to the expenditure on fixed inputs) and total variable cost (due to the expenditure on variable inputs). Of course,

the total fixed cost does not vary over the short run—only the total variable cost does. It is important for the firm also to calculate the cost per unit of output, called the "average cost." The average cost also is made up of two components—the average fixed cost (the total fixed cost divided by the number of units of the output) and the average variable cost (the total variable cost divided by the number of units of the output). As the fixed costs remain fixed over the short run, the average fixed cost declines as the level of production increases. The average variable cost, on the other hand, first decreases and then increases—economists refer to this as the U-shaped nature of the average variable cost. The U-shape of the average variable cost (curve) occurs because, given the fixed inputs, output of the relevant product increases more than proportionately as the levels of variable inputs used increase—this is caused by increased efficiency due to specialization and other reasons. As more and more variable inputs are used in conjunction with the given fixed inputs, however, efficiency gains reach a maximum—the decline in the average variable cost eventually comes to a halt. After this point, the average variable cost starts increasing as the level of production continues to increase, given the fixed inputs. First decreasing and then increasing average variable cost leads to the U-shape for the average variable cost (curve). The combination of the declining average fixed cost (true for the entire range of production) and the U-shaped average variable cost results in the U-shaped behavior of the average total cost (curve), often simply called the average costs.

AVERAGE COST AND ECONOMIES OF SCALE. Economies of scale are defined in terms of the average cost per unit of output produced. When the average cost is declining, the producer of the product under consideration is reaping efficiency gains due to economies of scale. So long as the average cost of production is declining the firm has an obvious advantage in increasing the output level (provided, there is demand for the product). Ideally, the firm would like to be at the minimum average cost point. However, in the short run, the firm may have to produce at an output level which is higher than the one that yields the minimum average total cost.

When a firm has to add to production capacity in the long run, this may be done by either duplicating an existing fixed input (for intance, a plant) or increasing the size of the plant. Usually, as the plant size increases, a firm is able to achieve a new minimum average cost point (lower than the minimum average cost achieved with the previous smaller capacity) plant. For example, in the case of Better Steel Corporation, the average cost per ton of steel at the minimum average cost point with the larger blast furnace may be 20 percent less than the average cost at the minimum average cost point with smaller blast furnace. Thus, in the long run, a firm may keep switching to larger and larger plants, successively reducing the average cost. One should, however, be warned that due to technological constraints the average cost is assumed to start rising at some output level even in the long run—that is, the average cost curve is U-shaped even in the long run.

Therefore, while looking at the average cost per unit of output is the key to understanding economies of scale, it is useful to remember that the average cost declines up to a point in the short run, and it may decline even more in the long run (also up to a point), as higher and higher levels of output are produced.

ECONOMIES OF SCALE AND OLIGOPOLY

It is interesting to examine how economies of scale lead to market forms such as **oligopoly** and monopoly, provide a reason for engaging in foreign trade, and are a factor in generating productivity gains. The existence of economies of scale in certain industries can lead to oligopolistic market structures in those industries. An oligopoly is a market form in which there are only a few sellers of similar products. Low costs of production (cost per unit or the average cost) can only be achieved if a firm is producing an output level that constitutes a substantial portion of the total available market. This, in turn, leads to a rather small number of firms in the industry, each supplying a sizable portion of the total market demand. In addition, economies of scale in production are often accompanied by economies of scale in sales promotion for the product under consideration, further strengthening the emergence of an oligopolistic structure in the industry.

The automobile industry has long been considered a good example of an industry that demonstrates economies of scale in production in the United States. According to a study by Joe Bain of the University of California, an automobile plant of a minimum efficient size can supply roughly ten percent of the total automobile demand of the domestic market. Thus, it is not economical to have a large number of automobile firms. It is conceivable that the U.S. auto industry can possibly have about ten firms or so, and still not lose productive efficiency—that is, the industry will, even with ten firms, be able to produce at the technologically feasible minimum average cost. However, the U.S. automobile industry can simply not afford to have 50 or 100 firms due to economies of scale. The U.S. automobile industry also provides a good example of an industry that experiences economies of scale in sales promotion. Sales **advertising** for automobiles can be considered in a manner similar to actually producing automobiles. For an effective advertising campaign, the sales promotion must be done on a large scale. As the scale of advertising increases, the advertising cost per unit of output (advertising cost per automobile in this example) declines, at least up to a certain level of output. In addition, buyers of cars generally like to deal with a firm that has a large and dependable network of dealers. Establishing a large and dependable dealership requires a lot of money. Since dealers are also attracted to more reputable and popular brands, smaller automobile manufacturers are put at a considerable disadvantage in the battle for better dealers.

ECONOMIES OF SCALE AND MONOPOLY

Economies of scale can also lead to a monopoly, a market structure in which there is only one seller of a particular product. As explained earlier, in economies of scale the average cost per unit of output declines as the level of production is increased. If the average cost of producing the product reaches a minimum at such an output level that it is large enough to satisfy the product demand of the entire market (at a price that leads to at least some profits), a firm that is supplying this product may become a monopolist. In such a case where the firm is experiencing economies of scale, it has an obvious incentive to keep expanding production until it produces enough to meet all of the market demand for the product—in the face of falling average cost of the product, it would be hard to come to any other conclusion but to expand production (provided that there are no legal impediments). Therefore, competition can simply not be maintained in such a case. Even if there are a number of firms in the industry, each firm will have the same natural desire to expand—an economic warfare is most likely to result under such circumstances. The most likely ultimate outcome of the economic rivalry will be the survival of a single winning firm, now a monopolist.

Cases where economies of scale lead to a monopolistic market structure are considered examples of "natural monopolies." There are many reasons why a monopoly may emerge. When a monopoly emerges due to economies of scale, it is considered defensible on the basis of the cost efficiency that it generates. However, since a monopolist may engage in an unfair pricing policy (due to lack of competition in the industry), the public often insists that the monopolist's pricing behavior be regulated by government.

The electric power industry provides an example of an industry that experiences economies of scale to such an extent as to lead to a natural monopoly. This industry experiences great economies of scale, with rapidly decreasing average costs of producing electrical energy. Fuel consumed per kilowatt hour of electric power is lower in larger-size power-generating plants. In addition, there are economies in combining generating units at a single location, rather than have them spread over different sites. Because of these factors, the propensity toward natural monopoly is great. As a result, there has been very little attempt to force competition in the electric power industry, since it would be economically wasteful. Instead, a monopolist producer of electrical power in each area is regulated by government.

It should be noted that the fact that an industry experiences economies of scale (declining average costs of production) does not imply that it will necessarily lead to a monopoly. The likelihood that the average cost per unit of output will decline up to a point that can satisfy the entire market demand depends also on the size of the market. The smaller the market, the more likely it is to lead to a natural monopoly. The case for the European Common Market was, at least partially, based on the premise that integrating markets across Europe would lead to great economies of scale in production. This, in turn, would make them more competitive internationally, and benefit the European consumers who would also benefit from lower average costs (as these would translate into lower retail prices paid by them).

ECONOMIES OF SCALE AND INTERNATIONAL TRADE

Participating in foreign trade is considered an important way to reap advantages of unrealized potential of economies of scale. Usually, foreign trade is based on specialization—each country specializing in production of goods and services in which it has the comparative advantage. With the possibility of the benefits from economies of scale, there are advantages in engaging in specialization and foreign trade even if there is no difference among countries with respect to the economic efficiency with which they produce goods and services. As an example, suppose that a country may experience economies of scale in producing a particular commodity (for instance, steel). However, this country is producing this commodity at such a low output level that the average cost per unit of the output is high. Due to the high average cost it does not have the comparative advantage in exporting this product to foreign countries. Now, assume that this country specializes in production of this commodity and exports to another country. The other country does the same—it specializes in the production of another product (say, aluminum) and exports to the first country. Thus, the first country specializes in the production of steel and the second country specializes in the production of aluminum. If economies of scale exist in both steel and aluminum industries, firms can serve the *combined* markets of both countries and supply both goods at lower prices (assuming some of the advantages of lower costs are passed on) than if they only reach their respective domestic markets.

This is a major argument for an international economic association such as the European Common Market.

In addition to the pure economies of scale in production, there are ''economies of scale'' in learning associated with specialization in the foreign trade context. In this the average cost per unit goes down as economic efficiencies increase due to learning. In the aircraft and machine tool industries, manufacturers are well aware of reductions in average costs due to learning. It has been estimated that the average cost per unit of new machine tools tends to decline by 20 percent each time the cumulated output is doubled, due to improvement in efficiency through learning by individuals and organizations. In an industry where learning is an important factor in causing economies of scale, there are advantages in one country specializing in the production of that product. In such a case, specialization can reduce average costs and retail prices to lower levels than if each nation attempts to be self-sufficient in the products subject to economies of scale in learning.

ECONOMIES OF SCALE AND PRODUCTIVITY GAINS

Productivity gains (increase in output per unit of labor) are crucial to the economic growth of a nation. John Kendrick in Understanding Productivity: An Introduction to the Dynamics of Productivity Change analyzes the productivity gains in the United States in detail, and mentions economies of scale as one of the important factors.

Economies of scale accompany economic growth as increasing specialization of workers, machines, plants, and firms occurs and as certain kinds of overhead functions (such as financial management) do not need to expand at the same rate as the growth in output. These generate cost savings as output expands. Furthermore, it is easier to innovate when the production capacity is increased rather than when the capacity is being replaced. Thus, a growth in production contributes to productivity gains through economies of scale and associated reductions in costs and prices.

Kendrick does, however, point out that the optimal rate of economic growth is determined by factors other than economies of scale, particularly the saving and investment propensity of the community (economy). As a result, a nation should not attempt to accelerate productivity gains (through economies of scale) by accelerating economic growth above the rate that is considered to be the optimal economic growth rate for that country. Nonetheless, Kendrick's analysis suggests that policy makers should attempt to achieve a steadier, higher economic growth rate since they will produce greater economies of scale. It must, however, be noted that the favorable effect of economies of scale accompanying economic growth would be partially offset by a decline in the average quality of land and other natural resources that are used in production processes. Kendrick, nevertheless, expects the net effect of economies of scale on productivity gains to be positive.

[Andrew P. Sahu]

FURTHER READING:

Bain, Joe. *Barriers to New Competition*. Harvard University Press, 1956.

Kendrick, John H. *Understanding Productivity: An Introduction to the Dynamics of Productivity Change*. The Johns Hopkins University Press, 1977.

Mansfield, Edwin. *Principles of Microeconomics*. 5th ed. W.W. Norton & Company, 1992.

ECONOMIES OF SCOPE

In terms of industrial organization, economies of scope are present in enterprises that develop and manufacture a variety of related products. Such corporations extend expertise in core competencies or technologies to the full range of products related to those core competencies or technologies. **Economies of scope** differ from economies of scale in that the enterprise enjoys a cost advantage from manufacturing generally limited quantities of a variety of products based on a core expertise, rather than concentrating that core expertise on manufacturing large quantities of one product.

General Motors Corp. provides an excellent example of a corporation with broad economies of scope. General Motors' core competency rests in the development and fabrication of products powered by gasoline- or diesel-fueled engines. The firm operates six automobile groups: Cadillac, Buick, Oldsmobile, Pontiac, Chevrolet, and Saturn. Each enterprise is engaged in the production of cars powered by internal combustion engines. This core competency is extended to larger vehicles through its GM Truck division—which manufactures small and medium-size utility trucks and larger semi-trailer tractors—and to railroad locomotives through its Electro-Motive division. In addition to conventional- and diesel-engine products, GM until recently enjoyed a position in a related propulsion technology, turbine engines, through its Allison division, which built a variety of turbojet engines for use in aircraft and power generation.

Ford Motor Co. was organized similarly across product lines, controlling the Ford, Lincoln, and Mercury automobile lines as well as the Ford Truck division. For a period during the 1930s, and again during World War II, Ford manufactured not only aircraft engines but also complete aircraft.

General Electric also achieved significant economies of scope around turbine engine technology, providing the company with significant positions in power-generating equipment, nuclear power, and jet engines.

During the 1980s, General Dynamics provided an example of economies of scope within defense technology, specifically as it related to defense electronics. General Dynamics controlled the nation's largest nuclear submarine company, Electric Boat, the former Chrysler battle tank division, and Convair, manufacturer of F-111 and F-16 aircraft and numerous rocket systems.

AT&T is a company initially organized solely around a single business, telecommunications technology, operating on the principle of economies of scale. Once the largest telecommunications company in the world, its recent forays into computer technology, wireless mobile telephone, and broadband data communications represent a transformation in which core competencies are being extended to related businesses.

Zenith Electronics Corp. provides an example of the opposite transformation. Once involved in television and radio production, computers, lighting systems, and cable communications, representing economies of scope, Zenith has shed all but its television and cable businesses, choosing to concentrate its expertise only in those areas where it is exceptionally competitive.

Like the condition of economies of scale, economies of scope provide an enterprise with opportunities for significant cost savings. Economies of scope achieve this, however, not through increases in the scale of manufacturing apparatus, but through increases in the scope of those applications into related fields. This situation provides numerous consumer benefits by enabling technological developments in one area to be tested and applied to other areas. The result is faster application of new technologies to a wider range of products and greater product value to the consumer.

[John Simley]

FURTHER READING:

Baumol, William J., and Alan S. Blinder. *Economics, Principles and Policy*. 2nd ed. New York: Harcourt Brace Jovanovich, 1982.

Fischer, Stanley, and Rudiger Hornbusch. *Economics*. New York: McGraw-Hill, 1983.

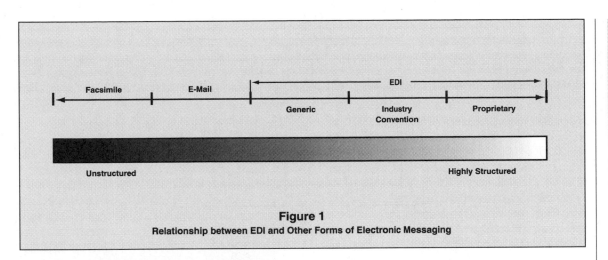

Figure 1
Relationship between EDI and Other Forms of Electronic Messaging

ECONOMISTS AND ECONOMICS

SEE: Macroeconomics; Microeconomics

ELASTICITY OF DEMAND

SEE: Microeconomics

ELECTRONIC DATA INTERCHANGE (EDI)

Electronic data interchange (EDI) is the electronic movement of data between or within organizations in a structured, computer-retrievable data format that permits information to be transferred from a computer program in one location to a computer program in another location without rekeying. EDI includes the direct transmission of data between locations; transmission using an intermediary such as a communication network; and the exchange of computer tapes, disks, or other digital storage devices.

EDI is only one of several ways to move data electronically. It is not facsimile (fax) nor **electronic mail**. As shown in Figure 1, facsimile transmission (fax) is the transfer of totally unstructured data. With fax, a digitized image of a paper document is transmitted. While mailing time delays are avoided, the receiver of a facsimile transmission would not be able to enter the image directly into a computer program without rekeying. Electronic mail (e-mail) also moves data electronically but is designed for person-to-person applications. It uses a free format rather than a structured format. A party receiving an e-mail pur-

chase order, for example, would not likely be able to automatically read it into an order entry program, and would most likely have to rekey the information.

Nor is EDI electronic order entry (EOE). With EOE, a customer keys an order into a seller's order entry system using a computer terminal located on the customer's premises. EOE is not computer-to-computer. It does not permit the customer to enter data automatically from the customer's inventory management or other order generating system.

EDI has two important subsets, illustrated diagrammatically in Figure 2.

Electronic funds transfer (EFT) is EDI between financial institutions. The result of an EFT transaction is the transfer of monetary value from one account to another. Examples of EFT systems in the United States are FedWire and Automated Clearing House (ACH) payments. FedWire is the same-day, real-time, electronic transfer of funds between two financial institutions using the communication network of the Federal Reserve Bank. ACH transfers are batch-processed electronic transfers that settle in one or two business days. An example of an ACH transfer is the direct deposit of payroll offered by many firms to their employees. Using the ACH network, the originating bank sends electronic payment instructions to each receiving bank. Another application of the ACH system is direct debits often used by consumers to make mortgage, utility, or insurance payments.

Financial EDI (FEDI) is EDI between banks and their customers or between banks when there is not a value transfer. For example, a firm may receive electronic reports from its bank listing all checks received the previous day. A bank may also send its monthly statement to a firm using FEDI. Some firms send FEDI payment orders to their banks to initiate supplier payments.

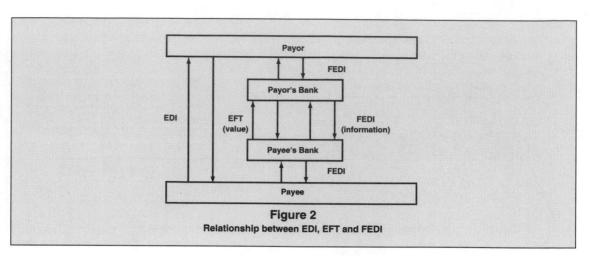

Figure 2
Relationship between EDI, EFT and FEDI

BENEFITS OF EDI

EDI was developed to solve the problems inherent in paper-based transaction processing and in other forms of electronic communication. In solving these problems, EDI is a tool that enables organizations to reengineer information flows and business processes. Problems with the paper-based transaction system are:

- Time delays. Delays are caused primarily by two factors. Paper documents may take days to transport from one location to another. In addition, manual processing delays are caused by the need to key, file, retrieve, and compare data.

- Labor costs. In non-EDI systems, manual processing is required for data keying, document storage and retrieval, sorting, matching, reconciling, envelope stuffing, stamping, signing, etc. While automated equipment can help with some of these processes, most managers will agree that labor costs for document processing represent a significant proportion of their overhead. In general, labor-based processes are much more expensive than nonlabor intensive operations involving **computers** and telecommunications.

- Errors. Because information is keyed multiple times and documents are transported, stored, and retrieved by people, non-EDI systems tend to be error prone.

- Uncertainty. Uncertainty exists in two areas. First, paper transportation and other manual processing delays mean that the time the document is received is uncertain. Once a transaction is sent, the sender does not know when the transaction will be received nor when it will be processed. Second, the sender does not even know whether the transaction has been received at all nor whether the receiver agrees with what was sent in the transaction.

- High Inventories. Because of time delays and uncertainties in non-EDI processing, inventories are often higher than necessary. Lead times with paper processing are long. In a manufacturing firm, it may be virtually impossible to achieve a just-in-time inventory system with the time delays inherent in non-EDI processing systems.

- Information Access. EDI permits users access to a vast amount of detailed transaction data—in a non-EDI environment this is possible only with great effort and time delay. Because EDI data is already in computer-retrievable form, it is subject to automated processing and analysis. Such information helps one retailer, for example, to monitor sales of toys by model, color, or customer ZIP code. This enables the retailer to respond very quickly to changes in consumer taste.

INFRASTRUCTURE FOR EDI

In order to have EDI, four elements of infrastructure must exist: (1) format standards are required to facilitate automated processing by all users, (2) translation software is required to translate from a user's proprietary format for internal data storage into the generic external format and back again, (3) value-added networks are very helpful in solving the technical problems of sending information between computers, and (4) inexpensive microcomputers are required to bring all potential users—even small ones—into the market. It has only been in the past several years that all of these ingredients have fallen into place.

FORMAT STANDARDS. To permit the efficient use of computers, information must be highly organized into a consistent data format. A format defines how information in a message is organized: what data goes where, what data is mandatory, what is optional, how many characters are permitted for each data field, how data fields are ordered, and what codes or abbreviations are permitted.

Early EDI efforts in the 1960s used proprietary formats developed by one firm for exclusive use by its trading partners. This worked well until a firm wanted to exchange EDI documents with other firms who wanted to use their own formats. Since the different formats were not compatible, data exchange was difficult if not impossible.

To facilitate the widespread use of EDI, standard formats were developed so that an electronic message sent by one party could be understood by any receiver that subscribes to that format standard. In the United States the Transportation Data Coordinating Committee began in 1968 to design format standards for transportation documents. The first document was approved in 1975. This group pioneered the ideas that are used by all standards organizations today. North American standards are currently developed and maintained by a volunteer organization called ANSI (American National Standards Institute) X12 Accredited Standards Committee (or simply ANSI X12). The format for a document defined by ANSI X12 is broad enough to satisfy the needs of many different industries. Electronic documents (called transaction sets by ANSI X12) are typically of variable length and most of the information is optional. When a firm sends a standard EDI purchase order to another firm, it is possible for the receiving firm to pass the purchase order data through an EDI translation program directly to a business application without manual intervention.

INDUSTRY CONVENTIONS. To satisfy users from many different organizations with vastly different needs, the ANSI X12 standards must remain very generic. Some industries have developed their own subsets of the more generic EDI formats. These formats may essentially be considered customized formats of the more generic standard EDI formats. For example, the ANSI X12 standard defines two-digit codes for more than 400 units of measure. The automotive industry does not need nearly that many so their industry convention documentation defines only a handful of units of measure. This makes EDI less confusing for implementers.

TYPES OF STANDARDIZED DOCUMENTS. There are currently generic standards for over 250 types of transactions including: purchase order, invoice, functional acknowledgment, purchase order acknowledgement, payment order, request for quote, insurance claim, inventory data, grade transcript, student loan data, freight invoice, bill of lading, lockbox receipt, load tender, library loan request, promotion an-

nouncement, advanced ship notice, material release, telephone bill, price/sales catalog, and claim tracer.

EDIFACT STANDARDS. Under the auspices of the **United Nations**, a format standard has been developed to reach a worldwide audience. These standards are called EDI for Administration, Commerce, and Transport (EDIFACT). They are similar in many respects to ANSI X12 standards but they are accepted by a larger number of countries. By 1996, all new ANSI X12 EDI documents will be developed using the EDIFACT format.

TRANSLATION SOFTWARE. Translation software makes EDI work by translating data from the sending firm's internal format into a generic EDI format. Translation software also receives a sender's EDI message and translates it from the generic standard into the receiver's internal format. There are currently translation software packages for almost all types of computers and operating systems.

VALUE-ADDED NETWORKS (VANS). When firms first began using EDI, most communications of EDI documents were directly between trading partners. Unfortunately, direct computer-to-computer communications requires that both firms (1) use similar communication protocols, (2) have the same transmission speed, (3) have phone lines available at the same time, and (4) have compatible computer hardware. If these conditions are not met, then communication becomes difficult if not impossible. A value added network (VAN) can solve these problems by providing an electronic mailbox service. By using a VAN, an EDI sender need only learn to send and receive messages to or from one party: the VAN. Since a VAN provides a very flexible computer interface, it can talk to virtually any type of computer. This means that to conduct EDI with hundreds of trading partners, an organization only has to talk to one party.

VANs also provide a security interface between trading partners. Since trading partners send EDI messages only through a VAN, there is no fear that a trading partner may dip into sensitive information stored on the computer system nor that a trading partner may send a computer virus to the other partners.

INEXPENSIVE COMPUTERS. The fourth building block of EDI is inexpensive computers that permit even small firms to implement EDI. Since microcomputers are now so prevalent, it is possible for firms of all sizes to deal with each other using EDI.

EXAMPLES OF EDI

The Bergen Brunswig Drug Company, a wholesale pharmaceutical distributor in Orange, California, is one of the most successful companies in using EDI

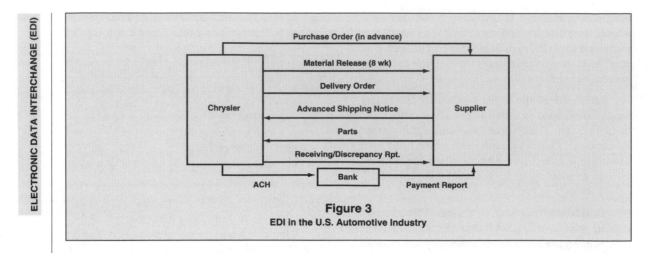

Figure 3
EDI in the U.S. Automotive Industry

for many of its business processes. To generate an order to Bergen Brunswig, a customer (pharmacist) uses a hand-held bar code scanner to capture the UPC (Universal Product Code) number on a shelf label for a product to be ordered. The pharmacist enters the quantity desired into a key pad on the scanner and moves onto the next item. All items in the pharmacy can be scanned in only a few minutes. A microcomputer next reads the information contained in the scanner and an electronic order is prepared for the pharmacist's review. The order is sent via EDI to a Bergen Brunswig distribution center where the order is analyzed and resequenced to match the product location in the distribution center. Within five hours, the order is delivered to the pharmacy. Bergen Brunswig has been able to eliminate all order takers, reduce errors to near zero, fulfill orders faster, reduce overhead costs, and build customer loyalty. The company also uses EDI for sending purchase orders to pharmaceutical manufacturers, receiving invoices, and handling charge backs.

PST Vans in Salt Lake City, Utah, is using EDI to receive load tenders from shippers and make confirmations back to them. Freight bills are also sent to shippers from PST's accounts receivable department. The application of EDI has resulted in more accurate shipping information, reduced paper storage requirements, and faster bill payment.

The automakers in the United States are also extensive users of EDI. Chrysler Corp., as illustrated in Figure 3, has applied EDI to reengineer its manufacturing processes. Once a contract has been negotiated with a parts supplier, Chrysler sends the supplier weekly electronic material releases specifying the intended use of parts over an eight-week horizon. Several days before the parts are needed, Chrysler sends an EDI delivery order to the supplier detailing precisely how many parts are needed for delivery on a certain date, where the parts are to be delivered, what bar coding is to be put on the containers, and when

delivery is expected. Some suppliers are told how to sequence the parts on the truck for most effective unloading. After the supplier loads the parts, an EDI advanced shipping notice is sent to Chrysler verifying that the delivery is on the way. Chrysler scans the parts in as they arrive and may send an electronic discrepancy report if there are problems. Payments are often made electronically on a settlement date specified in the contract. No invoice is used in this reengineered process. In this environment Chrysler needs very little inventory and, in fact, has been able to shave approximately $1 billion from its parts inventory.

Use of EDI is spreading to many different types of organizations. The insurance industry is beginning to use EDI for health care claims, procedure authorization, and payments. Universities are using EDI for sending grade transcripts, inter-library material requests, and student loan information. Even the U.S. court system is looking into the use of EDI for filing certain data-intensive documents such as bankruptcy information.

STATUS OF EDI

EDI appears to be entering into a rapid growth phase. According to an extensive market survey completed by the EDI Group Ltd. in 1993, 45 percent of U.S. firms with over 5,000 employees are using EDI. This is up from 41 percent in 1992. The largest increases, however, came in smaller firms. Medium-sized firms (501-5,000 employees) grew to 31 percent usage in 1993 from only 20 percent in 1992. Usage in small firms (500 or fewer employees) grew to 18 percent from only 10 percent in 1992. There was also a significant drop in the percentage of firms having no plans for implementing EDI. In 1993, only 29 percent said they had no plans, considerably down from the 63 percent who were not considering EDI in 1992.

It appears that EDI is destined to become more and more important as a data communication tool that will enable organizations to more efficiently design internal processes and external interactions with trading partners.

FURTHER READING:

Emmelhainz, Margaret A. *EDI: A Total Management Guide.* 2nd ed. New York: Van Nostrand Reinhold, 1993.

Hill, Ned C., and Daniel M. Ferguson. "Electronic Data Interchange: A Definition and Perspective." *EDI FORUM: The Journal of Electronic Data Interchange.* March, 1989, pp. 5-12.

Hill, Ned C., and Michael Swenson. "Bergen Brunswig: An Update on an Industry EDI Leader." *EDI FORUM: The Journal of Electronic Data Interchange.* August, 1993, pp. 60-63.

In the words of one business seer quoted in a magazine article, "In a few years, everyone will assume you have an E-mail address." Of course, that person could be expected to have a positive view of E-mail since he is also the executive director of the Electronic Mail Association. Still, judging from the number of computer and modem owners who are starting to use computer electronic mail, bulletin board services, on-line research and "real time chat" services, his prediction is likely to come true.

Strictly defined, "electronic mail" is the process of sending or receiving a computer file or message by computer modem over telephone wires to a preselected "mail box" or "address." The message can be a simple letter, or material many pages long such as a book chapter or detailed contract. It can even send a graphics file of photographs or artwork. Newer innovations include the ability to send sound recordings over the wires so music lovers with the properly set up computers can download the songs of their favorite musical group.

The mail box is an electronic version of what it sounds like. It has an address, usually a combination of numbers or key words selected by either the company operating the E-mail service or the E-mail customer. The address describes what service carries the mailbox and where on that service to send the message.

The typical E-Mail message might be comprised of a memo from the **CEO** duplicated in every mail box in every desktop computer operated by a corporation in all of its locations around the world. Or, the message could be delivered to a single computer, just as a person would send a letter to a business prospect or acquaintance in another part of the world.

The difference between electronic mail and real mail is that the electronic message never sees envelope or stamp. The difference between electronic mail and facsimile mail is that the message passes between two computers without ever being put onto paper, unless the person receiving it sends it to a printer. One wrinkle on this definition: some services will convert E-mail into fax mail if the sender wants the receivers to get a paper copy. An example of this would be if the sender was not sure that all intended receivers of a message actually had an E-mail address, such as when a corporation wants to send the same press release to a large number of news media outlets, but there is no practical way of learning their E-mail addresses.

Electronic mail can be delivered 24 hours a day, or at preselected times when phone rates are the lowest. The big advantage is that it is instant. No waiting for the delivery man to come, no worrying about rain, snow, or gloom of night, no rushing to package draft documents in time to make the airplane for the next-day delivery service.

The history of E-mail is quite young. Most providers have been in the business for less than 10 years, although the Internet, the unrestricted, global network of on-line services and computer bulletin boards, has had varying versions of E-mail for a while longer. Only in recent years have two different types of standardized E-mail providers emerged.

HOW E-MAIL IS DELIVERED

One type of company is strictly an E-mail provider. Represented by MCI Mail, AT&T EasyLink or SprintMail, these firms provide E-mail and services such as E-mail to fax conversion and electronic data interchange (constant, heavy computer contact between corporations to accomplish such tasks as regularly ordering inventory or paying invoices by computer). These providers can make their E-mail look like regular mail, including scanning in a company's letterhead and signature of the sender then matching them to personalize the E-mail message.

Other companies such as CompuServe, Prodigy, America Online, GEnie and Delphi mainly provide access to on-line services such as research databases and real-time chat lines, with access to an E-mail address as an additional benefit. These companies have been experiencing rapid growth through the mid 90s as more home computer owners purchase modems and the software companies make the devices easier to use.

Besides the E-mail capabilities provided by these companies, they also have numerous "bulletin board systems" or BBS as they are known to regular users, and "real-time chat lines" where users can discuss virtually any subject that interests them. The BBS are similar to E-mail boxes except they are more like the bulletin boards. Computer users with questions post their request and computer users with the answers post their responses. Even software and job openings in particular companies may be posted on the BBS then downloaded by people calling the board.

The chat lines have proven to be popular for computer users. People with common interests reach the chat lines through their on-line services then join the conversation on whatever discussion group they have joined. The process is similar to joining a cock-tail party conversation by keyboard.

USE OF E-MAIL AWAY FROM THE USUAL PROVIDERS

While each E-mail provider operates its own proprietary system, savvy users can communicate across all the systems using software that automatically handles any differences. These same languages allow E-mail users to communicate with corporations operating their own **Local Area Networks (LANs)** or networks of computers linked together within the building) or on the Internet. To reach these other mailboxes, the E-mail provider operates a ''gateway'' that allows access to the Internet.

Most of the major on-line services and many low-profile local access companies now provide access to the Internet through their gateways. The process of navigating the Internet can be difficult. The Internet was conceived and is still dominated by computer techies who never saw the need to make it simple to use since everyone they knew understood how to figure out its technical eccentricities. Now with America Online and CompuServe subscribers tentatively venturing forth, the Internet regulars are being forced to share their once-private services with increasing numbers of people new to on-line services.

The Internet regulars have not made it easy for the neophytes. When the regulars become offended at something newcomers have done or written on the Internet, they sometimes ''flame'' the newcomers' mail boxes, sending them useless, sometimes obscene, always angry, messages that fill the mail box to capacity, rendering it useless until emptied by the newcomer.

E-MAIL CUSTOMS AND THE NEED FOR SECURITY

Traditionally, the Internet has been free of advertising. Since it has always been funded by government and universities, there has never been any need to sell things to keep it in service. More commercially-oriented newcomers have been known to broadcast messages to mail boxes advertising everything from legal services to computer products.

The ability to offend is not the only concern among on-line service or E-mail users. Security is a big question. For example, messages sent over the corporate E-mail system could technically belong to the corporation, even if they were meant to be seen only by certain people within that corporation. This means that managers could conceivably read their employees' E-mail. There is no legal reason to prevent them from so doing. In cases over the past several years, employees have been fired for denigrating their bosses in E-mail messages. The bosses found out how their employees felt when they delved into the mailboxes.

Important to the corporation are cases in which E-mail messages have been subpoenaed by the court. Depending on the sophistication and complexity of the E-mail system, messages once thought to have been erased may still exist. At least one company sells itself on the ability to retrieve supposedly erased E-mail messages from the bowels of the corporate mainframe. In one case involving a woman who claimed she was wrongfully fired, the corporation's attorney produced E-mail messages showing how all procedures were followed in terminating the woman's employment. The woman's attorney, using earlier E-mail messages that had been retrieved from the system, showed that the woman was wrongfully fired. Her boss had created the later E-mail messages in order to look good in court.

In other cases, plaintiffs have sued companies involving product development or liability. E-mail messages between engineers and designers have been subpoenaed. The result has been that sometimes serious, sometimes frivolous, E-mail messages have taken on new meanings when presented in an open court.

The message is clear for both corporations and individuals using electronic mail. While E-mail may be secure from most prying eyes, it may never be 100 percent secure unless other preventive measures are taken. Particularly in a corporation, E-mail can be read by people sophisticated enough to get into the system.

FUTURE OF E-MAIL

E-mail is still in its infancy, but the next ''toddler'' step may be one of the most amazing aspects of its young life still to come. Engineers are now working on practical wireless data networks. While voice cellular phones account for almost all wireless communications today, one telephone company has predicted that data communications could account for up to one-third of the wireless traffic by the turn of the century.

Visionaries predict that laptop computers and personal digital assistants (such as the before-its-time Apple Newton) will soon be routinely sending and receiving messages without the need for hooking up to telephone wires. Instead of telephones, the PDAs will use existing cellular communications towers, or perhaps a system of satellites orbiting the Earth. This means that salespeople will be able to download their E-mail messages while driving to their next appointment; that investors can get stock tips while soaking up the beach sun, and that no one need ever be out of touch with their computer system again.

[Clint Johnson]

EMBARGO

An embargo is a state-sponsored prohibition on the movement of goods between nations. It is an integral part of economic warfare. Embargoes can be selective or universal, and they can cover both imports to a country and the **exporting** of goods from that country. Regardless of their scope, embargoes are primarily punitive in nature; their purpose is not to protect home markets (which is the function of a tariff) but rather to punish a foreign country.

Although embargoes are economic sanctions, most often they are used for achieving political goals. The United States's embargo of Cuba is meant to punish that island nation for having an anti-American communist government and for exporting its communist revolution to Africa and Latin America. By denying Cuba American markets and American goods and services, it is hoped that the embargo will contribute to the downfall of the communist regime.

In spite of its punitive nature, an embargo is not a military act of war. An embargo is different from a blockade, which is a military obstruction of trade by one country against two or more other countries and which can be construed as an act of war. A boycott is an embargo of sorts on purchases, but it is usually conducted by private groups with specific social goals rather than nations with political ends. Some of the more well-known 20th century embargoes have been the American- and English-sponsored oil embargo against Japan in 1940, the aforementioned American embargo against Cuba, the American wheat embargo against the former Soviet Union during Jimmy Carter's administration, and the United Nations sanctioned embargoes against South Africa and Iraq.

The most famous embargo in U.S. history was Thomas Jefferson's embargo of 1807 in which he sought to punish Great Britain and France by withholding American raw materials and finished goods and by suspending European exports to the Unted States. This was in retaliation for French threats against American vessels and British impressment of American sailors into service.

As Richard Ellings points out in his book *Embargoes and World Power*, embargoes have their advantages and disadvantages. Embargoes are less risky and less expensive than armed intervention. Generally they are deemed to be less noxious to neutral or third parties and, therefore, are preferable compromises between going to war and taking no action. Embargoes, however, often have drawbacks. The target countries may consider a country using an embargo in place of military action as lacking resolve. Many target countries respond with their own counter-embargoes. Furthermore, other countries must cooperate with the embargo for it to be truly effective. During the American wheat embargo of the former Soviet Union, for example, that country quickly turned to South America for its grain and cereal needs.

SEE ALSO: Trade Barriers, Foreign Trade Zones

[Michael Knes]

FURTHER READING:

Ellings, Richard. *Embargoes and World Power: Lessons from American Foreign Policy*. Westview Press, 1985.

Wiles, P. J. D. "Economic Wars," in *The New Palgrave Dictionary of Economics*. London: MacMillan, 1987.

EMBEZZLEMENT

Embezzlement is a form of fraud that involves misappropriation of money or property by someone who has been entrusted with it by virtue of their position or employment. Larceny and theft, on the other hand, involve taking money or property that belongs to someone else by trespass or force.

Depending on the amount of money or value of property involved, embezzlement is a misdemeanor or felony and a statutory crime punishable by fine and/or imprisonment. However, according to one profile, the typical embezzler is not usually prosecuted, usually does not receive a jail sentence upon conviction, and usually does not repay the victim or pay court costs.

An embezzler may be a public official or someone employed in a fiduciary capacity. Such a person is entrusted with funds or property by virtue of his or her position. When they use funds or property belonging to another person or business for their own account, they are guilty of embezzlement. While virtually any business can be the victim of embezzlement, the crime most often occurs in financial institutions, healthcare companies, and a variety of small businesses.

Examples of embezzlement include bookkeepers stealing from their employers' accounts by making false journal entries, altering documents, and manipulating expense records. Embezzlement may take the form of making payments to "dummy" suppliers and vendors. Employees of financial institutions may attempt to embezzle by diverting funds from legitimate accounts into "dummy" accounts.

The criminal act of embezzlement usually involves three distinct phases. At each stage the embezzler leaves indications that a crime has occurred; unlike many other crimes, however, there often is little hard evidence to indicate that a crime has been committed. The first phase of embezzlement is the criminal act itself, taking money or property manually, by computer, or by telephone. Once the crime has been committed, the embezzler attempts to conceal it. Making a phony payment, falsifying a document, or making misleading journal entries are some of the ways that embezzlers try to hide their crime. Finally, the third phase of criminal activity involves converting the stolen assets into cash and spending it.

At each step the embezzler is subject to detection. The act itself must be witnessed in order for the embezzler to be caught at the first stage. Concealment of the act results in altered records or miscounted cash that can be detected by auditors. Conversion usually results in lifestyle changes that can be noted by fellow employees.

In order to protect themselves from embezzlement, companies need to develop a program to recognize signs of employee fraud. One aspect of such a program is recognizing accounting irregularities. Embezzlers usually alter, forge, or destroy checks, sales invoices, purchase orders, and similar documents. Examination of source documents can often lead to the detection of embezzlement.

Internal controls are another important aspect of a fraud prevention program. A company's internal control system should be examined for weaknesses. Internal controls are designed to protect a company's assets. If they are weak, then the assets are not safe. Typical controls that help prevent embezzlement include segregating duties, regular or programmed transfers of employees from department to department, and mandatory vacations. In the banking industry, the Office of the Controller of the Currency requires all bank employees in the United States to take at least seven consecutive days of vacation per year. Many cases of fraud have been discovered while employees were on vacation and unable to cover their tracks.

Other recognizable signs of embezzlement include anything out of the ordinary, such as unexplained inventory shortages, unmet specifications, excess scrap material, larger than usual purchases,

significantly higher or lower account balances, excessive cash shortages or surpluses, and unreasonable expenses or reimbursements. Finally, embezzlers often reveal themselves through noticeable lifestyle and behavioral changes. Embezzlers are often first-time criminals whose guilt feelings cause them to act erratically and unpredictably. They usually spend the money they have embezzled rather than saving it. A successful fraud prevention program should include incentives for employees to report unusual behavioral and lifestyle changes in fellow employees.

[David Bianco]

EMERGING MARKETS

The term "emerging markets", while commonly used, is difficult to define. From the perspective of the United States, an emerging market would be one to which a previously untapped potential for U.S. exports or investment might be anticipated.

In 1994, the U.S. Department of Commerce identified 10 nations as "Big Emerging Markets" or those which were predicted to have promising prospects for substantial incremental gains in exports from the United States. Included among these were: the Chinese Economic Area, Indonesia, India, South Korea, Mexico, Argentina, Brazil, South Africa, Poland, and Turkey. These nations carry such favorable prospects as emerging markets precisely because of such factors as changing political relationships with the United States, privatization of key sectors, changes in foreign investment opportunities and rapid economic growth.

While no such list could be definitively argued as complete, other nations commonly included as emerging markets for U.S. exports along with the 10 identified by the Commerce Department are Chile, Vietnam, Malaysia, Thailand, the Czech Republic, and Hungary.

Riskier markets still presenting notable business opportunities in previously less developed markets would also include Uruguay and Paraguay—the two Mercosur nations (nations belonging to a fairly young South American customs union) not listed on the Department of Commerce list. Russia and several of the newly independent states of the former Soviet Union—though riddled with political instability, economic confusion, a weak technological infrastructure, and a lack of business expertise—could still be included as potentially emerging markets. This is because Russia and the newly independent states are all markets receptive to U.S. products that have never before been tapped by U.S. exporters. Additionally, the wrenching shift away from central planning places them in considerable need of business services and expertise of the sort readily available from the United States.

The reasons each of these nations is likely to be considered an important emerging market. One possibility is improved trade relations with the United States along with a strong economy. The liberalization of trade between the two countries would consequently create a marked rise in demand for U.S. exports. This liberalization of trade relations could reflect a change in U.S. policy toward the emerging market. For example, the lifting of various U.S. trade embargoes against South Africa has created a marked potential for U.S. exports following the elimination of that nation's Apartheid policies. South Africa has for years been Africa's strongest economy, but the overwhelming response to the political situation in that nation stunted U.S. exports until fairly recently. The formal opening of relations between Vietnam and the United States in August 1995 would also fall into this category.

Identification as an emerging market could also reflect a change toward U.S. trade within the policy of another established market. This liberalization of trade previously restrictive to U.S. exports could thus inspire new and rapid demand for formerly unavailable U.S. products. The creation of economic zones within the People's Republic of China, for example, made it considerably easier than in past years for U.S. exports to enter China. This, coupled with the liberalization of central control in the designated free economic zones, has led to rapid development. Indeed, Guangdong province (next to Hong Kong) would be the world's fastest growing economy were it treated as an independent state.

Similarly, the post-Communist governments of eastern European nations as well as the newly independent states represent the opening of markets previously walled off from most U.S. exports. While many of these nations remain unstable or economically undeveloped, the stability of nations such as Poland (the first of the Warsaw Pact nations to throw off a communist- or Soviet-influenced government) or the strong manufacturing base of Hungary or the Czech Republic make them potentially promising as emerging markets.

Political factors from abroad have helped some nations emerge as U.S. export and investment destinations. Turkey's active role as an alternative Moslem economic system to such fundamentalist Islamic models of Iran have helped it emerge as a major regional player in the Islamic states of the former Soviet Union, such as Kazakhstan and Turkmenistan. Additionally, Turkey's trade ties with Europe and its repeated attempts to join the European Union (rebuffed for several political reasons unrelated to its

economy) have added further to its aura of stability as an emerging market.

Political factors of another nature have affected the view of U.S. exporters and investors regarding South Korea. In an about-face of decades of earlier practice that discouraged the purchase of foreign goods as "luxury" items, Korea has begun to actively encourage the purchase of U.S. (and European) goods to defuse political pressure from U.S. governmental officials concerned over the **trade deficit** with Korea.

The mutual lifting of restrictions in trade simultaneously from both the United States and from another nation could also earmark that nation as an emerging market for U.S. goods. The North American Free Trade Agreement (NAFTA), for example, represented a lifting of trade restrictions in Mexico and the United States taking place in both countries at the same time. This free trade allowed Mexico, already an important destination for U.S. exports, to "emerge" as an even more important export destination.

An emerging market could also reflect the potential for the rapid economic development of another nation with no change in existing trade restrictions directed against the United States or directed against that nation by the United States. For instance, the massive economic reform program begun in July 1991 in India, and still ongoing, has helped to transform its previously stagnant economy. India's moves to deregulate lending rates and bank reserve requirements, its plans to privatize such public services as the telephones, its revamping of foreign investment regulations, and its reduction of many tariffs, have created strong economic growth. With this comes a related U.S. export potential of goods and services directed toward India's steady economic strength.

Similarly, the actions of the post-Allende governments in Chile have succeeded first in stabilizing and then in encouraging significant growth in both mining and manufacturing. Chile's emphasis on a free market economy has led it to be considered the most likely fourth partner to the North American Free Trade Agreement. Moreover, its economic stability has acted as an incentive to foreign investors. Indeed, Chile was the first Latin American country in a decade to have received a regular commercial bank loan, an occurrence that has not been lost on U.S. investors in the region.

Rapid growth has also marked Indonesia, Malaysia and Thailand as prime emerging markets. Investment from the United States and other nations has flowed into these three southeast Asian nations as all three have freed up investment opportunities, encouraged the development of their natural resources, and capitalized on growing labor costs in Japan and Korea to significantly increase their industrial base and export volume. In turn, they have grown almost between three- and five-fold over the last 25 years and become a major destination of U.S. exports.

Finally, the free trade inroads made following the creation in 1991 of the South American customs union, Mercosur, have strengthened the economies of its four signatory nations Argentina, Brazil, Uruguay, and Paraguay. Mercosur, which formally took effect on January 1, 1995, has added a source of economic strength independent of trade outside of South America. While both Argentina and Brazil would have remained "emerging economies" regardless of their participation in Mercosur, the trade union arrangement has added considerable leverage to the economies of Uruguay and Paraguay. Indeed, both nations are undergoing an economic boom directly linked to the trade liberalization. For example, Paraguay, a major producer of cotton, has traditionally exported only as raw material 90 percent of its cotton to Brazil. Following the formation of Mercosur, it has been able to export manufactured cotton products such as thread and cloth to Brazil without paying duties. The result has been a boom in textile manufacturing in Paraguay that had not existed before. Similarly, the position of Uruguay directly in the path between Buenos Aires and Sao Paulo has strengthened the nation's role as a transportation center due to duty free trucking. The result is the current proposal to build the 47 kilometer bridge over the Rio de la Plata connecting the Uruguayan border city with the Argentine capital on the opposite bank. The bridge—when completed—would be the longest of its type in the world—and would reinforce Uruguay's position as a commercial crossroads. Additionally, the bridge, unthinkable before Mercosur, would substantially cut the transportation time between Mercosur's two greatest industrial centers. The stability linked to Mercosur, coupled with a decade of economic austerity measures and with less protectionist trade policies, have also resulted in increased U.S. export opportunities. The calming of political turmoil, economic austerity measures, and debt-equity swaps have enhanced Brazil as the largest of the Latin American emerging markets. Finally, Argentina's currency reform—tying the newly coined peso to the U.S. dollar—as well as its elimination of exchange controls and import quotas have added considerably to its reputation as Mercosur's most attractive emerging market for U.S. investment.

No list of emerging markets is ever stable. Once an emerging market does remain consistent, it is no longer "emerging"; rather it is an "established" market. Earlier emerging markets such as Greece, Spain, and Portugal have long-since become established. Other markets have come to seem too established to include in a list of "emerging" markets although they may have grown to the level of "established" only recently (for example, Singapore). Some potentially important markets may not be fully justified in being labeled as "emerging" markets—yet. These future or nascent emerging markets are myriad. One could argue for including Gabon, for example, since it has the world's fastest growing **gross national product** at the time of this writing, but it has little **infrastructure** for capitalizing on its rapid growth. One could argue for countries such as Colombia or Venezuela, but their internal political unrest arguably makes them somewhat suspect despite their economic strengths. Similarly one could argue that the tremendous economic activity in Taiwan should it as an emerging market, but that nation's current political situations would preclude its otherwise strong economy from most lists. Thus, any list of emerging markets should not be viewed as definitive but rather as continually evolving.

[David A. Victor]

EMPLOYEE ASSISTANCE PROGRAMS (EAPS)

Employee Assistance Programs (EAPs) were established in the late 1960s with the goal of maintaining **productivity**. EAPs provide employees with counseling and referral services for such problems as alcohol and substance abuse and other mental health problems. As EAPs evolved they began to deal with a wider range of employee concerns, including health, marital, family, financial, alcohol, drug, legal, emotional, and stress-related problems. A specific EAP may focus on one or more of these problem areas or be open to treat them all.

A wide range of businesses throughout the United States and abroad have EAPs. More than 90 percent of the Fortune 500 companies have Employee Assistance Programs. They are also commonplace in many other English-speaking nations. An EAP may offer employees the services of psychiatrists, clinical psychologists, clinical social workers, rehabilitation counselors, psychiatric nurses, and support personnel, among others. In practice EAP counselors may have a variety of educational and professional backgrounds.

While all EAPs are workplace-based, there are several different models. Internal EAPs' counselors work for the business or organization they serve. They may have their own department or be part of the company's human resources or personnel department. In external EAPs, an external provider, such as a mental health organization or hospital, contracts with a business or organization to provide counseling. In larger corporations an EAP may be set up with corporate EAP personnel providing managerial supervision and support for contracted EAP professionals.

An important element of an EAP is confidentiality. EAP counselors work under strict confidentiality whether or not they are employed by the same company or organization as the employees they are counseling. They may not reveal an employee's concerns or problems to the employee's supervisor or manager, or anyone else outside of the EAP. Even the fact that an employee has contacted an EAP counselor usually remains confidential.

In organizations with an EAP, employees are encouraged to contact an EAP counselor whenever they have a problem they would like to discuss, especially if it is a problem that is affecting their ability to function on the job. In some programs EAP counselors meet face-to-face with troubled employees. In other programs they may provide telephone consultation only. All EAP services are generally paid for by the employer and are considered a benefit for the employee.

During the initial and early meetings, the EAP counselor attempts to assess the employee's needs and problems. The EAP counselor listens and talks to the employee until the nature of the problem can be assessed. Some programs may offer a maximum number of sessions, such as two or three, while others may not impose a limit on the number of counseling sessions. During these sessions the EAP counselor may determine whether or not any of the employee's immediate family should also be included in further counseling.

Once the problem has been assessed, the EAP counselor may provide a variety of services depending on his or her qualifications and the nature of the company's EAP. The EAP counselor may provide short-term counseling and/or therapy. If it is apparent there is a crisis, the EAP counselor may be required to intervene. In EAPs limited to telephone consultation, the EAP counselor provides problem assessment over the telephone along with limited counseling and resource referral.

In cases requiring additional professional services, the EAP counselor serves as a link to professional and community resources for the employee. The EAP counselor may refer the employee to other managed care services for appropriate diagnosis, treatment, and assistance. After an employee has been referred for treatment, there may be additional sessions during which the EAP counselor provides follow-up assessment and counseling to help the employee maintain his or her productivity and well-being on the job.

EAPs have been widely accepted by business and industry and their employees. Employers have recognized that EAPs benefit all concerned—employees, their families, and their employers. By responding to a wide range of employee problems, EAPs serve business and industry by providing for a more productive workforce.

SEE ALSO: Human Resource Management

[David Bianco]

EMPLOYEE BENEFITS

Employee benefits are an indirect means of compensating workers. Rather than simply providing an economic benefit, as does cash compensation, benefits foster economic security and stability by insuring beneficiaries against uncertain events. In addition, some benefits programs serve to insure the income and welfare of American families. A common delineation between direct forms of employee compensation, such as wages, and indirect compensation, or benefits, is that the former creates an employee's standard of living, whereas indirect compensation, or benefits, protects that standard of living.

BACKGROUND

Rudimentary employee benefit programs were brought over from Europe and implemented in the colonies. In fact, one of the first recorded benefit programs in American history was the Plymouth Colony settlers' military retirement program, which was established in 1636. Subsequent benefit programs of note incuded: Gallatin Glassworks' **profit sharing** plan (1797); American Express Co.'s private employer pension plan (1875); Montgomery Ward's group health, life, and accident insurance program (1910); federal tax incentives to employers sponsoring **pension plans** (1921); and Baylor University Hospital's group hospitalization program (1929).

Despite the implementation of several different types of benefit programs in both the government and private sectors, employee benefits before the 1930s were negligible by current standards. The Great Depression, however, provided an impetus for the formation of more advanced and substantial social mechanisms that could provide economic stability. Of import were the retirement provisions of the Social Security program enacted at the federal level in 1935. Tax-favored status for compensation received by employees during sickness or injury was added in 1939.

After World War II, federal government initiatives caused a variety of benefits to become more popular with private sector employers. For example, health insurance premiums were made tax-deductible to employers and became nontaxable to employees. As a result, health insurance and other benefits became extremely cost-effective forms of compensation in comparison to wages and salaries. Furthermore, tax-favored benefits became a popular bargaining tool for unions seeking to improve their total pay package. As living standards increased, moreover, people in industrialized nations began to view health insurance and other benefits as necessities, and even entitlements or individual rights.

Largely as a result of government policies, employee benefits in the public and private sectors exploded during the 1950s, 1960s, and 1970s. Government mandates required that employers supply their workers with benefits like **workers' compensation**, Social Security, and Medicaid. And new tax laws prompted a smorgasbord of optional benefits such as pension plans, life insurance, stock bonuses, dental care, **child care**, cafeteria plans, and many more. The rampant proliferation of private-sector benefits ebbed during the late 1970s and 1980s, as the post-war U.S. economic expansion slowed and a new corporate cost-consciousness emerged. Nevertheless, by the late 1980s the federal government estimated that employee benefits represented about 36 percent, or $814 billion, of all wage and salary payments in the United States.

TYPES OF BENEFITS

Employee benefits are any kind of compensation provided in a form other than direct wages and paid for in whole or in part by an employer, even when it's provided by a third party (*Employee Benefits Plain and Simple*, Collier Books, 1993). An example of a third party is the government, which disburses social security benefits that have been paid for by employers.

Benefits fall into one of three principal categories: Mandatory, supplementary, and time-oriented. Mandatory benefits are required by law, and serve to provide economic security for employees related to lack of income for workers and dependents as a result of **unemployment**, old age, disability, poor health, or other factors. Supplementary benefits include the major voluntary benefits of value, like insurance and stock bonuses. Most of those instruments can be classified as: Fully taxable; tax-preferred; tax-deferred, meaning that taxes are not incurred on the benefit until it is accessed; or tax-exempt. They serve many of the same basic functions as mandatory benefits, but also include perks designed simply to attract and please workers. Finally, examples of time-oriented benefits are vacations and sick days, which typically offer company's an inexpensive means of providing attractive employee perks. Some time-oriented benefits possess a tax-favored status.

Major benefits included in each category are listed below:

MANDATORY BENEFITS

Medicaid

Basic Medicare

Public Assistance

Social Security Retirement

Social Security Disability

Supplemental Security Income

Unemployment Insurance

Workers' Compensation

SUPPLEMENTARY BENEFITS

Fully Taxable

Cash bonuses and awards

Non-qualifying stock bonuses

Non-qualifying stock ownership and profit-sharing programs

Severance Pay

Tax Preferred

Life insurance

Long-term disability insurance

Sickness and accident insurance

Tax Deferred

401(k) arrangements (retirement plan)

Deferred profit-sharing plans

Employee stock ownership plans

Most types of qualified pension plans

Stock bonus plans

Thrift savings plans

Tax-Exempt

Cafeteria facilities and meals

Dental and vision insurance

Dependent care

Education assistance

Flexible spending accounts

Health insurance for employees and retirees

Legal assistance

Parking

Supplementary Medicare premiums

TIME-ORIENTED BENEFITS

Flexible shifts

Maternity and paternity leave

Other leave (funeral, jury duty, etc.)

Overtime

Paid lunch

Rest periods

Sabbaticals

Sick days

Vacations and holidays

CHIEF ROLE OF BENEFITS

Benefits are an important means of meeting employees needs and wants. They are often used as perks to attract and keep good workers, for example, or to boost employee morale. However, the chief role of employee benefits is to provide various types of income protection to groups of workers. It is this income protection that delivers the individual security and societal economic stability alluded to in the introduction. Five principal types of income protection delivered by benefits are: 1) disability income replacement; 2) medical expense reimbursement; 3) retirement income replacement; 4) involuntary unemployment income replacement; and 5) replacement income for survivors. Different mandatory and voluntary elements of each of these categories are typically combined to deliver a benefits package to a group of workers that complements the resources and goals the of the organization supplying the benefits.

DISABILITY

Benefits that provide disability income replacement include programs such as Social Security and workers' compensation. The bulk of these benefits are mandatory, although numerous supplementary plans, most of which are tax-favored, exist. Most organizations seek to assemble a disability package that will provide an adequate safety net, yet not act as a disincentive to return to work. A common objective is long-term income reimbursement of 60 percent of pay, which is preceded by higher levels of reimbursement, usually as much as 100 percent during the first six months of disability. Long-term disability pay typically ends at retirement age (when pension payments begin), or when the worker recovers or finds another job.

Other disability related incentives may include sick pay, including cash awards for unused sick days at the end of the year. Employers may vary the quality of their disability package with different copayment options, limits on payments for voluntary coverage, and extended coverage for related health insurance, life insurance, and medical benefits related to the disability.

MEDICAL

Medical expense reimbursements are typically one of the most expensive and important of the voluntary benefits. The two primary types of voluntary medical coverage options are fee-for-service plans and prepaid plans. In addition to voluntary plans, government-backed health care plans, such as Medi-

care and Medicaid, serve as safety nets to furnish medical coverage to select groups of society and to those least able to afford other types of health insurance.

Under traditional fee-for-service plans, the insurer pays the insured directly for any hospital or physician costs for which the insured is covered. Under a prepaid plan, insurance companies arrange to pay health care providers for any service for which an enrollee has coverage. The insurer effectively agrees to provide the insured with health care services, rather than reimbursement dollars. Prepaid plans offer the advantages of lower costs, which results of reduced administrative expenses and a greater emphasis on cost control. The most commony type of prepaid plan is the health maintenance organization (HMO).

Most plans cover basic costs related to: hospitalization, including room and board, drugs, and emergency room care; professional care, such as physician visits; and surgery, including any procedures performed by surgeons, radiologists, or other specialists. More comprehensive plans provide higher dollar limits for coverage or cover miscellaneous services not encompassed in some basic plans, such as medical appliances and psychiatric care. The most inclusive plans eliminate deductible and coinsurance requirements, and may even cover dental, vision, or hearing care.

There are several specific methods that companies can use to vary the level of voluntary benefits provided in their medical benefits package. For instance, insureds may select a high deductible as a way of lowering the cost of a plan (the deductible is the amount of initial costs covered by the insured before reimbursement begins). Likewise, different levels of coinsurance and copayments are usually available. For example, a beneficiary may be required to cover 10 percent of all costs incurred after the deductible amount up to a total of $100,000 (for a total disbursement by the insured of $10,000). A more expensive plan may reduce the beneficiary's share of those costs to five percent, or even zero. The total limit on insurer payments can also be adjusted; an individual lifetime maximum of $250,000 to $1 million is common.

Auxiliary medical-related employee benefits include wellness programs that teach and encourage exercise, weight control, how to stop smoking, and similar health benefits. Many companies also provide financial incentives for workers that achieve specific health-related goals, such as a certain height-to-weight ratio.

RETIREMENT

Companies provide retirement-related employee benefits through three avenues: Social Security, pension plans, and individual savings. Social Security mandates that workers and employers jointly fund an account that is managed by the federal government. The combined contribution totals about 15 percent of a worker's total salary. The money is placed in the fund, and most of it is spent by the federal government to fund unrelated programs. However, the government backs the fund with what amounts to a promise to replenish the fund, with interest, and pay benefits to beneficiaries when they reach retirement age. The amount of expected benefits varies by age, with younger contributors expected to receive at least a meager portion of their and their employer's total contribution.

Pension plans are primarily financed by employers. Unlike the Social Security fund, funds created by private employers are subject to strict government controls designed to ensure their long-term existence. The two major categories of pension funds are defined benefit and defined contribution. The former represents the traditional approach; workers are assured a determined income level (given expected Social Security disbursements) at retirement. The company finances the worker's account and manages the investments. In contrast, defined contribution plans utilize savings techniques such as money purchase plans, stock ownership plans, and profit sharing. Companies make regular contributions to workers' accounts through those different instruments, and may also integrate employee contributions. The beneficiary simply receives the value of the contributions, with interest, at retirement. The obvious benefits are deferred taxes and flexibility in comparison to defined benefit programs.

The third type of retirement benefit offered by many employers is supplementary individual savings plans. These plans include various tax-favored savings and investment options. Employers may also provide retirement benefits such as retirement counseling, credit unions, investment counseling, and sponsorship of retiree clubs and organizations.

UNEMPLOYMENT

Most employers choose to offer some form of protection against involuntary termination as a benefit to employees. In addition, termination benefits are required under various circumstances by collective bargaining agreements and state and federal laws. A common unemployment benefit is severance pay, which may take the form of a lump sum or continuing payments. In addition, some industries provide supplemental unemployment pay plans. These are employer-funded accounts designed to ensure adequate and regular payments to workers, usually members of labor unions, during periods of inactivity.

Because of the increase in employee layoffs caused by restructuring during the 1980s and early 1990s, many companies have initiated benefit plans that help their terminated workers to find new jobs. These programs help workers to develop new skills, learn job-seeking techniques, relocate to new regions, and pay for professional outplacement assistance. At the executive level, some workers receive "**golden parachute**s," or the equivalent thereof. Those instruments ensure that if the executive is terminated as a result of a hostile takeover or some other unforeseen event, he or she will receive a pre-set sum or allowance.

SURVIVORS

Like disability compensation, benefits for the survivors of deceased employees are comprised primarily of mandatory Social Security and workers' compensation benefits. Eligiblity for such mandatory benefits is determined by factors such as age, marital status, and parental responsiblities. In addition, however, a plethora of different privately financed benefits are available for employer, most of which have a tax-favored status. Most plans are set up to make payments to a beneficiary designated by the employee. Payment levels are usually contingent on the cause of death. For example, a worker killed while on the job would likely receive much more than an employee who died at home or on vacation. A common survivorship benefit is some form of term life insurance that takes advantage of tax preferences and exemptions. Those plans often allow employees to contribute, thus significantly raising the expected payoff at death.

[Dave Mote]

FURTHER READING:

Briggs, Virginia L., Michael G. Kushner and Michael J. Schinabeck. *Employee Benefits Dictionary*. The Bureau of National Affairs, Inc., 1992.

Briggs, Virginia L., Michael G. Kushner and Michael J. Schinabeck. *Employee Benefits Dictionary; An Annotated Compendium of Frequently Used Terms.*

Foster, Jr., Ronald M. *The Manager's Guide to Employee Benefits*. Facts on File Publications, 1986.

Fundamentals of Employee Benefit Programs. Employee Benefit Research Institute, 1990.

Gomez-Mejia, Luis R., ed. *Compensation and Benefits.* The Bureau of National Affairs, Inc., 1989.

Jenks, James M. and Brian L.P. Zevnik. *Employee Benefits Plain and Simple.* Collier Books, 1993.

Williams, Stephen J., and Sandra Guerra. *Health Care Services in the 1990s.* Praeger Publishers, 1991.

EMPLOYEE DISMISSALS

Employee dismissals are terminations rendered by an organization against the will of the employee. Two basic types of dismissals discussed below are behavior-related terminations and reductions in force (RIF). Although employees may also be terminated for no reason whatsoever, legal risks make such firings the exception.

BACKGROUND

In 19th century England, the master and servant relationship was regulated by law—employers could not fire workers unless their conduct was unsatisfactory, and workers could not quit without providing sufficient notice. That system was adopted early in the United States as well, but it was abandoned beginning in the middle 1850s in favor of a more Laissez-faire approach. In a landmark 1849 case a federal court upheld the firing of a riverboat pilot without cause (*Turesdale v. Young*). And in 1877, Horace Gay Wood published his renowned *Law of Master and Servant*, which spelled out the "employment-at-will" doctrine that was emerging in the nation.

The employment-at-will doctrine was applied in both state and federal courts throughout the late 1800s and early 1900s. Among the most concise interpretations of the creed was that penned by the California Supreme Court in 1910: "Precisely as may the employee cease labor at his whim or pleasure, and, whatever be his reason, good, bad, or indifferent, leave no one a legal right to complain; so, upon the other hand, may the employer discharge, and whatever be his reason, good, bad, or indifferent, no one has suffered a legal wrong."

Although employees retained their employment-at-will rights, employers' rights to terminate workers at their discretion began to erode in the 1930s. In 1935, the federal Wagner Act of 1935 made it illegal for companies to fire employees because of union activity. Subsequent laws and court decisions during the mid-1900s reflected increasing concern about "wrongful discharge," implying that circumstances do exist in which it is legally wrong for a company to fire a worker. During the 1960s and 1970s, particularly, a number of new laws and regulations were enacted to protect workers from wrongful discharge in all types of cases, including those related to bias, whistle blowing, and trait-related factors.

Employment-at-will remained theoretically intact during the 1980s and early 1990s. A company could legally fire an employee without any reason whatsoever, or even for some arbitrary reason that had nothing to do with the worker's performance. Doing so, however, would likely leave the company open to legal action on the grounds of age, disability, race, or sex discriminition(or some other type of discrimination against a legally protected minority) or for defamation of character, breaking an implied contract, or some other infraction that could be construed by the courts as constituting wrongful discharge. As a result, the employee dismissal process has become more complex and more formalized in most organizations.

BEHAVIOR-RELATED TERMINATIONS

Behavior-related dismissals represent a termination of an employer-worker relationship by the employer as a result of the actions of the employee. Common behaviors that lead to terminations, in rough order of prevalence, include: absenteeism and tardiness; unsatisfactory performance; lack of qualifications or ability; changed job requirements; and misconduct, particularly drug abuse. The term "behavior-related" distinguishes this type of termination from trait-related dismissals, which are based on immutable characteristics of the employee, such as color of skin or physical disability. Trait-related terminations may be legal if the employer can prove that the trait keeps the employee from performing a job satisfactorily. However, they are much less common.

Employers are generally allowed by law to terminate workers based on any type of behavior they deem unacceptable (or, technically, for no reason at all) However, laws and court decisions have protected some types of behavior when the employer's retaliatory action is deemed: 1) a violation of public policy; 2) a violation of an implied contract between the employer and the employee; or 3) an act of bad faith. An act of bad faith is vaguely defined, and is simply a recognition of an employer's duty to treat employees fairly. For example, it might be considered illegal for a company to fire a worker because he refused to engage in an activity that a reasonable person would consider excessively dangerous or hazardous.

One illustration of a public policy violation would be a company that fired a worker because he refused to engage in an unlawful act, such as falsifying public financial documents or giving false testimony in court. Another public policy violation would be the firing of an employee because he exercised a statutory right, such as voting in an election or worshipping at a church. A third type of infraction in this category would be dismissal of an employee for reasons stemming from his exercising a right to perform an important public obligation. Known as "whistle-blower" laws, legislation passed during the late 1900s serves to protect workers who expose corporate wrongdoing for public, not personal, interests. For instance, it would be illegal for a company to fire an employee that alerted authorities to the illegal dumping of toxic wastes.

Violations of implied contracts occur when a company dismisses a worker despite the existence of an insinuated promise. For example, if an employer conveys to a worker that he will receive long-term employment in an effort to get the employee to take a job, it could be liable if it fired the worker without what the courts deem just cause or due process. As another example, one court ruled that an employer had broken an implied contract when it terminated a poorly performing employee after 18 years of good service because it deprived the worker of pension benefits. Implied contracts often emanate from interviews, policy manuals, or long-term patterns of behavior by the employer in a relationship with an employee.

Even when an employer acts in good faith and does not violate the public trust or an implied contract, it can be legally liable for dismissing a worker for other reasons. Specifically, an employer may be found liable if it can't prove that: 1) its decision to dismiss an employee is not founded on bias against a protected minority; or 2) the firing does not produce inequitable results. Suppose, for instance, that a company decided to fire all managers who did not have a college degree. Doing so, however, resulted in the dismissal of a disproportionate number of legally protected minorities from its work force. The company could be held liable if it could not show that having a college degree was necessary to effectively execute the duties of the position.

Partially because of the legal risks inherent in dismissing employees, most companies terminate workers only after administering a progressive disciplinary and counseling process. Besides legal reasons, studies show that most companies try to correct behavior out of a perceived moral obligation to the employee. Furthermore, many employers benefit economically from correcting employee behavior, rather than terminating workers because of the high costs of employee turnover.

Procedures that companies use that may result in termination vary, especially if a labor union is involved. However, most companies employ some process of progressive disciplinary action that involves four basic steps: counseling, written reprimands, final written warnings, and dismissal. During counseling, an employee's superior brings the unacceptable behavior to the attention of the worker and suggests methods of correction. If that fails, the superior issues a written reprimand, which serves to communicate the seriousness of the situation and to officially record management's good faith in rectifying the behavior. The written warning typically includes a description

of prior counseling, defines expectations, and sets a time limit for the employee to rectify the problem.

If a written reprimand fails, a superior issues some form of final written warning to the worker. The written warning may include: copies and summaries of previous admonishments; specific behaviors that need to be corrected; a time limit to make corrections; and a formal statement that specifies the actions that will be taken if the worker fails to reform. If the final warning(s) do not produce the desired results, the manager or some other authority will terminate employment in writing. Often, an exit interview is conducted before the termination is finalized to give the employee a final chance to bring to light any factors neglected by management. The employee may be given notice or, as is often the case, told to gather belongings and immediately leave the premises to avert theft or destruction of property. Depending on laws and company policies, the company may provide severance pay, career and placement counseling, ongoing health insurance, or other post-termination benefits.

REDUCTIONS IN FORCE (RIF)

Reductions in Force (RIF), or work force reductions, may include a number of methods of eliminating worker hours, including layoffs. Dismissals are usually the result of surplus labor caused by economic factors, changing markets, poor management, or some other factor unrelated to worker behavior. Because layoffs make a company vulnerable to many of the same legal risks inherent in behavior-related terminations, companies usually lay off workers by means of a carefully planned and documented process. The process is typically conducted in two stages, the first of which entails selecting the workers to be fired and then firing them, and the second of which is outplacement.

Selecting and firing employees is handled carefully because most profit-maximizing organizations are obviously concerned about losing talent or diluting the effectiveness of the company. But care must also be taken to ensure that the layoffs do not violate state and federal laws. As with behavior-related terminations, the layoffs can't be based on bias against protected minorities, or even unintentionally result in an inequitable outcome for a protected group. In fact, extensive legislation exists to protect disabled workers, racial minorities, workers over the age of 40, women, and other groups.

In addition to bias-related laws, moreover, companies must comply with a battery of laws specifically directed at corporate layoffs. For example, the federal Worker Adjustment and Retraining Notification (WARN) Act of 1988 requires companies with 100 or more employees to file at least 60 days prior notice before conducting mass layoffs or work force reductions. Among other stipulations, the notice must be in writing and addressed to employees and specified government workers.

The second stage of the layoff process, outplacement, is also heavily influenced by legislation aimed at protecting employees. But it is also used to maintain the morale of the work force and to enhance the public image of the company conducting the layoffs. Outplacement usually includes two activities: counseling and job search assistance. Counseling occurs on both the individual and group levels. Both are necessary to help the displaced worker: 1) develop a positive attitude; 2) correctly assess career potential and direction, including background and skills, personality traits, financial requirements, geographic constraints, and aspirations; 3) develop job search skills, such as resume writing, interviewing, networking, and negotiating; and 4) adjust to life in transition or with a new employer.

Many companies assist with the job search by hiring a job-search firm to help their fired employees find new work. In addition to providing some or all of the counseling services described above, job-search companies act as brokers, bringing together job hunters and companies looking for employees. Job-search companies can expedite the job hunting process by eliminating mismatches from the interview process and by helping both parties to negotiate employment terms. In some cases, the former employer will reimburse job hunting costs as part of the severance package of benefits.

COURT CASE EXAMPLES

Among the most well-known precedent-setting cases affecting employee dismissal was *Griggs v. Duke Power Co. of 1971*. Duke Power required all of its workers, except maintenance personnel, to have a high school diploma. Because far fewer blacks than whites had diplomas, almost all of the better jobs in the company were held by whites. The Supreme Court found that possession of a diploma was not necessarily a valid requirement for many of the jobs from which blacks without diplomas were being excluded. Therefore, Duke was forced to abandon its policy and to begin hiring blacks into its management ranks. According to the court, ''Congress had directed the thrust of the 1964 Civil Rights Act at the consequences of employment practices, not simply the motivation.'' This ruling has also been applied to wrongful termination cases.

More recently, McDonnell Douglas Corp. laid off one-quarter of its employees in the St. Louis area during a 1990-1991 RIF. Although the company followed a RIF plan that it deemed impartial, the end result of the layoff was that 900 of 10,000 employee

that were forced to quit or retire were more than 55 years old. Under **Equal Opportunity Employment Commission (EEOC)** mandates, McDonnell should have shed 370 fewer workers from that age group. Demonstrating the risk inherent to layoffs, McDonnell was ordered to rehire 200 of the former employees, give a total of $10 million in cash to the 900 workers, and add $10.1 million to the pensions of those workers based on their age and experience. In addition, McDonnell incurred large legal bills in an effort to settle the disputes.

A case decided in favor of the employer demonstrates the application of the employment-at-will doctrine. In 1979 a former employee of Ortho Pharmaceutical Corp. filed suit against the company. She claimed that it had fired her for refusing to test children with a drug that had a high saccharin content. She argued that her discharge was wrongful because it was a violation of public policy—Ortho had fired her for not engaging in behavior that she believed would harm society. The New Jersey court determined that her case did not qualify as an exception to the employment-at-will doctrine: ''. . . the employer's legitimate interest in conducting his business and employing and retaining the best personnel available cannot be unjustifiably impaired. Thus it cannot change the present rule which holds that just or good cause for the discharge of an employee at will or the giving of reasons therefore is not required.''

[Dave Mote]

FURTHER READING:

Blustain, Harvey. *Company Policy Manual: Special Report—Outplacement in Times of Organizational Change.* Panel Publishers, 1993.

Cascio, Wayne F. *Human Resource Planning Employment & Placement.* Bureau of National Affairs, 1989.

Coulson, Robert. *The Termination Handbook.* The Free Press, 1981.

Milkovich, George T. and John W. Boudreau. *Personnel/Human Resource Management: A Diagnostic Approach.* Business Publications, Inc., 1988.

Werther, William B., Jr. and Keith Davis. *Human Resources and Personnel Management,* 3rd ed. McGraw-Hill Book Company, 1989.

EMPLOYEE MOTIVATION

For centuries supervisory personnel have sought an answer to the question, ''How do I get my workers to do what I want them to?'' Hundreds of years later, the question might be phrased, ''How do I motivate my employees?'' In the intense competitive environment businesses face today, employee motivation is a genuine concern for modern managers.

The advent of **labor unions** forced **management** and labor to cooperate and secured worker rights. Over the decades, nonunionized environments also experimented with factors hoped or perceived to motivate employees toward more **productivity**. Even today, the combinations of variables hoped to bring about effective motivation of employees are ever-changing in their scope and appropriateness for different organizations.

WHAT MOTIVATES?

One view has been to approach motivating factors as ''add-ins'' to an individual's job. Endless mixes of **employee benefits** such as health care and life insurance, **profit sharing**, **employee stock ownership plans (ESOP)**, exercise facilities, subsidized meal plans, **child care** availability, company cars and more have been used by companies in their efforts to maintain happy employees in the belief that happy employees are motivated employees.

Many modern theorists, however, propose that the motivation an employee feels toward his or her job has less to do with material rewards such as those described above, and is more dependent upon the design of the job itself. Studies as far back as 1924 show that simplified, repetitive jobs, for instance, fostered boredom and the taking of frequent, unauthorized breaks by those who performed them. In 1950 a series of attitude surveys found that highly segmented and simplified jobs resulted in lower employee morale and output. Other consequences of low employee motivation include **absenteeism** and high turnover, both very costly for any company. ''Job enlargement'' initiatives began to crop up in major companies in the 1950s, with one champion of the cause being Thomas Watson, Sr., founder of IBM. On the academic front, Turner and Lawrence proposed task attributes that comprise jobs that motivate.

Turner and Lawrence suggest that there are three basic characteristics of a ''motivating'' job:

1. *It must allow a worker to feel personally responsible for a meaningful portion of the work accomplished.* An employee must feel ownership of and connected to the work he or she performs. Even in team situations, a successful effort will foster an awareness in an individual that his or her contributions were important in accomplishing the group's tasks.

2. *It must provide outcomes which have intrinsic meaning to the individual.* Effective work that does not lead a worker to feel that his or her efforts matter will not be maintained. The outcome of an employee's work

must have value to himself or herself and others in the organization.

3. *It must provide the employee feedback about his or her accomplishments.* A culminating factor to the two above points is feedback. A constructive, believable critique of the work performed is crucial to a worker's continuance or improvement of that which has already been performed.

In 1971 Hackman and Lawler designed a test of these ideas. Using a telephone company as a test site, they surveyed 200 employees to determine relationships between employee attitudes and behavior and the characteristics of the employee's job. The study also assessed whether an employee's reaction to his or her work is dependent upon particular kinds of satisfactions valued by the employee. Positive correlations were found to exist between the quality of an employee's job, with quality jobs meeting the three criteria above, and positive employee attitudes and behavior. Further, ''doing well'' at a job was interpreted by the employee as having put in a high quality performance, rather than a high quantity performance. Employees feel positively when they have accomplished something they feel is meaningful, and will strive to do so if given an encouraging opportunity.

While terminology changes, the tenets of employee motivation remain relatively unchanged from findings over half a century ago. Today's buzzwords include ''**empowerment**,'' ''**quality circles**,'' and ''teamwork.'' All three demonstrate the three characteristics of motivating jobs set forth in the theory of Turner and Lawrence. Empowerment gives autonomy and allows an employee to have ownership of ideas and accomplishments, whether acting alone or in **teams**. Quality circles and the increasing occurrence of teams in today's work environments gives employees the opportunities to reinforce the importance of the work accomplished by an organization's members as well as receive feedback on the efficacy of that work.

MYRIAD OF MOTIVATION

The methods of motivating employees today are as numerous and different as the companies operating in the global business environment. What is the nature of the company and its industry? Is it small or big? What kind of culture is fostered? Is it conservative or innovative? What is important to the employees? What steps have been taken to find out?

The best employee motivation efforts will focus on what the employees deem to be important. It may be that employees within the same department of the same organization will have different motivators. Many organizations today find that flexibility in job design and reward has resulted in employees' increased longevity with the company, increased productivity, and better morale. Although this "cafeteria-plan" approach to the work-reward continuum presents variety, some strategies are prevalent across all organizations striving to improve employee motivation.

EMPOWERMENT. Giving employees more responsibility and decision-making authority increases their realm of control over the tasks for which they are held responsible and better equips them to carry out those tasks. Trapped feelings arising from being held accountable for something one does not have the resources to carry out are diminished. Energy is diverted from self-preservation to improved task accomplishment. Empowerment brings the job enlargement of the 1950s and the job enrichment that began in the 1960s to a higher level by giving the employees some of the power to expand their own jobs and create new, personally identified challenges.

CREATIVITY AND INNOVATION. At many companies, employees with creative ideas do not express them to management for fear of jeopardizing their jobs. Company approval and toeing the company line have become so ingrained in some working environments that both the employee and the organization suffer. When the power to create in the organization is pushed down from the upper echelon to line personnel, employees are empowered and those who know a job, product, or service best are given the opportunity to use their ideas to improve it. The power to create motivates employees and benefits the organization in having a more flexible **workforce**, using more wisely the experience of its employees and increasing the exchange of ideas and information among employees and departments. These improvements also create an openness to change that can give a company the ability to respond quickly to market changes and sustain a first mover advantage in the marketplace. Minnesota Mining and Manufacturing, Co., better known as 3M Company, has fostered companywide creativity for decades. Its relentless support of new ideas has paid off in profitability and loyal employees who are so motivated that they have the most nimble and successful new product development system in the industry. MCI, too, encourages employees to develop new ideas and take chances with them. A top manager there stated, "We don't shoot people who make mistakes around here, we shoot people who don't take risks."

LEARNING. If employees are given the tools and the opportunities to accomplish more, most will take on the challenge. Companies can motivate employees to achieve more by committing to perpetual enhancement of employee skills. Accreditation and licensing programs for employees are an increasingly popular and effective way to bring about growth in employee

knowledge and motivation. Often, these programs improve employees' attitudes toward the client and the company, while bolstering self-confidence. Supporting this assertion, an analysis of factors which influence motivation-to-learn found that it is directly related to the extent to which training participants believe that such participation will affect their job or career utility. In other words, if the body of knowledge gained can be applied to the work to be accomplished, then the acquisition of that knowledge will be a worthwhile event for the employee and employer.

QUALITY OF LIFE. The number of hours worked each week by American workers is on the rise again and many families have two adults working those increased hours. Under these circumstances, many workers are left wondering how to meet the demands of their lives beyond the workplace. Often, this concern occurs while at work and may reduce an employee's productivity and morale. Companies that have instituted flexible employee arrangements have gained motivated employees whose productivity has increased. Programs incorporating flextime, condensed workweeks, or job sharing, for example, have been successful in focusing overwhelmed employees toward the work to be done and away from the demands of their private lives.

MONETARY INCENTIVE. For all the championing of alternative motivators, money still occupies a rightful place in the mix of motivators. The sharing of a company's profits gives incentive to employees to produce a quality product, perform a quality service, or improve the quality of a process within the company. What benefits the company directly benefits the employee. Monetary and other rewards are being given to employees for generating cost-savings or process-improving ideas, to boost productivity and reduce absenteeism. Money is effective when it is directly tied to an employee's ideas or accomplishments. Nevertheless, if not coupled with other, nonmonetary motivators, its motivating effects are short-lived. Further, monetary incentives can prove counterproductive if not made available to all members of the organization.

OTHER INCENTIVES. Study after study has found that the most effective motivators of workers are nonmonetary. Monetary systems are insufficient motivators, in part because expectations often exceed results and because disparity between salaried individuals may divide rather than unite employees. Proven nonmonetary positive motivators foster team spirit and include recognition, responsibility, and advancement. Managers who recognize the "small wins" of employees, promote participatory environments, and treat employees with fairness and respect will find their employees to be more highly motivated. One company's managers brainstormed to come up with 30 powerful rewards that cost little or nothing to implement. The most effective rewards, such as letters of commendation and time off from work, enhanced personal fulfillment and self-respect. Over the longer term, sincere praise and personal gestures are far more effective and more economical than awards of money alone. In the end, a program that combines monetary reward systems and satisfies intrinsic, self-actualizing needs may be the most potent employee motivator.

[Richard C. Cuthie]

FURTHER READING:

Clark, Catherine S., Gregory H., Dobbins, and Robert T. Ladd, "Exploratory Field Study of Training Motivation," *Group & Organization Management*. September, 1993, pp. 292-306.

Coates, Joseph F., and Jarrett, Jennifer. "Workplace Creativity." *Employment Relations Today*. Spring, 1994, pp. 11-22.

Herzberg, Frederick. "One More Time: How Do You Motivate Employees?" *Harvard Business Review*. January-February, 1968, pp. 53-62.

Kennish, John W. "Motivating with a Positive, Participatory Policy." *Security Management*. August, 1994, pp. 22-23.

Peters, Tom. "Get Innovative or Get Dead, Part II." *California Management Review*. Winter, 1991, pp. 9-23.

EMPLOYEE OUTPLACEMENT

Before the 1980s, there hardly seemed a need for the service that today is called employee outplacement. For years, opportunities abounded and large salaries were common for executives, managers and supervisors. It wasn't unusual for such individuals to devote their entire working lives to one company. Then came a downward turn in the economy. Private- and public-sector industries lost vast capital, and reacted by reevaluating their entire workforce. Variously called "restructuring," "downsizing," or "cost-cutting," the turn toward mass layoffs and dismissals affected organizations that were once considered safe havens. The cycle of layoffs and retrievals was a familiar one to the blue-collar workforce. But from the defense industry to Wall Street, the decline of American industry created a new category of the unemployed—the executive class.

"Once out the door, displaced managers are confronting a much harsher world than they faced just a few years ago," *Fortune*'s David Kirkpatrick reported in 1991. "There are many more of them competing for jobs—400,000 managers and professionals, by one count—and fewer companies are hiring." This is where outplacement comes in.

Employee outplacement refers to career counseling services offered to employees at the time they are laid off. An outside or in-house outplacement team provides counseling, interviewing tips, networking leads, and even (in the case of high-level clients) cubicles or offices with phones, fax machines, word processors, and secretarial support. The sponsoring company pays for these services, usually at a rate of 12 percent to 15 percent of the dismissed employee's salary.

ADDRESSING MANY NEEDS

For the employees, outplacement represents a bridge between the shock of sudden dismissal and the daunting prospect of future employment. For the sponsoring company, the service is an altruistic gesture toward good workers who through no fault of their own have been caught in an unfortunate circumstance—plus, outplacement provides some measure of security against those employees possibly considering a lawsuit against the company.

The widely regarded pioneer in this field, James E. Challenger, saw the potential in such a service as far back as the 1960s. As he wrote in his book *Outplacement* "I perceived that while there were numerous assistance programs for the disadvantaged who were discharged, nothing was being done for the individual who was not disadvantaged. That person underwent the same emotional trauma and stress as his or her less privileged counterpart upon losing a job and, in my opinion, deserved no less in the way of assistance."

Challenger's first outplacement service—then called Executive Retrieval—consisted of a grassroots door-to-door campaign of calling on corporations to promote the idea of helping out the executive on the street. Acceptance came slowly, as Challenger recalled in his book: "When I first approached companies with the concept, I was often ushered out of the executive suite. 'Why in the world,' they asked, 'should we help someone we are discharging?' I continually explained how it was to the mutual benefit of the company and the individual. . . . [to turn] a negative situation for the company into one which put the firm into a favorable light in terms of public opinion. It assuaged internal corporate guilt . . . [and] it prevented unwise or hasty action by the individual that would damage a future career and provided the job search knowledge and tools for the person to find new employment."

Executive Retrieval evolved into the firm of Challenger, Gray & Christmas. The company grew from a three-member team to what is today the oldest and one of the leading outplacement firms, with 1992 revenues around $16 million. As Michael Barrier quoted Challenger in *Nation's Business*, the Chicago-based company can dispatch a counselor "anywhere in the country on 24 hours' notice" when someone is about to be fired. But what happens when a counselor and client meet is the subject of controversy.

THE COUNSELING CONTROVERSY

Most outplacement firms work essentially the same way. They "are very big on putting everyone through psychological testing to help them figure out what they should do with their lives," noted Dyan Machan, reporting for *Forbes*. Machan's article concerned a typical client who had lost his marketing job, signed up with an outplacement firm that, after 50 hours of counseling and testing, gave the client "a keen grasp of the obvious: He was told he should stay in marketing or perhaps should be a consultant."

This sort of cookie-cutter counseling approach is the biggest charge clients have against outplacement firms. Another complaint: people who are promised perks such as private cubicles and phones often must wait for such services due to the sheer volume of displaced clients. "The facility may have only 80 spaces, and if, say, 100 axed managers show up—not an unusual situation after a big layoff—20 are left without a cubicle for the day," as Machan wrote, though she added that "higher-level executives generally do better and get something more like a private office."

For another view of outplacement, consider the experience of publishing executive Betsy Carter. Carter found herself out of a job when her magazine folded; as a senior ranking executive, she was offered six months' outplacement service with America's largest outplacement firm, Drake Beam Morin. Carter called her counselor "unrelentingly optimistic," and in a *Working Woman* piece reported that she herself "loved taking the tests and plowing through the workbook exercises to glean what my 'career anchor' is . . . It was reassuring to have a place to go between appointments. In the mornings, I'd check in with the receptionist, who always called me by my first name, then go to my desk. It was easy to distinguish between the Drake Beam employees and my fellow unemployees. The former were exceedingly chipper, quick to smile and offer some pleasantry. The latter—mostly displaced male executives—rarely met my eyes, much less smiled."

Carter also noted that among the spate of aptitude tests and psychological counseling, she was informed that she had "most in common with photographers, musicians and chefs and the least in common with emergency medical technicians and Air Force enlisted personnel. These findings were not exactly surprising. My mother could have told me all this for free."

PERFORMANCE APPRAISAL

So does employee outplacement really work? The answer often lies within the client's own initiative and attitude. Carter stayed with Drake Beam Morin and eventually found herself with a promising job

offer and a chance to work as an independent contractor. Other outplacement clients report that the impersonal testing and competition for cubicles and phones makes outplacement no more appealing than striking out on one's own in the job hunt. As Machan pointed out, "Unlike just about every other industry, there's little accountability here. That's because the buyer is not the user. An employer, understandably concerned about sinking morale, wants minimal contact with the newly axed. There's typically no follow-up by the company of the former employees."

But as Challenger noted in his book, outplacement is not meant to be an employment service, but a support service. And as for the by-the-numbers counseling, that's a given as well. "Good outplacement counseling is a generic process built around the uniqueness of the client," Challenger wrote. "Professions do not really matter. My staff has no nuclear physicists or microbiologists on its staff and yet we successfully counseled several in one year."

For those who might find the "generic process" too limiting, Machan gave this suggestion: "Look for smaller or specialized firms. Harris, Heery, of Norwalk, Conn., for example, specializes in marketing managers. Stanley Herz & Co., of Stamford, Conn., specializes in finance and information services." And, she added, "this much is clear: Companies may feel they are getting their money's worth using outplacement firms as litigation insurance and as sops to the consciences of the higher-ups who do the firing. But it is not easy to find firees who feel they have gained much from outplacement services."

[Susan Salter]

FURTHER READING:

Barrier, Michael. "Lighting a Fire under the Fired." *Nation's Business*. July, 1992, pp. 55-56.

Carter, Betsy. "My Life and (Surprisingly Good) Times at an Outplacement Center." *Working Woman*. September, 1992, pp. 65-67+.

Challenger, James E. *Outplacement*. Apex Publishing Co.

Kirkpatrick, David. "The New Executive Unemployed." *Fortune*. April 8, 1991, pp. 36-48.

Machan, Dyan. "Meet the Undertakers." *Forbes*. November 11, 1991, pp. 384-88.

EMPLOYEE PUBLICATIONS

Employee publications are the newsletters, newspapers, magazines, magapapers or possibly electronic forms of communications produced by a company that allows **management** to communicate with its employees. Recent surveys show that more than half of employee publications are simply produced newsletters, followed by 24 percent of companies producing more expensive magazines. Just over 14 percent of the companies surveyed produce magapapers, which is a cross between a magazine and a newspaper in a larger format than the magazine.

Over the past decade, another form of employee communication has emerged that is replacing the company magazine in some firms; employee television is evident in several forms. The simplest form looks like the familiar cable TV announcement "crawl" with continuous listings of the important news of the day, such as the time and place for employee meetings. This type of employee communication can be created with little more than simple computer software and the placement of TV monitors in areas where employees gather.

Larger companies may have their own TV production studios where they prepare broadcast-quality shows that can be replayed on videotape, or even sent by satellite to remote company locations. This type of communication can be used to reach all employees instantly with the same message. It is particularly valuable when used to announce new products and **marketing** campaigns, or to control the spread of rumors.

Electronic mail (distributing news over a computer network) is a growing, but still limited, means of communicating with employees. It is confined to companies where employees work from computer terminals, and would be impractical in any company where most employees do not regularly utilize them.

The history of the very first employee publication is unknown, but the increased use of written communication most likely evolved from bulletin board announcements as management realized that companies were growing too large to distribute important news through just one medium.

DEVELOPMENT OF EMPLOYEE COMMUNICATIONS

Over the last 100 years, almost every company of any size has developed its own publication. Once known as "house organs," a now-outdated term among employee editors, these publications are intended to fulfill several purposes. Most important is to alert employees to news that concerns them and to give management the ability to reach employees on a one-to-one basis. To a lesser extent, employee communications have also been used to entertain employees. Some top managers believe that keeping employees informed about each other's social activities will reinforce the "work family" environment.

Achieving these employee publication goals is not as easy as it might sound. A 1991 study conducted in cooperation between Industry Week magazine and the International Association of Business Communicators (IABC, a 2,500-member professional association that includes employee publication editors) found that **CEO**s, employees, and publication editors frequently have widely divergent views on what is important to the company.

According to the study, CEO concerns revolve around product quality, cutting costs, the company's long-term plans, regulatory compliance, **competition**, and employee drug use. Employee concerns include the company's future, competition, reasons behind recent corporate decisions, product development, **employee benefits**, product quality, and recent financial results.

Editors, on the other hand, appear to have a different agenda. A study of the top ten stories published in their magazines concerned current programs or activities, community relations, personal news (such as number of years service of long-term employees), employee benefits, the company's future and goals, human interest stories about employees, employee recreation news, product quality and the organization's strength and stability.

The study found that of every 100 articles published in employee magazines, only 25 were on the CEO's top worry list. Employees, for whom the publications are written, faired little better. Of the top ten subjects covered in the publications, only five (employee benefits, company's future, organization's goals and direction, quality improvement, and the company's strength and stability) were considered important by the employees. Only one other subject favored by employees, product development, accounted for more than three percent of the first 100 articles published.

The implication of the research was that employee publication editors have not been paying much attention to their dual audience. They are not addressing the concerns of the CEOs, who fund their publications. Neither are they writing about what their fellow employees want to know.

Surveyors speculated that editors were doing one of two things. They were either publishing the news that readership surveys told them employees wanted to see in magazines, or they were writing "safe" articles in the attempt to avoid painful issues that could pit management and employees against each other. Editors, apparently, do not want to bring up issues such as downsizing or product quality problems.

A second IABC survey taken two years after the first seemed to show a change in editors' attitudes. This survey revealed a better understanding among editors of the need to directly relate management's goals to employees. More than half of the editors surveyed said they ran articles on **strategy** and issues. More than 12 percent reported more frequent contact with management. However, only nine percent said they had changed the approach of the content of their magazine. That seems to show either a tremendous change in editorial content in just two years, or a continuing misunderstanding among editors about what their CEOs wanted to see in the magazines.

Whatever the change, editors reported that management still supported the need for continuing employee publications. Nearly three-quarters of the editors said their company had not consolidated publications; 18 percent said their publication had increased frequency of publication, while only ten percent had reduced frequency. More than 35 percent of the editors reported their companies were spending more money on employee communications while 21 percent experienced a decline.

The implication is that while top management has concerns that are not always expressed in the employee magazine, the CEO believes that communication has to remain open. The best way to do that is through an employee publication, or possibly over the company's own closed-circuit television network.

[Clint Johnson]

EMPLOYEE RECRUITING

The employee recruitment process begins with the identification of a job opening by either a human resource plan or on request by a manager. Once job openings have been identified, the recruiter, who usually works in the human resource department, uses a job description and/or job specification to identify key information about the job. By integrating this information with specialized knowledge about recruitment channels and other factors, recruiters locate potential applicants. Interested applicants complete a job application form to signal the end of the recruiting process. Job application forms identify applicants according to a consistent and formal information gathering process and within legal and ethical boundaries that protect the applicant from discrimination in the selection process.

JOB DESCRIPTIONS AND SPECIFICATIONS

At the heart of the recruitment process lies the general concept that a company needs to hire someone to complete a certain task or series of tasks within the organization. The description of this job is contained within the job description and/or job specification. A job description is functionally and descriptively stated while a job specification is usually intended for organizational use and may reflect a more quantitative

approach to the tasks at hand. Recruiters rely on clear and concise job descriptions and specifications to construct advertising and to effectively use other recruitment channels. Job descriptions and specifications include known duties and responsibilities, required education and experience, salary and benefits, and information regarding the work environment. Helpful details address required travel, normal work schedule, general physical conditions, geographic location, union status, bonuses, and any other information directly pertinent to the job. These details provide the recruiter with valuable and applicable information for use in locating potential applicants.

KEY FACTORS

In addition to the fundamental job description and job specification, other key factors affect recruiting. Corporate employment policies and plans, environmental conditions, and money or budgetary constraints are primary considerations. Current issues and trends in the workplace and population also significantly affect recruiting practices. Within a company, specific plans and policies regarding recruitment are often in place. For example, companies with internal promotion policies prefer to use in-house employees when possible. This policy affects the strategy and tactics of a recruiter when locating potential applicants for the job. Likewise, policies that address company-wide compensation and salary levels, preferences for full-time or part-time employees, and restrictions on international hiring also figure into the recruiter's plan of action. Some human resource plans reflect desired personnel staffing levels. For example, affirmative action plans reflect ideal demographic mixtures that guide and direct recruiting activities.

Environmental factors such as the economic and legal conditions of the current environment also affect recruitment. High costs of living and inflation dilute recruitment efforts when salary constraints are inflexible. High or low unemployment rates, both locally and nationally, may also affect recruiting activities. Legal requirements, too, influence recruitment in a variety of ways. The **Fair Labor Standards Act of 1938** specifies minimum wage requirements and child labor restrictions. The Immigration Reform and Control Act addresses illegal aliens and their employment. The **Americans with Disabilities Act** outlines employment requirements for workers defined as disabled. And, the National Labor Relations Act details employment issues and union status. These federal laws, in conjunction with applicable state and local laws, require recruiters to conform to prescribed expectations and actions in the recruitment process.

Finally, costs and incentives may limit or expand recruiting options and activities. Costs have a direct effect as in the case of a newspaper advertising rate or the overall cost of an actual hire. Recruiters take action and make decisions within a limited budget. Incentives or inducements allow recruiters to attract a higher quality and/or higher volume of potential applicants. Fast-food companies such as McDonald's or Burger King offer educational incentives to encourage youths to apply and stay employed with a particular chain. Eastman Kodak Co. offers a similar incentive called Kodak Scholars. Others offer child care or elder care services. Apple Computer, Inc. provides an on site day care center while Johnson and Johnson coordinates referrals and placements in a local day care provider. Effective inducements of this nature are a direct result of a changing workforce and workplace.

CURRENT ISSUES AND TRENDS

The workforce and the workplace change in response to demographic, social, and economic changes. Recently, more women, minorities, and aging workers have entered the workforce, whie the workplace has reflected an increase in professional, technical, service, and sales jobs and a decrease in manufacturing and agricultural jobs. Combined, these trends signal fewer qualified applicants, fewer traditional candidates, and more candidates with different motivational needs. The changing workforce and workplace challenges recruiters to respond with effective strategies.

Demographically, aging workers represent a significant portion of the employable population. In the last hundred years, the portion of the population over age 65 rose from four percent to twelve percent. Companies such as Days Inn are well-known for their innovative and effective strategies with older workers. More than a quarter of their total staff were seniors in 1989. In conjunction with the Americans with Disabilities Act, disabled persons emerged as an employable category that had often been previously ignored. Persons with disabilities represent a strong demographic pool in recruitment since, by some estimates, almost 68 percent of this pool of applicants are considered employable. Women and minorities continue to increase the overall employment pool. Nationwide Insurance implemented a plan called Women in Nationwide Sales (WINS) to encourage the development of female sales agents. Likewise, Franklin Life Insurance doubled its number of female agents within three years with the same targeted approach. More systematic changes included Deloitte and Touche's long-term training and career development program to reduce turnover among female managers and to increase promotion of women to partnership positions. These programs attempt to defeat a phenomenon known as the "glass ceiling" in which women attain a limited role in the organization and fail to reach the highest management positions. Minority recruitment increases workplace diversity and represents an attempt to focus on yet another segment of society as part of the recruitment pool. In one innovative program, Ryder joined with the National Urban League to enhance minority recruiting in Los Angeles.

Social changes in the workplace and society at large center around literacy. Literacy is defined as the ability to functionally read and write. Current workplace changes require applicants with reading and writing skills. Additionally, problem-solving and computer skills are also increasing in importance. Many companies such as AT&T, General Motors Corp., IBM, and Aetna Life & Casualty offer classes to increase literacy and computer competencies among workers. In spite of these efforts and others, however the pool of potentially qualified applicants is decreasing for many recruiters. Illiteracy remains a significant problem when attempting to fill more professional, technical, service, and sales positions.

Economically, more and more workers are hired on a part-time basis without benefits. This reflects an indirect effect of costs on recruitment. It also reflects demographic and social changes. Many seniors or youths are only interested in working part-time and already have health benefits through parents or retirement. Part-time and flexible working schedules such as job sharing, compressed work week, and flextime appear to accommodate individual preference while often reducing costs for the employer, such as by reducing employee turnover.

RECRUITMENT CHANNELS

Recruiters identify potential applicants by receiving unsolicited application materials or providing job announcement information to a targeted recruitment source. Unsolicited applicants enter the application process randomly. Solicited application methods are more controlled and require proactive invitation via a recruitment source. Employer sources, referral sources, and institutional sources are all methods employed to solicit applications.

Employer sources include both employee referral channels and advertising. Employee referral systems can quite successfully extend the applicant pool without direct cost and attract applicants with potentially similar work habits and ethics. It can also lead to a homogenous work environment when overused or abused. Advertising offers another traditional method of soliciting job applications. The most common type of advertising is the help wanted ad. Targeting help wanted ads to appropriate publications commonly increases response rate. Display advertisements can sometimes increase response rate, as well.

Referral sources such as state employment agencies, private placement firms, and professional search firms use banks of job applicants to identify potential referrals. While the state employment office agency, often called the unemployment office, aids applicants and businesses without a fee, private placement firms and professional search firms charge varying fees. A private placement firm is a matching service for applicant and job description; a fee of up to ten percent of the first year's salary is charged. A professional search firm offers more specialized and executive services with fees often running into several thousands of dollars.

Institutional sources comprise agencies such as schools, professional associations, labor associations, military units, and governmental agencies. Each offers a more specialized and focused channel to reach potentially qualified applicants. Recruiting at colleges and universities is a long-standing tradition that has waned in recent years due to costs and difficulties in mapping job requirements to academic preparation. Professional associations and their publications present another means of reaching highly qualified and specialized applicants. Other institutions such as labor, the military, and municipalities serve as valuable resources in identifying recruits. In one example, the Job Training Partnership Act of 1982 formalized monies and programs for local communities to create institutional sources as necessary. These communities and programs offer yet another means of identifing potential job applicants.

Other sources for recruitment include temporary agencies, leased employees, departing employees, job fairs, open houses, and direct mail. Temporary agencies typically provide short-term or substitution stays while leased employees are generally employed for a longer term. Departing employees can often provide recommendations while job fairs and open houses act as valuable arenas for the marketing of employment opportunities.

APPLICATION FORMS

Applicants in the recruiting process complete an application form to signal interest in employment with a particular company. There are several common elements to an application form. First, personal data such as name and address are required to uniquely identify applicants. Questions to identify an applicant's sex or race or other non-job related information are discriminatory and prohibited. Application forms also request a minimum of information on education and skills, work history, and references. Education and skills information indicates the applicant's formal schooling and skill inventory. Work history documents previous employer, periods of employment, and job description. Military experience may be addressed in a separate category to aid in the identification of preferential veteran's status. Awards and honors may provide additional pertinent insight into an applicant's abilities.

References detail other people willing to discuss the applicant's skills, abilities, and experiences. A signature compels applicants to personally verify the accuracy of the form's contents.

Application forms extend and reinforce the recruiting activities of the organization in both function and design. The functions of an application form are to aid in pre-selection sifting, gather data for reporting requirements, and build a resource file for future vacancies. Application forms that are well-designed graphically and easy to complete expedite the application process. Some companies, such as Pinkerton, also require the completion of an honesty questionnaire to supplement the application form.

[Tona Henderson]

FURTHER READING:

Arthur, Diane. *Recruiting, Interviewing, Selecting & Orienting New Employees*. New York: AMACOM, 1991.

Cullen, David. ''Minority Recruiting: Strength in Diversity.'' *Fleet Owner*. April, 1993, pp. 74-76.

''Ensuring Effective Recruitment: Developments in the Use of Application Forms.'' *Industrial Relations Review & Report* March 1994.

Gilbert, Evelyn. ''Nationwide Targets Female Market.'' *National Underwriter*. August 15, 1994, pp. 3, 21.

Goss, David. *Principles of Human Resource Management*. New York: Routledge, 1994.

Hand, Shirley, and Robert A. Zawacki. ''Family-Friendly Benefits: More Than a Frill.'' *HR Magazine*. October, 1994, pp. 79-84.

Milkovich, George T., and John W. Boudreau. *Human Resource Management*. Boston: Irwin, 1991.

Rogers, Charles S. ''The Flexible Workplace: What Have we Learned?'' *Human Resource Management*. 31:3, pp. 183-199.

Sorohan, Erica Gordon. ''Advancing Women in the Workplace.'' *Training & Development*. September, 1993, pp. 9-10.

Smith, Bob. ''Pinkerton Keeps Its Eye on Recruitment.'' *HR Focus*. September, 1993, pp. 1, 6.

Storey, John. *Management of Human Resources*. Oxford: Blackwell, 1992.

Thomson, Rosemary. *Managing People*. Oxford: Butterworth-Heinemann, 1993.

Wanous, John Parker. *Organizational Entry: Recruitment, Selection, Orientation and Socialization of Newcomers*. New York: Addison-Wesley, 1992.

Werther, William B., and Keith Davis. *Human Resources and Personnel Management*. New York: McGraw-Hill, 1993.

EMPLOYEE RIGHTS

Employee rights can be broken down into four primary categories: rights relating to **labor union** organizing and collective bargaining; rights relating to working hours and pay; rights relating to workplace safety and workers' compensation; and rights relating to **discrimination** in hiring or in the workplace. Contemporary employee rights were established primarily through legislation. Workers also secured rights through collective bargaining, but these rights were themselves established largely through legislation.

Many contemporary employee rights were established by federal legislation. Prior to this legislation, however, **labor-management relations** were regulated at the state level, primarily by courts on a case-by-case common law basis. The earliest labor organizations in the United States were the workers' associations, begun in the late eighteenth century. Until the middle of the nineteenth century, state courts generally ruled that it constituted an unlawful conspiracy for workers to organize on the basis of minimum pay rates for members.

An 1842 ruling by the Massachusetts Supreme Court affirmed the right of workers to organize, and other state courts also came to recognize this right. The states continued to vary widely, however, in restrictions on labor unions' activities. Some states recognized the right of workers to strike but not to picket in support of their strike, on the grounds that picketing interfered with employees who wished to work and with employers' operations. Other states that recognized the right to strike and picket often restricted these activities on the basis of the so-called ends/means test. That is, the right of unions to strike and picket could be curtailed if a court did not approve of the purpose or conduct of the strike. Product boycotts of employers involved in a labor dispute were occasionally ruled to be unlawful.

Collective bargaining agreements were held to be valid and binding in many states. Yet employers were under no obligation to bargain or enter into collective bargaining agreements. A strike undertaken with the intent to compel an employer to sign a contract could be enjoined by the courts on the grounds that such a strike interfered with the employer's right to enter into a contract solely on a voluntary basis. After the passage of the federal Sherman Antitrust Act of 1890, the federal courts also acted to curtail strikes and **boycotts** on the grounds that such activities constituted a conspiracy or combination in restraint of the free flow of trade.

FEDERAL LEGISLATION

The first comprehensive federal labor law was the Railway Labor Act of 1926. The act recognized the right of railroad workers to organize and engage in collective bargaining and was extended to include airline workers in 1936. The Norris-LaGuardia Act of 1932 declared the unlawfulness of the ends/means test, preventing a judge from enjoining a strike on the basis of the strike's purposes or methods.

A key piece of legislation for the rights of workers was the National Labor Relations Act (NLRA) of 1935, commonly referred to as the Wagner Act. Wagner was enacted during the Great Depression as part of the Roosevelt administration's New Deal. The act was groundbreaking in a number of respects. It protected the rights of workers to join unions and to engage in collective bargaining. The act also prohibited employers from engaging in what it termed unfair labor practices, including interfering with a worker's right to join a union and engage in union activities. Wagner established procedures by which unionized workers elected their representatives and required employers to bargain in good faith with these representatives. Largely as a result of the Wagner Act, union membership in the United States increased from 4 million in 1935 to 12 million in 1947.

The Wagner Act provided for the establishment of the **National Labor Relations Board (NLRB)**. Congress's motive in establishing the NLRB was to circumvent the courts, which had traditionally ruled in favor of employers. The NLRB remains the key government agency mediating labor-management relations in the United States.

The **Fair Labor Standards Act of 1938**, commonly known as the Wage-Hour Law, established a minimum wage, restricted the use of child labor, and required employers to pay a 50 percent premium for all hours worked in excess of 40 per week.

The Labor Management Relations Act of 1947, commonly referred to as the **Taft-Hartley Act**, significantly amended the National Labor Relations Act of 1935. Whereas the Wagner Act was pro-labor, Taft-Hartley reflected employers' interests. Mirroring the provisions of Wagner, the Taft-Hartley Act prohibited what it defined as unfair labor practices on the part of unions. Unions were also required to bargain in good faith. Taft-Hartley permitted states to enact what came to be called "Right-to-Work" laws that prohibited the union shop, in which all workers in a shop were required to be dues paying union members. Right-to-work laws made it more difficult for unions to organize, and they are still opposed by organized labor today.

The National Labor Relations Act was also amended by the Labor Management Reporting and Disclosure Act of 1959, commonly referred to as the Landrum-Griffin Act. Landrum-Griffin established a so-called Bill of Rights for union members, regulating union elections and the disclosure of the financial records of unions, union representatives, and employers. The act also eliminated the so-called "hot cargo" clauses of the original National Labor Relations Act, which prohibited one employer from doing business with others for whom workers were either on strike or nonunionized.

The Postal Reorganization Act of 1970 put postal workers under the jurisdiction of the National Labor Relations Board and gave them the right to engage in collective bargaining. As federal employees, postal workers did not have the right to strike. The Reorganization Act prohibited the union shop for postal workers and, in contrast with the National Labor Relations Act, provided for binding arbitration in cases of otherwise unresolvable labor disputes.

The National Labor Relations Act was modified once again in 1974 by the Health Care Amendments, which covered workers in nonprofit hospitals. Only workers in for-profit hospitals had previously been covered. In 1980, the Religious Belief Exemption established for hospital workers by the Health Care Amendments was extended to include all workers. The Religious Belief Exemption provided that if workers had religious objections, they need not join unions or pay union dues as a condition of employment.

The National Labor Relations Board's jurisdiction is limited to preventing unfair labor practices and administering union elections as provided for in Sections 8 and 9, respectively, of the NLRA. The U.S. Department of Labor and the **Equal Employment Opportunity Commission (EEOC)** are the other federal government agencies that administer labor law. The Department of Labor oversees the Fair Labor Standards Act, the Occupational Safety and Health Act, and parts of the Landrum-Griffin and Employee Retirement Income Security Act of 1974 (ERISA). The EEOC oversees Title VII of the Civil Rights Act of 1964, the Equal Pay Act of 1963, the Age Discrimination in Employment Act, and the **Americans with Disabilities Act**.

SPECIFIC EMPLOYEE RIGHTS

Collective bargaining has to be undertaken by what the NLRB deems an appropriate bargaining unit. Appropriate units are required to have a distinct community of interest. Thus employees across a firm's plants can bargain collectively if their interests are not at odds with each other. In recent years, the NLRB has tended to look with increasing favor on larger bargaining units. The requirement of a distinct community of interest means that certain types of employees are excluded from the bargaining units of regularly employed workers. Among excluded employees are supervisors and managers, part-time and temporary workers, independent contractors, and family members of employers.

Elections addressing union representation can take place during a strike. The eligibility of workers to vote during a strike depends on a number of factors. Workers striking on the grounds of unfair labor practices can continue voting regardless of how long they have been on strike, and replacements for such strikers are not allowed to vote. Workers striking on economic grounds who are replaced can vote for up to one year after the beginning of a strike, and their replacements are permitted to vote. Laid-off employees are also eligible to vote provided that they are likely to be recalled at some point.

Employers are barred from engaging in a number of practices in the face of unionization efforts. Employers are prohibited from using the threat of reprisal or force as well as from promising benefits if workers choose not to unionize. Employers are also barred from hindering the distribution of union literature, from engaging in the interrogation or surveillance of employees' union activities, from using fraudulent documents, from giving a speech to employees on company time within 24 hours of an election, and from otherwise interfering with the NLRB's administration of an election. If employers violate these regulations, the NLRB can call for a new election or, in cases of extreme violation, can compel employers to bargain with the union even if the union lost the election.

Unions that are certified as bargaining agents by the NLRB have the right of exclusive representation. That is, employers are prohibited from dealing with any other employee representatives on issues involving wages, working hours, and other conditions of employment. Employers are prohibited from providing most types of assistance to the union and from dominating unions. Unions dominated by employers are considered company unions, which are prohibited by the Wagner Act. Unionized workers have the right to have a shop steward present at any questioning by the employer that could lead to dismissal. (During the 1980s, however, the NLRB weakened its position on the reinstatement of workers who were dismissed as a result of unlawful questioning). The NLRA prohibits employers from discriminating against workers based on their union activities, whether this discrimination takes the form of firing, denying promotion, assigning less desirable work, or reducing benefits. Employers are also prohibited from discriminating against workers who file charges or provide testimony under the NLRA.

Both employers and union representatives are required to bargain in good faith. To go through the motions of bargaining without the intent to come to an agreement is unlawful "surface bargaining." Items negotiated in contracts are categorized as mandatory or permissive. Mandatory items include wages, working hours, and working conditions, and are the items for which employers and union representatives are required to bargain. Unions can strike based on disagreement over mandatory items only. Employers and union representatives can agree to bargain over permissive items, which include issues not directly related to wages, hours, and working conditions. Unions also have wide-ranging rights to company information relevant to the negotiation process.

The replacement of striking workers is one of most contentious issues in the field of employee rights. A distinction is made between workers striking over an employer's alleged unfair labor practices or over wages, benefits, and other economic issues. Employers are able to freely replace workers striking over economic issues. Workers striking over unfair labor practices can't be permanently replaced, however, unless they find equivalent employment elsewhere or their jobs are eliminated and they are unqualified to fill remaining openings. Though employers have had the legal right since 1935 to replace workers striking on economic grounds, they rarely chose to do so until the 1980s. The proposed Workplace Fairness Act would have prohibited employers from hiring permanent replacements for striking workers. The act was blocked for a second time in July 1993 by a Republican filibuster.

Civil rights became an important component of employee rights with the passage of the Civil Rights Act of 1964. Employee rights are addressed in Title VII of the act, which prohibits employment discrimination on the basis of race, color, religion, sex, or national origin. (The Equal Pay Act of 1963, an amendment to the Fair Labor Standards Act of 1938, was a predecessor to Title VII that established the principle of equal pay for equal work for male and female workers.)

Title VII does not provide criminal penalties for noncompliance, but rather offers a conciliation process that is administered by the Equal Employment Opportunity Commission (EEOC). Along with the Johnson Administration's Executive Orders, the Civil Rights Act of 1964 has become the foundation for affirmative rights programs. The Johnson Administration also established the Office of Federal Contract Compliance (OFCC), which covers firms contracting with the federal government. The Age Discrimination in Employment Act of 1967 (amended in 1986) provides protection from employment discrimination to older workers.

The EEOC was strengthened by the Equal Employment Opportunity Act of 1972, which enables the agency to file class action suits in addition to its conciliation role. Though **affirmative action** programs came under attack during the Reagan and Bush Administrations, their legality was reaffirmed by the **Civil Rights Act of 1991**. This act also enables minority and female victims of intentional discrimination to be awarded up to $300,000 in compensatory damages. The Civil Rights Act of 1964, in contrast, had only provided for backpay and restitution. Disabled Americans were extended protection from employment discrimination by the Americans with Disabilities Act of 1990.

WORKERS' COMPENSATION AND SAFETY

Workers' compensation laws were established at the state level between the 1910s and 1940s. These laws vary substantially across states, but have central features in common. Employers are required to pay medical expenses, disability benefits, and compensation for lost working time for all work-related injury and illness. In exchange, workers are prohibited in many circumstances from suing employers for such injury and illness. Along with its attempts to overhaul the health care system in the United States, the Clinton Administration sought to transfer the administration of workers' compensation from the states to the federal government.

At the federal level, the key piece of industrial safety legislation is the Occupational Safety and Health Act of 1970. The act established the **Occupational Safety and Health Administration** (OSHA) and the National Institute of Occupational Health and Safety (NIOSH), which play important roles in protecting the safety rights of employees. OSHA issues safety standards covering industrial accidents and health standards covering the more long-term effects of work hazards. In 1983, OSHA issued the Hazard Communication Standard, which requires that employers identify dangerous materials in the workplace and inform workers of these dangers and train them in their safe use.

Since the mid-1970s, legislation has been introduced in the U.S. Congress that requires employers to give workers advance notice of plant closures and large-scale **layoffs**. Finally passed in the late 1980s as the Worker Adjustment and Retraining Notification Act, the law requires employers to give 60 days to 6 months prior notice, depending on firm size, of plant closings or mass layoffs.

Under the Clinton Administration, the U.S. Department of Labor implemented the Family and Medical Leave Act OF 1993 (which took effect in August of that year). The act requires all firms with more than 50 employees to provide up to 12 weeks of unpaid leave in the event of a family emergency.

THE FUTURE

A large share of **labor law** focuses on the rights of workers to organize unions and bargain collectively. It has been argued that this focus has become problematic with the dramatic decline in union membership in recent years, from a peak of 35 percent of private nonagricultural workers in 1955 to just over 10 percent in the 1990s. In his 1993 volume *Rights at Work*, Richard Edwards wrote ''Collective bargaining was—and, where it still exists, is—a subtle blend of legal requirement and voluntary contract, of local flexibility and general impact, and of public policy and private accommodation. Nonetheless . . . collective bargaining no longer provides a useful framework for a generalized system of workers' rights. Put simply, this is because unions today represent far too few workers to serve as the centerpiece for workers' rights.''

In 1993, the Clinton Administration established the Commission on the Future of Worker-Management Relations. This was commonly referred to as the Dunlop Commission after its chairman, John Dunlop, Secretary of Labor during the Ford Administration. The main purpose of the Commission is to consider reforms to labor law. The last attempt to significantly reform labor law was in 1978, under the Carter Administration. These reforms narrowly failed passage.

Representatives of employers and workers both argue the need for labor law reform. Employer representatives hold that the overtime premiums established by Fair Labor Standards Act hinder some employers' desire to introduce less regular work schedules and that the Wagner Act's prohibition of company-dominated unions interferes with the introduction of **quality control** circles and other labor-management cooperation programs. Labor representatives argue that labor law needs to accommodate the rapidly growing number of part-time and temporary workers and to facilitate their participation in collective bargaining. Labor representatives also have lobbied to make union organizing easier and to prohibit the permanent replacement of striking workers.

The Dunlop Commission issued its recommendations in January of 1995. The commission proposed speeding up the election process that determines whether a workplace can become unionized in an effort to facilitate organizing. The commission also proposed easing restrictions on labor-management committees so that these committees can deal "incidently" with issues of wages and work schedules.

SEE ALSO: Sex Discrimination

[David Kucera]

FURTHER READING:

Bacow, Lawrence. *Bargaining for Job Safety and Health*. MIT Press, 1980.

Dworkin, Ronald. *Taking Rights Seriously*. Harvard University Press, 1977.

Edwards, Richard. *Rights at Work: Employment Relations in the Post-Union Era*. The Brookings Institution, 1993.

Ewing, David. *Justice on the Job: Resolving Grievances in the Nonunion Workplace*. Harvard Business School Press, 1989.

Feldacker, Bruce. *Labor Guide to Labor Law*. Third edition. Prentice Hall, 1990.

Kochan, Thomas (ed.) *Challenges and Choices Facing American Labor*. MIT Press, 1985.

Manegold, Catherine. "For 2nd Time, Senators Block Bill to Bar Replacement of Strikers." *New York Times*. July 14, 1994.

Noble, Barbara Presley. "At Work; Labor Management Rorschach Test." *New York Times*, June 5, 1994.

Noble, Barbara Presley. "At Work; Unions Call Out Their Troops." *New York Times*. June 6, 1993.

Sandver, Marcus Hart. *Labor Relations: Process and Outcomes*. Little, Brown and Company, 1987.

Uchitelle, Louis. "Panel on Labor to Urge Changes Aiding Unions and Employers." *New York Times*. January 6, 1995.

Uchitelle, Louis. "A Call for Easing Labor-Management Tension." *New York Times*. May 30, 1994.

EMPLOYEE STOCK OPTIONS AND OWNERSHIP

In recent years, employee stock ownership plans (ESOPs) have emerged from relative obscurity and have become one of the more popular types of qualified employee benefit plans. More than 10,000 ESOPs already exist in the United States, and some 400 new ones are started each year. ESOPs are defined contribution plans—which were created by the **Employee Retirement Income Security Act of 1974 (ERISA)**—designed to invest primarily in the **stock** of the corporation sponsoring the plan or an affiliate of the corporate sponsor.

ESOPs may be used by both publicly owned and **closely held corporations**. Historically, ESOPs were primarily adopted by corporations whose stock was publicly traded. In recent years, however, ESOP legislation has primarily benefited closely-held corporations. To establish a plan, the company sets up a trust to hold the assets and makes contributions of company securities. Company contributions to the ESOP are tax deductible in an amount up to 25 percent of the total payroll of the eligible employees in the plan. The stock contributed to, or purchased by, the trust is allocated to the accounts of employees who have met the eligibility requirements of the ESOP. Participants are not taxed on the income earned by the plan, contributions to the plan, employer stock, or other amounts added to their accounts until the time of distribution.

ESOPs may be classified as leveraged, leverageable, and nonleveraged. In a leveraged ESOP, the plan borrows funds from a financial institution to purchase the securities of the employer firm. In turn, the employer firm makes contributions to the ESOP in order to make the interest and principal payments due the financial institution. Employee ownership of the shares accrues according to the rate at which loan principal is repaid. In a leverageable ESOP, the plan is authorized but not required to borrow funds to purchase the employer securities. Under this plan, cash or securities are contributed to the plan according to a defined formula. A nonleveraged ESOP is not authorized to use borrowed funds to purchase shares.

USES OF ESOPS

Many business owners are using ESOPs to cash out part of their ownership and establish a pension plan for employees. ESOPs generally are employed in smaller and medium-sized businesses and may be used to: (1) create an additional employee benefit, (2) provide a tax-favored market for the shares of a retiring owner of a closely held firm, and/or (3) borrow money at a lower interest rate.

Owners of small and medium-sized businesses have increasingly turned to ESOPs when they are ready to sell their companies. An ESOP allows a business owner to be compensated for his or her efforts while the continuity of the business is maintained and employees are given power to work as owners. ESOPs may be of particular benefit to retiring minority shareholders who, absent the presence of a ready and able buyer, may be forced to choose between retaining unmarketable, closely held stock, or selling such shares to the remaining shareholders at a substantial discount. As a result, approximately half of all ESOPs are used to provide a market for the shares of a departing owner of a profitable, closely held company. Most others are used either as a supplemental employee benefit plan or as a means for companies to borrow money in a tax-favored manner with the company repaying the loan in pretax dollars. Only in a small minority of cases are ESOPs used as a legal defense against a takeover or to save a failing company.

Successful ESOPs have several components. First, employees receive regular contributions of stock. Second, management seeks to involve employees in **decision making**. Finally, companies share information about performance with employee-owners.

TAX INCENTIVES

The Tax Reform Acts of 1984 and 1986 made ESOPs much more attractive by providing major new income and estate tax incentives. The major tax incentives for ESOPs include: (1) company contributions to the ESOP are tax deductible; (2) **dividends** paid on ESOP stock are tax deductible to the paying company; (3) tax on stock sold to the ESOP may be deferred; and (4) qualified lenders may exclude 50 percent of interest on **loans** to the ESOP.

Like other qualified employee benefit plans, ESOP contributions are deductible, within allowable limitations, by the sponsoring employer. While contributions to ESOPs used to repay the principal portion of an exempt loan are deductible in the amount of 25

percent of compensation, ESOP contributions used to repay interest on an exempt loan are deductible in full. As a result, ESOP sponsors have the opportunity to make contributions to the ESOP and deduct a significantly greater amount than if contributions were made to another type of plan.

Generally, an employer may deduct from income the amount of dividends paid to an ESOP to the extent the dividends are either used to make payments on the principal portion of an exempt loan or paid in cash to participants.

The principal benefits to shareholders from the adoption of an ESOP is their ability to sell stock to the ESOP and defer taxation on the gain from the sale. No gain on the sale of qualified securities to an ESOP will be recognized so long as the proceeds are reinvested in qualified replacement property. Therefore, income taxes may be deferred on a sale of qualified securities until the selling shareholder disposes of the qualified replacement property.

For this regulation to be applicable, however, the ESOP must hold at least 30 percent of (1) each class of outstanding stock of the corporation that issued the qualified securities or (2) the total value of all the corporation's outstanding stock immediately after the sale of qualified securities to an ESOP. Furthermore, the ESOP must hold the requisite percentage of stock for a period of at least three years following the sale.

Perhaps the most significant benefit afforded ESOP sponsors is the ability to borrow money at lower interest rates than are customarily available from conventional third-party lenders. Fifty percent of the interest received by a bank or another lender used with respect to a securities acquisition loan is exempt from taxes. A securities acquisition loan includes a loan to the ESOP.

ESOPs have become an important element of corporate acquisitions in recent years, particularly in **leveraged buyouts** in which a large indebtedness is required. The combination of the lender interest exclusion, which reduces the costs of borrowing, and the allowable deductions for ESOP contributions and dividends, which permit the deduction of the principal portion of debt repayments, provides substantial tax benefits that often translate into increased earnings and cash flow. The combined tax benefits often permit the acquiring corporation to pay a higher price for a target corporation's stock than would otherwise be the case.

LIMITATIONS AND DRAWBACKS TO ESOPS

On the other hand, ESOPs have a number of limitations and drawbacks. These include: high start-up costs and the ongoing expenses of administering the plan, the necessity of financial disclosure to employees, and exclusion from **S corporation** status. Thus, ESOPs cannot be used in partnerships or professional corporations. These disadvantages must be weighed against the tax and corporate performance benefits that ESOPs can offer.

ESOPs must also comply with specific investment and distribution requirements. A qualified participant who is at least 55 years old with ten or more years of plan participation can elect to have up to 25 percent (increasing to 50 percent in the participant's final election years) of his or her account balance invested in assets other than employer stock. The ESOP may meet the diversification requirement either by offering at least three investment options to the participant, or it may distribute the portion of the account balance elected for diversification. This diversification requirement may place cash flow burdens on the ESOP if participants are likely to diversify to reduce risk or the employer stock is not publicly traded. In addition, participants who receive distributions of stock in a closely held firm must be given an option to sell the stock to the employer (a put option). With this option, a participant may require the employer or the ESOP to repurchase the shares at fair market value within 60 days of distribution.

Many closely held corporations prefer to limit control over the affairs of the corporation to a key group of employees. Regardless of management's desires, plan participants must be given voting rights on shares of voting stock allocated to their accounts. If the stock is not publicly traded, however, the voting rights of participants may be limited to mergers, recapitalizations, and similar corporate control transactions.

EMPLOYEE STOCK OPTIONS

Stock price is typically viewed as the single most important long-term performance measure for shareholders. In recent years, both the **Securities and Exchange Commission** (SEC) pay disclosure rules and the **Internal Revenue Service (IRS)** tax laws have been modified in an attempt to encourage a linkage between executive compensation and corporate performance. The SEC has mandated displaying total shareholder return (dividends plus stock price appreciation) in annual proxy statements. Under Internal Revenue Code Section 162, companies are unable to deduct executive compensation in excess of $1 million unless the compensation is linked to the attainment of performance objectives adopted by the board's compensation committee. In order to relate executive pay to share price performance, companies grant executives employee stock options. By offering stock options, companies are providing executives with the opportunities for large gains. Many managers receive annual stock options worth more than their salaries. In addition, companies are encouraging executives to purchase and hold stock by adopting stock ownership guidelines, usually as a multiple of the executives's salary.

Employee stock option plans may be classified into two basic categories: investment plans and appreciation plans. Under investment plans, executives are given the opportunity to purchase shares of **common stock** at a fixed price over a specified period. Under appreciation plans, the employee is awarded the increase in share price, measured by fair market value or some formula, from the date of award to some future date. The executive is not required to make any investment.

INVESTMENT PLANS. The two most common types of investment plans are nonqualified stock options and incentive stock options. With nonqualified stock options, the executive is allowed to purchase common stock at a fixed price for a specified period, typically ten years. The option price is generally equal to the fair market price at the time of grant, although it may be more or less. When the manager buys the stock, he or she is taxed at ordinary income tax rates on the difference between the grant price and the fair market value at the time of exercise. If there is subsequent appreciation between the time of exercise and the eventual sale of the shares, the employee will pay taxes on this gain at the **capital gains** rate. There is no charge to the earnings of the corporation unless the option price is not fixed or less than 100 percent of fair market value at the date of grant. The company is also allowed to deduct income recognized by the employee.

Incentive stock options provide for the purchase of common stock at a fixed price for a period of up to ten years, and can qualify for capital gains treatment. The option price must be equal to or greater than the fair market value at the time of grant. The executive will receive long-term capital gain treatment when the stock is sold provided the shares are held for two years after the options are granted and one year after the date of exercise. The company does not take a charge to earnings and forgoes the tax deduction.

A new variation on the incentive stock option is the performance accelerated option. With these vehicles, the executive receives options that will eventually vest according to a schedule irrespective of company performance. The vesting accelerates, however, if the company meets certain long-term goals. Another innovation is the performance contingent option. These options only become exercisable if the company attains certain objectives.

Critics of executive stock options have objected to the granting of long-term options at the current market price since the long-term upward trend in the stock market is likely to make the options profitable, irrespective of company performance. Accordingly, some firms, such as Procter and Gamble and Walt Disney, have granted premium options. These options require the executive to pay an exercise price for the premium options that is significantly higher than the current market price at the grant date.

APPRECIATION PLANS. Stock appreciation rights provide an executive with the appreciation in the market value of the stock, usually in return for surrendering a stock option. Stock appreciation rights may be paid in cash, shares, or a combination of the two. The appreciation in fair market value is charged to earnings each period.

Full value plans give the executive the full value of shares of common stock, or a specified dollar amount. No investment is required on the part of the executive in these types of plans. Three common forms of full value plans are performance shares, performance units, and restricted stock awards.

Performance share plans provide rewards for satisfying long-term performance goals. Contingent shares are granted at the beginning of each performance period, generally every three to five years. At the end of the performance period, the employee earns a portion or multiple of the original shares allotted, based upon the extent to which the performance goals have been met. A minimum threshold level of performance must be attained, however, before an award is paid. Otherwise, the performance shares lapse. Performance shares may be paid out in cash, stock, or a combination of the two. The executive pays taxes on the gain at ordinary income rates. The company charges the value of performance shares against earnings to the extent that the performance goals are attained over the performance period, adjusted to reflect the value of the shares at the end of the performance period. Performance unit plans are similar to performance share plans, except contingent units with a specified dollar value are granted rather than performance shares.

Shares of stock that vest only after a specified restriction period are termed restricted stock awards. The employee receives voting and dividend rights immediately. If, however, the executive terminates before the end of the restriction period, he or she must return the shares to the granting company. In contrast to the other forms of incentive compensation the executive receives both dividends and capital gains.

Some companies, such as Ameritech, have combined restricted stock and performance shares making the eventual vesting of the restricted stock contingent on the firm achieving specified objectives.

[Robert T. Kleiman]

FURTHER READING:

Carey, James F. ''Employee Stock Ownership Plans as a Restructuring Option.'' In *Corporate Restructuring: A Guide to Creating the Premium Valued Company*, edited by Milton L. Rock, and Robert H. Rock. New York: McGraw-Hill, 1990.

Chingos, Peter T. ''Executive Compensation Issues in a Restructuring.'' In *Corporate Restructuring: A Guide to Creating the Premium Valued Company*, edited by Milton L. Rock, and Robert H. Rock. New York: McGraw-Hill, 1990.

Theisen, Barbara A., and Robert T. Kleiman. ''Employee Stock Ownership Plans: The Right Choice for Closely Held Corporations?'' *The Tax Advisor*. January, 1991, pp. 40-49.

EMPLOYEE TURNOVER

Employee turnover is the voluntary leaving of significant numbers of employees from a business, usually, but not always, against the wishes of the employer. Turnover is expressed as an annual percentage of the total **workforce**. For example, 25 percent employee turnover would mean that one-quarter of a company's work force at the beginning of the year has left by the end of the year. Turnover should not to be confused with layoffs, which involves the termination of employees at the employer's discretion in response to business conditions such as reduced sales or a merger with another company.

The severity of turnover varies widely by type of business and the economic health of the region where companies are located. The ''hottest'' software companies and most successful manufacturers frequently experience low turnover rates while fast food restaurant managers expect turnover to be as high as 50 to 75 percent. Coal mining companies in sparsely populated regions experience lower rates of turnover because there are few other job opportunities.

CAUSES OF EMPLOYEE TURNOVER

Better pay being offered by competitors is a major turnover problem, particularly in low-paying jobs such as fast food restaurants. If workers discover that competing restaurants are paying 25 cents per hour more than their present employer, they might move to the higher paying job if they perceive no other benefits from staying with their present employer.

Another cause is dissatisfaction with the employer's **management** style. Few employees, in high- or low-paying jobs, enjoy working for companies they do not like. If opportunities open at competitors and the pay scale is close, a company with management tyrants could suffer high turnover.

Retirement of experienced employees can cause high rates of turnover and extreme loss in **productivity**, particularly in industries where there is little competition. For example, the National Aeronautics and Space Administration has expressed concern about its future launch capability as thousands of 1970s-era "space race" engineers simply age out of the workforce.

Work stress experienced at particular types of jobs can also create turnover. Child-care workers watching over constantly crying children, waiters dealing with demanding dinnertime customers, police officers in high-crime areas, and truck drivers facing long hours and heavy traffic are all in job categories experiencing high levels of turnover.

Even seasonal changes such as the beginning of a school year can cause high turnover when part-time, school-age employees return to their classrooms. In this case, however, turnover is less likely to be unexpected by management. For instance, summer tourist-area restaurants likely staff up with college-age waiters knowing that they will leave by August.

EFFECTS OF EMPLOYEE TURNOVER

Turnover is a particularly troubling concern for those companies that have small staffs, pay low wages, and regularly deal with the public. Small companies that represent all three of those elements can be destroyed by high turnover. For example, if both of the cashiers of a T-shirt shop on the beach quit the day before the July 4th weekend, the owner of the shop has experienced a 100-percent staff turnover and a potential economic disaster. The T-shirt shop manager has to immediately find two honest cashiers who will not steal money or merchandise, who know how to run registers and count change, who are willing to hang T-shirts, and who are able to keep a cheery disposition during retail hours. They have to be willing to do all this for not much more than minimum wage.

The cost of turnover varies with the difficulty of the job to be performed. For example, in a food-processing company, showing someone how to put jars of jam into a cardboard box may take five minutes, so the cost of training someone to handle this job would not be high. If, however, the tyrannical manager of the food processing line at the company kept driving away food cookers and quality-control workers, the cost of constantly training employees in this critical area could be high.

Reducing high employee turnover saves money. Estimates on the costs of recruitment, selection, and training of employees range into the billions of dollars on a national basis so the effect on a company's finances is obvious. Money saved from not having to find and train replacement workers can be used elsewhere, including the bottom line of the company's profit statement. The U.S. Department of Labor estimates that it costs about 33 percent of a new recruit's salary to replace a lost employee. In other words, it could cost nearly $11,000 in direct training expenses and lost productivity to replace an experienced employee making $30,000.

Even low-paying jobs can require a great deal of training. While "burger flipping" is often denigrated as a dead-end job by workforce critics, these employees have to know how to properly prepare food to kill food-borne diseases, how to operate computerized cash registers, and how to juggle several tasks at once.

Some research studies have found that turnover from transient workers has lasting effects on loyal employees who stay with a company. One recent research study tested productivity among workers who were exposed to a management-planted person who quit in the middle of a task, citing dissatisfaction with the job and the company. A second group of employees worked with another planted person who had to leave the task because of illness. The group exposed to the employee who quit had lower productivity levels than the group exposed to the ill employee. The employees apparently took the complainer's statements to heart while the ill employee had nothing bad to say about the company.

High turnover can sometimes be useful. Employers who are poor interviewers may not discover that new employees are actually poor employees until after the workers have been on the payroll for several weeks. Rather than go to the trouble and documentation of firing these underperforming workers, some companies rely on turnover to weed out the bad employees.

[Clint Johnson]

FURTHER READING:

Gardner, James S. *Stabilizing the Workforce: Corporate Guide to Controlling Turnover*. Quorum Books, 1986.

Sheehan, Eugene. "The Effects of Turnover on the Productivity of Those Who Stay." *The Journal of Social Psychology*, October 1993, pp. 699-707.

White, Gerald. "Employee Turnover: The Hidden Drain on Profits." *HR Focus*. January 1995, pp. 15-18.

EMPLOYMENT

Information on employment is usually provided by citing the **unemployment** rate which, in turn, is expressed in percentage terms. The unemployment rate itself is defined as the percentage of labor force unemployed. The labor force is composed of individuals unemployed and employed. A person is considered unemployed if the person is out of work, but is actively seeking work. If a person is not working and is also not seeking work, then the person is voluntarily unemployed. A voluntarily unemployed person is not considered by the government as part of the labor force and is thus not counted as being truly unemployed. The division of the labor force into employed and unemployed individuals provides the direct and clear linkage between employment and unemployment rates, even though information is often provided in terms of the unemployment rate—an 8 percent rate of unemployment implies that the remaining 92 percent of the labor force is gainfully employed. The sum of unemployment rate and the associated employment rate must always, by definition, be equal to 100. Thus, the traditional use of the unemployment rate to describe the state of employment in an economy should not cause any confusion.

The concept can be illustrated with the help of recent statistics. In 1993, a total of 129.5 million people were in the U.S. labor force, of which 8.7 million people were unemployed. These two numbers yielded the unemployment rate of 6.7 percent for *all workers*. It is customary to make a distinction between *civilian workers* and *all workers*. The labor force in terms of all workers is made up of civilian workers and those in the U.S. armed forces. It is often considered that the civilian unemployment rate provides the truer picture of the underlying strength of the economy, as it captures the employment provided by the market forces. As a result, the unemployment rate quoted in the popular and financial media is almost invariably the civilian unemployment rate. The 1993 U.S. unemployment rate for civilian workers was 6.8 percent. As is the case with the 1993 example, the difference between the unemployment rates for *all workers* and *civilian workers* is pretty small.

FULL EMPLOYMENT

On the surface, full employment may appear to be equivalent to a zero unemployment rate. However, official statistics do not treat the full employment level in this manner. Full employment is officially defined as a mere six percent unemployment rate. Six percent is currently considered to be the *full employment rate of unemployment*. The use of the 6 percent bench mark is based on the fact that it is not realistic to expect the unemployment rate to drop to zero even under best of circumstances—there will be some unemployed people seeking jobs at any point of time. One may appreciate this seemingly odd convention if one understands the different kinds of unemployment that may be prevalent at different points of time. There are mainly four kinds of unemployment: seasonal, frictional, structural, and cyclical.

SEASONAL UNEMPLOYMENT. Seasonal unemployment results due to a variation in employment pattern as seasons change during a year. Thus, certain industries witness higher levels of unemployment during slack seasons whereas they may even experience a labor shortage during the peak seasons. For example, during harvesting season, employment in the agricultural sector increases drastically. Similarly, the construction industry experiences higher unemployment during winter and increased employment during summer months. In cold weather regions, construction workers may be laid off for months at a time. So, why are these workers in such a high risk industry? While the average unemployment rate in the construction industry is quit high, the industry attracts workers because the average wage rate is also high. Agricultural workers are not so lucky. Wage rates for workers harvesting crops quite low. As a result, migrant workers from Latin America, who are enthusiastic to raise funds to take back home, often end up with the lowest paying agricultural jobs.

It may, however, be noted that seasonal variations in unemployment can only happen if a region experiences a change in season. Thus, employment in the construction industry in California may not vary much across the year due to seasonal factors. While a particular region of the economy may be unaffected by seasonal factors, for the nation as a whole, seasonal variations in employment pattern are easily detectable.

FRICTIONAL UNEMPLOYMENT. In 1993 the U.S. labor market comprised about 130 million individuals. The labor market is in a constant state of flux, even when the economy is in equilibrium. Millions of people are entering the labor force or leaving it at any time. Moreover, millions are seeking gainful employment at any point in time (roughly nine million by the end of 1993).

The very complexity of the labor force itself becomes a cause for a temporary unemployment, called frictional unemployment. For example, if a housewife notes that the economy is doing quite well and speculates that there may be a good chance of getting a decent job, she might start actively searching for a job, thereby entering the labor force for the first time. Once part of the labor force but not yet employed, she will be counted in government statistics as being involuntarily unemployed. Let us assume that she finds an acceptable job after three months of being in the labor force. For these three months, she is a part of what is known as the frictionally unemployed labor force. Similarly, if a software programmer quits his current job due to inadequate pay or unsatisfactory work conditions, for example, and starts searching for a better job, he is also part of the frictionally unemployed labor force. Similar norms apply to a worker who re-enters the labor force. A new mother, for example, may leave her job to take care of her child for a few years and come back to look for a job when the child can go to preschool. When she re-enters the labor force, she joins the group of frictionally unemployed workers.

One can thus summarize that the frictional unemployment occurs during the normal job search process by individual workers. Since frictional unemployment occurs in the normal process of *turnover* in the labor market, it is also called turnover unemployment. While, the frictional unemployment for any one individual is a temporary phenomenon, for the economy as whole there are always a good number of people that are frictionally unemployed. Any economy is expected to have a modest amount of frictional unemployment. For a number of reasons, the United States seems to have a higher level of frictional unemployment than some other developed countries. The system of unemployment compensation in the United States is considered one of the factors leading to higher than necessary frictional unemployment. It is argued by critics of the unemployment compensation policy that the system induces higher overall unemployment.

STRUCTURAL UNEMPLOYMENT. Structural unemployment occurs in the economy when it undergoes structural changes. The structural changes lead to a mismatch: skill requirements and/or the geographical location of existing jobs do not match the present skills of workers seeking jobs or the geographical location of unemployed workers. Since the structural unemployment involves this mismatch between skills and/or locations, it is also called *mismatch unemployment*. There are a number of factors that account for the mismatch between skills, locations or both.

Mismatches between current skills of workers and skill requirements of available jobs arise when workers to meet specific skill requirements of vacant jobs. If an office wants to hire a secretary who knows the filing system employed in that office, having general skills such as typing will not suffice. Sometimes, the skill gap may be due to much higher technical skills required at emerging jobs (job openings for computer programmers, for example). These vacancies cannot be filled with workers that only know word processing.

Structural changes, often triggered by technological changes, lead to job losses in some industries. For example, with a rise in wages and advancements in technology, the United States' economy no longer has a comparative advantage in producing labor intensive products. One such example is the decline of the U.S. shoe industry. The American shoe industry could not compete with workers in developing countries because workers in those countries possess the skills needed in shoe manufacturing and their wage rates are

much lower. As a result, the American Shoe industry is fighting a losing battle. A similar situation has already occurred in the textile industry. American textile jobs have been lost to developing countries. This phenomenon is by no means unique to the United States—the Japanese textile industry suffered a similar fate.

The steel industry is also having a difficult time. The reason again is the technological change, but of a slightly different sort. The U.S. steel industry is quite old and thus while it embodies the best technology available at the time these steel plants were built, they have been made obsolete by later developments in steel manufacturing technology. Thus, the late-starting less-developed countries (LDCs) possess a technological edge and are thus able to out-compete the U.S. steel manufacturers. Now, suppose a worker who has lost his job in the steel industry goes looking for a job. Clearly, it is most unlikely that the worker would find many steel industry jobs waiting—he or she would have to find a job in another industry. This is a classic case of structural unemployment. Retraining to acquire new skills is the only remedy available for this worker.

A mismatch of locations occurs when job vacancies and unemployed workers are distributed unequally across geographical regions. During the 1980s, when the New England economy was booming, the Texas economy went bust. The bursting of the economic bubble in the Texas economy was due to a collapse in oil prices. A lot of oil industry and related jobs were lost. The New England economy, on the other hand, was booming due to an increased demand for computer and financial services. Thus there were unemployed workers in Texas and a surplus of jobs in New England. Why didn't the unemployed workers move to New England? There are at least three factors that accounted for the reluctance of Texas workers to move to New England. First, job requirements for the two kinds of jobs were probably very different. Second, a preponderance of two-worker families implied that each family would need to find two jobs, not one, to make moving feasible. Finally, most people are reluctant to move across country in search of work—they would rather stay near friends and family.

Structural unemployment tends to last much longer than frictional unemployment, as it takes much longer to acquire new skills or to move to a new location to begin a job search. Several solutions have been suggested to deal with structural unemployment. Economists have suggested that the government should provide better public education, provide subsidies to firms that train workers, and initiate government financed training programs to solve the problem of low skills. One of the suggestions to deal with the mismatch in locations is for the government to subsidize the cost of relocation. Another suggestion to deal with the problem calls for the establishment of tax incentives-based **enterprise zones**.

FULL EMPLOYMENT. As mentioned in the beginning, at the six percent rate of unemployment, the economy is considered as good as being fully employed. The six percent level is called the bench mark unemployment, full employment rate of unemployment, or the natural rate of unemployment. This number is arrived at by adding the three components of unemployment discussed above—seasonal, frictional and structural unemployment. The six percent level is the current estimate of these three components. With the increasing complexity in the U.S. labor market, this bench mark unemployment rate has been steadily revised upward over time—it was four percent during 1952-58, 4.5 percent in 1970 and 4.9 percent in 1977, and it is six percent at the current time.

CYCLICAL UNEMPLOYMENT. Cyclical unemployment can be considered to be determined residually as the difference between the actual and natural rates of unemployment. Thus, if the current rate of unemployment is 7.5 percent, 1.5 percent is attributable to cyclical unemployment. What causes cyclical unemployment?

Cyclical unemployment is the result of variations in the level of aggregate demand in the economy. If the aggregate demand level falls short of that necessary to maintain full employment, cyclical unemployment is the result and the unemployment rate goes above the six percent bench mark level. The higher the deficiency in aggregate demand, the higher the unemployment rate climbs above the six percent mark. As fluctuations in the aggregate demand are considered to be cyclical, the unemployment caused by demand deficiency (i.e., those not attributable to natural factors) is called cyclical unemployment. It is the cyclical unemployment that is the focus of government **macroeconomics** policies.

HOW THE GOVERNMENT COLLECTS UNEMPLOYMENT DATA

Unemployment (especially cyclical unemployment) is the focus of government policies. Thus, collection of unemployment data by the government on a continuous basis is of great importance for policy purposes and is collected every month. The government needs to know not only the prevailing unemployment rate at the national level, but also its geographical and demographic break. Of course, collecting unemployment data every month by contacting everyone in the labor force would be a very time consuming and costly affair, as there are about 130 million people in the labor force. As a result, the government uses a cost efficient, but scientifically de-

signed, alternative known as the survey method. Each month Census Bureau workers interview about 66,000 households regarding their employment status. In particular, they are asked if they are working for pay (full or part-time), are actively looking for jobs, are temporarily absent from work or are on layoffs. Each month one-fourth of the households in the sample are replaced by new households in order to gradually update the sample. While the data obtained from the survey are not as good as those based on contacting all workers in the labor force, they are pretty close.

FLAWS OF OFFICIAL UNEMPLOYMENT DATA

The official unemployment rate data do not represent the true extent of unemployment in the economy. They suffer from several flaws that undermine the use of the unemployment rate as guide of labor market conditions. These will be briefly discussed to warn the readers of the shortcomings of the official unemployment rate statistic. First, the unemployment rate does not capture the effects of discouraged workers dropping out of the labor force. For example, say a female worker keeps looking for a job for about a year and does not find one. She is so discouraged about the prospect of landing a job that she quits searching. The moment she quits actively searching for a job, she is no longer considered a part of the labor force and is thus not counted among unemployed in official statistics. As a result, if there is a poor job market from which a lot of workers drop out, the official unemployment rate may actually go down because those people aren't looking anymore. Suppose, for the purpose of illustration, that there are 100 persons in the labor force, 10 of whom are unemployed, yielding an unemployment rate of 10 percent. Assume now that 3 discouraged workers drop out of the labor force—the labor force declines to 97 and the number of unemployed reduces to 7. The official unemployment would drop from 10 percent to about 7 percent. One thus observes a rather backwards response of the unemployment rate statistic to a discouraging labor market condition. An opposite phenomenon occurs when the economy is doing very well and the labor market shows a lot of promise to aspiring workers. People who are not yet in the labor market feel encouraged to enter the job market. Even if they find jobs ultimately, they raise the number of unemployed temporarily. This can result in higher official unemployment rate even when the economy is doing better than before.

Another drawback of the unemployment statistic is that it does not distinguish between part-time and full-time employment. While working the 2:00 a.m. to 4:00 a.m. night shift at a convenience store is not a dream job, the government statistics would count that person as being employed. This naturally inflates the extent of true employment in the economy.

Even if somebody is employed full-time, that person might be working a minimum wage job with no fringe benefits or job security. Such a job may be unable to provide the worker with enough income to support a family. Workers employed in this manner are often called the working poor.

The above mentioned drawbacks of the official unemployment statistics provide adequate warning not to take the unemployment rate literally without asking additional questions. While the unemployment rate data are not without flaws, the government relies on them to a large degree to gauge the labor market.

GOVERNMENT POLICIES AND THE FULL EMPLOYMENT GOAL

Unemployment of labor essentially amounts to a waste of productive labor resources. It also leads to a number of undesirable outcomes, such as lower incomes, lower standards of living, greater social tension, and greater welfare expenditures. Thus, we need to consider not only the economic costs (billions of dollars in lost output) but also the human costs associated with increased unemployment. With respect to economic costs, researchers have estimated that every percentage point increase in the unemployment rate above the natural rate leads to a loss in output equivalent to 2.5 percent of the year's **gross domestic product** (the main gauge of the nation's economic activity). This implies that if the unemployment rate was seven percent in 1993, it was equivalent to an output loss of about $625 billion in 1993 prices.

Researchers have also found that the human costs of unemployment are quite tragic. Estimates by two economists (Bluestone and Harrison in *The Deindustrialization of America*) suggest that for every one percent increase in the unemployment rate, 920 more people commit suicide, 650 more commit homicide, 500 more die from heart and kidney disease, 4000 more are admitted to state mental hospitals, and additional 3300 individuals are sent to state prisons.

Both economic and human costs, in addition to probably the political motivations, are the reasons behind the use of active government policies to reduce the unemployment rate to the full employment level. The government uses two sets of macroeconomic policies to reduce the unemployment rate—monetary and fiscal policies. These policies attempt to reduce unemployment by increasing aggregate demand for goods and services in the economy. Greater demand for goods and services leads to higher production, requires a larger number of workers to be employed in the production process. This, generally, reduces the unemployment rate.

THE UNEMPLOYMENT AND INFLATION RATES

While reducing the unemployment rate sounds desirable, the process is not without complications. A lowering of the unemployment rate leads to higher **inflation**, especially when the economy is at or near the full employment level. So, the macroeconomic policies have to strike a balance between acceptable unemployment and inflation rates. Normally fiscal policy, conducted by the U.S. Congress and the White House in the United States, tends to have pro-employment bias. Monetary policy, conducted by an independent central bank (called the **Federal Reserve System** in the United States), on the other hand, tends to have anti-inflation bias. In general, the purpose of both monetary and fiscal policies is to strive to achieve high employment consistent with low and stable inflation.

[Anundi P. Shau]

FURTHER READING:

Branson, William H. *Macroeconomic Theory and Policy*, 2nd edition. Harper & Row Publishers, 1979.

Froyen, Richard T. *Macroeconomics: Theories and Policies*, 4th edition. Macmillan Publishing Company, 1993.

Gordon, Robert J. *Macroeconomics*, 6th edition. Harper Collins College Publishers, 1993.

Hall, Robert E. "Why is the Unemployment Rate So High at Full Employment?" *Brookings Papers on Economic Activity*. Volume 3, 1970.

Sommers, Albert T. *The U.S. Economy Demystified*. Lexington Books, 1985.

EMPOWERMENT

Empowerment in business means knowing how to "humanize" the work environment so **management** and employees work together to enhance **productivity** and achieve greater personal and professional success. An empowered company understands and appreciates that the "human factor" can add or subtract from the bottom line. Empowerment is a companywide commitment to respect all employees as intelligent and responsible human beings.

Empowerment is an entire company mind-set for successfully doing business in a global marketplace. Businesses are now asking: What exactly is an empowered workplace? And, how do we know when we have achieved an empowered **workforce**?

Highly successful companies encourage team members to worktogether for the betterment of the whole company. A commitment to empowerment influences and nurtures individuals to become active participants in the successes and challenges of the entire company. Empowerment is both an individual and a team effort.

An empowered company begins with self-empowerment. Owners and managers cannot empower others to perform their best until they are empowered themselves. Empowered management begins by hiring leaders who possess healthy self-esteem, superior people skills, and the willingness to share their expertise to bring out the best in their employees. Empowerment is a skill and can be learned. Managers can begin by reading empowering materials; attending seminars and workshops aimed at the ''whole person''; taking time to rejuvenate their own mind, body and spirit; learning to manage time and energy effectively; and participating in empowerment training. Effective management **teams** must have a firm grasp on the latest business technique as well as understanding the importance of human potential and high self-esteem.

Promoting and maintaining consistently high self-esteem in managers and employees is a vital ingredient to a highly empowered workforce. High self-esteem within the company is achieved by encouraging creativity, individuality, problem solving, and an open and honest exchange of ideas among all the employees in a nonthreatening environment. The opposite of an empowered workforce is one riddled with negativity, low morale, and a distrust of management. A disempowered workforce is an unproductive workforce.

Empowerment involves a companywide program based on promoting clarity of the company goals, high morale, fairness, recognition, teamwork, active participation, extensive communication, and a purposeful working environment. Empowerment is a total commitment to doing business in a productive and positive way.

Managers and workers have the basic need to feel they are contributing and making a difference. Employees who consistently feel enthusiastic about what they are doing, do a good job. An empowered company encourages employees to actively look out for and solve problems. The main benefit to the empowered company is quality improvement. Empowered workers feel responsible for the industry reputation and consumer perception of their company. Empowered employees take pride in their work.

An empowered management team does not manage by iron-fisted control. Successful managers promote an environment of sharing, openness, growth, and reward. The morale and productivity of a workforce are a direct reflection of the attitudes and values of the management team.

Empowerment requires flexibility. Adaptability is vital to implementing any empowerment program.

Employees will quickly lose enthusiasm and interest if a program in such a way that makes it inflexible, threatening, or unworkable.

Promoting a sense of importance and fair play is as important to success as any business plan or marketing campaign. Business success begins with each individual in the company, and empowerment begins by empowering everyone who can contribute to the success of the business. If employees have low self-esteem and a bad attitude, the company suffers. Since a company is known by the attitude of its employees, the impression of company competency expressed to the outside world begins with the image displayed by each employee.

Empowerment training benefits everyone in the organization. When employees feel good about themselves, they want to share their enthusiasm by helping the business succeed. An overall positive employee attitude minimizes infighting and back-stabbing and keeps morale consistently high. Empowerment in the workplace involves empowering workers with the skills and self-confidence they need to achieve their personal and professional best.

An empowered company begins with empowered management, so empowerment training should begin at the top. Lasting empowerment is a process of building trusting relationships and partnerships between management, employees, and customers.

Education, training, and positive reinforcement are critical to the success of any empowerment program. Part of building trust between employees and management is giving workers the tools they need to make an empowerment program successful. An effective empowerment program requires a sincere commitment to learn and assimilate new professional, personal, and technical skills. Empowerment includes self-development opportunities such as seminars and tape programs. A library of empowering resources is a valuable and positive resource that a company should not overlook.

Valuing the opinions and ideas of every employee is another foundation of empowerment. Workers should be encouraged to fine-tune their problem-solving skills. Learning to problem solve often involves trial and error. Patience and encouragement by management will produce a quality conscious, self-sufficient workforce.

Being a valued part of work **teams** is what empowerment is all about. Management and employees must work together to develop a common vision and compatible goals. Employees at all levels want to feel respected and valued. Working as a team to make the company's vision a reality encourages worker involvement and mutual respect and trust.

Employees want clear, consistent goals and direction. In today's competitive business world, most companies have good wages and working conditions. An empowered company adds trust, respect, education, and positive direction to their list of benefits. They reward a job well-done by providing for intellectual and emotional growth. They know how to make all the employees part of the successes, as well as partners in facing the challenges. Empowered companies have a strong corporate sense of community.

A feeling of belonging to a corporate community is important. The lines of communication must be well defined and open. Extensive and honest communication may even help employees do their job better. Fear of the unknown can be demoralizing and destructive.

An empowered environment encourages the best from all the team members. By providing empowerment opportunities, the company in return has a right to expect the employees to work smart and commit themselves to bettering their jobs and themselves. No one in an empowered company should be unproductive. When people find their work rewarding, they work harder and smarter. Empowerment encourages job satisfaction to become a top priority.

Empowerment does not happen overnight. It takes time to see the results of empowerment training. A belief that employees want to do a good job is essential. Working with individuals to set their professional goals will enhance the empowerment process. People will generally set higher goals for themselves than we would set for them. Empowerment involves management taking a proactive approach soliciting suggestions and ideas. Workers have many valuable time management and money-saving ideas. Most people are willing to share their observations and thoughts if they feel safe enough to do so. Management must nurture an environment in which employees are encouraged to use their own judgement and common sense.

An empowered environment is reflected in the overall attitude, production level, customer satisfaction, and profitability of a company. Top management has the responsibility of setting the tone for lasting empowerment. Empowerment is more than a "buzzword," it is a commitment to the entire company working together as a team. Management and employees must open the lines of communication to efficiently and effectively empower one another to greater success. Empowerment in business is built on a trusting, competent relationship between management and employees and between employees and customers.

[Sharon A. Michaels]

FURTHER READING:

Byham, William C., and Jeff Cox. *Zapp! The Lightening of Empowerment.* Fawcet Columbine, 1988.

Case, John, and Michael P. Cronin. "The Best Small Companies to Work For in America." *Inc.* November, 1992, pp. 88-95.

Finegan, Jay. "People Power." *Inc.* July, 1993, pp. 62-63.

Glaser, Connie, and Barbara Steinberg Smalley. *Swim with the Dolphins.* Warner Books, 1995.

Katayama, Danny. "A Success Story: Power to the People." *Jackson (TN) Sun Newspaper.* August 28, 1994.

Plunkett, Lorne C., and Robert Fournier. *Participative Management (Implementing Empowerment).* John Wiley & Sons, 1991.

Ruoff, Mary. "Business Forms Firm Empowers Its People." *Williamsport (PA) Sun-Gazette Newspaper.* September 4, 1994.

Tracy, Diane. *The Ten Steps to Empowerment: A Common Sense Guide to Managing People.* William Morrow, 1990.

EMPOWERMENT ZONES

An empowerment zone is an economically distressed American community that receives tax incentives and grants from the federal government under the Empowerment Zones and Enterprise Communities Act of 1993. The act provided for the designation of nine empowerment zones nationwide—six urban and three rural—as well as 95 enterprise communities, which receive similar benefits on a smaller scale. The term "empowerment zone" comes from the program's goal of providing resources and opportunities that will empower poor persons to become self-sufficient.

In order to be designated as an empowerment zone, a community had to meet a series of eligibility criteria based on its economic distress and its development potential. It then had to apply for consideration by submitting a detailed strategic plan outlining the coordinated public and private efforts that would contribute to its renewal and growth. The nine empowerment zones receive a number of tax incentives designed to stimulate **employment** and business investment in the region. In addition, each zone receives a block grant of $100 million over two years toward social service and economic development programs. About 500 communities applied for a coveted spot in the $3.8 billion empowerment zone program by the June 1994 deadline. The six urban U.S. empowerment zones, which were announced in December 1994, are Atlanta, Baltimore, Chicago, Detroit, New York City, and a joint effort between Philadelphia and Camden, New Jersey. The designation lasts for ten years.

IDEA EVOLVED OVER 15 YEARS

The main ideas behind empowerment zones—using tax incentives to encourage business investment, improve employment opportunities, and stimulate economic growth in certain geographical areas—originated in the late 1970s. Sir Geoffrey Howe, a member of the British Parliament, announced the first ''enterprise zones'' in 1978 to help improve economic conditions in the dock districts of London. The system implemented in England reduced government restrictions in order to encourage the formation of new businesses in impoverished areas. It met with limited success, however, because it did not include provisions for improving the infrastructure of the urban areas, which was found to be necessary for the new businesses to succeed.

In the United States, the zone concept gained its first supporters among leaders of the Republican party, which advocated an overall reduction of government influence. In the early 1980s, Ronald Reagan included enterprise zones in the urban policy platform for his presidential campaign, and Senator Jack Kemp introduced the first bill featuring enterprise zones in Congress. The idea gradually expanded its base of supporters to include more liberal members of Congress, like Democrats Robert Garcia and Charles Rangel of New York, as well as the leaders of prominent minority organizations, such as the National Urban League and the National Association for the Advancement of Colored People (NAACP).

The first enterprise zone legislation enacted in the United States came in 1987, with the passage of Title VII of the Housing and Community Development Act. Rather than providing tax incentives, the act was intended to relax federal regulations and coordinate the efforts of existing programs in the designated zones. Although the U.S. Department of Housing and Urban Development (HUD) received applications from 270 distressed communities for assistance under the program, it never designated any **enterprise zones**. When George Bush became president, he also voiced his support for the idea of creating enterprise zones to revitalize urban areas. Several bills were introduced during his administration, but Bush vetoed the two that passed because they included tax increases. This development meant that no federal enterprise or empowerment zones were created in the United States during the 1980s, despite widespread support for the idea.

In the meantime, many states adopted the enterprise zone idea and started their own programs. According to Marilyn Marks Rubin in *Public Administration Review,* 37 states had enacted some variation of the enterprise zone concept by July 1993, and 25 of these states claimed that their programs had created jobs. The state programs all differed in their eligibility criteria, types of incentives, and methods for measuring success or failure. Consequently, evaluating and comparing the state programs was problematic.

President Bill Clinton supported the idea of empowerment zones during his campaign, but he proposed several changes to the plans put forth by previous administrations. Most significantly, the Clinton plan combined tax incentives, to lure new businesses to the zones, with grants—or ''targeted government investment''—to help improve the zones' social and economic infrastructure. The Clinton plan also differed in that it provided for two tiers of assistance by designating nine empowerment zones and 95 enterprise communities. The Democrat-controlled Congress passed the Empowerment Zones and Enterprise Communities Act in May 1993.

SPECIFICS OF THE CLINTON PLAN

For a community to be considered for designation as an empowerment zone under the act, it had to demonstrate economic distress. Some of the measures of economic distress include high levels of **unemployment**, a poverty rate of at least 20 percent, a declining population, and a pattern of disinvestment by businesses. In addition, an empowerment zone community had to show the potential for **economic development**. Communities could meet this requirement by having public and private resources available to aid in the renewal process, and by involving various community groups and other interested parties in developing and implementing the strategic plan.

Once a community met the economic distress and development potential criteria, it had to apply for the program with the help of its local and state governments. The application for the empowerment zone designation required communities to submit a strategic development plan—incorporating the input of all affected members of the community, from business and government to church groups and community organizations—and identify sources of private funds and support for the renewal effort. Finally, the community had to develop baseline measurements and **benchmark** goals to evaluate the success of the program.

The nine communities that were designated as empowerment zones receive a number of tax incentives to help stimulate business activity. In order to create jobs for area residents, employers receive a 20 percent wage **credit** for the first $15,000 paid to a resident of the empowerment zone, in addition to tax breaks for any expenses incurred to train these workers. In order to encourage investment in the zones, the act allows businesses to exclude from taxation 50 percent of any capital gains from such investments. It also provides tax-exempt bond financing for the purchase of certain properties within the zones, and increases the allowance for depreciating such properties by $10,000 to $20,000 in the first year (which has the effect of reducing taxes). In contrast to empowerment zones, which receive all of these benefits, enterprise communities are eligible only for tax-exempt bond financing.

Each empowerment zone also receives a block grant of $100 million over two years toward the economic development programs included in its strategic plan. Such programs might focus on reducing drug abuse and crime or providing affordable housing. Each enterprise community receives a block grant of $2.8 million. Another provision of the act was to establish a Specialized Small Business Investment Company (SSBIC) in each empowerment zone. An SSBIC is a private lender that receives matching funds from the **Small Business Administration (SBA)** for its investments in empowerment zone businesses. The SSBICs are intended to become "one-stop capital shops" and distribute $300 to $400 million in **loans** and **equity** investments to zone businesses over a five-year period.

[Laurie Collier Hillstrom]

FURTHER READING:

Bates, Timothy. "A Bad Investment," *Inc.* January 1995, pp. 27-28.

"Empowerment Zone Applications Being Taken," *Practical Accountant.* March 1994, p. 16.

James, Jeffrey K. "Empowerment Zones, Enterprise Communities, and Rural Development Investment Areas," *CPA Journal.* July 1994, pp. 66-67.

Lloyd, Fonda Marie. "Time to Live Up to the Hype," *Black Enterprise.* June 1994, p. 27.

McCoy, Frank. "Can Clinton's Urban Policies Really Work?," *Black Enterprise.* June 1994, pp. 178-186.

Rubin, Marilyn Marks. "Can Reorchestration of Historical Themes Reinvent Government? A Case Study of the Empowerment Zones and Enterprise Communities Act of 1993," *Public Administration Review.* March/April 1994, pp. 161-169.

ENTERPRISE ZONES

Since the War on Poverty in the 1960s, both the private sector and the government have tried several programs to reverse the economic decline in some of the major cities of the United States. One such program is the development of a system of designated enterprise zones.

Enterprise zones are economically depressed areas, specifically defined and denoted by each state. They involve the application of tax incentives and the alleviation of regulations to encourage private sector investment and redevelopment in these geographic districts. The concept of enterprise zones was developed by British Professor Peter Hall in 1977, as an effort to revive decaying inner cities in Great Britain. The idea moved to the United States in the early 1980s and was adopted by many states.

The main goal of enterprise zones is to improve economically troubled areas and to create job opportunities, especially for individuals living within the zone boundaries. The enterprise zone concept lessens government intervention by removing regulatory obstacles that restrict market entry. Ideally, the private sector would be encouraged to establish businesses within the territory, thereby generating revenue, which would be utilized to revitalize the existing neighborhoods and create new employment opportunities.

By 1990, 37 states and the District of Columbia had certified enterprise zones. Twenty-six of those states, according to a U.S. Department of Housing and Urban Development report, had developed 3,172 enterprise zones. Louisiana led the way with the most zones, 1,553, while Arkansas followed with 458 zones. Within all zones, 11,658 businesses were taking part in the numerous state programs.

The eligibility requirements for a geographic region to be selected as an enterprise zone vary from state to state, but an overwhelming number of states require high unemployment, low income levels, widespread poverty, and population decline as the primary eligibility criteria. The states offer a variety of tax incentives to firms that are located within the enterprise zones. The most frequently offered incentives include employer tax credit, sales or use tax credit, and property tax credits. Advocates of these tax policies argue that tax breaks stimulate free enterprise and business growth.

POSITIVE ASPECTS. During the 1970s and 1980s, the inner cities of many major urban areas experienced significant losses of residents and jobs. Observers of these older urban areas argued that something needed to be done to develop economic activity within these regions. Supporters of enterprise zones believe they are a viable tool to spur economic development in these depressed areas. Proponents contend that tax incentives and the reduction of red tape will make these older sections more competitive with other municipalities in the metropolitan area. Advocates also suggest that the creation of enterprise zones will expand minority **entrepreneurship** and help bring jobs, prosperity, and ownership to people who are today locked into poverty and despair.

While acknowledging that tax incentives for enterprise zones could decrease revenue, supporters of the enterprise zone system cite two conceivable benefits. First, the increased investment and employment stimulated by enterprise zone tax incentives may produce sufficient profits to balance the sacrifice of the tax preferences, and perhaps build positive tax revenues. Second, the economic lives of people who live and work in depressed geographic areas will be improved. By steering investment and employment to geographic areas that have had significant economic declines, rather than existing, flourishing regions, it is reasonable to contest that society as a whole would profit.

POSSIBLE DISADVANTAGES. If the capital equipment purchased and the structures built or rehabilitated within the zone do not employ the labor of enterprise zone citizens, there will be few direct benefits from this capital infusion. While there are additional incentives for employing residents of enterprise zones, there are methods to hire outside the zones under specific situations. If an employer concludes that the efficiency of enterprise zone residents will be lower than that of nonresidents, he or she can employ a well-off, nonresident worker and still collect significant tax advantages. Furthermore, many small businesses are unable to take advantage of the tax incentives since they experience difficulties in obtaining the capital necessary for expansion.

The U.S. Department of Housing and Urban Development acknowledges that more than a tax break is needed to make the zones work. For enterprise zones to be successful, zone residents may require job training and work skills. In addition, social problems within the zone boundaries must also be dealt with.

Modest tax incentives and deregulation by themselves do not produce sufficient inducements to compensate for the discouragements of locating in afflicted neighborhoods. Other considerations such as the availability of a skilled labor force, proximity to transportation and markets, local amenities, and the physical security of the location, play a more significant role when businesses contemplate relocation or expansion in a given area. High unemployment, poverty, and crime weigh against investing in afflicted areas, as do run-down infrastructures and mediocre services and amenities.

Although enterprise zones are subsections of large metropolitan areas, tax breaks and deregulation apply only to the zones. It follows that the subsidies accompanying classification may lessen the competitiveness of businesses lying outside the perimeters of the zone, which in numerous instances may be equally depressed. While tax incentives for businesses locating in the enterprise zone would likely escalate economic activity in the defined area, the entire effect of the program may not lead to a net gain in tax revenues and employment. Increases in investment, employment, and productivity in enterprise zones might be offset by reduced investment, employment, and productivity in other areas.

EMPOWERMENT ZONES

The **empowerment zone** program represents the biggest federal attempt to revitalize America's decaying cities since the War on Poverty in the 1960s. Seventy-four cities competed for the lucrative urban empowerment zone prizes, which each awarded $100 million for employment and antipoverty programs and approximately $200 million in tax breaks for businesses in the zone that employ zone residents over a two-year period.

Atlanta; Baltimore; Detroit; Philadelphia/Camden; New Jersey; Chicago; and New York were the six cities selected as urban empowerment zones. In addition, 95 "enterprise communities" were supposed to get $3 million each. HUD then created two new categories of awardees. Supplemental Empowerment Zones worth $125 million and $90 million, respectively, went to Los Angeles and Cleveland. These cities will get economic development grants through the Department of Housing and Urban Development, but no new tax breaks. Enhanced Enterprise Communities worth $25 million each went to Boston; Houston; Oakland, California; and to a joint application from Kansas City, Missouri and Kansas City, Kansas.

Each city will get $50 million in social service block grants for each of the next two years. The funds be used for drug treatment, job training, public works, child development, and other social service programs. The U.S. Department of Health and Human Services is administering the awards. Half the money—$50 million—was available during fiscal year 1994, which ended September 30, 1995. The remainder will be available during fiscal year 1995, which runs October 1, 1995, through September 30, 1996.

Other assistance is also available to the empowerment zone. Employers in the zone qualify for tax credits for each worker who lives in the zone, up to 20 percent of the first $15,000 in wages and certain training costs. The zone also qualifies for up to $20 million in tax-exempt bonds for business expansion.

In contrast to past urban redevelopment programs, the hands-on approach from the federal government is designed to result in a higher degree of accountability. Critics of the program, however, argued that the notion that government can reduce poverty by developing the community from within and stimulating the creation of jobs in the immediate neighborhood had not worked successfully in the past.

[Robert T. Kleiman]

FURTHER READING:

Cordtz, Dan. "Mainstreaming the Ghetto." *Financial World.* September 1, 1992, pp. 22-25.

Cowden, Dick, and Sarah Eilers. "Will Enterprise Zones Make It to the End Zone." *Business & Society Review.* Summer, 1991, pp. 58-61.

Levitan, Sara A., and Elizabeth I. Miller. ''Enterprise Zones Are No Solution for Our Blighted Areas.'' *Challenge*. May-June, 1992, pp. 4-8.

ENTREPRENEURSHIP

An entrepreneur is one who organizes a new business venture in the hopes of making a profit. Entrepreneurship is the process of being an entrepreneur, of gathering and allocating the resources—financial, creative, managerial, or technological—necessary for a new venture's success. One engages in entrepreneurship when one begins to plan an organization that uses diverse resources in an effort to take advantage of the newly found opportunity. It involves hard work, long hours, and, usually, the hope of great financial return. More importantly, entrepreneurship is characterized by creative solutions to old or overlooked problems; ingenuity and innovation are the entrepreneur's stock in trade. By taking a new look at difficult situations, the entrepreneur discerns an opportunity where others might have seen a dead end.

Entrepreneurship is a source of more entrepreneurship. The American economy has always been fueled by the innovations and new products entrepreneurs bring to the market. All big businesses started out small, usually as one man or woman with a good idea and the willingness to work hard and risk everything. While it is true that about half of all new businesses fail, the ones that succeed contribute a great deal to the creation of other new ventures which leads, in turn, to a dynamic national economy.

Successful entrepreneurship depends on many factors. Of primary importance is a dedicated, talented, creative entrepreneur. The person who has the ideas, the energy and the vision to create a new business is the cornerstone to any start-up. He or she is the glue that holds the pieces together. But the individual must have ready access to a variety of important resources in order to make the new venture more than just a good idea. He or she needs to develop a plan of action, a road map that will take the venture from the idea stage to a state of growth and institutionalization. He or she needs to put together a team of talented, experienced individuals to help manage the new venture's operations. Entrepreneurship also depends on access to capital, whether it be human, technological, or financial. In short, entrepreneurship is a process that involves preparation and the involvement of others in order to exploit an opportunity for profit.

ENTREPRENEURSHIP DEFINED

One of the biggest problems among those who are interested in entrepreneurship is defining it. The multiplicity of the entrepreneur's motivations and goals leads to questions aimed at distilling the essence of entrepreneurship. To what or to whom does one refer when one uses the word? Is there any difference between a person who opens yet another dry cleaning establishment, sandwich shop, or bookstore and the entrepreneur? If so, what is it that separates the two? What characteristics define an entrepreneur and entrepreneurship itself? Historians and business writers have struggled with providing the answers. Even today, there is no widely accepted definition, but the variety of possibilities provides important clues as to what makes entrepreneurship special.

One of the first American writers to investigate the work of the entrepreneur in the national economy was Joseph Schumpeter. The Harvard professor argued that the defining characteristic of entrepreneurial ventures was innovation. By finding a new ''production function'' in an existing resource, a previously unknown means through which a resource could produce value, the entrepreneur was innovating. The innovation was broadly understood; an innovation could take place in product design, organization of the firm, marketing devices, or process design. Nevertheless, innovation was what separated the entrepreneur from others who undertook closely related endeavors.

Arthur Cole, another Harvard professor, defined entrepreneurship as purposeful activity to initiate, maintain, and develop a profit-oriented business. The important part of this definition is the requirement that individuals must create a new business organization in order to be considered entrepreneurial. Cole's entrepreneur was a builder of profit-minded organizations. Moreover, that organization must seek *financial* gain. Whereas Cole's definition was concerned primarily with the monetary profits of the business world, Schumpeter made room for all organizational activities by broadly defining profits. That is, according to Schumpeter, profits do not have to come in dollars and cents.

Shapero and Sokol (1982) argued that all organizations and individuals have the potential to be entrepreneurial. They are at odds with those who try to describe entrepreneurship in terms of what makes an entrepreneurial organization different than others. Rather than focusing on the nature of an entrepreneurial organization, the object of Shapero and Sokol's study was the range of entrepreneurial activities themselves. They focused on what happens when an individual or an organization acts like an entrepreneur. Shapero and Sokol contend entrepreneurship is characterized by an individual or group's initiative taking, resource gathering, autonomy, and risk taking. Their definition could theoretically include all types and sizes of organizations with a wide variety of functions and goals. By defining an "entrepreneurial event" instead of entrepreneurship itself, Shapero and Sokol avoid the pitfalls inherent in trying to delineate what types of organizations can or cannot be entrepreneurial.

In his book *Innovation and Entrepreneurship*, Peter F. Drucker took the ideas set forth by Schumpeter one step further. He argued that Shumpeter's type of **innovation** can be systematically undertaken by managers to revitalize business *and* nonbusiness organizations. By combining managerial practices with the acts of innovation, Drucker argued, business can create a methodology of entrepreneurship that will result in the institutionalization of entrepreneurial values and practice. Drucker's definition of entrepreneurship—a systematic, professional discipline available to anyone in an organization—brings our understanding of the topic to a new level. He demystified the topic, contending that entrepreneurship is something that can be strategically employed by any organization at any point in their existence, whether it be a start-up or a 200-year-old business. Drucker understood entrepreneurship as a tool to be implemented by managers and organizational leaders as a means of growing a business.

ENTREPRENEURSHIP IN THE NATIONAL ECONOMY

Entrepreneurship is a catalyst for economic growth. Drucker suggested that the work of entrepreneurs drives free market economies. Yet economists have been slow to recognize the central role played by entrepreneurs in driving growth. As creators of new organizations, entrepreneurs are giving others across the nation good jobs and a chance to become part of growing organizations. To appreciate the enormous contributions made by entrepreneurs and their companies to national growth, one must look at how entrepreneurship and innovation positively influence the economy.

Entrepreneurs drive the economy because they create wealth through innovation. Drucker argued that, "innovation is the specific instrument of entrepreneurship. It is the act that endows resources with a new capacity to create wealth." Innovation takes place when an individual or a group recognizes a new application for the resources available to them. An entrepreneur adds wealth (or at least the potential for gain) to the economy when he or she presents the economy with new ways to use the resource as a means of gaining some kind of value. By discovering and exploiting a resource's previously hidden capacity for wealth creation, entrepreneurs are catalysts for economic growth. In addition to natural resources such as plants, animals, and minerals, the resource could be a physical thing, such as a new polymer or a piece of computer hardware. A resource could also be an intellectual concept such as a technological breakthrough, a patent for a drug, a trademark, or special expertise in a certain area such as **marketing** or **advertising**. Furthermore, the resources that can be leveraged in an entrepreneurial endeavor may include selling processes, distribution networks, or manufacturing techniques.

Innovation, then, involves finding new, creative applications for existing resources. It involves finding new profit opportunities for an existing product or introducing a new product or service to a new or existing market. The innovation may come as a result of seeing an existing resource in a new light or as a result of a technological discovery. Or the innovation may come in the way the resource is marketed, manufactured, or processed. Ray Kroc and McDonald's, the company he created, may be the perfect example of an innovator and an entrepreneurial organization. The company that he built based upon a few key innovations was a source of great economic wealth. Before Kroc, hamburgers were well known; you could find them in restaurants across America. But Kroc applied innovations in the process by which hamburgers were made and sold. He standardized production and training, and focused on high quality and consistency in his products. Because of Kroc's innovations, none of his competitors were able to completely match McDonald's prices and quality. He introduced a new way of doing business that laid the groundwork for vast expansion and growth for his company. In addition, he provided an example of a new way of doing an old business, opening up opportunities for competitors interested in trying to match his success.

McDonald's basically created the fast food industry, one which has become a huge part of the American economy. Kroc's innovation led to more innovations and more profit opportunities. The drive-through window, value meals, and a slew of new food products were introduced in the wake of his initial innovations. After seeing that Kroc and McDonald's profited from their innovations, competitors spent money trying to copy his techniques so they could try to copy his profits. The first improvement, the first creative step led to more profits and growth not only for his organization but also for a host of imitators.

Growth and wealth grew from the early entrepreneurial work of Kroc and his staff. Likewise, other innovations are keys to economic growth. The development of sophisticated computer circuitry led to smaller, more affordable **computers** for home users. The rise of the personal computer has led to a massive market for products and services that relate to it. The multibillion dollar personal computer **software** industry was very small before innovations in computer technology lead to computers that individuals could purchase relatively cheaply.

Innovation and entrepreneurial work are major factors in the growth and vitality of an economy. Innovation turns old products and methods into better, more valuable products and methods by exposing new dimensions of utility. By finding new applications for existing resources, entrepreneurs can stimulate demand for them, making them seem like suddenly more valuable resources. As well, by exposing profit opportunities in otherwise untried areas, entrepreneurs can stimulate investment in the means by which the new profit opportunity is exploited. Competitors, wanting the same chance for profit, will invest the capital necessary to pursue the profit.

ENTREPRENEURSHIP AND THE PERSONALITY OF THE ENTREPRENEUR

Jeffry Timmons, one of the most respected commentators on the topic of entrepreneurship, has defined the term in his book *The Entrepreneurial Mind* as "the ability to create and build something from practically nothing." His definition captures the spirit of the word, the sense that entrepreneurs are like magicians, creating thriving organizations out of good ideas and a lot of sweat. Timmons's words hint at the myths inherent in the common understanding of entrepreneurship. They bring to mind the great entrepreneurs who have become American icons, national celebrities because of their ability to almost magically create their business success. Men and women of popular lore such as King Gillette, Mrs. Fields, Colonel Sanders, Ray Kroc, Steven Jobs, Mary Kay, Ben and Jerry, and Bill Gates have taken a place in the spotlight of American business mythology.

Many businesspeople believe that entrepreneurs have a personality that is different than everyone else's. Entrepreneurs have "the right stuff." But what does that consist of? While it is hard to generalize about what it takes to be a successful entrepreneur, some personality traits seem to be more important than others. Of course, entrepreneurs need to have a large amount of courage. And they certainly need to be driven to succeed. But there are other, less obvious, personality characteristics that an entrepreneur should develop as a means of further ensuring their success. In his book *Entrepreneurship: Texts, Cases, Notes*, Robert C. Ronstadt indicated some of the traits that help entrepreneurs build thriving organizations. Chief among these, Ronstadt numbered creativity and the ability to tolerate ambiguous situations.

Creative solutions to difficult problems may make or break the young and growing business; the ability of an entrepreneur to find unique solutions could be the key to his or her success. One of the most vexing situations entrepreneurs face is the allocation of scarce resources. For instance, owners of new ventures need to be able to decide how to best use a small advertising budget or how best to use the computer available to them. Furthermore, they must be creative in their ability to find capital, team members, or markets. Entrepreneurs bank their businesses on their ability to make do with the limited resources available to them.

In addition to being creative, an entrepreneur must be able to tolerate the ambiguity and uncertainty that characterize the first years of a new organization. Inevitably, business or market conditions are going to change, causing uncertainty for the venture and for the entrepreneur. Being creative enables entrepreneurs to more successfully manage businesses in new and ambiguous situations, but without the ability to handle the pressure that uncertainty brings upon an organization, the entrepreneur may lose sight of his or her purpose.

Often, personal or work history has led individuals to be more open to taking the risks involved with undertaking a new venture. For instance, individuals who know successful entrepreneurs may be stimulated to try their hand at running their own business. The successful entrepreneurs act as role models for those thinking about undertaking a new venture, providing proof that entrepreneurship does not always end in bankruptcy. Furthermore, Robert H. Brockhaus, Sr. pointed out that dissatisfaction with previous employment is "closely related to the entrepreneurial decision." Those who have been dissatisfied with working for others or who have had negative work experiences are more likely to be willing to tolerate the ambiguity that characterizes new ventures. Personal experience and work history work in conjunction with personality traits to bring out the entrepreneurial spirit in individuals, pushing them towards the process of entrepreneurship.

THE PROCESS OF ENTREPRENEURSHIP

The myths that have grown up around the great entrepreneurs in America have focused more on the personality of the individual than on the work that he or she did to create a prosperous organization. What sticks in our memories are the qualities of a great entrepreneur, those personality traits that "make" a great businessperson. Successful entrepreneurs, however, work hard to build their organizations, starting from little and undertaking a process that results in a thriving business. Even the best ideas were profitable only because the entrepreneur went through the steps necessary to build a company from scratch. Successful new ventures do not appear magically out of the swirl of the market—they are planned, created, and managed.

It is important to understand some of the stages a businessperson must go through in order to create a successful entrepreneurial venture. All entrepreneurs go through three very general stages in the process of creating their ventures: a concept formation stage where ideas are generated, the innovation and opportunity are identified, and the business begins to take shape; a resource gathering stage where necessary resources are brought together to engage in the optimization of the opportunity; and a stage where the organization is actually created. The three stages can overlap and there may be times when an entrepreneur may be doing all three stages at one time. Moreover, the stages do not necessarily follow sequentially. Nevertheless, the decisions made in the first stage tend to lay the framework for the rest of the organizational activity.

Before any business opens its doors, it must make crucial decisions about the way the business will be run. The first step in the entrepreneurial process is the concept formation stage, the time when the entrepreneur generates ideas about the opportunity he or she will pursue and on what innovations the organization will be based. The first stage is where the entrepreneur determines what kind of potential market exists for the business and forms a rough idea of how to penetrate that market. During the concept formation stage, the entrepreneur must answer hard questions about the potential business. As well, the entrepreneurs should examine their own motivations and ask why they want to go into business. The answers to these questions will provide the framework for future planning, growth, and innovation.

There is a great deal that is unknown to the entrepreneur before he or she starts out. The viability of the venture depends on the individual's ability to lessen that which is unknown and maximize that which is known. The central question an entrepreneur should ask him or herself during the idea generation stage is whether there is actually an opportunity for a successful venture. That is, will starting a new business enable the entrepreneur to accomplish things or meet goals he or she might not otherwise meet? Some entrepreneurs want to make a certain return on their efforts and investment or are looking to run a business that will afford them a certain lifestyle. Others are looking to capture a certain percentage of the market. Still others go into business for themselves because it would afford them the independence and freedom that working for someone else would not. Before taking the plunge, prospective entrepreneurs should investigate the extent to which their envisioned business will give them an opportunity to meet their goals.

A new business can be opened by anyone with the capital and time to do it. Nevertheless, businesses that will be successful, that will remain viable for years and employ others, must be strong financially.

Among the first questions an entrepreneur should ask are those that explore the potential profitability of the venture. The entrepreneur should be able to estimate sales and selling expenses as well as other costs of doing business. In order to develop a sense of the economic feasibility of a venture, the entrepreneur should ask: How big is the potential market for the product or service? Is it a regional or national market? Are businesses currently making money in the market? How much capital will it take to get the business up and running? Who are the competitors? Quantitative analysis of the opportunity is a vital part of the conceptualization of the business. The results of "running the numbers" and creating a set of figures with which the future can be planned, will enable the entrepreneur to determine whether the potential business will be profitable.

The first stage of the entrepreneurship process should give the individual enough information to make the "go/no go" decision. The concept formation stage should enable the individual to decide whether there is an opportunity for a viable business and whether the opportunity is attractive enough to pursue. Once the decision has been made, the entrepreneur either begins looking for a new opportunity or moves into another step in the process, that of gathering the necessary resources. Without a sufficient supply of resources the opportunity might never be turned into a business that makes money for the entrepreneur. In the resource gathering stage the entrepreneur begins to assemble the tools that he or she will need to profit from the opportunity. In general, a person has to gather three types of primary resources: capital, human/managerial, and time. Capital can be financial (in the form of cash, stock ownership, or loans), intellectual (**patents**, trademarks, **brand names** and **copyright**s), and technical (innovations in design or production that competitors can not or will not duplicate). Human resources refers to the individuals who will help the entrepreneur take advantage of the opportunity, either as employees of the new organization or as paid and unpaid counselors. Therefore, resources could mean anything from a Small Business Administration loan, to signing contracts with distributors or sales representatives, to signing a lease on office space. Because it is intellectual capital, a patent could be a resource. A computer systems manager or a marketing manager or a good accountant could also be resources, tools that the entrepreneur will use to build his or her business team. In order to create a viable organization an individual entrepreneur has to be ready and able to manage the resources at his or her disposal, bringing them together in ways that are advantageous and efficient.

Of the resources available to an entrepreneur, one of the most important is time. When an opportunity becomes apparent, most people realize it will not last forever. There is a "window of opportunity" that will close at some time in the future. For instance, a business based on a patented technological innovation has a certain amount of time to operate before the patent expires and competitors can duplicate the innovation. When the patent expires, the competitive advantage held by the business is diminished or gone. Other businesses may be based on selling to a new or unique market. The entrepreneur who runs the business has a certain amount of time before potential competitors notice that the business is (or will be) profitable. In that time frame—the window of opportunity—the entrepreneur who found the opportunity must manage resources so that the business is established and protected from the threat of competition. The time which is available to exploit the opportunity is another dimension, another resource, which the entrepreneur must manage. The entrepreneur must try to exploit the opportunity while the "window" remains open.

The first two stages may overlap. An entrepreneur may begin gathering resources while defining the concept for the venture. Likewise, the entrepreneur may have to redefine the concept or fine-tune it a bit after gathering resources. The activities that characterize the first two stages will also continue to some extent as the new venture moves into the third stage. After the entrepreneur has decided to undertake the new venture, he or she enters a third stage of entrepreneurship: new venture management. The entrepreneur goes from being just a visionary to a visionary-with-a-business-to-run and so his or her activities become even more varied. The entrepreneurial process demands that the activities of the entrepreneur change to meet the needs of a dynamic business.

One way to examine the changing managerial activities of the entrepreneur is to look at the different roles filled by the entrepreneur as the business develops. In her book *Entrepreneurial Behavior*, Barbara J. Bird examined entrepreneurial roles and their place in the management of ventures. The first role most entrepreneurs fill is that of the organization creator. As the instigator of the organization, the entrepreneur sets the philosophy of the organization, establishes the strategic focus and educates new employees. In this role, the entrepreneur lays the groundwork for the emerging corporate culture. Another role Bird argued most entrepreneurs must fill is the promoter role. They must act as the new venture's chief salesperson in contacts with financial backers, prospective clients, employees, suppliers, and others. In many cases, the entrepreneur acts as a role model or a mentor to others in the organization. As founders (or founding team members) of organizations, entrepreneurs are often called upon to provide counsel or advice to community members or employees. The roles that an entrepreneur must fill demand flexibility and creativity. In order to successfully manage a new venture, an entrepreneur must be comfortable in all the roles.

Even more important than being able to juggle the multiple entrepreneurial roles, entrepreneurs must be able to balance the activities of leadership and his or her managerial duties. In short, leaders are trying to make important strategic decisions. They are attempting to do the things they believe will lead to a successful organization. Managers, on the other hand, are more concerned with the day-to-day operations of the business. Bird argued that managers are resource driven and leaders are opportunity driven. It is a precarious relationship, but entrepreneurs must be both managers and visionary in order to build their organizations. A successful entrepreneur has to avoid getting caught up in the details of management such that he or she loses sight of the larger mission that guides the new venture.

The mission of the new venture can only be fulfilled if the entrepreneur remains entrepreneurial throughout the life of the organization. That is, innovation has to be a primary strategy of the venture. Drucker pointed out that the venture must be receptive to innovation and open to the possibilities inherent in change. Change must be seen as a positive for a business to remain entrepreneurial. Therefore, management of an entrepreneurial organization requires policies that encourage innovation and rewards those who innovate. If the venture is to remain dedicated to entrepreneurship, management has to take the lead in establishing the patterns that will lead to a dynamic, flexible, and vital organization.

[Jim Cuene]

FURTHER READING:

Bird, Barbara J. *Entrepreneurial Behavior*. Glenview, IL: Scott, Foresman and Co., 1989.

Brockhaus, Robert H., Sr. "The Psychology of the Entrepreneur." In *Encyclopedia of Entrepreneurship*, edited by Calvin A. Kent, Donald L. Sexton, and Karl H. Vesper. Englewood Cliffs, NJ: Prentice-Hall, 1982.

Casson, Mark, ed. *Entrepreneurship*. Brookfield, VT: Edward Elgar Publishing, 1990.

Cole, Arthur. "An Approach to the Study of Entrepreneurship." In *Exploration in Enterprise*, edited by Hugh G. J. Aiken. Cambridge, MA: Harvard University, 1965.

Cole, Arthur H. *Business Enterprise in Its Social Setting*. Cambridge, MA: Harvard University, 1959.

Drucker, Peter F. *Innovation and Entrepreneurship*. New York: Harper & Row, 1986.

Drucker, Peter F. "Our Entrepreneurial Economy." *Harvard Business Review*. January-February, 1984, pp. 59-64.

Kent, Calvin A., Donald L. Sexton, and Karl H. Vesper, eds. *Encyclopedia of Entrepreneurship*. Englewood Cliffs, NJ: Prentice-Hall, 1982.

Ronstadt, Robert. *Entrepreneurship: Texts, Cases & Notes*. Dana Point, CA: Lord Publishing, 1985.

Schumpeter, J. A. *History of Economic Analysis*. New York: Oxford University, 1954.

Schumpeter, Joseph A. *The Theory of Economic Development*. Cambridge, MA: Harvard Economic Studies, Harvard University, 1934.

Timmons, Jeffry A. *The Entrepreneurial Mind*. Andover, MA: Brick House Pub. Co., 1989.

ENVIRONMENTAL MARKETING

SEE: Green Marketing

ENVIRONMENTAL LAW AND BUSINESS

Observers have called 1970 the "year of the environment." On April 22, 1970, the first celebration of "Earth Day" took place. Also that year, the National Environmental Policy Act was passed by the United States Congress, the United States **Environmental Protection Agency (EPA)** was created, and the **Occupational Safety and Health Administration** was established. Various U.S. environmental laws predate 1970, but since that year, those laws have been developed extensively, and the enforcement of those laws has changed the way business "does business." Every business in this country is affected by environmental laws. On a daily basis most businesses deal with one or more environmental laws and the administrative agencies that enforce them. For example, businesses must inform and educate their employees about hazardous materials in the workplace as required by the Occupational Safety and Health Administration (OSHA), and they must inform their communities about such materials on their premises pursuant to 1986 amendments to the **Comprehensive Environmental Response, Clean Up, and Liability Act (CERCLA) of 1980 (Superfund)** legislation. Businesses must apply for and adhere to permits from the federal EPA for their air emissions and their effluents discharged into waterways. Businesses generating hazardous wastes must comply with the EPA's manifest system (a record-keeping system), and the disposal of hazardous and non-hazardous waste is regulated extensively. Businesses are being required to clean up or pay for clean up of environmental contamination caused by their past acts and practices. Further, businesses are now being required to monitor their production methods and seek ways to prevent pollution. The list of the ways in which environmental law affects the daily operations of business goes on.

Therefore, for any business person, it is helpful to be familiar with the problems addressed by our environmental laws, the provisions of those laws, and the kinds of mechanisms and administrative agencies through which those environmental laws are enforced.

Environmental laws deal with myriad pollution problems. Pollution or contamination of the environment is found within the walls of factories and other business facilities as well outside the walls of those facilities. Environmental law deals with contamination of our air, surface waters, drinking water, ground waters, and land. Those affected include workers and their families as well as other members of their communities. And, as U.S. business people increase their participation in a global market place, it is becoming increasingly clear that environmental contamination extends beyond local and regional concerns; its effects are international and even global. As illustrated along the U.S.-Mexican border, environmental contamination does not recognize political boundaries.

The United States is clearly a "legalistic" society in that its people rely on its legal system to "do something" about injuries to individuals as well as social problems affecting large numbers of people. Thus, it is not surprising that individuals as well as groups of concerned citizens rely on our legal system to "do something" to compensate individuals who suffer harm due to exposure to environmental contamination (toxic substances), to provide a mechanism for clean up of environmental contamination, to protect citizens from exposure to toxic (hazardous) substances and to prevent further contamination of the environment.

In recent decades, there has been an increase in what lawyers call "toxic tort" litigation. Toxic tort litigation refers to the use of tort law to seek compensation for illness, injury or death resulting from exposure to hazardous substances or to seek an abatement of hazardous conditions. (Tort law includes causes of action such as negligence, trespass, nuisance, or strict liability for hazardous products or activities.) One well-known example is the Love Canal case. Love Canal is a community near Niagara Falls, New York, where beginning around 1970 families realized that they were suffering from unusually high rates of cancer and other illnesses as well as birth defects. Investigation revealed that the families' homes and even an elementary school for their children had been built on top of tons of chemical wastes that had been deposited in a ditch and covered over. In one of various legal responses to the disaster, the residents sued the Occidental Petroleum Corp. based on tort law and recovered millions of dollars in damages.

Love Canal was a well-publicized case revealing the extensive damage associated with hazardous waste from industrial disposal sites and industrial plants throughout the United States. But, the case was not unique. Other well known toxic tort cases have arisen from such contamination in Woburn, Massachusetts; Times Beach, Missouri, and elsewhere. Thousands of cases have been brought against businesses based on similar, even if less extensive, contamination at hazardous waste disposal sites and industrial facilities throughout the United States.

Such cases are expensive for the businesses being sued as well as the plaintiffs bringing the suit, as is illustrated by the "Woburn, Massachusetts" case. Parents of eighteen children who contracted leukemia (plus one adult victim) became convinced that their disease could be traced to industrial solvents in the water supply. After years of investigation and months of trial (which was only partially completed), the case was settled. Defendant W.R. Grace & Co. said that it had spent $2.5 million in defense and investigation costs. Although an exact amount was not revealed to the public, the settlement paid by W.R. Grace & Co. was said to total $9 million to nine of the victims (and their survivors) with additional amounts going to other victims.

The Love Canal and Woburn, Massachusetts toxic tort cases were heavily publicized by the news media. Public awareness was raised in the 1970s and 1980s by reports of numerous toxic tort cases and of contamination such as PCB in New York's Hudson River, and a pesticide (Kepone) which had been dumped into the James River near Hopewell, Virginia. Therefore, it is easy to see why the country has taken substantial steps during the past two decades to move away from the "reactive" approach of tort law, which is used to compensate victims after harm has occurred. A proactive approach to environmental problems through which future contamination is prevented and existing contaminated sites are cleaned up can save substantial amounts of money for businesses and society as a whole in the long run.

In recent decades society has relied increasingly on a statutory approach to environmental law. A statutory (or regulatory) approach to law represents a proactive approach in dealing with a set of specific societal problems. Administrative (or regulatory) agencies have been assigned many missions designed to deal with our environmental problems. Such an agency is created by Congress. Then, through a statute (or statutes) called "enabling legislation" the agency is charged with planning, creation of regulations (or standards), and enforcement of those standards. Thus, when in 1970 Congress created the Occupational Safety and Health Administration (OSHA), OSHA was charged with doing what is "reasonably necessary or appropriate to provide safe or healthful employment and places of employment." OSHA has created and enforces thousands of regulations designed to carry out that directive. Similarly, in 1976,

Congress passed the **Resource Conservation and Recovery Act (RCRA)**, assigning to the **Environmental Protection Agency (EPA)** the task of controlling solid waste management practices with the objective of protecting the public health. Pursuant to that enabling act and subsequent amendments to it, the EPA has established and currently enforces an extensive regulatory program controlling the activities of generators of waste, transporters of that waste, and owners or operators of waste disposal (storage) sites.

ADMINISTRATIVE AGENCIES

The federal Environmental Protection Agency (EPA) and its state counterparts are the primary enforcers of environmental laws in the United States. Each of the fifty states has an administrative agency which serves as a counterpart to the federal EPA. The state agency is often the primary environmental law-enforcing agency with which business deals on a daily basis.

However, it must be recognized that environmental law is not exclusively the domain of the EPA. Various other administrative agencies, both state and federal, enforce laws that are related to the environment. Further, the EPA often coordinates its enforcement efforts with those of other administrative agencies whose missions complement or even overlap with those of the EPA. Table 1 lists various federal administrative agencies which are engaged in such environmentally related missions.

TABLE 1: MAJOR FEDERAL ADMINISTRATIVE AGENCIES THAT WORK WITH THE EPA

Agencies Within the Department of Labor

- Occupational Safety and Health Administration

Regulates to protect health and safety of workers within workplaces. (Excludes mining.)

- Mine Safety and Health Administration

Regulates to protect health and safety of workers in mines and to protect public from hazards associated with mining.

Agencies Within the Department of Interior

- Bureau of Land Management

Created in 1946. Manages federally owned lands, which total over 350 million acres. Manages resources on those lands including timber; oil, gas and minerals; rivers and lakes; plants, animals, and fish and their habitats.

- U.S. Fish and Wildlife Service

Manages the National Wildlife Refuge System which was created in 1983 and now includes at least 472 national wildlife refuge areas.

- National Park Service

Administers the U.S. National Parks, which cover over 80 million acres.

Agencies Within the Department of Agriculture

- U.S. Forest Service

Manages wilderness areas covering 33.6 million acres. Decisions regarding use of resources for lumbering, mining, farming, and grazing.

Agencies that are Independent or Within Other Government Organizations

- Council on Environmental Quality (CEQ)

Oversees compliance with National Environmental Policy Act (NEPA) by agencies throughout federal government.

- Consumer Product Safety Commission

Charged with enforcement of various enabling acts designed to protect consumers. Includes responsibility for protecting consumers from toxic (hazardous) chemicals. Independent agency.

- Food and Drug Administration

Charged with enforcement of statutes designed to protect the public from harmful food or drugs. Works with the EPA to protect the public from hazards associated with pesticide residues in food. Independent agency.

- Nuclear Regulatory Commission

Regulates nuclear facilities and handling and disposal of nuclear materials.

- Federal Energy Regulatory Commission

Regulates dams and hydroelectric power.

- Federal Maritime Commission

Certifies that ships carrying oil and hazardous materials have ability to cover costs of any spills.

- Army Corps of Engineers

Regulates construction projects on navigable waters; coordinates administration of Superfund cleanups; engages in construction projects to protect wildlife on shorelines and in navigable waters; and other projects.

- National Institute for Occupational Safety and Health (NIOSH)

Under jurisdiction of Centers for Disease Control (CDC). Conducts research on effects of toxic substances on humans. Results of NIOSH research are used by OSHA, EPA, and other agencies.

KINDS OF REGULATION

One of the nation's first environmental laws was the National Environmental Policy Act (NEPA) of 1970 which requires that all federal administrative agencies "consider" the environment by preparing an Environmental Impact Statement (EIS) before undertaking any major action which is likely to have a significant effect on the environment. Although the utility of the EIS in protecting the environment has been debated by scholars in law and economics, the high ideals represented by NEPA have earned the statute the label, the "Environmental Magna Carta." Other statutes regulating the activities of business were passed in the 1970s soon after NEPA's enactment. A look at the history of environmental regulation in the United States reveals that various kinds of regulatory mechanisms have been developed and implemented over the past twenty-five years. Various kinds of regulation have been developed to deal with varying environmental concerns, ranging from clean up of past mistakes, to record-keeping detailing where toxic wastes are being placed, to efforts to protect citizens from exposure to toxic materials being used daily in industry.

PROTECTING CITIZENS FROM EXPOSURE TO TOXIC MATERIALS

One major area of concern is to protect workers and other citizens from toxic materials used by industry. In the 1970s, the majority of environmental regulation applied to business facilities could be described as "command and control" regulation. Such regulation, most of which is still in effect, consists of detailed standards set down by an administrative agency. For example, if a business applies for an emissions permit pursuant to the **Clean Air Act** or an effluent permit pursuant to the Clean Water Act, the EPA will base the terms of that permit on EPA regulations (standards) for that chemical. The permit will specify what can be emitted (e.g. benzene or perchlorethylene) and how much can be emitted. If a business exceeds the limits of its permit, it is subject to civil or criminal penalties.

Closely related to "command and control" regulation is the concept of "end of pipe" regulation. "End of pipe" regulation requires treatment of waste or pollutant just before it is emitted. For example, companies use "scrubbers" on smokestacks to reduce the amount of a pollutant emitted such as sulphur dioxide. "End of pipe" regulation was relied on heavily during the 1970s and continues to be used extensively today.

During the 1980s, "command and control" regulations began to be supplemented by a new kind of regulation of known as "Right to Know." In the early 1980s, workers advocated the adoption of Worker

Right to Know (RTK) laws. Such laws are designed to give workers access to information about the presence of and identities of toxic chemicals in the workplace. Such laws were first enacted by various local and state governments. OSHA promulgated (made into law) its Hazard Communication Standard (HCS), creating Worker RTK across the nation in 1984, and by 1989 its coverage had been extended to protect workers in all public businesses. Following the example of workers, environmentalists began to advocate Community Right to Know (RTK) laws during the 1980s. Such laws were first adopted in various states; Community RTK on the federal level was created through the 1986 Superfund Amendments and Reauthorization Act. Such laws give citizens access to information about chemicals located on the premises of businesses in their communities.

Worker RTK and Community RTK place duties on employers and businesses to provide information to workers and communities through documents called Material Safety Data Sheets (MSDS), which describe chemicals, their properties and the hazards associated with their use. Further, the Community RTK program requires that a business inventory toxic materials on its premises and document all releases into the environment of such materials. That information, in turn, is made available to citizens and various committees and regulatory bodies. Thus, RTK is primarily an information policy. Citizens including, but not limited to, workers may be able to make better-informed decisions about dealing with toxic (hazardous) materials in their workplaces and in their communities.

As a result of greater citizen awareness of the presence of toxic materials and the hazards they create, citizens in the 1990s are demanding that more be done to reduce those hazards. In response to citizens' concerns, a third type of environmental laws regulating businesses' activities is being advocated and enacted in various states and on the federal level. Pollution Prevention Laws, which are also known as Toxics Use Reduction Laws, have been enacted in at least twenty-six states. In addition, Congress passed the Pollution Prevention Act of 1990, which is not as stringent as most of the state laws but takes some important steps to require pollution prevention. Pollution prevention statutes are designed to prompt business facilities to examine their production processes and change those processes and their products to reduce their use of toxic chemicals. Comprehensive state pollution prevention statutes include provisions imposing planning and reporting requirements on business facilities with respect to toxic chemicals used. Such statutes also cover: (1) protection of the business' proprietary interests; (2) worker and community involvement in planning processes; (3) technical assistance and research to assist business facilities and funding for such programs; and (4) enforcement

mechanisms and penalties for non-compliance. The Federal Pollution Prevention Act of 1990 provides matching grant money for state programs to assist businesses in reducing their use of toxic substances.

Because such programs are relatively new, their long-term effectiveness cannot yet be assessed. Yet, it is clear that such laws are causing some businesses, especially in the chemical industry, to examine their production practices carefully. Many firms such as the E.I. Du Pont de Nemours & Co., the 3M Company, and the Emerson Electric Company in North Carolina are finding that toxics use reduction makes good business sense. Elimination of wastes saves money immediately and will continue to save those companies money in the long run as the costs of meeting the increasingly more stringent requirements of "command and control" regulations rise.

OTHER KINDS OF REGULATION

There are other kinds of environmental regulation in addition to those described above. Laws such as the Federal Insecticide, Fungicide, and Rodenticide Act (FIFRA) and the Toxic Substance Control Act (TOSCA), regulate the manufacture of economic poisons and other chemicals. Such laws require approval and licensing by the EPA before a chemical product can be produced and marketed.

The Comprehensive Environmental Response, Clean Up, and Liability Act (CERCLA) of 1980 (Superfund) provides for programs to identify hazardous waste sites, evaluate and prioritize them, and clean up or contain hazardous wastes at such sites. Thus, it deals with "cleaning up" our past mistakes. The program relies on public funds, taxation of the chemical industry, and a polluter pays principle (collection of clean up costs from those who contributed hazardous wastes to the site) as funding sources.

To prevent the creation of future "Superfund" sites, the Resource Conservation and Recovery Act (RCRA) requires licensing and close monitoring of hazardous waste generators, transporters, and disposal or treatment sites. The program uses a "Manifest" system which creates a "cradle to grave" written record of each and every batch of hazardous waste produced by a business facility in the United States.

LOOKING AHEAD

As businesses enter the twenty-first century, they will deal increasingly with the environmental laws of other countries and with the ramifications of international treaties dealing with both trade and the environment. For example, the environment is one of the major areas of public debate regarding the **North American Free Trade Agreement**. That agreement, which took effect on January 1, 1994, was approved by the U.S. Congress only after the addition of an "Environmental Side Agreement." Former U.S. EPA Administrator William K. Reilly has observed that it is "the most environmentally sensitive free trade agreement ever negotiated anywhere." Expanded industrialization in (currently) underdeveloped countries resulting from such trade pacts is accompanied by serious concerns about the environmental effects of such industrialization. In 1994, such concerns were included in what are known as the "Uruguay Round" of negotiations regarding the **General Agreement on Tariffs and Trade (GATT)**. Further, President Clinton's administration has already called for a future "Green Round" of the GATT at which various environmental concerns would be addressed. Such concerns include the need for upward harmonization of health, safety, and environmental standards as well as the need to adopt dispute resolution processes that will result in rulings that are more protective of the environment than those currently in effect.

Overall, consideration of the environment and adherence to environmental laws and regulations have become important in the day-to-day conduct of business in the United States and throughout the world. Businesses, workers, environmentalists, and government officials need to work together to find economically sound ways of reducing the amounts of toxic substances released into our environment.

[Paulette L. Stenzel]

FURTHER READING:

Stenzel, Paulette L. "*The Crucial, Yet Difficult, Partnership Between Science and Law in Litigation and Regulation Related to Toxic Substances*," in Selected Readings on Business and the Law, 1994.

Kubasek, Nancy K., Gary S. Silverman. "*Environmental Law.*" Prentice-Hall, 1994.

Stenzel, Paulette L. "*Toxics Use Reduction Legislation: An Important 'Next Step' After Right to Know*," 1991 Utah Law Review, pp. 707-748.

Stenzel, Paulette L. "*Right to Act: Advancing the Common Interests of Labor and Environmentalists*," 57 Albany Law Review, pp. 1-40.

ENVIRONMENTAL PROTECTION AGENCY (EPA)

The federal Environmental Protection Agency (EPA) was created on December 2, 1970 by executive order of President Richard Nixon to "permit coordinated and effective government action on behalf of the environment." Fifteen different environmental programs from various federal offices were combined and placed under the jurisdiction of the newly created EPA. The EPA was designed to serve as an "umbrella agency" through which most federal environmental laws, regulations, and policies would be administered.

The creation of the EPA was one of several significant events with respect to the environment that took place in 1970, with the first Earth Day commemorations having been held in April of that year and the implementation of the National Environmental Policy Act (NEPA), which had been passed by Congress the previous year. NEPA was a result of the environmental movement of the 1960s, and, although it was not the first of our federal environmental protection laws, it was viewed as the proclamation of a new era in this country's efforts to protect the natural environment. NEPA's purpose was to reform governmental decision-making processes concerning natural resources and the environment, and NEPA included the requirement that all federal agencies "consider the environment" and prepare an Environmental Impact Statement (EIS) before pursuing any "major" federal project which may have a significant effect on the environment. Creation of the EPA was, therefore, one among various steps taken by our government in 1970 to promote more vigorous and effective protection of our environment.

OBJECTIVES, POWERS AND PROGRAMS

The EPA's powers and programs are established through legislation passed by Congress. (Such legislation delegating powers to an agency is known as "enabling" legislation.) Today the EPA is charged with the administration of a myriad of federal environmental laws dealing with air and water pollution, drinking water quality, radioactive wastes, pesticides, solid wastes, and noise pollution. Those environmental statutes include, for example, the **Clean Air Act**, the **Clean Water Act**, the **Resource Conservation and Recovery Act (RCRA)**, the **Comprehensive Environmental Response, Clean Up, and Liability Act (CERCLA-the Superfund Program)**, the Toxic Substances Control Act (TOSCA), and the Nuclear Waste Policy Act (NWPA). In general, the EPA develops standards or regulations pursuant to environmental statutes; enforces those standards, regulations, and statutes; monitors pollutants in the environment; conducts research; and promotes public environmental education.

The main office of the EPA, which is located in Washington, D.C., oversees implementation of national environmental laws and programs, oversees the EPA's regional offices and laboratories, and submits budget requests to Congress. Research is conducted through the EPA's main office and at its regional field laboratories. There are ten regional EPA offices and field laboratories which work directly with state and local governments to coordinate pollution control efforts. The EPA uses a portion of its federal funding to provide grants and technical assistance to states and local governmental units that seek to prevent pollution.

The EPA is organized to fulfill five main objectives, which are called "core functions." The first is "Pollution prevention," which is also know as "source reduction." The second is "Risk Assessment and Risk Reduction," which is the task of identifying those risks which pose the greatest risks to human health and the environment and taking action to reduce those risks. The third is "Science, Research, and Technology," which involves research designed to develop innovative technologies to deal with environmental problems. Fourth is "Regulatory Development." That involves developing standards for operations of industrial facilities, including, for example, standards for air emissions of pollutants pursuant to Clean Air Act permits and standards for discharge of effluents under Clean Water Act permits. Fifth is "Environmental Education," pursuant to which the EPA develops educational materials and provides grants to educational institutions.

EPA'S ORGANIZATION

The Administrator of the EPA is appointed by the President of the United States and approved by the United States Senate. Also appointed by the President and approved by the Senate are a deputy administrator, nine assistant administrators, an inspector general, and a general counsel. The inspector general is responsible for investigating environmental crimes, and the general counsel provides legal advice.

Within the EPA there are four "program" offices. They are (1) Air and Radiation; (2) Water; (3) Pesticides and Toxic Substances; and (4) Solid Waste and Emergency Response. There is also an office for Research and Development which works in coordination with each of the four program offices.

COORDINATION WITH OTHER FEDERAL ENVIRONMENTAL PROGRAMS

The EPA works closely with state and local governments in their pollution control efforts. During the early 1980s, there were efforts by the Reagan and Bush administrations to implement what has been called the "New Federalism." The New Federalism refers to efforts to "downsize" federal government and hand over more responsibility for enforcement of regulatory programs to state and local governments. In the area of environmental law, this has been implemented in programs in which states are encouraged to pass their own statutes and regulations which meet or exceed the requirements of the federal statutes such as the Clean Air Act, the Clean Water Act, RCRA, and CERCLA. Upon certification by the federal EPA,

such states take over day-to-day enforcement of a specific statutory program such as the Clean Air Act and of the regulations implementing that program. As a result, business people in many states find that their day-to-day contact with enforcement officials regarding environmental statutes and regulations is with a state counterpart to the EPA rather than with the federal EPA itself. For example, in Michigan a business applies to the Michigan Department of Natural Resources (MDNR—Michigan's counterpart to the EPA) for emissions permits under the Clean Air Act and effluent permits under the Clean Water Act; it files its "hazardous waste manifests" required by RCRA with the MDNR; and it deals with the MDNR with regard to identification of and clean-up of a contaminated site under the Superfund program. However, even when a state has been certified to administer such a program, the federal EPA continues to oversee the state's enforcement activities. It provides assistance to state officials and sometimes participates directly in major enforcement actions against violators of environmental laws.

The EPA works closely with other federal environmental control agencies such as the National Oceanic and Atmospheric Administration and the United States Coast Guard. The National Oceanic and Atmospheric Administration engages in long-range research on pollution problems, especially problems affecting the ocean and the atmosphere such as the hole in ozone over Antarctica, which is currently of great concern to scientists and citizens throughout the world. The EPA works with the United States Coast Guard on flood control, dredging activities, and shoreline protection. Since 1970, the EPA has worked closely with the Council on Environmental Quality (CEQ), a relatively small executive agency which was created pursuant to the NEPA. Its mission is to advise the President on federal policy and action in the environmental area and to ensure that other federal agencies comply with NEPA. Compliance with the NEPA includes the requirement that any federal agency pursue environmentally sound policies and that it prepare an Environmental Impact Statement (EIS) before undertaking any major action which might significantly affect the environment. In conjunction with reorganization of the EPA and proposed legislation which would elevate the EPA to Cabinet-level status, as of 1994, the CEQ has been reduced to a skeletal staff and is operating under a severely reduced budget. At the end of the Bush Administration, the EPA had a staff of forty people and a budget of $2.5 million. The CEQ was reduced to a staff of five people with a budget of $375,000 for fiscal year 1994.

HISTORY AND ADMINISTRATORS

The image and effectiveness of the EPA throughout its existence have been closely tied to its Administrator. When the EPA was created in 1970, it was headed by William Ruckleshaus, a loyal member of the Republican party who earned a reputation as a skilled administrator who was able to work effectively with environmentalists as well as business people.

The EPA faced little criticism until the early 1980s. Anne Burford Gorsuch was appointed by President Reagan and took control of the agency in 1980. Early in 1983, the EPA came under criticism from the public and Congress. There were allegations of mishandling of Superfund monies, conflicts of interest related to ties between EPA officials and regulated businesses, manipulation of the Superfund for political purposes, and lax enforcement against polluters. Observers were concerned to see that under Gorsuch the number of environmental crime cases referred by the EPA to the United States Justice Department for prosecution declined from 255 in 1979 to 97 in 1982. Gorsuch became known by her colleagues and the public as "the Ice Queen" as a result of her comportment within the EPA and her arrogance and cold public demeanor during an ensuing Congressional investigation. As a result of the investigation, Gorsuch and twenty other EPA officials resigned from their positions; one of those officials, Rita LaVelle, went to prison after being convicted of perjury in her testimony on the affair before Congress. As a result of that affair, dubbed "Sewergate" by the newsmedia, public confidence in the EPA plummeted.

Upon Gorsuch's resignation in March, 1983, President Ronald Reagan asked William Ruckleshaus to serve as interim EPA administrator. Ruckleshaus agreed to do so, serving until the appointment of his successor, Lee Thomas, in November of 1984.

The EPA and the environment were issues during the 1988 presidential elections, when then-candidate George Bush campaigned with a pledge to be the "Environmental President." Upon his election, he named William K. Reilly, a former head of the Conservation Foundation and the World Wildlife Fund, to be the EPA's new administrator. In doing so, Bush chose a moderate environmentalist. The Conservation Foundation is known for conservative reports and is not considered by other environmental groups to be politically active. In fact, the Foundation has been called "the Vatican of the environmental movement" due to its conservatism. Yet as a moderate environmentalist within the Bush administration, Reilly was viewed as an "out-and-out zealot." Overall, the Bush Administration achieved a mixed environmental record. Reilly helped push through the first revision of the Clean Air Act in thirteen years, resulting in the 1990 Clean Air Act Amendments. The Bush administration agreed to phase out asbestos use by 1997 and supported a ban on importation of ivory products from Africa. But, the administration and the EPA were criticized for failing to commit to timetables or spe-

cific measures to deal with global warming and for failing to take action to preserve wetlands. Bush was sharply criticized for proposing a $400 million cut in water-pollution programs after his campaign promises to clean up Boston Harbor. Further, new EPA standards for pesticides were criticized as being too flexible and for giving too much weight to economic factors in deciding whether to take a pesticide off the market. During his administration, President Bush endorsed legislation that would elevate the EPA to Cabinet-level status, but such legislation did not pass during his administration.

The current chief Administrator of the EPA, who was chosen by President Clinton in December of 1992 shortly after his election, is Carol Browner. Ms. Browner came from the position of Secretary of Environmental Regulation for the State of Florida. She is considered to be prominent among a new group of environmentalists who view environmental protection and economic development as compatible objectives. Thus, her views are compatible with the Pollution Prevention Act of 1990, which directs the Administrator of the EPA to develop and implement strategies to promote "source reduction." "Source reduction" refers to pollution prevention practices designed to reduce the amount of any hazardous substance entering the environment or any waste stream. Ms. Browner strongly supports pollution prevention as an alternative to the EPA's former emphasis on "command and control" methods of regulation, which focus on regulating only that which comes from the "end of the pipe," such as the emissions coming from a smokestack. Leading the EPA in another departure from its past practices, Ms. Browner instituted a plan in 1993 to strengthen the EPA's Office of Enforcement by reconsolidating it and adding some staff. (It had been divided into different offices under the Reagan administration.) The Office has been directed to target entire industries rather than focus only on individual companies breaking environmental laws. Because the EPA has been criticized in recent years for failing to enforcement anti-pollution laws, Browner's moves to revamp the EPA's Enforcement Office are viewed as a positive step toward making the EPA more effective.

As of 1994, legislation giving the EPA cabinet-level status is pending before the United States Congress. Such legislation is supported by President Bill Clinton. The main purpose of the legislation is to give the EPA the same status as the Education, Housing and Urban Development, and other departments within federal government. In addition, the legislation is viewed as an important mechanism for promoting better interagency communication, increased stature for the EPA with respect to foreign governments, and more efficiency within the EPA itself.

Meanwhile, the EPA faces tremendous challenges as it moves into the twenty-first century. It is widely agreed that the EPA must find more efficient and more cost-effective ways to clean up the environment and protect the public from further contamination than those it has used so far. For example, many business people and environmentalists believe that the Superfund law doesn't work. Between its passage in 1980 and 1993, EPA had identified over 1,200 "national priority" sites for clean up, yet, after spending nearly $20 billion by 1993, only a small number of those sites had actually been cleaned up. In the mid-1990s, the EPA and Congress will face major challenges as they deal with issues related to revision of Superfund and The Clean Water Act, deal with constitutional issues involved when property owners are denied permission to develop land due to federal wetlands-protection lawsand policies, and work with foreign governments to study and to develop mechanisms to deal with global warming.

[Paulette L. Stenzel]

FURTHER READING:

Adler, Jerry. " 'Ice Queen' Under Fire," *Newsweek*. Feb. 21, 1983, p. 24.

Bukro, Casey. "EPA Chief Ties Ecology to Economy," *Chicago Tribune*. Feb. 13, 1993, pp. 1-2.

"Bush and Congress Get Low Grades," *Congressional Quarterly*. Jan. 27, 1990, p. 235.

Cahan, Vicky. "Can the EPA Chief Clean Up Bush's Image?," *Business Week*. Dec. 11, 1989, pp. 135-6.

Gabriel, Trip. "Greening the White House," *The New York Times Magazine*. Aug. 13, 1989, p. 25.

"How 'Sewergate' is Paralyzing the EPA," *Business Week*. Feb. 28, 1983, pp. 73-4.

EQUAL EMPLOYMENT OPPORTUNITY COMMISSION

Becoming operational on July 2, 1965, the Equal Employment Opportunity Commission (EEOC) was established to enforce provisions of Title VII of the Civil Rights Act of 1964. Title VII forbids discrimination in the workplace based on race, age, handicap, religion, sex, or national origin. Title VII covers all phases and aspects of employment including but not necessarily restricted to hiring, termination of **employment**, **layoffs**, promotions, wages, **on-the-job training**, and disciplinary action. Encompassed by Title VII are employers in the private sector with 15 or more employees, educational institutions, state and local governments, **labor unions** with 15 or more members, employment agencies, and, under certain circumstances, labor-management committees. Not covered under the provisions of Title VII are government-owned corporations, Indian tribes, and federal employees. Originally federal employees were protected from discriminatory practices by Executive Order 11478 which was administered and enforced by the U.S. Civil Service Commission. In 1978, however, federal equal employment functions were transferred to the EEOC. Title VII was amended by the Equal Employment Opportunity Act of 1972, the Pregnancy Discrimination Act of 1978, and the **Civil Rights Act of 1991**.

The EEOC is also responsible for enforcing the Equal Pay Act of 1963, the Age Discrimination in Employment Act of 1967, the Rehabilitation Act of 1973, and the **Americans with Disabilities Act** of 1990.

Title VII and the EEOC trace their beginnings to World War II federal defense contracts. Under the threat of a "Negro march" on Washington protesting discrimination in hiring of defense contract workers, President Roosevelt issued Executive Order 8802 in 1941. This order called for the participation of all U.S. citizens in defense programs regardless of race, creed, color, or national origin. The order also established the Fair Employment Practices Committee (FEPC) which by 1943 was processing 8,000 employment discrimination complaints. The FEPC while discouraging discrimination in relation to defense contract workers lacked power of enforcement. Presidents Truman and Eisenhower established committees on government contract compliance but again enforcement power was absent. President Kennedy created the President's Committee on Equal Employment Opportunity which for the first time did have enforcement powers, albeit limited. These various committees and programs, however, dealt with discrimination only in relation to workers and government contracts, not workplace discrimination in the overall private sector. The Civil Rights Act of 1964 which included Title VII changed this by addressing discrimination in all areas of employment. The act was signed into law July 2 by President Johnson.

Anyone who feels that he or she has suffered workplace discrimination because of his or her race, age, handicap religion, sex, or national origin is eligible to file a complaint with the EEOC. Complaints or charges are generally filed at an EEOC office by the aggrieved party or by his or her designated agent. All charges must be filed in writing preferably but not necessarily on the appropriate EEOC form within 180 days of the occurence of the act that is the reason the complaint is being filed. There are 50 district, area, local, and field EEOC offices throughout the United States.

Upon receiving a discrimination charge the EEOC defers that charge to a state or local fair employment practices agency. This agency, depending on a number of factors, has either 60 or 120 days to act on the complaint. If no action is taken on the state or local level within that time the charge reverts back to the EEOC which processes the charge on the 61st or 121st day which becomes the official filing day of the complaint. Within 10 days of the filing date the EEOC notifies those parties charged with discrimination. The EEOC investigates the charge and if a determination is reached that discrimination has taken place the EEOC attempts to bring both parties to a voluntary agreement. The reaching of a voluntary agreement signals closure of the case. If a voluntary agreement cannot be reached, the EEOC has the option of filing suit in court or the aggrieved party may file suit on his or her own. If no violation of Title VII is found, the EEOC removes itself from the case leaving the charging party still free to file suit in court within a specified time.

The EEOC has filed and won numerous precedent setting cases in the federal courts. Some of the more notable include:

- *Diaz v. Pan American World Airways*, 442 F 2d 385 (5th Cir 1971)—Customer preference of a particular sex is not justification for discrimination based on gender.

- *Phillips v. Martin-Marietta*, 400 US 542 (1971)—Mothers with pre-school age children cannot be denied employment without ample business justification.

- *Local 53, Asbestos Workers v. Voegler*, 407 F2d 1047 (5th Cir 1969)—If a workforce or union membership is primarily Caucasian, preferential hiring of relatives and friends of union members is unlawful.

- *Rosen v. Public Service Electric Co.*, 409 F2d 775 (3rd Cir 1973)—Different retirement ages for men and women as provided in pension plans is unlawful.

- *Rosenfeld v. Southern Pacific Railroad*, 293 F Supp. 1219, (C D Cal 1968)—State laws which limit the number of hours a woman may work or the maximum amount of weight she may lift are invalid when they are deemed to discriminate rather than protect.

The commission has numerous programs designed to inform the public of EEOC activities and responsibilities. The Voluntary Assistance Program is a one-day educational seminar for unions and small and midsize employers. This program highlights the rights of employers and employees under Title VII. The Expanded Presence Program sends contact teams to areas that would otherwise have little immediate accessibility to the EEOC. The contact teams provide information to the interested public on the EEOC. The EEOC also sponsors a Federal Dispute Resolution Conference, aids state and local fair practices employment agencies, and has liaison programs with unions,

civil rights organizations, and various federal, state and local government agencies.

[Michael Knes]

FURTHER READING:

U.S. Equal Employment Opportunity Commission. *The First Decade*. Washington D.C.: GPO, 1974.

EQUAL OPPORTUNITY

Equal opportunity refers to the equality of access to jobs, promotions, and other opportunities in corporations, associations and nonprofit organizations. Historically, first blacks and later women were the objects of equality of opportunity. More recently, persons with disabilities, veterans, and the aged have fallen under the protection of equal opportunity. These groups or classes of individuals are termed a protected class, defined as persons who have suffered the effects of employment discrimination. The history of equal opportunity is traced through a continuum of federal legislation, executive orders, government agency decisions, and court cases. Corporations and organizations have developed separate offices or units to deal with the various aspects of equal opportunity and spend a significant part of their budgets to ensure equal access.

Equal opportunity relates directly to equal access, an access that has grown and continues to grow in order to cover a vast array of areas beyond jobs. These include recruitment, hiring, training, layoffs, discharge, recall, promotions, responsibility, wages, sick leave, vacation, overtime, insurance, retirement, pensions, and various other benefits. In order to provide and protect equal opportunity, the federal government as well as state governments have established offices and agencies to provide guidelines, education, and programs for employers and employees. More recently, corporations and other associations/organizations have followed the government's example to create a workplace environment where equal opportunity is an accepted and common practice.

Equal employment opportunity (generally termed EEO) policies should be administered and communicated to provide an effective and efficient work environment for all employees and job applicants. Such communication needs to start with supervisory personnel through employee handbooks and manuals, forms, handouts, training sessions and films, meetings and retreats, and a variety of other means of educating supervisory personnel. Some of the major issues to be covered include federal and state laws which relate to equal opportunity; the employer's specific EEO policies and how they relate to addressing and solving employment discrimination concerns; selection procedures used for hiring, promotion, training, and termination decisions; and employee procedures for handling complaints of discrimination in any form. A few examples of employer practices promoting EEO and affirmative action principles serve to demonstrate how some firms have addressed the issues. Exxon Research and Engineering Company conducted an employee survey of affirmative action practices which indicated the firm's underutilization of women and minorities. As a result, an internal training program using women and minorities was organized in order to educate supervisors on cultural differences and their impact on the workplace as well as emphasizing EEO and affirmative action objectives. The Stanley Works, a tool manufacturer, formed a group named Women in Management, which was aimed at fostering the advancement of women—their professional advancement, career development, and upward mobility. The group sponsors education and training programs and serves as a support system for women in management positions. Finally, Aetna Life & Casualty established the consulting pairs program as part of a broader effort to eliminate barriers to advancement for minorities and women. The program paired employees of different racial, ethnic, and even gender groups in order to address the issue of workplace diversity. The "pairs" had three weeks of off-site intensive training relating to racial and sexual employment issues. The original pairs then worked with additional pairs who were experiencing similar problems on the job. The consulting pairs also served an awareness role to raise consciousness among other workers on issues of cultural differences and tolerance, as well as sharing new ideas with supervisors and managers. These and other employer-initiated programs are generally financed by the company but are usually cost-effective in helping to eliminate employment discrimination and other illegal practices which, in the end, prove expensive for the employer.

HISTORICAL DEVELOPMENT OF EQUAL OPPORTUNITY LEGISLATION

Although most would consider equal opportunity a recently developed concept, the true beginning of the idea can be traced to the Fourteenth Amendment (1868). This landmark constitutional doctrine did not address equal opportunity directly, but it did provide for equal protection of the law. The provisions of the Fourteenth Amendment would be circumvented for years but lawmakers, attorneys, and civil rights advocates would constantly seek the shield of its protection. In 1933, Congress passed the Unemployment Relief Act, which forbade discrimination in employment on the basis of race, color, or creed. During World War II Congress again entertained and discussed equal opportunity and fairness in employment

legislation. These early efforts to eliminate discrimination in employment gained little steam but nevertheless continued to build toward significant federal programs. National attention was diverted first by the Great Depression, the war, the perceived threat of global war and the cold war, McCarthyism, and finally the revolution in civil rights after the Supreme Court's *Brown v. Board of Education* decision of 1954. The "new frontier" of the Kennedy administration marked the initial steps of the revolution in equal opportunities.

In early 1961 President John F. Kennedy signed Executive Order 10925, establishing the President's Committee on Equal Opportunity. This set the concept of equal opportunity in motion not only for government employment but also for employees in government contracts, a step which would provide leverage for enforcing equal employment opportunities. The next stage was the passage of the Civil Rights Act of 1964, signed by President Lyndon Johnson, who sought to continue Kennedy's New Frontier with the Great Society.

The Civil Rights Act of 1964 is not only the linchpin of twentieth-century civil rights legislation and Johnson's Great Society, but it is also the foundation of equal opportunity in employment. Title VII of 1964's Civil Rights Act is aimed at eliminating employment discrimination based on the usual litany of race, religion, sex, or national origin. The law became effective in July 1965, one full year after its passage, and originally applied only to employers of 100 or more individuals. It now applies to employers of 15 or more workers. Title VII has been amended on numerous occasions in the past 30 years, including the enactment of the Equal Employment Opportunity Act of 1972, the Pregnancy Discrimination Act of 1978, the Civil Rights Reformation Act of 1987, the **Civil Rights Act of 1991**, and the Family and Medical Leave Act of 1993. Title VII was also the basis of what has become the sweeping **affirmative action** programs brought about by Executive Order 11246 (1965). The **Equal Employment Opportunity Commission (EEOC)** was also provided for under Title VII. A five-member presidential-appointed federal commission, the EEOC's function is to administer employment provisions and guidelines under Title VII. Since 1979, federal restrictions on discrimination against the aged and disabled in employment have been vested in the EEOC, these having previously been administered by the U.S. Civil Service Commission.

Like the agencies and programs established under Title VII, the Civil Rights Act of 1964 has been the constant target of employers, contractors, and detractors of the federal government's role in employment issues. The breadth of protection and remedies under Title VII have resulted in an endless number of court cases, and many states have followed the congressional example in attempts to provide employee protection. With the passage of the Civil Rights Act (and Title VII), the words "equal opportunity" and "affirmative action" became extremely important concepts in employment and race relations in the United States.

Affirmative action has become the cornerstone of a great deal of equal opportunity in the employment arena. Established by Executive Order 11246, affirmation action programs are a remedy to discriminatory hiring practices. Since inception, affirmative action has evolved into other personnel issues, such as recruitment, transfers, pay scales, and training opportunities. Generally, federal courts or the EEOC have enforced affirmative action remedies, and the number of groups covered by these programs has expanded.

The primary goal of affirmative action remedies has been correcting employers' underutilization of certain groups in employment—mainly African Americans and, to a lesser degree, women. Such remedies may also take the form of back pay or retrospective awarding of seniority rights. For federal contractors with 50 or more employees, written affirmative action plans are required, and successive federal legislation has included provisions for the utilization of qualified handicapped individuals, veterans and disabled veterans, and other protected classes.

The Equal Pay Act of 1963 amended the **Fair Labor Standards Act of 1938** in order to bar employers from paying members of one sex less than the opposite gender when job skills are the same or similar in nature. The act protects executive, administrative, professional, and sales employees. The EEOC is the agency charged with the enforcement of the Equal Pay Act.

Other federal acts have complemented the Civil Rights Act of 1964 by extending employment protection to various groups. The Age Discrimination in Employment Act of 1967 (ADEA) prohibited discriminatory practices in hiring, promotion, demotion, compensation, and transfers based on the age of the employee. The act also covered benefit plans and retirement incentives. Persons aged 40 to 65 were protected by ADEA; this protection was extended to age 70 under 1978 amendments, and simply to persons over 40 in 1986. Employers of 25 or more workers were covered in the original legislation; this changed to 20 or more employees in 1974. There are several categories of exemptions, most notably when an employer can demonstrate age is a legitimate qualification. The EEOC is charged with enforcement of the ADEA. In 1975, Congress passed the Age Discrimination Act, prohibiting age discrimination by recipients of federal financial assistance.

The Education Amendments of 1972 included employment protection in Title IX, which prohibited **sex discrimination** in educational programs or activities at institutions that received federal aid—in reality, most colleges and universities. Although not having the same impact on employment as other federal legislation, Title IX is nevertheless significant. Numerous women's advocacy groups have cited Title IX in justifying support of women's collegiate sports programs—programs that often include job opportunities for women. Recent court decisions and out-of-court settlements support their development, but not without considerable discussion and often bitter disputes.

Another key ingredient in the evolution of equal opportunity legislation was the Rehabilitation Act of 1972, which prohibited discrimination against qualified individuals with disabilities by employers whose federal contracts exceed $10,000. Government contractors who employ 50 or more persons and have contracts totaling $50,000 or more were required to develop affirmative action programs to protect qualified disabled employees. Section 504 of the Rehabilitation Act extended coverage to employers receiving federal financial assistance.

The act defined persons with disabilities as those with a physical or mental impairment that caused substantial limits to the individual's "major life activities." Important wording added that employers were required to make reasonable accommodations for employees with disabilities—wording that, like much federal legislation focusing on equal opportunities in employment, has often created a furor among employers. Reasonable accommodations may include toilet facilities fitted for the disabled, computer adaptations for the blind, or telephones accommodating the hearing impaired, to mention only a few examples. The Office of Federal Contract Compliance Programs (OFCCP) in the U.S. Department of Labor is charged with enforcement of the provisions of the law. Much of the **Americans with Disabilities Act** (1990) reinforced and extended protection under the Rehabilitation Act.

Following the Vietnam War, Congress passed the Vietnam Era Veterans' Readjustment Assistance Act of 1974 to add Vietnam-era veterans to a growing list of protected classes. Under this law, federal contractors or subcontractors with contracts of $10,000 or more had to take affirmative action measures to hire, train, and promote disabled and Vietnam veterans. The act provided that all job vacancies paying up to $25,000 be listed with local employment services and gave veterans priority referrals. Contractors with 50 or more employees and federal contracts in excess of $50,000 had to develop written affirmative action plans in order to improve the employment status of veterans. The OFCCP was charged with enforcing this law. Still another federal act aimed at protecting a specific class in employment is the Immigration Reform and Control Act (1986), by which employers of three or more persons were prohibited from discrimination on the basis of national origin or citizenship. Protected were U.S. citizens, permanent resident aliens, refugees, and recently legalized aliens who had filed to become U.S. citizens.

An often overlooked policy is the 1978 Uniform Guidelines on Employee Selection Procedures which apply to employers regulated by Title VII or Executive Order 11246 (affirmative action). The purpose of these guidelines was to eliminate discrimination based on employment and selection tests. Such tests had to meet validation standards and if found to have an adverse effect on any race, sex, or ethnic group, the tests were ruled illegal. As a general rule of thumb, if the selection rate of a protected group is less than 80 percent of that for the group with the highest selection rate, the test or practice is considered discriminatory. Known as the ''4/5ths'' or ''80 percent'' rule, these guidelines are followed by the EEOC and the federal departments of Labor, Justice, and the Treasury.

The sweeping Civil Rights Act of 1991 enhanced the rights of employees in discrimination in employment suits. The law reversed parts of seven U.S. Supreme Court decisions that had found against the discriminatory affect employer and, in so doing, expanded remedies available under Title VII. Provisions of the act included allowing for compensatory and punitive damages for victims of intentional discrimination based on sex, religion, or disability—damages previously available only to racial and ethnic minorities. Jury trials were also provided and damage award amounts could range from $50,000 to $300,000, depending on the total **workforce** of the employer. ''Race norming'' of employment test scores, or adjusting employment-related test scores on the basis of sex, race, religion, or national origin, was eliminated. The EEOC was required to establish the Technical Assistance Training Institute in order to provide training and education programs for the victims of longstanding job bias. Interest payments for delayed awards against federal and nonfederal employers were approved. The EEOC had to notify complainants when ADEA charges were dismissed. In addition, the Glass Ceiling Commission was created to study artificial barriers to the advancement of women and minorities in top-level management positions. The commission was further charged with making recommendations to Congress to eliminate the **glass ceiling**. The Glass Ceiling Commission made its initial report in March 1995, but recommendations were not expected before November 1995.

The Rehabilitation Act of 1972 was augmented with the Americans with Disabilities Act (ADA), passed in 1990 to go into effect on July 26, 1992. This broad act prohibited discrimination against qualified persons with disabilities. Employers are required to make ''reasonable accommodations'' for employees who are otherwise qualified for a position unless these accommodations would create undue hardships for the employers. The act initially was imposed on companies in an industry affecting commerce with 25 or more workers. ADA prohibited discrimination in hiring, training, promotion, compensation, or discharge, and made illegal non-job-related employment or selection tests. Provisions of the ADA have to be conspicuously posted. Beyond the employment issue, ADA required businesses to make services and facilities accessible to disabled persons, ordered that buses and trains be made accessible, and forbade discrimination in state and local government services on the basis of disabilities. Remedies were provided following Title VII guidelines and the EEOC was charged with ADA enforcement.

Although not having the impact on equal opportunity employment law as the aforementioned legislation, the Family and Medical Leave Act of 1993 (FMLA) has had a significant impact on equal protection under the law. The act guarantees up to 12 weeks of unpaid leave in case of family medical emergencies, childbirth, or adoptions. As important is the FMLA provision that employees taking leave under the law return to the same (or equivalent) job at the same pay and with the same benefits. The law covers employees who have been on the job at least 12 months for companies with 50 or more workers. The unpaid leave can be taken in hour increments if necessary. If state law provides more generous protection, those laws prevail. FMLA has already had an impact on employment law.

SIGNIFICANT EQUAL OPPORTUNITY COURT CASES

In addition to the federal agencies charged with enforcement of these laws and executive orders, the courts have seen literally thousands of cases litigated under protection of landmark acts such as the Civil Rights Act of 1964 and affirmative action. Although it is not possible to enumerate and describe even a small fraction of cases focusing on equal employment opportunities, what follows are brief descriptions of several representative cases unique to one form of protection or another—racial discrimination, age discrimination, religious discrimination, or others.

Perhaps the most widely recognized employment opportunity case is the 1989 *Wards Cove Packing Co., Inc. v. Antonio*, where the U.S. Supreme Court concluded statistical evidence alone pointing to a racial imbalance between one segment of a workforce population and another was not enough to make for a case of racial discrimination. A firm's selection practices cannot have a disparate impact on nonwhites if the absence of minorities in skilled positions reflects a lack of qualified nonwhite applicants, which is not the company's fault, the court said. In a religious discrimination case, the Supreme Court ruled in 1986 that once an employer provided reasonable accommodation for an employee seeking to exercise his religion, there was no further obligation to effect employee-suggested remedies. The case centered on a school teacher who cited the need to observe six holy days during the school year. The employer provided for three days for religious observance and allowed use of up to three days of sick leave as religious holidays. The teacher filed suit under Title VII but was denied relief (*Ansonia Board of Education v. Philbrook*).

In 1987 the U.S. Eighth Circuit Court of Appeals held that a government agency's decision not to hire a woman with a long history of alcoholism did not violate her rights under the Rehabilitation Act of 1973. While alcoholism was defined as a handicap under the act, the appeals court ruled the employer had the right to rule the woman an employment risk, especially since she refused to enter a rehabilitation program, thus making it impossible for the government to provide reasonable accommodation (*Crew v. U.S. Office of Personnel Management.*)

While these cases represent instances when the courts have ruled against claims of discrimination, the vast majority of case law generally provides for relief of discrimination. In two cases from the early 1980s, the Supreme Court and a second district court ruled that in situations of sex discrimination in compensation, protection is afforded under Title VII and the Equal Pay Act of 1963. The Equal Pay Act prohibited wage differentials for men and women doing the exact same job, while Title VII provided remedies in cases where intentional discrimination for comparable jobs is involved, a rather liberal interpretation of the law (*Gunther v. County of Washington*, 1981; and *Connecticut State Employees Association v. State of Connecticut*, 1983).

In *Metz v. Transit Mix, Inc.* in 1987, the Seventh Circuit Court of Appeals ruled that a financially stressed company could not lay off a 54-year-old manager and replace him with a 43-year old worker who made one-half the salary of the manager. Citing protection under the ADEA, the court ruled such a cost-cutting move was discriminatory. A state of California court recently ruled in favor of an asthmatic employee who filed under ADA. Ruling sensitivity a disability, the court mandated a smoke-free workplace when steps taken to accommodate the employee had failed (*County of Fresno v. FECH*, 1993).

TRENDS IN EQUAL EMPLOYMENT OPPORTUNITY

The agency charged with enforcement of most equal opportunity in employment legislation is the EEOC, and charges filed with that agency continue to increase. For 1994, the EEOC received in excess of 90,000 new discrimination charges, up nearly 6 percent for a three-month period (October to December, 1993) compared to the same period one year earlier. The increase in discrimination charges filed from 1992 to 1993 was an extraordinary 16.5 percent, up from 72,302 (1992) to 87,942 (1993). The EEOC concluded that most of this significant increase was due to filings under ADA and the Civil Rights Act of 1991. Expanding coverage under ADA protections, which began in July 1994, account for the latest increase. Whatever the reasons for charges filed with the EEOC, the conclusion is that discrimination is increasing as measured by complaints filed with the EEOC. Since 1991, when the EEOC received 63,898 discrimination charges, the increase is nearly astronomical (up 40.8 percent from 1991 to 1994).

Using the October to December 1993 quarterly data, 60 percent of EEOC charges were filed under Title VII of the Civil Rights Act of 1964, and 20 percent were ADA claims. ADEA accounted for 18.3 percent of the charges, thus these three statutes represent nearly all of the charges filed. Using the same statistics, ADA charges increased significantly and ADEA charges decreased, but sexual harassment increased 12.5 percent (under Title VII protection). The message to employers is clear—avoid discriminatory practices and address them immediately when they arise. The EEOC estimated, however, that by the end of 1994, the agency would face a 17-month backlog.

OFCCP data for 1994 also shows an increase in numerous categories, although most are negative records. For example, in 1994 the OFCCP ordered nearly 40 million dollars ($39,644,000) in back pay, settlement dollars, and contract debasement. The 1994 figure represents an increase of more than $5 million from 1993. These monetary awards benefited 10,986 individuals in back benefits. A total of five firms were debarred from federal contracts (thus could no longer receive federal contracts), a somewhat alarming figure since only four companies were debarred in the prior six years. Other statistics reveal improving conditions in equal employment opportunities. There were 4,179 compliance reviews in 1994, down from 4,456 in 1993—both figures representing a significant decrease from a high total of 6,232 in 1989. Complaint investigations in 1994 reflected a record low, 802. The OFCCP has collected data since 1982.

EQUAL EMPLOYMENT OPPORTUNITY POLICIES AND PROGRAMS IN BUSINESS

Given the excessively high cost of litigation and the various costs associated with labor turnover, most employers find that awareness of equal employment issues is a must. As part of personnel practices in any work setting, employers and managers look to survey data to assist in shaping the means of communicating such awareness. A Bureau of National Affairs (BNA) 1986 survey of 114 employers provided keen insight into related personnel policies affecting equal employment opportunities and revealed the concern these employers have for communicating such policies. All 114 employers communicated equal opportunity statements to employees and job applicants. Most employers communicated these statements in more than one way—88 percent included such policies in the personnel manual, 75 percent posted equal opportunity policies on a bulletin board, and 7 percent of the employers included such statements in the employee handbook. Bulletin boards were used by 81 percent of nonmanufacturing businesses and 85 percent of manufacturing firms, and the figures for using policy manuals were similar (84 percent for nonmanufacturers, 85 percent for manufacturers).

Written **affirmative action** plans were maintained by 74 percent of the firms surveyed although a quarter of these businesses were not required to do so. These written plans were updated annually at 77 percent of the firms which maintained them. Fifty-eight percent of the respondents had goals and timetables for hiring individuals from protected classes and 68 percent of those indicated they would continue to maintain goals and schedules even if no longer required to do so. Nonmanufacturing firms tended to have a higher percentage supporting affirmative action programs.

Most of the surveyed businesses (93 percent) were required to file either federal or state equal opportunity reports. Slightly over one-half (58 percent) of the respondents had federal contracts or subcontracts and were regulated by OFCCP guidelines. Almost one-half (47 percent) of those had OFCCP compliance reviews, but only 13 percent were conducted due to employee complaints. All complaints were corrected by minor changes in employment policies and none were debarred from holding federal contracts.

The BNA survey also indicated the person usually responsible for EEO/affirmative action policies was the top personnel manager (66 percent) or an individual who reported to the personnel manager. Nearly all of the EEO administrators were charged with compliance to equal opportunity regulations. Their duties included reviewing complaints, conducting investigations, and reviewing hiring decisions. Seventy-two percent of responding firms had internal procedures to handle complaints and 75 percent of those found such dispute resolutions beneficial. Only 16 percent had internal committees to address equal opportunity issues—most in unionized firms. In order to comply with EEO policies, four-fifths of the firms had hiring and promotion decisions reviewed by ei-

ther the personnel manager, the EEO officers, or some member of the top management team. Two-thirds offered EEO training and education for supervisors and managers. Such programs generally covered employment laws, human relations skills, and problems related to sexual harassment in the workplace. A final survey item focused on employees with disabilities, where 66 percent provided forms for self-identification for reporting handicaps or disabilities. Forty-two percent of respondents had provided modifications or special equipment and furniture to accommodate employees with disabilities, ranging in cost from $50 to $60,000.

CURRENT CONTROVERSIES AND FUTURE TRENDS

Equal opportunity in employment is now fully entrenched in American life. Not only does the federal government have numerous agencies directly charged with employee protection in employment, there are offices in virtually every state with similar duties. In addition, states have enacted legislation which in many instances complements federal law in providing remedies in cases of employment discrimination. Both federal and state case law is riddled with equal opportunity litigation, although the courts have proved that frivolous suits are easily dismissed and employees often find themselves losing out in cases where employment practices are involved. ADA case law alone multiplies daily. Yet equal opportunity is not without its critics and controversial issues as we head into the twenty-first century. A conservative Supreme Court poses a threat to legislation passed in a more liberal-minded America. The issue of gays in the military has expanded into employment law as gay advocates and groups look to the federal government for protected class status. AIDS victims have looked to legislation such as ADA for relief. The pending recommendations of the Glass Ceiling Commission will most assuredly be challenged. Perhaps the most unsettling issue is the future of affirmative action. Never without critics, affirmative action programs are now the subject of Supreme Court deliberations which may bring an end to the controversial system. Labor analysts predict the EEOC and the courts will be at the center of civil rights employment activities. The OFCCP is the target of potential budget cuts. And in the states, California's Proposition 187 has already had an impact on the future of alien employment protection. If this hotly debated legislation stands the test of the courts, other states may find following a similar pattern is a viable solution for answers to difficult employment questions. With three major pieces of employment legislation enacted since 1990 (the Civil Rights Act of 1991, the Americans with Disabilities Act, and the Family and Medical Leave Act, it is easy to conclude equal opportunity protection is in an evolving stage subject to major changes with significant implications for additional employer expenses. Many law firms and consulting agencies now specialize solely in employment issues. With so many unsettling issues, the future of equal opportunity is as uncertain as the past.

SEE ALSO: Age and Employment; Minority Businesses; Women in Business

[Boyd Childress]

FURTHER READING:

Belton, Robert. *Remedies in Employment Discrimination*. John Wiley & Sons, 1992.

Commerce Clearing House. *Human Resources Management. Equal Employment Opportunity*. Vol. 3. CCH, 1981-.

Gold, Michael Evan. *An Introduction to the Law of Employment Discrimination*. ILR Press, 1993.

Larson, Lex K. *Employment Discrimination*. 2nd ed. Bender, 1994-.

Player, Mack A. *Federal Law of Employment Discrimination in a Nutshell*. West Publishing Company, 1992.

Sedmark, Nancy J. *Primer on Equal Employment Opportunity*. 6th ed. BNA Books, 1994.

ERGONOMICS

Ergonomics is the study of work, more specifically, the study of the relationship between the work performed and those who perform the work. The word was formed from a blending of two others: the Greek word *ergon* or work, and *economics*, which originally meant household management.

The **Occupational Safety and Health Administration** (OSHA) of the U.S. Department of Labor defines ergonomic disorders (EDs) as a range of health disorders arising from repeated stress to the body. These disorders may affect the musculoskeletal, nervous, and neurovascular systems. EDs include the various occupationally induced cumulative trauma disorders, cumulative stress injuries, and repetitive motion disorders.

Ergonomics focuses not on the work product, but on how the producer could be better served. Today's ergonomics students analyze the workplace environment and tasks to determine how those components can or should be modified to better fit the needs and abilities (usually the physical aspects) of workers who perform those tasks in those environments.

The interest in ergonomics arose out of the industrial revolution specialization of the worker. On the assembly line, the worker repeats one task, using one particular part of the body in one type of motion, for the entire work day. On the farm, the worker performed many chores in the course of a day and lessened the impact of any one motion on any one part of the body.

Since the mid 1980s ergonomic disorders have accounted for 60% of reported occupational illnesses. The subsequent cost to employers in terms of **workers' compensation**, medical payments, and work hours lost has greatly increased the interest of all parties in this subject. In 1984 the American Academy of Orthopedic Surgeons estimated that repetitive motion disorders alone cost the American public $27 million a year in lost earnings and medical expenses.

As of January 1994, OSHA was in the process of drafting a rule requiring ergonomic protection for employees in the workplace. One of the goals of the standard will be to reduce the severity and prevalence of the risk for musculoskeletal disorders.

[Joan Leotta]

ERROR ANALYSIS

The analysis of errors in statistical models involves the application of formulas to identify and gauge the seriousness of incorrect information and, rather than dismiss that information, develop measures for correcting or adjusting the model so that the effect of subsequent errors may be minimized.

Errors that occur in models commonly result from imprecise measurement. In fact, some aspects of error analysis have their origin with astronomers who had difficulty accurately charting the paths of comets. The crude nature of telescopes and measuring equipment suggested that the comets took highly erratic paths, tacking north, then south, then north again as they traversed across the sky.

Early in the nineteenth century, mathematicians developed a solution to these measurement errors in the **least squares** criterion, a method for determining the true path of a comet by factoring out errors to the greatest extent possible. When a theoretical path was charted, astronomers knew where to look for the elusive objects and dismiss others that were not in question.

But even at this stage, astronomers were "eyeballing" their predictions. While their observations could be improved, they still had difficulty training their telescopes accurately. They required a system that would govern the spread about the predicted path of the object in which the object was most likely to be spotted. This may be thought of as a band straddling the path wherein the object is most likely to be sighted.

Again, a mathematical solution was used. A statistical analysis of the deviations of sightings from the path was employed to determine the dispersion of observations—or width of the band. Observations were charted, showing their deviation from the predicted path. In most cases, these formed a classic bell-shaped curve from which other information could be established.

This charting showed that an object should appear within a specific distance from the predicted path, and was more likely to be spotted closer to that path.

This analysis indicated not errors in the path of the comet (we assume comets do not make turns while barreling through space), but rather errors in the accuracy of the astronomer's *measurement*. One notable exception occurs when observed objects do, in fact, take turns in space, suggesting the presence of another unseen but gravitationally significant object. This is how the planet Pluto was discovered.

Another type of error may arise from poorly structured *parameters*. For example, rocket scientists concerned with delivering a nuclear warhead to a specific point on the Earth may consider a series of factors, including trajectories and speed, rotation of the Earth, gravity, and the weight of the warhead. But hundreds of other factors also may influence the re-entry path of a warhead from space, including atmospheric winds and humidity, the shape of the warhead, and even the position of the moon. If these factors are not considered, errors will arise that may cause the warhead to land several miles from its computed impact site, frustrating or completely negating the effect of the warhead, e.g. destroying the target.

These two types of errors, from inaccurate measurement and ill-considered parameters, translate directly to economic analysis.

Unfortunately, economics is a science rife with measurement error; how can an analyst accurately gauge highly intangible concepts like value, utility, and demand? Worse yet, economic data is extremely complex, providing dozens of individual considerations by millions of people. An attempt to simplify this information has led to a division of economics into often contradictory approaches.

The proliferation—and tolerance—of errors in economic analysis has deprived the discipline of status as a natural science. The types and degrees of error common in economics are abhorred by mathematicians and engineers. Cynically stated, in economics, 2 + 2 sometimes equals 5.

The English political philosopher Jeremy Bentham is credited with conceiving the idea of measuring utility in his 1789 book, *An Introduction to the Principles and Morals of Legislation*. Bentham suggested that the utility of public policies could be measured by summing numerical "degrees of good tendency" determined by the population of individuals. But the subjective nature of this approach left tremendous room for measurement error.

The Italian economist Vilfredo Pareto sidestepped the metaphysical problem of measuring utility in 1927, when he theorized that degrees of utility may be derived from observations of tangibles such as quantity, price, and income. This, he maintained, would greatly reduce the degree of error in measuring utility.

However, it was Ragnar Frisch who first developed a formula for the quantification of errors in variables in 1934. Frisch suggested a relationship wherein a dependent variable Y is determined by an independent variable X and a coefficient β, plus a "random disturbance," or error ϵ.

$$Y = X\beta + \epsilon$$

There are several sources for the introduction of errors into an analysis. Errors in variables may occur when the spread of data about the mean is especially wide or unusually distributed. In addition, errors may result from regressions that are heteroskedastic—and may contain a correlation between error ϵ and one of the variables—or where there is no relationship between variables.

Error analysis is often misapplied because results are misinterpreted and changes are introduced that increase the number and magnitude of errors. Problems of this sort are common in economics, where solutions only exacerbate errors, until the parameters of the situation can be restated.

One famous example of a misapplication of error analysis was developed by W. Edwards Deming. In this model, a supervisor measures the occurrence of faulty products produced by two workers on a theoretical assembly line. Deming asked two participants of his seminar to blindly draw 10 beads from a shoebox which is filled with 800 white beads, representing perfect products, and 200 red beads, representing defective products.

Of the 10 beads, one "worker" draws four that are red, while the second draws only one. The supervisor assumes that the first worker produces a higher rate of faulty products, 40 percent. Meanwhile, because only 10 percent of the second worker's products are faulty, the supervisor assumes that his defect rate is lower. The supervisor punishes the first worker for his poor performance by docking his wages, and rewards the second for his good performance by giving him a bonus.

The test is then repeated. This time, the first worker draws no red beads, and the second draws three. Now the first worker's defect rate has fallen to zero while the second worker's has risen to 30 percent. The supervisor assumes that his punishment of the first worker has inspired that worker to do better. Meanwhile, the second worker has grown lazy from his bonus, causing him to do worse. Now the first worker is rewarded for his improvement and the second is punished.

The test is repeated a third time, and the first worker draws two red beads, while the second draws only one, causing the supervisor to reverse the reward and punishment yet again.

After several dozen iterations of this contest, it becomes apparent that the amount of each worker's bonuses roughly equal his pay reductions; his good performance is almost exactly cancelled out by his poor performance. More importantly, each worker's average defect rate is quite close to 20 percent.

In fact, the workers' performance has absolutely nothing to do with the rate of defective products. Because the workers are drawing beads from a box that contains exactly 20 percent red beads, they will draw, on average, two red beads per contest.

What Deming illustrates is the pointlessness of reward systems where the fault rate is determined by some factor other than the workers' performance. If the supervisor ignores the possibility that he should be looking elsewhere for the cause of product defects, he may introduce solutions that worsen and further obscure the nature of the errors. As the error rate climbs, he becomes even more confused about the system.

In dealing with highly complex economic problems, where the relationships between dozens of variables is not known, it is common for policy makers to measure the strength of these relationships by purposely adjusting certain variables to see what happens. While seemingly haphazard, it is highly practical because hypotheses may be tested through actual application. When the relationships between variables can be quantified, the analysis may be extended to the identification and dynamics of errors in models.

[John Simley]

FURTHER READING:

Eatwell, J., ed. *The New Palgrave Dictionary of Economics.* London: Macmillan, 1987.

Johnson, Robert R. *Elementary Statistics*, 3rd ed. North Scituate, MA: Duxbury Press, 1980.

Kazmier, Leonard J. *Basic Statistics for Business and Economics.* New York: McGraw-Hill, 1990.

Monks, Joseph G. *Statistics for Business.* Science Research Associates, 1988.

ESCALATOR CLAUSES

Purchase contracts, transportation contracts, commercial leases, and collective bargaining agreements are among the different types of contracts that may contain escalator clauses. When included in such contracts, escalator clauses indicate that both parties have agreed that the base prices, wages, or rents in the original contract may increase over time under certain conditions. Typically, escalator clauses provide for increases based on similar increases in an agreed-upon index or other indicator. For example, a collective bargaining agreement may contain an escalator clause that provides for an increase in wages when the **Consumer Price Index** rises by a certain amount. Such wage increases are called cost of living adjustments (COLAs).

Escalator clauses tend to be used more frequently when inflation rates or expectations are high. Industrial purchasers use escalator clauses to protect themselves from sharp price increases. From the suppliers' point of view, escalator clauses allow them to pass on those cost increases that were caused by inflation. For commercial property owners, escalator clauses can keep their rental income from being eroded by higher prices.

According to a 1993 survey by *Purchasing* magazine, contracts using escalator clauses accounted for an average of 13 percent of all goods purchased in 1993. That compared with 16 percent in 1989 and 24 percent in 1981. The relatively lower percentage for 1993 was explained as a combination of lower inflation expectations and fewer purchasers relying on escalator clauses as a tool to control sharp price increases. Approximately four of every ten surveyed purchasing professionals believed they were effective.

When escalator clauses are included in a contractual agreement, both parties must agree on which index or indicator is to be used. The most commonly used indicators are one or more of the U.S. Bureau of Labor Statistics' (BLS) indexes, such as the Consumer Price Index (CPI). However, it is critical that the selected index bear some relation to or accurately reflect the prices in the contract. Since the CPI is unrelated to industrial prices, industrial purchasing contracts may rely on various Producer Price Indexes or industry data as the relevant indicator for their escalator clauses. In some cases it may not be possible to find an appropriate index.

Other problems associated with indexing prices include the fact that data may be outdated by the time it is published or otherwise becomes available. Many industrial purchasers feel that escalator clauses send the wrong message to suppliers and that they may not watch their costs as closely as they should. As an alternative to escalator clauses, industrial purchasers may favor developing long-term, partnering relationships with suppliers to control price increases.

Another problem associated with escalator clauses is that the agreed-upon indexed prices may in fact rise above market prices. For example, oil price increases tend to drive the BLS industrial commodities index higher. However, when oil prices decline, the index does not go down at the same rate. As a result, contract prices may increase substantially above market prices, if they contain escalator clauses.

Recent developments in industrial purchasing contracts have allowed purchasers to shift the risk of price increases to the supplier's ability to cut costs and improve quality. Long-term contracts may contain a market price limiter, which lets the buyer retain the option of paying either the market price or the indexed price according to the terms of the escalator clause. In other cases, floors and ceilings are written into escalator clauses to place a cap on price increases.

Different indexes may favor one or the other of the contracting parties. In the transportation industry, for example, the Railroad Cost Recovery (RCR) Index is the one most commonly used by railroads in negotiating escalator clauses with shippers. While the RCR measures certain railway industry expenses, it does not measure productivity improvements realized by railroads. That is, the index reflects the cost of resources, but not how much transportation is provided by each unit of resource. As a result, shippers do not share in the benefits from a railroad's productivity increases when escalator clauses are based on such an index.

The **Interstate Commerce Commission (ICC)** has developed a Railroad Cost Adjustment Factor (RCAF) that can be used as an index in escalator clauses. In addition, the ICC developed a Productivity Adjustment Factor to be used in conjunction with the RCAF. While the RCAF indexes the cost of inputs, the Productivity Adjustment Factor indexes the cost of output. Thus, any productivity improvements would be reflected in the Productivity Adjustment Factor. If the Productivity Adjustment Factor were used in an escalator clause, it would have the effect of allowing shippers to share in the productivity gains realized by railroads and other carriers.

Escalator clauses must be carefully negotiated if they are to fairly protect the contracting parties from inflation and unexpected price increases. In addition to the basic escalator clause, contracts may contain a variety of other escalator mechanisms and provisions to add further protection. A key factor in successfully negotiating escalator clauses is finding an appropriate index that accurately reflects the costs involved and that is fair to both parties in the contract.

[David Bianco]

ESTATE TAXES

Estate taxes are one form of death taxes, the origins of which extend back to ancient Egypt, Greece, and Rome. Estate taxes are distinct from inheritance taxes, in that the former are levied on a decedent's estate before any distributions are made, whereas the latter are imposed on the estate's heirs—the recipients of those distributions. Additional forms of death taxes include levies on gifts of cash, land, or other **assets** made by a decedent before his or her death.

In the United States, estate taxes were first adopted during the early twentieth century, when they were used as a means of generating revenue for the nation's participation in World War I. Today, not only does the federal government levy estate taxes, but all of the nation's states except Nevada levy estate taxes, inheritance taxes, or both.

At federal and state levels alike, these taxes are generally structured in progressive fashion, according to the size of the estate and any applicable exemptions. Federal estate taxes, for example, are calculated at rates ranging from 3 to 77 percent; state taxes, at rates ranging from 3 to 23 percent.

Over the decades, estate taxes have been subject to various tax reform measures and regulations. The federal Economic Recovery Tax Act of 1981 (ERTA), for instance, provided exemptions for estates valued below $600,000 and for the transfer of property between spouses; it also eliminated taxes on gifts of $10,000 or less. Even with the unification of the estate tax and the gift tax at the federal level, numerous exemptions and deductions make estate planning a complicated endeavor.

Although estate taxes account for only a small portion of total tax revenues in the United States, their socioeconomic significance has been the subject of widespread and continuing debate, with some arguing for stricter taxes to help redistribute wealth and others maintaining that these taxes adversely affect individuals' rights to ownership of and investment in property.

[Roberta H. Winston]

FURTHER READING:

Downes, John, and Jordan Elliot Goodman. *Barron's Finance and Investment Handbook*. Hauppauge, NY: Barron's, 1986.

Scott, David L. *The Guide to Tax-Saving Investing*. Old Saybrook, CT: Globe Pequot Press, 1995.

ETHICS

SEE: Business Ethics

EUROBOND MARKET

The Eurobond market is the group of investors, **banks**, borrowers, and trading agents that deals in the issuing and buying of Eurobonds. Eurobonds are **bonds** created for a foreign borrower and issued simultaneously in several nations at once. Eurobonds are generally denominated in U.S. dollars but are also denominated in Japanese yen, German deutsche marks, and Dutch guilders.

Eurobonds are a type of foreign bond. A foreign bond is a bond issued by a foreign investor in a domestic market in the domestic currency. A Eurobond differs from other foreign bonds in that it is issued in several foreign markets at one time. Domestic governments treat Eurobonds differently than domestic or foreign bonds by having different tax and issuing laws. Generally, Eurobonds face lower issuing restrictions and interest payments are not taxed. At the same time, Eurobonds are subject to less government control and are therefore more risky than domestic or other foreign bonds.

The Eurobond market is a complex market made up of several players. Not all players are involved in every deal but here is a brief rundown of the players and their roles. First there is the borrower who needs to raise funds by selling bonds. The borrower, which could be a bank, a business, an international organization, or a government, approaches a bank and asks for help in issuing their bonds. This bank is known as the lead manager and may ask other banks to join them to form a managing group that will negotiate the terms of the bonds and manage issuing the bonds. The managing group will then sell the bonds to an underwriter or directly to a selling group. The underwriter will actually purchase the bonds at a minimum price and assume the risk that it may not be possible to sell them on the market at a higher price. The underwriter (or the managing group if there is no underwriter) sells the bonds to a selling group that then brings the bonds to market.

Once the bonds are issued, a bank, acting as a principal paying agent, has the responsibility of collecting interest and principal from the borrower and disbursing the interest to the investors. Often the principal paying agent will also act as fiscal agent, that is, on the behalf of the borrower. If, however, a principal paying agent acts as a trustee, on behalf of the investors, then there will also be a separate bank acting as fiscal agent on behalf of the borrowers appointed.

Eurobonds are bearer bonds meaning that whoever physically holds the bond is entitled to the interest payment. This differs from many domestic bonds that are registered to a particular investor.

Eurobonds are traded over-the-counter which means there is not one physical place where they are all traded but rather they are traded by telephone and computer between banks and brokerage firms. Major markets for Eurobonds are in London, Frankfurt, Zurich, and Amsterdam.

SEE ALSO: Capital Markets

[Judith A. Zimmerman]

FURTHER READING:

Grabbe, J. Orlin. *International Financial Markets*. Elsevier Science Publishing Co., 1986.

Walmsley, Julian. *The Foreign Exchange and Money Markets Guide*. John Wiley & Sons, 1992

EUROPEAN BANK FOR RECONSTRUCTION AND DEVELOPMENT

The European Bank for Reconstruction and Development (EBRD) is a financial institution created to further develop capitalist interests in central and eastern Europe. The EBRD has a 23-member board of directors and is run by five vice presidents and one president. The Articles of Agreement for the EBRD were signed on May 29, 1990, in Paris and the EBRD formally began operations on March 28, 1990.

The EBRD was first proposed by the French government in 1989. Initially, the European Economic Community (EEC) members were not interested in such a bank and some were even opposed to the idea. Despite initial resistance, the French government was able to negotiate an agreement to establish the EBRD within only five months. This compares to nearly three years of negotiations that were needed to establish the World Bank.

The main goals of the EBRD are to promote economic development, market-oriented economies, and private entrepreneurial ventures. The EBRD is an organization designed to help the former communist states make the transition to capitalist economies. Members of the EBRD hope that the bank will help develop a strong European economy that brings together both the current western European economy and the growing eastern European economy that is replacing communism.

The majority (60 percent) of the bank's funds are designated specifically for the development of private businesses or the conversion of state-owned firms to private concerns. The remaining 40 percent is set aside for the development of much-needed infrastructure projects, such as improved roads and railroads, to better link the newly developing economic centers.

The bank member countries are: Albania, Australia, Austria, Belgium, Bulgaria, Canada, Cyprus, Czechoslovakia, Denmark, Egypt, Finland, France, Germany, Greece, Hungary, Iceland, Ireland, Israel, Italy, Japan, South Korea, Liechtenstein, Luxembourg, Malta, Mexico, Morocco, Netherlands, New Zealand, Norway, Poland, Portugal, Romania, Spain, Sweden, Switzerland, Turkey, the United Kingdom, and the United States. The institutions of the European Community and the European Investment Bank are also members.

The EBRD's capital is denominated in European Currency Units (ECU). The bank's capital is set at 10 billion ECUs (about $12.6 billion). The United States is the bank's largest shareholder with 10 percent of the capital. The European Community (EC) and its member countries together hold 51 percent of the capital. The former republics of the Soviet Union hold 6 percent.

The bank began its lending operations in April 1991. In the first year of operations, the bank loaned approximately $780 million for a total of 19 projects. The initial agreement called for a borrowing limit on the former USSR. This three-year minimum was equal to the USSR paid-in capital. However, after the breakup of the USSR, members decided that a limit was no longer prudent. Therefore, the majority of the EBRD's funds (60 percent) have been disbursed to Central and East Europe nations and the Baltic states (as of the end of 1994).

The bank's first years were not without controversy. Most controversial of all was the first president of the EBRD, Mr. Jacques Attali. Attali, an economist, a former adviser to the French President, and author of 16 books, had no banking background. He was criticized for creating a top-heavy management and for ignoring the interests of the non-EC members of the EBRD. However, the bank owed much of its existence to Attali's passionate views of a strong, unified European economy.

[Judith A. Zimmerman]

FURTHER READING:

"Fact Sheet: European Bank for Reconstruction and Development." *US Department of State Dispatch*, August 1992, p. 21.

Meredith, Mark. "EBRD: A New Banking Hybrid." *The Accountant's Magazine*, June 1991, p. 30.

Mistry. "Who Needs the EBRD?" *The Banker*, January 1991, p. 9.

Porter, Janet. "New European Bank Will Target Savings." *Journal of Commerce and Commercial*, March 21, 1991, p. 5.

EUROPEAN ECONOMIC COMMUNITY (EEC)

SEE: European Union

EUROPEAN FREE TRADE ASSOCIATION

The European Free Trade Association of the Seven (EFTA) is a trading bloc that was established by the Convention of Stockholm in response to the establishment of the European Economic Community (EEC). Signed January 4, 1960, the treaty became effective May 3rd of that year. Membership in EFTA has fluctuated since its inception. The original signers of the accord were: Austria, Denmark, Great Britain, Norway, Portugal, Sweden, and Switzerland. Since the founding, Finland, Iceland, and Liechtenstein have joined while Portugal, Denmark, and Great Britain have resigned. Iceland joined in 1970 and Finland and Liechtenstein became full members in 1986 and 1991, respectively. Denmark and Great Britain resigned to join the European Communities in 1973, as did Portugal in 1986.

Headquartered in Geneva, EFTA is administered by a secretary general and a Council of Ministers. The council consists of one delegate from each member nation and is responsible for implementing policy especially the mandated system of tariffs. Although there is no official language the working language of EFTA is English. Funding for EFTA comes from assessments determined as a fixed allocation proportional to the **gross national product** (GNP) of member countries. The 1991-92 allocations were as follows: Austria 17.27 percent, Finland 14.47 percent, Iceland 1.74 percent, Liechtenstein .6 percent, Norway 12.2 percent, Sweden 24.94 percent, and Switzerland 28.78 percent. EFTA's operating budget for 1991-92 was 48.5 million Swiss Francs.

EFTA is not a common market nor does it aspire to one day becoming a supranational state. The purpose of EFTA is to promote nonagricultural economic development of its member states by doing away with barriers to nonagricultural trade. Unlike its powerful economic counterpart the European Economic Community (ECC), EFTA has never advocated a common external tariff. The impetus for the formation of EFTA came after negotiations to form an all-inclusive European common market broke down prior to 1960. EFTA was formed by its original seven members as a bargaining and economic counterbalance to the EEC—as much as for intra-EFTA economic cooperation.

EFTA's goal of barrier-free nonagricultural trade between its member states was realized by 1966. By the mid-1970s EFTA was expanding its sphere of activities to include cooperative agreements on natural resources, the free movement of labor, and cooperative monetary planning. In 1977 there were two controversial EFTA meetings. The February meeting sponsored by the Consultative Committee of EFTA's discussed the need for an all-encompassing economic plan that would go far beyond the original intent of the association. In May another meeting resulted in the Vienna Declaration which again called for a multilateral economic master plan. A 1984 Luxembourg Declaration paved the way for future cooperation between EFTA and the European Community (EC). The meeting also explored the creation of a joint economic coalition between EFTA and EC to be called the European Economic Space.

Throughout the 1980s and into the 1990s there were many other meetings between EFTA and the EC. The EC is an umbrella organization covering the European Coal and Steel Community (ECSC), the EEC, and the European Atomic Energy Community. EC has 12 members: Belgium, Denmark, France, Germany, Great Britain, Greece, Ireland, Italy, Luxembourg, the Netherlands, Portugal, and Spain. The three organizations comprising the EC are collectively administered by the Common Institutions. These meetings concluded with agreements on customs forms, judicial enforcement of commerce regulations, and continued plans for a joint economic union to be called the European Economic Area (EEA). There are, however, many roadblocks to the formation of the EEA: EFTA farmers fear a 20 to 40 percent price reduction if their agricultural products remain unprotected, EFTA members fear diluted economic influence in Europe, and a Swiss referendum in 1993 rejected a Swiss role in the proposed union.

For further information, contact: European Free Trade Association, 9-11 rue de Varembé, CH-1211, Geneva, 20 Switzerland. The EFTA publishes a bulletin, which is available in English, French, German, and Norwegian-Swedish.

SEE ALSO: European Union

[Michael Knes]

EUROPEAN MONETARY SYSTEM

In the early 1970s the United States was just emerging from a recession and the dollar was plagued by a ballooning American deficit, a rapid increase in the price of gold, and continued unemployment and "stagflation." The Nixon administration, wishing to fund domestic programs, refused to devalue the dollar. Dollars were flooding into Europe and Central European banks could not continue to buy dollars in order to stabilize their own currencies whose value was pegged to the dollar. This led to increased speculation against the dollar, driving its value down even further.

In 1978 the European Council, which was a principal policy-making organ of the European Community (now **European Union** agreed on a new monetary system in an effort to protect European currencies from a depreciating dollar and what was viewed as an inadequate American fiscal policy. This new system, the European Monetary System (EMS) was an outgrowth of the Barre Plan (Hague Summit, 1969), the Werner Report (1971), and the so called "snake systems" (1972-78) all of which were monetary cooperation plans. The EMS had new regulations covering exchange rate stabilization procedures and central bank practices. France, Ireland, Italy, Germany, Denmark, and the **Benelux** countries were charter members with Great Britain joining soon after.

An integral part of the EMS is the body of rules governing **central bank** intervention in order to stabilize exchange rates. This procedure is known as the exchange rate mechanism (ERM). Intervention is mandatory when the exchange rate between two currencies varies by more than plus or minus 2.25 percent from the centrally established rate of exchange. Central banks of countries having strongest of the two respective currencies are compelled to buy the weaker currencies. Likewise, central banks from countries having the weakest of the two respective currencies are obligated to sell the currencies to the corresponding central bank.

Another important part of the EMS is the European currency unit (ECU) originally called the European unit of account when it was created in 1974. The unit is backed by a pooling of specified amounts of member nation currencies and is used as a unit of exchange. The amount of currency deposited by each member country is related to the economic strength of that country. In 1990, 30 percent of the ECU pool or basket was in deutsche marks, 19 percent in French francs, 12 percent in pound sterling, and 10 percent in Italian lira. The balance of the basket came from the remaining EMS countries. The ECU represents a stable unit of exchange and can be used in commercial transactions and payrolls.

The EMS has generally been viewed as a success not only in achieving its goals but also in what it portends for the future. The EMS is credited with helping to stabilize exchange rates, reducing **inflation**, and coordinating monetary policy set by the various central banks. It is also seen as a firm beginning towards the European Monetary Union envisioned by the **Maastricht Treaty** of 1992 that called for a European Central Bank and establishment of the ECU as the single currency of Europe by 1997. The ECU is supported by those who feel its implementation will improve trade and be a major step towards the political unification of Europe. Others, such as former British Prime Minister Margaret Thatcher opposed the plan. Thatcher felt that if the ECU became the standard European currency, Britain would lose much of its sovereignty. Although the ECU was supported by leaders of her cabinet, Thatcher was staunchly opposed, and the issue led to her resignation as prime minister in November 1990.

Although monetary integration was not an original goal of the European Community, the concept seemed to gain support with each European monetary crisis. By 1994, 11 countries including Belgium, Denmark, France, Greece, Ireland, Italy, Luxembourg, Netherlands, Portugal, Spain and the United Kingdom, had ratified the Maastricht Treaty. Monetary unification now appears to be a goal of the Community and the Maastricht Treaty is viewed as a means to that end. Germany, however, has not signed the treaty because of constitutional obstacles, and the Bundesbank's tight anti-inflationary monetary policies have had a deliterious impact on the currencies of other European nations, especially Britain, Italy and Spain. Germany's actions, coupled with the deep recession of 1993 have derailed Maastricht's timetable.

[Michael Knes]

FURTHER READING:

Britton, Andrew. *Achieving Monetary Union in Europe*. Sage Publications, 1992.

Claassen, Emil-Maria. *International and European Monetary Systems*. Praeger, 1990.

Eichengreen, Barry, and Jeff Frieden. *The Political Economy of European Monetary Unification*. Westview Press, 1994.

Gros, Daniel. *European Monetary Integration*. Longman, 1992.

Kondonassis, A. J., and A. G. Malliaris. "Toward Monetary Union of the European Community." *The American Journal of Economics and Sociology*, July, 1994.

Lieberman, Sima. *The Long Road to a European Monetary System*. Lanham, 1992.

Torres, Francisco, and Francesco Giavazzi. *Adjustment and Growth in the European Monetary Union*. Cambridge University Press, 1993.

EUROPEAN UNION

Since the signing of the Treaty of Rome in 1957 which created the European Economic Community (EEC), there has been continual impetus for the community to expand far beyond the scope of an economic union. The ultimate goal is the creation of a European Union (EU). Features of the EU would include a single monetary system, the abrogation of frontiers between member states, unimpeded movement of EU citizens between member states, the right to vote and hold political office in countries other than the one of origin, and a harmonized defense and foreign policy. The existing economic mandates of the EEC would remain in place or be further liberalized. Standing in the way of the EU are issues of national identity and national sovereignty.

From the legions of ancient Rome to the armies of the Third Reich, there have been aspirations to unite the diverse peoples and countries of Europe under a single banner, by force if necessary. Until the Treaty of Rome and the creation of the EEC, however, there was no cooperative framework from which such a union could evolve. The EEC is a voluntary organization and, at first, functioned solely as an economic common market without explicit supra-national intentions.

The EEC soon joined the European Atomic Energy Community (EAEC) and the European Coal and Steel Community (ECSC) to form the European Community (EC). Expanding into areas outside of the original economic and free trade sphere and following its preamble which calls for "an ever closer union," the EEC held a meeting in Paris, France in 1972 to discuss a future union. Convened by the EEC's Heads of State and Government, the meeting proposed the establishment of a European Union by 1980. In a 1983 meeting in Stuttgart, Germany, the EEC reaffirmed its goal of a European Union although implementation was behind schedule. In 1984 the European Parliament of the EEC called for the establishment of the EU by 1992, and in 1989 it issued a resolution calling for member states to prepare for union treaty ratification.

In February of 1992, the twelve member states of the EEC signed the Treaty on European Union in Maastricht, the Netherlands. The **Maastricht Treaty** was the single greatest step towards European unification since the 1957 Treaty of Rome. The Maastricht accord called for the EC to expand its activities and responsibilities to include health care, consumer protection, common industrial planning and environmental protection. It also proposed a trans-European transport system and common visa policy.

The treaty also moved the EC into social policy formulation. While stopping short of creating a European police authority, it mandates a cooperative judicial system and moves certain policy decisions and responsibilities from national parliaments to the European Parliament, an EC organ. The treaty encourages a lessening of disparity between wealthy and less wealthy countries through a fund for economic and social cohesion as well as other organizations, such as : the European Social Fund, the European Regional

Development Fund, the European Agricultural Guidance and Guarantee Fund, and the European Investment Bank. Mechanisms for enhancing harmonious foreign policy and security decision making as well as the goal of a common currency and common union citizenship by 1999 are also included in the Maastricht Treaty.

In anticipation of the treaty, an economic policy coordination effort began between the EC member states in mid-1990. This effort, which was eventually incorporated into the treaty, envisioned a convergence of monetary policies beginning in 1994. A focal point of the European Union would be price and currency stability. To achieve this, the treaty mandates the creation of a European Monetary Institute and a European Central Bank. Also planned is a European System of **Central Banks**; this system is supposed to as a liaison between the newly created European Central Bank and the long established central banks of each member country. Planners hope that a single monetary policy will emerge from this union. Ideally, the policy will be free of partisan political influence, it will not extend credit to countries with large deficits, and it will demand the issuance of warnings and fines to countries with excessive deficits and/or excessive rates of inflation.

Throughout 1992 as national parliaments debated, ratification opposition began to emerge. Although the reasons for resistance to the treaty varied from country to country, fear of losing national sovereignty was the overriding theme of dissent. Opposition often cut across partisan lines with the French communists and the conservative neo-Gaullists opposing the treaty. In Great Britain and Germany, the prospect of a single European currency (European Economic Unit) was met with disagreement.

By late 1992, an economic summit in Edinburgh, Scotland produced a series of compromises that speeded up ratification. Great Britain did not have to adopt the European Economic Unit and was able to modify border crossing strictures. Denmark also opted out of using the single unit of currency, participation in certain defense mandates, a common European citizenship, and certain judicial and internal affairs policies. There was also a compromise on the EC budget. Under the new plan the 1993 and 1994 EC budget would be equal to 1.2 percent of the gross domestic product (GDP) of EC members. The budget would rise incrementally to 1.27 percent of joint GDP by 1999. It is estimated the budget will be 84 billion European Currency Units ($105 billion) through 1999. As a result of these compromises, in October 1993, Germany became the 12th and last EC member country to ratify. The Treaty of Maastricht went into effect November 1, 1993.

[Michael Knes]

FURTHER READING:

Heater, Derek. *The Idea of European Unity.* Leicester University Press, 1992.

Office for Official Publications of the European Communities. *Towards European Union.* 1992.

Werts, Jan. *The European Council.* North-Holland, 1992.

EXCESS PROFITS TAX

An excess profits tax, also sometimes referred to as a windfall profits tax, is a corporate income tax that is levied on profits above a specified level. It is assessed in addition to any corporate **income tax** already in place. It typically takes effect when corporate profits reach a certain level above what is considered normal. Historically in the United States, an excess profits tax has been put into effect by the federal government during periods of war. In addition, an excess profits tax was assessed on oil producers during the 1980s when the price of a barrel of crude oil went above a certain specified level.

The federal government of the United States put an excess profits tax into effect around the time of World War I (1917-1921), World War II (1940-45), and the Korean War (1950-53). The purpose of the tax was to return to the government the profits private businesses realized as a result of high government spending caused by the wartime situation. The World War II excess profits tax, for example, was set at 95 percent of all corporate income in excess of what was considered normal.

Historically the excess profits tax has been difficult as well as expensive to administer and collect. Disputes arose between private corporations and the government over a variety of **accounting** practices and treatments that affected corporate profits. Among the accounting practices that were argued over were the treatment of borrowed capital, accumulated deficits, new business, and invested capital. Since the tax was relatively expensive to administer, its net yield was often less than anticipated.

The excess profits tax enacted during the Korean War, effective July 1, 1950, was intended to raise $4 billion annually. The target of the tax was corporate profits that were inflated by government expenditures related to the Korean War. As originally enacted, the law imposed a 30 percent tax on all corporate profits that exceeded 85 percent of the average three highest years since 1946. Subsequent legislation modified the terms of the tax, which expired on December 31, 1953.

The only non-wartime excess profits tax in the United States was enacted in 1980 under President

Carter. Commonly referred to as the windfall profits tax, it was assessed against the excess profits of oil producers that resulted from an energy crisis. Internal upheaval in Iran had caused the price of oil to soar, and Americans were waiting in lines to fill their cars with gasoline. It was perceived that oil producers were enjoying excess profits as a result of the situation, so the federal government enacted an excess profits tax.

The excess profits tax on oil producers was levied when the price of a barrel of crude oil hit a certain level, ranging from $19 to $29 depending on the oil's classification. The tax rate varied from 30 to 70 percent of the oil producer's revenue above the trigger price. The oil industry had many disputes with the government over the tax, and in fact the industry regarded it as an excise tax on revenues rather than as an excess profits tax. In 1994, Amoco Corporation was awarded a $440 million refund from the Internal Revenue Service for overpayment of the tax. Amoco's dispute was based on a variety of accounting treatments, including what kinds of expenses could be allocated to an oil well.

The excess profits tax on oil producers was repealed in 1988 under President Reagan as part of a wide-ranging trade bill. At that time the price of crude oil was approximately $15 per barrel, well below the trigger price. The government had not collected any significant revenues from the tax since 1986, when the price of crude settled below the tax's trigger price. According to the oil industry, it was costing oil producers approximately $100 million annually to comply with the recordkeeping requirements of the law. During the eight years it was in effect, the excess profits tax on oil producers generated about $77 billion in tax revenue for the federal government.

[David Bianco]

EXCISE TAX

An excise tax is a type of tax that is applied to a specific commodity or type of goods, such as cigarettes, gasoline, and alcoholic beverages. While the excise tax is assessed on and paid by the manufacturer, the actual tax burden is usually passed along to the consumer by incorporating the amount of the excise tax into the final selling price of the product. Excise taxes are assessed in the United States by federal and state governments as well as by local governments when permitted by state law, often on the same commodities.

In the United states excise taxes are usually assessed on a per unit basis (e.g., per gallon of gasoline or per package of cigarettes). In some cases the excise tax may be an ad valorem tax, or one that is a fixed percentage of the selling price. The excise tax is typically paid by purchasing tax stamps from the government, which must then be affixed to the product before it can be sold. The tax stamps affixed to alcoholic beverages and packages of cigarettes indicate that the excise taxes have been paid by the manufacturer.

Like other sales taxes, an excise tax is generally considered regressive. That is, individuals and families with lower incomes pay a greater proportion of their income toward such taxes than people with higher incomes. Products that have excise taxes levied on them, such as cigarettes, gasoline, and alcoholic beverages, generally account for a declining percentage of individual or family expenditures as incomes rise. In most cases, the amount of the tax is incorporated into the product's final selling price and is ultimately paid for by the consumer.

Because of the regressive nature of excise taxes, governments may be reluctant to use them unless they serve some legitimate social or economic purpose. Excise taxes are frequently used to limit consumption of a product and to regulate consumer behavior. Goods such as cigarettes and alcoholic beverages carry a high level of excise tax, since it is considered socially beneficial to limit their consumption. Similarly, legal gambling activities frequently have an excise tax, in part because it is considered desirable to limit such activities. Excise taxes that are designed to discourage consumption of a particular commodity for the benefit of society are known as sumptuary taxes, or more commonly as ''sin taxes.''

Excise taxes that are applied to gasoline are not designed to limit consumption. Such taxes are typically applied to the building and maintenance of highways and roads. This type of excise tax can easily be justified as a user charge on the basis of the benefit principle. It is reasoned that only those individuals who benefit from road and highway construction and maintenance have to pay the gasoline excise tax.

Excise taxes are an important source of revenue for state governments in the United States. The three major sources of state tax revenue—general sales taxes, excise taxes, and individual income taxes—accounted for approximately 80 percent of state tax revenue in 1989, with corporate income and other taxes accounting for the remaining 20 percent. Of those, excise taxes accounted for approximately 16 percent of state tax revenue, with general sales taxes accounting for 33 percent and individual income taxes accounting for approximately 31 percent. By comparison, excise taxes account for only five percent of federal tax revenue and three percent of local government tax revenue.

The trend in state tax revenue since World War II has been for individual income taxes and general sales taxes to account for an increasing percentage of state tax revenue relative to excise taxes. In 1948, for example, excise taxes accounted for 38 percent of all state tax revenue, with general sales taxes contributing 22 percent and individual income taxes contributing approximately 7.5 percent. Since that time, sales and individual income taxes have grown to become more significant revenue sources, leaving excise taxes to account for a smaller portion of state tax revenue.

[David Bianco]

EXECUTIVE DEVELOPMENT

There was a time in the not-too-distant past when successful business executives were considered to have been born, not made. For the most part, business owners considered executive skills unnecessary. Almost anyone could become a manager. What mattered more was whom the executive knew, e.g., a father, uncle, or other family member. It was not until the early 1900s that business owners and academicians took a serious look at executive development. Once they did, the course of business history changed dramatically.

EXCEPTIONS TO THE RULE

Of course, not all business owners looked upon well-developed managerial skills as helpful, but not required. There were business leaders who learned early in their careers that home-grown talent could enhance their companies' chances of success. One such person was Eliphalet Adams Bulkeley, founder of Aetna Life & Casualty, in Hartford, Connecticut.

Bulkeley and his successors believed firmly in developing managers and promoting executives from within. Eliphalet set the tone early by developing his son, Morgan Gardner Bulkeley, to assume the presidency when he retired or died. He passed on in 1872, the same year Morgan joined the company as a member of the Board of Directors. Morgan did not have the desired managerial experience at the time, so he had to wait. In the interim, Thomas O. Enders assumed the company's presidency. He stepped down in 1879. By that time, Morgan was ready. He became Aetna's third president and remained in office for 45 years.

When Morgan Bulkeley assumed Aetna's presidency, he was well versed in the company's operations. Bulkeley offered proof to the efficacy of in-house executive development. He, in turn, was succeeded by Eliphalet's grandson, Morgan Bulkeley Brainard.

Brainard served two years as a legal apprentice in the law office of Aetna's general counsel. In 1905, he became Aetna's assistant treasurer. Two years later, he moved up to treasurer. In 1910, he was promoted to vice president, a position which put him in a close working relationship with Morgan Gardner Bulkeley. It was not until 1922, when Bulkeley died, that Brainard assumed the company's presidency. He remained in that position until 1955. In its first 101 years in business, Aetna had had only four presidents, all developed internally, and the company had grown considerably. Aetna's experience proved that the system of self-developed executives could—and did—work. Other companies utilized the same approach with success. For the most part, though, companies did not place undue emphasis on executive development.

Right up until World War II, business experts were decrying the lack of well-trained business leaders in the United States. In 1931, Wallace B. Donham, then Dean of the Harvard University Graduate School of Business Administration, wrote in his book *Business Adrift*:

> We need the leadership of far-sighted men who can think out the effects of conditions of flux on our business and political policies and make plans which shall affect these policies. . . . The danger in our situation lies in the lack of effective business leadership.

Donham, a former banking executive, believed firmly that American business executives were trained poorly. He was not alone in thinking so. Many of his contemporaries in business and academia agreed. In fact, some business leaders such as Henry Ford believed that managers were unnecessary.

Ford believed that any business could be run by an owner-entrepreneur and his helpers. He was not above firing any of his subordinates who made decisions without Ford's input. Perhaps his opinion may have had some merit in the early days of business when companies tended to be small and one person could make all decisions, but as businesses grew in size and complexity, leaders began to realize that competent executives were crucial if companies were to survive. So, executives like Alfred P. Sloan, Jr., who was appointed president of General Motors Corp. in the 1920s, and Chester Barnard, president of New Jersey Bell Telephone Company at about the same time, argued that executive development was necessary to a business' success. Nevertheless, there was no major push to implement executive training programs on a major scale.

PRE-WORLD WAR II EXECUTIVE DEVELOPMENT

One of the problems regarding formal management training centered around the executive's role in the business world. There were still people who believed as Ford did that executives were not a necessary cog in the company structure. That did not mean, of course, that management training could be ignored. There was a cadre of early researchers who had sought ways to train managers to motivate their workers to produce more. People like Frederick Taylor, Frank and Lillian Gilbreth, and Henry L. Gantt presented radical (for the time) ideas to increase productivity and improve managers' skills.

Taylor, a mechanical engineer, performed studies aimed at defining the one best way to do each job. The Gilbreths did extensive research on how to eliminate wasted hand and body motions in routine tasks such as bricklaying. They were among the first researchers to use motion pictures to study body motions. Gantt, like Taylor, an engineer, developed a chart managers could use to show the relationship between work planned and completed on one axis and time elapsed on the other. By and large, though, these researchers were practitioners, not academic theorists. They were not connected to educational institutions, which had traditionally eschewed any concentration on management courses, largely because many people thought they were unnecessary.

There were two schools of thought about the need for formal management training at the college level. One group felt that the best way to learn to manage was to manage. In their eyes, the best management training program was on-the-job experience. Others disagreed. They believed that managers' jobs were too complex to be left to trial and error. They argued that budding executives would be better served if they combined experience and formal education, with the emphasis on the latter. The debate continued. Meanwhile, the little management training that was available at the college level prior to the 1930s was geared primarily to undergraduates. It concentrated exclusively on theory. Most of the schools concentrated more on business skills than management. If management was taught at all, it was more than likely presented in specialized fields such as production engineering or personnel practices.

The Wharton School of Finance, the first collegiate school of business established in the United States, typified colleges' approach to management training in the first part of the twentieth century. The curriculum concentrated on undergraduate training. The courses the school offered were not considered entirely practical even by the late 1920s. Only two universities in the country, Harvard and Stanford, sponsored schools that dedicated themselves entirely to graduate students of business. Many business people saw the lack of concentration at the graduate level as a severe deficiency in the educational system. Some business executives and educational administrators sought to remedy that situation. Enter Wallace B. Donham.

Donham took over as dean of the Harvard Business School at a time when people were beginning to look at business as a profession. The role of business was changing considerably. Until World War I ended, business had been conducted on a small scale and mostly in the small community. As the 1920s came to a close, business was becoming bigger and its local flavor was fading. Business leaders and educators saw a need for a new approach to teaching business. Donham reacted to the need by introducing the business case history approach to the curriculum. The change revolutionized management training.

Donham emphasized that since more college graduates find careers in business than in any other field, training should neither be strictly theoretical nor restricted to colleges necessarily. His goal was to widen business students' overall knowledge of business theory and its practical application. The Harvard Business School's role was not to train specialists per se. It was more to develop students' capacities to examine as many of the constantly changing facts and forces surrounding administrative situations in business as they could, and to use their acquired knowledge imaginatively in determining current policies and action. To accomplish this goal, Donham introduced the case history approach as a way of developing students' capacities.

Donham felt strongly that case histories developed students' essential habits, skills, and capacities to form judgements on diverse factual situations, as well as their initiative. His innovative approach did just that. Students who dealt with actual case experiences to test their analytical, problem-solving, and decision-making abilities were better prepared to assume management roles in actual business situations. Students of business were few in number compared to the quantities growing businesses required in the years leading up to World War II. The war decreased the supply even more.

WORLD WAR II'S IMPACT ON BUSINESS

Many business people, managers and subordinates alike, entered the armed forces between 1941 and 1945, creating a shortage of management talent. Ironically, the demands of the armed forces created a business boom at a time when there were too few executives to manage the increased production and sales. There was a positive side to the irony, however: people began to appreciate the importance of well-trained managers in the workforce. Consequently, there was a renewed emphasis on executive development once the war ended.

OLD-TIME EXECUTIVES DID NOT DISAPPEAR

Even though more attention was paid to executive development after World War II, the "old school" managers did not disappear entirely. Company histories abound with stories of presidents and chief executive officers whose styles were a bit unorthodox but who were outstanding leaders. Take the case of Joe T. LaBoon, CEO of Atlanta (Georgia) Gas Company.

LaBoon proved that pre-World War II management styles could still be effective in the 1950s and beyond. He epitomized the idea that a company's commitment to managers who worked their way up through the ranks could be beneficial to shareholders, customers, and employees alike.

LaBoon began work with Atlanta Gas in 1939 as a cooperative education student from Georgia Tech. He rose through the ranks gradually, taking on greater responsibilities such as Vice President in the Rome and Atlanta divisions (1962-69) and Senior Vice President of Operations (1974-76) before assuming the company's presidency in 1976—after 39 years with the company. He was elected CEO in September 1980. LaBoon was the consummate CEO who recognized the value of the company's employees and strong public relations.

LaBoon was a nontraditional CEO who fostered an open environment in which employees at all levels became part of the decision-making process. He expanded the company's training programs, raised pay scales, improved facilities and buildings, and upgraded the gas delivery system. In short, LaBoon positioned Atlanta Gas Light Company to grow bigger and more financially secure during his eight-year tenure as CEO. By the time he died in 1988, he had served the company for 49 years. His success explained in part why businesses placed new emphasis on executive development after World War II.

MANAGEMENT BECOMES A PROFESSION

After World War II, business owners and academicians began to think of management as not just a complex and demanding job, but as a profession which required well-developed college-trained people to fill executive positions. Thus, there grew a new emphasis on college degrees as a first step toward managerial training. However, companies also recognized that they had to develop their own training programs to supplement college training. First, though, they had to define exactly why executive development programs were necessary.

WHY STRONG EXECUTIVE DEVELOPMENT PROGRAMS ARE NECESSARY

There were a number of changes in the workplace that prompted a different approach to executive development after World War II. For instance, technology began changing at an unprecedented rate. Workers expected more autonomy on the job. Executives could no longer be autocrats. They had to find new ways to motivate their employees. Labor unions grew in size and importance after World War II. These changes created a major reason for implementing new styles of management and management training.

Another significant reason for a new approach to executive training was continuity. Business leaders such as Bulkeley and LaBoon were prime examples of the advantages of continuity. Not only had their predecessors, who were also their mentors, groomed them well, but they had done the same for their successors. As time passed, it became more and more obvious to business leaders that continuity in management was necessary if a company were to survive and prosper.

Another issue prompting the new approach centered around strategy. The new corporate environment emerging after World War II suggested that companies would have to change their strategies in order to remain competitive. No longer were domestic companies the only businesses providing goods and services to Americans. A number of foreign competitors were entering the marketplace on a worldwide basis. They brought with them different styles of management, more efficient means of production, and a host of new ideas that threatened to change the way American companies did business. So, if American business executives were not aware of the new management theories, production techniques, etc., they would be unable to manage effectively. The best way to instill the new theories was through revamped and constant training.

A fourth reason involved corporate structure. Many American companies had grown too large and unwieldy to be managed by a limited number of bureaucrats. General Motors Corp. was a typical example of a mechanistic organization, a.k.a. a bureaucracy, a business structure that is built on complexity, formalization, and centralization. Corporate leaders after World War II recognized the need to reorganize, to simplify their companies' structures as much as possible. Doing so required a new breed of executive who could engineer change with an eye toward reducing the levels of bureaucracy and enhancing productivity. The question facing business leaders was where they could find executives who could accomplish this task. The answer lay in training. They realized, however, that they could not provide this training by themselves and turned to the world of academia for help.

A PARTNERSHIP BETWEEN BUSINESS AND ACADEMIA

Educational leaders were happy to work closely with their business counterparts to develop new management theories and training programs. The two entities formed a symbiotic relationship from which they both profited. Business schools produced well-trained, albeit somewhat inexperienced, management specialists. Companies provided funds, equipment, and executive expertise to help schools build up their facilities and programs. Special programs such as Masters of Business Administration (MBA), cooperative education, and internships grew by leaps and bounds.

In cooperative education (co-op) programs, students attended school and worked in paid or unpaid assignments simultaneously. By the time they graduated and entered the workforce, they were well versed in theory and practical application. Internship programs were similar, but they generally involved unpaid apprenticeships. The close relationship between education and business paid off handsomely for the two. However, they still had one major question with which to grapple as the partnership developed.

One of the first questions to be asked about executive development was simply what skills should be developed. Theorists emphasized the need for executive development in such areas as managers' knowledge and awareness of their organization and environment and their self-awareness. They took a close look at executives' tasks and skills. Academicians broke management down into its basic components, which had actually been determined by Henri Fayol, the managing director of a large French coal-mining firm, in the early 1900s: planning, organizing, leading, and controlling. They differentiated between management (simply getting things done) and leadership (getting things down by influencing other people). They studied the different specialized areas of management, e. g., marketing, financial, operations, human resources, and information. Basic management skills drew increased attention.

Academicians and business leaders recognized that in order to be successful, managers needed to develop their technical, human relations, and conceptual skills. To teach these skills, schools offered courses in every aspect of management. Learning became a never-ending process for many executives. Once they graduated from college, which became the most common source of supply for businesses, they continued with (MBA) programs or other business-related curricula. Businesses left nothing to chance. Most companies established their own in-house training programs to supplement academic programs. There were two reasons for this: to ensure that executives had access to current theories and practices and to help develop in-house employees. This was in recognition of the fact that colleges could not supply all of the potential executives companies needed to operate.

Executives and academicians did not overlook the importance of experience. They realized that there existed a great deal of executive potential in some employees who had not had the benefit of college training. Therefore, companies operated training programs to help develop these employees. The new philosophy of executive development was simple. While college training was helpful to give aspiring executives the theory of management they needed to start their careers, it could not be substituted entirely for experience. Their philosophy reflected the point Henry David Thoreau made in his book *Walden*, when he wrote, "To my astonishment, I was informed on leaving college that I had studied navigation!—why, if I had taken one turn down the harbor I should have known more about it." Executive development training became cyclical. It was a case of education, experience, more education, more experience, and so on.

Organizational behavior specialists developed a wide variety of theories to explain workers' behavior and develop their potential. Names like Maslow (Hierarchy of Human Needs), McGregor (Theory X and Theory Y), and Ouchi (Theory Z) became prominent in organizational behavior circles. Managers adopted their theories and implemented many of them in the workplace. (See the glossary for a brief description of these theories.) They developed programs for: reinforcement and punishment; management by objectives; participative management; and job enrichment and design, quality circles. The extensive list went on. Executive development was almost becoming a science.

Executive preparation encompassed three distinct parts: training, education, and development, all of which could occur simultaneously. Training referred to on-the-job learning aimed at helping incumbents perform better in their current positions. Education was more formal in nature. It prepared people for future positions. Development concentrated on programs designed to prepare individuals for new jobs required by organizational or industry change. The idea was that no employee could advance up the career ladder without adequate development. But, much of that training had to be completed by executives in an informal setting.

THE IMPORTANCE OF SELF DEVELOPMENT

One of the keys to successful executive development is that the higher a person progresses up the corporate ladder, the more he or she needs to rely on personal development to manage successfully. For several years after World War II, management development programs operated under the pretext that companies could control the entire development process. However, this philosophy changed as the years went by when it was discovered that not all managers "cloned" by development programs were successful in their jobs. Theorists began to understand that individual development is influenced as much by personal environment and life style as it is by other people's ideas and experiences. They introduced a new approach to executive development: on-the-job versus off-the job development.

On-the-job development included such facets as experience, mentoring, job rotation, and assignments to special projects, task forces, and committees. The idea was to give budding executives exposure to as many different experiences and environments as possible. There were drawbacks to this on-the-job training, though. For example, it was sometimes too narrow in focus and taught only current production methods and techniques. Off-the-job training, on the other hand, presented more diverse approaches to executive development.

In the 1960s, theorists introduced a large number of new ideas to enhance executive development. They concentrated on three approaches to management: process, system, and contingency. The process approach was proposed as a way to synthesize the diversity in management. It was simply a rehash of Fayol's steps of planning, organizing, leading, and controlling. The systems approach recognized the interdependency of internal activities within the organization and between the organization and its external environment. Finally, the contingency approach argued that different situations required different managerial responses. These approaches blended well with new styles of training that companies began including in their development programs, e.g., role playing, sensitivity training, conference training, and simulation. The emerging use of computers was particularly helpful in simulation.

Simulation enhanced managers' decision-making abilities and provided experience in teamwork. Computer-generated games created hypothetical companies and scenarios which tested students' skills. The simulated situations asked students to make decisions about production, costs, sales, inventories, and research and development problems. In this respect, simulation differed somewhat from role playing, which involved human resources problems for the most part. Often, the participants formed teams which competed against one another to formulate the best answers to problems. This gave them the chance to develop their teamwork skills, which prepared them for the emergence of quality circles and participative management. Thus, the introduction of the computer marked an important step in executive development.

Companies were quick to adopt the new techniques as they were introduced—and as they fit into their own cultures. For example, Boeing Corporation concentrated on mentoring, special courses, participation in the increasing number of professional societies, and university courses as keys to its executive development program. The Goodyear Tire and Rubber Company focused on job rotation and special internal and external courses. Which techniques companies used varied from firm to firm. Specialists recognized that there was no one executive development approach that worked better than any other. The key was for each company to utilize executive development approaches which worked well in their particular culture. That practice has continued to this day.

Another major innovation of the 1960's was provided by W. Edwards Deming. He introduced a comprehensive system that became the model for **Japanese management techniques**. Deming emphasized the use of statistics to analyze variabilities in the production process. At first, American manufacturers were reluctant to adopt his ideas, which focused on rigorous quality standards on the initial design of products, seeking constant and ongoing improvements in production and service operations, and thorough training for employees in all facets of management and production. Eventually, American managers incorporated his ideas, particularly those regarding training.

THE 1970S

As the 1970s began, the focus on executive training changed somewhat. In fact, change was the issue of the decade. Two management specialists in particular spearheaded the issue: Rosabeth Moss Kanter and Tom Peters. Kanter produced a book, *The Change Masters*. In it, she told executives that they had to become adept at anticipating the need for, and leadership in, productive change. Peters asserted that past management practices were outdated. He said that the unprecedented rate of change in business mandated that managers respond to constant innovations in areas like computer and telecommunications technologies if they wanted to remain competitive. He encouraged management to focus on self-managing teams and simplified organizational structures. The ideas of Kanter and Peters found their way into executive training programs quickly. Speed in adopting new ideas became essential in executive training, especially for companies that wanted to survive in the fast-paced business environment of the 1970s and 1980s.

THE 1980S

The decade of the 1980s created a new focus on executive training. College and business training programs began to emphasize communication and interpersonal skills. The programs included such heretofore overlooked skills as listening and nonverbal communication. Executives received training in effective feedback and delegation skills. Training programs addressed new communications media such as electronic mail and information networks. New programs placed increased emphasis on cross-cultural insights into the communications process. These were influenced in part by the ever-growing global economy, in which business executives from many different countries were liable to be involved in a variety of projects.

Executives required training in foreign cultures, languages, and business practices. They had to grasp the realities of intercultural business dealings in which the simple act of a handshake could make or break a deal. They had to learn entire new ways of doing business, which included responding to a rising emphasis on public policy. Executives had to become aware of a plethora of governmental regulations and social issues influencing their business strategies and tactics. In many industries, the role of the **CEO** became one of dealing exclusively with government officials and stakeholders, i.e., non-company employees who had any type of interest in a business' operations. CEOs left day-to-day operations to their subordinates, which influenced training programs. Executive training involved diverse specialized courses such as Business and Society, and Ethics. Society had a major influence on the direction and content of executive training programs. The programs of the 1980s carried over into the 1990s with the usual changes.

THE 1990S

Business in the early 1990s was marked by major restructuring changes. Corporations began downsizing, which resulted in the loss of millions of jobs. Executive development programs included enhanced concentration on topics such as sensitivity training, ethics, **affirmative action**, and **sexual harassment**. Universities and in-house training programs alike changed as rapidly as necessary in order to include courses on the topics affecting society and the workplace, not only nationally but internationally. The changes had a definite impact on what companies were looking for in executives—and the training they provided.

THE FUTURE OF EXECUTIVE TRAINING

The need for executive development programs will increase throughout the 1990s and beyond. Companies that do not respond to this need will be unable to survive in the rapidly changing, highly competitive, global environment. Executives will have to be aware of changes in public policy and governmental regulations at home and abroad that will impact the ways they manage. To ensure a continuity in **management**, businesses and universities will need to maintain a close working relationship. Businesses will also continue to operate their own training programs. Corporations that do not establish and maintain intensive executive development training are destined to become obsolete—which is one thing executive development can never afford to be.

GLOSSARY

Hierarchy of Human Needs - describes the five levels of human needs in order of ascending importance, i.e., physiological, security, social, esteem, and self-actualization, which people must fulfill on an ascending basis before they can become fulfilled.

Management by Objectives - An approach to management control and employee motivation in which a manager and an employee cooperatively establish goals against which the employee is subsequently evaluated.

Participative Management - A method of increasing employees' job satisfaction by giving them some say in how they do their own jobs and how the company is managed.

Theory X - A management approach based on the belief that people must be forced to be productive because they are naturally lazy, irresponsible, and uncooperative.

Theory Y - A management approach based on the belief that people want to be productive because they are naturally energetic, responsible, and cooperative.

Theory Z - A management approach commonly found in American companies that have adapted Japanese techniques that employs consensual decision making, lifetime employment, slower evaluation and promotion, informal control, a moderately specialized career path, and holistic concern for the employee.

[Arthur G. Sharp]

FURTHER READING:

Donham, Wallace B., *Business Adrift*. New York: Whittlesey House, 1931.

Drucker, Peter F. *Management: Tasks, Responsibilities, Practices*. New York: Harper & Row, Publishers, 1974.

Kanter, Rosabeth Moss. *The Change Masters: Innovation for Productivity in the American Corporation*. New York: Simon & Schuster, 1983.

London, Manuel and Edward M. Mone, eds. *Career Growth and Human Resource Strategies*. New York: Quorum Books, 1988.

Mailick, Sidney, Ed., Solomon Hoberman, and Stephen J. Wall. *The Practice of Management Development*. New York: Praeger, 1988.

Peters, Tom. *Thriving on Chaos*. New York: Alfred Knopf, 1988.

Sharp, Arthur G. *American Champions: A History of Business Success, Part I*. Morrisville, Pennsylvania: International Information Associates Publishers, 1991.

Sharp, Arthur G., and Elizabeth O. Sharp. *The Business-Education Partnership*. Morrisville, Pennsylvania: International Information Associates Publishers, 1992.

EXIT STRATEGIES

Exit strategies are techniques used by companies to abandon products, divisions, or even entire industries. Exit strategies are implemented only after a company has decided that it is no longer beneficial to remain active in a given market or industry. For example, a company that manufactures men's suits may determine that it wants to jettison its leisure suit division because of declining sales and a vanishing market. Or, a U.S. electronics producer might decide to exit the entire industry because of pressure from less-expensive imports.

Exit strategies have traditionally received little attention in the **management** field. Instead, most research and management practice has been focused on keeping products and businesses alive, despite exit pressures. The decision to exit has often been viewed as succumbing to failure or "giving up." Nevertheless, attitudes toward exiting began to change in the 1960s and 1970s for several reasons. Importantly, markets became much more competitive and complex than they had been earlier in the century because of increased production capacity and an increasingly global economy. As a result, more companies began to view exiting as a viable and profitable alternative within their overall corporate **strategy**.

Evidencing the increased emphasis on exit strategy was research conducted during the mid-1960s through the mid-1970s that analyzed the exit process and created a framework that business decision makers could use to determine when and how to exit. For example, Conrad Berenson posited an exit model in 1963 that identified five categories of criteria used to evaluate a product abandonment decision: (1) financial security, which entails determining if the minimum return on investment is being met for the firm; (2) financial opportunity, or calculating the return on alternative uses of the firm's resources; (3) **marketing strategy**, which determines the value of the product above pure financial profit, such as brand-name worth and the value of established distribution channels; (4) social responsibility, or criteria that encompass the firm's responsibilities to customers, employees, suppliers, etc.; and (5) organized intervention, which takes into account actions by government, society, or labor groups as a result of the decision to exit.

In addition to Berenson's criteria for determining the value of an exit decision was a model developed in 1964 by R.S. Alexander. Among other things, Alexander's model identified six major telltale signs that suggest that a firm may have to consider exiting a market: falling sales; deteriorating prices; declining profitability; an increase in the popularity of substitute products, such as margarine instead of butter; obsolescence of a product or idea; and increasing consumption of management resources to keep the product viable. Although Alexander's model was based on relatively simple concepts, it provided a systematic approach for periodically searching for and selecting products, services, or divisions to abandon.

Philip Kotler complemented Berenson's and Alexander's work in 1965. His model incorporated Alexander's six points, but was more detailed. He added such exit impetuses as alternative opportunities, product contribution in relation to other products, and the impact of the product on the company's image or on sales of other products. For example, Kotler pointed out that while a product may still be profitable viewed independently, it may be cannibalizing sales of other products in a company's line or consuming resources that could be used to a greater advantage to promote other products or divisions. Kotler also devised a system for using more and better **accounting** data to help managers' develop exit strategies.

Other models relating to exit decisions and strategies were developed in the 1970s by researchers such as Robert W. Eckles, Parker Worthington, Edward M. Mazze, and William G. Browne. The primary benefit of most of this research was that it helped to establish more financially quantifiable tools and techniques for determining when and how to exit a market or industry. Those techniques increasingly found application during the late 1970s and early 1980s as domestic market growth in the United States slowed and foreign competition, particularly from Japan, proliferated.

BASIC EXIT DECISIONS AND STRATEGIES

A number of different exit strategy models and theories have been applied by companies seeking to abandon products or industries. In general, they all recognize basic elements of the exit decision process. Of import is the widely accepted product life-cycle theory. That theory holds that most new products (and companies) go through a cycle of: (1) introduction and acceptance; (2) growth; (3) maturity; and (4) decline. In some cases a company may choose to exit during an early stage of the cycle because, for example, the product is worth more to another firm, or because it can use its limited resources more effectively elsewhere. But it is usually during the decline phase that an entity must face the fundamental exit decision; should it exit before the product (or company) declines too far, or should it try to revitalize?

In determining whether or not to exit, the company usually takes into account many of the considerations identified in the exit models highlighted above. The decision of whether or not to exit basically boils down to a simple question of profitability: will the company be better off in the long run, from a profit standpoint, if it exits the market or industry. For example, suppose that a food company introduces a new garlic potato chip product. After one year the product fails to meet sales expectations. Even if the new item is losing money the company may decide to continue to sell it for reasons not related to the profitability of that particular product. For instance, it may determine that the cost of alienating customers who like the chip could damage the reputation of other products sold under the same brand name.

Now suppose that the new garlic chip was very successful and exceeded expectations. The company may decide to abandon the product for any number of reasons. For instance, it may determine that the resources required to promote and distribute the product could be used more profitably to promote a new item that is even more successful. Or, it may be able to sell the product to a competitor with a more established distribution network that is willing to pay more for the product than the originator expects to make from it. Likewise, as suggested above, the chip may be cannibalizing market share from the potato chip products that have higher profit margins, thus damaging overall profitability.

Once an organization determines that it does wish to exit a market or industry, it usually faces three basic exit options: sale, **spin-off**, and employee ownership. The advantage of the first option, an outright sale, is that it allows a company to quickly jettison a product or division and it provides an injection of **capital** that can be invested elsewhere at a higher return. The typical strategy for selling a product, division, or company is simple: find companies that are structured in such a way that they could make better use of the abandoned subject and solicit bids. In some cases a suitable buyer for an entire operation may not exist. Therefore, a company may choose to liquidate the operation in pieces, simply walk away and absorb the loss, or spin it off.

A company spins off a division by creating a separate company or subsidiary in which it sells shares to a potential buyer. A spin-off amounts to a sale of the operation over a period of time. It is a useful technique when the purchasing company has inadequate resources or is hesitant to buy the entire operation outright. For example, General Electric exited the computer business by spinning its computer division off to Honeywell. Honeywell Information

Systems was formed as a joint operation—GE retained 18 percent of the stock, which it sold over a period of three years. In some instances the original owner may retain its equity or even eventually buy back the product or operation.

A third exit option is selling an operation to employees. The advantage of selling a business or division to employees is that it generates capital for the parent company and places the ultimate responsibility for achieving profitability on the employees. For example, B.F. Goodrich Co. was failing to meet its profit goals in its tire and appliance stores. It felt that it could get a better return on its resources by investing them in its profitable chemical businesses. So, Goodrich sold, or franchised, many of the stores to the managers and employees that ran them, and it invested the capital in its chemical operations to greater profitability. An interesting result of the exit process was that the profitability of the stores increased because managers suddenly had a personal stake in the success of the business.

[Dave Mote]

FURTHER READING:

Alexander, R. S. "Death and Burial of 'Sick' Products." *Journal of Marketing*. april, 1964, pp. 1-7.

Bereson, Conrad. "Pruning the Product Line." *Business Horizons*. Summer, 1963, pp. 63-70.

Brown, William G., and Patrick S. Kemp. "A Three Stage Product Review Process." *Industrial Marketing Management*. 1976, Vol. 5, pp. 333-42.

Eckles, Robert W. "Product Line Deletion and Simplification." *Business Horizons*. Ocotober, 1971, pp. 71-74.

Guth, William D. *Handbook of Business Strategy*. New York: Warren, Gorham & Lamont, 1985.

Hamelman, Paul W., and Edward M. Mazze. "Improving Product Abandonment Decisions." *Journal of Marketing*. April, 1972, pp. 20-26.

Kotler, Philip. "Phasing Out Weak Products." *Harvard Business Review*. March-April, 1965, pp. 107-18.

Lambert, Douglas M. *The Product Abandonment Decision*. Hamilton, Ontario: National Association of Accountants, 1985.

Rothschild, William E. *Strategic Alternatives: Selection, Development, and Implementation*. New York: Amacom, 1979.

Wheelen, Thomas L., and J. David Hunger. *Strategic Management and Business Policy*. Reading, MA: Addison-Wesley Publishing Co., 1992.

Worthington, Parker M. "The Assessment of Product Deletion Decision Indicators." In *Fortran Applications in Business Administration*. University of Michigan, 1971.

EXPECTED VALUE

Expected value is a statistical concept that is applied to many business situations. Often, the term may be loosely used. Nevertheless, whenever some-one mentions expected profit or expected loss from a business venture—that is, the expected value of the likely magnitude of profit or loss from the business under consideration—the term has a rigorous mathematical foundation.

DEFINING EXPECTED VALUE

The expected value concept uses two main mathematical concepts—random variables and **probabilities**. To understand a *random variable*, let us assume that an experiment results in a certain number of outcomes and each of the outcomes is assigned a numerical value. A random variable then is a numerical description of the outcome of an experiment. Suppose a coin is tossed. In this case, there are two possible outcomes: heads or tails. One can assign a numerical value of 1 with the outcome heads and a value of 0 with outcome tails. Thus, if we consider the number of possible outcomes on a single toss as a random variable (often given a generic mathematical name "x"), it takes two values: x = 0, 1. In a more complicated case, a random variable can take a large number of values—sometimes even an infinite number of values.

The notion of probability is quite widely used and refers to the chance of an event occurring. The probability of an event (denoted as p) lies between 0 and 1. That is, 0 is less than or equal to p and p is less than or equal to 1. In the above example of coin tossing, the probability of heads turning up on a toss is 0.5 and the probability of tails turning up is also 0.5.

One may be able to assign a probability value to every value a random variable takes. In the preceding example, one can say that the probability that x = 1 is 0.5. Mathematically, it can be said that p(x) = 0.5 when x = 1 (when heads turns up). Similarly, one can say that p(x) = 0.5 when x = 0 (when tails turns up).

A mathematical expression for the expected value of a random variable (x) can now be given as:

$$E(x) = \Sigma x * p(x)$$

In this expression, the notation Σ is the Greek letter capital sigma. Mathematicians use the Σ notation to indicate sum of a number of items. E(x) is used as a notation for the expected value of the random variable x, and p(x) is the probability that the random variable x takes a particular value. The above expression thus holds that in order to compute the expected value of a discrete random variable, one must multiply each value of the random variable by its corresponding probability and then add all the resulting products. For the tossed coin example, the expected value (that is, the expected number of heads on a toss) can be

calculated as follows using the above expression: 1 * 0.5 + 0 * 0.5 = 0.5. Here, the random variable takes two values: 1 (a head) and 0 (a tail) with probabilities 0.5 each. The expected value calculation implies that the expected number of heads on a single toss is 0.5. This means that if one tosses a coin 100 times, one would expect to see 50 heads on the basis of the expected value concept.

Since the coin example is a rather simple one, a more realistic example follows. Suppose that we have data on the number of children that American families have (call it the random variable x). The minimum number of children a family had was 0 and the maximum number of children a family had was 5. Thus, the random variable x takes six values: x equals 0, 1, 2, 3, 4 and 5. Based on the number of families with different numbers of children, one has data on the probability of a family having a certain number of children. These data are provided in the first two columns of Table 1:

Table 1

x	p(x)	x * p(x)
0	.18	0 * .18
1	.39	1 * .39
2	.24	2 * .24
3	.14	3 * .14
4	.04	4 * .04
5	.01	5 * .01

The first two columns of Table 1 show that the probability of a family having 0 number of children is equal to 0.18 or 18 percent. Similarly, the probability of a family having 1 child is equal to 0.39 or 39 nine percent; the probability of a family having 2 children is equal to 0.24 or 24 percent; the probability of a family having 3 children is equal to 0.14 or 14 percent; the probability of a family having 4 children is equal to 0.04 or 4 percent; and the probability of a family having 5 children is equal to 0.01 or 1 percent. The last column of the table multiplies the different values of x by its corresponding probability, according to the previously given mathematical expression, to compute the expected value of the number of children in those households to whom the above data apply. When all the six products are added, the expected value of the number of children (that is, the expected value of the random variable x) turns out to be 1.5. One can interpret the expected value of 1.5 as the mean number of children for the households considered. In more concrete terms, we can say that if a family was picked at random from among the families considered, it would be expected to have 1.5 children.

The application of the expected value concept to business can be illustrated using the following example. Suppose a business firm has the option of building a large, medium, or small sized plant. Profits from each plant size depend on whether demand is low or high. Assume that the firm knows the probabilities of low and high demands. Based on these probabilities and corresponding profit/loss figures, the firm can calculate the expected profit for each plant size. The firm should build the plant that generates the largest expected profits.

[Anandi P. Sahu, Ph.D.]

FURTHER READING:

Anderson, David P., Dennis J. Sweeney and Thomas A. Williams. *An Introduction to Management Science: Quantitative Approaches to Decision Making.* 7th ed. West Publishing Company, 1994.

Anderson, David P., Dennis J. Sweeney and Thomas A. Williams. *Statistics for Business and Economics.* 5th ed. West Publishing Company, 1993.

EXPENSE ACCOUNTS

Expense accounts, also called expense allowances, are plans under which companies reimburse employees for business-related expenses. These expenses include travel, entertainment, gifts, and other expenses related to the employer's business activity. Of particular interest to businesses and their employees is the tax treatment of business-related expenses, what types of expenses an employer will allow to be reimbursed, and how those reimbursements are administered.

For tax purposes a company's expense account plan is either accountable or nonaccountable. An accountable plan must meet the following requirements of the **Internal Revenue Service (IRS)**: there must be a business connection; expenses must be substantiated; and any amount received by an employee in excess of actual expenses must be returned to the employer. Substantiation means that the employer must be able to identify the specific nature of each expense and determine that the expense was business-related. Expenses may not be aggregated into broad categories, and they may not be reported using vague terminology.

If the company's plan is in fact an accountable plan, then all money received by an employee under the plan is excluded from the employee's gross income. It is not reported as wages or other compensation, and it is exempt from withholding.

Companies that fail to require employees to substantiate their expenses or allow employees to retain amounts in excess of substantiated expenses are considered by the IRS to have nonaccountable plans. Funds that employees receive under nonaccountable plans are treated as income, subject to withholding, and such expenses are deductible by the employee only as a miscellaneous itemized deduction (which must exceed two percent of the employee's Adjusted gross income).

The tax laws affecting business-related expenses change from time to time. Starting in 1994, for example, allowable meal expenses were reduced from 80 percent to 50 percent. Other types of business-related expenses affected by changing tax laws include deductions for spousal business travel and dues and memberships in certain types of clubs.

Employees who find they are incurring business-related expenses need to determine from their employer exactly what types of expenses are reimbursable. In an effort to control spiraling travel and other business-related expenses, some companies have developed reimbursement policies that spell out in detail what expenses qualify for reimbursement. For example, companies may require employees to book their travel in a certain way or from certain vendors.

Because of the IRS's substantiation requirement, employees need to carefully document all business-related expenses. Receipts are normally required for all expenses. If it is not possible to obtain a receipt, the amount of the expense should be noted along with the date, place, and reason for the expense.

[David Bianco]

EXPERIENCE AND LEARNING CURVES

Learning curves graphically portray the **costs** and benefits of experience when performing routine or repetitive tasks. Also known as experience curves, cost curves, efficiency curves, and productivity curves, they illustrate how the cost per unit of output decreases over time as the result of learning and experience. That is, as cumulative output increases, learning and experience cause the cost per unit to decrease. Experience and learning curves are used by businesses in production planning, cost forecasting, and setting delivery schedules, among other applications.

Learning curves are geometric curves that can be graphed on the basis of a formula. Typically the X (horizontal) axis measures cumulative output, and the Y (vertical) axis measures the cost per unit. The curve starts with a high cost per unit at the beginning of output, decreases quickly at first, then levels out as cumulative output increases. The slope of the learning curve is an indication of the rate at which learning becomes transformed into cost savings.

An 80 percent learning curve is standard for many activities and is sometimes used as an average in cost forecasting and production planning. An 80 percent learning curve means that, for every doubling of output, the cost of new output is 80 percent of prior output. As output doubles from one unit to two units to four units, etc., the learning curve descends quite sharply as costs decrease dramatically. As output increases, it takes longer to double previous output, and the learning curve flattens out. Thus, costs decrease at a slower pace when cumulative output is higher.

One can explain the shape of learning curves another way. When a new task or production operation begins, a person or system learns quickly, and the learning curve is steep. With each additional repetition, less learning occurs and the curve flattens out. At the beginning of production or learning, individuals or systems are said to be "high" on the learning curve. That means that costs per unit are high, and cumulative output is low. Individuals and systems "move down" the experience or learning curve by learning to complete repetitive tasks more efficiently, eliminating hesitation and mistakes, automating certain tasks, and making adjustments to procedures or systems.

Some theorists believe that learning curves are not actually curves, but more like jagged lines that follow a curving pattern. They assert that learning occurs in brief spurts of progress, followed by small fallbacks to previous levels, rather than in a smooth progressive curve. Such a model of learning, however, does not affect the usefulness of learning curves in business and production applications.

System changes that affect how tasks are accomplished cause disruptions in learning curves. Every change has costs and, presumably, benefits that can be graphed by overlaying the learning curve based on the new way of doing things with the old learning curve. When the change is introduced, a new learning curve starts at a point above the current learning curve. The new learning curve soon intersects the old learning curve as cumulative output increases. The graphic area above the old learning curve and under the new learning curve represents costs associated with the change. Once the new learning curve intersects the old learning curve, the area under the old learning curve and above the new learning curve represents benefits associated with the change. Optimally, no new changes would be introduced until change benefits exceed change costs.

[David Bianco]

EXPERT SYSTEMS

Expert systems combine computer equipment, software, and specialized information to imitate expert human reasoning and advice. As a branch of **artificial intelligence**, expert systems assist less knowledgeable humans by providing advice and explanation. While artificial intelligence is a broad field covering many aspects of computer-generated thought, expert systems are more narrowly focused. Typically, expert systems function best with specific activities or problems and a discrete database of digitized facts, rules, cases, and models. While **computers**, **software**, and information are all required for an expert system, many consider computer equipment to be a standing prerequisite. Thus, although expert systems may require a computer with sufficient processing and storage power to be effective, expert systems are more frequently defined as software programs. As a software program, the expert system integrates a searching and sorting program with a knowledge database. The specific searching and sorting program for an expert system is frequently called the inference engine. The inference engine contains all the systematic processing rules and logic associated with the problem or task at hand. Mathematical probabilities often serve as the basis for many expert systems. The second component—the knowledge database—stores necessary factual, procedural, and experiential information representing expert knowledge. Through a procedure known as knowledge transfer, expertise (or those skills and knowledge that sustain a much better than average performance) passes from human expert to knowledge engineer. The knowledge engineer actually creates and structures the knowledge database by completing certain logical, physical, and psychosocial tasks. For this reason, expert systems are often referred to as knowledge-based information systems. By widely distributing human expertise through expert systems, businesses can realize benefits in consistency, accuracy, and reliability in problem-solving activities.

Early expert systems appeared in the mid-1960s as an offshoot of research in artificial intelligence. While artificial intelligence encompasses general areas such as engineering, sociology, and psychology, expert systems are specific in nature. Many early systems (GPPS and DENDRAL at Stanford University, XCON at Digital Equipment Corp. (DEC), and CATS-1 at General Electric) pioneered the concept of a computer expert, but one, MYCIN, most clearly introduces two essential characteristics of an expert system: modularity and justification. MYCIN was developed at Stanford University as an expert system to aid in the diagnosis of bacterial meningitis. As it was developed, MYCIN emerged as a product of modular design with a facility to explain its own advice. Modular design refers to the concept and practice of developing software as stand-alone sets of programming code and informational materials. Each set connects as a module or self-contained capsule to other modules. This idea of modular design led to the further advance of expert shells. An expert shell program simplifies the development of an expert system by providing preexisting inference engines and module knowledge database components. The frontward and backward chaining effects of MYCIN (its ability to recount the steps it took to arrive at any recommendation), still influence the design of expert systems. As a result, the ability to explain or justify is a standard facility on commercially produced expert systems and programs. Perhaps the most important discovery for MYCIN and other early expert systems was the importance of the human expert in the expert system.

The basic role of an expert system is to replicate a human expert and replace him or her in a problem-solving activity. In order for this to happen, key information must be processed from a human expert into the knowledge database and, when appropriate, the inference engine. Two different types of knowledge emerge from the human expert: facts and procedural or heuristic information. Facts encompass the definitively-known data and the defined variables that comprise any given activity. Procedures are the if-then of information through any given activity. Through a formal knowledge acquisition process that includes identification, conceptualization, formalization, implementation, and testing, expert databases develop. Interviews, transactional tracking, observation, case study, and self-reporting choices are common means of extracting information from a human expert. Using programmatic and physical integration of logic, data, and choice, expert systems integrate the examination and interpretation of data input with specific rules of behavior and facts to arrive at a recommended outcome. Four interactive roles form the activities of the expert system. Expert systems can diagnose, interpret, or predict—based on the query at hand,—the information available, and the relevant rules of behavior or **decision making**. The fourth interactive role of an expert system, instruction, emerges as a result of the expert systems justification system. Synthesizing feedback with various combinations of diagnostic, interpretative and predictive curriculum, the expert system can become a finely—tuned personal tutor or a fully-developed and standardized group class. Computer aided instruction (CAI) thrives as a field of inquiry and development for businesses.

Uncertainty is an underlying consideration in the overall conceptualization, development, and use of an expert system. One popular treatment of uncertainty uses fuzzy logic. Fuzzy logic divides the simple yes-

no decision into a scale of probability of yes-no. This extension of probability criteria allows the expert system to accommodate highly complex problems and activities in an attempt to more closely model human expert assistance and interaction. Probabilities of uncertainty differ according to the activity of an expert system.

In its diagnostic role, an expert system offers to solve a problem by analyzing yes or no with the likelihood of correctly identifying a cause of a problem or disturbance. By inferring difficulties from past observations, the expert system identifies possible problems while offering possible advice and/or solutions. Diagnostic systems typically infer causes of problems. Applications include medicine, manufacturing, service, and a multitude of narrowly-focused problem areas. As an aid to human problem solving, the diagnostic system or program assists by relying on past evidence and problems. By inferring descriptions from observations rather than problems, the expert system takes an interpretive rather than diagnostic role. Interpretive systems explain observations by inferring their meaning based on previous descriptions of situations. The probability of uncertainty is quantified as the likelihood of being an accurate representation. In a predictive role, the expert system forecasts future events and activities based on past information. Probabilities of uncertainty are emphasized as chances or the likelihood of being right. Finally, in an instructive role, the expert system teaches and evaluates the successful transfer of education information back to the user. By explanation of its decision-making process, supplemental materials, and systematic testing, the instructive system accounts for uncertainty by measuring the likelihood that knowledge transfer was achieved. Regardless of the role of an expert system or how it deals with uncertainty, its anatomy is still similar. The inference engine forms the heart of the expert system. The knowledge database serves as the brain of the expert system.

The inference engine churns through countless potential paths and possibilities based on some combination of rules, cases, models, or theories. Some rules, such as predicate logic, mimic human reasoning and offer various mathematical arguments to any query. A decision tree or branching steps and actions synthesize probability with rules and information to arrive at a recommendation. Probabilities mirror the human expert's own experience with an activity or problem. Other models or cases structure some systematic movement through a problem-solving exercise in different ways. Case-based reasoning uses specific incidents or models of behavior to simulate human reasoning. Other inference engines are based on semantic networks (associated nodes and links of association), scripts (preprogrammed activities and responses), objects (self-contained variables and rule sets), and frames (more-specialized objects allowing inheritance). In all cases, the inference engine guides the processing steps and expert information together in a systematic way.

The knowledge database provides the fuel for the inference engine. The knowledge database is composed of facts, records, rules, books, and countless other resources and materials. These materials are the absolute values and documented evidence associated with the database structure. If-then procedures and pertinent rules are an important part of the knowledge database. Imitating human reasoning, rules or heuristics use logic to record expert processing steps and requirements. Logic, fact, and past experience weave together to make an expert database. As a result of knowledge transfer, significant experiences, skills, and facts fuse together in a representation of expertise. This expert database, or knowledge-based information system, is the foil for the inference engine. As such, the knowledge database must be accurately and reliably conceived, planned, and realized for optimum performance. Additionally, the knowledge database must be validated and confirmed as accurate and reliable. Expert databases containing inaccurate information or procedural steps that result in bad advice are ineffective and potentially destructive to the operation of a business. When, however, the inference engine and knowledge database synchronize correctly, many businesses realize gains in productivity and decreases in costs.

Some benefits of an expert system are direct. Loma Engineering reduced its staff requirements from five engineers to a 1.5 equivalent by using an expert system to customize machine specifications. Other benefits are more indirect and may include improved managerial functions. The Federal Aviation Administration uses the Smartflow Traffic Management System to better coordinate air traffic activities. The American Stock Exchange also put expert systems to use in monitoring insider trading. Retail giants such as J.C. Penney and small entrepreneurs alike use expert systems to provide customer service and improve customer satisfaction. In manufacturing, expert systems applications are frequent and successful perhaps due to the extremely quantifiable nature of many manufacturing operations. Computer integrated manufacturing (CIM) is a growing field that specifically combines computers and manufacturing operations. Increasingly, CIM and expert systems are integrated to improve the manufacturing process. It would be difficult to find a significant U.S. business that has not or is not using some expert system to improve performance and quality. Performance of expert systems in general, however, is inconsistent. Some estimates place successful implementation as low as 10-20 percent due to failures in knowledge transfer, system design, and resource configurations. Regardless, expert systems

enjoy wide distribution and use in the American business community.

The cost of an expert system may vary considerably. For large companies and complex activities, sufficiently powerful computer hardware must be available. When the system is intended to be complex, expensive machinery must be purchased, therefore expert systems can become costly. Additionally, expert systems do not learn independently as other artificial intelligence systems may. The knowledge database must be updated frequently to gain relevance and timeliness. Thus, expert systems are often expensive to maintain. Using an expert shell (predesigned inference engine and database structure) is one way to reduce the costs of obtaining an expert system. The expert shell simplifies the expert system by providing preprogrammed modules and inference engine. New companies such as Attar Software, Bendata Management Systems, The Malloy Group Inc., AI Corp., and Aion Corp, provide expert shells that support business and industrial operations. Increased costs may also appear with the identification and employment of an expert or a series of experts. Retaining an expert involves the potentially expensive task of transferring expertise to a digital format. Depending on the expert's ability to conceive and digitally represent knowledge, this process may be lengthy. Because the expert system is so narrowly focused and tailored, **economies of scale** rarely appear. Expert systems suffer, as well, from the systematic integration of preexisting human biases and ignorances into its original programming.

Expert systems benefit companies, as well. Expert systems capture scarce expert knowledge and render it archival. This is an advantage when losing the expert would be a significant loss to the organization. Distributing the expert knowledge enhances employee productivity by offering necessary assistance to make the best decision. Improvements in reliability and quality frequently appear when expert systems distribute expert advice, opinion, and explanation on demand. Expert systems are capable of handling enormously complex tasks and activities as well as an extremely rich knowledge-database structure and content. As such, they are well suited to model human activities and problems. Expert systems can reduce production downtime and, as a result, increase output and quality. Additionally, expert systems facilitate the transfer of expertise to remote locations using digital communications. In specific situations, ongoing use of an expert system may be cheaper than the services of a human expert.

Businesses may or may not differentiate between a **decision support system (DSS)** and an expert system. Some consider each one, alternately, to be a subcategory of the other. Whether or not they are one in the same, closely related, or completely independent is frequently debated in trade and professional literature. Like expert systems, the DSS relies on computer machinery, software, and information to function effectively. The debatable distinction, however, between an expert system and a DSS seems to lie in its practical application. Decision support systems are used most often in specific decision making activities while expert systems operate in the area of problem-solving activities. No one specific criteria for separating decision-making and problem solving is valid or in popular-use. For this reason, investigation of an expert system includes research on DSS as well.

SEE ALSO: Management Information Systems

[Tona Henderson]

FURTHER READING:

Anthes, Gary H. "FAA Expert System Aims Sky High." *Computerworld*. March 7, 1994, pp. 73, 75.

Grabowski, Martha, and William A. Wallace. *Advances in Expert Systems for Management*. JAI Press Inc., 1993.

Heichler, Elizabeth. "Expert System Keeps UK TV Ads in Line." *Computerworld*. December 20, 1993, p. 30.

Lucas, Henry C., Jr. "Market Expert Surveillance System." *Communications of the ACM*. December. 1993, pp. 27-34.

May, Kenneth M. "Companies Get Smart with Smart Systems." *National Underwriting*. August 9, 1993, pp. 2, 18.

Partridge, Derek, and K. M. Hussain. *Artificial Intelligence and Business Management*. Ablex Publishing Corporation, 1992.

Turban, Efraim. *Decision Support Systems and Expert Systems: Management Support Systems*. Macmillan, 1993.

Turban, Efraim, and Jay Leibowitz. *Managing Expert Systems*. Idea Group Publishing, 1992.

Watkins, Paul R., and Lance B. Eliot. *Expert Systems in Business and Finance: Issues and Applications*. John Wiley & Sons, 1993.

Winkler, Connie. "Redrawing Design Process Cuts Repetition at Loma." *Software Management*. April, 1994, pp. 101-103.

EXPORTING

Exporting refers to the act of producing goods or services in one country and then selling or trading them abroad. Exporting is usually conducted by the company that manufactures the product or provides the service, through either direct or indirect channels. Exporting is just one of several methods that companies use to participate in economies outside of their home country.

Exporting has played an important role in global trade throughout history, and the United States in particular, has always been heavily dependent upon exports. Even before its Declaration of Independence, the United States relied on exports of cotton, tobacco, and other agricultural products to Europe for much of its commerce. United States merchants were penalized by English duties and restrictions in Europe and the West Indies after the Revolutionary War. But those impediments prompted new trade ties with overseas buyers in Africa, India, and East Asia, laying the groundwork for a legacy of U.S. trading overseas.

Despite America's significant cross-border activity during its first 100 years, it was not until the industrial revolution in the late 1800s that exporting began to proliferate rapidly. Export growth was largely a corollary of technological advancements in communications, manufacturing, transportation, and food preservation techniques. It was during that period—the late 1800s and early 1900s—that the United States made the transition from a supplier of agrarian products to a manufacturer of industrial goods, such as ships, railroads, clothes, and cars.

Importantly, global trade during the early 1900s was also characterized by a rise in protective **trade barriers** and restrictions created by countries to further their own trade interests. In the United States, elements of the Sherman Antitrust Act of 1890, the Federal Trade Commission Act of 1914, the Trading with the Enemy Act (1917), the Smoot-Hawley Tariff Act of 1930, and many other laws were used to protect domestic industries and give local firms an advantage in trade. Unfortunately, though, the adversarial and repressive trade environment that emerged is credited with helping push the world into depression during the 1930s.

Realizing the importance of a more cooperative world trade climate, the United States and other nations worked to reduce trade barriers during the mid- and late 1930s. The Reciprocal Trade Agreements Act of 1934 in the United States led an international movement toward lower tariffs and duties imposed on imports. Likewise, the **Most Favored Nation (MFN)** trading program extended the benefits of any bilateral tariff reductions negotiated by the United States to all MFNs.

In addition to gains achieved through reduced trade barriers, World War II served to bolster U.S. exports. Warring nations that were forced to turn to the United States for supplies began to recognize the fledgling industrial power as a source of high-quality goods. After the war, moreover, the United States emerged as the undisputed international trade leader, as devastated European and Japanese manufacturing sectors scrambled to rebuild. In fact, between the late 1940s and the mid-1960s, the U.S. trade surplus (defined as the value of U.S. exports less the value of imports into the country) ballooned at a rate of 20 percent annually.

U.S. exports continued to rise rapidly, swelling from about $43 billion in 1970 to nearly $225 billion by 1980. However, increased competition, particularly from Western Europe and Japan, began to erode U.S. international market share during the 1970s. In the 1980s, in fact, U.S. exports were overshadowed by imports as the national trade deficit plunged to more than $160 billion annually by the late 1980s. Although much of that deficit was the result of oil imports, the improved manufacturing prowess of Japan was also a major factor. Nevertheless, increasing internationalization of markets and a continued move toward lower trade barriers vastly expanded global trading. Going into the 1990s, annual U.S. exports were rapidly approaching $400 billion and the total global export market outside of the United States was estimated to be more than $2 trillion.

BENEFITS OF EXPORTING

The chief goal of any company's exporting endeavor is usually to maximize profits by exploiting opportunities in foreign markets that don't exist in domestic markets. For example, products that have become obsolete in U.S. markets, such as washboards, can sometimes be marketed abroad very successfully. Thus, by increasing a product's life span, a manufacturer is able to reduce new product development costs and capitalize on learned efficiencies particular to the product related to production, distribution, and marketing.

Likewise, when markets for products that are still viable in the United States begin to mature and become saturated, many producers are able to continue to achieve steady sales and profit gains through cross-border sales. Because markets in other countries are often less mature and less competitive, exporters can typically achieve faster sales growth and higher profit margins. Foreign markets often provide relief not only from maturing domestic markets, but also from intensifying competition from imports. In addition, as manufacturing volume grows, benefits related to economies of scale may improve the exporter's competitiveness in both foreign and domestic markets.

Besides profit opportunities related to untapped markets, another major benefit of exporting is market risk diversification. In other words, a company can generally lessen its vulnerability to cyclical economic downswings or regional disturbances by extending its geographic reach. For instance, companies that were active in both the United States and Western Europe during the late 1980s likely benefitted from the lag between the U.S. recession and the European Community economic slump that peaked several months later, just when the United States was beginning to cycle out of its downturn. Geographic diversification also lessens risks affiliated with seasonality inherent to some products (like fishing tackle) and increased competition in individual regions.

EXPORT ROUTES

The typical export arrangement is a company-owned export department, whereby a manufacturer sells products directly to companies or consumers in foreign countries. The company has almost total control over the marketing and distribution of its goods and services, and coordinates research, distribution, sales, marketing, pricing, legal, and other efforts in-house. This stereotype, however, is not representative of the export systems utilized by most U.S. exporters. In fact, most companies depend on one or a mix of specialized export channels outside of their organization.

Aside from company-owned exporting operations, the two major routes an individual company can take to become an exporter are indirect and direct. Indirect exporting entails selling goods through home-based proxies or resellers. Direct exports are sold through foreign-based parties. Both methods can be conducted through either merchants or agents, the delineation being that merchants actually assume ownership of the goods while agents simply represent the manufacturer or owner. Manufacturers may also trade their goods abroad through barter. Finally, firms that export certain services are generally classified separately. For example, an engineering firm might provide design services for a dam in India; it would likely bid on the job, perform the services at home and in India, and then bill its foreign client.

INDIRECT AGENTS

A company exports its goods indirectly when it utilizes a home-based merchant or agent to essentially find, and deliver goods to, foreign buyers. Indirect exporting represents the least expensive and lowest-risk method of participating in foreign markets because it is relatively easy to initiate and requires a meager up-front capital investment. Indirect exporting agents essentially act as intermediaries, matching exporters and customers and facilitating the flow of goods.

A common type of indirect agent is an export management company (EMC). EMCs typically represent several companies within one or many industries. They profit by charging domestic companies fees or commissions. In return, they offer the manufacturer instant access to foreign channels of distribution and to in-depth knowledge about markets. EMCs often act as a division of the manufacturer, even utilizing its letterhead and negotiating with buyers on its behalf. They may also perform services such as billing and credit management, pricing, and complying with various trade restrictions. EMCs are particularly beneficial for small and medium-sized firms that are unable to launch an export program in-house. The obvious disadvantage of EMCs is that their compensation may substantially reduce profit margins for exporters.

A second class of indirect export agencies is Webb-Pomerene Associations (Webb-Pomerene Act of 1918), of which about 40 existed in the United States in the early 1990s. They are organizations comprised of competing U.S. manufacturers formed for the purpose of exporting. The benefit of the associations is that they are exempt from U.S. **antitrust laws**, including restrictions related to price setting, discounting, and sharing of customer information. Members may also combine efforts toward **market research**, product development, and distribution.

Export trading companies (ETCs), or American Trading Companies, were initiated in the United States in 1982 (Export Trading Company Act of 1982) by the federal government to help exporters compete against powerful Japanese trading conglomerates. ETCs provide many of the advantages of both EMCs and Webb-Pomerene Associations, but usually on a larger scale. Although ETCs were still in their infancy in the early 1990s, several major U.S. manufacturers, such as General Electric and Bank of America, were utilizing them effectively.

Another form of indirect export agency is the export commission house, or commission agent. Commission agents represent buyers in foreign countries. When the foreign buyer places an order, the commission agent solicits bids from domestic manufacturers. The agent usually awards the lowest bidder with the order and is compensated by the foreign buyer with a fee or commission. The advantage of this arrangement for the exporter is that payment is usually received almost immediately and there is very little effort required to complete the sale. However, the bidding process sometimes diminishes profit opportunities. An arrangement similar to the commission agent is the resident buyer, which differs in that resident buyers usually do not require bids. Instead, they build relationships with preferred suppliers and simply provide ongoing local representation for their foreign sponsor.

Among the many other forms of indirect trading agents, some of the most popular include: foreign freight forwarders, which simply manage overseas shipments of goods to foreign ports in return for a fee or product discount; brokers, which only bring buyers and sellers together and are removed from handling or distributing the exported goods; and export agents, who represent the manufacturer, act under their own name, and generally contract for two years or less.

INDIRECT MERCHANTS

Direct exporting occurs when an intermediary takes title to a company's products (or services) and trades the goods under its own name. A common indirect exporter of this type is the export merchant, which buys the goods and then resells them to its foreign contacts at a markup. Thus, the export merchant essentially acts in the same role as a domestic wholesaler. A class of export merchant is the export vendor, which specializes in purchasing surplus or poor quality goods that producers can't profitably sell domestically. Similarly, overseas military market representatives specialize in selling to U.S. military post exchanges around the world. The representatives typically buy in bulk from producers and receive commissions from the government.

Another means of indirect merchant exporting is **cooperatives**. Cooperative exporting, or piggybacking, takes place when a company with an established distribution channel for its own products contracts to export the goods of a noncompeting foreign manufacturer. For instance, a Japanese maker of consumer electronics might contract with a U.S. producer of home appliances to market and distribute its appliances in Japan. As another example, a U.S. producer of electronics that exports its goods to Europe may contract to market the same appliance manufacturer's wares through its established European channels.

DIRECT AGENTS

Several types of agents serve U.S.-based companies from foreign countries. Foreign sales representatives, for example, are paid by U.S. firms through commissions, work on a contract basis, and usually do not simultaneously represent competing products. The exporting firm may train the representative and supply him or her with literature with which to sell its goods. The exporter benefits from the representatives knowledge of, and access to, local markets.

Purchasing agents are similar to commission agents and resident buyers, described above. They are sent to a foreign country to purchase goods for a company or government in their homeland, and are paid fees or commissions by the foreign sponsor. They are different from commission agents in that they are sent for a short time period (to buy heavy equipment for a large project for instance) and then leave the United States.

DIRECT MERCHANTS

Direct merchant exporters are organizations in foreign countries that buy goods in the United States, or some other country, and then resell them domestically. Export distributors, for example, buy goods from U.S. manufacturers and resell them for a markup in their own country. They typically provide complementary services to their buyers, such as maintenance, parts sales, and technical assistance. The export distributor often has a close relationship with the exporter and secures exclusive rights to sell and service its goods.

Sometimes a U.S. exporter will sell its goods directly to a foreign retailer, such as a department store chain. The retailer may buy/order from catalogs or sales literature, or through an order taker representing the exporter. Similarly, export ''jobbers'' in foreign countries serve exporters by determining exact customer needs, buying the goods abroad, and then reselling to their customers.

BARTER TRADING

Although **barter**ing is not a distinctly different channel of exporting, it represents a departure from conventional indirect and direct exporting arrangements in that it does not involve the use of money. Instead, goods and services are traded for other goods and services in another nation. Such an arrangement may reduce trade barriers, minimize tax burdens, or result in a more lucrative swap for both parties. Although bartering has traditionally been utilized in command economies that discouraged the exchange of currency, it gained popularity in the 1980s and early 1990s in many free markets.

There are four primary forms of barter. ''Counterpurchase,'' or pure barter, arrangements entail an equal exchange between traders of goods. For instance, a timber manufacturer may trade logs for tractors of an equal value. ''Switch trading'' is similar to counterpurchase, but more parties are involved— Cash and goods are effectively exchanged between three or more parties until an equitable trade is achieved. A ''clearing agreement'' involves the long-term exchange of goods between two governments, and factors exchange rates into the value of the trade. It is useful for a trade in which one party receives goods long before the other party. Finally, in a ''buy-back barter'' a company buys capital equipment, such as an earth moving machine, through the output created by the equipment. For example, a coal mining firm might pay for its earth mover by supplying coal to the foreign heavy equipment manufacturer.

GOVERNMENT EXPORT BARRIERS AND SUPPORTS

Governments have erected a wide array of different barriers to the export and import of goods. The barriers are designed to serve a number of purposes, such as protecting specific industries, maintaining national employment levels, discouraging dumping of foreign products at prices below manufacturing cost, and improving the national trade balance. Despite an effort by the United States and several other nations to reduce trade barriers, many leading industrial countries, particularly Japan, sustain an intricate network of restrictions that severely impact the world export market.

The two major classes of trade restrictions are tariff and nontariff. Tariffs equate to duties that are imposed on goods leaving or coming into a country. In addition to the goals listed above, tariffs may be used to ensure that the prices of imported goods are equivalent to domestic substitutes, or simply to garner revenue for the government. In addition, tariffs are often used to penalize other countries for trade or political actions. The United States, for instance, may elect to impose a tariff on cars imported from France as a way of punishing France for erecting a large tariff on wine imported from the United States.

Nontariff barriers include restrictions such as quotas, taxes, and exchange rate controls. They can be classified into six major categories:

1) Specific trade limitations, such as quantity limits (quotas), price limits, embargoes, and license requirements;

2) customs and administrative entry restrictions, which encompass miscellaneous entry fees and documentation requirements;

3) standards, which generally include qualitative mandates related to safety, minimal quality standards, and packaging;

4) government participation, which refers to government buying policies, taxes, and export subsidies;

5) import charges, such as deposit requirements, administrative fees, and credit discrimination; and

6) miscellaneous categories, such as voluntary export agreements and formal agreements between trading partners.

Besides the mass of trade barriers, most governments also engage in various global export initiatives designed to foster free trade. The **General Agreement on Tariffs and Trade (GATT)**, for example, was agreed to by 117 nations in 1993. It effectively calls for a reduction of both tariff and nontariff barriers on a worldwide scale. It incorporates the United States' Most Favored Nation principal, which extends the best trade terms to all GATT members. Other recent agreements include: the Asian-Pacific Economic Cooperation Forum (APEC), signed in 1989: the **North American Free Trade Agreement (NAFTA)** of 1993; and the European Economic Community, or **Common Market**, which aims to eliminate trade barriers between member European nations. Other supranational supports include programs sponsored by political organizations, such as the **International Monetary Fund (IMF)**.

On the national level, most governments support specific industries or companies through: financial assistance, such as lower tax rates, **loans**, or even direct grants to companies that enter new overseas markets or export certain products; state-sponsored trading companies, like American Trading Companies; and government research and information services, particularly services that help exporters identify potential markets and the risks inherent to those markets.

SEE ALSO: Global Strategy

[Dave Mote]

FURTHER READING:

Branch, Alan E. *Elements of Export Marketing and Management*, 2nd ed. London: Chapman and Hall, 1990.

Jain, Subhash C. *International Marketing Management*. Boston: PWS-Kent Publishing Company, 1990.

Nagel, Jr., Walter H. and Gaston. *Export Marketing Handbook*. New York: Praeger, 1988.

Renner, Sandra L. and W. Gary Wingnet. *Fast-Track Exporting: How Your Company Can Succeed in the Global Market*. New York: AMACOM, 1991.

Sandhusen, Richard L. *Global Marketing*. Hauppauge, NY: Barron's Educational Series, Inc. 1994.

Terpstra, Vern. *International Marketing*, 4th ed. New York: The Dryden Press, 1987.

EXTERNALITIES

Externalities, or "spillover effects," are the effects of actions which are external to, or do not directly affect, the entity performing the act. These effects may be either positive or negative. Examples of negative externalities would be an increase in pollution because of a new **manufacturing** process, or increased traffic because of a plant expansion. The costs of the increased pollution, or of the increases in road maintenance, fuel costs, and lost time due to increased traffic, would not ordinarily be borne by the firm. Examples of positive externalities would include reductions in traffic from a city bus system, or a reduction in pollution due to a new manufacturing process. The savings in road maintenance, fuel costs, and time, and the benefits of reduced pollution, would not be captured by the bus system and the firm.

While externalities are easily overlooked, consideration of externalities is an important part of planning. First, while the planning entity may not be directly affected, there is often a change in goodwill (or badwill) toward the entity. This may cause an indirect or secondary effect, as the planning entity may face **boycotts** or decreased cooperation from the affected group. Second, externalities may lead to direct effects in the future. Examples are imposition of pollution reduction requirements, or an increase in **taxes** to offset external effects. Third, in some cases, the firm can recapture some of the externalities through bargaining with the affected parties, through such means as tax reduction or direct payments. Finally, examination of externalities is also important for ethical considerations. Goodwill or badwill aside, the adoption of a project which is profitable to the initiating entity may have effects on others which preclude its acceptance on ethical grounds.

Externalities have been described as market failure, and used to support an argument in favor of government intervention. These interventions may take the form of limitations or other regulations, such as limits on power plant sulfur emissions. **Subsidies**, such as tax reductions to attract new industries, are another form of intervention. This political approach is not favored by economists, who tend to suggest various market mechanisms to re-internalize externalities.

Externalities are often used to justify adoption of public projects such as the Tennessee-Tombigbee Waterway, or various space programs. It can be argued that for public entities there are no externalities, i.e., since the public entity exists for the good of all, all effects must be taken into account in public planning. In the example of the bus system, it would not be economically correct to shut down the system on the basis of the fares not covering the costs. Further, it would not be economically correct to simply set the fares on the basis of covering costs. The proper fare structure would instead be one which maximized the sum of all benefits to all citizens. If there are externalities, setting fares below cost to attract more users may be the best economic action.

[David E. Upton]

FURTHER READING:

Bromley, Daniel W. *Environment and Economy*. Basil Blackwell Ltd., 1991.

Cornes, Richard, and Todd Sandler. *The Theory of Externalities, Public Goods, and Club Goods*. Cambridge University Press, 1986.

Cowen, Tyler. *The Theory of Market Failure*. George Mason University Press, 1988.

F

FACILITY MANAGEMENT

Facility management encompasses all activities related to keeping a complex operating. Facilities include sports complexes, jails, office buildings, hospitals, hotels, retail establishments, and all other revenue-generating or government institutions. Responsibilities include providing janitorial services, security, engineering services, managing telecommunications and information systems, and many other duties. It is the job of the facility manager to create an environment that encourages productivity, is safe, is pleasing to clients and customers, meets government mandates, and is efficient.

Facility management has traditionally been associated with janitorial services, mailrooms, and security. Since the mid-1900s, though, facility management has evolved into a demanding discipline. Factors driving the complexity of the facility manager's job are numerous. For example, facilities have become much larger and more complicated, often relying on computerized and electronic support systems that require expertise to operate and repair. Furthermore, a newfound corporate cost-consciousness that emerged during the 1980s has generated an emphasis on operational efficiency.

In addition, a proliferation of government regulations and court decisions has forced facility managers to consider all kinds of factors related to handicapped access, hazardous materials (e.g. CFCs in the air-conditioning system), and legal liability for the safety of the people that enter the premises. Indeed, as government oversight at the federal, state, and local level

mushroomed between the 1960s and early 1990s, many establishments became overwhelmed by complex rules and restrictions. Almost every industry was barraged with a separate set of regulations aimed at its niche.

Hospitals, for example, were forced to comply with thousands of mandates related to waste disposal, malpractice liability and protection, and safety. But even general regulations that apply to all facilities have ballooned. Churches, schools, and factories alike must comply with stringent laws regarding staffing, employee and civil rights, patron and employee safety and comfort, recycling and energy conservation, and pension and health benefits. Adding to those are a profusion of environmental laws related to factors such as indoor air quality, grounds maintenance, and hazardous emissions.

The end result of new technology, efficiency pressures, and government regulations has been an expansion of the facility management role. Facility managers in the 1990s are often highly trained and educated and must wear several hats. Depending on the size of the complex, he (she) will likely be responsible for directing a facility management and maintenance staff(s). In addition to overseeing the important duties related to standard janitorial, mailroom, and security activities, he may also be responsible for providing engineering and architectural services, hiring subcontractors, maintaining computer and telecommunications systems, and even buying, selling, or leasing real estate or office space.

For example, suppose that a company has decided to consolidate five branch offices into a central computerized facility. It may be the facility manager's job to plan, coordinate, and manage the move. He may have to find the new space and negotiate a purchase. And he will likely have to determine which furniture and equipment can be moved to the new office, and when and how to do so with a minimal disruption of the operation. This may include negotiating prices for new furniture and equipment or balancing needs with a limited budget. The facility management department may also furnish engineering and architectural design services for the new space, and even provide input for the selection of new computer and information systems. Of import will be the design and implementation of various security measures and systems that reduce the risk of theft and ensure worker safety.

The manager will also be responsible for considering federal, state, and local regulations. For example, he will need to ensure that the complex conforms with strict new mandates imposed by the Americans with Disabilities Act (ADA) and the new Clean Air Act (CAA). The ADA dictates a list of requirements related to disabled employee and patron access with which most facilities must comply, and the CAA imposes standards for indoor air quality and hazardous emissions. Similarly, other laws regulate energy consumption (e.g. lighting systems), safety, smoking, and other factors that fall under the facility manager's umbrella of responsibility.

CONTRACT FACILITY MANAGEMENT

A facility manager may be an employee of the company which owns and operates a facility, or, as is increasingly the case, s/he may work for a specialized facility management company that operates the complex for the owner on a contract basis. The latter arrangement has become more common as the scope and complexity of facility management has exceeded the capability of building occupants. Companies that hire contract managers prefer to focus on other goals, such as producing a product or providing a service. Many of those firms find that outsourcing facility management duties to a specialist reduces costs and improves operations.

Contract facility managers may be hired to manage an entire complex or just one part of a large operation. For example, some companies hire contract managers that specialize in operating mailrooms or providing janitorial services. In any case, the company expects to benefit from the expertise of the manager it hires. A contractor that manages data processing systems, for example, may bring technical know-how that its employer would have great difficulty cultivating in-house. Likewise, a stadium owner that employees a facility manager specializing in the operation of sport complexes may benefit from the contractor's mix of knowledge related to groundskeeping, accounting and reporting, and sports marketing, among other functions.

Besides expertise and efficiency, several other benefits are provided by contract facility managers. For example, they reduce the owner's or occupant's liability related to personnel. By contracting a firm to manage one of its factories, for instance, an organization can substantially reduce headaches related to staffing, training, worker's compensation expenses and litigation, employee benefits, and worker grievances. It also eliminates general management and payroll responsibilities—rather than tracking hours and writing checks for an entire staff, it simply pays the facility management company. In addition, a company that hires a facility management firm can quickly reduce or increase its staff as it chooses without worrying about hiring or severance legalities. In other words, a large portion of the benefit provided by contract managers is not directly related to facilities management.

An example of a specialized facility manager is Wackenhut Corrections Corp., of Florida, which is a subsidiary of Wackenhut Corp. Established in the early 1980s, Wackenhut Corrections Corp. is a leading international provider of prison design, construction, and management services. It designs prison facilities, hires workers to staff them (including guards, social workers, doctors, and cooks) and manages inmate education programs, among other tasks. In 1994, Wackenhut managed 10 prisons in the U.S., two in Australia, and one in England.

[Dave Mote]

FURTHER READING:

Becker, Franklin. *The Total Workplace: Facilities Management and the Elastic Organization*. New York: Van Nostrand, 1990.

Cornacchia, Anthony J. ''Facility Management: Life in the Fast Lane,'' *The Office*. June, 1994.

Eyerdam, Rick. ''Wackenhut Goes Abroad for Prison Work,'' *South Florida Business Journal*. February 18, 1994.

Macknight, Diane. ''Facility Management in the'90s,'' *The Office*. January, 1993.

Managing the Office Building. Institute of Real Estate Management, 1985.

Sopko, Sandy. ''Smaller Staffs and Budgets Boost FM Outsourcing,'' *The Office*. August, 1993.

FACTOR ANALYSIS

Factor analysis is a statistical technique that is used to determine the extent to which a group of measures share common variance. Factor analysis is sometimes termed a *data reduction* technique because the method is frequently used to extract a few underlying components (or factors) from a large initial set of variables. It is extensively used in psychological research concerned with the construction of scales intended to measure attitudes, perceptions, motivations, and so forth. Business-related applications are numerous and examples include the development of scales used to measure customer satisfaction with products and employee work attitudes. Factor analysis, however, has applicability outside of the realm of psychological research. It may be used, for example, by financial analysts to identify groups of stocks in which prices fluctuate in similar ways. There are many different methods of factor analysis and the mathematical theory underlying it is quite complex. The basic elements of factor analysis, though, are relatively simple to understand.

An example of the use of factor analysis might involve research designed to construct a scale of employee job satisfaction. Initially, a researcher or consultant may assemble a large set of questionnaire items that seem to be related to job satisfaction. These items will generally be presented to subjects along with some type of numeric or verbal scale.

The job satisfaction questionnaire may include several dozen such questions. What is really of interest, however, are employee views regarding underlying dimensions of job satisfaction. Typically, there are only a few such dimensions, which are psychological states that cannot be directly measured Such dimensions are called *factors* and factor analysis is used to assess them indirectly.

In this case, the basic factor analysis model assumes that employee responses to each of the job satisfaction items in the questionnaire can be condensed into one or more underlying factors. Sometimes the researcher will have some expectation as to the number of factors, although such an assumption is not necessary. The factors are assumed to be related to the score of each item on the questionnaire in a linear manner. Suppose that a researcher thought that all of the answers to the job satisfaction items derived from two underlying factors, plus some random element (perhaps due to measurement error). If so, then a respondent's answer to a particular item could be decomposed into those basic factors according to the following equation: where: $score_i$ = subject's score on questionnaire item i; a_{1i} = coefficient relating factor 1 to $score_i$; $factor_1$ = value of the first factor for the subject; a_{2i} = coefficient relating factor 2 to $score_i$; $factor_2$ = value of the second factor for the subject; random = random error.

The underlying factors can be thought of as the subject's true feelings with respect to his or her job. The researcher, however, only has the subject's answers to specific questions regarding the characteristics of the employee's job. Since these are measured with some error, there is also a random component to the observed value. Separate equations can be written

for all of the items in the questionnaire. For each item, the coefficients (a_{1i} and a_{2i}) will probably be different. These coefficients are usually referred to as *factor loadings*. While the factors cannot be measured directly, it is possible to estimate factor loadings indirectly. Estimates of factor loadings are derived from the matrix containing the intercorrelations of all of the observed scores for a large number of subjects. Each subject in the sample answers all of the questionnaire items and the matrix contains all possible correlations between pairs of these items. The mathematics of this process is beyond the scope of this article (though is discussed in the references included at the end). Most general statistical programs, such as the *Statistical Package for the Social Sciences* (SPSS) contain factor analysis modules.

Factor analysis methods can extract as many or as few factors from a given correlation matrix as the researcher wishes. The researcher may have some predetermined notion of the number of factors that correspond to a particular set of items. In that case, the researcher would direct the program to extract that number of factors and examine the resulting pattern of factor loadings to see if these conformed to expectations. Alternatively, the researcher might not have strong expectations as to the number of underlying factors and may experiment with different numbers of factors until some configuration that makes sense emerges. The number of factors extracted cannot exceed the number of observed items. Since factor analysis is a data reduction technique, however, the number of factors extracted is normally much smaller than the number of observed items.

Unlike many other statistical methods, most approaches to factor analysis do not have tests of statistical significance that can be used to infer that the correct number of factors has been extracted. Consequently, the researcher must often rely on professional judgment in this process (although rules of thumb have been developed to aid in this process). In recent years, more sophisticated factor analysis methods have been developed that allow hypothesis testing, but these methods are only useful in certain cases. One such method is called *confirmatory factor analysis*.

The basic output from a factor analysis is a table listing all estimated factor loadings for all observed (measured) items. An example of a factor loading table in presented in Table A. The first column lists the observed items. In this case, these would be the employee's satisfaction with several aspects of the job (pay, fringe benefits, intellectual challenge, etc.). The second column gives factor loadings for Factor 1 and the third column gives factor loadings for Factor 2. There will be as many columns of factor loadings as there are factors extracted in the analysis. Factor analysis methods derive factor loadings in such a way that groups of variables that are highly interrelated tend to load on the same factor. Loadings are in the range −1.0 to 1.0 and the higher the absolute value of a loading, the more closely linked an observed item is to a factor.

The observed pattern of factor loadings in generally used as a way of interpreting the underlying factors. This pattern will depend on a number of decisions made by the researcher, including the number of factors extracted and the factor extraction methods specified. Usually, factor loadings of greater than .70 (or less than −.70) are considered indicative of a close association between a factor and an observed item. In the hypothetical example, relatively strong factor loadings are highlighted. Factor 1 appears to be associated mainly with the economic aspects of the job, while Factor 2 is associated mainly with the job's more intrinsic qualities. This may lead the researcher to conclude that there are two principal dimensions to employee job satisfaction and name the factors accordingly.

It is also possible to estimate the proportion of variance in an observed item that is explained by underlying factors. This is called an item's communality. Of course, some variables may fall through the cracks. This is the case with "level of stress," which loads weakly with both factors. The communality of the stress variable is also going to be low. The researcher might conclude that stress represents an independent dimension and exclude it from the analysis.

One of the most important aspects of factor analysis is that the technique is widely used in developing scales and can serve to establish both scale reliability and validity. Once the factors have been extracted, further mathematical techniques can be used to compute *factor score coefficients*. These are weights that are applied to scores of the observed items to construct scales that correspond to the underlying factors. A simple scale could be constructed by adding a group of items together (for example, the items that define the first factor). Implicitly, that approach assumes each item has a weight of 1.0. Factor analysis is more precise and weights an item in proportion to its importance in defining a factor. The technique helps establish scale reliability; items with low communalities are generally removed from the analysis, as they do not contribute to scale reliability. Finally, if factor loading patterns conform to expectations, this helps to establish the construct validity of the scale.

[John J. Lawler]

FURTHER READING:

Kim, Jae-on, and Charles W. Muller. *Factor Analysis: Statistical Methods and Practical Issues*. Beverly Hills, CA: Sage Publications, 1978.

Norusis, Marija J. *SPSS for Windows: Professional Statistics (Release 6.0)*. Chicago: SPSS, Inc., 1993.

Overall, John W., and C. James Klett. *Applied Multivariate Analysis*. New York: McGraw-Hill, 1972.

FACTORING

Obtaining secured short-term **credit** involves offering specific **assets** of the firm as collateral to protect the lender in the event of loan **default**. Because accounts receivable are among the most liquid of all the firms assets lenders consider them to be an attractive form of collateral for a secured loan. The two primary methods for obtaining short-term credit using accounts receivable as collateral are pledging or factoring. If receivables are pledged, they are used as collateral for a loan arrangement. In this arrangement, the receivables are still the property of the firm, and it is the firm which evaluates the quality of a proposed credit and either accepts or rejects. There are two essential differences between pledging and factoring. First, when receivables are factored they are actually sold to the "factor." Second, the factor normally assumes the credit evaluation role, in effect serving as the credit department of the borrowing firm. An example of factoring is the use of a credit card, in which the credit card issuer becomes the owner of the receivable. There are a wide variety of arrangements within this basic framework.

TIME OF CASH FLOW

In maturity factoring the firm does not receive the proceeds until the normal time of collection, or at specified periods. In this case the factor is providing a credit service only. An alternative arrangement is advance factoring. In advance factoring the factor provides a line of credit for the firm. This line of credit has a limit that is typically 80% of the value of the factored receivables, so as to provide a cushion against uncollectible accounts.

NOTIFICATION AND RECOURSE

Under factoring, the customer customarily, but not always, receives notification of the sale of the receivable. In many cases the customer is instructed to remit directly to the factor, rather than to the firm itself. Factoring may occur with or without recourse. Factoring with recourse means that the firm is ultimately responsible for the payment of the receivable, and must pay for uncollectible receivables. Factoring without recourse means that the factor takes full responsibility for collection, with the firm having no obligation to make good on the receivable.

COSTS OF FACTORING

Factoring is generally considered an expensive source of cash. The factor charges a fee for the credit appraisal which may range from 1 to 3 percent of the amount of the receivable. There is also a factoring fee for the accepted credits, and this may be 1 or 2 percent on a monthly basis. The advance is in the form of a loan ranging 2 to 4 percent above the **prime rate**, if advance factoring is used.

ADVANTAGES OF FACTORING

Factoring has a number of advantages which may offset its high cost, particularly for smaller firms. The firm avoids the necessity to maintain a credit department, and the function may be more effectively handled by an experienced factor. It is not surprising that factoring is widely used in international trade, where smaller firms might find the credit function prohibitively expensive or overly risky.

[David Upton]

FAIR LABOR STANDARDS ACT OF 1938 (FLSA)

The Fair Labor Standards Act of 1938 (FLSA) is one of the landmark pieces of legislation of President Franklin Delano Roosevelt's New Deal. Provisions of the FLSA established for the nation a minimum Wage, a maximum number of hours for the work week, set standards for wage and hour record keeping, and forbade the employment of children. The law applied then—as it does now—to employees of firms whose business operations span the borders of more than one state (engage in interstate commerce) and whose business operations are of a certain size, or whose employer is a public agency.

The constitutional basis for allowing federal regulation of work in private industry at this level is based on the ability of the federal government to regulate interstate commerce. The original provisions of the bill provided for a 25 cents per hour minimum wage and limited the work week to 44 hours per week and did not apply to public agencies. In 1940 the work week was reduced to its current 40 hours per week by an amendment to the FLSA. The FLSA set standards for the payment of overtime and for wage and hour record keeping by employers.

The Act also banned (and still does) the **employment** of minor children under the age of fourteen except for agriculture and some theatrical and family business exceptions. Children under eighteen are banned from taking any job deemed "hazardous," including mining and certain factory jobs.

The FLSA has been amended more than twenty times since its inception. Many of those amendments simply raised the minimum wage. Others, such as the Equal Pay Act of 1963, extended the scope of the law's protections. The provisions of the Equal Pay Act, according to WH publication 1282, "prohibit wage differentials based on sex, between men and women employed in the same establishment, on jobs which require equal skill, effort, and responsibility, and which are performed under similar working conditions."

Today the FLSA affects over 80 million full-time and part-time workers in the private sector and in federal, state, and local governments. Coverage, as stated in U.S. Department of Labor publication WH 1318, revised August 1991, extends to all employees of certain enterprises having workers engaged in interstate commerce, producing goods for interstate commerce or handling, selling, or otherwise working on goods or materials that have been moved in or produced for such commerce by any person. Those enterprises included are those whose related activities are performed through a unified operation or common control by person(s) for a common business purpose and whose gross volume of sales is not less than $500,000; those engaged in the operation of a hospital; or those whose activity is that of a public agency.

In 1981, for the first time, the FLSA recognized a "training" wage, setting forth a strict set of criteria which must be met before this wage—which is below the minimum wage—may be paid in lieu of the minimum wage. Special situations which may apply to learners, apprentices, students, and handicapped workers are covered in section 14 of the FLSA. Employers wishing to use this provision must apply to the U.S. Department of Labor for a certificate of exemption (except for institutions of higher education). Special rules also apply to state and local governments, employment involving volunteers, compensatory time in lieu of cash overtime pay, and jobs where tips are calculated as part of the wages.

Enforcement of the FLSA, with a few exceptions, is a part of the responsibility of the U.S. Department of Labor's Employment Standards Administration, Wage-Hour Division. These Wage-Hour investigators have the authority to take complaints, conduct investigations, and gather data on wages, hours, and other employment practices and conditions to determine compliance with the FLSA. If violations are found, they may also recommend changes in employment practices and recommend fines in addition to repayment of wages lost.

The amendments of 1985 brought legal protection from job discrimination and firing for those who bring complaints against their employers under the FLSA.

The Equal Pay Act of 1963 prohibited **discrimination** in the payment of wages by employers subject to the FLSA on the basis of sex. The enforcement of this part of the Act was transferred from the U.S. Department of Labor to the **Equal Employment Opportunity Commission (EEOC)** in 1979.

The Wage-Hour Division has many local offices. To obtain information or to file a complaint, look for the Wage and Hour Office under the U.S. Government Heading, Department of Labor, in your local telephone book to determine if there is an office in your immediate area. More detailed information on the Fair Labor Standards Act of 1938 and its amendments, and the location of Wage-Hour field offices may be obtained by writing to: U.S. Department of Labor, 200 Constitution Ave. NW, Washington, DC 20210, c/o Wage-Hour Division. Request WH publication #1282, revised May 1992 for general information on the FLSA. Sensory impaired individuals may contact the Wage-Hour Division by calling Voice phone (202) 219-8743 or for TDD Phone, 1-800-326-2577.

SEE ALSO: Child Labor, Compensation Administration, Sex Discrimination

[Joan Leotta]

FURTHER READING:

WH Publication 1282, U.S. Department of Labor, May 1992.

FAMILY LEAVE

In the latter half of the twentieth century, the American family and the American workforce underwent two changes that impacted the workplace significantly. The cost of living rose dramatically, making it more and more common for both parents to work outside of the home, and the family became less likely to be comprised of two parents, working or nonworking. Where one adult headed a household, that adult worked. In addition, these adults became increasingly responsible not only for the care of young children, but also for the care of older adults—those over age 55. These shifting family responsibilities impacted the workforce in terms of scheduling to spend more time with children and older adults, especially when one of the persons being cared for by a worker became ill. While most workplaces offered paid sick leave for illnesses of the worker, few offered any kind of assistance when a worker had to take off time to tend to the needs of another family member.

"Family leave" is the term applied to leave taken for the care and assistance of another member of the family or a person in the care of the family. The term itself does not imply anything about the pay status of this leave. In other words, the leave may be paid or unpaid, nor does it imply a reason for taking the leave—such as pregnancy, maternity leave, care for the elderly, adjustment to adoption, etc.

In the 1980s many employers saw the need for the workplace to adapt to the changing circumstances of the American family. Some employers built on-site day care centers for children and even for the elderly. Employers began to experiment with alternative work programs such as job sharing, flextime, flexi-place, and other arrangements that would allow employees to deal more conveniently with personal responsibilities without taking time from the workday. Unions negotiated further arrangements including the right to take large blocks of unpaid time off with the guaranteed right to return. This concept of taking time off from work to meet emergencies and be guaranteed a right to return to one's job became more important in the tight economy of the late 1980s and early 1990s when finding a new job was becoming increasingly difficult. More employees wanted this right and finally, Congress passed a law putting these rights "on the books" for the majority of public and private employees.

The Family and Medical Leave Act of 1993 (FMLA) is a landmark piece of legislation designed to resolve the gap between the needs of the U.S. workforce and the development of high performance, economically healthy workplace organizations. FMLA entitles eligible employees in the private and public sectors to take up to 12 weeks of unpaid job-protected leave each year for law-specified family and medical reasons. One of the key provisions of the bill is that during the time of unpaid leave, the employer maintains any pre-existing health insurance under any group health plan for the duration of the leave and at the level and under the same conditions that the coverage was provided prior to the commencement of the leave. The law is administered and enforced by the Wage and Hour Division (WH) of the U.S. Department of Labor's Employment Standards Administration.

According to WH publication 1421, "The FMLA is intended to balance the demands of the workplace with the needs of families. . . ." The need for such a law has been documented in many ways. Fact Sheet No. 86-4 from October 1986 documents the role of the working American woman in the care of children and the elderly. Fact Sheet 93-2 on American Women Workers documents that in 1992 women represented nearly 45 percent of all persons in the civilian labor force in the United States. Working wives contribute substantially to family income. In March of 1992, according to the U.S. Department of Labor, 59 percent of wives in married couple families were in the workforce. In 1991 the median income for families with the wife in the labor force was $48,169 and for families without the wife in the paid labor force, the income was $30,075. Women who maintain families alone had the lowest median income ($16,692) of any group in the labor force.

Of the 34 million women who had children under the age of 18 in March of 1992, 67 percent were in the labor force. 58 percent of the 9.6 million women with children under the age of six were in the workforce in March of 1992. At the same time there was a great growth in the number of elderly who needed care. The Department of Labor figures showed that overwhelmingly it was the women who gave care, despite or in addition to their participation in the workforce. The Department of Labor Fact Sheet 86-4 reports:

> Those caring for functionally impaired elderly family members are predominantly females, with adult daughters providing 29 percent of the long term care and wives providing 23 percent. Three-fourths of the caregivers live with the care recipient and the majority provide assistance seven days a week, an average of four hours a day. About one-fourth of the daughters and one-third of the other female care givers have competing family obligations. . . . The burden for workers responsible for both children and elderly relatives, however, is expected to be especially great in the years of the next century when the baby boom cohort largely constitute the members of the elderly population. Many persons then ages 45-49 will have to support both an aged parent or parents often over 70 years and children of college age or younger.

One of the salient points of the FMLA is that it applies to both males and females, recognizing the fact that while by tradition the responsibilities fall more often on the female there are certainly many cases in which the male is the caregiver and some in which the male would like to be the caregiver. The right to take leave under FMLA applies equally to male and female workers.

Coverage is not universal and the right to take up to 12 weeks of unpaid leave does not apply to all circumstances, only to 'legitimate' reasons as recognized by the FMLA. The FMLA provides that when the cause of the leave is "foreseeable", as in the birth or adoption of a child, the employee must give the employer at least 30 days notice. The employer, under some circumstances, has the right to include paid leave days as part of FLMA leave. It must also be noted that if a State's benefits are more generous than those of the FMLA, then the State's benefits supersede those of the FMLA. Fact Sheet 93-1 notes: "The Act does not supersede any State or local, collective bargaining agreement, or employment benefit plan providing greater employee family leave rights, nor does it diminish the capacity to adopt more generous family leave policies."

Not everyone is entitled to apply for leave under the FMLA. Teachers are subject to special rules when leave coincides with the end of a school term. A husband and wife who are working for the same firm cannot each take 12 weeks of leave; they must split the time except in cases of rare illness in the immediate family. The highest paid 10 percent of a company's salaried employees may be denied job restoration. An employer can require a person to provide an additional medical opinion from its own physician list about the need for leave. If for some reason a person decides not to return to the job after the leave, the employer has the right to bill for the cost of all of the health benefits paid during the absence.

The law excludes any persons employed at a worksite that has fewer than 50 employees, if the total number of persons employed by the employer within 75 miles of the worksite is fewer than 50.

The law also specifies the way in which leave may be taken. It may be taken intermittently or on a schedule that reduces the usual number of hours per workday, subject to employer approval.

Public and private sector employees eligible for the leave must have been employed by the employer for one year and have worked at least 1,250 hours. The 12 weeks of leave may be taken only once in any 12 month period. The law specifies that a leave may be taken for these reasons: birth or adoption of a child; acquiring a foster child; the serious illness of a child, spouse, or parent, and the serious illness of the employee.

Employee rights are enforceable through civil actions. Complaints of violations must be brought to the attention of the Department of Labor no later than two years after the date of the last event constituting the alleged violation or within three years of the last event if the violation is willful. Complaints are filed with the Department of Labor's Employment Standards Administration (ESA). The many local offices of the Wage and Hour Division of ESA may be found in the local telephone directory under Labor Department in the section of the telephone book that contains Federal Government phone numbers or may be obtained by writing to the U.S. Department of Labor Wage and Hour Division.

Both employers and employees wishing to know more about the Act should contact the U.S. Department of Labor, Office of the Secretary, NW Washington, DC and request Fact Sheet 93-1 of the Women's Bureau and WH Publication 1421, Compliance Guide to the Family and Medical Leave Act printed in June 1993.

[Joan Leotta]

FAMILY-OWNED BUSINESSES

Family-owned businesses are recognized today as an important and distinct organization in the world economy. Family-owned businesses now operate in every country and may be the oldest form of business organization, only within the last decade have their unique benefits been identified and studied. Family businesses have been described as unusual business entities due to their concern for the long term over generations, their strong commitment to quality which usually stands behind their own family name, and their humanity in the workplace where the care and concern for employees is often likened to that of an extended family.

Recognizable businesses which are still managed by a family member today include: Benneton, Beretta, Estee Lauder Inc., Tootsie Roll, Playboy, Gucci, Carnival Cruise Lines, Harley-Davidson, Inc., U-Haul, Ford Models, Forbes Inc., and Ford Motor Co. They vary widely in regards to the overlap of family and business issues, and much can be learned from studying their experiences.

Family businesses provide the only setting for an unusual social phenomenon, the overlap of family issues and business issues. The family business offers two separate but connected systems of family and business with uncertain boundaries, different rules, and differing roles. Family businesses may include numerous combinations of family and business, including husbands and wives, parents and children, extended families, and multiple generations in roles of stockholders, board members, working partners, advisors, and employees.

The two systems in a family business, described as the interaction of two separate but connected systems, are often shown as two overlapping circles depicting the unclear boundaries of family and business. (See Figure 1).

THE PROS AND CONS OF FAMILY BUSINESS

Family businesses provide a number of advantages to family members with the most common being freedom, independence, and control. In addition, they also offer many lifestyle benefits such as flexibility, prestige, community pride, and creativity. Family businesses normally provide for closer contact with management, are less bureaucratic, have a built-in trust factor with established relationships, and provide for hands-on training and early exposure of the next generation to the business.

On the other hand, family businesses also bring a unique set of challenges. Family businesses are often recognized in the popular press as a source of difficulty when it comes to succession issues, identity development, and sibling relationships. Succession is one of the largest challenges facing family businesses and in most cases the process is resisted. Succession becomes an issue when the senior generation does not allow the junior generation the necessary room to grow, effectively develop, and eventually assume the leadership of the business. Often business relationships among siblings or between parent and child deteriorate due to an underlying difficulty in communication within the family. This behavior erupts into criticism, judgments, conservatism, lack of support, and lack of trust which often affect the business.

ROLES IN THE FAMILY BUSINESS

The most successful families in business have clearly defined roles and responsibilities for individuals in the family and in the business. Most often these roles have fallen along gender lines. The most common form of family business is one in which a husband and wife are both involved. Often the business is referred to as ''his'' business and the wife sees her role as ''helping out.'' Women are often in the office, on the computer, or doing the bookkeeping and have been described as ''invisible.'' These same women, however, often become ''instant entrepreneurs'' when their husbands are ill or die, or an economic crisis forces them to assume the husbands' role.

The role of a father who is also the boss of his children is more often a difficult one to balance. One father shared the story about his second son who was always late for work and provided a bad example for other employees. He called him aside one day and said, ''Son, as your boss, I have to tell you, 'you're

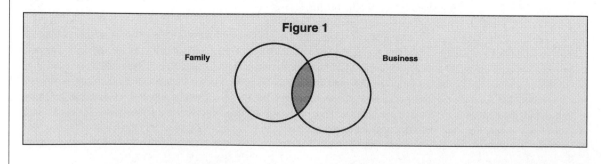

Figure 1

Family   Business

fired!' and as your father, 'I am sorry to learn you have just been fired.' "

Research indicates adult children describe their fathers as bosses in many different ways. One son's statement relates the patterns that repeat in families and therefore carry over to the business, "I'm stubborn just like him, and it is like looking in a mirror." In the ideal case, the father serves as a role model and trainer for the next generation. He treats both his sons and daughters equally and exposes them to various aspects of the business. He listens to their ideas and lets them make their own mistakes. He views the business as a team project rather than an individual effort and turns over the leadership reins before the children are thirty-five.

Mothers are influential whether they work in the business or not, and their roles need to be recognized. Traditionally mothers have worked behind the scenes supporting their husbands and maintaining the home. The changing roles of women have brought them challenges when trying to balance home and business. One woman said she wished she was more like Mrs. Cleaver, which seemed to reflect her confusion about not being a mother like her own, yet also not being comfortable in a leadership role in a business. Often women do not get equal credit in the role they choose. Just like the case of the fathers, these roles also carry over into the next generation and influence both daughters and sons.

Brothers and sisters usually disagree in their views of their mother, but agree in their views of their father. This might be explained by the fact that fathers are seen primarily as the leaders in the business, while the mothers play a variety of roles, and sons and daughters describe the role they are most comfortable with. For example, one son describes his mother as always being at home for him, while the daughter described her active role in the business.

FAMILY BUSINESSES AS A TRAINING GROUND

Perhaps the best job training programs throughout history have been family businesses. Research indicates that over two-thirds of all people starting businesses today grew up in a family business environment. Many share stories from as early as three years old when they stayed at the family store, rode on the delivery trucks, or went to visit customers with their parents. This early exposure enables them to hear, see, observe, and absorb the business environment. This experience can teach children about the value of money, customer relations, dealing with employees, and how an organization operates.

A number of factors have been found which predispose children to be interested in the family busi-

ness. The first is time spent with their father in the business. Most family businesses currently operating in the United States were started after World War II and most were founded by men. As more women start businesses, children will also benefit in business from spending time with their mother.

Exposure to various aspects of the business positively affects children. As they grow they assume new and varied roles, developing skills in the business as they take on each new role. With encouragement and a positive attitude from the parents about the business, their interest is heightened. Along the way, as children work in the family business, their individual contribution to the team needs to be recognized on a regular basis.

Lastly, an opportunity to join the company needs to be presented to the children as a career option. Not all children will join the family business, but they should know how to fully take advantage of the opportunity if they so choose. Throughout this training process children and parents who see each other as peers have an optimal relationship.

Daughters have special needs when it comes to developing as leaders in family businesses. They normally spend less time in the business, develop fewer skills, and face a major obstacle right from the start in family businesses because fathers typically consider sons and not daughters to be successors. The process of preparing daughters to join the business is often overlooked. A report from the family business workshops held at Wharton School of Business over a three year period showed that among female Wharton business students, only 27 percent planned to enter the family business and only 22 percent studied business in college.

Research shows a number of surprising factors which influence the leadership interest of women. Women show an interest in leading the family business when their brothers are not strong leaders, when they do not have a spouse or children of their own, and when they are asked by the father to join the company. Women are found to be held back from leading the company when they lack skills and knowledge, experience constraints from their own family, or have little encouragement from their father or husband. Women who are not at all interested in the family business have not developed an identity in the business, have found better opportunities elsewhere or are dependent on their spouse to satisfy their financial needs.

When it comes to sons, researchers found that the quality of the work relationship between fathers and sons varies as a function of their respective life stages. When sons are between 17 and 22, and they are in the process of establishing identity and separating from the family, poor communication is common. At this time, the father is in his forties and is also re-establishing his identity and appraising his life. Here fathers want to give their life meaning and exert power and control, which is the opposite of what the sons need at this time. As the father reaches his fifties, and the son matures from 23 to 33, the father has become less competitive and with his experience he may have the inclination to teach. Sons during this time feel an urgency to focus their lives and settle in, reappraising the past and considering the future. They strive for competence, and desire recognition and advancement. By 40 the goals of competence, recognition, advancement, and security become pressing, and the son struggles with authority if the father is still involved in the business. The father, in his sixties, is reminded about retirement and often death, which leads to a problematic relationship should he try to hang on to the business. There are numerous cases of sons in their fifties with fathers in their seventies and eighties who still are in control of the family business. This becomes a mistake for both individuals as well as the business.

Sibling relationships in the family business are important since these are the vehicles by which social skills are learned, and siblings often go on to work together. These relationships play a significant part in identity development, yet research is sparse in this general area. Sibling accommodation in the family business occurs when they agree on their relative positions of responsibility and power.

EXTENDED FAMILY

Extended family members can have a wide range of roles in the family business. Family businesses become more complicated in multiple generations when all of the family members stay involved in some manner. For example, a husband and wife start a business and involve their three children. These three children have six children each for a total of 18. These 18 have a total of 29 children between them. Within 50 years over 50 direct decedents could now have involvement, and that does not include in-laws.

In-laws are controversial in family businesses. Some businesses have a rule not to involve in-laws in either ownership or management, others involve them to varying degrees. In either case it is best to have clearly defined rules when it comes to the role and responsibility of in-laws, and clear expectations of the consequences of a death, divorce or involvement of the children. In one case, the son-in-law was asked to stay on in a management capacity in the business after the daughter divorced him, which caused friction between the father and his daughter for the next 20 years.

THE PLANNING PROCESS

Planning is more crucial to family business than to other types of businesses because most families have a majority of their assets tied up in their business. Estate planning becomes essential and is intertwined with succession planning, business planning, and family planning.

ESTATE PLANNING. Estate planning involves the financial and tax aspects of the company. Families plan to minimize taxes at the time of the owners death so the resources can stay within the company. Tax laws today provide disincentives for families wishing to continue the business.

BUSINESS PLANNING. Business planning often guides the entire planning process and sets the agenda for the future regarding operations of the business. This process is often overseen by a board of directors, an advisory board, or professional advisors. Owners must ask themselves where they want the company to be in 5, 10, or 20 years, including the level of family involvement. Owners often have a mental picture of this, but unless a business plan for financing purposes is necessary, it is usually not down on paper.

SUCCESSION PLANNING. Succession planning is a long process that owners normally wait too long to address. The grooming and training and development of talent in the next generation should start in the preadolescent years.

Most family businesses do not have a succession plan. This becomes crucial in the event of a sudden death. Often the remaining family members do not know where to begin to pick up the pieces. This is the reason most family businesses do not succeed to the next generation. The issues involved in succession are too numerous to leave to chance, and without planning, it is likely the family will not remain involved.

The lack of planning, particularly in first to second generation businesses, is often the fault of the founder himself. Usually the business is such an extension of his life that he has few outside interests and can not imagine letting go of the helm. As a result his business dies with him. Others who recognize these issues too late in life hastily turn over the business to an ill prepared child, only to have him fail.

FAMILY PLANNING. Family planning takes into account the needs and interests of all family members involved with the business. The formation of a group called a family council often guides the communication process between family members and management. They address issues such as rules for entry, conduct, and community relations.

SYSTEMS FOR PLANNING IN THE FAMILY-OWNED BUSINESS

There are numerous systems which can aid planning in the family-owned business. Estate planning is normally handled by a team of professional advisors which includes a lawyer, accountant, financial planner, insurance agent, and perhaps a family business consultant. Estate planning normally begins with the success of the enterprise and is continually updated as the business and family change.

A professional family business consultant can be a tremendous asset when confronting these planning issues. The consultant is a neutral party who can stabilize the emotional forces within the family and bring the expertise of working with numerous families across many industries. Most families believe theirs is the only company facing these difficult issues, and a family business consultant brings a refreshing perspective. He or she can be involved at many levels, including working through the succession process. This may involve a variety of issues, such as training the children, selecting a successor, involving non-family management, and facilitating the transition process. In addition, the family business consultant can establish a family council and advisory board and serve as a facilitator to those two groups.

Often the firms attorney and accountant may see planning problems coming, are not prepared to face them directly for many reasons. Some do not feel they have the specialized understanding of family dynamics and others fear they could lose a client when dealing with sensitive issues. Instead, they may make the recommendation to bring in an outside family business consultant for an interim period of time.

A family council is a system which encourages family involvement and communications. It allows for a regular meeting where family members can voice their opinions and plan for the future in a structured way. Ultimately a more organized and strengthened family will emerge. Children gain a better understanding of the opportunities in the business, learn about managing resources, and inherit values and traditions. Conflicts can be discussed and settled.

Topics brought to family councils can include: rules for joining the business, treatment of family members working and not working in the business, role of in-laws, evaluations and pay scales, stock ownership, ways to provide financial security for the senior generation, training and development of the junior generation, image in the community, philanthropy, opportunities for new businesses, and diverse interests among family members.

These family meetings evolve and change as the business evolves. A businesses in the first generation usually only involves a nuclear family, whereas, a business in the second generation with a sibling team faces additional issues of family harmony, equal treatment, and the involvement of multiple children in the business. A family business in its third generation or beyond may include cousins, in-laws, and family members not working in the business. Issues in this case become much more complicated and may include commitment, traditions, community image, and resource allocation.

Family members who participate in family councils find it a good forum to voice their opinions. They feel more like a team, and they see progress being made. Leadership of the family council can be on a rotating basis, and the family business consultant may leave the facilitating role once the forum is well established and emotions are under control. Stepping out too early, however, can lead to a collapse of the entire system.

Advisory boards can be established to advise the president or board of directors. These boards consist of five to nine non-family members who meet regularly to provide advise and direction to the company. They too can take the emotions out of the planning process and provide objective input. Advisory board members should have business experience and the capabilities of assisting the business to get to the next level of growth. For example, a company now doing five million dollars in annual sales should seek advisors who have experience with seven to ten million dollar companies. In most cases, the advisory board is compensated in some manner.

As the family business grows, the family business consultant may suggest many different options for the family. Often professional non-family managers or an outside CEO are recruited to play a role in the future growth of the business. Some families operate with few or no family members in the business and simply retain ownership. The family can retain ownership by serving on the board of directors or setting up a holding company which may manage several companies and investments for the family.

One second generation family in the steel business recognized a declining market for their product and decided to sell off their divisions and liquidate the remaining assets. The dollars generated from this process led to the sibling team staying together and forming an investment company. Today they are in the business of buying other family businesses and putting in professional managers to operate them. They now manage eight such companies in a variety of industries throughout the United States.

THE FUTURE OF FAMILY BUSINESSES

Family businesses will continue to play a greater and greater role in world economies into the next century. They will become more recognized as business organizations, and studied and written about even more. Schools and colleges will recognize the family business as a career option of choice and provide direction and resources for students to pursue opportunities there.

Over fifty percent of the family businesses in the United States think their businesses will be owned and managed by two or more of their children, so the future looks bright. Even in Eastern Europe entrepreneurs are emerging and rekindling family businesses of years ago. They are starting family businesses for the next generation, and others are using family support systems to launch new enterprises. In Italy, family businesses are so common that the Chamber of Commerce tracks each family member and their position in the firm along with the traditional business information which is regularly collected. Asians have a legacy of passing on the family traditions in business and all working together with a central business focus. The next century will bring more research on how ethnicity affects families in business.

RESOURCES

There are a growing number of resources now available to families in business. The Family Firm Institute is a group of close to 1000 professional advisors serving the field. Located in Boston, they publish a free directory (617-738-1591). The Family Business Network is headquartered in Switzerland and holds an annual convention (41 21 6180335).

University programs which include credit and non-credit activities are now available at over fifty institutions. They are normally offered through the Business Department or Department of Continuing Education. The following educational products are also available:

Family Business Leadership Series, Craig Aronoff and John Ward, Business Owner Resources, Georgia, 1993. (Includes booklets on Succession, Family Meetings, Preparing Successors, Working Together, and Compensation)

[Cynthia Iannarelli]

FURTHER READING:

Benson, Benjamin. *Your Family Business*. Homewood, IL: Business One Irwin, 1990.

Carver, John. *Boards that Make a Difference*. San Francisco: Jossey Bass, 1990.

Cohn, Mike. *Passing the Torch*. New York: McGraw Hill, 1992.

Danco, Leon. *Beyond Survival*. Cleveland, OH: Center for Family Business, 1982.

Hausner, Lee, and Jermey Tarcher. *Children of Paradise*. 1990.

Jaffe, Dennis. *Working with the Ones You Love*. Emeryville, CA: Conari, 1990.

Lea, James. *Keeping it in the Family*. NY: John Wiley and Sons, 1991.

Poza, Ernesto. *Smart Growth*. San Francisco: Jossey Bass, 1989.

FASCISM

The term ''fascism'' characterizes any movement, ideology or government that advocates extreme nationalism, hatred of one or more minorities, a distrust of democracy, the subordination of the individual to the government or state, and force as a legitimate means to achieve its ends. In economic terms, fascism can be understood to mean economic self-sufficiency (or autarky), a distrust of foreign trade and foreign investment, and government control (but not ownership) of the economy to achieve political goals. Like **communism**, fascism is considered to be ''totalitarian'' in that fascist ideologies, as well as the proponents of fascism, advocate a system of government that is all controlling and that suppresses dissent of all kinds, usually by forceful means.

Fascism is a phenomenon of the twentieth century. Certainly throughout history, fascist elements have been evident (the use of force to achieve political ends, suppression of dissent and minorities, and the subordination of the individual to the state). However, not until the twentieth century did it become possible for a political party or dictator to exercise total control, thanks to modern communications and rapid transportation. A fascist movement or government attempts to harness extreme nationalism to gain followers or to stay in power. The love of one's country, rather than of the region in which one was born and raised, is also a modern phenomenon linked to the development of modern means of transportation and communication.

While modern fascism first appeared in Western Europe because it was the most highly developed area of the world, fascism was by no means confined to Europe. The most advanced country in Asia, Japan, would also succumb to fascist control in the 1930s. Fascism, of course, did not gain widespread popularity in all highly developed countries. Fascist ideas, which negate the individual and are anti-democratic, gained widespread popularity in countries where democracy and democratic traditions were weak or non-existent. Moreover, fascism became popular at time of great national suffering. Italy was the first country in history to succumb to a fascist government during the political and economic chaos in the aftermath of World War I. In Germany, the Nazis came to power in 1933, at the height of the Depression. The fascists in both Italy and Germany accomplished what the previous liberal, parliamentary governments in both countries had seemed incapable of doing: restored order, brought back prosperity to the businessmen whose businesses had failed, and gave full employment to previously unemployed workers. In both Italy, Germany and Japan, democratic traditions were weak, so the satisfied businessmen and workers ignored the price they paid for a return to order and prosperity: government control of the economy, the subordination of the individual to the state, and the government's suppression of political and civil liberties. The fascists' glorification of the nation plunged Italy, Germany and Japan into World War II, which brought tremendous suffering to their citizens.

Both communism and fascism are modern phenomena, and during World War II, communists and fascists were on opposite sides. Despite theoretical differences, in practice both are totalitarian (hence, anti-democratic), nationalistic, and advocate the use of force to achieve political ends. The principal difference between a communist and fascist government is the degree of control over the economy: in a communist state, the government is the owner of all means of production; in a fascist state, business remains in private hands, but private enterprise is severely circumscribed. In Italy, the first country to succumb to fascist control, the government organized a system of 22 state ''corporations'' that enabled the government to serve as a watchdog over the workers, businessmen, and industrialists. Inefficient industries often were propped up by government support, and goods in Italy were often shoddy. In Nazi Germany, when the first Volkswagens (or ''People's Car,'' to emphasize that this was an automobile that every worker could afford) rolled off the assembly lines in the 1930s, all of them went to the use of the army. The Volkswagen factories were privately owned, but the government determined the output and market, set prices and wages, and in both Italy and Germany, forbade trade unions and strikes, similar to the World War I years. In Germany, military spending leaped 60 percent in only three years (1935-1938), and government functionaries set economic targets according to ''four year'' plans. Incidentally, German fascists inserted the word ''socialist'' in their party's name to win the support of German workers, who after World War I, favored socialist and communist parties.

[Sina Dubovoy]

FURTHER READING:

Brooker, Paul. *The Faces of Fraternalism: Nazi Germany, Fascist Italy, and Imperial Japan.* Clarendon Press, 1991.

De Grazia, Victoria. *How Fascism Ruled Women: Italy, 1922-1945.* Univ. of California Press, 1992.

Fletcher, William Miles. *The Search for a New Order: Intellectuals and Fascism in Prewar Japan.* University of North Carolina Press, 1982.

Renneberg, Monika, Walker, Mark (eds). *Science, Technology and National Socialism.* Cambridge University Press, 1994.

Sternhell, Zeev, et al. *The Birth of Fascist Ideology: From Cultural Rebellion to Political Revolution.* Princeton University Press, 1994.

Tanin, O. and Yohan, E. *Militarism and Fascism in Japan.* Greenwood Press, 1973.

FEDERAL COMMUNICATIONS COMMISSION (FCC)

The Federal Communications Commission (FCC) was created as a result of the Communications Act of 1934, which called for a government agency to be established for the purposes of regulating interstate and foreign communications by wire and radio in the public interest. The FCC obtained additional regulatory responsibility under the provisions of the Communications Satellite Act of 1962, and today regulates the following interstate and foreign communications: radio, television, wire, satellite, and cable (telephone and telegraph; two-way radio also).

The FCC is primarily responsible for the organized development and subsequent operation of broadcast services, as well as assuring that ''rapid, efficient nationwide and worldwide telephone and telegraph services are provided at reasonable rates,'' (U.S. Government Manual). The U.S. government has also charged the FCC with the responsibility of the use of communications for promoting the safety of life and property and for strengthening the national defense.

ORIGINS OF THE FCC

The origins of the FCC can be traced back to the early 1900s, when radio, or audio communication, was new. The Wireless Ship Act of 1910 preceded the Radio Act of 1912, which in turn preceded the Dill-White Radio Act of 1927. Each of these acts was established to regulate the ever-evolving broadcasting business. The Radio Act of 1927 was more similar to its eventual legislative successor (Communications Act of 1934) than either the Wireless Ship Act of 1910 or the Radio Act of 1912. The Radio Act of 1927, created at the insistence of President Calvin Coolidge, helped to regulate the interference caused by a rapid growth of AM radio stations. The radio air waves had become almost a ''free-for all'' for the various broadcasters.

An outcome of the Radio Act of 1927 was the creation of the Federal Radio Commission, which was established to eliminate or control the overall confusion existing within the radio broadcast band. This ultimately resulted in the loss of broadcast licenses to many operators, simply because there were too many stations operating.

The communications industry in America continued to expand and grow, and at the urging of President Franklin Delano Roosevelt, a special government-appointed committee was given the task of studying electronic communications and offering recommendations on the best method of monitoring this rapidly growing business. It was the recommendation of the committee that Congress "establish a single agency to regulate all interstate and foreign communication by wire and radio, including telephone, telegraph, and broadcast" (U.S. Government Manual). This agency was to be called the Federal Communications Commission (FCC).

WHAT IS THE FCC?

The FCC is an independent government agency with a direct "reporting" relationship to the U.S. Congress. Its regulatory jurisdiction includes the United States, District of Columbia, Guam, Puerto Rico, and the Virgin Islands.

FCC Commissioners are appointed by the President, confirmed by the Senate, and generally serve 5-year terms. Presently there are five Commissioners directing the FCC, reduced from seven in 1983. The Chairman of the FCC is also appointed by the President (chosen from one of the five Commissioners), and may remain Chairman during his term for as long as the President chooses. The FCC makes every effort to insure against partisan politics and conflict of interest among its Commissioners. The maximum number of Commissioners allowed to serve on the FCC from the same political party is three, and none of the Commissioners are permitted to have a financial interest in any Commission-related business.

The FCC is divided into four major operating bureaus: Mass Media, Common Carrier, Field Operations, and Private Radio. In addition, there are seven staff offices, consisting of Managing Director, General Counsel, Engineering and Technology, Plans and Policy, Congressional and Public Affairs, Administrative Law Judges, and the Review Board.

Specific FCC functions include assigning frequency, power, and call signs for radio; allocating spectrum space for AM and FM radio, as well as VHF and UHF television broadcast services; designating sign-on/sign-off times and operating power for broadcast stations. Although the FCC is prohibited by law from censoring program content and material, it does however, possess many regulatory responsibilities in the programming area. Licensees are required by the FCC to "attempt to serve the programming needs and interests of their communities" (U.S. Government Manual).

Another important role of the FCC is to require its licensees to allow for equal opportunity for the use of broadcast facilities by political parties and candidates, to state a position or serve up a rebuttal. The FCC also conducts regular inquiries and investigations, subjecting licensees to sanctions, including loss of license and fines of up to $20,000 for violations of FCC statutes, rules, or policies.

The FCC limits the number of broadcasting outlets that may be owned by an individual or corporation

to a total of twelve (either AM, FM, or TV stations). The FCC licenses television stations for five-year terms, and radio stations for seven-year terms.

[Art DuRivage]

FEDERAL DEPOSIT INSURANCE CORPORATION (FDIC)

The Federal Deposit Insurance Corporation (FDIC) is an independent U.S. government agency that insures deposits up to $100,000 in most U.S. banks and **savings and loans** (S&Ls). The FDIC also regulates and examines **banks** and S&Ls and provides financial assistance to failing institutions. The FDIC is run by a five member board of directors. Three of the directors are appointed by the President. The Comptroller of the Currency and the Director of the Office of Thrift Supervision balance out the board.

The FDIC was created in 1933 as part of the Glass-Steagall Act in an effort to restore faith in the U.S. banking system following events which led to the Great Depression. At the time of its creation, the FDIC only insured deposits in banks, not savings and loan associations. Those deposits until 1989 were insured by the Federal Savings and Loan Corporation (1934). The FDIC was created amidst much controversy. Proponents of the new corporation felt it would prevent bank runs, facilitate the national check clearing system, and add much needed safety and liquidity to bank deposits. Opponents of the FDIC feared it would over-regulate banks and that bank customers, knowing their deposits were fully insured, would favor high interest-bearing accounts in high risk banks rather than lower interest accounts in safer institutions. Although bank failures were relatively rare through the 1970s (approximately 10 per year) the savings and loan debacle of the late 1980s bore out the fears of those opposed to deposit insurance for customers of institutions making high risk loans. Initially, deposit insurance covered only the first $2500. By 1934, it had quickly risen to $5000 By 1980 the cap was $100,000. In some cases, the FDIC took the controversial position of ignoring the $100,000 limit on deposit insurance.

When confronted with a bank failure, the FDIC can do one of three things. The corporation can "pay off the bank," which means it will reimburse the depositors for whatever amount was in their accounts up to $100,000. The FDIC can also assist in selling the bank or merging it with another institution, or it can stop the bank from failing with a bailout. If there is a bailout the FDIC has the option to invoke its controversial "too big to fail" doctrine. This procedure came about largely as a result of the Continental

Illinois Bank fiasco in Chicago in 1984. The FDIC argued that the failure of a large and important financial institution, such as Continental, would rock the foundations of the American banking system. Thus, in order to keep Continental solvent, all deposits, regardless of size, would be covered. This practice, it was argued, encouraged large investors to patronize major banks at the expense of smaller banks. Subsequent legislation never completely did away with this practice, but it did make the "too big to fail" procedure more difficult to invoke. In addition to the FDIC, the approval of the U.S. Treasury Department and the **Federal Reserve** is now needed to invoke the "too big to fail" procedure. As a result of the savings and loan bailout of the 1980s and the subsequent **bankruptcy** of the Federal Savings and Loan Insurance Corporation, the FDIC began providing insurance on S&L accounts in 1989.

Another result of the savings and loan debacle was the FDIC Improvement Act of 1991. Amidst much opposition from the banking industry, the new legislation gave even greater regulatory powers to the FDIC concerning intervention, executive salaries, performance, and lending practices. The FDIC in an effort to forestall a bank failure can intervene in a bank's operations at an early date and force the bank to liquidate assets and reduce **dividends** and staff in order to raise cash to keep the institution solvent. The FDIC can also limit executive salaries, bonuses, and renumerations in troubled institutions, regulate **real estate** loans, and invoke regulatory guidelines on earnings.

The FDIC is independent of partisan political influence largely because it does not depend on the government for funding. The FDIC receives operating income from assessments on insured banks as a percentage of deposits ($\frac{1}{12}$ of 1 per cent of domestic deposits in 1986), interest from FDIC investments in government securities, and, when necessary, money borrowed from the U.S. Treasury. Money borrowed from the U.S. Treasury must be used only for carefully proscribed purposes.

In addition to insuring deposits and regulating banking practices the FDIC can help finance mergers and acquisitions of failing institutions, regulate their closings and re-openings, and—with appropriate warning and publicity—terminate an institution's deposit insurance. In relation to banks that are not part of the Federal Reserve System, the FDIC performs periodic **audits** and regulates mergers and acquisitions, locations of branch and main office facilities, changes of ownership, loans made to banks by other institutions, and bank security. In addition to its headquarters in Washington D.C., the FDIC has eight regional offices in Atlanta, Boston, Chicago, Dallas, Kansas City, Memphis, New York, and San Francisco.

[Michael Knes]

FURTHER READING:

Federal Deposit Insurance Corporation: The First Fifty Years - A History of the FDIC 1933-1983. Federal Deposit Insurance Corporation, 1984.

Henderson, David R., ed. *The Fortune Encyclopedia of Economics*. Warner Books, 1993.

Seidman, L. William. *Full Faith and Credit: Great S & L Debacle and Other Washington Sagas*. Times Books, 1993.

Sprague, Irvine H. *Bailout*. Basic Books, 1986.

The United States Government Manual. Washington, D.C.: United States Government Printing Office, 1993.

FEDERAL HOME LOAN MORTGAGE CORPORATION

The Federal Home Loan Mortgage Corporation (FHLMC) was established pursuant to Title III (Federal Home Loan Mortgage Corporation Act) of the Emergency Home Finance Act of 1970. FHLMC is an independent agency sponsored and regulated by the federal government. Prior to 1989 the FHLMC was managed under the auspices of the Federal Home Loan Bank Board. The FHLMC now has an eighteen member board of governors and comes under the purview of the U.S. Department of the Treasury and the U.S. Department of Housing and Urban Development. The primary function of the FHLMC is to act as a secondary market for conventional home mortgages. However it is considering expansion into related fields such as home equity lending and senior citizen housing.

The FHLMC operates by buying mortgages at a **discount rate** from primary lending institutions such as **savings and loan associations**. The S & L profits from fees for the original processing of the mortgage and initial loan payments. By selling the mortgage the original lending institution also increases its liquidity. The FHLMC, upon buying the mortgage, pools it with similar mortgages it has purchased and—using the pool as collateral—sells pass-through securities to individual and **institutional investors**. This system benefits the original mortgage holder, the FHLMC and the home buyer because of the fluid pool of mortgage funds. The system is an example of government use of the private sector to implement public policy, in this case home ownership especially for lower and middle income families.

The FHLMC issues two kinds of certificates: Participation Certificates and Guaranteed Mortgage Certificates. Guaranteed certificates represent undivided interests in conventional residential mortgages and pay interest semi-annually. Participation Certificates are freely transferable and holders receive monthly payments on pooled mortgages including prepayments and interest.

There are also FHLMC swap transactions by which Participation Certificates are traded to lending institutions for mortgages.

The FHLMC, like its sister institution the Federal National Mortgage Association (Fannie Mae), is in a symbiotic relationship with the federal government. Until 1984 the FHLMC was considered to be a governmental instrumentality and as such it was not subject to state, local or federal taxes. That status was revoked and in 1985 the FHLMC was subject to federal taxation. However the FHLMC by virtue of its being a quasi-independent agency receives a non-cash "subsidy" worth billions of dollars. Even though the FHLMC and its securities are not backed by the "full faith and credit" of the U.S. Government there is an implied backing nonetheless. This makes it possible for the FHLMC to borrow at preferred discount rates and pay lower **interest rates** to investors because of the aura of risk free investment.

This association, however, also carries with it government regulation and scrutiny. In 1992 Congress passed the Federal Housing Enterprises Financial Safety and Soundness Act. This legislation increased regulation of government-sponsored enterprises such as the FHLMC. The act mandates closer federal "examination and evaluation" of FHLMC activities, strict compliance to purchasing a fixed percentage of low, moderate, and minority mortgages, and tighter capital provisions.

[Michael Knes]

FURTHER READING:

Munn, Glenn G. *Encyclopedia of Banking Finance.* Bankers Publishing Company, 1991.

FEDERAL LABOR RELATIONS AUTHORITY

The Federal Labor Relations Authority (FLRA) is an independent agency of the executive branch of the U.S. federal government. Established under the authority of Reorganization Plan No. 2 of 1978 (5 U.S.C. app.), it became effective January 1, 1979 pursuant to Executive Order 12107. The duties and the authority of the FLRA are detailed in title VII (Federal Service Labor-Management Relations) of the Civil Service Reform Act of 1978 (5 U.S.C. 7101-7135).

The purpose of the FLRA is to administer provisions of the Federal Service Labor-Management Statute which prescribes the relationship between certain federal agencies and the bargaining units representing employees of those agencies. The FLRA is involved in virtually every aspect of the labor-management relationship. The FLRA establishes guidelines and policies, acknowledges the legitimacy of bargaining units, oversees union elections and voting procedures, implements arbitration decisions, and resolves disputes. In essence, the FLRA is a liaison between the Federal Service Labor-Management Statute, affected federal agencies, collective bargaining units, and workers falling under the purview of the statute.

The FLRA is divided into three offices: the Authority, the General Counsel, and the Federal Service Impasses Panel. Attached to the FLRA is the Foreign Service Labor Relations Board and its adjunct the Foreign Service Impasses Disputes Panel. These last two offices were established by the Foreign Service Act of 1980.

The Authority determines the appropriateness of bargaining units, conducts and certifies elections, resolves issues dealing with consultation rights, and oversees adherence to the concept of "bargaining in good faith." The Authority also resolves charges of unfair labor practices, exceptions to arbitration awards, and administers relevant portions of the Civil Service Reform Act of 1978. The Authority has three officers from at least two different political parties. They are appointed to five year terms by the President of the United States with the advice and consent of the Senate. One member is designated by the president as Chairman of the authority and serves as the chief administrative officer of the FLRA.

The General Counsel is also appointed by the president with the advice and consent of the Senate to a five year term. The Counsel operates independently, investigates charges of unfair labor practices, and presents and, if necessary, prosecutes such cases before the Authority. Under the supervision of the General Counsel are eleven regional FLRA offices. Each office is headed by a Regional Director who is responsible for processing cases arising in his/her district.

The Federal Service Impasses Panel is charged with settling an impasse in negotiations between a federal agency and a bargaining unit. The Panel generally seeks to resolve the impasse through factfinding. The Panel is headed by a chairman and six other members, all appointed by the President. Appointment to the Panel is based on experience in labor-management relations.

The Foreign Service Act of 1980 established a labor-management statute affecting foreign service employees of the (U.S. Information Agency, the Agency for International Development, and the U.S. Departments of State, Agriculture and Commerce.) This statute resulted in the creation of the Foreign Service Labor Relations Board (FSLRB). The FSLRB is responsible for implementing relevant portions of the Foreign Service Act. The FSLRB acts much like the Authority in overseeing labor-management relations between bargaining units, the federal government, and foreign service employees of the five agencies. There is also a Foreign Service Impasse Disputes Panel which resolves impasses arising during collective bargaining.

The Federal Service Labor-Management Relations statute covers all employees of the executive branch of the government, the Library of Congress and the Government Printing Office. It does not include aliens or non-citizens holding a federal position outside of the United States (exceptions are made for Panama Canal Commission employees and others working in the Republic of Panama), members of the uniformed services, and those of supervisory or management level. (Also excluded are employees of the Foreign Service assigned to the U.S. Department of State, the Agency for International Development, or the International Communication Agency.)

For further information contact: Federal Labor Relations Authority, 607 Fourteenth St. NW, Washington D.C. 20424; (202)482-6560. The FLRA publishes annual reports as well as a guide to the statute which created it.

[Michael Knes]

FEDERAL MEDIATION & CONCILIATION SERVICE

The Federal Mediation and Conciliation Service (FMCS) is an independent agency of the federal government established by the Labor Management Relations Act of 1947 to promote harmonious labor/management relations throughout the United States. The director of the FMCS, appointed by the President of the United States with the advice and consent of the Senate, leads the agency towards this goal by providing government mediators to help resolve labor management disputes affecting interstate commerce. In its Office of Arbitration Services, the FMCS maintains a roster of professional arbitrators. An Office of Technical Services acts as the educational arm of FMCS and conducts arbitration seminars and labor relations programs for labor, management, and other interested groups.

When labor management negotiations reach an impasse, both sides may resort to voluntary and non-binding mediation in an effort to resolve the dispute. Both parties must agree to mediation although it may be requested by only one. Throughout the mediation process, the mediator seeks to bring both parties of the dispute to a voluntary agreement, although neither side is obligated to comply with the final decision.

FMCS mediators, known as commissioners, staff 75 district offices throughout the country, concentrated mostly in industrialized areas. As required by the Labor Management Relations Act as amended, if the parties to the labor contract fail to reach an agreement 30 days prior to the termination or reopening of the contract, they must notify the appropriate district FMCS office. FMCS district directors review all notices sent to their offices. If the FMCS director believes the dispute falls under FMCS guidelines, a mediator is assigned to the case, who will assist in negotiating an agreement with the parties concerned. The FMCS will not likely become involved if the dispute has minimal impact on interstate commerce or if state or other conciliation services are available.

MEDIATION VERSUS ARBITRATION

Through its Office of Arbitration Services, the FMCS provides a panel or list of arbitrators chosen from the FMCS roster to both sides of a labor dispute. The two sides then follow a stipulated procedure to strike names from the list until only one name remains. The remaining person on the list will arbitrate the dispute. Unlike FMCS mediators, the arbitrators are not federal employees, but private citizens qualified to settle labor disputes.

Decisions made through arbitration are almost always binding. Occasionally, however, disputing parties participate in non-binding or "advisory" arbitration. Grievance arbitration usually involves disputes over language in pre-existing contracts. Interest arbitration, on the other hand, takes place while a contract is being negotiated.

The FMCS offers the services of its mediators without charge. They are salaried employees of the Federal government although their positions are exempt from Civil Service eligibility requirements. Likewise there is no charge for the FMCS to provide a panel of arbitrators. The arbitrator's fees, however, are paid by the disputing parties.

For further information contact: Federal Mediation and Conciliation Service, 2100 K Street NW, Washington DC 20427; (202)653-5290.

SEE ALSO: Arbitration & Mediation

[Michael Knes]

FURTHER READING:

"Policies, Functions and Procedures." Washington Federal Mediation and Conciliation Service, Office of Arbitration Services, 1979.

FEDERAL NATIONAL MORTGAGE ASSOCIATION

The Federal National Mortgage Association (FNMA) is a creation of the Reconstruction Finance Corporation and was originally called the National

Mortgage Corporation. The National Mortgage Corporation was established by the National Housing Act of 1938. The corporation was re-chartered under the Housing Act of 1954 and became part of the Housing and Home Finance Agency until 1965 when it came under the purview of the U.S. Department of Housing and Urban Development. In 1968 under the authority of Title VIII of the Housing and Urban Development (HUD) Act, the FNMA assumed its present name and became a government sponsored private corporation. The purpose of the FNMA is to make housing in the United States more accessible by providing a secondary market for home **mortgages**. The FNMA is commonly referred to as Fannie Mae and is under the joint oversight of the U.S. Treasury and Housing and Urban Development Departments.

Although the FNMA is sponsored by the federal government it is a profit oriented public corporation that issues stock which is traded on the New York Stock Exchange. Fannie Mae raises funds by selling **stock** and short term securities to the public. The FNMA functions by buying mortgages from original lenders (banks, thrifts etc.) when funds are scarce and selling mortgages when money is more plentiful. The FNMA also packages mortgages of like characteristics and uses these packages or pools as collateral for the securities it sells. These pass-through securities are in essence **mortgage backed securities**.

Fannie Mae and its brother institution Freddie Mac (Federal Home Loan Mortgage Corporation) have come under criticism from many parts of the private sector because of their relationship with the federal government. Although the securities issued by both corporations are not federal obligations there is on the part of the public and financial institutions a sense of implied government guarantees. This aura of low risk creates a financial climate in which the FNMA can borrow at discount rates and pay lower interest on its obligations. The FNMA also has minimal capital requirements and as a government instrumentality the FNMA is exempt from state and local taxes (except for taxes on real property). The Secretary of the Treasury also has the discretionary authority to purchase FNMA obligations under certain conditions.

There are also regulatory drawbacks to being a private corporation issuing what are classified as federal agency securities. The Secretary of Housing and Urban Development has the authority to assure FNMA compliance with its charter and to require the FNMA to purchase mortgages on low and moderate income housing. Stock issues, their rate of interest and maturity dates must also be approved by HUD and the U.S. Treasury Department. HUD also has limited authority over stock dividends and the **debt/capital** ratio that the FNMA must maintain. Originally the FNMA could only purchase federally insured mortgages but since 1970 its been allowed to purchase conventional mortgages which today constitutes most of Fannie Mae's purchases.

In 1992 the Office of Federal Housing Enterprise Oversight (OFHEO) was created as part of the Housing and Community Development Act. The purpose of the OFHEO is to serve as a watchdog over both Fannie Mae and Freddie Mac. It was felt that both corporations needed closer scrutiny than HUD could provide. Especially important to the OFHEO is implementation of legislation mandating 30 percent of all mortgage purchases made by the two corporations be for mortgages on low and moderate income housing. In response Fannie Mae started the Community Home Buyers Program in 1992. This program helps finance mortgages in low and moderate income and minority neighborhoods and allows mortgages with as little as five percent down. In 1993 another program was started which eased regulations for re-financing residences where the **equity** is as low as five percent. This plan is for neighborhoods where declines in housing values have also caused a decline in home owner's equity.

For further information contact: Federal National Mortgage Association, 3900 Wisconsin Ave. NW, Washington D.C. 20016; (202)752-7000.

[Michael Knes]

FURTHER READING:

Federal National Mortgage Association. A guide to Fannie Mae. Federal National Mortgage Association. 1979.

Federal National Mortgage Association. Background and History of the Federal National Mortgage Association. 1969.

Fish, Gertrude ed. *The Story of Housing.* Macmillan. 1979.

Vidger, Leonard Perry. *The Federal National Mortgage Association, 1938-1957.* 1960.

FEDERAL RESERVE SYSTEM

The Federal Reserve System is the central bank of the United States. "The Fed," as it is also known, is exclusively a banker's bank and does not conduct commercial banking activities such as maintaining personal checking accounts or extending loans to qualified individuals.

The Federal Reserve's goal is to attain stable economic growth in the nation, and through its actions, influence the flow of money and credit in the economy. Specifically, the Fed is responsible for

1. formulating monetary policy;

2. acting as lender of last resort for the nation's banks and depository institutions;

3. facilitating the collection and clearance of checks;

4. regulating and supervising banks and other financial institutions;

5. acting as fiscal agent for the United States Treasury;

6. distributing coin and currency to the public through depository institutions; and

7. implementing certain regulations of consumer credit legislation.

The system is composed of the Board of Governors of the Federal Reserve System, the Federal Open Market Committee, twelve Federal Reserve Banks and twenty five branches, member financial institutions, and advisory committees.

THE FORMATION OF THE FEDERAL RESERVE

The historical roots of the Federal Reserve System extend back to 1791. Alexander Hamilton, Secretary of the Treasury under George Washington, advocated the establishment of the First Bank of the United States. Hamilton believed the nation needed a central bank for several reasons. First, a central bank would facilitate the creation of banking establishments throughout the United States and generate a greater supply of bank credit to aid economic growth. Second, the monetary and fiscal responsibilities of

Congress as enumerated in the Constitution were so great that a central bank was needed to carry out those activities. Finally, a central bank could serve the Treasury in its revenue collection and distribution functions. Although Secretary of State Thomas Jefferson opposed Hamilton's plan, the twenty-year charter for the First Bank of the United States passed in 1791.

The First National Bank of the United States proved to be a successful and profitable institution, but a bill to recharter the bank was defeated in Congress. Opponents, primarily the state-chartered banks, argued the bank had monopoly power and was under the influence of foreign owners. The bank ceased operations in 1811, and America's banking system was thrown into a tailspin. The number of state-chartered private banks increased dramatically, creating a hodgepodge of bank notes and disrupting the system of interregional payments. With the outbreak of the War of 1812, the federal government's finances fell into disarray. At this time, many Americans thought the monetary activities of the nation's banks required federal regulation. As a result of these conditions, a bill to charter the Second National Bank of the United States was introduced and passed by Congress in 1816, the final year of James Madison's presidency.

The Second National Bank developed a powerful and effective system of monetary regulation under the leadership of Nicholas Biddle (1786-1844), its president from 1823 to 1839. Biddle hoped to expand the bank's role in America's economy, but as the bank became more powerful, many citizens feared it was a threat and menace to democracy. President Andrew Jackson distrusted the central bank's authority, believing it was an instrument of the rich and powerful. The 1832 bill to recharter the bank passed both houses of Congress, but Jackson vetoed the bill. Nicholas Biddle resigned as president in 1839 and the bank finally ceased operations in 1841.

In the absence of a central bank authority, the state-chartered banks once again filled the gap with a patchwork system subject to violent fluctuations in the monetary system. The United States Treasury assumed some central banking responsibilities such as open market securities purchases. Clearinghouse associations also performed some responsibilities normally under the jurisdiction of a central authority. The associations issued clearinghouse loan certificates, which became a important type of ''emergency currency'' for banks during financial panics. Regulatory activities, such as controlling member banks' interest rates on deposits and conducting member bank examinations, were also carried out by the associations.

The National Banking Act (formerly the National Currency Act) of 1863 instituted a system of nationally chartered banks subject to strict capital requirements. Three types of national banks were recognized: country banks, reserve city banks, and central reserve city banks. The country banks were required to keep a portion of their reserves in vault cash and the remainder with a national bank in a reserve or central reserve city in the form of vault cash. Reserve city banks had to keep a portion of their reserves as vault cash and the remaining portion as a deposit in a national bank at a central reserve city. The central reserve city banks in New York, Chicago, and St. Louis were required to keep all their reserves as vault cash.

Under this system circulating bank notes had to be backed by the holdings of United States government securities. State bank notes eventually ceased circulating, but state banks continued to thrive. Checking accounts rather than bank notes provided the revenue these banks required to operate.

The primary weaknesses of the national banking system were an inelastic supply of currency and the immobile reserves. The currency supply did not expand and contract as appropriate with the cycle of business, and the pyramid structure of country, reserve city, and central reserve city banks meant reserves were not readily available when needed. As a result the economy suffered wild cycles of boom and bust.

Congress passed the Aldrich Vreelad Act of 1908 after the financial panic of 1907. One of the most important provisions of the act was the creation of the National Monetary Commission. Under the direction of its chairman, Senator Nelson W. Aldrich of Rhode Island, the commission studied the nation's financial system over three years. The final report, known as the Aldrich Plan, recommended the creation of a central banking system.

Acting on the findings of the Aldrich plan, Representative Carter Glass (1858-1946) of Virginia and H. Parker Willis(1874-1937), an expert adviser to the House Committee on Banking and Finance, drafted the Glass-Willis proposal and presented it to President Woodrow Wilson. Initial opposition to the bill was voiced by Secretary of State William Jennings Bryan. Bryan argued the proposal allowed bankers too much influence over the system and failed to weaken the Wall Street "money trust," a small group of finance leaders with vast control over the nation's money and credit. He also believed the government and not the reserve banks, as the Glass-Willis proposal specified, should be empowered to issue currency. Other opponents included city bankers and agrarian leaders. After many changes and compromises, the revised bill was introduced by Glass and Senator Robert Owen of Oklahoma in the House and Senate.

Eventually the Owen-Glass bill passed both houses of Congress, and the Federal Reserve Act became law December 23, 1913. The law enumerated three primary purposes of the Federal Reserve System: to provide an elastic supply of currency, a means to discount commercial credits, and a system of supervision and regulation over the nation's banks.

The responsibility of implementing the system, as designated by the law, fell to the Reserve Bank Organization Committee. The Committee consisted of the Secretary of the Treasury William G. McAdoo, the Secretary of Agriculture David F. Houston, and the Comptroller of the Currency John Skelton Williams. After many meetings across the nation with various leaders of banking, finance, and government, the committee completed its task and the Federal Reserve Banks opened for business November 16, 1914.

The structure of the Federal Reserve System is based on five components: the Board of Governors of the Federal Reserve System, the Federal Open Market Committee, the Federal Reserve Banks, member banks, and advisory committees. Figure one illustrates the organizational relationship of these components.

THE BOARD OF GOVERNORS AND THE FEDERAL RESERVE SYSTEM

The Board of Governors, frequently called the Federal Reserve Board, represents the ultimate authority of the Federal Reserve System. Located in Washington, D.C., the board consists of seven members, mostly professional economists, appointed by the President of the United States and confirmed by the Senate. The full term of a member's appointment is fourteen years, and it is not possible to be re-appointed. The terms are staggered to provide a system of checks and balances so one member's term expires every even-numbered year. Members usually retire before completing the term. The board's chairman and vice-chairman, appointed by the president with the advice and consent of the Senate, serve four-year terms and their positions may be renewed provided they have not exceeded their terms as Board members. The Chairman is the most well-known and visible representative of the Federal Reserve System.

The primary responsibility of the board is the determination and implementation of monetary policy. However, the board devotes the most time to regulatory and supervisory activities. The board exercises ultimate supervisory and regulatory authority over Reserve Banks, bank holding companies, and Federal Reserve System banks. As part of these responsibilities the Board decides the percentage of deposits member banks must hold as reserves. It also reviews and approves the rate of interest, or the **discount rate**, charged to member banks for Federal Reserve loans. The Board works with other federal agencies to determine the maximum interest rates offered by member banks on savings and time deposits.

Additionally, the board supervises a wide variety activities in areas such as bank mergers, consolidations, acquisitions, international banking operations in the United States, operations of member banks in foreign countries, and interest regulation on time and savings deposits. Other responsibilities include supervision of the nation's payment system and regulatory implementation of consumer credit and community affairs laws such as the Truth in Lending Act and the Community Reinvestment Act. The board also approves all presidents and vice-presidents of the twelve Federal Reserve Banks.

The board reports to Congress, and its chairman acts as one of the principal economic advisers to the president and Congress. Detailed statistics and other information about the system and the Board's activities are available through publications such as *The Federal Reserve Bulletin* and the board's annual report.

THE FEDERAL OPEN MARKET COMMITTEE

The Federal Open Market Committee (FOMC) consists of seven members from the Board of Governors and five presidents from the twelve Federal Reserve Banks. The Chairman of the Board of Governors also serves as the Chairman for the Committee. Four of the five slots occupied by bank presidents rotate on a yearly basis, and the fifth slot is permanently held by the New York Bank president. Those presidents not currently serving on the Committee usually attend and participate in meetings but do not vote. Traditionally, the president of the New York Bank is elected Vice-Chairman of the Committee. Meetings are usually held eight times a year, but the committee may consult as needed between these dates.

The most important function of the Federal Open Market Committee is to determine and direct the open market operations for the Federal Reserve. Open market operations are purchases or sales of securities in the nation's open money and bond markets that affect the level of reserves financial institutions hold. The FOMC's operations also extend to the international exchange market where foreign currencies are traded. Each Federal Reserve Bank may not execute open market operations for the sole benefit of the individual bank but must work in coordination with the FOMC. Banks may engage in open market transactions in foreign exchange following the review and regulation of the Federal Open Market Committee.

The Federal Reserve Bank presidents play an important role on the FOMC. Although every president does not vote at every meeting, the presidents provide a sense of balance in the direction of open market operations. As representatives of their individual districts, their presence ensures the Fed will remain a decentralized entity as the original architects intended.

THE FEDERAL RESERVE BANK

The twelve Federal Reserve Bank branches are located in Boston, New York, Philadelphia, Cleveland, Richmond, Atlanta, Chicago, St. Louis, Minneapolis, Kansas City, Dallas, and San Francisco. The branch banks and boundaries of the Federal Reserve districts for each Reserve Bank are shown in figure two. The stock of each Federal Reserve Bank is owned by the respective district member banks as required by the membership guidelines. However, stock ownership does not confer the privileges of financial or controlling interest as does common stock ownership.

Each Reserve Bank has its own board of nine, part-time outside directors that supervises the general operations of each bank and elects each bank's officers. The directors are classified as either Class A, B, or C directors. Class A directors, representing commercial banks from their districts, are elected to the position by the district member institutions. Three Class B directors are also elected by district member

banks, but Class B directors may not be employees, officers, or directors of any bank. Class B directors must be active representatives of commerce, agriculture, labor, or other industrial sectors within the district. The remaining three directors for each bank, the Class C directors, are appointed by the Board of Governors. The Class C directors may also not be employees, officers, directors, or stockholders of any bank. One of the Class C directors is designated the chairman of the bank's board and one is designated deputy chairman. Small, medium, and large member banks each vote for one Class A and Class B director to maintain a system of checks and balances and prevent the interests of large institutions from dominating the board. All directors are elected for three year terms on a staggered basis.

A president, first vice president, and other officers for each bank are appointed by the board at each Federal Reserve Bank with the approval of the Board of Governors of the Federal System. The president receives a five year term. Many activities fall within the authority of the twelve Federal Reserve Banks. Among the most important are: first, each bank's board establishes the discount rate subject to the approval of the Board of Governors; second, the banks act as depository and fiscal agents for the United States Treasury and other government agencies; third, the Banks act as regional clearinghouses and collection agents for depository institutions collecting checks and other instruments; fourth, reserve or clearing balances for depository institutions are held at the Reserve Banks in accordance with the Monetary Control Act of 1980; fifth, the Federal Reserve Banks act as representatives of their districts to the Federal Reserve System by providing information concerning local business and financial conditions. This information is critical to the decision-making process of monetary policy. The Banks also act as representatives of the Fed in their respective business communities.

MEMBER BANKS

As of December 31, 1991 approximately 39,449 commercial banks were members of the Federal Reserve System accounting for nearly 62% of all commercial banks in the United States. National banks, chartered by the Comptroller of the Currency, are required to be members of the Federal Reserve System. State-chartered banks may become members if certain requirements, established by the Board of Governors, are met and the board gives final approval. As a member of the Federal Reserve System, each institution is required to hold stock in its respective Federal Reserve Bank and is subject to the supervision of the Reserve Banks. Member institutions elect six of the nine members to each Federal Reserve Bank's board and receive an annual dividend on the Reserve Bank stock.

Prior to 1980 many state-chartered banks opted not to become members of the Federal Reserve System because of the relatively high reserve requirements imposed by membership in the system. Non-member banks only had to meet the lower reserve requirements imposed by their state authorities. The Monetary Control Act of 1980 established that all depository institutions, regardless of their status as members or non-members, are subject to the reserve requirements of the Federal Reserve System. The act also expanded access to the Federal Reserve services, which were previously restricted to member institutions, with explicit fees for various services.

ADVISORY COMMITTEES

Several advisory committees and councils facilitate the flow of operations and communication within the Federal Reserve System. The Federal Reserve Act created the Federal Advisory Council consisting of one member from each Federal Reserve District. Members are selected by the board of directors at each Reserve Bank on an annual basis and are usually prominent bankers in the district. The council meets at least four times a year in Washington, D.C. to discuss general business issues and monetary policy matters with the Board of Governors.

The Consumer Advisory Council also meets with the Board of Governors at least four times each year. Composed of thirty members, the group represents the interests of consumers and creditors. Its function is to advise the Board of Governors on such matters related to the Fed's authority in the areas of consumer and creditor laws.

The Thrift Institutions Advisory Council, established in 1980 with the Monetary Control Act, provides information related to issues and concerns of thrift institutions. The council is composed of representatives from savings banks, savings and loan associations, and credit unions. It meets at least four times every year.

A Small Business and Agricultural Advisory Committee exists at each Federal Reserve Bank. The committee advises each bank on business conditions within its respective area. Some members of these committees meet with the Board of Governors each year.

The Fed's overall goal is to promote the stable growth of the nation's economy, ensuring that monetary and financial markets remain relatively safe and sound. The functions and responsibilities under the Fed's authority all work to attain this goal, but it is important to remember that the Fed does not operate in isolation. Many other factors, such as current United States government fiscal policy objectives and consumer expectations, also influence the condition of the nation's credit and financial markets.

MONETARY POLICY

Considered the most important responsibility of the Federal Reserve, monetary policy refers to the actions undertaken to influence the availability, cost, and release of reserves at depository institutions to influence bank lending and investing as it relates to consumer and business spending. The primary tools of monetary policy are the discount rate, open market operations, and reserve requirements. The discount rate is the interest rate charged by each of the Federal Reserve Banks on loans made to financial institutions. Each bank's rate is reviewed and approved by the Federal Reserve Board of Governors. An institution with reservable deposits may borrow from the "discount window" for short-term purposes on a limited basis, and the rates are usually similar across districts. High rates tend to result in decreased borrowing for reserves, and low rates tend to result in increased borrowing depending on the level of reserves institutions hold.

Open market operations are purchases or sales of securities in the open money and bond markets. The Federal Reserve Bank of New York acts as the Fed's agent by executing the operations as directed by the Federal Open Market Committee on a continuous basis. These operations directly affect the level of reserves held by depository institutions at Federal Reserve Banks and, as a result, affect the nation's **money supply**. The money supply is an important factor in determining the availability of credit, interest rates, prices, and other important measures of financial condition. A purchase of securities ultimately results in an increased reserve level at depository institutions and increased economic growth through the payment for these securities by the Fed. Conversely, the selling of securities reduces the level of reserves and tends to reduce growth.

All depository institutions in the United States are required to hold reserves against certain accounts at their institutions. The reserves may be held as either vault cash or deposits at a Federal Reserve Bank as a determined percentage of deposit liabilities. The **Banking Act of 1933** extended the authority of the Federal Reserve to vary these reserve requirements, and under the Monetary Control Act of 1980 the Board of Governors may impose these requirements on transaction deposits and on nonpersonal time deposits for the sole purpose of executing monetary policy. Changes in the reserve requirement affect the supply of money in the economy. Raising the reserve requirement decreases any excess reserves an institution may hold by transforming the reserve's status from excess to required. Thus, raising the requirement limits a bank's ability to expand deposits.

LENDER OF LAST RESORT

In its role as lender of last resort, the Federal Reserve makes loans to financial institutions in times of crisis when funds are not available through any other means. It is an important tool to help avoid monetary panics and ensure the nation's financial stability.

CHECK CLEARING

Each Federal Reserve Bank acts as a regional clearinghouse to exchange or "clear" checks deposited at one institution but written on another institution. The Fed also "settles" checks by moving the funds as required from payee to payor institution. Other Fed payment services include wire transfers and automated clearinghouse services using magnetic tapes.

REGULATION AND SUPERVISION

The Federal Reserve System shares its regulatory and supervisory responsibilities with many other federal agencies and state authorities. A few of the supervisory powers include oversight of state chartered banks which are members of the Federal Reserve System, supervision and regulation of foreign banking operations in the United States, and regulation of United Stab commercial banking activities in foreign countries.

UNITED STATES TREASURY FISCAL AGENT

The Federal Reserve is independent of the U.S. Treasury, but the Federal Reserve works with the Treasury in formulating economic policy and carrying out the day-to-day fiscal tasks as Treasury's "bank." The Treasury has an account with the Federal Reserve to transfer funds and to handle the payment and clearance of Treasury obligations.

DISTRIBUTION OF CURRENCY AND COIN

The Federal Reserve Banks utilize the depository institutions within their respective districts to enter or remove coin and currency from circulation. Each institution's account at the bank is credited if excess cash is returned or charged if additional cash is requested. The banks also remove worn and damaged currency from circulation through this mechanism.

CONSUMER CREDIT LEGISLATION

The Consumer Credit Protection Act assigned certain responsibilities to the Federal Reserve System. The most important pieces of legislation included in the act were the Truth in Lending Act, the Fair Credit Billing Act, the Equal Credit Opportunity Act, and the Electronic Funds Transfer Act (EFTA). The Fed is responsible for writing regulations and implementing the laws to ensure the provisions of the acts are followed and enforced. The Fed is also involved in implementing and supervising community related acts such as the Community Reinvestment Act and the Home Mortgage Disclosure Act.

THE FEDERAL RESERVE SYSTEM AND THE FEDERAL GOVERNMENT

The architects of the Federal Reserve Act sought to create a central banking authority free from the political and industrial pressures which may try to influence the course of its operations. Therefore, the Federal Reserve is not under the jurisdiction of any department and is an independent agency within the federal government. Although the member institutions own stock in the Federal Reserve Banks, members do not control or own the Fed. The President and Congress do possess some influence over the Fed, and many sections of the system maintain close relationships with other federal departments on a formal and informal basis.

SEE ALSO: Interest Rates; Macroeconomics

[Paula M. Ard]

FURTHER READING:

Board of Governors of the Federal Reserve System. *The Federal Reserve System Purposes & Functions.* 7th ed. Board of Governors of the Federal Reserve System, 1984.

Broaddus, Alfred. *A Primer on the Fed.* Federal Reserve Bank of Richmond, 1988.

Johnson, Roger T. *Historical Beginnings . . . The Federal Reserve.* Federal Reserve Bank of Boston, 1977.

Kemmerer, Edwin and Donald L. Kemmerer. *The ABC of the Federal Reserve System.* Harper & Brothers Publishers, 1950.

Mayer, Thomas, J.S. Duesenberry, and R.Z. Aliber. *Money, Banking, and the Economy.* 3rd ed. W. W. Norton & Company, 1988.

Trescott, Paul. "Central Banking," in *Encyclopedia of American Economic History: Studies of the Principal Movements and Ideas,* edited by Glenn Porter. Charles Scribner's Sons, 1980.

Woolley, J.T. *Monetary Politics: The Federal Reserve and the Politics of Monetary Policy.* Cambridge University Press, 1984.

FEDERAL TRADE COMMISSION (FTC)

The Federal Trade Commission (FTC) was established as an independent administrative agency pursuant to the Federal Trade Commission Act of 1914. The purpose of the FTC is to enforce the provisions of the Federal Trade Commission Act, which prohibits "unfair or deceptive acts or practices in commerce."

The Clayton Antitrust Act (1914) also granted the FTC the authority to act against specific and unfair monopolistic practices. The FTC is considered to be a law enforcement agency, and like other such agencies it lacks punitive authority. Although the FTC cannot punish violators, it can issue cease and desist orders and argue cases in federal and administrative courts. The FTC is administered by a five-member commission, each commissioner being appointed by the President for a seven-year term with the advice and consent of the Senate. The commission must represent at least three political parties and the President chooses from its ranks one commissioner to be chairperson. The chairperson appoints an executive director with the consent of the full commission; the executive director is responsible for general staff operations.

The FTC was created amidst public outcry against the abuses of monopolistic trusts of the 1800s. The Sherman Antitrust Act of 1890 proved inadequate in limiting trusts, and the issue of misuse of economic power was a factor in the election of Woodrow Wilson in 1912. Wilson's State of the Union Message of 1913 called for **antitrust laws** that resulted in the passage of two acts. The first was the Federal Trade Commission Act, which created and empowered the FTC to define and halt "unfair practice" in trade and commerce. Next, the Clayton Antitrust Act covered specific activities of corporations, such as mergers which inhibited trade by creating monopolies. The FTC began operating in 1915 and the Bureau of Operations, which had previously monitored corporate activity for the federal government, was folded into the FTC.

The FTC is empowered to enforce provisions of both acts following specific guidelines. The offense must fall under the jurisdiction of the various acts and must affect interstate commerce. The violations must also affect the public good; the FTC does not intervene in disputes between private parties. As noted, the FTC lacks authority to punish or fine violators, but if an FTC ruling—such as a cease and desist order—is ignored, the FTC can seek civil penalties in federal court and seek compensation for those harmed by the unfair or deceptive practices.

Since 1914 both the Federal Trade Commission Act and the Clayton Act have been amended numerous times, thus expanding the legal responsibilities of the FTC. Some of the more notable amendments are:

Webb-Pomerene Export Trade Act of 1918: This act promoted exports by encouraging cooperative activities.

Robinson-Patman Act of 1936: This act strengthened the Clayton Act and dealt with pricing practices of suppliers and wholesalers.

Wool Products Labeling Act of 1939: This act ensured the purity of wool products.

Lanham Trademark Act of 1946: This act required the registration and protection of trademarks used in commerce.

Fair Packaging and Labeling Act of 1966: This act legislated against unfair or deceptive **labeling** and **packaging**.

Truth in Lending Act of 1969: This is a consumer act which requires full disclosure of credit terms, limits consumer liability concerning stolen credit cards, and regulates **advertising** for **credit** services.

Fair Credit Reporting Act of 1970: This act regulates the practices of credit reporting agencies.

Magnuson-Moss Warranty-Federal Trade Commission Improvement Act of 1975: This act expanded the authority of the FTC by allowing it to seek redress for consumers and civil penalties for repeat offenders. It also increased the FTC's authorization to pursue violations "affecting commerce" rather than violations "in commerce," an important distinction. Under the act manufacturers are not required to warrant their products but if they do they must specify whether their warranties are "full" or "limited" and limitations on **warranties** must be explained in writing.

Three bureaus of the FTC interpret and enforce jurisdictional legislation: the Bureau of Consumer Protection, the Bureau of Competition, and the Bureau of Economics. The Bureau of Consumer Protection is charged with protecting the consumer from unfair, deceptive, and fraudulent practices. It enforces congressional consumer protection laws and regulations issued by the Commission. The Bureau is involved in federal litigation, consumer, and business education and conducts various investigations under its jurisdiction. The Bureau has divisions of advertising, marketing practices, credit, and enforcement.

The FTC's Bureau of Competition is responsible for antitrust activity and investigations involving restraint of trade. The Bureau of Competition works with the Antitrust Division of the U.S. Department of Justice, but while the Justice Department concentrates on criminal violations, the Bureau of Competition deals with the technical and civil aspects of competition in the marketplace.

The Bureau of Economics predicts and analyzes the economic impact of FTC activities especially as these activities relate to competition, interstate commerce, and consumer welfare. The Bureau provides Congress and the Executive Branch with the results of its investigations and undertakes special studies on their behalf when requested.

The FTC becomes aware of alleged unfair or deceptive trade practices as a result of its own investigations or complaints from consumers, business people, trade associations, other federal agencies, or local and state governmental agencies. These complaints become known as "applications for complaints" and are reviewed to determine whether or not they fall under FTC jurisdiction. If the application does fall under FTC jurisdiction the case can be settled if the violator agrees to a consent order. This is a document issued by the FTC after a formal, and in some cases, public hearing after which the offending company or person agrees to discontinue or correct the challenged practices. If an agreement is not reached via a consent order, the case is litigated before an FTC Administrative Law Judge. Following a decision either the FTC counsel or the respondent can appeal the decision to the Commission. The Commission may either dismiss the case or issue a cease and desist order. If a cease and desist order is issued, the respondent has sixty days to accede or begin an appeal process through the federal court system. For further information contact: Federal Trade Commission, Pennsylvania Avenue at Sixth Street NW, Washington, D.C. 20580; phone: (202) 326-2222.

[Michael Knes]

FURTHER READING:

Rosch, J. Thomas. *Manual of Federal Trade Commission Practice*. Bureau of National Affairs, 1989.

United States Federal Trade Commission Annual Report. Federal Trade Commission, U.S. Government Printing Office.

A Guide to the Federal Trade Commission. Federal Trade Commission, 1987.

Your Federal Trade Commission: What It Is and What It Does. Federal Trade Commission, 1975.

FIDUCIARY DUTY

A fiduciary duty is one of complete trust and the utmost good faith. A fiduciary is a person, committee, or organization that has agreed to accept legal ownership and control and management of an asset or group of assets belonging to someone else. While fiduciaries take legal title to **assets**, they do not take equitable title. The assets do not belong to fiduciaries. Rather, legal title allows fiduciaries to administer and manage the assets. The assets are the fiduciary's only for a temporary period and only for a specific purpose. Fiduciaries must not derive any direct or indirect profit from their position, and they may not place their own interests above those of the beneficial owners of the assets.

In taking control of another's assets fiduciaries also agree to manage the assets in accordance with the wishes of the individual who established the fiduciary relationship. The powers and duties of fiduciaries are often established in a document that creates the fiduciary relationship. The conduct of fiduciaries is also governed by common law as well as specific federal and state laws. The Uniform Fiduciary Act and the Uniform Trustees' Powers Act serve as models for state legislation.

Banks, through their trust departments, often act as fiduciaries. A federally chartered bank that wishes to exercise fiduciary powers must file a special application with the Comptroller of the Currency. State laws typically allow state-chartered banks and specially formed trust companies to exercise fiduciary powers. Banks often act as fiduciaries with regard to trusts and estates and may assume such roles as trustee, executor, administrator, registrar of stocks and bonds, guardian of estates, assignee, receiver, and managing agent.

Corporate directors have a fiduciary duty to their shareholders. They are accountable not only for the safekeeping of assets but also for their efficient and effective use. Directors may not profit personally at the expense of, or contrary to, the corporation's shareholders. Corporate directors must place the interests of shareholders above their own interests.

Other examples of fiduciary relationships include those between attorneys and clients, stockbrokers and clients, and agents and principals. In all cases the interests of the beneficial owners must come before those of their fiduciaries, whether the fiduciaries are attorneys, stockbrokers, or agents.

ESTATES AND TRUSTS

The most common forms of formal fiduciary relationships involve estates and trusts, where fiduciaries act as trustees, executors, or personal representatives for beneficial owners. Such fiduciaries are different from agents in that they take legal title to the assets. Where agencies typically depend on the existence of the parties involved, trusts and estates are more impersonal in nature.

In the case of estates fiduciaries are known as executors if there is a will, administrators if there is no will. Both are also known as personal representatives. The conduct that executors must follow is determined by the will. In the case of administrators, they must follow state law. Reports may need to be made to probate courts, and the assets must be administered and finally distributed as directed by the will or state law.

In the case of trusts fiduciaries serve as trustees. Their conduct is determined by a written instrument that created the trust. If there is a testamentary trust, or one that was included in a will, then the trustee's directions should be part of the decedent's will that established the trust. Trust instruments do not necessarily have to be recorded in public records. Trustees are primarily responsible to the beneficiaries of the trust.

Fiduciaries have all the powers "necessary and appropriate" to accomplish the purposes of the estate or trust. These powers may include some that are not specifically given in the trust document. The trust instrument may also prohibit certain powers to fiduciaries. In general fiduciaries have the power to sell property, whether specifically granted or not. Unless it is specifically stated in the trust instrument, however, fiduciaries do not have the power to borrow against property. In some cases the courts may grant such powers to fiduciaries in order to preserve the assets and if it seems consistent with the grantor's probable intent. Fiduciaries may also incur reasonable expenses in the administration of the assets. They may make improvements to property when necessary. In short, their powers are very broad, subject to general rules and any specific instructions.

Every privilege has a corresponding responsibility, and fiduciary powers also involve fiduciary duties. All fiduciaries must exercise the care and skill of a "reasonably prudent person." The reasonably prudent person rule is one that is based in common law. In the United States it was first articulated in an 1830 case, *Harvard College v. Amory*. Such a rule, for example, prohibits trustees from speculating. The rule guides the conduct of fiduciaries in terms of preserving **capital** and producing **income** from a trust's or estate's assets. Federal and state legislation may serve to enhance the prudent person rule and set forth additional guidelines regarding permissible conduct. In addition to acting prudently, fiduciaries are expected to exercise any special skills they might have for the benefit of the estate or trust.

Thus, the major objectives for fiduciaries in the case of estates and trusts are to preserve the estate's assets and to use them to produce income. Fiduciaries also have a duty to keep their own funds and assets entirely separate from those of the trust. They are not allowed to make loans to the trust or estate, nor can they accept loans from it. They are not allowed to accept any compensation from a third party for their actions in connection with the trust or estate.

Fiduciaries have a duty to examine the instrument that created the trust or estate, to determine the property and assets involved as well as the identity of the beneficiaries. They must examine the instrument to determine what their own duties are as fiduciaries, and they must administer their office in accordance with the terms of the trust or estate document.

Fiduciaries must exercise reasonable diligence in locating the property and assets of an estate or trust. They must take tangible or real property into possession without undue delay. They must also take possession of any documents representing intangible assets.

They are allowed to employ agents as needed to accomplish these duties. In caring for the assets and property fiduciaries must use reasonable care and prudence. Their duties may include recording deeds, carrying adequate insurance, renting a safe deposit box, inspecting property from time to time, supervising all investments, paying off encumbrances and taxes that might jeopardize title, and keeping property in good repair.

In many estates and trusts fiduciaries have an additional duty to make the assets produce income. Fiduciaries may have to develop an investment plan for generating income. They may have to sell off nonproductive assets, if such power has been granted, and reinvest the proceeds in more productive assets.

Fiduciaries must administer their office solely for the benefit of the beneficiaries or beneficial owners. Fiduciaries may not take a position that could be considered adverse to the beneficiaries. They may not obtain a personal advantage at the expense of the beneficiaries. They are under a duty of absolute loyalty to the beneficiaries.

EMPLOYEE BENEFIT PLANS

Employers that establish employee benefit plans, such as **401(k) plans** or other types of **pension plans**, have a fiduciary duty to their employees. The **Employee Retirement Income Security Act of 1974 (ERISA)** regulates and sets standards for employee benefit plans. ERISA confirmed the prudent person rule found in common law, but it also set higher standards of fiduciary duty for individuals who have control over a plan's assets.

In spelling out fiduciary duties with regard to employee benefit plans, ERISA covers the duty of loyalty, the duty to use prudence, and the duty to comply with the plan. The duty of loyalty means that fiduciaries must act in the best interests of the plan and its participants. If fiduciaries are also plan participants, they must subordinate their own interests to those of the plan. In cases where plan participants form a diverse group with different interests, it may be difficult to balance the interests of all concerned.

ERISA expands the concept of prudence beyond that found in common law. Section 404(a)(1) of ERISA states that a fiduciary shall discharge his duties with respect to a plan "with the care, skill, prudence, and diligence under the circumstances then prevailing that a prudent man acting in a like capacity and familiar with such matters would use in the conduct of an enterprise of a like character and with like aims." Thus, fiduciaries of employee benefit plans must discharge their duties with adequate expertise. The courts have found that fiduciary duties were breached when nonexpert laypersons failed to seek independent qualified counsel when making decisions affecting plan assets. Plan fiduciaries are under an obligation to not only use their special skills and expertise, they must engage qualified advisers and managers if they lack the expertise themselves.

The prudent person standard, as expressed in ERISA, also requires that fiduciaries "diversify the investments of the plan so as to minimize the risk of large losses, unless under the circumstances it is clearly prudent not to do so." ERISA also makes note of prohibited transactions. Additional specific duties of plan fiduciaries may be set forth in the plan document, and fiduciaries have a duty to administer the plan "in accordance with the documents and instruments governing the plan." Fiduciary duties outlined in the plan document must be consistent with ERISA.

A much-discussed aspect of ERISA is that it established personal liability for breaches of fiduciary duty. That is, fiduciaries of employee benefit plans can be held personally liable for any breaches of their duties as spelled out in ERISA. ERISA expanded the concept of fiduciary to cover named fiduciaries as well as anyone who has the power to manage, acquire, or dispose of any assets of a plan. Thus, even if they are not named specifically as fiduciaries, **chief financial officers**, **controllers**, and management accountants can be held to ERISA's standards of fiduciary duty if they have the power to manage, acquire, or dispose of the plan's assets.

SEE ALSO: Employee Benefits

[David Bianco]

FINANCE

The field of finance encompasses numerous corporate and governmental activities. In the most basic sense, the term **finance** can be used to describe the activities of a firm attempting to raise **capital** through the sale of **stocks, bonds**, or other **promissory notes**. Similarly, public finance is a term used to describe government capital-raising activities through the issuance of bonds or the imposition of taxes. The theory of finance, in the broadest sense, can be defined as an integrated body of knowledge constructed around the goal of maximizing shareholder wealth and the principles of the time value of money, leverage, diversification, and an investment's expected rate of return versus its risk.

Within the discipline of finance, there are three basic components. First, there are financial instruments. These instruments—stocks and bonds—are recorded evidence of obligations on which exchanges of resources are founded. Effective **investment man-**

agement of these financial instruments is a vital part of any organization's financing activities. Second, there are financial markets, which are the mechanisms used to trade the financial instruments. Finally, there are banking and financial institutions which facilitate the transfer of resources among those buying and selling the financial instruments.

In today's business environment, **corporate finance** addresses issues relating to individual firms. Specifically, the field of corporate finance seeks to determine the optimal investments that firms should make, the best methods of paying for those investments, and the method by which to manage daily financial activities to ensure that firms have adequate cash flow. Finance influences all segments of corporate activity, both for profit oriented firms and non-profit firms. Through the acquisition of funds, the allocation of resources, and the tracking of financial performance, finance provides a vital function for any organization's activities. Furthermore, finance provides stockholders and other interested parties with a tool with which to assess management activities.

Like other business disciplines, the study of finance was originally part of the field of economics. By the turn of the century, However, the Industrial Revolution had changed the existing business environment so drastically that there was an increased need to study detailed business problems and processes. Thus, corporate finance was born with the purpose of describing and documenting the quickly evolving financial instruments, markets, and institutions. During the 1930s and the Great Depression—the field of finance underwent a series of meaningful changes. Due to the circumstances of the time, individuals involved in the field became increasingly focused on activities surrounding **bankruptcy**, liquidation, reorganization, and government regulation. During the 1940s and early 1950s, finance continued to exist as a descriptive field focusing on fund raising and on activities concerning stockholders' equity and liabilities.

In the mid-1950s, finance underwent additional changes. The field of finance evolved from a purely descriptive discipline to a proactive field allowing managers to make choices regarding their firms' financial operations. Much of these changes can be attributed to the work of Joel Dean, who furthered the understanding of the area of capital budgeting and sought to make it a major discipline within the field of finance. With this advancement, there was increased understanding of the cost of capital and the valuation of financial assets. Furthermore, these changes led to more interest in the theory of **capital structure**, security analysis, and **portfolio management**. The field of finance continues to evolve even today; it is constantly reacting to activities in the economy and to new theoretical ideas. For instance, because of today's volatile, global business climate, managers must be able to react swiftly to economic downturns and to better understand the operations of firms abroad.

[Kathryn Snavely]

FURTHER READING:

Brealey, Richard A., and Stewart C. Myers. *Principles of Corporate Finance*. 4th ed. New York: McGraw-Hill, 1991.

Cooper, S. Kerry, and Donald R. Fraser. *The Financial Marketplace*. Reading MA: Addison-Wesley Publishing Co., 1986.

Gallinger, George W., and Jerry B. Poe. *Essential of Finance: An Integrated Approach*. Englewood Cliffs, NJ: Prentice Hall, 1995.

Petty, J. William, Arthur J. Keown, David F. Scott, Jr., and John D. Martin. *Basic Financial Management*. 6th ed. Englewood Cliffs, NJ: Prentice Hall, 1993.

Spiro, Herbert T. *Finance for the Nonfinancial Manager*. 3rd. ed. New York: John Wiley & Sons, 1988.

FINANCIAL ACCOUNTING STANDARDS BOARD

The Financial Accounting Standards Board (FASB) is one branch of the Financial Accounting Foundation (FAF), an independent, nonprofit corporation currently based in Norwalk, Connecticut. The Financial Accounting Standards Board bears responsibility for establishing generally accepted accounting principles (GAAP) for the private sector.

HISTORY AND BACKGROUND

The impetus for the Financial Accounting Standards Board dates back to the economic boom of the 1920s, the stock market crash of 1929, and the Great Depression that followed. By the mid-1930s, both the financial community and the federal government had responded to the obvious need for uniform accounting standards, particularly for the **financial statements** of public corporations traded on the stock exchange. The New York Stock Exchange and what is now the American Institute of Certified Public Accountants (AICPA) ventured preliminary guidelines in the jointly published *Audits of Corporate Accounts* of 1934. The congressional **Securities Act of 1933** and the **Securities Exchange Act of 1934** threatened to supersede such efforts by establishing the **Securities and Exchange Commission** (SEC), which is authorized, among other functions, to prescribe standards for the preparation of financial reports. In 1938, however, the SEC voted to forgo this prerogative and allow the private sector to regulate its accounting practice—a policy that the commission has maintained to date.

The AICPA's Committee on Accounting Procedure (CAP) assumed the financial accounting stan-

dard-setting role in 1939. The AICPA shifted this responsibility to its Accounting Principles Board (APB), equipped with its own research staff, in 1959. Even so, the APB's main contribution—*Basic Concepts and Accounting Principles Underlying Financial Statements of Business Enterprises*, published in 1970—was criticized as achieving too little, too late. In 1971, a special committee of the AICPA suggested that the association turn over the standard-setting role to an autonomous body. In 1973, therefore, the Financial Accounting Standards Board within the Financial Accounting Foundation was established. Soon thereafter, the SEC ratified the FASB's role in promulgating financial accounting and reporting "principles, standards, and practices."

STRUCTURE OF THE FASB

The Financial Accounting Foundation's 16-member board of trustees appoints the chair and members of the Financial Accounting Standards Board. For the sake of efficiency, the FASB is restricted to seven members. These board members are drawn from the professional community of **certified public accountant**s; financial analysts, executives, and educators; investment bankers; and government bureaucrats. To ensure objectivity, members are employed exclusively by the FAF at professional salaries, and are subject to strict conflict-of-interest standards (including the termination of all prior business affiliations). Board members serve staggered five-year terms, and may be reappointed for a consecutive term.

FUNCTIONS OF THE FASB

The Financial Accounting Standards Board is responsible for establishing, updating, clarifying, and publishing both the broad principles and the specific practices that constitute acceptable private-sector financial accounting. Individual businesses, accounting and industry associations, and government agencies, among other sources, request findings from the FASB on issues ranging from the consolidation of subsidiaries to post-employment benefits. The FASB operates through a process of research projects, discussion memoranda, public hearings, comment letters, and proposal drafts. The FASB's ultimate findings on agenda items are published as *Statements of Financial Accounting Standards*.

An extensive research and technical staff and special task forces generally appointed by the chair assist the FASB in its standard-setting function. The Financial Accounting Standards Advisory Council (FASAC), a separate branch of the FAF, routinely advises the FASB on fulfilling its complex mission, particularly in the setting of agenda priorities. For public-sector accounting, the FASB and the FASAC are complemented within the FAF by the Government

Accounting Standards Board (GASB) and the Government Accounting Standards Advisory Council (GASAC). Pronouncements by various government agencies (particularly the SEC) and professional bodies (particularly the AICPA's Accounting Standards Division) also supplement the work of the Financial Accounting Standards Board.

[David Sprinkle]

FURTHER READING:

Kay, Robert S., and D. Gerald Searfoss, eds. *Handbook of Accounting and Auditing*. 2nd ed. Boston: Warren, Gorham & Lamont, 1989.

Miller, Paul B. W. *The FASB: The People, the Process, and the Politics*. 3rd ed. Burr Ridge, IL: Irwin, 1994.

Minter, Frank C. *Handbook of Accounting and Auditing*. 2nd ed. 1995 Update. Boston: Warren, Gorham & Lamont, 1995.

Original Pronouncements: Accounting Standards. 1990/91 ed. Norwalk, CT: Financial Accounting Standards Board.

FINANCIAL ENGINEERING

Financial engineering is the design and construction of a new financial contract or the packaging of existing financial instruments to meet very specific risk and return requirements of the client initiating the contract. It is analogous to the engineering function in building construction. For example, the building construction contract may include specifications regarding size, number of rooms, adequate plumbing and heat, quality of materials to be used, and a completion date. The financially engineered contract may also include specifications of size (or dollar amount), the types of securities that will be used, the cash flows that they will generate, the risk associated with those cash flows, and the date upon which the contract will be renewed or will expire.

This very general definition of financial engineering includes many contracts that are now considered commonplace. For example, **banks** sustained large losses in the early 1980s when their cost of funds rose sharply with **interest rates**. These banks had made large, long-term, fixed interest rate loans to families purchasing homes. They found that the moderate fixed interest charges they received on these loans were not sufficient to cover the interest expense that was incurred to attract new funds to the bank. Hence, banks began to write adjustable-rate loans that would vary interest charges to borrowers commensurate with fluctuations in the cost of funds to the bank.

Another common example of financial engineering is the **mutual fund**. Individual investors realized that there were benefits in terms of risk reduction if they could invest in a broad array of securities. Most individuals, however, had limited resources and found it very expensive to purchase small amounts of many securities. A basic mutual fund is a portfolio of securities that can be as diverse and numerous as the client demands. The creation of these funds allowed individuals to purchase shares of an already diversified portfolio and establish an investment with lower risk and at more moderate cost than they could achieve otherwise.

The two previous examples illustrate the ubiquitous nature of financial engineering. Financial contracts that are now considered standard were designed and constructed to meet the needs of a particular set of clients. Financial engineering still responds to those needs but now frequently incorporates more complex combinations of securities including foreign currencies and derivative securities. Before describing some of these more complex examples of financial engineering, a brief review of the fundamentals of the individual elements that are used in their construction is useful. This review begins with basic financial **assets** themselves: **stocks**, **bonds**, and various indexes. This will be followed by a description of various **derivative securities**, so named because their value is derived from the value of another security. **Options**, forward contracts, and **futures contracts** are in this category.

BASIC FINANCIAL ASSETS

BONDS. Shares of stock and bonds represent claims on current and future earnings of a corporation. Bonds represent a **debt** or liability on the corporation's (or government's) **balance sheet** and typically oblige the firm to make periodic interest payments to bond holders. Bonds eventually mature and at that time the principal amount of the loan that the bond represents must be returned to the holder. The holder of a bond may passively collect interest payments over the duration of the bond's life and then receive the principal at maturity or the holder may elect to sell the bond at any time prior to maturity. Since the bond represents a claim on a series of future payments, the bond's value can be estimated at any point as the discounted present value of those payments. Thus, when the bond holder offers the bond for sale, the interest rate used to discount the remaining payments will be the primary determinant of its value. This interest rate can also be interpreted as the potential buyer's required rate of return. This required rate will be determined by a variety of factors including expectations of **inflation**, the default risk associated with the corporation, and interest rates offered on similar securities. This description culminates in two observations regarding the value of bonds. First, the higher the required rate of return, the lower the discounted value of the bond's required payments and hence, its value. In other words, as interest rates go up, bond prices go down.

Conversely, as interest rates fall, bond prices rise. Second, these interest rates are determined in a competitive market and they will fluctuate continuously. Therefore, the market value of the bond will change constantly.

STOCKS. Stock represents a claim on residual earnings of the corporation. Since there may be no earnings available after all other claims have been satisfied and since those earnings may be retained by the firm rather than directly distributed to stockholders as **dividends**, the value of stock is inherently more volatile than the value of bonds. The value of stock is also related to expected future cash flows: dividends and future selling price. Nevertheless, these future cash flows are much more difficult to forecast. Obviously, as the market's assessment of the level of these future cash flows improves or deteriorates, the stock's price will rise or fall.

MARKET INDEXES. There are also a variety of market indexes that measure overall price movement of the U.S. stock market (e.g., Dow Jones Industrial Average, Standard & Poor's 500), interest rate sensitive instruments such as bonds (e.g., Salomon Brothers Bond Indexes), and the level of interest rates themselves (e.g., yields on various securities issued by the U.S. Treasury, the federal funds rate, and the London interbank offered rate (LIBOR). There are comparable indexes for every major financial market throughout the world (e.g., the Financial Times 100 index in England and the Nikkei 225 index in Japan). These market indexes play an important role in financial engineering. **Contracts** can be tied to the value of a specific index and can thereby be used to initiate cash flow movements between contracting parties. In this way, a contract can simulate rates of return for an index without the obligation to buy and hold the securities actually included in the index.

DERIVATIVE SECURITIES

Stocks, bonds, and market indexes represent the fundamental set of building blocks that can be used to engineer a financial contract. Such derivative securities as **options**, forward contracts, and **futures contracts** comprise the next level.

OPTIONS. An option is a contract that provides the holder with the right to purchase or sell a security at a predetermined price regardless of the prevailing market price. To obtain such a contract, the potential holder must buy it from a seller who has assessed the risk associated with the potential gains and losses on the contract. The option to buy is referred to as a call and the option to sell is a put. For example, suppose an individual paid $5 to purchase a call option on XYZ stock with an exercise price of $60 and the stock subsequently rose to $72. This individual could exer-

cise the option to buy at $60 and, ignoring brokerage fees and taxes, resell the stock for $72 for a gross profit of $12. When the initial cost of the option is factored in, the net profit to the call buyer is $7. If XYZ's price had gone higher the profit would have been even greater. On the other hand, if XYZ's price had fallen to $57, the call buyer would not elect to exercise the right to buy at $60. The maximum loss at any price below $60 would be limited to the initial cost of the option, $5 in this case. So, the call option buyer has unlimited potential for gains while losses are limited to the price, or premium, initially paid. Conversely, the seller of the option has limited gains, but the potential for significant losses.

Contrast the position of the call buyer with that of the put buyer. Suppose an individual buys a put option on XYZ's stock for $4 with an exercise price of $60. This individual now has the right but not the obligation to sell XYZ for $60. If the price falls to $55, the put holder can buy the stock in the market and sell it for $60 by exercising the put option. This produces a gross profit of $5 and a net profit of $1 when the original put premium is factored in. The gains to the put buyer will increase as the value of XYZ continues to fall, but will diminish if the price rises. If the price is above the exercise price of $60, the put buyer will not exercise the option and will incur a net loss of $4, the amount of the put premium. Therefore, the put buyer has significant potential for gains if XYZ's stock price falls significantly, but losses are limited to the amount of the put premium. Again, the converse is true for the put seller. The seller incurs significant losses if XYZ's value falls materially, but gains are limited to the amount of the premium.

Since there must be a buyer for every seller, both must agree to the initial price or premium. This premium will be influenced by the difference between the current price for the stock (or other asset) and the exercise price on the contract. Options are essentially a ''zero-sum'' game. This means that what the buyer gains, the seller loses. Only one party to the contract will have made the proper assessment. However, both parties will agree that stocks with greater potential for large price movements are worthy of higher option premiums than those with more stable prices. Also, options have an expiration date and buyers are willing to pay more for an option that has longer to live.

While these examples have centered on stock options, there are also many actively traded contracts on various government bonds, market indexes, **commodities** (e.g., corn, oil, gold), and foreign currencies.

FORWARD CONTRACTS AND FUTURES CONTRACTS. Forward and futures contracts are typically derived from price levels for various market indexes, interest rate sensitive securities such as bonds, commodities, and foreign currencies. These contracts are designed to transfer the risk associated with the price level of the underlying asset from one party to the other. Forward contracts represent an agreement to make or take delivery of a specific asset at a specific future date for a price that is also predetermined. For example, suppose A, a U.S. businessperson, has an obligation denominated in French francs (FF) that is due in six months. A's major concern is that the dollar will weaken with respect to the franc. If the current rate of exchange is $0.20 per Fr, then a weaker dollar might produce an exchange rate of $0.22 per Fr in six months. This means that A will have to pay more dollars for the same number of francs. Conversely, if the dollar strengthens and the exchange rate moves to $0.18 per Fr, then A can meet the franc-denominated obligation with fewer dollars. A's concern is exchange rate risk. One way to avoid this risk is to buy French francs on the forward market. Suppose that A can enter into an agreement to take delivery of the necessary francs in six months for a price of $0.21 per Fr. That forward price is fixed, eliminating exposure to subsequent fluctuations in the exchange rate, favorable or unfavorable. This practice is referred to as **hedging**.

Who will sell the French francs to A using the forward contract? There are two possibilities. B is a French businessperson who has an upcoming obligation denominated in U.S. dollars. B is also subject to exchange rate fluctuations and may be willing to sell francs at $0.21 per Fr in six months. B's willingness to sell francs can also be interpreted as an interest in buying dollars in the forward market. In this example, both A and B are hedging to eliminate exchange rate risk. If B is not interested or available to accept the other side of this contract, there is another possibility. C is a speculator in exchange rate movements. C believes that the current rate of $0.20 per Fr will be stable for the next six months and is therefore willing to agree to sell to A at $0.21 per Fr in six months. Again, A has eliminated concern with exchange rate fluctuation. C expects to be able to buy francs for $0.20 and sell them to A for $0.21 earning $0.01 per franc. If the rate rises to $0.22 per Fr, C will lose $0.01 per franc. However, if the dollar strengthens and the rate falls to $0.18 per Fr, C will earn $0.03 per franc. C is willing to speculate on the future exchange rate of dollars for francs. Exchange rate risk has not been eliminated, only transferred from A, the hedger, to C, the speculator.

While forward contracts can be customized to meet the very specific needs of the parties involved, they also create counterparty risk. Counterparty risk is an important underlying concept in all financially engineered contracts. It represents the potential that one of the parties to the contract will not follow through on its obligation. For example, if A entered into a forward contract to purchase five million French francs from C six months from now and C failed to deliver, A would be obliged to purchase the necessary francs at the prevailing market price. Conversely, after six months, A may find that the market price for French francs is favorable to the price specified in the forward contract and renege on the promise to purchase from C. Although the contract itself can (and does) penalize each party for deviations in promised performance, it may be inconvenient and costly to enforce these provisions.

Futures contracts are similar to forward contracts in that they represent an agreement to engage in a transaction at some future date. Futures contracts, however, are standardized with respect to size, expiration date, and many other relevant features. This means that hedgers may not be able to obtain the exact contract parameters to completely eliminate risks associated with price movements. Nevertheless, it also means that buyers (who agree to take delivery of an **asset**) and sellers (who agree to make delivery) of futures contracts are pricing identical contracts. This allows all trades to be funneled through a clearinghouse that can assume all counterparty risk. It also means that traders can quickly purchase or sell additional contracts to perfect a hedged position or to amplify a speculative one. Likewise, positions in the futures market can be "unwound" by selling contracts to offset previous purchases or by buying contracts to offset previous sales.

Another important distinction between forward and futures contracts regards the timing of the cash exchange between the parties. In a forward contact, the cash flow from the buyer to the seller of the asset occurs at the end of the contract period. With a futures contract, the buyer and seller agree on a price for future delivery at a future time, but that future price is changed continuously. If the price for future delivery rises in a given day, the buyer is now holding a claim that is more valuable than it was previously. The seller now finds it more costly to fulfill the contract. To adjust for this change, an amount equivalent to the aggregate change in value is transferred from the seller's account to the buyer's account. Likewise, if the price for future delivery falls during the day, funds are transferred from the buyer's account to the seller's account. This process is repeated daily for the life of the contract and is called marking to market". As a result, at the contract's expiration, all favorable or unfavorable movements in the market price of the asset to be delivered have already been accounted for. If the buyer of the contract opts to take delivery of the asset at this point, the transaction occurs at the prevailing market price.

The **derivative securities** discussed previously can correctly be considered as products of financial engineering. These contracts were invented, and in some cases, standardized, in order to provide clients with a more effective vehicle for avoiding particular types of risk or of speculating on specific price movements. In the next section, these securities will be included as some of the primary building blocks for more complex financially engineered contracts.

COMPLEX FINANCIAL ENGINEERING CONTRACTS

PORTFOLIO INSURANCE. One prominent example of financial engineering to meet the needs of clients is portfolio insurance. Portfolio insurance is essentially a strategy of **hedging**, stabilizing, or reducing the downside risk associated with the market value of a portfolio of financial assets such as stocks and **bonds**. There are a variety of techniques to protect the value of such a portfolio. As an example, suppose a portfolio manager wants to build a floor under the current value of a well-diversified portfolio. Furthermore, suppose that this portfolio is currently valued at $1,594,000, and its changes in value closely correspond with changes in the Standard & Poor's 500 (S&P 500) index. Ideally, the manager would like to reap the benefits of further increases in portfolio value, but wants to assure investors that the value will not fall below a certain, specific level. One solution is to purchase put options on the S&P 500 index. These options exist and are heavily traded at a variety of exercise prices. If the current level of the S&P 500 index is 455.56 and the manager wants to ensure that the value of his portfolio does not fall by more than 10 percent, put contracts with an exercise price of 410 (10 percent below the current level) can be purchased. The manager must purchase enough put option contracts so that the underlying value of the optioned asset is equal to the value of the portfolio. In this example, the portfolio value is approximately 3,500 times the current value of the S&P 500 index. Therefore, if the manager could buy puts on 3,500 "units" of the index, the position could be fully hedged. In reality, a single S&P 500 put contract represents 500 units of the index. So, the manager would purchase seven put contracts. Subsequent to the purchase, if the S&P 500 index (and the portfolio) rises in value, the manager will not exercise the put. Gains to the portfolio will be reduced by the modest amount of the put premium that was paid. On the other hand, if the index and the portfolio dropped in value by 20 percent, the put could be exercised at a significant profit that would generate a net loss for the position of approximately 10 percent. If the index value fell even lower, the profit from the put would be even greater and always provide a net loss of 10 percent.

Other techniques of portfolio insurance use **futures contracts** on stock and other market indexes. In the previous example, the manager could "synthetically" sell some or all of the portfolio by selling futures contracts on the S&P 500 index. If the portfolio subsequently fell in value along with the S&P 500 index, the futures position would generate profits that would partially or entirely offset the loss. If market prices rose, the portfolio would rise in value but the futures position would generate a loss that would tend to offset the gain. Note that this technique not only stabilizes the value of the stock portfolio, but also allows the manager to create a position with profits and losses that is equivalent to a smaller stock portfolio. This lower risk position is achieved without the significant expense of actually selling a portion of each individual stock position within the portfolio. Technically, this is an example of hedging, or maintaining a particular market value for a period rather than ensuring a minimum value while retaining the opportunity for upside gains. Nevertheless, it is possible to sell the proper number of S&P 500 index futures in order to mimic the overall profits of the put insured portfolio described above. This would require periodic adjustment to the hedge, or the number of futures contracts sold, as prices changed and the time to expiration of the contracts diminished.

SWAPS. Another broad category of contracts that result from financial engineering are referred to as swaps. Swaps represent exchanges of cash flows generated by distinct sets of assets or tied to distinct measures of value. An early example of an engineered swap is the currency swap. In this example, consider two firms in different countries each having continuing financial obligations in the other's country. More specifically, consider a French firm with a U.S. subsidiary that requires dollars to operate and a U.S. firm with a French subsidiary that has need for French francs. One alternative is to borrow the funds in the home country and exchange them for the foreign currency needed by the subsidiary. Another alternative is for the subsidiary to borrow the needed funds in the local currency. This second alternative will provide needed funds for the subsidiary and avoid the costs associated with foreign exchange transactions. It is also likely, however, that the subsidiary is at a disadvantage when negotiating the rate on a loan in the local currency. For example, the U.S.-based subsidiary of a French corporation may not have the perceived creditworthiness of a U.S. corporation with foreign subsidiaries and as a result will be forced to pay a higher rate of interest on the dollar-denominated loan.

If each firm becomes aware of the other's needs, they can do the following. First, each parent corporation should borrow an equivalent amount in their home currencies. These amounts will be equal based on the current exchange rate between dollars and francs. Second, they will simultaneously transfer the proceeds of the loan to the other firm's subsidiary (i.e., the French parent will transfer the borrowed francs to the U.S. firm's French subsidiary and the

U.S. parent will transfer the borrowed dollars to the French firm's U.S. subsidiary). As interest payments become due, the French-based subsidiary pays the French parent and the U.S.-based subsidiary pays the U.S. parent. Finally, when the term of the loans expires, each subsidiary will repay the other's parent. Note that this financially engineered contract has (1) effectively exploited each firm's ability to borrow at more favorable rates in its home country and (2) avoided all need for foreign currency exchange.

Obviously, the crucial factor in the formation of such a mutually advantageous contract is the identification of two parties with offsetting needs. In recent years, many financial intermediaries have developed services to fill this need. Swap dealers and brokers have developed the expertise to serve a broad variety of needs by matching the interests of counterparties and by engineering contracts that are mutually advantageous to the contracting parties and profitable for the intermediary.

A second common swap agreement is the interest rate swap. This typically takes the form of an exchange of a fixed-rate interest payment for a floating-rate interest payment. Suppose a bank has made a large number of loans at a fixed rate, but most of its liabilities are floating-rate obligations. If interests rise materially, its expenses will rise but its revenues are fixed. Profitability will suffer. If the bank can swap its 12 percent fixed-rate loans for a comparable amount of floating rate obligations that generate the yield on 30-year U.S. Treasury Department bonds plus 4 percent, it has materially reduced the influence of interest rate fluctuations on its profitability. In this example, once the bank has found a willing swap partner, the parties will agree to a notional principal amount. That is, the counterparties will agree on the amount of interest-generating capital that will be used to design the agreement. Typically, the parties will not exchange these notional amounts because they are identical. As time elapses, the bank will swap interest payments with its counterparty. For example, if the Treasury bond rate is 9 percent during a particular period, the agreement mandates that the bank receive 13 percent while it pays 12 percent. The swap agreement will only require that the net difference be exchanged, 1 percent paid to the bank in this case. If the Treasury bond rate drops to 6.5 percent, then the bank is obligated to pay the net difference between 10.5 percent (or 6.5 percent + 4 percent) and 12 percent, or 1.5 percent to the counterparty. If the Treasury bond rate remains at 8 percent, the fixed and floating rates are equivalent and no cash exchange would be necessary. Since there was no need for an actual exchange of the identical principal amounts at the beginning of the swap, none is required to close the positions at expiration of the agreement.

More complex swaps could involve trades of fixed- and floating-rate payments denominated in different currencies. Others could involve swaps of the income from debt instruments for the income generated by an equity investment in a specific portfolio such as the S&P 500. Swaps can also provide the basis for engineering a more efficient method of diversifying risk or allocating assets across asset classes. Consider this well-documented example. A chief executive officer (CEO) of a major corporation has accumulated a significant equity stake in his firm. While the CEO has other investments, he is not effectively diversified since he has an enormous amount of his own firm's stock. The CEO can contact a swap dealer who will arrange to swap the cash flows generated from the CEO's stock (**capital gains** and/or dividends) for a cash flow generated by an identically valued investment in a broadly diversified portfolio or market index. In this example, the CEO has (1) avoided the cost of selling his stock and any capital gains taxes that may result from the sale; (2) retained the voting rights of his stock; and (3) created a "synthetic" portfolio that is much less sensitive to the fluctuations in value of any particular company.

The swap can also be engineered to provide immediate international diversification. Suppose two portfolio managers, one in the United States and another in Japan, manage purely domestic portfolios. They may agree to swap notional values that would generate returns on their own managed portfolios or generate cash flows commensurate with an investment in a market index. For example, the U.S. manager may agree to provide the cash flow generated by a $100 million investment in the S&P 500 in exchange for returns generated from a similar-sized investment in the Nikkei 225 index. This would provide instant international diversification without the sizable cost of purchasing a large number of individual foreign securities. In addition, many countries impose fees or taxes on returns to foreign owners. A properly engineered swap agreement can avoid most or all of these expenses.

OTHER FINANCIALLY ENGINEERED INSTRUMENTS

There are a myriad of other examples of financial instruments or **contracts**. Many of these instruments are new and trade infrequently. They are often referred to as "exotics." For example, it is possible to use combinations of puts and calls on interest rate instruments to create caps, floors, and collars on interest payments. A cap represents the maximum rate that a floating interest rate position can obtain, a floor is the minimum rate, and a collar is the combination of a cap and a floor. Another unusual option feature is the lookback option. A call option with the lookback feature allows the holder to purchase the asset at the most favorable (lowest) price that prevailed over the life of the option. A put option with this feature allows the holder to sell the asset at the highest price over the option's life. These options set the exercise price at the end of the option's life rather than at the beginning. Closely related are Asian, or average-rate, options. These options set the exercise price at expiration as the average asset price during the option's life span. Barrier options are options that are activated, canceled, or exercised if a particular price condition is met. For example, a "down and out" option is canceled if the asset price falls below the exercise price while a "down and in" option is activated if the same price trigger is breached. Conversely, "up and out" and "up and in" options are canceled or activated when the exercise price is exceeded. Since these options are inert for large ranges of their underlying asset's price, they are less expensive than ordinary options and have generated interest among hedgers and speculators.

In summary, financial engineering is the design and construction of new financial contracts. These contracts are typically assembled from a modest number of basic financial instruments and indexes including stocks, bonds, options, forward contracts, and futures contracts. The need for properly engineered financial contracts is motivated by the client's interest in reducing risk, reducing costs associated with foreign exchange or other market transactions, and to provide the potential to enhance returns. Many financial intermediaries have developed specialized services in the area of financial engineering. As they have done so, the markets where elaborate and specialized contracts can trade efficiently have expanded and are likely to continue to do so.

[Paul Bolster]

FINANCIAL INSTITUTIONS

The financial market is composed of a number of financial institutions that perform a variety of functions. In most contexts, financial institutions can be considered synonymous with financial intermediaries in the financial markets. In a nutshell, financial intermediaries are the financial institutions that pool resources and channel funds from savers/lenders to spenders/borrowers. Smooth functioning of these institutions is very important for an efficient financial market and for the conduct of fiscal and monetary policies. Due to their crucial importance, almost all financial intermediaries are regulated—some are subjected to very tight regulations whereas others operate under less stringent regulations.

FINANCIAL INTERMEDIARIES

A large number of financial institutions serve as financial intermediaries. The essential economic function of the financial markets is to channel surplus funds from individuals who have saved from their incomes to individuals who want to finance their consumption or businesses that need funds to finance capital investments. There are two ways in which funds are channeled from savers/lenders to spenders/borrowers. The first is called direct finance. In direct finance, lenders lend to borrowers directly. A saver, for example, has $10,000 saved and buys a $10,000 General Motors (GM) bond maturing in ten years, paying an interest rate of 9.5 percent per annum—in this transaction, the saver has essentially *directly* lent $10,000 to General Motors for ten years. The second way in which funds are channeled is called indirect finance. It is in indirect finance that financial institutions called financial intermediaries are involved. In this case, a financial intermediary stands between savers/lenders and spenders/borrowers—it obtains surplus funds from savers and lends them to borrowers of its choice. A commercial bank is a common example of a financial intermediary—a commercial bank receives savings and checking deposits from individuals, and uses them, for instance, to make mortgage loans.

There are a large number of financial institutions that serve as financial intermediaries. According to Frederic Mishkin, the author of *The Economics of Money, Banking and Financial Markets*, financial intermediaries themselves are subdivided into three broad categories: (1) depository institutions (commonly referred to as banks); (2) contractual savings institutions; and (3) investment intermediaries. The division of financial intermediaries into these three groups is based on their primary sources of funds and how they use these funds. Based on Mishkin's book, each of these three categories and the financial institutions that fall under these categories are briefly discussed below.

DEPOSITORY INSTITUTIONS

Depository institutions are generally referred to as banks. The term "depository institution" originates from the fact that a banking-type financial intermediary accepts deposits from individuals and businesses, and makes loans. Depository institutions are made up of four kinds of banking institutions: commercial banks, **savings and loan associations, credit unions**, and mutual savings banks. The key characteristics of these four kinds of banking institutions are briefly described in what follows.

COMMERCIAL BANKS. Commercial banks are financial intermediaries that raise funds primarily by issuing (1) demand and other checkable deposits (deposits by businesses or individuals on which checks can be written to make payments); (2) savings account deposits (they carry interest payments, but can not be used to write checks on and are usually maintained by households and individuals); and (3) certificates of deposit (CDs) or time deposits (they earn interest and have fixed terms to maturity and are opened by both individuals and businesses). Commercial banks use the resources so raised (within limitations imposed by the nation's central bank, the Federal Reserve Bank) to make loans to consumers (for instance, to buy durable goods, such as automobiles), to businesses (for example, to invest in a plant expansion), and to home buyers (mortgage loans). They also investment their funds in U.S. Treasury bonds, and state and local government bonds (municipal bonds). Commercial banks are like other businesses—they profit from the difference between the reward for lending and the cost of borrowing.

There are approximately 12,000 commercial banks in the United States, a number that is much larger than in most other industrialized countries. As a group, they are the largest financial intermediary in the United States. Most of them, however, are very small—almost 72 percent of commercial banks in the United States have assets of less than 100 million dollars, and another 22 percent of them have assets between 100 and 500 million dollars. Only a little over three percent of the banks have assets over one billion dollars. Despite the large number of banks in the U.S. banking industry, larger banks do hold a giant share of the industry assets. Based on 1992 data, the top 3.3 percent of banks (with assets of 1 billion dollars or more) hold nearly 70 percent of all bank assets. Based on 1993 data, Citicorp (New York), is the largest U.S. commercial bank, followed by Bank-America Corp. (San Francisco).

In most other industrialized countries, there are far fewer banks—typically, five or fewer banks dominate the banking industry. The latter is true for countries such as Great Britain or Canada, where a small group of commercial banks accounts for most of the banking business. By contrast, in the United States, based on 1993 data, the ten-largest banks together hold only about 30 percent of the industry assets. This characteristic of the banking industry sets it apart from other industries in the United States. The automobile industry in the United States, for example, is dominated by only three firms. Almost the same is true for mainframe computers. Does this mean that the U.S. banking industry is more competitive than, for instance, the auto industry? Surprisingly, this is not the case. The answer lies in the banking regulation embodied in the McFadden Act of 1927, which has effectively prohibited branching across state lines.

Commercial banks are very heavily regulated. They are often subject to multiple layers of regulation. They are either chartered by states or the federal government (the U.S. Department of Treasury), and they are thus regulated by their chartering institution. Many commercial banks are members of the **Federal Reserve System** and are regulated by the Federal Reserve. In addition, as most commercial banks buy deposit insurance (in which an account with a bank is insured up to $100,000) from the **Federal Deposit Insurance Corporation** (FDIC), they are also regulated by this agency. Nevertheless, the U.S. banking industry is undergoing a period of rapid transformation with the passage of deregulation legislation in the mid-1990s.

SAVINGS AND LOAN ASSOCIATIONS (S&LS). Except for some minor differences, **savings and loan associations** (S&Ls) look like commercial banks. The main difference lies in the way S&Ls obtain their funds and use these funds to make loans. Like commercial banks, they also obtain their funds by issuing checkable deposits, savings account deposits, and time deposits. Traditionally, however, savings deposits have played greater role for savings and loan associations. The funds obtained through different kinds of deposits have traditionally been used to make mortgage loans—in contrast, business and consumer loans dominate commercial banks' loan portfolios. Also, there are some subtle differences between commercial banks, and savings and loan associations. For example, savings deposits issued by S&Ls are often called shares

Until 1980 government regulations did not allow savings and loan associations to establish checking accounts. They were also restricted to making mortgage loans. The S&Ls were allowed, however, to pay somewhat higher **interest rates** (compared to commercial banks) on their savings deposits, so as to attract funds that could be used to make mortgage loans. This arrangement landed savings and loan associations in deep trouble. During the 1950s and early 1960s, interest rates were relatively low and S&Ls grew faster than commercial banks—they had a comfortable margin between the cost of their funds and the interest they received on their mortgage loans. Interest rates, however, rose quite sharply from the late 1960s to the early 1980s. The high interest rate of these years meant that the S&Ls were raising funds at higher costs. Many of their mortgage loans, however, were made years before at very low interest rates, and these were long-term fixed-rate mortgages, with maturity exceeding over 25 years. As a result, savings and loan associations' incomes from mortgages fell short of the cost of acquiring new funds, a phenomenon known as the profit squeeze. Partly due to this reason, many savings and loans suffered large losses and had to go out of business.

Through the Banking Deregulation Act passed in 1980, the restrictions on savings and loan associations' activities have been substantially eased. They were allowed to issue checkable deposits, make consumer loans, and to participate in other activities that were hitherto restricted to commercial banks. Through the 1980 act, however, S&Ls were also made subject of the same Reserve requirements that are applied to commercial banks. As the result, the distinction between commercial banks and savings and loan associations has been blurred. More and more, these two kinds of depository institutions look alike and behave in a similar fashion. To many people, it may make virtually no difference whether they bank with savings and loan associations or commercial banks.

Similar to commercial banks, savings and loan associations are also subject to multiple layers of government regulation. Federally chartered savings and loan associations are regulated by the Office of Thrift Supervision (OTS), a bureau within the federal Treasury. Federal deposit insurance for S&Ls is provided by the Savings Association Insurance Fund (SAIF), a subsidiary of the Federal Deposit Insurance Corporation.

CREDIT UNIONS. Credit unions are also depository institutions, but they are structured as cooperative lending institutions—they are organized around a particular group, such as employees of a company or an institution, members of a **labor union**, or members of a particular branch of armed forces. Credit unions, like commercial banks and savings and loan associations, acquire funds by issuing different kinds of deposits (often called shares) and primarily make consumer loans. The 1980 Banking Deregulation Act also eased restrictions on credit unions—this act allowed them to issue checkable deposits, as well as to make mortgage loans in addition consumer loans. For all practical purposes, members of a credit union can consider it as a bank. Membership in the credit union is not, however, as open as commercial banks—one must belong to the particular group, in some way, to qualify for the membership of the relevant credit union.

There are large number of credit unions in the United States, about 13,000. As a group, in terms of sheer numbers, they are larger than commercial banks. Most credit unions, however, are quite small—most have assets of less than $10 million. As credit unions are intimately tied to a particular group (a company, an institution, or an industry), they lack the diversification of a commercial bank, making them vulnerable. If a large number of workers in an industry are laid off and thus have trouble making loan payments, this can easily endanger the credit union in that industry. Recent regulatory changes have attempted to reduce this risk of credit union failures by allowing them to cater to a more diverse group of individuals. This has induced an increase in the size of credit unions.

Like commercial banks, and savings and loan associations, deposits up to $100,000 (on a per-account basis) are insured, and they are subject to regulations. Credit unions are chartered either by state banking authorities or the federal government. Nearly half of all credit unions are federally chartered. Charters are issued by a federal agency known as the National Credit Union Administration (NCUA), which regulates federally chartered credit unions through establishment of minimum capital requirements, periodic examinations of credit unions' books, and the requirement that these institutions submit periodic reports on their activities. Federal deposit insurance is provided by a subsidiary of the NCUA called the National Credit Union Share Insurance Fund (NCUSIF). NCUSIF provides insurance both to federally chartered and state-chartered credit unions. When a state-chartered credit union buys insurance from the NCUSIF, it becomes subject to regulation by the NCUSIF, in addition to the regulation by the relevant state banking authority. Similar to commercial banks, this leads to multiple layers of regulations.

The interstate branching laws do not apply to federally chartered credit unions. A federally chartered credit union can open branches wherever its members are. In some cases, it literally leads to a worldwide branching. Members of the U.S. Navy and Marine Corps belong to the Navy Federal Credit Union. As these servicepersons are also stationed at locations outside the United States, the Navy Federal Credit Union has branches across the world.

Credit unions have not faced the problems that rocked the savings and loan industry. This is because most of the loans made by credit unions are to consumers, and consumer loans have much shorter maturity periods than mortgage loans (the primary assets of savings and loan associations).

MUTUAL SAVINGS BANKS. Mutual savings banks are the smallest group of financial intermediaries among depository institutions. They are quite similar to savings and loan associations. Also, one can consider them as hybrid between a savings and loan and a credit union. Like savings and loan associations, they acquire funds by issuing different kinds of deposits and make, primarily, mortgage loans. Like credit unions, however, they are organized as cooperatives, known as mutuals, in which depositors own the bank.

Like savings and loan associations, mutual savings banks were restricted to making mortgage loans until the restrictions were relaxed by the 1980 banking act. As a result, mutual savings banks also experienced profit squeeze from the late 1960s to the early 1980s. They can now issue checking deposits and make consumer and other loans, in addition to making mortgage loans.

There are only about 500 mutual savings banks in the United States, and most of them are concentrated in New York State and New England. They can also be chartered either by states or the federal government. Nearly half of mutual savings banks are chartered by the states. A majority of them have deposit insurance from the Federal Deposit Insurance Corporation (FDIC). As in case of other categories of depository institutions, each account is insured up to $100,000. Because of buying the deposit insurance from the FDIC, most mutual funds are also subject to regulations by the FDIC.

THE BLURRING OF DISTINCTIONS AMONG DEPOSITORY INSTITUTIONS

Two acts—the Depository Institutions Deregulation and Monetary Control Act of 1980, and the Garn-St. Germain Depository Institutions Act of 1982—blurred the distinction among the four kinds of depository institutions discussed above. These acts expanded the ability of noncommercial banks to participate in activities from which they were hitherto barred. For example, all four kinds of depository institutions were allowed to issue checking accounts.

There is one area of regulation, branching regulations, where the old restrictions imposed by the Mc-Fadden Act of 1927 (prohibition against branching across state lines) are still in place. Due to the McFadden Act, there are a large number of commercial banks in the United States. Crises in the savings and loan industry during the 1980s induced some banks to purchase failed savings and loan associations spread over several states, effectively implying branching across states in these instances. Technological changes (especially the widespread use of automated teller machines, **ATMs**) and the use of ''**holding companies**'' (where a holding company owns banks in different states) have dealt a further blow to branching restrictions imposed by the 1927 act. There is a widespread belief that the Mcfadden Act has long been obsolete. Congress is now in the process of removing the restrictions against branching across state lines.

CONTRACTUAL SAVINGS INSTITUTIONS

Contractual savings institutions are financial intermediaries that acquire funds periodically on a contractual basis and invest them (lend them out) in such a way that they have financial instruments maturing when their contractual obligations have to be met. In general, they can predict their liabilities fairly accurately, and thus they (unlike depository institutions) do not have to worry as much about losing funds. As a result, they mainly invest their resources in longer term securities, such as, corporate stocks and bonds, and mortgages. Three major categories of contractual savings institutions—life insurance companies, fire and casualty insurance companies, and pension funds and government retirement funds—are briefly discussed below.

LIFE INSURANCE COMPANIES. Life insurance companies sell life insurance policies that protect the beneficiaries of a policyholder against financial hazards that follow the death of the insured person. Life insurance companies also sell annuities in which an insurance company contracts to make annual income payments to the annuity buyer upon his or her retirement. These insurance companies acquire funds through payments of premiums by individuals who pay to keep their policies in force. Life insurance companies can calculate their liabilities with a fair degree of accuracy using mortality tables. As a result, they use their funds to buy longer term securities—primarily corporate bonds and mortgages. While corporate **stocks** are also long-term securities, life insurance companies are restricted in the amount of stocks they can hold. This government restriction is based on the perception that stocks are risky, and they may thus jeopardize the insurance companies' ability to meet their liabilities. With about two trillion dollars in assets, life insurance companies are the largest segment among contractual savings institutions.

FIRE AND CASUALTY INSURANCE COMPANIES

Fire and casualty insurance companies (also called property and casualty insurance companies) are in the insurance business like the life insurance companies. They insure policyholders against the risk of loss from a variety of contingencies, such as fire, flood, theft, or accidents. An individual buys car or home insurance, for example, from a property and casualty insurance company. Like life insurance companies, fire and casualty insurance companies acquire funds through payments of insurance premiums from their policyholders. Unlike life insurance companies, however, the property and casualty insurance companies are subject to greater uncertainty with respect to their liabilities—there is no way to pinpoint as to when major disasters may happen. Two major hurricanes, Hugo in 1989 and Andrew in 1992, hit U.S. states, which multiplied the claim payments by the property and casualty insurance companies to policyholders manifold. Due to this kind of uncertainty, these insurance companies buy more liquid assets (shorter-term securities) than life insurance companies. Municipal bonds constitute the largest fraction of their total assets. They also, however, invest in corporate stocks and bonds, and Treasury securities.

PRIVATE PENSION FUNDS AND GOVERNMENT RETIREMENT FUNDS

Private pension funds and government retirement funds receive periodic payments of contributions from employers and/or employees that participate in the program. Employee contributions are either automatically deducted from their pay or made voluntarily by them. The pension and retirement funds' liability is to provide retirement income, generally in the form of annuities, to individuals covered by these pension plans. As the liabilities of private pension and government retirement funds are fairly certain with respect to timing and are of a long-term nature, they invest their resources in long-term financial instruments, such as corporate stocks and bonds.

The federal government has encouraged growth in pension funds through legislative actions that mandate establishment of pension plans, as well as through tax incentives to individuals that lower their costs of contributing to the pension plans. The federal 403(b) provision is an example of the federal tax incentive.

INVESTMENT INTERMEDIARIES

Most, though not all, investment intermediaries facilitate investments in financial assets by individuals and institutions by pooling resources and investing them according to stipulated objectives. The financial intermediaries included under this category are: mutual funds, money market mutual funds, and finance companies.

MUTUAL FUNDS. **Mutual funds** are financial intermediaries that raise funds through sale of shares to many individuals and institutions, and pool these to buy a diversified portfolio of stocks, bonds, or a combination of stocks and bonds. The number of mutual funds in the United States has grown rapidly. Now, there are more mutual funds than the number of stocks on the New York Stock Exchange. With the growth in the mutual fund industry, characteristics of mutual funds have also undergone changes. At the present time, a specific mutual fund is organized around an investment philosophy. In selling shares to perspective participants, the mutual fund is expected to state its investment philosophy, and follow it (generally) in investing pooled resources. A mutual fund, for example, may be a broadly diversified stock fund that picks stocks from among all available domestic stocks. A stock fund may also, however, concentrate on a narrow range of stocks, such as small capitalization stocks, over-the-counter stocks, blue-chip stocks, depressed stocks, stocks that pay high dividends, or stocks of a particular sector of the economy. Thus, one must carefully interpret a mutual fund's investment into a diversified portfolio of, for instance, stocks—

the diversified investment is subject to the investment philosophy of the relevant mutual fund. Also, different investment philosophies and levels of diversifications carry different levels of investment risk. Even when a mutual fund specifies an investment philosophy, it may not be fully invested—it may keep, for example, some cash on hand for investment opportunities that may open in the future or to meet redemptions.

Similar to stock mutual funds, there are bond mutual funds. Once again, a bond mutual fund follows an investment philosophy—it may invest its funds in, for example, a diversified portfolio of bonds, in long-term Treasury bonds, higher-quality corporate bonds, lower-quality corporate bonds (the so-called **junk bonds**), or bonds of state and local governments (called municipal bonds or munis). Bond mutual funds are generally considered less risky than stock mutual funds. As mentioned earlier, some mutual funds also invest their funds in a combination of stocks and bonds.

In general, mutual funds permit an individual to participate in a more diversified portfolio of financial instruments than would have been possible if the individual tried to make the investment on his or her own—the use of a mutual fund reduces the **transaction costs** for the individual. In addition, as mutual funds are expected to be managed by experts, the individual participating in a mutual fund can expect better returns. In addition to these benefits, mutual funds provide liquidity to individuals participating in these funds—they can redeem or sell their shares at any time. The value of their shares, however, will depend on the value of the mutual fund's portfolio (which, in turn, will depend on the conditions in the markets for the securities in which the mutual fund is invested). This obviously implies that an individual is not guaranteed to receive the principal amount back. Also, mutual fund shares, unlike deposits at a depository institution, are not insured by a federal agency.

MONEY MARKET MUTUAL FUNDS. Money market mutual funds are like ordinary **mutual funds** with some added characteristics. The most important difference between mutual funds and money market mutual funds is that the latter invest in money market financial instruments (securities that have maturities of less than a year). Because of the kind of securities they invest in, assets of a money market fund are considered very liquid and are unlikely to generate losses to those that participate in these funds. Shareholders in a money market mutual fund receive investment income based on the earnings of the security holdings of the fund. A key characteristic of a money market mutual fund is that participants in these funds have limited check-writing privileges on their shareholdings—frequently, checks cannot be written for less than $500.

FINANCE COMPANIES. Finance companies acquire funds by issuing commercial papers (short-term corporate debt instruments), stocks and bonds. They use these funds to make loans to consumers to finance home improvements or to purchase a consumer durable (such as cars or furniture), and to small businesses for various purposes. Sometimes, a finance company helps to sell a particular product. GMAC or Ford Motor Credit company are examples of finance companies that perform such a function.

[Anandi P. Sahu]

FURTHER READING:

Mishkin, Frederic S. *The Economics of Money, Banking and Financial Markets.* 4th ed. HarperCollins Publishers, 1995.

Ritter, Lawrence S., and William L. Silber. *Principles of Money, Banking and Financial Markets,* 6th ed. Basic Books, 1989.

FINANCIAL PLANNING

In the 1980s, financial planning became the buzzword for an overview of one's financial situation. Through sound and thoughtful planning and the use of basic financial techniques such as savings and investing, financial planning practitioners help consumers achieve financial goals such as a comfortable retirement, college education for their children, or tax reduction.

The need for financial planning or coordination for one's overall financial affairs grew from constantly-changing and complex tax laws which affect short-term and long-term goals. Another influence is the growth and complexity of insurance and investment products.

Financial planning can be described as figuring out, both literally and figuratively, where one is, where one wants to go, and how one is going to get there. Financial planning involves reviewing one's total financial picture: **budgeting**; cash reserves; college funding; **debt**; estate plans (including wills and **trusts**); insurances (including automobile, homeowners, life, and disability); investments, including debt investments (notes, **bonds** and other loaned **assets** that pay interest and provide safety and income) and **equity** investments (**stocks**, **real estate**, precious metals, coins, antiques and other collectibles that offer growth but are evaluated on a risk/reward basis); **retirement** plans; and **taxes**.

Financial planning practitioners begin the financial planning process by gathering quantitative and qualitative data to establish one's current financial situation. Items to be addressed include health status and family data, personal and invested assets, **liabili-**ties, annual income and living expenses, insurance and investment products currently owned, and retirement benefits. Step two in the financial planning process is to establish tentative financial goals in terms of realistic objectives. These goals should be specifically geared to an individual's financial attitude and capabilities. Personal goals include: increasing one's standard of living; achieving financial security at retirement; increasing net worth; reducing tax burden; paying for children's college education; providing for one's family in the event of death or the death of one's spouse; purchasing a house; minimizing the cost of probate and **estate taxes**; controlling the distribution of assets to one's heirs; and planning for long-term or nursing home care.

The financial planning practitioner processes and reviews the information to determine what strengths and weaknesses currently exist. This process includes preparation of **financial statements**, such as a statement of financial position (net worth) or **cash flow statement** (one's annual income and expenses) and a projection of cash flow. Additionally, the financial planning practitioner will review existing insurance policies, tax returns, wills and other information. At this point, the financial planner and client can determine if the tentative goals are realistic or need to be revised.

Assuming the goals are realistic, the financial planner will recommend appropriate techniques for achieving objectives. This process can include alternate investment vehicles, insurance products, and/or income and estate tax planning strategies. A review of the recommendations will be made to determine their overall effectiveness and then implemented with the assistance of other allied professionals. The use of financial planners does not replace the need for specialists, but rather they can act as coordinators.

Furthermore the plan will be reviewed periodically, to reflect changes in economic conditions, regulatory laws, objectives and product performance.

There are two categories of financial plans: the single-purpose plan and the comprehensive plan. A single-purpose plan is problem-oriented and centers on a particular concern, such as tax planning or estate planning. This process accomplishes its goal by isolating that problem or question and focusing on how it affects a particular individual.

The comprehensive financial planning process involves six distinct steps:

(1) clarify one's present situation by collecting and assessing all relevant personal and financial data, including assets and liabilities, tax returns, records of securities transactions, insurance policies, wills, trusts, and **pension plans**;

(2) decide where one wants to be by identifying both financial and personal goals and objectives;

(3) identify financial problems that may create barriers to achieving financial goals;

(4) provide a written plan;

(5) implement the agreed-upon recommendations; and

(6) review and revise the plan periodically.

Financial planners are generally compensated one of five ways: fee-only; commission-only; fee-offset; combination fee/commission; and salary. A fee-only financial planner is compensated entirely from fees for consultation and/or financial plan development. Commission-only or combination fee and commission financial planners are compensated through the products they sell when implementing a financial plan, such as trust services, tax-advantaged investments, securities, real estate or insurance. Financial planners using a fee-offset approach receive their compensation in the form of commissions from the sale of financial products which, in turn, offset the fees associated with the planning process. Some financial planners work on a salary basis for financial service institutions including banks and credit unions.

The Institute of Certified Financial Planners (ICFP) is a national, non-profit professional association for financial planners. Membership is limited to those who have earned the Certified Financial Planner (CFP) designation; individuals who are actively enrolled in a CFP curriculum approved by the International Board of Standards and Practices for Certified Financial Planners, Inc. (IBCFP), allied credentialed professionals who are eligible to take the CFP examination, as well as academician and paraplanners are eligible for ''Affiliate'' status in the ICFP. Institute members are required to meet continuing education, ethics, examination, and experience prerequisites set by the IBCFP. The ICFP is located at 7600 E. Eastman Avenue, Suite 301, Denver, CO 80231, (800)282-7526 or (303)751-7600.

The International Association for Financial Planning (IAFP) is the leading association representing financial professionals who help clients manage and invest their money to reach their financial goal and objectives. Founded in 1969, the IAFP has over 11,000 members who reside in all 50 states and 22 countries. IAFP members either work with clients in the areas of personal and/or corporate financial advice or provide services and products to whose who work directly with clients. The IAFP is located at Two Concourse Parkway, Suite 800, Atlanta, GA 30328, (800)945-4237.

The IAFP sponsors the Registry of Financial Planning Practitioners. The Registry defines standards and qualifications for professionals in the financial planning industry. Criteria include education, experience, practice, plus passage of a three-section Practice Knowledge Examination.

SEE ALSO: Investment Management; Securities and Investments

[Susan Bard Hall]

FURTHER READING:

''Your Right to Financial Independence,'' *The Daily Market Digest.* Greater Chicago Society of the Institute of Certified Financial Planners, 1986.

''Overview of Financial Planning,'' Institute of Certified Financial Planners.

''Fact Sheet,'' Institute of Certified Financial Planners.

''Selecting A Qualified Financial Planning Professional: Twelve Questions To Consider,'' Institute of Certified Financial Planners.

''Financial Planning: A Common Sense Guide for the 1990s,'' Institute of Certified Financial Planners.

''A Profile: The International Association for Financial Planning,'' International Association for Financial Planning.

''Consumer Guide to Comprehensive Financial Planning,'' International Association for Financial Planning. pp. 5, 7.

FINANCIAL RATIOS

There are many financial ratios used by analysts to assess various attributes of a company's financial strength or operating results. They all involve the comparison of elements from a **balance sheet** or **income statement**, and are crafted with particular points of focus in mind. Financial ratios can be broken down into four main categories with several specific ratio calculations prescribed within each:

1. **Profitability** or Return on Investment

   a. Gross profitability: Gross Profits/Net Sales - measures the margin on sales the company is achieving. Can be a measure of **manufacturing** efficiency, or **marketing** effectiveness.

   b. Net profitability: Net Income/Net Sales - measures the overall profitability of the company; how much is being brought to the bottom line. Strong gross with weak net profitability may indicate a problem ''below the line'' with indirect operating expenses, such as G&A expense, or non-operating items, such as interest expense.

   c. Return on assets: Net Income/Total **Assets** - indicates how effectively the company is deploying its assets.

d. Return on investment 1: Net Income/ Owners' Equity - indicates how well the company is utilizing its equity investment. Due to leverage, this measure will generally be higher than return on assets.

e. Return on investment 2: **Dividends** $+/-$ Stock Price Change/Stock Price Paid - from the investor's point of view, measures the gain (or loss) reaped from placing an investment over a period of time.

f. **Earnings per share**: Net Income/No. of Shares Outstanding - states profits in terms of per share basis; helpful in further comparison to market price of stock.

2. **Liquidity**

a. Current ratio: Current Assets/Current **Liabilities** - measures the ability of an entity to pay its near-term obligations. Current usually is defined as within one year.

b. Quick ratio (or "acid test"): Quick Assets/Current Liabilities, where "quick assets" consist of cash, marketable securities and receivables - measures a more strict definition of the company's ability to make payments on current obligations.

c. Cash to total assets: Cash/Total Assets - measures the portion of a company's assets held in cash or marketable securities. Although a high ratio may indicate some degree of safety from a creditor's viewpoint, excess amounts of cash may be viewed as inefficient.

3. **Leverage**

a. Debt/equity ratio: Debt/Owners' Equity - indicates the relative mix of the company's investor-supplied capital. A company is generally considered safer if it has a low debt to equity ratio, that is a higher proportion of owner-supplied capital.

b. **Debt** ratio: Debt/Total Assets - measures the portion of a company's capital that is provided by borrowing. A debt ratio greater than 1.0 means the company has negative net worth, and is technically bankrupt. This ratio is similar, and can easily be converted to, the debt to equity ratio.

c. Interest coverage: Earnings Before Interest & Taxes/Interest Expense - indicates how comfortably the company can handle its interest payments.

4. **Inventory and Receivables Management**

a. Inventory turnover/year: Cost of goods sold for Year/Average Inventory - shows how efficiently the company is managing its production, warehousing and distribution of product, considering its volume of sales. Generally, higher ratios are thought to be better.

b. Inventory holding period: 365/Inventory Turnover/Year - calculates the number of days, on average, that elapse between finished goods production and sale of product.

c. Inventory to assets ratio: Inventory/Total Assets - shows the portion of assets tied up in inventory. Generally, the lower the better.

d. Accounts receivable turnover: Net (credit) Sales/Average Accounts Receivable - gives a measure of how quickly credit sales are turned into cash. Alternatively, the reciprocal of this ratio indicates the portion of a year's credit sales that are outstanding at the particular point in time.

e. Collection period: 365/Accounts receivable turnover - measures the average number of days the company's receivables are outstanding, between the dates of credit sale and collection of cash.

[Christopher Barry]

FINANCIAL STATEMENTS

Financial statements are considered to be a major feature of financial reporting, and the principal method of communicating financial information about an entity to parties outside an entity. In a technical sense, financial statements are a summation of the **accounting** process reflecting a tabulation of account titles and amounts of money that reports the financial position of an entity and changes therein at a moment in time and during a period of time. The basic purpose of financial statements is to communicate information about economic decisions made to external and internal parties.

General purpose financial statements are designed to meet the needs of many diverse users, particularly present and potential owners and creditors. Financial statements result from simplifying, condensing, and aggregating masses of data obtained primarily from the financial system. They are an output of the accounting system.

FINANCIAL REPORTING

The **Financial Accounting Standards Board**, in its *Statements of Financial Accounting Concepts*, asserted that financial reporting includes not only financial statements but also other means of communicating information that relates, directly or indirectly, to the information provided by the accounting system. Financial reporting is the process of communicating financial accounting information about an enterprise to its external users. Financial statements provide information useful in investment and credit decisions and in assessing cash flow prospects. They provide information about an enterprise's resources, claims to those resources, and changes in the resources.

Financial reporting is a broad concept encompassing financial statements, notes to financial statements and parenthetical disclosures, supplementary information (such as changing prices), and other means of financial reporting (such as management discussions and analysis, and letters to stockholders). Financial reporting is but one source of information needed by those who make economic decisions about business enterprises.

The primary focus of financial reporting is information about earnings and its components. Information about earnings based on accrual accounting usually provides a better indication of an enterprise's present and continuing ability to generate positive cash flows than that provided by cash receipts and payments.

MAJOR FINANCIAL STATEMENTS

The basic financial statements of an enterprise include the (1) balance sheet (or statement of financial position), (2) **income statement**, (3) cash flow statement, and (4) statement of changes in owners' equity or stockholders' equity. The **balance sheet** lists all the **assets**, **liabilities**, and stockholders' equity (for a corporation), of an entity as of a specific date. The balance sheet is essentially a financial snapshot of the entity. The income statement presents a summary of the revenues, gains, expenses, losses, and net income or net loss of an entity for a specific period. This statement is similar to a moving picture of the entity's operations during a period. The cash flow statement summarizes an entity's cash receipts and cash payments relating to its operating, investing, and financing activities during a particular period. A statement of changes in owners' equity or stockholders' equity reconciles the beginning of the period equity of an enterprise with its ending balance.

For an item to be recognized in the financial statements, it should meet four fundamental recognition criteria, subject to cost-benefit constraint and a materiality threshold. These criteria are:

- Definitions: The item meets the definition of an element of financial statements.

- Materiality: It has a relevant attribute measurable with sufficient reliability.

- Relevance: The information about it is capable of making a difference in user decisions.

- Reliability: The information is representational faithful, verifiable, and neutral.

Items currently reported in financial statements are measured by different attributes (for example, historical cost, current cost, current market value, net reliable value, and present value of future cash flows). While historical cost has traditionally been the major attribute assigned to assets and liabilities, the Financial Accounting Standards Board expects to continue to use different attributes.

Notes to financial statements are informative disclosures appended to financial statements. They provide information concerning such matters as **depreciation** and inventory methods used, details of long-term debt, pensions, leases, income taxes, contingent liabilities, method of consolidation, and other matters. Notes are considered an integral part of the financial statements. Schedules and parenthetical disclosures are also used to present information not provided elsewhere in the financial statements.

Each financial statement has a heading, which gives the name of the entity, the name of the statement, and the date or time covered by the statement. The information provided in financial statements is primarily financial in nature and expressed in units of money. The information relates to an individual business enterprise. The information often is the product of approximations and estimates, rather than exact measurements. The financial statements typically reflect the financial effects of transactions and events that have already happened (i.e., historical).

Financial statements presenting financial data for two or more periods are called comparative statements. Comparative financial statements usually give similar reports for the current period and for one or more preceding periods. They provide analysts with significant information about trends and relationships over two or more years. Comparative statements are considerably more significant than are single-year statements. Comparative statements emphasize the fact that financial statements for a single accounting period are only one part of the continuous history of the company.

Interim financial statements are reports for periods of less than a year. The purpose of interim financial statements is to improve the timeliness of accounting information. Some companies issue comprehensive financial statements while others issue summary statements. Each interim period should be viewed primarily as an integral part of an annual period and should generally continue to use the generally accepted accounting principles (GAAP) that were used in the preparation of the company's latest **annual reports**.

Financial statements are usually audited by independent accountants for the purpose of improving the level of confidence in their reliability.

ACCOUNTING ASSUMPTIONS

Accounting statements are prepared on the assumption that each enterprise is a separate entity, that all transactions can be expressed or measured in dollars, that the enterprise will continue in business indefinitely, and that statements will be prepared at regular intervals. These assumptions provide the foundation for the structure of financial accounting theory and practice, and explain why financial information is presented in a given manner.

ACCOUNTING PRINCIPLES, PROCEDURES, AND POLICIES

GAAP are the conventions, rules, and procedures necessary to define accounting practice at a particular time. The Financial Accounting Standards Board (FASB), created in 1972, is currently the independent nongovernmental body in the United States that develops and issues standards of financial accounting. The seven members of the FASB serve full time and are paid for their services. Pervasive accounting principles include the recording of assets and liabilities at cost, and recognizing **revenue** when it is realized and when a transaction has taken place (generally at the point of sale) and expenses according to the matching principle (costs to revenues). Modifying conventions include conservatism and materiality. Conservatism requires that uncertainties and risks related to a company be reflected in its accounting reports. Materiality requires that anything that would be of interest to an informed investor should be fully disclosed in the financial statements.

Accounting procedures are those rules and practices that are associated with the operations of an accounting system and that lead to the development of financial statements. Accounting procedures include the methods, practices, and techniques used to carry out accounting objectives and to implement accounting principles.

Accounting policies are those accounting principles followed by a specific entity. Information about the accounting policies adopted by a reporting enterprise is essential for financial statement users and should be disclosed in the financial statements. Accounting principles and their method of application in the following areas are considered particularly impor-

tant: (1) a selection from existing alternatives, (2) areas that are peculiar to a particular industry in which the company operates, and (3) unusual and innovative applications of GAAP. Significant accounting policies are usually disclosed as the initial note or as a summary preceding the notes to the financial statements.

QUALITATIVE CHARACTERISTICS OF ACCOUNTING INFORMATION

Qualitative characteristics of accounting information are those properties of information necessary to make it useful in making economic decisions. To be useful, accounting information should be understandable to users who have a reasonable knowledge of business and economic activities and who are willing to study the information with reasonable diligence. Decision usefulness is the underlying qualitative characteristic when judging the quality of accounting information. Relevance and reliability are the primary decision-specific qualities of accounting information. Relevance is the capacity of information to make a difference in a decision by helping users to form predictions about the outcomes of past, present, and future events or to confirm or correct prior expectations. Reliability of information assures that information is reasonably free from error and bias and faithfully represents what it purports to represent. A secondary qualitative characteristic of accounting information is comparability (including consistency)—the quality of information that enables users to identify similarities in and differences between two sets of economic phenomena. Consistency refers to conformity from period to period with unchanging policies and procedures. Two constraints to the hierarchy of qualitative characteristics can be used to identify what accounting information should be disclosed in financial statements: a benefit/cost constraint and the materiality constraint. The benefit/cost constraint refers to the premise that the cost of collecting, processing, auditing, and communicating the information will not exceed the benefits to be derived from its use. The materiality constraint provides a quantitative threshhold referring to the magnitude of an omission or misstatement of accounting information that would make it likely that the judgment of a reasonable person relying on it would have been influenced by the omission or misstatement.

ELEMENTS OF FINANCIAL STATEMENTS

The Financial Accounting Standards Board (FASB) has defined the following elements of financial statements of business enterprises: assets, liabilities, equity, revenues, expenses, gains, losses, investment by owners, distribution to owners, and comprehensive income. According to FASB, the elements of financial statements are the building blocks with which financial statements are constructed—the broad classes of items that financial statements comprise. FASB concepts statement No. 3, ''Elements of Financial Statements of Business Enterprises'' defined the interrelated elements that are directly related to measuring performance and the financial position of a business enterprise:

- Assets are probable future economic benefits obtained or controlled by a particular entity as a result of past transactions or events.

- Comprehensive income is the change in equity (net assets) of an entity during a period from transactions and other events and circumstances from nonowner sources. It includes all changes in equity during a period except those resulting from investments by owners and distributions to owners.

- Distributions to owners are decreases in net assets of a particular enterprise resulting from transferring assets, rendering services, or incurring liabilities to owners. Distributions to owners decrease ownership interest or equity in an enterprise.

- Equity is the residual interest in the assets of an entity that remains after deducting its liabilities. In a business entity, equity is the ownership interest.

- Expenses are outflows or other using up of assets or incurring of liabilities during a period from delivering or producing goods or rendering services, or carrying out other activities that constitute the entity's ongoing major or central operation.

- Gains are increases in equity (net assets) from peripheral or incidental transactions of an entity and from all other transactions and other events and circumstances affecting the entity during a period except those that result from revenues or investments by owner.

- Investments by owners are increases in net assets of a particular enterprise resulting from transfers to it from other entities of something of value to obtain or increase ownership interest (or equity) in it.

- Liabilities are probable future sacrifices of economic benefits arising from present obligations of a particular entity to transfer assets or provide services to other entities in the future as a result of past transactions or events.

- Losses are decreases in equity (net assets) from peripheral or incidental transactions of an entity and from all other transactions and other events and circumstances affecting the entity during a period except those that result from expenses or distributions to owners.

- Revenues are inflows or other enhancements of assets of an entity or settlement of its liabilities (or a combination of both) during a period from delivering or producing goods, rendering services, or other activities that constitute the entity's ongoing major or central operations.

SUBSEQUENT EVENTS

A subsequent event is an important event that occurs between the balance sheet date and the date of issuance of the annual report. Subsequent events must have a material effect on the financial statements. A subsequent event does not include the recurring economic fluctuations associated with the economy and with free enterprise, such as a strike or management change. A subsequent event is considered to be important enough that without such information the statement would be misleading if the event were not disclosed. The recognition and recording of these events requires the professional judgment of an accountant or external auditor.

Events that effect the financial statements at the date of the balance sheet might reveal an unknown condition or provide additional information regarding estimates or judgments. These events must be reported by adjusting the financial statements to recognize the new evidence.

Events that relate to conditions that did not exist on the balance sheet date but arose subsequent to that date do not require an adjustment to the financial statements. The effect of the event on the future period, however, may be of such importance that it should be disclosed in a footnote or elsewhere.

SEGMENTS

A segment of a business is a part of an entity whose activities represent a major line of business or class of customer. A segment is a part of an enterprise that sells primarily to outsiders for a profit. Examples of a segment include a subsidiary, a division, a department, a product, a market, or other separations where the activities, assets, liabilities, and operating income can be distinguished for operational and reporting purposes. Accountants require that financial statements be supplemented with information concerning the industries and geographic areas in which an enterprise operates. Information about segments of a business, is useful to investors of large, complex, heterogeneous, publicly traded enterprises in evaluating risks, earnings, growth cycles, profit characteristics,

capital requirements, and return on investments that can differ among segments of a business. The need for segment information is the result of many environmental factors, including the growth of conglomerates, acquisitions, diversifications, and foreign activities of enterprises.

A reportable segment is determined by the following procedures: (1) identifying the enterprise's products and services, (2) grouping the products and services into industry segments, and (3) selecting the significant industry segments by applying various tests established for this purpose.

Segment information that must be disclosed in financial statements includes an enterprise's operations in different industries, foreign operations, export sales, and major customers. Detailed information must be disclosed relating to revenues, the segment's operating profit or loss, and identifiable assets along with additional information. Segment information is primarily a disaggregation of the entity's basic financial statements.

CONSOLIDATED FINANCIAL STATEMENTS

Consolidated financial statements are produced by the parent company when the financial statements of a parent and a subsidiary or **subsidiaries** are added together so that they portray the resulting financial statements as if they were the financial statements of a single company, i.e., a single economic entity. A subsidiary is a separate legal entity whose outstanding **common stock** is more than 50 percent owned by another company.

Consolidated financial statements are prepared primarily for the benefit of the shareholders and creditors of the parent company. There is a presumption that consolidated statements are more meaningful than the separate statements of members of the affiliation. Nevertheless, subsidiary creditors, minority shareholders, and regulatory agencies must rely on the statements of the subsidiary to assess their claims. The usual condition for consolidating the statements of an affiliated group of companies is ownership, directly or indirectly, of over 50 percent of the outstanding voting shares of another company. Generally accepted accounting principles (GAAP) in the United States require that all subsidiaries be consolidated unless control is lacking or is likely to be temporary.

Accounting for consolidations requires (1) the summation of the parent and subsidiary accounts to prepare the parent's consolidated statements and (2) the elimination of intercompany items. When a parent company owns less than 100 percent of the subsidiary's stock, the part owned by outside investors is referred to as minority interest.

INTERNATIONAL TRANSACTIONS AND OPERATIONS

International business transactions and operations relate to activities across national boundaries. When business occurs between companies in different countries, a common problem is the translation of foreign currency amounts into dollars, accomplished through a foreign currency exchange rate. Changes in exchange rates can cause companies to have foreign currency transaction gains and losses on credit transactions. These gains and losses must be accounted for and disclosed in the financial statements.

Consolidation of a foreign subsidiary's financial statements maintained in a foreign currency requires that they be translated into the parent company statements and be adjusted to reflect GAPP in the United States. The translation process can create a translation adjustment that must be reported in stockholders' equity.

PERSONAL FINANCIAL STATEMENTS

The reporting entity of personal financial statements is an individual, a husband and wife, or a group of related individuals. Personal financial statements are often prepared to deal with obtaining bank loans, income tax planning, retirement planning, gift and estate planning, and the public disclosure of financial affairs.

For each reporting entity, a statement of financial position is required. The statement presents assets at estimated current values, liabilities at the lesser of the discounted amount of cash to be paid or the current cash settlement amount, and net worth. A provision should also be made for estimated income taxes on the differences between the estimated current value of assets. Comparative statements for one or more periods should be presented. A statement of changes in net worth is optional.

Personal financial statements should be presented on the accrual basis. A classified balance sheet is not used. Assets and liabilities are presented in the order of their liquidity and maturity, respectively (not on a current/noncurrent basis). A business interest that constitutes a large part of an individual's total assets should be shown separate from other assets. Such an interest would be presented as a net amount and not as a pro rata allocation of the business's assets and liabilities. A statement of changes in net worth would disclose the major sources of increases and decrease in net worth. Increases in personal net worth arise from **income**, increases in estimated current value of assets, decreases in estimated current amount of liabilities, and decreases in the provision for estimated income taxes. Decreases in personal net worth arise from expenses, decreases in estimated current value of assets, increases in estimated current amount of liabilities, and increases in the provision for income taxes.

DEVELOPMENT STAGE COMPANIES

An enterprise is a development stage company if substantially all of its efforts are devoted to establishing a new business and either of the following is present: (1) principal operations have not begun, or (2) principal operations have begun but revenue is insignificant. Activities of a development state enterprise frequently include financial planning, raising capital, **research and development**, personnel recruiting and training, and market development.

A development stage company must follow generally accepted accounting principles applicable to operating enterprises in the preparation of financial statements. In its balance sheet, the company must report cumulative net losses separately in the equity section. In its income statement it must report cumulative revenues and expenses from the inception of the enterprise. Likewise, in its cash flow statement, it must report cumulative cash flows from the inception of the enterprise. Its statement of stockholders' equity should include the number of shares issued and the date of their issuance as well as the dollar amounts received. The statement should identify the entity as a development stage enterprise and describe the nature of development stage activities. During the first period of normal operations, the enterprise must disclose in notes to the financial statements that the enterprise was but is no longer in the development stage.

COMPANIES IN FINANCIAL DISTRESS

Businesses are experiencing increasing financial distress reflecting both financing and operating problems. Financing problems can be identified in situations where the company experiences liquidity deficiency, equity deficiency, debt default, and funds shortage. Operating problems are expressed in terms of continued operating losses, doubtful prospective revenues, jeopardization of the ability to operate, incapable management, and poor control over operations. An examination of the financial statements along with evidence obtained from management and other sources can provide a person with a basis for evaluating the going-concern condition of an enterprise. As a general rule, the assumption is made that the entity is a **going concern** in the absence of evidence to the contrary.

During the auditing process, the auditor may raise questions concerning the going-concern possibilities of the company. The auditor considers whether management's plans for dealing with the conditions and events concerning the uncertainty are likely to negate the problem. If, after evaluating management's plans, substantial doubt still exists, the auditor should either add explanatory language to his or her qualified report or disclaim an opinion. The audit report must explicitly include the phrase ''substantial doubt about the entity's ability to continue as a going concern.''

FRAUDULENT FINANCIAL REPORTING

Fraudulent financial reporting is defined as intentional or reckless reporting, whether by act or by omission, that results in materially misleading financial statements. Fraudulent financial reporting can usually be traced to the existence of conditions in either the internal environment of the firm (e.g., inadequate internal control), or to the external environment (e.g., poor industry or overall business conditions). Excessive pressure on management, such as unrealistic profit or other performance goods, can lead to fraudulent financial reporting.

The accounting profession generally is of the opinion that it is not the responsibility of the auditor to detect fraud, beyond what can be determined with the diligent application of generally accepted auditing standards. Because of the nature of irregularities, particularly those involving forgery and collusion, a properly designed and executed audit may not detect a material irregularity. The auditor is not an insurer and the auditor's report does not constitute a guarantee that material misstatements do not exist in the financial statement. The legal system generally defines the auditor's responsibilities associated with the detect of fraudulent reporting by a company.

In 1977, Congress enacted the **Foreign Corrupt Practices Act** to deter various illegal activities including illegal foreign political contributions, bribes, kickbacks, and other violations. Specifically, the act makes it a criminal offense to offer a bribe to a foreign official, foreign political party, party official, or candidate for foreign political office for the purpose of obtaining or retaining business from, or directing business to any person.

Certain fraudulent activities have been tried under the Racketeer Influenced and Corrupt Organizations Act of 1970 (RICO). This act covers most patterns of criminal activities. The main features of the legislation require that the fraud must involve an organization (two or more persons) and a pattern of criminal activities (two or more crimes). A U.S. attorney must obtain permission from the U.S. Department of Justice before prosecuting a case under RICO. The maximum sentence that can be given is 20 years and a $250,000 fine on each count. Triple damages are allowed under certain circumstances.

AUDITING

The preparation and presentation of a company's financial statements are the responsibility of the management of the company. Published financial statements are audited by an independent **certified public**

accountant. During an audit, the auditor conducts an examination of the accounting system, records, internal controls, and financial statements in accordance with generally accepted auditing standards. The auditor then expresses an opinion concerning the fairness of the financial statements in conformity with generally accepted accounting principles (GAAP). The auditor's standard opinion typically includes the following statements: the auditor is independent; the audit was performed on specified financial statements; the financial statements are the responsibility of the company's management; the opinion of the auditor is the auditor's responsibility; the audit was conducted according to generally accepted auditing standards; the audit was planned and performed to obtain reasonable assurance about whether the financial statements are free of material misstatements; the audit included examination, assessment, and evaluation stages; the audit provided a reasonable basis for an expression of an opinion concerning the fair presentation of the audit; and the signature and date by the auditing firm.

An unqualified opinion contains three paragraphs: an introductory paragraph, a scope paragraph, and the opinion paragraph. In addition to the unqualified opinion, an auditor may issue a qualified opinion, an adverse opinion, or a disclaimer of opinion.

GLOSSARY

- Investing activities: Cash flows that include lending and collecting loans and acquiring and disposing investments and productive long-lived assets.

- Liquidity: An indication of the nearness to cash of the asset and liabilities of an enterprise.

- Minority interest: A subsidiary company's equity that is owned by stockholders other than the parent company.

- Operating activities: Cash flows that include the cash impacts of transactions that are related to net income for the period

- Parent company: An investor company that owns more than 50 percent of the voting stock of a subsidiary company.

- Statement of cash flows: A basic financial statement that provides information about the cash receipts and cash payments of an enterprise during a period, classified as operating, investing, and financing activities. The statement reconciles the beginning and ending cash balances or net income with cash from operating activities (the indirect method).

- Subsidiary company: An investee company in which a parent company owns more than 50 percent of the voting stock.

SEE ALSO: Audits and Auditing

[Charles Woelfel]

FURTHER READING:

Beams, F. A. *Advanced Accounting.* 5th ed. Englewood Cliffs, NJ: Prentice Hall, 1992.

———. *FASB No. 14: Financial Reporting for Segments of a Business Enterprise.* Stamford, CT.: FASB, 1976.

Financial Accounting Standards Board. *Statements of Financial Accounting Concepts.* Homewood, IL: Irwin, 1987.

Harrison, W. T., Jr., and C. T. Horngren. *Financial Accounting,* 2nd ed. Englewood Cliffs, NJ: Prentice Hall, 1995.

Hendriksen, E. S., and M. F. Van Breda. *Accounting Theory,* 5th ed. Homewood, IL: Irwin, 1992.

Jarnagin, B. D. *Financial Accounting Standards.* Chicago, IL: Commerce Clearing House, 1992.

Kieso, D. E., and J. J. Weyugandt. *Intermediate Accounting.* New York: John Wiley & Sons, 1995.

Nikolai, L. A., and J. D. Bazley. *Intermediate Accounting.* 5th ed. Boston: PSW-KENT, 1988.

Woelfel, C. J. *Financial Statement Analysis.* Chicago, IL: Probus, 1994.

Wolk, H. I., and others. *Accounting Theory: A Conceptual and Institutional Approach.* Cincinnati, OH: South-Western, 1992.

FINANCIAL STATISTICS

Financial statistics include all numerical data that summarize past behavior or forecast future behavior of an individual financial security or a group of securities. It is useful to first categorize these statistics into one of three areas. Global or national statistics examine the behavior of business or economic conditions that influence the value of securities in general. Market or industrial statistics track the activity of a specific set of securities linked by a common trading market or industry classification. Company-specific statistics examine performance of individual firms.

GLOBAL/NATIONAL FINANCIAL STATISTICS

ECONOMIC INDICATORS. One broad class of global or national statistics is the series of economic indicators. These indicators assess where the economy stands within the current business cycle and provide information useful to forecast the likelihood of improvement or deterioration, or to confirm the economy's current status. The National Bureau of Economic Research tracks several hundred measures of economic activity that are correlated with the status of the national economy. Economic indicators are typically split into three categories. Leading indicators correlate with patterns of future economic activity. For example, the and profit margins formation of new businesses tend to improve or deteriorate in advance of other symptoms of a change in the overall status of the economy. Coincident indicators assist in confirming the economy's current status. Examples of these indicators are comprehensive levels of employment and industrial production. Finally, lagging indicators confirm that the economy has passed through a particular phase of the business cycle. Such indicators react after the change in economic condition has already been established. The average duration of **unemployment** is one example of a lagging indicator.

GROSS DOMESTIC PRODUCT. There are many other examples of global economic statistics that have immediate relevance to financial analysis. One commonly followed statistic is the forecasted growth rate in **gross domestic product** (GDP). As an aggregate measure of overall output of a national economy, GDP growth is a highly anticipated figure. Many of the subcategories of GDP, such as government spending and exports, are closely followed as well.

EXCHANGE RATE STATISTICS. A more pervasive and continuous source of financial information is found in exchange rate statistics. An exchange rate is the price of one country's currency in terms of another's. For example, if the U.S. dollar can be exchanged for 5 French francs, then residents in either country can quickly assess the value of real or financial assets in the other country. Since this data is so important to international trade and capital flows, exchange rate statistics are widely reported in many periodicals and newspapers on a daily basis.

INTEREST RATES. Another set of statistics that are broadly followed in financial markets throughout the world are those associated with **interest rates**. Interest rates represent the price of money in a particular currency. This price includes a premium for expected inflation and another premium for risk of default. One common method of reporting interest rates is the yield curve. The yield curve represents the relationship between the maturity of a debt instrument, typically bonds, and the rate of return implied by its current price. A yield curve represents a relevant comparison of yields between different securities with different maturities only if the securities have similar default risk. As a result, the most common yield curve statistics relate to government bonds within a particular country. These statistics are frequently reported in tabular form with yields on various securities sorted by maturity. The same information is also commonly depicted in a graph. For example, early 1995 yields for U.S. Treasury bonds with maturities of 1, 5, 10, 20, and 30 years are 7.24 percent, 7.85 percent, 7.92 percent, 8.02 percent, and 7.90 percent respectively.

With the exception of the 30 year bond, this pattern is indicative of an upward sloping yield curve. This is the most common pattern, but inverted and humped yield curves have also been observed during the past two decades. Similar statistics can be graphed for corporate bonds with similar default risk ratings.

MARKET/INDUSTRIAL FINANCIAL STATISTICS

The second broad category of financial statistics assess the behavior of security markets. Most countries with well-developed financial markets have a variety of indexes that track overall market activity or activity of a specific market segment. Examples of these indexes in the United States are the Dow Jones Industrial Average, the Standard & Poor's 500, and the New York Stock Exchange Composite. Other examples include the Financial Times 100 in England, the Nikkei 225 in Japan, and the CAC 40 in France. Each of these widely followed indexes tracks general market conditions. Market indexes can be distinguished by their method of construction or the sample of securities they comprise.

There are three basic techniques for construction of market indexes. A price-weighted index basically reports the average price per share for a sample of securities. A value-weighted index monitors changes in the aggregate market value of all shares outstanding for a sample of securities. An equally weighted index determines the change in value for each security separately and then reports the average change for all securities. Value-weighted and equally weighted indexes are expressed as a proportion of some base value determined at a particular point in time. The proportion is often multiplied by a number such as 100 before it is reported.

The Dow Jones Industrial Average (DJIA) is an example of a price-weighted index. This means that the index tracks and reports the average price per share of a sample of securities. The DJIA has been in existence since 1885 when it was first constructed by Charles Dow. He selected 20 "blue chip," or well-established, companies and tracked the average price per share. In the late 1920s, the number of stocks was increased to 30. During the more than 100 years of its existence, many DJIA stocks have split (i.e., issued two new shares to replace one old share) when management felt that their share price had become exorbitant. In addition, some firms have gone bankrupt or merged with other firms and thus trading in these securities has been eliminated. A price-weighted average accounts for such changes by altering the divisor to render the event neutral. This technique means that the divisor of the DJIA which was 30 in the late 1920s has fallen far below 1 by 1995.

As statistics of aggregate market behavior, price-weighted averages suffer from several biases. For example, a high price-per-share stock has greater influence over the index than a lower price-per-share stock even though there may be many more shares of the lower priced stock outstanding. In addition, stocks split to reduce price per share and make them more affordable to investors. It does not alter the collective value of the stock (i.e., 100 shares at $10 are worth the same as 200 shares at $5), but it does reduce the impact of that stock on the overall index. This is relevant since it is the stocks with the highest growth that have the greatest propensity to split and implies that price weighted averages are downwardly biased indicators of market performance. The DJIA in particular is frequently criticized for its small sample of purely industrial firms. This suggests that it may be a poor proxy for overall market behavior. Statistical analysis indicates, however, that it is highly correlated with other, broader measures of market activity.

The Standard & Poor's 500 (S&P 500) is a value-weighted index that comprises a sample of 400 industrial, 20 transportation, 40 utility, and 40 financial firms. It is constructed by multiplying the current share price by the number of shares outstanding for each of its 500 firms. The sum of these products is divided by a similar sum constructed using stock prices from the period from 1941 to 1943. This ratio represents the cumulative growth of this portfolio of 500 stocks from that base period to the current period. Unlike the price-weighted average, stock splits are neutral events since the aggregate value of all shares of a firm is not changed by the split. Bankruptcies, mergers, and other events that stop public trading of a firm's stock will require adjustment of the index. While the S&P 500 comprises a much larger sample of securities, larger firms have a greater influence on its behavior. To see this more specifically, imagine ranking all 500 firms by value. Clearly, the largest firm will represent a much larger portion of the aggregate value of the entire sample of 500 firms than will the smallest.

The development of an equally weighted index is an attempt to eliminate the bias just described in the value-weighted index. The idea behind an equally weighted index is to generate a ratio, or growth factor, for an individual firm by measuring its stock price today and dividing by its stock price during some base period. This process is repeated for a sample of stocks and then an average growth factor is reported. One such index that represents 1,700 U.S. stocks is the Value Line Index. Equally weighted measures are considered a better measure of the behavior of the typical security during any period of time.

While this discussion has focused on stock indexes for the overall market, there are many other indexes that examine other classes of securities or specific industries or segments of the market. For example, the New York Stock Exchange also tracks a value-weighted average of its listed firms in the categories of industrials, utilities, transportation, and finance. Many publications use an even finer breakdown of industrial classifications. There are also a broad variety of indexes that examine various categories of **bonds** and **mutual funds**.

FIRM-SPECIFIC FINANCIAL STATISTICS

A final category of financial statistics are those that are firm specific. These statistics include bond ratings, price-to-earnings ratios, and other various indicators of risk and return.

HISTORICAL STATISTICS. It is useful to begin by considering statistics constructed from historical measures. For example, an analysis of periodic prices and cash payments from a historical period provides the data needed to construct statistics of risk and return. Historical returns can be reported as an arithmetic average (computing rate of return for a series of sequential periods and averaging) or a geometric average (computing the annualized compound interest rate that the investor would have received). Additionally, this data will allow for construction of risk statistics such as variance and standard deviation.

To illustrate the computation of these historical statistics, consider the following example which uses data for Apple Computer. Table A contains the closing price for a share of Apple stock at the end of September for five consecutive years. It also contains the dividend per share that Apple paid during each year and the one-year holding period return—the rate of return an investor would have achieved during that particular period.

Table 1

Date	Price	Dividend	Holding Period Return
Sept. 1990	$29.75	$0.44	
Sept. 1991	49.25	0.48	0.672 or 67.2%
Sept. 1992	46.25	0.48	-0.051 or -5.1%
Sept. 1993	24.75	0.48	-0.455 or -45.5%
Sept. 1994	34.50	0.48	0.413 or 41.3%

The holding period return (HPR) for each one-year period is computed using the following formula:

$$HPR = (\text{Ending Value} - \text{Beginning Value} + \text{Dividends})/\text{Beginning Value}$$

In other words, the overall return from stock appreciation and dividend income from 1990 to 1991 was 67.2 percent. Similar interpretations can be derived from the calculation for subsequent years. We can average, or annualize these returns by adding the one-year HPR and then dividing by the number of returns—four in this example:

Arithmetic mean return = (0.672 − 0.051 − 0.455 + 0.413)/4
= 0.145 or 14.5 percent per year

The other interesting observation that can quickly be drawn from the table of holding period returns is their significant volatility from year to year. This can be formally measured as variance or standard deviation, both important measures of risk. Variance of these returns can be computed by calculating the deviation of each individual annual holding period return from the mean return computed above, squaring this difference, adding the squared differences together and finally dividing by the number of years in the sample. The Apple Computer data allows the following computation of variance:

[(0.672 − 0.145)2 + (−0.051 − 0.145)2 + (−0.455 − 0.145)2 + (0.413 − 0.145)2]/4 = 0.1870

The variance is an aggregate measure of dispersion away from the mean return. It is commonly restated as a standard deviation by computing its square root. In this example, the standard deviation of Apple's returns is 0.432 or 43.2 percent. Equipped with a mean to measure the security's return and a standard deviation to assess its risk, meaningful comparisons can now be made with other securities that have been subjected to similar analysis.

While the statistical measures constructed in the preceding example are valid, it is important to consider their purpose. If an investor was interested in performance over some prior time interval to answer questions such as "How well did my investment perform?" or "How much risk was I exposed to?," then these statistics are clear indicators. On the other hand, if investors want to know "How will this security perform?" or "How risky is this stock?," then the statistics must be interpreted quite differently. In the second case, the historical statistics are valuable only if it is reasonable to expect future performance to correlate to past performance. It is usually reasonable to use historical risk as a proxy for expected risk. This is because risk is a function of exposure to broader economic forces and firm-specific characteristics such as financial structure and operating-cost structure. These influences are not likely to change, or changes are reasonably predictable. Nevertheless, it is frequently more difficult to use historical return as a proxy for expected future return.

The measure of risk can be refined by dividing total risk, as measured by standard deviation, into two parts. The first part is the variation in a stock's return that results from general market movements and is referred to as systematic risk. The second component is the variation that results from factors unique to the individual firm and is referred to as unsystematic risk. There is considerable interest in the systematic risk component of a stock's overall risk because the unsystematic risk can be minimized by holding a variety of securities together in a portfolio. Systematic risk is measured by the statistic beta (b). Beta represents the volatility of an individual security relative to the average market volatility. Therefore, the average security beta is 1. Beta can be derived statistically by computing the ratio of the covariance of the individual security's returns with those of the market by the variance of the market's returns. It can also be derived by the regression procedure where the equation of the line that best fits a scatter of points, each representing return for the security and the market at a particular time, is determined statistically. The slope of this line represents the security's beta. Beta is a useful statistic in portfolio management because it allows managers to actively position their portfolios in an above-average, average, or below-average risk position by choosing securities with an average beta of above 1, exactly 1, or below 1, respectively.

FINANCIAL RATIOS. A final category of firm-specific statistics refers to the **financial statements** that the firm has generated in the past and allows forecasts of future financial performance. **Financial ratios** comprise another family of relevant statistics that are frequently used to assess the financial health and development of individual firms. While some of the more prominent financial ratios relate to profitability (e.g., net profit margin, return on equity), others can be used to assess other characteristics of a firm that ultimately pinpoint potential reasons for the resulting profitability. These other measures can be categorized into several areas. Liquidity ratios assess the firm's ability to meet its short-term financial obligations with its most liquid assets. Activity ratios measure how effectively the firm is able to use various categories of assets to generate sales revenues. Leverage ratios examine how the firm's assets are financed and how the firm's financing structure is likely to influence profits. Finally, there are many ratios that attempt to relate market values of the firm's assets to their financial statement counterparts. Collectively, these ratios can be monitored over time to detect trends in firm performance or they can be examined in relation to industry average ratios. In either case, the statistics can be very useful for probing, explaining, and forecasting a firm's financial performance.

[Paul Bolster]

FISCAL YEAR

Most corporations are required by law or by their own bylaws to report on the results of operations once a year. This one-year **accounting** period is known as the company's fiscal year. In most cases the fiscal year corresponds with the calendar year, starting on January 1 and ending on December 31. A business is allowed, however, to establish the dates of its fiscal year as it pleases. A business may choose to make its fiscal year correspond with its natural business year. For example, retailers commonly end their fiscal year on January 31 so as to take into account post-holiday sales and returns.

The end of the fiscal year marks the end of an accounting period for the purposes of reporting results to the public and to the company's shareholders. At the end of the fiscal year the company closes its books and balances all of its accounts. It issues an annual report containing, among other items, a balance sheet reflecting the financial condition of the company at the end of its fiscal year. Companies also usually take a physical inventory at the end of their fiscal year.

SEE ALSO: Inventory Accounting

[David Bianco]

FIVE TIGERS

If, as economists have forecast, the 21st century belongs to Asia, such a scenario will have come about mainly through the growing clout of the "Five Tigers" driving the Asian economic boom: Taiwan, South Korea, Singapore, Hong Kong, and Thailand.

Economic prospects during the 1990s may look anemic at best—except in East Asia. The five tiger economies represent among the fastest growing trading nations, amassing **manufacturing** profits and foreign reserves as Western investors looking for the highest return on their money flock to the region.

The five tigers may have suffered of late during the 1990s from the current global economic downturn, but they are gaining ground in the world market. Each in their turn followed Japan in the push for riches during the last two decades. As with Japan, they first took advantage of low-wage labor and high savings rates to make low-quality products which they then sold in world markets. But with resulting success, the tigers are increasingly exporting quality products—most prominently electronic gadgets, but also computer chips and other hi-tech goods—manufactured in modern Japanese factories situated throughout East Asia in tiger economies.

The tigers certainly have done well trading with the West. But even more revealing, nearly half of their trade during the 1990s has taken place within the region as an Asian economic bloc rises to challenge rival blocs in North America and the European Union. This came about during the second half of the 1980s when Japan invested billions in the tiger economies to build factories where for centuries only farmers and water buffaloes had stood. Furthermore, the original tigers have—again following Japan's example—begun investing in other regional markets like Malaysia, Indonesia, and India. Of course the tigers began their climb to prosperity from low levels of **economic development**, but they are securing newfound affluence for at least some of their citizens at the same time that they ship their products to eager Western consumers.

Massive **infrastructure** projects are being planned as governments in the region look to the future are luring foreign firms to bid on **contracts**. In 1992, Taiwan announced a US$300 billion six-year infrastructure plan to build highways and subways. All the tiger economies are spending billions to fit themselves with modern **telecommunications**. Furthermore, while Japan may have negligible military power, East Asia represents the largest market for military hardware in the world.

The Tokyo stock exchange may still cause jitters following its steep 1990 plunge. Smaller bourses in tiger markets have not followed suit, however. They have instead posted steep share price gains in recent years, albeit after wild rollercoaster rides for daring investors.

Aside from growing economic clout, political question marks hang over the five tiger nations. Their problem is that they no longer fit the stereotype of developing nations with only very rich and very poor people. Instead recent and unprecedented economic growth under authoritarian, often military regimes has produced growing middle classes who yearn for political reform and participation. Moreover, some 70 percent of the population in the tiger nations is under 30 years of age, and many of them dream of the 3 C's—cars, condominiums, and credit cards. Their ambition gains push from flimsy social safety nets in tiger economies and pull from the drive to achieve and amass personal **wealth**. The result is that as in the case of Thailand and its 1992 military coup, military leaders deeply entrenched in the country's private economy have been loathe to throw off the vestiges of crony **capitalism** and allow economic and political progress to grow hand in hand.

Only Hong Kong has never known an authoritarian military regime that pushed its economic levers.

South Korea experienced a military coup as did Thailand before its current government could establish a degree of stability. Even today, however, concern for North Korea's apparent nuclear capability offers unwelcome instability to investors with a foothold in, or at least an eye on, South Korea's growing economy. Taiwan experiences continuing political isolation as its trading partners juggle loyalties to Taipei and Beijing, China. On the other extreme, Singapore's government appears as strong politically as the economy it steers. Stability may well be returning to Hong Kong as its 5.8 million inhabitants appear to reconcile themselves to reverting to the control of China in 1997. This, while Hong Kong's 28th governor, Chris Patten—and probably its last—tries in vain to introduce significant democratic institutions to the British colony.

For all the tiger nations, securing real and consistent economic growth will only come if each turns the strains of modernization to advantage and spreads the spoils of prosperity around. Otherwise, the sense of community that often gives way to modernization and its emphasis on individual enterprise will threaten a growing faith in opportunity, encourage tensions between rich and poor, and ultimately leave the social fabric in shreds. The one certainty for the five tigers, however, is that economic growth in future years is assured, whatever the bumps in the road ahead.

[Etan Vlessing]

FURTHER READING:

Armstrong, Larry. "South Korea and Taiwan and Roaring." *Business Week.* August 11, 1992, p. 41.

Haoli, Victor. "The World's Biggest Boom." *World Monitor.* December 1991, pp. 26-30.

Kraar, Louis. "Ten to Watch Outside Japan." *Fortune.* Fall 1993, pp. 25-27.

van Wolferen, Karel. *The Enigma of Japanese Power.* New York: Vintage Books, 1990.

FIXED ASSET ANALYSIS

The analysis of fixed **assets** determines if there is sufficient maintenance of productive assets to ensure current and future earning power, and the relative profitability contributed by fixed assets and fixed asset acquisitions.

A decrease in operational efficiencies and productivity results from the lack of required repairs and/or replacement of obsolete assets. Asset analysis examines the age and condition of each major asset category, as well as the costs of replacing old assets to determine the output levels, downtime, and temporary discontinuances. The measure of efficiency involves the calculation of these ratio:

- Fixed asset acquisition to total assets
- Repairs and maintenance to fixed assets
- Repairs and maintenance to sales
- Sales to fixed assets
- Net income to fixed assets

DEPRECIATION

The analysis of depreciation helps to clarify the useful life of an asset. The comparison of the **depreciation** rate to the industry norm will underscore the findings of the repairs and maintenance ratios.

To determine the adequacy of the depreciation charge, do the following:

1. calculate the trend in depreciation expenses to fixed assets

2. determine the trend in depreciation expenses to sales

3. compare the book depreciation to tax depreciation

If the trends are declining, depreciation charges may be inadequate. If sales are decreasing as **capital** expenditures are increasing, the company may be over-expanding, and lifting its bottom line through large write-offs rather improved than operating margins. Unwarranted changes in the lives or **salvage values** of fixed assets will increase depreciation expenses, and thus overstate earnings.

INTANGIBLE ASSETS

Intangible assets have a 40-year amortization period. If not closely adhered to, companies may overstate or understate their intangibles. In addition, changing trends in consumer buying habits and the quality of competitors' products may eliminate the earning power of the goodwill on the books. Therefore, the level of intangibles to total assets needs to be studied in light of market trends and conditions.

Trends for the following ratios are applicable to analysis of intangible assets:

- Intangible assets to total assets
- Intangible assets to stockholders' equity
- Intangible assets to sales
- Intangible assets to net income
- Changes in intangible assets to changes in net income
- Questionable intangible assets, like good will, to total assets.

[Roger J. AbiNader]

FLEXIBLE MANUFACTURING

According to the U.S. Department of Commerce, the conceptual terms flexible **manufacturing** or flexible manufacturing system (FMS) jointly refer to production techniques that integrate the elements of three industrial processes: (1) numerically controlled machine tools linked by (2) automated materials handling systems whose operation is administered by (3) a centralized computer control system. That said, however, the problem of arriving at a satisfactory definition for FMSs has remained elusive. Reflective of the systems themselves, a plethora of varying definitions and interpretations abound, with differences emanating mainly from the production environment where FMSs have been implemented. For instance, small and mass producers have maintained different viewpoints regarding standard notions of "flexibility" as well as the appropriate degree of automation. Yet when all is said and done, FMS production techniques are functionally similar even when their configured layouts escape easy generalization.

In general, the flexibility of an FMS is characterized by how rapidly it responds to changes in product design and production schedules. The degree to which it does this is in turn determined by the scope of FMS design. FMSs vary in terms of their level of complexity, configuration, and range of size. Output produced by FMSs also varies from small precision components used in instrumentation and auto assembly to very large structural components of construction and aerospace equipment.

While acknowledging the inherent difficulties encountered when trying to compose a definition for FMSs, Nigel R. Greenwood, an author with expert background on the subject, put forward a provisionally tenable definition in his book *Implementing Flexible Manufacturing Systems*. Accordingly, an FMS:

> "through the careful combination of computer control, communications, manufacturing process and related equipment, enables a section of the production-orientated aspects of an organization to respond rapidly and economically, in an integrated manner, to significant changes in its operating environment. Such systems typically comprise: process equipment (for example, machine tools, assembly stations, **robotics**, etc.) material handling equipment (for example, robots, conveyors, automated guided vehicles, etc.) a communication system and a sophisticated computer control system."

Though somewhat lengthy and abstract, Greenwood's definition avoids the subjectivist tendencies of other definitions that simply define FMSs by virtue of a particular process technology associated with particular products and production environments. In an economic climate where quick responses to change are the norm, narrowly subjectivist definitions of FMSs are hardly able to withstand the passage of time.

THE BASICS OF FMSS

Although each FMS is unique in configuration and process, an abstract description of overall operations in outline form is possible. First, numerical control programs and computer aided process planning are utilized to develop the sequence of production steps for each machined part. Next, based on inventory, orders, and computer simulations of how an FMS can run most economically, a schedule is established for parts that are going to be produced on that day. Following that, material and required tooling are retrieved either automatically or manually from storage and loaded into the system. Once loaded, the FMS begins machining operations. According to the process plan, robots, conveyors, and other automated material handling devices transport the workpiece between workstations. Should any tool breakdown during the production cycle, an FMS can reroute the workpiece to other tools within the system. In general, the essential characteristics that comprise a workable "part family" are common shape, size, weight, and tolerance range.

A key concept central to any discussion of FMSs is the term "workstation," which refers to an individual processing unit. Furthermore, the term "processing unit" refers to the sum of operations performed within a particular factory area containing several pieces of process equipment meant to carry out individual or multiple operations on various products. Indeed, different workstation distinctions mark the divide between two FMS subsystems—the flexible manufacturing module (FMM) and the flexible manufacturing cell (FMC). The module comprises a standalone numerically controlled machine tool (NCMT), automatic material handling device (such as a robot or automatic pallet changer,) and an automated monitoring system to control for tool breakage, equipment depreciation, automatic measuring and related diagnostics. FMMs constitute the first step in the automation of the loading and unloading of parts to and from an NCMT. For machining centers, automatic pallet changers make it possible for unmanned attended machining to occur for up to six hours.

The flexible manufacturing cell, on the other hand, comprises two or more machine tools which may or may not include NCMTs. Similar to FMMs, the FMC incorporates a material handling device (such as a robot) servicing several machine tools arranged in a circle or line. Automatic pallet changers are also used in conjunction with automatic conveyor systems linking NCMTs. Compared to an FMM, information flow to and from an FMC is integrated into a larger monitoring control system. FMCs are less flexible than FMMs. Usually FMCs are applied to a "family," as opposed to some broader grouping of components—for instance shafts within a prescribed size range. Because each FMC is designed to meet the specialized requirements of different customers, standardization is not a universal feature. In fact just the design phase requires considerable consultation and information exchange between the specific user and FMC supplier. It should be noted that early versions of FMCs and FMSs initially functioned below their anticipated performance level. Problems arose due to the technical difficulties involved when linking product flows with different machines. As a result, demand for FMCs is initially limited to a few large firms with enough financial clout to undertake the risky investment the systems represented.

With the above subsystems in mind, FMSs can be distinguished by the following characteristics: the flow of tools and parts between different machine groups is automated; material handling is mostly, but not exclusively, performed by automated guided vehicle systems (AGVS), and not, as in the case of FMCs, industrial robots. This is explained by the fact that FMSs consist of machining centers mostly involved with the production of, geometrically speaking, prismatic parts, while material handling robots work in conjunction with computer numerically controlled (CNC) lathes that machine rotational parts. To a far greater extent FMSs also incorporate the use of conveyors and rail guided transport systems. And, in comparison with their subsystems, FMSs have a lower rate of labor utilization, higher labor productivity, and, in certain cases, higher capital productivity. FMSs are usually equipped with a "hot standby" feature. This alludes to a computer control system comprising two computer units. Should one fail to operate, the other automatically kicks in to keep the FMS running.

In terms of joint characteristics, FMSs and their subsystems, share most if not all of the following:

1. Machine flexibility: refers to the ease of making the changes necessary to manufacture a specific set of part/product types.

2. Process flexibility: the capacity to manufacture a given set of part/product types in a variety of ways, each possibly using different materials.

3. Product Flexibility: the systematically unique condition to change over to produce a new set of parts or products economically and quickly.

4. Routing flexibility: the capability to cope with breakdowns and continue manufacturing a given set of part/product types using alternative routes.

5. Volume flexibility: the ability to operate profitably across a range of different production volumes.

6. Expansion flexibility: the potential to expand in a modular fashion.

7. Production flexibility: the variable domain of part/product types that a system can produce.

Besides true FMSs and their subsystems, are two other manufacturing concepts distinguished more for their comparatively higher level of **automation** and lower level of flexibility. These are the flexible transfer line and fixed transfer line. Between these two systems and FMSs a trade-off, or "productivity dilemma," is said to exist. Accordingly, the higher the level of automation, the greater the manufacturer efficiency in terms of productivity and lower unit costs. But the efficiency advantage held by non-FMS related systems is said to be achieved at the expense of losing a certain degree of innovative flexibility.

The flexible transfer line comprises workstations utilizing numerous automated general or special purpose machine tools joined by an automated workpiece flow system according to line principle. The flexible transfer line is capable of simultaneously or sequentially machining different workpieces running along the same path. A fixed transfer line, by contrast, utilizes a number of special purpose machine tools (as opposed to general ones) initially designed to produce one product only. After a considerable period of set-up time though, it can accommodate a different variant of the product, as in the case of different sized cylinderheads.

From an economic standpoint, if the number of variants is high (from 500 or more variants) but produced in relatively small annual amounts, the use of stand-alone NCMTs (a portion of which included FMMs) is considered appropriate. Progressing to larger annual production of fewer variants, FMCs, followed by FMSs, become optimal strategies. FMSs then, occupy a middle ground between highly automated and highly flexible manufacturing systems. Based on several empirical studies conducted in the 1980s, the respective variants range for FMSs stands between 4 to 100, for FMCs between 40 and 800. For workpieces of different types ranging from 2 to 8, flexible transfer lines are used, and for 1 or 2, fixed transfer lines.

More than a few manufacturing experts have taken issue with the so called "productivity dilemma" as described above, countering that it is at best a transitory trend. They look instead to the further development of **computer aided manufacturing**

(CAM) as the potential solution for reversing the short term opposition between cost efficient but inflexible production units. Computer-based technology, they have argued, reverses the trend towards specialized hardware and replaces it with specialized **software**. Thus general purpose machines utilized in flexible transfer lines can be programmed with special purpose software to achieve the flexibility once attributed to an earlier but narrowly conceived definition of a FMS. Simply by reprogramming a general purpose machine, the switch to a new product variant can be accomplished without having to rip out and replace the machine, as was the case in earlier times. Also unlike times past, this task can be completed in a matter of hours instead of weeks.

COMPUTER SIMULATION. One of the outstanding features of FMSs is computer simulation. Thirty years after their introduction, a plethora of microcomputer-based simulation packages are available for simulation analysis. There are also many mainframe simulation packages now available in a microcomputer format. Unlike their mainframe forerunners, microcomputer simulation packages are considered user-friendly and do not require the presence of highly skilled individuals. Subsequent developments introduced sophisticated color graphics in conjunction with several advances in computer mainframes that allowed software developers to create even more complex programs that retain their user-friendly orientation. A noteworthy advance is the incorporation of animation techniques. In the opinion of Nigel Greenwood, had simulation analysis been available in the early days of FMSs, their success rate would have been greatly enhanced.

Computer simulation exercises are performed to identify system bottlenecks—the utilization of fixed resources such as machine tools and variable resources such as operators, tools, and material transporters. Utilization of resources is measured in terms of busy, idle, down, and blocked time. Simulation results then provide information to FMS designers about work in progress, production rates, and the impact of equipment failure, all relevant factors that determine how well a particular FMS works. When computer simulation packages first appeared, many experienced production engineers questioned their usefulness. Having been schooled in a ''hard modelling'' simulation background that used scale layout, pieces of paper, drawing pins, and the like to represent personnel and pallets, experienced engineers are skeptical of computer simulation modelling. The substantial advantages of computer simulation and the influx of new engineers with computer trained backgrounds has alleviated this initial skepticism.

One critical limitation of computer simulation resides in the fact that computer simulation modelers are unable to accurately depict a specifically designed FMS facility, so that the possibility of an informational discrepancy between FMSs project designers and simulators is real. Heightened communications between these two groups ensures that discrepancies are minimized. It is also expected that further developments in microcomputer-based packages will help minimize discrepancies.

In the evolution of an FMS during its multiphase design process, computer simulation is of great assistance. During the conceptual design phase, if given a hypothetical array of workstation configurations, a computer simulation is able to determine their respective throughput times to a high degree of reliability. It is also used to calculate initial financial analysis and to animate prospective configurations. During the detailed design phase, computer simulation makes it possible for suggested system improvements to be incorporated and tested in an FMS model to analyze their impact.

MATERIAL TRANSPORT TASKS AND COMPUTER CONTROL SYSTEMS. The principal motivation for developing and implementing an FMS is to ensure that the transformation of processed and unprocessed raw materials to finished parts is as rapid, efficient, and well-conceived as possible. Of the three elementary FMS processes, material handling devices and computer control systems offer the greatest potential for improved performance results. The other element of FMSs—the manufacturing process—has experienced significant progress in terms of speed, reliability, and efficiency, which led to a sizable reduction in overall product throughput time. In turn, a greater emphasis on the implementation of automated material handling systems to increase the overall efficiency of FMSs is paramount. It has been estimated that close to one-third of an FMS product's total manufacturing cost is absorbed by the expense of successive material handling tasks.

FMSs incorporate four major types of material transport tasks: transport between different systems; transport between different subsystems within the same FMS; transfers between workstations within various subsystems; and transfers within the workstations themselves. From the standpoint of an FMS designer, it would be ideal to address these tasks in their totality, but the incompatible variety of the tasks or load types makes this impossible.

Given their relatively versatile property and high load capacity, automated guided vehicle systems figure prominently in most FMSs. They are battery-driven, bidirectional vehicles designed to automatically transport material from one location to another along a predefined route or set of routes. Programming is accomplished using microprocessor controls or wire guided systems. Of the two, wire guided vehicles are preferred. Transport instructions from a central computer are received via a wire buried an inch below the shop floor through inductive sensors located on either side of the vehicle. Loading and unloading operations are performed by hydraulic lifts or in manner similar to traditional fork-lifts.

Considered less flexible and unable to duplicate the high load capacity of an AGVS, conveyors are thought to be just as reliable, relatively less expensive, and battery-free. Conveyors are useful for frequent transportation tasks. Because of their mechanical simplicity, conveyors can transfer loads efficiently using a large number of sensors connected to a conveyor control system. Conveyors are available in wide variety of sizes, speed capabilities, and forms. Among some of the more common industrial types are overhead monorail, carry and free, power and free, underfloor drag chain, floor slat, gravity feed, and plastic chain link.

Rail guided transport represents a blend of conveyor and AGVS systems. Instead of being guided by a underground wire, above-ground rails determine routing direction. Compared to an AGVS, rail guided transport moves more rapidly along straight distances that typically range from 30-50 meters, but do not have as much route flexibility. Because of their relatively unsophisticated control systems and battery-free operation, rail guided transfer systems have many of the advantages attributed to conveyors.

Within FMS subsystems, robot and gantry loaders predominate. Robots are mostly used for tasks directly related to the manufacturing process rather than material handling. Under the appropriate circumstances, they can be used for material transport, as their inherent flexibility often offsets their relatively high cost. Programmable logic controller gantry loaders combine the advantages of robots with conveyors. Indeed many of these are simply an overhead rail-mounted robot or a robot arm moving along a rail. This gives them a speed advantage over robots, but being mounted on a fix path (albeit with several stopping points) reduces their flexibility. Manual material loading or fork-lift operations are the most inexpensive material handling and versatile form of transport. The advantage held by automated systems however, is their continuous operation and accurate and consistent performance.

Computer control systems account for the largest single risk factor within FMSs. Between 50-75 percent of the total risk involved in FMS implementation is attributed to the control system, which includes both the computer hardware and associated software. In overall cost terms, computer hardware ranges from 10-15 percent while its associated software represents 15-30 percent.

This high risk factor is associated with several problems, the most pronounced of which is the fact that the "mechanics" of many FMSs are designed by machine-tool inclined engineers, while the software is designed by persons who have little background in the manufacturing environment they are attempting to create products for. An additional problem is that FMS software is extremely difficult to evaluate prior to being installed and tested. If found to be inadequate, corrective steps are expensive.

The principal objectives of an FMS computer control system are fourfold: to facilitate the transmission of support software to material handling systems and manufacturing process equipment; coordination of the material handling system to allow the manufacturing process equipment to function at it highest level of utilization; to facilitate data entry, control, operation, and monitoring of the FMS as a whole; and to guide the return of the system to its complete operational status following a failure.

At the turn of the twentieth century, one of the most active areas of FMS development is directed at producing a "generic" computer control system to replace customized systems. While the prospects for success are mixed, incremental progress is being made in reducing the costs and risks associated with software developments.

EARLY FMSS AND HISTORICAL ANTECEDENTS

In the early 1970s, after a period of initial euphoria, disappointment set in when FMSs failed to live up to their potential. Since the early 1980s, however, FMSs proved to be technically feasible, reliable, and cost-effective. Indeed, by the 1990s, it is widely accepted that production principles once thought to be applicable only at the level of the small job-shop (a small manufacturing facility typically engaged in making a small batch of a wide variety of different parts for a large customer) were equally successful in mass production operations.

The Wealth of Nations, Adam Smith's famous analysis of the division of labor and its impact on specialization, productivity, automation, and product flow, marked one of the first recorded commentaries on changing production techniques in the early modern era. Nearly 130 years later, thanks to Henry Ford, the **assembly line method** of mass production represented the perfect illustration of Smith's ideas. Yet because Ford's highly automated assembly line operated with only the slightest degree of product variation, it represented the virtual antithesis of flexible manufacturing. Between the two World Wars, the automated assembly line dominated the industrial sector because of its unsurpassed efficiency and productivity.

Two developments following World War II proved critical in the development of flexible manufacturing systems. These are the manufacturing philosophy of group technology and the introduction of numerical control machine tools (soon to be followed by the related development of computer numerically controlled—CNC—machine tools and other applications). Both developments are instrumental in narrowing the gap between the increased variety characteristic of FMSs and the efficiency associated with assembly line automation.

GROUP TECHNOLOGY. Group technology was based on the principle of using the common properties of similar parts to rectify shared design and manufacturing problems. This involved the creation of a coding system to classify parts into groups given their shape, overall dimension, required accuracy, surface finish, manufacturing requirements, and material composition. Afterwards, an analysis is performed to determine all the major components a firm might manufacture. The acquired information is then sorted into major categories, such as processes or products, to indicate common production groupings in order to determine the appropriate set of machine tools necessary for their manufacture.

Initially, because the set of machine tools used for producing these parts was kept to a minimum, a small scale manufacturing shop was able to produce the parts more efficiently than a larger manufacturing unit. The connection between group technology and FMSs stems from the sorting process that occurred within group technology. Sorting parts into well-defined groups, performing an analysis, selecting the parts, and determining the most appropriate machine grouping—all of these steps are necessary to derive the maximum benefits from a FMS investment.

The cost-saving impact of group technology was illustrated in a 1986 study. Components produced by one large U.S. manufacturer required over 100 operations and had a throughput time (a measure of a component's processing time from start to finish) averaging five months, during which time they travelled some three miles on the shop floor. Following the implementation of group technology, the number of operations decreased from 100 to 10, throughput time fell to just days, and the distance travelled on the shop floor decreased to 200 feet. A factor critical to the success of group technology was the willingness of the workforce to acquire a multiskilled background that reduced the number of shopfloor skill levels from 11 to 2.

NUMERICAL CONTROLLED MACHINE TOOLS. Numerical control machine tools, on the other hand, first emerged in 1952. Parallel developments are undertaken at the Massachusetts Institute of Technology and by Alfred Herbert in the United Kingdom. Initially, these continuous-path machines proved unreliable and it was 1956 before more reliable machines were developed.

It is largely the aerospace industry that encouraged the development of NCMTs because it frequently required "copied" components that could only be produced repetitively using relatively inaccurate hand-made templates. The computer equipment used to control machines engaged in manufacturing aerospace components was at first cumbersome and expensive, but advancements in computer technology in the area of complex integrated circuits ushered in the era of computer controlled machine tools. Compared to their numerical control predecessors, small minicomputers had far more versatile and reliable control devices. They were less expensive, incorporated computer-aided programming, and featured sophisticated editing components. These benefits meant machine tools were more flexible, more programmable, and easier to set-up when producing a variety of components. Developments in computer numerically controlled machine tools culminated in machining centers, which incorporated automatic tool changers, tool storage systems, automatic work transfer, and off-line programming capabilities.

The development of CNC machine tools provided the major technological foundation upon which early FMS versions are built. The tools made it possible for a computer, instead of a skilled operator, to control a manufacturing process. At first computer numerical control was applied only to machine tools. Later it is broadened to a wide variety of manufacturing processes. Further developments in CNC applications led to the creation of advanced industrial robots. Among other tasks, robots are used for material handling purposes, arc and spot welding, and paint spraying. The combination of CNC technologies and advances in computer technology allowed FMS designers to introduce such breakthrough tools as programmable logic controllers (PLC), automated guided vehicle systems (AGVS), and automated storage and retrieval systems (ASRS). Yet despite these advancements, FMSs encountered difficulties when it came time to smoothly integrate these major elements into a dependable working system while minimizing the costs and risks attributed to once-off control software.

The first FMS (albeit rudimentary) was installed in England in 1968. Some authorities dispute this however, arguing that Project Tinkertoy, carried out under the auspices of the U.S. National Bureau of Standards in 1955, represented the first FMS. The English FMS is developed by D.T.N. Williamson of the Molins Machine Tool Company; it was known as "System 24." The confluence of several factors prompted its development: the advancements made in machine tool technologies, theoretical progress surrounding the area of job-shop scheduling, the growing influence of group technology in different manufacturing environments, and the increasing demands placed upon larger manufacturing establishments to produce components economically in small batches.

Similar to later FMS developments, System 24 is designed to feature three specific qualities: the ability to produce a large variety of components virtually at random; the ability to both load and unload tools and workpieces automatically; and the ability to operate without manned attendance over an extended period. The eventual demise of System 24 came about due to the system's unreliability and the fact that the light flat alloy components market for which it is developed did not expand as had been predicted. As a result, the development of FMS techniques in England was abandoned for nearly ten years; FMS research and development pressed onward in the United States and Japan.

In their early phase, many FMSs encountered a common set of difficulties that were eventually corrected. First, process equipment initially proved to be insufficiently flexible to meet the varied production requirements. Second, many supporting technologies also proved inadequate. For instance, sensors built into early systems were usually limit switches. Experience had demonstrated that limit switches are highly unreliable, yet they were included in FMSs in such a manner that their failure prompted the entire FMS to cease operation.

Additionally, most early FMSs were overly machining center oriented. This bias resulted from the fact that advances in machining centers outdistanced those of other machine tool types. Systems typically associated with cubic component workpieces progressed the quickest in design and implementation, computer control systems, and pallet and tool changers; systems associated with rotational workpieces lagged considerably behind.

Lastly, some early FMS projects are motivated for questionable reasons, such as securing a government grant to simply jump on the technology bandwagon. This meant many projects were neither serious nor well thought out. As a result of these early difficulties, many production engineers hastily concluded that FMSs did not represent a significant manufacturing technique of the future. In their rush to judgement, these engineers did not allow enough time to pass so that FMSs could be debugged and allowed to demonstrate their effectiveness.

FMS AND LABOR RELATIONS

Given the technological orientation of FMS literature, an often overlooked aspect is the impact that FMSs have had in three areas: (1) workplace organization; (2) their tendency to de-skill the workforce; and (3) their significant employment/labor-saving component at the company level.

Two persistent, parallel, and interconnected economic forces figured largely in the development of

FMSs, which in turn prompted a substantial reorganization of the workplace environment. First, competitive pressures to lower unit costs are typically achieved by boosting productivity through the introduction and diffusion of technological change. This applied just as readily to FMS production techniques as it did to other groundbreaking techniques. And, as is true in previous times, active periods of technological change usually entail a significant de-skilling component.

Second, in terms of changes in market demand, a heightened presence of market uncertainty (rapid demand surges followed by just as rapid declines) stimulated FMS development. The impact of increased market uncertainty required that workers respond in a manner consistent with changing demand conditions, which in turn gave rise to the notion of labor flexibility. With respect to the organization of the workplace, this notion contained three potential policy scenarios related to flexibility: functional; numerical; and financial.

Functional meant the ease with which tasks performed by workers could be adjusted to meet changes in technology, markets, or company policy. Functional flexibility further grouped skill backgrounds into core, dual, and multiskill classifications. Core skill referred to cases where the practice of an existing craft or trade continued but, as the need arose, performance of unrelated tasks was required. Dual skill meant retention of the existing skill but also the requirement that the worker become proficient at a second task, for instance a machine operator undergoing training in hydraulic systems in order to maintain industrial robots. Multiskill referred to workers who had obtained skill proficiency in three or more tasks.

Numerical flexibility referred to the ease with which the number of workers could be adjusted to meet demand fluctuations using alternative types of employment contracts. These included annual hours, various forms of job sharing, part-time, and minimum/maximum hours working arrangements.

Financial flexibility captured the degree to which the structure of pay encouraged and supported functional and numerical flexibility. By the 1990s, while only a handful of FMS firms had incorporated the full complement of labor flexibility components as describe above, it was widely expected that, in time, they were to become the norm. Several case studies suggested that functional flexibility was more likely to be found in capital-intensive FMS firms, while numerical and financial flexibility practices were growing among relatively more labor-intensive ones.

As concerned the de-skilling impact of FMSs, Edquist and Jacobsson (1988) conducted research in Sweden that indicated that the diffusion and displacement of conventional machine tools by NCMTs led to a significant reduction in the skills per worker needed to operate NCMTs, as well as in the number of people required to learn these skills. They reported that the maximum time required for an unskilled person with a technically oriented secondary education to become proficient with a NCMT ranged from six to twelve months. For skilled operators using conventional machines, by contrast, five years experience was often necessary to acquire proficiency. Productivity gains ranging from 50 to 60 percent were reported by substituting semiskilled computerized numerically controlled (CNC) machine operators for skilled conventional operators. Increases were reported, however, in newly skilled NCMT and CNC support workers, such as setters, programmers, and repair and maintenance engineers. All emerged with the spread of nonconventional machine tools and were not previously required as support labor to operate convential machines. But estimates for a long-term trend indicated that the number of newly skilled support workers would fall far short of compensating for the loss of skilled machine tool workers once required to operate conventional machine tools.

FMSs wholly integrate NCMTs, CNC machine tools, various automatic transport handling equipment, and CAD systems, which numerous studies have indicated all individually exhibit significant labor savings/replacement effects. Extrapolating from this data as well as their own measures, Edquist and Jacobsson calculated that nearly 10,000 workers were replaced worldwide by the end of the 1980s. As FMSs continue to spread, it is expected that the number of replaced workers will continue to grow.

[Daniel E. King]

FURTHER READING:

Browne, J., D. Dubois, K. Rathmill, S.P Seithi, and K.E. Stecke. "Classification of Flexible Manufacturing Systems." *FMS Magazine*. April, 1984.

Bolwijn, P.T., T. Kumpe, et al. *Flexible Manufacturing: Integrating Technological and Social Innovation*. Elsevier Science Publishers, 1986.

Economic Commission for Europe (ECE). *Production and Use of Industrial Robots*. United Nations, 1986.

Ediquist, C. and Jacobsson. *Flexible Automation: The Global Diffusion of New Technology in the Engineering Industry*. Basil Blackwell, 1988.

Greenwood, Nigel R. *Implementing Flexible Manufacturing Systems*. Halsted Press, 1988.

Jaikumar, R. "Postindustrial Manufacturing." *Harvard Business Review*. No. 6, 1986, pp. 69-76.

Jha, Nand, K. ed. *Handbook of Flexible Manufacturing Systems*. Academic Press, 1991.

Kusiak, Andrew, ed. *Flexible Manufacturing Systems: Methods and Studies*. Elsevier Science Publishers, 1986.

Stecke, K. E., and S. Rajan, eds. *Flexible Manufacturing Systems: Operations Research Models and Applications*. Elsevier Science Publishers, 1986.

U.S. Department of Commerce. *A Competitive Assessment of the U.S. Flexible Manufacturing Systems Industry*. Washington, DC: Government Printing Office, 1985.

Tidd, J. *Flexible Manufacturing Technologies and International Competitiveness*. Pinter Publishers, 1991.

FLOW CHARTS

Flow charts are graphical representations of a process that detail the sequencing of steps needed to perform the output of the process. The sequencing of steps needed to complete or perform a process may include the sequencing of operations, machines, materials, or information. Flow charts are an important tool for the improvement of processes. They help project teams to identify the different elements of a process and understand the interrelationships among the different steps. Flow charts may also be used to gather information and data about a process or process performance that will greatly aid in **decision making** regarding the process.

Flow charts can also help project teams to understand the process for further analysis and improvements and for identifying problems associated with the process or its performance. They can also be used to analyze and properly define the scope of the process.

Constructing flow charts requires the use of different symbols. The main symbols that are used to construct flow charts are shown in Figure 1. They are:

- Starting and ending activities are indicated by a rounded-edge rectangle. These are sometimes referred to as terminal activities.

- Activities or steps are indicated by a rectangle. Each step or activity is indicated by a single rectangle. These symbols are called activity or process symbols.

- Decisions are indicated by a diamond. They are called decision symbols. The question or decision to be made or answered is written inside the diamond. The answer determines the path that will be taken as a next step.

- The progression or transition from one step to another are indicated by *flow lines*.

Written information or documents related to the activity or the process are indicated by a *document symbol*.

To construct a flow chart, the following main steps are required:

1. Define the process and identify the scope of the flow diagram.

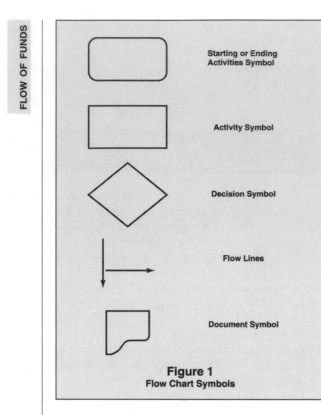

Figure 1
Flow Chart Symbols

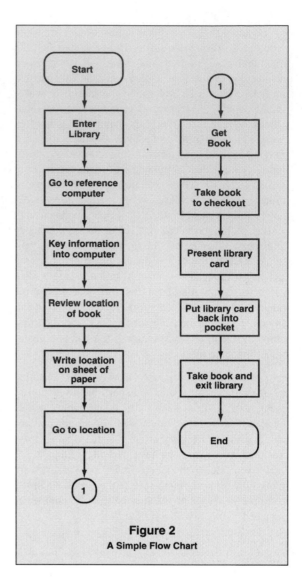

Figure 2
A Simple Flow Chart

2. Identify project teams members that are to be involved in the construction of the process flow diagram.

3. Define the different steps involved in the process and the interrelationships between the different steps. All team members should develop and agree on the different steps for the process.

4. Finalize the diagram. Get other concerned individuals involved as necessary. Modify the diagram as needed.

5. Use the flow diagram and continuously update as needed.

An example of a flow diagram is shown in Figure 2.

[Ahmad K. Elshennawy, Ph.D.]

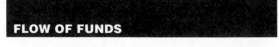

FLOW OF FUNDS

The working definition for *funds* is "net working capital." The *flow of funds* is the dynamic portrayal of the *changes* in net working capital that occur during a period, the *sources of the additions* to net working capital, and the *uses* resulting from any decrease to net working capital. Statements of changes in net working capital generally start with the amount of net working capital at the beginning of the period, the changes occurring during the period, and the net results at the end of the period. In public reporting, companies provide supplemental information detailing the beginning and ending balances of the individual assets and current liabilities.

Statements depicting net changes in working capital have alternative titles. Commonly used are: *Statement of Sources and Uses of Funds, Statement of Sources and Applications of Funds*, and *Statement of Changes in Financial Position*. Stated in cash and cash-equivalents, the statement of changes in financial position demonstrates either the sources and uses of working capital and changes in each working capital account, or changes in cash.

APB OPINION NUMBER 19

In 1963 the Accounting Principles Board (APB)of the American Institute of Certified Public Accountants (AICPA) issued Opinion No. 3 *suggest-*

ing inclusion of the Statement of Changes in Financial Position (SCFP), as a supplement in financial reports. By 1972 Opinion No. 19 noted that regulatory agencies required the preparation of funds statements because the information contained therein was essential to financial statement users. Opinion No. 19 required presentation of such a statement each time a company presented a **balance sheet** and **income statement**. Also, the opinion mandated that companies prepare fund statements in accordance with the all-financial-resources concept under the title of "Statement of Changes in Financial Position."

APB No. 19 provides for the summarization of financial and investing activities along with funds generated from operations during the period. It also requires the complete disclosure of changes in financial position. To be meaningful, a statement needs to focus on a specific aspect or dimension of a financial position (e.g., cash, working capital, net assets, monetary assets) because a statement cannot portray, in an understandable way, all effects of all activities on all possible measures of financial position.

When a company uses the all-financial-resources concept, it reports on the effects of all transactions with outsiders. This includes cash or working capital changes, as well as those material items that are not defined as cash or working capital but which affect a company's financing activities.

The **Financial Accounting Standards Board (FASB)** which was formed to succeed the APB in 1973, issued FASB 95 requiring that a *statement of cash flow* accompany the **annual reports**. Furthermore, it calls for separate reporting of certain information related to noncash investments and financing transactions. The statement of cash flows classifies cash receipts and cash payments resulting from operating, investing, and financing activities. Thus, a statement of cash flow shows a company's cash receipts and cash payments made during a period along with a *reconciliation between* net income and cash flow from operations. With the change in cash and cash equivalents shown, the statement of cash flow and its supplements provide essentially the same information as the SCFP.

PRESCRIBED FORMAT

The APB's requirement to include a SCFP according to a prescribed format is meant to assist financial statement users in answering a number of essential questions about a company's profitability, liquidity, and quality of management. Some of these questions refer to:

- The level or existence of dividends
- The utilization of profits

- The impact of losses on the level of dividends
- The relationship between level of assets and profitability
- The need for an increase in financing
- The application of funds raised from the sale of assets or securities
- The ability to meet debt obligations and retire debt
- The financing of a deficit in working capital

The prescribed format declares that companies should:

1. Prepare statements in such a manner as to express the financial position in terms of cash, cash and temporary assets, quick assets, or working capital. The statement should utilize the all-financial-resources concept, and give the most useful portrayal of financing and investing activities.

2. Disclose the net change in the cash, cash and temporary investments, quick assets, or working capital, depending upon the form of presentation.

3. Disclose outlays for long-term assets, net proceeds from the sale of long-term assets, conversion of long-term debt or preferred stock to common stocks, issuance and re payments of debts, and issuance and repurchases of capital stock and dividends.

The prescribed format allows the formats, terms, and contents of changes in financial position to vary according to the objective of the company. A survey of annual reports by the AICPA indicated that more than half of publicly owned companies issued SCFPs which highlighted the changes in working capital. Less than ten percent "balanced" the statement by reporting the increase in cash or working capital as a use of funds (or a decrease in cash or working capital as a source of funds); and about one-third used a format which reported the ending balance of cash or working capital as the final amount.

Opinion No. 19 also states that net changes in each element of working capital should be disclosed for at least the current accounting period either in the SCFP itself or in a supporting exhibit. This disclosure applies to all formats. Therefore, a company must disclose changes in current assets (other than cash) and current liabilities which constitute sources and uses of cash. A company presents the effect of other financing and investing activities separately. The SCFP should disclose all important changes in financial position for the period covered so that users may determine period changes of relative importance.

IMPORTANCE OF MEASURING FUNDS FLOW

Investors and creditors are interested in determining how effectively management plans and controls the quantity and types of its resources, and in what method it engages to finance them. The design of the SCFP assists users in evaluating the financial operations of a company and the results of the company's financial management policies. Users of **financial statements** employ comparative analysis of this data over a number of years to better evaluate a company's performance and to enhance their ability at predictive decision making. Users analyze the trends to determine the degree to which funds, derived from operations, contribute to the growth of the company. When using the statements in conjunction with the balance sheet and the income statement, users are better equipped to budget future cash flows and changes in resource allocations.

INCOME STATEMENT VERSUS SCFP. The income statement and the SCFP are complementary approaches to evaluating business performance. The income statement is concerned with profitability, matching each period's revenues and expenses to document changes in the long run. The SCFP depicts changes in financial structure and liquidity, summarizing each period's events in terms of their short-run effects. Both statements are necessary, but neither answers all the questions of the period's activities.

Income. The income statement reports the success or failure of management in choosing to invest funds (*outflows* of cash) in various assets used in production, marketing, research and development, administration, outside investments, and so forth. The *inflow* of funds represents a type of disinvestment by selling assets, including inventory, and borrowing new funds through long-term financing. While the funds statement reports the sources and amounts of the inflows and outflows, the income statement shows whether the use of the in-flowing funds was profitable.

Profit. Profit is not synonymous with flow of funds or cash flow. Profit is a term given to the change in a company's net assets resulting from the analysis of selected operating, financing, and investing activities. Yet, profit is not a physical thing that can be disposed of, retained, or paid out. Although it is a change in the net assets, profit is not an asset. Even though a company states profit in monetary terms, profit is not actual money. Profit is not able to explain what happens to a company's cash since the income stream is not the same as funds flow. Therefore, the income and financial position statements do not give an adequate picture of the funds flow.

A company uses an SCFP to identify changes in funds flow where there is no corresponding change to income and profit. For example, while sales and income may be rising and an increase in profit is expected, large capital investments could seriously drain available cash. Only a statement of cash receipts and payments provides the needed information about this change in the cash position.

INVESTING AND PLANNING USES. Stockholders and creditors find funds flow helpful in understanding the changes in assets and asset sources which are not readily evident in the income statement or the financial position. The funds statement explains how the company used additional resources derived from profitable operations, and point out the financial strengths and weaknesses of the business. This additional information helps in evaluating managerial performance and in making investment decisions. Creditors are more able to determine how the business uses credit and the debt capacity of the business.

Within the company managers rely upon funds statements particularly in planning and budgeting. From analyzing a series of funds statements over the years, management is better able to project cash requirements needed for growth, identify and plan the efficient use of idle funds, determine working capital requirements, ease the impact of insufficient cash balances, and plan the payment of interest to creditors and dividends to stockholders.

FLOW OF FUNDS STATEMENT

The SCFP classifies cash receipts and cash payments resulting from operations, investments, and financing activities. *Operations* generate most of the funds *flowing into* a company through such activities as sales, leasing, and fees. Since cash flow from operations measures the cash impact of translations affecting the profit computation, the SCFP also includes collections on accounts receivable, cash received from settlements, insurance reimbursements, and interest and dividends revenue. Operational *outflows* of funds are typically material purchases, labor, merchandise, supplies, taxes, penalties and fines, charitable contributions, and returns and allowances.

The *outflow* of funds as *investments* make loans and purchase property, plant, equipment, and securities of other companies. The *inflows* to the company come as debt collections, the sale of securities, and the sale of property, plant, and equipment.

The *financing* activities of a business entity involve the securing of equity funds, providing owners with a return on their investments, the issuance of corporate debt, and the paying off of such debt. Cash *inflows* from financing activities include funds obtained from issuing debt and equity securities. *Outflows* decrease funds on hand through dividend pay-

Table A
Working Capital Adjustments to Net Operating Income (loss)

Income Element	Adjustment
Depreciation of plant assets	Add
Amortization of intangible assets	Add
Deferred income tax	Add, or Subtract — if amount of the deferral is negative
Sale of noncurrent asset If a Gain If a (Loss)	 Subtract Add
Undistributed affiliate earnings	Subtract
Early extinguish of debt If a Gain If a (Loss)	 Subtract Add
Interest expense Long-term premium amortized Long-term discount amortized	 Subtract Add

ments, principal payments for long-term debt, and purchases of treasury stock.

In some instances an outlay of cash may relate to more than one business activity. The purchase of equipment may be essential for generating cash from operations. However, equipment purchases (prevailing tax-treatment aside) are durable goods and, therefore, long-term assets. A company usually classifies them by their main characteristics – *investments*.

DIRECT AND INDIRECT METHODS

A company uses what is called the *direct method* of calculating the SCFP when it reports cash flows from operating activities by major classes of receipts and payments, and by the resulting net amount. Included are only those items which either generate or utilize cash. The SCFP begins with cash from operations, adds cash provided by financing and investing activities, and ends with the change in cash and the current cash balance.

The direct method follows the cash-flow format which reflects a more short-term orientation than working capital because it focuses on immediate cash-paying ability not readily apparent from working capital. For example, net changes in working capital often change the cash position, but do not change total working capital. Sales of inventory increase cash while working capital does not change.

Source of Funds. There are four main categories for sources of funds:

1. current operations, if profitable (unprofitable operations result in a negative source of cash);

2. borrowing, except for trade credit;

3. issuance of capital stock; and

4. sale of business assets and investments.

Use of Funds. A company's use of funds is related to satisfying its commitments to its sources of funds.

1. financing current operations;

2. debt servicing and extinguishing debt;

3. repurchase of stock and payment of dividends; and

4. purchase of noncurrent assets and investments.

The *indirect method* works through a series of adjustments to net income (loss) from operating activities to report the net cash flow from operations. The statement for the period begins with income (or loss) before extraordinary items, if any, and adds back (or deducts) items recognized in determining income or loss but which did not use (or provide) working capital or cash.

Table A presents a number of adjustments made to net operating income (loss) to derive working capital.

Table B
Consolidated Statement of Cash Flows
Strader Wingnut Company and Subsidiaries
For the years ended December 31, 1993, 1992, and 1991 (in millions)

	1993		1992		1991	
	Wingnut	Financial Services	Wingnut	Financial Services	Wingnut	Financial Services
Cash and cash equivalents at January 1	$3,504	$3,182	$4,958	$3,175	$4,599	$2,168
Cash flow from operating activities (Note 15)	6,862	7,145	5,753	5,762	3,341	4,780
Cash flow from investing activities						
Capital expenditures	(6,714)	(100)	(5,697)	(93)	(5,723)	(124)
Proceeds from sale and leaseback of fixed assets	884	·	263	·	619	·
Acquisitions of other companies	0	(336)	0	(461)	0	860
Proceeds from sales of subsidiaries	173	0	52	0	273	0
Acquisitions of receivables and leased investments	·	(163,858)	·	(134,619)	·	(124,606)
Collections of receivables and leased investments	·	142,844	·	123,144	·	117,581
Purchases of securities	(100,493)	(13,741)	(50,437)	(12,877)	(56,141)	(11,876)
Sale of securities	101,927	12,426	49,629	12,169	52,795	14,450
Proceeds from sales of receivables	·	4,794	·	6,465	·	4,533
Loans originated net of principal payments	·	(1,466)	·	(938)	·	(321)
Investing activity with Financial Services	(117)	·	709	·	837	·
Other	(69)	389	(92)	372	(175)	555
Net cash used in investing activities	(4,409)	(19,048)	(5,973)	(6,838)	(7,515)	(668)
Cash flow from financing activities						
Cash dividends	(1,086)	·	(977)	·	(927)	·
Sale of Preferred Stock	0	·	1,104	·	2,252	·
Issuance of Common Stock	394	·	221	·	371	·
Changes in short-term debt	(66)	6,065	(426)	2,739	117	(3,931)
Proceeds from issuance of other debt	424	22,128	1,865	13,382	4,808	13,889
Principal payments on other debt	(376)	(13,791)	(1,598)	(13,122)	(2,477)	(9,981)
Financing activity with Wingnut	·	117	·	(709)	·	(837)
Changes in customers' deposits, excluding interest credited	·	(3,861)	·	(3,418)	·	(1,875)
Receipts from annuity contracts	·	821	·	703	·	46
Issuance of subsidiary company preferred stock	·	375	·	283	·	0
Other	(124)	(76)	79	(10)	3	12
Net cash (used in)/provided by financing activities	(834)	11,778	268	(152)	4,147	(2,677)
Effect of exchange rate changes on cash	17	25	(220)	(47)	(35)	(7)
Net transactions with Wingnut/Financial Services	527	(527)	(1,282)	1,282	421	(421)
Net increase/(decrease) in cash and cash equivalents	2,163	(627)	(1,454)	7	359	1,007
Cash and cash equivalents at December 31	$5,667	$2,555	$3,504	$3,182	$4,958	$3,175
Total cash and cash equivalents		$8,222		$6,686		$8,133

Source: Annual Report 1993

An SCFP, based on the indirect method and following the all-financial-sources concept, shows at least one change on the left side of the following equation, and at least one change on the right side. These changes affect at least one current element and one noncurrent element on the balance sheet.

$$\begin{array}{c} \text{Change in} \\ \text{Working} \\ \text{Capital} \end{array} = \begin{array}{c} \text{Change in} \\ \text{Noncurrent} \\ \text{Liabilities} \end{array} + \begin{array}{c} \text{Change in} \\ \text{Owner's} \\ \text{Equity} \end{array} - \begin{array}{c} \text{Change in} \\ \text{Noncurrent} \\ \text{Assets} \end{array}$$

The APB notes in Opinion No. 19 that, with either method, a company would clearly label the resulting amount of working capital or cash as "Working capital provided from [used in] operations for the period, exclusive or extraordinary items." Immediately after this total, a company would indicate working capital or cash provided or used by income or loss from extraordinary items, if any. A company also would adjust extraordinary income or loss that did not provide or use working capital or cash during the period.

DIRECT METHOD: STRADER WINGNUT COMPANY.
The "Consolidated Statement of Cash Flows" for the fictional Strader Wingnut Company and its subsidiaries, depicted in Table B, demonstrates the direct method.

Following Opinion No. 19's alternative format, Strader Wingnut begins with cash and cash equivalents from operations. It only includes items which directly affect the use of cash. It disregards write-offs such as depreciation, and changes in the valuation of quick assets which required no change in the cash position. The company has substantially increased it cash flows from operating activities 1991 through 1993.

Table C
Consolidated Statement of Cash Flows
Wolverine Steel Limited
Annual Report 1993

Year ended December 31, in millions	1993	1992	1991
OPERATING ACTIVITIES			
Net income (loss)	($104)	($112)	($36)
Adjustments to determine cash from operating activities:			
Depreciation	443	449	429
Deferred income taxes	(54)	(87)	33
Equity income - net of dividends	31	(4)	(46)
Change in receivables	41	114	163
Change in inventories	144	245	142
Change in payables	(18)	(139)	(96)
Change in income and other taxes payable	(21)	37	(84)
Change in deferred changes, receivables and credits	6	41	139
Changes in operating working capital due to:			
Deferred translation adjustments	(55)	(93)	(6)
Acquisitions, disposals and deconsolidations	12	(18)	2
Other - net	19	32	19
Cash from operating activities	444	465	659
FINANCING ACTIVITIES			
New debt	414	588	636
Debt repayments	(382)	(389)	(262)
	32	199	374
Short-term borrowings - net	(124)	(266)	2
Common shares issued	5	7	15
Preference shares issued	•	150	•
Preference shares redeemed	•	(9)	•
Shares issued by subsidiary companies	•	•	21
Dividends - Wolverine shareholders (including preference)	(85)	(124)	(212)
- minority interests	•	(1)	(3)
Cash from (used for) financing activities	(172)	(44)	197
INVESTMENT ACTIVITIES			
Property, plant and equipment	(251)	(389)	(891)
Investments	(119)	(85)	(61)
	(370)	(474)	(880)
Sales of fixed assets and investments	31	24	23
Cash used for investment activities	(339)	(450)	(857)
Effect of exchange rate changes on cash and time deposits	(1)	(8)	6
Increase (decrease) in cash and time deposits	(68)	(37)	5
Cash of companies desconsolidated	–	(19)	–
Cash and time deposits - beginning of year	149	205	200
Cash and time deposits - end of year	$81	$149	$205

The company next shows that this cash was generously employed in capital expenditures and financial services. The other activities were minor in comparison. Strader turned over its securities portfolio and sold or leased productive assets. Opinion No. 19 allows for the consolidation of minor and immaterial items under "Other."

The company's financing activities indicate that the Wingnut area needed very little outside financing, in terms of stock and debt, to meet its operational and investing needs. At period's end, the area substantially increased its cash position. On the other hand, Financial Services obtained long- and short-term debt to close the gap between cash flow and investing activities such that it decreased its cash position by period's end for the first time in three years.

INDIRECT METHOD: WOLVERINE STEEL LIMITED. The "Consolidated Statement of Cash Flows" for the fictional Wolverine Steel Limited, depicted in Table C, demonstrates the indirect method.

The statement begins with a summary of changes in the area of operations. Wolverine first states, in this case, a net loss from operations as calculated for the income statement. In order to determine the actual *cash* derived from operations, it adjusted the net loss for write-offs which did not affect the cash position. Added back to the net loss were depreciation, equity income (net of dividends), and the changes in the quick assets. On the other hand, Wolverine incurred a decrease in deferred liabilities, and subtracted deferred income taxes to indicate the unavailability of that cash. Finally, the company presented changes in operating working capital resulting from translation adjustments, and changes due to reorganization of operations. Immaterial items are consolidated under "Other - net." The net loss for 1993 was $104 million while the actual cash from operations was $444 million.

Wolverine's cash from operating activities decreased about one-third, by some $215 million, between year-end 1991 to 1993. However, in the section summarizing financing activities, the company shows a decrease in new debt to a net of $32 million from $374 million. Dividends declined, as well as cash raised through the issuance of equities and debt instruments. For 1993, it used more cash flow for financing activities than it had cash raised through the issuance of common shares.

In the third section, "Investment Activities," Wolverine indicates continued investment in property, plant, equipment, and other investments. It slightly increased the sale of fixed assets and investments. Overall, however, investment activities have decreased. From the data presented for preceding years, it appears that the company drew down its savings, accumulated prior to 1991, to help finance its apparent restructuring and expansion.

These examples of a consolidated statement of cash flows are only small, albeit significant, parts of their company's annual reports, and would be better understood in conjunction with all other financial statements, the voluminous notes and explanations, and the narrative in the annual reports.

SUMMARY

The statement of changes in the financial position is both an alternative and a complementary report to the income statement and statement of working capital. Because the SCFP shows the sources and uses of a company's funds, it provides both insiders and outsiders the means to better evaluate the firm's management of its finances and the profitability of its operations. Furthermore, the SCFP is a powerful planning tool in projecting cash flow and financing needs.

SEE ALSO: Income Statement; Working Capital

[Roger J. AbiNader]

FURTHER READING:

APB Opinion No. 19, Reporting Changes in Financial Position. Accounting Principles Board, AICPA, 1971.

Black, Homer A., John E. Champion, and Gibbs U. Miller Accounting in Business Decisions: Theory, Method, and Use. Prentice-Hall, 1973.

Bierman, Harold, Jr., and Seymour Smidt. Financial Management for Decision Making. Macmillan Publishing Company, 1986.

Meigs, Robert F., and Walter B. Meigs Accounting: The Basis for Business Decisions, 8th ed,. McGraw-Hill, 1990.

Welsch, Glenn A. Budgeting: Profit Planning and Control. Prentice-Hall, 1976.

FOCUS GROUPS

Focus groups have become one of the most popular ways to gather market research data. In 1992 more than 100,000 different focus group sessions were conducted. As a research technique they are used by marketing managers, product managers, and market researchers. Businesses find them useful for staying close to consumers and their ever-changing attitudes and feelings. Focus groups provide qualitative information from well-defined target audiences; the information can be used for decision making and developing marketing strategies and promotional campaigns.

Focus groups are essentially discussion groups. They generate output that tells businesses and other clients who utilize them what their target audience feels or thinks about certain concepts, which are known as test concepts. This type of **market research** is known as qualitative research. Unlike quantitative research, which provides hard numbers on which to base conclusions, qualitative research provides the kind of information that cannot be put into numbers. Other types of qualitative research techniques include in-depth interviews conducted with one or two individuals and expert panels. These methods are to be contrasted with quantitative techniques, such as behavioral and attitudinal surveys, which generate quantifiable data. Quantitative data can also be generated from different types of advertising studies and product tests that use representative population samples.

APPLICATIONS

As focus groups became more popular in the 1980s and 1990s, they became more widely used for applications outside of their traditional ones. For example, pharmaceutical companies have convened focus groups consisting of medical professionals to test concepts related to new drug products. The legal profession has used focus groups to improve the quality of their cases. Nonprofit organizations have used focus groups to test fundraising campaigns. Focus groups have been used in industrial settings by business-to-business marketers. Companies have set up employee focus groups to learn more about employee motivation.

Traditionally, focus groups have been used to gather qualitative data from target groups of consumers. They are frequently used in new product development to test consumer reaction to new product concepts and prototypes. Focus groups are also used to test communications programs and can provide an indication of how consumers will react to specific advertising messages and other types of marketing communications. Focus groups can generate output that helps advertising and promotion managers position a particular product, service, or institution with respect to their target audience. Reactions to new types of product packaging can also be determined.

Focus groups are also used to discover more about consumer habits and product usage. They can reveal how different products and services are used by consumers. In addition they can be used to find out more about consumer attitudes toward products and services. Quality of service can be evaluated through the use of focus groups. Public relations agencies often use focus groups to gather information about consumer attitudes and perceptions.

Idea generation is another area in which focus groups are useful to businesses. Participants are encouraged to talk about their problems and unfulfilled needs. From this type of focus group new ideas can be generated concerning possible new products and services.

CHARACTERISTICS

A key factor in determining the success of focus groups is the composition of the group in terms of the participants' age, gender, and product usage. Product usage, or nonusage in some cases, means that participants are selected on the basis of their use, knowledge, attitudes, or feelings about the products, services, or other test concepts that are the subject of the focus group. In selecting participants, the objective is to find individuals who can discuss the topics at hand and provide quality output that meets the specified research objectives.

The most common method of selecting participants for focus groups is from some type of database that contains demographic, psychographic, and lifestyle information about a large number of consumers. Such databases are available from a variety of commercial vendors. A list of desired characteristics is drawn up and matched with the database to select participants for focus groups. These characteristics may include purchase behavior, attitudes, and demographic data such as age and gender. The goal is to select participants who would likely be in the target audience for the products, services, or concepts being tested.

There is no absolute ideal in terms of the number of participants. Different moderators are comfortable with different sizes of focus groups. A full group usually includes from eight to ten participants. Minigroups consist of four to six individuals. Full groups offer several advantages over smaller groups, but in some cases it is not possible to convene a full group.

Full groups of eight to ten participants provide a sufficient amount of output that smaller groups may not be able to offer, especially if one or two individuals either dominate the discussion or tend to be withdrawn and shy. There is usually better interaction, or group dynamics, in full groups. Participants in full groups are not made to feel like experts, as may be the case in minigroups; they participate as average consumers and provide more reliable output.

Groups that include more than ten participants are usually more difficult for moderators to control. Group interaction is also more difficult, and moderators have a harder time stimulating discussion. Similarly, it is more difficult for a moderator to spend time probing one individual when there are too many participants.

Focus groups that are homogeneous in terms of age, gender, and product usage generally work better than mixed groups. When it is desirable to obtain data from different age and gender groups, most experts recommend scheduling a series of focus groups using homogeneous participants. There are several reasons homogeneous groups work better than mixed groups. One is that it is easier to evaluate output from homogeneous groups. It would not be possible in a mixed gender group, for example, to distinguish male and female attitudes toward a certain topic. To do so would require two separate, homogeneous groups, one consisting of males and one of females.

Another reason homogeneous groups work better is that group dynamics tend to become inhibited in mixed gender or age focus groups. In addition, specific topics can be explored in greater depth when there is homogeneity among the participants with regard to usage of or attitudes toward the products being tested.

The most successful focus groups, then, are those that contain approximately eight to ten members who are representative of individuals who would use the product or service being discussed. Ideally they would be of the same gender and age group. If individuals chosen for a focus group do not represent the target audience for the concepts being tested, then the group is likely to provide misleading information.

MODERATORS

Moderators play an important role in determining the success of focus groups. Well-trained moderators can provide a great deal of added value in terms of their past experience, skills, and techniques. Poorly trained moderators are likely to fail to generate quality output from their focus groups. In addition to professional, full-time focus group moderators, other types of individuals who serve as focus group moderators include professional researchers, academicians, marketing consultants, psychologists or psychiatrists, and clients themselves.

Focus group moderators serve as discussion leaders. They try to stimulate discussion but say as little as possible. They are not interviewers. They usually work from a guide that provides them with an outlined plan of how the discussion should flow. The guide includes topics to be covered together with probes that can be used to stimulate further discussion. Moderators try to include everyone in the discussion. They allocate available time to make sure the required topics are covered. When the discussion digresses, it is up to the moderator to refocus the group on the topic at hand.

SESSIONS

When setting up a focus group session, careful attention should be paid to the physical setting where the session or sessions will take place. It is important that the location be one that encourages relaxed participation and informal spontaneous comments. The focus group facility must be of adequate size and have comfortable seating for all of the participants. Living room and conference room settings both provide good settings for focus groups. Public places, such as restaurants and auditoriums, do not.

In selecting a focus group site it is also important to make it geographically convenient for the participants. Locations that are hard to find or located in out of the way places may cause delays and scheduling problems.

The facility should also be relatively soundproof, to minimize outside noises and distractions. While focus group sessions are almost always audiotaped and many are videotaped, clients usually like to observe their focus groups firsthand. The ideal focus group facility would be equipped with a one-way mirror that allows clients to observe without intruding. An alternative viewing arrangement would be to use a remote video hookup that would allow clients to view the proceedings on a video screen. Having clients in the same room as the focus group is the least desirable arrangement.

Once the facility, moderator, and participants have been selected, typical focus group sessions begin with an introduction. During the introductory part of the session the moderator welcomes the participants, informs them of what will take place during the session, and generally sets the stage for the discussion to follow. Prior to the main discussion there is usually a warm-up phase. The warm-up is designed to make the participants feel at ease. During the warm-up participants generally introduce themselves to the group. General topic discussions, usually related to the specific topics that will be covered later, also form part of the warm-up stage. These general discussions help participants focus their attention. They also provide the moderator with some insight into the different participants and allow the moderator to disguise the specific objectives of the focus group.

Gradually the moderator moves the level of discussion from general topics to more specific ones. The moderator may present different concepts for discussion. These include the test concepts for which the group was convened. The moderator may choose to use props to focus the group's attention. Typical props include product samples, actual or concept ads, concept statements that participants read together, photographs and showing television commercials.

Once all of the test concepts have been discussed and evaluated by the group, the moderator moves the discussion into a wrap-up phase. During this phase the best concepts are identified and their strengths and weaknesses discussed. Participants may be asked to write down their reactions to what they have seen and discussed. During this final phase any outstanding issues that were omitted are covered.

When all of the substantive discussions have been completed, the moderator closes the session by thanking the participants and giving them any final instructions. Participants should leave with a positive feeling about the experience and the client, if the client has been identified. After the participants have left, it is standard practice for the moderator and the client observers to have a postgroup discussion.

Following the conclusion of the focus group or series of focus group sessions, the moderator may prepare a report for the client. The report generally provides a written summary of the results of the session or sessions as interpreted by the moderator. Focus group reports may be summary in nature or more detailed. In some cases the client may not require a written report.

ADVANTAGES

Focus groups have become a widely used market research tool because of the advantages they offer. With respect to other qualitative research methods, such as in-depth interviews with one or two individuals at a time, focus groups are much faster and more cost effective. It takes much less time to generate output from focus groups than from one-to-one interviews. Focus groups also allow clients to participate by viewing the discussions, something which is usually not possible with in-depth interviews.

The group dynamics of focus group discussions also provide many benefits. The synergy, or combined effect, of group interactions results in more output than would be obtained individually. Group discussions often snowball, or build on previous statements, to reach a level of output that does not occur individually. Participants are likely to be more spontaneous in focus groups than in one-to-one interviews, and their informal comments may produce unexpected results.

[David Bianco]

FURTHER READING:

Greenbaum, Thomas L. *The Handbook for Focus Group Research*. Rev, ed. Lexington Books, 1993.

Greenbaum, Thomas L. *The Practical Handbook and Guide to Focus Group Research*. D. C. Heath, 1988.

Krueger, Richard A. *Focus Groups: A Practical Guide for Applied Research*. Sage Publications, 1988.

FORECASTING

Forecasting can be broadly considered as a method or a technique for estimating many future aspects of a business or other operation. There are numerous techniques that can be used to accomplish the goal of forecasting. For example, a retailing firm that has been in business for 25 years can forecast its volume of sales in the coming year based on its experience over the 25-year period—such a forecasting technique bases the future forecast on the past data.

While the term "forecasting" may appear to be rather technical, planning for the future is a critical aspect of managing any organization—business, nonprofit or other. In fact, the long-term success of any organization is closely tied to how well the management of the organization is able to foresee its future and to develop appropriate strategies to deal with likely future scenarios. Intuition, good judgment, and an awareness of how well the economy is doing may give the manager of a business firm a rough idea (or "feeling") of what is likely to happen in the future. Nevertheless, it is not easy to convert a feeling about the future into a precise and useful number, such as next year's sales volume or the raw material cost per unit of output. Forecasting methods can help estimate many such future aspects of a business operation.

Suppose that a forecast expert has been asked to provide estimates of the sales volume for a particular product for the next four quarters. One can easily see that a number of other decisions will be affected by the forecasts or estimates of sales volumes provided by the forecaster. Clearly, production schedules, raw material purchasing plans, policies regarding inventories, and sales quotas will be affected by such forecasts. As a result, poor forecasts or estimates may lead to poor planning and thus result in increased costs to the business.

How should one go about preparing the quarterly sales volume forecasts? One will certainly want to review the actual sales data for the product in question for past periods. Suppose that the forecaster has access to actual sales data for each quarter over the 25-year period the firm has been in business. Using these historical data, the forecaster can identify the general level of sales. He or she can also determine whether there is a pattern or trend, such as an increase or decrease in sales volume over time. A further review of the data may reveal some type of seasonal pattern, such as peak sales occurring before a holiday. Thus by reviewing historical data over time, the forecaster can often develop a good understanding of the previous pattern of sales. Understanding such a pattern can often lead to better forecasts of future sales of the product. In addition, if the forecaster is able to identify the factors that influence sales, historical data on these factors (or variables) can also be used to generate forecasts of future sales volumes.

FORECASTING METHODS

All forecasting methods can be divided into two broad categories: qualitative and quantitative. Many forecasting techniques use past or historical data in the form of time series. A time series is simply a set of observations measured at successive points in time or over successive periods of time. Forecasts essentially provide future values of the time series on a specific variable such as sales volume. Division of forecasting methods into qualitative and quantitative categories is based on the availability of historical time series data.

QUALITATIVE FORECASTING METHODS

Qualitative forecasting techniques generally employ the judgment of experts in the appropriate field to generate forecasts. A key advantage of these procedures is that they can be applied in situations where historical data are simply not available. Moreover, even when historical data are available, significant changes in environmental conditions affecting the relevant time series may make the use of past data irrelevant and questionable in forecasting future values of the time series. Consider, for example, that historical data on gasoline sales are available. If the government then implemented a gasoline rationing program, changing the way gasoline is sold, one would have to question the validity of a gasoline sales forecast based on the past data. Qualitative forecasting methods offer a way to generate forecasts in such cases. Three important qualitative forecasting methods are: the **Delphi technique**, scenario writing, and the subject approach.

DELPHI TECHNIQUE. In the Delphi technique, an attempt is made to develop forecasts through "group consensus." Usually, a panel of experts are asked to respond to a series of questionnaires. The experts, physically separated from and unknown to each other, are asked to respond to an initial questionnaire (a set of questions). Then, a second questionnaire is prepared incorporating information and opinions of the whole group. Each expert is asked to reconsider and to revise his or her initial response to the questions. This process is continued until some degree of consensus among experts is reached. It should be noted that the objective of the Delphi technique is not to produce a single answer at the end. Instead, it attempts to produce a relatively narrow spread of opinions—the range in which opinions of the majority of experts lie.

SCENARIO WRITING. Under this approach, the forecaster starts with different sets of assumptions. For each set of assumptions, a likely scenario of the business outcome is charted out. Thus, the forecaster would be able to generate many different future scenarios (corresponding to the different sets of assumptions). The decision maker or business person is presented with the different scenarios, and has to decide which scenario is most likely to prevail.

SUBJECTIVE APPROACH. The subjective approach allows individuals participating in the forecasting decision to arrive at a forecast based on their subjective feelings and ideas. This approach is based on the premise that a human mind can arrive at a decision based on factors that are often very difficult to quantify. "Brainstorming sessions" are frequently used as a way to develop new ideas or to solve complex problems. In loosely organized sessions, participants feel free from peer pressure and, more importantly, can express their views and ideas without fear of criticism. Many corporations in the United States have started to increasingly use the subjective approach.

QUANTITATIVE FORECASTING METHODS. Quantitative forecasting methods are used when historical data on variables of interest are available—these methods are based on an analysis of historical data concerning the time series of the specific variable of interest and possibly other related time series. There are two major categories of quantitative forecasting methods. The first type uses the past trend of a particular variable to base the future forecast of the variable. As this category of forecasting methods simply uses time series on past data of the variable that is being forecasted, these techniques are called time series methods.

The second category of quantitative forecasting techniques also uses historical data. But in forecasting future values of a variable, the forecaster examines the cause-and-effect relationships of the variable with other relevant variables such as the level of consumer confidence, changes in consumers' disposable incomes, the interest rate at which consumers can finance their spending through borrowing, and the state of the economy represented by such variables as the unemployment rate. Thus, this category of forecasting techniques uses past time series on many relevant variables to produce the forecast for the variable of interest. Forecasting techniques falling under this category are called causal methods, as the basis of such forecasting is the cause-and-effect relationship between the variable forecasted and other time series selected to help in generating the forecasts.

TIME SERIES METHODS OF FORECASTING. Before discussing time series methods, it is helpful to understand the behavior of time series in general terms. Time series are comprised of four separate components: trend component, cyclical component, seasonal component, and irregular component. These four components are viewed as providing specific values for the time series when combined.

In a time series, measurements are taken at successive points or over successive periods. The measurements may be taken every hour, day, week, month, or year, or at any other regular (or irregular) interval. While most time series data generally display some random fluctuations, the time series may still show gradual shifts to relatively higher or lower values over an extended period. The gradual shifting of the time series is often referred to by professional forecasters as the trend in the time series. A trend emerges due to one or more long-term factors, such as changes in population size, changes in the demographic characteristics of population, and changes in tastes and preferences of consumers. For example, manufacturers of automobiles in the United States may see that there are substantial variations in automobile sales from one month to the next. But, in reviewing auto sales over the past 15-20 years, the automobile manufacturers may discover a gradual increase in annual sales volume. In this case, the trend for auto sales is increasing over time. In another example, the trend may be decreasing over time. Professional forecasters often describe an increasing trend by an upward sloping straight line and a decreasing trend by a downward sloping straight line. Using a straight line to represent a trend, however, is a mere simplification—in many situations, nonlinear trends may more accurately represent the true trend in the time series.

Although a time series may often exhibit a trend over a long period, it may also display alternating sequences of points that lie above and below the trend line. Any recurring sequence of points above and below the trend line that last more than a year are considered to constitute the cyclical component of the time series—that is, these observations in the time series deviate from the trend due to cyclical fluctuations (fluctuations that repeat at intervals of more than one year). The time series of the aggregate output in the economy (called the real gross domestic product) provides a good example of a time series that displays cyclical behavior. While the trend line for **gross domestic product** is upward sloping, the output growth displays a cyclical behavior around the trend line. This cyclical behavior of gross domestic product has been dubbed **business cycles** by economists.

The seasonal component is similar to the cyclical component in that they both refer to some regular fluctuations in a time series. There is one key difference, however. While cyclical components of a time series are identified by analyzing multiyear movements in historical data, seasonal components capture the regular pattern of variability in the time series within one-year periods. Many economic variables display seasonal patterns. For example, manufacturers of swimming pools experience low sales in fall and winter months, but they witness peak sales of swimming pools during spring and summer months. Manufacturers of snow removal equipment, on the other hand, experience the exactly opposite yearly sales pattern. The component of the time series that captures the variability in the data due to seasonal fluctuations is called the seasonal component.

The irregular component of the time series represents the residual left in an observation of the time series once the effects due to trend, cyclical, and seasonal components are extracted. Trend, cyclical, and seasonal components are considered to account for systematic variations in the time series. The irregular component thus accounts for the random variability in the time series. The random variations in the time series are, in turn, caused by short-term, unanticipated and nonrecurring factors that affect the time series. The irregular component of the time series, by nature, cannot be predicted in advance.

TIME SERIES FORECASTING USING SMOOTHING METHODS. Smoothing methods are appropriate when a time series displays no significant effects of trend, cyclical, or seasonal components (often called a stable time series). In such a case, the goal is to smooth out the irregular component of the time series by using an averaging process. Once the time series is smoothed, it is used to generate forecasts.

The moving averages method is probably the most widely used smoothing technique. In order to smooth the time series, this method uses the average of a number of adjoining data points or periods. This averaging process uses overlapping observations to generate averages. Suppose a forecaster wants to generate three-period moving averages. The forecaster would take the first three observations of the time series and calculate the average. Then, the forecaster would drop the first observation and calculate the average of the next three observations. This process would continue until three-period averages are calculated based on the data available from the entire time series. The term "moving" refers to the way averages are calculated—the forecaster moves up or down the time series to pick observations to calculate an average of a fixed number of observations. In the three-period example, the moving averages method would use the average of the most recent three observations of data in the time series as the forecast for the next period. This forecasted value for the next period, in conjunction with the last two observations of the historical time series, would yield an average that can be used as the forecast for the second period in the future.

The calculation of a three-period moving average can be illustrated as follows. Suppose a forecaster wants to forecast the sales volume for American-made automobiles in the United States for the next year. The sales of American-made cars in the United States during the previous three years were: 1.3 million, 900,000, and 1.1 million (the most recent observation is reported first). The three-period moving average in this case is 1.1 million cars (that is:

$$[(1.3 + 0.90 + 1.1)/3 = 1.1]$$

Based on the three-period moving averages, the forecast may predict that 1.1 million American-made cars are most likely to be sold in the United States the next year.

In calculating moving averages to generate forecasts, the forecaster may experiment with different-length moving averages. The forecaster will choose the length that yields the highest accuracy for the forecasts generated.

It is important that forecasts generated not be too far from the actual future outcomes. In order to examine the accuracy of forecasts generated, forecasters generally devise a measure of the forecasting error (that is, the difference between the forecasted value for a period and the associated actual value of the variable of interest). Suppose retail sales volume for American-made automobiles in the United States is forecast to be 1.1 million cars for a given year, but only 1 million cars are actually sold that year. The forecast error in this case is equal 100,000 cars. In other words, the forecaster overestimated the sales volume for the year by 100,000. Of course, forecast errors will sometimes be positive, and at other times be negative. Thus, taking a simple average of forecast errors over time will not capture the true magnitude of forecast errors; large positive errors may simply cancel out large negative errors, giving a misleading impression about the accuracy of forecasts generated. As a result, forecasters commonly use the mean squares error to measure the forecast error. The mean squares error, or the MSE, is the average of the sum of squared forecasting errors. This measure, by taking the squares of forecasting errors, eliminates the chance of negative and positive errors canceling out.

In selecting the length of the moving averages, a forecaster can employ the mean squares error measure to determine the number of values to be included in calculating the moving averages. The forecaster experiments with different lengths to generate moving averages and then calculates forecast errors (and the associated mean squares errors) for each length used in calculating moving averages. Then, the forecaster can pick the length that minimizes the mean squared error of forecasts generated.

Weighted moving averages are a variant of moving averages. In the moving averages method, each observation of data receives the same weight. In the weighted moving averages method, different weights are assigned to the observations on data that are used in calculating the moving averages. Suppose, once again, that a forecaster wants to generate three-period moving averages. Under the weighted moving averages method, the three data points would receive different weights before the average is calculated. Generally, the most recent observation receives the maximum weight, with the weight assigned decreasing for older data values.

The calculation of a three-period weighted moving average can be illustrated as follows. Suppose, once again, that a forecaster wants to forecast the sales volume for American-made automobiles in the United States for the next year. The sales of American-made cars for the United States during the previous three years were: 1.3 million, 900,000, and 1.1 million (the most recent observation is reported first). One estimate of the weighted three-period moving average in this example can be equal to 1.133 million cars (that is,

$$[\{ (3/6) * (1.3) + (2/6) * (0.90) + (1/6) * (1.1) \} / 3 = 1.133]$$

Based on the three-period weighted moving averages, the forecast may predict that 1.133 million American-made cars are most likely to be sold in the United States in the next year. The accuracy of weighted moving averages forecasts are determined in a manner similar to that for simple moving averages.

Exponential smoothing is somewhat more difficult mathematically. In essence, however, exponential smoothing also uses the weighted average concept—in the form of the weighted average of all past observations, as contained in the relevant time series—to generate forecasts for the next period. The term "exponential smoothing" comes from the fact that this method employs a weighting scheme for the historical values of data that is exponential in nature. In ordinary terms, an exponential weighting scheme assigns the maximum weight to the most recent observation and the weights decline in a systematic manner as older and older observations are included. The accuracies of forecasts using exponential smoothing are determined in a manner similar to that for the moving averages method.

TIME SERIES FORECASTING USING TREND PROJECTION. This method uses the underlying long-term trend of a time series of data to forecast its future values. Suppose a forecaster has data on sales of American-made automobiles in the United States for the last 25 years. The time series data on U.S. auto sales can be plotted and examined visually. Most likely, the auto sales time series would display a gradual growth in the sales volume, despite the "up" and "down" movements from year to year. The trend may be linear (approximated by a straight line) or nonlinear (approximated by a curve or a nonlinear line). Most often, forecasters assume a linear trend—of course, if a linear trend is assumed when, in fact, a nonlinear trend is present, this misrepresentation can lead to grossly inaccurate forecasts. Assume that the time series on American-made auto sales is actually linear and thus it can be represented by a straight line. Mathematical techniques are used to find the straight line that most accurately represents the time series on auto sales. This line relates sales to different points over time. If we further assume that the past trend will continue in the future, future values of the time series (forecasts) can be inferred from the straight line based on the past data. One should remember that the forecasts based on this method should also be judged on the basis of a measure of forecast errors. One can continue to assume that the forecaster uses the mean squares error discussed earlier.

TIME SERIES FORECASTING USING TREND AND SEASONAL COMPONENTS. This method is a variant of the trend projection method, making use of the seasonal component of a time series in addition to the trend component. This method first removes the seasonal effect or the seasonal component from the time series. This step is often referred to as de-seasonalizing, the time series.

Once a time series has been de-seasonalized it will have only a trend component. The trend projection method can then be employed to identify a straight line trend that represents the time series data well. Then, using this trend line, forecasts for future periods are generated. The final step under this method is to reincorporate the seasonal component of the time series (using what is known as the seasonal index) to adjust the forecasts based on trend alone. In this manner, the forecasts generated are composed of both the trend and seasonal components. One will normally expect these forecasts to be more accurate than those that are based purely on the trend projection.

CAUSAL METHOD OF FORECASTING. As mentioned earlier, causal methods use the cause-and-effect relationship between the variable whose future values are being forecasted and other related variables or factors. The widely known causal method is called regression analysis, a statistical technique used to develop a mathematical model showing how a set of variables are related. This mathematical relationship can be used to generate forecasts. In the terminology used in regression analysis contexts, the variable that is being forecasted is called the dependent or response variable. The variable or variables that help in forecasting the values of the dependent variable are called the independent or predictor variables. Regression analysis that employs one dependent variable and one independent variable, and approximates the relationship between these two variables by a straight line is called a simple linear regression. Regression analysis that uses two or more independent variables to forecast values of the dependent variable is called a multiple regression analysis. Below, the forecasting technique using regression analysis for the simple linear regression case is briefly introduced.

Suppose, a forecaster has data on sales of American-made automobiles in the United States for the last 25 years. The forecaster has also identified that the sale of automobiles is related to individuals' real disposable income (roughly speaking, income after income taxes are paid, adjusted for the inflation rate). The forecaster also has available the time series (for the last 25 years) on the real disposable income. The time series data on U.S. auto sales can be plotted against the time series data on real disposable income, so it can be examined visually. Most likely, the auto sales time series would display a gradual growth in sales volume as real disposable income increases, despite the occasional lack of consistency—that is, at times, auto sales may fall even when real disposable income rises. The relationship between the two variables (auto sales as the dependent variable and real disposable income as the independent variable) may be linear (approximated by a straight line) or nonlinear (approximated by a curve or a nonlinear line). Assume that the relationship between the time series on sales of American-made automobiles and real disposable income of consumers is actually linear and can thus be represented by a straight line.

A fairly rigorous mathematical technique is used to find the straight line that most accurately represents the relationship between the time series on auto sales and disposable income. The intuition behind the mathematical technique employed in arriving at the appropriate straight line is as follows. Imagine that the relationship between the two time series has been plotted on paper. The plot will consist of a scatter (or cloud) of points. Each point in the plot represents a pair of observations on auto sales and disposable income (that is, auto sales corresponding to the given level of the real disposable income in any year). The scatter of points (similar to the time series method discussed above), may have an upward or a downward drift. That is, the relationship between auto sales and real disposable income may be approximated by an upward or downward sloping straight line. In all likelihood, the regression analysis in the present example will yield an upward sloping straight line—as disposable income increases so does the volume of automobile sales.

Arriving at the most accurate straight line is the key. Presumably, one can draw many straight lines through the scatter of points in the plot. Not all of them, however, will equally represent the relationship—some will be closer to most points, and others will be way off from most points in the scatter. Regression analysis then employs a mathematical technique. Different straight lines are drawn through the data. Deviations of the actual values of the data points in the plot from the corresponding values indicated by the straight line chosen in any instance are examined. The sum of the squares of these deviations capture the essence of how close a straight line is to the data points. The line with the minimum sum of squared deviations (called the **least squares** regression line) is considered the line of the best fit.

Having identified the regression line, and assuming that the relationship based on the past data will continue, future values of the dependent variable (forecasts) can be inferred from the straight line based on the past data. If the forecaster has an idea of what the real disposable income may be in the coming year, a forecast for future auto sales can be generated. One should remember that forecasts based on this method should also be judged on the basis of a measure of forecast errors. One can continue to assume that the forecaster uses the mean squares error discussed earlier. In addition to using forecast errors, the regression analysis uses additional ways of analyzing the effectiveness of the estimated regression line in forecasting.

[Anandi P. Sahu]

FURTHER READING:

Anderson, David P., Dennis J. Sweeney, and Thomas A. Williams. *An Introduction to Management Science: Quantitative Approaches to Decision Making.* 7th ed. West Publishing Company, 1994.

Anderson, David P., Dennis J. Sweeney, and Thomas A. Williams. *Statistics for Business and Economics.* 5th ed. West Publishing Company, 1993.

FOREIGN CORRUPT PRACTICES ACT

In the mid-1970s, and in the wake of the Watergate scandal, stories began to surface in the U.S. media about U.S. corporations paying favors to officials in foreign countries. Companies from many nations had long engaged in secret payments to public officials, but U.S. Congress and the public demanded action after the **Securities and Exchange Commission** (SEC) solicited (and received) voluntary disclosure from over four hundred American companies that they had paid hundreds of millions of dollars in secret bribes to foreign public officials.

The result was the Foreign Corrupt Practices Act (FCPA), passed by Congress and signed into law by president Jimmy Carter in 1977. The act prohibits U.S. companies (incorporated in or having a principal place of business in the United States) from making payments, promises, or offers to give anything of value to foreign officials or anyone else if the purpose is to obtain or retain business, or direct business to any person. These are the anti-bribery provisions. In addition, the Act imposes two basic **accounting** requirements on U.S. companies:

(1) Financial records and accounts must be kept that, "in reasonable detail, accurately and fairly reflect the transactions and dispositions of assets" of the business.

(2) The business must create and maintain internal accounting controls "sufficient to provide reasonable assurances" that transactions are being done in accordance with proper authorization from **management**.

Violations of the anti-bribery provisions require some element of knowing or intent to corrupt, while a violation of the FCPA's accounting requirements can take place without any corrupt intent. The FCPA's coverage includes any officer, director, employee, agent, or stockholder acting on behalf of a U.S. company. The intent and effect of these provisions is to correct the widespread earlier practice of making secret payments to foreign officials and accounting for them as commission payments, payments for services, or other business expenses, then deducting those payments on U.S. income tax returns.

The act has been controversial from the start. No nation has followed the lead of the United States and created its own foreign corrupt practices act. U.S. businesses are thus at a disadvantage in obtaining and retaining business in foreign countries where public officials are prone to ask for or accept gifts or payments in return for favorable consideration. Many have also questioned the ethics of imposing U.S. standards of morality in other parts of the world, though it must be mentioned that the bribery endemic to Italy and Japan eventually undermined the dominant political parties in each country. The FCPA had no causal relation to these political falls from grace—the corruption itself, once made public, was enough to convince many people in each country that wholesale changes in power were due.

During the 1980s, considerable pressure developed to make the FCPA more amenable to the legitimate needs of U.S. companies doing business abroad. In 1988, Congress amended the FCPA in response to this pressure. First, payments that are lawful in the foreign country are not unlawful under the FCPA. Second, certain "reasonable and bona fide" (good faith) payments may be made to foreign officials when they are directly related to promoting or demonstrating products. If, for example, a foreign official in charge of purchasing tanks were to be given travel expenses for coming to the United States for a demonstration, the payment could be accounted for as a business expense and would not be categorized as a bribe under the FCPA.

The 1988 amendments also increased the criminal penalties for companies violating the antibribery provisions of the FCPA to a maximum of $2 million. Individuals may be fined up to $100,000 and/or be sentenced to up to five years in prison. A successful prosecution under these provisions must overcome three principal areas of ambiguity: the *routine governmental action* exception, the *corruptly* requirement, and the *knowing* requirement.

The first of these ambiguities involves ministerial or clerical actions for which "gratuity" or "grease" payments may be "routine." U.S. executives have to guess whether the payment is "routine" or not. For example, in the case where a customs official grants licenses to every applicant, and payment is made to expedite the processing time, the FCPA is not violated. Payments to higher level officials with discretion to grant or deny a privilege, license, or contract are far riskier.

The second of these ambiguities is the statutory use of the word "corrupt." A Negligent or unsophisticated businessperson who naively makes payments to a local foreign agent without realizing that part of the payment is going to a public official will probably not have the requisite "corrupt" state of mind prohibited by the anti-bribery provisions. Yet the *knowing* requirement imposes a duty to make reasonable inquiries; failing to ask about what you have reason to believe you would discover will satisfy the *knowing* requirement. Thus, a very large payment made by your agent to a government official would be reviewed by U.S. authorities to discover whether you knew or should have made inquiries about the payment and its ultimate disposition.

[Don Mayer]

FOREIGN CREDIT INSURANCE ASSOCIATION (FCIA)

The Foreign Credit Insurance Association (FCIA) is an independent association of **stock** and mutual insurance companies that issues export **credit** insurance to exporters of American goods. The FCIA was established in 1961 during the Kennedy administration and acts as an agent of the Export-Import Bank of the United States, a federal agency. The FCIA was created to help rectify America's trade imbalance by absorbing some of the risk inherent in the export market. This enhances the sale of American goods abroad. In essence, the exporter is able to purchase insurance against a foreign buyer defaulting on payments because of commercial or political reasons.

When goods are sold to a foreign interest, it is advantageous for the exporter to receive payment in advance. This is a risk-free method of financing exports, but a foreign buyer will seldom agree to it. Exports such as consumer goods, agricultural products, chemicals, etc. are referred to as short-term exports and are usually financed for periods between 90 and 180 days. Medium-term exports may be financed for up to five years and include large durable items such as machine tools or mainframe **computers**.

Between the time that goods are shipped by the seller and the final payment is made by the buyer, the exporter is at risk of not being paid in full. If the buyer defaults, it is usually because of political or commercial circumstances. Political reasons can include wars, revolutions, civil upheavals, nationalization policies, or currency inconvertibility. Commercial defaults are associated with insolvency, cash flow problems, economic downturns, or unstable market demands. Because the exported goods and the purchaser are in a foreign country, recovery through litigation can be complicated, time consuming, expensive, and less than fruitful.

Through its export credit insurance the FCIA absorbs much of the risk inherent in foreign trade. Depending on the circumstances of the exchange, the FCIA may choose to issue Multi-Buyer, New to Export, Single-Buyer or Umbrella policies. Multi-Buyer policies are written for experienced exporters with multiple buyers in one or more foreign countries. These policies can be written for both short and medium-term contracts. The New to Export policies are for new or inexperienced exporters and cover only short-term transactions. Single Buyer policies cover short and medium-term contracts for exporters with a single foreign customer. Umbrella policies are written for short-term contracts when a third party administrator is involved. Often an inexperienced exporter will seek outside administrative assistance to prepare and process the necessary paperwork. In these situations, the FCIA policy is written to the administrator, not the exporter.

The FCIA writes comprehensive policies covering a variety of political and commercial scenarios or it may write a policy covering only specified political risks. Regardless of the policy coverage, the FCIA aids the exporter by not only absorbing risk but also making the exporter more competitive. Because of the FCIA insurance the exporter is generally able to grant more generous terms to a foreign buyer and is able to bargain for more favorable borrowing terms at home.

The exporter pays premiums to the FCIA, of course, and must abide by the stipulations in each policy. The premiums are based on the experience and credit worthiness of the exporter and the circumstances of the transaction. The exporter must also follow such stipulations as ceasing shipment if the borrower should **default** beyond a specified number of days. The exporter must also be able to cover any risk not covered by the FCIA, make attempts at recovery, and provide assistance to FCIA recovery actions.

The FCIA also writes policies insuring U.S. **bank**ing **loans** to foreign purchasers of American goods and policies insuring against foreign noncompliance with letters of credit to U.S. banks. In 1990, the FCIA insured $4 billion of U.S. goods exported by 1,100 American companies.

[Michael Knes]

FOREIGN EXCHANGE

Foreign exchange is the process of trading the currency of one country for the currency of a different country. This process is necessary for international trade to take place in a world of different currencies. Those conducting international business need to complete purchases by making payment in the local currency. Only through trading their own currency for the foreign currency can this transaction be completed. Currencies are traded in the foreign exchange market. The amount of currency needed to purchase a unit of a foreign currency is called the exchange rate. You can think of the exchange rate as the price of purchasing foreign currency.

For as long as trade between countries with different currencies has taken place, foreign exchange has been in existence. According to Julian Walmsley, author of *The Foreign Exchange and Money Markets Guide*, although foreign exchange has existed since before biblical times, a formal global market for foreign exchange did not develop until the 1800s with cable transfers taking place between London and New York.

The foreign exchange market is not located in one specific place but rather is made up of the thousands of businesses and individuals throughout the world that buy and sell currency. The players in this market include **central banks**, portfolio managers, foreign currency brokers, and commercial banks. Some of these organizations deal in currencies as an investment. Others sell the currency to their own customers, such as multinational corporations, importers, and exporters, who need foreign currency to conduct their businesses. For example, a U.S. importer of Italian leather goods would need to change U.S. dollars to Italian lire in order to pay his or her Italian supplier. He or she could go to a commercial bank and have his or her dollars converted to lire.

The foreign exchange market determines the exchange rates. When demand for the currency of one country goes up the exchange rate goes up. Some of the factors that increase demand for a country's currency are an increase in exports (more currency is needed to pay for these exports), an increase in **interest rates** (the currency now earns more for the holder), and anything that improves political stability (the risk of holding that currency has decreased).

Historically governments have set exchange rates themselves to improve a country's trade position. If a country sets its exchange rate low, relative to others, people can purchase more of that country's currency and therefore purchase more of that country's goods and services. This improves the country's trade position relative to other countries but often leads to trade wars as each country struggles to improve its trade position. Since the early 1970s, however, most major currencies have been allowed to "float." Floating is allowing exchange rates to be determined by **free trade**. Most countries still fine tune the exchange rates by keeping a reserve of foreign currencies that they buy and sell to stabilize their own currency when necessary.

Most newspapers list the daily exchange rates for major currencies. Two exchange rates are listed for each country reflecting the currency trade in either direction. For example, you can buy British pounds with U.S. dollars or you can buy U.S. dollars with British pounds. Both exchange rates are listed. Exchange rates show how many units of one currency you can buy with one unit of another currency and vice versa. Here are two examples of how to use the exchange rate information.

Example 1: You are going on vacation to London and want to have enough British pounds to pay for your hotel. You know the hotel will cost you roughly $500 for the week you will be there. You look in the paper and see the following:

	U.S.	Foreign
British (pound)	1.527000	.654879

These figures show that you can buy 1.527 of a dollar with one pound, and you can buy .654879 of a pound with one dollar. Therefore, when converted, your $500 will be worth 327.44 pounds.

$$\$500 \times .654879 = 327.44 \text{ pounds}$$

Example 2: When you get back from your trip to London, you still have 100 pounds left over. You want to get this changed back to dollars. Using the information from the paper you know you will get 1.527 of a dollar for one pound so your 100 pounds will be changed to $152.70.

$$100 \text{ pounds} \times 1.527 = \$152.70$$

Foreign exchange is quite simply the act of buying one currency with another. It is one of the most commonplace of monetary transactions, but at the same time one that is vital to the smooth operation of international trade.

[Judith A. Zimmerman]

FURTHER READING:

Grabbe, J. Orlin. *International Financial Markets*. Elsevier Science Publishing Co., 1986.

Walmsley, Julian. *The Foreign Exchange And Money Markets Guide*. John Wiley & Sons, 1992.

FOREIGN INVESTMENT

Foreign investment in the United States grew steadily during the 1970s, but experienced a surge during the middle and late 1980s. The high levels of foreign investment led to concerns about a loss of control over domestic economic activity, or "economic sovereignty," and the effect of foreign ownership on national security. With the economic slowdown of the early 1990s, and a dropoff in the rate of foreign investment these concerns became muted. Attitudes toward foreign investment changed somewhat as localities vied to attract investment for its economic stimulus. These concerns are still evident, however, as the rate of investment has accelerated once again. It may be that changing political pressures in the United States may result in pressures against the free flow of investment.

REASONS FOR FOREIGN INVESTMENT

The increase in foreign investment took place during a period in which international trade of all types was expanding. Free trade agreements such as that between the United States and Canada, and the creation of the **North American Free Trade Agreement**, make investment within the United States more attractive and expedient. Further, multinational operations provide opportunities for tax avoidance through transfer pricing policies which shift accounting profits to lower tax areas. The foreign investment decision is, however, largely a function of microeconomic variables affecting the firm. Unless the firm can achieve some competitive advantage, it is likely to choose **exporting** rather than **direct investment**. Foreign investment activity, for instance, tends to be concentrated in technology-intensive industries in which **research and development** are important. Characteristically, foreign manufacturing investments have larger-than-average plant sizes and are more capital intensive than domestic firms. Although foreign manufacturing investments tend to have higher hourly production wages, this is offset by higher labor productivity.

IMPACT OF FOREIGN INVESTMENT

The impact of foreign investment is complex and unclear. Fears of loss of economic sovereignty are sometimes countered by noting that foreign investment, though involving large sums, is still only a very small portion of the U.S. economy. The overall figures can hide specific impacts, however, and in some industries foreign-owned enterprises account for more than half of U.S. production.

On a global basis, and over a long time, a free flow of **capital** is beneficial since it promotes an efficient allocation of resources. For shorter periods, and within a given country or region, the impact is mixed. The most immediate impact is the creation of more jobs within the immediate locality. Beyond this, however, the increased competition, capital-intensive nature, and higher productivity may lead to a net loss of employment. Foreign-owned enterprises also tend to have a higher import content than domestic firms. The technologically intensive nature of foreign investment is suggested as indicating a transfer of technology to the United States, but this is countered by the reverse flow of technology from acquired firms. It appears that there is no overall answer, and that individual analysis is required.

[David E. Upton]

FOREIGN TRADE ZONES

Free Trade Zones are known in the United States as Foreign Trade Zones (FTZ). Foreign Trade Zones are secured areas, usually located adjacent to a port and within the zone a country's customs regulations are suspended. Foreign Trade Zones are meant to encourage international trade and commerce. Foreign Trade Zones were established in the United States pursuant to the Foreign Trade Zone Act of 1934. The act was subsequently amended in 1950 to allow manufacturing and exhibition of merchandise within the zone. Free Trade Zones have existed in Europe since the 1800s, the most notable being the free port of Hamburg, Germany. In the United States however the concept was opposed by owners of bonded warehouses and protectionists who felt the establishment of a free port would be a precursor to lower tariffs and detrimental trade liberalization laws. All of this changed in early 1937 when a 92 acre parcel of land and water on Staten Island, NY was formally opened as U.S. Foreign Trade Zone No. 1. By 1956 other Foreign Trade Zones were established in New Orleans, LA, San Francisco and Los Angeles, CA and Seattle, WA.

New York Congressman Emanuel Cellar who spearheaded efforts to establish the first American FTZ described these zones as ''. . . a neutral, stockaded area where a shipper can put down his load, catch his breath and decide what to do next.'' While slightly tongue-in-cheek, this is an apt description. In a Foreign or Free Trade Zone operations involving legal foreign or domestic merchandise may take place free of customs regulations. These operations include but are not necessarily restricted to storage, sale, exhibitions, breaking up, repackaging, assembling, sorting, grading or cleaning merchandise. This merchandise may also be mixed with other foreign or domestic goods. All health and safety laws must be adhered to and retail sales are not allowed. There are also restrictions on the manufacture of goods subject to internal revenue taxes such as alcoholic beverages. Merchandise which cannot be legally imported to the United States is prohibited but merchandise which cannot legally enter the United States may be stored in a Foreign Trade Zone until such time as it may legally be entered. This situation is often applied to merchandise subject to quotas. When the quota is lifted or reopened the stored merchandise may then be released.

There are many advantages to a shipper or importer moving merchandise through a Foreign Trade Zone. Customs duties are only paid when the merchandise is moved out of the FTZ not when it enters the U.S., and while goods are being stored they are not subject to U.S. excise taxes. Security is also very tight around these zones and U.S. Customs procedures are held to minimum requirements. There are also tax advantages to performing various operations on goods while they are in the FTZ and merchandise may be stored indefinitely. These advantages generally enhance cash, flow, reduce insurance costs, and reduce, defer or eliminate various taxes and duties. In some cases certain operations performed on goods while they are in a Foreign Trade Zone allow the addition of a ''Made in U.S.A.'' label to the finished product. Foreign Trade Sub-Zones are also allowed under certain conditions. These sub-zones are established inland from an FTZ usually at the site of a foreign owned manufacturing operation and generally have a single or special purpose application. The Volkswagen manufacturing facility in Westmoreland, PA is one such example.

The Foreign Trade Zones Board is the authority for administering the Foreign Trade Zone Act. The chairman and executive officer of the Board is held by the Secretary of Commerce. The other two board members are the Secretary of the Treasury and the Secretary of the Army. The Army is involved because it was originally felt that the Army Corps of Engineers would be involved with the construction of port facilities. While the Board administers the FTZA the U.S. Customs Service remains responsible for enforcing the Tariff Act and other customs regulations that relate to Foreign Trade Zone activities. For further information contact: Executive Secretary of the Foreign Trade, Zone Board, U.S. Department of Commerce, Washington D.C. 20230; phone: (202)377-2862. National Association of Foreign Trade Zones, 1825 Eye Street NW, Suite 400, Washington D.C. 20006; phone: (202)429-2020.

[Michael Knes]

FURTHER READING:

Thoman, Richard S. *Free Ports and Foreign Trade Zones.* Cornell Maritime Press, 1956.

U.S. Customs Service Foreign Trade Zones: U.S. Customs and Procedures. Washington D.C. Dept. of the Treasury, U.S. Customs Service, 1979.

U.S. Customs Service U.S. Customs Foreign Trade Zone Manual. Washington D.C. Dept. of the Treasury, U.S. Customs Service (Supt. of Documents, U.S.G.P.O.) 1991.

401(K) PLANS

A 401(k) plan is a tax-deferred, defined-contribution retirement plan. The name comes from a section of the Internal Revenue Code that permits an employer to create a retirement plan to which employees may contribute a portion of compensation on a pretax basis. This section allows the employer to match employee contributions with tax-deductible company contributions. Earnings on all contributions are allowed to accumulate tax-deferred. In early 1995, 401(k) plans ranked among the most popular and fastest-growing types of retirement plans in America.

HISTORY

The 401(k) provision was created in 1978 as part of that year's Tax Revenue Act, but went largely unnoticed for two years until Ted Benna, a Pennsylvania benefits consultant, devised a creative and rewarding application of the law. Section 401(k) stipulated that cash or deferred-bonus plans qualified for tax deferral. Most observers of tax law had assumed that contributions to such plans could be made only after income tax was withheld, but Benna noticed that the clause did not preclude pretax salary reduction programs.

Then a benefits consultant with the Johnson Cos., Benna came up with his innovative interpretation of the 401(k) provision in 1980 in response to a client's proposal to transfer a cash-bonus plan to a deferred profit-sharing plan. The now-familiar features he sought were an audit-inducing combination then—pretax salary reduction, company matches, and employee contributions. In January 1980, the answer came, according to Benna, literally in response to a prayer. He called his interpretation of the 401(k) rule "Cash-Op," and even tried to patent it, but most clients were wary of the plan, fearing that once the government realized its tax revenue-reducing implications, legislators would pull the plug on it.

Luckily for Benna and the millions of participants who have utilized his idea, the concept of employee savings was gaining political ascendancy. Ronald Reagan had made personal saving through tax-deferred **individual retirement accounts**, or IRAs, a component of his campaign and presidency. Payroll deductions for IRAs were allowed in 1981 and Benna hoped to extend that feature to his new plan. He convinced his superior at Johnson Cos. to establish a salary-reducing 401(k) plan even before the **Internal Revenue Service (IRS)** had finished writing the regulations that would govern it. The government agency surprised many observers when it provisionally approved the plan in spring 1981 and specifically sanctioned Benna's interpretation of the law that fall.

401(k)s quickly became a leading factor in the evolving retirement benefits business: from 1984 to 1991, the number of plans increased more than 150 percent, and the rate of participation grew from 62 percent to 72 percent. The number of employees able to participate in 401(k) plans rose to more than 48 million by 1991 from only 7 million in 1983, and Benna's prayerful breakthrough earned him the appellation "the grandfather of 401(k)s." The government soon realized the volume of salary reductions it was unable to tax and tried to quash the revolution: the Reagan administration made two attempts to invalidate 401(k)s in 1986, but public outrage prevented the repeal.

The advent of 401(k) plans helped effect a philosophical shift among employers, from the provision of defined-benefit pension plans for employees to the administration of defined-contribution retirement plans. In the past, companies had offered true pension plans which guaranteed all individuals a retirement benefit. But after 1981, rather than providing an employer-funded pension, many companies began to give employees the opportunity to save for their own retirement through a cash or deferred arrangement such as a 401(k).

THE BASICS OF 401(K) PLANS

In benefits parlance, employers offering 401(k)s are sometimes called ''plan sponsors'' and employees are often known as ''participants.'' Most 401(k)s are qualified plans, meaning that they conform to criteria established in the Economic Recovery Tax Act of 1981 (ERTA). ERTA expanded upon and refined the Employee Retirement Income Security Act of 1974 (ERISA), which had been enacted to protect participants and beneficiaries from abusive employer practices and created guidelines that were intended to ensure adequate funding of retirement benefits and minimum standards for pension plans.

Basic eligibility standards were set up with this legislation, including a minimum age of 25 years and a predetermined length of service before contributions were made. Some union employees, nonresident aliens, and part-time employees were excluded from participation.

The new 401(k)s incorporated many attractive features for long-term savers, including tax deferral, flexibility, and control. Taxes on both income and interest were delayed until participants began receiving distributions from the plan. Rollovers (direct transfer of a 401(k) account into another qualified plan, such as a new employer's 401(k), an IRA or self-employed pension plan) and emergency or hardship **loans** for medical expenses, higher-education tuition, and home purchases, allayed participants' fears about tying up large sums for the long term. While there are restrictions on these loans' availability, terms, and amounts, the net cost of borrowing may be quite reasonable because the interest cost is partly offset by the investment return. Employees may also receive lump sum distributions of their accounts upon termination. If an employee elects to take his or her distribution in cash before retirement age, the employer is required by law to withhold 20 percent of the distribution. If the account is rolled over into another qualified plan, nothing is withheld. Employees' self-determination of investments has allowed tailoring of accounts according to individual needs. For example, younger participants may wish to emphasize higher-risk (and potentially higher-return) investments, while employees who are closer to retirement can focus on more secure holdings. These features have been refined over the years through legislation, especially after the government realized the tax revenue losses engendered by the popular plans.

The Tax Equity and Fiscal Responsibility Act of 1982 (TEFRA) reduced maximum contribution limits that had been set by ERISA, introduced the ''top heavy'' concept, and revised the rules for federal income tax withholding on plan distributions. Most plans allowed employees to defer 1 percent to 10 percent of current compensation, but such internal limitations have been bound by compensation and contribution ceilings enumerated in TEFRA and subsequent legislation. These limits have made senior executives and other highly paid employees the big losers under 401(k) plans. In 1986, the amount an employee could defer annually under such programs was reduced from $30,000 to $7,000. In addition, the compensation that could be considered in determining an employee's deferral was limited to $200,000. The $200,000 limit, which had previously been increasing on an annual basis through a cost of living adjustment, was limited to $150,000 per year under the 1993 tax law. Mandatory ''top heavy'' tests that prevent 401(k) programs from favoring highly-compensated employees restrict the amount that highly paid employees can contribute to 401(k) plans.

Known as ''nondiscrimination tests'' in the benefits industry, top heavy rules separate employers and employees into two groups: those who are highly compensated and all others. The amounts that the highly paid employees may defer is based upon what the lower-paid employees deferred during the year. A simplified example helps illustrate this concept: if the average lower-paid employee only contributed 2 percent of his or her compensation to the corporate 401(k), high-paid employees may only divert 4 percent of their pay. This test adds a second level of limitation on the amount that highly paid employees can defer, often lessening it from legally established limits. Benefits and tax specialists have, of course, devised strategies to circumvent these restrictions, such as 401(k) wrap-arounds, ''rabbi trust arrangements,'' and other ''non-qualified'' plans that consciously and legally operate outside the bounds of ''qualified'' 401(k)s.

The Deficit Reduction Act of 1984 (DEFRA) continued the government's revenue-raising—and often 401(k)-limiting—provisions. The Retirement Equity Act (REACT or REA) of that same year helped protect spouses of plan participants by requiring that qualified plans provide numerous survivor benefits. REA also reduced the age at which employees became eligible to contribute to a 401(k) from 25 to 21. The Tax Reform Act of 1986 (TRA 86) incorporated some of the most extensive, revenue-raising changes in 401(k) criteria since ERISA by imposing new coverage tests and accelerating vesting requirements. Although much of this legislation was intended to benefit employees, it has also been cited as the principal cause of the voluntary termination of thousands of pension plans—a total of 32,659 between July 1987 and September 1988. These terminations eliminated future pension benefits for hundreds of thousands of workers.

During the 1980s, many plan sponsors offered employees only two investment options for their 401(k) account: an insurance company's **guaranteed income contract (GIC)** and a profit sharing plan. Insurance companies often had full-service capabilities in place and the GICs, with their high interest rates, garnered the lion's share of plan sponsors and participants. Statistics from the Employee Benefit Research Institute and the U.S. Department of Labor showed that about 40 percent of the assets in 401(k) plans was invested in GICs, which placed the burden of performance on employers and their fiduciary agents. But a rash of insurance company failures late in the decade prompted many portfolio managers to increase the number of investment alternatives.

A new provision, ERISA rule 404(c), that went into effect January 1, 1994, stipulated several changes in the ways employers administered their programs. First, plans were required to offer at least three distinctly different investment options that spanned the entire investment spectrum, in addition to the employer's stock. Qualified plans were also compelled to educate participants by providing adequate information about each investment option, thereby enabling employees to make informed choices among them. Finally, employers and their 401(k) administrators were obliged to make more frequent performance reports and allow more frequent changes in investments. These changes have shifted the responsibility for choosing investments from employer to employee, thereby limiting the potential liability of employers for investment results. Although 404(c) was not mandatory, industry observers predict that many plan sponsors would comply with the new provisions in the interest of happier, more financially secure employees.

It was anticipated that the enactment of provision 404(c) would trigger an investment shift among 401(k)s from GICs and employer stocks to **mutual funds**. As of the end of 1992, mutual funds held about 24 percent of the then-$410 billion 401(k) market, but that percentage was expected to grow dramatically by the end of the century. Mutual funds were seen as an easy way for employers to comply with 404(c) because of the benefits and services they afforded, including access to top professional money managers, instant diversification, portfolios managed according to specified investment objectives and policies, liquidity, flexibility, and ease and economy of administration.

At the end of 1993, surveys showed that approximately 70 percent of eligible workers, or 16 million people, participated in a 401(k) plan, and **assets** invested in such programs exceeded $440 billion as of January 1994. Defined-contribution plans overall, including 401(k), profit-sharing and thrift savings plans, are expected to grow threefold, to more than $1 trillion, by the end of the century.

The shift from defined-benefit plans to defined-contribution plans such as 401(k)s has had both positive and negative ramifications for both employees and employers. On the downside, employees have been compelled to shoulder more of the financial burden for their retirement, and employers have had a larger responsibility to report their application of pension funds. But most observers have applauded the movement. Employees have gained greater control over their retirement assets. The plans provide immediate tax advantages as the contributions are not subject to federal income taxes nor to most state and local taxes. They also provide long-term tax advantages, as earnings accumulate tax-free until withdrawal at retirement when withdrawals can receive favorable tax treatment. Employers have been able to share or even eliminate their pension contributions. And if employers do choose to contribute, they too get a tax deduction. 401(k)s have evolved into a valuable perk to attract and retain qualified employees. Employers can even link contributions to a profit sharing arrangement to increase employee incentive toward higher **productivity** and commitment to the company.

SEE ALSO: Profit sharing; Retirement Planning

[April Dougal Gasbarre]

FURTHER READING:

Bedsole, Andrew J., III. "Pension Turmoil Causes Thousands of Plan Terminations." *Pension World*. February, 1990, pp. 30-32.

Burzawa, Sue. "Companies Add Funds, Educate Employees." *Employee Benefit Plan Review*. January, 1994, pp. 10-12.

"How a 401(K) Plan Works." *Management Accounting*. November, 1993, p. 62.

Jenkins, Gary E. "401(k) Wrap-Arounds: Attempting to Restore the Executive Nest Egg." *Pension World*. Janary, 1994, pp. 10-12.

Solomita, Anthony F. "A New Generation of Plans: Banks with Mutual Funds Bidding for 401(k) Assets." *Pension World*. Janary, 1994, 18-20.

Vosti, Curtis. "Creator Faced Long Struggle." *Pensions & Investments*. October 28, 1991, pp. 17,24.

Vosti, Curtis. "401(k) 'Clarification': a Crossroads." *Pensions & Investments*. October 28, 1991, pp. 17, 24.

Wilcox, Melynda Dovel. "Why New Rules Worry the Founder of 401(k)s." *Kiplinger's Personal Finance Magazine*. December, 1993, p. 130.

Williams, Gordon. "Fiddling with 401(k)s." *Financial World*. Febuary 1, 1994, pp. 64-68.

FRANCHISING

People who drive down the main street of any town, regardless of its size, will more than likely do much of their shopping in franchised stores. That is because franchise operations have taken over much of the United States economy in the past 30-40 years and are becoming more popular in other countries around the world. In the process, they have created some controversy over their value to the economic and social fabric of society. On the other hand, they have provided opportunities for people who otherwise might never have had the chance to start their own businesses. Opportunity and controversy aside, franchises continue to grow and prosper.

The impact of franchises on the American economy is significant. Franchise businesses accounted for slightly over 34 percent of all retail sales in the United States in the early 1990s. According to figures compiled by the International Franchise Association (IFA), American franchises generate $716.4 billion in sales of goods and services annually in the United States. In 1994, retail sales from franchising exceeded the trillion-dollar level. By 2000, they will account for over 50 percent of total retail sales.

Since 1980, sales from franchised businesses have grown at an average annual rate of 8 percent, compared to an overall economic rate of only 2 percent. One out of every three dollars spent by Americans for goods and services is spent in a franchised business. More importantly, franchises create 300,000 new jobs per year. Each new franchise generates 8-10 new jobs, and a new franchise opens every 17 minutes. In 1994 there were more than 500,000 franchise operations in the United States.

Franchising is not restricted to the United States. Over 400 U.S.-based franchise companies operate 35,000 outlets overseas, and that number is rising dramatically. In fact, the IFA reported that the number of overseas outlets increased by 10.8 percent between 1986 and 1988 alone. It is no wonder, then, that franchising experts predict a steady growth in the number of outlets throughout the world in the near future.

FRANCHISING DEFINED

Franchising is a vehicle for marketing products and services. In its simplest definition, it is authorization granted by a manufacturer or service provider to a distributor or dealer to sell its products. Each party gives up some legal rights to gain others. The idea is that both parties to the agreement gain something. The franchisor (the owner of the name or trademark), also known as the company, increases its number of outlets and gains additional income. The franchisee (the individual who purchases the right to use a business' name or trademark) opens a business which is almost guaranteed success. Franchising offers people a chance to own, manage, and direct their own business without having to take all the associated risks. This aspect has allowed many people to open businesses of their own who might never have done so otherwise.

Franchising has opened the door of opportunity for women, families, and minorities. Women have discovered that operating franchises often allows them to spend more time with their families. In many cases, families pool their resources and time to operate outlets—and often use the profits to create their own mini-chain of stores. Minorities have benefited, too. They have been able to locate establishments in urban areas which at one time lacked minority ownership. Significantly, some franchisors such as Burger King and the Southland Corporation, owner of the 7-11 convenience stores, provide special financial programs for minority owners. They also work closely with organizations like the National Association for the Advancement of Colored People (NAACP) to recruit more minority owners. In this respect, franchises have been a boon for society.

No matter who owns a franchise outlet, the franchisee and the franchisor share the risks and the responsibilities, although not always equally. Since both parties have a financial investment at stake, the risk can be costly—extremely so at times.

COSTS OF FRANCHISING

Franchise costs depend to some extent on the nature of the business. For example, a person who wishes to open a franchised employment service operation, such as Talent Force, based in Atlanta, Georgia, can get away with as little as a $7,500 fee, plus one year's starting capital investment of $50,000 to $110,000. On the other hand, start-up costs for a company like J.O.B.S., based in Clearwater, Florida, can be as little as $45,000, including a $30,000 franchise fee. These figures pale in comparison to food franchises.

A Popeye's Famous Fried Chicken and Biscuits, Inc., outlet will cost the franchisee a minimum of $200,000—with no financing assistance available. (Some franchisors do offer financial assistance either from within or through outside sources.) A Perkins Restaurants, Operating Co., L.P. franchise costs between $959,000 and $1,500,000. An individual's initial cash investment would be about $150,000. Initial costs such as these can present serious obstacles to some people trying to purchase a franchise.

FUNDING THE FRANCHISE

There are several sources of financial backing for potential franchisees. Financial assistance from franchisors is rare. Therefore, people rely primarily on their own funds, family support, and the traditional sources such as financial institutions, banks, and private investors. The more money a franchise costs, the harder it is for potential operators to raise the necessary funds. However, the search does highlight another positive aspect of franchising: it involves a cadre of specialists (e.g., bankers, lawyers, and accountants), who earn all or part of their salaries from their involvement with franchise operations.

For people with limited cash or access to it, franchising may not be the easiest career path for prospective business operators, then. However, for many people who have made the investment, franchising has paid substantially from both the company and outlet owner standpoint, as history suggests.

HISTORY OF FRANCHISING

Franchise operations, as we know them, are not very old. The boom in franchising did not take place until after World War II—and it has not abated since.

The earliest franchises date back to the Middle Ages when the Catholic Church granted them to tax collectors, who retained a percentage of the money they collected and turned the rest over to the church. The practice ended around 1562 but spread to other endeavors. For example, in seventeenth century England franchisees were granted the right to sponsor markets and fairs or operate ferries. There was little growth in franchising, though, until the mid-19th century, when it appeared in the United States for the first time.

One of the first successful American franchising operations was started by an enterprising druggist named John S. Pemberton. In 1886, he concocted a beverage comprising sugar, molasses, spices, and cocaine (which is ostensibly no longer an ingredient, although the recipe is still a carefully guarded secret). Pemberton licensed selected people to bottle and sell the drink, which is now known as Coca-Cola. His was one of the earliest—and most successful—franchising operations in the United States.

The Singer Company implemented a franchising plan in the 1850s to distribute its sewing machines. The operation failed, though, because the company did not earn much money even though the machines sold well. The dealers, who had exclusive rights to their territories, absorbed most of the profits because of deep discounts. Some failed to push Singer products, so competitors were able to outsell the company. Under the existing contract, Singer could neither withdraw rights granted to franchisees nor send in its own salaried representatives. So, the company started repurchasing the rights it had sold. The experiment proved to be a failure. That may have been one of the first times a franchisor failed, but it was by no means the last. (Even Colonel Sanders did not initially succeed in his Kentucky Fried Chicken franchising ef-

forts.) Fortunately, the Singer venture did not put an end to franchising.

Other companies tried franchising in one form or another after the Singer experience. For example, several decades later, General Motors Corporation established a somewhat successful franchising operation in order to raise capital. Perhaps the "Father of Modern Franchising," though, is David Liggett. In 1902, Liggett invited a group of druggists to join a "drug cooperative." As he explained to them, they could increase profits by paying less for their purchases, especially if they set up their own manufacturing company. His idea was to market private label products. About 40 druggists pooled $4,000 of their own money and adopted the name "Rexall." Sales soared, and "Rexall" became a franchisor. The chain's success set a pattern for other franchisors to follow.

Although many business owners did affiliate with cooperative ventures of one type or another, there was little growth in franchising until the early 20th century, and what franchising there was did not take the same form as it does today. As the United States switched from an agricultural to an industrial based economy, manufacturers licensed individuals to sell automobiles, trucks, gasoline, beverages, and a variety of other products. The franchisees did little more than sell the products, though. The responsibility sharing associated with contemporary franchising arrangement did not exist to any great extent. Consequently, franchising was not a growth industry in the United States.

It was not until the 1960s and 1970s that people began to take a close look at the attractiveness of franchising. The concept intrigued people with entrepreneurial spirit. (Actually, true entrepreneurs would not be interested particularly in owning individual franchises, since they would have to relinquish too much control. True entrepreneurs like to control their operations and assume most of the risks. They would be more likely to establish and operate franchising companies, like those of Ray Kroc, Dave Thomas, and Famous Amos.) However, there were serious pitfalls for investors, which almost ended the practice before it became truly popular.

Since there was no regulation of franchises to speak of, a number of hucksters involved themselves in the field. Many of them initiated get-rich-quick schemes which cost investors countless dollars. As a result, franchising became a bad word to some people. In 1970 alone, over 100 franchisors went out of business. Concomitantly, thousands of franchisees lost their businesses and their money. Fortunately, public and private sector watchdogs helped to restore franchising's good name and launch its way to a prominent place in the American economy.

Some franchisors formed the IFA in 1960 to police the franchising industry and eliminate the hucksters. Individual states began passing laws to regulate franchise activities. By 1979, the **Federal Trade Commission** (FTC) initiated a franchise trade rule requiring disclosure of pertinent information to prospective franchise owners. The watchdogs did their jobs. Franchising became a respectable word again, and the practice flourished, aided by the efforts of early franchisors like Ray Kroc and Dave Thomas.

Kroc, the founder of the highly successful McDonald's hamburger chain, called franchising the "updated version of the American Dream." He established his franchising operation in 1955. Fifteen years later, the chain included 1,500 outlets.

Wendy's founder Dave Thomas believed that McDonald's hamburgers were skimpy and decided he could improve the basic hamburger. In 1968, Thomas received $1.7 million as his share of the sale of four chicken stores by Hobby House Restaurants, for whom he was a manager. He invested most of it into a new chain of hamburger stands. By the end of 1972, he had nine outlets with annual sales of $1.8 million. By June 1975, he opened the 100th Wendy's restaurant. Less than two years later, the number jumped to 1,000. In 1978 alone he opened 500 outlets. Thomas proved that there was plenty of room in the franchising world.

Ironically, one of the people he met in the Fort Wayne, Indiana restaurant was "Colonel" Harlan Sanders, who was in the initial stages of forming his Kentucky Fried Chicken chain. Sanders was unfamiliar with mass marketing techniques, so he was trying to find local restaurant owners who would buy his franchises. He managed to persuade Thomas that his idea was viable, but few others saw the merit in it. Eventually, Sanders succeeded, as did many other entrepreneurs who entered the franchising arena in a variety of businesses.

THE SPREAD OF FRANCHISING

Franchising grew slowly during the 1940s and 1950s. The majority of the outlets were placed in the suburbs or along highways as people moved out of the cities and into rural areas. The now familiar "strips" lined with franchises started changing Americans' eating and shopping habits. Spurred by the success of the early franchisors, others entered the competition for the shoppers' dollars.

Franchise chains in virtually every business category started operations. Their stores were not always well received, especially in urban areas. Individuals and community groups protested the arrival of franchises, but their efforts were generally unsuccessful. Even today, many community groups and individuals protest the arrival of well-known franchise outlets—sometimes successfully. For example, activists in Williamsburg, Virginia, prevented Wal-Mart from opening a store in their community in 1994. Wal-Mart has experienced similar problems elsewhere, as have other large franchising chains such as Home Depot.

Some franchise detractors believe that chains such as Wal-Mart and Home Depot undercut small, locally owned business owners' prices so drastically that they drive the independent owners out of business. They suggest that the franchises come into a community, price their products artificially low, eliminate local competitors, and then raise their prices to gouge customers. Whether these arguments hold water or not is debatable—as are the merits of franchises themselves. By and large, though, franchises have become the driving force in the American economy, particularly since they have become more diverse than ever.

Today, franchises are active in a wide range of categories. They exist in lawn, garden, and agricultural supplies and services, maid and personal services, security services, tools and hardware, weight control, and many types of food products, including baked goods, donuts and pastry, popcorn, ice cream, yogurt, and fast foods. As the economy and consumers' preferences change, technology advances, and new products are introduced, existing franchises will likely continue to grow, change, and innovate in response.

More than 95 percent of the franchise chains in existence today started operations in the last four decades. Most of them formed between 1965 and 1985. Their growth was phenomenal. For example, Century 21, the real estate operation, began in 1972 and grew to include 7,400 outlets by 1980. It took McDonald's only 25 years to establish its 6,200th store. There is hardly a community anywhere that does not have at least one franchise operation.

WHY FRANCHISES HAVE GROWN

Picture the typical family driving into an unfamiliar community. They are tired, hungry, and in need of a hotel. The family will likely choose a Texaco, Mobil, or Amoco Corp. gas station at which to fuel the car. They will stop at McDonald's, Denny's, Pizza Hut, or Olive Garden to eat rather than take a chance at the locally owned burger emporium. Finally, they will register at a Holiday Inn or Sheraton. Why? They have confidence in the names of the establishments and the consistency of the food and service they will receive. This explains one of the biggest reasons for the success of franchising: name recognition.

A franchisee who advertises a well-known name on the company marquee dramatically reduces the risks associated with starting a new business venture. That is not the only benefit to a franchise, however.

Franchisees reduce their personal investments in their business, because the franchisor is sharing the risks involved in a start-up operation. Actually, there are very limited risks involved in opening a franchise. According to the U.S. Department of Commerce figures, between 1971 and 1988, less than 5 percent of franchised outlets have been discontinued per year. In 1986, just 3.3 percent of franchise-owned outlets went out of business. Often, the reasons had nothing to do with business failure. These statistics alone help explain the growth of franchising.

Another factor involved in the popularity of franchising centers around financing. If a prospective franchisee needs to borrow money to help with business-related costs, financial institutions are more willing to lend if a well-known franchisor is backing the applicant. (The franchisor's name itself does not guarantee loan approval, though. Applicants must meet other strict criteria.) This is especially true if the franchisor is well established, rather than based on a new concept.

Other benefits to the franchisee include training, national advertising, cost-saving bulk purchase capability, management consulting and assistance, new products and services, and a protected territory. These come at a price, since the franchisee must pay a certain percentage of the business' profits to the franchisor. This is a minor disadvantage, though, when compared to the benefits franchisees derive from their associations with the franchisors. But, it is only one of several disadvantages.

THE DISADVANTAGES

In addition to the payment of fees and royalties, franchisees give up some control over their own businesses, as well as lose their own identity. Most patrons do not know who owns their local McDonald's, Burger King, or MAACO auto painting and body repair establishment. So, many franchise outlet owners are relegated to anonymity—which can be a drawback.

Franchisees are often subjected to tight supervision by the franchisor. They cannot pick out their own business name, buy products and services from whom they choose, or select the location at which they will do business. Some franchisors control their outlets so tightly they even tell business operators when to empty their trash cans, how to dress their employees, where to dispose of food, what color to paint their fences, etc. As a result, some franchisees may become totally dependent on their franchisors. This can be detrimental in that this may make it more difficult for franchisees to sever their ties with the franchisor.

Another problem with franchising is that franchisees may fall victim to the company's problems. While a particular business owner may be doing well, the chain itself may encounter financial problems due to mismanagement, a failing economy, or any other reason which impacts operations. This can result in increased fees or royalties or a switch in suppliers which can lead to reduced quality of goods and services. In extreme cases, the franchisor can go out of business completely. A final problem for potential franchisees is how to select the right company with which to affiliate.

As the number of franchisors increases, the method of choosing which franchise is right for a particular individual becomes more complex. Even if a potential franchisee knows which type of business to enter, the selection of a franchisor may pose a challenge.

The person who wants to open a fast-food franchise has to decide what type of food it will serve: pizza, hamburgers, yogurt, full meals, etc. Other matters to consider include fees required, royalties, governmental regulations, and whether the particular business is part of a growing industry. Such choices are closely tied in to public policy and governmental regulation today.

GOVERNMENTAL REGULATION IN FRANCHISING

Franchising can be broken down roughly into two broad categories: retail and service. Many of the businesses in both categories are subject to extensive government regulations today, which can increase both the franchisors' and franchisees' responsibilities and financial investments. For example, franchisors in personal services, such as water conditioning and pest control experts, have to be aware of **Environmental Protection Agency** (EPA) regulations governing the use of pesticides and toxic products and the added costs associated with them. The same holds true for automotive retail franchises. Questions must be answered regarding where and when used batteries, replaced oil, rusted mufflers, etc., can be disposed.

These are generally matters to be resolved by the franchisor, but franchisees must be aware of current and impending local and state laws before opening their operations.

Governmental involvement in franchising is not new. For instance, the State of California enacted the first pre-sale franchise disclosure law in 1970. The law addressed two broad areas: full and accurate pre-sale disclosure to prospective franchisees of information about the franchisor and the contract, and the fairness of the contract itself. Several other states passed similar laws shortly afterward. The first federal law was passed in 1979 under the aegis of the Federal

Trade Commission (FTC).

Since many companies operated in several states, it was inevitable that the federal government would involve itself in franchise regulation. That became the FTC's role. The agency required every franchisor to provide each potential franchisee with a detailed disclosure document which protects everyone involved in a possible agreement. The document contains twenty different categories of information about the franchise. Included is information about required fees, basic investment, bankruptcy, and the franchisor's litigation history. There are also inclusions concerning how long the franchise will be in effect, the franchisor's financial statement, and earnings claims (if they are available). The financial disclosure laws had a major impact on franchising.

The laws made it clear that franchisors were in business not only to make a profit, but to supply their clients with services and products that made their ownership easier. The laws corrected any imbalance in franchise agreements that were tipped in the franchisors' favor. Under the laws, franchisors had to reveal all the information potential franchisees needed to make a decision on whether or not to open an outlet. The companies had to reveal how long they had been in business, the number of unit failures, lawsuits in which they were involved, either currently or in the past, and supporting information to back up any claims they made about their operations. This protection stands potential franchisees in good stead and eliminates possible fraud on the part of franchisors.

It is imperative to note that the financial disclosure laws do not protect potential franchisees completely. For instance, the FTC does not certify any information provided. The individual must verify information provided by franchisors. The key is that laws exist to protect people interested in franchises, which is a far cry from the early days of franchising when caveat emptor was the watch word for franchisees. Because there was a great deal of risk involved in dealing with franchisors in those days, there was considerable controversy over the benefits of franchising. Much of that controversy remains, although it has changed in focus somewhat.

THE CONTROVERSY OVER FRANCHISING

As successful as franchising has been in the United States, there are critics who suggest that it has been detrimental to the country's economy. One argument is that franchise employees receive low wages. This is partly because the majority of the workers are part-time employees who do not receive any benefits. Because of the low wages and lack of benefits, franchise owners have a hard time attracting and retaining quality workers. One of the solutions to this problem would be union organization. However, labor unions in general have lost their power in recent years, so they are more reluctant than ever to organize franchise workers in deference to focusing on unionizing larger and more stable employers. Without union representation, workers may not organize and wages may remain low.

A second argument suggests that chains detract from the aesthetics of a community. They may locate in residential neighborhoods and erect huge unsightly signs. Some communities have eliminated these problems through strict zoning laws and signet legislation. Often, these laws are ''grandfathered,'' which means existing businesses are unaffected. So, if urban blight is to be eliminated, it will not happen for years to come.

Opponents of franchises also cite the distribution of franchise revenues. Much of the money franchisers take in goes to the franchisor. Thus, it is removed from the local economy. A locally owned firm's revenues would stay in the community. But, since chains drive out local owners, much of a community's revenues are lost.

Certainly, there are arguments that support the existence of franchises, too. Regardless of the controversy, franchising has had a major impact on the American economy, and is impacting foreign countries as well.

FRANCHISING GOES INTERNATIONAL

The growth of franchising in the United States has been phenomenal. Not only has it encompassed virtually every aspect of American business, but it has spread abroad. Canada in particular has proven lucrative for American franchisors. In fact, it has the second highest number of franchise outlets in the world. That is due primarily to the common language and similar culture the two countries share. Canada is by no means the only target of U.S. franchisors, though.

American companies are expanding their operations into countries as diverse as the Dominican Republic, Saudi Arabia, and Japan. Ironically, Japan, even thought it is culturally dissimilar form the United States, represents a prolific market for American franchisors.

Currently, franchises account for only about four percent of all retail sales in Japan. However, some American franchisors such as the Southland Corporation have made large inroads. In fact, one Japanese franchisee operates 3,800 7-11 stores. McDonald's and Toys 'R' Us run a joint venture in Japan. Certainly, not every American franchisor can function well there. For example, Gymboree, which franchises developmental programs for preschoolers and their parents, had to turn down Japanese investors due to a lack of space in which to erect equipment.

Another problem American franchisors faced in Japan was the working conditions. The concept of part-time work puzzled the Japanese. They are accustomed to lifelong, full-time employment for which workers receive adequate wages. So, when Kentucky Fried Chicken entered the Japanese market, it had to change its wage policy and upgrade working conditions. Otherwise, the company would not have survived. Other companies have faced similar problems in Japan and elsewhere, but they have overcome them, survived, and grown.

Occasional setbacks aside, American franchisors are moving ahead aggressively to gain a toehold in other countries. Century 21, for example, has established franchises in Canada, France, Japan, and the United Kingdom. Jani-King International, Inc., a commercial janitorial company, has operations in Canada, Japan, Australia, and the United Kingdom. Hardee's Food Systems has outlets in Costa Rica, the Netherland Antilles, Singapore, Korea, Japan, Thailand, and Hong Kong. There is apparently no geographical limit to where franchisors can—or will—go.

THE FUTURE OF FRANCHISING

Based on the success companies have enjoyed since the franchising boom began in the 1950s, the future of franchising is positive. The U.S. Department of Commerce predicts that a more slowly growing American population, population shifts to new metropolitan areas, and the introduction of new technology will create new opportunities for franchises. Mergers and acquisitions will increase as larger franchisors take over smaller ones. Schools and universities are adding franchising studies to their business curricula. These factors, combined with the low rate of franchise failure, stability in the industry, and a considerable return on everybody's investment, have made franchising a major force in the American economy to this point. There is no reason to believe it will not continue to grow in importance.

[Arthur G. Sharp]

FURTHER READING:

Coltman, Michael M. *Franchising in the U.S.: Pros and Cons.* Self-Counsel Press, 1988.

Dicke, Thomas S. *Franchising In America.* The University of North Carolina Press, 1992.

International Franchise Association. *What You Need to Know to Buy a Franchise.* International Franchise Association, 1988.

Kinch, John E. *Franchising: The Inside Story.* TriMark Publishing Company, Inc., 1986.

Kursh, Harry. *The Franchise Boom.* Prentice-Hall, Inc., 1969.

Luxenberg, Stan. *Roadside Empires: How the Chains Franchised America.* Viking Penguin, 1985.

Smith, Brian R. and Thomas L. West. *Buying A Franchise.* The Stephen Greene Press, 1986.

FREE TRADE

Free trade refers to the absence of restrictions on international trade between two nations. As a commercial policy affecting international trade, free trade is the opposite of protectionism. Where protectionism calls for tariffs and duties on imports to "protect" a country's domestic producers, free trade is a policy of allowing imports and exports to flow freely between nations without any restrictions.

In the 18th century, economist Adam Smith (1723-90) wrote *The Wealth of Nations* to explain the benefits of free trade. What he proposed has come to be called unilateral free trade. That is, he called on nations to unilaterally practice free trade by allowing unrestricted free access to their domestic markets. In addition he recommended a nation neither hold back nor subsidize its own exports. His response to the practice of **dumping**, for example, would have been to welcome foreign goods that were being sold below cost or fair market value, rather than to impose antidumping **duties** on them. He argued that domestic industries would respond to dumping by shifting their resources to the production of different goods that would benefit the nation's economy.

The doctrine of free trade holds that interventions in international trade, such as tariffs and duties, only serve to reduce the overall wealth of all nations. In practice, Victorian England in the 19th century has been the only country where unilateral free trade was an official policy. It has never been the policy of the United States. The imposition of tariffs and duties has always been a source of revenue for the U.S. government. In the mid 19th century, for example, tariffs on imports accounted for more than 90% of total federal revenue. In the mid 20th century it was less than 1%, due in large part to other sources of federal tax revenue.

It was 19th century economist David Ricardo (1772-1823) who put forth the doctrine of comparative advantage, which showed how free trade between nations benefits each nation involved. Though one nation may enjoy an absolute advantage over another nation in terms of being able to produce goods more inexpensively, Ricardo demonstrated that such an absolute advantage is irrelevant in determining whether trade can benefit two trading partners. He showed that even when one country enjoys an absolute advantage over another country in two industries, for example, each nation will have a comparative advantage in only one of the industries.

On that basis, both nations can enjoy benefits from exchange and from specialization. That is, the nation that enjoys a comparative advantage in one industry benefits by exporting more goods from that industry and also by shifting more resources to producing goods in that industry. In addition, the reallocation of labor and other resources increases the overall production of goods in those industries by both nations. As a result nations are economically motivated to engage in international trade.

U.S. commercial policy has always been a mixture of free trade and protectionism. After tariffs and duties reached a peak in the early 1930s, the United States began to reduce tariffs and duties on imports substantially by negotiating bilateral trade agreements with other countries. In the years following World War II, the **General Agreement on Tariffs and Trade (GATT)** took effect. It provided for multilateral trade agreements to be negotiated in a series of ''rounds,'' the most recent of which was the Uruguay Round that concluded in 1993.

The principles of free trade form the basis for regional free trade agreements and economic communities. In the European Community (EC), for example, member nations enjoy a form of free trade when trading with other member nations. The **North American Free Trade Agreement** (NAFTA) calls for the reduction and, in many cases, the elimination of duties and tariffs on goods flowing between Canada, Mexico, and the United States. Such agreements and economic communities have given rise to the phenomenon of large trading blocs, which may act collectively to impose restrictions on imports from nations who are not part of the trading bloc. For example, the EC has generally increased tariffs and duties on imports from non-EC countries since 1975.

Trade wars can erupt when nations believe that the principles of free trade have been violated. Protectionist measures may be taken to reduce imports and protect a nation's industries. Such measures are usually met with retaliatory measures. If one country imposes an unusually high tariff on the exports of another country, it is likely that additional tariffs will be levied on some of the exports of the first country. International trade agreements, such as GATT, are designed in part to prevent the escalation of such trade wars and ensure that international trade is conducted for the benefit of all nations.

[David Bianco]

FREE TRADE PROTECTION AND AGREEMENTS

The international free trade systems that exist today—the World Trade Organization and various regional free trade groupings such as the **North American Free Trade Agreement** (NAFTA) or the **European Union**—developed from the experience of the Great Depression and World War II. The prevailing belief at the end of World War II was that war had found its roots in the Depression, and that the dire economic conditions of the Depression had been exaggerated (if not caused by) national policies that placed protectionist trade barriers between nations. Protectionist policies prior to the Depression had, at the very least, ignored the economic wisdom of comparative advantage through **free trade**, a theory advanced by English economist David Ricardo (1772-1823) in *Principles of Political Economy and Taxation*, published in 1817.

After World War II, the victorious Allied nations envisioned a global system of institutions (including the **United Nations**, the **International Monetary Fund**, and an International Trade Organization) to promote and protect global security, development, and trade. The International Trade Organization (ITO) never came into being; the 1947 **General Agreement on Tariffs and Trade (GATT)** served for many years as an organization promoting tariff reductions among member nations. In 1993 the Uruguay Round of Multilateral Trade Negotiations of GATT trade negotiations was concluded among 124 nations, and in 1995 the World Trade Organization (WTO) came into being. The WTO will have many of the powers originally conceived for the ITO. As with GATT, the overall purpose of the WTO is to promote free trade, with each participating nation making some economic trade-offs in order to assure greater global economic prosperity overall.

GATT AND THE WORLD TRADE ORGANIZATION

The foundation of global free trade since World War II has been the General Agreement on Tariffs and Trade, better known as GATT. GATT has been the only global and multilateral agreement on terms of trade, and functions as a forum for the member nations to negotiate reductions in trade barriers and discuss trade distortions affecting the free flow of goods among member nations. In 1995 GATT was joined by the World Trade Organization, with has significantly greater power in resolving trade disputes among signatory nations.

The major purpose of GATT has been to ''liberalize world trade'' by means of three basic principles. First, international trade should be conducted on the basis of nondiscrimination. Second, governmental restraints on the movement of goods should be kept to a minimum. Third, the conditions of trade should be agreed upon within a multilateral framework.

The principle of nondiscrimination is furthered in Article I of the GATT, which requires that member states undertake to grant each other **most-favored nation status**, such that any bilateral tariff reduction between member countries is automatically extended to all other GATT members.

The second manifestation of GATT's nondiscrimination principle is the obligation of contracting parties, once an imported product has cleared customs, to treat both foreign and domestic products equally. Article III states the national treatment principle, in which contracting parties agree to treat foreign and domestic products equally if they have met tariffs and other import requirements. This second principle—keeping governmental restraints to a minimum—has as a corollary the notion that governmental restraints should in general be reduced over time rather than increased.

The third principle—multilateral trade action—has been realized in continuing negotiations under Article XXVIII. GATT's tariff structure developed through a series of negotiating rounds in which member countries lowered tariffs through reciprocal concessions. In the first 20 years of GATT, six general negotiations were held. The seventh round was formally initiated in 1973; this so-called ''Tokyo Round'' of Multilateral Trade Negotiations focused on the elimination of nontariff barriers and ended in 1979. This round produced a series of specialized codes dealing with subsidies and countervailing duties; discrimination against foreign goods in government procurement and product quality specifications that hindered the importation of foreign goods; and unified rules on dumping. In 1986 preparations were begun for a new round of multilateral trade negotiations which would address restraints on trade in services such as insurance, banking, and transportation. This new round become known as the Uruguay Round of Multilateral Trade Negotiations, since the 1986 negotiations began in Uruguay, at Punta del Este. This round, concluded after eight years of negotiating, made important advances in further reducing tariffs by about 40 percent, extending intellectual property protection worldwide, and tightening rules of investment and trade in services.

NONTARIFF BARRIERS AND SUBSIDIES. In addition to the three basic principles described above, the GATT contains two important subsidiary restrictions: (1) no prohibitions or restrictions other than tariffs are allowed, and (2) subsidies on exports, while not entirely prohibited, are disapproved and limited. This second subsidiary principle is in accordance with generally accepted **economic theory** that export subsidies may have a distorting effect comparable to a tariff on the import side.

The first subsidiary principle means that quantitative restrictions such as quotas—or complete bans—are inconsistent with GATT; Article XI makes this prohibition plain. Quotas and bans—along with discriminatory tariffs—are seen as inconsistent with the

free flow of goods, the operation of comparative advantage, and an efficient allocation of global goods.

Other than quotas or bans, however, a variety of nontariff barriers may impede global **free trade**. National governments may generate performance standards or specifications; grant government contract preferences for domestic suppliers; impose health or safety standards, language requirements, or country of origin labeling; or require elaborate customs inspections. The Uruguay Round was to have addressed such issues, and, in part, did so, but much room for negotiating remains.

EXCEPTIONS ON THE PROHIBITION OF QUANTITATIVE RESTRICTIONS. GATT allows four exceptions to the general rule prohibiting the use of quantitative import restrictions. A nation may impose restrictions for protection of domestic agricultural support systems, to help a serious balance of payments problem, for economic development, or for reasons of national security. The balance of payments and economic development exceptions are designed primarily to aid developing nations, for whom strict application of free trade principles may be a developmental disadvantage.

EXCEPTIONS FOR HEALTH, ENVIRONMENT, AND HUMAN SAFETY. Limited exceptions to GATT's basic and subsidiary principles are provided for in Article XX. Two of the exceptions, Articles XX(b) and XX(g), permit measures necessary to protect human, animal, or plant life or health, or to conserve exhaustible natural resources. In GATT panel disputes however, these exceptions have been read narrowly, and panels have been wary of barriers that may be used to disguise protectionist impulses.

In a major GATT panel dispute, Mexico and the European Union challenged the United States's quotas on imported tuna. Under the U.S. Marine Mammal Protection Act, the Mexican tuna fishing fleet could not catch yellowfin tuna using dolphin-unsafe purse seine netting techniques or export to the United States more than one and one-half times the amount of such ''dolphin unsafe'' tuna than the U.S. tuna industry. Mexico argued that the United States could not discriminate against Mexico's tuna based on an environmentally unsound production or processing method, and the GATT panel agreed. Moreover, the panel noted that the attempt by the United States to use trade barriers to preserve dolphins or anything else outside U.S. territory was impermissible under GATT obligations. Neither the GATT nor the subsequent WTO treaty mentions the word ''environment,'' nor do their provisions make any allowance for member countries to impose any tariffs on imports to ensure better conservation of a natural resource or to compensate domestic industries for the imposition of costs for environmental protection.

DISPUTE RESOLUTION. As noted above, trade disputes between GATT signatory nations have sometimes been serious enough that a GATT dispute resolution panel has been necessary. Yet nations are free to effectively veto GATT panel rulings. The new WTO sets up a more powerful dispute resolution system—with three-person arbitration panels, expedited hearing schedules to be strictly adhered to, and automatic adoption by the WTO. For signatory nations such as the United States, the new procedures are a double-edged sword: while the United States could block or delay implementation of the GATT panel ruling on the U.S.-Mexico tuna/dolphin dispute, it could not obtain effective relief through GATT after winning a panel's decisions against European subsidies for soybeans and other produce, since the European Union managed to block the decisions.

NULLIFICATION AND IMPAIRMENT. Dispute resolution under GATT or the WTO begins when one nation that believes that free trade benefits are being nullified or impaired by the policies of other signatory nations. If a panel determines that an offending nation has interfered with another nation's benefits under GATT, the panel may authorize the petitioning nation to take defensive action (trade sanctions) on its own, or the nation may be authorized to withdraw or suspend a concession previously made to the other party. Nations who impose trade sanctions in retaliation for benefits impaired will, under the WTO, risk a reprimand as well as remedies authorized by the WTO.

SAFEGUARDS FOR DOMESTIC INDUSTRY. Within the GATT regime, it is permissible for signatory nations to have some safeguards for protecting domestic industries. Under the guise of free trade, businesses from one nation may penetrate another nation's markets either by "dumping" goods below cost in order to gain a foothold in the market, or by offering subsidized goods at injuriously competitive prices. Under U.S. law, a countervailing duty may be levied to raise the price of an imported good that has benefitted from a government subsidy, bounty, or grant in the country of origin. But the duty can only be imposed where the International Trade Commission (an independent U.S. federal agency) has determined that there is "material injury" to a U.S. industry or "material retardation" to establishing an industry in the United States.

Antidumping duties may be imposed in a similar manner. The International Trade Commission will make an injury determination as to whether the goods are being sold at less than fair value or below cost. If the answer seems to be that they are, then sales of those goods in the United States are suspended. The importer must then post a bond equal to the estimated antidumping duties.

Trading partners of the United States have often been critical of the extent to which U.S. government and industry has imposed countervailing and antidumping duties. Quicker action on trade dispute resolution by the WTO will likely challenge some below-cost conclusions and subsidy calculations used in the process of imposing countervailing and antidumping duties.

REGIONAL FREE TRADE AREAS

There are other important free trade regimes, such as the **North American Free Trade Agreement** (NAFTA), which includes Canada, the United States, and Mexico. In North America, the Cartagena Agreement of 1969 began the Andean Common Market (ANCOM) which includes Bolivia, Venezuela, Colombia, Ecuador, and Peru. Chile withdrew from ANCOM in 1977, but has been interested in joining with the United States in a "Western Hemisphere" free trade zone.

The purpose of these other regimes is to lower tariff and nontariff barriers to the free movement of people, goods, and services among the member states even more than is required under GATT or the WTO. This seemingly contradicts the most-favored-nation provisions of the WTO, since granting additional trade concessions within a regional free trade group entails not granting those concessions to countries outside the group. But Article XXIV of GATT seems to allow the formation of "a customs union" or "free trade area" among a small number of GATT members with the sole proviso that the "parties to such union or agreement" may not impose duties and other regulations on nonparties that are "higher or more restrictive" than existed prior to the union or agreement.

THE FUTURE OF FREE TRADE

With the WTO, global free trade has entered a new stage. The WTO's more binding dispute resolution mechanisms will sooner or later test the limits of national sentiments in major trading nations. Dispute panels will have power to assign trade sanctions against losers in WTO arbitration. In significant cases, nationalist sentiment may find much to quarrel with, and occasional calls for a nation's withdrawal from the WTO are inevitable. In the past, GATT cooperation has relied largely on consensus; to move from consensus to confrontation and binding resolution poses a stronger legal order with which many will feel uncomfortable. Notably, the U.S. Congress saw fit to make clear that it reserved the right to withdraw from the WTO on six months' notice, and the United States is setting up its own panel of judges to review WTO decisions.

Much remained unresolved in the Uruguay Round of Multilateral Trade Negotiations. Negotiating accords in financial services and basic telecommunications proved elusive, and agricultural trade barriers remained. Moreover, labor leaders in the United States and elsewhere continue to express concern that minimum standards were not set in such areas as child labor, convict labor, wage scales, and labor union protection. For developing countries, where workers generally do not enjoy the same rights as in the industrialized countries, these complaints ring of potential trade barriers or discrimination against nations that depend on providing low-cost labor to compete in the global market. Yet human rights activists are alarmed at the growing number of laborers—many of them children—who work in conditions comparable to slavery, and insist that trade under such conditions may be free but is not fair. Among some Asian countries, the counter-complaint has been that the developed West was seeking to impose its own cultural and ethical norms on other countries.

Similar clashes have developed in the area of environmental protection. In 1992 a global summit on environmental sustain ability took place in Rio de Janeiro (the Earth Summit), and numerous countries declared their allegiance to the concept of sustainability. Yet for some developing countries, the need for hard currency and the hope of further development seem to hinge on the rapid depletion of natural resources within their boundaries or the degradation of their natural environment. Some environmentalists in the industrialized nations have proposed debt-for-nature swaps and the imposition of a tariff on rainforest timber, proceeds from which would be dedicated to buying and preserving rapidly dwindling rainforest resources. Such notions have been denounced as invasions of sovereignty or self-determination, and as barriers to free trade. The rapid depletion of U.S. natural resources in the history of its economic development is often cited by developing nations that might be affected by tariffs designed to promote sustainable production practices and punish nonsustainable ones.

On legal grounds, the GATT tuna/dolphin dispute panel made clear that tariffs placed on imported items based on their production or processing methods would not be permissible under GATT principles. But the issue of sustainable business and economic practices will remain, given the growing economies in a world which is not growing in finite resources.

The value differences on issues of labor and environment are accompanied by value differences on issues on intellectual property and nontariff barriers. A long and large trade dispute between the United States and Japan over automobiles and auto parts highlights, among other things, very different approaches to marketing and distribution systems. U.S. automakers contend that the Japanese market is effectively closed because of traditional ways of doing business, ways allegedly supported by the Japanese government. But proving state action may be difficult. In the early days of GATT, finding specific tariffs and setting goals and timetables for their reduction was relatively easy. The process of focusing on subsidies and legal structures that impede free trade is proving far more difficult and contentious. In matters such as these, as well as the labor and environmental questions that remain, it can be fairly said that the continued success of free trade depends to a great extent on the gradual emergence of some global consensus over what kinds of business activities are both economically appropriate and ethical.

[Joan Leotta]

FURTHER READING:

"General Agreement on Tariffs and Trade: Dispute Settlement Panel Report on United States Restrictions on Imports of Tuna." *I.L.M.* 30. 1594, 1991.

Jackson, John H. *The World Trading System.* Cambridge, MA: MIT Press, 1989.

Mayer, Don, and David Hoch. "International Environmental Protection and the GATT: The Tuna/Dolphin Controversy." *American Business Law Journal.* 31. 1993, pp. 187-244.

FREE-LANCE EMPLOYMENT

Free-lance employees, also known as independent contractors, are individuals who work on their own, without a long-term contractual commitment to any one employer. A free-lance employee usually performs services or completes work assignments under short-term contracts with several employers, or clients, who have the right to control only the final result of the individual's work, rather than the specific means used to get the work done. Examples of positions held by independent contractors range from doctors and programmers of **computers** to maids and farm workers. Free-lance employment can offer a number of advantages to individuals, including flexible work arrangements, independence, variety, and some tax deductions. It can also hold some pitfalls, however, such as assuming **risk** in business dealings, paying **self-employment** taxes, and taking personal responsibility for health insurance, disability, and **retirement** coverage.

Individuals who are classified as independent contractors can deduct work-related expenses for tax purposes. In contrast, the first 2 percent of expenses are not deductible for those classified as employees, plus the deduction is phased out above $55,900 in **income**. In addition, independent contractors often qualify for tax deductions for using part of their home as an office and for salaries paid to other people, while employees usually do not. Independent contractors also have the benefit of sheltering 15 percent of their annual income, or up to $30,000, for retirement, while employees are limited to $9,500 annually. Finally, independent contractors must pay the full amount of Social Security and Medicare taxes and make quarterly estimated tax payments to the federal government. Employers must withhold taxes for their employees and pay half of their Social Security and Medicare taxes.

Free-lance employment boomed in the United States during the 1980s, as many companies sought to reduce their payroll **costs** in order to remain competitive. Instead of hiring new employees and paying an additional 30 percent or more in payroll taxes and benefits, many companies chose to make "work-for-hire" arrangements with independent contractors. Businesses, and especially **small businesses**, can gain several advantages from such arrangements. For example, employers are not responsible for paying taxes for free-lance employees, and they avoid the high costs of providing health insurance, paid vacation and sick leave, and other benefits often granted to regular, full-time employees. Instead, employers simply file Form 1099 with the government to report the total compensation paid to each independent contractor for the year.

FREE-LANCE TREND CAUSES CONTROVERSY

The boom in free-lance employment led to increased scrutiny by the U.S. **Internal Revenue Service (IRS)** in the early 1990s. Section 1706 of the Internal Revenue Code provides a 20-part test to determine whether workers are employees or independent contractors. The IRS began using this test to reclassify many independent contractors—particularly those engaged in high-paying professions—as employees in order to eliminate tax deductions and increase tax **revenues**. This practice "leaves virtually everyone angry, and that includes the IRS," according to David Cay Johnston in the *New York Times.* "The agency is trying to apply tax laws that were largely written for an age of manual work and factories to an era of intellectual labor, often conducted in **home offices.**" The IRS would argue that the law also protects individuals from unfair treatment by employers—such as being fired and then rehired as an independent contractor without benefits—but few of the reclassifications have involved exploited low-wage laborers, because they generate minimal tax revenues. Since the issue could potentially affect up to five million self-employed Americans, Johnston called it "the most contentious employment tax issue in the nation today."

Although the controversy surrounding free-lance employment has received increased attention in recent years, it is not new. As early as the 1960s, the IRS started looking more closely at household employees—such as maids, nannies, and gardeners—who often received income "under the table" and thus did not pay taxes. The main cause of dissention over current application of the law, according to the *New York Times,* is that it often tends to penalize individuals who wish to be classified as independent contractors and take advantage of tax breaks (as well as the small businesses that depend on them), while it often fails to protect individuals who should be classified as employees and be eligible for benefits. For example, the IRS would be likely to review the case of a highly paid engineer who markets her services to several companies as an independent contractor and deducts various expenses of doing business. However, the IRS would be unlikely to review the case of a migrant farm worker who is employed by a large producer but, as an independent contractor, makes less than minimum wage and receives no disability or old-age benefits.

ELEMENTS OF THE IRS TEST

The IRS applies a 20-part test in order to determine whether a certain worker should be classified as an employee or an independent contractor. The main issue underpinning the test is who sets the work rules: employees must follow rules set by their bosses, while independent contractors set their own rules. The hours during which a job is performed is one determination of work rules. For example, if the employer dictates an individual's work hours or pays an individual by the hour rather than by the job, that individual is likely to be considered an employee rather than an independent contractor. Likewise, if the employer requires that an individual work full-time or not be employed by another company simultaneously, that individual would appear to be an employee. On the other hand, an individual who sets his own hours, receives payment by the job, and divides his time between work for several different employers would probably be classified as an independent contractor.

Other criteria involve who provides the tools and materials needed to complete the work. For example, an individual who works at an employer's facility and uses the employer's equipment would be considered an employee, while one who works at a separate location and provides her own equipment would be classified as an independent contractor. Another element of the IRS test involves termination of the work relationship. Employees can usually quit their jobs at will, and can also be fired by their employers. However, a free-lance employee would have a contractual obligation to complete a specific amount of work for an employer, and neither party could break the agreement without cause. Finally, an independent contractor usually pays his own expenses of doing business and takes the risk of not receiving payment when work is not completed in accordance with a contract, while an employee is usually reimbursed for business-related expenses by the employer and receives a paycheck whether his work is completed or not.

Despite such specific guidelines, the IRS test has generated criticism. "This 20-factor test has frustrated both the IRS and the small-business owner," said an accountant quoted in *Crain's Small Business Detroit.* "Ten different revenue agents could review the same case, and ten different responses could result." The IRS recognized that the test was sometimes applied inconsistently, and was evaluating whether to modify or eliminate it. However, the agency had no plans to reduce its efforts to reclassify certain independent contractors as employees because of the potential gains in tax revenue. Reclassification can cost small businesses that rely on free-lance employees huge sums in penalties, back taxes, and interest—and can even force some out of business. In Michigan alone, the IRS reclassified 51,000 independent contractors in 1993 and assessed a total of $100 million in back taxes.

[Laurie Collier Hillstrom]

FURTHER READING:

Brodsky, Ruthan, and Marsha Stopa. "Sneak a Tax," *Crain's Small Business Detroit.* July 1994, pp. 1-8.

"Employee vs. Independent Contractor," *IRS Publication No. 937.* Washington, D.C.: Internal Revenue Service, 1994.

Johnston, David Cay. "Are You Your Own Boss? Only if the IRS Says So," *New York Times.* March 19, 1995, p. F13.

Saunders, Laura. "Attention, Income Hiders," *Forbes.* March 2, 1992, p. 64.

Spragins, Ellyn E. "Protecting Independent Contractor Status," *Inc.* March 1992, p. 98.

Szabo, Joan C. "Contract Workers: A Risky Business," *Nation's Business.* August 1993, p. 20.

FUTURES/FUTURES CONTRACTS

A futures contract is a commitment to make or take delivery of a specific quantity and quality of a given commodity at a predetermined place and time in the future. All terms of the contract are standardized and established beforehand, except for the price, which is determined by open outcry in a pit or ring on the exchange trading floor of a regulated **commodity exchange**. All contracts ultimately are settled either through liquidation (by offsetting purchases or sales) or by the delivery of the actual, underlying physical commodity. Delivery occurs in less than one percent of all contracts traded.

Futures markets provide the medium whereby producers, processors, and users of raw or basic **commodities** can hedge their price risk. By using the futures markets effectively, businesspeople can minimize their risk, which in turn, lowers their cost of doing business. This savings can be passed along to consumers in the form of lower prices.

An option is the right, but not the obligation, to buy or sell a futures contract at some predetermined price at anytime within a specified time. An option to buy a futures contract is known as a call option, while an option to sell a futures contract is known as a put option. The predetermined futures price at which the futures contract may be bought or sold is called the strike or exercise price. The amount paid for the option is called the premium.

Anytime before the option expires, the option buyer can (1) exercise the option; (2) convert the option into a futures contract at the strike price; (3) sell the option to someone else; or 4) do nothing and let option expire.

The option seller receives the premium from the option buyer at the time of the option transaction. If the option buyer exercises the option, then the option seller is obligated to take the opposite futures position at the strike price.

When it was first established on April 3, 1848, the Chicago Board of Trade (CBOT) was a centralized cash market, formed in response to the need for a central marketplace that would bring together large numbers of buyers and sellers, thus providing liquidity, as well as providing a place with rules for ethical trading practices and reliable standards of weights and measures. Soon after the founding of the exchange, grain brokers began trading in "cash forward contracts," in order to assure buyers a source of supply and sellers the opportunity to sell 12 months a year. As the use of the cash forward contracts escalated, the futures contract, as it is known today, evolved. Because of its many economic benefits, the futures market has expanded to include numerous and varied commodity groups throughout the world.

On September 8, 1981, the **Commodity Futures Trading Commission** (CFTC) adopted a comprehensive set of regulations to govern exchange trading of options on futures contracts under a controlled and monitored three-year pilot program. On August 31, 1982 the CFTC designated the first contract markets for options on futures contracts. These markets included options on sugar futures traded at the Coffee, Sugar, and Cocoa Exchange, Inc.; options on gold futures at the Mid-America Commodity Exchange; options on gold futures at the Commodity Exchange, Inc. (COMEX); and options on U.S. Treasury Department bond futures at the CBOT.

Futures trading has been an attractive investment vehicle because of its low margins, high leverage, and frequently volatile prices; also, the need for hedgers to manage price uncertainties inherent in business creates opportunities for profit. Futures trading gained in popularity in the 1970s when traditional approaches such as savings accounts and stocks couldn't keep pace with inflation.

Futures offer investors the ability to buy or sell a contract for five to 18 percent of its underlying value. This leverage capability offers the investor a potentially high rate of return for a relatively small investment. However, substantial risk can accompany this potential for high rates of return. If the market moves in a direction contrary to the investor's position, he or she could lose the entire initial investment, as well as be liable for any additional losses that result from the adverse move.

When investors place orders to buy or sell futures contracts, they are required to post a performance margin, which is a financial obligation to ensure that they fulfill their financial obligations. Margins are set by the commodity exchanges on which the contract trades, but the brokerage firm, futures commission merchant, or introducing broker through which investors decide to trade and open their trading accounts may require a larger margin than what the exchange requires. The initial amount investors must deposit into their trading accounts is called the initial margin. On a daily basis, the margin is debited or credited to the investors' open position, based on the close of the day's trading session, known as marking-to-the-market. Investors must maintain a set minimum margin known as a maintenance margin. If a market movement against the investors' position reduces the equity in their trading accounts to where the accounts fall below the maintenance margin level, the customers will be required to add funds to their accounts in order to return the accounts to the initial margin level, before they may buy or sell additional contracts. Funds in the accounts in excess of the required margins may be withdrawn by the customers.

In addition to low margins and leverage, futures markets provide the opportunity for an investor to profit both from buying a futures contract and having it rise in value, as well as selling a futures contract and having it decline in value. The ability to make money on both the long or buying side as well as the short or selling side makes futures trading an attractive investment vehicle.

Futures markets also are known for their volatility or price movement. This allows investors to enter and exit the marketplace quickly, which provides opportunity for profit as well as the ability to limit losses.

Lastly, **hedging** has been referred to as the major economic justification for futures markets. Since futures trading began, hedgers and speculators or outside investors have interacted to determine commodity prices. The hedger uses the futures market to protect against the risk of unfavorable price movement, while the speculator, using risk capital, assumes risk in the hope of making a profit by correctly forecasting future price movement.

In 1993, a total of 339,075,626 futures contracts were traded on U.S. commodity or futures exchanges. An additional 182,326,764 options were traded on U.S. futures and U.S. securities exchanges in 1993.

For 1993, U.S. futures volume by commodity group is as follows, with the percentage of total trading also provided: Interest Rate: 173,768,387 (51.25 percent); Ag Commodities: 56,724,601 (16.73 percent); Energy Products: 45,618,438 (13.45 percent); Foreign Currency/Index: 30,816,446 (9.09 percent); Equity Indexes: 14,996,787 (4.42 percent); Precious Metals: 14,683,066 (4.33 percent); Non-Precious Metals: 2,064,629 (0.61 percent); and Other: 403,272 (0.12 percent).

Also in 1993, options on futures volume on U.S. futures by commodity group is as follows, with the percentage of total trading also provided: Interest Rate: 47,458,153 (57.98 percent); Ag Commodities: 9,766,714 (11.93 percent); Foreign Currency/Index: 9,588,967 (11.71 percent); Energy Products: 8,966,434 (10.95 percent); Equity Indexes: 2,965,862 (3.62 percent); Precious Metals: 2,888,520 (3.53 percent); Non-Precious Metals: 146,594 (0.18 percent); and Other: 77,391 (0.09 percent). Options on securities indexes and foreign currencies by commodity group is as follows for 1993: Equity Indexes: 87,302,403 (86.90 percent); Foreign Currency/Index: 13,101,365 (13.04 percent); and Interest Rate: 64,361 (0.06 percent).

SEE ALSO: Discount Broker; Stock Market; Stocks.

[Susan Bard Hall]

FURTHER READING:

Best Commodities Services, Inc. *Introduction to Futures: Who Makes Money and Why*. Chicago, 1983, p. 1.

Chicago Board of Trade. *From Beans to Bonds: A Brief Look at the Chicago Board of Trade*. Chicago, 1992, pp. 2, 10.

Chicago Board of Trade. *Options on Agricultural Futures - A Home Study Course*. Chicago, September, 1989, pp. 5, 17.

Commodity Futures Trading Commission. *Commodity Futures Trading Commission Annual Report 1993*. Washington, pp. 15-16.

Futures Industry Association. *Preface to An Introduction to the Futures Markets*. Washington, D.C., 1982.

Futures Industry Association. *Options Volume on U.S. Futures & U.S. Securities Exchanges by Commodity Group*.

Futures Industry Association. *U.S. Futures Volume by Commodity Group* Washington, D.C., 1994.

National Futures Association. *Understanding Opportunities & Risks In Futures Trading*. Chicago, 1990, p. 45.

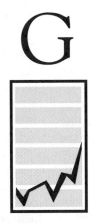

G

Game theory is a science in which players develop behavioral strategies in order to compete for a specific limited benefit with optimal prospects for success. Its starting point consists of a series of assumptions that are either given or conditional upon the actions of other players. These assumptions, and the strategies they form, may be modified to meet changing conditions as the game is played.

It is called "game theory" because its application is limited to hypothetical situations where assumptions may be tested without real consequences. Its purpose is to develop logic skills within established frameworks so that players may be trained for subsequent games or real world situations.

As a scientific discipline, game theory emerged early in the twentieth century as the result of efforts to apply quantitative analysis to abstract cognitive dilemmas. Because of poorly developed methodologies and a lack of demonstrably consistent application to more widely useful purposes, it was largely ignored until the 1940s.

However, during the early years of the Cold War, significant breakthroughs were made that legitimized it as a science with testable proofs. As a result, certain aspects of game theory could be applied to war games and global military strategy, economic and pricing strategies, social questions, and even labor bargaining issues.

Like **econometrics**, game theory continues to be treated as something less than a pure natural science. This is due to the fact that many of the variables in a game proof are irrational or apparently random, and therefore impossible to quantify with predictive reliability. As a result, every outcome is likely to be unique and answers are often defined only in terms of probabilities.

Game theory frequently has created difficult marriages of behavioral and mathematical assumptions that yielded such ridiculously mechanical computations as "megadeaths" in military **strategy**, where certain scenarios for nuclear war could be extrapolated into forecasts of how many millions of people would be killed.

In other areas, however, the capabilities of the science were limited to simple marketing programs for products such as cigarettes, automobiles, and toothpaste. Here, applications of game theory could be tested for validity while certain shortcomings could be readily identified, and adjustments made.

Game theory may be considered a modeling technique that is used to anticipate the actions of all agents involved in a **competition** and to test and determine the relative optimality of different strategies. Its primary applications are in linear programming, statistical **decision making**, operations research, and military and economic planning. Recent extensions of game theory include sociological and ethical dilemmas.

THE PRINCIPLES OF GAME THEORY

The language of game theory can seem confusing and difficult to the uninitiated. It consists of summations, sets, "n-tuples" and other specialized notation that is beyond the scope of this essay. Rather than provide a tutorial on the execution of game theory, this discussion will be confined to game theoretical approaches.

Game theory first developed out of attempts to quantify logical processes in complex situations where outcomes were dependent on a series of decisions, each of which affected the conditions of the next and all others that followed. Whether theories pertaining to these processes were applied to games or real world situations was irrelevant; the goal was to gain insights into strategies and establish anticipatory consistency among variables.

A good example is provided by board games like chess. In chess, two opponents each control 16 pieces which compete on a board of 64 spaces. Each of the pieces has different capabilities, but all can remove, or "take," any opposing piece. Chess is therefore analogous to a battle situation, where degrees of skill or effectiveness are reflected in the capabilities of the pieces, but any one can kill off any opposing piece.

Pieces are afforded opportunities to strike at opposing pieces in turn. Therefore, defensive strategies are just as critically important as offensive ones. Indeed, defensive strategies can lure attackers into traps, where they can be taken. Players may choose to sacrifice less important pieces in order to remove opposing pieces that are strategically more valuable.

Contests between subsets of pieces occur all over the board. While one player is developing an attack, he may be unaware of an attack forming elsewhere on the board. As a result, offensive moves may occur at the expense of more crucial defensive ones. If all this information is not fully calculated by the players, opportunities may be missed and mistakes made.

Just as the game may be divided into contests between subsets of pieces, it may also be divided into sub-games. At the lowest level, each move may be considered a sub-game. Combinations of moves may constitute a larger sub-game where the objective is to take a certain piece.

Keeping in mind that some pieces may move only a certain number of spaces and only in specified directions, that there are a finite number of pieces and spaces, and that moves are taken in turn, the number of ways a game may progress are tremendous.

In a simplified example, the number of movements made by only one side may be expressed mathematically as $(16^y)^n$, where 16 is the number of pieces, y represents the number of ways those pieces may move, and n represents the number of moves. If each piece may move an average of, say, 6 ways, after only three moves, one player may have any one of nearly five sextillion situations on the board. After six moves, the possibilities increase to more than 22 dodectillion—and this number doesn't even represent the actions of the opposing player.

Clearly, chess players cannot consider every play option for every piece for any number of moves. Instead, players dismiss certain options—or ignore areas—that have no strategic immediacy, and concentrate only on the sub-games that do. Of course, ignoring too much has consequences as well.

A skilled chess player will adopt a style of play that combines offensive strategies with defensive ones. This requires the player to anticipate opposing moves by thinking not only for himself, but also for his opponent; at each stage the player asks, "If I were him, what would I do?" These processes make the game even more complex by duplicating the number of considerations each player must process.

People familiar with military strategy—or its close cousin, competitive **marketing**—will recognize that chess combines virtually all the same strategic considerations as prosecuting a war or introducing a new product. In fact, chess and games like it were invented specifically to hone the skills of battle strategists and improve their ability to defeat enemies, simply by training them how to recognize opportunities for attack, where to retreat, what to sacrifice and, perhaps most importantly, what to ignore.

The example of chess is a good starting point, but other games can be more complicated. For instance, what if there are more than two players, an unlimited playing surface, a less exhaustible source of pieces, and the capability to form teams among players? These situations introduce strategic considerations that more closely represent a wider range of real world competitive situations and more thoroughly demonstrate the value of game theory.

Chess provides an example of a two-person zero-sum game, where a gain by one player comes at the expense of the other and all forms of cooperation—other than a draw—are counterproductive. The first theorem developed for zero-sum games was propounded in 1913 by Zermelo, who argued that games like chess are strictly determined because all information in the game is immediately revealed and prescribed rules govern the actions of all players. Chess is not individually rational because no player may force a draw when under threat of losing—such as in tic-tac-toe, where stalemates are easily attained.

Harold Kuhn expanded on Zermelo's theorem by arguing that strategies in sub-games will be in equilibrium if decisions made by the players are rational. These equilibria may be extended to combinations of sub-games, and even to the game as a whole, removing the limitation that games be zero-sum and individually rational. Another extension of the theory was made by Rufus Isaacs, who established the concept of the differential game, where perfect information may not exist.

These developments appear to be only logically semantic, but they provided bases for application of earlier theorems to a wider range of problems. For example, a game such as poker contains opportunities to drive the decisions of opponents with misinformation by injecting doubt into the observations of other players—a strategy called bluffing. Negative influences of this type are qualitative rather than quantitative, and serve to frustrate logical decisions based solely on a given theory of play.

The economist Oskar Morgenstern recognized the interactive nature of economic intercourse—that each person's decisions depend on the decisions of every other person's. Morgenstern and John von Neumann developed applications of game theory to the problems raised by interactivity in their seminal work *The Theory of Games and Economic Behavior*, published in 1944.

Morgenstern and von Neumann provided a basis for new concepts in game theory, including the idea of cooperative and noncooperative games. A cooperative game is one in which sets of players are bound by agreements to work in mutual, rather than individual, interest—even when noncooperative play would be more beneficial.

In a game of Monopoly, for instance, where there are six players, each player may purchase and hold certain properties to deny other players a monopoly on the group to which that property belongs, thereby precluding the placement of houses and hotels by opponents. However, a group of two players might find it advantageous to cooperate by trading properties that the other wants, enabling each to build greater threats to other players.

As the game progresses, the other four players—who are in strategically weaker positions—are likely to be victimized by this strategy and bankrupted. At this point, the purpose of the cooperation has run its course and the two players begin oppositional noncooperative play.

Cooperative games remain cooperative only as long as the conditions of their agreement remain enforceable and effective. They become noncooperative when prospective individual rewards overwhelm the basis for cooperation.

Coalitional games are related to concepts of cooperation, particularly in parliamentary forms of government. Where an election denies a party an absolute majority, it may form coalitions with other parties to achieve a majority. These coalitions are based on agreements to pool interests—an unstable situation, given that parties in a coalition have appreciable conflicts. If a smaller coalition partner feels it has been ill-served by the coalition, it may dissolve its partnership and bring down the government.

John Nash dealt extensively with noncooperation, particularly in cooperative games where subversion is a strategic consideration. In 1951 he provided applications of the von Neumann-Morgenstern interdependency theorem, previously used most in military strategy, to economic problems.

Central to Nash's approach is the concept of individual rationality, where each player may determine when it is best to abrogate an agreement. Nash said an equilibrium is established in any noncooperative game where agreements are self-enforcing; where the benefits of cheating a partner are outweighed by future retribution. The Nash equilibrium is observed in games where players adopt mixed strategies, or pursue a course of play with two or more different, but related, goals.

Nash equilibria may be said to make noncooperative games cooperative, and games featuring it are therefore quite predictable, not to mention boring. But they illustrate another facet of game theory, that of Pareto efficiency, named for Italian economist Vilfredo Pareto. Cooperative players will negotiate an alliance that is individually Pareto-optimal; their payoff will be less, but their chances of winning something are better.

In a market of 12 suppliers, there are many opportunities for noncooperative activity, each is trying to exploit weaknesses in every other, and competition is varied and fierce. Because noncooperative behavior is expected, a Nash equilibrium is unlikely.

But if there were only two suppliers, a cooperative strategy may prove more beneficial. This is because the benefits from cooperation (a duopoly) outweigh the potential consequences of cut-throat competition. In mapping out the terms of their cooperation, either implicitly or explicitly, each will seek a strategy that is Pareto-optimal.

A precondition to cooperation and noncooperation is that the reward, or ''payoff,'' have transferable utility—that is, that every player values the reward equally. Likewise, each player must equally value the threats associated with losing. If there are differences in either case, player motivations will differ accordingly, possibly affecting the terms of agreement between players.

Players may gain an indication of a payoff profile from solution concepts, which are simply sets of likely outcomes. They cannot predict what will happen, but what might happen. For example, a five-player voting game will reward all who cooperate with a share of $15, perhaps $3 each. The stable set provides the following imputation: (3,3,3,3,3), or $3 for each player. However, assuming that it takes three players to *dominate* or win the game, three players may gang up on the other two and divide the reward among themselves—(5,5,5,0,0).

Players 4 and 5, hoping to minimize losses or deny other players a payoff, may strike a separate deal with one of the first three, offering to split the reward in such a way that provides an even greater benefit to that player—(0,0,7,4,4).

Another example is provided in the **prisoner's dilemma**, first defined by Al Tucker. Tucker used the example of two suspects who participated in crime. Prosecutors have sufficient evidence to prove both are accomplices, but cannot prove which was the leader. They offer each suspect a proposition: either testify against the other or remain silent.

If both prisoners remain silent, they go to jail for one year. If they implicate each other they go to jail for two years. But if prisoner A plea bargains and implicates prisoner B, and prisoner B remains silent, prisoner A gets no jail time and prisoner B gets six years. The reverse applies if B implicates A and A remains silent. The dilemma may be expressed in a matrix (see Figure 1).

	Prisoner A	
	Confess	Stay Silent
Prisoner B		
Confess	A:2 B:2	A:6 B:0
Stay Silent	A:0 B:6	A:1 B:1

Figure 1

The dilemma Tucker identified is whether each prisoner should confess or stay silent. If each wishes at all costs to avoid spending 12 years in jail, he will be motivated to confess and may get as few as one or as many as six years in jail, depending on whether his accomplice confesses. But if one of these players wishes only to minimize his time in jail, he may risk being silent and hope his partner stays silent as well, and settle for three years behind bars.

The cooperative dilemmas facing players in both examples become more complex when they are not limited to single "one-shot" games, but are extended to additional rounds. These dynamic games, including stochastic and repeated games, provide players with a basis of knowledge—namely, the behavior of other players—that may be employed in future contests. This knowledge is defined in the Folk Theorem, which states that abrogation of cooperative agreements may be dealt with in subsequent games; Quislings will be punished next time around. The Nash Theorem suggests that risk-averse players will be rewarded more often for cooperating than for not cooperating.

The prisoner's dilemma seems rudimentary, but the dynamic may be applied to more complex situations. Consider that five airline companies are competing in a three-city market. The matrix thus expands to three sets, or dimensions, of five-by-five matrices, yielding 75 possible outcomes. Add the dimension of time, and the number of decisions is multiplied at every period in question.

In dealing with outcomes indicated by matrices, a player may seek to maximize opportunities to finish ahead of his opponents by adopting a strategy wherein the sum of his minimum payoffs is greater than the sum of his opponents' sum of minimum payoffs. This is called the minimax criteria, and ensures that this player's outcomes will exceed, or dominate, his opponents'.

By its nature, minimax is risk-averse. In various types of tests it has proven more successful in guaranteeing a dominant outcome.

Simple game theory models are deeply frustrated by the existence of incomplete information among players. John Harsanyi postulated that in such differential or asymmetric games, each player is certain only about his own utility function, but must speculate about other players' utility functions and, more importantly, other players' conception of every other players' utility functions.

Simply put, each player must know his own payoff probability, guess other players' payoff probabilities, and also guess what other players' are guessing about his own payoff probability. Furthermore, the player must guess what other players are guessing about his guesses about them, forming an infinite regress.

The complexity of these assumptions is illustrated in chess, poker, and Monopoly; no player can be expected to know precisely what the other is trying to achieve at every stage. However, the motivations of other players—constituting a type—can be revealed during play or in repeated games. Players unwittingly offer indications of their type by voluntarily demonstrating their motivations through play.

Asymmetric games occur all the time in economics, where some "players" simply know more than others and this knowledge is expressed as a competitive advantage. In an enormous market of 100 million consumers, no single player may be expected to assert appreciable influence. This is called the equivalence principle, where competition generally ensures that allocations are equally distributed.

An exception arises if a significant number of players pool interests to form a group specifically to extract greater bargaining power. Assume a market where 100 people each have two jars of peanut butter and another 100 each have two jars of grape jelly. Each would be expected to trade one jar of peanut butter for one jar of jelly, and vice versa, establishing a market equilibrium.

This equilibrium yields an empty core; which is to say that nothing is left over, or the market has fully cleared.

Now assume that a group of people with peanut butter band together to demand a more favorable ratio of trade, say, three jars of jelly for every two jars of peanut butter. By organizing a **cartel**, they may exercise greater influence over the market of many individually insignificant players; they are transformed into a functionally significant bloc that may determine a balance of trade through cooperative or noncooperative bargaining.

The example illustrates that, if it is assumed everyone is trying to make peanut butter and jelly sandwiches, some players will be left with peanut butter to trade, but the market has no jelly to offer in exchange. Meanwhile, some players will be left with no jelly with which to trade for peanut butter. This condition, where an amount of one product remains disproportionally underutilized (in this case, jelly), yields a nonempty core.

If the situation is repeated, however, the jelly holders may form their own cartel, threatening to withhold *all* jelly unless they receive more favorable trade terms. Although simple, it is not difficult to see how simple disputes such as this can escalate into full fledged international trade wars.

One way in which game theory demonstrates its ability to outperform more strictly mathematical methods of computation is in its capacity to include irrational decisions. Game theory assumes that irrationality may be a factor in player decisions. As a result, when a player makes an irrational move, game strategies may adjust, where strict formulas might collapse into invalidity.

Game theoretical approaches are extremely versatile and accommodating because they are based on logical constructs rather than rigid formulas with given values. Economists are trained to accept a regime of market equilibrium as given, studying how that equilibrium may affect price, supply, and demand. Game theorists, on the other hand, investigate the forces that created the equilibrium to determine whether it is valid in the first place.

Therefore, the game theorist approach is to take an economic problem, translate it into a game format, find a game-theoretic solution, and convert the solution back into the format of the economic problem. In economics and other social science methodologies, solution sets are directly applied to a formal model.

Thus, game theory provides useful perspective by ignoring where given information may lead, and instead asking why that given information exists in the first place.

[John Simley]

FURTHER READING:

Eatwell, J., Ed. *The New Palgrave Dictionary of Economics.* London: Macmillan, 1987.

Fischer, Stanley and Rudiger Hornbusch. *Economics.* NY: McGraw-Hill, 1983.

Johnson, Robert R. *Elementary Statistics*, 3rd Ed. MA: Duxbury Press, 1980.

Warsh, David. "Game Theory Plays Strategic Role in Economics' Most Interesting Problems," *Boston Globe*, July 24, 1994.

GENDER AND LEADERSHIP

Gender and leadership is a subject that is concerned with two main questions: (1) What are the determinants of male/female differences in the "who assumes **leadership** positions" and in leadership behavior? and (2) How is leadership a gendered concept?

Social scientists distinguish between "gender" and "sex." Sex refers to the basic, biologically given physiological differences between males and females. Gender refers to a culture's social construction of differences between the sexes. These include the different traits, roles, behaviors, attitudes, and aptitudes males and females are expected to display. Gender displays reinforce claims of membership in a sex. Expressions such as "gendered practices," "gendered language," and "gendered jobs" are used to emphasize the tenet that gender involves a process of social construction, and to make gender a more central explanation of organizational behavior phenomena such as leadership.

The term "leaders" refers to persons holding formal positions of leadership in complex organizations in industry, government, education, politics, the arts, sciences, and professions. Historically, sex precluded most females from becoming leaders in such organizations; as a result, the assumption that males were better suited than females for leadership roles was, until recently, rarely questioned. Since the early 1970s, the foundation of that assumption has been shaken by the large number of women who, according to *Bass and Stogdill's Handbook of Leadership*, have been (1) elected prime minister (in Britain, Canada, India, Pakistan, Philippines, Norway, Sri Lanka) and to other high government offices; (2) elevated to managerial positions in business organizations; and (3) earning Master of Business Administration (MBA) degrees. In addition, the assumption that leaders are to be men has come under scrutiny by a growing body of scholarly writing on the subject of gender and leadership.

Interest in gender and leadership started in the United States in the early 1970s, when women slowly began to seek and gain entry into **management**. Two types of literature sought to aid women's advancement. Practical, "how to" advice books warned that the predominantly male corporate world was, for women, akin to foreign, hostile, enemy territory: to be successful, women needed to learn and adapt themselves to the local language, dress, and customs. This theme is reflected in titles such as *The Managerial Woman: The Survival Manual for Women in Business*, by Margaret Hennig and Anne Jardim; *Games Mother Never Taught You*, by Betty L. Harragan; and *Making it in Management: A Behavioral Approach for Women Executives*, by Margaret Fenn.

The other body of literature—more academic in its content and research—provided the rationale for eliminating barriers (such as discriminatory policies) to women's progress in organizations and management. It argued that differences between women's and men's ability to carry out responsible jobs are minimal, once women attain the appropriate job qualifications. Women, thus, deserved equal opportunity in early childhood as well as higher education, and equal access to all types of job training and development. Women would then be able to compete with men for leadership positions and other jobs.

Other books and articles in the 1970s assailed society's loss of talent from the large pool of motivated females prohibited from many jobs simply because of their sex. These "**human capital**" theorists argued that such a gross underutilization of resources was wasteful, irrational, and disadvantageous to a firm's profitability and competitiveness. Both the equal opportunity and human capital arguments are based on the assumption that when a woman's advancement in a career is based on merit alone, she will be able to excel and advance into management and leadership positions if she desires.

The human capital theory presaged an argument that emerged in the middle 1980s: that a company's profits could be bolstered by the special qualities women possess: their proclivity for cooperative **decision making**, ability to share power and communicate well, experience in nurturing the development of others, and comfort with less hierarchical organizations. Increased foreign competition had made U.S. companies aware of the failings of the traditional, military, authoritarian leadership style, and thus the utilization females' talents was seen as a possible source of competitive advantage. This theme is reflected in the titles of books and articles such as *The*

Female Advantage: Women's Ways of Leadership, by Sally Helgesen; "Women as managers: What they can offer to organizations," by Jan Grant; and *Feminine Leadership or How to Succeed in Business Without Being One of the Boys*, by Marilyn Loden.

At the same time the idea that females possess a natural leadership advantage over males gained popularity in both academic and management circles, some scholars voiced a more critical view. They maintained that the idea of extracting the value of feminine skills and qualities in the global marketplace was exploitative. Such a plan is part of a managerialist ideology that dehumanizes and subordinates all workers, not females only. These writers were less concerned with the relationship between gender and leadership *per se*. Their primary interest was the issue of power, and how the gender categories "male" and "female" are part of a system of power relations that empowers some and exploits others.

WHY SO FEW WOMEN LEADERS?

Why are there differences between males and females in who becomes a leader? This is one main question of concern to writers in the area of gender and leadership. Though the situation has improved recently for women in the United States and other western countries, throughout human history women have not traditionally been found as leaders, outside the family, in complex organizations—those corporations, legislatures, universities, and financial institutions which greatly influence society.

Several reasons are cited for the low proportion of women leaders. One is that females' life aspirations are diminished by their early childhood socialization in the nuclear family. Generally the nuclear family transmits definitions of appropriate gender behavior to children. For girls, this includes submissiveness, passivity, avoidance of aggression and competition, reticence to take risk, and other qualities our culture considers "feminine." Research shows that even when high school boys and girls have the same college and career aspirations, the boys receive significantly more parental encouragement to pursue their goals.

One result of this childhood socialization is the tendency for adult women to be stereotyped as less well-suited than men for leadership roles. Several studies have shown that people perceive successful managers to have the characteristics typically associated with men, though the actual qualities successful managers possess are a combination of masculine (e.g., forcefulness, self-confidence, task orientation, and initiative) and feminine (e.g., concern for people, feelings, and relationships) traits. An obvious consequence of this is that a man is more likely to be selected for a leadership position than is a woman of equal qualification. Thus, a woman who aspires to leadership positions must overcome both her childhood socialization, which discouraged development of some essential qualities, and a popular perception of the maleness of leadership—both of which tangibly reduce the chance she will be judged qualified. In addition to socialization and stereotyping, other barriers to females' upward mobility into leadership positions are (a) discrimination against them in personnel decisions involving promotion, selection, and **supervision**; (b) a dearth of women and men willing to mentor women; (c) management development opportunities that are based on job rotation: geographic mobility can create difficulties for a woman's children and destroy her spouse's career; (d) coincidence of the biological clock and some professions' ''up or out'' policies, such as professors' tenure clock and lawyers' partner clock; and (e) the perception of women as ''outsiders'' due to their physical differences, stereotyping, and exclusion from some social clubs and activities where important networks are built and maintained.

Other reasons women ascend to leadership positions less frequently than men are that women most frequently inhabit managerial positions with little power, little advancement opportunity, or where other women are so rare that their presence is attributed to their sexuality or **affirmative action**, or it is used as a symbol of the organization's enlightenment. Outside their paid jobs, women usually have significant responsibility for the care of their families and home, thereby depleting the energy they might otherwise devote to the pursuit of leadership positions of consequence.

DO MALE AND FEMALE LEADERS BEHAVE DIFFERENTLY?

Though females' early socialization and other obstacles may impede them from becoming leaders, those who do ascend do not behave significantly differently from men in the same kinds of positions. Some studies have been able to discern differences in leadership style and managerial behavior, but most have not.

Studies have examined male/female differences in three main types of managerial behavior. The first is task accomplishment style, which is how much the leader initiates, organizes, and defines work activities and processes. The second is interpersonal style, which is how much the leader builds morale, relationships, satisfaction, and commitment in the organization. The third is decision-making style, which is how much the leader encourages a participative, democratic approach as opposed to an autocratic approach.

Some studies find differences between males' and females' task accomplishment styles and interper-

sonal styles. Males tended to be more task-oriented; females tended to be more relationship-oriented. These differences, however, have been observed only in men and women subjects of laboratory experiments, that is, people asked to speculate how they would behave if they were leaders. Differences disappear in studies where actual managers are compared: most conclude that women do not behave differently from men in the same or similar kind of leadership position. Moreover, experienced women managers show no differences in leadership abilities from experienced male managers. These women, in fact, are likely to more resemble their male counterparts in drive, skills, temperament, and competitiveness, than the average woman in the population.

Some difference has been found in males' and females' decision-making styles. According to Gary N. Powell's comprehensive study, *Women and Men in Management*, women tend to employ a more democratic, participative style while men tend to take a more autocratic, directive approach. This difference has appeared in both laboratory studies and observations of real leaders. Some scholars, thus, argue that women's tendency to negotiate, mediate, facilitate, and communicate is the more effective leadership style than men's emphasis on power and control; and because this ''feminine'' style reduces hierarchy, satisfies subordinates, and achieves results, it should be the norm to which men are compared. There is some evidence that this is occurring: most mainstream writers now urge managers to adopt a caring, cooperative, collaborative, nurturing, connective, servant leadership style.

HOW IS LEADERSHIP GENDERED?

The other main question of concern to writers in the area of gender and leadership is whether ''leadership position'' is implicitly a gendered concept. To answer this question, first one has to understand how organizations, including their leadership positions, are one place where gender is produced. In her article ''Gendering Organizational Theory,'' Joan Acker argues that gender is part of the logic used in organizations to determine what practices will be adopted. Organizations profess themselves to be gender-neutral, for example with their practice of filling an abstract job with a person who possesses the requisite qualifications. But when the ''job description'' for a leadership position includes twelve-hour days, business meetings and social events on weekends, and little time for non-job-related obligations, many women (and, increasingly, men) cannot qualify because of their family responsibilities. The ostensibly gender-neutral job, then, is not. It and the organization in which it exists are part of the gendered substructure of society. They assume and thereby replicate conventional gender roles: man working full-time for a lifetime in a job outside the home; woman working in the home to take care of him, the family, and any spillover from his job.

In this view, all social practices are structured in relation to gender. This includes the social practice of organizing businesses, schools, governments, and the like, and including leadership positions in the design of these organizations. Because social practices replicate the reproductive division of people into male and female, they are said to be "gendered." Thus, gender becomes a property of institutions and the human and historical processes that create them. It becomes a characteristic of not individual people but collectivities. To think of gender—and leadership—in this way is a considerable advance. Doing so provides an explanation for the difficulties women traditionally have experienced ascending to leadership positions and performing leader roles with comfort and ease.

SEE ALSO: Discrimination (Employment); Sex Discrimination

[Nanette Fondas]

FURTHER READING:

Acker, Joan. "Gendering Organizational Theory," *Gendering Organizational Analysis*, by Albert J. Mills and Peta Tancred. Sage Publications, Inc., 1992, pp. 248-260.

Bass, Bernard M. *Bass and Stogdill's Handbook of Leadership: Theory, Research, and Managerial Applications*. Third Edition. The Free Press, 1990.

Billing, Yvonne Due, and Mats Alvesson. "Four Ways of Looking at Women and Leadership," *Scandinavian Journal of Management*, 5 (1), 1989, pp. 63-80.

Calas, Marta B., and Linda Smircich. "Dangerous Liaisons: The 'Feminine-in-Management' Meets 'Globalization'," *Business Horizons*, March-April, 1993, pp. 71-81.

Connell, Robert W. *Gender and Power*. Polity Press, 1987.

Fagenson, Ellen A. "Perceived Masculine and Feminine Attributes Examined as a Function of Individuals' Sex and Level in the Organizational Power Hierarchy: A Test of Four Theoretical Perspectives," *Journal of Applied Psychology*, 75, 1990, pp. 204-211.

Fagenson, Ellen A. (Ed.) *Women in Management: Trends, Issues, and Challenges in Managerial Diversity*. Sage Publications, Inc., 1993.

Fenn, Margaret. *Making it in Management: A Behavioral Approach for Women Executives*. Prentice-Hall, 1978.

Fletcher, Joyce K. "Castrating the Female Advantage: Feminist Standpoint Research and Management Science," *Journal of Management Inquiry*, 3 (1), March, 1994, pp. 74-82.

Fondas, Nanette. "The Feminization of American Management," *Academy of Management Best Paper Proceedings*. Academy of Management, 1993, pp. 358-362.

Grant, Jan. "Women as Managers: What They Can Offer to Organizations," *Organizational Dynamics*, Winter, 1988, pp. 56-63.

Goodale, J.G., and Douglas T. Hall. "Inheriting a Career: The Influence of Sex, Values, and Parents," *Journal of Vocational Behavior*, 8, 1976, pp. 19-30.

Harragan, Betty Lehan. *Games Mother Never Taught You*. Warner Books, 1977.

Hearn, Jeff, and Wendy P. Parkin. "Women, Men, and Leadership: A Critical Review of Assumptions, Practices, and Change in the Industrialized Nations," *International Studies of Management and Organization*, 16, 1986/1987, pp. 33-59.

Helgesen, Sally. *The Female Advantage: Women's Ways of Leadership*. Doubleday/Currency, 1990.

Hennig, Margaret and Anne Jardim. *The Managerial Woman: The Survival Manual for Women in Business*. Pocket Books, 1976.

Kanter, Rosabeth Moss. *Men and Women of the Corporation*. Basic Books, 1977.

Loden, Marilyn. *Feminine Leadership or How to Succeed in Business Without Being One of the Boys*. Times Books, 1985.

Lorber, Judith and Susan A. Farrell (Ed.). *The Social Construction of Gender*. Sage Publications, Inc., 1991.

Mainiero, Lisa. "Coping with Powerlessness: The Relationship of Gender and Job Dependency to Empowerment Strategy Usage," *Administrative Science Quarterly*, 31, 1986, pp. 633-653.

Mills, Albert J. and Peta Tancred. *Gendering Organizational Analysis*. Sage Publications, Inc., 1992.

Powell, Gary N. *Women and Men in Management*. Second Edition. Sage Publications, Inc., 1993.

Radtke, H. Lorraine and Henderikus J. Stam (Ed.). *Power/Gender: Social Relations in Theory and Practice*. Sage Publications, Inc., 1994.

Rosener, Judy B. "Ways Women Lead," *Harvard Business Review*, November-December, 1990, pp. 119-125.

Schein, Virginia E. "The Relationship between Sex Role Stereotypes and Requisite Management Characteristics," *Journal of Applied Psychology*, 57, 1973, 95-100.

GENERAL ACCOUNTING OFFICE (GAO)

The General Accounting Office (GAO) serves as the investigative arm of Congress. Its overall mission is to examine and report on all matters relating to the receipt and disbursement of public funds. It was established by the Budget and Accounting Act of 1921 to independently audit government agencies. Since that time Congress has expanded the GAO's audit authority, adding new responsibilities and duties and strengthening its ability to operate independently. The GAO operates under the direction of the Comptroller General of the United States, who is appointed by the President with Senate confirmation and serves for a term of 15 years.

In pursuit of its mission, the GAO conducts a wide variety of activities. These range in practice from auditing the management of the National Aeronautics and Space Administration (NASA) to commenting on airport site selections and the diversity of computer software. The GAO in recent years has issued reports critical of the Federal Aviation Administration's (FAA) ocean traffic system, insurance reserves of the Veterans Administration (VA), contractor accountability in U.S. Department of Energy

(DOE) contracts, and the royalty collection system of the Minerals Management Service. On the positive side it has given government-operated Amtrak's finances approval after a thorough audit.

Audits and evaluations of government programs and activities form a major part of the GAO's work. The GAO may conduct such audits in response to requests from committee chairpersons in Congress as well as from individual members of Congress. Some audits are required by law and others are conducted on the basis of standing commitments to congressional committees. In addition the GAO may undertake audits independently in accordance with its basic responsibility to support Congress.

The GAO also supports Congress by providing it with current, accurate, and complete financial management data. It prescribes accounting principles and standards for the executive branch of government. It advises other federal agencies on fiscal and related policies and procedures. It also prescribes standards for auditing and evaluating government programs. The works with the Secretary of the Treasury and the Director of the Office of Management and Budget (OMB) to develop standardized information and data processing systems.

The GAO also provides legal advice and services to members of Congress. The Comptroller General may issue legal advice concerning government programs and activities as well as for proposed legislation. The GAO also functions to resolve bid protests that challenge the awarding of government contracts. It provides legal services to help adjudicate claims against the government and to assist government agencies interpret laws covering the expenditure of public funds. GAO investigators may assist auditors when they encounter possible criminal and civil misconduct in the course of their work.

The GAO may report its findings by giving testimony before congressional committees, giving members of Congress oral briefings, and issuing written reports. All of the GAO's unclassified reports are available to the public. Every month a list of reports issued or released by the GAO during the previous month is given to the members and committees of Congress. Copies are also furnished to a wide range of interested agencies, state and local government officials, foreign governments, members of the press, libraries, and nonprofit organizations.

The GAO is located at 441 G Street NW, Washington, DC 20548. Copies of GAO reports may be ordered from the U.S. General Accounting Office, P.O. Box 6015, Gaithersburg, MD 20884-6015. The rules and regulations of the GAO are contained in Title 4 of the Code of Federal Regulations.

[David Bianco]

GENERAL AGREEMENT ON TARIFFS AND TRADE (GATT)

The General Agreement on Tariffs and Trade (GATT) is an agreement between nations to promote international economic growth, consisting of legally binding rules by which economic parties trade. The GATT seeks to improve market access through the elimination of trade barriers and regional, preferential economic blocks such as those seen in international commerce during the 1930s. The most recent GATT was officially signed in Marrakesh, Morocco, on April 13, 1994, by 121 countries.

The roots of the GATT organization are in the Bretton Woods Conference of 1944, from which emerged a supranational body, the International Trade Organization (ITO). The role of the ITO was to monitor **economic policy**—that is, tariffs and trade—among economic partners in the West. In 1947, the GATT organization was established. In the immediate aftermath of World War II and the debilitating economic nationalism that preceded it, the United States in particular anticipated the creation of a new economic order and an international treaty and institution to monitor economic policy.

The original GATT membership consisted of 23 nations, but it soon swelled to 84. Under the GATT, trade barriers were to be torn down through multilateral negotiations. As barriers came down, international trade and production would supposedly increase. The GATT first secured these gains through **reciprocity**, i.e. where one country lowers its tariffs to another country's exports so that the other country will in turn lower its tariffs. Second, GATT implemented the "most-favored-nation" status, which is accorded to member countries that do not grant one member or a group of members preferential trade treatment. Trade negotiations since World War II have indeed reduced average tariffs on manufactured and semi-manufactured goods from 40 percent in 1947 to less than ten percent by the mid-1970s. During the early 1990s, that tariff figure dropped to approximately five percent. These reductions helped world trade to surge from $94 billion in 1955 to over $2 trillion in 1980.

Since the late 1970s, however, global trade output has grown at a much slower pace. The early-1990s recession hindered trade cooperation between GATT member countries. During this time three preferential trading blocks arose: the **European Union**, the **North American Free Trade Agreement**, and ASEAN in Southeast Asia. These trading blocks indicated future foreign policy tensions. For example, the United States and Europe, original framers of the GATT, now impose protectionist measures on entire industrial sectors like steel, chemicals, and electronics at the time that formerly protectionist nations of the developing world embrace free market principles and look to join GATT's supposedly open international trading system. Thus despite GATT's aims and past accomplishments, anti-dumping and countervailing-duty measures of member countries—especially through the increasing use of Section 301 of the U.S. Trade Law as well as tariff walls thrown up around the European Community—have resulted in not less but more protectionism since the 1980s.

The latest round of multilateral trade negotiations, launched in 1986 as the Uruguay Round, was designed in large part to reconcile the newfound protectionist principles of GATT member nations with the newfound free market principles of developing nations. These negotiations were a long, drawn-out process, with the concerns of developing nations that wanted to join GATT and attain export-led economic growth often ignored. Instead, the United States fought long and hard to secure significant reforms of Europe's Common Agricultural Policy, which originally aimed to protect the continent's farmers against hardship but which led in time to massive over-production of food and growing government subsidies. Although agriculture is only a small part of economic production among developed nations of the West, the United States saw multilateral farm trade reform—or progressively cutting support and protection of farm sectors—as the litmus test to the success of eventually liberalizing trade in services and especially in protecting **intellectual property**. If the West could liberalize its farm and textile sectors, the United States reasoned, developing countries would in turn open their markets to services and capital of developed economies and offer better protection for intellectual property. If such an agreement could be negotiated, the **World Bank** forecast a $300 billion annual boost to global income.

As many predicted, once American and European Union negotiators reached their own private agreement on trade reform in Brussels on December 15, 1993, the GATT of April 13, 1994, was possible. The final agreement signed in Marrakesh was voluminous, calling for a new World Trade Organization to settle trade disputes as well as tougher anti-dumping rules and sanctions. Four new areas were for the first time covered under GATT: agriculture, textiles, services, and intellectual property rights.

[Etan Vlessing]

GENERAL SERVICES ADMINISTRATION (GSA)

The General Services Administration (GSA) is an agency of the United States federal government and was created in 1949 pursuant to section 101 of the Federal Property and Administrative Services Act. Impetus for creation of the GSA came from a presidential commission's recommendation to Congress. Simply stated the GSA functions as the business agent for the federal government. Structured as a corporation, the GSA is responsible for most of the government's internal business, including purchasing supplies, building construction and maintenance, and various record keeping services. The GSA has more than 37,000 employees and has an annual budget of over $8 billion.

In maintaining the physical plant and meeting the service needs of the federal government, the GSA is involved in a myriad of activities. One of the largest responsibilities of the GSA is maintaining the buildings controlled by the federal government including office structures, warehouses, and laboratories. In total the GSA, through its Public Buildings Service, is responsible for more than 7,200 buildings comprising 250 million square feet of space. The Public Buildings Service is also responsible for the design and construction of new buildings, purchase and sale of real estate, property management and safety, physical security, planning the long-range needs of the government, and procurement and management of the public utilities that service the buildings. Various activities and responsibilities of the Public Buildings Service were strengthened by Presidential Executive Order 12512 (1985), which dealt with the development of a property management information system, and by the Public Buildings Act of 1959 and the subsequent Public Buildings Amendment of 1972, which expanded authority over new construction projects. The Public Buildings Cooperative Use Act of 1976 allowed the Public Buildings Service to lease space in federally owned buildings to commercial tenants and also dealt with the renovation and federal use of historic buildings.

In addition to the Public Buildings Service there are numerous other GSA offices responsible for a wide variety of activities. These offices include:

- The Office of Business, Industry and Governmental Affairs serves a troubleshooting function. This office manages the GSA Ombudsman Program, the Customer Outreach Program and the Business Advisory and Client Advisory Boards.

- The Office of Acquisition Policy is responsible for acquisition programs, establishing and meeting acquisition goals and objectives, overseeing major contracts, and dealing with contractors who default on their obligations. The office is also responsible for administering the Federal Acquisition Regulation, which covers acquisition programs for all federal agencies. The Civilian Agency Acquisition Council, the Federal Acquisition Institute, the Federal Procurement Data System and the Multiple Awards Schedule Program all fall under the purview of the Office of Acquisition Policy.

- The Office of Small and Disadvantaged Business Utilization is responsible for preferential procurement programs. These responsibilities include the Women in Business, Small Business and the Minority Business Enterprise programs.

- The Federal Information Center Program is an information referral program for all facets of federal activity. The center attempts to answer questions relating to federal programs, not just GSA programs.

Other offices include Child Care and Development Programs, Board of Contract Appeals, Information Security Oversight, Information Resources Management Service, Governmentwide Information Resources Management, Agency Management Assistance, Information Resources Management Policy, Information Resources Procurement, **Telecommunications** Service, and the Internal Information Systems Management Service.

[Michael Knes]

FURTHER READING:

U.S. General Services Administration. *What is GSA?* Washington, D.C.: GPO, 1988.

U.S. General Services Administration. *Who is GSA?* Washington, D.C.: GPO, 1980.

U.S. General Services Administration. Office of General Counsel. *Basic Laws and Authorities of the General Services Administration.* Washington, D.C.: GPO, 1987.

GEOGRAPHIC INFORMATION SYSTEMS

Geographic information systems (GIS) are computer-driven methods for integrating digitized data with automated mapping techniques. GIS use this data in displaying the spatial relationships that exist between the features of a landscape—both natural features and cultural features. The study and understanding of these spatial relationships is the essence of geography. These features and their relationships influence a plethora of human endeavors from city planning to retail location to environmental awareness. GIS store data which digitally represent these features and manipulate it onto a mapped format. Once this data is portrayed graphically it can be interpreted for a variety of purposes.

Landscape features exist in time and place and exert influence over one another. Natural features are phenomena such as canyons, lakes, or hills. Cultural features are man-made and may have a physical reality (such as towns, roads, airports, and buildings) or a symbolic reality (such as political boundaries and real estate plats). There is a constant interplay between the features of a landscape. Rain and water from underground springs run down hillsides, collect in low places, and begin to move as creeks or streams. The streams co-mingle and form a river. Using the river as part of a transportation network, people settle on its banks and a town evolves. An entrepreneur buys a piece of riverfront property, has it surveyed and registered, and erects a dock and a warehouse. Eventually, in an effort to increase its freight traffic, a railroad builds a bridge over the river and runs a spur into the town and alongside the warehouse. An understanding of this microcosm of human and natural interactions and activities is incomplete without an understanding of the influence these features and activities have on one another.

Information relating such scenarios as the one above can be collected, digitized, and stored in a database. A GIS can produce a base map of the area and overlay it with information from the database. This information can include facts such as topography, demographic data from census files, soil types, and transportation routes. GIS also have the ability to surround this data with boundaries such as zip codes or land use zones. In essence any information that can be digitized can be reproduced spatially in a map format by a GIS.

Like most other computer operations, the advantage of a GIS is its speed and efficiency. Maps have of course been produced for centuries and overlays can be produced on sheets of transparent polyester film. With GIS, however, the scale of the map and the overlays can be removed or added almost instantaneously. Another key advantage of GIS is the ability to store easily updated data and integrate this data with different forms of information. GIS can take information from such diverse formats as satellite imagery, air pollution analysis, and census statistics and integrate it into a meaningful whole.

Geographic information systems were originally used and appreciated by scientists, especially those in the earth and life sciences. From there GIS quickly migrated into fields concerned with planning, especially city and transportation planning. GIS is now starting to be used in various business fields as diverse as **banking** (mortgage lending, branch locations) and retailing (service areas, store locations). The utility of GIS is best posited by Star and Estes's Four Ms: GIS measures parameters of phenomena, produces maps, monitors changes, and aids in the production of models.

FURTHER READING:

The Local Government Guide to Geographic Information Systems: Planning and Implementation. ICMA, 1991.

Star, Jeffrey, and John Estes. *Geographic Information Systems: An Introduction.* Prentice-Hall, 1990.

U.S. Deptartment of the Interior. U.S. Geological Survey. *Geographic Information Systems.* Washington, D.C., 1991.

GERMAN ECONOMIC, MONETARY & SOCIAL UNION (GEMSU)

The German Economic, Monetary & Social Union (GEMSU) was one of four accords that brought about the reunification of the German state. Signed May 18, 1990, it represented an economic, monetary, and fiscal agreement between the Federal Republic of Germany (West Germany) and the German Democratic Republic (East Germany). Because it was the first of four treaties to be signed, GEMSU laid the groundwork for the others. The other three agreements were the East-West Election Treaty (August 20, 1990), the Unification Treaty (August 31, 1990), and the final reunification accord, the Two-Plus-Four Treaty on the Final Settlement with Respect to Germany (September 12, 1990). GEMSU dealt with establishing an economic basis for reunification between the two countries while the other treaties addressed social and political issues.

Following Germany's defeat by the allied powers in World War II, the country was divided into two states: West Germany (occupied by Great Britain, France, and the United States) and East Germany (a satellite of the former Soviet Union). Both Germanys became sovereign states, but West Germany prospered under a capitalist market economy with a strong western orientation while East Germany stagnated under communist rule. By the 1980s the annual **gross national product** (GNP) of West Germany was over $800 billion while the GNP of East Germany was only $207 billion. Throughout the cold war, the two Germanys remained ideological foes, but the concept of a unified Germany still lived in the minds of many German citizens and political leaders. There were two major roadblocks to reunification, however: the former Soviet Union was unalterably opposed to a single German state, and East Germany remained just strong enough to resist reunification out of fear of being economically overwhelmed by its richer neighbor to the west. Furthermore, given Germany's penchant for military adventurism, many other European states,

most notably France and Poland, were content with the status quo.

All of this changed with the coming to power of Mikhail Gorbachev, the subsequent dissolution of the former Soviet Union, and its loss of authoritarian control of eastern Europe. In 1989 when Erich Honecker was forced to resign as head of faltering East Germany, its citizens began streaming into West Germany in unprecedented numbers. On November 9, 1989, the East German government began dismantling the Berlin Wall, long a symbol of a divided Germany. The United States gave diplomatic credence to the concept of a single German state, and a reunited Germany seemed suddenly imminent.

With the rapid crumbling of political stability and the social infrastructure of East Germany, Chancellor Helmut Kohl of West Germany was forced to act quickly to prevent the German Democratic Republic from slipping into total chaos. By early 1990, the Kohl administration moved toward economic union. Although it was more than a year ahead of schedule, the administration believed economic union (albeit a hurried one) would serve to stabilize East Germany, integrate it into various West German fiscal and monetary institutions and practices, and serve as a symbol of West German commitment to helping its eastern neighbor.

The German Economic, Monetary & Social Union treaty established the West German deutsche mark as the official unit of currency in the central German bank, and made the Deutsche Bundesbank the sole authority for monetary policy. East Germany would also adopt an economy featuring private ownership, marketplace economics, competition, and the free movement of labor and capital. The German Democratic Republic would also begin a general privatization of its economy. The German economic unity treaty allowed East Germans a one-for-one exchange ratio between privately held East German marks and West German deutsche marks (up to 4,000 marks). Pension benefits and wages also would remain on a one-for-one basis. Other holdings of East German marks could be exchanged at a ratio of two-for-one. East Germans would begin paying West German taxes, including taxes for unemployment benefits and social security. The East Germans would conversely be eligible for West German unemployment and pension benefits. The treaty also had provisions covering limits on East German borrowing, real estate purchases in East Germany by western commercial interests, and West German medical benefits and housing subsidies for East German citizens.

The German Economic, Monetary & Social Union was signed in Bonn by the German Democratic Republic's Finance Minister, Walter Romberg, and the Federal Republic of Germany's Finance Minister,

Theo Waigel. GEMSU was a precursor to the Two-Plus-Four Treaty which resulted in the almost total economic, social, and political absorption of the German Democratic Republic by the Federal Republic of Germany.

[Michael Knes]

FURTHER READING:

Neckermann, Peter. *The Unification of Germany*. East European Monographs/Columbia University Press, 1991.

Pond, Elizabeth. *Beyond the Wall: Germany's Road to Unification*. Brookings Institution, 1993.

GLASS CEILING

The "glass ceiling" is the term used to describe barriers that prevent women and other minorities from advancing to management positions in corporations and organizations. The phrase was first used about 1985 or 1986. Statistics provided by the U.S. Department of Labor indicated only 2 percent of top level management jobs and 5 percent of corporate board positions were held by women as of 1987. The failure of more women and minorities to crack the upper levels of corporate management is due to the glass ceiling. The **Civil Rights Act of 1991** created a Glass Ceiling Commission to address these inequities, just as the Glass Ceiling Initiative, created in 1989 by the Department of Labor (DOL) under the leadership of secretary Lynn Martin had done.

Statistics prove beyond doubt that a glass ceiling existed long before the term was introduced. These barriers to minority progress had previously defied clear definition but, in the late 1980s, the glass ceiling became part of the language of management literature. Several articles in publications such as the *Wall Street Journal* detailed the increase of women in administrative and management level jobs, from 24 to 37 percent over a period from 1976 to 1987. Yet the glass ceiling blocked women from rising to top management positions as mentioned above. On March 24, 1986, a special 32-page section of the *Wall Street Journal* did much to define the glass ceiling for women. The inclusion of other minorities would follow. This report did much to bring full light to the ceiling in the corporate world. Using interviews and data to highlight the issues, the *Journal* report was the first landmark publication of a powerful voice in employment equity. Another significant work was published in 1987. Sponsored by the Center for Creative Leadership and written by Ann Morrison, *Breaking the Glass Ceiling* did much to synthesize the data and attitudes on the invisible barriers as well as outline the problems, provide a formula for success, and describe the pattern of future progress in breaking the ceiling. The conclusions of the study pointed to few true differences between men and women in psychological, emotional, or intellectual qualities, but contradictions in the expectations for women were a major factor in the glass ceiling. Women were expected to be tough but not display "macho" characteristics; they were expected to take responsibility yet be obedient in following orders; and expectations were for women to be ambitious yet not to expect equal treatment. Also, the glass ceiling applied to women as a group, not just individuals.

DOL data supported the independent conclusions of the findings of the Center for Creative Leadership team and those of the Catalyst, a New York-based research organization which advised corporations on how to foster the careers of women. The DOL's analysis of 94 corporate headquarters of *Fortune* 1000 companies for a three-year period indicated of a total of nearly 150,000 employees, 37.2 percent were women and 15.5 percent were minorities. Of 31,184 management-level employees, 5,278 (16.9 percent) were women and 1,885 (6 percent) were minorities. At the executive level, women represented only 6.6 percent and minorities an even smaller 2.6 percent. Other studies identified similar statistics, another factor that reinforced other findings and eventually led to greater DOL involvement. In a separate study, the Catalyst also identified a glass wall, a restriction on women's lateral mobility, so necessary for gaining relevant corporate experience. The organization studied employment and advancement trends for women in financial services, manufacturing, food and beverage industries, fashion retail merchandising, and high-technology corporations. Women face this glass wall early in their careers and miss opportunities for progressive training. Following the wall, the glass ceiling naturally limits upward advancement.

THE GLASS CEILING INITIATIVE

The glass ceiling spreads beyond the corporate environment. Among the first institutions to recognize the existence of the invisible barriers was the federal government. Recognition of dramatic changes in the economy and the workforce appeared in a formidable report published by the DOL in 1987. *Workforce 2000* was a 117-page document which helped to increase awareness of the role of women and minorities, it also defined the so-called "glass ceiling" with its various barriers. Out of *Workforce 2000* developed the Glass Ceiling Initiative, a DOL program intended to survey corporate America to identify the problems, causes, and solutions to the ceiling. The driving force behind the initiative was Elizabeth Dole, Secretary of Labor in the Bush administration. The Glass Ceiling Initiative called for an investigation set to begin in the fall of 1989. Nine *Fortune* 500 companies (representing a broad range of businesses) would be selected at random for review. Independent compliance reviews were conducted to explore the glass ceiling fully. Stated goals were to promote a diverse work force; to promote corporate conduct conducive to cooperative problem solving; to promote **equal opportunity**; and, to establish a DOL blueprint for future reviews at all management levels. The department's Office of Federal Contract Compliance Programs (OFCCP) was charged with conducting the reviews.

The initiative had four major components, including: (1) to educate DOL officials; (2) to conduct reviews; (3) to promote efforts to remove barriers to minority advancement; and (4) to reward contractors who demonstrated exemplary efforts. The program was designed to produce specific results—including identifying barriers, eliminating the problems, and increasing awareness of these barriers and the resulting discrimination. In February 1991 Lynn Martin replaced Elizabeth Dole and inherited the leadership of the Glass Ceiling Initiative. The first report from the extensive studies was issued on August 8, 1991.

None of the nine companies under review were cited for discriminatory practices, but a number of them failed to comply fully with all affirmative action requirements. The DOL realized a review of such a small sample was not an especially scientific study but there was ample evidence that the progress of women and minorities in management positions was blocked by considerably more than qualifications and career directions. The initiative found organizational and attitudinal barriers as strong obstacles to minority advancement. These barriers included three major categories. First was recruitment practices which centered on word-of-mouth and referral networking. Additionally, executive search firms and job referral firms used by the companies ignored many affirmative action/equal employment opportunity requirements. Secondly, several career advancement opportunities were often unavailable to women and minorities. These included credential-building experiences such as advanced education, developmental practices, and assignments essential to career enhancement. The report went further to conclude that if there was not a glass ceiling, there was a point beyond which women and minorities had not advanced. Minority advancement was seen as more restrictive than that of women. Corporations generally ignored responsibility for monitoring equal access and opportunity for advancement as well as compensation systems. Research data did not generally support placement patterns and, finally, there was a serious lack of adequate record keeping. The report also found the ceiling existed also at a lower level than previously assumed. In summary, the barriers to advancement for women and minorities created a glass ceiling, and the DOL was determined to ensure promotion of advancement opportunities guaranteed by law.

Response to the Glass Ceiling Initiative was predictable—criticisms of flaws in methodology and the small sample size. But the DOL stood by the conclusions and urged change and compliance. Almost immediately, the department continued the compliance reviews in a second round of follow-up reviews. The report of this series of OFCCP, *Pipelines of Progress*, was published in August 1992. *Pipelines of Progress* had a good news/bad news approach—numbers of minorities and women participating in higher levels of management had shown an increase, but the future of change was still limited by the ever present ceiling. Corporations had adopted diversity training and equal opportunity had received a renewed emphasis. Yet the same employers had failed to recruit for top management from a diverse candidate pool and had not provided training for minorities and women. Women with equal or superior educational attainments earned less on average than men in top level positions. Corporate leadership lacked a firm commitment to organizational responsibility for equal employment opportunity. Women expressed concern over access to mobility cited as necessary for climbing the corporate ladder and being held to different expectations of performance measures. Finally, *Pipelines of Progress* identified creative measures that worked. These included tracking the progress of women and minorities with advancement potential, ensuring equal access to corporate developmental opportunities, creating an environment for a bias-free workplace, and a conscious effort to hire qualified women and minorities in entry-level professional positions. The DOL once again confirmed its commitment to identify and eliminate the glass ceiling.

In the same year, a second edition of Morrison's *Breaking the Glass Ceiling* was published, citing progress made in hurdling the barriers but still criticizing corrective measures not yet enacted. But the most significant event after the work of the Glass Ceiling Initiative was the passage of the sweeping Civil Rights Act of 1991 which included legislation designated the Glass Ceiling Act of 1991. Sponsored by, among others, Kansas senator Robert Dole, the Glass Ceiling Act followed up the initial findings of the initiative by creating the Glass Ceiling Commission.

THE GLASS CEILING COMMISSION

Taking impetus from the Glass Ceiling Initiative, the Glass Ceiling Commission was established to study how businesses filled management and decision-making positions, corporate policies intended to provide career and skill enhancing opportunities, and current compensation programs and packages. The purpose of the studies was to develop recommendations aimed at eliminating the barriers to furthering the careers of women and minorities—simply stated, to break the glass ceiling. Almost unnoticed was the fact of increased awareness and the legislative body of the United States admitting there was a glass ceiling. Membership of the commission included 21 members—6 appointed by the President, 6 more selected by a joint decision of the Speaker of the House and the Senate Majority Leader, 1 member each appointed by the majority and minority leaders of the House and Senate, 2 House and 2 Senate members; it was chaired by the Secretary of Labor. Consideration was given to appointing representatives of women's and minority organizations, business leaders recognized as having positive attitudes on equal employment opportunity, and academics or others with expertise on employment issues, all intended to create a workable balance. The commission was to hold at least five open meetings in order to hear from a broad constituency base. These meetings were set up for the purpose of information gathering on all issues affecting women and men in employment issues. While having no subpoena power, information from federal agencies was made available for its use. Consultants and experts could be utilized within the budgetary power of the commission. The act set a date of 15 months for submission of a report to the president and Congress but at the same time gave the commission a four-year life span. Considering the past history of a lack of sympathetic understanding and awareness of the employment concerns of women and minorities, establishment of the Glass Ceiling Commission was indeed a remarkable event.

Even before the initial commission meeting, the scope of the body became more clearly defined. First, the promotion of workforce diversity was considered to be part of the group's function. As interviews for commission members proceeded, the task was expanded to include small and medium-sized businesses and a working relationship with the **Small Business Administration (SBA)**. Small business operations employed 54.3 million Americans. Statistics showed that women had started new businesses at twice the rate of men in recent years, an indirect benefit of the glass ceiling to women in business. Black-owned businesses had grown by about 40 percent, those owned by Hispanic Americans by 80 percent, and Asian American-owned businesses had increased over 90 percent. *Pipelines of Progress* had identified a trend that women and minorities were judged on what they had done, while men were evaluated on what they could do. The findings of the Glass Ceiling Initiative combined with the data and various hypotheses as the basis for the work of the commission.

By September 1992 commission members appointed included blacks, women, a Hispanic American, and Henry Tang, an Asian American and vice president of Solomon Brothers in New York. Two of the more outspoken members were Carol Cox Wait, president and chief executive officer of the Committee for a Responsible Federal Budget and head of a consulting group, and J. Alphonso Brown, founder of Brown Consulting Group. Senator Dole was also a member. Prior to the first commission session, Secretary of Labor Martin, as chair, sought input from the management of media outlets such as the New York Times Company, and Time Inc., and 20 college presidents. She also indicated a third round of OFCCP compliance reviews would target a media organization and an institution of higher education.

The initial meeting was held in Washington on October 2. Brown immediately questioned the balance of women's issues outweighing minority concerns. Before an audience of mostly white women, Martin assured him the commission would attempt to be sensitive to all groups. Tang warned of the far-reaching economic impact of the effects of the glass ceiling. Future meeting sites included Kansas City, Atlanta, Los Angeles, Dallas, and New York, with others possible. In November, compliance reviews were expanded to include health-care providers, financial services institutions, and law firms. Martin resigned her cabinet post with the new administration, and was replaced by Robert Reich, who named Joyce Miller as executive director of the Glass Ceiling Commission in April of 1993. Miller had previously been vice president and director of social services for the Amalgamated Clothing and Textile Workers Union, and she aggressively continued to expand the commission's focus. In June a wider range of jobs other than top management positions was added to the studies, especially those at the "mud floor," or dead-end, low-status, low-wage jobs.

Other agencies and organizations held their own hearings or conferences on the glass ceiling. In June 1993 the Small Business Committee in Congress scheduled a hearing and, at the Women's National Democratic Club the same month in Washington, a glass ceiling forum met with more revelations about women in employment. For many women, stereotypes about female employees and differences in their work-related learning patterns contributed to the ceiling. Stereotypes led to a narrow band of acceptable behavior for women and they pursued work-related learning differently. A survey showed that a greater percentage of women had a stronger tendency toward personal development than men, but more emphasis was needed in technical styles of learning. These and other conclusions moved the ceiling beyond awareness and toward household recognition. The Senate subcommittee on Employment and Productivity had held extensive hearings as early as October 1991. Awareness was seldom mentioned again as a problem.

The first commission meeting under new President Bill Clinton was in late June 1993. In addition to reiterating a commitment to eliminating barriers, the commission recognized a subtle but meaningful change, based on the premise that the glass ceiling was built first and lower for minorities than for women. The wording of the phrase women and minorities was altered to minorities and women to reflect this emphasis.

A pivotal hearing was held in Dallas in early December. Covenants were introduced as a new strategy for penetrating and breaking the ceiling. The covenant was a corporate organizational agreement to disclose how women and minorities were advancing into top management positions. The city government of Dallas had encouraged over 200 businesses with contracts with the city to go public in relation to minority advancement, and a women's covenant was the next target. Mentoring programs were cited as a working solution to minority advancement. Other directions included summer intern programs for minorities and women as well as recruiting at traditionally African-American universities and colleges. While noting slow progress, the commission heard from a broad range of businesses, from professional basketball to law firms. Commission members did agree on one key ingredient to success—commitment from top management. In a post-hearing interview, director Miller pointed to solutions, not the problem. She said the focus had changed since initial DOL involvement to include anyone who wanted to move up in the workforce. Native Americans and disabled workers were part of the focus. Since 64 percent of new entrants into the job market were women or minorities, the ceiling would eliminate a great many talents and abilities of a large army of workers. Only a diversity program would ensure the breaking down of barriers in employment—what Miller termed ''smart business.'' Although uncertain of new legislative proposals developing from the commission's report, she did cite the need for increased enforcement.

The April 1994 hearing was held in Cleveland, where the commission was told that shattering the glass ceiling was indeed a daunting task. One witness reported the barriers were stronger than ever in retailing. Engineering was seen as another area where progress lagged far behind expectations. Minorities and women hired at the same entry-level pay as men rapidly fell behind in a field (engineering) dominated by paternalistic attitudes. Evidence was introduced that there was no equity in professional sports. The OFCCP deputy director pointed out that generally the **chief executive officer**s now understood the goal and compliance reviews would number 40 in 1994 with an equal number primed for 1995.

In June Miller resigned as executive director to become an adviser on health-care reform to Labor Secretary Reich. Rene Redwood was named to the director's post in May 1994. Redwood's prior experience included work as a consultant and district office director to District of Columbia congresswoman Eleanor Holmes Norton. At the commission's August meeting in Atlanta, Redwood announced the commission would report by January 1, 1995. She commented the report would be pragmatic and implementable and would not be shelved away to ignore. At the final meeting in September, Secretary Reich repeated earlier statements that the elimination of the glass ceiling had to start at the top of organizations. He compared the ceiling to the imposing architectural presence of the Capitol Dome in Washington employment circles. Despite the series of open forums and various testimonies representing numerous minority interests, many members of the Glass Ceiling Commission felt they still lacked substantial information necessary for their report to Congress on the causes of discrimination. Member Carol Cox Wait expressed concern over wasting three million taxpayer dollars by failing to identify the root causes of the problem. Tang agreed, citing the lack of new knowledge. Several commission members wanted to retain the January 1995 reporting date, but still be able to provide additional materials and information at a later time.

During the fall of 1994, several important awards aimed at perpetrators of the glass ceiling were announced. In September, Georgia Power, Marriott International, and WordPerfect Corp. all agreed to pay nearly $500,000 to 68 women and minority employees who were paid a lower wage than others doing comparable work. The Atlanta-based Georgia Power agreed to pay over $210,000 to 23 individuals, Marriott awarded $167,000 to 40 top-level staff members, and WordPerfect made payments of approximately $140,000 to only 5 employees. These awards followed upon a September 1993 settlement of almost $600,000 paid to a group of 52 women by Fairfax Hospital in northern Virginia. Another significant jury award in November 1994 paid $343,000 to a woman employed by Hondo Inc., of Chicago, a franchisee of Coca-Cola Co. The woman, an 18-year manager with Hondo, had been passed over for promotions on numerous occasions and was, as her attorney concluded, a victim of the ''old boys network.''

On March 8, 1995 the commission voted to accept the final report. Nineteen members voted in the affirmative, one did not indicate a vote, and another withdrew from the commission due to time constraints. The report, *Good for Business: Making Full Use of the Nation's Human Capital*, was released on March 16. Criticisms of the ceiling dominated the report, which indicated 60 percent of the country's population is represented in 7 percent of the jobs. The report labeled progress discouragingly slow despite recognition by America's corporate leadership of the existence of a glass ceiling, a ceiling the final report characterized as firmly in place as a barrier to the advancement of women and minorities in upper management positions at three levels—government, business, and society. Minorities and women expressed dismay and anger at the ceiling, despite corporate promises to correct the problems. In order to provide positive examples of breaking the glass ceiling, the report included brief descriptions of dozens of practices used by some companies to advance minorities and women.

The initial report was disappointing to the extent that recommendations were not included. The Glass Ceiling Commission, after four years, still faces the task of agreeing on recommendations to eliminate the barriers. Those recommendations are expected by the end of November 1995, but if they follow a course similar to the commission's report, it may well be into 1996 before recommendations are made public. One member said this was the difficult work to be done.

The Glass Ceiling Initiative was the catalyst for the Glass Ceiling Commission. Encountering barriers at all angles, women and minorities still have to overcome ingrained obstacles to career fulfillment and potential. Expectations for solutions in the commission's report ran high, but the future remains uncertain beyond the glass ceiling.

[Boyd Childress]

FURTHER READING:

Bureau of National Affairs. *Daily Labor Report.* 1995.

Bureau of National Affairs. *Good for Business: Making Full Use of the Nation's Human Capital.* 1995.

Morrison, Ann M., and others. *Breaking the Glass Ceiling: Can Women Reach the Top of America's Largest Corporations?* Addison-Wesley, 1987.

Morrison, Ann M., and others. *Breaking the Glass Ceiling: Can Women Reach the Top of America's Largest Corporations?* 2nd ed. Addison-Wesley, 1992.

U.S. Department of Labor. *Pipelines of Progress: An Update on the Glass Ceiling Initiative.* Washington, DC: GPO, 1992.

U.S. Department of Labor. *A Report on the Glass Ceiling Initiative.* Washington, DC: GPO, 1991.

GLOBAL STRATEGY

Global strategy on the micro level pertains to the allocation of a company's resources in a manner that will take advantage of profit opportunities outside of domestic markets. In its broadest interpretation, that definition encompasses activities such as overseas manufacturing, foreign investing, and importing. This text, however, views global strategy primarily within the context of marketing-related activities, such as **exporting**, **licensing**, and partnering in foreign countries to sell goods and services abroad. In general, global marketing strategies encompass three basic decision areas faced by individual organizations: 1) whether or not to engage in foreign trade; 2) what specific markets should be served, including product, geographic, and demographic markets; and 3) how to participate in chosen markets, including strategies related to product planning, financing, promotion, distribution, and price.

On the macro level, global strategy is used by regions, countries, trading partners, and other entities to accomplish broad economic objectives related to foreign trade and competition. For example, most countries impose a variety of tariffs, quotas, and other restrictions on incoming goods. Likewise, groups of nations often form self-serving trade agreements that exclude other countries or global regions. And nations or states may engage in strategies, through tools such as tax incentives or government-sponsored promotions, intended to improve global competitiveness of help companies in their locale. All of these macro-level initiatives influence strategy at the micro level.

Discussed below are three basic theories of global trade, the chief benefits of global marketing, influences that dictate global strategies, and the four fundamental approaches to participating in foreign markets.

BACKGROUND

The international exchange of goods has been conducted for thousands of years through voluntary trade and by means of military conquest. However, the mercantilist era, which lasted from about 1500 to 1750, laid the foundation for, and continues to have a strong influence on, the modern practice of international trade. It was during that period that the philosophy of nationalism emerged, thus diminishing tribal and regional rivalries and creating unified nations-states. Nationalism gave rise to the view that trade was integral to the national interest, and should therefore be controlled by the government. Foreign trade was generally viewed as a form of rivalry similar to war—one nation gained at the expense of another.

Another ideology that characterized mercantilism was that a nation's wealth is measured in gold and silver, which implied that more bullion should come into the country than should go out. This idea is reflected in modern trade theory by the notion that a country is succeeding in the global trade arena only if it has a favorable trade balance, or exports more than it imports. The contrasting creed, exampled in the 20th century by both Soviet and Nazi regimes, held that a country should seek to import more goods than it exports as a means of increasing aggregate national wealth. A pivotal difference between the two tenets was that the triumphant mercantilist philosophy is more amenable to individual firms, which seek to maximize sales and thus benefit from increased exports.

Many of the negative elements of mercantilism were diminished during the late 18th and 19th centuries. The belief that gold was the purest measure of wealth, for example, was debunked by the advent of modern economic theory. The superseding wisdom held that a nation's money, or gold, is less of a measure of wealth than it is a determinant of price levels. For instance, the quantity theory posited that as a country's trade balance improved, its prices would rise. As a result, exports would decline in volume and imports would rise because of their comparatively lower price, which would have a balancing effect. Such theories contributed to abandonment of the gold standard by the United States and other nations during the middle 1900s.

A second negative concept of mercantilism—that trade is adversarial by nature and necessitates government control—was largely obliterated by Adam Smith's *Wealth of Nations*. That treatise postulated the "invisible hand" theory of market forces, which essentially displaced mercantilism. It served to reduce government control of foreign trade and foster a less confrontational trade climate. In addition to evolving economic paradigms, global trade strategy was particularly impacted by the events of the middle 20th century that effectively made world markets more accessible—technological advances related to communications, transportation, refrigeration and preservatives, and manufacturing combined to reduce many of the logistical barriers to international trade. Technological advances also served to minimize cultural and political differences between countries.

Evidencing the notable trend toward trade cooperativeness were numerous efforts by European nations between the 1950s and early 1990s to form trade agreements and establish economic unity. These included the Organization for European Economic Cooperation (OEEC) of 1948, the European Coal and Steel Community (ECSC) in 1952, the **European Free Trade Association (EFTA)** in 1960, and continuing efforts to cement the European Economic Community. Major initiatives highlighting this trend in other parts of the world during that period were: the **Organization of Petroleum Exporting Countries (OPEC)**: the **North American Free Trade Agreement** (NAFTA); the New International Economic Order (NIEO), a consortium of 77 poor countries; and attempts to enact the sweeping **General Agreement on Tariffs and Trade** (GATT), which would reduce tariffs and other political **trade barriers** reminiscent of the mercantilist era.

As a result of overall trade trends, global strategy at the macro level became a vital link to economic progress for many nations during the latter half of the 20th century. Furthermore, these trends were augmented in the 1970s and 1980s by a simultaneous slowdown in U.S. domestic market growth and the resurgence of former manufacturing powers in Europe and Japan. The overall implications of these developments for the United States, and for many other industrialized nations, was a vastly heightened impact of imports and exports on lifestyles and living standards. Thus, global strategy received greater emphasis on both the micro and macro levels.

GLOBAL TRADE THEORY

There are at least three major theories that explain the dynamics behind macro-level global strategies: classical, proportion, and product life cycle. The classical theory of international trade is based on the notion of economic advantage, which suggests that countries naturally emphasize foreign sales of products (and services) that they can produce cheaper or better—all other factors aside, a nation acting in its best interest will only import products that it has the greatest advantage in producing. The three types of advantages encompassed by classical theory are absolute, comparative, and equal. These advantages are the impetus behind international trade and price differences, and demonstrate the role of exchange rates as defined by the quantity theory.

A nation has an absolute advantage over another country when it is able to produce a product(s) at a lower price or higher quality level. Absolute advantages may be acquired, such as advanced technological abilities, or natural, such as access to natural resources. A comparative advantage exists when a country has an absolute advantage over a trading partner in many products, but the advantages are comparatively different. In this case, the country at a disadvantage may still be able to benefit (because of exchange ratio dynamics) by specializing in, and exporting, the product(s) in which it maintains the least disadvantage. Finally, an equal advantage exists when one country has an absolute advantage in all products. In this case, the countries cannot theoretically gain by trading because exchange ratios would cancel any economic gain.

The second global trade theory is factor proportion. It goes further than the classical theory in explaining the reasons behind prices and costs. It asserts that price levels differ amongst countries primarily because of factors related to the supply of natural resources. Thus, a country will generally export goods for which it has an abundant and accessible amount of an input, and it will import goods for which inputs are relatively inaccessible. This theory assumes relatively equal levels of production and technological prowess amongst competing countries.

The third trade theory, product life cycle, gained appeal during the late 1900s. It takes into account factors like technology and innovation to explain foreign trade forces, and places less emphasis on the role of prices and exchange rates. The product life cycle encompasses four phases. During the first, a new product is manufactured in the home country and succeeds partially because of local advantages, such as ease of distribution and marketing. During the second phase, the originating country benefits as the product gains familiarity in other countries (despite localized competitive disadvantages) because of its uniqueness. As a result, manufacturers in other countries begin copying the product. The third phase is characterized by competition, which increases as countries with competitive advantages, such as low labor costs, begin exporting the good or service. Finally, the country that originated the product succumbs to more competitive foreign producers that cannibalize its global and domestic market share. By that time, the product is often considered a commodity.

PRACTICAL GLOBAL BENEFITS

While theories help to provide a framework for the causes and dynamics of global trade, most countries and companies engage in strategic global initiatives to take advantage of very tangible benefits. Nations and regions pursue global trade primarily to capitalize on opportunities related to specialization and advantages, as described above. Individual companies that strive to expand globally may do so for a number of reasons related to improving profits.

A primary and obvious benefit for companies that sell products in foreign countries is access to new markets. Indeed, when markets for many products in the United States began to mature and become saturated in the 1970s and 1980s, many producers found that they could continue to achieve steady sales and profit gains through cross-border sales. This provided relief not only from maturing domestic markets, but also from intensifying competition from Europe and Japan. Because markets in other countries are often less mature and less competitive, companies can typically achieve rapid sales growth and higher profit margins. For example, although Coca-Cola received less than 40 percent of its revenues from foreign sales in the early 1990s, nearly 60 percent of its total profits came from those sales.

Another impetus for firms to engage in a global strategy relates to product life-cycles. Goods that have become obsolete in U.S. markets, for example, can sometimes be marketed abroad very successfully. By increasing a product's life span, a company is able to reduce new product development costs and capitalize on learned efficiencies particular to the product related to production, distribution, and marketing. Like-

wise, global selling often provides various tax benefits. Many countries, in fact, strive to attract foreign business activity by offering reduced import, property, or income taxes. Furthermore, companies are often able to allocate revenues, costs, and profits in such a way that reduces their overall tax burden.

Another major benefit of an integrated multinational approach is market risk diversification. In other words, a company can generally lessen its vulnerability to cyclical economic downswings or regional disturbances by extending its geographic reach. For instance, companies that were active in both the United States and Western Europe during the late 1980s likely benefitted from the lag between the U.S. recession and the European Community economic slump that peaked several months later, just when the United States was beginning to cycle out of its downturn. In addition, geographic diversification lessens risks affiliated with product cycles, seasonality inherent to some products (such as ski equipment), and increased competition in individual regions.

Besides benefits related to marketing goods and services (on which this text focuses), global strategy also offers benefits related to overseas manufacturing, partnering with foreign firms to develop or market products, foreign investing, **hedging** exchange rates, or importing goods or services to augment domestic efforts. For example, firms can often profit by moving their production facilities to areas that have lower labor costs, cheaper natural resources, less government regulation, more efficient access to neighboring export markets, or other advantages that bolster productivity. Or, they may be able to benefit from the effects of diversification through foreign investments—an insurance company, for example, could potentially reduce its financial risk by investing surplus funds in Japan or Germany.

EXTERNAL INFLUENCES ON GLOBAL STRATEGY

Three realms of influence outside of the control of a country or organization affect the determination of global strategy on the both the micro and macro levels: economic and competitive, political and legal, and cultural.

ECONOMIC AND COMPETITIVE INFLUENCES

Among the most fundamental precepts of global strategy is market concentration. Companies and countries striving to develop a successful global trade or marketing strategy realize, sooner or later, that they should focus their efforts on a small segment of the global market. For instance, although they contain only 20 percent of the world's population, Japan, Europe, and the United States make up a hefty 75 percent of the global economy. Furthermore, within each of those countries the majority of the wealth is controlled by a small fraction of the population. Therefore, a company can become truly dominant on a global scale by focusing on a few key markets. Conversely, it can easily fail by spreading its efforts too thin regionally.

Among the most important considerations for a company selecting regions to consider for trade is stage of economic development. Aside from political and social risks, countries at relatively mature stages of industrialization are most likely to offer healthy export markets. They generally have a more equitable distribution of buying power and possess societies that are more amenable to new products and technologies. In addition, industrial and post-industrial nations offer other key benefits, such as: a stable fiscal and monetary infrastructure; currency stability, which reduces risks associated with the rapid rise or fall of the value of investments in the host country; communication **infrastructure**, which eases marketing efforts; and transportation systems necessary for the efficient distribution of goods and services.

Influences ancillary to the economic environment include competitive forces that help to dictate global strategy. Although industrial societies typically offer better opportunities for global marketing, they also usually entail more acute competitive pressures. For instance, different countries may sport different levels of competition for various products ranging from a monopolistic country or product environment, which would be inaccessible, to pure competition. A company may also be able to compete, and even benefit from, a more oligopolistic environment in which a few major companies dominate the regional market.

Other competitive forces to consider include the threat of new entrants into the market. If barriers to entry are low and a company has few proprietary advantages, competitive risks may be elevated. The product or service is also vulnerable if it can be easily replaced by a substitute when market conditions change. For example, buyers might switch from boxed cereal to oatmeal to save money during a recession. Also of import is the bargaining power of buyers and suppliers in the host country. If a company is in a relatively weak bargaining position, particularly in relation to its competitors, its profitability could become overly dependent on supply and distribution channels. Existing competition is also a concern, as established brands and products can wreak havoc on the profitability of a new entrant.

POLITICAL AND LEGAL INFLUENCES

The chief consideration facing a company in choosing to enter a foreign market, or a country trying to determine trade policy, is the political stability and

legal environment of the host country. A third world nation with a history of revolt and instability, for example, would likely make a poor prospect for trade. Even an advanced industrialized nation could be a poor prospect, however, if its legal and political environment is generally hostile toward foreign competitors.

Most governments establish restrictions or **trade barriers** on foreign **competition**, most of which are designed to protect domestic industries and companies. These controls often dictate a firm's level of activity in an oversees market. A common control is license requirements, which force importers (exporters) to obtain a license before they can move the product into (out of) a country. For instance, a country may restrict the exporting of goods deemed to have military value. Or, the host may refuse to license goods for import that compete with a domestic industry that it is trying to support.

A second type of control is tariffs, or **taxes**, on imports. Like **license agreements**, tariffs are often used to protect domestic companies and industries from competition. However, tariffs may also be used to ensure that the prices of imported goods are equivalent to domestic substitutes, or to garner revenue for the government. In addition, tariffs are often used to penalize other countries for trade or political actions. The United States, for instance, may elect to impose a tariff on trucks from Japan to punish it for erecting a large tariff on rice imported from the United States.

A quota is simply a provision that limits the amount of a specific product that can be imported. Like tariffs, quotas may be established for a number of reasons. "Absolute" quotas provide a definite import quantity that can't be exceeded. "Tariff" quotas subject import volumes above a specified level to increasingly higher tariffs. Finally, "voluntary" quotas, or voluntary export restraints (VERs), are used to protect domestic companies from a particular competitor or in a special situation in which an industry is trying to regain it ability to compete.

Besides licenses, tariffs, and quotas, other control mechanisms include: special taxes, such as excise or processing taxes on certain products; qualitative restrictions, which specify minimum standards of quality or safety that must be achieved before the country will accept it for import or export; and exchange controls, which effectively limit the amount of foreign currency that an importer can obtain to pay for goods purchased, or that an exporter can hold for goods sold to another country.

Besides controls and restrictions that affect global trade strategies, most countries also engage in promotional activities designed to foster foreign exchange. These policies can hurt exporters competing against subsidized products, or help them if their country is doing the promotion. The two principal types of promotions are state trading and subsidies. State trading entails direct government involvement in buying and selling activities. State trading is practiced most vigorously by countries with command-type economies, like Russia. Subsidies, like tariffs and quotas, are often used to help an industry. They include benefits such as lower taxes, lower transportation rates, manipulation of exchange rates in favor of the exporter, or even direct government grants.

CULTURAL INFLUENCES

The third major external factor influencing macro and micro global strategy is the cultural and social environment, including elements such as social class, family structure and decision-making, market segmentation, and consumption patterns. Because a grasp of culture is so integral to the marketing process, companies that try to conduct business in a foreign country typically seek the counsel of someone close to that culture. Or, they will simply form some type of partnership or legal arrangement to have their product or service marketed by a local company.

Of primary concern to the global strategist is the level of material culture in each considered region. For instance, societies with less advanced material cultures, particularly non- or semi-industrialized nations, will generally necessitate more limited product lines, less sophisticated distribution systems, simpler advertisements, and a greater amount of time to accept a new product or service. Likewise, language differences can pose another formidable barrier to multinationals. Even within a diverse country, such as Spain or China, several different languages or dialects will impact a comprehensive sales strategy.

Another major cultural influences is aesthetics, which refers to a society's artistic sense. This element is particularly important for decisions related to advertising, packaging, and product design. Similarly, the general educational level of a society will dictate the sophistication of products, packaging, and promotions. But it may also impact strategy relating to supply and distribution channels that must be staffed by locals. Other social influences include religion, family organization, and consumer attitudes about risk-taking, material gain, and other factors.

Even when a company strives to assimilate its overall sales strategy into another culture, failure can result. Among the most blatant mishaps was General Motors Corp.'s attempt in the 1970s to market the Nova automobile in Mexico—the Spanish translation of "nova" is similar to "no go." A similar misadventure was undertaken by Braniff Airlines when it was advertising its leather-covered seats to Mexican travelers. Braniff's promotional slogan, "Sentando en cuero," translates into "sit naked." A less conspicuous error was Pepsodent's effort to market its teeth-whitening paste in Southeast Asia, where black or yellow teeth are often considered status symbols.

GLOBAL STRATEGIC OPTIONS

There are four basic avenues that companies can take to market their products or services globally: exporting, contractual agreements, joint ventures, and **manufacturing**. The course, or combination of routes, a company elects to pursue is contingent on internal industry and company influences, as well as the external factors described earlier. Important internal company influences include company goals, product lines, size and financial strength, knowledge of and access to specific foreign markets, and proprietary competitive advantages and technological strengths. These and other influences dictate which basic route a firm should take to market its offerings abroad.

EXPORTING

Exporting can represent a relatively inexpensive, low-risk means of participating in foreign markets because it is easy to initiate and requires a meager up-front capital investment. It can also be a complex endeavor, depending on the type of exporting in which a firm engages: indirect or direct.

Indirect exporting entails simply selling goods for resale in foreign countries, and involves relatively little management or strategy. A common indirect exporting method is selling goods in the home country that the buyer then ships and markets to a foreign market. For instance, a mining company in South Africa might maintain a procurement office in the United States to export its heavy equipment. Similarly, a domestic dealer might act as a middleman, buying the equipment and then selling it to overseas customers. Although it entails little risk or investment, this technique offers few expansion opportunities.

Another common indirect means of exporting is utilizing intermediate exporters, such as export management companies. EMCs are trading entities that specialize in exporting goods for domestic suppliers, either through commission arrangements or by purchasing and then reselling the goods. EMCs give a company slightly more control over its global marketing efforts, provides instant access to knowledge about foreign markets, and offers entry to established distribution channels. The EMC may even use the company's letterhead, serve as a proxy in negotiations, process orders, and handle credit and exchange matters.

Direct exporters sell products directly to companies or consumers in foreign countries. They enjoy greater control over the marketing and distribution of their products than do indirect exporters, and they avoid the cost of paying an EMC. However, the company usually must coordinate research, distribution, marketing, pricing, legal, and other efforts in-house, which typically involves a significant financial commitment. Massive responsibilities include establishing a direct **sales force**, financing customers and hedging exchange rates, **packaging** and shipping, providing technical support, establishing prices, and dealing with **taxes**, tariffs, quotas, and other restrictions.

CONTRACTUAL AGREEMENTS

A viable option, or complement, to exporting is **contracting**, whereby a multinational reaches an agreement with a company in the host country to handle one or several facets of its strategy in that nation or region. A common type of agreement is contract manufacturing, in which a manufacturer in the host country agrees to manufacture goods at the discretion of the multinational firm. This type of agreement is most advantageous for firms whose competitive advantage lies in marketing or distribution. Importantly, it cuts costs related to shipping goods and building manufacturing facilities, and effectively diminishes investment-related risks. In addition, contract manufacturing may allow the multinational to bypass certain trade restrictions because it is bringing money and jobs into the host country. The main drawback is that the multinational often loses control over the production process (i.e. quality), and may even find itself training its future competitor.

A second popular contract agreement is **licensing**, whereby a multinational company (the licensor) gives a local firm (the licensee) the rights to trademarks, **patents**, copyrights, or **proprietary information**. In return, the licensee typically agrees to produce and market the licensor's products, and to pay the licensor a fee, which is usually based on sales volume. The chief delineation between licensing and contracting is that the licensor's role is much greater than that of the contractor. Licensing works well for firms, particularly smaller ones, that want to enter a market quickly and inexpensively and are seeking to avoid exacting trade restrictions erected by the host government. However, licensing entails a loss of control over the product, and often results in the licensor becoming the licensee's prime competitor when the agreement expires.

Other types of contractual agreements include turnkey agreements, wherein a company in the host country agrees to build a manufacturing facility, train personnel, and execute initial production runs for another company. Similarly, under coproduction agreements a contractor in the host country agrees to build a factory in exchange for some of the output. Those agreements are most common in command economies where multinational's are forced to barter for goods and services in the host nation. Finally, management

contracts represent a type of service export; a company agrees to export its expertise to another country, to build and operate a hospital for example, until local people acquire the expertise to assume control of the operation. In return, the company receives a fee.

Examples of U.S. companies that utilize contractual agreements include tobacco manufacturers. Because many overseas countries, particularly in Europe, maintain tobacco monopolies, they are forced to license their brand names to the monopolistic producer. Another example that demonstrates the potential detriments of licensing is Westinghouse. In the 1970s, Westinghouse licensed Framatome, a relatively insignificant French concern, to use its patents to engage in the atomic power industry. When the agreement expired, Framatome became Westinghouse's second strongest global competitor by utilizing processes designed around Westinghouse patents.

JOINT VENTURE

After exporting, joint ventures are the next most common means of getting goods into foreign countries. In a joint venture, a multinational teams up with a company in a host country to share risks and complementary capabilities. Although contractual agreements are similar to joint ventures, the latter differ in the amount of input and control the companies share. The company in the host country may provide important access to local channels of distribution, government contracts, and supply sources. Or, it may bring technological or marketing skills to the table, or serve as a source of capital. Often times, a joint venture allows the multinational to bypass trade restrictions and overcome nationalistic barriers to success in the foreign country.

The primary risk inherent to joint ventures is that the interests of both parties might conflict. This usually occurs because the local company is viewing the operation within a local context, while the multinational is looking at the venture as just one element of an overall global program. Discrepancies often arise over how much profit to plow back into the operation, how to handle transfer pricing issues (how much affiliated companies should charge each other for various goods and services), and product and market decisions. In a worst case scenario, the partnership deteriorates to the point where one or both partners fail to benefit. For this reason, most successful joint ventures have a definite leader that maintains more control, and assumes more risk, in the venture.

An example of a successful joint venture that later soured involves Xerox Corp. In an effort to broaden its global presence, Xerox entered into a 50-50 joint venture in the 1950s with Rank Organization of the United Kingdom. Xerox signed an agreement that essentially gave Rank-Xerox the exclusive rights to manufacture and sell Xerographic machines outside of North America. As time progressed, Xerox outgrew its markets in North America and wanted to sell its machines in other countries. Because it had signed away its valuable rights to conduct business overseas, it was forced to slowly buy back those rights at an estimated cost of $300 million over twenty years.

MANUFACTURING

The fourth approach to getting goods into foreign markets is through wholly owned manufacturing facilities. This route represents the most comprehensive and risky avenue to global trade. It usually entails a large investment and leaves the company much more vulnerable to the whims of the government in the host country. However, it can also provide the biggest payoff and ensure the greatest degree of control over production activities.

Two cardinal options are acquisition and construction. A multinational that acquires existing facilities in the host country benefits from faster access and existing management that is familiar with local supply and distribution channels. On the other hand, building a new production facility is often necessary because the government will not allow a company to sell existing operations or because the multinational cannot find a company willing to sell. Sometimes the host country simply does not possess facilities of the magnitude or sophistication needed by the multinational.

The risks associated with wholly owned operations is evidenced by Union Carbide Corp.'s efforts in the Bhopal, India market. When a poisonous gas leak killed 2,000 people and permanently disabled thousands more, the Indian government became enraged, shut down the facilities, and exacted severe penalties on Union Carbide.

[Dave Mote]

FURTHER READING:

Albaum, Gerald, Jesper Strandskov, Edwin Duerr, and Laurence Dowd. *International Marketing and Export Management.* Addison-Wesley Publishing Company, 1989.

Jain, Subhash C. *International Marketing Management.* PWS-Kent Publishing Company, 1990.

Nagel, Jr., Walter H. and Gaston. *Export Marketing Handbook.* Praeger, 1988.

Nelson, Dr. Carl A. *Global Success: International Business Tactics for the 1990s.* Liberty Hall Press, 1990.

Sandhusen, Richard L. *Global Marketing.* Barron's Educational Series, Inc. 1994.

Terpstra, Vern. *International Marketing,* 4th ed. The Dryden Press, 1987.

GOAL SETTING

Goal setting is the process of setting targets for accomplishment. Goals can be used by both individuals and groups to outline what, how, and when to do things. Besides providing a target against which performance or results may be measured, goals can be used as a tool to motivate workers.

Goal setting is a process that has been used by individuals and groups to measure performance and results since the beginning of mankind. However, it is only since the mid-1900s that formal theories were posited and models were developed to explain the role and value of goals and to establish a framework for creating and using them in organizations. Of import to the study of goals was Abraham Maslow's (1908-1970) renowned theory of the hierarchy of needs, postulated in the early 1940s, which helps to explain the importance of goals to humans. That theory identified five levels of human needs, the most important of which include those related to physical and social welfare, such as food, safety, and love.

When these basic needs have been met, humans seek to meet other needs, including those related to self esteem and self actualization. Indeed, human nature seeks to fulfill needs for recognition, a sense of accomplishment, and maximizing potential. Satisfaction of those needs, according to Maslow, leads to self-confidence, pride, and a sense of value and importance. Thus, Maslow's theory implies that humans are goal-seekers by design—they have an innate need to set standards and objectives and then meet those marks. Maslow's theory also has implications for group goal setting and attainment because it recognizes people's intrinsic need for acceptance and a sense of belonging.

David McClelland punctuated Maslow's theories of motivation with his theory of need achievement, which gained acceptance during the 1960s and 1970s. That theory helps to explain how and why people set goals. In essence, the need achievement theory recognizes three basic human motivators: 1) achievement, or the desire to achieve in relation to a set of standards (i.e. goals); 2) power, or the need to influence others; and 3) the desire for cooperation and interpersonal relationships.

McClelland found that "high achievers," or workers with the greatest motivation, were those with a very high need to accomplish goals. His research also demonstrated that high achievers tend to set moderate goals that they know that they can reach, as opposed to easier goals that provide no challenge. Likewise, goals that are too difficult to realize are counter-productive—they reduce the achiever's control of the situation because he or she is gambling on being able to meet the objective. In addition to needing reachable yet challenging goals, achievers also need constant and concrete feedback on their performance so that they can adjust their behavior for success.

McClelland's individual need achievement theory also had numerous implications for managers seeking to set and work toward goals in a group setting. In fact, his research simulated the findings of Edwin A. Locke during the late 1960s and 1970s about the use of goals in organizations. Locke's research demonstrated that goals are the greatest single motivator for workers excluding financial compensation. Locke found that workers have a need for clearly defined, moderate goals. In addition, the goals must be accepted and supported by all members of a group. Acceptance of goals is contingent upon such factors as trust in management, perceived fairness, legitimacy, and the moral value of the objectives. The important requirement of acceptance, Locke's research suggested, can be met through participative goal setting techniques in which employees help managers shape the objectives.

Locke also discovered that goals that are specific are more likely to be achieved. For example, instead of setting a goal of "making the best ball bearings we can make," a manager should set a goal of "making ball bearings with 99 percent inspection approval." In addition, he found that groups and individuals need constant feedback to determine whether or not they are moving toward their goals. Without that feedback they can become frustrated and lose their motivation. Furthermore, incentives can be used to increase the likelihood of goal achievement. Incentives provided for achievement of goals include monetary as well as nonfinancial rewards, such as recognition, approval, and greater responsibility.

Research concerning the importance and use of goals in organizations culminated in a heightened interest during the mid- and late 1900s in using goals at the individual and group level to attain overall organizational objectives. Corporate goal setting initiatives have most often take the form of management by objectives (MBO), a technique first publicized by management guru Peter F. Drucker (1909-). In essence, MBO is an approach to enhancing organizational effectiveness that is based on goals. Besides motivating workers, MBO creates an environment in which the performance of managers can be evaluated on the basis of results rather than on personality or perceived effectiveness.

MBO programs take many forms. In general, though, they are designed to ensure that each worker has a set of goals that reflects the attributes described above. They typically encompass a four-step process used at both the individual and group levels: 1) deter-

mination of understandable goals; 2) formulation of realistic plans to meet the goals; 3) feedback, or constantly monitoring performance and relating results to workers and groups; and 4) behavior adjustment.

THE FUNCTION OF GOALS

Goal setting for individuals is the third of five stages in the motivation cycle: 1) the individual has an unsatisfied need, such as the need for food or recognition; 2) the a person begins to want to fill that need; 3) the individual sets a goal that, if achieved, will likely fulfill the desire; 4) the person acts to meet the goal; and 5) the person analyzes feedback to determine whether or not the goal was achieved. For example, suppose a woman gets hungry. She wants food. She decides to find a hamburger. She attempts to meet her goal by going to a restaurant and eating a hamburger. When she is finished eating, her stomach will tell her if she has fulfilled her original need for food. If she is still hungry she will have to change her behavior (or set a new goal). She may, for example, order another hamburger.

Goal setting for groups is part of the planning process in which strategies are developed to achieve specific organizational goals. Goal setting occurs at three basic management levels: top, middle, and line. Top managers are charged with setting long-term goals that define the overall objectives and missions of the organization. Middle managers carry out the goals of their superiors and, in doing so, set goals that direct the groups and individuals whom they lead—an example of a middle manager's goal might be to achieve a 14 percent increase in sales within 12 months. Finally, line managers strive to accomplish the goals of middle managers. To do so, they, in turn, create goals that address the day-to-day needs of the operation—a line manager may set a goal of reorganizing a stock room.

An example of this process may be that top executives at a car factory set a goal of producing the highest quality, least expensive truck engine in the world. Middle managers in the production division decide that accomplishment of that goal requires that they set specific goals for their departments, such as increasing productivity by 20 percent within 12 months, or lowering the defect rate to one per 1000. Finally, line managers would have to determine how to achieve those goals and who would do the actual work. They might decide to of reduce salaries and increase bonuses as a reward to those workers who produced the highest quality products.

As suggested above, goal setting at any level will generally involve basic attributes such as clarity and feedback. More specifically, organizational goals should be concrete and quantifiable, meaning that they can be measured against preset, preferably quantitive standards. They should also be time-oriented, in that they are devised with intermediate and final deadlines in mind. The goals should also be logistically attainable—insufficient resources or physically impossible goals can thwart motivation and result in underperformance. Finally, goals should be mutually supportive, meaning that plans made in one part of an organization should complement company-wide objectives.

SEE ALSO: Performance Appraisal & Standards

[Dave Mote]

FURTHER READING:

Cherrington, David J. *Organizational Behavior: The Management of Individual and Organizational Performance*, 2nd ed. Allyn and Bacon, 1994.

Ivancevich, John M. and Michael T. Matteson. *Organizational Behavior and Management*, 2nd ed. Richard D. Irwin, Inc., 1989.

Mescon, Michael H. *Management*, 3rd ed. HarperCollins College, 1989.

Plunkett, Warren R. and Raymond F. Attner. *Introduction to Management*, 4th ed. PWS-Kent Publishing Company, 1992.

Schermerhorn, Jr., John R., James G. Hunt and Richard N. Osborn. *Managing Organizational Behavior*, 4th ed. John Wiley & Sons, 1991.

Wren, Daniel A. and Dan Voich, Jr. *Management: Process, Structure, and Behavior*, 3rd ed. John Wiley & Sons, 1984.

GOING CONCERN

One of the most basic **accounting** assumptions is the concept that a business is a going concern. Unless there is significant evidence to the contrary, it is assumed that a specific business enterprise will continue to operate for an indefinite period—long enough both to meet its objectives and fulfill its commitments. Importantly, while the going concern concept assumes that the firm will continue to operate indefinitely, the concept in no way implies that the firm will make a profit.

GENERALLY ACCEPTED ACCOUNTING PRINCIPLES

The practice of accounting is based on generally accepted accounting principles (GAAP). These are assumptions, practices, and concepts that provide the foundation for measuring and reporting the results of business activities. As logic would dictate, they greatly influence the reported financial position of a firm; thus, simultaneous audits of the same firm can produce widely varying valuations for assets, liabilities, and equity if the audits are based on different fundamental accounting assumptions. Two concepts inherent in GAAP are historical valuation of assets and liabilities and the concept of going concern.

HISTORICAL VALUATION AS SUPPORTED BY THE GOING CONCERN CONCEPT

The assumption that a business is a going concern supports the practice of valuing assets and liabilities at their historical cost. The principle of historical cost dictates that assets and liabilities must be entered into accounting records at the cost the company paid for them when they were initially acquired, even if the market value changes significantly. For example, if a firm purchases land for $300,000, **assets** totalling that amount of money would appear on its **financial statements**. If the value of the land increased to $400,000, the historical valuation concept would dictate that the value of the land would continue to be carried on the books at $300,000.

Historical valuation is founded on the assumption that a business is a going concern. When a firm buys assets—such as land, machinery, or buildings—it does this with the assumption that using these assets will produce income; in other words, the firm does not intend to discontinue its operations and resell these assets. Moreover, it is assumed that the firm will be in existence long enough to fully use these assets and derive the complete benefit inherent within them. Thus, the prices at which the resources could be sold at the market value (after a period of use) would only be significant to financial reports if the business expected to cease operations at once and liquidate its assets. Assuming that the firm is a going concern, it is logical that the firm values these assets at their historical costs and does not adjust them for any subsequent change in value. It follows that the current liquidation value of these assets is not important and that the firm uses the original, or historical, costs of assets and liabilities on its financial statements.

For example, on any given day, a textile manufacturer has shirts at various stages in the production process. If the business were liquidated, the partially completed goods would have little value. Accounting does not attempt to value the firm's work-in-process at its current worth. Rather, accounting assumes that the business is a going concern and that the process will be completed; thus, the amount for which the partially completed shirts could be sold is irrelevant.

GOING CONCERN DOUBT

In 1988, a significant change occurred in the auditing standards with the imposition of a new requirement relating to the going concern assumption. This change requires auditors, in every **audit**, to evaluate whether there is substantial doubt about a company's ability to continue as a going concern over the coming year. If the auditor has such doubt, he or she must state that opinion in the audit's report paragraph.

In infrequent cases, the auditor may be unable to express an opinion about the company's ability to remain a going concern and, thus, may issue a disclaimer to that effect. This situation can occur if limitations are imposed on the scope of the audit by the company's management. Aside from a disclaimer, the auditor can also write an adverse opinion, if he or she concludes that the financial statements do not present the firm's situation fairly. Auditors write adverse opinions if the company does not use GAAP or if the firm is no longer a going concern. Disclaimers and adverse opinions are serious situations and usually result in suspension of trading in the firm's securities.

[Kathryn Snavely]

FURTHER READING:

Anthony, Robert N., and James S. Reece. *Accounting: Text and Cases*. 8th ed. Homewood, Il: Irwin, 1989.

Diamond, Michael A., Eric G. Flamholtz, and Diana Troik Flamholtz. *Financial Accounting*. 2nd ed. Boston, MA: PWS-Kent Publishing Company, 1990.

Eskew, Robert K., and Daniel L. Jensen. *Financial Accounting*. 4th ed. New York: McGraw-Hill, 1992.

Solomon, Lanny M., Larry M. Walther, and Richard J. Vargo. *Financial Accounting*. 3rd ed. New York: West Publishing Company, 1992.

GOLDEN PARACHUTE

A golden parachute is an **employment contract** between a corporation and one of its top executives that provides the executive with compensation in the event that he or she is dismissed as a result of a change in ownership of the corporation. Like most executive-level severance agreements, a golden parachute is intended to provide the manager with a source of **income** while he or she searches for a new job. The benefits often include a generous salary and bonus payment, in addition to vested status in **retirement** and **stock** plans. Many corporations believe that offering such contracts enables them to attract and retain top executive talent, because golden parachutes allay the executives' fears about losing their jobs if the corporation should become the target of a takeover. In addition, some corporations feel that adding a golden parachute provision to the corporate bylaws acts as a deterrent to unwanted takeover attempts, since these executive payments make it very expensive for a new owner to change the corporation's **management team**.

The term golden parachute came into existence in the 1980s, when hostile **takeovers** became common-

place in American business. The first formal guidelines for this type of severance agreement were established by the U.S. Congress as part of the Deficit Reduction Act of 1984 (DEFRA). Golden parachute provisions are also covered in Sections 280G and 4999 of the Internal Revenue Code. The formal guidelines state that two circumstances must be present for a golden parachute clause to be activated: there must be a change in ownership or effective control (defined as the acquisition of 20 percent of the voting stock by a single entity within one year) of the corporation or a substantial portion of its **assets**; and the executive must be terminated without cause, forced to relocate, or faced with a significant reduction in responsibilities as a result of the change in ownership. The tax code allows an executive to claim a "reasonable" amount of severance pay as compensation, but applies an excise tax to additional amounts—usually anything above three times the executive's base salary and bonus—it determines to be "excess" parachute payments.

A 1994 survey published in *HR Focus* revealed that a majority of companies provide some sort of "change-in-control" protection, or golden parachutes, for their top three tiers of executives. The top tier in most companies includes **chief executive officer**s, **chief financial officer**s, chief operating officers, and the heads of large divisions. The second tier consists of executives reporting directly to the top tier, while the third tier is made up of middle managers reporting to the second tier. In some companies, golden parachutes cover over 100 executives earning from $100,000 to more than $300,000 per year. According to the survey, top-level executives commonly receive their golden parachutes through special change-in-control plans, clauses in their retirement plans, clauses in their individual employment contracts, or regular severance plans. One criticism of golden parachute agreements is that they occasionally act as a reward for poor performance by a top executive. Compensation experts stress that these contracts must be worded carefully so that the board of directors retains the right to fire an executive for poor performance without activating his or her golden parachute.

[Laurie Collier Hillstrom]

FURTHER READING:

Fiore, Nicholas J. "Payment Based on Oral Agreement, Received by Executive in Connection with Merger, Was Golden Parachute," *Tax Adviser*. December 1994, pp. 777-78.

"In Event of Change, Executives Still Have Golden Parachutes," *HR Focus*. September 1994, p. 11.

Johnson, Riva T. "Severance Packages Protect Bank Executives," *Texas Banking*. July 1994, p. 12.

Rindler, Michael E. "Use and Abuse of Golden Parachutes," *Trustee*. February 1994, pp. 18-19.

Stahl, David. "Beating Back the Sharks," *Savings and Community Banker*. June 1994, p. 15.

GOVERNMENT CONTRACTS

The U.S. government is the largest purchaser of goods and services in the world. In 1992, government procurement rose to an all-time high of $200 billion, despite the fact that the Cold War was over. Nearly $18 billion alone was earmarked for the purchase of general purpose **computers**. Compare this to the $3.5 billion worth of procurements on the part of the entire **United Nations** system, considered one of the world's largest purchasers and consumer of goods and services. Moreover, government contracts are doled out not just to the huge, wealthy companies that make the news, but also to the smallest business run by only one person. Yet of the approximately 20 million small businesses in this country, barely 10 percent do business with the U.S. government.

Government contracts precisely spell out the goods or services that the government needs and the exact terms of payment. Therefore a contract is not the same as a grant, which is an outright award of money that the government makes to a grantee, with no expectation of a particular product or service in return. A government contract for a sum smaller than $25,000, moreover, is issued by means of a purchase order and is much less onerous to apply for than a large contract. Purchase orders are so common in government that their exact amount has not been determined. Therefore the aggregate of government contracting of goods and services is only approximate; it could well be above $200 billion, and is undoubtedly not below that figure.

Despite the occasional revelations of grossly overpriced goods that a government agency may have bought, or mistaken payments to vendors who had never sold the government anything, these are exceptional incidents. Government procurement always has been and still is guided by a few basic principles: as a rule, contracts are always awarded to the lowest bidder; in addition, government contracts are open to all and are far more competitive than private contracts; and contrary to popular perception, favoritism also is less pronounced than in the private sector. The typical wooing of a client over cocktails and a fine meal is not possible in doing business with the government. Moreover, the government is required by law to set aside contracts for small, disadvantaged businesses.

THE ADVANTAGES OF GOVERNMENT CONTRACTS FOR BUSINESSES

Because the lowest bid is usually the one awarded a contract, many businesses in the private sector cite low profit margins as the reason for not pursuing government contracts. Those who tena-ciously seek business with the government, however, do so because of the distinct advantages; the stability and reliability of the government, and that the size of a government contract can often be significant for a small enterprise, dwarfing all other business contracts. Furthermore, a business can often pick up multiple purchase orders, which do not require bidding, for procurements under $25,000.

The rule of thumb in government contracting is that the government buys everything that ordinary people buy, only in gigantic quantities. While traditionally government contracts have fallen into two categories—military and civilian—there is much crossover, since both sectors purchase many similar items. There are more procurement agencies within the civilian sector than in the military, and these in turn are not always centralized. Moreover, purchasing needs change frequently. In April 1993 President Clinton issued an executive order that stipulated that all government agencies had to purchase vehicles that used either alternative fuels or electricity. Another executive order required that the government use only recyclable paper. Since it is the biggest consumer of paper in the world, the recyclable paper industry was overjoyed.

Not only is the government market huge and changeable, there are literally countless government agencies located throughout the United States. The government is divided into ten regions; each of these has its own procurement needs, and in turn, they are subdivided into smaller units. More often than not, these regional offices and units are mandated to issue contracts to local businesses.

Aside from the 12 executive departments, there are the Library of Congress, the Government Printing Office, and the General Accounting Office (GAO)—considered to be under the legislative wing—that have huge procurement needs. Besides all of these, there are at least 60 independent agencies that answer to the federal government. Because almost all of these government departments and agencies are downsizing, often with only a skeletal staff to manage an office, there is greater need than ever for contracting for services: writers, translators, analysts, plumbers, and mechanics, to name just a few, are increasingly being hired on a contractual basis.

The government contracts with everyone, without regard to size or importance of the business. In fact, an agency often prefers placing a small order with a small firm, which will make it a priority, as opposed to a large enterprise. Government agencies are required by law to earmark a percentage of their contracts (those totaling over $100 million) to small enterprises. Currently, about one-quarter of government contracts fall to small business. In 1993, the U.S. Department of Defense, one of the largest government contractors, required prime contractors doing more than a half million dollars worth of business to invite small businesses to apply as subcontractors.

The **Small Business Administration (SBA)** also advises small businesses on how to acquire government contracts. In its many regional offices, the SBA makes pertinent databases available and offers seminars on government contracting. An important aspect of government contracting that is especially appropriate to small businesses is subcontracting from a prime contractor (and at times, a "prime subcontractor" also farms out subcontracts). The SBA and many business libraries maintain the *Small Business Subcontracting Directory*, published by the U.S. Government Printing Office, and a valuable source of current opportunities with subcontracting. Lastly, the SBA marketing representative can get a firm's name and address added to a database, Procurement Automated Source System (PASS), which makes it easier for a government purchasing office to locate and to contact the right small business. Like all aspects of government, contracting with the public is becoming increasingly electronic. By the turn of the century, all government procurement is expected to be carried out electronically.

Many prominent businesses got their start with government contracts; indeed, sometimes it is the government that turns out to be the best customer for a product, especially a new one, since the government is mandated to encourage technological innovation. That is how Teflon nonstick cookware got its start, as well as Tang, the instant orange juice drink, and such companies as IBM, McDonnell Douglas, and the clothing retailer Haggar.

THE GOVERNMENT CONTRACTING PROCESS

Obtaining any government contract begins with targeting the relevant agency or agencies that use the particular product or service, becoming familiar with the names of the procurement officers in charge of contracts, and establishing personal contact with them by phone or letter. The handiest source for obtaining information about procurement offices within the vast government jungle, with names and addresses of contracting officers, is the *United States Government Manual* or the *U.S. Government Purchasing and Sales Directory*, found in business libraries, or obtainable from the Government Printing Office and its outlets.

There are two basic types of government contracts: direct purchase (DP) contracts for purchases under $25,000, that are usually paid for out of a petty cash fund, and the competitive contract, which requires an elaborate application procedure. DP contracts are usually simple purchase orders that can begin with a phone call to the relevant purchasing officer or a visit to a procurement office.

Competitive contracts, for goods and services over $25,000, require submitting bids that entail a multitude of government forms, regulations, and procedures. To find out about these more lucrative procurements, one needs to be placed on a mailing list, which each procurement office maintains. After obtaining and mailing back Standard Form 129 (the "Solicitation Mailing List Application"), one is placed on a list, or on more than one. These lists are divided according to the needs of a particular agency: there is a computer list, a list for technical writing, office equipment, etc. In theory, these mailing lists are supposed to guarantee that one finds out about bid opportunities in one's specialty; in practice, notices are sent out erratically. Hence being placed on a mailing list will not get one informed of all contracting opportunities.

Relevant government periodicals, rather than newspapers, inform the prospective vendor of contracting opportunities. The most complete list of all upcoming competitive (over $25,000) and non competitive grant opportunities is contained in the *Commerce Business Daily* (CBD) obtainable in most libraries and at the SBA. Besides containing notices of upcoming contracts, divided into categories of goods and services, the CBD also informs the reader of grants already awarded, to whom, and the amounts, a useful indicator of the types of goods and services getting contract awards. Lastly, the CBD contains information about upcoming meetings of interested contractors and contracting officers, which is the way to do networking with the U.S. government.

Often by the time one sees a notice in the CBD, there is very little time to apply for the contract. For this reason, the *Federal Register* is a useful indicator of the kinds of goods and services the government will be needing in the near future. Like the CBD, the *Federal Register* is a daily publication and obtainable at libraries. Besides informing the public of all new federal laws and regulations, the publication also contains proposals for upcoming ones. Knowing which way the wind is blowing helps to make the future vendor aware of opportunities that will eventually materialize in the CBD.

The next stage in applying for a government contract requires one to write to the agency listed in the CBD announcement, asking for the requisite application materials (or "solicitation document"). All contracts for purchases over $25,000 are considered competitive contracts. If the contract is for a tangible product such as stationery, office furniture, or certain computer equipment, the solicitation document will require a detailed description of the items and the bidding price. The government procurement office then evaluates these bid offers and usually the lowest bid price is accepted, and announced publicly. For goods and services that are difficult to define in detail, the procurement agency requires a proposal in writing, referred to as a "sealed bid," since these are not announced in public and are considered to be negotiated contracts. Applying for these is time consuming and difficult, and the largest firms employ a proposal writing staff that does nothing but work on government contract proposals full time. The government evaluation process for written proposals takes longer and requires the prospective vendor to be interviewed. The great majority of written proposals are rejected because they fail to address the precise need of the government, despite the fact that a contracting officer is always available for specific information. A vendor can appeal a rejected proposal to the Government Accounting Office, which will investigate and adjudicate the matter.

Government contracting is controlled by a multitude of strict rules that are known as Federal Acquisition Regulations, or FARs. These in turn are codified in the Code of Federal Regulations. Any slight divergence from them disqualifies an applicant from obtaining a government contract. While this would appear to daunt any but the biggest firms and the most hardy, the reward of obtaining a sizable government contract appears to make up for the red tape. In addition, there is always plenty of advice and assistance from the contracting officers or, if it is a small business, from the SBA.

Despite the end of the Cold War, government spending has not declined significantly, unless perhaps for defense contracting. Currently there is much agitation in Congress for procurement reform, largely because of Vice President Al Gore's "reinventing government" initiatives. There is much dissatisfaction with the multitude of FARs, and a widespread belief that they can be streamlined or reduced in number, although this has never been done. The greatest impact on government contracting—finally streamlining the process—will come from computerization, as the government moves towards electronic purchasing and inventorying of needs and suppliers.

[Sina Dubovoy]

FURTHER READING:

Austin, Stephen. *Strategies and Tactics for Winning Government Contracts.* Santa Ana, CA: Global Engineering Documents, 1987.

Crowner, Clinton L. *Selling to Uncle Sam: How to Win Choice Government Contracts for Your Business.* New York: McGraw-Hill, 1993.

Nash, Ralph. *The Government Contracts Reference Book: A Comprehensive Guide to the Language of Procurement.* Washington, DC: George Washington University, 1992.

Porterfield, Richard L. *The Insider's Guide to Winning Government Contracts.* New York: Wiley & Sons, 1993.

Rowh, Mark. *Winning Government Grants and Contracts for Your Small Business.* New York: McGraw-Hill, 1992.

GOVERNMENTAL ACCOUNTING STANDARDS BOARD (GASB)

The Government Accounting Standards Board (GASB) was created in 1984 to establish generally accepted accounting principles (GAAP) for state and local government entities. Prior to 1984, issues in public sector accounting were addressed by the National Committee on Governmental Accounting (NCGA) of the Government Finance Officers Association (GFOA). As provided for in the GASB charter, an extensive review was conducted of the GASB's performance after five years. The 1989 report, while making several recommendations for change, concluded that the GASB had performed well in the public interest.

The GASB is one of two boards that establishes GAAP. The other is the **Financial Accounting Standards Board (FASB)**. While the GASB has jurisdiction over financial reporting by governmental entities, the FASB establishes rules for private sector accounting. Both boards are independent, nongovernmental bodies whose members are appointed by the trustees of the Financial Accounting Foundation (FAF). The FAF is an independent, nongovernmental body that is responsible for the basic structure for establishing accounting principles. With respect to the GASB, the FAF appoints GASB members, raises funds, and provides general oversight of governmental accounting standards-setting. Both the FAF and GASB are assisted by the Government Accounting Standards Advisory Council (GASAC).

The GASB consists of five members. As originally organized, the GASB had a full-time chairperson with the vice-chair and three other members being part-time. Following the 1989 review, it was decided to make all members full-time if sufficient funding was available. GASB members' five-year terms are now staggered so that they do not expire at the same time.

When it was first established in 1984, the GASB's first statement affirmed the authority of all previous rules established by the NCGA as well as certain state and local government accounting and reporting guidelines of the American Institute of Certified Public Accountants (AICPA). The existing rules were collected and published as the *Codification of Governmental Accounting and Financial Reporting Standards.* Revisions to existing rules and new rules are announced periodically by the GASB.

Two key issues have arisen concerning the relationship between the GASB and FASB. While the jurisdictional boundaries of the two boards were clearly spelled out, a jurisdictional question that became a source of potential conflict occurred with respect to special entities. A special entity is one that could be either publicly or privately owned, such as a utility, a hospital, or a college or university. Since some special entities are government owned and others are privately operated, it became possible for two similar entities to be governed by two different sets of GAAP. While the matter of which standards would apply to special entities was given considerable attention in the five-year review, the proposal that finally settled the issue simply charged the GASB to be mindful of the need (with regard to special entities) for comparison between public and private sector financial statements. That is, special entities that are privately owned continue to be subject to FASB rules, while special entities that are government owned remain subject to GASB rules.

The other issue that arose during the first five years of GASB was known as the hierarchy issue. The hierarchy issue refers to the applicability of FASB rules to government entities when the rules cover areas that have not been addressed by the GASB. As originally conceived, government entities would be subject first of all to all GASB rules, then to FASB rules if no GASB rule applied. During its first five years, the GASB denied the applicability of two FASB rules to state and local government entities. Following the five-year review, the FAF adopted the recommendation that government entities would not have to comply with FASB rules unless the GASB designated them as mandatory.

[David Bianco]

GRAPHICAL USER INTERFACE (GUI)

A graphical user interface (GUI, pronounced ''gooey'') is a type of computer display format that represents directions, programs, and files with pictures. Instead of laboriously typing commands at a prompt to tell the computer what to do, the user can simply choose commands by activating the pictures with an input device, such as a keyboard or mouse. GUIs make **computers** ''user friendly'' by simplifying tasks and decisions, and by creating a visual representation of a computer system to which people can more easily relate.

The term ''interface'' was added to the English language in the late 1800s as a noun defined as ''a surface lying between two portions of matter or space, and forming their common boundary.'' The term was adopted early in the computer industry, during the 1950s, to describe computer video displays, or ''user interfaces.'' Early user interfaces, such as the one employed by the Whirlwind Computer developed at MIT in 1950, consisted of simple cathode ray tubes (CRTs) that displayed simple input prompts. They facilitated crude interaction and a dearth of graphical representation. Users had to flawlessly enter complicated commands and typically had to commit the commands to personal memory or refer to user manuals.

During the 1960s more advanced displays were developed that offered more advanced interactive capabilities, meaning that the user could provide input to the computer more easily and efficiently. Among the earliest advanced interactive systems were systems developed by Ivan Sutherland, including his Sketchpad drawing system. Among other innovations, Sutherland created a graphical interaction method that allowed computer users to provide input using a light pen (a hand held pointing device that sensed objects on a cathode ray tube). His research laid the groundwork for more advanced systems that emerged during the mid- and late 1960s, including **computer aided drawing** (CAD) and **computer aided manufacturing** (CAM) systems that used styli to draw forms and choose commands.

Computer systems that utilized graphical interface technology were implemented in the commercial sector during the late 1960s and early 1970s, but only by the most technologically advanced enterprises—the General Motors Corp. engineering department, for example, was among the first organizations to use graphical interaction technology for product design. During the remainder of the 1970s and particularly during the 1980s, a multitude of technological advancements spawned improved graphic interfaces, or ''graphical user interfaces.'' Pivotal breakthroughs that facilitated GUIs included the desktop or personal computer (PC), raster graphics and bit map technology, the concept of desktop and window relationships, and the mouse.

As the cost of GUI technology dropped, especially for PCs, GUI became the standard. Apple Computer, Inc. popularized the GUI concept with its Macintosh personal computers. The Macintosh rejected the traditional command-driven approach pioneered by International Business Machines Corp. (IBM) in favor of a menu-driven, object-oriented interface. The Macintosh's user friendly interface was designed to mimic the top of a desk. Programs and files were accessible through pictures, or icons, of files on the computer screen. Likewise, other commands and choices were represented by icons of trash cans, chalkboard erasers, diskettes, and other applicable symbols. Importantly, the Macintosh incorporated a mouse (a hand-operated device that can be used to ''point and click,'' or select, screen icons).

Although many purists initially denounced the Macintosh GUI as simplistic and juvenile, Macintosh became the computer of choice for many businesses that sought to reduce training expenses and simplify their PC systems. IBM eventually followed suit with its introduction of OS/2, an operating system that supported a GUI similar to Apple's. Likewise, Microsoft Corp. developed Windows, an ''overlay'' GUI for the popular command-driven disk operating systems utilized by IBM PCs. Windows is an adjunct to DOS that creates a GUI very similar to that found on Macintosh computers. The release of Windows 95 in August 1995 signalled a shift to more advanced PC GUIs.

THE GUI CONCEPT

The primary benefit of GUIs is that they create a visual representation of a computer system and structure that is more natural and easier for users to comprehend and conceptualize, hence the idiom ''user friendly.'' Because computer files, programs, and commands are represented by familiar icons, the user is effectively able to operate in an affable environment. In contrast, traditional command-driven interfaces force users to remember commands or search for the proper directives in ''help'' text or manuals. Using a command-driven interface is analogous to telling somebody how to repair a car engine over the telephone, while a GUI effectively lets you look at the engine and fix it yourself without having to carefully recall and verbalize specific instructions.

In addition to facilitating visualization, a major and obvious benefit of GUIs is that they allow users to quickly accomplish object-oriented tasks, such as drawing lines and shapes, repositioning or resizing pictures and text, and other graphical manipulations. Such tasks are usually accomplished through peripheral input devices such as a mouse, stylus, or joy stick. A less obvious GUI benefit is that applications (software programs) developed for use on GUIs are device-dependent. That means that as an interface changes to incorporate new peripheral devices, such as a printer or memory device, applications can utilize those peripheral devices with little or no modifications. Command-driven interfaces, in contrast, might require the user to supply commands that would tell the software exactly what the peripherals are and how they should be used.

While GUIs have many ''spatial'' advantages, they also incorporate conventional ''linguistic'' interface techniques used by command-driven systems. For example, an architect or engineer may benefit from being able to draw lines and shade regions using a mouse. But technical drawings require that he or she be able to tell the computer precisely, perhaps within 1/1000th of an inch or less, where to place a point or coordinate. This requirement brings to the light an advantage command-driven systems have over some GUIs; verbal commands are often more precise than point-and-click visual directives. Therefore, GUIs are generally an amalgam of object-oriented and command-driven technologies.

GUI TECHNOLOGY

As noted earlier, GUI is made possible by technology innovated and implemented commercially during the 1970s and popularized during the 1980s. Most important, perhaps, was the concurrent development of extremely powerful microprocessors and exceptionally efficient memory storage apparatus. New microprocessors delivered the processing prowess necessary to handle the complex mathematical demands of GUIs, and powerful memory devices accommodated the massive amounts of code needed to run GUIs.

Besides advancements in processing and storage, however, progress related to graphical displays contributed to the gradual dominance of GUIs. Of import is raster graphics technology. Raster video displays use bit maps (arrays of dots, or pixels, on a computer screen) to form graphics. A simple bit map represents each pixel with a bit (binary digit represented by 0 or 1) of information. The bit map is made up of a rectangular array of pixels, each of which is independently addressable by the computer. The value of each bit in the array can be changed to cause corresponding pixels to become white or black. Systems that assign multiple bits to each pixel create advanced bit maps called ''pixel images.'' Pixel images assign different shades of grey, or even different colors and intensities, to each pixel.

GUIs use raster displays to form text and graphics on a computer screen because the array of pixels can be manipulated to create forms (i.e. text and pictures) that, when viewed from a distance, are seemingly contiguous. Raster displays were developed as an alternative to vector displays, which create graphics using solid lines. Raster displays are much more amenable to graphic applications because, besides allowing more acute manipulation of images, they make it easier for the user to create shades and colors.

[Dave Mote]

FURTHER READING:

Barry, John A. *Technobabble*. The MIT Press. 1993.

Foley, James D. with van Dam, Feiner, Hughes and Phillips. *Introduction to Computer Graphics*. Addison-Wesley Publishing Company. 1994.

Scott, Joan E. *Introduction to Interactive Computer Graphics*. John Wiley & Sons. 1982.

Vince, John. *Computer Graphics for Graphic Designers*. Knowledge Industry Publications, Inc. 1985.

GRAY MARKET

The gray market refers to those goods that are legitimately imported from abroad, carry a recognizable trademark or brand name, and are sold at significant discounts outside of the manufacturer's normal distribution channels. The practice of gray marketing has affected a wide range of consumer and other products, including personal computers, automobiles, perfume, cameras, film, and semiconductors. The profits of gray marketers are sensitive to international exchange rates, and they tend to thrive during times when the U.S. dollar is strong in relation to other world currencies.

While gray market goods are legally imported from abroad, the importer is typically not one of the manufacturer's authorized distributors. The importer then turns around and sells them at substantial discounts outside of the manufacturer's authorized distribution channels. Gray market goods are not counterfeit goods; their trademarks are genuine. Purchasing gray market goods can result in substantial savings for consumers, but the practice also has its risks. Consumer products such as automobiles that are manufactured outside of the United States may have been built to different specifications and with different materials. Imported gray market automobiles, for example, must be modified by **Environmental Protection Agency (EPA)** approved independent commercial importers to meet federal emission standards.

Gray market goods are typically sold without any of the original manufacturer's warranties. Some independent companies have stepped in and offered to sell warranties for selected gray market products. Other problems a consumer may encounter include being unable to obtain factory service and other support from the original manufacturer.

The essential feature of gray market goods is that they are sold outside of the manufacturer's authorized distribution outlets. In 1984 IBM was the victim of gray marketers who accounted for as much as 10 percent of the company's personal computer sales. These gray marketers were high-volume purchasers who received a substantial discount from IBM, then resold the computers to unauthorized dealers. IBM sought to trace the gray marketers using serial numbers on the computers and cut off sales to them.

Gray marketers have been the target of litigation on the part of manufacturers for the past decade and longer. Even though court decisions have generally failed to outlaw the practice, a group of authorized distributors formed the Coalition to Preserve the Integrity of American Trademarks (Copiat) in 1984 to challenge gray marketing. That year an estimated $7 billion of discounted gray market goods entered the United States.

[David Bianco]

GREEN MARKETING

Environmentally-responsible or "green" marketing refers to the satisfaction of consumer needs, wants, and desires while promoting preservation and conservation of the natural environment. Considered an oxymoron by many environmentalists (because it still promotes consumption, albeit *responsible* consumption), green marketing manipulates the four elements of the marketing mix (product, price, promotion, and distribution) to sell products and services offering superior environmental benefits in the form of reduced waste, increased energy efficiency, and/or decreased release of toxic emissions. These benefits are frequently estimated using life cycle analysis (LCA) studies, which measure the environmental impact of products over their entire life cycle—resource extraction, refining, manufacturing, transportation, use, and disposal.

BEGINNINGS OF ENVIRONMENTALISM

Environmental concern in the United States has ebbed and flowed with the times. The first wave of environmentalism began in the late 1800s and was hallmarked by the preservationist-conservationist debates between naturalist John Muir (1838-1914) and Gifford Pinchot (1865-1946), first Chief of the U.S. Forest Service. In 1962, Rachel Carson's (1907-64) monumental book on the harmful effects of the pesticide DDT, *Silent Spring,* touched off another wave which took hold in the turbulent 1960s and lasted until the early 1970s. Much of our current environmental legislation stems from concerns raised during this period. In 1976, marketing scholars Karl E. Henion II, and Thomas C. Kinnear introduced the concept of *ecological marketing*, "... concerned with all marketing activities (1) that have served to help cause environmental problems and (2) that may serve to provide a remedy for environmental problems." Shortly thereafter, the nation was hit by hard economic times and little attention was paid to either the impact of business on the environment or ecological/green marketing strategies for the remainder of the decade.

In the late 1980s, a renaissance of environmental concern swept through the country, sparked by fears of global warming, loss of the earth's protective ozone layer, destruction of tropical rain forests, and changing perceptions of mankind's place in the world. This "third wave" of environmentalism differs from earlier periods in two significant aspects: 1) The most pressing environmental problems are now global, rather than local, in scope and 2) Businesses are responding much more proactively and much less antagonistically than in former times. Many businesses believe long-term success in the twenty-first century will require increased attention to environmental issues.

Green marketing emphasizes environmental stewardship. Alma T. Mintu and Hector R. Lozada define green marketing as: "... the application of marketing tools to facilitate exchanges that satisfy organizational and individual goals in such a way that the preservation, protection and conservation of the physical environment is upheld." Walter Coddington defines *environmental marketing* as "... marketing activities that recognize environmental stewardship as a business development responsibility and business growth responsibility ..." Others have focused more on strategic dimensions in defining green marketing; for example, Martin Charter defines it as "... a holistic and responsible strategic management process that identifies, anticipates, satisfies and fulfills stakeholder needs for a reasonable reward, that does not adversely affect human or natural environmental well-being." Finally, Robert D. Mackoy, Roger Calantone, and Cornelia Dröge differentiate among three aspects of green marketing, which they identify as *demarketing* (managing demand to maintain optimal long-term profitability), *green marketing* (addressing the needs and wants of a segment of consumers expressing environmental concerns), and *social marketing* (adapting marketing tactics and strategies to the development and promotion of social goals).

All of these definitions enlarge the traditional objective of business to maximize profits, by including some notion of maintaining the integrity of the natural environment. Operationally, green marketing seeks to satisfy the needs and wants of individual consumers while simultaneously seeking to improve environmental quality of life for society as a whole. Environmental concerns thus act as *constraints* on business operations, echoing a passage from the Great Law of the Iroquois Confederacy: "In our every deliberation, we must consider the impact of our decisions on the next seven generations."

THE GREENING OF BUSINESS

A number of factors have caused business firms to behave more responsibly towards the natural environment. Perhaps foremost among these is the possibility of capitalizing on opportunities from the sale of environmental services and/or "earth-friendly" products. Environmental-protection spending has grown three times faster than the U.S. **gross domestic product (GDP)** since the late 1960s and is currently esti-

mated at $170 billion, or 2.8 percent of GDP. It is expected to increase to 3.1 percent of GDP by the year 2000, an amount approximately equal to the anticipated defense budget at that time (Bezdek 1993). "Green" consumers have arisen with preferences for products made from recycled materials or products whose use entails reduced environmental impact. Oftentimes such products command premium prices.

As landfills fill up and public opposition mounts against opening new ones (the NIMBY, or "Not In My Back Yard," syndrome), waste treatment and disposal costs rise. Storage, transport, and disposal of hazardous wastes is quickly becoming unaffordable for many firms, stimulating a search for less-toxic alternative processes. Furthermore, liability and litigation costs for environmental damages are skyrocketing with little sign of abatement. At the time of the first Earth Day in April 1970, there were approximately 2,000 federal, state, and local environmental regulations. Today there are approximately 100,000 such rules, and more than 90,000 changes are expected over the next four years.

Faced with a growing environmental consciousness, many business firms are adopting a pro-environment stance in hopes of improving credibility with the public. Unfortunately, some companies have been a bit overzealous with their environmental claims, prompting cries of "greenwashing" from critics. Another impetus causing business to embrace environmental concerns is to attract better employees and/or improve working conditions. Many young people entering the workforce today exhibit greater social concerns than those of ten years ago, and many wish to join firms perceived to be making a positive contribution to society.

Environmental regulations are increasing in both number and complexity. Some firms have identified opportunities in this changing legal environment and are making changes to drive regulation for purposes of competitive advantage. Because many regulations require use of the "best available technology," firms actively involved in developing and implementing new technologies may achieve the benefits of monopoly status for a short while.

Companies are also becoming more environmentally responsible as part of an overall commitment to **Total Quality Management** and/or sustainable development. Sustainable development involves meeting the needs of the present without compromising the ability of future generations to meet their own needs.

CRITICISMS OF THE CONSUMPTION CULTURE

Traditional marketing attempts to identify and meet latent, current, or future consumer needs by manipulating the price, promotion, product, and/or place (distribution) channels. These objectives have historically been identified with efforts to increase consumption of material goods and services, practices not particularly compatible with a sustainable society. Environmentalists have criticized various aspects of the consumption culture. Mackoy, Calantone, and Dröge identify six categories of critiques:

1. Puritan: Consumption distracts individuals from appreciation of nature and corrupts not only our natural but spiritual habitat.

2. Quaker: Consumption is wasteful and ignores the true costs of production and disposal.

3. Republican: Consumption encourages environmental irresponsibility. Individuals have a duty to behave in an environmentally responsible manner so as to ensure future generations the same opportunities they have enjoyed.

4. Marxist: Consumption exacerbates differences between rich and poor and imposes environmental inequities on the lower classes.

5. Aristocrat: Consumption destroys areas of natural beauty which have intrinsic value and which should be preserved.

6. Systems: Consumption strains already fragile natural and social ecosystems and threatens wholesale collapse.

Managers should keep these critiques in mind when creating green marketing strategies. Green marketing is compatible with the Quaker, Republican, Aristocrat, and Systems critiques, but has limited application in addressing concerns voiced by those holding Puritan and Marxist views. Marketing managers meet the needs of consumers expressing these various beliefs by manipulating the "4 Ps" of the marketing mix—product, price, promotion and place (or distribution). The following sections describe strategies and methods used in the promotion of more environmentally responsible consumption.

GREEN PRODUCTS

There is no widespread agreement on what, exactly, makes a product green. According to Elkington, Hailes, and Makower a green product is one which:

1. Is not dangerous to the health of people or animals.

2. Does not cause damage to the environment during manufacture, use, or disposal.

3. Does not consume a disproportionate amount of energy and other resources during manufacture, use, or disposal.

4. Does not cause unnecessary waste, due either to excessive packaging or to a short useful life.

5. Does not involve the unnecessary use of or cruelty to animals.

6. Does not use materials derived from threatened species or environments.

Charter has compiled a list of five "Rs" contributing to greener products, either by extending product life or by increasing the efficiency of resource utilization. These are: (1) *Repair*: the repair of one or more parts, (2) *Reconditioning*: a complete overhaul to replace worn-out parts, (3) *Re-use*: designing products for multiple uses, (4) *Recycling*: collecting, sorting, and reprocessing materials for use in other products and (5) *Remanufacture*: producing new products from used ones. A sixth "R," *reduction* (buying fewer products) provides the greatest benefit of all, though most firms are reluctant to advocate this approach. A notable exception is Esprit Corporation, a clothing manufacturer who urges customers to consume more responsibly and notes: "We believe this could best be achieved by simply asking yourself before you buy something (from us or any other company) whether this is something you really need. It could be you'll buy more or less from us, *but only what you really need*."

A great deal of work on this area is concerned with a product's environmental impact at various stages of its useful life. *Life cycle analysis* (LCA) and/or *product line analysis* (PLA) studies measure the environmental impact of products over their entire life cycle-resource extraction, refining, manufacturing, transportation, use and disposal—that is, from the "cradle to the grave." Such studies track resource use, energy requirements, and waste generation in order to provide comparative benchmarks enabling manufacturers and consumers to select products involving the least impact upon the natural environment. Though useful, LCA studies have been criticized for their subjectivity in setting analysis boundaries and for difficulties in establishing comparable impacts across environmental media, e.g. "How many tons of carbon dioxide emissions equal the release of one picogram of dioxin?"

Information from these studies and additional consumer research is being used to develop new products and to redesign existing products and services in order to reduce environmental impacts. *Design for the environment*, *design for durability*, and *design for disassembly* have become watchwords for companies seeking to prevent waste and manage material flows more efficiently. Products and packaging are being redesigned to use less materials or to be easily disassembled so high-value components can be recycled or refurbished more readily. Of course, numerous trade-offs must be made weighing health and safety attributes and consumer desires for convenience against packaging, energy use, and recycling requirements.

GREENER PRICING

A central concern of many environmentalists is that product prices do not reflect total environmental costs. Waste disposal costs, for instance, are frequently incurred on a fixed-fee basis, regardless of how much waste is actually generated. Similarly, the national accounting systems of most countries do not incorporate the costs of environmental degradation or depletion. After-the-fact expenditures on pollution control and remediation are included, albeit as **income**. The 1989 Exxon Valdez oil spill in Alaska's Prince William Sound increased the United States's gross domestic product by approximately $2 billion—the cost of the cleanup. Greener pricing decisions are based on the premise that goods and services associated with greater environmental damage should cost *more*.

A number of companies have undertaken audits of their production processes to identify hidden environmental costs and to provide better information for pricing decisions. Emissions charges, carbon taxes, and increased fines are possible methods governments might use to implement better environmental costing. European firms have been particularly proactive in this area, developing a method of environmental auditing (the *ecobalance*) bridging the gap between standard **accounting** practice, in which data is expressed solely in monetary terms, and qualitative environmental impact reports.

Research conducted by the Roper Organization (1990) identified five different groups of environmental consumers with varying degrees of commitment to purchasing environmental products. Willingness-to-pay for perceived environmental benefits varied widely from about three percent for the least-committed group to approximately 20 percent for individuals espousing the highest level of commitment. Across the board, consumers indicated a willingness to pay an average premium of approximately seven percent for products with positive environmental attributes. Attitudes do not always translate into action, of course, but environmental attributes do seem to be "tie-breakers" for customers faced with a choice between two products offering similar benefits and prices.

GREEN PROMOTION

Perhaps no area of green marketing has received as much attention as promotion. In fact, green advertising claims grew so rapidly during the late 1980s that the **Federal Trade Commission (FTC)** issued guidelines to help reduce consumer confusion and prevent the false or misleading use of terms such as "recyclable," "degradable," and "environmentally friendly" in environmental advertising (FTC 1992).

The FTC offers four general guidelines for environmental claims:

1. Qualifications and disclosures should be sufficiently clear and prominent to prevent deception.

2. Environmental claims should make clear whether they apply to the product, the package, or a component of either. Claims need to be qualified with regard to minor, incidental components of the product or package.

3. Environmental claims should not overstate the environmental attribute or benefit. Marketers should avoid implying a significant environmental benefit where the benefit is, in fact, negligible.

4. A claim comparing the environmental attributes of one product with those of another product should make the basis for the comparison sufficiently clear and should be substantiated.

The FTC report provides additional guidance for a number of specific claims including "Degradable/ Biodegradable/Photodegradable," "Compostable," "Recyclable," "Recycled Content," "Source Reduction," "Refillable," and "Ozone Safe/Ozone Friendly." They strongly recommend avoidance of overly general claims such as "environmentally friendly."

ECO-LABELING. Environmental certification or labeling programs attempt to increase consumer awareness and knowledge of environmental issues. Marketers use eco-labels to convey information about a product's environmental benefits and to differentiate among competing products. Eco-labels may identify a product's contents, e.g. the triangular arrangement of arrows on recycled paper and plastic products, or highlight other benefits, e.g. reduced water usage or increased energy efficiency. Germany's "Blue Angel" program is the oldest and most successful eco-labeling program. Introduced in 1977 by the Federal Minister and Ministers for Environmental Protection of the various German states, it now appears on more than 4,000 different products. The Blue Angel is awarded on the basis of comparisons with similar products, and is designed to guide consumers in their purchasing decisions. For instance, a product may have particularly low pollutant or noise emissions, entail less wastes in its production, or be designed for easier recycling than its competitors. The Blue Angel has proven to be a useful selling tool in Germany's ecologically-conscious society. A few other countries have established eco-labels, though none has yet had as great an impact as the Blue Angel.

In the United States, two private firms, Scientific Certification Systems and Green Seal, have developed guidelines to identify environmentally preferable products. Scientific Certification Systems, a private testing concern, awards a "Green Cross" for products meeting very specific criteria, e.g. X% recycled content, less than Y% pesticide residues, etc. Green Seal, a nonprofit organization, is engaged in more ambitious efforts using life cycle analysis to identify a product's impact on the environment at all stages of its life.

Eco-labeling programs increase awareness of environmental issues, set high standards for firms to work towards, and help reduce consumer uncertainty regarding a product's environmental benefits. They have also been criticized as confusing, misleading, overly simplistic and prone to manipulation by firms with less-than-honorable intentions. Thus far, the U.S. government has resisted instituting an officially-sanctioned eco-label program.

ECO-SPONSORING. Another avenue for companies to promote their ecological concern is to affiliate themselves with groups or projects engaged in environmental improvements. In eco-sponsoring's simplest form, firms contribute funds directly to an environmental organization to further the organization's objectives. Another approach is to "adopt" a particular environmental cause, e.g. a community recycling program, demonstrating the company's willingness to put its money and its reputation on the line. Sponsoring educational programs, wildlife refuges, and clean-up efforts communicates a firm's commitment to finding environmental solutions. Partnerships with environmental organizations can open lines of communication and provide new perspectives on "business as usual."

In considering an eco-sponsorship, firms must address the problems of legitimacy and believability. Not all environmental sponsorships are legitimate or appropriate for a particular company's needs. Chemical firms, for instance, may find it difficult to support Greenpeace's anti-chlorine campaign. Believability is even more critical. Business firms consistently rate lowest in surveys of credibility with consumers. Eco-sponsoring should not be used as an alibi for a firm's day-to-day actions.

GREENER DISTRIBUTION

Logistics and transportation costs are coming under greater scrutiny due to rising fuel prices, congested highways, and global-warming concerns. Package redesign for lighter weight and/or greater recyclability reduces waste while simultaneously reducing costs. In some countries, marketers must also consider two-way flows, as governments pass legislation requiring manufacturers to take back products at the end of their useful life ("reverse logistics)." Germany is again the world leader in this arena; it has already passed ordinances targeting the electronics, automobile, and packaging industries.

Faced with the undesirable option of accepting used packaging from consumers, German manufacturers banded together in 1990 to create the "Dual System"—an alternative, country-wide waste management system which guaranteed the collection and recycling of various packaging materials. Administered by the *Duales System Deutschland* (DSD), a consortium of retailers, distributors, manufacturers, waste haulers, and recycling firms, the system requires manufacturers to pay a small fee for the right to display a green dot (*grüner Punkt*) on their products, indicating that the packaging is eligible for recycling by the DSD. Despite numerous setbacks and logistical difficulties, the DSD met nearly all its recycling targets in 1993.

Green marketing strategies are also reducing inventory and production costs. Standardization and identification of product parts and packaging materials benefits the environment by reducing complexity and improving efficiency. Substituting electronic or computer controls for analog devices improves quality and reduces waste.

STRATEGY AND TACTICS

Green marketing as a subdiscipline is only a few decades old, and much remains to be learned about consumer preferences, product substitutions, and environmental tradeoffs. Nonetheless, a few principles useful in developing a green marketing strategy have emerged.

In reacting to environmental constraints required by green marketing, managers should apply the *Precautionary Principle.* Environmental issues are fraught with scientific and social uncertainties. There is significant debate, for example, regarding the effects of global warming and thinning of the ozone layer. In designing new products and services, marketers should choose a strategy providing benefits even if the environmental issue proves inconsequential. For example, improving energy efficiency reduces carbon dioxide emissions, a primary factor in global warming. It also reduces energy use and saves money, making it a "no regrets" decision, even if global warming is not as severe a problem as some environmentalists suggest.

Governments are increasingly adopting the *Polluter Pays Principle*, establishing environmental liability for manufacturers and businesses engaged in polluting activities. Neither environmental legislation nor waste cleanup costs are likely to decrease in the coming decades, suggesting that a proactive strategy aimed at reducing waste and pollution at the source will yield both financial and environmental benefits. Indeed, *pollution prevention* is recommended by the U.S. Environmental Protection Agency as the most appropriate course of action for dealing with environmental problems. Firms needing an extra nudge towards this position might consider the draconian features of the federal government's Comprehensive Environmental Response, Compensation, and Liability Act (CERCLA) of 1980 (Superfund), which assigns *retroactive* and *joint and several* liability to owners, transporters, and generators of hazardous wastes violating its requirements.

The *Principle of Cooperation* advises marketers to interact more closely with communities and governments in addressing environmental problems and communicating their respective expectations and concerns. Failure to work together on a voluntary basis may lead to additional regulations and requirements. For example, the Chemical Manufacturers' Association, a trade organization representing approximately 90 percent of basic industrial chemical production in the United States, requires its members to subscribe to the principles of *Responsible Care*, a program deliberately designed to improve communication about environmental, health, and safety issues between workers and communities. The **European Union**'s Eco-Audit program, also administered on a voluntary basis, shows promise in creating greater opportunities for communication and cooperation between industry, communities, and governments.

Numerous product success stories are associated with the implementation of these strategies. Low-phosphate detergents, CFC-free refrigerators, high-efficiency light bulbs, low-emissions gasoline, lighter-weight packaging, powder paint sprays, and high-quality clothing made from recycled soda bottles are among many examples which might be mentioned. Partnerships between environmental groups and business organizations, such as the Environmental Defense Fund's work with the McDonald's fast-food restaurant chain, have increased communication and fostered better understanding of each group's objectives.

CONCLUSION

Green marketing is based on the premise that businesses have a responsibility to satisfy human needs and desires while preserving the integrity of the natural environment. That this latter concern has been ignored throughout most of recorded human history does not mean it will be unimportant in the future. Indeed, there are significant indications that environmental issues will grow in importance over the coming years and will require imaginative and innovative redesign and reengineering of existing marketing efforts on the part of many businesses. Solutions to our environmental problems can be characterized into roughly three categories: ethical, legal, and business (economic and technological) solutions. Long-term sustainability of the planet is likely to require some rather distinct changes in the ethical behavior of its human population. Barring a crisis, these changes will probably be a long time coming (at least in the developed world). Legislation is a useful tool for effecting social change; it has a tremendous advantage over moral persuasion in terms of speed and efficacy of implementation, although its results are not always what was intended. In the short term, business solutions—the enlightened self-interest of commercial enterprises finding new ways to incorporate technology and carry on exchanges with greater concern for heretofore unpriced environmental goods and services—offer particular promise. Green marketing and the promotion of responsible consumption are part of that solution.

[Mark A. White]

FURTHER READING:

Bezdek, Roger. "Jobs and Economy: What's the Bottom Line?." *Environment.* September, 1993, pp. 7-11, 23-32.

Bruno, Kenny. *The Greenpeace Book of Greenwash.* Washington: Greenpeace, 1992.

Charter, Martin. "Greener Marketing Strategy." *Greener Marketing*, edited by Martin, Charter. Sheffield, UK: Greenleaf Publishing, 1992, pp. 141-168.

Coddington, Walter. *Environmental Marketing.* New York: McGraw-Hill, 1993.

Elkington, John, Julia Hailes, and Joel Makower. *The Green Consumer.* New York: Penguin Books, 1990.

Federal Trade Commission. *Guidelines for the Use of Environmental Marketing Claims.* Washington: U.S. Government Printing Office, 1992.

Henion, Karl E., II, and Thomas C. Kinnear. "A Guide to Ecological Marketing." *Ecological Marketing*, edited by Karl E. Henion, II, and Thomas C. Kinnear, Chicago: American Marketing Association, 1976, pp. 1-2.

Hopfenbeck, Waldemar. *The Green Management Revolution.* Hertfordshire, UK: Prentice Hall International, 1993.

Mackoy, Robert D., Roger Calantone, and Cornelia Dröge. "Environmental Marketing: Bridging the Divide Between the Consumption Culture and Environmentalism." *Advances in Environmental Marketing*, edited by Michael J. Polonsky, and Alma T. Mintu-Wimsat. Binghamton, NY: Haworth Press, forthcoming.

Mintu, Alma T. and Héctor R. Lozada. "Green Marketing Education: A Call For Action." *Marketing Education Review.* Fall, 1993, pp. 17-23.

Office of Technology Assessment. *Green Products by Design: Choices for a Cleaner Environment.* Washington: U.S. Government Printing Office, 1992.

Ottman, Jacquelyn A. *Green Marketing.* Lincolnwood, IL: NTC Business Books, 1993.

Rehak, Robert. *Greener Marketing and Advertising: Charting a Responsible Course.* Emmaus, PA: Rodale Press, 1993.

The Roper Organization. *The Environment: Public Attitudes and Individual Behavior.* Survey commissioned by S. C. Johnson & Son, 1990.

Salzhauer, Amy L. "Obstacles and Opportunities for a Consumer Ecolabel." *Environment.* November, 1991, pp. 10-15, 33-37.

GREENMAIL

Greenmail can be loosely defined as a type of legal blackmail. In the business world, the term relates to business **takeovers** and describes the type of leverage used when a party attempting a hostile takeover agrees to withdraw the takeover if his or her controlling shares are bought at a high price. The "green" in "greenmail" refers to the color of money.

In a hostile takeover, one person or group of persons decide to take over the stock majority of a company without that company's consent and, in the early stages, without their knowledge. The suitor, also called a "raider," begins by buying up shares of the company's stock. If the targeted firm realizes what is happening, it often tries to fend off the takeover by buying back its own stock. The raider sells, but often at an inflated price, thus greenmail.

The October 30, 1989 issue of *Forbes* documented a $2 million case of greenmail wherein the stockholders of Transtech were about to resist the greenmail until they realized that an obscure tax law would cause them to owe 60 percent of their gross income to the government if they did not buy back the stock. They paid the greenmail ransom to save their company from death by taxation.

[Joan Leotta]

FURTHER READING:

"Greenmail," *Economist.* December 10, 1988, pp. 63-64.

Hannon, Kerry. "Hoist by Their Own Greenmail," *Forbes.* May 29, 1989, pp. 156-157.

King, Ralph, Jr. "What's Wrong with Greenmail?" *Forbes.* March 6, 1989, p. 64.

McMenamin, Brigid. "Political Greenmail," *Forbes.* May 27, 1991, p. 72.

GROSS DOMESTIC PRODUCT

A country's gross domestic product (GDP) is similar to its **gross national product** (GNP), except that GDP excludes net income from foreign sources.

Like GNP, GDP is a measure of the value of a country's production of goods and services for a specific period, usually one year. Comparisons of GDP or GNP from year to year, when measured in constant dollars, indicate changes in a country's overall production and the direction of its economy. In general, economic policy makers look to the size and growth of the GNP or GDP as an indication of the well-being of the country's economy.

As reported by the U.S. Bureau of Economic Analysis in *Survey of Current Business*, the United States's GDP is calculated as the sum of the four components of aggregate demand: consumption, investment, government purchases, and net exports. Personal consumption expenditures are broken out for durable goods, nondurable goods, and services. Gross private domestic investment includes fixed investment and changes in business inventories. Net exports include the value of all goods produced in the United States but sold abroad, minus the value of goods produced abroad and imported into the United States. Government purchases are reported for federal, state, and local governments. All government purchases are considered as final purchases for the purpose of calculating the GDP.

Once the GDP has been calculated, the Bureau of Economic Analysis obtains the nation's GNP by adding all receipts of factor income from the rest of the world and subtracting payments of factor income to the rest of the world. Factor income refers to income received by various factors involved in the production of goods and services, such as employees, business owners, and investors. Factor income from the rest of the world consists largely of receipts by American residents of interest and **dividends** and reinvested earnings of foreign affiliates of American corporations. Payments of factor income to the rest of the world consist largely of payments to foreign residents of interest and dividends and reinvested earnings of American affiliates of foreign corporations.

The difference between the United States's GNP and GDP is relatively small. Where the GDP for 1992 was reported at $6,038.5 billion for 1992, the GNP was $6,045.8. Net income from foreign sources was only $7.3 million in a $6 trillion economy.

[David Bianco]

GROSS NATIONAL PRODUCT

A country's gross national product (GNP) is a measure of the value of its production of goods and services for a specific time period, usually one year. Comparisons of GNP from year to year, when measured in constant dollars, indicate changes in a country's overall production and the direction of its economy. In general, economic policymakers look to the size and growth of the GNP as an indication of the health of the country's economy. In a sense, it is the single most important measure of how an economy is functioning.

The term GNP was probably first used in print by Clark Warburton in his article entitled "Value of the Gross National Product and Its Components, 1919-1929," *Journal of the American Statistical Association,* December 1934.

GNP can be measured in at least two different ways, both of which yield the same result. One way of measuring the GNP is from the buyer's point-of-view, or in terms of aggregate demand. Also known as the expenditure approach to measuring GNP, this method calculates the value of the GNP as the sum of the four components of GNP expenditures: consumption, investment, government purchases, and net exports.

The expenditure method accounts for the source of the monetary demand for products and services. The largest component, consumption, includes the value of all the goods and services purchased by consumers during the year. (As a general rule, consumption expenditures account for approximately 65 percent of GNP in the United States). The investment category includes the production of buildings and equipment as well as the net accumulation of inventories. Financial investments, which involve only transfer payments rather than the production of capital goods, are not counted. Government purchases include only expenditures for goods and services, not transfer payments such as social security. Net exports include the value of all goods produced in the United States but sold abroad, minus the value of goods produced abroad and imported into the United States.

Since every transaction involves a buyer and a seller, the GNP can also be calculated from the seller's point-of-view, which focuses on where money payments go. The method, also known as the income approach, measures GNP as the sum of all the incomes received by all owners of resources used in production. Such income payments are known as factor payments, because they are paid to various factors involved in the production of goods and services. These include employee compensation, rental income, proprietary income, corporate profits, interest income, **depreciation**, and indirect business taxes.

Employee compensation includes all payments relating to labor, including fringe benefits and taxes paid on labor. In the United States, employee compensation accounts for approximately 60 percent of GNP. Rental income is paid for the use of capital goods. Proprietary income represents payments to owners of

business firms. Corporate profits are earned by the shareholders of a business. Interest income is received for lending financial resources. Depreciation is a charge against **assets** used in production. The indirect business tax refers to **sales tax**, which represents part of the payments for goods and services that are not paid to any of the income recipients.

The measurement of GNP is fairly complex and follows a set of rules that, while generally agreed upon, may nevertheless appear somewhat arbitrary. For example, housing is treated in a manner that protects GNP calculations from changes in the rate of home ownership. All occupant-owned housing, as opposed to rental housing, is treated in the GNP accounts as if rented. Thus, the rental value of occupant-owned housing is included as a service in the GNP along with the rental value of houses that are actually rented.

GNP measures the value of final products and services, so it is necessary to avoid double-counting the many intermediary products that are bought and sold in the economy. Products and services are counted as part of the GNP when they reach their final form.

Some important final products are actually excluded from the GNP. Many household activities are excluded, as are all illegal goods and services. In the case of housework, the services of a hired maid are considered part of the GNP, but not if the same services are performed by a member of the household. The exclusion of domestic chores has a greater effect on the calculation of the GNP of lesser-developed countries, where households may produce their own food and clothing to a greater extent than in the United States.

The treatment of government expenditures also affects GNP calculations. All government expenditures are considered final; there is no attempt to categorize them as intermediate and final. The effect of this rule is an upward bias in the GNP. In addition, all government expenditures are considered as current consumption rather than as investments; they are only measured once, in the year in which they occur. Finally, government goods and services, which are usually not sold in the marketplace, are valued at cost in the GNP.

In the United States the GNP is reported at an annual rate every quarter by the U.S. Department of Commerce's Bureau of Economic Analysis. That is, the quarterly figures represent what the GNP would have been for the year had the same rate of production continued for the entire year.

GNP is usually reported in current dollars. To obtain a comparison with past GNPs, the real GNP is calculated in constant dollars using what is known as the GNP deflator. While the reported GNP of the

United States grew from approximately $288 billion in 1950 to $5201 billion in 1989, the real GNP as measured in constant 1982 dollars only grew from $1204 billion to $4118 billion. During that period real GNP increased less than four times over, while GNP as measured in current dollars appeared to increase by approximately 15 times. The difference between reported GNP and real GNP is due to price increases rather than increases in the production of goods and services.

[David Bianco]

FURTHER READING:

Carson, Carol. "The History of the United States National Income and Product Accounts: The Development of an Analytical Tool," *Review of Income and Wealth*. June, 1975, p. 162.

GROUPTHINK

Groupthink occurs when group pressure causes poor group decision making, usually resulting in bad decisions and bad outcomes. Psychologist Irving Janis defines groupthink as: "a quick and easy way to refer to a mode of thinking people engage in when they are deeply involved in a cohesive in-group, when the members' striving for unanimity override their motivation to realistically appraise alternative courses of action. Groupthink refers to a deterioration of mental efficiency, reality testing, and moral judgment that results from in-group pressures." It can also refer to the tendency of groups to agree with powerful, intimidating bosses. As Janis says, "Sometimes the main trouble is that the chief executive manipulates his advisors to rubber-stamp his own ill-conceived proposals." The term "groupthink" was coined by Janis to explain some startlingly bad decisions made by governments and businesses, which he calls "fiascoes." He was particularly interested in situations where group pressure seemed to result in a fundamental failure to think.

Social science has a long history of interest in group pressure on individual rational processes—for example, the early work of G. Le Bon on crowd behavior and Emile Durkheim's work on altruistic suicide, first published in 1898. Individual judgment "caves in" under group pressure, and, as Durkheim says, "The weight of society is thus brought to bear on him to lead him to destroy himself."

Although not focusing on groups in particular, Stanley Milgram was interested in the concept of submission to authority, a phenomenon similar to that which occurs when groups agree not to create disharmony in the face of powerful bosses. Jerry Harvey noted similar results—groups doing things of poor quality which no one really wanted to do—and called it the Abilene Paradox. Barbara Tuchman called poor decisions "folly" in her 1984 book, *The March of Folly*. She was more interested in decision results than in the group process which drove them, but she falls within the group of thinkers exploring poor quality decisions.

The study of **decision making** is complex. There is the decision itself, how it is made, and the results of the decision. A crude decision formula is: $R = D + I$ (results equals decisions plus implementation). There are many factors that can affect a result other than the group's decision, including events that happened after the decision was made and faulty implementation. Even bad decisions sometimes have good results if opponents make even worse decisions.

The concept of groupthink provides a summary explanation of reasons groups sometimes make poor decisions. Indeed, groups are supposed to be better than individuals at making complex decisions, because, through the membership, a variety of differing perspectives are brought to bear. They not only serve to bring new ideas into the discussion but also act as error-correcting mechanisms. Groups also provide social support, which is especially critical for new ideas.

But when new perspectives are rejected (as in the "not invented here" syndrome), it is hard to correct errors. And if the social support was geared toward supporting the group's "accepted wisdom," the elements that can make groups better decision makers than individuals become inverted, and make them worse. Just as groups can work to promote effective decision thinking/making, the same processes which enhance the group's operation can backfire and lead to disastrous results.

Janis identified seven points on how groupthink works. First, the group's discussions are limited to a few alternative courses of action (often only two), without a survey of the full range of alternatives. Second, the group does not survey the objectives to be fulfilled and the values implicated by the choice. Third, the group fails to reexamine the course of action initially preferred by the majority of members from the standpoint of the nonobvious risks and drawbacks that had not been considered when it was originally evaluated. Fourth, the members neglect courses of action initially evaluated as unsatisfactory—they spend little or no time discussing whether they have overlooked nonobvious gain. Fifth, the members make little or no attempt to obtain information from experts who can supply sound estimates of gains and losses to be expected from alternative courses of action. Sixth, selective bias is shown in the way the group reacts to factual information and relevant judgments from experts. Seventh, the members spend little time deliberating about how the chosen policy might be hindered by bureaucratic inertia or sabotaged by political opponents; consequently, they fail to work out contingency plans.

While these kinds of problems can stem from many sources, they are common to groupthink situations. Tuchman surveys history from the incident of the Trojan Horse to Vietnam, while Janis looks at situations such as Watergate and the Iranian rescue mission. Numerous examples from business could be cited as well.

Three general problems seem to be at work: overestimation of group power and morality, closed mindedness, and pressures toward uniformity. Groupthink occurs when a group feels too good about itself. The group feels both invulnerable and optimistic. The group feels morally right. As one business leader has said, "We thought we were golden." Linked to this attitude of perfection is a correlative closemindedness. Warnings are ignored. Messengers of difference are dismissed. Negative, stereotypic views of opponents are created and used. Finally, there is pressure for uniformity. A certain amount of self-censorship occurs. If individuals have questions, they keep them to themselves. This lack of dissent results in what Janis calls an "illusion of unanimity." If any difference does occur, group pressure is applied to bring the dissident into line. Janis also mentions "the emergence of self appointed mindguards—members who protect the group from adverse information that might shatter their shared complacency."

If these precipitating problems support tendencies to groupthink, there are predisposing conditions as well. Janis suggests four antecedent conditions that create the predisposition to groupthink: cohesiveness, group isolation/insulation, leader intimidation, and an absence of decision-making procedures.

As a group "hangs together" and members grow to like each other, there will be greater pressure not to introduce disturbing information and opinion that might tear at that cohesiveness. Maintaining the good feelings that come from such cohesion become part of the group's "hidden agenda." The insulation of the policy-making group is another factor. Frequently groupthinking groups are removed from interaction with others, perhaps because of their position at the top of the organization.

Lack of impartial **leadership** is a third contributing cause. When powerful leaders want to "get their way" they can overtly and covertly pressure the group into agreement. Indeed, such pressure has become in many quarters a shorthand definition of groupthink itself—capitulation to power. Brian Dumaine wrote about some of these tough bosses in *Fortune*: "In an era of endless restructuring, cutting heads like Robespierre is just average. These leaders inflict pain by messing with your mind." When your boss screams at you for several minutes, as Steve Jobs was reported to have done to a hapless subordinate, groupthink is virtually inevitable.

Finally, the group did not have a template or protocol for decision making, and norms for such a procedure were also missing, what Janis calls "the lack of norms requiring methodological procedures for dealing with decision making tasks."

There are several things businesspersons can do to avoid groupthink: follow good meeting procedures, including the development of agenda; aim for proper and balanced staff work; and present competing views and attend to correlative meeting problems like exhaustion. A template for discussion might also be useful. One suggestion is to use (step #1) an "options memo technique" in which information is presented as a problem statement (step #2) a list of options and (step #3) a preliminary recommendation. The group then looks at the preliminary recommendation with at least four questions in mind: (1) is the logic correct? (in selecting the preliminary recommendation from among the options); (2) is the judgment correct? (the logic may be fine, but the judgment may be poor); (3) are there any problems or errors remaining in the preliminary recommendation?; (4) can the preliminary recommendation be improved? Janis and L. Mann provide a template that proceeds with the following six questions: (1) need; (2) alternatives; (3) gains and losses to self and others; (4) overall pros and cons; (5) commitment to action (decision), (6) implementation.

Resolving the template issue is one thing. Securing norms that support its use is another. Both are needed. In addition, work is needed to prevent group isolation. This can be achieved through bringing in new participants on a regular basis, using outside experts (both specific experts and experts on the meeting/decision process), and inviting the group to meet off-site so that changes in settings and surroundings are a stimulant.

It is vital for the chairperson, or leader, to become a statesperson, an orchestra conductor, instead of a partisan virtuoso. Leadership almost always involves getting work done through others. High-quality decisions are not made through intimidation, intentional or unintentional. Many bosses lack a sufficiently developed "observing ego" to see how much they intimidate others. Some bosses have no idea why people do not speak up, while the reason they do not is because they are likely to be attacked. Bosses are best if they can alert their groups to the kind of review they want. A boss can say "I have made this decision. If anyone wants to comment, that's fine, but it is a done deal;" or "I am going to make this decision. I would like your input, but I am not promising I will follow the alternatives you develop here." Or a boss can say, "I am going to make this decision and want your input. I will be shaped by it, and you will see that in the result;'' or '' I would like you to make this decision, but here are my parameters in term of time, cost, etc.'' If the leader can be clear, and temperate, there is a great likelihood that norms of disagreement will develop.

Finally, there is the cohesion process itself. Decision making tears at the fabric of group cohesion, and it is the desire to preserve cohesion that is an underlying dynamic of groupthink. Decision fiascoes are nondecisions, or a decision masked by fake agreement. It is clear that decision making will rupture cohesion. But if decisions lower group cohesion it is not necessary to avoid decisions; an alternative is to rebuild it each time. One way to accomplish this rebuilding is to complete decision making by about 65 percent of the way through the meeting, then move on to brainstorming, ''blue-sky'' (future-oriented) items for the last 20-30 percent of the meeting. People who have differed before have a chance to continue to interact, now around less threatening, future-oriented items. It allows for decompression, and for rebonding the group.

Because of the flaws of individual decision making—selective perception, excessive self-interest, limited knowledge, limited time—most important decisions today are made in groups. And groups can do a spectacular job; but they often do not. Meetings, the place where groups do their decision-making work, have a ''bad press,'' largely because of processes such as groupthink. Groupthink is the result of flawed procedures, poor leadership, insulation, and an unmanaged desire for the maintenance of group cohesion and its good feelings. These can be addressed positively, and group decision making improved, while groupthink is kept to a minimum.

SEE ALSO: Policy Making

[John E. Tropman]

FURTHER READING:

Durkheim, Emile. Suicide. New York: The Free Press, 1950.

Entrepreneurial Systems for the 1990s. Westport: Quorum Books, 1989.

Goodman, Paul S., and Associates. Designing Effective Work Groups. New York: Jossey-Bass, 1986.

Groupthink. Video recording. Carlsbad, CA: CRM Films, 1991.

Harvey, Jerry. ''The Abilene Paradox.'' Organizational Dynamics. Summer, 1974, pp. 63-80.

Hart, Paul. Groupthink in Government. Amsterdam and Rockland, Mass.: Swets & Zeitlinger, 1990.

International Studies Quarterly. 38 (supplement) April, 1994, pp. 101-107.

Janis, I. Crucial Decisions. New York: The Free Press, 1989.

Janis, I. Groupthink: Psychological Studies of Policy Decisions and Fiascoes. Boston: Houghton Mifflin, 1983.

Janis, I., and L. Mann. Decision Making: A Psychological Analysis of Conflict, Choice, and Commitment. New York: The Free Press, 1977.

Kleindorfer, Paul R. Decision Sciences: An Integrated Perspective. New York: Cambridge University Press, 1993.

Le Bon, G. The Crowd. London: Unwin, 1986.

March, James G., and H. Simon Organizations, New York: Wiley, 1958.

Milgram, Stan. Obedience to Authority. New York: Harper & Row, 1974.

Plous, Scott. The Psychology of Judgment and Decision Making. New York: McGraw Hill, 1993.

Sims, Ronald. ''Linking Groupthink to Unethical Behavior in Organizations.'' Journal of Business Ethics. September 11, 1992 pp. 651-652.

Tropman, John E. Effective Meetings. Sage Publications, 1995.

Tropman, John E., John Erlich and Jack Rothman, eds. Tactics and Techniques of Community Intervention. 3rd ed. Itasca, IL: F. E. Peacock, 1995.

Tuchman, Barbara. The March of Folly. New York: Knopf, 1984.

Weick, Karl, and Karlene Roberts. ''Collective Mind in Organizations: Heedful Interrelating on Flight Decks.'' Administrative Science Quarterly. 38, 1993, pp. 357-381.

Zander, Alvin. Making Groups Effective. San Francisco: Jossey-Bass, 1982.

GUARANTEED INVESTMENT CONTRACTS

Guaranteed investment contracts (GICs) are a type of financial instrument available to investors. Based on an article by Kleiman and Sahu in the American Association of Individual Investors Journal, key characteristics, advantages and disadvantages of owning guaranteed investment contracts are explained in this essay.

BACKGROUND AND SOME KEY CHARACTERISTICS OF THE GICS

Guaranteed investment contracts are one type of financial instrument with certain special characteristics regarding the rate of return on the instrument. Guaranteed investment contracts are similar to certificates of deposit issued by commercial **banks**, **savings and loan associations**, and **credit unions**, except that they are marketed by insurance companies, which are considered nonbank financial institutions. With GICs, corporations and individuals pay money in exchange for a contract that ''promises'' them the return of their principal at maturity plus an investment yield (i.e., the return on the investment) in line with prevailing money market rates at the inception of the contract. The yields or returns on GICs are generally higher than those on bank CDs by one-half of a percent to one percentage point at the time of purchase.

Guaranteed investment contracts are one of the most popular choices of participants in 401(k) retirement plans, who collectively hold $200 billion of the GIC securities. Roughly two-thirds of all **401(k) plans** offer guaranteed investment contracts as an investment option, and GICs account for more than 50 percent of the invested financial **assets** of these retirement plans. GICs bought for 401(k) plans usually permit deposits to be timed throughout the purchase year so that they coincide with employees' deferred income plans.

When employees of a company join their firm's 401(k) retirement plan, they are offered at least four options for investing their pension contributions—typically a money-market **mutual fund**, the company's own **common stock**, one or more equity (stock) mutual funds, and a GIC. For the portion of 401(k) retirement plan contributions allocated by employees to GICs, the company's pension plan manager shops for the best deal among the insurance companies that offer GICs, looking for attractive **interest rates** and maturities. Furthermore, in order to diversify the risk, fund managers may sign contracts with as many as 20 issuers of guaranteed investment contracts, although a recent study by Buck Consultants suggested that the typical large employer purchased GICs only from seven different carriers. The insurance companies that receive funds through the issuance of GICs, in turn, invest GIC money in a variety of investment vehicles—residential mortgages; government bonds, corporate bonds and riskier high yield bonds (junk bonds); and private placements. The yield or return that an employee receives on his or her investment represents the blended rate of return from the various GICs selected by the employee's company.

There are two basic types of GICs: participating and nonparticipating. With the first variety of GICs, investors receive a variable rate of return, and thus they literally *participate* in the risks and rewards resulting from the fluctuations in the interest rate. On the other hand, on participating GICs offer a fixed rate of return. When current market interest rates are high, it may make sense to buy a nonparticipating GIC and lock in the high fixed rate of return for the life of the investment contract. However, if interest rates are expected to rise in the future, it may instead be preferable to invest in a participating GIC, so as to benefit from the expected rise in the interest rate.

GIC contracts bought for defined contribution pension plans are generally quite large. A standard transaction might involve a sum of $10 million or more. The contracts generally have a maturity period between one and seven years. When the term of the GIC contract is up, the employees' pension fund recovers the principal from the maturing contracts and either reinvests it in another GIC or returns it to employees who are either retiring or cashing out of the plan.

THE "GUARANTEE" IN GICS. Unsophisticated investors are very likely to ask why they even need to worry about of the loss of principal in a GIC contract. After all, aren't these investments guaranteed? The answer to the puzzling question lies in the fact that the "guarantee" refers only to the rate of interest that the issuer of the financial instrument promises to pay for the life of contract. As the holders of GICs issued by the Executive Life and Mutual Benefit Life insurance companies were reminded recently, the principal invested is very much at risk if the issuer of the GIC fails.

In contrast to bank CDs, GICs are backed only by the financial health of the insurance company issuing the contract, not by the federal government. Bank CDs are almost invariably insured by a federal agency called the **Federal Deposit Insurance Corporation** (FDIC); CDs issued by savings and loans, and credit unions are insured by similar federal deposit insurance agencies. Therefore, a GIC is only as good as the insurance company that issues the contract. Recently, some insurance companies burdened with investments in high-risk junk bonds and nonperforming real estate loans, have seen their credit worthiness deteriorate considerably. The well-publicized failures in 1991 of the two insurance companies mentioned above, Executive Life and Mutual Benefit Life, have forced pension fund managers and 401(k) plan members to take a harder look at GICs and to re-evaluate the risk associated with them.

Of course, the chance that big insurance companies will go bankrupt and cost employees their 401(k) retirement money is quite remote. Moreover, since the GICs included in an individual company's pension plan are most likely to be composed of contracts issued by a number of insurance companies, the failure of one insurer would not necessarily cause a significant decline in the value of the pension plan's total assets. In addition, many major insurance companies that market GICs hold only small amounts of noninvestment grade, or junk, bonds. It is important to note that approximately 50 percent of the **junk bonds** owned by the life insurance industry are held by ten companies, and few of these companies sell GICs.

Does an investor lose the principal amount if the insurance company that issued a GIC goes bankrupt? The bankruptcy courts are now in the process of deciding this issue. The current laws in most states stipulate that holders of guaranteed investment contracts come after the policyholders of the insurance company in question, should the insurance company go bankrupt. Other than Louisiana, all states in the United States maintain a guaranty fund to compensate insurance policyholders in the event an insurance company fails. However, not all state guaranty funds cover the GIC obligations of insurance companies. Almost half of the states are not explicit regarding their intent towards compensating holders of GICs.

NEWER VARIETIES OF GUARANTEED INVESTMENT CONTRACTS

The traditional GIC issued by insurance companies promises to pay a rate of return based on the earnings of the company's assets. The principal amount, however, is backed by the company's own ability to pay, as embodied in its credit worthiness. This, in turn, implies that a guaranteed investment contract is as good as the insurance company that issues it. Thus, as concerns regarding the financial soundness and robustness of insurance companies have mounted, new versions of the standard guaranteed investment contracts have emerged in the financial markets to address the aforesaid concerns.

With investments of more than $200 billion in GICs, a loss of confidence in insurance companies could potentially lead to a gigantic outflow of cash from the insurance companies participating in the GIC market. Although most insurance companies have solid asset bases especially those that are not threatened by risky real estate **loans** or a heavy concentration in junk bonds and are most likely to keep much of their customer base, many types of financial institutions are rushing to provide alternative financial instruments to calm the nerves of worried pension fund managers.

Basically, the new varieties of guaranteed investment contracts carry additional protection against default by issuers of the contract. The improved versions of guaranteed investment contracts include bank investment contracts (BICs), which are issued by financial institutions such as Bankers Trust and J.P. Morgan, and GIC "alternatives," which are sold by major securities firms such as Merrill Lynch and Shearson Lehman Brothers. It is useful to examine the nature of extra protection built into the newer instruments.

THE ADDED SECURITY OF THE NEWER INSTRUMENTS. In contrast with the holders of guaranteed investment contracts issued by insurance companies, buyers of contracts marketed by banks and investment firms purchase the underlying securities outright. The relevant securities are then held in a trust fund for investors. This arrangement seems to clearly put the securities beyond reach of the banks' and investment firms' creditors in the event that these institutions default or go bankrupt. Thus, the arrangement spreads the risk beyond the issuer of the contract. Some institutions have taken added precautions—some banks deposit additional securities as collateral to make up for any shortfall in the market value of the original

investments in case of a default, while some investment firms guarantee the book value of the newer versions of the standard GIC by obtaining a letter of credit that cannot be revoked.

Investors in the contracts sold by banks might be tempted to assume that BICs would be protected by FDIC insurance, which insures bank deposits up to $100,000. Because, bank investment contracts (BICs) are like bank deposits in principle, they too can be federally insured for as much as $100,000. However, this insurance should not be assumed automatically— it is up to the banks issuing BICs to decide whether FDIC insurance is offered for those contracts. At present few banks offer FDIC insurance on bank investment contracts. The cost of the premium is the key deciding factor—the premium is about 0.25 percent of the deposit, which would make the new instrument less competitive with non-FDIC insured GICs if the increased cost is passed on to buyers of the contract, and less profitable to the financial institutions if it is absorbed by the issuers. Therefore, some investors, lured by somewhat higher returns, are continuing to stick with traditional GICs issued by the most credit worthy of insurance companies.

SYNTHETIC GICS. While BICs have pulled in more than $20 billion, they face tough competition from a number of other GIC alternatives. These alternative instruments have been dubbed as SynGICs or synthetic GICs—sometimes referred to as "participating" or "separate-account" GICs.

With synthetic GICs, an employer is allowed to examine what is in the portfolio of investments and, in some cases, is permitted to choose the specific assets that would back the contract he or she is buying for the employee pension fund. Thus, rather than relying on all assets in the portfolio of an insurance company, the investor could, for instance, pick mortgages backed by Fannie Mae or Treasuries, which are considered virtually risk-free with respect to the repayment of the principal. Under this arrangement, the assets earmarked for the guaranteed investment contracts are transferred back to the pension fund in the event that the insurance company goes bankrupt.

Although synthetic GICs are designed to shift the credit risk away from the insurance company, investors do pay for the sense of added security in other ways. The synthetic guaranteed investment contracts no longer embody the long-term guaranteed rate of return. Instead of a guaranteed rate, these new securities are subject to annual interest rate adjustments. In addition, buyers of synthetic GICS assume at least some of the default risk associated with the underlying investments. If an investment backing a synthetic GIC sours, the investor's return would also be reduced.

Several securities firms are promoting the alternative instrument known as synthetic GICs. Moreover, insurance companies themselves have joined the fray, issuing several varieties of the synthetic GICs. Insurance companies such as Metropolitan Life are offering a version of synthetic GICs that spreads credit risk by placing underlying securities in an account that is separate from the insurance company's general assets. By placing the securities in a separate account for the purposes of GICs, default risk is essentially designed to be passed on to the issuers of the underlying securities. This arrangement also puts the underlying assets out of reach of the insurer's creditors, in case the insurer goes bankrupt. Under this arrangement, the issuers of the underlying securities would have to default in order to jeopardize the GIC investor's principal. The aforesaid arrangement, however, is not without difficulties. Some legal experts question whether the arrangement will withstand challenges in courts, since the insurance companies continue to maintain the legal ownership of the securities, which is also the case with traditional GICs. In other words, some believe that a mere separation of accounts may not be enough to keep the underlying securities from the reach of the insurer's creditors.

Rising concern about the financial soundness of insurance companies has prompted some pension fund managers to re-examine the wisdom of GIC investments. A survey by Buck Consultants suggested that a majority of employers are considering, or have already made changes, such as examining vendors of GICs more closely, raising required credit standards, or adding other fixed-income options to their retirement plans. In fact, the proportion of company retirement plans offering GICs and BICs has also declined, according to a study by Greenwich Associates.

INVESTMENT PERFORMANCE OF GICS/BICS

As mentioned earlier, a guaranteed yield is one of reasons for growth in GICs (and now BICs). Some experts, however, question whether GIC/BIC yield levels are adequate to be suitable investments for retirement plans (note that a pension or retirement plan is, by nature, a longer term investment, and the return over the long period should be attractive enough to warrant inclusion of a financial instrument into the pension plan portfolio). The study by Kleiman and Sahu in the *AAII Journal* examined average yields for GICs/BICs from 1989-91. They found that the average rate of return on three-year GICs/BICs was 8.24 percent per annum. The Kleiman-Sahu study also suggested that, as with other fixed rate financial investments, the yields increased as the term to maturity increased—the average yields on five- and seven-year GICs/BICs were 8.62 percent and 8.78 percent, respectively. In addition, their study found that yields increased as the size of the GIC contract increased—the average yield on $1 million denomination GIC/

BIC contracts was 8.49% over the time period studied, whereas the comparable figures for $5 million and $10 million denominations were 8.56 percent and 8.59 percent, respectively.

Are these yields on GICs/BICs high enough to warrant investment? As Kleiman and Sahu reported in their study, the yields on GICs/BICs were only slightly higher than those prevailing on U.S. Treasury securities of comparable maturities. Based on data compiled by Fiduciary Capital Management, the average spread between GICs/BICs and Treasury instruments widened during the 1989-1991 time period—from 0.74 percent in 1989 to 1.07 percent in 1991. This increase is likely due to the well-publicized financial difficulties encountered in 1991 by insurance companies such as Executive Life and Mutual Benefit Life. Over a longer time period covering 1975 to 1990, guaranteed investment contracts yielded an average of 9.2 percent annually, which outperformed the 8.9 percent return achieved by the average Treasury bond fund with a two-year maturity by mere 0.3 percent.

DO GICS/BICS BELONG IN PENSION PLANS? Given that GICs only marginally outperform Treasury securities, the investor can question whether the added risk of guaranteed investment contracts (in relation to risk-less Treasury bonds) is commensurate with the extra return on GICs/BICs. Moreover, in concentrating only on the credit and market risks associated with guaranteed investment contracts, investors in these instruments may be overlooking the mortality risk. Mortality risk essentially measures the possibility that the annual long-term returns on a retirement portfolio will not be sufficient to provide retirement benefits that a participant in the pension plan will not outlive. In other words, a pension fund participant's benefits may run out before his or her death.

Financial experts feel that, even if a GIC is performing well, an investor under 40 years of age who has more than 20 percent of his/her pension fund portfolio in guaranteed investment contracts can probably afford to take greater levels of market risk (the risk of fluctuations in the market value of the investment portfolio). The main rationale for undertaking greater market risk by younger investors is based on the potential for greater reward offered by alternative investment vehicles which, in turn, will result in reduced mortality risk. Many alternative investment mediums yield far greater returns over a long period of time. Investments in a well-diversified, equity-oriented portfolio are generally considered the best bet for relatively young investors (40-years-old or under). Common stocks, of course, are considerably volatile and thus risky. They have, however, yielded returns commensurate with the risk—approximately 6.5 percent per annum inflation adjusted real rate since 1920. More recently, a diversified portfolio of common stocks has yielded a compounded annual return of roughly 15 percent over the 1975-1990 time period. For an initial investment of $10,000, the difference between the investment in common stocks yielding 15 percent per annum and the 9 percent return from a non-participating GIC is almost $45,000 over a 15-year investment period, quite a noticeable amount. Younger investors should therefore consider putting between 70 percent and 80 percent of their retirement portfolios into common stocks.

One must, however, remember that the returns on common stocks are also considerably more volatile than those on guaranteed investment contracts. This volatility can adversely affect the retirement funds of participants who are close to retirement. Thus, for individuals closer to retirement, financial experts advise a gradual shift of their pension fund resources into fixed-income securities (such as GICs, CDs, short-term Treasuries, etc.) until these securities constitute the vast majority of their portfolios (perhaps 90 percent or more) at age 65. Such a retirement strategy will have the benefit of portfolio growth fueled by the stock market when the investor can afford to take greater risk during younger days and the safety of fixed-income instruments at the time of retirement, when taking chances with stock market volatility may be too risky to be worthwhile.

THE FUTURE OF TRADITIONAL AND SYNTHETIC GICS

The news on both traditional and synthetic guaranteed investment contracts continues to be mixed. According to Julie Rohrer (*Institutional Investor*), rising interest rates and declining concerns about the credit worthiness of insurance companies has led to a resurgence of the traditional single-maturity guaranteed investment contracts in the last few years. Synthetic GICs also seem to be riding a wave of popularity, despite the adverse effect of rising interest rates on the investment performance of underlying bond portfolios. Antony Michels reported in *Fortune* in 1994, that, after losing ground since 1990, sales of guaranteed investment contracts were up nearly 36 percent in the second quarter of 1994 versus the same period in 1993.

The return of guaranteed investment contracts to favor was not confined to sales growth alone—the recent investment performance of GICs was also quite noticeable. According to the *Pension & Investments Performance Evaluation Report* (PIPER), eight of the top 10 performing PIPER commingled funds in the second quarter of 1994 were guaranteed investment contracts stable value funds, while 7 of the top 10 commingled funds for the 12 months ended June 30, 1994 were GIC funds. Note that stable value funds are essentially a new class of guaranteed investment contracts (GIC), under the broad category commonly known as synthetic GICs—they guarantee a stable value, but do not invest underlying assets in a single insurance company's general account; instead, they are "owned" by the pension plan sponsor.

The news regarding GICs is, however, not uniformly good—uncertainties regarding the financial soundness of contract issuers continue. *Barron's* reported on September 5, 1994 that a Canadian insurer, Confederation Life Insurance Co., had failed. Its demise created some doubt as to the status of nearly $2.4 billion in guaranteed investment contracts that the company's U.S. subsidiary had sold to pension plan managers across the United States. The Confederation collapse is very unsettling, as there were few outward signs of major financial problems before the insurance company was seized by Canadian regulators in August 1994. Confederation has already stopped making principal and interest payments on its GIC obligations and is not expected to make any payments until an arrangement is worked out to liquidate or rehabilitate the company's American operations. Experts are inclined to believe that the Confederation situation will most likely accelerate the trend toward alternatives to traditional GICs—synthetic GICs and other similar financial instruments.

GROWTH OF SYNTHETIC GICS. According to William Fred in *Pensions & Investments*, two financial services firms, Aldrich, Eastman & Waltch and ITT Hartford Life Insurance Companies, have introduced stable value investment vehicles with some new twists designed to appeal to the growing interest in alternatives to the traditional guaranteed investment contracts.

Jim Connolly emphasized the growth of synthetic GICs in *National Underwriter*. He reported two recent surveys issued by LIMRA that reported investments in stable value products for 1993 reaching an estimated $47 billion to $48 billion. The survey showed that synthetic products accounted for more than one quarter of all stable value products sold in 1993, compared with 15 percent during 1992.

THE LIKELY FUTURE OF GUARANTEED INVESTMENT CONTRACTS. Not everyone feels comfortable about the move away from the traditional GICs. Charles Clinton (in *Benefits Quarterly*), for example, expressed his disappointment that many pension plan sponsors were moving away from traditional GICs for the wrong reasons—they believed that the products were flawed. Clinton also believed that traditional GICs were flawed only if they were managed by a financially weak insurance company. The Confederation collapse demonstrated that logic was flawed.

[Andrew Sahu]

FURTHER READING:

Clinton, Charles A. "Traditional GICs Are Here to Stay." *Benefits Quarterly*. Second Quarter, 1993, pp. 17-21.

Connolly, Jim. "GIC Shifts Noted in '93 Sales Totals." *National Underwriter*. [Life/Health/Financial Services], July 11, 1994, p. 3, 23.

Kleiman, Robert T., and Sahu, Anandi P. "The ABCs of GICs for Retirement Investing." *AAII Journal*. March, 1992, pp. 7-10.

Michels, Antony J. "The Return of the GIC." *Fortune*. September 5, 1994.

Rohrer, Julie. "GIC Revival." *Institutional Investor*. August, 1994, pp. 119-120.

Williams, Fred. "GIC Managers Score Best in PIPER Rankings." *Pensions & Investments*. September 5, 1994, pp. 19-20.

Williams, Fred. "Stable Value Funds Feature New Twists." *Pensions & Investments*. August 8, 1994, p. 2.

GUARANTEES

SEE: Warranties and Guarantees

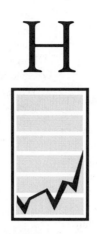

H

HANDBOOKS AND MANUALS

Handbooks and manuals are the most common form of documentation in the business environment. They are required for virtually every type of activity. Many are computerized today, but in whatever form they appear, they must be available. Without them, employees would lose a valuable reference source and businesses would suffer from a variety of problems, ranging from untrained workers to costly lawsuits. Simply put, business offices cannot function efficiently without the myriad of handbooks and manuals lining their shelves.

HANDBOOKS AND MANUALS: THEY ARE NOT THE SAME

Some people use the terms handbook and manual interchangeably. There is a subtle difference between the two. A handbook is a concise manual or reference book providing specific information or instruction about a topic. A manual is a larger document that contains a broader range of information. Subtle differences aside, the terms are used interchangeably throughout this article. Whichever term is applied, handbooks and manuals are extremely important documents in the business world.

THE IMPORTANCE OF HANDBOOKS AND MANUALS

Business people need handbooks and manuals to keep employees, suppliers, customers, shareholders, and anyone else who has an interest in their business apprised of policies, procedures, and regulations. The documents in some cases represent the company's survival. In today's litigious society, companies often become the target of lawsuits that can cost them millions of dollars. Some of these lawsuits, e.g., those regarding **sexual harassment** and **product liability**, can be avoided if companies include in their handbooks information that explains their policies regarding those issues. And, without adequate documents, employees would be at a loss regarding a company's culture, i.e., the way it does things, mission, grievance procedures in short, anything that affects employees and their work environment. Not all of the documents are related strictly to the company, though. They address a variety of topics.

For example, a company that purchases machinery of any type, from punch presses to computers, needs manuals to explain to the people who will be using it how the equipment operates, when it is to be serviced, etc. Likewise, if a company purchases **software** for its operations, it must also acquire manuals which explain how the software operates and provide instructions to employees on how to use it. **Manufacturing** concerns need extensive documentation to stay abreast of government regulations, safety standards, and other issues legislated by local federal, and state agencies. Documentation is used for other purposes, too.

Handbooks and manuals are used in training programs. It is not enough in many situations to simply distribute a policy handbook to all employees, for example. Many of the policies included, particularly those that have a direct impact on the employee and the company, may require follow-up training. Such topics might include sexual harassment policies and codes of ethics. Also, computer users may require in-class training on different functions of computer hardware and software, **customer relations**, etc. Thus, handbooks and manuals are integral parts of in-house training programs. There is seemingly no end to the number and types of documents needed to support a company's operations. Fortunately, the proliferation of computers has facilitated the process considerably.

COMPUTERS IN THE DOCUMENTATION PROCESS

Computers have greatly facilitated the production of manuals and handbooks. They can incorporate graphics with text, print multiple copies of documents in color or black and white, and make the change process simple. They enhance the artwork included in manuals and utilize a wide range of type fonts that improve the appearance of documents. Computers have made it possible for virtually anyone who can use a computer to produce the text and graphics that comprise handbooks and manuals. At the same time, they have created new job opportunities for technical writers and graphics artists, the specialists who produce manuals and handbooks. More importantly, computers have reduced the costs involved in producing quality manuals and handbooks and have made documents of all types more accessible.

WHO PRODUCES HANDBOOKS?

Handbooks and manuals are written by anyone from entry-level custodians to the chief executive officers of corporations. Who writes particular documents depends on the size of the corporation, the expertise of the employees, the purpose of the manual, etc. There are also specialists who are employed full time or on a contract basis to produce manuals. Many of them fall under the broad headings of technical writers and graphics artists.

Graphics artists produce the illustrations that accompany the text in handbooks and manuals. Technical writers specialize in producing scientific or industry-specific information in readable form for lay persons. "Scientific" in this case can mean anything from data processing language to engineering terms to astrophysics. Often, scientists rely on technical writers to translate the special terminology they use in their fields of expertise into understandable terms for non-scientists or product users. There is often a mystique attached to technical writing. In truth, technical writing is no different than any other type of writing.

The purpose of technical writing is to reduce to understandable terms language that might be hard for the average person to comprehend. For example, data processing technical writers produce a wide range of manuals. They might produce user manuals for computer users and systems manuals for programmers and analysts. Technical writers in scientific fields might produce research proposals for professors and consul-

tants or a procedures manual for a geological team to follow. But, not all manuals and handbooks are written by technical writers.

An administrative assistant might be asked to write a handbook explaining to co-workers or temporary workers how to use a switchboard or a computer. The chief executive officer of a small corporation may put together an informal handbook for managers on how to supervise people, handle customer returns, etc. Generally, who writes the manuals is not important. What is important is whether the manual serves a practical purpose, i.e., teaches employees, customers, and other audience members about a procedure, policy, technique, etc.

THE ART OF MANUAL WRITING

Handbooks and manuals are only as effective as the manner in which they are presented. The same rules that apply to any form of writing apply to manuals and handbooks. They must be written clearly, concisely, consistently, and accurately. If they are not, the audience for whom they are intended will ignore them, which can lead to problems for some companies.

Document writers must define three things before they write a manual or handbook: audience, purpose, and scope. Once they have defined each, they can begin the writing process.

The audience is important because different groups of people have varied levels of understanding about certain topics. Or, the audience may not be fluent in the language in which the manual is being written. This is particularly true in today's emerging **global market** environment.

Many products being sold in the United States today have been manufactured in foreign countries. It is not uncommon for a company based in Taiwan, for example, to include with its products instructions written in hard-to-understand English. That is one of the pitfalls of the global market. Often, handbooks and manuals are written by people who are not fluent in foreign languages. In such cases, the documents will be useless to consumers. This can lead to lost sales and/or customer dissatisfaction. Even if the writer and the audience do speak the same language, there is a need for audience definition.

For example, if a writer is producing a manual for a group of second graders on how to play a computer game, the document can not be written with a high fog level. (A fog level measures the understandability of a piece of writing. The higher the level, the more difficult the writing will be to understand.) By the same token, the manual need not be written at the "Dick and Jane" level, e.g., "Dick has a computer. You can play a game on it. Here is how." It is up to the writer to decide at what level of understandability the manual should be written.

Defining the audience is only the first step in producing a manual. The writer must also understand the manual's purpose. Is it meant to be instructional? Informative? Does it present the solution to a problem? The manual's intention dictates to a great extent how its contents will be presented. For example, if it is instructional, the writer must be able to perform the procedures contained in the manual. A "how to" writer who is unfamiliar with the procedure being documented is doomed to failure. Worse, there will be inevitable errors in the manual that will defeat its purpose. Errors can also arise if the writer does not define the scope of the report.

One of the keys to the success of any manual or handbook is conciseness. Readers do not want to read any more than is absolutely necessary in order to learn how to perform a procedure, accept or evaluate a proposal, or assimilate information. If a writer is responsible for producing a manual on how to shingle a roof, it is unnecessary to include the history of roofs and shingles. The idea is to reduce the scope to its narrowest focus and produce the manual based on those parameters.

The next step the writer must consider is clarity. The language used should consist of commonly used words, rather than complex, seldom used words that will confuse the readers. One of the quickest ways to lose an audience is to use words they do not understand. In some cases, the words used may be familiar to no more than a few audience members. For instance, technical writers may use jargon known only to a few members of the audience. This procedure inhibits the presentation of the overall message and defeats the purpose of the manual.

Another factor to be considered is consistency. Manuals should be consistent in terminology, format, and presentation. If a writer chooses to use the Dewey Decimal System to number paragraphs and sections, the system should remain in place throughout. If visual aids such as charts, graphs, and diagrams, which are used to enhance, clarify, and supplement, the material, are placed intermittently throughout the text, and do not refer to the contents of the manual, they, too will be distracting. And, terminology must be used consistently.

A writer who uses the word "star" in one part of an astronomy manual to define a celestial body and then switches to "a self-luminous, self-containing mass of gas in which the energy generated by nuclear reactions in the interior is balanced by the outflow of energy to the surface, and the inward-directed gravitational forces are balanced by the outward-directed gas and radiation pressures" in another section is inconsistent. In the first instance, the writer has defined a celestial body in a context which most audience members can grasp. The second use is a definition more appropriate for astronomers. Consistency in usage is important in any handbook or manual—as is the use of definitions.

Many handbooks and manuals produced in the business world contain terminology that might not be familiar to all users. This is particularly true in scientific documents. Therefore, it is imperative that document writers define terms whenever they feel that it is warranted. Definitions can be presented through symbols, sentences, or extensions. Generally, business terms can be defined in one or two words. Technical terms, however, may require more extended definitions. In any case, manual producers must pay attention to the audience and the need for definition, paying attention to even the most basic terms included in a document.

For instance, in a banking manual using the word "poor" to denote a certain class of people, it might be prudent to define "poor." Some audience members might construe the word as used in a certain context to define an economic class of people. Others might see it as an attempt to elicit sympathy for certain people. Therefore, ordinary terms, if not defined exactly, can confuse the audience. It is always the writer's decision regarding definitions, e.g., what words to define, when to define them, and how extensive the definitions should be. Clear, consistent use of definitions has a major impact on the overall quality of a manual or handbook.

Manuals should also be as complete as possible. A writer should make every effort to include *all* the information that is required by the audience to understand the topic or follow instructions. For instance, if a manufacturer encloses with a product a manual explaining how to assemble it, unpack it, install it, or maintain it, it is a wise idea to include as much relevant data as possible. Such information might include a complete list of all parts, tools required, dangers involved in the installation or set-up . . . in short, anything that might facilitate the job to be done.

Completeness also involves the writers' knowledge of the subject or process. A technical writer who is unfamiliar with the installation process for a spreadsheet package, for example, might omit a crucial step or two in the instructions. Not only will such an omission lead to frustration among the software installers, but it can lead to lost sales and customers. It is true in hardware and manual production, just as it is in other phases of business communication, that the manual represents the company. Disgruntled customers who are displeased with a producer's instructional manuals may judge the entire organization on that one basis. They, in turn, might tell other potential customers. This can be damaging to a company's reputation, sales—and profits. It is for this reason that completeness is an integral part of the document process. The definition of completeness in this case goes beyond the use of terminology and omission of steps in instructional processes. There must also be a judicious use of illustrations in business documents.

HANDBOOK AND MANUAL ILLUSTRATIONS

Illustrations are important components of manuals and handbooks. They can be produced in a variety of fashions and in any step of the documentation process. Computers and cameras are particularly helpful in producing illustrations.

Illustrations in many forms can be used. They can range from simple hand-drawn charts and graphs to three-dimensional computer-generated designs. They can be produced by engineers, graphics artists, freelance artists, or secretaries working with computer graphics software packages. Illustrations can be changed at any stage of the production process, especially when computers are used to create them. Technical illustrations have been around a lot longer than computers, however.

A BRIEF HISTORY OF TECHNICAL ILLUSTRATION

Early Greek and Egyptian engineers provided drawings with their plans and designs. They were basic, to say the least. For example, the engineers could not combine in one view the height, depth, and width of objects. It was not until the 15th and 16th centuries that technical illustrators were able to use drawing as a thinking tool.

Leonardo da Vinci is generally credited with refining the use and application of technical illustration. It was he who used drawing as a way of describing technical, medical, and engineering principles. There were slight improvements in the art of technical illustration over the next few centuries, but it was not until the start of the Industrial Revolution in the late 1700s that any appreciable refinements occurred. It was during this period that standards were set, conventions accepted, and techniques developed. The drawings still lacked any real three-dimensional depth, however.

The next noticeable change in technical illustration came in the 19th century, when artists learned to give more realistic views of objects. The technical illustrators learned techniques such as line shading, line weight changes to show solidity, and selective use of hidden lines. The techniques were used extensively in patent drawings and other industrial sketches. Once again, there was a period of constancy. It was not until the start of the Second World War that illustrators learned more advanced techniques, which they improved on starting in the 1950s in response to the demands of the emerging space industry. There has been steady improvement since. Many of the new techniques are included in contemporary manuals and handbooks in virtually every business discipline.

Technical illustrations are particularly important as accompaniments to foreign-produced goods. For example, a French manufacturer which exports pieces of furniture that require assembly might find it easier to include as many pictures as possible in the instruction manual to alleviate the number of mistakes American consumers might make if they had to follow the ''how to's'' written in French. There are simply too many words in some languages that cannot be translated into others. The inclusion of instructions in as many as six languages on packages containing computers, printers, industrial machinery, and other products sold in America today demonstrates the need for a way to supplement foreign-language instructions. So, with the advent of expanded global trade, technical illustrations may play a more important role in consumer manuals.

Illustrations are certainly easier to produce today, but they are still dependent to a large extent on humans' capabilities. Computers are very helpful, but they cannot produce illustrations by themselves. Not only are they incapable of generating their own drawings, but they are expensive to purchase and operate. Granted, they do produce reproduction-quality illustrations and facilitate changes to drawings. There is still room, though, for humans in the illustration process. In fact, the more people learn about computer-generated technical illustration, the more valuable they become in the handbook and manual production process. They can use computers as faster, smarter pencils that enhance documentation of all types—and there are a lot of different types.

TYPES OF HANDBOOKS AND MANUALS

From the moment employees are hired to the time they leave a company, they will be using different types of handbooks and manuals. When they are initially hired, for example, they will be handed an orientation manual that includes extensive information they will need to fit into the corporate culture. Upon retiring, they will be given a handbook that spells out everything from benefits to payment schedules and how to ease the transition between work and retirement. In between, they will use many other handbooks and manuals, some of which are discussed below.

ORIENTATION HANDBOOKS

Orientation handbooks are provided to new employees of corporations. They are often combined with employee handbooks. These documents contain a wealth of information regarding the corporation. For example, they might include the company's mission statement, history, and code of ethics. Many corporations pay particular attention to these three categories.

The mission statement is a broad declaration of the basic, unique purpose and scope of operations that distinguishes the organization from others of its type. It serves several purposes, all of which are essential to the overall organization, which is why the statement is included in the handbook.

Employees must know from the beginning of their careers with employers what their roles within the organization will be. The mission statement defines that role. It also defines a common purpose, encourages company loyalty, and creates a sense of community among workers. The mission statement also provides managers a benchmark against which they can measure individual and organizational success. Finally, the mission statement provides insight into the company's operation for investors, customers, and anyone else who has an interest. Since most employers want to inculcate the company's culture in employees at the beginning of their careers, they see the orientation handbook as the proper place to start the process.

Of equal importance is the employer's Code of Ethics, which is a document prepared to guide organization members when they encounter an ethical dilemma. This is sometimes a stand-alone document given to each company employee. In some cases, employees must sign a statement acknowledging that they have read, understand, and agree to abide by the code. Nearly three-quarters of the major corporations in the United States have written Codes of Ethics.

A company history is a common inclusion in an orientation handbook. The philosophy behind the history is to provide employees with an insight into the company's growth and importance to the community. This is particularly important to older firms such as Procter and Gamble Co., which has been around since 1837, and Dexter Manufacturing, which opened its doors in 1767. Both of these companies have gone through major changes in their history and will no doubt go through more. Employees should be made aware of the companies' vicissitudes and the sacrifices their predecessors have made to ensure the firms' futures. Eliciting a feeling of belonging can be done through company histories, which explains why orientation handbooks often include them.

Orientation handbooks include a variety of other information that human resources and management specialists consider necessary to the starting employee. This information can range from the location of local banks and grocery stores to a description of the employers' physical plant layouts. The contents of

such handbooks vary from company to company, but their intent is always the same: to welcome new employees and help them fit into the company's culture and workforce as quickly as possible.

EMPLOYEE HANDBOOKS

Employee handbooks are logical extensions of orientation documents. They are intended to present more in-depth information for employees who have been with the employer for a while and who are expected to stay for the foreseeable future. Employee handbooks are a wealth of information for employees.

These documents may contain some of the information included in orientation handbooks. For instance, they, too, might include the company's mission statement and Code of Ethics. For the most part, however, they are designed to keep employees informed of many other topics of continuing and significant interest.

Employee handbooks may contain information on employers' work hours, benefit programs, affirmative action policies, grievance procedures, counseling programs, etc. They may also include information pertinent to such things as company-sponsored social activities, location of company stores, restaurants, and fitness centers, local business firms that provide discounts for employees . . . there is no end to the list. The contents of employee handbooks are often dictated by the size of the company, number of employees, and other factors. Regardless of the scope of the handbook, however, it is always intended to be as complete a compendium as possible regarding information employees need to function effectively within the corporate environment. These documents may be considerably larger in union environments.

HANDBOOKS AND MANUALS IN A UNION ENVIRONMENT

Companies which have agreements with **labor unions** are likely to have a broader range of material included in employee handbooks. Sometimes union agreements are stand-alone documents. Some employers, however, prefer to include essential union-related information in employee handbooks and treat the union contract as a separate document. Whichever approach companies use, there is a great deal of documentation that must be included. Both management and labor representatives maintain extensive handbooks and manuals to monitor one another's activities.

There exist manuals which include descriptions of virtually every activity covered under contract administration. There are sections addressing discipline, incentives, work assignments, individual personnel assignments, hours of work, supervisors performing production work, production standards, working conditions, subcontracting, past practice, rules, etc. These manuals might also include the actual contracts negotiated between labor and management. It is essential that both sides have copies of these documents—and that they adhere to the information therein.

It is particularly important that management have on hand readily accessible union contracts and relevant documentation. Union stewards, the elected or appointed shop floor union representatives responsible for interpreting the contract for union members and processing grievances, are generally extremely knowledgeable about the contents of labor contracts. Management should be equally knowledgeable. Historically, however, that is not the case. Managers who do not pay attention to union contracts can hurt themselves and their employers. That is why it is of utmost importance that *both* sides possess and read contract-related documents.

There are other documents extant in union environments. For example, there are bargaining books, which are cross-referenced files enabling negotiators to determine quickly what contract clauses would be affected by involved parties' demands. These books contain information like the general history of specific contract terms and a code to indicate the proposals' relative importance to management. Many bargaining books today are automated and keyed to **spreadsheets**. This allows negotiators to answer ''what if'' questions immediately and calculate the cost implications of demands and concessions.

Such books contain much valuable information. For example, they include the history and text of the particular clause as it was negotiated in previous contracts, comparisons of the company's experience with that of other companies in the industry, the company's experience with the particular clause, both in operation and the grievances, and legal issues pertaining to the clause. These books are invaluable to management. In fact, manuals and handbooks in general are valuable to management in union environments. They are no less valuable in non-union workplaces. That is why many companies produce and distribute supervisors' and managers' handbooks.

SUPERVISORS' AND MANAGERS' HANDBOOKS

Some companies produce these handbooks separately. Others will combine them. In some cases, firms will produce three separate handbooks, one for each level of management. Those distributed to senior-level executives might deal exclusively with topics like public policy, government regulation, etc. These are issues not likely to affect middle- and first-level managers to any great extent. How the documents are produced and for which levels of management they are intended is dependent on a company's size, num-

ber of employees, etc. In large companies, however, they are frequently produced separately, particularly for the middle- and first-level managers, since there is a fine line between supervisors' and managers' responsibilities.

Not all managers are responsible for subordinates. Managers are not necessarily leaders of people, whereas supervisors are. In general, supervisors are responsible for production in a workplace. They are the first-line supervisors. Managers are generally considered to be middle level. More often than not, they manage other managers, including supervisors. Therefore, the contents of a supervisor's manual may differ greatly from those of a manager's manual.

The distinction may be blurry at times. A general overview of the two types of manuals reveals that they may contain information like how to handle grievances, enforce company policies concerning issues like work hours and dress codes, administer discipline, reward and motivate employees, and recognize employees' personal problems such as substance abuse, financial difficulties, etc., that might have an impact on their work performances. In the contemporary workplace, managers and supervisors must be much more aware of a broader set of issues than were their counterparts a few years ago. To them, supervisor and manager handbooks are invaluable. The same holds true for personnel manuals.

PERSONNEL MANUALS

Personnel manuals are traditionally the corporate bible. They contain information that explains the rules, policies, procedures, etc., that govern a company's day-to-day operations. Without them, no company can survive.

The list of topics included in personnel manuals is seemingly endless. The issues discussed cover *every* facet of a company's operations. In many cases, the manuals are so thick that they can be maintained only at certain locations within a company. They are too cumbersome and expensive to produce and to distribute them to every employee. Thus, they may be maintained only in the human resources department, on selected executives' desks, or in the company library. Wherever they are housed, they must be accessible to all employees at all times. More importantly, they must be updated frequently.

Human resource management is the management of various activities designed to enhance the effectiveness of an organization's work force in achieving organizational goals. The activities include functions like planning, staffing, employment development and evaluation, compensation, and maintaining effective work force relationships. Manuals must reflect these activities.

A basic personnel manual is likely to include job descriptions, job specifications, organizational charts, **affirmative action** rules, job posting procedures, employee selection guidelines, **training and development** policies, compensation and benefit schedules, sexual harassment guidelines, and **employee assistance policies**. This list is by no means inclusive of all the topics that might be covered in personnel manuals.

The key to maintaining personnel manuals is constant updating. Often, personnel manuals and/or employee handbooks are considered legal contracts to which the corporation is liable for violations of company policies, procedures, and rules. It is important to note that the three terms are not synonyms.

A policy is a general guide that specifies the broad parameters within which organization members are expected to operate in pursuit of organizational goals. A procedure is a prescribed series of related steps to be taken under certain recurring circumstances. A rule spells out specific actions to be taken or not taken in a given situation. The company may have some flexibility in each of these areas, but if nothing regarding policies, procedures, and rules is written in some type of readily accessible document, it may be subject to legal action from disgruntled or displaced workers. In light of this, it is important that personnel manuals be updated to reflect the most recent changes in company policies, procedures, rules, and outside influences that might impact its operations.

For example, it is crucial that companies update affirmative action guidelines and sexual harassment policies immediately if changes to them should be necessary. It is especially important to update policies dictated by local, state, or federal governments. Once again, companies that do not document such changes and make available copies to *every* employee are leaving themselves open to costly and disruptive legal action. The expense incurred in updating personnel manuals is minor compared to the possible costs of lawsuits filed by disgruntled parties.

SUBSETS OF PERSONNEL MANUALS

Occasionally, personnel manuals are simply too extensive to distribute to every staff member. Therefore, it is prudent to produce mini-manuals which include the issues that workers are most interested in. These might include benefits handbooks, job posting handbooks, employee assistance handbooks, etc. (These subsets illustrate clearly the subtle difference between a manual and a handbook. In this case, the personnel manual includes all the relevant human resources topics. The handbooks are dedicated to a limited number of those topics individually or in combination.)

There are several advantages to personnel handbooks. Employees have immediate access to them.

That also makes it more likely that employees will become aware of critical changes in pertinent issues as soon as they are distributed. For example, if an employer distributes a Grievance Procedure Handbook which includes sexual harassment and Affirmative Action guidelines, any changes to one or all of the policies will reach employees' attention immediately. This can save companies problems, since some employees may be inclined to plead ignorance of certain guidelines on occasion. Occasionally, companies may ask employees to acknowledge changes by signing distribution forms that act as contracts. This is one way of ensuring that employees read and understand critical handbooks. Of course, that is not always necessary, since many manuals and handbooks are simply "for your information" in nature or basic "how to's." This is often the case with electronic data processing (EDP) manuals and handbooks.

DATA PROCESSING HANDBOOKS AND MANUALS

Documentation is particularly important in EDP operations. Virtually every aspect of a data processing system is documented. For example, there is extensive documentation involved in the EDP life cycle. Developing an EDP system comprises several stages: analysis and design (when the basic concepts of the system are laid out by analysts and designers), development (when the programs are being written), integration (when the programs are assembled into a cohesive system), implementation (when the system is up and running), and maintenance and enhancement (making sure the system runs smoothly to its logical demise). There is a considerable amount of documentation produced in each stage. There is also the ultimate document to be produced in the EDP arena: the user manual.

Users are often unfamiliar with many of the concepts used in EDP. Their sole interest at times is simply to acquire an end product that will facilitate their operations. Generally, they have a representative on the system development team, but often just in an advisory capacity. The system developers themselves may not be too eager to produce reams of documentation. The ultimate responsibility, then, rests on the shoulders of technical writers. They are generally the people responsible for producing the large number of manuals and handbooks that are natural by-products of EDP projects.

However, the manuals produced by EDP developers are by no means restricted to in-house users and other people. Software developers and hardware manufacturers must produce concise, easy-to-understand handbooks and manuals for purchasers of computers. More and more people are buying computers today for home use. Each computer and its software must be accompanied by a user manual instructing users how to install and use them. This is a daunting task for technical writers, since many home computer users are not EDP experts. This same idea applies to other instruction and information manuals produced by manufacturers for consumers.

BUSINESS MANUALS FOR CONSUMERS

Virtually every manufacturer that sells products to consumers today must include as part of the package a manual or handbook outlining how to use the product, the hazards associated with it, and other valuable information. For instance, every new car comes equipped with an owner's manual which describes the function of virtually every part of the vehicle, presents maintenance schedules, and provides instructions on how to perform basic repairs. Cellular phones and coffee makers are replete with lengthy manuals that describe how to use and maintain the products. There are few consumer products in existence today that are not accompanied by user manuals of some kind.

Much of the information contained in these consumer manuals is mandated by various governmental agencies. These documents must be written clearly with the audience in mind. They must include all the possible hazards associated with each product and contain numbers where consumers can talk to company representatives. Many of the documents provided by manufacturers are included simply to protect the companies as much as possible from consumer lawsuits. Regardless of why they are included, without them, many consumers would have no idea of how to use the particular products. As noted earlier, there are problems in this regard, especially with the expansion of the global market.

THE INFLUENCE OF GOVERNMENT AGENCIES ON HANDBOOKS AND MANUALS

Many handbooks and manuals are the direct result of government legislation and policies. Companies must maintain a variety of documentation dealing with federal and state regulations regarding clean water, clean air, noise pollution, workplace safety, etc. Such manuals are especially prevalent in the industrial section of the business environment.

The increased involvement of society and government in business affairs has necessitated a greater demand for laws to protect the environment and increase worker safety. Chemical manufacturers, for example, must adhere to strict federal and state environmental pollution guidelines which are part of various clean air and water acts. In order to do so, they must maintain comprehensive manuals and handbooks outlining policies, fines for violating the acts, reporting regulations, etc. This simply adds one more

level of documentation to be managed by businesses—and increases their costs besides for everything from production to storage.

STORAGE OF HANDBOOKS AND MANUALS

Today, handbooks and manuals can be stored in a variety of mediums. There are still large numbers of them in hard copy resident on employees' desks. Some companies prefer to store them in collections at central points such as libraries and selected department offices. There has been a trend toward storing documents on-line via computer. People who want access to them can gain it via computer. Other companies store all or part of their handbooks and manuals on microfiche. Regardless of which medium is used, handbooks and manuals will not go out of style.

THE FUTURE OF HANDBOOKS AND MANUALS

The proliferation of manuals and handbooks in the business world will continue. Companies see a greater need to keep their employees informed of policies, procedures, government regulations, etc., via handbooks and manuals. The increasing use of computers in the business world and private sector has increased the demand for clear, concise, complete documentation. Handbooks and manuals are the lifeblood of businesses' information stream. They have been for years—and will no doubt continue to be.

[Arthur G. Sharp]

FURTHER READING:

Beach, David P., and Torsten K. E. Alvager. *Handbook for Scientific and Technical Research*. Englewood Cliffs NJ: Prentice Hall, 1992.

Duff, Jon M. *Industrial Technical Illustration*. Montery CA: Brooks Cole Engineering Division, 1982.

Simmonds, Doig., and Linda Reynolds. *Computer Presentation of Data In Science*. Dordrecht, Netherlands: Kluwer Academic Publishers, 1989.

Vatavuk, William M. *Marketing Yourself with Technical Writing*. Boca Raton FL: Lewis Publishers, 1992.

Wieringa, Douglas, Christopher Moore, and Valerie Barnes. *Procedure Writing: Principles and Practices*. Columbus OH: Battelle Press, 1993.

Young, Matt. *The Technical Writer's Handbook*. Mill Valley CA: University Science Books, 1989.

HAWTHORNE EXPERIMENTS

The Hawthorne experiments were groundbreaking studies in human relations that were conducted between 1924 and 1932 at Western Electric Company's Hawthorne Works in Chicago. Originally designed as illumination studies to determine the relationship between lighting and productivity, the initial tests were sponsored by the National Research Council (NRC) of the National Academy of Sciences. In 1927, a research team from the Harvard Business School was invited to join the studies after the illumination tests drew unanticipated results. Two additional series of tests, relay-assembly tests and bank-wiring tests, followed the illumination tests. The studies assumed the label Hawthorne experiments or studies from the location of the Western Electric plant. Concluded by 1932, the Hawthorne studies, with emphasis on a new interpretation of group behavior, were the basis for the school of human relations.

In the early 1920s Chicago's Western Electric Hawthorne Works employed 12,000 workers. The plant was a primary manufacturer of telephones, and, in 1924, the company provided a site to cooperate with the NRC on a series of test room studies to determine the relationship between illumination and worker efficiency. The basic idea was to vary and record levels of illumination in a test room with the expectation that as lighting was increased, productivity would too. In another test room, illumination was decreased, again with the expectation that efficiency would also decrease. The electric power industry provided an additional impetus for these tests, hoping to encourage industries to utilize artificial lighting in place of natural light. The Illuminating Engineering Society's Committee on Research also supported the tests and cooperated with the NRC. From the fall of 1924 to spring, 1927, three series of tests were conducted and carefully monitored. Three departments at the Hawthorne plant were involved—relay assembling, coil winding, and inspection. Workers were notified of the tests in order to attempt to control interference from human factors. When production increased in each test period, researchers looked to other factors such as increased supervision and a sense of competition that developed between the test and control groups. But the one conclusion the impressive team of industrial specialists and academics discovered was the lack of a consistent correlation between lighting levels and product output. No further tests were planned originally, but researchers were surprised at the unanticipated results.

NRC representatives and the engineers involved drew several conclusions. First, illumination was one factor in output but not the most important. More important to the tests was the realization there was not a simple answer to the issue of illumination and worker productivity and that other factors that were not controlled presented a problem to test results—the issue of human factors. In retrospect, researchers from the NRC and the Illuminating Engineering Society (which together formed the Committee on Industrial Lighting) stated they were not surprised by the test results. They even predicted other factors impacting upon the tests, but their mandate was to isolate other variables, and the Hawthorne studies continued.

In order to observe the impact of these other factors, a second set of tests was begun before the completion of the illumination studies on April 25, 1987. The relay-assembly tests were designed to evaluate the effect rest periods and hours of work would have on efficiency. Researchers hoped to answer a series of questions concerning why output declined in the afternoon—whether the operators tired out, if they needed brief rest periods, the impact of changes in equipment, the effects of a shorter work day, and worker attitudes. Hawthorne engineers led by George Pennock were the primary researchers for the relay-assembly tests, originally intended to take place for only a few months. Six women operators volunteered for the study and two more joined the test group in January, 1928. They were administered physical examinations before the studies began and then every six weeks in order to evaluate the effects of changes in working conditions on their health. The women were isolated in a separate room to assure accuracy in measuring output and quality as temperature, humidity, and other factors were adjusted. The test subjects constituted a piece-work payment group and efforts were made to maintain steady work patterns. The Hawthorne researchers attempted to gain the women's confidence and to build a sense of pride in their participation. A male observer was introduced into the test room to keep accurate records, maintain cordial working conditions, and provide some degree of supervision.

The women were employed in assembling relays or electromagnetic switches used in switching telephone calls automatically. The women assembled the more than 35 parts of the relay by hand. The relays were then carefully inspected. The entire process was highly labor intensive and the speed of assembly had an obvious effect on productivity.

Initially, the women were monitored for productivity, then they were isolated in a test room. Finally, the workers began to participate in a group payment rate, where extra pay for increased productivity was shared by the group. The other relay assemblers did not share in any bonus pay, but researchers concluded this added incentive was necessary for full cooperation. This single difference has been historically criticized as the one variable having the greatest significance on test results. These initial steps in the relay-assembly studies lasted only three months. In August, rest periods were introduced and other changes followed over the rest of the test period, including shortened work days and weeks. As the test periods turned from months into years, worker productivity continued to climb, once again providing unexpected results for the Hawthorne team to evaluate.

Productivity increased in excess of 30 percent over the first two-and-a-half years of the studies and remained steady for the duration of the tests. The physicals indicated improved worker health and absenteeism decreased. By their own testimony, the women expressed increased satisfaction with all aspects of their jobs. Researchers tentatively concluded performance and efficiency improved due to the rest periods, relief from monotonous working conditions, the wage incentive, and the type of supervision provided in the test environment. After additional study and consideration, the first two factors were rejected and further tests were conducted in an attempt to verify the effects of incentives, and working conditions. The results were still not totally conclusive. Finally, researchers realized worker attitudes within the group were influential as was the more personal atmosphere of the test room. They concluded factors such as lighting, hours of work, rest periods, bonus incentives, and supervision affected workers, but the attitudes of the employees experiencing the factors were of greater significance. As a result, the Hawthorne team decided not to pursue similar studies. Almost as significant during the relay-assembly tests was the introduction of a team of academics from the Harvard Business School into the experiments. Led by professors Elton Mayo and F.J. Roethlisberger, this new group of researchers would have an enormous impact on the Hawthorne studies and the future of human relations in the workplace.

Mayo's contributions became increasingly significant in the experiments during the interviewing stages of the tests. Early results from the illumination tests and the relay-assembly tests led to surveys of worker attitudes, surveys not limited to test participants. From 1928 to 1931, more than 21,000 individuals were interviewed to survey worker morale in an attempt to determine specific features of their jobs workers either liked or disliked. The objective was to identify areas where reasonable improvements might lead to greater job satisfaction and thus increased efficiency and productivity.

The initial conclusions were disappointing. Interviewers looked for factors concerning job satisfaction, working conditions, and supervision. What they found was a complex battery of attitudes influenced by outside factors such as conditions at home or within the community, as well as one's social situation at work. Researchers began to conclude that prior life experience had an important influence on worker attitudes, and that manipulation of lighting, pay, supervision, and working conditions could not solely bring about a desired change. The one consistent conclusion was that employees felt more positive about the work environment when an interviewer or listener showed interest. This interviewing technique, the nondirective method, proved useful to later researchers at Haw-

thorne and eventually led to an employee counseling program, now widely practiced in personnel management circles.

The final stage of the studies was the bank-wiring tests, which began in November of 1931. The foreman of the bank-wiring department resisted the intrusion of observers into his work space and a bank-wiring test room was set up. The test room housed nine wirers, three solderers, and two inspectors. All were male between the ages of 20 and 25. Their job was to wire conductor banks, a repetitive and monotonous task. The banks were one of the major components of automatic telephone exchange. Between 3,000 and 6,000 terminals had to be wired for a set of banks. The work was tiring and required the workers to stand for long periods of time. Pay incentives and productivity measures were removed, but a researcher was placed into the test room as an observer and the workers were interviewed. The purpose of the bank-wiring tests was to observe and study social relationships and social structures within a group, issues raised by two other significant members of the research team, W. Lloyd Warner and William J. Dickson. Warner was on Mayo's Harvard team, trained as an anthropologist and primarily interested in Hawthorne from an entirely different perspective, that of an observer of the social behavior of a group. Dickson was a Hawthorne employee, with an even keener interest in the tests than the Harvard team; he remained with the company until retiring in 1969. Their contributions were to adapt social anthropology research methods to industrial conditions. Dickson conducted the interview phase of the tests. Perhaps the most revealing aspect of the bank wirers was the workers combined to slow down production—a clear indication of the need for analysis of the social relationships of workers. Research showed the most admired worker among the group was the one who demonstrated the greatest resentment of authority by slowing down production the most.

The bank-wiring tests were shut down in the spring of 1932 in reaction to layoffs brought on by the deepening depression. Layoffs were gradual, but by May the bank-wiring tests were concluded. These tests were intended to study the group as a functioning unit and observe its behavior. The study findings confirmed the complexity of group relations and stressed the expectations of the group over an individual's preference. The conclusion was to tie the importance of what workers felt about one another to worker motivation. Industrial plants were a complex social system with significant informal organizations that played a vital role in motivating workers. Employees had physical as well as social needs, and the company gradually developed a program of human relations including employee counseling and improved supervision with an emphasis on the individual workers.

The results were a reinterpretation of industrial group behavior and the introduction of what has become human relations.

The Hawthorne studies were conducted in three independent stages—the illumination tests, relay-assembly tests, and the bank-wiring test. Although each was a separate experiment, the second and third each developed out of the preceding series of tests. Neither Hawthorne officials nor NRC researchers anticipated the duration of the studies, yet the conclusions of each set of tests and the Hawthorne experiments as a whole are the legacy of the studies and what sets them apart as a significant part of the history of industrial behavior and human relations.

The tests challenged prior assumptions about worker behavior. Workers were not motivated solely by pay. The importance of individual worker attitudes on behavior had to be understood. Further, the role of the supervisor in determining productivity and morale was more clearly defined. Group work and behavior were essential to organizational objectives and tied directly to efficiency and, thus, to corporate success. The most disturbing conclusion emphasized how little the researchers could determine about informal group behavior and its role in industrial settings. Finally, the Hawthorne studies proved beyond certainty there was a great deal more to be learned about human interactions in the workplace, and academic and industrial study has continued in an effort to understand these complex relationships.

Beyond the legacy of the Hawthorne studies has been the use of the term "Hawthorne effect" to describe how the presence of researchers produces a bias and unduly influences the outcome of the experiment. In addition, several important published works grew out of the Hawthorne experience, foremost of which was Mayo's *The Human Problems of an Industrial Civilization* (Boston: Division of Research, Harvard Business School, 1933). Roethlisberger and Dickson's *Management and the Worker* was published by the Harvard University Press in 1939. Other books focused on the various parts of the experiments, and researchers have authored countless analyses and histories of the Hawthorne studies.

The Hawthorne studies have been described as the most important social science experiment ever conducted in an industrial setting, yet the studies were not without their critics. Several criticisms, including those of sociologist Daniel Bell, focused on the exclusion of unionized workers in the studies. Sociologists and economists were the most commanding critics, defending their disciplinary turf more than offering serious criticisms. For his part, Mayo called into question research findings of both economists and psychologists. More serious questions were raised by social scientists who termed the studies bad science due

to Mayo's conservative views. Others expressed serious concerns of undue pressure from corporate interests and called Mayo and his colleagues "servants of power." Despite these critical views, the flow of writings on the Hawthorne studies attests to their lasting influence and the fascination the tests held for researchers. The studies had the impact of defining clearly the human relations school. Another contribution was an emphasis on the practice of personnel counseling. Industrial sociology owes its life as a discipline to the studies done at the Hawthorne site. This, in part, led to the enormous growth of academic programs in organizational behavior at American colleges and universities, especially at the graduate level.

[Boyd Childress]

FURTHER READING:

Gillespie, Richard. *Manufacturing Knowledge: A History of the Hawthorne Experiments*. Cambridge University Press, 1991.

Landsberger, Henry A. *Hawthorne Revisited*. New York State School of Industrial and Labor Relations, 1958.

Mayo, Elton. *The Human Problems of an Industrial Civilization*. Macmillan, 1933.

Roethlisberger, F. J., and Dickson, W.J. *Management and the Worker: An Account of a Research Program Conducted by the Western Electric Company, Hawthorne Works, Chicago*. Harvard University Press, 1939.

Whitehead, T. N. *The Industrial Worker: A Statistical Study of Human Relations in a Group of Manual Workers*. Harvard University Press, 1938.

HEALTH CARE COSTS ON BUSINESS, IMPACT OF

Throughout 1993 and most of 1994 there was no escaping intense, detailed discussion of the cost of health care. President Bill Clinton guaranteed he would veto any health care bill set before him that did not include universal coverage for every American. He called for every employer to offer company-paid health insurance for every employee. He pledged to pay for increased government costs by finding savings in Medicare, by cutting the cost of insurance compliance, and by taxing cigarettes to help cover the uninsured.

In response to President Clinton's plan, Republican and Democratic Congressional leaders sent up trial balloons putting forth dozens of ideas to lower costs, raise taxes, cover all employees, increase deductibles, and put all companies into health care buying alliances. Every plan was supposed to fix health care and slow rising costs without breaking the system or the people who would have to pay for it.

For the most part, professional politicians, whose health insurance is paid for by taxpayers, debated the issue of health care while business leaders, who were expected to pay for the new health coverage, were delegated to a minor role. When asked, "big business," which perceived that it would pay less for coverage, was usually for the plan. "Small business," which perceived it would pay much more, was usually against it. What many observers think was the most dramatic moment in the televised public debate over health care reform came when the president of Godfather's Pizza told the president of the United States that his company could not afford to provide paid health coverage for all his employees. The U.S. president, who had never run a business, thought for a moment, then presented his solution to Godfather's problem: "Just raise the price of your pizza."

Thus went the debate between business and government over the impact of providing health care to all Americans. Although "health care reform" was pulled from Congressional debate in September 1994, business analysts are sure it will return. At issue then will be the same issue as before, how can government and private business pay for increased annual health care costs estimated to be at least $40 billion.

Health care costs have a huge direct impact on American business. Spending on health care is almost one trillion dollars a year, 13.4 percent of the U.S. **gross national product** (GNP). Canada spends 10 percent of its GNP on health care and Japan only 6.6 percent.

Those percentages are often used with other figures that show that while the United States leads in the development of health care technology, not everyone pays for it or receives it. Depending on the research source, up to 37 million Americans do not have any health insurance, either because they have lost it because of layoff, it was not offered when they were hired, or they choose not to pay or cannot afford to pay the extra costs out of their own pocket. One study estimates that 85 percent of the people without health insurance are low-income workers. Others are primarily young and healthy people who have opted out of the system, gambling that they will not become ill and if they do the government will treat them.

Businesses, acting independently of government plans, are working on their own to cut their health care spending. They are doing it by cutting access to insurance. According to the Employee Benefit Research Institute, 55.6 percent of Americans had employer-provided health insurance in 1992, down from 59.7 percent in 1988, a downward trend from President Clinton's original dream of 100 percent employer-provided coverage.

Though some individual companies are trying to save money by cutting their insurance responsibilities, industry as a whole still picks up the tab. According to a 1993 U.S. Bureau of Labor Statistics report, em-ployers are already paying more than $17 billion in an unofficial "subsidy" to cover the costs of uninsured or uncompensated medical care. Another study found that nearly 20 percent of the nearly $2 billion hospitals that carry as "bad debt" comes from uninsured workers, and almost $13 billion is "shifted" among workers when the dependents of well-insured workers' are carried on the well-insured workers' insurance plans (with more benefits), rather than on the other lesser plans offered by the dependents' smaller employers.

Companies that offer insurance to employees are looking at a number of opportunities to lower their costs and the health care industry also appears to be helping. Several research studies have found that the rate of health care cost increases is slowing. The rate of growth was eight percent in 1993, the first below-double-digit increase since 1987. Analysts credit companies requiring higher deductibles, the increased use of health maintenance organizations (HMOs), and corporations asking their employees to be more cost conscious consumers of health care.

Asking employees to be cost conscious of health care may prove to be a winning effort for businesses. Successful companies freely tell stories of how employees are cooperating to reduce the cost of health care to the company. One company has tried to bring market competition into play by developing a fee schedule of more than 11,000 medical procedures. Employees are encouraged to use the schedule to check what their doctor is charging for an operation compared to what the fee schedule lists as a fair payment.

More companies are creating "wellness" programs, where employees take responsibility for living healthier and more risk-free lifestyles. This emphasis can be important to reducing the later cost of health care since medical costs for high-risk employees can be 75 percent higher than for other employees.

One company has its own in-house cardiac rehabilitation program that has saved it more than $1 million. Another has its own in-house prenatal program that has reduced the number of premature births experienced by women in its **workforce**. Another company offers $600 bonuses to employees who wear seat belts and who control four identified risk factors: blood pressure, weight, cholesterol, and smoking. Another bonus is paid into a pool if health care costs come in under budget. Since 1989 the company's health costs increases have averaged just one percent a year and in 1993 it spent only 68 percent of its health care budget, leaving a $67,000 rebate that was divided among employees.

What do the nation's employees want? One poll says 76 percent want everyone to have access to universal health insurance. They do not necessarily want the insurance to be paid by the employer, but they want to feel that insurance will be there when it is needed.

[Clint Johnson]

HEALTH INSURANCE OPTIONS

Health insurance, like other forms of insurance, serves to spread the consequences of a loss that would normally fall upon a single individual over members of a large group. It also ensures that health care providers will be paid for services that an uninsured individual may otherwise not be able to afford. The two primary types of U.S. health plans addressed in this article are: (1) fee-for-service plans, which encompass traditional indemnity insurance; and (2) prepaid plans, which include popular managed care options such as health maintenance organizations (HMOs).

In addition to the two principal types of plans, government-backed health care plans, such as Medicare and Medicaid, serve as safety nets to furnish medical coverage to select groups of society and to those least able to afford other types of health insurance. Furthermore, a significant segment of the American population elects to provide or pay for their own health care for personal or religious regions.

BACKGROUND

Although the concept of insurance dates back over 2,000 years, the first form of health insurance in the United States can be traced back to the 1800s. At that time, merchant seamen could pay a modest premium and then obtain health care as they traveled from port to port. Health insurance as it is known today, however, is a relatively new concept that has its roots in the Great Depression. In fact, the first major managed care, or prepaid, plan was started in the 1930s by Henry J. Kaiser and Sidney Garfield to provide medical care for San Francisco shipyard workers. That same plan was offered to the public at large in the 1940s.

The popularization of private health insurance in the United States is a phenomenon of the post-World-War-II economic expansion. After the war, federal government initiatives caused fee-for-service health insurance to become a popular benefit for employees. Health insurance premiums became tax deductible to the employer and were not taxable to the employee. Therefore, health insurance became a cost-effective form of compensation, and health care benefits became a popular bargaining tool for **labor unions** seeking to improve their total pay package. Furthermore, as living standards increased, people in industrialized nations began to view health insurance as a necessity, and even an entitlement or individual right.

During the 1960s the health insurance industry in the United States grew massively in proportion to other types of insurance. A primary impetus for that growth was the advent of modified agreements, which shifted a greater amount of health care risk to the employers that offered employee insurance plans. Under these agreements, insurers, employees, and health care providers had little reason to control health care costs, because the employers, as policyholders, were paying the insurance bill. In fact, one result of these agreements was that insurance company profits increased in proportion to the rise in the cost of medical care. These circumstances resulted in unprecedented growth in group health insurance, which averaged 15 percent per year in the 1970s and early 1980s.

Although traditional fee-for-service plans remained the dominant health care option into the 1980s and early 1990s, managed care plans similar to the Kaiser plan were formed during the 1950s and 1960s, and they became widely available to the general public in the 1970s. It was during that time that society began to address the dilemma of spiraling health care costs. The federal Health Maintenance Organization Act of 1973 stimulated the growth of the industry by providing grants and loans that expanded existing plans and spawned new HMOs. Although a few companies, such as Kaiser and Group Health of Puget Sound, offered managed care plans in the early 1970s, fewer than 3 percent of Americans were enrolled in them.

By the late 1970s, changes in the American economy began to dictate a transformation of health insurance. As economic stagnation exerted downward pressure on company profits and a new corporate cost-consciousness developed, employers began to shift more of the insurance burden to their employees. Likewise, insurance companies were battling new economic and regulatory forces; skyrocketing **inflation**, deregulation of financial institutions in the early 1980s, and public pressure to cap rising insurance rates all contributed to a decline in insurance company profitability. All of these forces combined to encourage the use of more cost-effective insurance instruments, particularly managed care.

Health care costs continued to spiral upward much faster than inflation throughout the 1980s and early 1990s: Between 1988 and 1993, moreover, aggregate U.S. health care expenditures rose 63 percent, to $889 billion. And from 1989 to 1991 the average employee contribution to company-sponsored health insurance plans increased 50 percent while the amount of services diminished and deductibles went up. Those trends resulted in fewer people having health insurance, and in a greater reliance on government-backed health care options. Those trends also helped to open the door to previously ignored health insurance alternatives, such as HMOs—by 1992 managed care plans were serving nearly 30% of the population and were rapidly gaining market share.

TYPES OF PLANS

Health insurance plans can be classified as prepaid or fee-for-service. Under traditional fee-for-service plans, the insurer pays the insured directly for any hospital or physician costs for which the insured is covered. Under a prepaid plan, insurance companies arrange to pay health care providers for any service for which an enrollee has coverage. The insurer effectively agrees to provide the insured with health care services, rather than reimbursement dollars. Service plans offer the advantages of lower costs, which results from reduced administrative expenses and a greater emphasis on cost control.

FEE-FOR-SERVICE. Fee-for-service health insurance plans remained the most popular form of health insurance in the United States during the early 1990s, though their popularity was waning. Two principal categories of fee-for-service health insurance plans are individual and group. Individual insurance covers people who are not part of an insured group, such as self-employed individuals. Group health insurance, on the other hand, insures a pool of enrollees and therefore offers benefits derived from **economies of scale**. Group insurance benefits generally include lower premiums and deductibles, more comprehensive coverage, and fewer restrictions.

Most fee-for-service plans cover basic costs related to: hospitalization, including room and board, drugs, and emergency room care; professional care, such as physician visits; and surgery, including any procedures performed by surgeons, radiologists, or other specialists. More inclusive health insurance plans are referred to as major medical insurance. Two types of major medical plans are: (1) supplemental, which provides higher dollar limits for coverage or covers miscellaneous services not encompassed in some basic plans, such as medical appliances and psychiatric care; and (2) comprehensive, which usually covers all costs covered by basic and supplemental plans, and may also eliminate deductible and coinsurance requirements. Basic, supplemental, and comprehensive plans usually do not insure dental, vision, or hearing care.

Most health care options related to fee-for-service plans relate to different degrees of coverage. For instance, insureds may select a high deductible as a way of lowering the cost of the plan—the deductible is the amount of initial costs covered by the insured before reimbursement begins. Likewise, different levels of coinsurance are usually available. For example,

the plan participant may agree to pay for 20 percent of all costs incurred after the deductible amount, up to a total of, say, $50,000 (for a total disbursement by the insured of $10,000). A more expensive plan may reduce the participant's share of those costs to 5 or 10 percent. The total limit on insurer payments can also be adjusted; an individual lifetime maximum of $1 million is not uncommon.

PREPAID PLANS. The second major category of health insurance is prepaid, or managed care, plans. Managed care plans typically arrange to provide medical services for members in exchange for subscription fees paid to the plan sponsor. Members receive services from physicians or hospitals that also have a contract with the sponsor. Thus, managed care plan administrators act as middlemen by contracting both with health care providers and enrollees to deliver medical services. Subscribers benefit from reduced health care costs, and the health care providers profit from a guaranteed client base.

Although they serve the same basic function as traditional health insurance, managed care plans differ because the plan sponsors play a greater role in administering and managing the services that the health care providers furnish. For this reason, advocates of managed care believe that it provides a less expensive alternative to traditional insurance plans. For instance, plan sponsors can work with health care providers to increase outpatient care, reduce administrative costs, eliminate complicated claims forms and procedures, and minimize unnecessary tests.

Managed care sponsors accomplish these tasks by reviewing each patient's needs before treatment, sometimes requiring a second opinion before allowing doctors to administer care; by providing authorization before hospitalization; and by administering prior approval of services performed by specialists. Critics of managed care claim that some techniques the sponsors use, such as giving bonuses to doctors for reducing hospitalization time, lead to undertreatment. Some plans also offer controversial bonuses to doctors for avoiding expensive tests and costly services performed by specialists.

Managed care plan sponsors also have more of an incentive to emphasize preventive maintenance procedures that avoid serious future health problems and expenses. For instance, they typically provide physicals and checkups at little or no charge to their members, which helps them detect and prevent many long-term complications. Many plans offer cancer screenings, stress reduction classes, programs to help members stop smoking, and other services that save the sponsor money in the long run. Some plans also offer financial compensation to members who lose weight or achieve fitness goals. For example, one plan offers $175 to overweight members who lose 10 pounds and gives $100 to members who participate in a fitness program.

Another difference between traditional insurance and managed care is that members typically have less freedom to choose their health care providers and have less control over the quality and delivery of care in a managed system. Members of managed care plans usually must select a "primary care physician" from a list of doctors provided by the plan sponsor.

Managed care plans can take many forms. The most popular plans are health maintenance organizations (HMOs) and preferred provider organizations (PPOs). Other services that mimic these two plans include point-of-service plans and competitive medical organizations. In addition to these established plans, many employers and organizations offer hybrid plans that combine various elements of fee-for-service and managed care options.

The most popular plan, the basic HMO, is the purest form of the managed care concept described above. A PPO is a variation of the basic HMO. It combines features of both indemnity insurance and HMO plans. A PPO is typically organized by a large insurer or a group of doctors or hospitals. Under this arrangement, networks of health care providers contract with large organizations to offer their services at reduced rates. The major difference from the HMO is that PPO enrollees retain the option of seeking care outside of the network with a doctor or hospital of their choice. They are usually charged a penalty for doing so, however. Doctors and hospitals are drawn to PPOs because they provide prompt payment for services as well as access to a large client base.

HMOs are differentiated by four organizational models that define the relationship between plan sponsors, physicians, and subscribers. Under the first model, called individual practice associations (IPA), HMO sponsors contract with independent physicians who agree to deliver services to enrollees for a fee. Under this plan, the sponsor pays the provider on a per capita, or fee-for-service, basis each time it treats a plan member. Under the second model, the group plan, HMOs contract with groups of physicians to deliver client services. The sponsor then compensates the medical group on a negotiated per capita rate. The physicians determine how they will compensate each member of their group.

A third model, the network model, is similar to the group model but the HMO contracts with various groups of physicians based on the specialty that a particular group of doctors practices. Enrollees then obtain their service from a network of providers based on their specialized needs. Under the fourth model, the staff arrangement, doctors are actually employed by the managed care plan sponsor. The HMO owns the facility and pays salaries to the doctors on its staff.

This type of arrangement allows the greatest control over costs but also entails the highest start-up costs.

[Dave Mote]

FURTHER READING:

Abromovitz, Les. *Family Insurance Handbook*. Blue Ridge Summit, PA: Tab Press, 1990.

Briggs, Virginia L., Michael G. Kushner, and Michael J. Schinabeck. *Employee Benefits Dictionary: An Annotated Compendium of Frequently Used Terms*.

Weiner, Edith. "The Changing Face of Health Care." *Best's Review*. Life/Health Edition. January, 1993.

Williams, Stephen J., and Sandra J. Guerra. *Health Care Services in the 1990s*. New York: Praeger Publishers, 1991.

Wolford, G. Rodney, Montague Brown, and Barbara P. McCool. "Getting to Go in Managed Care." *Health Care Management Review*. Winter, 1993.

HEDGING

Hedging has been referred to as the major economic justification for futures markets. By definition, hedging is the act of taking a temporary position in the futures market that is equal to, yet opposite one's position in the cash market in order to protect that cash position against loss due to unfavorable price fluctuations.

Since futures trading began, hedgers and speculators have interacted to determine commodity prices. The hedger uses the futures market to protect against the risk of unfavorable price movement, while the speculator, using risk capital, assumes risk in the hope of making a profit by correctly forecasting future price movement.

Futures markets exist only in relation to cash markets, which are the underlying primary markets in which actual physical **commodities** are bought and sold. In many basic commodities, price volatility is inherent and that volatility is a source of significant financial risk for those who produce, market, process, or ultimately consume these commodities and any products which are derived from them. The hedger uses the futures market to protect against the risk of unfavorable price movement.

The first organized **commodity exchange**s in the United States date back to the 1800s; the Chicago Board of Trade (CBOT), founded in 1848, is the oldest existing U.S. futures exchange. When first established, the CBOT was a centralized cash market, formed in response to the need for a central marketplace that would bring together large numbers of buyers and sellers, thus providing liquidity, as well as providing a place with rules for ethical trading practices and reliable standards of weights and measures. Soon after the founding of the exchange, grain brokers began trading in "cash forward contracts," in order to assure buyers a source of supply and sellers the opportunity to sell 12 months a year. As the use of the cash forward contracts escalated, the **futures contracts**, as they are known today, evolved. Futures contracts differed from cash forward contracts in that they specified the price at the time the contract was made, as well as the quantity, quality, and delivery time.

There are two types of hedges: the long or buying hedge and the short or selling hedge. In a long or buying hedge, futures contracts are purchased in anticipation of making a purchase in the cash market sometime in the future. The long hedge is utilized by individuals who want to protect the cost of a cash commodity that they intend to buy at a later date. Anyone who uses or merchandises raw commodities is a potential long or buying hedger.

In a short or selling hedge, futures contracts are sold equal to the cash position to be hedged. The short hedger generally tries to sell futures contracts in the month that most closely corresponds to the anticipated sale in the cash market. For example, if a farmer plans to sell wheat in the cash market in November, he or she would hedge the commodity by selling December wheat futures contracts. The owner of a commodity would use a selling hedge to protect against inventory losses due to adverse price changes.

The difference between the cash price of a commodity at a particular time and place and the price of that commodity on the futures market is called the basis. Basis generally refers to the difference between the current local cash price and the nearby futures contract price. Basis is important in hedging because basis risk is generally more tolerable than outright price risk. As an example, the cash price may fluctuate one cent during a specific period, the futures price may change ten cents, while the basis may change only five cents.

Grain elevator operators might use a short or selling hedge to protect their eventual grain sale. On September 15, the elevator operators anticipate selling 20,000 bushels of wheat in November, and feel that during this two-month period, the price of wheat will fall. On September 15, the price of wheat in the cash market is $4.04. The elevator operators sell four December wheat futures contracts (each contract is 5,000 bushels so it takes four contracts to equal 20,000 bushels) at a price of $4.35 per bushel. The basis here is 31 cents.

On November 15, the elevator operators sell 20,000 bushels of wheat at a cash price of $3.85, or 19 cents less than the price they could have commanded had they sold the wheat back on September 15 at $4.04 per bushel. However, during the two-month period, their four futures contracts, which they had sold on September 15 at $4.35 per bushel, have declined in value as well. They are able to buy four wheat futures contracts to offset the four they sold earlier, this time at $4.16 per bushel, giving them a gain of 19 cents per bushel. The 19 cents per bushel they gained in the futures markets offsets the 19 cent per bushel loss in the cash market. The basis is still 31 cents—the difference between the futures price of $4.16 per bushel and the cash price of $3.85 per bushel.

In this scenario, the grain elevator operators' futures market gain offset the loss they would have sustained in the cash market. The hedgers made exactly what they expected when they placed the hedge, and the basis at 31 cents was they same when they placed the hedge as when they lifted it, which produced a perfect hedge. Perfect hedges rarely occur in actual market conditions. However, even with an imperfect hedge, the hedgers have protected themselves against the losses that they would have sustained in the cash market had they not hedged at all.

Grain elevator operators might also use a long or buying hedge because they anticipate buying wheat in 60 days to fill a forward contract they have made with a wheat processor. On September 15, the elevator operators anticipate buying 20,000 bushels of wheat in November, and feel that during this two-month period, the price of wheat will rise. So on September 15, they buy four December wheat futures contracts at $4.35 per bushel; wheat is selling for $4.04 per bushel in the cash market. Again, the basis is 31 cents. On November 15, the elevator operators buy 20,000 bushels of wheat at $4.10 per bushel, six cents more per bushel than they would have paid had they purchased the wheat they required back on September 15. However, during this same two-month period, the price of their futures contract rose from $4.35 per bushel to $4.41 per bushel, producing a six cent gain. Therefore, the six cents they gained in the futures market offset the six cent higher price they were required to pay in the cash market. The basis remained at 31 cents—the difference between the futures price of $4.41 per bushel and the cash price of $4.10 per bushel. Although perfect hedges like this rarely occur, the example illustrates that opposite positions in the cash and futures markets protect the long or buying hedgers against the risk of rising prices.

[Susan Bard Hall]

FURTHER READING:

Chicago Board of Trade. *Speculating in Futures*. Chicago, 1990, pp. 1-3, 16-17, 19-22.

Chicago Board of Trade. *CBOT Financial Instruments Guide*. Chicago, 1994, p. 4.

HIGH YIELD BONDS

SEE: See Junk Bonds

HISTOGRAMS

In many situations, it is important to collect data and desirable and represent it in a meaningful way in order to make needed conclusions. This section looks at different ways of data representation, with particular emphasis on histograms.

A histogram is essentially a bar graph in which categories are classes. They are a powerful tool for statistical process control. Histograms are also used for basic analysis of data. They illustrate the variation of a process and other useful conclusions about its performance. A histogram is also used to show measures of central tendency, to illustrate whether or not specifications are met for the purpose of process capability analysis. A histogram can also be used to identify the nature of the underlying distribution of the data. In descriptive statistics, is there are basically two different ways for data representation.

1. Numerical measures for describing data

2. Graphical methods for visualizing data

The proper procedure to be used for presenting data depends on type of data. In many engineering and business applications, data may be categorized into discrete data (attributes) and continuous data (variables or measurements).

NUMERICAL METHODS FOR DESCRIBING DATA. Analytical measures are those numbers computed from a data set to help create a meaningful interpretation of a large number of observations. These measures fall into two categories:

1. Measures of central tendency or central location

2. Measures of variation or dispersion

Numerical descriptive measures computed from sample data are normally referred to as statistics. Those numerical descriptive measures of the population are called parameters. The three most commonly used measures of central tendency are the mean, the median, and the mode. The three most commonly used measures of variation are the range, the variance, and the standard deviation.

GRAPHICAL METHODS FOR DESCRIBING DATA. The most popular means of achieving graphical representation of data sets are:

1. *Bar graphs* may be in a vertical or horizontal orientation. Frequency (or relative frequency) corresponding to each category height (or length) of bar is proportional to category frequency (or relative frequency)

2. *Pie charts* divide a complete circle into slices such that one slice corresponds to each category. Central angle of slice is proportional to the category relative frequency.

3. *Frequency histograms*, or frequency distributions, are most commonly used in describing data graphically.

FREQUENCY HISTOGRAMS. In a frequency histogram (relative frequency histogram), the heights of bars are determined by the class frequency (class relative frequency).

Histograms are mostly used in scientific publications to describe quantitative data sets, they are better suited to the description of large data sets. A stable histogram has the following characteristics:

1. Most of the data points are near the centerline, or average.

2. The shape of the histogram is symmetrical.

3. It exhibits a bell-shaped distribution.

Figure 1 (see next page) shows the common shapes of histograms.

[Ahmad K. Elshennawy]

FURTHER READING:

Ishikawa, Kaoru. *Guide to Quality Control.* Hong Kong: Asian Productivity Organization, 1982.

Gitlow, H., S. Gitlow, A. Oppenheim, and R. Oppenheim. *Tools and Methods for the Improvement of Quality.* Homewood, IL: Irwin, 1989.

Juran, Joseph. *Quality Control Handbook.* 4th ed. New York: McGraw-Hill Book Company, 1988.

Juran, Joseph, and Frank Gryna. *Quality Planning and Analysis*, 2nd ed. New York: McGraw-Hill Book Company, 1980.

HOLDING COMPANIES

A holding company is a corporation that is organized for the purpose of owning stock in other corporations. A company may become a holding company by acquiring enough voting stock in another company to exercise control of its operations, or by forming a new corporation and retaining all or part of the new corporation's stock. While owning more than 50 percent of the voting stock of another company ensures control, in many cases it is possible to exercise control

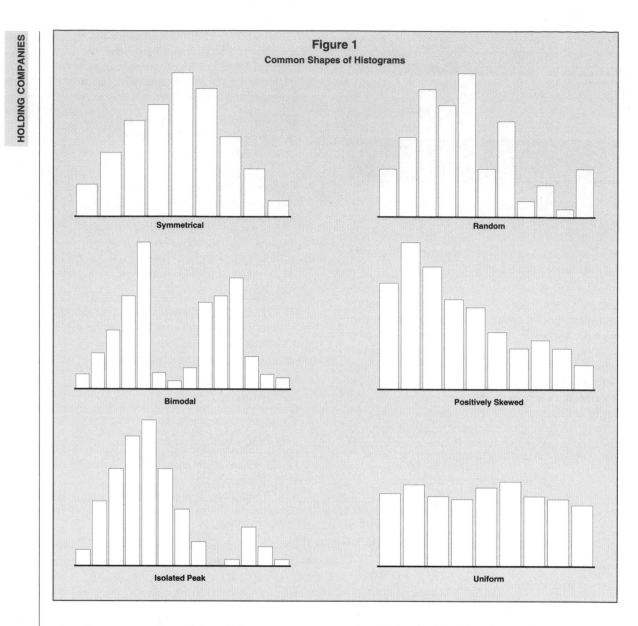

Figure 1
Common Shapes of Histograms

Symmetrical

Random

Bimodal

Positively Skewed

Isolated Peak

Uniform

of another company by owning as little as ten percent of its stock.

Holding companies and the companies they control have a parent-subsidiary relationship. When a holding company owns a controlling interest in another company, the holding company is called the parent company and the controlled company is called the subsidiary. If the parent owns all of the voting stock of another company, that company is said to be a wholly-owned subsidiary of the parent company.

Holding companies and their **subsidiaries** can establish pyramids, whereby one subsidiary owns a controlling interest in another company, thus becoming its parent company. While three to five levels are common in corporate pyramid structures, as many as 60 levels have been known to exist in practice. In the case of public utility holding companies, regulations of the **Securities and Exchange Commission** allow

only two levels of holding companies in addition to the operating subsidiaries.

A holding company is said to be a ''pure'' holding company if it exists solely for the purpose of owning stock in other companies and does not engage in business operations separate from its subsidiaries. If the parent company also engages in its own business operations, then it is said to be a ''mixed'' holding company or a holding-operating company. Holding companies whose subsidiaries engage in unrelated and uncomplementary lines of business are called conglomerates.

There are many advantages to establishing a holding company. From a financial point of view, it is usually possible to obtain control of another company with less investment than would be required in a merger or consolidation. A holding company only needs a controlling interest in the acquired company, not complete interest as in the case of a merger or consolidation. Consequently, it is possible to obtain control over large properties with less investment than would otherwise be required in a merger or consolidation.

Another advantage is that shares of stock in the subsidiary company are held as **assets** on the books of the parent company and can be used as collateral for additional debt financing. In addition, one company can acquire stock in another company without approval of its stockholders; mergers and consolidations typically require stockholder approval. Holding companies and their subsidiaries are considered separate legal entities, so that the assets of the parent company and the individual subsidiaries are protected against creditors' claims against one of the subsidiaries. However, holding companies and their subsidiaries may be considered a single economic entity, and consolidated financial statements are then prepared for the entire structure.

For tax purposes, the parent company must own at least 80 percent of the voting stock in another company in order to be able to file a consolidated tax return. The tax advantage here is that losses from one subsidiary can be used to offset profits from another subsidiary and reduce the overall taxable corporate income on the consolidated tax return. A significant disadvantage occurs when a company holds less than 80 percent of the subsidiary's voting stock; in that case separate tax returns must be filed for the parent and the subsidiary, and intercorporate dividends are subject to an additional tax.

From a management point of view, the parent-subsidiary relationship of holding companies and their subsidiaries allows for decentralized management. Each subsidiary retains its own management team, and the subsidiaries become responsible to the parent company on a profit and loss basis. Unprofitable subsidiaries can more easily be sold off than can divisions of a consolidated business. Subsidiaries retain their corporate identities, and the holding company benefits from any goodwill and recognition attached to the subsidiary's name. Parent companies may provide specialized staff services for the benefit of any of their subsidiaries.

Holding companies in certain industries are subject to special regulations. Public utility holding companies are subject to the Public Utility Holding Company Act of 1935 and must meet special SEC requirements. Railroad holding companies are regulated to some extent by the **Interstate Commerce Commission**, although statutory authority has been filled with loopholes. Bank holding companies are subject to regulation by the Board of Governors of the **Federal Reserve System**.

In addition, the acquisition of new subsidiaries and the formation of new holding companies are subject to the prenotification requirements of the Antitrust Improvement Act of 1976, which provides that the U.S. Department of Justice and the **Federal Trade Commission** (FTC) be notified in advance of all proposed **mergers and acquisitions**. Finally, corporations must specifically be granted the power to acquire stock in another corporation, through their corporate charter as well as through state laws of incorporation. The first state to grant corporations the power to acquire stock in other corporations was New Jersey in 1889.

[David Bianco]

HOME OFFICES

It may be a corner of a spare bedroom and nothing more than a desk. Or, it could be one whole floor of the house filled with the latest computer and communications devices. Whatever its size, the home office is common in American business today. Because many professionals maintain two offices, growing number are equipping their home computer with a modem that allows them access to their office computer files.

As many as 30 million people work from their home, with most of them being self-employed. A growing number of corporations are expanding experiments in telecommuting, which allows employees to use modem-equipped computers just as they would in the office.

While the home office may be considered a new wrinkle in business, the truth is that working away from home is the new wrinkle. For years farmers have used the kitchen table for their record keeping, and pub owners and shopkeepers lived on the second floor of their building. It has only been in the last two centuries that professions such as lawyers, doctors, and accountants have moved from their home offices into office buildings.

HOME OFFICE CONSIDERATIONS

There is nothing complicated about setting up a home office. Today, most have a computer equipped with a variety of **software** and a high quality computer printer. Other helpful tools include a fax machine (or fax-modem board in the computer), multi-line business telephone, and sometimes a photocopier.

The most important aspects of setting up a home office are the potential **tax** and legal implications. Home office operators may claim a deduction for those offices on **IRS** Form 8829 (Expenses for Business Use Of Your Home), which is filed along with Schedule C (Profit or Loss From Your Business). There are restrictions, however, which are covered in IRS Publication 587 *(Business Use of Your Home).* Failing to abide by these restrictions may put a red flag on a home office user's return, which could result in an **audit**.

In general, a home office deduction is allowed if the home is the principal place of business, is the place where the business owner meets to deal with clients and customers as part of the normal business day, or if the place of business is a separate structure on the property, but is not attached to the house or residence. The deduction is figured on the size of the home office as a percentage of the total house or residence. For example, if the total house size is 2,400 square feet and the home office is 240 square feet, ten percent of the total house is considered used for business. That would allow the homeowner to take a 10 percent deduction on the electricity, real estate taxes, mortgage interest, etc., used as a business expense.

Be warned, however, that the home office deduction cannot be used by everyone who has a home office. A recent U.S. Supreme Court decision has made the home office deduction more difficult to apply outside these very carefully worded restrictions. In a tax court case, a doctor worked in three different hospitals, but had no office in any of them so he claimed a home office deduction that he said was necessary to keep up with his billing and patient records. The Court ruled that since he spent most of his day visiting patients, the hospitals were his principal place of work, so his home office deduction was denied.

This ruling, which more narrowly defined the concept of ''principal place of business'' affected a large number of people, particularly professionals such as sales agents who see customers at the customers' places of business. Since the demonstration and sale of the merchandise occurs away from the home office, the IRS ruling is that those offices are not critical to conducting that business. If the income-producing activity takes place away from the office, a deduction is not allowed. On the other hand, a second job conducted exclusively from the home office may qualify for the deduction. The key is that the income must be generated from the home office.

A home office deduction is still possible, if it is set aside exclusively to meet clients or customers, even if it is not always the principal place of business. The IRS uses an example of a lawyer who works three days in an office and two days at home in an office set up so clients come to his home. The last test for an unchallenged home office deduction is that it can be a separate structure such as a studio or garage apartment

that is essential for running the business, for example, a floral shop owner who runs a greenhouse on his property.

The IRS maintains a myriad of rules about home offices, including depreciation of home, depreciation of equipment, how to recover that depreciation if the home is sold, etc. One important thing to note is that the monthly residential telephone charge cannot be deducted, even if most of the calls pertain to the business. However, long distance business related calls can be deducted. Consult a tax advisor to stay within the law on home office deductions.

Besides the IRS regulations, some municipal governments have zoning laws that restrict and/or license home offices. Originally designed to protect residential neighborhoods from becoming commercial zones, the zoning laws have sometimes been strictly interpreted to keep residents from conducting any sort of business from their home, even if it doesn't have a commercial impact on the rest of the neighborhood. People wishing to set up home offices should check with their city's zoning office and licensing board for restrictions that may apply to the city, or even to their particular neighborhood.

[Clint Johnson]

HOURS OF LABOR

In the twenty-four hours of a day, time is divided among many activities. The portion of hours that are hours of labor, by U.S. Department of Labor designation, has varied throughout United States and world history, settling in the twentieth century into the current U.S. standard of eight hours per day. The federal government defines a full workweek as forty hours of work, not including lunch time. This is the standard to which federal workers are held and to which the federal government holds employers in the private sector when applying laws dealing with overtime pay.

There are many variations of the workweek in several sectors of the economy, especially sectors such as public safety and health that require 24-hour coverage. The concept of the forty-hour week spread over five days no longer held by the end of the twentieth century for the retailing and the service industry, either, where weekend and evening hours came about for the convenience of the populace. These and other industries use shift work and overtime to schedule their hours of operation. When workers are not covered by the federal pay hour standards, the workweek can and does often exceed forty hours.

Tasks can be accomplished by hiring a few people to work long hours for bigger paychecks and little leisure time, or tasks can be accomplished by hiring many people for shorter workdays with smaller paychecks and more leisure time. The number of work and nonwork hours is a cultural and economical balance between work goals and leisure goals.

The measurement of hours of labor is important in calculating productivity, and projecting the direction of the economy. According to the August 1994 issue of the *Monthly Labor Review*, "The amount of time people spend at their jobs can be an important social and economic indicator."

The American labor movement's efforts to secure the forty-hour week or eight-hour day standard in America is traced in thorough detail by David R. Roediger and Philip S. Foner in *Our Own Time*. According to Roediger and Foner, as early as the Middle Ages the London weaver's guild attempted to cut the working hours of apprentices. In colonial America, this British concern for the workday persisted and a free man's workday generally ran from sunup to sundown with rest on the Sabbath.

As the Industrial Revolution progressed in England, craftspeople began to ask for shorter hours. According to Roediger and Foner, workers in shops and in the new factories viewed control over hours as part of the larger issues of control over work product, their own lives, and work conditions.

During and after the Civil War, labor unions focused on the goal of an eight-hour day to give the worker more free time. This issue remained central until the 1930s and has since dropped from view as a primary issue in labor negotiations. Average weekly hours dropped from 59 in 1900 to 40.6 in 1972.

In 1938 the **Fair Labor Standards Act of 1938** became a part of federal law. The act banned the employment of children under most circumstances and set a minimum hourly wage for workers in certain establishments.

Two common methods of measuring work hours are payroll hours and work diary. In the first method, firms and industry provide the U.S. Bureau of Labor Statistics (BLS), with data based on payroll, or paid employee hours. Gross calculations of productivity can then be compared by one industry on total hours paid. These figures do not cover sectors of the economy such as the self-employed, nor do they identify the total number of hours one worker may have put in, for instance, someone who has more than one job. The other method, work diary, is a more intensive and elaborate method. It separates the hours paid from hours worked and provides more detail. This method uses an individual sample that requires the keeping of a work diary in which all workers record activities of work and nonwork for a single week or more.

Despite a 4.3 percent increase in productivity in America from 1991 to 1992, many workers now voluntarily work more hours than the standard forty. Reasons often cited for this increase in the workday are union negotiations for greater benefits for each employee, and workers putting in more overtime hours due to the decline of the real dollar. Increased fringe benefits are thought to make employers reluctant to hire new employees, and instead cause them to fill in the gaps with temporary employees or with overtime when the workload peaks. In *The Overworked American*, Juliet B. Schor posits that in the 1980s and 1990s Americans began to spend more time on their jobs—despite an increase in productivity—in order to earn more and to be able to buy more goods.

The number of housewives who joined the job market grew from 15 percent in 1904 to 66 percent in 1992. The work hours they take on are often in addition to the hours spent working on homemaking tasks. Policy issues in the workplace in the late twentieth century focus on the creation of flexible arrangements for child care, job sharing, flextime, and part-time work. The length of the workday has become secondary to the right to take paid and unpaid leave for family emergencies, flexible hours and work sites, and **child care** and **elder care**.

SEE ALSO: Family Leave

[Joan Leotta]

FURTHER READING:

Robinson, John P., and Ann Bostrom. "The Overestimated Workweek?" *Monthly Labor Review*. August, 1994.

Roediger, David R., and Philip S. Foner. *Our Own Time*. New York: Verso Books, 1989.

Schor, Juliet B. *The Overworked American*. New York: Basic Books 1991.

US Department of Labor. Wage and Hour Division. *Handy Reference Guide to the Fair Labor Standards Act*. Washington, D.C. 1992.

HUMAN CAPITAL

The concept of human capital refers to the education, **on-the-job training**, and work experience of the labor force. It is analogous to other forms of capital in that investments in human capital yield income and other benefits over a long time. An investment in human capital means investing in education or some form of on-the-job training to improve workforce quality. Such investments provide returns to the individual as well as to the economy as a whole. Individuals benefit from higher earnings, and the economy as a whole benefits from higher productivity.

Human capital theory is concerned with finding ways to measure human capital and the rate of return on investments in human capital, both to the individual and to the economy as a whole. The quality of the labor force, or investment in human capital, can be measured in different ways. One way is to measure expenditures on education and training. Since the overall health of workers also affects productivity, investments in medical care are sometimes considered human capital expenditures.

Another method of measuring the quality of a country's labor force is to determine its occupational composition. In the United States, for example, the percentage of laborers and unskilled workers has decreased over time, while the percentage of professionals, managers, executives, and technical workers has increased. These changes during the twentieth century indicate that the quality of the labor force has risen. Such a change can be quantified to determine how rapidly the average skill level of the labor force has risen over time.

Studies have shown that investments in human capital are essential for sustaining economic growth over time. The law of diminishing returns suggests that investments in physical capital and land eventually fail to result in economic growth. Yet, countries such as the United States, Japan, and many European nations have sustained economic growth over the past century. Heavy investment in the training of workers and a better-educated labor force are given credit for much of the growth in per capita incomes and economic productivity. A comparison of modern, educated farmers with farmers in traditional economies shows the need for educating workers to help them cope with changing technologies.

While economists have been able to demonstrate a statistical relationship between education and earnings, they have not been able to conclusively show a cause-and-effect relationship. That is, while higher earnings are associated with more education, it has yet to be conclusively shown that more education leads to higher earnings. The theory that more education is a causative factor in higher earnings has been attacked on two points. One is the ability problem, or the fact that more-highly educated individuals are also likely to have the ability, self-discipline, and motivation that also result in higher earnings. Such individuals tend to do well in the labor market, it is argued, not because of their education, but because of other abilities.

A second critique of the human capital theory is the screening hypothesis, which states that higher levels of education serve to grade and label individuals in the job market. That is, higher levels of education do not necessarily make individuals more productive, they simply give people credentials which are then associated with higher-paying jobs. If this criticism is valid, then it can be argued that greater social expenditures on education may not result in as much increased economic productivity as the human capital model would suggest.

The concept of human capital can be applied to the individual firm as well as to the economy as a whole. The expertise of a company's employees is often referred to as its intellectual capital. It may include such intellectual assets as patents, processes, **management** skills, technologies, information systems, and customer knowledge. Like human capital, intellectual capital is difficult to measure, and companies that recognize its benefits are seeking ways to manage and codify it.

Companies can invest in intellectual capital, just as countries invest in human capital, through training programs and hiring practices. Social investment in human capital is a matter of public policy. Examples of policies that tend to increase a country's stock of human capital include using the human capital of women, investing in higher education, supporting dropout prevention programs, and encouraging highly skilled immigrants to enter the workforce.

[David Bianco]

FURTHER READING:

Becker, Gary S. *Human Capital.* National Bureau of Economic Research, 1964.

HUMAN RESOURCE INFORMATION SYSTEM

A *human resource information system* (HRIS) is defined as a computer-based application for assembling and processing data related to the **human resource management** (HRM) function. As in other types of information systems, an HRIS consists of a *database*, which contains one or more files in which the data relevant to the system are maintained, and a *database management system*, which provides the means by which users of the system access and utilize these data. The HRIS thus contains tools that allow users to input new data and edit existing data; in addition, such programs provide users with the opportunity to select from an array of predefined reports that may either be printed or displayed on a monitor. Reports may address any of a number of different HRM issues (e.g., succession planning, compensation planning, equal employment opportunity monitoring). HRISs also generally include tools by which users or system administrators may generate ad hoc reports and select specific cases or subsets of cases for display.

In order to understand the types of applications available to HRIS users, it is best to consider the evolving nature of human resource information systems applications over the past ten to 20 years. In general, the HRM field has lagged behind a number of other functional areas of management in the utilization of computer applications and it has only been since the mid-1980s or so that extensive use of sophisticated applications began to appear. Prior to that time, manual record systems often dominated in personnel or human resource departments. Computer applications used in the field were generally limited to basic record keeping and payroll management systems. Virtually all such systems were based on mainframe computers and required extensive support from information systems professionals. Thus, human resource managers had little opportunity to design sophisticated reports and computer-based analytical tools to aid in managerial decision making. In general, uses of the computers in HRM fell into the category of electronic data processing (EDP) applications, which generally involve the automation of relatively routine tasks (e.g., calculating pay and printing checks).

Beginning in the mid-1980s, a number of trends seem to have contributed to a growing reliance on **computers** as information-processing and decision-aiding tools in HRM. The emergence of the human resource management field (versus personnel administration) gave the human resource function greater credibility within the managerial hierarchy, necessitating more sophisticated use of information, especially as related to the strategic management function. At the same time many firms were experiencing increased competitive pressures, which translated into greater cost containment demands from upper management, leading to greater automation of the record-keeping function in the HRM field. The ready availability of **microcomputers** and relatively user-friendly software meant, that to an increasing extent, human resource managers were no longer dependent on information system professionals to develop and implement applications (which might be assigned a lower priority than other management functions). Many HRM departments in larger organizations also developed internal information system capabilities, so that HRIS units were established.

Another important factor has been the development of numerous HRIS products by external vendors. There are several full-featured, HR-dedicated database management systems available, both for mainframe and micro platforms. Specialized applications, intended to supplement the database management systems are also widely available. These include modules to aid in such areas as succession planning, benefits administration, applicant tracking, job evaluation, employee performance evaluation, grievance handling, and labor relations. These products, coupled with declining costs of computer systems (especially microcomputer systems) and the increasing user-friendliness of computer applications, have meant that the use of HRISs is increasingly attractive to practitioners.

In the future human resource departments are increasingly likely to rely on microcomputer systems as the preferred platform for all but the largest applications. The expanding power and simplicity of such systems, combined with limited costs, make microcomputer-based HRISs very attractive. More of these systems will use Windows-like operating environments. Moreover, networking will mean that very large databases can be maintained via distributed database management systems. Another likely development is the increasing use of client-server configurations, again as part of networks (both **local area networks (LANs)** and wide area networks (WANs). More sophisticated applications are also likely, such as the use of artificial techniques and expert systems.

[John J. Lawler]

FURTHER READING:

Ceriello, V., with C. Freeman. *Human Resource Management Systems: Strategies, Tactics, and Techniques.* Lexington, MA: Lexington Books, 1991.

Frantzreb, R. B. *The Personnel Software Census.* Roseville, CA: Advanced Personnel Systems, 1993.

Lawler, J. Computer-mediated Information Processing and Decision Making in Human Resource Management. *Research in Personnel and Human Resources Management,* edited by G.R. Ferris and K. M. Rowland. Volume 10. Greenwich, CT: JAI Press, 1992 pp. 301-345, 1992.

Walker, A. *Handbook of Human Resource Information Systems: Reshaping the Human Resource Function with Technology.* New York: McGraw-Hill, 1993.

HUMAN RESOURCE MANAGEMENT

Human resource management (HRM), or human resource development, entails planning, implementing, and managing recruitment; and selection, training, career, and organizational development initiatives within an organization. The goal of HRM is to maximize the productivity of an organization by optimizing the effectiveness of its employees. But HRM also encompasses personal development, the attainment of altruistic goals, and compliance with employment-related laws.

HISTORY

HRM dates back to the beginning of mankind. Mechanisms were developed for the selection of tribal leaders, for example, and knowledge was recorded and passed on to youth about safety, health, hunting, and gathering. More advanced HRM functions were developed as early as 1000 and 2000 B.C. Employee screening tests have been traced back to 1115 B.C. in China, for example. And the earliest form of industrial education, the apprentice system, was started in ancient Greek and Babylonian civilizations before gaining prominence during medieval times.

The need for an organized form of HRM emerged during the industrial revolution, as the manufacturing process evolved from a cottage system to factory production. Along with manufacturing efficiencies came several shortcomings related to working conditions. These problems included: tasks, long hours, and unhealthy work environments.

The direct cause of employers seeking better HRM programs was not poor working conditions, but rather the protests and pressures generated by workers and organized **labor unions**. Indeed, labor unions, which had existed as early as 1790 in the United States, became much more powerful during the late 1800s and early 1900s. There were two other particularly important contributing factors to the origination of modern HRM during that period. The first was the industrial welfare movement, which represented a shift in the way that managers viewed employees—from non human resources to human beings. That movement resulted in the creation of medical care and educational facilities. The second factor was Frederick W. Taylor's (1856-1915) *Scientific Management*, a landmark book that outlined management methods for attaining greater productivity from low-level production workers.

The first corporate employment department designed to address employee concerns was created by the B.F. Goodrich Company in 1900. In 1902, National Cash Register formed a similar department to handle worker grievances, wage administration, record keeping, and many other functions that would later be relegated to HRM departments at most large U.S. companies. HRM as a professional discipline was especially bolstered by the passage of the Wagner Act in 1935, which remained the basic U.S. labor law into the mid-1990s. It augmented the power of labor unions and increased the role and importance of personnel managers.

During the 1930s and 1940s the general focus of HRM changed from a focus on worker efficiency and skills to employee satisfaction. That shift became especially pronounced after World War II, when a shortage of skilled labor forced companies to pay more attention to workers' needs. Employers, influenced by the famous Hawthorne productivity studies and similar research, began to emphasize personal development and improved work conditions as a means of motivating employees.

In the 1960s and 1970s the federal government furthered the HRM movement with a battery of regu-

lations created to enforce fair treatment of workers, such as the Equal Pay Act of 1963, the **Employee Retirement Income Security Act of 1974 (ERISA)**, and the Occupational Safety and Health Act of 1970. These regulations created an entirely new legal role for HRM professionals. Also during the 1970s, HRM gained status as a recognized profession with the advent of human resource programs in colleges.

By the end of the 1970s, virtually all medium-sized and large companies and institutions had some type of HRM program in place to handle recruitment, training, regulatory compliance, dismissal, and other related issues. HRM's importance continued to grow during the 1980s for several reasons. Changing workforce values, for example, required the skills of HRM professionals to adapt organizational structures to a new generation of workers with different attitudes about authority and conformity. Shifting demographics forced changes in the way workers were hired, fired, and managed. Other factors contributing to an emphasis on HRM during the 1980s and early 1990s were increasing education levels, reductions in middle management, more women in the work force, slower domestic market growth, greater foreign competition, and new federal and state regulations.

THE FOCUS OF HRM

The three major resources employed by most organizations are: physical, such as materials and equipment; financial, including cash, credit, and debt; and human. In its broadest sense, HRM refers to the management of all decisions within an organization that are related to people. In practice, however, HRM is a tool used to try to make optimum use of human resources, to foster individual development, and to comply with government mandates. Larger organizations typically have an HRM department and its primary objective is to optimize human resources.

In *Human Resource Development*, R. Wayne Pace identifies seven underlying assumptions that provide a foundation and direction for HRM. First is the acknowledgement of individual worth, suggesting that an entity can be judged by how it recognizes and values individual contributions. Second is that employees are resources involved in learning new skills and ideas, and preparing to occupy new positions in the organization. Third is that quality of work life is a legitimate concern, and that employees have a right to safe, clean, and pleasant surroundings. A fourth assumption is the need for continuous learning; talents and skills must be continually refined in the long-term interests of the organization.

A fifth assumption supporting the existence of an organized HRM within a company or institution is that opportunities are constantly changing and the entity needs a tool to facilitate continual adaptation. Sixth is employee satisfaction, which implies that humans have a right to be satisfied by their work and that employers have a responsibility and profit motivation to try to match a worker's skills with his or her job. The final assumption is that HRM encompasses a much broader scope than technical training—employees need to know more than the requirements of a specific task in order to make their maximum contribution.

THE ROLE, POSITION, AND STRUCTURE OF HRM DEPARTMENTS

Paul S. Greenlaw and John P. Kohl in *Personnel Management* describe three distinct, interrelated fields of interest addressed by the HRM discipline: human relations, organization theory, and decision areas. Human relations encompasses matters such as individual motivation, leadership, and group relationships. Organization theory refers to job design, managerial control, and work flow through the organization. Decision areas encompass interests related to the acquisition, development, rewarding, and maintenance of human resources. Although the method and degree to which those areas of interest are handled vary among different HRM departments, a few general rules characterize the responsibilities, positioning, and structure of most HRM divisions.

HRM department responsibilities, other than related legal and clerical duties, can be classified by individual, organizational, and career areas. Individual management entails helping employees identify their strengths and weaknesses, correct their shortcomings, and then make their best contribution to the enterprise. These duties are carried out through a variety of activities such as performance reviews, training, and testing. Organizational development focuses on fostering a successful system that maximizes human, and other, resources. This important duty also includes the creation and maintenance of a change program, which allows the organization to respond to evolving outside and internal influences. The third responsibility, career development, entails matching individuals with the most suitable jobs and career paths.

The positioning of HRM departments is ideally near the theoretic organizational center, with maximum access to all divisions and management levels. In larger organizations the HRM function might be headed by a vice president, while smaller entities will have a middle-level manager as head of HRM. In any case, because the HRM department is charged with managing the productivity and development of workers at all levels, the top HRM manager ideally has access to, and the support of, key decision makers. In addition, the HRM department should be situated in such a way that it has horizontal access, or is able to effectively communicate with all divisions within the company. Horizontal access allows HRM to integrate,

educate, and train the work force, and to facilitate changes that affect one division and indirectly influence other segments of the company or institution.

The structure of HRM departments differs according to the type and size of the organization that they serve. But many large organizations (including governments, institutions, manufacturing companies, and service firms), organize HRM employee development functions around the clusters of people to be helped—they conduct recruiting, administrative, and other duties in a central location. Different employee development groups for each department are necessary to train and develop employees in specialized areas, such as sales, engineering, marketing, or executive education. In contrast, some HRM departments are completely independent and are organized purely by function. The same training department, for example, serves all divisions of the organization.

HRM ACTIVITIES

To fulfill their basic role, as described above, HRM professionals and departments engage in a variety of activities that can be categorized in a number of different ways. Greenlaw and Kohl in *Personnel Management* break HRM activities into four functional groups, each of which includes related legal responsibilities: acquisition, development, reward, and maintenance.

ACQUISITION. Acquisition duties include human resource planning for employees, which includes activities related to analyzing employment needs, determining the necessary skills for positions, identifying job and industry trends, and forecasting future employment levels and skill requirements. These tasks may be accomplished using such tools and techniques as questionnaires, interviews, statistical analysis, building skill inventories, and designing career path charts. Four specific goals of effective human resource planning include: sustaining stable work force levels during ups and downs in output, which can reduce unnecessary employment costs and liabilities and increase employee morale that would otherwise suffer in the event of layoffs; preventing a high turnover rate among younger recruits; reducing problems associated with replacing key decision makers in the event of an unexpected absence; and making it possible for financial resource managers to efficiently plan departmental budgets.

The acquisition function also encompasses activities related to recruiting workers, such as designing evaluation tests and interview methods. Ideally, the chief goal is to hire the most-qualified candidates without encroaching on federal regulations or allowing decision makers to be influenced by unrelated stereotypes. HRM departments at some companies may choose to administer honesty or personality tests, or to test potential candidates for drug use. Recruitment responsibilities also include ensuring that the people in the organization are honest and adhere to strict government regulations pertaining to discrimination and privacy. To that end, human resource managers establish and document detailed recruiting and hiring procedures that protect applicants and diminish the risk of lawsuits.

DEVELOPMENT. The second major HRM function, human resource development, refers to performance appraisal and training activities. The basic goal of appraisal is, to provide feedback to employees about their performance. This allows them to comprehend the appropriateness of their behavior in the eyes of their coworkers and managers, correct weaknesses, and improve their contribution. HRM professionals must devise uniform appraisal standards, develop review techniques, train managers to administer the appraisals, and then evaluate and follow up on the effectiveness of performance reviews. They must also tie the appraisal process into compensation and incentive strategies, and work to ensure that federal regulations are observed.

Training and development activities include the determination, design, execution, and analysis of educational programs. Orientation programs, for example, are usually necessary to acclimate new hires to the company. The HRM training and education role may encompass a wide variety of tasks, depending on the type and extent of different programs. In any case, the HRM professional ideally is aware of the fundamentals of learning and motivation, and must carefully design effective training and development programs that benefit the overall organization as well as the individual. Training initiatives may include apprenticeship, internship, job rotation, mentoring, and new skills programs.

REWARD. Reward, the third major HRM function, refers to HRM duties related to compensating and providing incentives for employees. HRM professionals are typically charged with developing wage and salary systems that accomplish specific organizational objectives, such as employee retention, quality, satisfaction, and motivation. Ideally, their aim is to establish wage and salary levels that maximize the company's investment in relation to its goals. This is often successfully accomplished with performance-based incentives. Importantly, HRM managers must learn how to create compensation equity within the organization that doesn't hamper morale and that provides sufficient financial motivation. Besides financial renumeration and fringe benefits, effective HRM managers also design programs that reward employees by meeting their emotional needs, such as recognition for good work.

MAINTENANCE. The fourth principal HRM function, maintenance of human resources, encompasses HRM activities related to employee benefits, safety and health, and worker-management relations. Employee benefits are nonincentive-oriented compensation, such as health insurance and free parking, and are often used to transfer nontaxed compensation to employees. The three major categories of benefits managed by HRM managers are: employee services, such as purchasing plans, recreational activities, and legal services; vacations, holidays, and other allowed absences; and insurance, retirement, and health benefits. To successfully administer a benefits program, HRM professionals need to understand tax incentives, retirement investment plans, and purchasing power derived from a large base of employees.

Human resource maintenance activities related to safety and health usually entail compliance with federal laws that protect employees from hazards in the workplace. Regulations emanate from the federal **Occupational Safety and Health Administration (OSHA)**, for instance, and from state worker's compensation and federal **Environmental Protection Agency (EPA)** laws. HRM managers must work to minimize the company's exposure to risk by implementing preventive safety and training programs. They are also typically charged with designing detailed procedures to document and handle injuries.

Maintenance tasks related to worker-management relations primarily entail: working with labor unions; handling grievances related to misconduct, such as theft or **sexual harassment**; and devising systems to foster cooperation. Activities in this arena include contract negotiation, developing policies to accept and handle worker grievances, and administering programs to enhance communication and cooperation.

MEASURING HRM RESULTS. One of the most critical aspects of HRM is measuring the results of its activities. Even the most carefully planned and executed HRM programs are meaningless without some way to judge their effectiveness and confirm their credibility. Larger human resource departments often use detailed, advanced data gathering and statistical analysis techniques to test the success of their initiatives. The results can then be used to adjust HRM programs or even to make organizational changes.

Michael Beer and others, in *Human Resources Management* posit four factors, the "four Cs," that should be used to determine whether or not an HRM department or individual program is succeeding: commitment, competence, cost effectiveness, and congruence. In testing commitment, the HRM manager asks to what extent do policies enhance the commitment of people to the organization? Commitment is necessary to cultivate loyalty, improve performance, and optimize cooperation among individuals and groups.

Competence refers to the extent to which HRM policies attract, keep, and develop employees: Do

HRM policies result in the right skills needed by the organization being available at the proper time and in the necessary quantity? Likewise, cost effectiveness, the third factor, measures the fiscal proficiency of given policies in terms of wages, benefits, absenteeism, turnover, and labor/management disputes. Finally, analysis of congruence helps to determine how HRM policies create and maintain cooperation between different groups within and outside the organization, including different departments, employees and their families, and managers and subordinates.

In addition to advanced data gathering and analysis techniques, several simple observations can be made that provide insight into the general effectiveness of a company's human resources. For example, the ratio of managerial costs to worker costs indicates the efficiency of an organization's labor force; in general, lower managerial costs indicate a more empowered and effective work force. Revenues and costs per employee, when compared to related industry norms, can provide insight into HRM effectiveness.

Furthermore, the average speed at which job vacancies are filled is an indicator of whether or not the organization has acquired the necessary talents and competencies. Other measures of HRM success include employee complaint and customer satisfaction statistics, health insurance and workers' compensation claims, and independent quality ratings. Importantly, the number of significant innovations made each year, such as manufacturing or product breakthroughs, suggest HRM's success at fostering an environment that rewards new ideas and is amenable to change.

LEGAL INFLUENCES

The field of HRM is greatly influenced and shaped by state and federal employment legislation, most of which is designed to protect workers from abuse by their employers. Indeed, one of the most important responsibilities of HRM professionals lies in compliance with regulations aimed at HRM departments. The laws and court rulings can be categorized by their affect on the four primary HRM functional areas: acquisition, development, rewards, and maintenance.

The most important piece of HRM legislation, which affects all of the functional areas, is Title VII of the Civil Rights Act of 1964 and subsequent amendments, including the **Civil Rights Act of 1991**. These acts made illegal the discrimination against employees or potential recruits for reasons of race, color, religion, sex, and national origin. It forces employers to achieve, and often document, fairness related to hiring, training, pay, benefits, and virtually all other activities and responsibilities related to HRM. The 1964 act established the **Equal Employment Oppor-**

tunity Commission (EEOC) to enforce the act, and provides for civil penalties in the event of discrimination. Possible penalties include forcing an organization to implement an **affirmative action** program to actively recruit and promote minorities that are underrepresented in a company's workforce or management. The net result of the all-encompassing civil rights acts is that HRM departments must carefully design and document numerous procedures to ensure compliance, or face potentially significant penalties.

In addition to the civil rights acts, a law affecting acquisition, or resource planning and selection, is the Equal Pay Act of 1963. This act forbids wage or salary discrimination based on sex, and mandates equal pay for equal work with few exceptions. Subsequent court rulings augmented the act by promoting the concept of **comparable worth**, or equal pay for unequal jobs of equal value or worth. The important Age Discrimination in Employment Act of 1967, which was strengthened by amendments in the early 1990s, essentially protects workers 40 years of age and older from discrimination. The Fair Credit Reporting Act also affects acquisition activities, as employers who turn down applicants for credit reasons must provide the sources of the information that shaped their decision. Similarly, the Buckley Amendment of 1974 requires certain institutions to make records available to individuals and to receive permission before releasing those records to third parties.

The major laws affecting HRM development, or appraisal, training, and development, are the civil rights act, the equal pay act, and the age discrimination in employment act. All of those laws also affected the third HRM activity, rewards, or salary administration and incentive systems. In addition, however, HRM reward programs must comply with a plethora of detailed legislation. The Davis-Bacon Act of 1931, for instance, requires the payment of minimum wages to nonfederal employees. The Walsh-Healy Public Contracts Act of 1936 ensures that employees working as contractors for the federal government will be compensated fairly. Importantly, the **Fair Labor Standards Act of 1938** mandates employer compliance with restrictions related to minimum wages, overtime provisions, child labor, and workplace safety. Other major laws affecting rewards include: the Tax Reform Acts of 1969, 1976, and 1986; the Economic Recovery Tax Act of 1981 (ERTA); the Revenue Act of 1978; and the Tax Equity and Fiscal Responsibility Act of 1982.

Perhaps the most regulated realm of the HRM field is maintenance, or benefits, safety and health, and employee/management relations. Chief among regulations in this arena is the Occupational Safety and Health Act of 1970, which established the Occupational Safety and Health Administration (OSHA). That act was designed to force employers to provide safe and healthy work environments and to make organizations liable for workers' safety. The sweeping act has ballooned to include thousands of regulations backed by civil and criminal penalties, including jail time and fines for company executives. Also of import are state **workers' compensation** laws, which require employers to make provisions to pay for work-related injuries, and forces HRM managers to create and document safety procedures and programs that reduce a company's liability. The Wagner Act (National Labor Relations Act of 1935) is the main piece of legislation governing union/management relations, and is a chief source of regulation for HRM departments. Other important laws related to HRM maintenance include; the Norris-Laguardia Act of 1932, the Social Security Act of 1935, the **Taft-Hartley Act** of 1947, and the Landrum-Griffin Act of 1959.

FORCES CHANGING HRM

In the early 1990s several forces were shaping the broad field of HRM. Chief among them were new technologies, particularly information technology that was allowing the decentralization of communications and the shake-up of existing paradigms of human interaction and organizational theory. Satellite communications, computers and networking systems, fax machines, and other devices were facilitating rapid change. In fact, it was those innovations that were driving many of the other forces causing changes in the HRM field.

A second important change affecting HRM was new organizational structures that began to emerge during the 1980s. Companies were scrapping traditional, hierarchical organizational structures in favor of flatter management systems—the end result was that fewer managers were involved in the decision-making process and companies were adopting more of a team approach to management. HRM professionals, as the agents of change, were charged with reorganizing workers and increasing their efficiency. A corollary of changing structures was the proliferation of part-time, or contract, employees, which required human resource strategies that contrasted with those applicable to full-time workers.

A third change factor was accelerating market globalization, which was increasing competition and demanding greater performance out of workers, often at diminished levels of compensation. To compete abroad, companies were looking to their HRM professionals to augment initiatives related to quality, productivity, and innovation. Other factors changing HRM include: an accelerating rate of change and turbulence, resulting in higher employee turnover and the need for more responsive, open-minded workers; rapidly changing demographics; and increasing income disparity as the demand for highly educated workers increases at the expense of lower-wage employees.

[Dave Mote]

FURTHER READING:

Beer, Michael, Bert Specter, Paul R. Lawrence, D. Quinn Mills, and Richard E. Walton. *Human Resource Management.* New York: The Free Press, 1985.

Greenlaw, Paul S., and John P. Kohl. *Personnel Management: Managing Human Resources.* New York: Harper & Row, 1986.

Pace, R. Wayne. *Human Resource Development: The Field.* Englewood Cliffs, NJ: Prentice Hall, 1991.

HYPOTHESIS TESTING

Hypothesis testing is the backbone of the positivist scientific method. A hypothesis is a proposition or statement about the world—derived from any source, from whim or fancy, from accumulated knowledge, from dominant or heretical ideas, from prejudices, or from guesses—that is capable of being confronted with facts and is thus capable of being refuted by those facts. In any field a science, from physics and chemistry to economics and sociology, the practitioners often pursue questions using this method, often referred to more generally as the scientific method. The overarching process involves the formulation of hypotheses (statements), testing them against the facts, and rejecting those that are refuted or reformulating them against the feedback of information gained from the testing.

HYPOTHESIS TESTING IN THE NATURAL SCIENCES

In many of the natural sciences, hypothesis testing takes place in the context of controlled laboratory experiments (so as to isolate a particular phenomenon or causal effect). For example, a medical researcher may wish to test the proposition that smoking causes lung cancer. In order to properly test the hypothesis he or she might try to look at identical individuals in identical environments, with the only difference being that one group smokes while the other group (the control group) does not. Assuming that all other factors could be controlled, if the group that smoked eventually developed lung cancer, the researcher could conclude that his or her hypothesis was confirmed.

HYPOTHESIS TESTING IN THE SOCIAL SCIENCES

By contrast, in the social sciences, investigators often resort to secondary analysis; Statistical methods are employed to analyze data because social phenomenon are rarely, if ever, amenable to laboratory-type experiments. Hypotheses are tested using statistical techniques in order to infer conclusions about a population from information obtained taken from a subset (or sample) of that population. Statistical inference (based on laws of probability) is then used to test whether a particular observed phenomenon is due to chance. For example, we might wish to test whether the observation that men's wages (on average) are significantly higher than women's wages is not a random event characteristic of a particular sample of the men and women we surveyed. To test this we would formulate a null hypothesis that the true mean wages of men and women are equal. Then, if we reject the null hypothesis we accept the alternative—that the differences are not due to chance. We could then discuss *why* this might be the case and this is where the controversy would arise. Hypothesis testing may indicate that there may be a connection between observed phenomenon, but the forces that generated these results might be accounted for by any number of explanations or theories.

In econometrics (the branch of economic statistics that most often deals with hypothesis testing), an investigator might assume some relationship between variables for purposes of statistical testing. For example, a **tax** on **corporate income** might be posited to be passed on to consumers in the form of higher prices. One way of testing this hypothesis would be to test the hypothesis that prices are correlated with the tax. Other common hypotheses tested are that the quantity of a good demanded depends on the price of the good. Another repeatedly confirmed hypothesis is that variation in the **money supply** in an economy is associated with variation in the price level of the economy. In all of these cases correlation is easily shown—that is to say, all of these hypotheses have been largely confirmed. The limits to this type of analysis is that while hypothesis tests can establish correlation between variables, it cannot explain how and why systems function as they do. For example, does a change in the money supply lead to a change in prices (does money *cause* price changes?)? Does a change in prices lead to a change in the money supply? Does some other variable, or variables, lead to a change in *both* the money supply and the price level? Differing reasonable explanations abound. Thus, while certain confirmed hypotheses might exhibit substantial predictive power, in order to gain a more complete understanding of any subject, empirical testing must be embedded in a larger context of historical and theoretical reasoning about the world.

Much of the research in the social sciences (and various business applications) relies on statistical methods that allow the researcher to make general statements about a population from information derived from a sample. These statistical methods then allow us to separate the effects of systematic variation of a variable from mere chance effects. As mentioned, this technique is especially useful in the social sciences because many phenomena cannot be isolated or controlled in a laboratory-type setting, as in the physical sciences. Many tests of economic hypotheses, for example, take the form of testing parameters of linear regression models. For example, suppose an economic relation is hypothesized to take the form

$$Y = XB + e$$

where Y is supposed to be observations of the dependent variable and X is supposed to be observations of explanatory (or causal) variables. The quantity B is a coefficient that expresses the relationship between the independent variables and the hypothesized dependent variables, while e is a vector of residual terms that are assumed to be independent of one another (or random). Hypothesis tests could then be formulated by placing restrictions on one or more of the coefficients and testing whether certain variables (alone or in concert) have an effect on Y. Thus, one might hypothesize that consumption expenditures are related to income, or wages, wealth, and certain other variables. We could then posit the null hypothesis that, for example, consumption is not a function of income, holding other variables constant (i.e., that the coefficient for B is zero) Then, if the null hypothesis is rejected, that would imply that a measurable portion of the variation in consumption expenditures (captured in the parameter B) is explained by the variation in income.

USES AND ABUSES OF HYPOTHESIS TESTING

In spite of claims that scientists are passive recipients of facts about the world, questions of how and which hypotheses are tested is, in fact, a complicated social process that involves issues of a particular society's collective or dominant values; our perceptions of the world shape our understanding of the world and our understanding of the world contributes to how we in turn act upon our world. In other words, the type of questions that are asked is itself a product of many factors, including the inherited historical knowledge, the dominant values and ideology of a particular society (e.g., the ancient Egyptians built pyramids, the United States sent men to the moon). Without doubt, this knowledge influences the society's technological and social trajectory. In the process, science (or ideas in general) shapes the world and the world shapes our understanding.

But the dominant notion of the scientist is one of the neutral observer trying to make sense of a complicated world. In their labors, scientists obtain information about the world and formulate propositions in the form of refutable hypotheses. The goal is to find regularities concealed by random disturbances. In this way, primary causal relations may be separated from those phenomena that are generated by chance. The accumulation of accepted hypotheses are then accretions to scientific knowledge. Often the people who test hypotheses are separate from those who think about and interpret the results of empirical tests. Thus, for example, one often finds theoretical physicists and theoretical economists as distinct from applied economists and applied physicists. In any case, it is the facts that speak to the observer. Not surprisingly then, one of the most fundamental notions of positivist science is the separation of analytical (often called metaphysical or logical) arguments (not directly observable) from testable (by definition empirical) statements. One of the crudest versions of this method elevates prediction as the best way to judge the validity of a theory, regardless of its assumptions. Whether prediction is the most desirable test of the validity of any theory is not, of course, a settled issue.

Thus, one of the philosophical tenets of the method of positivist science puts forward a view of the scientific investigator as the neutral observer of historical and physical phenomena, one who is given the role of selecting and testing facts. Of course, facts always require interpretation, and by subsuming these interpretations under a scientific method, asserting passive acceptance of natural laws, and claiming that the facts speak for themselves, the scientist merely ignores an important aspect of the scientific endeavor, or according to Robert Heilbroner ''acquiesces before whatever viewpoint establishes its facts.'' In other words, some would argue, one cannot separate science from ideology (everyone speaks from a point of view), but one can openly recognize perspectives for what they are. By accepting the scientist as neutral observer (existing outside of the world that he or she studies), we allow the positivist to smuggle in an interpretation (which by definition embodies a perspective, whatever that perspective may be) through the back door.

Within any particular natural or social science, hypotheses that have been confirmed (by replication and verification) and accepted are often elevated to the status of laws. Laws are valued because they have substantial predictive power and because they can account for certain regularities in nature or society. These laws, however, do not explain the regularities, the facts; they only describe them. In other words, to explain why a phenomena occurs we turn to a larger context, typically to abstract forces for which often no direct observational evidence exists but which may be discerned by the array of phenomena generated by these forces. For example, one cannot observe gravity directly but one can observe (measure, test etc.) the phenomena that the force of gravity generates in different contexts (e.g., a person jumping off a building will fall at a particular speed, the Moon revolving around Earth will travel a particular path at a particular speed). The strength of hypothesis testing lies in its ability to glean patterns in an apparently chaotic world, thereby directing the researcher towards which facts to look for and which questions to ask about the world.

[John A. Sarich]

FURTHER READING:

Broad, William, and Nicholas Wade. *Betrayers of Truth: Fraud and Deceit in the Halls of Science*. Simon & Schuster, 1982.

Connerton, Paul, ed. *Critical Sociology*. Penguin Books, 1976.

Heilbroner, Robert. *Marxism: For and Against*. W. W. Norton & Company, 1980.

Hempel, Carl G. *Philosophy of Natural Science*. Foundations of Philosophy Series. Prentice Hall, 1966.

Kennedy, Peter. *A Guide to Econometrics*. 2nd ed. MIT Press, 1987.

Lewontin, Richard. *Biology as Ideology*. Harper Perennial, 1993.

Pindyck, Robert S., and Daniel L. Rubinfeld. *Econometric Models and Econometric Forecasts*. 2nd ed. McGraw-Hill, 1981.

Popper, Karl. *The Logic of Scientific Discovery*. Basic Books, 1959.

I

ILLITERACY IN THE WORKPLACE

"Workplace illiteracy" refers to the inability of an employed person to carry out the functions of his or her job because of an inability to read or write. While illiteracy technically occurs at any job level, illiteracy is most prevalent among clerical and traditional blue-collar industrial workers. Contrary to popular perceptions, illiteracy in the workplace is not a result of large numbers of immigrants in the work force. Moreover, while the perception of illiteracy in the workplace has increased recently it does not mean that employees were more literate or better educated in the past.

Strictly defined, illiteracy means the inability to read and write (some experts would include the inability to perform simple arithmetic). This kind of serious illiteracy does exist in this country, it constitutes a serious problem. Statistics that gauge the level of serious illiteracy vary in the extreme with estimates ranging from 5 million to 27 million of the nation's adult population. Within this broad range, very few people are totally illiterate (that is, they have no knowledge of the alphabet). Nonetheless, the fact that millions of adults in the workforce are unable to read and write is cause for public alarm.

According to a **United Nations** survey of worldwide adult literacy, of the 158 member nations that make up that body, the United States ranks 49th. The real illiteracy problem in the workplace is not total, illiteracy, but rather, functional illiteracy. Once again, this classification varies as to definition and specific numbers.

A National Adult Literacy Survey conducted in the early 1990s revealed the startling fact that at least 47 percent of adults in the United States, (some 90 million people), could be classified as functionally illiterate—i.e., they could do only minimal reading and writing. There is some general agreement on what constitutes functional illiteracy—reading and writing below the sixth grade level. In 1993, the U.S. Department of Education determined that as many as 30 percent of unskilled and semiskilled industrial workers (approximately 14 million), were below even a fourth grade level of reading and writing. This would make it almost impossible to read required safety manuals, product labels, and even written warning signs. A recent case documented a tragedy involving an illiterate worker taking a cigarette break: unable to read the danger sign on the door of an empty room, the worker set off a lethal explosion after he entered the room and ignited his cigarette.

Since a high school level of literacy is usually necessary in order to read newspapers and magazines fluently, some experts insist that anyone who reads and writes below secondary school level is functionally illiterate. If one accepts this broad definition of functional illiteracy, then as many as 72 million adults are affected, making functional illiteracy a truly gargantuan problem in this country. Perhaps most alarming is the fact that the highest levels of functional illiteracy can be found among the young, specifically, in the 18- to 30-year-old age bracket.

The majority of this age group has already entered the workplace or hopes to become employed. Job applications have exposed the high level of illiteracy in the current adult population. In the early 1990s, the U.S. Department of Labor conducted its own poll of 5700 job seekers who were receiving some form of assistance from the department and found that a majority of them were functionally illiterate. In the state of Nevada, it was estimated in 1994 that two out of three recently hired employees had at most an eighth grade reading level. In 1990, Southwestern Bell received 15,000 job applications; of these, only 800 could pass the company's basic skills test.

Illiteracy—which in this essay will be considered functional illiteracy—has always existed in this country and cannot be blamed on immigrant labor. The industrial **manufacturing** sector of the economy has been employing immigrants since the early nineteenth century. While newly arrived immigrants for the most part read and write English poorly or not at all, the majority—over 50 percent—are literate in their own native languages and do not require literacy programs as much as they do ESOL (English as a Second Language) training.

Hence at the heart of the illiteracy problem in this country is rapidly changing technology, and most importantly, the computerization of business and industry. As recently as the 1960s, what mattered in most industrial jobs was physical endurance. Nowadays, even auto mechanics rely on computers and must study repair manuals written in advanced English; a welder in the days before computers merely had to know the variety of metals and how to use a torch. Nowadays, welders must master the repair of robot welders, which do the actual work.

It is not only computerization that has changed the workplace, however. Thirty years ago, business and industry for the most part had to contend only with domestic competitors. Nowadays, with **trade barriers** falling all over the globe, international **competition** has grown intense. Only the most streamlined, cost-efficient, and quality-conscious companies will survive and make a profit. Competition from Japan in particular has compelled American businesses to become more productive and create new products. Moreover, the internal structure of many businesses is changing. For decades, a company would be neatly divided between managers, who did the thinking, and the rank-and file-employees, who carried out management's ideas and plans. Nowadays, input, and especially creative thinking, is sought at all levels. Meeting these challenges necessitates a literate, if not highly literate, work force.

A Senate Labor Committee report in 1990 maintained that while a fourth grade education had always been sufficient for most skilled and unskilled jobs ever since World War II, current working conditions demanded that high school or the equivalent be the new minimum required level of education for the marketplace. Unfortunately, nearly two million students graduating from high schools annually are functionally illiterate. To American business and industry, which must pay high property taxes to support the public education system, this is a frustrating reality.

How is it that students can graduate from high school, while reading and writing far below the 12th grade level? One reason is the fact that students are often automatically promoted to the next grade even if they have not learned to read. Additionally, more inner-city counterparts students graduate functionally illiterate then do students at suburban schools. Hence illiteracy is also caused by economic disparity and social breakdown; students who have not learned to read very often come from broken and impeverished homes. Students from minority groups are far more likely to be semiliterate than caucasians. At least 40 percent of young minority persons under 18 are believed to be functionally illiterate. Educational studies have failed to prove that merely keeping a student behind a grade or two has helped him or her learn to read.

The toll illiteracy takes on business is high: illiterate workers make costly mistakes for themselves and the firms that employ them. The turnover of functionally illiterate workers, as well as those lacking other job-related skills, averages 20 percent nationwide. Moreover, illiterate or semiliterate workers earn the least of any wage earners, and hence, cannot become significant consumers.

Despite these large-scale problems, few employees seek out the help offered by literacy programs, even if they are free and easily accessible. This phenomenon has been closely studied by literacy experts, who posit that the social stigma of illiteracy is far greater than it is for drug or alcohol abuse. Moreover, should an older man or woman enroll in a literacy class, more often than not, he or she has to use materials geared for high school or even grade school-aged children, clearly inappropriate for older adults. Lastly, even if he or she is lucky to have adult-level learning materials, an illiterate person is often daunted at the length of time it takes to learn to read fluently— often several years, sometimes even longer. For this reason alone, most adults who are functionally illiterate bluff their way through their job by greatly exaggerating their reading and writing abilities.

Given the fact that rank-and-file employees (the backbone of companies) are poorly educated and trained and reluctant to seek out the help of community-based literacy programs, more and more companies are looking inward for solutions. The result is that by 1995, American companies will be spending more than $100 billion annually for education and training programs to increase the quality of their work force. Not only do these programs attempt to reach the functionally illiterate worker, but also the worker who has been on the job for years and needs to and upgrade job knowledge and skills (which often includes literacy).

Currently, at least one in five organizations (businesses as well as nonprofit concerns) sponsor and pay for programs that teach basic literacy skills. This translates into only 20 percent of organizations with a minimum work force of 100 employees. Of the 80 percent without such programs, almost all require testing to ensure job applicants have the appropriate, job-related skills. Most companies want to weed out the semiliterate applicants and hire only those who are fully qualified, this is increasingly becoming a luxury. According to the 1990 population census, America is headed for a serious shortage of workers, skilled as well as unskilled. To pass up intelligent, hardworking and ambitious applicants because of deficient skills is running the risk of running out of applicants altogether. This was the conclusion, in 1987, of the far-sighted chairman of Xerox Corp., David Kearns, who acknowledged even then the necessity of hiring unqualified employees if the company was to expand. According to Kearns, businesses throughout the United States could end up hiring upwards of one million entry-level employees annually who were unable to read or write.

The larger the company, the more apt it is to implement some kind of on-the-job training to combat declining skills, including the fundamentals—basic reading, writing, and math skills. Polaroid led the way in establishing the first on-the-job basic skills program more than 20 years ago. Since then, other companies have followed; nonetheless, 90 percent of American companies still lack such job training programs. An exception is Hershey Foods in Pennsylvania, which automatically sends any employee without a high school diploma to GED classes; it also provides employees desiring extra math and science training with tutors. In 1993, more than half of the 1,340 firms in Illinois responded positively on a questionnaire asking if their employees needed to upgrade their skills; only 24 percent of these firms provided training courses.

The cost of implementing such programs can be prohibitive. Start up costs can range anywhere from as low as $2,500 to a high of $100,000. Not all companies can afford to pour into basic literacy programs the $35 million that Motorola, Inc. had expended by 1993. By then, Motorola had decided that the time had come to turn away job applicants whose reading and writing skills fell below the seventh grade level. While even an eighth grade literacy level increasingly disqualifies one for the growing demands of the work place, nonetheless, training employees at this level requires much less time, and therefore, saves the company more money.

When Magnavox was faced with an increase in the number of immigrants seeking and obtaining work in the early 1990s, the firm installed a pilot literacy program that also included English as a second language courses. To mitigate the prohibitive cost of this program, Magnavox turned to the Department of Education's National Workplace Literacy Program for matching grant funds (the Education Department allocates the funds to the states, which in turn make them available to qualified applicants). In this way, the pilot program became a permanent success story emulated by other companies. However, the state governments administering the literacy grants are overwhelmed with applications each year, leading to stiff competition. Between fiscal years 1990-1994, the budget for literacy programs in the state of Illinois alone increased from $119,000 to nearly half a million dollars, but the number of grant applications still exceeded the budget.

The literacy program at Magnavox initially offered literacy classes in the evenings, but the company discovered, not surprisingly, that employees were far more encouraged to take these classes if they were conducted during work time. Despite the time lost in productivity, the long-term gain to the company offset the loss. Fortunately, many workplace literacy programs for adults have advanced beyond "Dick and Jane" readers. Nowadays, innovative products include tapes of adult-level reading material, which students listen to until they can recognize and read the corresponding text, and interactive computer software that simulates the work environment and challenges some adults to overcome their fear of computers. What used to take several years to master in some cases can now take as little as ten months. Workplace literacy programs offered during work hours have provided the most effective incentive to eradicate serious as well as functional illiteracy, when compared to community-based programs.

So many benefits accrue to companies that implement on-the-job literacy training programs that they become a form of investment, rather than an extraneous expense. For instance, there are improvements in job morale, in company loyalty (reducing the **employee turnover** rate), and in overall productivity. Some experts predict that by the years 2000, most jobs will demand a literacy level of more than 13 years of education, which is at least community college level. Even general literacy at this rate does not eliminate the need for on the job training and improvement. "Upgrading" now is being viewed by the business sector as a permanent necessity for the modern company, rather than as a temporary expedient.

[Sina Dubovoy]

FURTHER READING:

Boyett, Joseph H. *Workplace 2000: The Revolution Reshaping American Business*. New York: Dutton, 1991.

Dolan, Edward F. *Illiteracy in America*. New York: Franklin Watts, 1994.

Ellsworth, J. ed. *Literacy: A Redefinition*. Hillsdale, NJ: L. Erlbaum Associates, 1994.

Hollenbeck, Kevin. *Classrooms in the Workplace: Workplace Literacy Programs in Small and Medium Sized Firms.* Kalamazoo, MI: Upjohn Institute for Employment Research, 1993.

Lund, Leonard. "Literacy in the Workforce." *Conference Board Report #947.* New York: Conference Board, 1990.

IMPLICIT PRICE DEFLATOR

Implicit price deflator is an **index** that is used to gauge the extent of price level changes or **inflation** in the economy. This index is essentially one of three different methods by which inflation in the economy is measured. Knowledge of two concepts, the notions of inflation and price index, is crucial to understanding the implicit price deflator.

INFLATION AND DEFLATION

Inflation is understood to be an increase in price level. It is actually defined as the rate of change in the price level. Thus, an inflation rate of five percent per annum means that the price level is increasing at the rate of five percent. However, inflation need not always be positive. It may be a negative number, in which instance the price level would be declining. Negative inflation rates, deflation, are very uncommon. Most economies face positive rates of inflation year after year.

PRICE INDEX AND THE MEASUREMENT OF THE INFLATION RATE

The inflation rate is derived by calculating the rate of change in a **price index**. A price index, in turn, measures the level of prices of goods and services at any point of time. The number of items included in a price index varies depending on the objective of the index. Usually three kinds of price indices are periodically reported by government sources. The first index is called the **consumer price index** (CPI). This index measures the average retail prices paid by consumers for goods and services. There are approximately 400 items included in this index. These items are selected on the basis of their inclusion in the household budget of a consumer. Each of the 400 prices is assigned a weight based on the importance of the item in the household budget. As a result, the consumer price index reflects the changes in the cost of living of a typical household (consumer). The CPI is considered the most relevant inflation measure from the point of view of the consumers, as it measures the prices of goods and services that are part of their budgets. However, the consumer price index will not measure the changes in the cost of living of every consumer precisely due to the differences in consumption patterns.

A second price index used to measure the inflation rate is called the producer price index (PPI). It is a much broader measure than the consumer price index, in that it measures the wholesale prices of approximately 3000 items. The items included in this index are those that are typically used by producers (manufacturers and businesses) and thus contain many raw materials and semifinished goods. A change in the producer price index reflects a change in the cost of production, as encountered by producers. Since producers may pass on part or all of the increase in the cost of production to consumers, movements in producer price index indicate future movements in the consumer price index. The producer price index can thus forewarn consumers of coming increases in the cost of living.

The implicit price deflator is the third measure of inflation. This index measures the prices of all goods and services included in the calculation of the current output of goods and services in the economy, known as **gross domestic product** (GDP). It is the broadest measure of the price level. This index includes prices of fighter bombers purchased by the Defense Department as well as paper clips used in common offices. Thus, the implicit price deflator is a measure of the overall or aggregate price level for the economy. Movements in the implicit GDP price deflator captures the inflationary tendency of the overall economy.

CALCULATIONS OF THE IMPLICIT PRICE DEFLATOR AND THE INFLATION RATE

Calculation of the consumer price index (CPI) and producer price index (PPI) is direct—indexes are calculated from price data on the items included. Implicit price deflator, on the other hand, is inferred indirectly from the estimates of gross domestic product in nominal terms (in current dollars) and in real terms (when the nominal value of gross domestic product is adjusted for inflation by re-evaluating the GDP in prices that prevailed during a chosen base year).

Currently, 1987 is being used to calculate the real value of gross domestic product in the United States. Thus, the 1993 U.S. output of goods and services is first evaluated at prices prevailing in 1993. Once this is done, 1993 output of goods and services is also evaluated at prices that prevailed in 1987 (thus, the terms gross domestic product in 1987 dollars or constant dollars). One can easily see how the ratio of gross domestic product in 1993 prices and gross domestic product in 1987 prices would yield a measure of the extent of the rise in price level between 1987 and 1993. According to the federal government statistics, this ratio is estimated at 1.242, or 124.2 when multiplied by 100 (as is customarily done to determine the extent of price increase more conveniently). The value of implicit price deflator of 124.2 implies that the price level increased by 24.2 percent over the 1987-1994 period (note that the base year, currently 1987, value of implicit price deflator is equal to 100).

This method of expressing nominal or current gross domestic product into its value in 1987 prices is routinely done every year (of course, sometimes the base year itself, may be changed to a later year to keep the data series closer to the current period). Thus, we have 1992, 1991, 1990 (and so on) gross domestic products expressed in 1987 prices. This helps to calculate the inflation rate between subsequent years. For example, the implicit price deflator stood at 121.1 at the end of 1992. Given that the deflator was at 124.2 at the end of 1993, we arrive at the annual inflation rate of roughly 2.6 percent during 1993 (1993 inflation rate = [(124.2 − 121.1) / 121.1] * 100).

Since the implicit price deflator is derived from the nominal and real values of the gross domestic product (GDP), it is also called implicit GDP price deflator. One should also notice that the term *deflator* is not used in consumer and producer price indexes. This is because, if one knows the implicit price deflator, for 1993, and the 1993 gross domestic product in current prices, one could arrive at the gross domestic product in 1987 prices by deflating the 1993 gross domestic product in current prices by the deflator for 1993 (expressed in plain ratio form, rather than the one multiplied by 100). Despite the use of term deflator, one should not lose sight of the fact the implicit price deflator is essentially a price index.

[Andrew Sahu]

FURTHER READING:

Froyen, Richard T. *Macroeconomics: Theories and Policies*. 4th ed. New York: Macmillan Publishing Company, 1993.

Gordon, Robert J. *Macroeconomics*. 6th ed. New York: Harper-Collins College Publishers, 1993.

Sommers, Albert T. *The U.S. Economy Demystified*. Lexington, MA: Lexington Books, 1985.

INCOME AND REVENUE

Income is an important concept in economics as well as **accounting**. Accountants prepare an **income statement** to measure a company's income for a given accounting period. Economists are concerned with measuring and defining such concepts as national income, personal income, disposable personal income, and money income versus real income. In each field the concept of income is defined in slightly different terms.

For accounting purposes, income is distinguished from revenues. A company's revenue is all of the money it takes in as a result of its operations. Another way of defining a company's revenue is as a monetary measure of outputs, or goods sold and services rendered, with expense being a monetary measure of inputs or resources used in the production of goods or services. On the other hand, a company's net income or profit is determined by subtracting its expenses from its revenues. Thus, revenues are the opposite of expenses, and income equals revenues minus expenses. For example a store may sell $300 worth of merchandise, for which it originally paid $200. In that example the company's revenue is $300, its expense is $200, and its net income or profit is $100. Other expenses that are typically deducted from sales or revenues include salaries, rent, utilities, **depreciation**, and interest expense.

When looking at a company's income statement, it is easy to distinguish between revenues, which appear at the top of the statement, and net income, which appears at the bottom. In other contexts, however, it is easy to confuse the two through improper usage. It is misleading to refer to revenues as income, for a company with revenues of $1 million is much different from a company with net income of $1 million.

Since revenues increase owners' equity in a company, and expenses decrease owners' equity, income can also be defined as the increase in owners' equity due to transactions and other events and circumstances from nonowner sources. If we recognize that income results in an increase in owners' equity, then it becomes clear that income is not the same as a company's cash receipts. For example, a company may increase its cash account by taking a loan from a bank. Such an increase in cash does not increase owners' equity, though, because there is also an increase in the company's liability to the bank.

For personal income tax purposes, gross income is money received by an individual from all sources. Many of the items that the Internal Revenue Code defines as income and that are called income on tax form 1040 are actually revenues, such as dividend income, investment income, and interest income. The Internal Revenue Code also provides for exclusions and exemptions as well as for nontaxable types of income to arrive at the concept of taxable income.

While accountants measure a single company's income for a specific accounting period, economists are concerned with the aggregate income for an entire industry or country. In looking at an entity as a whole, economists define its gross income as the total value of all claims against its output. That is, when goods are produced and services are rendered by the entity, workers, investors, the government, and others have a claim against those goods and services. Workers are paid wages or salaries, investors receive interest payments for their investment, and the government collects **taxes**. The total value of these claims represents the entity's gross income and is equal to the total value added through activities that have contributed to the production of the entity's goods and services.

In looking at the economy as a whole, economists view gross national income as the total of all claims on the **gross national product**. These include employee compensation, rental income, net interest, indirect business taxes, capital consumption allowances, incomes of proprietors and professionals, and corporate profits. National income includes all compensation paid to labor and for productive property that is involved in producing the gross national product. In addition, about 20 percent of national income includes such items as depreciation or capital consumption allowances, indirect business taxes, subsidies less surpluses of government enterprises (such as the U.S. Postal Service), and business transfer payments to employees not on the job.

Personal income includes all payments received by individuals, including wages, transfer payments such as sick pay or vacation pay, and the employer's contribution to Social Security. Personal income differs from national income in two important aspects: (1) some national income is received by entities other than individuals, and (2) some individuals receive personal income from social insurance programs that are not connected with producing the current gross national product.

Disposable personal income is the amount of personal income that remains after an individual's taxes have been paid. It is estimated that approximately 70 percent of the gross national income ends up as disposable personal income. The remaining 30 percent includes such items as depreciation, retained corporate profits, and the government's net tax revenue.

Economists also distinguish between money income and real income. While money income is measured in terms of the number of dollars received, real income is measured by the purchasing power of those dollars. After all, what is important is not how much money you earn, but how much you can buy with that money. Economists use a deflator based on a **price index** for personal goods and services to calculate an individual's real income from his or her money income. Since rising prices reduce the dollar's purchasing power, real income provides a truer measure of buying power than does money income.

[David Bianco]

INCOME STATEMENT

An income statement presents the results of an entity's operations for a given reporting period. The statement reflects the extent to which and the way in which the **equity** of the entity increased or decreased (from all sources other than transactions with owners) during the period. A company's net income for an accounting period is measured as follows:

$$\text{Net income} = \text{Revenues} - \text{Expenses} + \text{Gains} - \text{Losses}$$

The statement provides information concerning return on investment, risk, financial flexibility, and operating capabilities. Return on investment is a measure of a firm's overall performance. Risk is the uncertainty associated with the future of the enterprise. Financial flexibility is the firm's ability to adapt to problems and opportunities. Operating capability relates to the firm's ability to maintain a given level of operations.

The current view of the income statement is that income should reflect all items of profit and loss recognized during the **accounting** period, except for a few items that would be entered directly under retained earnings on the balance sheet, notably prior period adjustments (i.e., correction of errors). The following summary income statement illustrates the income statement currently considered to represent generally accepted accounting principles:

Revenues	$1,000,000
Deduct expenses	(400,000)
Gains (losses) that are not extraordinary	(100,000)
Other gains and (losses)	20,000
Income from continuing operations	520,000
Gains (losses) from discontinued operations	75,000
Extraordinary gains (losses)	20,000
Cum. effect of changes in accounting principles	10,000
Net income	$ 625,000
Pre-tax Earnings per share (2,000 shares)	$3.13

The Financial Accounting Standards Board (FASB) provides broad definitions of revenues, expenses, gains, and losses that appear on the income statement in its Statement of Concepts No. 6. Revenues are inflows or other enhancements of **assets** of an entity or settlement of its **liabilities** (or both) during a period, based on production and delivery of goods, provisions of services, and other activities that constitute the entity's major operations. Examples of revenues are sales revenue, interest revenue, and rent revenue. Expenses are outflows or other uses of assets or incurrence of liabilities (or both) during a period as a result of delivering or producing goods, rendering services, or carrying out other activities that constitute the entity's ongoing major or central operations. Examples are cost of goods sold, salaries-expense, and interest expense.

Gains are increases in owners' equity (net assets) from peripheral or incidental transactions of an entity and from all other transactions and events affecting the entity during the accounting period, except those that result from revenues or investments by owners. Examples are a gain on the sale of a building and a gain on the early retirement of long-term **debt**. Losses are decreases in owners' equity (net assets) from peripheral or incidental transactions of an entity and from all other transactions and events affecting the entity during the accounting period except those that result from expenses or distributions to owners. Examples are losses on the sale of investments and losses from litigations.

Discontinued operations are those operations of an enterprise that have been sold, abandoned, or otherwise disposed. The results of continuing operations must be reported separately in the **income** statement from discontinued operations, and any gain or loss from the disposal of a segment must be reported along with the operating results of the discontinued separate major line of business or class of customer. Results from discontinued operations are reported net of income **taxes**.

Extraordinary gains or losses are material events and transactions that are both unusual in nature and infrequent in occurrence. Both of the following criteria must be met for an item to be classified as an extraordinary gain or loss:

- Unusual in nature: The underlying event or transaction should possess a high degree of abnormality and be of a pe clearly unrelated to, or only incidentally related to, the ordinary and typical activities of the entity, taking into account the environment in which the entity operates.

- Infrequency of occurrence: The underlying event or transaction should be of a type that would not reasonably be expected to recur in the foreseeable future, taking into account the environment in which the entity operates.

Extraordinary items could result if gains or losses were the direct result of any of the following events or circumstances: (1) a major casualty, such as an earthquake, (2) an expropriation of property by a foreign government, and (3) a prohibition under a new act or regulation. Extraordinary items are reported net of income taxes.

Gains and losses that are not extraordinary refer to material items which are unusual or infrequent, but not both. Such items must be disclosed separately above "income (loss) before extraordinary items," and would be not be reported net of tax.

An accounting change refers to a change in accounting principle, accounting estimate, or reporting entity. Changes in accounting principles result when an accounting principle is adopted that is different from the one previously used. Changes in estimate involve revisions of estimates, such as the useful lives or residual value of depreciable assets, the loss for bad debts, and warranty costs. A change in reporting entity occurs when a company changes its composition from the prior period, as occurs when a new subsidiary is acquired.

Net income is the excess of all revenues and gains for a period over all expenses and losses of the period. Net loss is the excess of expenses and losses over revenues and gains for a period.

Generally accepted accounting principles require disclosing **earnings per share** amounts on the income statement of all public reporting entities. Earnings per share data provides a measure of the enterprise's management and past performance and enables users of financial statements to evaluate future prospects of the enterprise and assess dividend distributions to shareholders. Disclosure of earnings per share for effects of discontinued operations and extraordinary items is optional, but it is required for income from continuing operations, income before extraordinary items, cumulative effects of a change in accounting principles, and net income.

Primary earnings per share and fully diluted earnings per share may also be required. Primary earnings per share is a presentation based on the outstanding common shares and those securities that are in substance equivalent to common shares and have a diluting effect on earnings per share. Convertible **bonds**, convertible **preferred stock**, stock option, and **warrants** are examples of **common stock** equivalents. The fully diluted earnings per share presentation is a pro forma presentation that affects the dilution of earnings per share that would have occurred if all contingent issuances of common stock that would individually reduce earnings per share had taken place at the beginning of the period.

The revenue recognition principle provides guidelines for reporting revenue in the income statement. The principle generally requires that revenue be recognized in the financial statements when: (1) realized or realizable and (2) earned. Revenues are realized when products or other assets are exchanged for cash or claims to cash or when services are rendered. Revenues are realizable when assets received or held are readily convertible into cash or claims to cash. Revenues are considered earned when the entity has substantially accomplished what it must do to be entitled to the benefits represented by the revenues. Recognition through sales or the providing (performance) of services provides a uniform and reasonable test of realization. Limited exceptions to the basic revenue principle include recognizing revenue during production (on long-term construction **contracts**), at the completion of production (for many **commodities**), and subsequent to the sale at the time of cash collection (on installment sales).

In recognizing expenses, accountants rely on the matching principle because it requires that efforts (expenses) be matched with accomplishments (revenues) whenever it is reasonable and practical to do so. For example, matching (associating) cost of goods sold with revenues from the interrelated sales that resulted directly and jointly from the same transaction as the expense is reasonable and practical. To recognize costs for which it is difficult to adopt some association with revenues, accountants use a rational and systematic allocation policy that assigns expenses to the periods during which the related assets are expected to provide benefits, such as **depreciation**, **amortization**, and insurance. Some costs are charged to the current period as expenses (or losses) merely because no future benefit is anticipated, no connection with revenue is apparent, or no allocation is rational and systematic under the circumstances, i.e., an immediate recognition principle.

The current operating concept of income would include only those value changes and events that are controllable by **management** and that are incurred in the current period from ordinary, normal, and recurring operations. Any unusual and nonrecurring items of income or loss would be recognized directly in the statement of retained earnings. Under this concept, investors are primarily interested in continuing income from operations.

The all-inclusive concept of income includes the total changes in equity recognized during a specific period, except for dividend distributions and **capital** transactions. Under this concept, unusual and nonrecurring income or loss items are part of the earning history of a company and should not be overlooked. Currently, the all-inclusive concept is generally recognized; however, certain material prior period adjustments should be reflected adjustments of the opening retained earnings balance.

FORMATS OF THE INCOME STATEMENT

The income statement can be prepared using either the single-step or the multiple-step format. The single-step format lists and totals all revenue and gain items at the beginning of the statement. All expense and loss items are then fixed and the total is deducted from the total revenue to give the net income. The multiple-step income statement presents operating revenue at the beginning of the statement and nonoperating gains, expenses, and losses near the end of the statement. However, various items of expenses are deducted throughout the statement at intermediate levels. The statement is arranged to show explicitly

several important amounts, such as gross margin on sales operating income, income before taxes, and net income. Extraordinary items, gains and losses accounting changes, and discontinued operations are always shown separately at the bottom of the income statement ahead of net income, regardless of which format is used.

Each format of the income statement has its advantages. The advantage of the multiple-step income statement is that it explicitly displays important financial and managerial information that the user would have to calculate from a single-step income statement. The single-step format has the advantage of being relatively simple to prepare and to understand.

GLOSSARY

Comprehensive income. The change in equity of a business enterprise during a period from transactions and other events and circumstances from nonowner sources.

Cost of goods sold. The cost of the inventory that the business has sold to customers.

Dual presentation. The presentation with equal prominence of two types of earnings per share amounts on the face of the income statement: one is primary earnings per share; the other is fully diluted earnings per share.

Earnings per share. The amount of earnings attributable to each share of common stock.

Gross margin. Excess of sales revenue over cost of goods sold.

Income from operations. Gross margin minus operating expenses.

Multiple step income statement. Under the multiple-step format, significant subtotals are presented, as illustrated here:

Sales

Deduct: Cost of goods sold

Gross profit (or loss)

Deduct: Operating expenses

Operating income

Other revenues and expenses

Income before income taxes

Deduct: Income taxes

Net income

Prior period adjustments. Adjustments related to prior periods that are excluded in the determination of net income for the current period and are reported as an adjustment of the opening balance of retained earnings on the retained earnings statement. They are primarily the correction of errors of prior periods.

Statement of retained earnings. A financial statement which reconciles the balance of the retained earnings account from the beginning to the end of the period, illustrated as follows:

Beginning retained earnings

Plus (minus): Prior period adjustments (net of income taxes)

Adjusted beginning retained earnings

Plus (minus): Net income (loss)

Minus: Dividends (specifically identified, including per share amounts)

Ending retained earnings

[Charles Woelfel]

FURTHER READING:

Financial Accounting Standards Board. *Statements of Financial Accounting Concepts.* Homewood, IL: Irwin, 1986.

Hendriksen, E. S., and M. F. Van Bred. *Accounting Theory.* Homewood, IL: Irwin, 1991.

INCUBATORS, BUSINESS

Business incubators are literally what they sound like, a warm nurturing environment for new, small, entrepreneurial businesses to start and grow. Incubators are usually located in older, sometimes abandoned offices or industrial buildings. Incubators give starting businesses inexpensive space to rent, shared office support such as telephone receptionists/secretaries, office services such as photocopiers, and most important, other people who are in the same situation of starting their own businesses. A budding entrepreneur can frequently walk a few steps to someone in the same situation to ask questions and advice.

The stakes are high as studies show that up to 90 percent of new **small business**es fail within five years of their founding. For that reason, some incubators also offer business advice from retired executives or consultants who agree to charge low fees to start-up companies.

Incubators are relatively new concepts, born in the late 1950s in Batavia, N.Y. when the city leaders decided to help businesses without much capital grow into job-producers. Over the last several years, the concept has taken off. In 1990 the National Business Incubation Association in Athens, Ohio reported there were 385 incubators in operation around the country. By 1994 that number had grown to more than 500.

The association estimates that U.S. incubators open at a rate of one per week.

The concept appears to be most popular in both rural areas, where farmers and other small town residents fill them when not working full-time on the farm, and in the inner city. According to the association, more than a quarter of the nation's incubators are in rural areas and almost half of those have opened since 1991. Urban-based incubators make up 62 percent of the total while suburbs (to where many of the former urban jobs moved) have just 12 percent.

The "big" business community has not yet embraced incubators as a way to build a network of vendors or as a system for developing future new products. Only eight percent of all incubators have a for-profit company as a sponsor. More than half of all incubators are sponsored by government agencies, sometimes as an effort to boost economic development in an area, or as a means of encouraging those laid off from "big business" to go into commerce for themselves. Four-year colleges and universities sponsor ten percent of the incubators, sometimes providing the schools a way to help showcase or market the research developed at the schools.

Business incubators shelter as many types of businesses as exist in the cold world outside them. A 1992 study conducted by the National Business Incubation Association found that 36 percent of all incubator companies were in the service industry, 20 percent were in light **manufacturing**, 16 percent were in technology products, and 11 percent were in **research and development**. Another eight percent acted as **wholesalers**/distributors for products.

One of the advantages of incubators is that the concept works in all size communities and in urban or rural areas. The incubator takes on the character of the community in which it is located. Rural-based incubators may launch companies based on the agriculture present in the area. For example, an incubator based in the heartland might build its expertise around turning grain and corn into products other than foodstuffs. An urban-based incubator in Miami might draw on the Cuban culture to produce ethnic foods. In both cases, the small business people in the community would know more about how to start and operate such businesses than major corporations that focus on mass production.

[Clint Johnson]

INDEPENDENT CONTRACTORS

SEE: Contractors; Free-lance Employment

INDEX/INDEXES

Various kinds of indexes or index numbers are used by the scientific and academic communities, and the popular media. In fact, some indexes are so commonly used that one does not even recognize that they are *index* numbers, not absolute values of the variable or the item of interest. Changes in stock prices associated with several stock markets, for example, are quoted in terms of index numbers. Thus, when the media reports that the Dow fell by 100 points on a particular day, the reference is to the fall in the value of the index representing 30 industrial stocks included in the Dow Jones Industrial Average index, sometimes called the Dow 30. Suppose that the Dow Jones Industrial Average was at the 4,000 mark before it fell by 100 points. This implies that the average price of the 30 stocks included in the Dow index fell by 2.5 percent in one day ([100/4,000]*100 = 2.5 percent). In order to understand index numbers, it is useful to have some idea of the methods of constructing indexes, and to be able to relate these methods to some common examples of index numbers.

THE WIDESPREAD USE OF INDEXES IN BUSINESS AND ECONOMICS

A wide variety of sources generate the various indexes in the fields of business and economics. Many government agencies in the United States regularly produce information in index number form on a variety of variables. The Bureau of Labor Statistics under the U.S. Department of Labor reports data on various price indexes that are used to measure the inflation rate in the economy. The U.S. Department of Commerce also reports economic data on a regular basis. In addition to government sources, economic data are also reported (many of them in index number form) by private sources, and partisan and nonpartisan research organizations. Most business-related indexes, can be categorized within two broad categories—those associated with the financial markets and those that describe the state of the economy.

INDEXES ASSOCIATED WITH THE FINANCIAL MARKETS. There are many indexes associated with the financial markets. These indexes measure different attributes of the financial markets at various degrees of depth and rigor. The majority of them track two major components of the financial markets: stock markets and bond markets.

Several index numbers measure the changes in stock prices at different levels of aggregation (that is, with respect to the number of stocks included in an index). The Dow Jones Industrial Average (an index of 30 industrial stocks), or DJIA, is one of the most commonly followed stock price indexes. It includes major U.S. industrial stocks (such as Coca-Cola, IBM, General Motors, du Pont, Eastman Kodak, Disney, Sears, Goodyear, Merck, and AT&T) listed on the New York Stock Exchange (NYSE). There are also index numbers that represent stock price changes at a particular stock exchange or a stock trading network. Thus, pertaining to the three trading mediums—NYSE based in New York, the American Stock Exchange also based in New York (popularly called AMEX), and the computer-linked stock trading network of the National Securities Dealers Association (called NASDAQ), there are separate indexes called NYSE, AMEX, and NASDAQ, respectively. In addition to these so-called exchange-based indexes, there are several other stock price indexes that include an increasing number of stocks. For example, the S&P100 index, maintained by Standard & Poor's, measures stock price movements of 100 important stocks. Similarly, the S&P500 index measures the change in the aggregate price level of 500 selected stocks. The Wilshire 5000 index measures the change in the aggregate price level of the 5,000 stocks it monitors—a large number of stocks are included in this index to give a better picture of the overall stock market, rather than a narrow group of stocks.

By contrast, the bond market has far fewer indexes. The most widely used bond price index is the Lehman Brothers' bond price index; it measures changes in prices of long-term bonds included in the index. Changes in bond prices convey information regarding changes in interest rates. Thus, the bond price index is also closely watched by financial market participants.

INDEXES ASSOCIATED WITH THE ECONOMY. Information and data on a large number of economic variables are regularly reported. Some of these data are reported in index number form. All price data in the economy are reported in index number form—as will be explained later, this is out of necessity, rather than choice. Three major price indexes are: consumer price index, producer price index, and implicit gross domestic product price deflator. Similarly, the Federal Reserve Bank computes the index of industrial production on a monthly basis to gauge the pace of industrial production.

Other regularly reported indexes that describe the state of the economy (current or future) include: index of leading indicators, which indicates the pace of economic activity in the economy in the near future; consumer confidence index, which captures consumer sentiment and thus suggests consumers' willingness to spend; housing affordabilty index, which track the cost of being able to afford a home. Some indexes are not reported regularly, but they occasionally crop up. For example, George Bush during his reelection campaign kept referring to the misery index, which captures the combined effects of inflation and unemployment.

THE NEED FOR AN INDEX. Most economic variables are measured in absolute terms. For example, 12 million cars were produced in 1994 in the United States, or the gross output of goods and services in the United States was estimated at $6.5 trillion during 1993. It is not possible, however, to measure the price associated with a group of commodities in absolute terms; it can only be done so long as we refer to one commodity. We thus can say that the average price of a loaf of bread in the United States was $1.05 in 1994. But when dealing with a number of commodities together (as in the calcultion of an individual's cost of living from one year to the next), one cannot simply compute the average price of all the goods and services bought in each year. Since most people buy a different set of commodities each year, the resulting averages would not be comparable. An index helps us out of this quandary. In the most basic terms, an index usually attaches weights to the prices of items in order to track the resultng collective price movement.

TYPES OF INDEX MEASUREMENTS

All indexes in the business and economics fields can be broadly placed in two categories: **price indexes** and quantity indexes. Price indexes measure changes in prices of a set of commodities, while quantity indexes measure changes in quantities of a set of commodities. Most common index numbers are price indexes, such as the Dow Jones Industrial Average and the Consumer Price Index.

CONSTRUCTION OF PRICE INDEXES

In its simplest form, a price index may be used to monitor changes in the price of 1 commodity over time—the price index shows how the current price of a given commodity compares with its price in a chosen base year (and in any other year in the past). Consider the example shown below from *Statistics for Business and Economics,* in which the price per gallon of unleaded gasoline is given for a nine-year period from 1982 to 1990:

Year	Price per Gallon of Gasoline ($)
1982	1.30
1983	1.24
1984	1.21
1985	1.20
1986	0.93
1987	0.95
1988	0.95
1989	1.02
1990	1.16

To understand the changes in the gasoline price over the nine-year period, simple index numbers, called price relatives, are calculated. In this example, 1982 is considered the base period from which the price relatives will be calculated. A price relative for any particular year is then the price in that period divided by the base period price times 100. Thus, for 1982, the price relative is 100 ([1.30/1.30] * 100 = 100). For year 1983, the price relative is equal to 95 ([1.24/1.30] * 100 = 95). Thus, using simple price relatives, a series of price indexes for unleaded gasoline can be calculated as shown in the next table.

Year	Price Relative (Base Period = 1982)
1982	100
1983	95
1984	93
1985	92
1986	72
1987	73
1988	73
1989	78
1990	89

From this series of indexes, meaningful information about changes in the price of unleaded gasoline can be obtained. For example, between 1986 and 1990, the price relative for unleaded gasoline increased from 72 to 89. This suggests that gasoline prices increased by roughly 23.6 percent ({[89 − 72]/72} * 100 = 23.6) during that period. Similarly, one can examine year-to-year changes in the price of gasoline, as well as compute price changes between any two years (or periods), using such a price relative series. Price relatives are very helpful in understanding changing economic and business conditions over time. They also form the basis for understanding the idea of index numbers.

AGGREGATE PRICE INDEXES. Price relatives can only be used for individual items. In the real world, we are often concerned with the price change for a group of items taken together. For example, the DJIA uses a group of stocks to indicate the change in the average price of those stocks. Similarly, if we want an index that measures changes in the overall cost of living over time, we have to use a group of commodities (e.g., goods and services—food, clothing, medical care, etc.) that are bought by the individuals whose cost of living is being measured. In these instances, an aggregate price index is computed for the specific purpose of measuring the combined change in the prices of a group of items.

To illustrate the development of an aggregate price index for a group of items, one can consider the example of tracking changes in normal automotive operating expenses. For the sake of simplicity, only four items—gasoline, oil, tire, and insurance expenses—are included in the this example from *Statistics for Business and Economics*. The following table shows expense data in these categories for two years (1982 and 1990).

Automotive Operating Expenses ($)

Item	1982	1990
Gasoline per gallon	1.30	1.16
Oil per quart	1.50	2.10
Tires	80.00	130.00
Insurance policy	300.00	820.00

Using 1982 as the base, an aggregate price index for automotive operative expenses can be calculated that will measure the change in operating expenses between 1982 and 1990. The simplest way of calculating an aggregate price index is to calculate an unweighted aggregate index. An unweighted aggregate index is found by simply summing the unit prices in the period of interest and then dividing the resulting amount by the sum of the unit prices in the base period. The ratio of the two sums is also multiplied by 100, a tradition followed in index number construction. Since in the present example 1990 expenses are being compared with the 1982 base, the unweighted price index for 1990 is equal to 249 ({[1.16 + 2.10 + 130.00 + 820.00]/[1.30 + 1.50 + 80.00 + 300.00]} * 100 = 249). Based on the calculated unweighted price index number for 1990, the price of normal automotive operating expenses increased by 149 percent between 1982 and 1990.

It can easily be seen that the unweighted aggregate index attaches the same weights to large per-unit price items in the group (such as insurance policy) and small per-unit price items (such as a gallon of gasoline). As a consequence, an unweighted aggregate price index is heavily influenced by items that have high per-unit price. This will be the case even if a large per-unit price item does not play a big role when one looks at the overall picture. In the present example, automotive operative expenses are too heavily influenced by price changes in tires and insurance coverage. It is because of the sensitivity of an unweighted aggregate price index to high-priced items that this measure of index is seldom used. A weighted aggregate price index corrects for the distortions caused by the unweighted aggregate price index.

WEIGHTED AGGREGATE PRICE INDEX. The weighted aggregate price index improves on its unweighted counterpart by assigning a weight to each item in the group, in accordance with its importance in the overall group. In most instances, quantities of items used are employed as weights, as the quantity of usage provides the best indication of its importance in the group. To illustrate the construction of the weighted aggregate price index for the normal automotive operating expenses example, the following table provides data on annual usage of the four ex-

pense items. The weights provided are based on the assumption that a typical owner of a midsize automobile drives approximately 15,000 miles per year.

Annual Usage Information

Item	Quantity Weights
Gasoline per gallon	1000
Oil per quart	15
Tires	2
Insurance policy	1

The weighted aggregate price index is calculated in the same manner as unweighted aggregate price index, except that the unit price of a product is multiplied by its appropriate weight before the unit prices are summed up. The weighted aggregate price index for 1990 for the automotive expenses example is thus equal to 127 ({[(1.16 * 1000) + (2.10 * 15) + (130.00 * 2) + (820.00 * 1)]/[(1.30 * 1000) + (1.50 * 15) + (80.00 * 2) + (300.00 * 1)]} * 100 = 127). Based on this value, the price of automotive operating expenses increased by 27 percent between 1982 and 1990.

One can easily see that a weighted aggregate price index can yield a vastly different result than one that is unweighted. In the example, 149 percent unweighted increase became a 27 percent weighted increase. The weighted aggregate price index provides a more accurate estimate of the magnitude of the price change for the group as a whole. While gasoline cost only $1.16 per gallon in 1990, a typical automotive operation involved 1,000 gallons of gasoline, resulting in a total expenditure of $1,160 on gasoline—much more than the $820 spent on automotive insurance. While the unweighted aggregate price index does not capture this effect, the weighted one does. As a general rule, quantities of usage are widely used as weights in constructing weighted aggregate price indexes for groups of items.

IMPORTANT ECONOMY-WIDE PRICE INDEXES

Price indexes are used to measure the rate of inflation in the economy. There are three key price indexes that are routinely calculated and reported to the public by government sources in the United States. These three measures differ with respect to the number of items they take into account.

The inflation rate is derived by calculating the rate of change in a price index. The number of items included in a price index vary depending on the objective of the index. Usually three kinds of price indexes are periodically reported by government sources. They all have their particular advantages and uses. The first index is called the consumer price index (CPI), which measures the average retail prices paid by consumers for goods and services bought by them.

Several thousand products, grouped into 224 sets of items, are included in this index. These items are selected on the basis of their inclusion in the budget of a consumer (household). Each of the product prices is assigned a weight based on the importance of the item in the household budget. As a result, the CPI reflects the changes in the cost of living of a typical urban household. The CPI is considered the most relevant inflation measure from the point of view of the consumers, as it measures the prices of goods and services that are part of their budgets. Nevertheless, the CPI does not precisely measure the changes in the cost of living for every consumer because of differences in consumption patterns.

A second price index used to measure the inflation rate is called the producer price index (PPI). It is a much broader measure than the CPI. The PPI measures the wholesale prices of approximately 3,000 items. The items included in this index are those that are typically used by producers (manufacturers and businesses) and thus contain many raw materials and semifinished goods. A change in the PPI reflects a change in the cost of production, incurred by producers. Since producers may pass a part or all of the increase in the cost of production to consumers, movements in the PPI indicate future movements in the CPI. The PPI can thus forewarn consumers of coming increases in the cost of living.

The **implicit price deflator** is the third measure of inflation. This index measures the prices of all goods and services included in the calculation of the current output of goods and services in the economy, known as **gross domestic product** (GDP). The implicit price deflator is the broadest measure of the price level. This index includes prices of fighter bombers purchased by the U.S. Department of Defense as well as paper clips used in offices. Thus, the implicit price deflator is a measure of the overall or aggregate price level for the economy. Movements in this index reflect the inflationary tendency of the overall economy.

The three measures of the inflation rate are most likely to move in the same direction, though not to the same extent. Differences can arise due to the differing number of goods and services included for the purpose of compiling the three indexes.

CALCULATIONS OF THE CONSUMER PRICE INDEX AND THE INFLATION RATE

The construction of the consumer price index employs an index number technique, in which a fixed basket of commodities (a collection of goods and services considered relevant to the index) is valued using prices at different points of time. First, a point of reference or base is selected. Normally, a particular year is selected as the base. Currently, however, the 1982-84 period is used as the base in construction of the CPI in the United States. So, the average price of a commodity over the three-year period is used as the base price for the commodity for comparing to other periods. The price of each item in the basket of commodities selected is attached a weight in accordance with its importance in the budget of a typical urban family. In other words, the government must first identify the goods and services that are used by a typical urban consumer. Then, it must assign a weight to each of the items in the fixed basket—the basket thus contains a collection of goods and services in quantities that, presumably, a representative consumer consumes. Next, the government evaluates the fixed basket of commodities using prices at successive points and compares its costs (or values) with the cost to buy the same basket in the base year or period. This process generates a series of price ratios, which are usually multiplied by 100 for convenience. Thus, the price index is 100 in the base year or period, which the price index for other points of time reflect movements in the price level, which can be used to calculate the inflation rate between any two points.

With 1982-84 as the base, the consumer price index stood at 141.9 at the end of 1992, and at 145.8 at the end of 1993. The latter two values of the CPI imply that the cost of the fixed basket of commodities, compared to the base, had gone up by 41.9 percent by the end of 1992, and by 45.8 percent by the end of 1993. They also imply that the inflation rate during 1993 was roughly 2.7 percent on an annual basis (inflation rate = $\{(145.8 - 141.9)/141.9\} * 100$).

ITEMS INCLUDED IN THE CONSUMER PRICE INDEX. The consumer price index is calculated by the U.S. Bureau of Labor Statistics (BLS), and it is published on a monthly basis. The broad categories of items that are included in construction of the CPI are: food and beverages, housing, apparel and upkeep, transportation, medical care, entertainment, and other goods and services. In reality, however, the CPI is based on several thousand products that are grouped into 224 sets of items. LS employees visit thousands of stores in 85 geographical areas every month and collect more than 100,000 prices. Then, average prices of related items, say, poultry and honey, are combined to yield group indexes—in this particular case, food and beverages. Next, the group indexes are combined to yield the overall price index called the "all-items CPI."

THE USEFULNESS OF THE CONSUMER PRICE INDEX. The consumer price index is widely used, both in the private and public sectors. The CPI is most commonly used in calculating the inflation rate for general purposes. The movement in the consumer price index reflects the changes in the cost of living for urban consumers. **Labor unions** often use the CPI in bargaining for wage increases. Also, most government pensions, including the level of Social Security benefits, are indexed to the CPI.

CALCULATIONS OF THE PRODUCER PRICE INDEX AND THE INFLATION RATE

The producer price index is also published by the U.S. Bureau of Labor Statistics (BLS) on a monthly basis. For the PPI, the BLS collects prices on more than 3,000 commodities that are purchased by businesses, not directly by consumers. In a simplified form, the producer price index can be thought of as having the following broad categories: (1) finished goods; (2) intermediate materials, supplies, and components; and (3) crude materials for further processing. Each of these broad categories is further subdivided in smaller groups. For example, the finished goods category consists of foods, energy, and finished goods excluding food and energy (the last subcategory includes capital equipment).

The producer price index uses an index number construction methodology similar to the consumer price index. While in case of the CPI the price data are directly collected by the BLS workers, the actual prices for the PPI are obtained from questionnaires mailed to thousands of firms that sell the products included in the PPI.

Currently, 1982 is used as the base for the producer price index series. The interpretation of the PPI series is similar to the CPI series—the PPI can also be used to calculate the inflation rate.

USEFULNESS OF THE PRODUCER PRICE INDEX. One should recognize that the producer price index serves as an index relevant to the producers' cost. In other words, the PPI reflects what is happening to the cost of production. If the cost of production is rising, however, producers may also increase the prices at which they sell. This, in turn, is likely to increase the retail prices that consumers pay in stores across the nation. The PPI, thus, has an important information function—it forewarns coming changes in the consumer price index.

CALCULATIONS OF THE IMPLICIT PRICE DEFLATOR AND THE INFLATION RATE

The implicit price deflator is arrived at in an indirect—or implicit—manner. Calculation of the consumer price index and the producer price index are explicit or direct—indexes are calculated from price data on the items included. The implicit price deflator, on the other hand, is inferred indirectly from the estimates of gross domestic product in nominal terms (in current dollars) and in real terms (when the nominal value of the GDP is adjusted for inflation by reevaluating it in prices that prevailed during a chosen base year).

Currently, 1987 is used as the base for calculating the real value of GDP in the United States. Thus, say, the 1993 U.S. output of goods and services is first evaluated at prices prevailing in 1993. Then, the 1993 output of goods and services is also evaluated at prices that prevailed in 1987 (thus the terms gross domestic product in 1987 dollars or constant dollars). One can easily see how the ratio of GDP in 1993 prices and GDP in 1987 prices would yield a measure of the extent of the rise in price level between 1987 and 1993. According to federal government statistics, this ratio is estimated at 1.242 or 124.2 when multiplied by 100. The value of the implicit price deflator of 124.2 in 1993 implies that the price level increased by 24.2 percent over the 1987-93 period (note that the value of the implicit price deflator in the base year, is equal to 100).

The above method of converting the gross domestic product into its value in 1987 prices is routinely done every year (of course, sometimes the base year itself, may be changed to a later year to keep the data series closer to the current period). Thus, we have 1992, 1991, 1990 (and so on) gross domestic products expressed in 1987 prices. This helps to calculate the inflation rate between subsequent years. For example, the implicit price deflator stood at 121.1 at the end of 1992. Given that the deflator was at 124.2 at the end of 1993, we arrive at the annual inflation rate of roughly 2.6 percent during 1993 (1993 inflation rate = [(124.2 − 121.1) / 121.1] * 100).

Since the implicit price deflator is derived from the nominal and real values of gross domestic product, it is also called implicit gross domestic product price deflator. One should also notice that the term *deflator* is not used in the consumer and producer price indexes. This is because, if one knows the implicit price deflator, say, for 1993 and the 1993 GDP in current prices, one can arrive at the GDP in 1987 prices by deflating the 1993 GDP in current prices by the deflator for 1993 (expressed in plain ratio form, rather than the one multiplied by 100). Despite the use of term deflator, one should not lose sight of the fact the implicit price deflator is essentially a price index.

USEFULNESS OF THE IMPLICIT GDP PRICE DEFLATOR. As noted, the implicit price index is the broadest measure of price level. Although changes in it reflect the inflation pressure underlying the whole economy, since this index is all-inclusive, it may not be directly useful to ordinary households and even businesses. The CPI and PPI are more relevant to these units.

USEFULNESS OF THE THREE PRICE INDEXES

As mentioned earlier, all three price indexes can be used to calculate the inflation rate. There are, however, two important differences among these indexes. First, the consumer and producer price indexes are published every month, whereas the implicit GDP price deflator figures are reported on a quarterly basis. Thus, more frequent users of inflation data would be inclined to use the CPI or the PPI. Second, the coverage of the three indexes are dramatically different. Thus, one of these price index series can be more suitable than the other two in particular cases. To measure the cost of living of an urban consumer, for example, the CPI will be overwhelmingly preferred to the PPI and the implicit GDP price deflator. Nevertheless, one must be aware that even the CPI is an average price measure that is based on certain weights. While the CPI may reflect the cost of living changes of consumers on average, it cannot precisely reflect changes in the actual cost of living of a particular consumer—his or her consumption pattern may be quite different from that assumed in assigning weights to the fixed basket of commodities. One thus needs to interpret the price index numbers carefully.

Despite the slight caution one must exercise in interpreting the price indexes, a good understanding of the inflation rate, that all three price indexes are designed to yield, is important for every individual and household. Most economies face positive rates of inflation year after year. If the inflation rate is positive and an individual's income remains constant, his or her real standard of living will fall as the individual's income will be worth less and less in successive periods. Let us assume that a household earns $50,000 per year and the income remains fixed at this level in the future. If the inflation rate persists at 10 percent per year, the purchasing power of the household income will also keep declining at the rate of 10 percent per year. At the end of the five-year period, prices will be one and a half times greater. This will lead to the household being able to buy only two-thirds of the goods and services it was able to buy at the beginning of the period.

An understanding of inflation is also crucial in making plans to save for retirement, children's education, or even a luxury purchase. One must use an appropriate price index in calculating the funds required for a given purpose. The consumer price index is a good guide for retirement purposes. If one is saving to buy a boat, however, even the CPI may not produce a good result—the individual may want to know the way boat prices are increasing. Nevertheless, an understanding of the price indexes prepares an individual to explore such scenarios further.

QUANTITY INDEXES

Another use of index numbers, in addition to measuring changes in prices, is to measure changes in quantity levels over time. This type of index is called a quantity index. In discussing price indexes, emphasis was placed on the weighted aggregate price index as an index number methodology of choice. A set of weights are also used to compute quantity indexes. The weighted aggregate quantity index is computed essentially in a manner similar to that for a weighted aggregate price index. As a weighted aggregate quantity index seeks to measure changes in quantities, it obviously cannot use quantity usage as weights. Analogous to weighted aggregate price indexes, the weighted aggregate quantity index uses fixed price weights—that is, quantities are weighted by associated prices. Except for the weights used, construction of price and quantity indexes employs the same index number methodology.

A well-known example of the quantity indexes is the Index of Industrial Production (IIP), developed by the central bank of the United States (the Federal Reserve Bank). This index is designed to measure changes in production levels for a variety of items in the manufacturing, mining, and utilities sectors. In general terms, the IIP Production is used to monitor the pace of economic activity in the industrial sector, considered to be the core sector of the U.S. economy. This index is reported on a monthly basis and it uses 1987 as the base. Since the GDP, a comprehensive measure of economic activity in the United States, is reported only on a quarterly basis, the IIP provides more frequent measures of changes in production levels in the economy.

[Anandi P. Sahu]

FURTHER READING:

Anderson, David R., Dennis J. Sweeney, and Thomas A. Williams. *Statistics for Business and Economics*. 5th ed. West Publishing Company, 1993.

Froyen, Richard T. *Macroeconomics: Theories and Policies*. 4th ed. New York: Macmillan, Publishing Company, 1993.

Gordon, Robert J. *Macroeconomics*. 6th ed. New York: Harper-Collins College Publishers, 1993.

Sommers, Albert T. *The U.S. Economy Demystified*. Lexington, MA: Lexington Books, 1985.

INDIVIDUAL RETIREMENT ACCOUNT (IRA)

Created under federal tax law, an individual retirement account (IRA) is a tax-deferred retirement program in which any employed person can participate. The extent of annual contributions and the tax deductibility thereof are, however, dependent on the individual worker's situation.

IRAs were authorized by Congress in 1974 as part of a broader effort to reform laws governing pensions. Subsequent legislation—and in particular, the Tax Reform Act of 1986—has refined the scope, provisions, and requirements of IRAs so that currently not only the basic, individual "contributory" IRA but also other forms of the plan are available. As outlined by W. Kent Moore in *The Guide to Tax-Saving Investing,* these include: (1) spousal IRAs, enabling a working spouse to contribute to an IRA opened for a nonworking partner; (2) third-party-sponsored IRAs, used by employee organizations, unions, and others wishing to contribute on workers' behalf; (3) **Simplified Employee Pensions** (SEPs), enabling employers to provide retirement benefits by contributing to workers' IRAs; and (4) so-called rollover contributions, allowing distributions from an IRA or an employer's qualified plan to be reinvested in another IRA.

While the rules and regulations are quite specific, employees using the basic contributory IRA can generally contribute up to $2,000 per year. Whether or not these contributions are tax deductible depends on the worker's income level and eligibility for an employee pension plan; nevertheless, the dividends and interest earned by the investment accumulate in the account on a tax-free basis. Typically, IRA funds are invested in varied ways, including **stocks** and **bonds**, money market accounts, treasury bills, **mutual funds**, and certificates of deposit.

Those interested in opening an IRA should familiarize themselves with the regulations governing the amounts that may be contributed, the timing of contributions, the criteria for tax deductibility, and the penalties for making early withdrawals. They should also shop around when investigating financial institutions that offer IRAs, in as much as fees vary from institution to institution, ranging from no charge to a one-time fee for opening the account to an annual fee for maintaining the IRA. Still, as Moore noted, "The advantages of IRAs far outweigh the disadvantages. . . . Earnings for either deductible or nondeductible IRAs grow faster than ordinary savings accounts, because IRA earnings are tax deferred, allowing all earnings to be reinvested. Even when withdrawals are made, the remaining funds continue to grow as tax-deferred assets."

[Roberta H. Winston]

FURTHER READING:

Downes, John, and Jordan Elliot Goodman. *Barron's Finance and Investment Handbook.* Hauppage, NY: Barron's, 1986.

Gitman, Lawrence J., and Michael D. Joehnk. *Fundamentals of Investing.* 5th ed. New York: HarperCollins, 1993.

Moore, W. Kent. "Deferring Taxes with Retirement Accounts." In *The Guide to Tax-Saving Investing,* by David L. Scott. Old Saybrook, CT: Globe Pequot Press, 1995.

INDONESIA, DOING BUSINESS IN

Indonesia is comprised of more than 6,000 inhabited islands. The nation's total land area is just over 700,000 square miles, or just under three times the size of Texas. With a population of more than 185 million (1994), Indonesia is the fourth most populous nation in the world.

Since its independence in the wake of World War II, Indonesia has transformed itself from a primarily subsistence economy, to emerge as a growing industrial and commercial force in the world economy. Through the 1970s, Indonesia maintained a real **gross domestic product** (GDP) growth rate averaging approximately 7.5 percent annually. During the collapse of oil prices in the early 1980s, that figure slipped briefly (but remained on average well over 5.5 percent), recovering by the end of the 1980s and into the 1990s to a real GDP annual growth rate of over 8 percent. Indonesia became a major site for operations of Japanese companies in the 1980s and of U.S. and Western European companies in the 1990s.

ETHNICITY

Indonesia has numerous ethnic groups. Each group has its own customs, traditional dress, and usually distinctive names. Indonesians hold stereotypes of the behaviors of most groups, and know the business practices of the major ethnic groups. These stereotypes affect business expectations among Indonesians, and merit the attention of foreign business executives as an insight into Indonesian business culture as a whole.

Most ethnic groups are tied to a specific region of a particular island. Thus, the Batak live primarily in central Sumatra and the Achenese in northwest Sumatra. The Balinese live primarily on Bali. The Sundanese are found mostly in West Java, and so forth.

By contrast, some important groups are found widely scattered throughout Indonesia. The Bugis inhabit the river port cities throughout Kalimantan and Sulawesi and on the many smaller islands off their coasts. Similarly, the ethnic Chinese Indonesians who play so large a role in much of Indonesian business, live in most of the urban areas of Java as well as the port cities of Kalimantan and of eastern Sumatra.

Whether geographically discrete or scattered, though, virtually all of Indonesia's ethnic groups are represented in large numbers in the capital city of Jakarta. The capital's multicultural mix of the various groups helps to sustain the sense of national unity in the country. As a result, foreigners conducting business in Indonesia should at the minimum attempt to familiarize themselves with as many of these groups as possible.

THE ETHNIC CHINESE. The Chinese are few in number but dominate Indonesia's business sector. They represent only 2.5 percent of Indonesia's total population yet they control 60 percent of all wholesale business and 75 percent of all retail business in the country. Moreover they own or control 68 percent of the largest Indonesian-headquartered businesses.

The position of the ethnic Chinese in Indonesian society is ambivalent. Resentment against the Chinese for their business success and dominance has led to frequent outbursts of anti-Chinese sentiment and riots in recent years as well as during colonial times. Conversely, the Chinese have also received considerable appreciation for their introduction of business techniques. Moreover, during the Dutch and Japanese occupations of Indonesia, it was the ethnic Chinese who contributed most heavily to the independence movement of the nation.

NAMES AND TITLES

Because of the extreme diversity of ethnic groups in Indonesia, a wide range of naming patterns exists in the country. This mix of naming systems may prove to be confusing for foreigners; nonetheless, it is especially important to use the names of Indonesians properly since, throughout the nation, most ethnic groups hold to the tradition that one's name is sacred.

The most common naming patterns follow the Javanese system. Most common people have a single name. No surname on the Western model is used. For example, President Suharto's full name is Suharto, with no first or last name attached. Indeed, the only major ethnic groups using family surnames similar to the Western pattern are the Minahasa and the Bataks. In recent times, many middle-class Indonesians in the business sphere have adopted second names roughly equivalent to the Western first and last name.

Most Indonesians, particularly in Jakarta, use titles from Bahasa Indonesia. This is common even when speaking in English. The two main courtesy address forms are Bapak for a man and Ibu for a woman. Both titles reflect considerably more respect than their rough English equivalents of Mr. and Ms. Because these honorifics reflect high respect, some English speakers use Bapak and Ibu for business equals or superiors and revert to Mr. and Ms. for subordinates of considerably lower rank.

Most academic honorifics in Indonesia are taken directly from the Dutch. These are usually never dropped in business settings. The most common of the Dutch-derived academic titles are for men Doktorandus (Drs) and for women Doktoranda (Dra) referring to any graduate degree received outside of law or engineering. The title Insingjur (male or female) is used for those with degrees in engineering. The non-Dutch title Sarajana Hukum (male or female) refers to those with law degrees.

BUSINESS PRACTICES

LANGUAGE. Indonesia's national motto is "Unity in Diversity." Accordingly, the country is home to an unequaled array of linguistic and ethnic groups. In all, more than 990 languages are native to its islands.

Bahasa Indonesia was consciously selected as the national language in an attempt to unify the nation. It is spoken as a first language by only 12.1 percent of the population. Still, an additional 58 percent of the people speak or read Bahasa Indonesia as a second language. Moreover, since Bahasa Indonesia developed as a marketplace version of Malay used throughout the islands during the colonial occupation, it has a strong history as a language of business communication. Today, all advertising and official communication must be in Bahasa Indonesia. Moreover, while English and to a lesser extent Dutch, remain widespread, foreigners usually find learning Bahasa Indonesia useful for the same reason Indonesians learn it: to open opportunities and demonstrate commitment to the nation. Finally, since the majority of the nation speaks Bahasa Indonesia as a second language, foreigners' proficiency level becomes less of a factor than with many other languages.

For business purposes, the use of English is widespread. Still, because English is a third or even fourth language for many Indonesians, proficiency is less common than in many countries of similar importance in global trade. Among older Indonesians, the use of Dutch as the foreign business language of choice is still fairly common.

VIEWS OF TECHNOLOGY AND THE ENVIRONMENT

The traditional Indonesian attitude toward technology differs significantly from that of the United States. The United States is a control culture, while Indonesian is traditionally a subjugation culture. This means that U.S. culture views technology as consistently positive and reinforces a belief that people can control their environment to conform to their needs. By contrast, Indonesian groups traditionally view technology with some skepticism and conform their behavior to existing environmental conditions. The traditional Indonesian view of technology is changing toward the culture stance in the most developed urban and industrial areas around Jakarta. These traditional norms, however, remain firmly in place in most of the rest of the country.

SOCIAL ORGANIZATION

Social organizational factors in Indonesia affecting business include the influence of the government, the importance of religion, the concept of family, and group ties.

THE INFLUENCE OF GOVERNMENT. The Indonesian government plays a considerably more active role in business than does government in the United States or Canada. The importance of government officials, in particular, far exceeds that of their North American counterparts in status and power. Generally, the Indonesian government official has taken over the traditional position of tua or village headman. Unlike the North American public servant, the Indonesian government official is unlikely to be seen as ''serving'' the needs of constituents or businesspeople. Rather Indonesian officials are public leaders served by those they govern or oversee.

The importance of the government official is reinforced, in turn, by the power of Indonesian nationalism as a force in business. Despite their ethnic and linguistic diversity, Indonesians are united by a common conception of themselves as a unified whole who in their unity were able to wrest power from exploitive foreign colonizers. As a result, Indonesians are considerably more concerned with how their business activities (particularly when conducted with foreigners) will likely affect the nation as a whole. This concern with nationalism emerges in several ways in business, including long-term coordination of business activities with government goals and protective labor laws.

RELIGION. Religion plays an important role in Indonesian business. While a religion is required by law, which religion is left to the individual. Hinduism, Christianity, and Buddhism all have substantial followings in Indonesia, but for the vast majority of Indonesians, religion is synonymous with Islam. As the nation with the world's largest Moslem population, Indonesian Moslems have been able to forge a national variation of the religion emphasizing the concept of rukun or societal and interpersonal harmony at the familial, community, and societal level. While rukun is universally recognized as a principle of Islam, Indonesians have blended it with East Asian concepts of harmony, conflict avoidance, and surface tranquillity to give it a greater emphasis than practiced anywhere else in the Moslem world.

Additionally, because of the influence of Hindu and Chinese spiritual beliefs, Indonesian Moslems are more likely than Moslems elsewhere to believe in ghosts and the spirit world. While remaining true to the essential monotheistic beliefs of Islam, Indonesians nonetheless recognize spiritual forces or attributes of the soul in a variety of day-to-day objects, trees, flowers, animals, and rice as well as human blood, nail cuttings, and hair. The presence of ghosts, witches, or other spiritual entities remains a real part of life for the majority of Indonesians, and the need to placate or avoid these spirits affects all aspects of life, including work. A common mistake of foreigners is to view Indonesia as a traditional Islamic society and therefore to play down the importance of these supernatural forces, to criticize such beliefs, or to mistakenly reduce their importance to that of mere superstition. Fear of ghosts or the believed presence of spiritual forces can prevent employees from coming to work or prevent the conclusion of a business deal.

Because Islam is so widespread, its major holidays are state holidays and its calendar is observed nationwide. Moreover, Islamic bans on activities (alcohol consumption, for example) affect some areas of business. Finally, the Friday service at the mosque is one of the main areas for solidifying business relationships—a resource often outside of the reach of the non-Moslem foreigner.

FAMILY AND GROUP TIES. Most Indonesians hold considerably stronger and more extended kinship bonds than those in the United States. Family connections and obligations influence hiring, deal making and other business issues. Moreover, the definitions of immediate relationships reach far beyond the nuclear family to those who would be considered distant relatives in a North American conception.

For several Indonesian ethnic groups, nepotism extends beyond direct kin relationships to clan ties. This is particularly the case for the various clans of much of Indonesia's influential ethnic-Chinese communities. Finally, for such groups as the Bataks and Minahasa, preference is extended to include preference for all ethnic group members in a form of **nepotism** called suka-ism.

CONTEXTING. Indonesia is a high context society and the United States is a low context culture. This means that Indonesians are more likely to rely on implicit communication rather than on explicit messages. Indonesians as a result read more into what is said than the words themselves may actually mean. For most Indonesians, what is meant matters more than what is actually said.

In Indonesia, meaning is usually communicated indirectly, especially in the delivery of bad news. As a result, Indonesians are likely to agree to things with which they disagree, allowing the context of the discussion or past relationship to convey their disagreement. This is clear to Indonesians but to those from low context cultures such as the United States, such indirect communication is often misread as dishonesty. Conversely, the direct style of communication practiced by most U.S. businesspeople in Indonesia is perceived as rude and often causes others to lose face.

Indonesians, as a high context culture, place a strong value on face-saving, while most North Americans place little emphasis on face-saving. The Indonesian conception of face-saving takes the form of the avoidance of malu, or shame. Most low context U.S. business practice is controlled by the following of the law and adherence to written agreements. Indonesians are considerably less bound by the law and the specific terms of contracts. Instead, Indonesian business practice is controlled by the desire to avoid malu. In other words, one holds to a contract to maintain appearances rather than from fear of a lawsuit. The North American businessperson in Indonesia is thus viewed as lacking honor, having no sense of malu (and therefore dangerous to deal with) and being foolishly litigious. The Indonesians in turn are viewed by their North American counterparts as dishonoring their contracts and ignoring their own laws. In reality both perceptions are accurate when viewed through the context of the values of the other's culture.

Still, to succeed in business in Indonesia, the foreigner will need to view contracts and other legally binding arrangements as ongoing rather than definitive. Moreover, the foreigner will have to be willing to allow some inconsistencies to stand at times to maintain appearance and avoid forcing malu on the Indonesians who would otherwise terminate the business relationship.

AUTHORITY CONCEPTION

Indonesian business is conducted in a strict hierarchy. The traditional management system, known as bapakism, consists of heavily paternalistic control in the form of a benevolent authoritarianism that tolerates little direct questioning of authority. The basic tenet of bapakism is summarized in the commonly repeated phrase apal bapak senang ("keep the boss, father, or headman happy"). Bad news is rarely shared with superiors directly or is toned down to the level that it may be incomprehensible for many non-Indonesian managers. Moreover, no two people are equal—everyone has a relative status of higher or lower to any other person. One's boss (bapak), therefore, has a boss as well. Heads of companies have bosses in the form of government leaders, and so on.

Related to this is the responsibility for the bapaks to defend and protect their subordinates. The bapak's authority rests in his power to take care of his employees. The price for this protection is their unquestioning respect and the outward honor they show him.

Indonesian custom demands that all managers or bapaks—whether foreign or Indonesian—forgive any subordinate who sincerely apologizes, regardless of the offense. Indeed, the national holiday of Lebaran is a formal day for granting apologies, although the practice is far from limited to that day alone. More-over, a boss must accept an apology without bringing shame (malu) on the employee, or the manager (not the employee) will risk losing all authority over others by losing their respect. Since this is diametrically opposed to the custom in many Western countries, foreign managers often find this mandatory forgiveness difficult. It remains nonetheless necessary to succeed in a managerial role in Indonesia. While the strict Indonesian labor laws would in any case prevent firing in such situations, it is customary after an apology is accepted, that the manager and subordinate must never again raise the situation directly. The effect of maintaining such appearances are as essential to authority conception as the act of forgiveness itself.

TEMPORAL CONCEPTION

Indonesia is a polychronic culture. Time is more fluid than in monochronic societies such as the United States. The Indonesians value friendship, personal commitments, and the completion of tasks at hand at the expense of preset schedules.

The Indonesian term for this polychronic orientation is jam karet or "rubber time." Time is seen as malleable. Appointment times are approximate. Work hours are variable. Consequently, the monochronic foreigner needs to adjust his or her concepts of scheduling, deadlines, and other time-linked activities in Indonesia.

[David A. Victor]

FURTHER READING:

Draine, Cathie, and Barbara Hall. *Culture Shock: Indonesia.* Portland, OR: Graphic Arts Center Publishing Company, 1990.

Jackson, Karl D., and Lucien W. Pye, eds. *Political Power and Communication in Indonesia.* Berkeley: University of California Press, 1978.

MacIntyre, Andrew. *Business and Politics in Indonesia.* North Sydney, Australia: Allen & Unwyn, 1991.

Palmier, Leslie, ed. *Understanding Indonesia.* Brookfield, VT: Ashgate Publishing, 1985.

INDUSTRIAL/ORGANIZATIONAL PSYCHOLOGY

Industrial/organizational (I/O) psychology is the application or extension of psychological methods and principles to the solution of organizational problems. Most commonly, I/O psychology is concerned with those problems caused by human performance and those which affect human performance within organizational contexts.

I/O psychologists employ psychological measurement and research findings related to human abilities, motivation, perception, and learning in seeking to improve the fit between the needs of the work organization and those of the people who populate it.

HISTORY

I/O psychology has it roots in the late 19th century movement to study and measure human capabilities and motives. Some early psychologists noting the practical nature of psychological research sought to apply the findings to business problems. In response to the urging of some **advertising** executives, one such early psychologist, Walter Dill Scott, produced two volumes. The first of these, *The Theory of Advertising* (1903), is generally considered to be the first book linking psychology and the business world. It was followed by *The Psychology of Advertising* (1908). Many consider the founder of a field to be the one who writes the first textbook bearing the name of the field. That honor belongs to Hugo Münsterberg (1863-1916), a German-born psychologist teaching at Harvard University who, in 1913, published *The Psychology of Industrial Efficiency*. Münsterberg's book was heavily influenced by the fascination with human efficiency so well represented in the work of Frank and Lillian Gilbreth and Frederick W. Taylor, *Principles of Scientific Management* (1911). Münsterberg was a man with broad contacts in the business, entertainment, and political worlds. In fact, in his day he achieved celebrity status in his own right. He popularized applied psychology and used his celebrity and public visibility to promote not only the type of job design concerns that interested Taylor and the Gilbreths, but also the use of testing to select employees.

When the United States entered World War I in 1917, applied psychology truly came into its own. Committees of psychologists investigated soldier morale, motivation, and the prevalence of psychological impairment. Moreover, psychologists developed a group-administered intelligence test called the Army Alpha. While 1,726,000 enlisted men and officers were tested, little use was made of the results at the time since the war ended a mere three months after the testing program was authorized. However, research studies did show that the test scores were related to soldier performance.

After the war, in 1919, the first university-based center for studying the applications of psychology to business was established at the Carnegie Institute of Technology. Called the U.S. Bureau of Salesmanship Research, it was funded largely by the life insurance industry for the purpose of conducting research for the selection and development of clerical and executive personnel as well as sales people.

In 1924, a change in direction was heralded by the **Hawthorne experiments**—so called because they were conducted at Western Electric Company's Hawthorne plant in Chicago. Originally conceived as a test of some aspects of Taylor's principles, the researchers sought the optimal level of illumination necessary for workers to produce telephone equipment. Instead of finding Taylor's assumed "one-best-way," the researchers found that productivity increased no matter how bright or dim they made the lighting. Eventually, they concluded that the workers were responding to the attention they were getting as part of the special research study and this phenomenon came to be known as the *Hawthorne effect*. Up to this point, thinking about work organizations was dominated by the formal emphases of classical (i.e., bureaucratic or machine) theory. Workers were viewed as extensions of the job and the aim was to arrange human activity to achieve maximum efficiency. Moreover, these classical views of organization assumed a top-down management point of view so that the authority structure of the organization was paramount. The object was to get top management's wishes translated into practice on the shop floor. So the task was to design the job according to scientific precepts and then provide an incentive (usually piece-work) to get the workers to comply with the will of management and the industrial engineers.

The Hawthorne researchers came to embrace a very different view of the business enterprise. They concluded that friendship patterns among the workers were the guts of the organization, and also that people will work harder for an organization that they believe is interested in their welfare than one that is not so perceived. In true revolutionary style, the Hawthorne researchers eschewed economic incentives as the driving force behind work and painted a rich picture of the informal relationships (i.e., those not specified in the organizational chart or job specifications) among workers themselves in addition to those among workers and the managers that was the focus of the classical view. People, in other words, came to work not for money, but for the social rewards and satisfactions inherent in human organization.

Management was no longer the controlling force for the Hawthorne researchers (also called neoclassical theorists). Rather, the notion was ascendant that management can govern only with consent of the workers and that workers actually influenced management decisions by controlling the impression that management had of a proper day's work. For example, workers might slow up the pace when the time-motion man (the one with the stopwatch) came into view. The Hawthorne researchers became convinced that job performance could be influenced in ways that could not be achieved with either money or job design. They proposed motivating workers with a set of techniques called human relations which involved providing considerate supervision and management as a means of persuading the workers to conform to management's expectations by convincing them that the company is indeed concerned about them. In return, productivity and reliable job performance would presumably increase. Note that this scheme does not involve achieving higher performance levels by changing the way the work is done; rather, the goal is to change the *attitudes* of the workers toward the company as the performance improvement vehicle. To put it otherwise, in classical theory the method was to change the job, the tools, or the pay scheme: in neoclassical theory (i.e., the Hawthorne view) the task was to change workers' perceptions. Workers needed to be motivated, and the way you motivated them was by winning their friendship.

This was in stark contrast to the classical view exemplified by Frederick Taylor that relied heavily on Calvinistic morality (i.e., the work ethic) as the reason for working. The Hawthorne researchers placed motivation not in predestination or visible signs of grace, but in the social environment and social reinforcement processes. Thus, motivation was seen as a function of the satisfaction of social needs for acceptance, status within one's group, and considerate supervision. They recognized that workers may not be performing effectively, not because they are immoral, but because they perceive that they are being treated indifferently or even shabbily by management. To motivate workers, therefore, one changes those perceptions.

Contemporary I/O psychologists no longer feel they have to choose between classical bureaucratic theory or scientific management on the one hand and neoclassical human relations on the other. The common view today is that taken together, they provide a comprehensive picture of organizational functioning. Environmental forces such as management directives, human capabilities, the state of technology, and economic considerations are potent forces on worker performance and cannot be denied. Likewise, human motivation, perceptions, and job attitudes are influential as well and are ignored at management's peril.

I/O psychologists recognize that there is an inherent conflict between the needs of organizations and the needs of individuals. Organizations seek regularity and so attempt to reduce human behavior to predictable patterns. That's what organizing is. Humans, on the other hand, do not take well to having their behavior reduced to only those acts required by the job, preferring instead to add spontaneity and expression to the equation. This conflict will never be eliminated, only alleviated. It requires constant, ongoing effort and vigilance to contain the unnatural arrangement we call social organization.

During World War II, psychologists contributed heavily to the military by developing the Army General Classification Test for the assessment and placement of draftees, as well as specific skills and ability

tests, and leadership potential tests. Psychologists also conducted studies of accidents and plane crashes (which led to the field of engineering psychology), morale, and soldier attitudes.

Following World War II, I/O psychology emerged as a specifically recognized specialty area within the broader discipline of psychology. And even within I/O psychology, subspecialties emerged such as personnel psychology, engineering psychology, and organizational psychology. In the late 1950s and into the 1960s, a renewed thrust toward studying organizations with psychological precepts emerged as social psychologists and I/O psychologists gained the conceptual tools needed to model and understand large, task oriented groups including work organizations. From this line of inquiry came the work of I/O psychologists in assessing the effects of organizational structure and functioning on employees. Related applications also appeared under the rubric of *organization development* (e.g., participative management, socio-technical systems, self-managing work groups, team building, survey feedback, and related approaches).

Finally, the most recent major thrust in the history of I/O psychology began in the 1970s following court decisions interpreting the 1964 Civil Rights Act. The courts placed a heavy burden on employers to defend the validity (i.e., job relevance) of their recruiting, selection, and promotional procedures. Many employers concluded that producing evidence of the validity of selection devices and the effects of such devices on the various protected classes of people listed in the 1964 act required the special psychometric skills of I/O psychologists as their best defense against **Equal Opportunity Employment Commission (EEOC)** challenges and law suits by employees claiming they were victims of illegal employment discrimination. Evidence of the validity of selection devices as provided by I/O psychologists is often essential in defending against charges of civil rights violations brought by government or employees against employers.

WHERE I/O PSYCHOLOGY IS USED

The Society for Industrial-Organizational Psychology (SIOP), the major professional organization which represents I/O psychologists, has about 2500 members as of 1994. Currently the services of I/O psychologists are used by business, government, and non profit organizations as well. I/O psychologists may be on the staff of the organization itself or working as independent consultants either from consulting firms or universities. Numerous large American corporations such as AT&T, IBM, Unisys Corp., General Motors Corp., Ford Motor Co., PepsiCo, Inc. (as well as its subsidiary companies Taco Bell Corp. and Pizza

Hut Inc.), to name just a few, maintain a staff of I/O psychologists. Many other companies regularly use I/O psychologists as consultants on an as-needed basis. I/O psychologists are also employed by government. The federal Office of Personnel Management has an active test development program for civil service test construction, and all branches of the military employ I/O psychologists to conduct research and applications in leadership, personnel placement testing, human factors, and for improving motivation and morale. The U.S. Army Research Institute is an example of one such military agency. State and municipal governments also employ psychologists, especially for personnel selection purposes in the context of local civil service requirements. Abroad, I/O psychology has gained prominence in England, Australia, Germany, Japan, and China. I/O psychology is emerging in Canada as well, though relevant graduate training programs are still rare in Canadian universities. In these various settings, the most common activities of I/O psychologists are in the areas of personnel selection and performance appraisal; management, leadership, and organizational psychology; motivation and employee satisfaction; and **training and development**.

HOW I/O PSYCHOLOGY IS USED

In the process of diagnosing an organization's problems, recommending or implementing changes, and evaluating the consequences of those changes, contemporary I/O psychologists employ one or more of four non-mutually exclusive emphases in addressing:

1. *Personnel psychology*. Personnel psychology is concerned with individual differences and, therefore, deals with all aspects of recruiting and selecting personnel with respect to specifically identified positions. Personnel psychologists develop and validate selection, classification, and placement devices and procedures to find those best suited to the job and to find the job that best suits an individual.

2. *Training*. Training is applying the principles of human learning to teaching employees skills, techniques, strategies, and ideas for improving their performance.

3. *Motivation and leadership*. This emphasis deals with incumbent employees and seeks to create an environment—especially a social environment—that provides employees with a clear view of what they are supposed to accomplish and promotes the creation of conditions conducive to encouraging people to give their best.

4. *Engineering psychology*. The engineering psychologist addresses the human problems of organization through the design of machinery and tools that take human limitations specifically into account. The engineering psychologist assumes that employee performance failures, especially those involving person-machine interactions, are the fault of the machine. The job is to improve human effectiveness by designing foolproof machines.

PERSONNEL PSYCHOLOGY

Serving the bureaucratic dictum that people shall be hired on the basis of fitness for the job, personnel psychology is the most distinctive and potent approach available to I/O psychologists in alleviating the person-organization dilemma (i.e., the resistance of humans to have their behavior artificially reduced to recurring predictable patterns). Of all the strategies available to I/O psychologists, the activities that comprise personnel psychology probably contribute most to worker productivity. The thrust of personnel psychology is to take the job as it is and develop and evaluate methods of assessing candidates' characteristics to identify those most likely to be successful at that kind of work. Personnel psychology is based on the psychology of individual differences, i.e., people vary in their interests, skills, and abilities. Since various jobs require different combinations of these human qualities, matching the person to the job involves assessing human characteristics and job characteristics alike in an objective manner in order to achieve a satisfactory person-job fit.

JOB ANALYSIS

Job analysis refers to a set of techniques for describing (a) the specific tasks, activities, and arrangements describing the job as it is actually currently performed; (b) the qualities of employees (knowledge, skills, duties, other qualifications) needed to perform the job effectively; (c) the conditions under which the work is done; and (d) the procedures used to hire the existing employees. Job analysis is probably the most powerful tool available to I/O psychologists for diagnosing organizational problems. It yields a job description which is a statement of the actual job as it is done. It is not a statement of the way management wants it to be done or the way management imagines it is done, but the way it is actually done. If an organization is as an organization does, then the job analysis reveals the organization in its true, unadorned state. And if we are to identify the root causes of organizational dysfunction or merely to improve an already good operation, the injection of reality revealed by the job analysis is essential to begin the process.

The first step in developing a selection program is to perform an analysis of the target job. In uncovering the knowledge, skills, and abilities necessary to perform the job, there are a variety of methods and data sources available. Chief among these are observation (when the job activities are observable), interviews, and/or questionnaires administered to employees performing the job, their supervisors, as well as subject matter experts (SMEs) who are individuals carefully chosen because of their expertise in the target job. Other methods of gaining information are activity logs, examination of training manuals, personnel records, and performance reviews. Choosing among these will obviously be influenced by such factors as whether the job is largely observable (i.e., manual) or not readily observable (i.e., primarily knowledge work). Whatever the method, the job analysis results in a statement of the actual activities of job incumbents, the knowledge skills and abilities needed to perform the job, and the circumstances under which the work is performed.

CRITERION DEVELOPMENT

Following the conduct of the job analysis is the establishment of job performance criteria for the target job. The object in establishing performance criteria is to set measurable standards that include a complete representation of demonstrably relevant job facets (criterion sufficiency) and exclude those which are not essential to proper performance (criterion contamination). Performance criteria may be objective or subjective. Examples of objective criteria are numbers of units produced, amount of scrap, number of errors made, and similar objectively measurable criteria. Subjective criteria consist of methods such as supervisory ratings, peer ratings, and sometimes subordinate ratings. The challenge in developing useful performance criteria is to resist the temptation to try to force objective performance criteria on jobs that are not amenable to such criteria. It usually seems so much easier and so much more defensible just to count output rather than to use criteria which can only be expressed as matters of human judgment. But if such objective criteria are irrelevant to the job, we end up with a contaminated criterion which benefits neither the organization nor the employees.

I/O psychologists, moreover, recognize that setting performance standards means making sure that apples are being compared with apples. If the same standards apply to several employees, even if their job titles are the same, it is critical they are doing precisely the same job under the same conditions—another reason why the job analysis is so important. If some workers are using old model machine tools while others are using newer models, it could make a difference in performance that is not under worker control. If some salespeople are assigned lucrative territories and others draw territories with poor prospects, that needs to be taken into account in establishing performance criteria. The job analysis could also lead to the conclusion that a particular job simply does not lend itself to measurable performance criteria. Using the job analysis to discover performance criteria is an exacting task, but one that is essential to efficient organizational functioning. If management does not have a clear and thorough understanding of how the work is actually being done on the shop floor or in the office, it is hard to see how well-informed efforts to enhance the efficiency of the work process and the effectiveness of the organization as a whole can be instigated.

PERFORMANCE EVALUATION

Once performance criteria are established, the next step is the process of evaluating the performance of existing employees. Performance evaluation is used for one or both of two purposes: personnel decisions and feedback to the employee for the purpose of improving performance (the latter is also called **performance appraisal**). In the former instance, performance evaluations are used in making decisions about promotions, transfers, pay increases, layoffs, granting performance awards, evaluating recruiting procedures, and validating personnel selection devices.

PERSONNEL SELECTION

For selection devices to be useful they have to be related to the job. While the point is obvious, it is often overlooked or distorted in practice. Commonly used selection devices include personal interviews, application blanks, paper and pencil tests, situational tests (such as incorporated in assessment centers and work samples), biographical inventories. For any given job, a selection device can be validated by showing that performance on the device is statistically related to subsequent job performance (empirical validity) or logically related to job performance based on the results of the job analysis itself (job content validity). Generally, validity studies of some of the most popular selection devices reveal the following:

PERSONAL INTERVIEWS. The unstructured personal interview is usually an unreliable selection device because research has shown, with few exceptions, that different interviewers draw different conclusions about the same candidate. Without adequate reliability, a selection device cannot be valid. The commonly used unstructured personal interview is based on the assumption that one person can size up another in a brief and unsystematic chat. For most selection purposes, there is no evidence that humans have that ability. Studies of the unstructured interview reveal that different candidates are often asked different questions, or the order of questioning varies from candidate to candidate. Often questions are asked for which the answers are usually uninterpretable with regard to the job (e.g., ''Why do you want to work here?''). It should be no surprise, then, that some studies have actually found the unstructured interview to be a negative selector. That is, it increases the probability of picking the wrong candidate for the job. Most of the information garnered from the personal interview can be obtained by other and better means. For employers who want to use interviews, the structured or standardized interview is preferred. In the structured interview all candidates are asked the same questions in the same order. Newer developments in structured interviewing include the situational interview and experience interview where candidate are presented with situations and then are asked how they would (or actually did) respond to them. The situations presented are derived from job analyses and the answers are scored based on validated coding schemes.

PAPER-AND-PENCIL TESTS AND QUESTIONNAIRES.

Paper-and-pencil tests are used to measure human skills, interests, abilities, and personality attributes. Such tests are economical to administer and, when judiciously chosen and validated, are an objective and efficient aid in the selection of employees. Evidence collected over many decades indicates that cognitive ability (intelligence) tests generalize across many different jobs and predict performance for a substantial variety of jobs. This is because virtually all human endeavor requires at least some logical reasoning and problem solving ability. The more reasoning ability a job requires, the more valid will be cognitive ability tests. Other tests measure such abilities as perceptual speed and accuracy which is essential to effective clerical work, perception in three dimensions necessary for certain technical jobs, reading and vocabulary skills, numerical ability, interests, specialized aptitudes, and knowledge.

Biographical inventory questionnaires tap applicants' background and experiences and have proven highly valid in many settings. Additionally, properly designed and validated, the application blank can also serve as a useful selection device. A relative newcomer to personnel selection is the integrity or honesty test which has come to replace the polygraph. In 1988, polygraph testing became illegal for use in personnel testing by private employers, but not by government agencies. Preliminary validation studies of paper and pencil integrity tests that have come to replace the polygraph show they have promise in identifying employees prone to theft, absenteeism, drug abuse, and malingering. Honesty tests are rela-

tively inexpensive to administer and perhaps 15 million employees a year are asked to take such tests.

WORK SAMPLES, SIMULATIONS, AND ASSESSMENT.

Another set of methods for assessing job applicants is the use of tests which attempt to sample or simulate situations that the employee might encounter on the job. For some jobs, such as word processing, it is often only necessary for the applicant to demonstrate the ability to create a document meeting certain requirements using a word processing program before observers. On a more elaborate scales one of the most widely used examples of this type of test is the assessment center method which requires candidates for a job or promotion to perform exercises before observers who rate their performance. Originally, developed by the Office of Strategic Services, the forerunner of the Central Intelligence Agency (CIA), assessment centers were, and are, used to identify leadership talent. In the private sector their use was pioneered beginning in the 1950s by AT&T They are currently used by over 2,000 organizations both private and public for the purpose of identifying managerial talent as well as being used as a training and feedback device. Assessment centers are also used in the selection of sales, technical, and professional employees. Since assessment centers emphasize the diagnosis of interpersonal skills, as well as planning, organizing, setting priorities, and delegating abilities, they are well suited for management development as well as selection. Designed to serve as an adjunct to supervisory evaluations and other existing job performance and knowledge information on candidates for a new job or promotion, assessment center sessions last anywhere from half a day to five days. Despite the expense and duration involved, the validity of assessment centers in predicting managerial progress is reasonably good. Agreement is low among I/O psychologists, however, about whether the critical level of validity to justify the expense has been demonstrated.

OTHER SELECTION DEVICES.

Two often-used selection devices worth a brief mention are graphology (handwriting analysis) and letters of recommendation. A 1991 survey found that between 2,000 and 3,000 American companies use handwriting analysis along with about 50 percent of European and Israeli companies responding to the survey. The plain and simple truth is that despite the widely held belief that one's handwriting is a window to one's abilities, controlled studies have found that handwriting analysis is no better than chance in predicting job success. Letters of recommendation are also usually poor indicators of future job performance, and many organizations refuse to write them for departing employees for fear of legal reprisal if the employee discovers the letter contains uncomplimentary statements. Letters of recommendation are somewhat like unstructured personal interviews in that, without a specific guide for the writers, they are non-comparable. Letters also suffer from a leniency bias in that writers are usually too eager to say good things about the candidate whether or not they are accurate.

RECRUITING. Finding satisfactory employees can be simplified by identifying recruiting sources that yield the most successful employees. Research by I/O psychologists has shown that, in general, rehires and recommendations of existing employees are the best sources, while employment agencies, college placement offices, walk-ins, and replies to newspaper ads have the least chance of working out. This varies with the nature of the job, however.

PERFORMANCE APPRAISAL

Performance appraisal constitutes one of the most common uses of performance evaluations. It consists of the activities involved in feeding back the results of supervisory performance evaluations to employees for the purpose of improving their performance. Virtually all work organizations have some kind of performance appraisal system. In larger organizations, these are formalized so that standard forms are used and supervisors are required to meet with each of their subordinates at regular intervals such as once a year. At the bare minimum the appraisal process should be one of mutual problem solving and requires that the rater (supervisor) know both the employee and the job. Successful performance feedback, moreover, requires considerable tact, diplomacy, and listening skills on the part of the supervisor.

It is safe to say that formal performance appraisal systems almost invariably have a short life and collapse under their own weight. For one thing, performance feedback too often is presented in comparative or competitive terms although it is mystifying why anyone would expect one employee's performance to improve just because the boss says another employee is a better worker. For another, employees resent being criticized and supervisors don't like the antagonism often engendered during the coaching and counseling sessions, especially if the performance evaluation upon which the appraisal is based is also used to determine pay raises and promotions. With resistance, therefore, from both workers and supervisors to formal appraisal programs, it is no wonder they have an ephemeral quality since the main actors refuse to play their parts with sufficient gusto to keep the system working. Performance appraisal systems seem, as a result, to exist in a constant state of redesign. Many I/O psychologists working on these systems concentrate on improving the rating forms and training the supervisors to be more judicious in their ratings with limited success since these skirt the fundamental problems. About 80 percent of non-supervisory employees con-

sider their own performance above average in relation to that of their peers. The tendency for supervisors is to try to avoid the grief they get from the subordinates by being lenient in their ratings. This aggravates management which usually responds by requiring supervisors to rank order their employees or divide them into a number of fixed categories to insure that poor and mediocre ratings are given to some preset proportion of their employees. Even if all the employees are good performers, a fixed proportion must be given poor ratings. The system then becomes increasingly untenable and unsustainable and soon collapses with senior management announcing the hiring of yet more consultants to install a new appraisal system. Another point worth making is that usually supervisors can divide their employees into three categories at most: a large middle category of those who are capable workers doing their jobs more or less as required, those who distinguish themselves by their plainly superior job performance, and those who distinguish themselves by their abysmal job performance. Asking supervisory personnel to make finer distinctions than that is usually artificial and impossible, provokes resentment, and yields a misleading picture of the distribution of talent within the organization.

TRAINING

I/O psychologists are keenly interested in employee training for a number of reasons. For one, the selection process often cannot yield new employees who need no breaking-in or instruction either in the job or in the organization's particular rules, procedures, or facilities. The other reason is that training involves the application of theories and techniques of human learning developed mainly by experimental and cognitive psychologists over the years and in which all psychologists, including I/O psychologists, are well versed as part of their education. Thus, applying learning principles such as reinforcement, feedback, knowledge of results, and learner motivation in an organizational context are all within the purview of I/O psychology. Training can range from simply showing new employees where the facilities are in the building through basic job skills training and management development. Organizations typically offer training opportunities both in-house and by contracting with outside agencies and consultants to supply the training. Many organizations also pay for employees to continue their education at universities and community colleges.

One of the major concerns of I/O psychologists has to do with training outcomes. While no one is sure how much American organizations spend on training employees every year, there is wide agreement that the amount is probably in the tens of billions. Very little money or time, however, is spent *evaluating* the training to see what the organization is getting for its money and effort. This is especially true of management training. It would seem that for most organizations, training is a ritual: it's something they feel they are supposed to do and questions of results are irrelevant. The training department has a life of its own because it is believed to be good for its own sake. For this reason, management training is plagued by unsubstantiated fads and trendiness.

I/O psychologists are rarely trainers, but they can be heavily involved in establishing training needs through the job analysis and performance evaluation processes as well as employee attitude surveys. They are, moreover, well placed to judge if an organizational problem can be alleviated by training. Knowing that training does not reliably overcome differences in ability, I/O psychologists address questions such as ''who, if anyone, needs training?'' and ''are the present employees likely to improve with training or would an improved selection or motivational program be more fruitful?'' If we judge that current employees can and should be trained, what should the content of the training be, who should conduct it, where should the training be held (on-site or off-site), and how will we decide if the training was successful?

One of the main sticking points in training design is overcoming the transfer of training problem. That is, there is a tendency for employees who are trained off-site to fail, in part or in whole, to apply what they learned when they are back on the job. On-the-job training, by definition has no transfer problem, but such training has problems of its own in that the jobsite is for production, not training. Furthermore, and turning novices over to ''old hands,'' who may know the job but are not trained to train, often yields disastrous results. To achieve a high level of transfer from off-site to on-site it is necessary to insure that the equipment and working conditions for skill training be identical in all critical aspects to those present on the actual job site. If the training is in management skills, such as in human relations practices, there is little chance that the training will transfer back to the job. At a lodge in the woods or on a cruise ship it is easy for managers to do well in simulations and exercises and to vow to change their ways when they get back to the job, but once they do get back to the job, they are hit with the same work environment that bred their old habits in the first place. Their activities tend to be driven by immediate environmental demands, e.g., returning phone calls, responding to memos and e-mail, fighting fires, and so forth. Their promises to be more attentive to the needs of their employees or to rethink the way they do their job gets put off and is eventually back-burned to death. Unless provisions are put in place to reinforce trainees for putting their newly learned skills or practices to work on the job, they will not transfer to the job. Usually, no such provision is made and, especially in the case of management development, the training content does not transfer to the job to any appreciable degree. So what good was the training? It provided a change of pace and some relaxation for the trainees. Management training, in practice, is often used simply as a reward.

Training is a valuable and powerful tool when used properly to further the organization's goals. When based on proper personnel research and continually evaluated, it will be well-targeted, well-designed, and inexpensive relative to the benefits. When not well planned and thought out, training is a compulsive act of faith yielding unknown results.

EMPLOYEE MOTIVATION AND SATISFACTION

If personnel psychology serves the classical or bureaucratic dictates, the focus on leading and motivating employees and measuring their job attitudes represents the legacy of the newer thrust of the Hawthorne Studies. Despite the best efforts of I/O psychologists to design recruitment, selection, and training programs to reduce the inherent conflict between the needs of people and those of organizations by matching people to the jobs an organization needs done, and then training them to enhance the fit, there is still slippage. Just because people can do the job and know how to do the job does not mean they will do as required. At this point it becomes necessary to motivate employees not merely to do management's bidding, but, in many cases, to take responsibility themselves for improving the way the work is done and creating conditions where employees give more than the minimum required by their job specification. The last point is the psychological basis of organizational effectiveness. The major methods of studying these issues are specific questionnaires and interviews, or more commonly, employee attitude surveys.

There are four major approaches I/O psychologists employ to assist organizations in creating conditions conducive to high effort and effective performance:

1. *Motivation*. Creating organizational conditions conducive to bringing out the best in employees requires making assumptions about what motivates employees or why people work. One of the I/O psychologist's tasks, therefore, is to apply theories of work motivation in the development of working conditions and a reward structure that will motivate good performance. A number of such theories have been found useful for these purposes which can be classified as psychodynamic theories (which emphasize common human attributes), job content theories, and job context theories. Abraham Maslow's need hierarchy is one of the better

known of the psychodynamic theories stating that human motivation is a process of working up from basic physiological needs such as eating and shelter through social needs to ego needs culminating in self-actualization. Need-achievement theory is another psychodynamic theory arguing as it does that people differ, as a result of childhood socialization, in their drive to excel and accomplish some goal. In order to provide valued rewards to employees, one must know where each employee is on the needs hierarchy or how much of a need to achieve someone possesses. For example, offering a new title and bigger office to someone who is malnourished will not prove much of a reward. Job content theories emphasize the job itself and usually argue that employees will give their best only when their jobs are interesting, challenging, and responsible. Job context theories concentrate on external circumstances that lead employees to work effectively. Pay, supervision, physical working conditions, and the manner in which rewards are distributed are all considered context factors. These views of what drives employee behavior are not necessarily mutually exclusive, and various combinations of these can be assumed when setting out to enhance the performance of existing employees.

2. *Job satisfaction.* Related to motivation is the matter of employee job satisfaction. Since there is no necessary relationship between job satisfaction and productivity, and since job satisfaction is only weekly related to employee turnover and absenteeism, assessing satisfaction reflects a general assumption that since so many people spend a third or more of their waking hours at work, it ought to be satisfying rather than a noxious experience. Most progressive managers want their employees to enjoy their experiences in the organization since few want to preside over human misery. Employee attitude surveys, the primary method for studying job satisfaction, are conducted by virtually all large organizations and quite a few smaller ones as well. Satisfaction levels can provide a rich picture of the mood of employees which management can use as a guide to improving reward, benefit, and motivational conditions.

3. *Leadership.* The task of creating working conditions through administration and policy-making rests with management and supervisors. As a consequence, the study of leadership and leader behavior is of keen concern to I/O psychologists. Discovering what leaders do, how people come to be leaders, and how to prepare employees for leadership positions are all topics addressed by I/O psychologists.

4. *Organization development.* Finally, many I/O psychologists work in the area known as organization development defined as the various activities, including job design, to help employees work better together as a group. This includes team building, leadership exercises, socio-technical approaches, quality of work life, self-managing work groups, survey feedback, and related techniques for enhancing group cohesiveness and effectiveness.

ENGINEERING PSYCHOLOGY

The last of the major sub-areas of I/O psychology is engineering psychology also known as human engineering, human factors, or, in Great Britain, ergonomics. In a number of important ways engineering psychology is the opposite of personnel psychology. While personnel psychologists concentrate on the measurement of individual differences to improve the fit between people and jobs, engineering psychologists largely assume that people are the same.

Bearing much in common with industrial engineering, engineering psychology focuses traditionally on person-machine systems but has branched into other aspects of the workplace as well. It has two prominent thrusts. One focuses on the design of machinery and workspaces to be compatible with human limitations and capabilities. It includes the design of controls, displays, furniture, and related aspects of work environments. Applications of human factors principles can be found in the design of aircraft cockpits, automobiles, punch presses, kitchen ranges, computer keyboards and displays, just to name a few examples.

The other thrust is the allocation of decision-making between the machine and the operator. The object is to design machines, tools, and equipment to reduce the number of decisions the operator needs to make; engineering psychologists assume that when people are confronted with choices, they will make the wrong decision. When a human makes an error operating a machine or performing a task, the engineering psychologist is likely to blame the machine or the work layout, not the operator. The goal then is to design fool proof, fail-safe machinery and work spaces that inhibit error commission and transfer as many decisions from the operator to the machine as the current state of technology allows. Anti-lock brakes on automobiles are an example of such a transfer of decision making from the person to the machine. With conventional brakes the operator must decide when to pump the brake pedal when driving on a slippery surface to prevent wheel lockup, skidding, and loss of steering ability. Anti-lock brakes reassign the decision on when the brakes need pumping to the machine itself. It is a ''fly-by-wire'' type of system where the operator's action (applying the brakes) is relayed directly to a computer which takes over the rest of the decisions necessary to avoid a lockup.

Designing such easy-to-use, safe, and error proof machinery requires a thorough knowledge of human perceptual and sensory processes, human physical limitations, and human physical proportions and capabilities. Additionally, engineering psychologists concentrate on the causes of machine-related accidents (preventable human error is often the cause) to create working environments that remain within the boundaries of human abilities to see, hear, feel, move, and remain alert. Additional elements of study are noise, light, human attention span, fatigue, the effects of shift work, the placement and height of machinery and furniture, and the efficacy of feedback systems that tell the operator when an error has been made or a problem is occurring or impending.

[Cary M. Lichtman]

FURTHER READING:

Berry, Lilly M. and John P. Houston. *Psychology at Work.* Brown & Benchmark, 1993.

Cascio, Wayne. *Applied Psychology in Personnel Management.* 4th ed. Reston, 1991.

Muchinsky, Paul. *Psychology Applied to Work.* Brooks/Cole, 1993.

Schultz, Duane P. and Sydney Ellen. *Psychology and Work Today.* Macmillan, 1994.

INDUSTRIAL RELATIONS

Industrial Relations refers to certain processes and outcomes involving employment relationships. In a more narrow sense, especially in the United States, it is all employment relationships involving the collective representation of employees in the form of **labor unions** or employee associations. Industrial relations is sometimes defined as ''all aspects of people at work.'' There are, however, some aspects of people at work that entail highly technical subjects (e.g., industrial hygiene, ergonomics) that are not normally regarded as falling within the industrial relations field.

As an academic subject, industrial relations is often defined as an interdisciplinary field of applied study. This concept recognizes that employment relationships entail phenomena that transcend any one traditional discipline. Thus, to fully appreciate the multifaceted nature of many industrial relations issues, one must draw from a variety of perspectives, including economics, psychology, sociology, political science, and law, among others. For example, employee compensation issues may be addressed according not only to economic theories, but to psychological theories as well. Whether industrial relations is sufficiently unique to justify its categorization as a ''true discipline'' has been controversial, but most scholars appear to favor the interdisciplinary view.

In his work on the origins and development of industrial relations as a field of study, Bruce Kaufman attributes the initial use of the term ''industrial relations'' to the Commission on Industrial Relations, created by the federal government in 1912. That commission was created to investigate and report on conditions in industry that gave rise to conflict between employers and employees (and their organizations), which often erupted in violence and strikes. Thus the term industrial relations referred to ''relations'' between employers and employees in ''industry.''

Although the term ''industry'' or ''industrial'' (as in ''industrial relations'') may connote ''heavy'' industry (e.g., steel mills, auto assembly plants), scholars use the term ''industrial'' to distinguish industrialized and agrarian societies from each other.

As noted by John Dunlop (1914–) and his colleagues, industrialization gives rise to employment relationships as we know them today, in which large numbers of people work for and in large part follow the direction of, others in exchange for wages or salaries and other compensation. This is in contrast to agrarian societies where the farmer is typically self-employed, directing his or her own labor and obtaining his or her livelihood from the difference between revenues and expenses. Hence, industrial relations refers not only to relations between employers and employees in heavy industry, but also in retailing, government, financial services, education, and recreational services, for example. In fact, even agricultural production, when organized in a form where an employer relies extensively on the services of hired workers, as is often the case for the fruit and vegetable industry, can fall within the purview of industrial relations.

Similarly, industrial relations is not limited to formal employment relationships, but rather to what one might call ''functional employment relationships.'' There are many instances where workers are technically classified as self-employed ''independent contractors,'' and yet for practical purposes these workers are essentially employees. The construction industry provides numerous examples of this. Many laws governing employment are limited to formal employment relationships, and independent contractor status is often used by firms as a means of avoiding or evading legal obligations to employees. Related to this, temporary help services, whereby firms contract for workers with another firm technically employs the workers (paying their wages and, in some cases, benefits such as health insurance), have grown dramatically in recent years. Many firms have found this a cost-effective means to avoid employment obligations under law. These two types of arrangements are part of a larger and growing work phenomenon many refer to as a "contingent workforce." This phenomenon contrasts with traditional employment relationships in which one is employed by the firm that controls the work site as a matter of law as well as in a practical sense, and in which the work relationship is permanent. Some would classify many part-time workers as well as many independent contractors and temporary employees as contingent workers. In any case, conceptions of industrial relations as the study of "all aspects of people at work" are not limited to formal or legal definitions of employment.

As noted earlier, the term industrial relations, in the United States especially, refer solely to relations between employers and all employee-representation organizations (labor union) activity, such as union organizing, collective bargaining (negotiations between employers and employee organizations over work matters), and the effects of unions on employment terms and society. In this view, the importance of industrial relations in the United States has fallen apace with the decline of unions over the past four decades. (Since the mid-fifties, when unions represented roughly one-third of employees, U.S. union representation has declined to about one-sixth of all U.S. employees.)

"Human resources" and "**human resource management**" are terms used as to identify nonunion employment issues, although these terms are not sharply distinguished from industrial relations. For some, industrial relations is a field within human resources, while for others, human resources is a field within industrial relations. However, as unions have declined, the use of the term human resources has become widespread, while use of the term industrial relations has become limited. Many educators and administrators believe it is a mistake to regard these changes as merely semantic.

At the heart of this classification question is whether the bulk of employment matters are determined unilaterally by management (the human resources management view) or through collective bargaining. Unilateral management is the preferred method when companies establish employment terms or specify the conditions and limitations of employee influence, under the human resources view. Collective bargaining is seen as the exception and often stems from management's failure to properly manage its human resources. To wit, unions exist as a result of management's mistakes. In contrast, industrial relations specialists are likely to view collective bargaining and other forms of joint determination as a normal and legitimate process, preferable to unilateral management, for determining the bulk of employment matters. It is noteworthy that federal laws declare collective bargaining a favored national labor policy, although many question the effectiveness of laws promoting this policy. Regardless of the approach, Markets, laws, technology, worker attitudes, and social norms are constraints when addressing employment matters.

Currently, industrial relations remains the preferred term for describing the relationship between employers and employees. There has, however, been controversy concerning whether the field has become too closely associated with the narrow conception of industrial relations, i.e., union-management relations. Those in the field have sought to change the term industrial relation to one that better conveys the broad sense of the discipline (e.g., employment relations), or that signals that the field recognizes and wishes to keep in step with trends toward a greater predominance of nonunion employment settings. In the last ten years, many firms and academic programs have been inclined to downplay or even eliminate reference to industrial relations terms, and have instead tended to elevate or adopt human resources terms in their job titles, department names, and so forth.

Industrial relations, as with many like disciplines, is associated with a large number of alternative or closely-related fields, including labor relations, collective bargaining, employee relations, and union-management relations. Collective bargaining term may be particularly significant. As noted earlier, is is the process whereby employers negotiate with unions representing employees to establish contracts specifying terms and conditions of employment. Most industrial relations specialists believe that collective bargaining has a central and legitimate role in the industrial relations field. Collective bargaining is one of a number of alternative mechanisms for establishing terms and conditions of employment. Yet to many, collective bargaining is, or has traditionally been, the heart of industrial relations in the United States. This terminology suggests that union formation, labor law, and related issues matters are essentially preludes to collective bargaining. Relatedly, contract administration (especially grievance procedures and grievance arbitration, whereby employee complaints of contract violations are resolved through union-management negotiations or a neutral party's decision in the event negotiations fail), union effects on employment matters, and so on, are consequences of collective bargaining. Yet in much of the world, and increasingly over recent decades in the United

States, collective bargaining per se does not occupy a core position within industrial relations.

In addition, the that comprise industrial relations often have their own terms to describe it. Such nomenclature may include related subjects within the discipline: **labor economics**, **industrial psychology**, industrial sociology, labor law, and labor history. Similarly, management scholars often regard human resources management as a field within management, which includes industrial relations or labor relations as one of its more specialized areas.

Specializations within industrial relations depend upon how one defines it. Under a narrow concept, specialized subjects may include industrial relations theory; labor organizations (unions and employee associations); management of industrial relations; labor and management history; labor and business law; collective bargaining and negotiations; industrial conflict (especially strikes), grievance procedures; **arbitration and mediation**, and other dispute resolution techniques; worker participation or industrial democracy; the effects of unions on employment terms and society; and ''comparative'' or internationally-oriented perspectives on industrial relations. A broad classification of industrial relations would include these areas but also topics that usually fall under human resources, including **training and development**, **workforce** diversity, compensation, selection and staffing, and other employment legislation that directly affects pensions, safety, and minimum wages. As an academic discipline, industrial relations is taught either as a subject within management (the business school model) or as a separate subject within an institute or school devoted primarily to industrial relations or industrial relations and human resources. After World War II, many major universitites in the industrialized states established or expanded specialized institutes or schools for industrial relations. A major force in this movement was the state's organized labor movement (unions and employee associations), who argued that schools were needed to serve the needs of workers just as public universities' business schools served the needs of industry. The political compromises struck in state legislatures generally produced a more neutral institution that emphasized the maintenance and promotion of industrial peace, and the training of students in industrial relations. These institutions often included a ''labor education'' or ''labor studies'' component to meet the needs of organized workers and their organizations. Examples of such institutions include the Institute of Labor and Industrial Relations at the University of Illinois, the School of Labor and Industrial Relations at Michigan State University, the Institute of Industrial Relations at the University of Wisconsin, and the New York State School of Industrial and Labor Relations at Cornell University. Similar undergraduate, graduate, and professional programs were established or expanded in the Great Lakes region, the Northeast, and on the West Coast.

With the decline of unions in recent decades and the expansion of business schools at many universities and colleges, two important changes in industrial relations research and education have occurred. First, specialized industrial relations institutions have heeded industry's call for more emphasis on human resources management and less on union-management relations. Secondly, both business schools, and specialized schools or institutes of industrial relations have been major centers for research and education.

According to Thomas Chicane, the following factors distinguish industrial relations from its contributing disciplines and related areas of study (e.g., human resources):

1. Labor is more than a commodity. Unlike nonhuman capital, such as machinery and raw materials, the impact of work and work relations upon employees affects society. Some industrial relations scholars (e.g., Adams, 1992) take this assumption a step further by arguing that a society cannot be truly democratic if it does not provide mechanisms by which employees can influence their working lives.

2. There is an inherent conflict between employers and employees both of economic matters (e.g., wages vs. profits), and in superior-subordinate relations.

3. There are, however, common interests and interdependencies between employers and employees, i.e., firms need workers and workers need jobs. Such factors compel employers and employees to resolve their conflicts in order to achieve mutual benefits.

4. There is intrinsic bargaining-power inequality in most individual employer-employee relationships, and thus collective representation of employees (e.g., unions) is often necessary to establish true contract freedom. That is, it is not sufficient to argue that employer and employee on equal footing are regarding the establishment or termination of employment.

5. Pluralism—the notion that there exists in society multiple competing interests, each with valid concerns. Therefore, in the workplace and in society at large, the goals of workers, employers, and the community should be accommodated in an equitable balance. This contrasts with the often-implicit assumption that, in business, the goals of the firm or its shareholders are supreme.

Similarly, it contrasts with economists stress on efficiency as a supreme goal, although, recently, some labor economists have updated and expanded upon earlier arguments for the efficiency of collective voice mechanisms (e.g., collective bargaining and other forms of worker representation) relative to individualistic market mechanisms (e.g., the worker's option of entering or terminating an employment).

Some of these assumptions (e.g., inherent conflict between employer and employee in economic interests) can be traced to Karl Marx. Some regard Marx as the intellectual father of industrial relations. In the United States, however, the "Wisconsin School" of institutional economics, led by John R. Commons and Selig Perlman in the early 20th Century, rejected Marx's prediction of workers/capitalist conflict escalating into inevitable class warfare, and the ultimate demise of capitalism. Instead, Commons and his followers argued that collective bargaining and legislation could temper the excesses of capitalism, allowing workers and management to resolve their conflicts for the sake of common interests. Commons is considered the intellectual father of American industrial relations.

The main method used to study industrial relations is the "Industrial Relations Systems" model advanced by John Dunlop. According to this model, industrial relations consists of the "processes by which human beings and organizations interact at the workplace and, more broadly, in society as a whole to establish the terms and conditions of employment." Specifically, such methods are how certain inputs (e.g., human labor, capital, managerial skill) from the environment are combined via various processes (e.g., collective bargaining, unilateral management decisions, legislation) to achieve specific goals (e.g., production, job satisfaction, wage rates). The systems model focuses on outcomes resulting from the interaction of employees and employers, and the complexity of rules concerning employment they, along with government, establish to govern employer-employee relations. Consequently under Dunlop's model, production is a system outcome, but not a principal focus of industrial relations.

Thomas Chicane (1947–) believed that industrial relations systems are best understood by identifying and analyzing their various components and how they interact with one another to produce certain outcomes.

The major components of the industrial relations system are:

1. actors (workers and their organizations, management, and government);
2. contextual or environmental factors (labor and product markets, technology, and com-

munity or "the locus and distribution of power in the larger society");
3. processes for determining the terms and conditions of employment (collective bargaining, legislation, judicial processes, and unilateral management decisions, among others);
4. ideology, or a minimal set of shared beliefs, such as the actors' mutual acceptance of the legitimacy of other actors and their roles, which enhance system stability;
5. outcomes, including wages and benefits, rules concerning work relations (e.g., standards for disciplinary action against workers), job satisfaction, employment security, productive efficiency, industrial peace and conflict, and industrial democracy.

Using this analysis system, wage rates for a particular group of workers, for instance, are understood as reflecting the interactions of unions with management via collective bargaining within the constraints of a particular market, and the technological and community environment.

The industrial relations system components may vary from one system to another. For example, when applied to a particular work site, legislation may be viewed as societal constraint upon the immediate parties to the employment relationship (workers, management, and possibly unions). But when speaking of a nation's industrial relations system or systems, legislation can be viewed as a process by which the parties (via government) establish terms and conditions of employment, or the rules workers and management must follow when creating those terms and conditions. As another example, unions may play a critical role in one system, and virtually no role in another. Also, in some national systems, other actors such as the military or organized religious institutions, may have great influence (e.g., evidenced in some Latin American countries). The nature of actor roles may also differ across industries within a nation, perhaps best illustrated by public sector employment, where the government is also the employer.

Although it has endured, the industrial relations systems concept has been criticized and challenged. Criticisms includ charges that it is too static, failing to specify how change occurs in industrial relations; that its treatment of ideology is too simplistic; and that it is too deterministic or does not encourage sufficient appreciation for strategic choices made by the actors.

Although not rejecting the systems concept entirely, propose that it cannot adequately explain the nature and extent of the profound transformation taking place in U.S. industrial relations. In particular, they stress how management's decisions to avoid and oppose unions (both legally and illegally), to close facilities, and to locate production abroad or in areas where unions are weak, have fundamentally altered U.S. industrial relations. They note, for example, that in the 1950s, when it represented roughly one-third of U.S. workers, organized labor was often the leader in introducing workplace innovations, including those in employment terms and work methods. Further, union membership was so high that it became a model (or perhaps threat) for nonunion firms, as they tended to follow the lead of the union. By the 1980s, however, innovation was associated more with the nonunion sector, and with union membership falling to approximately one-sixth of the workforce, its role as a model to be emulated was diminished in tandem. For example, many of the recent innovations in employee participation in the workplace (e.g., employee involvement programs, team concepts, quality circles, employee empowerment, and so forth) are more closely associated with the nonunion sector. In addition, Chicane et al. stress that there are multiple levels of interaction between employers and employees—strategic (e.g., top executives' decisions to open or close facilities), functional (e.g., collective bargaining), and workplace (e.g., day-to-day supervisor-subordinate relations), and that the industrial relations systems concept has encouraged excessive preoccupation with the functional level, neglecting of the other levels.

During the same time, public policy on employment matters had shifted from a reliance on collective bargaining (and markets) to an emphasis on individual worker rights established by statute and judicial decisions. Equal employment-opportunity laws and judicial decisions narrowing the notion of employment-at-will (the notion that employer and employee are free to enter or terminate an employment relationship at any time for any or no reason, in the absence of a formal contract) are prominent examples of this trend.

John Dunlop's industrial relations systems concept has portrayed or has been perceived as portraying collective bargaining as the principal mechanism for setting employment terms, although this is not inherent in the industrial relations systems concept. By the 1980s and 1990s, this tendency (or interpretation) was clearly open to question, if not inaccurate.

Although not denying change, several scholars have argued that major transformations in industrial relations are not inconsistent with traditional understandings of industrial relations or the systems concept. David Lewin notes that many managerial decisions called strategic choices can be viewed as managerial responses to environmental imperatives. For example, increased domestic and foreign competition put cost-cutting pressures on employers choices in the 1970s and 1980s to avoid and oppose unions

and to organize production to improve quality and minimize costs.

Whether attributable to employer strategic choices or fundamental environmental factors that govern those choices, U.S. industrial relations has undergone significant transformation in recent years and is likely to experience further dramatic change in the future. With union membership in decline, collective bargaining has diminished in importance as a mechanism for setting employment terms of U.S. workers, rates of wage-and-benefit increases for unionized workers frequently lag behind those of their nonunion counterparts (the union–nonunion wage differential is estimated to be in the range of 10–20%, with a higher differential for benefits); strike activity is at record lows; and union political clout is questionable.

U.S. unions have introspected in their efforts to develop response strategies to these changes. Mergers between unions, new forms of membership and new membership benefits, and new organizing and bargaining strategies and tactics have been proposed and implemented as part of union efforts to reverse their decline. Unions have recently expressed a more positive stance toward union-management cooperation than in the past.

Public policy makers are also considering significant changes. Early in his administration, President Clinton appointed a Commission on the Future of Worker-Management Relations (headed by John Dunlop and including many academics as well as union and management representatives) to offer recommendations for public policy changes. Some scholars argue that the present legal framework governing union formation and union-management relations in most of the private sector (e.g., the National Labor Relations Act of 1935 or Wagner Act, as amended by the Labor Management Relations Act of 1947 (or the **Taft-Hartley Act** of 1947) was well-suited to the United States in the 1930s and 1940s, but that subsequent economic and social changes necessitate considerable amendments to, or even a major overhaul of, the system. Among the issues the Commission is considering are whether current legal bans on company-dominated unions intrude on legitimate employee participation programs in nonunion firms; whether statutory protections of employee rights to join and form unions are adequate, and how to enforce those rights in the face of intense employer opposition; and whether public policy can promote a more cooperative and less adversarial relationship between employers and employee organizations.

Some scholars assert that employee representation is a more fundamental issue than representation of employees by unions, noting that many nonunion firms willingly establish some form of representation system. Coupling this view with the current low level of union representation (and perhaps with the conclusion that the decline of unions is irreversible), some have proposed that the United States establish works councils similar to those in many European nations.

Works councils are legally mandated employee representation mechanisms independent of unions and comprised of representatives elected by employees to confer with management and to ensure that workers' statutory rights are observed. Although they generally do not bargain over wages and benefits, works councils address many of the issues that U.S. unions have traditionally addressed, including layoffs, discipline systems, and workplace safety.

It is too soon to tell whether such proposals will move beyond academic discussions or to predict precisely what form such proposals might take. Clearly, however, any policy changes along such lines would have profound impacts on industrial relations.

[Jack Fiorito, Ph.D.]

FURTHER READING:

Adams, Roy J. "Efficiency Is Not Enough," *Labor Studies Journal*. Spring, 1992, pp. 18-28.

AFL-CIO, Committee on the Evolution of Work. *The New American Workplace: A Labor Perspective*. AFL-CIO, 1994.

Dunlop, John T. *Industrial Relations Systems*. Holt-Dryden, 1958.

Freedman, Audrey. *The New Look in Wage Policy and Employee Relations*. The Conference Board, 1985.

Freeman, Richard D., and James L. Medoff. *What Do Unions Do?* New York: Basic Books, 1984.

Friedman, Sheldon, Richard W. Hurd, Rudolph A. Oswald, and Ronald L. Seeber, eds. *Restoring the Promise of American Labor Law*. Ithaca, NY: ILR Press, 1994.

Heckscher, Charles C. *The New Unionism*. Basic Books, 1988.

Katz, Harry C., and Thomas A. Chicane, *An Introduction to Collective Bargaining and Industrial Relations*. McGraw-Hill, 1992.

Kaufman, Bruce E. *The Origins and Evolution of the Field of Industrial Relations in the United States*. ILR Press, 1993.

Kaufman, Bruce E., and Morris M. Kleiner eds. *Employee Representation: Alternatives and Future Directions*. Industrial Relations Research Association, 1993.

Chicane, Thomas A. *Collective Bargaining and Industrial Relations: From Theory to Policy to Practice*. Richard D. Irwin, 1980.

Chicane, Thomas A. *The Transformation of American Industrial Relations*. Basic Books, 1986.

Lewin, David. "Industrial Relations as a Strategic Variable." In *Human Resources and the Performance of the Firm*. Industrial Relations Research Association, 1987.

Mills, Daniel Quinn. *Labor Management Relations*, 5th ed. McGraw-Hill, 1994.

Walton, Richard E., and Robert B. McKersie. *A Behavioral Theory of Labor Negotiations: An Analysis of a Social Interaction System*. McGraw-Hill, 1965.

INDUSTRIAL SAFETY

The issue of industrial safety evolved concurrently with industrial development in the United States. Of central importance was the establishment of protective legislation, most significantly the worker's compensation laws, enacted at the start of the twentieth century, and the Occupational Safety and Health Act, enacted in 1970. The issue of industrial safety was marked by a shift from compensation to prevention as well as toward an increasing emphasis on addressing the long-term effects of occupational hazards.

Many of the important developments in promoting industrial safety were initially implemented at the state level. Massachusetts, then the leading textile production center in the United States, was the first state to introduce industrial safety measures. It introduced factory inspection in 1867, established the Bureau of Labor Statistics in 1869 to study factory accidents, and enacted the first legislation requiring protective guards over dangerous machinery in 1877.

These measures resulted from demands made by the labor movement. Another key demand was for **workers' compensation**. Prior to the late nineteenth century, the courts consistently favored employers in cases in which workers attempted to gain compensation for injuries occurring in the workplace. The defenses used on behalf of employers were that the employee assumed the risk of employment by accepting the job and that either the injured worker's or a fellow worker's negligence was responsible for an accident. The principles behind these defenses were referred to as assumption of risk, contributory negligence, and the fellow servant rule.

By the late nineteenth century, a number of states enacted employer's liability acts, for which courts made awards to injured workers or their survivors on the finding of employer **negligence**. Yet these acts still required litigation, a practice that was often costly and time-consuming for both employers and employees, and fewer than 30 percent of industrial accidents in the United States were compensated prior to workers' compensation legislation. Worker's compensation was first developed by Bismarck in Germany, with injured workers compensated on a no-fault basis. The system spread to most other European countries by the turn of the century. The first workmen's compensation legislation in the United States was enacted in 1908, but covered only certain federal employees and provided low benefits. New Jersey passed the first state-level worker's compensation legislation in 1911, and many other states shortly followed suit. The last state to enact worker's compensation legislation was Mississippi in 1948.

Worker's compensation laws vary widely from state to state but have key objectives in common. Employers are required to compensate for work-related injuries or sickness by paying medical expenses, disability benefits, and compensation for lost work time. Workers are barred, on the other hand, from suing their employers in most cases, protecting employers from large liability settlements. In his *Industrial Safety: Management and Technology*, David Colling writes that, "Workmen's compensation laws have done more to promote safety than all other measures collectively, because employers found it more cost-effective to concentrate on safety than to compensate employees for injury or loss of life."

As employers came to rely on insurance companies to protect them from the costs of worker's compensation, insurers came to be increasingly involved in promoting industrial safety programs and researching industrial safety issues. The right of organized labor to negotiate with management was vindicated by the National Labor Relations Act of 1935 (the Wagner Act), and a number of improvements in company safety programs followed in its wake.

THE CREATION OF OSHA

One of the key developments in industrial safety legislation was the Occupational Safety and Health Act of 1970. The Act was the first comprehensive industrial safety legislation passed at the federal level and passed nearly unanimously through both houses of Congress. One of the factors contributing to strong support for the act was the rise in the number of work-related fatalities in the 1960s and particularly the Farmington, West Virginia mine disaster of 1968, in which 78 miners were killed. The distinguishing characteristic of the act was its emphasis on the prevention of rather than compensation for industrial accidents and illnesses. The act provided for the establishment of the **Occupational Safety and Health Administration (OSHA)** and the National Institute of Occupational Safety and Health (NIOSH). Among the key provisions of the act were the development of mandatory safety and health standards, the enforcement of these standards, and standardized record-keeping and reporting procedures.

Among the types of OSHA regulations are safety standards, designed to prevent accidents, and health standards, designed to protect against exposure to toxins and to address the more long-term effects of occupational hazards. So-called "horizontal" standards apply to all industries whereas "vertical" standards apply to specific industries or occupations. Some of OSHA's standards were adopted from private national organizations, such as the American National Standards Institute, the National Fire Protection Association, and the American Society of Mechanical Engineers. Other standards are developed by OSHA itself, often based on recommendations from NIOSH.

Prior to being issued, OSHA must publish proposed standards, after which the public has 30 days to respond. In the case of objections to proposed standards, OSHA holds public hearings to determine whether the standard should be issued or withdrawn. Court rulings upheld OSHA's enforcement of standards through surprise inspections. Given the high ratio of workplaces to OSHA inspectors, however, the agency often is compelled to inspect worksites after an accident has occurred. A program of voluntary compliance was also developed in which employers invite OSHA inspectors to provide assistance in identifying and correcting violations of standards. OSHA's Office of Cooperative Programs expected to make about 30,000 visits to jobsites at the request of employers in fiscal year 1994.

OSHA's effectiveness in reducing industrial injury and illness has been debated since its earliest years. There was a 27 percent decline in the actual number of workplace fatalities from 1974 to 1986 and a 40 percent decline in the rate of fatalities over these same years. However, in his *Cooperation and Conflict in Occupational Safety and Health*, Richard Wokutch cites several studies that argue that these declines are not readily attributable to OSHA's actions. Consistent with the anti-regulatory agenda of the Reagan Administration, OSHA suffered substantial cutbacks in the 1980s. In the budget for fiscal year 1982, OSHA funding fell to $195 million, down from $205 million in fiscal year 1981, and the number of funded positions was reduced by 19 percent.

Right-to-know laws were an important development in industrial safety legislation. The first of these laws was OSHA's Hazard Communication Standard, enacted in 1983. The **Environmental Protection Agency (EPA)** is also engaged in the administration of Right-to-know laws as a result of the Superfund Amendments and Reauthorization Act of 1986. Right-to-know laws require that dangerous materials in the workplace be identified and that workers be informed of these dangers as well as trained in their safe use.

Under the Clinton Administration, OSHA began issuing higher fines and increasing its finding of "willful violation." OSHA also proposed a 15 to 20 percent increase in the number of inspectors in 1994. OSHA fined General Motors Corp. $1.9 million and Bridgestone/Firestone Inc. $7.5 million in 1994. In both cases, a worker was killed when the machine he was repairing turned on accidently. OSHA regulations require that power be disconnected from all machines being serviced.

Worker fatality rates were nearly ten times higher in 1910 than in 1980 and declined by 50 percent from

1974 to 1994. Nonetheless, worker injury and illness rates remained essentially the same from 1974 to 1994. OSHA estimated that deaths and injuries in the workplace would cost businesses $115 billion in 1994. There was a substantially higher number of worker fatalities at small firms from 1988 to 1992. An analysis of 500,000 federal and state inspection records for these years revealed that 4,337 workers died while working for firms with fewer than 20 employees, whereas 127 died while working for firms with more than 2,500 employees.

One of the important aspects of industrial safety programs is the identification of hazards. Managers typically determine hazards by the examination of accident records, interviews with engineers and equipment operators, and the advice of safety specialists, such as OSHA or insurance companies.

Approximately one-fourth of worker's compensation claims result from the handling of materials, including not only manual handling, but also semi-automated handling and material handling with powered equipment, such as forklifts. Fully 80 percent of injuries resulting from the handling of materials are injuries to the lower back. Most back injuries result not from a single incident, but from prolonged repetition. The development of automatic palletizing machinery has eliminated one of the tasks most responsible for causing lower back injury.

Based on a NIOSH study, the Kaiser Aluminum and Chemical Corporation undertook a safety program for forklift operators. One of Kaiser's and NIOSH's findings was that most forklift accidents occurred when operators were backing up. After identifying this hazard, Kaiser developed an operating procedure that required a redesign of the exhaust systems on their propane-fueled forklifts, such that forklift operators could improve their visibility when backing up without breathing in exhaust.

About one-tenth of industrial accidents result from operating machinery, and these accidents often result in severe injury. Among the most dangerous types of machinery are power presses and woodworking tools, which most commonly cause injury to the hands. A number of mechanisms have been developed to safeguard against such injuries. The simplest of these are barrier guards, in which the moving parts of machinery are enclosed in a protective housing. These safeguards are typically used in conjunction with sensors so that the machine cannot be operated without them. Other types of safeguards include those which prevent a machine from operating unless a worker has both hands properly in place, automated material feeding devices, warning labels, and color coding.

LONG-TERM PROBLEMS GAINING ATTENTION

One of the effects of the establishment of OSHA, NIOSH, and the Right-to-Know laws was a shifting emphasis from traditional industrial safety issues to more long-term health issues. Among the common types of occupational illnesses are skin disorders, "repeated trauma" disorders such as carpel tunnel syndrome, hearing loss, respiratory problems, cancer, and diseases of the nervous system. More generally, industrial health hazards are typically categorized into three classes: chemical hazards, in which the body absorbs toxins; ergonomic hazards, such as those resulting from improper lifting or repetitive stress; and physical hazards, in which the worker is exposed to temperature extremes, atmospheric pressure, or excessive noise.

Toxins are most commonly ingested through inhalation, and the most commonly inhaled substances are dust, fumes, and smoke. Toxins are also commonly absorbed through the skin. Skin disorders result in approximately 200,000 lost working days each year. The most common of these disorders is dermatitis, which is particularly problematic in the food preparation and chemical industries.

Among the most commonly-used toxins are industrial solvents. The toxicity of solvents varies widely by type, but the most toxic of these are carcinogens and can cause permanent damage to the nervous system through prolonged occupational overexposure. In addition, organic solvents, such as those made from petroleum, are often highly flammable. Tightly-fitted respirators with activated charcoal filters are used to protect against inhalation of organic solvents, particularly in spraying applications in which solvents are atomized. Ventilation systems comprised of fans and ducts are also used to control airborne toxins of all types. Rubber gloves are commonly used to prevent skin absorption of organic solvents.

One of the most rapidly-growing types of reported occupational injury is what the U.S. Bureau of Labor Statistics refers to as "disorders associated with repeated trauma." These conditions result from repeatedly performing the same tasks over a prolonged period of time. For the manufacturing sector, they accounted for 47 percent of worker's compensation claims in 1986, up from just 20 percent in 1976. By 1994, repetitive stress disorders accounted for fully 60 percent of all workplace injuries. This increase results at least in part from the fact that a number of these disorders, such as carpel tunnel syndrome, have only recently been diagnosed and compensated. Workers suffering from these disorders have also filed claims under the **Americans with Disabilities Act**. Joseph Dear, who became the head of OSHA in 1993, stated that protecting workers from repetitive stress injuries was a top priority for the agency.

SEE ALSO: Comprehensive Environmental Response, Compensation & Liablity Act of 1980 (Superfund)

[David Kucera]

FURTHER READING:

"BFS Plans to Fight OSHA Citations," *Modern Tire Dealer*, May 1994.

"Clinton Plan Boosts MSHA and OSHA Funding," *Pit and Quarry*, March 1994.

Colling, David A. *Industrial Safety: Management and Technology*. Prentice Hall, 1990.

Dallabrida, Dale. "OSHA Targets Injury from Repeated Motion," *USA Today*, November 23, 1993.

Feder, Barnaby. "A Spreading Pain, and Cries for Justice," *New York Times*, June 5, 1994.

"GM Fined $1.9 Million After Oklahoma Death," *Washington Post*, April 8, 1994.

"LOTO Penalties: OSHA's 'Wake-up'," *PIMA*, July 1994.

Marsh, Barbara. "Workers at Risk: Chance of Getting Hurt is Generally Far Higher at Small Companies," *Wall Street Journal*, February 3, 1994.

Noble, Barbara Presley. "At Work; Breathing New Life into OSHA," *New York Times*, January 23, 1994.

"OSHA: Clinton Administration Comes Out in Favor of Reform of the Occupational Safety & Health Administration (OSHA)," *Cosmetics and Toiletries*, May 1994.

"OSHA: Injuries, Deaths Cost Firms $115 Billion a Year," *Journal of Commerce and Commercial*, May 3, 1994.

"OSHA to Get Tough on Safety and Ergonomic Standards," *Meat Processing*, February 1994.

"Small-Business Owners Get Cleanup Tips from OSHA," *Wall Street Journal*, July 12, 1994.

Wokutch, Richard E. *Cooperation and Conflict in Occupational Safety and Health: A Multination Study of the Automotive Industry*. Praeger, 1990.

INFLATION

Inflation is commonly understood as an increase in the price level. Formally, it is defined as the rate of change in the price level. Thus, an inflation rate of five percent per annum means that the price level is increasing at the rate of five percent. However, inflation need not always be positive. It could be a negative number, in which case the price level would be declining. Of course, a negative inflation rate, termed deflation, is very uncommon. Most economies face positive rates of inflation year after year.

If the inflation rate is positive and an individual's **income** remains constant, his or her real standard of living will fall as the individual's income will be worth less and less in successive periods. Let us assume that a household earns $50,000 per year and the income remains fixed at this level in the future. If the inflation rate persists at ten percent per year, the **purchasing power** of the household income will also keep declining at the rate of ten percent per year. At the end of the five year period, prices will be one and a half times greater. This will lead to the household being able to buy only two thirds of the goods and services it was able to buy at the beginning of the period.

MEASUREMENT OF THE INFLATION RATE

Inflation rate is derived by calculating the rate of change in a **price index**. A price index, in turn, measures the level of prices of goods and services at any point of time. The number of items included in a price index vary depending on the objective of the index. Usually three kinds of price indices are periodically reported by government sources. They all have their particular advantages and uses. The first index is called the **consumer price index** (CPI), which measures the average retail prices paid by consumers for goods and services bought by them. About 400 items are included in this index. The second price index used to measure the inflation rate is called the producer price index (PPI). It is a much broader measure than the consumer price index because it measures the wholesale prices of approximately 3000 items. The items included in this index are those that are typically used by producers (manufacturers and businesses) and thus contain many raw materials and semifinished goods. The third measure of inflation is the called the **implicit price deflator**. This index measures the prices of all goods and services included in the calculation of the current output of goods and services in the economy, known as **gross domestic product** (GDP). It is the broadest measure of the price level.

The three measures of the inflation rate are most likely to move in the same direction, even though not to the same extent. Differences can arise due to the differing number of goods and services included for the purpose of compiling the three indices. In general, if one hears about the inflation rate number in the popular media, it is most likely to be the one based on the CPI.

[Anandi P. Sahu]

FURTHER READING:

Froyen, Richard T. *Macroeconomics: Theories and Policies*. 4th ed. New York: Macmillan Publishing Company, 1993.

Gordon, Robert J. *Macroeconomics*. 6th ed. New York: HarperCollins College Publishers, 1993.

Sommers, Albert T. *The U.S. Economy Demystified*. Lexington, MA: Lexington Books, 1985.

INFOMERCIALS

An infomercial is a 30- or 60-minute broadcast commercial where the emphasis is on delivering extensive sales messages in a natural format. It differs from the typical television commercial in respect to amount of time, amount of information, and amount of reality. Although the infomercial format has been around for several years, the modern-day infomercial bloomed in 1984 when deregulation freed television stations and cable networks to sell entire half-hour blocks of air time for **advertising**. What they sold initially were "remnants," the unprofitable, late-night slots that had been the domain of 1950s horror flicks and test patterns.

The historical evolution of infomercials is certainly one of the more interesting stories in modern business. In 1987, for example, American Telecast Corp. of Pasli, PA, produced "Where There's a Will There's an A" with John Ritter as host. Since then, more than a million audio and videocassettes of the study program have been sold for $60 to $90 apiece. Similarly 70-year-old fruit-juice fanatic Jay Kordich was nothing more than an oddity at local trade shows until Trilium Health Products of Seattle put him in an infomercial as its "Juiceman" and launched a nationwide juicing craze. Finally, Mike Levy went from obscurity to self-proclaimed most-watched man on television with his "Amazing Discoveries" infomercials. Among his more amazing feats: selling more than $40 million each year of tooth whitener and car wax.

In the early 1990s, infomercials earned the interest and respect of a more upscale audience. Companies such as Volvo, IBM, AT&T, and Time-Life have all made infomercials. Further, traditional ad agencies such as Foote, Cone and Belding, Ketchum Communications, and Hal Riney have either established their own infomercial departments or have formed partnerships with infomercial production houses.

Three interrelated reasons have been proposed for this growth in infomercials. The first is cost. Infomercials became attractive because of the cheap air time, as few as a few hundred dollars per half-hour, and the relatively small amount they cost to produce, usually somewhere between $150,000 and $500,000 for 30 minutes. A second reason is a result of the tremendous need for alternative programming as the nation's cable system expands to a capacity of as many as 150 channels apiece by the mid-1990s. A third reason is increased strategic credibility. As better companies have become involved with infomercials, an improvement in product quality and implementation has resulted. Celebrity endorsements also provide credibility. Vanna White has cashed in on her famous smile by endorsing Perfect Smile teeth whitener. She helped generate over $20 million in sales for the product in just a few months. A mid-range celebrity can make $25,000 an infomercial, plus up to five percent of gross sales. Consumers see that the stars are using the products and they naturally want to emulate that person. Consequently, infomercials are more and more viewed as a legitimate part of a company's communication strategy.

The mid-1990s do not bode well for infomercials, according to some experts. An increasingly crowded market is pushing up the cost of airtime and crimping bottom lines. Major marketers are leaving. The boom hasn't gone bust yet: infomercial revenue—estimated at $900 million in 1993, up 20 percent from 1992—could top $1 billion in 1994. Today, about one in seven shows prove successful.

Along with the growth of infomercial credibility, there have also been positive changes in the profile of the infomercial viewer. The old perception of the infomercial buyer was the same as the perception of the home-shopping buyer: somebody who has nothing better to do at three in the morning but buy something they don't need at a price they can't afford. According to a 1993 study conducted by National Infomercial Marketing Association, the results reveal a majority are married women, ages 26 to 45, with incomes of $25,000 to $50,000. But 31 percent are men, and 11 percent have incomes of more than $75,000. Among other findings, 92 percent said they are satisfied or very satisfied with the products they bought; 95 percent said they would buy more products from infomercials; and 66 percent said they are more likely to buy a product from a 30-minute infomercial than a shorter TV commercial.

In conclusion, infomercials are in a transition from early skepticism and junk products to quality products sold by major manufacturers and retailers. Although the future looks bright, potential problems remain.

[John J. Burnett]

FURTHER READING:

Haley, Kathy. "The Infomercial Begins a New Era as a Marketing Tool for Top Brands," *Advertising Age*. January 25, 1993, p. M-3

Marin, Rick. "Infomercials," *New York Times*. October 4, 1992, pp. 1, 11-12.

Miller, Annetta. "Highbrow Goes Lowbrow," *Newsweek*. April 5, 1993, pp. 48-49.

Zoglin, Richard. "It's Amazing! Call Now!," *Time*, June 17, 1991, p. 71.

INFORMATION MANAGEMENT AND PROCESSING

Information is the fuel that is driving business in the late twentieth century. Those organizations that can best manage the information resources available to them will be the more successful organizations in their respective industry sectors. Information management and processing itself is concerned with a number of components. First there is the information that the organization produces internally—such as reports, correspondence, financial data, and statistical information—which may be used only within the organization or both within and outside the organization. The second component is information that is external to the organization but important and useful. This kind of information falls into a number of subcategories such as competitor intelligence, trade and industry association data, government information, business literature, and other information that may not be of a specific business nature but still has relevance for anorganization. But knowing that these different kinds of information exist is only the beginning. The third component involves the format in which information can be found: print, electronic, microfilm, audio and/or video, on some combination of these. Or, if the information in question deals with the organization's culture, it may exist as oral tradition, passed along from one organizational generation to the next. The last two components, organizing and retrieving information, deal with how the organization processes information. More specifically, this involves organizing the information so it can be retrieved when it is necessary. All the information in the world will not make an organization successful if the right piece of information can not be found efficiently and effectively when it is needed.

INTERNAL INFORMATION

Internal information is created by the organization both for its own use (a policy or procedure manual) or for distribution outside the organization (a product catalog or corporate annual report). Depending upon the organization's own philosophy of information management—as well as reporting requirements of federal, state, local, or foreign government agencies and data needed by trade or professional associations and similar bodies—abroad or narrow view as to which internal information should be retained, organized, and retrieved can be adopted. Furthermore, depending on the ''information investment'' made by the organization, the information management function is usually performed by one (or a combination) of three groups: (1) the corporate library or information center, (2) the records management department, or (3) the **management informa-**

tion systems (MIS) department (or its equivalent). For those organizations with all three of these groups, a **chief information officer** (CIO) is usually responsible for coordinating the information function of the organization.

EXTERNAL INFORMATION

External information is that body of information not created by the organization itself, but which the organization needs to function more effectively. This information can range from a subscription to the *Wall Street Journal* providing general business news, to a subscription to a trade or professional publication providing more industry-specific information, to purchasing a market research report providing very detailed, market-specific information. Organizations manage this kind of information by one of two methods or combination thereof. The first method of managing external information is through a library or information center. This method tries to ensure that all necessary information is accessed by the organization in the most efficient and cost-effective manner possible. The trade-off is the cost of maintaining this kind of operation. The second method of accessing external information is to use commercial information services, also called information brokers, to retrieve external information as it is needed. This eliminates the ongoing costs of maintaining an information center, while trying to ensure access to needed information. If the organization uses a lot of external information, however, this method can get very expensive. Some organizations fail to employ any method to manage external information. This usually leads to not having the desired information when it is needed, and it also leads to a good deal of duplication of the same information, as different people within the organization acquire information that the organization already has.

INFORMATION FORMAT

The primary concerns involving format deal with the format in which the information is originally found, the format in which the information may be stored, and the format in which the organization needs the information for use. A major part of processing and managing information in today's environment is using appropriate information technologies to deal with format issues. Information that is originally in print may need to be scanned or otherwise digitized for storage in electronic format, only to be retrieved and incorporated into a multimedia format for presentation.

ORGANIZATION OF INFORMATION

This area perhaps represents the biggest challenge to information management. For many organizations it is no longer a question of trying to determine if information exists on a certain topic; the challenge is sorting through all the information available to find the most useful information. By organizing the information in the most appropriate manner, the organization can help ensure the required information will be at hand when needed.

The guiding principle in organizing information resources is utility—what information will be used, how will the information be used, how often will the information be used, by whom will the information be used, and where will the information be used? Knowing the answers to these questions will allow the organization to adopt an organizational scheme that will be both useful and usable. The organization should not feel it has to use an organizational scheme that already exists if there are unique responses about how or who is using the information that would nullify the benefits of those existing systems. Additionally, the organization may find that due to different formats of the information, different users of the information—or similar concerns—different organizational schemes may be necessary for different types of information or even for the same information that is used in different ways.

A key element in establishing the organizational scheme to be used is how the information will be indexed. This in turn will depend on the kind of information in question and how it will be accessed. Indexing systems range from the very rudimentary that allow for only one or two possible access points, to very sophisticated systems that index virtually every word in a document and provide what is known as full-text retrieval.

INFORMATION RETRIEVAL

The true test of any information management system is its ability to retrieve relevant information when it is needed. Regardless of where the information was created, in which format it is found, and how easy or difficult it is to locate, if the needed information can be accessed then the organization's information management system is successful. Depending upon the kind of information to be retrieved, as well as the organization's needs, there are three types or levels of retrieval an information management system should provide. One system may provide all three levels, or an organization may employ a different system for each type of retrieval.

The first type of retrieval is known as reference retrieval. This system is designed to provide the requester with references to the actual information that is being sought. With this kind of system, retrieval is a two-step process, first accessing the references and second accessing the information itself. This system needs basic indexing that allows access by one or two key elements at a time. The next level of retrieval is known as information retrieval. This system is designed to provide the requester with the specific information sought in a one-step process. This type of retrieval system is good for factual information, as well as financial and other numeric information (such as census data). The indexing to support this kind of retrieval is usually more detailed than for reference retrieval, depending on the number of elements or parameters used in searching for the needed information. The final type of retrieval is known as item retrieval because the system provides the actual document sought, again in one step. This kind of retrieval is based on more-sophisticated indexing that allows searching the full-text of the document itself or searching an abstract that describes the contents of the document.

CONCLUSION

Systems to manage and process information can be highly complex or extremely simple depending on the needs of the organization. At one end of the spectrum is the one person in the organization who just "knows" where everything is. The organizational scheme is in this person's head. The drawback to this is its dependence on just one person and when that person is gone (either temporarily or permanently) the system collapses. If a different person can come in and institute a new system that works just as well, however, the long range result is the same. The other end of the spectrum can take many different scenarios—from a system that is so complex it inhibits use, to a system that is usable by people throughout the organization regardless of their technological expertise. As the amount of information increases and the technologies for information management continue their rapid development, organizations will be challenged to keep their information needs in clear focus. This will allow an organization to develop a system that enhances its productivity and profitability by providing an uninterrupted flow of useful information.

SEE ALSO: Database Management Systems; Proprietary Information

[William Fisher]

INFORMATION TECHNOLOGIES

Information technologies encompass a broad spectrum of technologies used to create, store, retrieve, and disseminate information. This information can be text, graphics, voice/audio, video, or some combination of these. One goal of most information technology is to make the transfer from one information format to another or the combination of information formats as seamless and transparent to the user as possible. Another goal is to be able to do this regardless of any differences in operating systems, **software** applications, or kinds of equipment used between where the information is coming from and where the information is going.

New information may be entered into a system using a variety of software, such as **word processing**, **spreadsheets**, or **database management programs**. Scanning devices may also be used if the information already exists in print. Other technologies allow access to information in the system, so it can be pulled out of the system for use elsewhere, merged into a different document or other information product, or used within the existing system. Computer simulation, for example, allows someone to run information through a number of different scenarios to get an idea of what could happen before an action actually takes place. Use of **computer networks** allows information to be easily exchanged among members of the network, as well as allowing simultaneous access to the information. Certain technologies such as **electronic mail**, fax systems, voice mail, and other **telecommunications** enhancements have become so widely used that some businesses could not function without them.

Information technologies are constantly changing. Enhancements to existing technologies continue to be introduced into the marketplace, while at the same time new technologies continue to be developed. For those who view humankind as a breed of innovators and entrepreneurs, the way in which we have embraced information technologies certainly substantiates that view.

SEE ALSO: Automation; Computer-Aided Design (CAD) & Computer-Aided Manufacturing (CAM); Computer Conferencing; Computers & Computer Systems; Desktop Publishing; Electronic Data Interchange; Geographic Information Systems; Graphical User Interface (GUI); Management Information Systems (MIS); Microcomputers in Business; Office Automation; Optical Character Recognition Devices

[William Fisher]

INFRASTRUCTURE

Infrastructure refers to a wide variety of systems in place to support the prevailing industrial society, in both the public and private sectors. The current definition encompasses a number of basic structures and services, including sewers, housing, education, and highways and roads. Recently, **communication systems**, **computer networks**, and information superhighways have also been included in the definition of infrastructure.

In the United States, the majority of public infrastructure activity, about 85 percent, has been undertaken by state and local governments. To build, oversee, and maintain the full range of public works, state and local governments provide fiscal, governmental, and technological services. Additionally, these governments sometimes enter into arrangements with private companies to help them perform these tasks. State and local investments in the infrastructure can be divided into three groups: (1) the core infrastructure (water supply facilities, sewers, and utility and transit systems); (2) buildings (schools and hospitals); and (3) water resource projects (especially flood control).

The U.S. infrastructure is arguably the most extensive in the world, and after years of technological development and construction, has become a tangible asset improving the quality of life for the nation's population. Most facilities and structures comprising U.S. infrastructure were built as a series of separate and distinct projects by federal, state, and local agencies, as well as by independent authorities and private corporations. Because many of the investments were made in earlier decades and because there was little coordination between the agencies involved, the U.S. infrastructure is aging, inefficient, and inadequate.

HISTORICAL ASPECTS

From 1929 to 1969, the investment in public infrastructure increased consistently. This increase can be attributed to rapid growth in the overall **gross national product** (GNP) as well as an increase in the percentage of GNP spent on infrastructure investments. The reason that a great deal of attention was given to infrastructure needs can be attributed to the demographic demands of the day. For example, during the 1950s and 1960s, U.S. investment in its infrastructure rose sharply, in part to meet the increased educational demands of the baby boom generation.

Since the 1970s, there has been a drastic decline in funding that supports the infrastructure of the United States, as well as in funding for other countries' infrastructures. In constant dollars, federal grants that support state and local efforts have remained stable, representing a decline in the real amount of federal funding. In the 1980s, this trend continued as most of the wealth of the United States was devoted to consumption rather than to the enhancement of the nation's infrastructure (or any other form of future investment). Thus, the current infrastructure has not kept pace with the growing population.

Some of this decline in spending was in response to budget pressures felt in all levels of government, but much of it can be attributed to an inattention to the importance of top-quality public amenities and to a shortsighted perspective about the value of investing in the future. This perspective began to change somewhat during the 1990s, a decade marked by the end of the Cold War. During this time, officials in the federal government started to discuss alternative ways to spend the funds formerly spent on the military, although these discussions were waylaid somewhat by the Persian Gulf conflict. There seemed to be a growing realization, however, that additional money should be devoted to repairing the existing infrastructure and adding to it.

ECONOMIC IMPLICATIONS

The state of the nation's economy plays a large role in infrastructure needs. Obviously, a very direct impact on the economy are the federal, state, and local tax bases available to pay for the needed infrastructure investments. Changes in the pace and areas of economic growth, however, are also very important—critical to both the demand for and the ability to support infrastructure investments. Economic growth has numerous effects on the demand for a nation's infrastructure. First, in a fast-growing economy, infrastructures are placed under great use, deteriorate quickly, and require replacement frequently. In slower economies, the opposite is true. Second, as the economy changes, modifications must be made to capital outlays. For example, as the U.S. economy changes from reliance on manufacturing to reliance on high-tech industries, the mix of infrastructure needs changes. Ensuring that an infrastructure is in place to facilitate communications may one day be as important as planning for highways. Third, changes in the economy cause shifts in the population that, in turn, require modified infrastructure investments. Thus, in some areas of the country, rapidly growing economies and populations strain existing infrastructures; at the same time, areas of the country experiencing minimal growth may have situations of overcapacity.

DECLINING INVESTMENTS: THE REAL IMPACT

In 1960 U.S. federal public spending on infrastructure was 5 percent of **gross domestic product** (GDP); by the mid-1990s, this figure was down to 2.5 percent. Similarly, the capital spending on the building of infrastructures worldwide has declined. The reasons behind this decline in spending can be attributed to numerous factors. First of all, many countries have experienced large budget deficits in recent years and thus do not have the extra capital to spend on their infrastructures. Second, tax revenues in many coun-

tries have been stagnant since the oil crisis of the 1970s. Third, many countries have increased their spending on welfare, using money usually spent on the public sector, and have underestimated the increasing burden that population growth and other societal changes place on existing infrastructures. The long delays in the planning and implementation of major projects is a fourth significant problem. Delays are caused by the increasingly complex nature of many of these major projects as well as by the increased scrutiny and opposition by environmental advocacy groups and landowners.

The decline in government spending, however, may not be as significant as it first seems. For instance, the prices associated with some aspects of major infrastructure projects have declined due to better technology. Furthermore, in some areas of the nation's infrastructure, new investments have been made by the private sector, especially in the areas of **telecommunications** and the generation and distribution of electric power. Indeed, in some places, there is actually overcapacity of substructure services.

As one may expect, however, the spending decline of the last two and one-half decades is not without negative consequences. In the 1990s, there was almost a certainty that the increasing population combined with other events, such as globalization and regional economic integration, would increase worldwide demand for transportation, telecommunications, waste disposal, energy, and other elements associated with infrastructure over the years to come. For example, in the United States, the increased use of automobiles led to congestion on public highways that was projected to cause traffic delays of four billion vehicle hours by the year 2005. In the European Union, similar traffic delays were projected as European borders continued to come down; in fact, travel between the EU countries was projected to grow about 130 percent by 2015. Similarly, studies projected that the use of the railroad system in Europe was likely to triple by 2005.

The financial implications of infrastructure investments necessary to meet projected demands was staggering. To meet the projected needs of the U.S. infrastructure until the turn of the century, in the mid-1990s the U.S. Congressional Budget Office projected that it would cost taxpayers approximately $800 billion. And the United States was not alone in these cost projections. In Europe and Asia, countries face proportionately large costs.

When finances are short, most infrastructure needs have to be met by the public sector. Governments all over the world are in debt, averaging 40 percent of GDP in countries belonging to the **Organization of Economic Cooperation and Development** (OECD). Although budget deficits were projected to decline in the latter part of the 1990s, there are other factors, such as the projected rising health costs associated with aging populations, that will require increased spending. Thus, governments in the United States and abroad are faced with the tasks of repairing existing infrastructures and building new ones to meet future needs, even though, economically, they will have a very difficult time meeting very basic needs.

[Kathryn Snavely]

FURTHER READING:

Gould, James P., and Andrew C. Lemer. *Toward Infrastructure Improvement.* Washington, DC: National Academy Press, 1994.

Munnell, Alicia H., ed. *Is There a Shortfall in Public Capital Investment?* Boston, Massachusetts: Federal Reserve Bank of Boston, 1991.

Organization for Economic Cooperation and Development. *Assessing Structural Reform: Lessons for the Future.* Paris, France: Head of Publications Service, OECD, 1994.

Organization for Economic Cooperation and Development. *Infrastructure Policies for the 1990s.* Paris, France: Head of Publications Service, OECD, 1993.

Organization for Economic Cooperation and Development. *Urban Infrastructure: Finance and Management.* Paris, France: Head of Publications Service, OECD, 1991.

Perry, David C. *Building the Public City.* New Park, California: Sage Publications, 1995.

Stein, Jay M., ed. *Public Infrastructure Planning and Management.* New Park, California: Sage Publications, 1988.

INJUNCTION

An injunction is a court order issued by a judge that prohibits an individual, business firm, labor union, or other type of organization from engaging in a specified action. An injunction is intended to protect the property rights of an individual or business from being violated. It is not used to punish violations of the law, although it may be used to enforce a breach of contract.

A preliminary injunction may be issued when a lawsuit is initiated to protect property rights while the litigation is in progress. Such an injunction is often issued on a temporary basis without a hearing. Preliminary injunctions are frequently sought in patent infringement cases, where the plaintiff alleging a patent violation obtains a preliminary injunction against the party who is charged with infringing on the plaintiff's patent rights. In such cases a judge may issue a preliminary injunction prohibiting the defendant from manufacturing or distributing the product or products alleged to be in violation of the plaintiff's patent rights. The effect of such an injunction may be to put the competitor out of business, especially if it is a smaller company and the patent suit takes a long time

to resolve. Consequently, judges may grant such preliminary injunctions only when there is a reasonable likelihood that the patent infringement claim will be successful.

In the early 20th century injunctions were frequently used by big business to prevent **labor unions** from going on strike. The Norris-LaGuardia Act of 1932 limited the ability of federal courts to issue injunctions in labor disputes. The Labor Management Relations Act of 1947, also known as the **Taft-Hartley Act**, allowed the president of the United States to seek an injunction when a labor dispute threatened national health or safety.

In the realm of contracts, an injunction may be used to enforce a negative covenant (an agreement not to perform certain acts or services) when there is a breach of contract. For example, a recording company may seek an injunction against a recording artist who is under contract to prevent the artist from recording for another label or performing in violation of specific articles of the contract.

SEE ALSO: Copyright

[David Bianco]

INNOVATION

Innovation is the act of introducing something new. Innovation in business differs from creativity in that the latter is generally associated with the generation of new ideas. In contrast, innovation refers to taking those new ideas and actually implementing them in the marketplace. Thus, creativity is simply one element of the innovation process in which new ideas are transformed into profits.

Characteristics of innovative individuals and organizations are identified below, as are opportunities for innovation. Innovation-based market strategies are reviewed and a well-known model used to foster innovation in organizations is described.

FUNCTION AND ATTRIBUTES OF INNOVATION

Entrepreneurs, scientists, and other innovators in business had always assumed that creativity and innovation were necessary to succeed and advance in a constantly changing world and marketplace. Evidencing this theory were hugely successful industrial pioneers, such as Henry Ford. Ford achieved great success by innovating mass production techniques that boosted productivity and output. But the Ford Motor Co. also demonstrated the results of failing to innovate—because Ford's organization failed to retain its creative edge, other manufacturers (i.e., General Motors Corp.) managed to exploit Ford's manufacturing breakthroughs with additional innovations of their own, eventually eclipsing the success of Ford.

To help explain the functions, causes, and effects of imagination and inventiveness, U.S. researchers began to apply scientific methods to the study of innovation and creativity during the mid-1900s. A plethora of research, particularly during the 1960s, served to highlight the importance of innovation in organizations, identify characteristics of innovative individuals and groups, and establish a framework for fostering creativity and inventiveness. For example, various research efforts quantified the link between creativity and risk-taking (McClelland; Glover and Sutter); examined characteristics of successful inventors (Chambers; Roe); measured the creativity levels of different professionals (MacKinnon); identified sources of innovation (Drucker); and brought to light other aspects of innovation, particularly as it applied to business.

In general, research has focused on two areas: 1) characteristics and cognitive abilities of creative individuals that lead to creative thinking; and 2) environments that foster creativity and innovation in organizations. Numerous models have been used to describe the personality traits of innovative individuals. In general, those models suggest that people that have a high level of creativity and innovative ability are open to new ideas and willing to take risks.

Creativity is similar to music ability in that theory and techniques that will enhance a person's ability to innovate can be learned and practiced. In addition, background and environment influence creative ability. For example, a positive correlation has been shown to exist between creative ability and an unpredictable, abnormal childhood. Indeed, the most creative individuals are often those that had a childhood punctuated by diversity and family conflict but combined with opportunities to learn.

Creativity is also related to mental aptitude, meaning that some innovators, like some musicians, have a greater capacity for inventiveness. For instance, research has revealed two important aptitudes characteristic of the most innovative thinkers: "opposition thinking" and "homospatial thinking." Opposition, or janusian, thinking refers to one's ability to conceptualize and integrate opposite or conflicting ideas simultaneously (the term "janusian" is derived from the Roman god Janus, who had a bearded face on two sides of his head). Homospatial thinking is the ability to conceive of more than one entity occupying the same space.

In addition to opposition and homospatial thinking, several other aptitudes and personality traits have been ascribed to people most likely to be good innovators. Different occupations and situations require different attributes for innovation. In general, though, people that score high on creativity tests are conceptually fluent, which means that they can generate large numbers of ideas rapidly for a variety of requests. They also have a high degree of conceptual flexibility, as indicated by their ability to easily discard paradigms and simultaneously accept different approaches. Likewise, an innovator's tendency to give unpredictable answers or unusual interpretations of events reflects creativity. Innovative individuals exhibit a preference for complexity and an independence of judgment—they tend to be more opinionated and stubborn. And they tend to view authority as temporary or not worthy of moral obligation. They are also apt to be impulsive.

While aptitude, background, and learned skills can all contribute to a person's ability to create and innovate, traits are inconsequential if they are not combined with hard work. Indeed, research has shown that one of the most common qualities possessed by notable innovative individuals is discipline and a commitment to see their ideas become reality. Consider, for example, the case of Howard Head, an aerospace engineer and ski enthusiast. Head invented metal skis in the 1940s and tried unsuccessfully to get professional skiers to embrace his skis for several years. Head became known as a fanatic who had become obsessed with a frivolous concept. After failing for seven years and eventually going broke, Head's skis finally achieved massive success in the marketplace and were credited with helping to create the ski boom of the 1950s.

GROUP TRAITS AND THE INNOVATION PROCESS

Like individuals, groups and organizations also exhibit certain characteristics that reflect a propensity to innovate. For instance, companies in which employees are given a lot of responsibility for initiating new projects tend to be more innovative, as do companies that offer their workers a high degree of job security (i.e. the freedom to make mistakes without fear of retribution). Minimal interference from superiors also enhances creativity. And the most innovative organizations successfully match the skills and interests of their workers to job tasks.

In general, companies in the United States that are more likely to be considered innovative are those that score highly in comparison to non-innovative firms in the following trait categories, in rough order of importance: freedom, risk taking, idea-support, time to generate ideas, freedom to debate and challenge, and trust. More specifically, ten stimuli to creativity have been identified (*Handbook for Creative and Innovative Managers*, McGraw-Hill, 1988).

The five most commonly occurring stimuli are: 1) freedom and control to get a job done with minimal supervision; 2) good project management, including the supervisor's ability to match individuals to tasks and protect the group from destructive outside intervention; 3) sufficient resources to realize ideas; 4) encouragement, or the support of upper management and peers to take risks; and 5) a corporate climate that is generally amenable to making suggestions and trying new things. Other important organizational attributes include recognition and feedback, sufficient time to execute ideas, and a challenging environment.

Although certain characteristics are important to facilitate innovation in organizations, the existence of the personal attributes described earlier do not necessarily have to be present in all workers for an atmosphere of innovation to exist. In fact, three particular personality types—risk takers, caretakers, and undertakers—are found in most groups, all of which can contribute positively to the organizational creative process. Most people lean toward one personality type but occasionally exhibit traits of all three categories.

Risk takers are the innovators in an organization. They possess the creative traits described earlier. Caretakers, in contrast, try to maintain the status quo. They tend to see changes as threats, rather than opportunities, and typically respond to outside influences only when forced to do so. Finally, undertakers are those people that are extremely resistant to change and are even willing to bury projects or sabotage ideas to maintain the status quo. They are often a detriment to the innovation process but may assume certain organizational roles that facilitate the innovation process.

Indeed, organizational innovation benefits from a diversity of personality types that fill different roles. After all, if every person in a company is extremely innovative, free-spirited, and nonconformist, the entity might lack balance and grounding. Thus, a multiplicity of personality types and traits can be accommodated by the five-step organizational innovation process. The first stage of the innovation process is idea generation, which involves thinking of new ideas, developing solutions for problems, and identifying opportunities. Idea generators are often experts in one or two fields and are therefore able to recognize niche opportunities. They often enjoy working alone and are able to think abstractly and conceptually.

Championing, the second stage of the organizational innovation process, entails selling the ideas to others in the organization and securing resources to execute ideas. Individuals that fulfill this function are referred to as "intrapreneurs." In contrast to idea generators, champions are more apt to possess a wide range of interests, have general knowledge about several areas of a company or industry, and like to work with and influence other people. They are also more likely to be very energetic and to take risks.

Project leading is the third step of the process. It encompasses activities such as leading teams, planning and organizing projects, and balancing project goals with available resources and organizational needs. Effective project leaders are good at working with other people and fostering group cooperation. They are also adept at company politics and have a broad knowledge of company functions, such as **finance**, production, and **marketing**.

Gatekeeping, the fourth stage of the innovation process, entails tracking influences outside of the organization through conferences, journals, friends at other companies, and similar sources. Gatekeepers pass the information on to others and serve as an information source, and sometimes critic, to idea generators, champions, and leaders. They facilitate group communication and project coordination. Good gatekeepers typically enjoy working with other people, are personable, and have a relatively high degree of technical competence. The gatekeeper role is one in which a noninnovative personality may still function to the benefit of the group.

Finally, the coaching phase of the organizational innovation process consists of encouraging and assisting team members, protecting the team from destructive outside forces (e.g. undertakers in other departments or groups), and securing the support of top-level management. Employees that fill the coaching role in the innovative process are usually good listeners. In addition, they tend to be less opinionated than their coworkers, a characteristic not ascribed to the stereotype creative personality. Effective coaches are also proficient at politicking and have proven experience sponsoring new ideas.

SOURCES OF INNOVATION

Innovation is occasionally the result of a stroke of genius. More often, though, it occurs in response to a problem or opportunity that arises either inside or outside of an organization. Management guru Peter F. Drucker has identified four internal and three external impetuses for innovation. Internal prompts include unexpected occurrences, incongruities, process needs, and industry or market changes.

Unexpected occurrences include mishaps, such as a failed product introduction. It is often through such unexpected failures (or successes) that new ideas are born from new information brought to light. For instance, Ford's failed Edsel gave the company new information about marketing that allowed it to achieve stellar gains with succeeding products. Unexpected occurrences can also take the form of accidents. For example, the hugely successful Nutrasweet artificial sweetener was created by an accident during a project completely unrelated to sweeteners.

Incongruities result from a difference in a company's or industry's perception and reality. For example, although the demand for steel continued to grow between 1950 and 1970 profits in the steel industry fell. This incongruity caused some innovators to develop the steel minimill, a less expensive method of making steel that was also more conducive to changing market demands.

Innovations inspired by process needs are those created to support some other product or process. For example, advertising was innovated as a means of making mass-produced newspapers plausible—to cover the expense of printing the newspapers on the new equipment that made such printing possible, newspaper publishers devised ads.

Industry and market changes, the fourth internal impetus to innovate, often result in the rise (and decline) of successful innovators. For example, innovation and business savvy allowed International Business Machines Corp. (IBM) to effectively dominate the computer industry during the 1970s and early 1980s. However, it failed to respond to a market switch during the 1980s from mainframes to smaller computer systems, particularly workstations and personal computer networks. As a result, IBM's share of the computer market plummeted and profits plunged as more innovative newcomers emerged.

External impetuses to innovate include demographic changes, shifts in perception, and new knowledge. Demographic changes affect all aspects of business. For instance, an influx of Asian and Mexican immigrants into the United States has created new market niches for companies. Likewise, an increase in the level of education of Americans has resulted in a dearth of qualified workers for some low-paying jobs, causing many companies to develop new automation techniques.

Changes in perception also open the door to innovation. For example, despite the fact that health care in the United States has continually gotten better and more accessible, people have become increasingly concerned about their health and the need for better and more accessible care. This change in perception has generated a huge market for health magazines, vitamin supplements, and exercise equipment.

Finally, one of the strongest external impetuses for innovation is new knowledge, or technology. When a new technology emerges innovative companies can profit by exploiting it in new applications and markets. For example, the invention of Kevlar, a synthetic material, has spawned thousands of new product innovations ranging from improved canoes and bullet-proof vests to better tires and luggage.

INNOVATION STRATEGIES FOR ORGANIZATIONS

Two types of strategies for innovation in business are internal and market-based. Internal strategies include programs and initiatives implemented by companies to foster a creative and innovative environment. Those strategies usually seek to develop and nurture the attributes of innovative corporations identified earlier. Specific approaches to encouraging innovation differ by company and industry. For example, an integral aspect of Dow Corning Inc.'s strategy is to form "research partnerships" with its customers that solicit creative input from consumers and help the company to benefit from new market opportunities. Other companies that employ customer partnering programs include Black & Decker Corp. and General Electric.

Rubbermaid, Inc. encourages innovation by requiring that 30 percent of its sales come from products developed during the past five years. An important element of its program is searching for new ideas in other industries, such as the automotive business. Similarly, researchers at Hewlett-Packard (HP) are encouraged to spend at least ten percent of their time toying with pet projects. HP also keeps its labs open 24 hours each day and utilizes small divisions and decentralized decision-making. Likewise, pharmaceutical giant Merck & Co., Inc. gives its researchers time and money to pursue high-risk, high-reward projects—a strategy which has profited the company handsomely.

One of the most innovative firms in the United States, 3M Company, sustains its creative environment by following a set of simple rules. Its keeps its divisions small; division managers must know the first names of all their subordinates, and groups are split up before they surpass $250 million to $300 million in sales. It tolerates failure by promoting risk-taking and experimentation. In fact, divisions must derive at least 25 percent of their profits from products developed during the past five years. 3M also ties salaries and bonuses to the success of new ideas and allows people that generate viable ideas to recruit an action team to develop them. In addition, 3M seeks customer input, shares technology throughout its different divisions, and never "kills" a project in which an employee has faith.

One of the best illustrations of the benefits of 3M's innovation program is Post-it notepads. The adhesive for the pads was developed by 3M researcher Spencer Silver. Unfortunately, the company was unable to find an application for Silver's new adhesive for five years. Company support slipped and his project was eventually abandoned. However, 3M allowed Silver to continue to spend 15 percent of his time looking for a way to use his creation. Finally, the adhesive was used to create one of 3M most successful consumer innovations, Post-it pads.

One of the most renowned strategies to generate innovation in organizations is the "Office of Innovation" model developed by Eastman Kodak Company in the late 1970s. It has since been implemented by several leading organizations, including Amoco Corp., Union Carbide, the U.S. Air Force, and Bell Canada. The Office of Innovation provides a mechanism for drawing people together to brainstorm on ideas that may not even be related to their department or expertise. In fact, its chief benefit is that it promotes cross-fertilization and free-flow of ideas within a company.

Although implementations vary, the model prescribes the use of a decentralized network of individual offices located in different functional areas, such as marketing, finance, and production. Staff members are encouraged to seek employees in other sectors who will come to the office and generate or provide feedback on new ideas. The process is founded on the importance of giving credence to workers' ideas. It involves a five-step process that mimics the five-stage innovation process detailed earlier: idea generation, initial screening, group review, seeking sponsorship, and sponsorship. Kodak estimated that in just one year its Office of Innovation program harvested ideas eventually worth more than $300 million.

MARKET-BASED STRATEGIES

Even companies with the most innovative organizational environments will languish if they fail to effectively market their innovations. For example, just because a firm improves its product doesn't mean that it should necessarily take the improvement to the market. From a strategic standpoint, the company could lose money if it has invested a lot of resources in marketing the original product because the improved version might cannibalize sales. On the other hand, if the company waits too long to introduce the improved version a competitor may innovate earlier and steal market share. Consider the inventors of items like the air conditioner or electric lamp. The innovators of those concepts died before their creations were widely accepted by the marketplace.

Although there are a number of product- and industry-specific strategies that companies may employ to promote their innovations, three basic market-based innovation strategies are leader, quick follow, and slow follow (or no follow). (*Strategic Alternatives*, Amacom, 1979.) A company that adopts a leadership strategy for its invention becomes the first to introduce the innovation to the market. The obvious risk of such a move is that the product or service will be rejected by the marketplace at a potentially enormous cost to the company. However, the leadership strategy may be employed to provide a variety of different benefits.

For instance, companies often introduce an innovation to an existing product or service, calling it "new" or "improved," to breathe new life into it. Or they may bring out an improved product to discourage the competition from trying to steal market share, or to "leapfrog" their competitors. In the case of completely new products or ideas, a company may introduce the innovation in an effort to establish market dominance and attain leadership status.

The quick-follow strategy is often used by established competitors that already lead an industry or market niche. Rather than assume the risk inherent to the leadership strategy, the company will simply wait for one of its competitors to introduce an innovation. Shortly thereafter, the company will follow the leader with a substitute or improvement of the innovation. Quick followers are usually relatively sure of their ability to crush the competition with their established reputation and marketing and distribution channels.

The risk of the quick-follow tactic is that the follower will be unseated by a hugely successful introduction, or that it will lose its reputation as an innovator over time. Other quick followers include smaller competitors that are simply trying to keep up with the competition. They may try to target select market niches. For example, a company may follow with a cheaper version of a new innovation in an effort to lure buyers that can't afford the leader's good or service.

A company that adopts a slow- or no-follow strategy may do so for a number of reasons. It may feel that existing competitive pressures or lackluster market growth make an investment in following an innovation unappealing. Or, the company may realize that it simply lacks the resources or technology necessary to compete with the new innovation. Some companies refuse to introduce or adopt an innovation because they fear that they will lose customers. For instance, a manufacturer of industrial air-conditioners may delay introducing a substantially different technology because it knows that its existing customers have made large capital investments in its existing product line and will be hesitant to buy new equipment. Finally, some companies are so strong in marketing or manufacturing that product innovation is simply not a chief concern—they would prefer to wait until the new innovation is accepted in the market before they follow.

[Dave Mote]

FURTHER READING:

Henry, Jane. *Managing Innovation*. Sage Publications, 1991.

Katz, Ralph. *Managing Professionals in Innovative Organizations*. Ballinger Publishing Company, 1988.

Kotter, John P. *The Leadership Factor.* The Free Press, 1988.

Kuhn, Robert L. *Handbook for Creative and Innovative Managers.* McGraw-Hill Book Company, 1988.

Mescon, Michael H. *Management: Individual and Organizational Effectiveness*, 2nd ed. Harper & Row, Publishers.

Rothschild, William E. *Strategic Alternatives.* Amacom, 1979.

Sayles, Leonard R. *Leadership: Managing in Real Organizations*, 2nd ed. McGraw-Hill Book Company, 1989.

Terkel, M. *Integrative Management, Innovation and New Venturing: A Guide to Sustained Profitability.* Elsevier, 1991.

INPUT-OUTPUT ANALYSIS

Writing in the *New Palgrave Dictionary of Economics,* Wassily Leontief (1906–), who was awarded the 1973 Nobel Prize in Economics for his pioneering work in the area, defined input-output analysis as a "practical extension of the classical theory of general interdependence." Input-output analysis, he further explained, "views the whole economy of a region, a country and even the entire world as single system and sets out to describe and to interpret its operation in terms of directly observable basic structural relationships."

The reference to "classical theory" in the above definition situates Leontief's mode of analysis within a bygone methodological approach practiced by the school of classical theory economists. During the eighteenth and first half of the nineteenth centuries the theoretical perspectives of classical school economists held sway in the field of economics. Many of its principal contributors resided or gained notoriety in England. In general, classical theory economists approached the study of economics from the vantage point of its systematic operation, attempting to understand the mutual interaction between parts and whole. This major distinction set them apart from the core theoretical approach taken by present day neoclassical economics which has dominated formal economic analysis since the 1870s. In direct contrast to classical theory, neoclassical theory builds from the level of individual economic agents and conducts its analysis in terms of the operation of individual markets.

The theoretical works of Adam Smith (1723-90) and David Ricardo (1772-1823) figure most prominently within the school of classical theory. And, while he was critical of and rejected some of their major theoretical propositions, Karl Marx (1818-83) duly acknowledged the contributions of Smith and Ricardo as instrumental to his own investigation into the systematic operation, as opposed to individual market analysis, of a capitalist economy.

While reviving the methodological approach analogous to classical theorists, Leontief's overriding concern focused on how economic systems were structured, the way an economy's component parts interrelate and mutually influence one another. To a limited extent, because input-output analysis deals with aggregate categories, it falls within the purview of **macroeconomics**. Yet because it is applied within the realm of observable and measured phenomena, input-output analysis is considered a branch of **econometrics**. As such, much of the existing literature on the subject is highly technical in nature. Practitioners of input-output analysis converse in a seemingly arcane language that few outside its profession know how to interpret. It draws heavily upon mathematics, especially matrix algebra, and, in the construction of input-output tables, strives to be in strict conformity with a bevy of statistical properties. For these reasons alone many students, academics, professionals, and other interested parties find input-output analysis intimidating. Yet the basic approach to the construction of input-output tables and their analysis is highly accessible.

A salient feature of Leontief's early input-output work resided in its highly disaggregated nature. This allowed for a comprehensively detailed, quantitative grasp of the structured linkages between an economic system's component parts. Parallel to his efforts of compiling a highly disaggregated database, Leontief formulated an equally disaggregated theoretical model. For its time, the empirical implementation of his model presented an unsurpassed challenge. Its numerical computations, both in terms of their complexity and scale, were virtually unknown within the field of economics or, for that matter, within any other empirically grounded social science discipline.

Ironically, around the same time Leontief was busy developing input-output tables, complete with their aggregative and disaggregative capabilities, the general direction of economic research, under the influence of John Maynard Keynes (1883-1946), became increasing dominated by an highly aggregative approach. The foremost concern of Keynesian economics was countering the effects of chronic **unemployment**. This cast a decade's long shadow over Leontief's pathbreaking efforts. Nevertheless, during a time when all the world's advanced capitalist economies were mired in the Great Depression, the emphasis on aggregates, at least from a public policy standpoint, made practical sense.

During the mid-1940s, Leontief acted as a consultant for the U.S. Bureau of Labor Statistics (BLS) when it undertook the first construction of a national input-output table. The effort culminated in the 1947 publication of a 50-sector table of interindustry relations followed shortly thereafter by a 200-sector table with more highly detailed industrial and sectoral classifications. One important practical result of the table was its projections for postwar employment growth until the year 1950 along with policy recommendations should the economy fall short of fullemployment.

Unfortunately, in the early 1950s, government appropriations for the BLS's continued development of input-output analysis ceased. A short time later, in 1953, the U.S. Department of Defense abandoned plans to conduct a departmental study using input-output analysis. These decisions were influenced by some businessmen who cast the BLS's program as a step toward socialist "push-button planning." No further work on government-sponsored input-output projects transpired until after the Census of Manufacturers of 1958. The interindustry results of the input-output study were eventually published in 1964.

Despite its languish in the United States, not long after World War II the use of input-output analysis began to gain an institutional presence throughout the world. Its application soon incorporated major traditional areas of economic analysis such as short-term **forecasting**, dynamic input-output modeling, income and employment multipliers, regional and interregional analysis, environmental impacts, international trade, underdeveloped economics, and social demography. By 1986, about 90 countries had constructed input-output tables.

HISTORICAL FORERUNNERS

The historical precursors to input-output analysis were in evidence as far back as the first half of the seventeenth-century. Most economic historians cite Francois Quesnay's (1694-1774) *Tableau Economique* as the earliest recorded examples to depict the importance of mutual interindustry flows or, in more modern parlance, systematic economic interdependence. Quesnay was one of the leading theoreticians whose work inspired the formation of a group of French agrarian social reformers called the Physiocrats. Though its central focus was on agriculture, the *Tableau* represents a basic working model of an economy and its extended reproduction. It highlighted the processes of production, circulation of money and **commodities**, and the distribution of **income**. And, despite having originally appeared in a cumbersome zigzag form, the *Tableau's* easy adaptability to Leontief's input-output or double-entry table format has been demonstrated.

The Physiocrats divided society into three classes or sectors. First, a productive class of cultivators engaged in agricultural production were solely responsible for the generation of society's surplus product, a part of which formed net investment. Second, the sterile class referred to producers of manufactured commodities. The term sterile was applied not because manufacturers did not produce anything of value, but because the value of their output (e.g, clothes, shoes, cooking utensils) was presumed to be equal to the necessary costs of raw materials received from the cultivators plus the subsistence level of the producer wages. According to the Physiocrats no surplus product or profits were thought to originate in manufacturing. Lastly came landlords or the idle class who through the money they received as rent consumed the surplus product created by the productive cultivators.

Of particular relevance to the contemporary method of input-output analysis is the *Tableau's* lengthy depiction of the three classes' transactions. Once the landlord class received their money rents, account was made of the transactions that lead to distribution of products between the agricultural and manufacturing sectors. In short, the *Tableau* illustrated the two sectors' interdependence as the output from each sector served as a necessary input for the other. These are exactly the type of interindustry relationships that form the core theoretical foundation upon which modern day input-output analysis rests. Here, money's role as a medium of circulation was also critical since it functioned to maintain a fluid means of product allocation. Finally, with the passage of one year, the *Tableau's* entire socioeconomic process came to an end and the transactions were aggregated. Given the *Tableau's* postulated assumptions, it could then be shown that the economy arrived back at its initial static state.

Some of the outstanding ideas expressed in Quesnay's *Tableau* were to exercise an enduring impact, even up to the present day, on the study of economics. Among these were: (1) the notion of productive and unproductive labor and their relationship to an economic surplus, (2) the mutual interdependence of production processes, and (3) the circular flows of money and commodities and the potential for economic crises that arise from the hoarding of money. Of these, the second point clearly resonates closest to the object of input-output analysis, while the concern raised by the third point has been addressed by the creation of central banking institutions. However, with the notable exception of two economists, Anwar Shaik and Ertugrul Amhet Tonak, little in the way of integrating the first and second point has been attempted. This is somewhat unsettling as once this distinction has been drawn, comparisons in the measurement of commonly used aggregate macroeconomic input and output variables estimated across the postwar period diverge both in terms of the direction and magnitude of their trends.

Though they were active in England instead of France, the economists who figured most prominently in the development of classical theory themselves drew heavily from theoretical insights of the Physiocratic school. Adam Smith's seminal work, *An Inquiry into the Nature and Causes of the Wealth of*

Nations, borrows wholesale, and proceeds to extend upon, the Physiocrats' major theoretical propositions. And, as Luigi Pasinetti indicated, the analytical roots of Ricardo's now widely used one sector corn model or two sector gold and corn model, depicting economic growth or capital accumulation, takes its notion of economic surplus from the Physiocrats. Both of Ricardo's models also emphasize the Physiocratic notion of production as a circular process, or, in accord with Leontief's definition, of an economy's "general interdependence."

Most of the economic history literature covering the early forerunners of input-output analysis contain a curious omission—hardly any mention of Marx's work. Indeed, of all the economists typically associated with developing the early groundwork out of which input-output analysis was to emerge, probably none spent more time in exploring the interdependence of economic life, along with a host of other related matters, than Marx.

For instance, all the material covered in Volume II of *Capital* (some 550 pages), analyzes the complete process by which one industry's output serves as another's input. Marx readily acknowledged the debt he owed to Quesnay's *Tableau.* Called the "reproduction schema," Marx divided total social reproduction into two basic departments: production of the means of production and production of the means of consumption. He then proceeds to elaborate a simple mathematical model to explore what happens when the entire surplus product is totally consumed or used for further accumulation, while in either case balance (equilibrium) between each department is maintained. Simple reproduction referred to the above case where the entire surplus product was consumed while extended reproduction designated the instance where a fraction or all of the surplus product was employed for accumulation purposes.

In his *Theories of Surplus-Value,* Parts I and III, Marx also devotes over 100 pages to a critique of Quesnay's *Tableau* and other issues related to Physiocratic theory. Both the *Theories of Surplus-Value,* and the three volumes of *Capital* contain much qualified praise for Quesnay's *Tableau* and other Physiocratic writings which, as Marx pointed out, were to form the theoretical foundation upon which Smith and Ricardo drew.

Leon Walras represents the last link in the chain leading up to Leontief's formulation of input-output analysis. Despite having worked within a neoclassical framework, Walras is credited with introducing the use of production coefficients, a concept that closely resembles one of the core ideas contained in Leontief's work. Yet unlike Leontief's approach, Walras's model of a pure exchange market economy's ability to arrive at an equilibrium state analytically trivialized the production sector. It treated production as nothing more than an intermediate phase sandwiched between simultaneous acts of utility maximization and the optimal allocation of exogenously given stock of scarce resources. Though it makes little sense to the uninitiated, Walras's use of production coefficients grafted onto this theory of a pure exchange equilibrium suffered from a major limitation. He erroneously treated the stock of resources as a flow variable that occurred within a current period and failed to take account of its existence from previous periods. As a result, Walras was never able to develop a coherent theory of capital accumulation.

LEONTIEF'S DEVELOPMENT OF INPUT-OUTPUT ANALYSIS

Born on August 5, 1906, in St. Petersburg (formerly Leningrad), Russia, Leontief received a degree of "Learned Economist" from the University of Leningrad. He received his Ph.D. in 1928 while attending the University of Berlin. Taking up an offer to join the staff of the prestigious National Bureau of Economic Research, Leontief arrived in the United States in 1931. Within a few months he had accepted an appointment at Harvard University where he was to remain and attain worldwide recognition for his invention and application of input-output analysis.

Growing impatient with the penchant of his economist peers for "implicit theorizing," Leontief set out to pursue a dictum that has served as a guiding thread throughout his career: that economic concepts were of little validity unless they could be observed and measured. He was convinced that not only was a well-formulated theory of utmost importance but so too was its application to real economics. To be of use, an economic theory must yield interesting behavioral predictions whose results were subject to verification. With this in mind, Leontief's early extensions of input-output analysis were intended to demonstrate that: (1) production coefficients, expressing relationships among the industrial sectors of an economy, lent themselves to statistical estimation; (2) that the estimated coefficients were sufficiently stable so as to be used in comparative static analyses, i.e., different equilibrium states; and, given the above two points, (3) that on a quantitative level, the merits of different economic policies could be evaluated by taking into consideration both their direct and indirect feedback effects (or multiplier impact) on interindustry flows.

At the time, Leontief's grandiose input-output efforts encountered two major stumbling blocks. First, only part of the information needed for his production coefficients was available (through the U.S. Census of Manufacturers) while the remainder had to be arduously gleaned from trade journals and other dispersed sources. Second, underlying Leontief's input-output method was the assumption that production coefficients remained largely constant for extended periods. This proposition was hard to reconcile with the dominant neoclassical theory of production that held that factors of production, (i.e., different quantities of labor and machines expressed in isoquants), were readily substituted for one another as their relative prices changed (i.e., the changing slopes of isocost curves).

Undaunted, around 1934 Leontief began to surmount these self-admitted difficulties. He compiled a 44-sector industrial table containing about 2,000 coefficients in addition to mapping out a plan for their analysis and tests for their validity. To ascertain the coefficients' stability, tables were constructed for the years of 1919 and 1929. The first test results on the coefficients' stability proved inconclusive. This lack of decisiveness was rectified in 1944, however, when Leontief calculated a table of coefficients for 1939, comparable in scope to his 1919 and 1929 tables. He arrived at a satisfactory degree of stability for most coefficients across the two decades.

In 1948, Leontief founded and became the director of the Harvard Economic Research Project established for the purposes of applying and extending the field of input-output analysis. During his 25-year tenure as its director, Leontief remained a driving force in developing interregional input-output analysis and in introducing capital-coefficient matrices meant to depict the investment response to changes in final demand. Given these developments, input-output analysis proved adept at generating an economic system's forecasted growth path as well as its various static equilibrium positions. Leontief's work at the project led to the publication of two books, *The Structure of American Economy 1919-1939,* in 1951, and *Studies in the Structure of the American Economy,* in 1953.

Other significant extensions of input-output analysis included estimates of the inflationary consequences of wage settlements, the direct and indirect impact of armament expenditures, estimates of capital requirements for economic development, and methods intended to forecast the individual growth-paths of industrial sectors in a developing economy. In more recent years input-output analysis has been applied to the issue of worldwide economic growth, its environmental consequences, its impact on the world's reserve of natural resources, and the political-economic ramifications for relations between the economies of developed and less-developed countries. Under a project funded by the **United Nations**, Leontief managed a study on the growth of the world economy until the year 2000. The multiregional input-output model extended across 15 regions consisting of 45 sectors each with balanced trading accounts.

The results were published in 1977 as *The Future of the World Economy.* Based on a broad set of reasonable assumptions, it provisionally concluded that only small progress would be made in closing the gap between rich and poor regions unless current policies dealing with international trade and finance were abandoned. As policy alternatives the study recommended a marked increase in multinational aid and a significant increase in the flow of imports from the Third World to the first.

BASIC DEVELOPMENTS AND EXTENSIONS

A standard input-output table contains an equal number of rows and columns. Tables can measure dollars or physical units of produced goods and services, such as tons of steel, bushels of wheat, or gallons of fuel. Following the construction of an annual input-output table, it is possible to derive a second table of input or technical coefficients. The term "technical coefficients" refers to the quantity of inputs required from each industry to produce one dollar's worth of a given industry's output. Because it represents the entire domain of wealth-producing activities, computation of the technical coefficients are restricted to the processing sector industries only. The coefficients can be denominated in either monetary or physical units.

Once a transaction table of direct and indirect coefficients (or a coefficients' matrix) has been obtained, several analytic exercises common to field of economics can be performed. The first concerns the use of static input-output tables to consistently forecast projections of both industry and final sector demands. Typically, for periods of up to two or three years, these are reliable short-term forecasts over which it makes sense to assume that the production coefficients change very little.

But the existence of stable technical coefficients within a longer term forecast is tenuous. Integration of disturbances related to relative input price changes, the appearance of new industries during the projection period, and the effects of technological change on technical coefficients, require more complex, dynamic models of input-output analysis. Around 1953 Leontief initially formulated a dynamic input-output model. Later, Copper Almon also achieved significant results working with dynamic input-output models.

A second area extending the use of input-output analysis concerns the use of income multipliers. Their construction requires appending the households row and column to a coefficient table followed by the calculation of their direct and indirect effects. While Keynes first introduced and applied multipliers as an concept central to the study of macroeconomics, it was R. S. Kahn who originated their theoretical development. Nevertheless, credit goes to input-output analysis for making it possible to disaggregate the highly aggregated multipliers in order to detail how multiplier effects ramify throughout an economic structure. If, for instance, it becomes a question as to whether a given level of public investment should be directed toward the construction or military industries, then, based on their different multiplier impacts, input-output analysis provides policy makers with a tool to evaluate the merits of either project. Or, in the area of international trade, should the problem concern easing import restrictions, input-output analysis can indicate how imports might affect industries supplying domestic inputs and outputs.

In short, when based on the assumption that each industry's output expands by the same amount, then input-output augmented multipliers reveal that varying amounts of income are generated by different industries. In general, for the case of international trade, the greater the degree of the domestic economy's interdependence, the greater will be the direct effects of income change. But in terms of both the direct and indirect effects the results could be reversed, neutralized, or strengthened.

Thirdly, the existence of an input-output table combined with a projected change in aggregate final demand also allows for the calculation of employment multipliers. Computation of employment multipliers differ from the method used for income multipliers. Two methods, the Isard-Kuene and Moore-Peterson approach, were the first to tackle the subject. The Isard-Kuene method sought to measure the total employment impact within a region based on the establishment of a new basic industry within it borders. It drew from national coefficients to estimate the inputs of both the basic industry and the accompanying industries expected to locate around the new industry. The Moore-Peterson method, by contrast, uses regional—instead of national—coefficients to estimate both the direct, indirect, and induced employment effects. Assuming a change in the final demand for the output of one or more industries within the region, calculation of total employment changes was performed across all industries.

Developments in both regional and interregional models of input-output studies have loomed large in the post-World War II era. During this time the trend in economics has moved to quantitative research, a task for which input-output analysis is well suited. The distinction between the two models is straightforward, a region comprises one geographical area while an interregional model spans several regions. From here two further complementary distinctions apply— that between a balanced regional and pure interregional model. A balanced regional model is constructed through disaggregation of a national input-output model into component regions. Conversely, a pure interregional model is designed by aggregating a number of regional tables, which may or may not include all the regions in a national economy.

Interregional models have been used to analyze regional **balance of trade** payments and interregional trade flows. Interregional models are more complex than either national or regional models. This stems from having to sort out interindustry and interregional economic flows. As a result many have tended to be highly aggregated since reliable data on industry sales and purchases by region are hard to come by.

Regional models cover geographic areas of varying size. Some have encompassed **Federal Reserve** districts, others, metropolitan areas, states, counties, or an area specified across two or more states. For the most part, regional input-output models are considered more ''open'' than a national economy model. The quality of openness derives from the tendency of regions to be more highly specialized in terms of their processing sectors, thus more inclined to transact exchanges from without.

[Daniel E. King]

FURTHER READING:

Almon, Clopper. ''Consistent Forecasting in a Dynamic Multi-Sector Model.'' *The Review of Economics and Statistics*. May, 1963, pp. 148-62.

Leontief, Wassily. *Input-Output Economics*. Oxford University Press, 1986.

Leontief, Wassily. *The Structure of American Economy, 1919-1939*. International Arts and Sciences Press, 1951.

Leontief, Wassily, and others. *Studies in the Structure of the American Economy*. International Arts and Sciences Press 1953.

Miernyk, William H. *The Elements of Input-Output Analysis*. Random House, 1965.

Miller, Ronald E. *Input-Output Analysis: Foundations and Extensions*. Prentice Hall, 1985.

Pasinetti, Luigi L. *Lectures on the Theory of Production*. Columbia University Press, 1977.

Phillip, Almarin. ''The 'Tableau Economique' as a Simple Leontief Model.'' *Quarterly Journal of Economics*. 1955, pp. 137-144.

Shaik, Anwar, and Ertugrul A. Tonak. *Measuring the Wealth of Nations: The Political Economy of National Accounts*. Columbia University Press, 1994.

Sohn, Ira, ed. *Readings in Input-Output Analysis: Theory and Applications*. Oxford University Press, 1986.

INSTITUTIONAL INVESTMENTS

An institutional investor is an organization, usually a corporation, that trades large volumes of securities on behalf of a collection of individual investors. Such an organization offers individual investors two primary benefits. First, by trading in aggregate—or utilizing the collective financial resources of many individual investors—the institutional investment firm may realize tremendous **economies of scale** in security trades. For example, such high-volume trades qualify the investment firm for discounts on commissions.

Second, the financial largesse of the **assets** of the investment firm enables the firm to retain highly qualified money managers, or professional investment advisers, who may devote greater time and attention to thorough investigation of investment opportunities than any single investor may be able to afford.

Institutional investment firms have their origin in investment trusts that came into being in European financial centers, principally London, Amsterdam, and Paris, during the eighteenth and nineteenth centuries. Such firms later formed in other financial centers, such as New York, Chicago, Hong Kong, and Frankfurt, and today may exist in virtually any city in the world.

Institutional investors include commercial **banks**, **savings and loan associations**, investment trusts, insurance companies, pension funds and, most notably in recent years, **mutual funds**.

The growth of institutional investment institutions was fueled to a great extent during the 1980s by growth strategies of firms that sought new sources of investment capital. By marketing new, more customized investment vehicles and services to smaller investors, institutional investment firms brought the benefits of participation in large financial markets to investors who previously lacked the financial critical mass necessary for cost-effective participation. As individuals, they lacked sufficient **capital** to enter markets or profit fully from trades in those markets. As members of investment collectives, however, various entry and operating costs could be widely distributed and reduced.

In fact, trades by institutional investment firms now account for about 90 percent of all trades in financial markets. This does not represent the waning of the individual investor, but merely a trend in which individual investors participate in markets through institutional investment intermediaries rather than as direct investors.

It has been suggested, particularly after the October 1987 market collapse, that the influence of institutional investors over markets is too strong. The collapse of 1987 resulted in a decline in the Dow Jones Industrial Average of more than 500 points, representing devaluation of about 20 percent.

At the time of the collapse, market values for shares was generally agreed to be inflated, and a correction was necessary. Nevertheless, the actions of institutional investors were governed largely by computer programs, set to sell in increasing volumes as market prices declined. Therefore, a small number of highly sensitive programmed trades caused the entire community to bail out of the market all at once. Market prices fell, but far beyond what was necessary for a proper correction. Regulatory safeguards were subsequently enacted to blunt the effect of programmed trading by institutional investors.

[John Simley]

FURTHER READING:

Vickers, Douglas. *Money, Banking, and the Macroeconomy.* Englewood Cliffs, NJ: Prentice-Hall, 1985.

INTANGIBLE ASSETS

Intangible assets are non-physical assets, including such things as trademarks, patent rights, copyrights (known collectively as intellectual property), franchise rights, goodwill, customer lists, leasehold interests, non-compete agreements, prepaid expenses, and deferred costs. Although they lack physical substance, intangible assets may represent a substantial, or even a major, portion of a company's total assets.

Intangible assets are usually shown on a company's balance sheet under noncurrent assets, falling after fixed assets and before or among other **assets**. Generally they are recorded at their historical cost, and amortized to expense over an appropriate period of time. Some examples of intangibles, how they arise and how they are treated follow.

Patent rights represent the rights to a 17-year monopoly to manufacture or use a certain product or process. The capitalized value of the intangible asset usually includes the legal costs involved with filing the patent application and perfecting and enforcing the patent rights. Research and development costs incurred in discovering the patent are typically excluded from the intangible asset, as accounting rules require such expenditures to be expensed in the year incurred. If part of the patent utility involves a cross-license arrangement with another company, any monies paid to that other company would be included in the capitalized value of the intangible asset. Although patents have a technical length of 17 years, as a practical matter, the subject invention is often superseded by technological advancement in much shorter periods. The amortization period should be the shorter of 17 years or until the patent no longer confers a competitive or marketable advantage.

Trademarks are the exclusive rights to proprietary symbols, names, and other unique properties of a product, such as packaging, style, and even color (in rare instances). The trademark is established by active use in the marketplace, and registration with the U.S. Patent and Trademark Office. Capitalized costs will include the original design work plus the legal expense and filing fees to record the trademark. Any costs incurred to enforce the exclusive use of the mark are included as well. Trademarks have an indefinite life, provided the owner continues to actively use them, and, therefore, are not necessarily amortized.

Copyrights represent the legal right, for a period of 50 years after the author's death, to sell, copy, and perform (etc.) a piece of literary, musical, or art work. This intangible asset will normally be recorded at its acquisition price, if the rights were bought, or simply the cost to file the copyright notice. This asset is amortized over its useful life, but not more than 40 years.

Goodwill equals the excess of the price paid for a company above the market value of its tangible assets. When a company is bought, the price paid will often be above the market value of its facilities, equipment, receivables, inventory, etc. This is because the company has a track record of operations over which it has established many beneficial relationships, including those with customers, distributors and suppliers. The specific manifestation of goodwill may be found in customer name mailing lists, trademarks, a manufacturing process, or license rights. In any event, it reflects the buyer's perception that the company as a whole is worth more on a going concern basis than the sum of the identifiable physical assets. Goodwill, as an intangible asset, is amortized for accounting purposes over no more than 40 years; current tax provisions do not allow a deduction for amortization of goodwill.

Sometimes in connection with the purchase and sale of a business, the former proprietor(s) will agree not to engage in a similar business within a defined geographic area and for a defined period of time (generally two to five years). Such agreements are called non-compete agreements. The parties may also agree to allocate a portion of the purchase price to the non-compete provision. In these circumstances, the amount allocated becomes the intangible asset, which is amortized over the prescribed non-compete period.

Deferred costs represent monies spent for some future benefit. Examples include capitalized drilling costs, loan acquisition costs, and capitalized interest. The intangible asset will be recorded at the amount of money disbursed and amortized over the appropriate period to which the benefit accrues.

Licenses are the contractual rights to use another's property, whether it be a patent, trademark copyright, real estate (usually called a lease), or exploration for natural resources. Often such licenses provide for ongoing payments assessed as a function of the utility gained by the licensee from the use of the property; these are known as royalties. In some cases, however, an up-front payment is extracted by the licensor, in which case that amount can be recorded as an intangible asset by the licensee. As with other intangible assets, its value should be amortized over the useful or contractual life, whichever is shorter.

SEE ALSO: Intangible Assets; Inventory Accounting; Licensing Agreements; Patent Law/Patents

[Christopher Barry]

INTELLECTUAL PROPERTY

The term intellectual property refers to items that represent the expression of ideas or intellectual pursuits and that are assigned certain rights of property. Intellectual property is an intangible creation of the human mind usually expressed or translated into a tangible form. Examples of intellectual property include an author's **copyright** on a book or article, a distinctive logo design representing a soft drink company and its products, or a patent on the process to manufacture chewing gum. Intellectual property law covers the protection of copyrights, **patents**, trademarks, and trade secrets, as well as other legal areas such as unfair competition. Intellectual property, frequently abbreviated IP, may also be referred to as industrial property.

The concept of intellectual property developed and evolved through its individual components. There is no history of intellectual property per se, but the history of trademarks, for example, extends back to the medieval period.

The laws protecting intellectual property in the United States exist at the state and federal level. State laws cover a broad spectrum of intellectual property fields from trade secrets to the right of publicity. The law differ somewhat from state to state. At the federal level, the Constitution and Congressional legislation authorized under the Constitution deal exclusively with patents, copyrights, and partially with trademarks and related areas of unfair competition.

In the late nineteenth century, intellectual property protection at an international level became an important issue in trade and tariff negotiations—and has remained so ever since. One of the first international treaties relating to intellectual property in the broadest sense was the International Convention for the Protection of Industrial Property or the Paris Convention. Written in 1883, the treaty created under the Paris Convention provided protection for such properties as patents, industrial models and designs, trademarks, and trade names. Over 100 countries have signed the Paris Convention treaty, and it has been modified several times. Two of the most important provisions of the treaty relate to the right of national treatment and the right of priority.

The right of national treatment ensures that those individuals seeking a patent or trademark in a foreign Convention country will not be discriminated against and will receive the same rights as a citizen of the country. The right of priority provides an inventor one year from the date of filing a patent application in his or her home country (six months for a trademark or design application) the right to file an application in a foreign country. The legal, effective date of application in the foreign country is then retroactively the legal, effective filing date in the home country provided the application is made within the protection period. If the invention is made public prior to filing the home country application, however, the right of priority in a foreign country is no longer applicable.

Enforcement and protection of intellectual property at the international level is extremely complex. Laws vary significantly from country to country, and the political climate within each country influences the extent of protection available. Separate legislation and treaties specifically address relevant procedures, conventions, and standards for each area within the scope of intellectual property such as copyright or trade secrets.

The value of intellectual property to an individual or corporation is not based on physical properties such as size and structure. Intellectual property is valuable because it represents ownership and an exclusive right to use, manufacture, reproduce, or promote a unique creation or idea. It is perhaps the most valuable asset a company or individual can own. For example, the apple silhouette logo of Apple Computer, Inc. not only identifies a computer as an Apple product but also represents the company and may be reproduced thousands of times in promotional documents and other printed or electronic mediums. Millions of people see the logo and instantly associate the item with Apple.

[Paula M. Ard]

FURTHER READING:

Foster, Frank H., and Robert L. Shook. *Patents, Copyrights & Trademarks*. New York: John Wiley & Sons, 1993.

McCarthy, J. Thomas. *McCarthy's Desk Encyclopedia of Intellectual Property*. Washington, D.C.: Bureau of National Affairs, 1991.

Miller, Arthur R., and Michael H. Davis. *Intellectual Property: Patents, Trademarks, and Copyright in a Nutshell*. St. Paul, MN: West, 1990.

"Protecting Intellectual Property: An Introductory Guide for U.S. Businesses on Protecting Intellectual Property Abroad." *Business America*. July, 1991, pp. 2-9.

Tabalujan, Benny. "Keeping the Fruits of Your Intellectual Pursuit to Yourself." *Business Times*. July, 1993, pp. 23-26.

INTEREST RATES

It is human nature to prefer immediate gratification. We dislike postponing consumption and, if we are requested to delay our satisfaction, we demand a reward. This reward often takes the form of increased consumption at the later time. This same idea applies to money. Money, it has been observed, is only as good as what you can use it for. Whether dollars, rubles, or drachmas, money is a measure of the ability to consume. If we give up the immediate consumption represented by money, i.e., if we lend the money, we expect a reward in the form of getting back more than was originally lent. In the case of money, the reward, or difference between what was lent and what is returned, is referred to as "interest."

MEASUREMENT

For reasons of comparability, interest is normally specified as an annual percentage rate of increase, rather than as an absolute amount. The "interest rate" is the percentage increase:

$$\text{percent interest rate} = \frac{\text{amount returned} - \text{amount lent}}{\text{amount lent}} \times 100$$

The specification of the interest rate is not complete unless the period over which the increase occurs is specified. The standard is an annual period, and if a different period is used it should be specified. The interest rate is also sometimes described in terms of "basis points," with one basis point being one hundredth of 1 percent. The difference between the interest rate of 10.25 percent and the interest rate of 10.00 percent is 25 basis points.

Interest is also normally assumed to be "compounded," i.e., at the end of each period the interest is assumed due. If not paid the interest is added to the "principal," or amount borrowed. Because unpaid interest is added to the principal, in subsequent periods there will be "interest on interest." For instance, if $10.00 is borrowed at 10 percent compounded annually, at the end of one year the lender is owed the original $10.00 plus $1.00 interest. At the end of the second year, the lender is owed a principal consisting of the original $10.00 plus the $1.00 interest from year one, plus the interest for year two. This interest for year two is on the increased principal, i.e., $1.00 interest on the original $10.00, plus $0.10 interest on the $1.00 interest owed from year one. Although the interest on interest for the second year is only $0.10, the interest on interest component compounds exponentially with the passage of time. It can become quite large and may rapidly dominate the original debt. After 20 years, for instance, the amount owed is $67.27: the original $10.00, $20.00 interest on the original $10.00, and $37.27 interest on interest.

The standard period for compounding is also one year. Different compounding periods are used, however, and quarterly, daily, or even continuous compounding is not unusual. Where the compounding period is shorter than one year, the realized or "effective" annual interest rate will be higher than the stated annual rate due to the interest on interest effect. If the above $10.00 had been lent at 10 percent compounded semiannually, at the end of six months half of the yearly interest, or $0.50 (one-half of 10 percent of $10.00), would be added to the principal. The interest over the second half of the year would be $0.525 (one-half of 10 percent of $10.50), of which $0.025 is interest on interest. The principal at the end of the year would be $11.025, and the "effective" annual interest rate would be 10.25 percent. The absolute difference in interest rate is not large, but over long periods the compounded amount can be significantly different. If the above $10.00 had been compounded semiannually at 10 percent for 20 years, the amount owed would be $70.40, an increase of $3.13 over the amount owed under annual compounding.

Although annual compound interest is the accepted normal measure of interest rates, there are some alternative measures. The yield or interest rate on bonds is normally computed on a semiannual basis, and then converted to an annual rate by multiplying by two. This is called simple interest, and does not include the one-year interest on interest effect. In our example, the simple annual interest rate would be twice the 5 percent semiannual rate, or 10 percent. Although this rate is incorrect it has become convention, a holdover from days of hand calculation. This is the approach used in calculation of the annual percentage rate (APR) required in interest rate disclosures. Another form of interest is "discounted in advance." In this form, the interest is deducted from the principal, and the borrower receives the net amount. This form can severely understate the interest rate. In our example, a one-year borrower would receive $9.00, or $10.00 principal less $1.00 interest for one year, and would owe $10.00 at the end of the year, effectively paying the interest at the time of borrowing. This is equivalent to paying $1.00 to borrow $9.00, a compound annual rate of 11.11 percent.

DETERMINANTS OF INTEREST RATE LEVELS

The level of interest rates is set by supply and demand—i.e., when the amount of money supplied is equal to the amount that other economic units wish to borrow. The interesting question, however, is what factors influence supply and demand. Since interest is in the nature of a reward for postponing consumption, a higher interest rate can be expected to result in a greater supply of funds. Under different conditions, however, a given interest rate may result in a differing supply. Attitudes toward consumption are important, as shown by the differences between savings rates in different countries. Uncertainty about the economy may prompt more saving, as shown by the different attitudes of the "depression generation" and their children. Demand, on the other hand, depends on the investments available, and will be downward sweeping since more investments are profitable at lower interest rates. In periods of high growth or technological advancement, there will be more acceptable investment and greater demand. Future economic growth is affected by the rate of increase of population, the workforce, and the educational and skill level. Economic conditions and production possibilities set the general level of demand for funds.

Economic and other variables set the interest rate as a rate of increase in ability to consume. This rate of increase in ability to consume is called the "real" rate of interest. The "nominal" or dollar rate of interest measures the increase in dollars. Money is a measure of ability to consume, but the yardstick itself changes over time due to **inflation**. Inflation is a decrease in the purchasing power, or amount of consumption that can be acquired per monetary unit. Since it is the real rate of interest that controls the supply and demand of funds, the nominal interest rate must include a premium that compensates for any expected loss of purchasing power. The stated or nominal interest rate is then expressed as the real rate of interest plus an inflation premium. If R_N is the nominal rate of interest, R_R is the real rate of interest, and I is the expected rate of inflation:

$$R_N = R_R + I + IR_R$$

For small rates of inflation the inflation rate itself is a good approximation of the premium required, and the last term is often ignored. For higher rates of inflation the last term becomes significant, and should be included. The higher level of interest rates in the early 1980s is partially due to the effects of actual or feared inflation. Interest rates are also affected by and are an instrument of government policy. The **Federal Reserve System** manages the amount of money in circulation, and affects the interest rates. Too rapid growth of the amount of money will have an immediate effect of decreasing interest rates, since supply is increased. Over the longer run, however, too rapid growth in the amount of money may result in inflation. Interest rates, reacting to the expectation of inflation, will increase. Too low a rate of growth in the amount of money, on the other hand, will result in a reduction of supply and higher interest rates. This in turn may hamper economic growth. If the economy stagnates, the eventual result may well be decreased interest rates.

Over time the Federal Reserve has placed varied emphasis on two policy targets. The first is the growth of the amount of money, while the second is interest rates. It would be incorrect to say that the Federal Reserve has "control" over either of these variables. This would be impossible in a dynamic economy such as that of the United States. Given the number of money-like arrangements, the definition of "money," much less its measurement, is difficult. The monetary tools of the Federal Reserve work most directly on short-term interest rates. Interest rates for longer maturities are indirectly affected through the market's perception of government policy and its economic effects. More recently, expectations of possible inflation have been a major concern to lenders and policy makers. Economic forces shape the level of interest rates, while governmental policies have some effect on economic forces. Foreign interest rates have become increasingly important. Major firms now routinely borrow in foreign markets, and lenders are increasingly willing to hold foreign debt. This forces some alignment of interest rates worldwide, and reduces the amount of control any nation has over its domestic conditions. There are many forms of borrowing, and thus many interest rates. Borrowing and lending arrangements include personal **loans**, credit cards, **mortgages**, various federal and municipal government obligations, corporate bonds, and multiple other forms. Investors borrow when they trade on margin, firms borrow by using **trade credit**. The interest rate on different borrowing arrangements will be different, which is why the plural is used here. While economic and other variables set the general level of interest rates, specific interest rates are affected by other variables. While there are a multitude of factors affecting interest rates, they are generally grouped under differences in maturity, quality, and tax status.

THE TERM STRUCTURE OF INTEREST RATES

Interest rates are also related to the maturity, or length of commitment, of the arrangement. The relationship is often described by a yield curve showing the interest rates for various maturities. There are several theories to explain term structures of interest rates. The first is called the expectations theory. This theory holds that interest rates over longer periods are dependent on the series of short-term interest rates expected over that period—i.e., lenders are indifferent to the length of commitment, but require the same expected ending wealth regardless of whether they lend money once for ten years or they make a series of ten one-year loan. The motivation here is that if this relationship did not hold, investors would prefer the alternative with the higher ending wealth, forcing a readjustment of interest rates.

Alternately, if the relationship did not hold, investors could **arbitrage**, selling the lower-yielding alternative and investing the proceeds in the higher-yielding alternative. This arbitrage would allow the arbitrager to make a return from a net zero investment. Under this theory, the yield curve would be upward sweeping if short-term interest rates were expected to increase in the future, and downward sweeping if short-term interest rates were expected to decrease in the future. A second approach, called the liquidity theory, suggests that investors are not indifferent as to the length of commitment. This argument suggests that lending for longer periods is more risky than short-term lending. The longer time makes prediction less accurate, and permits more opportunities for negative results. Investors prefer more liquid, shorter term lending, and will not commit the funds for longer periods unless given a liquidity premium to compensate for this higher risk. Under this approach, the yield curve would be upward sweeping at all times. Empirical observation of decreasing yield curves does not refute this theory, however, if it is combined with other theories. If the liquidity premium is superimposed on the expectation that short-term interest rates will decrease in the future, the result can be a yield curve that is still downward sweeping but less steep. A third approach is called the segmented markets theory. As we have noted, interest rates depend on supply and demand. Segmented markets builds on this obvious statement, adding the idea that lenders and borrowers will have a "preferred habitat," or length of commitment. This preferred habitat comes about because of the desire of lenders and borrowers to reduce risk by matching the maturity of **assets** and **liabilities**. A lender with a liability that will come due in ten years, for example, avoids risk by lending with a maturity of ten years; a borrower whose use of the funds will pay off in ten years will borrow with a maturity of ten years. Borrowers and lenders are thus reluctant to leave their preferred maturity, and will not arbitrage. As a result, the interest rate for any given maturity will depend on the supply and demand for that given maturity. In actuality, all of these theories are to some extent correct. Empirically, since World War II the yield curve has been predominantly upward sweeping, although downward sweeping yield curves have occurred.

THE QUALITY STRUCTURE OF INTEREST RATES

The quality structure of interest rates describes the effect of uncertainty about receiving the specified reward. In the face of uncertainty about payments, lenders will demand a higher rate of return or risk premium. The interest rate to a particular borrower will be the sum of a risk-free rate plus the risk premium. Default risk is not simply the failure to pay principal, but is rather a matter of degree. There are many possibilities short of complete loss, sometimes as small as a skipped or late payment. Loan arrangements with little likelihood of a problem are said to be of high quality.The higher the severity and probability of a problem, or the lower the quality, the higher will be the risk premium. Treasury obligations, which are direct obligations of the U.S. government and assumed to have no default risk, are of the highest quality. **Bonds** issued by agencies of the government, which are not direct government obligations, are of only slightly lower quality since it is assumed the government would assume the responsibility. State and local bonds, called municipals, vary widely in quality depending on the characteristics of the security and the issuer. The same variation is true of corporate bonds. These securities are sometimes rated as to quality by independent firms such as Standard & Poor's, Moody's Investors Service, Duff & Phelps, and Fitch Investors Service. These ratings are widely used to classify bonds and are important factors in the interest rate, or yield, provided to investors. Bonds below a certain rating are often referred to as **junk bonds**, and carry a higher interest rate.

The **prime rate** is the rate charged to large customers with established relationships. Borrowers with less admirable credit records (or smaller accounts which are comparatively more expensive) will pay a higher rate. Collateral is also important. Unsecured personal loans, such as credit card credit, will ordinarily pay a higher rate than car loans, which will in turn pay more than home mortgages. An important characteristic of loan arrangements is liquidity. An asset that can be converted to cash quickly at a fair price is liquid; if price concessions are required for rapid sale the asset is illiquid. Many loans have been relatively illiquid, so that once the loan is made the creditor was locked in. This lack of freedom of action increased the risk of the lender, resulting in higher interest rates. More recently, a number of classes of loans have been ''securitized'' by being bundled into portfolios against which securities are issued. This added liquidity reduces lender risk and lowers the interest rate on the underlying loan classes.

TAX STATUS

The interest rate on bonds issued by state and local governments, called municipal bonds, are below the interest rates on corporate bonds of the same quality. The reason for this difference is that the interest on these debt obligations is generally exempt from federal taxation. They are also often exempt from taxes of the state of issue. The real rate of increase in purchasing power from taxable federal and corporate debt instruments will be reduced by the taxes:

$$\text{After Tax Rate of Return} = \\ (\text{Pre-Tax Rate of Return}) \times (1 - \text{Tax Rate})$$

Since interest rates reflect the real rate or increase in purchasing power, taxable and nontaxable debt will have the same after-tax rate of return. This equilibrium will not hold for all investors because of differing tax rates. For investors with high tax rates, the after-tax rate of return on municipals may be higher, while for investors with low tax rates the return on corporate debt may be higher.Another tax effect comes about because of the tax deductibility of some interest payments on personal taxes. The tax deductibility of interest on home mortgages effectively lowers the interest rate. This is reflected in the rapid increase in mortgage-based loans after interest on consumer debts was no longer tax deductible.

[David E. Upton]

INTERNAL AUDITING

Internal auditing, an independent appraisal function, is performed in a wide variety of companies, institutions, and governments. What distinguishes internal auditors from governmental auditors and public accountants is the fact that they are employees of the same organizations they **audit**. Their allegiance is to their organization, not to an external authority. Titles other than ''internal auditor'' are sometimes used for those performing an internal audit function. Internal auditors have been named control analysts, systems analysts, business analysts, internal consultants, evaluators, or operations analysts. Regardless of the position title, it is the characteristics of the service being performed that would classify it as internal auditing.

Because internal auditing evolved only within the last few decades, the roles and responsibilities of internal auditors vary greatly from one organization to another. Internal audit functions have been structured based on the differing perceptions and objectives of owners, directors, and managers. While some companies have very sophisticated internal audit functions providing a broad array of services, other organizations have only one or two internal auditors performing routine inspections. Despite the diversity in roles and responsibilities of practicing internal auditors, the Institute of Internal Auditors (IIA) is a governing body for internal auditors that brings some uniformity and consistency to the practice. An international association, the IIA by 1995 had grown to 52,000 members and 210 chapters operating in more than 100 countries. The IIA provides general standards for performing internal audits and serves as a source for education and information.

In its *Standards for the Professional Practice of Internal Auditing*, the IIA defines the internal auditing function in the following way:

> Internal auditing is an independent appraisal function established within an organization to examine and evaluate its activities as a service to the organization. The objective of internal auditing is to assist members of the organization in the effective discharge of their responsibilities. To this end, internal auditing furnishes them analysis, appraisals, recommendations, counsel, and information concerning activities reviewed.

The ''members of the organization'' considered in this definition include both management and the **board of directors**.

There is theoretically no restriction on what internal auditors can review and report about within an organization or its components. In practice, internal auditors work within an approved plan. In this way internal auditing resources are coordinated with the goals and objectives of the organization. Internal auditors perform a variety of audits including compliance audits, operational audits, program audits, financial audits, and information systems audits. Internal audit reports provide management with advice and information for making decisions or improving operations. When problems are discovered, the internal auditor serves the organization by finding ways to prevent them from recurring. A preventative approach is also possible. If the internal auditor evaluates a situation noting potential risks and notifies management, presumably management could then prevent the problem from occurring in the first place.

HISTORY AND BACKGROUND

The double-entry bookkeeping system invented in the thirteenth century provided the means for those engaged in commerce to control transactions with suppliers and customers, and check the work of employees. Historical records suggest that internal auditors were being utilized prior to the fifteenth century. These auditors were employed by kings or merchants and were charged with detecting or preventing theft, fraud, and other improprieties. Control techniques to detect and prevent improprieties, such as separation of duties and independent verification, are thought to have originated during that time.

During the Industrial Revolution, English auditing methods migrated to the United States. Managerial control through auditing continued to gain favor up to and through the twentieth century. Many events contributed.

The economy of United States was growing rapidly after World War I and required better techniques for planning, directing, and evaluating business activities. Unfortunately, the growth was accompanied by a rise in price-fixing, interlocking directorates, stock manipulations, and false statements of business performance. Regulatory actions followed and auditing was used as a means to confirm that laws were being followed. After the **Federal Trade Commission** (FTC) had been created in 1914, the Great Depression and the 1930s brought more regulatory action for publicly traded securities: the **Securities Act of 1933**, the **Securities Exchange Act of 1934**, the Public Utility Holding Company Act of 1935, and the Investment Company Act of 1940.

As the need for auditing grew, corporations realized that they could no longer rely solely on external auditors from public accounting firms. Corporations began hiring auditors as their own employees to verify financial transactions and test compliance with accounting controls. Many of these internal auditors were hired from the external auditing firms. They brought to the companies that hired them auditing methods used in public accounting and a financial statement focus. These internal auditors concentrated on financial auditing. Further, management viewed these internal auditors as a means to reduce external audit fees while maintaining the same level of financial audit coverage. Within some organizations this perception of internal auditing has remained strong.

Internal auditing began emerging as a function distinctly different from external auditing about the middle of the twentieth century. In 1941 the Institute of Internal Auditors (IIA) was founded in New York by a small group of practicing internal auditors. The group recognized that they had many commonalities in the way they worked despite the fact that they worked in different businesses and industries. They agreed that merely applying external auditing techniques internally was not sufficient. They felt the need for a formal approach to sharing and organizing their body of knowledge and their mutual concerns. They began the long process of achieving an identity for internal auditing as a distinct profession concerned with providing independent appraisals for all activities within an organization. The first textbook in the United States for the practice, *Brinks Internal Auditing*, was published in 1941. A technical journal for the field, *Internal Auditor*, distributed its first issue in 1943. The IIA developed the first version of a *Statement of Responsibilities* in 1947 and has continued to revise it (1957, 1971, 1976, 1981, 1990) as internal auditing practices have matured. In 1974 the IIA began a certification program. Candidates passing a two-day examination covering a variety of subjects receive the designation of "certified internal auditor" (CIA). In 1978 the IIA published the *Standards for Professional Practice* to serve as the primary source of reference for directing an internal audit function. The institute has continued to modify or amend these standards by issuing *Statements on Internal Auditing Standards and Administrative Directives.*

A significant event bringing internal auditing to the forefront was the federal Corrupt Practices Act of 1977. The act was the government's response to outcries as news of corporate wrong-doings increased. The act was passed to prevent secret funds and bribery. It specifically prohibited the offering of bribes to foreign officials. Further, it required organizations to maintain adequate systems of internal control and maintain complete and accurate financial records. While the act did not specifically call for an internal auditing function, internal auditors were poised to help management fulfill the requirements of this act. Testing and evaluation of internal controls increased significantly and the role of internal auditors gained importance.

In the mid- to late 1980s there were a number of large business failures and financial statement frauds. On several occasions external auditing firms failed to detect those frauds. The issue of fraudulent financial reporting was examined by a group of private sector organizations which included the American Institute of Certified Public Accountants (AICPA), the American Accounting Association (AAA), the Financial Executives Institute (FEI), the Institute of Internal Auditors (IIA), and the National Association of Accountants (NAA). This group of organizations known as the Treadway Commission issued its final recommendations in 1987, several of which were of great significance to internal auditors. Among other recommendations, the commission's report directed companies to maintain adequate internal control systems, effective internal audit functions staffed with adequate qualified personnel, and objective internal audit functions; and to coordinate internal auditor involvement with the external audit of the entire financial reporting process. The commission's report also directed internal auditors to consider whether their findings of a nonfinancial nature could have implications on figures reported in the organization's **financial statements**. The Treadway Commission further directed its sponsoring organizations to develop guidance on internal control. They did so by issuing a report, *Internal Control—Integrated Framework*, in 1992 which again emphasized the importance of internal controls in organizations.

INTERNAL AUDITING AND INTERNAL CONTROL

The manner in which internal auditing has evolved has linked it directly to the concepts and objectives of internal control. The IIA clearly advocates an internal control focus when it defines the scope of internal auditing: "The scope of internal auditing should encompass the examination and evaluation of the adequacy and effectiveness of the organization's system of internal control and the quality of performance in carrying out assigned responsibilities." At the most basic level, internal controls can be identified as individual preventive, detective, corrective, or directive actions that keep operations functioning as intended. These basic controls are aggregated to create whole networks and systems of control procedures which are known as the organization's overall system of internal control.

The IIA's *Standards of Professional Practice* outlines five key objective's for an organization's system of internal control: (1) reliability and integrity of information; (2) compliance with policies, plans, procedures, laws and regulations; (3) safeguarding of assets; (4) economical and efficient use of resources; and (5) accomplishment of established objectives and goals for operations or programs. It is these five internal control objectives that provide the internal auditing function with its conceptual foundation and focus for evaluating an organization's diverse operations and programs.

KEY ASSUMPTIONS ABOUT THE INTERNAL AUDIT FUNCTION

There are three important assumptions implicit in the definition, objectives, and scope for internal auditing. First is the assumption that internal auditors are independent from the activities they audit and can evaluate them objectively. Internal auditing is an advisory function, not an operational one. Therefore, internal auditors should not be given responsibility or authority over any activities they audit. They should not be positioned in the organization where they would be subject to political or monetary pressures that could inhibit their audit process, sway their opinions, or compromise their recommendations. Independence and objectivity of internal auditors must exist in both appearance and in fact, otherwise the credibility of the internal auditing work product is jeopardized.

Related to independence is the assumption that internal auditors have unrestricted access to whatever they might need to complete an appraisal. That includes unrestricted access to plans, forecasts, people, data, products, facilities, and records necessary to perform their independent evaluations.

Second is the assumption that the internal auditing function is staffed with people possessing the necessary education, experience, and proficiency to complete their work competently, in accordance with internal auditing standards. An understanding of good business practices is essential for internal auditors. They must have the capability to apply broad knowledge to new situations, to recognize and evaluate the impact of actual or potential problems, and to perform adequate research as a basis for judgments. They must also be skilled communicators and be able to deal with people at various levels throughout the organization. An in-depth study of knowledge and skills needed by internal auditors was completed and published by the IIA in 1992. It identified 334 competencies in 20 different disciplines needed by practicing internal auditors. The study, *A Common Body of Knowledge for the Practice of Internal Auditing*, lists those disciplines in the following order of perceived importance: reasoning, communications, auditing, ethics, organizations, sociology, fraud, computers, financial accounting, data gathering, managerial accounting, government, law, finance, taxes, quantitative methods, marketing, statistics, economics, and international knowledge.

Third is the presumption that the evaluations and conclusions contained in internal auditing reports are directed internally to management and the board, not to stockholders, regulators, or the public. Presumably, management and the board can resolve issues that have surfaced through internal auditing and implement solutions privately, and before problems get out of hand. Management is expected to acknowledge facts as stated in reports, but has no obligation to agree with an internal auditor's evaluations, conclusions, or recommendations. After internal auditors report their conclusions, management and the board have responsibility for subsequent operating decisions—to act or not to act. If action is taken, management has responsibility to ensure that satisfactory progress is made and internal auditors later can determine whether the actions taken have the desired results. If no action is taken, internal auditors have responsibility to determine that management and the board understand and have assumed any risks of inaction. Under all circumstances, internal auditors have the direct responsibility to apprise management and the board of any significant developments that the auditors believe warrant management and the board's consideration or action.

INTERNAL AUDITING VS. EXTERNAL AUDITING AND INDUSTRIAL ENGINEERING

The industrial engineer analyzes and measures methods of performing work, suggests improvements, designs and installs work systems, and evaluates the results of those systems. Internal auditors do use some of the analytical techniques belonging to industrial engineers but do not focus on them. Further, internal auditors do not design and install systems.

Internal auditors and external auditors both audit, but have different objectives and a different focus. Internal auditors generally consider operations as a whole with respect to the five key internal control objectives, not just the financial aspects. External auditors focus primarily on financial control systems that have a direct, significant effect on the figures reported in financial statements. Internal auditors are generally concerned with even small amounts of fraud, waste, and abuse as symptoms of underlying operational issues. But the external auditor may not be concerned if the incidents do not materially affect the financial statements—which is reasonable given the fact that external auditors are engaged to form an opinion only on the organization's financial statements. Internal auditors are concerned with such practices as ill-conceived business expansions, management override of internal controls, mismanaged contracts, and employee unrest, which can cause far greater loss and not be immediately reflected in financial data. Lawrence B. Sawyer in *Sawyer's Internal Auditing* summarized the differences in focus succinctly and emphatically:

Management controls over financial activities have been greatly strengthened throughout the years. The same cannot always be said of controls elsewhere in the enterprise. Embezzlement can hurt a corporation; the poor management of resources can bankrupt it. Therein lies the basic difference between external auditing and modern internal auditing; the first is narrowly focused and the second is comprehensive in scope.

True, the external auditor performs services for management and submits letters to management which recommend improvement in systems and controls. By and large, however, these are financially oriented. Also, the external auditor's occasional sally into nonfinancial operations may not benefit from the same depth of understanding as does the resident internal auditor, who is intimately familiar with the organization's systems, people, and objectives.

This comparison of internal auditing to external auditing considers only the external auditors' traditional role of attesting to financial statements. During the 1990s a number of the large public accounting firms began establishing divisions offering "internal auditing" services in additional to existing tax, actuarial, external auditing, and management consulting services. There is little information at this time to predict whether this new public accounting service will grow. Predictably the event has caused a flurry of debate among auditors about independence, objectivity, depth of organizational knowledge, operational effectiveness, and true costs to the organization.

TYPES OF INTERNAL AUDITS

Various types of audits are used to achieve particular objectives. The types of audits briefly described below illustrate a few approaches internal auditing may take. The examples are not to be considered all-inclusive.

An operational audit is a systematic review and evaluation of an organizational unit to determine whether it is functioning effectively and efficiently, whether it is accomplishing established objectives and goals, and whether it is using all of its resources appropriately. Resources in this context include funds, personnel, property, equipment, materials, information, space, and whatever else may be used by that unit. Operational audits can include evaluations of the work flow and propriety of performance measurements. These audits are tailored to fit the nature of the operations being reviewed.

A system analysis and internal control review is analysis of systems and procedures for an entire function such as information services or purchasing. Those systems and procedures are appraised with respect to one or more or the five key internal control objectives already mentioned.

An ethical business practices audit assesses to what extent employees follow established codes of conduct, policies, and standards of ethical practices. Policies that may fall within the scope of such an audit include procurement policies, conflicts of interest, gifts and gratuities, entertainment, political lobbying, patents and licenses, use of organization name, speaking engagements, fair trade practices, and private use of the organization's facilities.

A compliance audit determines whether the organizational unit or function is, or is not, following particular rules or directives. Such rules or directives can originate internally or externally and can include one or more of the following: organizational policies; performance plans; established procedures; required authorizations; applicable external regulations; relevant contractual provisions; and federal, state, and local laws. Characteristic of compliance audits is the yes/no aspect of the evaluation—for each event or transaction examined, either it follows the rule or does not.

A financial audit is an examination of the financial planning and reporting process, the conduct of financial operations, the reliability and integrity of financial records, and the preparation of financial statements. Such a review includes an appraisal of the system of internal controls related to financial functions.

A systems development and life cycle review is a unique type of information systems audit conducted in partnership with operating personnel who are designing and installing new information systems. The objective is to appraise the new system from an internal control perspective and independently test the system at various stages throughout its design, development, and implementation. The approach intends to identify and correct internal control problems before systems are actually put in place because modifications made during the developmental stages are less costly. Sometimes problems can be avoided altogether. There is risk in this approach that the internal auditor could lose objectivity and independence with considerable participation in the design and installation process.

A program audit evaluates whether the stated goals or objectives for a certain program or project have been achieved. It may include an appraisal of whether an alternative approach can achieve the desired results at a lower cost. These types of audits are also called performance audits, project audits, or management audits.

A fraud audit investigates whether the organization has suffered a loss through misappropriation of assets, manipulation of data, omission of information, or any illegal or irregular acts. It assumes that intentional deception has occurred.

A participative audit enlists the auditee to perform a self-assessment and otherwise assist in the audit process. In effect this become a problem-solving partnership between the internal auditor and auditee. This can be cost-effective but is not without risk. The internal auditor must retain the right to independently test any positions taken by the auditee.

INTERNAL AUDIT PLANNING

Knowing what areas to audit and where to commit resources is an integral part of the internal audit function. A long-range audit plan provides a complete view of audit strategy and coverage in relation to the relative significance of functions to be audited. The goal is to plan an audit strategy that is cost-effective and emphasizes audit projects that have high impact or address areas of significant risk. The person directing the internal audit function is usually the one responsible for creating a comprehensive multiyear audit plan. It is customary that the plan is reviewed and sanctioned by executive management and submitted to the board for approval.

An in-depth understanding of the organization and how it operates is a prerequisite for the audit planning process. Developing the plan first requires identifying and listing all auditable units or functions. (This is frequently called the "audit universe.") Next, a rational system must be devised to assign significance and risk to each auditable unit or function. Based on perceived significance and estimated risk, the audit priorities and strategies are documented in the audit plan. The planning process is not fixed, however. Departure of key people, changes in markets, new demographics, and other factors affect organizations. Drastic upheavals in the business environment are possible, changing the total character of operations. Organizational processes and existing internal control systems may become obsolete with new technology. Laws and regulations may change, as do attitudes about the degree of enforcement that is necessary. Consequently, risks and significance rankings, the audit universe, and audit strategies will change.

SEE ALSO: Compliance Auditing

[Aldona Cytraus]

FURTHER READING:

Albrecht, W. Steve, James D. Slice, and Kevin D. Stocks. *A Common Body of Knowledge for the Practice of Internal Auditing*. Alamonte Springs, FL: Institute of Internal Auditors, 1992.

Committee of Sponsoring Organizations of the Treadway Commission (COSO). *Internal Control-Integrated Framework: An Executive Summary*. Ernst & Young, 1992.

Institute of Internal Auditors. *Professional Internal Auditing Standards Volume. Standards for the Professional Practice of Internal Auditing*. Alamonte Springs, FL: Institute of Internal Auditors, 1992.

Price Waterhouse. *Improving Audit Committee Performance: What Works Best*. Alamonte Springs, FL: Institute of Internal Auditors Research Foundation, 1993.

Sawyer, Lawrence B. *Sawyer's Internal Auditing*. Alamonte Springs, FL: Institute of Internal Auditors Research Foundation, 1988.

Schiff, Jonathan. "A Report from the Conference Board and KPMG Peat Marwick." *In New Directions in Internal Auditing*. Research Report no. 946. New York: 1990.

Willson, James D., and Steven J. Root. *Internal Auditing Manual*. Boston: Warren, Gorham, & Lamont, 1989.

INTERNAL REVENUE SERVICE

The Internal Revenue Service (IRS), part of the U.S. Department of the Treasury, is mandated by federal law to enforce the tax laws of the United States. In addition to collecting income tax revenue from individuals and corporations—the largest source (55 percent) of the government's income—the IRS also collects such major revenues as Social Security **taxes**, excises (taxes on **commodities**), gift taxes, and **estate taxes**. Internal revenues derived from the sale of alcohol, tobacco, and firearms are no longer collected by the IRS.

For the most part, the revenue history of this country has consisted of tariffs levied on imported goods, and, in colonial times, of various property taxes. The extreme reaction to "taxation without rep-resentation" might have been due to the abhorrence of taxation in general. Raising revenue to fund George Washington's army turned out to be a thankless task; when Americans finally installed a government that represented them in 1781, they made sure that the Articles of Confederation deprived the central government of all right to levy taxes.

The stinginess of the state treasuries and obvious need for revenue led the founding fathers to insert into the new federal constitution a clause (Article I, Section 8) granting the federal government the right to raise taxes. As the first Secretary of the Treasury, Alexander Hamilton (1755-1804) exerted every effort to strengthen the taxing power of the government, and thanks to his initiative, Congress passed the first revenue bill in U.S. history, the Revenue Act of 1791. This created the office of the commissioner of Revenue, ancestor of today's IRS. The commissioner was empowered to collect the excise tax not only on distilled liquor, but excises on all manner of other goods, as well as a progressive tax on property.

Judging from the fierce opposition to these taxes, especially the one on liquor, taxation with representation proved to be every bit as unpopular as without it. Thomas Jefferson, who became president in 1801 and had led the opposition to the Revenue Act, helped to repeal the act and disband the commissioners office. The federal government subsequently relied on the lucrative revenues derived from tariffs, and the Treasury recorded surpluses annually until the eve of the Civil War.

The War of 1812 necessitated levying a new internal tax, which resembled a **sales tax** on purchased goods. The Office of Commissioner of Revenue was restored. When the war ended in late 1814, Treasury Secretary Albert Gallatin hoped the taxes would continue, but Congress abolished them, as well as the commissioner's office, in 1817. There was enough money in the treasury to fund the Mexican War 29 years later without an internal tax.

The real birth of the IRS, or the U.S. Bureau of Internal Revenue as it was originally called, had to wait until the Civil War. With $2 million per day going to fund the **public debt**, the need for more revenue was desperate. In July 1862, President Lincoln signed the largest revenue bill in U.S. history. Once again, it revived the office of Commissioner of Internal Revenue. The commissioner was empowered to establish a system to collect a progressive income tax based on income withholding (a tax return form was duly created), as well as to collect numerous other internal taxes. For the first time, failure to comply with the tax laws could result in punishment: prosecution and confiscation of assets in the most extreme cases. Tax returns had to be signed under oath.

Operating in a tiny room in the U.S. Treasury building in Washington, the new commissioner, George S. Boutwell, read every letter from anxious new taxpayers and kept his office open day and night to accommodate the crush of inquiries. The income tax forms seem simple by today's standards, but were complicated to most new taxpayers then: even Abraham Lincoln failed to understand his form and unnecessarily overpaid (the sizable refund arrived posthumously). By the end of **fiscal year** 1863, the new revenue bureau took in, through its assessors and collectors, nearly $40 million.

By war's end, the Bureau of Internal Revenue had grown from 1 employee to over 4,000. Despite the revenue garnered, the public deficit stood at an unprecedented $3 billion in 1865. Surprisingly, the income tax was discontinued after the Civil War, including the lucrative inheritance tax. The bureau, however was not dismantled along with the taxes. Until 1913, most of the nation's revenue derived from taxes on fermented and distilled liquor and tobacco. The bureau was put in charge of collecting the liquor and tobacco taxes, and a rather odd tax on oleomargarine that Congress levied in 1886 to protect the butter interest. In 1890, to control the sale of opium, a tax slapped on this "product," was also collected by the bureau.

How is it that the Bureau of Internal Revenue became identified almost exclusively with the income tax? In 1894, a bill restoring the progressive income tax passed Congress, in response to the agitation and lobbying efforts of Populists, Greenbackers, and other reformers who believed the rich should pay their dues to society. The next year, the U.S. Supreme Court, in *Pollock v. Farmers Loan and Trust Co.*, struck down the income tax as unconstitutional, to the dismay of reformers. The newly created Income Tax Division of the Bureau of Internal Revenue was duly disbanded.

Lobbying on behalf of a progressive income tax intensified after 1895. The vast majority of Americans would be exempt from paying income tax, with only the well-to-do expected to pay. President Taft (1909-13) supported the idea of an amendment to the constitution that would specifically allow the government to implement such a tax. The amendment he supported was swiftly accepted by the states, and in February 1913, the sixteenth Amendment, inaugurating the income tax, became part of the Constitution. In October followed a revenue bill establishing a progressive income tax for those earning over $3,000, only 1 percent of the population. Corporations also were subject to a tax on net income. Almost immediately, the Income Tax Division, heir to the one dismantled in 1895, was revived.

World War I, which cost the nation nearly $35 billion, was financed in part (33 percent) by internal revenues. Even before the United States became involved in the war, the Revenue Act of 1916 enlarged the number of taxpayers and created other internal taxes. The bureau was charged, for the first time, with publishing income tax statistics.

Following the 1916 tax law, other laws were swiftly passed to raise revenue for the war. The War Revenue Act of 1917 created new excess profits and estate taxes, and other revenue measures. The bureau was a beneficiary of some of this windfall, its budget increasing from $8 million in 1917 to nearly $15 million in 1918. In that same period, revenue collectors in the field increased from 4,500 to 7,400.

During World War I, the bureau for the first time made a determined effort to educate the public about the patriotism of paying taxes. Clergymen were encouraged to preach the morality of income tax filing from the pulpit. The bureau also established its first Intelligence Division, with specially trained officers to detect tax fraud (a system of withholding tax money from paychecks had been repealed by Congress in 1916, undoubtedly making evasion easier).

Postwar exigencies maintained the need for revenue, so that by 1920, the bureau collected a record $5.5 billion in revenue, compared to $350 million in 1913. From a total of 4,000 employees in 1913, its bureaucracy increased to 15,000 seven years later.

In 1919, the Nineteenth Amendment, outlawing alcoholic beverages, became part of the Constitution. Prohibition occasioned the establishment of a Prohibition Unit in the Bureau of Internal Revenue. Oddly, the Prohibition Law of October 1919, gave the Commissioner of Internal Revenue the authority to enforce the criminal aspects of the ban on liquor. Although distilleries were illegal, they were subject, if detected, to prosecution for tax evasion. The Bureau of Internal Revenue in 1925 alone made over 77,000 arrests, besides seizing and impounding property. After 1930, the U.S. Department of Justice took over these duties. When the Nineteenth Amendment was repealed in late 1933, the bureau switched to collecting liquor revenues again.

In that year, the Great Depression reached its height. The trauma of that experience ushered in the New Deal, which was committed to the philosophy that the government should spend money, even at the risk of an unbalanced budget, to get people back on the job. Another concern in those desperate times was the elderly indigent, whose plight resulted in the Social Security Act of 1935. Two years later, the Social Security Tax Division was up and running in the Bureau of Internal Revenue.

By 1941, the number of employees at the bureau, thanks to the New Deal, rose to an all-time high of 27,000. Because of five major tax cuts in the 1920s, revenues stood at only $1.6 billion in 1933. In 1941, because of government spending, tax revenues of necessity increased to a record $7.4 billion. Four years later, the cost of war had driven revenues up to $45 billion.

Despite the $7.4 billion collected by the IRS in 1941, still only a segment of the U.S. population filed income tax returns—at most eight million, including corporations. The huge demands of the World War II changed that. More and more individuals earning modest salaries, previously excluded from taxation, were required to pay. While in 1939, those earning less than $5,000 made up only 10 percent of the taxpayers, by 1948, these accounted for at least 50 percent. After 1941, therefore, the number of taxpayers increased greatly (from 8 million in 1941 to 60 million in 1945), and unlike the decade following World War I, there would not be a reduction in taxation after 1945.

The final building block to the creation of a modern revenue state was the reintroduction (after it was repealed in 1916) of tax withholding in July 1943. This money was sent directly from the place of employment to the Bureau of Internal Revenue. A year later, the "standard deduction" came into force for the first time also. Such a massive number of tax returns were coming into the bureau (the agency introduced an abbreviated tax form in 1941), that the bureau was collapsing under the strain, and tax refunds were taking over a year to be processed. This gave rise to bitter public criticism.

The result of the 1951 House subcommittee investigation of the bureau was the 1952 Reorganization Plan No. 1, inaugurating the most extensive restructuring of this agency in its history. All politically appointed posts within the bureau, except for commissioner and deputy commissioner, were replaced by civil service positions. The agency was significantly decentralized, with headquarters in Washington determining policy, while field offices were given wide latitude in **decision making**. In addition, electronic machines—predecessors of the computer—were introduced to speed up processing of forms, which in turn were further simplified. Lastly, the name of the agency was changed officially to the Internal Revenue Service.

The organization of the IRS has remained basically unaltered since 1952. Below the level of national headquarters, which is housed in its own building in Washington, there are 7 regional IRS offices, headed by a regional commissioner, and 64 district offices headed by a district director. It is at the district level that the tax laws are interpreted and applied, and often no two districts apply the laws alike. Ever since the U.S. Bureau of Alcohol, Tobacco and Firearms became a separate division within the Treasury Department in 1972, the IRS has no longer been responsible for collecting revenue on these items.

Tax collection is uncomplicated: most pay their taxes through payroll deductions. Tax returns are sent not to any one of the IRS administrative offices but to separate processing centers, where a computer scans each one for errors. For error-free returns, this is the end of the line, with the exception of processing a refund for those so eligible. Unlike Sweden, where the majority of tax returns are audited, in the United States, only a small number—10 percent of nearly 200 million—are audited, mainly because of the expense involved. If tax fraud is discovered through an audit, any one of a range of 150 penalties can be assessed against the taxpayer. The severest is the seizure of one's property. In 1990, nearly three million seizures took place. Taxpayers have the right to appeal such seizures.

Detecting such fraud is an important, expensive pursuit on the part of the IRS, requiring specialized computer equipment and employees who can sit for days researching, for instance, the most suspicious looking bank accounts to determine whether certain taxpayers have declared all of their income. The IRS has the legal authority to request information from any bank, and to inquire into any type of vehicle registration or business activity. This uncovers a huge range of information on a business, individual, or married couple, and this information in the future will expand as computers become ever more sophisticated. The IRS predicts that by the turn of the century, it will become virtually impossible for any person with a bank account to elude the IRS.

The IRS can also legally transmit taxpayer information to a variety of other government agencies. In this way, a person who has defaulted on a student loan, or who has failed to pay child support, can be ferreted out and forced to pay.

The right to demand such intimate details of one's finances, which inevitably discloses much about one's life and lifestyle, is authorized by Congress. Such power is not without its critics: no government agency is as pervasive as the IRS; none is as invasive of one's privacy; anyone with the smallest bank account can be tracked down.

Since the vast majority—over 95 percent—of eligible taxpayers in the United States faithfully file their taxes, resulting in $1 trillion for the U.S. treasury (up from $50 billion in 1951), the need to educate taxpayers is no longer a major task for the IRS. In addition, since the early 1990s, it is possible to file one's taxes electronically, which simplifies and speeds tax collection as never before. Hence the greatest challenge of the IRS has become not the collection and processing of taxes, or the educating of taxpayers, but rather, the pursuit of the "under reporter," or tax evader. The vast **underground economy** (estimated in the billions of dollars) continues to bedevil the IRS.

Detecting underreporting moonlighters (those who earn additional income outside their regular job) and many other potential underpayers of taxes has become a main goal of the IRS. Those hiring independent contractors and the self-employed will be particular targets in future. In the early 1990s, the IRS estimated that there were 500,000 self-employed people, earning incomes of $25,000 and more, who did not even file tax returns.

Achieving the formidable goal of near-perfect tax compliance (i.e., reporting of all income on the part of every single wage earner) would be unthinkable without the aid of computers. While a consequence of the 1952 reorganization of the IRS was a switch to electronic processing of tax forms, this was not computerization, which did not get underway until 1959. Two years later, the National Computer Center in Martinsburg, Virginia, was established—still the IRS's main brain center. Since 1984, $8 billion have been invested in modernizing IRS computers and programs in the agency's "Tax Systems Modernization" program. In 1995, it will be possible for the IRS to scan 17,000 tax form—including handwritten ones—per hour.

The sophisticated imaging and scanning equipment of the 1990s allows the IRS to conduct "targeted" searches of businesses, bank accounts, and licenses. One such search focused on California doctors and other professionals, 150 of whom were discovered to have underpaid their taxes. In a targeted search of commercial fishing licenses in Maine, nearly 2,600 holders of such licenses underreported earnings. The IRS regularly taps into the "Currency & Banking Retrieval System" database to examine casH transactions of $10,000 or more, and then match those transactions with tax returns.

Critics of the IRS abound. One critic, David Burnham, whose book on the IRS, *A Law unto Itself: The IRS and the Abuse of Power* created a stir when it was published in 1989, revealed many disturbing aspects of this agency. He claimed the IRS is almost completely unregulated and arbitrary in its **decision making** (decisions are made at the district level—no two IRS district offices need to apply a tax law in the same way). Burnham also questioned the right of the IRS to assess penalties in view of the fact that no two tax lawyers can come up with the same results on the same tax form.

[Sina Dubovoy]

FURTHER READING:

Anthes, Gary H. "IRS Turns to Imaging to Improve Performance: Tax Systems Modernization Project." *Computerworld.* April 11, 1994, p. 1.

Burnham, David. *A Law unto Itself: The IRS and the Abuse of Power.* New York: Vintage Books, 1989.

Doris, Lillian, ed. *The American Way in Taxation: Internal Revenue, 1862-1963.* Englewood Cliffs, NJ: Prentice Hall, 1963.

Gottschalk, Earl C., Jr. "There's Still Hope for Those Who Can't Pay." *Wall Street Journal.* February 18, 1994, p. C1.

Novack, Janet. "You Know Who You Are, and So Do We." *Forbes.* April 11, 1994, p. 88.

Treasury Deptartment. Internal Revenue Service. *Income Taxes, 1862-1962: A History of the Internal Revenue Service.* Publ. no.447. Washington, DC: GPO, 1962.

INTERNATIONAL ACCOUNTING STANDARDS COMMITTEE (IASC)

The International Accounting Standards Committee (IASC) was founded in London in 1973 by representatives of professional accounting societies of nine countries.

The purpose of the IASC in its own words is to "... formulate and publish in the public interest, standards to be observed in the presentation of audited financial statements and to promote their worldwide acceptance and observance."

The IASC is not the first organization on either a national or international scale that attempted to harmonize accounting standards. The English Institute of Chartered Accountants (1942) and the Committee on Accounting and Auditing Research of the Canadian Institute of Chartered Accountants (1946) studied harmonization on a national level, and the Accountants International Study Group, which was sponsored by American, Canadian, and British professional accountants, viewed standardization from a global perspective and compared the accounting practices and procedures of the three countries. In 1977, the International Federation of Accountants (IFAC) was created by members of the IASC, with which it is closely allied.

By 1991, professional accounting organizations representing 78 countries belonged to IASC. Although membership is worldwide (including the United States), most support for the IASC comes from the nations of western Europe. The IASC has a governing board that meets three times a year and consists of representatives of professional accounting organizations from member countries. In the United States, IASC membership is sponsored by the American Institute of Certified Public Accountants (AICPA) and Canadian membership is sponsored by the Canadian Institute of Chartered Accountants (CICA). The IASC is administered by a secretary-general who heads the Secretariat. Policy is set by the Consultative Group and various topic related steering committees. The IASC works closely with various national and regional accounting organizations, such as the African Accounting Council and the Inter-American Accounting Association. IASC activities are financed by board membership dues and the International Federation of Accountants.

In a lengthy study on the survivability of the IASC, IASC research fellow R.S. Wallace felt that the IASC lacked "de jure" institutional legitimacy. He concluded that the IASC lacked the authority to mandate standards to member countries, nor has any national member sought to grant that power to the IASC. In the United States, for example, accounting standards are largely set by the Securities and Exchange Commission, the **Financial Accounting Standards Board (FASB)**, and the **Government Accounting Standards Board (GASB)**, not the American Institute of Certified Public Accountants (which sponsors United States membership in IASC). Likewise, the IASC does not have a mandate from international organizations such as the United Nations to impose international standards. In essence, the IASC lacks the implicit and explicit authority to do more than offer and promote accounting standards to member countries. In his report, Wallace did feel that the IASC would continue to be influential in harmonizing financial statement standards largely because of a growing world economy. Common standards make the review and interpretation of financial statements, audits, and annual reports easier and more accurate. Other factors influencing IASC viability is its policy of dealing with general rather than industry or country specific issues, and a lack of competing organizations.

[Michael Knes]

FURTHER READING:

Skinner, Ross M. *Accounting Standards in Evolution*. Holt, Rinehart and Winston of Canada, 1987.

Wallace, R.S. "Survival Strategies of a Global Organization: The Case of the International Accounting Standards Committee." *Accounting Horizons*, June 1990, pp. 1-22.

INTERNATIONAL ARBITRATION

The term "international arbitration" covers dispute resolution where the dispute can be characterized as "international," such as when two parties to a dispute have places of business in different nations. For several reasons—notably speed, economy, privacy, and informality—many businesses prefer to arbitrate disputes rather than litigate them. For international business transactions, the reasons are somewhat different, but still compelling.

Even in the domestic context, some of the traditional advantages of arbitration are less evident. In the early history of arbitration, the typical claim would involve a relatively simple dispute between merchants over the quality or quantity of goods delivered under a contract. A trusted third party would be consulted for advice and counsel (in mediation) or for a final and binding decision (in arbitration) that was prompt and private. Yet more and more complex issues are being presented for arbitration, including resolution of claims based on statutes (including securities, antitrust, racketeering claims under RICO [Racketeer Influenced and Corrupt Organizations], and employment discrimination claims), and, increasingly, the arbitration process is being formalized to ensure greater due process. Yet despite arbitration's increasing complexity, disputes are still handled privately rather than publicly, with the arbitral award often being made known only to the parties. The award is final, with very limited bases of appeal open to the losing party.

These beneficial aspects (privacy, finality) apply with equal force in international arbitration, although the aspects of speed, economy, and informality are less evident. Still, there is a vital reason businesses prefer international arbitration to international litigation: where a dispute involves parties from different nations, there is no international court empowered to deal effectively with all international commercial disputes, and a judgment in one nation's courts will not automatically be honored in another country.

In Japan, for example, the judgment of a U.S. court will not be valid (and thus enforceable) unless (1) the U.S. court's jurisdiction did not contravene Japanese statutes or treaties; (2) there was proper notice; (3) the judgment does not violate Japanese policy or morals; (4) the U.S. court would also recognize a Japanese judgment (that is, there is reciprocity); and (5) the judgment was final (rather than "interlocutory" or intermediate). In short, if you believe you have a strong claim against a Japanese company with assets only in Japan, your U.S. judgment for money damages against that company would have to be "recognized" for enforcement (collection) in Japan; otherwise, you have only a piece of paper ordering the Japanese company to pay you, and do not have the money you seek.

How does international arbitration make a difference? In the typical international arbitration case, the two companies (1) have agreed contractually to arbitrate, either before a dispute arose or (less often) after; (2) an arbitrator or arbitral panel (usually three arbitrators) has made a decision and "rendered" an "award" determining who owed what to whom; and (3) national laws and international conventions assist in recognizing and enforcing the award in most trading nations.

INTERNATIONAL ENFORCEMENT

Although arbitration operates independently of the court system, it relies on a complex system of laws and on national court systems. The 1958 United Nations Convention on the Recognition and Enforcement of Arbitral Awards (the New York Convention) had a slow start, but as of 1995 over 85 nations have ratified the convention, including almost all nations active in international trade. In the signatory nations, the convention is the equivalent of a multilateral treaty, binding on citizens of the country adopting its provisions. The basic thrust of the New York Convention is to make arbitral awards rendered in one nation enforceable in any nation which has ratified the convention.

The New York Convention also provides for enforcement of agreements to arbitrate, even if the agreement to arbitrate is made prior to any actual dispute between the parties. The winning party can attach property of the loser located in any country that has ratified the convention. Thus, if a U.S. company agrees ahead of time to arbitrate any subsequent dispute arising out of its contract with a German company, and the two companies subsequently have a disagreement, either party can use the New York Convention to obtain a court order to (a) force the other party to arbitrate, and/or (b) enforce the award in any signatory nation without reopening the dispute.

The courts of a signatory nation will generally not examine the merits of the dispute prior to ordering arbitration, nor will they generally second-guess the decision of the arbitrator or arbitral tribunal after an award is made. This situation has some obvious advantages for the winning party: there is no rehearing of the dispute before a judge or jury. Under the New York Convention, as under the U.S. Federal Arbitration Act, there are very few grounds to effectively appeal an arbitral award, so a reluctant or unreasonable defendant cannot (as so often happens in litigation) prolong the inevitable by successive appeals to higher appellate courts.

THE ARBITRAL PROCESS

The arbitral process has essentially three parts. First, there must be an agreement by the parties to refer disputes to arbitration. The agreement may take place either before or after the dispute arises. Second, the arbitral tribunal must make a decision (not just a recommendation) that is final, but a decision which is within the scope of its authority. Third, with very few exceptions that provide a basis to appeal an award, the award can generally be enforced through court orders if the losing party does not voluntarily satisfy the terms of the award.

THE AGREEMENT TO ARBITRATE. An arbitration agreement establishes by mutual consent the parties' willingness to be bound by an arbitrator's decision, and also defines the issues on which an arbitrator may render an award. The parties may determine the number of arbitrators (usually one or a panel of three), the place of arbitration, the rules under which the arbitration will take place, and the applicable law. There are two basic types of arbitration agreements. The most common is an agreement to submit future disputes to arbitration (a predispute arbitration agreement); generally, this will be a relatively short clause in the more general contract between the parties. For example, the Balfour Corporation, based in Massachusetts, might contract with Mitsubishi Heavy Industries, based in Japan, using a single paragraph agreeing to submit to arbitration any future disputes relating to the contract. For example:

> The parties to this contract agree that, in the event of any dispute or disagreement of any kind arising out of this contract or matters pertaining to this contract, that such disputes be settled by arbitration before a panel of three arbitrators in Geneva, Switzerland, under the auspices of the International Chamber of Commerce.

If there is no predispute arbitration agreement and a dispute arises, the parties may draw up a set of questions to be decided along with procedural rules specifically suited to the dispute at hand to guide the arbitral tribunal. This is called a "submission." More often, however, the agreement to arbitrate precedes any dispute, and it is usual to incorporate the procedural rules of an institution such as the American Arbitration Association (AAA), the Inter-American Commercial Arbitration Association (IACAC), the International Chamber of Commerce (ICC), the International Center for the Settlement of Investment Disputes (ICSID), or the London Court of International Arbitration (LCIA). By incorporating the rules of these institutions, parties adopt an administering agency to assist the arbitral process.

As an example, consider the above predispute arbitration agreement between Balfour and Mitsubishi. Among other contingencies, the ICC's Court will (1) decide if there appears to be a binding arbitration agreement under which the ICC is authorized to act; (2) decide whether there should be one or three arbitrators, if the parties have not specified the number; (3) appoint arbitrators in accordance with its rules; (4) determine the place of arbitration, if not already agreed upon by the parties; (5) set time limits; (6) review the draft of the arbitral tribunal's award; and (7) administer issues of fees and expenses of the arbitrators. The reader is cautioned, however, that arbitrations conducted under institutional auspices may be more expensive than an arbitration where the rules and procedures have been crafted by the disputants to ensure the greatest efficiency.

Where the parties do not incorporate a set of institutional rules, an arbitration clause should—at a minimum—contain the following:

1. The place of arbitration (naming a certain city or nation). This will have the effect of establishing which nation's laws will govern the formation and maintenance of the arbitration. The law of the place of arbitration—or *lex arbitrii*—controls a number of key issues, including the validity of the arbitration agreement, appointment or removal of arbitrators, time limits, interim protective measures, and form of the arbitral award.

2. The number of arbitrators (whether one or three).

3. The choice of substantive law to be applied to any issue between the parties; in contrast to the *lex arbitrii*, the choice of a substantive or proper law for the arbitration is meant to reach the merits of the controversy to invoke some rule of decision.

4. The issues to be decided and any time limits for the award to be rendered.

Where parties to a dispute are unlikely to agree on such details after the dispute has arisen, making reference to arbitral institutional rules is nearly essential.

THE ARBITRATOR'S POWERS AND THE ARBITRAL DECISION. The arbitral tribunal—whether it be a single arbitrator or a panel—gets its power from the agreement to arbitrate and the willingness of a legal system to enforce that agreement or any arbitral award made pursuant to that agreement. Hence, if the arbitrator or arbitral panel decides a matter that is beyond the scope of the arbitration agreement, recognition and enforcement of the award may be refused. Also, certain kinds of agreements to arbitrate may be invalid under national law. For many years, U.S. courts refused to honor agreements to arbitrate certain kinds of disputes, such as claims based on violations of federal securities or antitrust statutes. Public policy, it was felt, was better served by having such federal law-based claims heard in the judicial system rather than by arbitrators. Gradually, however, the U.S. Supreme Court led the way in allowing arbitration of such claims. At present, arbitration of claims based on federal employment discrimination, antitrust, racketeering, and securities laws are all arbitrable. Few, if any, restrictions remain in U.S. law as to the kinds of controversies that can be arbitrated.

In other countries, however, the kinds of disputes that can lawfully be arbitrated may be limited. In Latin America, for example, commercial arbitration has not been generally accepted. A government contract may not be arbitrable in some countries unless a statute expressly allows it, and there are sometimes difficult issues involved in holding a particular government to its agreement to arbitrate disputes arising under a contract; issues of sovereign immunity and its waiver are often involved.

Even when there is little doubt about the arbitrability of a particular kind of claim, there may yet be some doubt as to whether the parties' predispute arbitration agreement was intended to cover certain issues. That is, the "scope" of the arbitrator's decisional powers as given by the parties may be contested. But predispute arbitration agreements are generally phrased rather broadly ("all disputes arising under or in relation to this contract") and are generally interpreted liberally by the courts. In any case, it is the arbitrator that makes the initial determination as to whether a particular issue or set of issues is within the scope of his arbitral authority, and not the court.

Much could be said about the arbitral hearing itself, and the kinds of evidence that are allowed and the kinds of procedures that are typical. But the reader is best advised to consult the more extended reference at the end of this article, and to bear in mind that, in general, arbitrations are often conducted with fairly strict time limits, that informality is the norm, that not all evidence is heard, and that the well-known judicial rights of cross-examination and discovery are largely absent under most international institutional arbitral rules. Moreover, by custom and law in many countries, the arbitrator has not been required to state the judicial equivalent of "findings of fact" or "conclusions of law"—it is sufficient that the arbitrator make a decision in writing, but not that he or she defend it.

This was probably appropriate in simple disputes where the arbitrator was called upon to render a prompt decision as to whether delivered goods did or did not correspond to a sample or to a known trade description or industry standard. Nevertheless, with the increasing complexity of arbitrations to include claims in securities, antitrust, employment discrimination, and the like, there is a discernible trend that favors giving reasons in awards. And since the arbitrator or panel has a duty to ensure that the award, once made, is valid and enforceable, the particular institutional rules (whether they are the UNCITRAL rules, the ICC rules, or some other set of institutional rules) must be consulted to see that the award is in proper form (and, thus, enforceable).

Under the UNCITRAL arbitration rules (formulated by the United Nations Commission on International Trade Law), for example, (1) the award must be in writing, (2) the reasons for the award must be stated, and (3) the award must be signed by the arbitrators and must bear the date and place of the decision. Under rules of the International Center for the Settlement of Investment Disputes (ICSID), there are additional requirements for a valid award, such as designating counsel for the parties, a summary of the proceedings, and a statement of facts as found by the tribunal.

The tribunal must issue its award within any time limits set forth in the submission or the institutional rules incorporated by the parties. For example, if parties submit a dispute to arbitration and require that a decision be made within 60 days, then any arbitral award taking place after 60 days would not be valid and enforceable. Under rules of the American Arbitration Association (AAA), the award must be made no later than 30-days from the close of the hearings; unless an extension had been obtained, an award dated beyond the 30-day period would not be valid and enforceable.

JUDICIAL REVIEW AND ENFORCEMENT OF ARBITRAL AWARDS. Once the arbitrator or arbitral tribunal has made its award it seldom has any further function with respect to the parties. The award, being final and binding, does have important legal consequences, and may be enforced against a nonpaying party or enforcement of the award may be delayed when the losing party seeks to "vacate" the award. But even if the losing party succeeds (which is relatively rare) the arbitrator or arbitral tribunal does not generally rehear the dispute unless the losing party (1) appeals to the courts in the country where the arbitration was held and (2) obtains an order requiring resubmission of all or part of the dispute. Almost always, however, the award marks the end of the tribunal's involvement with the parties on that particular dispute.

After the arbitration, the winning party may wish to register or deposit the award with a court in the country where the arbitration took place. In theory, this should not be necessary: the parties have agreed that an arbitrator should render a final and binding award, and implicit in that agreement is that no further action needs to be taken by the winning party. But not all awards are promptly and voluntarily paid; the losing party, after all, is likely to disagree with the tribunal's decision, and may well be looking for grounds on which to resist enforcement of the award. Registration or deposit of the award with a court of competent jurisdiction can in some cases put additional psychological pressure on the losing party to comply sooner rather than later, and in some cases, registration or deposit may be a necessary prerequisite to enforcement.

The winning party can often use the award to put pressure on the losing party, whether through explicit or implicit threats of commercial reprisal or noncooperation, or through the threat of adverse publicity. If such pressure fails, the winning party may have to seek execution by court proceedings on the bank accounts or other assets of the losing party. If the award has been deposited or registered, it may thereafter be enforced as though it were a judgment of the court. In many countries, however, and as envisioned by the New York Convention, a final and binding award may be enforced in a country other than where the arbitration took place, provided that the two countries are both signatories to the New York Convention.

A losing party can comply with the award, use it as a basis for negotiating a settlement, or may challenge the award. The bases for challenge, however, are few indeed. Aside from showing bias or favoritism on the part of arbitrators, the principal means of successfully challenging an award deal with procedural issues. Challenges on procedural issues may be made, for example, where the arbitrator failed to decide an issue submitted by the parties, failed to allow continuance of the hearing even though good cause was shown, or considered and decided issues beyond the scope of the agreement or submission by the parties. It is abundantly clear as of 1995 that, internationally, challenges to arbitral awards based on the merits (in contrast to procedural challenges) are fairly fruitless. In some countries, a tribunal's decision that is in manifest disregard of the law may be set aside by judicial review. This is not, however, a generally recognized basis for setting aside an arbitral award in the United States.

An award may be challenged in at least two ways. One way is for the losing party to ask a court to modify or set aside the award, while another way is to ask the court to remit the award to the arbitral tribunal for reconsideration and revision. If an award is set aside, the award loses its legal validity in the country where it was made, and also any country adopting the New York Convention (under which the setting aside of an award in the country of origin is grounds for refusing to recognize and enforce that award).

Under the New York Convention, recognition and enforcement of the award may be refused where the losing party offers proof:

1. That the agreement on which the arbitration is based involves one or more parties with a legal incapacity, or that the agreement is not valid under the proper law of the contract or the *lex arbitrii* (the law of the country where the award was made).

2. The losing party was not given proper notice of the appointment of the arbitrator or of the arbitration proceedings or was otherwise unable to present his case.

3. The award contained decisions on matters beyond the scope of the tribunal.

4. The composition of the arbitral tribunal was not in accordance with the agreement of the parties.

5. The subject matter of the decision is not capable of settlement by arbitration under the law of the country where the arbitration is held.

6. Recognizing and enforcing the award would be contrary to the public policy of the country whose court is asked to enforce the award.

These objections are largely procedural; none of them attacks the correctness of the particular decision (such as "Was delivery of the goods timely? And, if not, what are appropriate damages to the buyer?"). Rather, these objections largely concern whether the tribunal exceeded the scope of its authority or ignored basic rules of procedural fairness or its own set of procedural rules. Only the last two bases numbers (5) and (6) invoke matters of substance. Yet these are substantive questions of policy, going beyond which of the parties is entitled to what. These larger limitations on arbitration serve to remind us that arbitration, domestic or international, does not operate with complete independence from the legal systems of which it is a part.

[Donald O. Mayer]

FURTHER READING:

Convention on the Recognition and Enforcement of Foreign Arbitral Awards (New York Convention). U.S. Code. Vol. 9, secs. 201-208 (1958).

Redfern, Alan, and Martin Hunter. *Law and Practice of International Commercial Arbitration.* 2nd. ed., London: Sweet & Maxwell, 1991.

INTERNATIONAL COMMUNICATION

SEE: Cross-Cultural/International Communication

INTERNATIONAL COMPETITION

International competition is a fact of life for today's companies. Manufacturers in the United States, for example, must compete not only with exports from other countries, but also with American **subsidiaries** of foreign corporations. The same is true for manufacturers and other companies in Japan and the European Union (EU). Newly industrialized countries (NICs) such as China, South Korea, Taiwan, Singapore, Brazil, and Mexico are also competing for a share of the international marketplace.

International trade in the 1990s is dominated by the United States, Japan, and the European Union (EU). Together they generate 80 percent of all world trade and account for 65 percent of all foreign **direct investment**. One sign of increased international competition is the growth of imports and exports. In the United States, for example, exports increased from less than 10 percent of manufacturing output in the 1960s to more than 20 percent in the 1990s. Similarly, imports of manufactured products increased from 5 percent of domestic output in the 1960s to more than 25 percent in the 1990s.

FOREIGN DIRECT INVESTMENT

The growth of foreign direct investment is another sign of increased international competition. Since the 1980s, foreign direct investment has increased four times faster than world output. Trade between parent companies and their foreign subsidiaries in the early 1990s accounted for approximately 80 percent of all trade between the United States and Japan, 40 percent of all trade between the United States and the EU, and 55 percent of all trade between the EU and Japan.

Foreign direct investment is a strategy used by multinational enterprises to create international production networks. Through an equity investment by a parent company in a branch, subsidiary, or affiliate located in another country, the parent company gains managerial control of an enterprise located in another country.

Foreign direct investment is primarily used by companies to establish foreign subsidiaries that will produce goods and services for sale in local and international markets. In the early 1990s U.S. subsidiaries of foreign companies accounted for approximately 20 percent of all U.S. exports and 33 percent of all U.S. imports. Foreign subsidiaries of U.S. parent companies accounted for approximately 33 percent of U.S. exports and 20 percent of U.S. imports.

There is a tendency toward regional clustering of foreign direct investment. That is, Japanese firms tend to invest in Asian countries, EU firms in other European countries, and U.S. firms in North and South American countries. Among the three dominant international trading groups, the United States is the principal direct investor in the EU and Japan, and the EU is the principal direct investor in the United States.

The elimination of trade and investment barriers can encourage foreign direct investment. The **North American Free Trade Agreement** (NAFTA), for example, involves the United States, Canada, and Mexico. It eliminates many of the trade and investment barriers that existed among the three signatories. With the adoption of NAFTA, it is expected that foreign direct investment by the United States will increase in Mexico, just as foreign direct investment by U.S. companies in Canada increased following the passage of the **U.S.-Canadian Free Trade Agreement** of 1989.

HOW BUSINESSES COMPETE IN FOREIGN MARKETS

There are three basic methods by which companies can compete in foreign markets: **exporting**, licensing and other contractual agreements, and investment. Each method has its own advantages and disadvantages. One method may be more appropriate for a certain line of business than another. For example, exporting works for best for physical goods. Licensing and other contractual arrangements are more appropriate for intangibles, services, and the transfer of technology. Investment involves the transfer of an entire enterprise to another country.

Exporting is limited to physical goods. When a company exports goods to another country, those goods are manufactured outside of the target market. Companies that export can use intermediaries located in their own country to facilitate exports, or they can use no intermediaries or only those located in the target country. International freight forwarders, banks, and other specialists can assist companies wishing to export by handling many of the details regarding documentation and financing.

Exporting is often the way a company initially becomes involved in international trade. Companies can gain valuable experience in international markets through exporting without being exposed to large capital losses. A recent variation on traditional exporting is mail-order exporting. Mail-order companies based in the United States, for example, have found that with the use of fax machines, international toll-free calls, credit cards, and air courier delivery, consumers in Europe, Japan, and elsewhere are willing to place orders from catalogs and other direct mail promotions.

International licensing is another way for domestic companies to compete internationally. Under an international licensing agreement, domestic companies provide foreign companies with rights to some of their intangible assets, such as their patents, trade secrets, know-how, trademarks, or even their company name and logo. Domestic companies often provide some type of technical assistance to make sure the licensed properties are used properly. Similar contractual agreements may include franchising, technical agreements, service or management contracts, and other variations.

Licensing and other contractual agreements are typically long-term associations between an international company and an entity in the host country. They typically involve the transfer of technology or human skills. Characteristically there is no equity investment by the international company in such agreements.

Licensing and other contractual arrangements can offer several advantages over or alternatives to exporting. Exports are often subject to another country's import barriers, such as tariffs and quotas. Licensing agreements can circumvent such barriers, since it is only intangible assets and services that are being exchanged. When exports are no longer profitable, companies can enjoy incremental income from licensing agreements. In some cases a country's currency may experience a prolonged devaluation, making exports no longer profitable. Licensing agreements can overcome some of the risks associated with such currency fluctuations. There is also less of a political risk with licensing, which avoids the risks associated with expropriation of the international company's investment by the host country's government. Licensing can also provide the host country with much-desired **technology transfer**, so that its government is likely to view such agreements as beneficial.

Investment is the third way in which companies can compete in other countries. Typically, foreign direct investment involves ownership by an international company of a manufacturing plant or other production facility in a target country. Investments may be sole ventures, with full ownership and control by the parent company; or they may be joint ventures, with ownership and control shared with one or more local partners. Investment may be in a new establishment, or it may involve the acquisition of an existing enterprise.

International companies generally make direct investments in foreign countries for one of three reasons. One reason is to obtain raw materials from the host country. Such investors are known as extractive investors. Very little of the extracted resource is sold in the host country. Most of it is either exported back to the international company's home country for use in manufacturing there, or sold on the world market. The steel, aluminum, and petroleum industries are examples of this type of investment.

A second reason for foreign direct investment is to source products at a lower cost. Sourcing investors establish manufacturing or assembly operations in a foreign country for the purpose of obtaining components or finished goods more cheaply than they could in their home country. These components or finished goods are then exported back to the investor's home country or shipped to other countries. In the U.S. consumer electronics industry, for example, assembled products are obtained by U.S. companies from Mexico, Taiwan, or elsewhere for sale in the United States.

The third and most prevalent reason for foreign direct investment is to penetrate local markets and compete internationally. As noted above, international companies use direct investment to establish a production base in another country for the purpose of competing in that country's marketplace.

FINANCING INTERNATIONAL TRADE THROUGH COUNTERTRADING

Countertrading is a type of contractual agreement in international trade that provides special arrangements for financing an exchange of goods and services. There are many forms of countertrading, ranging from simple barter agreements to complex offset deals that involve the exporter agreeing to compensatory practices with respect to the buyer. Countertrading commonly takes place between private companies in developed nations and the governments of developing countries, although countertrading also occurs between developed nations. It has become popular as a means of financing international trade to reduce risks or overcome problems associated with various national currencies.

Buy-backs are a common form of countertrading that typically take place between a private corporation from a developed country and the government (or government agency) of a developing nation. Under the first contract of a buy-back arrangement, the exporting private corporation agrees to provide a production facility or other type of capital goods to the developing nation. Then, under the second contract, the developing nation repays the exporting private corporation with output produced at the facility or derived from the originally exported capital goods. The exporter, in effect, buys back the output of the facility it has constructed.

Buy-backs are used to finance direct investment in developing countries. They are popular because they meet the needs and objectives of both parties. From the developing country's viewpoint, buy-backs expand the country's export base, provide employment, and help it meet its goals for industrialization and development. From the point of view of a private corporation, the buyback may help it gain a market presence in the country and provide it with a source of products it can use or sell. If the particular output of the facility is not needed by the corporation, it can involve a third party to help it meet its countertrade obligations.

Another type of countertrade is the compensation trade. An exporter and importer agree to make reciprocal purchases of specific goods. The exchange is covered under a single contract. It may or may not take place simultaneously. Each delivery is invoiced in an agreed currency, with payments going either to the supplier or to a clearing account. A third party may be involved to fulfill the purchase commitment of one of the parties.

There are many other types of countertrading; it has become firmly established as a method of financing international trade. For developing countries that have hard currency shortages, or whose national currencies are not readily convertible to other types of foreign exchange, countertrading offers them a means of financing imports.

International companies from developed countries who are willing to countertrade have found that it provides them with a competitive edge. By being flexible in the type of payment they are willing to receive, companies that are willing and able to countertrade have a stronger position in competitive bidding for projects involving emerging markets in developing countries. Many such companies are eager to find outlets for their products in emerging markets such as China and Mexico, for example.

POLITICAL FACTORS IN INTERNATIONAL COMPETITION

International competition can be affected by political policies beyond the control of international companies. While various international trade agreements have served to reduce or eliminate **trade barriers**, such barriers continue to exist. The most common form of trade barrier in international trade is a tariff or duty that is usually imposed on imports. There is also a category of nontariff barriers that also serve to restrict global trade and affect international competition.

Governments can give international companies based in their own countries significant advantages by establishing trade barriers. Protecting domestic producers against foreign competitors—especially infant industries—improving a nation's terms of trade, reducing domestic unemployment, and improving a nation's balance-of-payments position are some of the reasons given for imposing import tariffs on foreign-made goods.

In addition to duties and tariffs, there are also nontariff barriers (NTBs) to international trade. These include quantitative restrictions, or quotas, that may be imposed by one country or as the result of agreements between two or more countries. Examples of quantitative restrictions include international commodity agreements, voluntary export restraints, and orderly marketing arrangements.

Administrative regulations constitute a second category of NTBs. These include a variety of requirements that must be met in order for trade to occur, including fees, licenses, permits, domestic content requirements, financial bonds and deposits, and government procurement practices. The third type of NTB covers technical regulations that apply to such areas as packaging, labeling, safety standards, and multilingual requirements.

In 1980 the Agreement on Technical Barriers to Trade, also known as the Standards Code, came into effect for the purpose of ensuring that administrative and technical practices do not act as trade barriers. By the end of 1988 the agreement had been signed by 39 countries. Additional work on promoting unified standards to eliminate these NTBs is being conducted by the **General Agreement on Tariffs and Trade (GATT)** Standards Committee.

Government subsidies are another way in which government policies can provide assistance to domestic companies involved in international trade. Export subsidies are given to domestic producers of goods that will be exported. Export subsidies may take the form of a variety of government benefits, including direct payments, support prices, tax incentives, and funds for training. Export subsidies are given on the condition that the goods being produced will be exported. In the European Union (EU), export subsidies are called variable subsidies. Rules affecting variable subsidies of EU countries are found in the Common Agricultural Policy of the EU.

GATT contains restrictions on the use of export subsidies. Developed countries are forbidden to use subsidies to support the export of most manufactured goods, for example. Under GATT, less-developed nations are permitted to subsidize manufactured goods that will be exported, provided the subsidies do not significantly damage the economies of developed countries. GATT also provides for remedies, such as countervailing duties, when it has been determined that one trading partner is unfairly using export subsidies.

THE FUTURE OF INTERNATIONAL COMPETITION

It is clear that many factors will contribute to the growth of international competition. These include technological and political factors as well as economic factors. Industries that are experiencing rapid technological advancements are already global in nature. Production facilities can and are being located virtually anywhere in the world. As a result, consumer demand in the different industrial countries is converging, so that consumers in Germany, for example, want the benefits of the same technologies as consumers in Japan.

Politically it seems clear that international and multinational trade agreements are being written for the purpose of facilitating international trade. The formation of the European Union, the North American Free Trade Agreement, and the General Agreement on Tariffs and Trade (GATT) indicate that political leaders not only have realized the benefits of less restricted international competition, they have also been able to convince their constituents of those benefits.

It is likely that international competition will continue to increase. Companies will continue to enter international markets through direct investment, licensing and other contractual agreements, and by exporting. International trade agreements will facilitate their efforts and hopefully make them more profitable. Consumers throughout the world will benefit with a higher standard of living from access to a wider range of goods and services.

[David Bianco]

FURTHER READING:

Nelson, Carl A. *Global Success: International Business Tactics for the 1990s.* Liberty Hall Press, 1990.

Root, Franklin R. *Entry Strategies for International Markets.* Rev. ed. Lexington Books, 1994.

INTERNATIONAL EXCHANGE RATE

A foreign exchange (FX) rate or international exchange rate is the price of one country's money (currency) in terms of another country's currency. Exchange rates are determined by the supply of and the demand for foreign currencies. Several factors influence exchange rates, including relative rates of **inflation**; comparative **interest rates**; growth of domestic money supply; size and trend of balance of payments; economic growth, as measured by the **gross national product**; dependency on outside energy sources; central bank intervention; government policy and political stability; and the world's perception of the strength of the foreign currency.

As nations and their economies have become increasingly interdependent, the FX market has emerged as a global focal point. With an estimated daily FX turnover exceeding $1 trillion, this is by far the world's largest market. In order to remain competitive in the world economy, it is vital to manage the risk of adverse currency fluctuations.

The largest users of the FX market are commercial **banks**, which serve as intermediaries between currency buyers and sellers. Corporations and financial institutions also trade currencies, primarily to safeguard their foreign currency-moninated assets and liabilities against adverse FX rate movement. Banks and fund managers trade currencies to profit from FX rate movements. Individuals also are subject to fluctuating FX rates, most commonly when a traveler exchanges his/her native currency for a foreign one before embarking on a business trip or vacation.

When the Chicago Mercantile Exchange introduced trading in foreign currency futures in 1972, it enabled all currency market participants, including individual investors, to capitalize on FX rate fluctuations without having to make or take delivery of the actual currencies. Foreign currency futures offer risk management and profit opportunities to individual investors, as well as small firms and large companies.

There are two types of potential users of foreign currency futures: the hedger and the speculator. The hedger seeks to reduce and manage the risk of financial losses that can arise from transacting business in currencies other than one's native currency. Speculators provide risk capital and assume the risk the hedger is seeking to transfer in the hope of making a profit by correctly forecasting future price movement.

Currently, **futures** and options on futures contracts are listed for trading in the following foreign currencies on the Chicago Mercantile Exchange: Australian dollar; British pound sterling; Canadian dollar; Deutsche mark; French franc; Japanese yen; and Swiss franc. The MidAmerica Commodity Exchange in Chicago lists the following futures contracts: British pound sterling; Canadian dollar; Deutsche mark; Japanese yen; and Swiss franc.

[Susan Bard Hall]

FURTHER READING:

An Introduction to Currency Futures and Options. Chicago Mercantile Exchange. January 1994, p. 4.

MidAm Foreign Currency Futures. MidAmerica Commodity Exchange. August 1993, pp. 3, 6.

Rolling Spot. Chicago Mercantile Exchange. August 1993.

INTERNATIONAL FINANCE

International finance is the examination of institutions, practices, and analysis of cash flows that move from one country to another. There are several prominent distinctions between international finance and its purely domestic counterpart, but the most important one is the role played by exchange rate risk. Exchange rate risk refers to the uncertainty injected into any international financial decision that results from changes in the price of one country's currency per unit of another country's currency. Examples of other distinctions include the environment for direct foreign investment, new risks resulting from changes in the political environment, and differential taxation of assets and income.

The level of international trade is a relevant indicator of economic growth worldwide. **Foreign exchange** markets facilitate this trade by providing a resource where currencies from all nations can be bought and sold. While there is a heavy volume of foreign exchange between some countries, such as the United States and Canada, other countries with little international trade may have only intermittent need for such transactions. Current exchange rates of one country's currency versus another are determined by supply and demand for these currencies. As an example of an exchange rate, consider a rate at which U.S. dollars (US$) could be exchanged for Canadian dollars (C$): US$0.74 per C$1. This implies that a Canadian dollar can be purchased for US$0.74 and conversely a U.S. dollar can be purchased for C$1.35 (or 1/0.74). These current rates are referred to as spot rates.

In addition to international trade, there is a second motivation for international financial activity. Many firms make long-term investments in productive assets in foreign countries. When a firm decides to build a factory in a foreign country, it has likely considered a variety of issues. For example: Where should the funds needed to build the factory be raised? What kinds of tax agreements exist between the home and foreign countries that may influence the after-tax profitability of the new venture? Are there any government-imposed restrictions on moving profits back to the home country? Do the forecasted cash flows of the new venture enhance the parent firm's exposure to exchange rate fluctuations or does it lessen this exposure? Are the economic and political systems in the foreign country stable?

The short-term motive for foreign exchange (trade) and the long-term motive (capital formation) are related. As an example, Japan has had a balance of trade surplus with the United States for a number of years. This is because Japan exports more to the United States than they import from the United States and represents a flow of funds from the United States to Japan. In recent years, Japan has made considerable investments in automobile plants in the United States. While there are several reasons for this strategic move, an important one is to provide a source for funds to flow from Japan to the United States. Japan invests much more in the United States than the United States invests in Japan. While the two motives for foreign exchange do not always offset, they typically do for major trading partners over longer periods.

THE NATURE OF EXCHANGE RATES AND EXCHANGE RATE RISK

Consider two developed countries, A and B. If A and B are trading partners and make investments in each other's country, then there must also be a well-developed market for exchange of the two currencies. From A's perspective, demand for B's currency will depend on the cost of B's products when compared with domestic substitutes. It will also depend on investment opportunities in B compared with those available domestically in A. Likewise, the supply of B's currency depends on the same issues when examined from B's perspective.

Ignoring everything else, A will demand more of B's currency if it can buy it more cheaply. For example, if the exchange rate moves from 2 B per 1 A to 3 B per 1 A, imports from B become cheaper since it costs A's residents fewer units of their own currency to buy them. Conversely, if the exchange rate moves to 1.5 B per 1 A, the cost of imports has risen and demand for B's currency will fall. The supply of B's currency will change for the same reasons, but the change will be in the opposite direction. If B's citizens can trade the same number of their own currency units for fewer units of A's currency, they will offer less currency for exchange. At some exchange rate, the supply of B's currency will exactly satisfy the demand and an equilibrium, or market-clearing rate, will be established.

This market-clearing exchange rate does not stay in one place. This is because of a variety of events including: (1) changes in the relative inflation rates of the two countries, (2) changes in the relative rates of return on investments in the two countries, and (3) government intervention. Examples of government intervention include quotas on imports or restrictions on foreign exchange. As a brief example of how the market-clearing exchange rate can move, suppose that the current equilibrium exchange rate is 2 B per 1 A. Next, consider new information indicating that investors can achieve a higher rate of return on investments in B while returns on investments available domestically in A remain the same. As investors in A realize this, they have greater interest in making investments in B. This increases the demand for B's currency and means that investors in A are now willing to pay more for a unit of B's currency. B's investors, however now see that investment in A is not as good as before. They are less interested in making these investments and will supply fewer units of B's currency in exchange for A's currency. The dual influences of A's investors becoming more eager to buy B's currency and the increased reluctance of B's investors to offer their currency indicates that the market-clearing exchange rate must be different than the prior rate of 2 B per 1 A. In this example, to reach equilibrium, the rate should move to a point where 1 unit of A's currency can be exchanged for less than 2 units of B's currency. This movement can be interpreted as a weakening of A's currency and a strengthening of B's currency.

Specific movements in the market-clearing exchange rate can be modeled by several economic equalities called parity conditions. Three specific parity conditions are commonly used to model exchange rate equilibrium. Purchasing power parity indicates that currencies experiencing high **inflation** are likely to weaken while those experiencing low inflation are likely to strengthen. The international Fisher effect indicates that currencies with high levels of interest will tend to strengthen while currencies with low levels of interest will weaken. A third parity condition, interest rate parity, indicates that exchange rates must move to a level where investors in either country cannot make a riskless profit by borrowing or lending a foreign currency.

EXAMPLES OF EXCHANGE RATE RISK

Since forecasts of future inflation rates, **interest rates**, and government actions are uncertain, exchange rates are also uncertain. This means that an investment that will pay its return in units of a foreign currency has an uncertain return in the home currency. For example, suppose an investor in A bought a security B for 100 B. This one-year investment has a guaranteed return of 10 B, or 10 percent. If the exchange rate remains at a constant 2 B per 1 A over the life of the investment, the investor must initially commit 50 A to exchange for 100 B to make the investment. After one year, the 110 B returned (including the 10 B in interest) is exchanged for 55 A. The profit of 5 A on an investment of 50 A represents a 10 percent return to the investor from A. If, however, the exchange rate moved to 1.8 B per 1 A during the year, the investor would now receive the same 110 B from the investment, but when converted to the home currency, 61.1 A is received. This represents a profit of 11.1 A on an investment of 50 A, or 22.2 percent. Note that the return is amplified because B's currency strengthened during the holding period. Likewise, if the exchange rate moved to 2.2 B per 1 A, the return of 110 B translates to 50 A and a rate of return of 0 percent.

As another example, suppose an importer in country A purchases a quantity of goods from an exporter in country B and agrees to pay 1,000 B in 90 days. The importer is now obligated to make a foreign exchange transaction and must purchase the units of B's currency at the exchange rate that prevails in 90 days. Since that rate is likely to be different from the current rate, the importer is exposed to exchange rate risk. One common method for reducing this exposure is to enter into a forward contract to buy B's currency. A forward contract is an agreement to trade currencies at a specified date in the future at an exchange rate determined today. By purchasing the needed currency through a forward contract, the importer can eliminate concern with exchange-rate volatility by locking in a specific rate today.

TYPES OF EXPOSURE TO EXCHANGE RATE RISK

Exposure to exchange-rate fluctuations can be placed into three categories: translational, transactional, and economic. Translation exposure refers to the changes in accounting profits that result from reporting requirements. Transaction exposure is created when the firm enters into agreements that will require specific foreign exchange transactions during the current period. The example of the importer in the previous paragraph would be classified as transaction exposure. Economic exposure is the need for foreign exchange transactions and exposure to exchange rate fluctuations that results from future business activities.

If a firm can measure its transaction exposure, it has the option to reduce or eliminate this risk by netting payments and receivables among foreign subsidiaries and other trading partners. Any exposures that cannot be eliminated by netting can be hedged by taking various positions in foreign currency forward or futures contracts. Suppose the importer used in a previous example had agreed to make payments in several different foreign currencies during the upcoming 90-day period. An initial measure of transaction exposure could be obtained by computing the value of each of the obligations using the spot exchange rate for each currency. The sum of these values, measured in the home currency, would provide a gross measure of transaction exposure. This measure, however, may overstate the true level of exposure if the importer also has receivables in these same currencies. Since foreign currency receivables offset payment obligations in the same currency, the more relevant measure of exposure is the net of payables less receivables.

Once a firm has properly measured its transaction exposure to exchange rate fluctuations, it can opt to reduce the risk by engaging in a practice called **hedging**. Hedging is a technique of eliminating or limiting losses due to unfavorable movements in exchange rates. For example, a United States importer with a large payment denominated in Canadian dollars due in 90 days may enter into a forward contract to purchase that currency when needed. A forward contract is an agreement to exchange currencies at a specific date in the future for a specific exchange rate determined now. Although the spot rate 90 days later may be materially different from the forward rate specified in the contract, both parties now know exactly what the other currency units will cost. In this way exchange rate risk can be effectively neutralized. Other financial instruments such as **futures contracts** and options can also be used to reduce transaction exposure. Foreign currency futures contracts are similar to

forward contracts but are more standardized and, as a result, can be purchased or sold very quickly. This means that futures contracts can be used when transaction exposure is likely to change. For example, if a firm agrees to purchase two million Canadian dollars using a futures contract and subsequently finds out that they will only need one million, they can quickly sell some of the contracts and reduce their protective hedge to the proper level. Forward contracts do not offer that flexibility. Foreign currency options can also be used to build a cap on the potential cost of an upcoming foreign currency purchase or a floor under the revenue from an upcoming payment.

Economic exposure to exchange rate fluctuations is often more difficult to manage. A prominent example of this exposure and its management is provided by the Japanese automobile manufacturer Toyota. This company developed a very sizable market in the United States by initially producing an inexpensive, fuel-efficient vehicle. As time passed, Toyota developed a broader line of products to expand its share of the United States automobile market. Beginning in the early 1980s, however, the yen began to appreciate relative to the dollar. Even with constant dollar sales in the United States market, Toyota's revenues began to drop significantly when converted back to yen. Since the majority of their production costs were already yen denominated, this hurt their profitability. Toyota was reluctant to raise the dollar price of their products because they feared that they would lose market share. The firm had significant economic exposure because a large proportion of its revenues were denominated in dollars while most of its costs were denominated in yen. Toyota responded to this problem by building manufacturing facilities in the United States. This generated dollar-denominated production costs that could be used to offset dollar revenues. The result was a reduced need for foreign exchange and more stable corporate earnings in Toyota's home country of Japan.

Note that economic exposure results from having revenue and cost streams that have different sensitivities to exchange rate changes. This is very different from measuring the need for foreign exchange transactions during an upcoming period and hedging the cost. Economic exposure to exchange rate fluctuations cannot be hedged with simple financial instruments. It must be managed more dynamically and requires actions such as relocating production facilities, borrowing in foreign countries, and developing product markets in a more diverse set of countries.

COUNTRY RISK

Layered on top of the other sources of risk that make international business decisions unique from a financial perspective are the concerns with country risk. Country risk can be divided into two parts: economic risk and political risk. Economic risk refers to the stability of a country's economy. It embodies concerns such as dependence on individual industries or markets, the ability to sustain a vibrant level of activity and to grow, and the supply of natural resources and other important inputs. Political risk is more concerned with the stability of the government that manages the economy. It encompasses concerns such as the ability to move capital in and out of the country, the likelihood of a smooth transfer of power after elections, and the government's overall attitude toward foreign firms. Obviously, these two branches of country risk overlap significantly. There are a variety of services that provide in-depth assessments of country risk for virtually every country; multinational firms make considerable use of these services to make their own decisions regarding international projects.

In summary, the basic objective of international finance is no different than that of its purely domestic counterpart. The firm should attempt to identify profitable business opportunities that will provide benefit to the owners of the corporation. When these opportunities traverse an international border, a variety of new complexities arise in the financial analysis. Many of the new concerns with this analysis stem from the risk that is introduced by the need for foreign exchange transactions in an environment of fluctuating exchange rates. Once these risks are identified, steps can be taken to address them. Short-term, specific sources of exchange rate risk can often be hedged using standard financial contracts. Longer-term exposure to exchange rate risk requires more strategic management. Additional risks arise due to the potential for major shifts in foreign economic or political climates. It is the recognition, assessment, and management of risks such as these that provides the unique character of financial decision making in an international context.

[Paul Bolster]

FURTHER READING:

Madura, Jeff. *International Financial Management*, 3rd ed. St. Paul, MN: West Publishing Company, 1992.

Shapiro, Alan C. *Foundations of Multinational Financial Management*, 2nd ed. Needham Heights, MA: Allyn and Bacon, 1994.

Solnik, Bruno H. *International Investing*, 2nd ed. Reading, MA: Addison-Wesley Publishing Co., 1991.

INTERNATIONAL LABOR ORGANIZATION (ILO)

Since its inception the International Labor Organization (ILO) has worked for worldwide improvements in working conditions and standards of living. The ILO believes such actions will eliminate the social injustice and social unrest that lead to conflict, social upheaval, and war. Since 1946 the ILO has been a Specialized Agency of the United Nations and is headquartered in Geneva, Switzerland, with regional offices responsible for Africa, the Arab states, Asia, the Caribbean, Europe, and Latin America.

During the 1800s there were numerous and largely unsuccessful efforts to establish an international labor movement in Europe. These short-lived and unaligned endeavors began as early as the Congress of Vienna (1814-15) and continued through the century, ending with international labor conferences in Berlin (1890), London (1896), and Zurich and Brussels (1897). In 1900 the International Association for Labor Legislation (IALL) was established, forming a loose coalition of government representatives, labor organizations, and private citizens interested in labor affairs. Although it lacked the wherewithal to institute sweeping labor reforms, the IALL had limited success in promoting better working conditions for women in certain industries. Headquartered at the University of Basel in Switzerland, the IALL served largely as a center for labor research and a clearinghouse for labor information before growing in influence and prestige. By 1912 its conference in Zurich attracted 22 government delegations and private delegates from 24 countries. The outbreak of war in Europe in 1914, however, brought a sudden end to IALL activities.

After World War I delegates to the Paris Peace Conference were mindful of agitation throughout Europe for an international labor organization. The Conference organized a commission headed by Samuel Gompers (1950-1924), then president of the American Federation of Labor, to study the issue. Rather than favoring an organization with legislative authority, the commission proposed an organization administered by representatives of government, labor, and industry which would make recommendations to national governments on issues of labor reform. The ILO was thus created pursuant to the Treaty of Versailles. In many respects the ILO was modeled after the now-defunct IALL and was designated soon therafter as an affiliated agency of the newly created League of Nations.

From its inception to the end of World War II, the ILO was involved in numerous legislative and research projects related to labor reform. During the 1930s it dealt with the worldwide economic depression and subsequent unemployment. With the end of the war, the ILO became the first Specialized Agency of the United Nations after overcoming initial objections from the United States and the former Soviet Union. Under an agreement with the United Nations, the ILO retained policy making and budgetary autonomy.

The ILO sets international standards concerning working conditions and labor activities and supervises the implementation of these standards. It also collects and disseminates information and, when requested, provides technical assistance on various projects. The ILO publishes the "International Labor Code," which sets forth the international standards of the organization, for the use of its members and other interested parties. The ILO, through its standards and policies, deals with a wide variety of issues including forced labor, discrimination in employment, wage structures, labor-management relations, occupational safety and health, working conditions, and social security and pensions.

The ILO holds an annual International Labour Conference which elects the Governing Body, the executive authority of the ILO. This body is comprised of 28 government representatives, 14 "workers," and 14 "employers." Day-to-day operations of the ILO are handled by the Secretariat and the administrative staff in Geneva. In 1969 the ILO received the Nobel Peace Prize. In 1991 the ILO had 150 member nations including the United States.

[Michael Knes]

FURTHER READING:

Morse, David A. *The Origin and Evolution of the ILO and Its Role in the World Community*. New York State School of Industrial and Labor Relations, Cornell University, 1969.

INTERNATIONAL LAW

International law comes from a variety of sources, including international organizations and nations. Since there is no unified "world government," there are multiple sources of rules and customs governing relations among nation-states, relations among individuals (including corporations) and foreign nations, and relations among individuals from different nations. The many rules that have evolved for these three different areas encompass most of what is generally known as international law.

Historically, international law began as the "law of nations." The recognition of separate nations and their reciprocal rights and duties toward one another has, at its core, the notion of national sovereignty. Each recognized government in the international community of nations is considered the political and legal ruler (sovereign) over a defined territory, economy, and population, and is entitled to self-determination in its political and economic affairs. Activities internal to

the nation are governed by the laws and values legitimated by the national government; international law recognizes that each sovereign has the power to prescribe and enforce laws within its boundaries.

RELATIONS AMONG NATION-STATES

Much of the law governing relations among nation-states developed from history, customs, and traditions that found their way into legal precedents. In cases where nations disagreed over their rights and duties toward one another, consensus developed slowly. For example, when a citizen attempted to bring a lawsuit in his home country against a foreign sovereign, the court would typically deny relief on the ground of foreign sovereign immunity as a generally recognized principle of customary international law.

Customary international law, however, could not serve all the needs of nation-states and their citizens. Agreements between nations were needed to improve alliances in pursuit of war, or to encourage trading relations in more peaceful times. A typical agreement for the United States is a treaty of "friendship, commerce, and navigation" (FCN). The purpose of such agreements is to define the reciprocal rights and duties of each nation in furtherance of each nation's self-interest. Most FCN treaties cover issues such as the entry of individuals, goods, ships, and capital into the other nation's territory, the acquisition of property, repatriation of funds, and protection of each nation's persons and their property in the treaty-partner's nation. At one time, when most nations discriminated in trade against other nations (by setting steep tariff barriers or enacting total embargoes on foreign goods), bilateral FCN treaties began the process of removing trade barriers.

Many treaties have more than two nations as signatories. These are "conventions," such as the U.N.-sponsored Convention on Contracts for the International Sale of Goods, or the Treaty of Rome, which began the Common Market (which eventually led to the European Community). Not all conventions are under the auspices of the **United Nations**, but the U.N., has sponsored and continues to encourage multi-lateral agreements among nation-states.

One organization within the United Nations has also encouraged the growth of international law: the International Court of Justice (ICJ). The ICJ hears and rules on disputes between nation-states but usually does so only where the respective nations agree that the ICJ should have jurisdiction. The ICJ also issues advisory opinions requested by agencies of the United Nations. The ICJ relies on customary international law, treaties, and conventions in making its decisions.

After World War II, when the United Nations was organized, it was envisioned that a **World Bank** and International Trade Organization (ITO) would also be established. The World Bank came into being as an international lending and development agency to which industrialized nations make contributions for the ostensible purpose of promoting development globally. But in 1948 the U.S. Congress had serious reservations about the wisdom of surrendering any of its sovereignty or discretion over trade matters to an international organization. Under powers delegated to the president in the Reciprocal Trade Agreements Act of 1934, the United States joined in the **General Agreement on Tariffs and Trade (GATT)**, which had been drafted in 1947 in Geneva. The basic purpose of GATT was to move the nations of the world toward lower trade barriers (free trade).

Under GATT, member nations obligated themselves to give "**most favored nation**" treatment to all goods originating in member countries. That is, trade concessions to one member nation would automatically be extended to all others. A series of negotiating "rounds" since 1947 has progressively lowered tariff barriers among GATT signatory nations. In the most recently concluded "Uruguay Round," both tariff and non-tariff barriers were further reduced. Moreover, the original vision of a global trade organization such as the ITO has been at least partially realized in agreement on a World Trade Organization (WTO) to replace the GATT. The WTO would have considerably more power to set and enforce standards than the current GATT secretariat in Geneva.

The institutionalization of free trade principles has been furthered by regional free trade arrangements, such as the European Community and the North American Free Trade Agreement (NAFTA). Nations who belong to either group are also members of the GATT, whose provisions allow that concessions given to other members of a regional trading block do not have to be given to other GATT-member nations.

RELATIONS AMONG INDIVIDUALS AND NATION STATES

One of the traditional principles of international law is that rights granted under international law are given to nations, not individuals. Violations of international law by nations which affect individuals (or corporations) must be raised, if at all, by a nation on behalf of its citizen.

A citizen of a country may mean either an individual or a corporation. While many corporations doing business globally tend to think of themselves as de-nationalized, or multi-national (having no particular allegiance or duties toward any particular country), corporations must often depend on national governments to protect their rights. For example, where patented or trademarked products are counterfeited, the company whose patent or trademark has been

misused will have to seek the protection of a certain country's laws. If that protection is not forthcoming, the company will often request that its home government (with whom it has the closest or most powerful connections) advocate its interests in treaty or convention negotiations. Protection of **intellectual property**, for example, was one of the principal areas of concern for industrialized nations in the recently concluded Uruguay Round of the GATT.

Similarly, where a corporation chooses to engage in foreign direct investment in a foreign country, political uncertainties and legal risk have frequently resulted in a loss of assets through expropriation or nationalization. In such cases, diplomatic efforts of the home country have been enlisted to recover adequate compensation. Or, if a corporation with a large number of employees in the United States experiences a serious competitive threat from products originating in another country, one time-honored strategy has been to seek protective legislation from the home country government.

The free trade movement has at least partially limited the success (or validity) of such efforts, but even the GATT has allowed exceptions for member nations to impose anti-dumping duties or countervailing duties where the country of origin has provided unfair subsidies for the product, or the product is being sold at below home country cost to establish a foothold in a new market.

Companies seeking to do business outside their home country have encountered many legal difficulties other than tariffs, anti-dumping duties, or countervailing duties. Technical and non-tariff barriers to trade often exist in the export market, barriers such as government procurement rules (requirements that a certain percentage of business must be given to home countries), Byzantine licensing and procedural requirements, and restrictions on the mobility of key personnel. Exports may also be limited by political and strategic considerations: since the 1950s, for example, the United States has had various statutes and executive orders establishing export controls for political reasons.

Some of the export control laws include the Export Administration Act of 1969, the International Emergency Economic Powers Act, the Trading with the Enemy Act, and various executive orders under each. When U.S. Embassy personnel were held hostage in Iran, President Carter ordered a cessation of all trade with Iran. A number of U.S. companies with contracts pending in Iran were adversely affected. Similarly, when President Bush ordered cessation of all business with Iraq after its invasion of Kuwait, a number of U.S. companies were affected.

When the Soviets invaded Afghanistan in 1980, U.S. companies with **subsidiaries** abroad were ordered by President Carter to cease doing business on the Soviet oil pipeline that was to serve Europe and bring much-needed hard currency to the Soviets. A French subsidiary of the U.S. company, Dresser Industries, had a pending contract with the U.S.S.R. Dresser U.S. was informed by the U.S. government that it must act to prevent its subsidiary from dealing with the Soviets. Dresser, its French subsidiary, and the government of France all resisted the application of U.S. law to a French company, and ultimately their resistance succeeded after the subsidiary was restructured to reduce formal control by Dresser U.S.

This incident illustrates a principal difficulty of international law: much of it is made by national legislatures and courts, and one nation's laws may reach beyond its own boundaries, or attempt to. When, for example, the U.S. public learned that many ''U.S.'' corporations were obtaining and retaining business in foreign countries by means of bribes or kickbacks, the U.S. Congress enacted the **Foreign Corrupt Practices Act (FCPA)**. The FCPA criminalized the act of making payments to foreign officials for the purpose of getting or keeping business. A U.S. company found to have made such payments could be prosecuted in the United Stats for actions taken outside U.S. territory; thus, the FCPA is an example of extra-territorial application of U.S. law.

Under customary international law, the basic principle of sovereign jurisdiction to prescribe and enforce law is territorial. International law also recognizes the nationality principle, the right of a sovereign to make and enforce law with respect to its citizens (nationals). Not only the FCPA, but also U.S. antitrust law, securities law, and employment discrimination law may apply to actions of U.S. companies outside U.S. territory. In the case of U.S. **antitrust law**, the action alleged to be a violation of the Sherman Act or the Clayton Antitrust Act must have a ''direct effect'' on the United States for extra-territorial application to be upheld. For employment discrimination cases, a U.S. company must adhere to the provisions of Title VII of the Civil Rights Act of 1964 (as amended) with respect to a U.S. citizen employed by that company overseas.

Conflicts between U.S. law and the law of foreign states has led to certain nations blocking the application of U.S. law by statute. Blocking statutes typically limit the extent to which U.S. plaintiffs can obtain evidence through discovery and make it difficult to enforce a U.S. judgment outside of the United States. Even where Congress clearly intends U.S. law to have extra-territorial application, U.S. courts are reluctant to apply it where doing so would raise a clear conflict or implicate foreign policy concerns in any way.

Where U.S. companies and individuals actually have an adversarial relationship with a foreign nation, either sovereign immunity or the Act of State Doctrine may apply. In the case of a claim in U.S. courts against a foreign sovereign, plaintiffs must show that the case fits one of the exceptions to sovereign immunity listed in the Foreign Sovereign Immunities Act of 1976 (FSIA). Under the FSIA, which adopts the restrictive theory of sovereign immunity (rather than the absolute theory), governmental activities are generally immune, whereas private or commercial kinds of activities are not. Under the FSIA, a foreign sovereign that engages in commercial activities in the United States or having a direct effect in the United States cannot avail itself of the sovereign immunity defense in U.S. courts. Most other industrialized nations follow the restrictive theory of sovereign immunity, either by statute or judicial precedents.

In certain cases, deciding a lawsuit in U.S. courts may require that the public act of a foreign sovereign (on its own territory) be declared invalid by the court. In such cases, the Act of State Doctrine may be invoked by the court to avoid coming to a decision on the merits in a way that would discredit the public act of the foreign sovereign. The Supreme Court has declared in numerous cases that it is not constitutionally proper for a U.S. court to decide a case in a way that would invalidate the public act of a foreign sovereign; this, it believes, would trench upon the proper prerogatives of the executive and legislative branches of U.S. government. For the Act of State Doctrine to apply, it is not necessary that the foreign sovereign be a named defendant; it is only necessary that the court be unable to find for a certain party without questioning the lawfulness of a public act of a foreign sovereign on its own territory.

RELATIONS BETWEEN INDIVIDUALS FROM DIFFERENT NATIONS

Quite apart from governing relations among states, or between individuals and nation-states, international law began centuries ago to develop rules for dispute resolution between citizens of different states. When Europe entered the Renaissance period, Roman and Germanic law were not adequate to handle the needs of a growing transnational commercial community. The guilds and merchant associations began forming their own customs and rules for fair dealing, and soon had their own courts. These rules, sometimes known as *lex mercatoria* (or Merchant Law), became influential and were eventually applied in both church and governmental courts. Many of the *lex mercatoria* concepts can be found today in the United Nations Convention on Contracts for the International Sale of Goods (CISG).

One of the common problems that arises in international commercial transactions is where a dispute between citizens of different states shall be heard. Without a contractual choice of forum, issues of personal jurisdiction often arise. For example, a Japanese company may find itself sued in a U.S. court for a small valve that was incorporated in a wheel by a Taiwanese manufacturer, then incorporated in a motorcycle by a different Japanese company. If the motorcycle is sold in the United States, and the wheel malfunctions, the tire valve manufacturer may find itself in a U.S. court. The U.S. Supreme Court has declared that, in fairness, a company must deliberately target the U.S. market to be held legally accountable in the United States. Mere predictability that its product may wind up in a certain market is insufficient to give the court valid personal jurisdiction over the nonresident corporation. Of course, if a company goes to another country to do business (either directly or through agents) and is sued there, courts generally will assume personal jurisdiction over the non-resident company.

For disputes between parties to a contract, the parties may have chosen to avoid any questions of personal jurisdiction by specifying the judicial forum where any disputes arising between them will be settled. Courts have typically upheld these ''choice of forum'' clauses in commercial contracts, as well as clauses that specify which law (e.g. German law, U.S. law, or Mexican law) will be applied in resolving the dispute.

International companies may entirely avoid judicial settlement of their dispute by choosing arbitration. This can be done prior to any disagreement by including a pre-dispute arbitration clause in the contract, or may be done after a dispute arises. In this way, a more neutral forum is often selected, so that the ''home court'' advantage does not favor either disputant. Often, the parties will have pre-selected a set of procedural rules to follow, such as those of the International Chamber of Commerce, or those of United Nations Commission on International Trade Law (UNCITRAL). This process is aided by the U.N.-sponsored United Nations Convention on Recognition and Enforcement of Arbitral Awards (sometimes known as the New York Convention), which has been ratified by most major trading nations. If a Japanese and German firm agree to arbitrate their dispute in Los Angeles, California for example, either party may proceed under the agreed-upon rules (even without the cooperation of the other party), obtain an arbitral award, and have it enforced in any signatory nation without the need to re-hear the facts and issues of the dispute. Companies dealing internationally with agencies of a national government may wish to include an arbitration clause in contracts with the foreign sovereign so as to secure a clear waiver of sovereign immunity.

Because international dispute settlement is often fraught with such considerations, sellers of goods may well choose to secure payment for full performance under a contract by securing a letter of credit from the buyer. A buyer must establish a line of credit with a bank (the issuing bank), and the bank issues a letter of credit in favor of the seller, who often specifies a corresponding bank in its own country. The letter of credit will specify that the seller will be paid by the corresponding bank upon presentation of certain documents, such as a clean bill of lading. If the entries on the documents correspond to the requirements of the letter of credit, the seller is promptly paid by the corresponding bank, regardless of whether the goods are delivered to the buyer in a timely fashion. Goods may be held up by forces of nature, acts of war, or may be damaged in transit due to no fault of the seller. The logic of the letter of credit is that the seller, having performed by delivery of documents entitling the buyer to receive the goods, is itself entitled to prompt payment.

[Don Mayer]

FURTHER READING:

August, Ray. *International Business Law: Text, Cases, and Readings*. Prentice Hall, 1993.

Hotchkiss, Carolyn. *International Law for Business*. McGraw-Hill, Inc., 1994.

Richards, Eric L. *Law for Global Business*. Richard D. Irwin, Inc., 1994.

Schaffer, Richard, Beverley Earle, and Filiberto Agusti. *International Business Law and Its Environment*. West Publishing Co., 1993.

INTERNATIONAL MANAGEMENT

The expansion of the global market has created a need for managers who are familiar with the nuances of international trade. There is no country in the world today that is—or can be—economically self-sufficient. Individual countries' economies are becoming increasingly interdependent. This trend toward a single global economy is shrinking borders, expanding markets, and providing unlimited opportunities for a new type of business specialist: the international manager.

THE GLOBAL MARKET DEFINED

The global market is best described as profit-related business activities conducted across international boundaries. The international character of business is reflected in the makeup of many of the products sold throughout the world. For instance, it is extremely difficult in today's business environment to identify exactly where specific products are manufactured. More and more products today are hybrids; they contain parts from many different countries. So, slogans such as "Made in America" or "Produced in Brazil" have no real meaning any more. This idea is made evident by the increasing number of businesses operating across international boundaries.

THE EMERGENCE OF THE GLOBAL ECONOMY

In the 1980s, the world's leading industrialized nations began an era of cooperation in which they capitalized on the benefits of working together to improve their individual economies. They continued to seek individual comparative advantages, i.e., a nation's ability to produce some products more cheaply or better than it can others, but within the confines of international cooperation. Countries negotiated trade pacts such as the **North American Free Trade Agreement (NAFTA)**, and the **General Agreement on Tariffs and Trade (GATT)**, or formed economic communities such as the **European Union**. These pacts and communities created new marketing opportunities for countries that were once independent from a business standpoint. They opened the door through which companies of all sizes and in various aspects of business entered the international market. The United States benefited extensively from the expanded global economic activity.

GATT promised to raise U.S. exports by $20 billion between 1994 and 2000. It also encouraged 122 other countries to lower their **trade barriers**. In addition, major U.S. retailers began expanding into new areas such as the former communist bloc nations, Asia, Latin America, and Mexico. For example, Wal-Mart opened 47 stores in Mexico and 122 in Canada. Toys'R'Us operated 288 stores in 17 countries. J.C. Penney planned 7 stores in Mexico and 1 in Chile. Penney also initiated sales of private-label men's clothing in Japan, Dubai, and Singapore.

As a result of GATT, U.S. producers were able to export a greater variety of American goods. Worldwide sales of U.S. snack chips rose from $26 million in 1988 to an estimated $225 million in 1994. The EU countries alone imported $28 million worth of American-made snacks in the first eight months of 1994, which was 76 percent more than in the same period in 1993. Japan imported 490 percent more snacks in 1994 than it did in 1993. In addition, U.S. companies in other industries also predicted increased exports. Beginning in 1995, American defense contractors predicted that at least 25 percent of their business would come from exports. However, business opportunities were not limited to exports.

Another benefit of GATT was that many foreign companies established plants in the United States. In Connecticut alone, foreign **direct investment** in 1993 reached $1.19 billion. (Direct investment is a form of organization for international business in which a domestic firm purchases or establishes a tangible asset in another country.) New York attracted $7.02 billion of foreign direct investment that same year; Texas acquired $4.1 billion, and Ohio received $818.8 million. Countries represented in the United States by their investments or business ownership included Denmark, Japan, the United Kingdom, Switzerland, and Sweden.

Economic activity between the United States and foreign countries increased considerably, and created a need for a more global approach to conducting business. Businesses engaged in a variety of innovative approaches to take advantage of the expanding global market.

TYPES OF INTERNATIONAL BUSINESSES

International businesses fall into several different categories. There are, for example, export/import businesses, independent agents, licensers, multinational corporations (MNC), generically labeled international businesses, and joint ventures. The differences among these companies are often subtle in nature.

For instance, an export firm is one that sells its domestically-made product(s) to a very small number of countries. In contrast, import firms import foreign-made goods into the country for domestic use. Often, export and import firms are operated by a small group of people who have close ties with the countries in which they do business. Some such firms may begin as export or import specialists, but eventually expand their operations to production of goods overseas. IBM and Coca-Cola Co. exemplify companies that have used that approach.

Independent agents are businesspeople who contract with foreign residents or businesses to represent the exporting firm's product in another country. Closely related are firms with **licensing agreements**, in which domestic firms grant foreign individuals or companies the right to manufacture and/or market the exporter's product in that country in return for royalties on sales. International firms are those that sell a significant part of their domestically designed and/or made products to a large number of countries. A **joint venture** is a merger of two or more companies that form a partnership with foreign firms in order to produce or market their products abroad.

Multinational firms are relatively new in the business world, yet they are becoming increasingly important. There is no specific definition of a MNC. Nor is it easy to differentiate an MNC from a company that simply operates internationally. Some experts define an MNC as a company that derives at least 25 percent of its sales from foreign sources. However, that is an arbitrary figure. Others define an MNC by its size. *Fortune* magazine, in its July 27, 1992, issue, included in its list of the world's 25-largest MNCs businesses such as General Motors Corp., which was ranked #1, Hitachi, #12, Unilever, #20, and Elf Aquitane, #25. Each of the four is based in a different country, the United States, Japan, Britain, and France, respectively. Yet, the top 25 also included companies based in Italy, Holland, Germany, and South Korea. The fact that eight countries are homes to the top-25 MNCs indicates that business on a global scale is increasing in scope, as is the demand for people to manage operations. Yet, however, companies doing business at the international level are defined, they all share one commonality: they are growing in number.

Experts predict that the numbers of MNCs, joint ventures, another international operations will rise as businesses seek to take advantage of **economies of scale**, growth of new markets and their proximity, etc., as a way of reducing costs and increasing profits. As the geographic boundaries over which individual companies operate become less defined, the need for people who are able to manage international activities becomes more acute. Thus, international managers are becoming more important in the business world, and their success can directly affect a company seeking to compete in the global market. Due to this, business leaders are placing increased emphasis on the development of managers with expertise in international management.

INTERNATIONAL MANAGERS NEED SPECIAL SKILLS

Contemporary international managers will need to demonstrate a higher level of skill than those exhibited by the traditional manager in the past. They must be multilingual, sensitive to cultural differences, and knowledgeable about current global **management** theory, philosophy, psychology, and their practical applications. Acquiring the skills needed to become a successful international manager is a demanding, albeit necessary, process—especially since the global market will continue to expand for the foreseeable future.

APPROACHES TO INTERNATIONAL MANAGEMENT

There are three approaches to international management: ethnocentric, polycentric, and geocentric. Each has its advantages and disadvantages. None of these theories can be successful, however, unless managers understand completely the nuances involved in their applications.

The ethnocentric approach is one in which management uses the same style and practices that work in their own headquarters or home country. Such an approach may leave managers open to devastating mistakes, because what works in the United States, for example, may not work necessarily in Japan. There are many cases in which companies made grievous errors when they attempted to transfer their management styles to foreign countries. For example, Procter and Gamble Co. lost $25 million in Japan between 1973 and 1986 because its managers would not listen to Japanese advisors. The company ran ads for its Camay soap in which a Japanese man meeting a Japanese woman for the first time compared her skin to that of a porcelain doll. That would never happen in Japan, which is exactly what an **advertising** advisor told Procter & Gamble's managers. Procter & Gamble, however, ignored the advice. They assumed that if a similar ad worked well in the United States and other countries (which it did), it would also be successful in Japan, which it was not. In fact, the ad infuriated the Japanese people, who refused to buy Camay. The Procter & Gamble executives learned a lesson, but at a high cost.

In contrast to ethnocentric management is the polycentric management theory. In this approach, management staffs its **workforce** in foreign countries with as many local people as possible. The theory is simple: local people know best the host country's culture, language, and work ethic. Thus, they are the ideal candidates for management. This approach works well in some countries. However, in countries without well-developed economies, it may not be the best approach because the workers may not always have the necessary business acumen or management skills.

The third style of international management is the geocentric approach. This theory holds that the best individuals, regardless of country origin, should be placed in management positions. This philosophy maintains that business problems are the same regardless of where in the world they occur. Therefore, competent managers who are able to apply logic and common sense to resolve them will be successful; specific cultural knowledge is not necessary. This is the most difficult of the three approaches to apply, since managers must be able to understand the local and global ramifications of the business.

The Boeing Corporation provides evidence that the geocentric approach can be successful. When sales of its 737 plane dropped precipitously in the early 1970s, Boeing's senior management asked a group of engineers to bolster sales of the plane. Management indicated that if they were unable to increase sales, production would be discontinued. The engineers seized the opportunity.

Their first step was to examine foreign markets for the aircraft. They recognized that what attracted buyers in the United States may not necessarily lure foreign buyers. So, they visited different countries to determine which characteristics might be useful to incorporate into the redesign of the 737. They found many differences in flight operations. For example, many foreign airports, especially those in developing countries, had shorter runways than those in the United States. Moreover, many were constructed of softer materials than concrete, the standard material used in the United States. As a result of their study, the engineers redesigned the plane's wings to allow for shorter landings on asphalt runways and altered the engines so takeoffs would be quicker. Finally, they designed new landing gears and switched to low-pressure tires. Shortly after they made the changes, 737 sales rose dramatically, and so did sales of Boeing's other models. In fact, the 737 eventually became the largest selling commercial jet in aviation history. The key to the engineers' success lay in their ability to think globally and assess the business environment in different parts of the world.

ASSESSING THE GLOBAL ENVIRONMENT

It is extremely important that managers involved in international business recognize the opportunities available in different countries. They must be prescient enough to recognize potential, as well as immediate opportunities. For example, there are three types of countries with which there are potential business opportunities: developed, less developed, and newly industrialized. Once managers have assessed which group a certain country belongs in, they must then analyze the country's **infrastructure**, too.

Developed countries, such as Australia, Canada, the United States, and Japan, are those that have a high level of economic or industrial development. Less developed countries, frequently called Third World countries, are relatively poor nations with low per capita income, little industry, and high birth rates. Many of these countries, however, have the potential to become lucrative trade partners, so international managers cannot afford to overlook them when analyzing business opportunities. Finally, there are countries labeled as newly industrialized, such as Taiwan, South Korea, and Vietnam. These countries are quickly becoming major exporters of manufactured goods. For example, the Hyundai Corporation has made great inroads into the United States through the sales of its cars. Hyundai's success provides ample evidence that more and more countries are taking their places in the industrialized world—and increasing the need for qualified managers who can oversee the business relations involved.

WHAT INTERNATIONAL MANAGERS NEED TO KNOW

Managers must be trained in facets of international business that are not normally the concern of domestic managers. On a broad scale, these issues include a knowledge of other countries' infrastructures, **balance of trade** (the difference between a country's exports and imports), and balance of payments (an account of goods and services, capital loans, gold, and other items entering and leaving a country). In addition, international managers must be knowledgable about exchange rates (the rate at which one country's currency can be exchanged for another's), and the legal-political and sociocultural elements of other countries. These skills are relevant in a variety of situations.

For example, there is the issue of ethics in international operations. Managers must know when they are confronted with the subtleties of legal and illegal payments, for instance. In some countries, bribes in the form of money or valuables given to influential people are common. So is extortion, or payments made to protect a business against some threatened action, such as the cancellation of a franchise. In such cases, international managers may be torn between U.S. law and foreign culture. However, there is an American law that provides guidance in such cases.

The **U.S. Foreign Corrupt Practices Act** prohibits most types of questionable payments involving American companies operating in other countries. The law in itself, however, does not make the international manager's job any easier when U.S. legislation and foreign cultures clash. Therefore, international managers are often faced with ethical dilemmas not common to their domestic counterparts. The solutions to these dilemmas can have a major impact on companies' operations and individual managers' careers—which is just one of the disadvantages of an international manager's job.

Politics are also an important aspect of the international manager's job. International managers must be able to assess political risks inherent in particular countries. Developed countries tend to be relatively stable from a political and an economic standpoint, while less developed countries may be more susceptible to political strife. Governments may come and go or may decide to nationalize companies. Such was the case in the 1960s when Chile's President Eduardo Frei "Chileanized" the country's copper mines. Many American companies lost their holdings, although they were compensated for their losses. International managers must also be prepared for similar events, such as expropriation.

Expropriation is not unheard of for American industries. For example, Iran seized an estimated $5 billion worth of American companies' holdings in

1970. The companies involved included Xerox Corp., R.J. Reynolds, and United Technologies. Events such as this mandate that international managers learn about the legal-political element of foreign business affairs. Their knowledge in this area must also include such things as **tariffs**, import quotas, and administrative protections (a type of **trade barrier** in the form of various rules and regulations that make it more difficult for foreign firms to conduct business in a particular country).

Equally important to the international manager are sociocultural elements. These include the attitudes, values, norms, beliefs, behaviors, and demographic trends of the host country. International managers must know how to motivate foreign workers, since motivational techniques differ among countries. They must also understood how important work is to individuals in different cultures. For example, researchers discovered in a 1986 poll that work is more important to the Japanese than Americans. The Dutch social scientist Geert Hofstede divided sociocultural elements into four categories: power distance, uncertainty avoidance, individualism-collectivism, and masculinity-femininity. International managers must understand all four elements in order to succeed.

Power distance is a cultural dimension that involves the degree to which individuals in a society accept differences in the distribution of power as reasonable and normal. Uncertainty avoidance involves the extent to which members of a society feel uncomfortable with and try to avoid situations that they see as unstructured, unclear, or unpredictable. Individualism-collectivism involves the degree to which individuals concern themselves with their own interests and those of their immediate families as opposed to the interests of a larger group. Finally, masculinity-femininity is the extent to which a society emphasizes traditional male values, e.g., assertiveness, competitiveness, and material success, rather than traditional female values, such as passivity, cooperation, and feelings. All of these dimensions can have a significant impact on a manager's success in an international business environment.

The inability to understand the concepts Hofstede outlined can hinder managers' capacity to manage—and their companies' chances of surviving in the international arena. Equally important is the manager's ability to choose the right strategy and organization applicable to individual companies operating in the international business arena.

INTERNATIONAL MANAGEMENT STRATEGY

There are four strategies involved in international management. They include globalization, rationalization, national responsiveness, and the multifocal approach. Whether or not these strategies are implemented depends on a company's size and the number of countries in which it operates. For example, a small export company is not likely to employ a rationalization program. On the other hand, an MNC might utilize all four strategies.

Globalization involves the development of relatively standardized products with worldwide appeal. Rationalization is the process of assigning activities to those parts of the organization best suited to produce specific goods or desired results, regardless of where they are located. National responsiveness allows **subsidiaries** latitude in adapting products and services to conform to the special needs and political realities of the countries in which they operate. Finally, the multifocal approach tries to achieve the advantages of globalization while attempting to be responsive to important national needs. Competent international managers must be able to analyze the business and political environments endemic to the countries in which they are operating and adapt the strategies, either individually or in combination, that best suit their needs. While strategy is important, so is organization.

INTERNATIONAL ORGANIZATION

Companies operating internationally tend to use the same types of organization they do domestically. They may operate functionally (by task), geographically (by country or region), or by product. Or, they may combine organizational strategies. Again, international managers will make those determinations based on their companies' products or services. Regardless of organizational strategy, international managers must pay particular attention to human resources issues, since there are vast cultural differences among citizens of different countries.

THE INTERNATIONAL MANAGER AND HUMAN RESOURCES

One of the most critical factors in the success of a company's international success is its hiring program. Generally, hiring production workers is not a major problem, companies recruit locals to perform the daily work. In all likelihood, first-level supervisors and possibly some of the middle managers will also be members of the local community. Hiring upper-level management, however, is another matter—one that must be handled with care and sensitivity.

International companies have several primary approaches to recruiting and assigning upper-level managers. For example, they can rely strictly on local residents or use expatriates (individuals who are not citizens of the countries in which they are assigned to work). If they assign expatriates to foreign operations, they must make sure those individuals relate well to

the local population. Relying strictly on employees' technical skills, to the detriment of interpersonal skills and sensitivity, can harm a company's reputation and destroy its operation in the process.

Another hiring tactic is to assign people to key managerial positions without regard to their native countries. For instance, they might place a foreign resident who was educated in the United States in a management position simply because that individual is best qualified for the job. Whichever options they choose, companies must be sensitive to local customs and cultures, lest they risk alienating the local community and inhibiting cooperation and productivity.

The bottom line is that international managers must be more cognizant of the differences in local social customs and work ethics than are their domestic counterparts. This is simply one more indication that companies involved in international operations must pay strict attention to the quality of the managers they assign to their overseas facilities. As the global economy expands, it is going to become even more critical that international managers be trained specifically for the special nuances involved in worldwide business activities.

HOW AMERICAN COMPANIES TRAIN INTERNATIONAL MANAGERS

Many U.S. companies sponsor special preparation programs for international managers. For example, IBM conducts internal executive development programs at its management development centers in Australia, Singapore, Japan, and Belgium. The company operates a six-week training program that includes a wide variety of international topics. Some companies use cultural assimilators, programmed learning approaches that expose members of one culture to some of the basic concepts, attitudes, customs, and values of another. Whatever approach individual companies use to prepare managers for overseas assignments, one thing is essential: the amount and intensity of training is proportionately related to the manager's success—and the company's.

THE FUTURE OF INTERNATIONAL MANAGEMENT

Individuals searching for careers in the field of international management will find numerous opportunities available to them. The field is becoming a specialty of its own. Virtually every management textbook being used in business curricula today has at least one chapter devoted entirely to international management. Colleges and universities are offering degrees ranging from associates to Ph.D.s in the field. As more and more companies enter the international business arena, the number of management opportunities will grow. International management is the wave of the future, because the global economy is a reality in the present.

SEE ALSO: Global Strategy

[Arthur G. Sharp]

FURTHER READING:

Adler, Nancy. *International Dimensions of Organizational Behavior*. Kent Publishing, 1986.

Daniels, John D., and Lee H. Radebaugh. *International Business*. Addison-Wesley, 1989.

England, George W., and Jyuji Misumi. "Work Certainty in Japan and the United States." *Journal of Cross-cultural Psychology*. December, 1986, p. 410.

Hodgetts, Richard M., and Fred Luthans. *International Management*. McGraw-Hill, 1991.

Ouchi, William G. *Theory Z*. Avon Books, 1981.

Robock, Stefan H., and Kenneth Simmonds. *International Business and Multinational Enterprises*. 4th ed. Homewood, IL: Irwin, 1989.

INTERNATIONAL MARKETING

International marketing occurs when a business directs its products and services toward consumers in more than one country. While the overall concept of marketing is the same worldwide, the environment within which the **marketing** plan is implemented can be drastically different. Common marketing concerns—such as input costs, price, advertising, and distribution—are likely to differ dramatically in the countries in which a firm elects to market. Furthermore, many elements outside the control of managers, both at home and abroad, are likely to have a large impact on business decisions. The key to successful international marketing is the ability to adapt, manage, and coordinate a marketing plan in an unfamiliar and often unstable foreign environment.

Businesses choose to explore foreign markets for a host of sound reasons. Commonly, firms initially explore foreign markets in response to unsolicited orders from consumers in those markets. In the absence of these orders, companies often begin to export: to establish a business to absorb overhead costs at home; to seek new markets when the domestic one is saturated; and to make quick profits. Marketing abroad can also spread corporate risk and minimize the impact of undesirable domestic situations, such as recessions.

While companies choosing to market internationally do not share an overall profile, they seem to have two specific characteristics in common. First, the products that they market abroad, usually patented, have high earnings potential in foreign markets; in

other words, the international sale of these products should eventually generate a substantial percentage of the products' total revenue. Also, these products usually have a price or cost advantage over similar products or have some other attribute making them novel and more desirable to end users abroad. Second, the management of companies marketing internationally must be ready to make a commitment to these markets. Further, they must be willing to educate themselves thoroughly on the particular countries they choose to enter and must understand the potential benefits and risks of a decision to market abroad.

MODERN U.S. HISTORY OF INTERNATIONAL MARKETING

Marketing abroad is not a recent phenomenon. In fact, well-established trade routes existed three or four thousand years before the birth of Christ. Modern international marketing, however, can arguably be traced to the 1920s, when liberal international trading was halted by worldwide isolationism and increased barriers to trade. The United States furthered this trend by passing the Smoot-Hawley Tariff Act of 1930, raising the average U.S. tariff on imported goods from 33 to 53 cents. Other countries throughout the world imposed similar tariffs responding to the United States's actions, and by 1932 the volume of world trade fell by more than 40 percent. These protectionist activities continued throughout the 1930s, and the Great Depression, to which many say protectionism substantially contributed, was deeper and more widespread than any other depression in modern history. Furthermore, according to the **United Nations**, this protectionism undermined the standard of living of people all over the world and set the stage for the extreme military buildup that led to World War II.

One result of the Great Depression and World War II was strengthened political will to end protectionist policies and to limit government interference in international trade. Thus, by 1944 representative countries attending the Bretton Woods Conference established the basic organizational setting for the post-war economy, designed to further macroeconomic stability. Specifically, the framework that arose created three organizations: the International Trade Organization (ITO), the **World Bank**, and the **International Monetary Fund**. Although negotiations undertaken for the ITO proved unsuccessful, the United States proposed that the commercial policy provisions that were originally be included in the ITO agreements should be temporarily incorporated into the **General Agreement on Tariffs and Trade (GATT)**. In 1947, 23 countries agreed to a set of tariff reductions codified in GATT. Although GATT was at first intended to be only a temporary measure, because ITO was never ratified, it became the main instrument for international trade regulation. As of 1995, 117 governments agreed to abide by the reductions in trade barriers proposed by GATT.

In the 1960s and 1970s, world trading patterns began to change. While the United States remained a dominant player in international trade, other less developed countries began to manufacture their own products. Furthermore, the United States became more reliant than ever on imported goods. For example, by 1982 one in four cars sold in the United States was foreign made and more than 40 percent of electronic products were produced or assembled abroad. To make matters worse, the United States consistently imported a sizable portion of its fuel needs from other countries. All of these elements created a U.S. dependency on world trade.

As free market policies continued to be the dominant political force concerning trade around the world, a host of new markets opened. Specifically, in the late 1980s, Central and Eastern European markets opened with the dissolution of the Soviet Union. By the 1990s, world trade began with China, as well as with countries in South America and the Middle East—new markets that looked quite promising. In spite of the changes in the world trading arena, the United States, Japan, and Europe continued to play a dominant role in world trade, accounting for 85 percent of the world's trade.

Interestingly, while the trend of opening new world markets continued, there was another trend toward regional trade agreements. These agreements typically gave preferential trade status to nations which assented to the terms of a pact over those nations that did not participate. Two examples are the creation of a single European Market and the ratification of the **North American Free Trade Agreement (NAFTA)**. Created in 1958, and renamed most recently in 1993, the **European Union** is a regional organization designed to gradually eliminate customs duties and other types of trade barriers between its members. Imposing a common external tariff against nonmember countries, EU countries slowly adopted measures which would unify and, theoretically, strengthen their economies. The current members are Belgium, France, Germany, Great Britain, Italy, Luxembourg, the Netherlands, Denmark, Ireland, Greece, Spain, and Portugal. Comprised of Canada, the U.S., and Mexico, NAFTA was passed by the U.S. House and Senate in November 1994. In total, 360 million consumers are subject to the agreement, with spending power of about $6 trillion. Therefore, NAFTA is 20 percent larger than the EU.

DEVELOPING FOREIGN MARKETS

There are four general ways to develop markets on foreign soil. They are: exporting products and services from the country of origin; entering into **joint venture** arrangements with one or more foreign companies; licensing patent rights, trademark rights, etc. to companies abroad; and establishing manufacturing plants in foreign countries. A company can commit itself one or more of the above arrangements at any time during its efforts to develop foreign markets. Each method has distinct advantages and disadvantages and, thus, no single method is best in all instances.

Companies taking their first steps internationally often begin by exporting products manufactured domestically. Since the risks of financial losses can be minimized, exporting is the easiest and most frequently used method of entering international markets. Achieving export sales can be accomplished in numerous ways. Sales can be made directly, via mail order, or through offices established abroad. Companies can also undertake indirect exporting, which involves selling to domestic intermediaries who locate the specific markets for the firm's products or services. While having numerous benefits, exporting can place constraints on marketing strategies. The exporter often knows little about typical consumer-use patterns or, if using an intermediary, may have little influence over product pricing.

International licensing occurs when a country grants the right to manufacture and distribute a product or service under the licenser's trade name in a specified country or market. Common examples are granting foreign firms rights to technology, trademarks, and patents. Although large companies often grant licenses, this practice is most frequently used by small and medium-sized companies. Often seen as a supplement to **manufacturing** and exporting activities, licensing may be the least profitable way of entering a market. It can be advantageous, however, because it allows domestic firms to avoid certain obstacles. To illustrate, companies can use licenses when their own money is scarce, when foreign import restrictions forbid other ways of entering a market, or when a host country is apprehensive about foreign ownership.

Two particular types of licensing are **franchising** and management contracts. Similar to franchising domestically, world franchising occurs most often in fast foods, soft drinks, hotels, and car rentals. The major benefit of this type of license is the ability to standardize foreign operations with minimal investment. A second type of licensing arrangement is referred to as a management contract, often resulting from external pressures from a host government. This contract can occur when the host government nationalizes strategic industries for political or economic purposes. Rather than banish the company completely, the country hires the foreign owner to manage the firm and to give technical and managerial knowledge to the local population.

A third way to enter a foreign market is through a joint venture arrangement, whereby a company trying to enter a foreign market forms a partnership with one or more companies already established in the host country. Often, the local firm provides expertise on the intended market, while the multinational firm is better able to accomplish general management and marketing tasks. Use of this method of international investing has accelerated dramatically in the past 20 years. The biggest incentive to entering this type of arrangement is that it reduces the company's risk by the amount of investment made by the host-country partner. Other potential advantages to a joint venture arrangement are that: (1) it may allow firms with insufficient capital to expand internationally; (2) it may allow the marketer to use the partner's preexisting distribution channels; and (3) it may let the marketer take advantage of special skills possessed by the host country partner. While this method of market entry often results in the loss of total control over business operations, it is the only method of foreign investment that some host governments (especially lesser developed countries) will allow.

A company can also expand abroad by setting up manufacturing operations in a foreign country. This method is optimal when the foreign demand for a product justifies the often costly investment required. Other benefits to manufacturing abroad can be the avoidance of high import taxes, the reduction of transportation costs, the use of cheap labor, and better access to raw materials. When a company chooses to manufacture abroad, the markets of the host country are serviced by that particular manufacturing facility. Moreover, often products from the same facility are sent to other countries—even back to the original home country—for distribution.

INCREASED UNCERTAINTIES ASSOCIATED WITH MARKETING ABROAD

Although firms marketing abroad face many of the same challenges as firms marketing domestically, international environments present added uncertainties which must be accurately interpreted. Like domestic marketing, international marketing requires managers to make decisions that are within the firm's control, such as which product to market, what price it should command, the optimal promotion strategy, and the best distribution channels. Furthermore, like firms marketing domestically, firms marketing internationally must be prepared to react to factors in the home country which might affect their ability to do business. Examples are domestic politics, competition, and **economic conditions**.

International marketers face a host of issues that are out of their direct control, both at home and abroad. For instance, although domestic policies on foreign trade cannot be controlled by individual businesses, firms marketing abroad must be aware of how domestic policies help or hinder their foreign trade activities. Firms marketing abroad must also be prepared for uncertainties presented solely by the business environment in the host country as well. Four very important issues to note in a host country are its laws, politics, economy, and competition. Other issues are the host country's geography, **infrastructure**, currency, distribution channels, state of technological development, and cultural differences.

The legal and political environments of the host countries are two of the most important variables faced by international marketers. First, companies operating abroad are bound by both the laws of their host and home countries; moreover, legal systems around the world vary in content and interpretation. These laws can affect many elements of **marketing strategies**, particularly when they are in the form of product restrictions or specifications. Also, politics can be a huge concern for companies operating abroad and is, perhaps, the most volatile aspect of international marketing. Unstable political situations can expose businesses to numerous risks that they would rarely face at home. When governments change their regulations, there are usually new opportunities for both profits and losses, and firms must usually make modifications to their existing marketing strategies in response. For instance, the opening of Central and Eastern Europe presented both high political risks and huge potential market opportunities for companies willing to take the risks.

Economic conditions, per capita **gross national product** (GNP), and levels of economic development vary widely around the world. Before entering a market, firms marketing abroad must be aware of the economic situation there; the economy—not to mention individual standards of living—has a huge impact on the size and affluence of a particular target market. Furthermore, marketers must educate themselves on any trade agreements existing between countries as well as on local and regional economic conditions. Being aware of economic conditions and the likely direction that those conditions will take can help marketers better understand the profitability of their potential markets.

Competition overseas can come from a variety of different sources as well. Further, it has the potential to be much more fierce than competition at home. Often, if a market is ready to accept foreign goods, numerous manufacturers—both indigenous and foreign-based—will be willing to risk entry into that market. Making the situation more intense, the gov-ernments of many other countries may subsidize their manufacturers to help them enter a particular market.

Obviously, the more foreign markets in which a firm enters, the more of these uncontrollable events the firm must consider. To make the situation more interesting, the solutions to problems occurring in one country are often inapplicable to problems occurring in a second country because of differences in the political climates, economies, and cultures. The uncertainties of different foreign business environments creates the need to closely study the environment within each new market entered.

SEPARATING CULTURAL VALUES

Culture is a very important aspect of international marketing because the elements that compose it affect the way consumers think. The language a population speaks, the average level of education, the prevailing religion, and other social conditions affect the priorities the inhabitants have and the way they react to different events.

With this in mind, it is easy to see that managers of firms operating only in the domestic market are often able to react to many market uncertainties correctly and automatically because they intuitively understand their own culture and the impact of changing conditions. In foreign markets, however, this is not the case. Because they were not raised in the country in which they are trying establish a market, managers abroad often do not fully understand the culture and lack the proper frame of reference. Thus, decisions that they would make automatically at home could be dramatically incorrect when operating abroad. Unless special efforts are made to understand the cultural meanings for activities in each foreign market, managers will likely misinterpret the events taking place and risk making the wrong decisions.

This problem is so real that some authorities in international marketing believe that unconscious references to a firm's domestic cultural values contribute to most international business problems. To overcome these potential disastrous decisions, firms must understand the cultural factors existing in both their domestic country and their host country. Business problems and goals must be defined totally in terms of the host country's culture. Being able to separate home-country norms from those in the host country can be a very challenging task. Often, the influence of one's own culture is underrated.

SEE ALSO: Africa, Doing Business in; China, Doing Business in; Eastern Europe, Doing Business in; Indonesia, Doing Business in; Japan, Doing Business in; Korea, Doing Business in the Republic of; Malaysia, Doing Business in; Mexico, Doing Business in; South America, Doing Business in

[Kathryn Snavely]

FURTHER READING:

Cateora, Philip R. *International Marketing*. 5th ed. Homewood, IL: Irwin, 1983.

Facts on File. Volumes 53, 54, 55. Library of Congress Catalog, Infobase Holdings Company, 1993, 1994, 1995.

Gibb, Richard, and Wieslaw Michalak, eds. *Continental Trading Blocs: The Growth of Regionalism in the World Economy*. New York: John Wiley & Sons, 1994.

Gowa, Joanne. *Allies, Adversaries, and International Trade*. Princeton, NJ: Princeton University Press, 1994.

Paliwoda, Stan. *The Essence of International Marketing*. New York: Prentice-Hall, 1994.

Phillips, Chris, Isobel Doole, and Robin Lowe. *International Marketing Strategy: Analysis, Development, and Implementation*. New York: Routledge, 1994.

Sletten, Eric. *How to Succeed in Exporting and Doing Business Internationally*. New York: John Wiley & Sons, 1994.

INTERNATIONAL MONETARY FUND

The International Monetary Fund (IMF) was founded as a result of the **United Nations** Monetary and Financial Conference held at Bretton Woods, NH in July of 1944. Representatives of 45 countries including the United States attended the conference and wrote the IMF charter known as the Articles of Agreement. By December of 1945 enough countries had ratified the charter to make the IMF a viable organization. The IMF, which is headquartered in Washington D.C., was created to promote international monetary cooperation and stability which in turn creates an atmosphere for fostering international trade and development.

One of the first and most important acts of the newly formed IMF was to establish a method for standardizing the par value of each member nation's currency. It was felt by many economists, most notably John Maynard Keynes (1883-1946) of Great Britain and Harry Dexter White of the U.S. Treasury, that the depression of the 1930s was exacerbated by currency inconvertibility. As a result of this belief, the IMF in late 1946 standardized the par value of the currencies of its members and developed a policy for easing currency convertibility. Par values were standardized using gold and the U.S. dollar as a base. This policy continued for nearly 25 years. It ended in the early 1970s when the Nixon administration ceased converting dollars for gold, other countries began floating their currencies and oil prices rose dramatically.

Nonetheless the IMF continues to function as an important international regulatory agency which promotes an environment for orderly and stable currency exchange arrangements. Although joining the IMF is voluntary, members are obliged to follow IMF standards for economic cooperation as they relate to currency exchange and **monetary policy**. IMF standards and policies are designed to adjust misaligned exchange policies and members are subject to close IMF scrutiny.

Following the elimination in the early 1970s of par value based on the U.S. dollar and the price of gold, it wasn't until 1978 that a modified standardization system became established. Members were still obliged to promote currency convertibility but they could choose from a number of standards by which to value their currency. These methods included allowing their currencies to float, pegging their currency to the value of another currency, or valuing their currency in relation to a basket of other currencies. Members, however, are not allowed to value their currency in relation to the price of gold. The Fund also holds annual consultations with members during which the countries adherence to IMF policies and standards are reviewed.

In addition to its regulatory functions the IMF is able to provide short and medium term financing to member states with balance of payment problems. These loans are available only to those countries willing to align their monetary policies with IMF policies. IMF programs emphasize a balanced mix of fiscal and monetary policy, appropriate interest and exchange rates and adherence to market economy precepts. These programs provide for a balanced and orderly adjustment of a troubled economy while enhancing development and credit-worthiness. A Special Drawing Rights program (SDR) was begun in 1969 to fund these programs. The SDR is an interest bearing international reserve of the IMF. Compulsory deposits to the SDR are based on each member's quota which in turn is based on the relative economic strength of each member country. The value of an SDR unit is based on a basket of currencies from five countries: the pound sterling, deutsche mark, French franc, U.S. dollar, and the yen. A nation's share of SDR may be held in account by the IMF, used in **foreign exchange** to purchase other currencies or transferred during various transactions.

An integral part of the IMF infrastructure is the quota system. Based on a country's economic strength, the quota system determines the voting power, contributions to various IMF funds, shares of SDRs and other IMF resources. Allocations are determined by the Fund's Board of Governors and may be paid in SDRs or the member country's currency. Total allocations in 1988 amounted to $117 billion (U.S. dollars).

IMF policy is set by the Board of Governors. Each member country is allocated one Governor and one alternate Governor. There is also a Board of Executive Directors (22 members) which oversees the Managing Director and the administrative staff. The

Managing Director and staff are responsible for day to day operations of the IMF. In conjunction with the Board of Executive Directors the administrative staff makes recommendations to the Governors, acts on requests for assistance from member countries, and consults with and reviews members monetary policies.

Since its inception the United States has been a member and strong supporter of the IMF. Six other large members (in terms of GNP) are: Canada, France, Germany, Italy, Japan, and the United Kingdom. Along with the United States these countries are referred to within the IMF as the major industrial countries. By 1992 membership had grown to 157 countries. The Soviet Union did not support the IMF but since its dissolution Russia has joined and in early 1994 was granted $1.5 billion (U.S. dollars) in loans. Membership in the IMF is a prerequisite for joining the **World Bank**, an organization the IMF is closely associated with.

[Michael Knes]

FURTHER READING:

International Monetary Fund. *The Role and Function of the International Monetary* Fund. Washington D.C., 1985.

Southard, Frank A. *The Evolution of the International Monetary Fund.* Essays in *International Finance,* Dept. of Economics. Princeton University, 1979.

INTERNATIONAL MONETARY MARKET

The International Monetary Market was established in May of 1972 by the Chicago Mercantile Exchange and provides a forum for trading in foreign currency futures. Impetus for its creation was fueled by the Nixon administration's devaluing of the dollar, discontinuation of converting dollars for gold and general turmoil in the international monetary system. This disarray created a need for hedge services among financial institutions and other borrowers and lenders. In essence, foreign currency was assuming the characteristics of other more familiar commodities such as grain, lumber and precious metals.

Commodities are sold in three ways: on the spot market, which calls for immediate delivery at an agreed upon price; the forward market, which calls for delivery on a pre-determined future date at an agreed upon price; and, finally, the futures market. The futures market is similar to the forward market except there are financial obligations, margin requirements, and exchange rules structuring and guaranteeing the future commitment. There are three reasons for dealing in futures contracts: price discovery, which helps predict future spot prices; hedging, which protects against future price declines and anticipates future

rising prices; and speculation. Futures contracts can be written against approximately 50 commodities including agricultural commodities (grain, fruit, cotton, lumber), precious metals (gold, silver, platinum), crude oil and interest bearing securities (U.S. **Treasury notes**, **bonds**, and **Treasury bills**). With the opening of the IMM, foreign currencies were added to the list of commodities.

When the IMM opened for trading it allowed 500 charter members; this number increased to a maximum of 750 in 1976. The membership charge at that time was $10,000. Monetary contracts and the contract size are: British pound sterling (50,000), Mexican peso (1,000,000), Canadian dollar (200,000), West German deutschemark (500,000), Swiss francs (500,000) and the Japanese yen (25,000,000). By 1976, Treasury bill futures were being traded on the IMM followed by Eurodollars and Certificates of Deposit. Trading hours are 8:30 a.m. to 1:15 p.m. to coincide with late hours at European banks and early hours at west coast banks. Delivery months are March, June, September, and December and delivery is on the third Wednesday of the contract month. Pounds, marks, francs, lira, and yen may be traded through the second business day proceeding delivery. Canadian dollars and the peso may be traded through the first business day preceding delivery. Delivery is the maturity date of the contract. By 1980 trades were totaling the equivalent of $1 billion (U.S. dollars) a day.

The IMM is governed by a 22 member board of directors and by a chairman, two vice-chairmen, a secretary, and a treasurer. There are also two public members who are not members of the exchange. There are 14 committees and an administrative staff of 45 who also are not members of the exchange. All futures trading is regulated by the **Commodity Futures Trading Commission**, a federal agency charged with enforcing the Commodity Exchange Act.

[Michael Knes]

FURTHER READING:

Chicago Mercantile Exchange. *Trading in International Currency Futures.* Chicago, 1975.

Powers, Mark. *Inside the Financial Futures Markets.* John Wiley & Sons, 1984.

Rothstein, Nancy H., *The Handbook of Financial Futures.* McGraw-Hill, 1984.

INTERNET (BUSINESS APPLICATIONS)

The Internet is an international system of interconnected computer networks of government, educational, nonprofit organization, and corporate **computers**. The computers and networks are connected to each other by high-speed data communications lines, and even dissimilar computers are able to exchange data with each other using a set of data communications protocols called TCP/IP (Transmission Control Protocol/Internet Protocol). TCP/IP supports Simple Mail Transfer Protocol (SMTP) to permit the sending of **electronic mail** (e-mail) messages, File transfer protocol (FTP) for moving files between computers, and telnet which makes it possible to log in and interact with a remote computer. TCP controls the transmission of data between computers, and IP controls the automatic routing of the data over what might be a chain of computers.

The Internet's structure is based on a predecessor network called ARPAnet, which was established by the U.S. Department of Defense's Advanced Research Project Agency (ARPA) in 1969 as an experiment to determine how to build a network that could withstand partial outages, such as from an enemy attack. Each computer on the network communicates with others as a peer instead of having one or a few central hub computers, which would be too vulnerable. In the late 1980s ARPAnet was replaced by NSFNET, run by the National Science Foundation, which expanded the network, replaced its telephone lines with faster ones, and funded more college and university connections to the network. Thus, educational institutions became the dominant users in the 1980s. Other organizations and corporations joined by linking their computers, **local area networks (LANs)**, and **wide area networks (WANs)** to the Internet and adopting TCP/IP to connect their computers. As a result, the Internet comprises some networks which are publicly funded and some of which are private and which charge network access fees. Consequently, different users pay different fees, or none at all, for the same services. In the 1990s corporations and consumers became the biggest users of the Internet.

In 1994 the Internet connected about 30,000 networks, of which the majority were run by businesses; covered over 140 countries; and had about 25 million users. In addition, non-TCP/IP networks are also connected to the Internet via "gateways," but only permit e-mail transfer. The United States still accounts for the majority of Internet usage.

Various informal information services have evolved on the Internet to take advantage of the large volumes of publicly available data on the computers on the Internet, and of the voluntary efforts of those individuals who use the Internet. These include moderated discussion groups or mailing lists on specific topics known as listservs, news and unmoderated discussion forums resembling electronic bulletin boards called USENET newsgroups, files available for public access at anonymous FTP sites, and a menu-based system for exploring Internet resources called Gopher. The newest system for information retrieval

over the Internet is called the World Wide Web, which is based on hypertext links between document files, known as "pages," on different computers. The use of certain World Wide Web graphical browsers, such as Mosaic and NetScape, also permits the access of graphics and sound. The World Wide Web, in particular, has greatly facilitated business use the Internet.

Large corporations have been linked to the Internet since the 1980s. Initially, however, it was only their **research and development** departments that would access the Internet, using it as a means to gain scientific and technical information from the government and the academic community. Corporate information systems staffs were the next to discover the value of the Internet, primarily the many USENET newsgroups that focus on computer hardware and **software**, whereby participants answer each other's technical questions. Soon thereafter computer product vendors, realizing that their products and those of their competitors were being discussed in the newsgroups, began to monitor the newsgroups as a means of gaining customer feedback, and participated in correcting false information. Later, as more corporations connected their internal local area networks to the Internet, e-mail became a practical means of long-distance communication between individuals from all departments of different companies. E-mail remains the most common use of the Internet.

The commercial potential of the Internet long went unrealized, due to the fact that most of the computers on the Internet were owned by governmental or educational institutions, and the network infrastructure was owned by the government. The use of the Internet to promote the sale of goods and services was thus considered unethical. Now that more of the computers and network infrastructure of the Internet are owned by corporations, commercial use is no longer an issue. Corporate-owned computers on the Internet may be used to disseminate commercial information, whereas nonprofit organizations continue to forbid the use of their Internet computers for commercial purposes.

Even when the Internet was still dominated by governmental and educational networks, job postings were considered a legitimate business use of the Internet, and they continue to be widely disseminated, especially through specific USENET newsgroups. A more recent business usage of the Internet is as a medium for **advertising** and **marketing**.

Advertising on the Internet differs from advertising in other media is that the user seeks out the advertisements. The World Wide Web pages are the leading means of advertising on the Internet, because the hypertext links between pages make it easier for the user find a given advertisement page, and the graphics supported by World Wide Web browsers permit more effective advertisements. Companies that have advertising on the World Wide Web include Chrysler Corp., Adolph Coors Co., MCA Records, MCI Communications Corp., and Bank of America, in addition to most computer companies. An advertiser can gain more user access to its page by establishing links from other pages. This is equivalent to buying advertising space from other publishers on the World Wide Web. *Wired* magazine and Time Inc. are among the publishing companies that sell graphical links from their World Wide Web pages to those of advertisers. New software and market research companies such as Digital Plant and Internet Profiles Corp. offer the services of analyzing data of World Wide Web page access to determine the effectiveness of the advertisements. Nielsen, the company that rates television viewing audiences, and the corresponding radio audience research firm Arbitron are also planning to enter the field of analyzing the Internet market.

There have been cases whereby small businesses or individuals have sent unsolicited advertising messages to subscribers of mailing lists and USENET newsgroups. While there are no rules or regulations to forbid this practice, it is considered obnoxious and damages the reputations of the sender of such messages. Most corporations steer clear of such practice.

Advertising on the Internet is more accurately a form of **direct marketing**, because it permits immediate response from prospective customers. A company can put the texts and graphics of all of its marketing literature, brochures, catalogs, press releases, and the like on the Internet. The prospective customer can then obtain as much or as little information as desired and may even take steps toward placing an order. The customer may also have the opportunity to participate in a market survey by filling out a computerized form. In this way a company can save telephone customer support and mailing expenses.

The final frontier in the commercial use of the Internet is its use to place actual purchase orders and conduct financial transactions. In addition to promoting consumer sales, the use of on-line catalogs, ordering, and payment on the Internet for large volume corporate clients can also have the advantage of shortening procurement cycles. The lack of sufficient data security, however, has prevented most companies from accepting orders in which the user transmits his or her credit card number over the Internet. Typically, the customer preregisters his or her credit card number or corporate purchase card number with the vendor through a different means, such as telephone, mail, or fax, in order to set up an account, after which purchase requests can be made over the Internet when desired. First Virtual Holdings Inc. is a company that plans to arrange customer accounts with credit card information off the Internet for subsequent use of a First Virtual account on-line for purchases from various

vendors. Otherwise, new or one-time buyers of goods or services offered over the Internet must download an order form from the Internet, fill out the form, and send it by another means, such as fax.

In the early 1990s a number of software companies were developing data encryption software which aimed at guaranteeing secure financial transactions over the Internet. The obstacles have not so much been the software technology itself, but regulations, especially in the United States, prohibiting the use of the most sophisticated encryption technologies for anything other than government security purposes. By 1995 some of this new software was being tested in actual purchases over the Internet. In January 1995 Wells Fargo became the first U.S. bank to conduct a customer's electronic data interchange payment over the Internet, using data encryption software provided by Trusted Systems Inc. The following month Wells Fargo began testing encrypted credit card purchases with a number of merchants that take orders over the Internet. MCI Communications Corp. introduced a "secure" World Wide Web shopping mall in April 1995, whereby shoppers enter credit card numbers on an electronically encrypted form decoded only by the bank. DigiCash BV of the Netherlands has developed an electronic payment system using what is called "e-cash." NetScape Communications Corp. and MasterCard also plan to jointly develop special digital credit cards for Internet purchases.

Although financial transactions are the leading demand for data encryption on the Internet, there are other business needs for security on the Internet. Security is needed for sensitive request for quotations, confidential bids, and collaboration on projects involving trade secrets. Once data encryption software proves sufficiently secure, these types of business exchanges are expected to become commonplace on the Internet. Thus the Internet can facilitate competitive bidding, which in turn allows companies to cut costs and permits suppliers to maintain lower inventories. Collaborative engineering, meanwhile, can shorten development cycles.

Another way the Internet is being used for business purposes is as a means for information service companies to distribute their data to paying clients. This may involve sending regular e-mail postings of information or granting passwords to access and search the company's databases by telnet. For example, the investment advisory firm Security APL Inc. of Chicago offers the Portfolio Accounting World-Wide service which provides subscribers connections to **Securities and Exchange Commission** archives, news, and on-line stock trading services. The company also offers a free stock quote information service as a means of attracting new clients. Travelogix Inc. of Austin, Texas, plans to introduce a World Wide Web version of its subscription service in 1996 that lets customers access the computerized reservation systems of airlines. Both traditional literature retrieval vendors, such as Knight Ridder's Dialog service, and newer services, such as Individual Inc.'s Newspage, offer subscribing customers the ability to search for and retrieve the full text of published journal articles on any subject. Newspaper publishers, such as *USA Today* and the San Jose *Mercury News*, offer subscription access to their articles over the Internet.

A final aspect of the business implications of the Internet is that something of an "Internet industry" emerged in the 1990s, comprising computer hardware, software, and service companies that supply products and services for use of the Internet. In this context, hardware refers to the computers and data communication devices dedicated for making files available on the Internet and does not include the use of computers merely to access the Internet. Software for the Internet includes both programs used by the computers dedicated to providing files for the Internet, known as servers, and programs used for accessing and navigating the Internet by users. The server software is by far the larger, because freeware versions of Internet navigation software are available. Internet service providers are companies that typically establish and maintain computer services enabling a corporation to establish its own server on the Internet, especially for the World Wide Web. Approximately half of the companies in the United States that have commercial World Wide Web pages outsource this work instead of using their own computer systems, according to a survey by ParaTechnology Inc. Finally, Internet-access providers are companies that sell dial-up access to their computers which are on the Internet.

There are varying estimates of the size of the Internet market, depending on how it is calculated. Volpe Welty & Co. analyst Gregory S. Curhan estimated that the Internet software market was $150 million in 1994 and projected it to grow to $1.6 billion by 2000, the Internet service provider market to grow from $60 million in 1994 to $750 million by 2000, and the Internet access market to grow from $150 million in 1994 to $2.5 billion in 2000. Forrester Research Inc., on the other hand, projected Internet-related revenue in 1995 to be $50 million for computer hardware, $143 million for software, $30 million for service providers, and $123 million for access providers.

[Heather Behn Hedden]

FURTHER READING:

Angell, David, and Brent Heslop. *The Internet Business Companion*. Reading, MA: Addison-Wesley, 1995.

Booker, Ellis. "Financial Services Spread across Web." *Computerworld*. May 15, 1995, p. 12.

Booker, Ellis, "IS Staffs Take the On-Line Plunge." *Computerworld*. May 15, 1995, p. 59.

Cronin, Mary J. *Doing More Business on the Internet*. New York: Van Nostrand Reinhold, 1995.

Ellsworth, Jill H., and Matthew V. Ellsworth. *The Internet Business Book*. New York: John Wiley & Sons, 1995.

Ellsworth, Jill H., and Matthew V. Ellsworth. *Marketing on the Internet: Multimedia Strategies for the World Wide Web*. New York: John Wiley & Sons, 1995.

Emery, Vince. *How to Grow Your Business on the Internet*. Scottsdale, AZ: Coriolis Group Books, 1995.

Flynn, Laurie. "Gauging Ad Audience in Cyberspace." *New York Times*. May 29, 1995, pp. 19, 22.

Krol, Ed. *The Whole Internet: User's Guide & Catalog*. 2nd ed. Sebastopol, CA: O'Reilly & Associates, 1994.

Mathiesen, Michael. *Marketing on the Internet*. Gulf Breeze, FL: Maximum Press, 1995.

Reeves, Scott. "Analyst Says Internet Set to Explode during Next 6 Years." *Dow Jones News Service*. May 15, 1995.

Sullivan-Trainer, Michael L. "Serving up the Web." *Computerworld*. May 15, 1995, p. 62.

"Wells Fargo, Virtual Vineyards are Open for Regular Business on the Internet" (press release). San Francisco, CA: Wells Fargo Bank, February 17, 1995.

INTERNSHIPS

In the last 30 years America's **workforce** has learned to live with a job market that is shrinking because of **automation** and corporate cost-cutting. Yet this shorter list of opportunities has had no corresponding effect on the number of college graduates. According to a *New York Times* column of June 18, 1995, the 1.17 million graduates who brought new qualifications into the workplace in 1994 represented a rise of almost two-thirds since 1960, when a mere 400,000 fresh diplomas were issued nationwide. Furthermore, decreased opportunities in the workplace are not the only problem these new professionals have. They also have to face the old conundrum of "no job without experience vs. no experience without a job," a drawback that forces some of them to accept work far below their level of education and talent.

BENEFITS OF INTERNSHIP

To avoid this unwelcome compromise, more and more students have learned to plot their job-hunting strategy during their undergraduate years. Rather than spending time at the beach during summer vacations or looking for part-time jobs with no relationship to the career they intend to pursue, they are mapping out their future financial security by applying for internships that pay them sparingly, if at all. The burgeoning popularity of this pay-now-benefit-later trend is underscored by the annual Lindquist-Endicott Report, Northwestern University's corporate job outlook survey, which pinpoints the 1994 intern figure at 26 percent of graduates nationwide, as against 9 percent just two years earlier. Almost universally interns find that internships bring handsome rewards, among them practical experience and good contacts for obtaining a full-time job after graduation.

COMPANY BENEFITS. Company benefits can be considerable. Interns give junior staff members their first taste of supervision and constructive criticism; they also bring with them the prospect of cheap (or free) labor. Later, such short-term employees may also point to a healthier company bottom line, since the intern who is later offered a permanent job saves the company the hefty costs of recruiting and training a completely untried worker.

Sometimes routine benefits come to companies in completely unexpected ways, as General Motors Corp. found. In 1992, looking for more effective ways to market their Geo automobile to college students, GM turned to their interns for advice. To the executives' surprise, the interns panned GM advertising for the car, and persuaded them to stop using the Chevrolet logo.

ITT Automotive, an ITT Corporation subsidiary, took the possibility of fresh perspective one step farther. Concerned that academic curricula for accounting did not give enough importance to the areas in which most graduates find corporate jobs, they decided that college teachers needed to retool the fit between their classes and the needs of the workplace. ITT's solution was to offer resident internships to college faculty members and give them practical experience of corporate challenges by assigning them specific problems to solve. This idea not only enriched academic courses for students, but also brought ITT Automotive a handsome dividend—ideas from seasoned academics, which were innovative enough to help the company streamline their financial operations. The liaison, as detailed in a *Management Accounting* article in July 1994, bridged the corporate-faculty communications gap, created a closer bond between college and corporate America, and ensured internship slots for many future management accountants.

COMMUNITY BENEFITS. A well-planned internship program can also be designed specifically to be of service to the wider community. After riots shattered Los Angeles in 1992, the *Los Angeles Times* implemented a corporate program targeting the angry inner-city youth. With the help of the city's Chinatown Service Center, the Korean Youth Center, the YMCA, and other ethnically-based groups, the newspaper crafted a schedule centering around the corporate need for workers of diverse backgrounds to get along together. Within three years the internship program became an established part of *Los Angeles Times's* operations, providing formerly inexperienced youths with eight weeks of full workdays consisting of 75 percent job training and 25 percent life skills. The program not only prepared them for the future, but gave them the wherewithal to pass their knowledge on to others.

[Gillian Wolf]

FURTHER READING:

Aldrich, Michael. "Breathing New Life into a Small-College Internship Program." *Journal of Career Planning*. Spring, 1993, pp. 6-7.

Bell, Justine. "Marketing Academic Internships in the Public Sector." *Public Personnel Management*. Fall, 1994, pp. 481-485.

Bounds, Wendy. "All Work and No Pay." *Wall Street Journal*. February 27, 1995, pp. R7-R11.

Edleson, Harriet. "Expanding the Talent Search." *HR Magazine*. July, 1991, pp. 39-41.

Epley, John S. "PRSA Members Witness History in Moscow." *Public Relations Journal*. February, 1992, pp. 17-29.

Gornstein, Leslie. "Heard at Downsized Firms: 'Hey! Let the Intern Do It!' " *Crain's Chicago Business*. September 5, 1994, pp. 4-40.

Hendricks, James A. "The Company and the Professor." *Management Accounting*. April, 1993, pp. 47-49.

Kaplan, Rochelle. "Hiring Student Interns." *Small Business Reports*. May, 1994, pp. 9-13.

Khalfani, Lynette. "Minority Program Is Making 'Inroads' in Wall Street Firms." *Wall Street Journal*. November 25, 1994, p. A5.

Kulesza, C. S. "The Faculty Internship Program at ITT Automotive." *Management Accounting*. July, 1994, pp. 43-44.

McMenamin, Brigid. "I Definitely Leapfrogged." *Forbes*. February 27, 1995, p. 140.

Moskat, Brian S. "A Few Good Crusaders." *Industry Week*. January 4, 1993, pp. 23-24.

Oldman, Mark, and Samer Hamadeh. *America's Top 100 Internships*. New York: Villard Books, 1994.

Peterson's Internships. Princeton, NJ: Peterson's Guides, 1995.

Pedersen, Laura. "Minding Your Business: Apprenticeships Abound for Students." *New York Times*. June 18, 1995.

Peters, Shannon. "Internship Program Helps Rebuild Los Angeles." *Personnel Journal*. September, 1993, pp. 120-129.

Warner, Fara. "Carmaker Goes Back to School." *Brandweek*. October 19, 1992, p. 3.

"Washington Update: Commerce Department Begins U.S.-Soviet Business Internships." *Journal of Accountancy*. February, 1991, pp. 20-21.

INTERSTATE COMMERCE COMMISSION (ICC)

The Interstate Commerce Commission (ICC) is the oldest federal administrative agency. It was established as an independent regulatory agency by the Interstate Commerce Act of 1887. The ICC was originally limited to regulating interstate commerce by railroad or by a combination of water and rail. Subsequent pieces of legislation serving to amend the original act broadened the regulatory powers of the ICC to include all surface transportation involved in interstate commerce and foreign commerce to the extent that it took place in the United States.

Surface transportation regulated by the ICC now includes railroads, trucking, buses, freight forwarders, water carriers, transportation brokers, and those pipelines that are not regulated by the Federal Energy Regulatory Commission (FERC). Since there are various exemptions from ICC regulations, in practice the ICC regulates approximately one-third of all interstate trucking operations and only about one-tenth of interstate water carrier operations. Exemptions apply to such areas as water transportation of products in bulk, school buses, hotel buses, national park buses, taxicabs, newspaper distribution vehicles, and vehicles incidental to air transportation.

While most legislation passed from 1903 to the early 1970s served to strengthen the ICC's authority and broaden its areas of jurisdiction, the Railroad Revitalization and Regulatory Reform Act of 1976 and subsequent legislation has served to provide for less regulation over carrier rates and practices. Responding to concerns of the railroad industry over the effect of ICC regulations on competitiveness, the Staggers Rail Act of 1980 eliminated many of the regulatory requirements of the ICC for railroads.

That same year the Motor Carrier Act of 1980 reduced the ICC's regulatory authority over the trucking industry. As a result the ICC no longer had as much control over such areas as entry into the trucking business, routes served, and commodities carried. Since part of the trucking industry was concerned about the negative impact of such deregulation, the law provided for phasing in regulatory changes gradually and formally reviewing the impacts of those changes. Other legislation in the 1980s provided for similar regulatory reforms affecting bus lines and surface freight forwarders.

Regulations of the ICC encompass transportation economics, transportation service, and consumer protection. In the area of transportation economics the ICC has regulatory power over rates and charges among regulated carriers, shippers, receivers of freight, and passengers, among others. It sets standards for reasonable rates and in recent years has been concerned with the practice of undercharging. It also has approval power over proposed mergers, acquisitions, and sales of regulated carriers. It administers laws, prescribes accounting rules, and awards reparations relating to railroad bankruptcy. In addition it has jurisdiction over a range of matters concerning railroad equipment.

The ICC regulates interstate transportation service by granting the right to operate railroads, trucking companies, bus lines, household goods transporters, freight forwarders, water carriers, and transportation brokers. The construction and abandonment of railroad lines must also be approved by the ICC.

Through its Office of Compliance and Consumer Assistance the ICC ensures that the public obtains the transportation services that are guaranteed by the Interstate Commerce Act. By law the general public is entitled to fair rates and reasonable service. Incidents of discrimination, preferential treatment, or prejudicial actions by regulated carriers are illegal.

The headquarters of the Interstate Commerce Commission are located at Twelfth Street and Constitution Avenue NW, Washington, DC 20423. The commission also maintains regional offices in Chicago, Philadelphia, and San Francisco. The rules and regulations of the ICC are contained in Title 49, Section XX, of the Code of Federal Regulations.

[David Bianco]

INVENTORY ACCOUNTING

The way in which a company accounts for its inventory can have a dramatic affect on its financial statements. Inventory is a current asset on the balance sheet. Therefore, the valuation of inventory directly affects the inventory, total current asset, and total asset balances. Companies intend to sell their inventory, and when they do, it increases the cost of goods sold, which is often a significant expense on the income statement. Therefore, how a company values its inventory will determine the cost of goods sold amount, which in turn affects gross profit (margin), net income before **taxes**, and hence taxes, and thus net income. Since inventory costing affects taxes, it affects a company's cash flow. Finally, since inventory affects net income, it will affect the retained earnings balance on the balance sheet. As you can see, how a company values its inventory causes ripple effects throughout its **financial statements**.

One may think that inventory valuation is relatively simple. For a retailer, inventory should be valued for what it cost to acquire that inventory. When an inventory item is sold, the inventory account should be reduced (credited) and cost of goods sold should be increased (debited) for the amount paid for each inventory item. This works if a company is operating under the Specific Identification Method. That is, a company knows the cost of every individual item that is sold. This method works well when the amount of inventory a company has is limited and each inventory item is unique. Examples would include car dealerships, jewelers, and art galleries.

Problems arise when a company owns a great deal of inventory and each specific inventory item is relatively indistinguishable from each other. For example, what if a company is a retailer and all they sell is blue jeans. There are various styles and sizes, but the inventory on the whole is similar. The retailer buys the inventory from a wholesaler or manufacturer. For example, let's assume that the retailer pays $3000 for 300 pairs of jeans. So the cost per pair is $10. If the cost never changes, then inventory costing is simple. Every pair of jeans cost the exact same amount. However, one can generally expect inflation and sometimes discounts or sales. So let's say that our retailer buys 100 pairs of jeans on Monday for $1000 ($10.00 per pair), and 200 pairs of jeans on Friday for $2150 ($10.75 per pair). A customer comes into the store on Saturday and purchases a pair of jeans. What is the cost of the jeans? Under the Specific Identification Method, the retailer would have to mark or code every pair of jeans, to determine from which purchase that particular pair of jeans came from. That is far too cumbersome. As a result, other inventory valuation methods have been developed.

Under the Weighted Average Method, a company would determine the weighted average cost of the inventory. In the example above, the weighted average cost would be $3150 / 300 pairs which equals $10.50 per pair of jeans. Therefore, every pair of jeans would be sold for $10.50, regardless of whether they were actually bought in the $10.00 purchase or the $10.75 purchase. This weighted average would remain unchanged until the next purchase occurs, which would result in a new weighted average cost to be calculated.

Another method used by companies is called the FIFO method (first-in, first-out). Under FIFO, it is assumed that the oldest inventory is always sold first. Therefore, the inventory that remains is from the most recent purchases. So for the given example, the first 100 jeans that are sold will reduce inventory and increase cost of goods sold at a rate of $10.00 per pair. The next 200 sold will be costed at $10.75 per pair. It is irrelevant whether a customer actually selects a pair of jeans from one purchase or another. Under FIFO, a company always assumes that it sells its oldest inventory first.

The final method that a company can use is the LIFO method (last-in, first-out). Under LIFO, it is assumed that the most recent purchase is always sold first. Therefore, the inventory that remains is always the oldest inventory. So for the given example, the first 200 jeans that are sold will reduce inventory and increase cost of goods sold at a rate of $10.75 per pair. It is irrelevant whether a customer actually selects a pair of jeans from one purchase or another. Under LIFO, a company always assumes that it sells its newest inventory first.

Among the four inventory methods mentioned, the most popular methods used are FIFO and LIFO. The Specific Identification Method is too cumbersome when large amounts of inventory items are on hand. The Weighted Average Method is not used very often, primarily because its valuation of inventory and cost of goods sold usually lie in-between the valuation derived under FIFO and LIFO.

The FIFO Method may come the closest to matching the actual physical flow of inventory. Since FIFO assumes that the oldest inventory is always sold first, the valuation of inventory still on hand is at the most recent price. Assuming inflation, this will mean that cost of goods sold will be at its lowest possible amount. Therefore, a major advantage of FIFO is that it has the effect of maximizing net income within an inflationary environment. The downside of that effect is that income taxes will be at their greatest.

The LIFO Method is preferred by many companies because it has the effect of reducing a company's taxes, thus increasing cash flow, and LIFO smooths income. However, these attributes of LIFO are only present in an inflationary environment. Under LIFO, a company always sells its newest inventory first. Given inflation, this will also be its most expensive inventory. So cost of goods sold will always be at its greatest amount, therefore, net income before taxes will be at its lowest amount, so taxes will be minimized. That is the major beneficial attribute of LIFO.

For example, in a footnote to General Motors Corp.' 1993 annual report, "the cost of substantially all U.S. inventories . . . (are) determined by the last-in, first out method. If the first-in, first-out method of inventory valuation had been used for inventories valued at LIFO cost, such inventories would have been $2,519.0 million higher at December 31, 1993." If you assume an average marginal tax rate of 35%, the choice of LIFO has saved General Motors $881.65 million in tax payments over the years. Of course, the downside is that net income before taxes has been $2,519.0 million lower over the years.

The other advantage of LIFO is that it can have an income smoothing effect. Again, assuming inflation and a company that is doing well, one would expect inventory levels to expand. Therefore, a company is purchasing inventory, but under LIFO, the majority of the cost of these purchases will be on the income statement as part of cost of goods sold. Thus, the most recent and most expensive purchases will increase cost of goods sold, thus lowering net income before taxes, and hence net income. Net income is still high, but just not as high than if FIFO had been used.

On the other hand, if a company is doing poorly, it will have a tendency to reduce inventories. To do so, the company will have to effectively sell more inventory than they acquire. Under LIFO, since a company sells its most recent purchases, the inventory that remains is older and inexpensive (given inflation). So when a company shrinks its inventory, it sells older, inexpensive inventory. Therefore, the cost of goods sold is lower, net income before taxes is higher, and net income is higher than it otherwise would have been. Once again, from the 1993 General Motors Annual Report, footnote 1, "as a result of decreases in U.S. inventories, certain inventory quantities carried at lower LIFO costs prevailing in prior years, as compared with the costs of current purchases, were liquidated in 1993 and 1992. These inventory adjustments improved pre-tax operating results by approximately $134.4 million in 1993 ... and $294.7 million in 1992."

A disadvantage of LIFO is the effect it has on the balance sheet. If a company always sells its most recent inventory, then the balance sheet will contain inventory valued at the oldest inventory prices. For instance, if a company were to switch from FIFO to LIFO in 1955, then unless the inventory was zeroed out at some point in time, there may be units of inventory valued at 1955 prices, even though the physical inventory is comprised of the most recent units. As a result, the inventory account can be dramatically undervalued if a company has adopted LIFO, and if during that time, the cost of inventory has increased. As noted above, the difference between LIFO and FIFO for General Motors as of December 31, 1993 was over $2.5 billion. Also, if General Motors were to switch from LIFO to FIFO, all of that old, inexpensive inventory would be the first items sold, resulting in cost of goods sold and net income before taxes being $2.5 billion lower and higher, respectively, than they otherwise would have been.

The LIFO Method is justified based upon the matching principle, as the most recent cost of inventory is matched against the current revenue generated from the sale of that inventory. However, FIFO does not distort the valuation of inventory on the balance sheet like LIFO can potentially do.

When examining financial statements, it is imperative that the inventory footnote be read carefully, to determine the method of inventory valuation chosen by a company. It is most likely that either FIFO or LIFO would have been chosen. Assuming inflation, FIFO will result in higher net income during growth periods and a higher, and more realistic inventory balance. In periods of growth, LIFO will result in lower net income and lower income tax payments, thus enhancing a company's cash flow. During periods of contraction, LIFO will result in higher income levels. LIFO also has the potential to greatly undervalue inventory over time.

[William H. Coyle]

INVENTORY CONTROL SYSTEMS

Inventory control systems maintain information about activities within firms that ensure the delivery of products to customers. The subsystems that perform these functions include selling or **marketing, manufacturing,** warehousing, ordering, and receiving. In different firms the activities associated with each of these areas may not be strictly contained within separate subsystems, but these functions must be performed in sequence in order to have a well-run inventory control system.

The general activities associated with marketing of products to customers is not strictly considered to be part of the inventory control function when an order is placed, however, the information becomes part of the system. The inventory control information collected at the point of the order or sale identifies the items that have been ordered by the customer. This information must be collected for use in other inventory activities. In manual ordering systems the information may be collected on paper documents and then transferred to either manual or computer-based system. Generally the information collected includes the quantities of each inventory item sold and the price charged. This is the most important point in the process because it is where inventory information is actually being created. If incorrect information is captured it can become very difficult to correct it later in the process. Therefore, firms have implemented three types of controls in an attempt to collect quality information.

The first control is quite simple and that is to require the information be collected on certain documents, usually a sales order or invoice. A well-designed document helps the person filling it out capture the correct information. A second control is the use of codes on the inventory items. These codes can be designed in many different ways but their basic function is to give the person selling inventory items a distinct set of characters that completely describe the product. Through the use of codes a salesperson may only have to place a few characters on the form rather than a complete description of the product. The final control that is probably the most significant is the application of various technological innovations in the capture of data at the point of sale. One of the most beneficial applications of technology to the inventory control function was to capture data machine-readable form as early in the process as possible. The first innovation was to place more sophisticated cash registers (i.e., terminals) at the point of the execution of the sale. Using one of these terminals a salesperson could collect the same information collected previously, but without it having to be reentered later. The next innovation required changes to both the products and the terminals. The information was placed on the product in machine-readable form and terminals equipped with laser wands or pads read the information on the product. Now the seller of the merchandise only had to drag a wand across the tag on the merchandise or move the product across the pad for the relevant information to be captured. Salespeople no longer had to create paper documents; they were created by the machine capturing the information. By moving the data capture for inventory control as early in the process as possible the information became more accurate. This also had an effect on the types of people that could work as salespeople. These people no longer had to be good at filling out forms but could concentrate on their selling activities.

After the sale or order information has been captured, the next step in the inventory control system is to update this information to the permanent inventory and customer records. In earlier manual systems this meant sending the documents to an individual responsible for inventory cards who posted the information. From a control standpoint this process required a great deal of verification so that the information was not entered incorrectly or to the wrong inventory card. These manual systems made it difficult to adequately monitor the movement of product on a timely basis. So one of the first steps in automating this step was to substitute a computer-based file for the manual inventory cards. The development of a master inventory file to maintain information about products meant that more information could be collected and saved and that this product information was useful to more people. For instance, information about the way in which products sold during a year or what products were sold together became more readily accessible.

Along with the computerization of inventory records came technological innovations that allowed the information captured at the point of sale to be updated to the file without any other transcription. This meant that the information was not only more likely to be correct but also more timely. This timeliness of the information contained in the inventory control system meant that certain other changes were now possible.

Once the order or sale has been updated to the inventory file a decision has to be about how to replenish the item. When information was maintained manually the decision about when to reorder was based on keeping enough on hand so that there were minimal stockout costs. In addition the decision about whom to acquire the product from was made as easy as possible; there was usually only one approved vendor. As the technological sophistication improved the timeliness of the information, the decision about when to reorder could be made closer and closer to the next time the item was needed. This also required the supplier of the product to be able to supply the product with less lead time. The end result of this reduction of lead time between sale and reorder is reflected in inventory control systems that use just-in-time ordering. In order to accomplish this, a change in the inventory control system's view of vendors also had to change.

Traditionally each part had an approved vendor and when parts were ordered the order was sent to that vendor. This selection of the best vendor for each part was usually based on the lowest-cost supplier. When the view of inventory control changed to an orientation that goods had to be delivered on time, a different relationship developed between suppliers and customers. Now it became critical to look at reliability of vendors and their ability to deliver products within a short period. Today, firms have reduced the size of their warehouses or in some cases eliminated them entirely as products move from supplier to seller and finally to the ultimate customer without being stored. This has changed the way in which inventory control systems maintain information. Certain sellers' inventory control systems are tied directly to the suppliers' systems so that orders are placed directly when the items are needed, with no time lost between the identification of the need for the product and the order. For manufacturing firms the change in inventory control systems has also changed the way in which materials are made available.

For manufacturing firms inventory control systems must monitor one additional step and that is the transformation of raw materials into products that are ready for delivery. The monitoring of inventory levels when a sale is made must take into account both the time it takes orders of raw materials to be received and the time it takes to convert them into a final product. The current approach to inventory control requires a system that can monitor this process closely as manufacturers attempt to reduce cost by keeping as small a raw materials inventory as possible. The emphasis is on receiving the raw materials just-in-time to be placed into production. In order to accomplish this, the relationship between supplier and purchaser discussed earlier must be monitored and continually evaluated by the inventory control system.

Inventory control systems have always been required to perform similar tasks regardless of the technology used to actually implement the system. The monitoring of sales (or removal of finished inventory) has always required processes to ensure that inventory stocks do not get too low and that orders are placed with the best vendor possible. As technology has been introduced into these systems the tasks can be performed more consistently and, as is the case with more advanced systems, the costs associated with ordering and warehousing either finished goods or raw materials inventory can be reduced.

SEE ALSO: Bar Coding; Electronic Data Interchange

[Graham Gal]

INVESTMENT ADVISERS ACT OF 1940

The Investment Advisers Act (IAA) was passed in 1940 in order to regulate those who, for a fee, advise people, pension funds, and institutions on investment matters. The Investment Advisers Act mandates that all persons and firms receiving compensation for serving as investment advisers must register with the Securities and Exchange Commission; it also defines the relationship between advisers and clients. A 1960 amendment to the act further empowers the **Securities and Exchange Commission**. The purpose of the act and subsequent amendments is to protect the public from fraudulent and unethical advisers. Many of the financial practices and outright chicanery that contributed to the stock market crash of 1929 and the subsequent Great Depression also influenced the 1940 legislation.

A hallmark of the IAA is the required registration of all investment advisers. The Act defines an investment adviser as: ''. . . any person who, for compensation, engages in the business of advising others, either directly or through publications or writings, as to the value of securities or as to the advisability of investing in, purchasing, or selling securities, or who for compensation and as part of a regular business, issues or promulgates analyses or reports concerning securities.''

Securities may be defined under the act as including but not necessarily limited to notes, **bonds**, **stocks** (common and preferred), mutual funds, money market funds, and certificates of deposit. They generally do not include commodity contracts, real estate, insurance contracts, or collectibles, such as works of art or rare stamps and coins.

Whether or not a person can be considered an investment adviser under the act generally depends upon three criteria: the type of advice offered, the method of compensation, and whether or not a significant portion of one's income comes from proffering investment advice. Related to the last criteria is the consideration of whether or not a person leads others to believe that he or she is an investment adviser, perhaps through television or print advertising, for example.

A person is generally considered to be an investment adviser under the act by offering advice or makeing recommendations on specific securities or securities as opposed to other types of investments. Even those who receive finder's fees for referring potential clients to investment advisers are considered to be investment advisers themselves. Generally excluded from coverage under the act are those professionals whose investment advice to clients is incidental to the relationship. This would generally include accountants, lawyers, and other financial professionals. Stock brokers and dealers are excluded from the act by statute. Banks, publishers, and government security advisers are also excepted from the act. People who call themselves financial planners may be considered investment advisers under the act and should at a minimum be familiar with Release 1092 of the SEC, which discusses the relationship between the IAA and financial planners. There are, however, three general exceptions to the registration requirement: investment advisers whose clients all reside in the same state as the adviser's business office and who does not provide advice on securities listed on national exchanges, investment advisers whose clients are solely insurance companies, and advisers who have fewer than 15 clients in any previous 12-month period.

If a person receives compensation for investment advice, that person is considered to be an investment adviser. The compensation may be defined as an advisory fee, a commission, or compensation for total services, of which investment advice is only a part. The adviser also need not be compensated by the actual advisee. Receipt of referral fees and finder's fees qualify one as an investment adviser. Nor does the compensation have to be in excess of the cost of the service. Additionally, a person must act as an investment adviser. That is, one must promote oneself as an adviser. Investment advice need not be one's major source of income or principal business to be considered an investment adviser under the act.

Under the act, investment advisers must register using Form ADV accompanied by a $150 filing fee. The form asks for information dealing with educational background, experience, exact type of business engaged in, assets, information on clients, past history of a legal and/or criminal nature, type of investment advice to be offered, etc. Registration under the act does not constitute an endorsement of the investment adviser nor can the person or firm advertise as such.

Advisers who are registered are required to annually update their ADV form and file operating reports with the SEC. The adviser must also provide to clients and prospective clients a written disclosure statement and allow SEC inspections of all records and books relating to investment advisory activities. Advisers generally cannot receive compensation based on the performance of the advisements, nor can they engage in excessive trading or profit from market activity resulting from their advice to clients. Investment advisers must also act in the best interest of their clients at all times concerning consideration of their client's financial position and financial sophistication. There are also many provisions in the act dealing with fraud in terms of advertising, control of client's assets, soliciting clients, and information disclosure.

[Michael Knes]

FURTHER READING:

Bernzweig, Eli P. *The Financial Planner's Legal Guide*. Prentice-Hall, 1986.

Regulation of Financial Planners in the 1980s: 1986. Practising Law Institute, 1986.

INVESTMENT ANALYSIS

In its broadest sense, investment means the sacrifice of current consumption for greater expected consumption. In finance and business, investors are willing to forego an identifiable stream of returns for uncertain future returns. When investors change their goals and objectives, they modify the allocation of their capital resources with the expectation that time will reward them with greater returns. Investors are willing to assume additional risk over time when they perceive profitable opportunities.

SECURITY ANALYSIS

A security is a financial asset representing a claim on the assets of the issuing firm and on the profits produced by the assets. The term security analysis pertains to the process of identifying desirable investment opportunities in such financial assets. In the case of corporate **stocks** and **bonds**, the analysis flows from the interpretation of **accounting** and financial data regarding operations, profitability, net worth, and the like. Investment alternatives are identified on (1) the investor's risk/reward ratio, (2) a specified time horizon, and (3) current market prices.

Security analysts, in essence, are the catalysts which drive the efficient market hypothesis. That is, "smart" money will logically and efficiently distribute itself in such a way that security prices reflect all available information. As new information becomes available, analysts assess it and recommend market price adjustments according to changes they anticipate for price levels. The cumulative impact of price adjustments moves the market to equilibrium so that the price of any security approximates true investment value.

Security analysts operate in three arenas, each reflecting a different set of goals and objectives. Investment banking and brokerage firms represent the "sell" side of security analysis. Their clients are fee and commission paying institutional and individual investors.

Investment management organizations conduct security analysis for the portfolios they manage. Since portfolio managers purchase securities, they represent the "buy" side of the street.

Finally, a number of investment publishing services provide security analysis for all investors subscribing to their reports. The most popular investment services are available through Value Line Inc., Standard's & Poor's, Moody's Investors Service, and **Dun & Bradstreet**.

METHODOLOGY

There are two basic methodologies: **fundamental analysis** and technical analysis. In their own way, each approaches investment decisions from the top-down and from the bottom-up.

THE TOP-DOWN APPROACH. The top-down approach, the traditional methodology, begins with a broad perspective and ends with a specific analysis of a stock or a bond. The top-down approach initially analyzes macroeconomic data, filters it into more specific sectors, and finally distills the results with respect to a specific security.

Analysts determine the important economic conditions and forces at work and their potential impact on the markets. Analysts examine corporate profitability, the direction and magnitude of **interest rates**, **money supply**, **fiscal policy**, **employment**, migration, export/import trends, etc., to evaluate the future performance of individual economic sectors and industries.

Security analysts also utilize the top-down approach to allocate available funds within portfolios between short-term and long-term investments, between risky and risk-free securities, and between stocks and bonds. Sector-to-sector and market-to-market comparisons purport to identify where investors should look for superior returns. Analysts recommend investing in favorable industries or sectors, and suggests specific stocks within each sector.

THE BOTTOM-UP APPROACH. A major drawback to the top-down approach is the likelihood of overlooking certain stocks that offer significant investment opportunities but which are outside the favorable sectors. To remedy this, analysts also utilize the bottom-up approach which identifies superior performers without regard to industry.

This approach identifies advantageous investments according to performance and financial criteria. The criteria are applicable across industry and sectors, establishing performance and financial benchmarks which companies must meet or exceed in order to be considered. Analysts also develop criteria to separate the top performers by various degrees of risk, e.g., conservative versus aggressive.

Once the screens have filtered out the appropriate securities, the analysts conducts a fundamental analysis of the company.

FUNDAMENTAL ANALYSIS

Fundamental analysts look for superior returns from securities which are mispriced by the market. To identify them the analyst engages in various calculations using data from **financial statements** to determine the future earnings and **dividends** of a company, the degree to which these exceed the expected average for the industry, and the potential for the stock to move closer to a correct or fair value. Fundamental analysts would recommend buying undervalued, or underpriced, stocks.

Stock values may also exceed their true/intrinsic value and, therefore, be overpriced or overvalued. A recommendation to sell or take a short position would be considered since the analyst would expect the market to correct the price in the future.

THE OPERATING ENVIRONMENT. Some of the external conditions affecting a company's performance are:

1. Demographic changes: sex, age, absolute numbers, location, population movements, educational preparation.

2. **Economic conditions**: employment level, regional performance, wage levels, spending patterns, consumer debt, capital investment.

3. Government fiscal policy and regulation: spending levels, the magnitude of entitlements, **debt**, war and peace, tax policies, environmental regulations.

4. **Competition**: market penetration and position, market share, commodity, **marketing strategies**, and niche products.

5. Vendors: financial soundness, quality and quantity of product, R&D capabilities, alternative suppliers, JIT capabilities.

Industry and firm specific characteristics important to the fundamental analyst are: profitability; market presence; productivity; product type, sales, and services; financial resources; physical facilities; **research and development**; quality of **management**.

The analyst approaches these indicators in two ways. First, as trends within an industry, and secondly as features of a particular firm. To do this, analysts use a series of ratios constructed from the financial statements. Ratios represent percentage or decimal relationship of one number to another. Ratios facilitate the use of comparative financial statements which provide significant information about trends and relationships over two or more years. Analysts compare a company's ratios to industry ratios, as well as cross-sectionally to other companies.

Structural analysis compares two financial statements in terms of the various items or groups of items within the same period. **Time series analysis** correlates ratios over time, measured in years or by quarters.

Since ratios are relative measures, they furnish a common scale of measurement from which analysts construct historical averages. Thus, analysts are able to compare companies of different sizes and from different industries based on performance and financial condition by (a) establishing absolute standards, (b) examining averages, and (c) using trends to forecast future results. To increase predictability, the analyst considers the impact of external factors on internal trends.

PIONEERS. In 1934 Benjamin Graham and David Dodd published *Security Analysis*. This book is considered the bible of fundamental practitioners. In the 1920s, Graham became a successful portfolio manager by stressing capital preservation by investing proportionately in high quality stocks and in low risk credit instruments. With Dodd, his student from UCLA, Graham laid out vigorous investment procedures in the aforementioned title.

Graham and Dodd primarily appraised stocks according to their earning power. They recommended an extensive list of **financial ratios** to measure a company's performance according to

1. Projected future earnings

2. Projected future dividends

3. A method for valuing expected earnings

4. The value of the asset.

In the belief that investors tended to overreact to near-term prospects, Graham and Dodd formulas designed to keep the disparity between P/E's for different companies within sharp focus. Analysts continue to apply these principles today.

FINANCIAL ANALYSIS. Financial analysis is necessary in determining the future value of a company. Financial analysis concentrates on the condition of the financial statements: the income statement, the **balance sheet**, the statement of changes in shareholders' equity, and the funds flow statements. From these the analyst determines the values of the outstanding claims on the company's **income**.

Financial analysts measure past performance, evaluate present conditions, and make predictions as to future performance. This information is important to investors looking for superior returns. Creditors use this information to determine the risk associated with the extension of credit.

RATIO ANALYSIS. The most common method used by analysts is financial ratios. Composition ratios compare the size of the components of any accounting category with the total of that category. For example, the percentage of net income to net sales. Composition ratios:

- Indicate the size of each of the components relative to their total and to each other.

- Make historic comparisons and trending possible.

- Point to cause-and-effect relationships between the individual components and their total.

FUNDAMENTAL WEAKNESSES. Although widely used, financial analysis does have some fundamental weaknesses. Since it is based on data from financial reports, its findings are subject to distortions resulting from **inflation**, wild business swings, changes in accounting practices, and undisclosed inner-workings of the firm. Management can manipulate important key ratios by changing inventory valuations, **depreciation** schedules, and expense recognition practices. Furthermore, since the financial statements are static, the analyst cannot account for the impact of seasonal variations. Finally, the ratios are meaningless unless compared to performance benchmarks.

TECHNICAL ANALYSIS

Technical analysis examines stock price trends in an attempt to predict future prices. Technical analysts believe that all the relevant information about economic fundamentals, of an industry and of a stock are reflected in the direction and volume of prices. Therefore, technical analysts look to the past, for they believe that markets are cyclical, forming specific patterns, and these patterns repeat themselves over time. They further believe that it is only necessary to compare short-term and intermediate price movements to long-term trends in order to predict market direction.

Two major techniques form the basis of technical analysis: the study of key indicators, and the charting of market activity.

KEY INDICATORS. Common key indicators utilized by technical analysts include the following:

1. Trading volume is based on supply-demand relationships and indicates market strength or weakness. Rising prices with increased buying generally signals uptrends. Decreasing prices with increasing demand, and increasing prices with decreasing volume, sig-

nal downtrends. Trading volume applies best to the short-term (three to nine months).

2. Market breadth examines the activity of a broader range of securities than do highly publicized indices such as the Dow Jones Industrial Average. The breadth **index** is the net daily advances or declines divided by the amount of securities traded. The breadth index is calculated by either the number of securities, the dollar volume, or nominal volume. Breadth analysis concentrates on change rather than on level in order to evaluate the dispersion of a general movement in prices. The slope of the advance/decline line indicates the trend of the breadth index. Breadth analysis points to the prime turning points in bull and bear markets.

3. Confidence indices evaluate the trading patterns of bond investors who are regarded as more sophisticated and more well-informed that stock traders and, therefore, spot trends more quickly. Other confidence theories measure the sentiment among analysts themselves, the breadth trends in options and futures trading, and consumer confidence. Analysts consider these to have predictive value in the near and intermediate term.

4. The put-call ratio divides the volume of puts outstanding by the volume of calls outstanding. Investors generally purchase the greatest number of puts around market bottoms when their pessimism peaks, thus indicating a turnaround. Call volume is greatest around market peaks, at the heights of investor enthusiasm—also indicating a market turn.

5. The cash position of funds gives an indication of potential demand. Analysts examine the volume and composition of cash held by **institutional investors**, pension funds, **mutual funds**, and the like. Because fund managers are performance driven, analysts expect them to search out higher returns on large cash balances and, therefore, will invest more heavily in securities, driving prices higher.

6. Short selling represents a bearish sentiment. Analysts in agreement with short sellers expect a downturn in the market. Analysts particularly watch the action of specialists who make a market in a specific stock. In addition, analysts look at odd-lot short sellers who indicate pessimism with increased activity. However, many technical analysts express a "contrarian" view regarding short sales. These analysts believe short sellers overreact and speculate because of the potential profits

involved. In addition, to close their positions, short sellers will purchase the securities in the future, thus putting upward pressure on prices. Short selling analysis is based on month-to-month trends.

7. Odd-lot theory follows the trends of transactions involving less than round lots (less than 100 shares). This theory rests on a contrarian opinion about small investors. The theory believes the small trader is right most of the time, and begins to sell into an upward trend. However, as the market continues to rise, the small investor re-enters the market as the sophisticated traders are bailing out in anticipation of a top and a pull back. Therefore, an increase in odd-lot trading signals a downturn in the market.

Odd-lot indices divide (1) odd-lot purchases by odd-lot sales, (2) odd-lot short sales by total odd-lot sales, and (3) total odd-lot volume (buys + sales) by round-lot volume.

CHARTING. Charting is useful in analyzing market conditions and price behavior of individual securities. Standard & Poor's *Trendline* is a well known charting service which provides data on companies. This data shows the trend of prices, insider sales, short sales, and trading volume over the intermediate and long-term. Analysts have plotted this data on graphs to form line, bar, and point-and-figure charts.

Chart interpretation requires the ability to evaluate the meaning of the resulting formations in order to identify ranges in which to buy or sell. Charting assists in ascertaining major market down-turns, upturns, and trend reversals.

Analysts use moving averages to analyze intermediate and long-term stock movements. They predict the direction of prices by examining the trend in current prices relative to the long-term moving average. A moving-average depicts the underlying direction and degree of change.

The relative strength of an individual stock price is a ratio of the average monthly stock price compared to the monthly average index of the total market or the stock's industry group. It informs the analysts of the relationship of specific price movements to an industry or the market in general. When investors favor specific stocks or industries, these will be relatively strong. Stocks that outperform the market trend on the upside may suddenly retreat when investors bail out for hotter prospects. Stocks that outperform in a declining market usually attract other investors and remain strong.

As analysts construct charts, certain trends appear. These trends are characterized by a range of prices in which the stock trades.

The lower end of the range forms a support base for the price. At that end a stock is a "good" buy and attracts additional investors, and thus forms a support level. As the price increases, a stock may become "unattractive" when compared to other stocks. Investors sell causing that upper limit to form a resistance level. Movements beyond the support and resistance levels require a fundamental change in the market and/or the stock.

RANDOM WALK THEORIES

Random-walk theorists do not believe in the cyclical nature of markets although they analyzed the same data as do chartists. **Random walk theory** maintains that technical analysis is useless because past price and volume statistics do not contain any information by themselves that bode well for success. Random walkers believe choosing securities randomly will result in returns comparable to technical and fundamental analysis.

Through a series of illustrations, academicians in the 1960s and 1970s demonstrated that there is no basis in fact to technical analysis. They found that price movements were random and displayed no predictable pattern of movement, as did the Frenchman Louis Bachelier at the turn of the century. Therefore, prices have no predictive value. Since all the studies indicated randomness in price, the proponents of this hypothesis called it the "random walk theory."

Random walkers use time-series models to relate efficient markets to the behavior of stock prices and investment returns. They believe that changes in prices are independent of new information entering the market, and that these prices changes are evenly distributed throughout the market. Since this means that the distribution of price changes is constant from one period to the next, investors are not able to identify "mispriced" securities in any consistent fashion. Experience and empirical evidence contradict this assumption, suggesting that the random walk properties of returns (or price changes) are too restrictive.

Technicians maintain the validity of their practices especially with regards to the timing of investments. Since computer-based trading programs incorporate some timing technique into their matrix, intraday trading has increasingly become characterized by dramatic movements in the indices. These movements represent a consensus among traders of the applicability of technical theories despite of the evidence of random walkers. A market driven by similarly configured indices, no matter what the basis, becomes more predictable over time.

In practice, computer programs execute trades not only in anticipation of a market move, but to provide fund managers the opportunity to change positions ahead of the others.

DOW THEORY

Although Charles Dow—publisher of the *Wall Street Journal*—was a fundamentalist, he published a series of articles which laid the foundation for William P. Hamilton's 1908 work that formalized the Dow Theory. Hamilton theorized that the stock market is the best gauge of financial and business activity because all relevant information is immediately discounted in the prices of stocks, as indexed by the Dow Jones Industrial Average and the Dow Jones Transportation Average. Accordingly, both averages must confirm market direction because price trends in the overall market points to the termination of both bull and bear markets.

Three movements are assumed to occur simultaneously:

1. A primary bull or bearish trend, typically lasting 28 to 33 months.

2. A secondary trend goes counter to the primary trend, typically lasts three weeks to three months, and reflects a long-term primary movement.

3. Day-to-day activity makes up the first two movements of the market, confirming the direction of the long-term primary trend.

The primary trend must be supported by strong day-to-day activity to erase the effects of the secondary trend, otherwise, the market will begin to move in the opposite direction. If day-to-day activity supports the secondary trend, the market will soon reverse directions and develop a new primary trend.

If the cyclical movements of the market averages increase over time, and the successive low become higher, the market will trend upward. If the successive highs trend lower, and the successive low trend lower, then the market is in a downtrend. Computer programs have full integrated Dow theory into their decision-making matrix.

SEE ALSO: Valuation

[Roger J. AbiNader]

FURTHER READING:

Alexander, Gordon J. and Jack Clark Francis. *Portfolio Analysis*, 3rd ed., Prentice Hall, 1986.

Dreman, David. *The New Contrarian Investment Strategy*. Random House, 1980.

Sharpe, William, F., and Gordon J. Alexander. *Investments*, 4th ed. Prentice Hall, 1990.

Shim, Jae K. and Joel G. Siegel. *Handbook of Financial Analysis, Forecasting, and Modeling*. Prentice Hall, 1988.

Shubik, Martin and Martin J. Whitman. *The Conservative Aggressove Investor*. Random House, 1979.

Welsch, Glenn A., Robert N. Anthony, and Daniel G. Short. *Fundamentals of Financial Accounting*. 4th ed. Homewood, IL: Irwin, Inc., 1984.

INVESTMENT MANAGEMENT

Investment management comprises a broad spectrum of topics ranging from the workings of **capital markets**, to valuation of financial securities, to the construction of portfolios of assets to meet the objectives of investors. Investment itself can be considered any activity that requires the commitment of current wealth to some set of specified assets for the purpose of enhancing future wealth. These assets can be either real (e.g., gold, art, **real estate**) or financial (e.g., **stocks**, **bonds**). The enhancement of future wealth can be derived from appreciation in the value of the asset itself, referred to as **capital gains**, or as **income** provided to the owner of the asset.

There are well-developed financial markets around the world that have evolved to assist in the transfer of funds from investors to individuals and organizations who have a need for capital. One useful way to dichotomize these markets is as primary and secondary. Primary markets represent the initial transfer of funds from investors to those with viable projects requiring additional cash. For example, a corporation may sell stock to the public in order to raise needed funds for an expansion of productive capacity, or to undertake new initiatives in new markets. This type of transaction is typically mediated by an investment banker who will assist the corporation in the sale of its securities. Other than the fee charged by the investment banker, the corporation actually receives the cash generated from the stock sale. The investor receives shares of stock representing partial ownership of the firm.

Secondary markets are resale markets where financial securities are traded among investors. Although corporations receive no additional cash flow from the purchase or sale of their securities in secondary markets, these markets provide the important ingredient of liquidity to investors. Liquidity refers to the ability to quickly exchange assets and cash at reasonable prices. The New York Stock Exchange (NYSE) is the largest example of a secondary market in the world. On the floor of the NYSE, traders exchange shares of corporations after agreeing on the proper price. Other major stock exchanges in the world are located in Tokyo, London, Frankfurt, Toronto, Paris, and in most other developed economies. In addition, there are significant markets that have no physical location. The over-the-counter (OTC) market in the United States, is one such example. This market is really a computer network of dealers who maintain inventories of various securities and serve as market makers. Each dealer posts a price at which they would be willing to purchase additional securities (the bid price) and one at which they would be willing to sell securities that they hold (the ask price).

Investors who want to buy or sell financial assets typically engage the services of a broker. The broker transmits orders to buy or sell to the trading floor of the appropriate exchange or views price quotes provided by dealers and executes the order at the best available price. Investors can submit either market orders or limit orders. A market order is an instruction to buy or sell at the current market price. A limit order carries conditions that must be met before the transaction can be carried out. These conditions relate to the price level of the security and the time period during which the order remains valid. Market orders are the most prevalent type processed by brokers.

Additionally, investors can hold a long position in a security, by purchasing a quantity and holding it, or a short position, by borrowing securities and selling them. While the motivation behind the long position is clear: the investor expects the value of the security to increase or expects it to provide income in the future, the motivation for a short position requires further explanation. By borrowing securities now, selling them at the current price, and agreeing to replace them at a later date, the investor is clearly **forecasting** a decrease in price. If the price does decline, then the investor can purchase securities at this lower price, repay the loan that is denominated in securities, not money, and profit from the decline. If the price rises after the initial sale, however, the investor will sustain a loss when the shares are eventually purchased and replaced. Brokers will assist in this transaction by locating shares that can be borrowed and sold.

Brokers will also lend funds to investors for the purchase of shares. This is referred to as margin trading. Current regulations in the United States allow an investor to borrow up to 50 percent of the value of securities purchased. Note that the investor's profits are amplified since only a fraction of the purchase was financed with personal funds. Likewise, losses will accumulate at a more rapid rate if the value of the securities purchased declines. If the drop in value is considerable, the investor will be contacted by the broker and instructed to provide additional cash in order to secure the position. This is referred to as a margin call.

There are a variety of financial assets for the investor to consider. Shares of **common stock**, often referred to as equity, represent a claim of ownership of the firm's future earnings. Common stockholders are the legal owners of a corporation and typically carry voting rights regarding matters of **corporate governance**. The shares have value if the firm is expected to generate significant future cash flows that will be sufficient to cover expenses and allow for a profit that can be distributed to shareholders. These future cash flows to shareholders can take the form of **dividends**, direct cash payments, or capital gains. Capital gains represent the change in the value of the shares themselves. This value will change as investors reassess the ability of the firm to generate future cash flows for shareholders. Closely related to common stock is a second category, **preferred stock**. This stock pays a dividend that is either fixed or varies with some indicator of **interest rates**. The term ''preferred'' refers to the fact that dividends must be paid to this class of shareholders before any dividend payments are made to common shareholders. While it is also considered equity, and its holders are also considered owners of the firm, preferred shareholders can vote on matters of corporate governance in only very limited circumstances.

A second category of financial assets is represented by **debt**. Debtholders are creditors of the firm, not owners. Therefore, an investment in a firm's debt is inherently less risky than an investment in its equity. All obligations to debtholders must be met before any payments can be made to preferred or common shareholders. Debt is often classified by the life of the liability it entails. At the shortest end of the maturity spectrum are highly liquid corporate and government obligations that must be paid within one year. Highly credit worthy corporations may issue commercial paper. Commercial paper carries a stated par, or face value, which represents the amount that the corporation agrees to repay when the obligation matures. This asset is sold at a discount, or for less than its face value. The return to the investor is the difference between this initial discount price and the face value. Similar instruments, called Treasury bills, **promissory notes** are issued by the U.S. Department of the Treasury and by governmental units of other foreign nations. Notes are medium-term obligations that typically have a life of more than one year and less than five years. Notes also have a face value and usually provide periodic payments of interest at a rate expressed as a percentage of the face value.

Bonds are the most prominent of the debt categories. They include any obligation with a life of more than five years. Bonds are commonly issued for 20-year periods. There are, however, many examples of 30-year bonds and the U.S. corporation, Disney, has issued bonds with a 100-year life. Regardless of longevity, bonds are similar to notes in that they make periodic payments of interest to holders. These payments are referred to as coupon payments and are typically expressed as a percentage of the bond's face value. For example, a 20-year bond with an 8 percent coupon rate and a $1,000 face value would make payments of $80 per year. Most coupon bonds commonly divide this interest payment into semiannual installments. There are many types of bonds that differ from the fixed-rate coupon bond just described. Floating-rate bonds have no fixed coupon rate. Instead, interest payments are adjusted to move with some broader indicator of interest rates. Zero coupon bonds pay no interest whatsoever. They are sold at some fraction of their face value and, unless resold, will generate no cash inflow until they mature. Convertible bonds are typically coupon-paying bonds that also provide the holder with the option of exchanging the bond for a specified number of shares of common stock. This option can be very valuable if the firm's stock price rises significantly.

Another class of financial assets is represented by **derivative securities**. These are securities whose value is directly tied to the value of another asset. One prominent example is the stock option. **Options** are traded securities that allow the holder to purchase or sell a specified quantity of shares of an individual stock for a predetermined price, called the strike or exercise price, during a specified period. The holder of a **call option** may purchase stock at the exercise price. Therefore, the call option becomes more valuable as the value of the stock itself increases. Conversely, the holder of a put option has the right to sell stock at the exercise price and will profit if the stock's value falls. A second prominent category of derivative securities is the futures contract. In a futures contract, the buyer agrees to take delivery of a specified commodity or financial instrument at a specified time and price. Therefore, the buyer profits if the value of the commodity rises above this price. The seller has incurred a loss since there is an obligation to deliver the commodity for a price that is lower than the current market price. The situation is reversed, however, if the value of the commodity falls below the price specified in the futures contract. In this case, the seller profits and the buyer loses. **Futures contracts** are used to hedge, or transfer, risk associated with the underlying commodity of the contract and they are used by speculators to take risky positions regarding the future price movements of the commodities themselves. Futures contracts are available on many agricultural **commodities** (e.g., corn, wheat, soybeans, cattle), industrial commodities (e.g., crude oil, copper), precious metals (e.g., gold, silver, platinum), interest rate sensitive securities (e.g., U.S. Treasury bonds, notes, and bills), foreign currencies, and a variety of market indexes.

Regardless of the assets chosen as investments, the investor must always consider the duality of **risk** and return associated with each. Rate of return refers to the percentage of wealth appreciation or depreciation associated with a particular investment. Rate of return can be considered in a historical or an expecta-

tional sense. That is, it can be measured for some prior period or it can be forecast for some upcoming period. Risk refers to the cloud of uncertainty surrounding the expected future return. It is common in investment analysis to use measures of historical return, such as an arithmetic average over multiple periods, and historical risk, such as statistical variance or standard deviation, to serve as a proxy for expected future returns and risk. But this is just a convenient starting point and investment analysis commonly modifies the forecast drawn from historical data to reflect more relevant information derived from a broader array of sources. So, it is the future risk and return that truly matters and it is reasonable to assume that as investors compare various alternatives, they will prefer higher expected returns and lower expected risk.

Analysis of individual investment alternatives is carried out in a variety of ways. One interesting dichotomy is the distinction between fundamental and **technical analysis**. Fundamental analysis is an attempt to build a model of security value by careful scrutiny of the characteristics of the firm (or government) that has issued the security. Such an assessment will draw upon **financial statements** of a corporation and other pertinent sources of information regarding the firm's activities. The assessment will also rely upon judgments made regarding the prospects of the industry in which the firm resides and on the outlook for the economy in general. The objective is to forecast the future cash flows that will be available to the various securityholders in the firm and to subsequently assess whether these expected cash flows will be sufficient to compensate the investor for the associated risk. Clearly, there is no one methodology for fundamental analysis even though there is a common objective.

Technical analysis attempts to forecast future security values by exploiting patterns in past security prices, and in the relationship between prices and other relevant variables. This technique requires careful identification and exploitation of trends that provide an unambiguous clue regarding future price movements. Technical analysts do not rely on information regarding financial characteristics of the firm itself, but instead examine both psychological and institutional determinants of supply and demand of the firm's stock. As with fundamental analysis, there is no one mode of technical analysis.

Acting as an umbrella over these two modes of investment analysis is the idea of market efficiency. A market is considered efficient if security prices fully reflect all available information. Furthermore, new and relevant information will be rapidly incorporated into the price. If there are many fundamental analysts searching for relevant information that can be used to value a security, then financial markets should be informationally efficient. On the other hand, if markets are imperfect and investors exhibit irrational behavior (e.g., systematically overreacting to bad news or exhibiting ''herd'' behavior), then markets will not be efficient. The question is really one concerning the level of efficiency. There are many studies that have scrutinized the predictive ability of past stock prices and other historical relationships. By and large, these studies have found no significant ''memory,'' or forecasting ability, using such data. Other studies have indicated that an unanticipated disclosure of information relevant to the future cash flow stream of the firm evokes a rapid and complete adjustment to a new price level for the firm's securities. There are small, yet undeniable, examples that suggest financial markets are not perfectly efficient and that investors sometimes act on information that should have no economic consequence. Nevertheless, it is reasonable to say that financial markets in most developed economies exhibit a high degree of informational efficiency.

Given well-functioning global security markets, a broad array of securities, and many sources of information for assessing alternatives, investors are presented with the difficult choice of what combination of securities to hold. The first step in addressing this fundamental problem requires an examination of investment objectives. A clarification of investment objectives and other relevant information regarding the investor's specific situation will lead to effective screening of investment alternatives, proper portfolio construction, and ultimately, a suitable set of investments for the investor. Investment objectives can be described in a number of ways. One useful scale is based upon risk and return.

Consider the following broad categories of investment objectives ranging from low to high risk: (1) preservation of capital, (2) growth and income, (3) capital appreciation, and (4) aggressive growth. The first category, preservation of capital, would consider only the highest-quality, lowest-risk, investment alternatives. Primary consideration is given to avoidance of loss, not to an increase in wealth. This objective could be met by holding Treasury bills, commercial paper, and other short-term, low-risk instruments. The second category, growth and income, would screen to find a set of securities that also have low risk, but which are expected to provide a reasonable level of current income. This would suggest a significant component of stocks paying a high dividend and coupon-paying bonds. In addition, the growth component of this objective may be met by holding a proportion of securities in industries that are expected to exhibit moderate growth over some upcoming period. Capital appreciation refers to an objective where current income is a minor consideration at best. Common stock (and possibly convertible bonds) in companies expected to exhibit average and above average growth would be appropriate to include. On the high-risk,

high-expected-return end of the spectrum is the aggressive growth objective. Here, an investor would screen out all but those firms expected to generate above-average growth. This portfolio may include stocks of relatively small companies in new industries, bonds from firms that are considered moderate to high credit risks, and derivative securities such as options.

In addition to these simple objectives, the investor's portfolio may be influenced by other characteristics. For example, an institutional investor managing a pension fund will have different concerns than an individual investor designing his or her own personal retirement plan. Other investors will want the portfolio to address their other sources of income, or lack thereof, tax status, age, need to provide for dependents, level of sophistication regarding investment alternatives, and many other attributes. These attributes and attitudes regarding risk will immediately exclude some investment alternatives and implicitly suggest others.

At this point, many investors—individual and institutional—will look toward **mutual funds** to provide them with a proper package of appropriate investments. Mutual funds are companies that hold portfolios of securities and sell shares in the portfolios that they hold. There are nearly as many mutual funds in the United States as there are publicly listed stocks. Mutual funds can be categorized by risk-return objective or by the subset of securities they hold. For example, there are many funds in each of the four categories previously described. In addition, there are sector funds (specializing in individual industries), country funds (specializing in the securities of an individual country), global funds, bond funds, real estate development funds, funds holding tax-exempt securities, and many others. Managers of these funds charge a fee, but relieve investors of the need to scrutinize individual investments.

After settling on an investment objective and screening the vast number of investment alternatives to a manageable number, there is still a major consideration that remains. **Portfolio management theory** indicates that an investor can reduce overall exposure to risk by holding a group of securities selected from a diverse set of industries or countries. This diversification of risk occurs because any individual security is subject to unique sources of risk. The unique sources of risk in one security, however, are distinct from the unique sources of risk in another security. This means that when the securities are held together, they tend to stabilize one another since unique surprises from one source are not compounded by similar surprises from another source. This lack of correlation among sources of risk for individual securities means that the investor can minimize, even eliminate, the risk unique to individual securities, by holding a large number of diverse securities. This set could span a number of different industries or regions of the world. This does not eliminate all risk for the investor, however. There is still risk that results from factors common to all securities in the sample. For example, all securities are subject to the risk of changes in overall economic conditions. An investor who wished to reduce risk further could choose securities that have lower sensitivity to such changes.

SEE ALSO: Diversification in Investments; Stock Market

[Paul Bolster]

FURTHER READING:

Bodie, Zvi, Alex Kane, and Alan J. Marcus. *Investments*. 2nd ed. Irwin, 1993.

Fabozzi, Frank J., and Franco Modigliani. *Capital Markets: Institutions and Instruments*. Prentice-Hall, 1992.